A NEW HISTORY OF IRELAND

UNDER THE AUSPICES OF THE ROYAL IRISH ACADEMY
PLANNED AND ESTABLISHED BY THE LATE T. W. MOODY

VII

IRELAND, 1921–84

A NEW HISTORY OF IRELAND

UNDER THE AUSPICES OF THE ROYAL IRISH ACADEMY
PLANNED AND ESTABLISHED BY THE LATE T. W. MOODY

* Already published

A NEW HISTORY OF
IRELAND

VII
IRELAND, 1921–84

EDITED BY

J. R. HILL

OXFORD
UNIVERSITY PRESS

OXFORD

UNIVERSITY PRESS

Great Clarendon Street, Oxford OX2 6DP

Oxford University Press is a department of the University of Oxford.
It furthers the University's objective of excellence in research, scholarship,
and education by publishing worldwide in

Oxford New York

Auckland Bangkok Buenos Aires Cape Town Chennai
Dar es Salaam Delhi Hong Kong Istanbul Karachi Kolkata
Kuala Lumpur Madrid Melbourne Mexico City Mumbai Nairobi
São Paulo Shanghai Taipei Tokyo Toronto

Oxford is a registered trade mark of Oxford University Press
in the UK and in certain other countries

Published in the United States
by Oxford University Press Inc., New York

British Library Cataloguing in Publication Data
Data available

Library of Congress Cataloging in Publication Data
Data available
ISBN 0-19-821752-8

1 3 5 7 9 10 8 6 4 2

Typeset 10.5/12pt MErhardt
by Kolam Information Services Pvt. Ltd., Pondicherry, India
Printed in Great Britain
on acid-free paper by
T. J. International Ltd, Padstow, Cornwall

PREFACE

THIS volume completes the text of the *New history* to 1984. The year 1984—in which the final report of the New Ireland Forum appeared—has been taken as the latest practicable date at which to end this volume. In selecting this date, we had to take into account the problems of dealing with Irish history so close to the present. In addition to the greatly increased flow of scholarly and other writing on this period since the compilation of the *New history* began, the course of events covered by later parts of the text has been subject to constant and dramatic change. The perspective in which the whole period appears has been similarly affected.

Coincidentally, the year 1984 was marked by the death on 11 February of T. W. Moody, without whom the development of Irish historiography in general since the mid 1930s would have been very different; and without whom the *New history* itself, in particular, would never have taken shape. His career, achievements, and personal qualities have received fitting recognition from F. S. L. Lyons and in obituaries by F. X. Martin, Helen F. Mulvey, and others whose work is listed in the bibliography to this volume, though a full account has not yet been written, and even an adequate tribute is impossible in the space available to us here.

Theo Moody launched the *New history* with the aim of making more widely accessible the fruits of a generation of specialist scholarship—partly to redress a shortage of good general histories of Ireland, partly to act as a stimulus to wider study and further research, and also because, in his own words, 'if history at its best is not made available to the educated public as a whole, it fails in one of its essential social functions'. In the years since he did so, the output both of good general histories (indebted in some degree to the example, even to the mere existence, of the *New history*) and of specialist research has increased to such an extent that a member of the educated public today may find it hard to appreciate the importance of his concept and his achievement. No one, however, should underestimate the extent to which the *New history*, as it now stands, depends on his personal investment of thought and effort. Up to his death, he was the impelling and directing force of the organisation that brought the work of scores of scholars together.

His successors as editors have tried to carry on what he established, and in doing so were perhaps more aware of his ideals than he was himself. The *New history* has certain characteristics, which were not the result of accident, serendipity, or fashion. One is the breadth of the work. This is best demonstrated by the inclusion of chapters on painting, architecture, and the decorative arts. The chapter on women's history in volume VII, we consider an extension that he would have approved. A further feature is an obsession with accuracy. It would be wrong to claim that the editors have checked every footnote and every detail in the text that was easily checkable, but they can say with a weary certainty that many, many details have been checked. They can also concede with regretful certainty that some details have escaped their vigilance. A third feature has been the consideration given to every aspect of the books' production. Whether it was the contents list, the lists of contributors, the illustrations, the index, or the dust-jacket, all received as much attention as the text and the scope and layout of the whole project. Among our achievements we include the attractive dust-jackets designed for us by Dr Edward McParland for all volumes since volume III; we must also mention the unique recognition given to the index of volume IV, prepared by Colm Croker, which was nominated for the Wheatley medal of the British Library Association in 1987.

To those who worked most closely with Theo, he was a constant and virtually inexhaustible source of energy, imagination, and sound judgement. For him the writing of history rested on a number of foundations that he not only set out for the *New history* but instilled in his students. His ideas for the *New history* were the local application of a philosophy of history that he propagated and inculcated. Briefly stated, the practice of history required four things. First, all the available sources should be used, and they should be critically appraised. Historiographical progress—advances in interpreting the past—could only come about as the result of new research, and that in turn required the historian to be steeped in as many of the sources as possible. Historians' views of the past did not depend on whimsy, changing orthodoxies, or convenient changes of viewpoint, but on the raw material of the story, which was constantly producing new characters and new plots. Secondly, the writing of history was done by making a series of generalisations that would stand the test of critical examination. Any new synthesis was likely to enjoy only the status of 'an interim report' (a phrase he often used). No interpretation of the past was so hallowed as not to be liable to change if new information came to light. Thirdly, writing should be clear, free from jargon, and purged of tendentious language. Fourthly, all conclusions had to be considered. There could be no suppression, invention, or misrepresentation. Facts, which in the nature of things were often more ambiguous than the enthusiastic would have wished, had to be faced. It was the rigour with which Theo adhered to these principles that made him such a formidable presence, whether directing a postgraduate seminar or chairing a meeting of the board of editors of the *New history*.

The *New history* could not have come into being without practical help from several quarters. Once again we acknowledge with gratitude the indispensable support of the late C. S. Andrews in setting the *New history* in motion; and the generous financial help provided by the late Dr John A.

Mulcahy, of New York, and the directors of the American Irish Foundation, which enabled us to carry out much-needed research in the early stages of work on the project.

In respect of volume VII, we take this opportunity of recording our debt to David Craig, Catriona Crowe, Nicholas Furlong, Seamus Helferty, Lar Joye, Mary Kelleher, Commandant Victor Laing, Bridget McCormack, James McGuire, Edward McParland, Theresa Moriarty, Helen F. Mulvey, Sarah Ward-Perkins, Jacinta Prunty, and Penny Woods. The contribution of Kevin B. Nowlan must be particularly acknowledged; he read the entire text and made many helpful suggestions. We also extend our thanks to our secretary, Richard Hawkins, and to our typist, Peggy Morgan, whose work for the *New history* to December 1994 completed over twenty-four years of invaluable service.

Finally, we record with sorrow the deaths of four scholars whose contributions to this volume have proved to be of lasting value, requiring little more than annotation to take account of work recently published—Vivian Mercier (3 November 1989), John Whyte (16 May 1990), Rex Cathcart (26 August 1994), and David Johnson (15 June 1998); and also the death (13 February 2000) of F. X. Martin, O.S.A., emeritus professor of medieval history, University College, Dublin, member of the board of editors since the foundation of this project, and its chairman since 1984.

F. J. BYRNE
W. E. VAUGHAN
ART COSGROVE
J. R. HILL
DÁIBHÍ Ó CRÓINÍN

Royal Irish Academy
November 2002

CONTENTS

VI NORTHERN IRELAND, 1920–25   by Brian Barton

VIII NORTHERN IRELAND, 1939–45
by Brian Barton

XII RECONCILIATION, RIGHTS, AND
PROTESTS, 1963–8   by J. H. Whyte

XIII THE NORTH ERUPTS, AND IRELAND
ENTERS EUROPE, 1968–72   by J. H. Whyte

XVI   LAND AND PEOPLE, *c*.1983
by Desmond Gillmor

XVIII   LITERATURE IN ENGLISH, 1921–84
by Vivian Mercier

CONTENTS xxv

XXI MUSIC IN INDEPENDENT IRELAND SINCE 1921
by Joseph Ryan

XXII MUSIC IN NORTHERN IRELAND SINCE 1921
by Roy Johnston

XXIII   THE MASS MEDIA IN TWENTIETH-CENTURY IRELAND
by Rex Cathcart with Michael Muldoon

XXV   HIGHER EDUCATION, 1908–84
by John Coolahan

XXVI   EMIGRATION AND IMMIGRATION IN THE TWENTIETH CENTURY: AN OVERVIEW

by J. J. Sexton

XXVII WOMEN, EMANCIPATION, AND POLITICS, 1860–1984

by Mary Cullen

CONTENTS <label>xxxv</label>

CONTRIBUTORS

Donald Harman Akenson	B.A. (Yale); Ed.M., Ph.D. (Harvard); F.R.S. (Can.); professor of history, Queen's University, Kingston, Ontario; Beamish research professor, University of Liverpool
Paul Arthur	B.A., M.S.Sc. (Q.U.B.); professor of politics and course director for postgraduate diploma/M.A. in peace and conflict studies
Jonathan Eric Bardon	B.A. (Dubl.), D.Phil. (Ulster), Dip.Ed. (Q.U.B.); lecturer in modern history, Queen's University, Belfast
Cyril Barrett	M.A., Ph.D. (Lond.); fellow of Campion Hall, Oxford; emeritus professor of philosophy, University of Warwick
Brian Edwin Barton	B.A., Dip. Ed. (Q.U.B.); M.A. (Ulster); Ph.D. (Q.U.B.); research fellow in politics, Queen's University, Belfast; lecturer, Open University
Neil Buttimer	M.A., Ph.D. (Harv.); statutory lecturer in modern Irish, University College, Cork
Hector Rex Cathcart	M.A., Ph.D., H.Dip.Ed., Dip.Geog. (Dubl.); Dip.Psych. (N.U.I.); professor of education, Queen's University, Belfast (died 26 Aug. 1994)
John Coolahan	B.A., M.A., H.D.E. (N.U.I.); M.Ed., Ph.D. (Dubl.); professor of education, National University of Ireland, Maynooth
Mary Cullen	M.A. (N.U.I.); research associate, Centre for Gender and Women's Studies, Trinity College, Dublin
Richard English	M.A. (Oxon.), Ph.D. (Keele); F.R.Hist.S.; professor of politics, Queen's University, Belfast

Sean Nial Farren	B.A. (N.U.I.), M.A. (Essex), D.Phil. (Ulster), H.Dip.Ed. (N.U.I.); senior lecturer in education, University of Ulster
Desmond Alfred Gillmor	B.A. (Mod.), M.A., Ph.D. (Dubl.); associate professor emeritus, Trinity College, Dublin
Brian Girvin	B.A., M.A., Ph.D. (N.U.I.); professor of comparative politics, University of Glasgow
Jacqueline Rhoda Hill	B.A., Ph.D. (Leeds); F.R. Hist. S.; associate professor of history, National University of Ireland, Maynooth
Michael Alan Hopkinson	M.A., Ph.D. (Cantab.); lecturer in history, University of Stirling
David Stuart Johnson	B.A., B.Phil. (Oxon.), senior lecturer in economic and social history, Queen's University, Belfast (died 15 June 1998)
Roy Johnston	B.A. (Dubl.), Ph.D. (Q.U.B.); Member of the Royal Musical Association
Liam Kennedy	B.Sc., M.Sc. (N.U.I.), D.Phil. (York); professor of economic and social history, Queen's University, Belfast
Dermot Francis Keogh	B.A., M.A. (N.U.I.), Ph.D. (E.U.I., Florence); professor of history, University College, Cork
Vivian Herbert Samuel Mercier	B.A., Ph.D. (Dubl.); emeritus professor of English and comparative literature, University of California at Santa Barbara (died 3 Nov. 1989)
Michael Muldoon	B.A., M.A. (Windsor, Canada); M.A. (Dublin Institute of Technology); senior lecturer and dissertation supervisor, Dublin Institute of Technology
Máire Ní Annracháin	M.A., Ph.D. (N.U.I.); senior lecturer, department of modern Irish, National University of Ireland, Maynooth
Eunan O'Halpin	B.A., M.A. (N.U.I.); Ph.D. (Cantab.); professor of contemporary Irish history, Trinity College, Dublin

Joseph J. Ryan   M.A., B.Mus., Mus.Dip., A.R.I.A.M.,
                              Ph.D. (N.U.I.); registrar, Athlone Insti-
                              tute of Technology

Jeremiah Joseph Sexton   M.Sc. (N.U.I.); professor, Economic and
                              Social Research Institute, Dublin

John Henry Whyte   B.A., B.Litt., M.A., Ph.D. (Oxon.); pro-
                              fessor of politics, University College,
                              Dublin (died 16 May 1990)

The maps have been prepared by Professor D. A. Gillmor. The index is the
work of Dr Helen Litton.

MAPS

LIST OF ILLUSTRATIONS
at end of volume

The originals of these illustrations were made available through the courtesy of the following, and are published by their permission: the National Museum of Ireland, plates 2, 3, 4, 5, 6, 7, 8, 9, 21, 28; the National Library of Ireland, plates 10, 11, 12, 13, 15, 16, 17, 18, 19, 44, 49; the Public Record Office of Northern Ireland, plates 23, 31, 33, 39, 42, 43, 54; Examiner Publications (Cork) Ltd, plates 29, 35, 46, 47, 61, 62; the Linen Hall Library, Belfast, plates 34, 51, 52, 53, 55, 56, 57, 58, 59; Mr Nicholas Furlong, plate 36; Mr James McGuire, plates 37, 50; Independent Newspapers (Ireland) Ltd, plate 38; Dr W. E. Vaughan, plate 41; Ms Mary Kelleher, R.D.S. Library, plate 45; Ms Janet Moody, plate 48; the Irish Times Ltd, plates 60, 63, 64, 65, 66; the Irish Architectural Archive, plates 67, 68, 69, 88; Mr Hugh Doran, plate 69; Bord Fáilte Éireann, plates 71, 84; Bank of Ireland Group, plates 72, 86; Mr Brendan Dempsey, plate 73; the National Gallery of Ireland, plate 74; the Hugh Lane Dublin City Gallery, plate 75, by courtesy of Felix Rosenstiel's Widow & Son Ltd., London on behalf of the estate of Sir John Lavery; the Ulster Museum, plates 76, 87; © The Estate of Jack B. Yeats 2003. All Rights Reserved, DACS, plate 76; the Crawford Gallery, Cork, plate 77; Mr Louis Le Brocquy, plate 78; Mr Patrick Scott, plate 79; Mrs Margaret Early O'Farrell, plate 80; Mr Campbell Bruce, plate 81; the James Joyce Museum, Sandycove, Co. Dublin, and the Dublin Writers Museum, Parnell Square, Dublin 1, plate 82; Dúchas The Heritage Service, plate 83; Mr Giollamuire Ó Murchú and Dr Brian Kennedy, plate 85; the estate of F. E. McWilliam, plate 87; the Bakery and Food Workers' Union, plate 89; Ms Deborah Brown, plate 90; Clongowes Wood College, plate 91; Eton College, plate 92; the Connacht Tribune Ltd, jacket illustration

ABBREVIATIONS AND CONVENTIONS

Abbreviations and conventions used in this volume are listed below. They consist of (a) the relevant items from the list in *Irish Historical Studies*, supplement I (Jan. 1968) and (b) abbreviations, on the same model, not included in the *Irish Historical Studies* list. Where an article is cited more than once in a chapter, an abbreviated form is used after the first full reference. Occasionally, however, the full reference is repeated for the convenience of the reader. Abbreviations that occur only within one chapter, where full details are given on first appearance, are not as a rule included in the following list.

a.	*ante* (before)
Adams, *Censorship*	Michael Adams, *Censorship: the Irish experience* (Dublin, 1968)
Anal. Hib.	*Analecta Hibernica, including the reports of the Irish Manuscripts Commission* (Dublin, 1930–)
Archiv. Hib.	*Archivium Hibernicum: or Irish historical record* (Catholic Record Society of Ireland, Maynooth, 1912–)
B.L.	British Library
B.L., Add. MS	——, Additional MS
Barton, *Brookeborough*	Brian Barton, *Brookeborough: the making of a prime minister* (Belfast, 1988)
Bodl.	Bodleian Library, Oxford
Bowman, *De Valera & Ulster question*	John Bowman, *De Valera and the Ulster question 1917–1973* (Oxford, 1982)
Brady, *Guardians of the peace*	Conor Brady, *Guardians of the peace* (Dublin, 1974)
Breifne	*Breifne: journal of Cumann Seanchais Bhreifne (Breifne Historical Society)* (Cavan, 1958–)
Buckland, *Factory of grievances*	Patrick Buckland, *The factory of grievances: devolved government in Northern Ireland 1921–39* (Dublin, 1979)
Bullán	*Bullán: an Irish studies journal* (Oxford, 1994–)

c.	*circa* (about)
C.S.O.	Central Statistics Office
Capuchin Annual	*Capuchin Annual* (40 issues, Dublin, 1934–77)
Clogher Rec.	*Clogher Record* ([Monaghan], 1953–)
Coogan, *I.R.A.*	Tim Pat Coogan, *The I.R.A.* (London, 1971 ed.)
Collect. Hib.	*Collectanea Hibernica: sources for Irish history* (Dublin, 1958–)
Cork Hist. Soc. Jn.	*Journal of the Cork Historical and Archaeological Society* (Cork, 1892–)
d.	died
Dáil Éireann deb, i [etc.]	*Dáil Éireann…, díosbóireachtaí páirliminte (parliamentary debates); tuairisg oifigiúil (official report)*, iml. i (vol. i), 1922 [etc.] (Dublin, Stationery Office)
Dáil Éireann treaty deb.	*Iris dhail Éireann, tuairisg oifigiúil, díosbóireacht ar an gconnradh idir Éire agus Sasana do signigheadh i Lundain ar an 6adh lá de mhí na Nodlag 1921; official report, debate on the treaty between Great Britain and Ireland signed in London on the 6th December 1921* (Dublin, [1922?])
Decies	*Old Waterford Society: Decies* ([Waterford], 1976–)
Dublin Hist. Rec.	*Dublin Historical Record* (Dublin, 1938–)
E.C.	European Community
E.E.C.	European Economic Community
E.H.R.	*English Historical Review* (London, 1886–)
Econ. & Soc. Rev.	*The Economic and Social Review* (Dublin, 1969–)
Econ. Hist. Rev.	*Economic History Review* (London, 1927–)
ed.	edited by, edition, editor(s)
Éire-Ireland	*Éire-Ireland: a journal of Irish studies* (Irish American Cultural Institute, St Paul, Minn., 1965–)

Études Irlandaises	*Études Irlandaises* (Lille, 1972–)
Fleischmann, *Mus. in Ire.*	Aloys Fleischmann (ed.), *Music in Ireland: a symposium* (Cork, 1952)
Galway Arch. Soc. Jn.	*Journal of the Galway Archaeological and Historical Society* (Galway, 1900–)
H.C.	house of commons papers
Hansard N.I. (commons), i [etc.]	*The parliamentary debates, official report, first series, volume i: first session of the first parliament of Northern Ireland, 12 George V, house of commons, session 1921* [etc.]; from 1958 the series is entitled *Parliamentary debates (Hansard)..., house of commons, official report* (Belfast, H.M. Stationery Office)
Harkness, *N.I. since 1920*	David Harkness, *Northern Ireland since 1920* (Dublin, 1983)
Hermathena	*Hermathena: a series of a papers... by members of Trinity College, Dublin* (Dublin, 1874–)
Hist. Ire.	*History Ireland* (Dublin, 1993–)
Hist. Jn.	*The Historical Journal* (Cambridge, 1958–)
Hist. Studies	*Historical Studies: papers read before the Irish Conference of Historians* (1958–)
Historical Studies	*Historical Studies, Australia and New Zealand* (Melbourne, 1940– ; from 1967, title *Historical Studies*)
Horgan, *Lemass*	John Horgan, *Seán Lemass: the enigmatic patriot* (Dublin, 1997)
I.B.L.	*The Irish Book Lover* (32 vols, Dublin, 1909–57)
I.E.R.	*Irish Ecclesiastical Record* (171 vols, Dublin, 1864–1968)
I.H.S.	*Irish Historical Studies: the joint journal of the Irish Historical Society and the Ulster Society for Irish Historical Studies* (Dublin, 1938–)
Ir. Archives	*Irish Archives: journal of the Irish Society for Archives* (Dublin, 1989–) [preceded

	by *Irish Archives Bulletin* (11 vols, Dublin, 1971–81)]
Ir. Booklore	*Irish Booklore* (4 vols, Belfast, 1971–80)
Ir. Builder	*The Irish Builder and Engineer* (Dublin, 1867–) [formerly *The Dublin Builder* (8 vols, 1859–66)]
Ir. Econ. & Soc. Hist.	*Irish Economic and Social History: the journal of the Economic and Social History Society of Ireland* ([Dublin and Belfast], 1974–)
Ir. Geneal.	*The Irish Genealogist: official organ of the Irish Genealogical Research Society* (London, 1937–)
Ir. Geography	*Irish Geography (bulletin of the Geographical Society of Ireland)* (vols i–iv, Dublin, 1944–63); continued as *The Geographical Society of Ireland, Irish Geography* (vol. v– , Dublin, 1964–)
Ir. Georgian Soc. Bull.	*Quarterly Bulletin of the Irish Georgian Society* (38 vols, Dublin, 1966–97) [continued as *Irish Architectural and Decorative Studies: the Journal of the Irish Georgian Society*, 1998–]
Ir. Jurist	*The Irish Jurist*, new series (Dublin, 1966–)
Ir. Political Studies	*Irish Political Studies* (Galway, 1986–)
Ir. Railway Rec. Soc. Jn.	*Journal of the Irish Railway Record Society* ([Dublin], 1947–)
Ir. Sword	*The Irish Sword: the journal of the Military History Society of Ireland* (Dublin, [1949]–)
Keogh, *Twentieth-century Ire.*	Dermot Keogh, *Twentieth-century Ireland: nation and state* (Dublin, 1994)
Kerry Arch. Soc. Jn.	*Journal of the Kerry Archaeological and Historical Society* ([Tralee], 1968–)
Kildare Arch. Soc. Jn.	*Journal of the County Kildare Archaeological Society* (Dublin, 1891–)
Léachtaí Cholm Cille	*Léachtaí Cholm Cille* (Maynooth, 1970–)

Lee, *Ire. 1912–85*	J.J. Lee, *Ireland 1912–1985: politics and society* (Cambridge, 1989)
Louth Arch. Soc. Jn.	*Journal of the County Louth Archaeological Society* (Dundalk, 1904–)
Lynn, *Holding the ground*	Brendan Lynn, *Holding the ground: the nationalist party in Northern Ireland, 1945–72* (Aldershot, 1997)
Lyons, *Ire. since famine*	F.S.L. Lyons, *Ireland since the famine* (London, *1973 ed.)
Macardle, *Ir. republic*	Dorothy Macardle, *The Irish republic: a documented chronicle of the Anglo–Irish conflict* (London, 1937; 4th ed., Dublin, 1951; American ed., New York, 1965; London, 1968)
MacEoin, *Survivors*	Uinseann MacEoin (ed.), *Survivors* (Dublin, 1981)
McMahon, *Republicans & imperialists*	Deirdre McMahon, *Republicans and imperialists: Anglo–Irish relations in the 1930s* (New Haven and London, 1984)
Mansergh, *Unresolved question*	Nicholas Mansergh, *The unresolved question: the Anglo–Irish settlement and its undoing 1912–72* (New Haven and London, 1991)
Meenan, *Ir. econ. since 1922*	James Meenan, *The Irish economy since 1922* (Liverpool, 1970)
Mil. Arch.	Military Archives
Mulcahy papers	Richard Mulcahy papers in U.C.D. archives department
N.A.I.	National Archives of Ireland
—, D.T.	Department of the Taoiseach (section of National Archives)
n.d.	no date
N.H.I.	*A new history of Ireland* (9 vols, Oxford, 1976–)
N.I.	Northern Ireland
N.U.I.	National University of Ireland
O.C.	Officer commanding

O'Malley notebooks/papers	Ernie O'Malley notebooks and/or papers, in U.C.D. archives department
O'Neill, *Ulster at the crossroads*	Terence O'Neill, *Ulster at the crossroads* (London, 1969)
p.	*post* (after)
P.R.O.	Public Record Office, London
P.R.O.I.	Public Record Office of Ireland (part of National Archives of Ireland)
P.R.O.N.I.	Public Record Office of Northern Ireland
Past & Present	*Past and Present: a journal of historical studies* (London, 1952– ; subtitle *A journal of scientific history*, 1952–8)
Phoenix, *Northern nationalism*	Eamon Phoenix, *Northern nationalism: nationalist politics, partition and the catholic minority in Northern Ireland, 1890–1940* (Belfast, 1994)
Q.U.B.	Queen's University of Belfast
R.I.A.	Royal Irish Academy
R.I.A. Proc.	*Proceedings of the Royal Irish Academy* (Dublin, 1836–)
R.I.A. Trans.	*Transactions of the Royal Irish Academy* (33 vols, Dublin, 1786–1907)
R.I.C.	Royal Irish Constabulary
R.S.A.I.	Royal Society of Antiquaries of Ireland
R.S.A.I.Jn.	*Journal of the Royal Society of Antiquaries of Ireland* (Dublin, 1892–)
R.U.C.	Royal Ulster Constabulary
Saothar	*Saothar: journal of the Irish Labour History Society* (Dublin, 1975–)
Seanad Éireann deb, i [etc.]	*Seanad Éireann, díosbóireachtaí páirliminte (parliamentary debates), tuairisg oifigiúil (official report)*, iml. i. (vol. i), 1922–3 [etc.] (Dublin, 1922–)
Seanchas Ardmhacha	*Seanchas Ardmhacha: journal of the Armagh Diocesan Historical Society* ([Armagh], 1954–) (title appears as *Seanchas Ard Mhacha* from vol. v, no. 1 (1969))

ser.	series
Stat. Soc. Ire. Jn.	*Journal of the Statistical and Social Inquiry Society of Ireland* (Dublin, 1861–)
Studies	*Studies: an Irish quarterly review* (Dublin, 1912–)
T.C.D.	(Library of) Trinity College, Dublin
T.D.	*Teachta Dála* (dáil deputy)
trans.	translated (by)
U.C.D.	University College, Dublin
——, A.D.	——, Archives Department
University Rev.	*University Review: official organ of the Graduates Association of the National University of Ireland* (5 vols, Dublin, 1954–69)
Whyte, *Ch. & state*	J. H. Whyte, *Church and state in modern Ireland 1923–1970* (Dublin, 1971; 2nd ed. (*1923–79*), 1980) [cite edition]
Younger, *Civil war*	Calton Younger, *Ireland's civil war* (London, 1968)

The solidus (/) is used to denote financial and academic years; e.g. 1949/50.

Some footnotes give the full pagination of an article (or similar source) and also draw attention to specific pages within it. Instead of the words 'especially' or 'at', a colon is used; e.g. 'pp 157–75: 163–4'.

INTRODUCTION

Ireland, 1921–84

JONATHAN BARDON and DERMOT KEOGH

THE backdrop of the scene in which Ireland was politically reshaped at the beginning of the period was the first world war. Developments that might have taken half a century, or longer, were telescoped into a few years of violence on a previously unimaginable scale. In that European civil war the contest was not only between imperial powers but also between rival nationalities and ethnic groups. The old central and eastern European empires had collapsed, and the peace negotiations in Paris presented statesmen with an opportunity to redraw the map of Europe to an extent not witnessed since the treaty of Vienna. In line with principles embodied in his 'fourteen points', Woodrow Wilson, president of the United States, encouraged the victors to give every nationality a state of its own. A glance at an ethnic map of Europe at the time indicated the extreme difficulty of putting this precept into practice even if another unwritten principle, that of rewarding the victors, is set aside.

Despite attempts by representatives of Dáil Éireann, the Paris peace conference did not play any part in the preparation of constitutional arrangements for Ireland in 1920–21. Yet the violence and passions of the first world war and the territorial adjustments following the conflict had a very profound impact on the political, social, and economic life of the island. This was especially true of Northern Ireland, created by the 1920 government of Ireland act,[1] and it could be said that every election in the region, whether local or provincial, or for the Westminster parliament, was dominated by support for or opposition to that act, even after the imposition of direct rule in 1972.

In 1914 Ireland had seemed on the brink of civil war, but the outbreak of a general European conflagration postponed internal conflict. Though rejected by both unionists and nationalists in 1914, partition was being considered by the Liberal government and the Conservative opposition. The experience of the first world war swept aside impediments to partition. Asquith enacted the third home rule bill in September 1914,[2] but in telling the commons that it would not be implemented till after the end of the war he also said to

---

[1] 10 & 11 Geo. V, c. 67 (23 Dec. 1920).   [2] 4 & 5 Geo. V, c. 90 (18 Sept. 1914).

members that the patriotic spirit of the Ulster Volunteer Force made the coercion of Ulster 'unthinkable'. The severity of the 36th (Ulster) Division's losses at the Somme did much to reinforce that commitment. The Easter rising a few months earlier had the effect of strengthening support for special treatment for Ulster at Westminster and of convincing a decisive majority in the Ulster Unionist Council to support partition, and of six rather than the nine counties of the historic province of Ulster. At the same time the formation of coalition governments from 1915 onwards brought into the administration men who had openly supported armed unionist defiance before the war.

The 1918 election demonstrated the extent to which Ireland's political landscape had been altered by the exigencies of war. The virtual elimination of the Irish parliamentary party by Sinn Féin was the most dramatic alteration, but an overdue redistribution of seats and the extension of the suffrage increased unionist representation from eighteen to twenty-six members. Just as significant was the shift in the balance of power in the Westminster commons: the continued premiership of Lloyd George disguised the fact that well over half the M.P.s were Conservatives, a shift of great assistance to the cause of Ulster unionism, particularly in view of—in Balfour's words— 'the blessed refusal of Sinn Féiners to take the oath of allegiance in 1918'.[3]

As the Anglo–Irish war got under way and intensified, the government of Ireland bill had a remarkably serene passage through Westminster. When it was put on the statute book just before the end of the year 1920, the act gave northern unionists almost everything they wanted. Northern Ireland, made up of the island's six north-eastern counties, was the maximum area that they could safely control with comfortable majorities and, though not part of the unionist programme, the devolved administration rapidly came to be viewed as a defence against future governments at Westminster seeking a form of reunification between north and south.

The government of Ireland act was rejected by Dáil Éireann, and the guerrilla fighting and reprisals continued. When the Anglo–Irish war concluded and negotiations began, northern unionists vigorously asserted that these deliberations had nothing to do with them. The uncertainty, however, magnified instability in Northern Ireland, and the 1921 Anglo–Irish treaty failed to assuage unionist fears, and raised the hopes of the nationalist minority by including provisions for a boundary commission.

The influence of territorial changes on the European mainland on the arrangements of 1920–21 for Ireland was greater than generally realised. Territorial partition of provinces had become a fully acceptable solution. The exact positioning of new frontiers in most cases was agreed only after holding

---

[3] Memo, 10 Feb. 1920, quoted in Michael Laffan, *The partition of Ireland 1911–1925* (Dundalk, 1983), p. 64.

plebiscites as, for example, was the case with Germany's borders under the treaty of Versailles in Upper Saxony, Schleswig, Marienwerder, and Allenstein. In some other cases frontiers determined in Paris by conference and treaty were subsequently altered by armed conflict as, for example, between Poland and Russia, and Greece and Turkey.

The cataclysm of total war in Europe made possible the most conscientious attempt ever undertaken to give every nationality its own state. In spite of this, only a very few of the new states emerging from collapsed empires had a fairly homogeneous ethnic composition. More than 25 million people, it has been estimated, found themselves as national minorities after the imposition of the postwar treaties. For example, only two-thirds of the inhabitants of Poland spoke Polish after the successful war against Russia in 1920–21. There were 4.6 million Germans, Poles, Ruthenes, and Magyars in Czechoslovakia out of a total population of 14.3 million.

In central Europe language was generally the badge of ethnic distinction, but not always. In the new Yugoslavia the four main ethnic groups—Serbs, Croats, Slovenes, and Muslims—were distinguished primarily by different religious affiliation and cultural traditions. This was the case in Ireland: despite its pivotal importance for nationalists, Irish was the native tongue of only a small minority. In Ireland religion was the ethnic divider, where the vast majority of protestants wanted to remain in the United Kingdom and, with the support of only a sprinkling of protestants drawn mostly from the intelligentsia, nearly all catholics sought a united Ireland independent of Britain. For British governments the compromise solution was to partition the island, giving dominion status on the Canadian model to the twenty-six counties of the Irish Free State and setting up a devolved administration in the remaining six counties of Northern Ireland.

Altered circumstances in the wake of the first world war may have enabled northern unionists to secure most of their demands, but a partitioned island fell far short of the ideals of nationalists of every variety, even during the period when a boundary commission seemed to promise substantial territorial alterations to the advantage of the Irish Free State. The Ulster Unionist Council in 1916 had decided to abandon those who had signed the Covenant in the counties of Monaghan, Cavan, and Donegal, to make certain that the electorate of Northern Ireland could never vote the region out of the union. However, the six north-eastern counties contained a very large minority, one-third of the population, who felt no allegiance to the devolved government in Belfast. Indeed, northern catholics felt their position had deteriorated substantially with the establishment of an administration that would be certain to be unionist for the forseeable future and beyond. Like Germans in Czechoslovakia and Poland, and Hungarians in Transylvania, the catholics of Northern Ireland wanted nothing less than the destruction of the state into which they had been placed. Protestants, who had only formed a majority in the historic province since 1871, therefore had their sense of deep insecurity nurtured rather than removed by the government of Ireland act. The political life of Northern Ireland was to be marked by two apparently contradictory features: rigidity, arising from highly predictable electoral outcomes; and instability, the consequence of inherited hostilities and fears sustained rather than reduced by the constitutional arrangements of 1920–21.

Blood continued to flow on the European mainland after the armistice, and during and after the Paris peace conference. Millions died of hunger and disease in the Russian civil war; brutal street battles fought between fascists and revolutionary socialists in northern Italian cities signalled the start of the collapse of democracy all over central Europe; Spartacists, Freikorps, and putschists delivered devastating blows to the November republic in Germany; and in the new central and eastern European states, deadly ethnic struggles raged. In these years Northern Ireland seemed to resemble states such as Poland and Greece rather more closely than the settled democracies of north-western Europe.

The violence in Northern Ireland between 1920 and 1922 exacted a heavier toll in blood than all the northern sectarian riots and affrays of the nineteenth century put together. The conflict was part of a wider struggle over the political future of the whole island, but it was at the same time a violent episode very different in character from the Anglo–Irish war in the other three provinces. Much more than is often acknowledged, in Ulster it was an ethnic conflict between people who, though they had intermarried for generations and could be distinguished neither by look nor dialect, felt themselves to be profoundly separate. The bitterness nourished over three centuries gushed to the surface, particularly along the invisible frontiers dividing catholic and protestant enclaves in Belfast and Derry.

The catholic minority reacted bitterly to the new political arrangements, while the protestant majority zealously fought to prevent their prize being taken from them by the I.R.A. and their allies. Even with the support of regular troops, the new administration in Belfast appeared to struggle to survive in the face of violence and dislocation. The Anglo–Irish treaty of 1921 magnified the conflict in Northern Ireland: protestants, particularly along the border, felt immediately threatened by possible boundary commission awards, while catholics, especially in the Belfast region, felt abandoned both by London and Dublin. Catholics living in areas with nationalist majorities such as Tyrone and south Armagh exulted in the likelihood of being assigned to the Free State, and some seized the opportunity to dislocate the local administration still further, believing that Northern Ireland could not long survive. The result was that the first six months of 1922 were the most violent of the period.

Any feelings of magnanimity expressed by Craig and his government were set aside as the violence increased: the unionist M.P.s voted for exceptional powers, created a heavily armed police force, and greatly expanded the exclusively protestant special constabulary in order to crush the threat from within. The threat from without was suddenly spirited away by the outbreak of civil war in the Free State in June 1922. Indeed, that conflict drew some of the most determined republican militants southwards to fight on both sides, and by the beginning of 1923 Northern Ireland was at peace.

Hopes and fears rose and dipped on steep gradients in Northern Ireland's first years, and by the end of 1925 it was clear that it was the expectations of catholics there that had been most comprehensively dashed. Civil war averted southern eyes from a regular viewing of their plight, and all but removed any ability to provide northern catholics with meaningful assistance. That conflict delayed the implementation of the boundary commission clauses of the Anglo–Irish treaty. When it was set up in 1924, the commission bore only a passing resemblance to those that operated in other parts of Europe immediately after the war: not one of the commissioners could be described as truly disinterested and, above all, there was no plebiscite— Balfour argued that referendums were only suited to defeated enemies: 'Ireland is not like a conquered state, which we can carve up as in central Europe.'[4]

The suppression of the commissioners' report, and the agreement between Dublin, London, and Belfast in December 1925, finally removed hopes and fears that the political arrangement of 1920 could be revised. This did produce quiescence, and in a region where the 'ordinary' crime rate was the lowest in the United Kingdom there was not one sectarian murder between 1923 and 1933. The outward calm did not, however, signal political contentment. Unionists, despite their victories, felt permanently threatened by such a large minority, which, it seemed, would seize the first opportunity to dislocate the economy and give succour to republican men of violence. At all levels of society, protestants remained constantly vigilant, and 'rotten Prods'—those who espoused nationalist or left-wing socialist ideals—were hardy souls indeed. Catholics, feeling abandoned by friends in the south and at Westminster, and oppressed by the devolved administration in Belfast, forlornly put their faith in an agitation against the partition of the island—a campaign that only rarely showed any prospect of success.

In its discontents, Northern Ireland resembled many of the states that had emerged from the wreck of the German, Russian, Austro–Hungarian, and Turkish empires. The region was, however, still part of a surviving empire and could call on the resources of the London government in times of difficulty. Unlike most central European states, Northern Ireland did not have to cope with the evils of landlordism; and like Czechoslovakia, but unlike most of the other successor states, the region had a well-developed industrial base

---

[4] Balfour to Lloyd George, 2 Nov. 1921, quoted ibid., p. 64.

and a middle class from which competent civil servants could be recruited. The middle class was smaller in proportion than in the Irish Free State, but (despite grave economic difficulties) living standards were marginally higher in the north-east than in the rest of the island. Nevertheless, the economic benefits of being part of the United Kingdom were limited during the inter-war years. The extraordinarily byzantine financial arrangements in the 1920 act had been finalised before the postwar boom had petered out. No one predicted that the traditional export industries would experience constant difficulties from the slump of the winter 1920–21 onwards. Elaborate provisions concerning 'excepted services', 'reserved services', and the 'imperial contribution' left the government of Northern Ireland in control of less than 20 per cent of its revenues. In addition, local government bodies shouldered only a fifth of 'domestic' expenditure in the region, and conservative attitudes prevailing throughout the community defeated most attempts to tackle local social problems by increasing the rates.

The period of intercommunal calm that began in 1923 gave the unionist government the opportunity to help heal both old wounds and new ones sustained during the intense unrest of 1920–22. With vivid recent reminders that one-third of the population sought the regime's downfall, and stung by mounting criticism in the British press, Craig's team was slow to attempt remedial action. The Northern Ireland government did not create the deep divisions in the community, but it did little to alleviate them. Unlike the great majority of states in central and eastern Europe, Northern Ireland remained a democracy, but corrupt practices inherited from the nineteenth century were allowed to survive and some were reinforced. Virtually no effort was made by government to ensure that the region had an all-embracing inclusive democracy.

Recalcitrance was demonstrated by both sides. In the nineteenth century, catholics in Ulster had been overwhelmingly confined to the lower rungs of the social ladder, and this situation had changed only marginally when the government of Ireland act was being implemented. The catholic minority, therefore, had a comparatively small pool of people with education and means from which political leaders could be drawn. The silver-tongued Joseph Devlin was an experienced parliamentarian, but in 1921 he was past his best, and he was not succeeded by anyone of his calibre till the middle 1960s. The catholic minority did not pull together politically: republicans were committed to abstention and non-cooperation, even when they suspended the armed struggle; and the nationalists were divided in their attitudes to repartition (apparently promised in the boundary commission) and then on whether or not their representatives should take their seats in the Belfast parliament. The prominent role of catholic clergy in nationalist politics helped to sustain protestant suspicion and was the natural outcome of the shortage of able lay leaders, particularly in rural areas.

The unionists took advantage of catholic divisions and reluctance to participate by abolishing proportional representation in local government elections in 1922[5] and then by meticulously revising electoral boundaries to their advantage. Proportional representation was abolished in elections for the Northern Ireland parliament in 1929;[6] though manipulation of boundaries was this time more restrained, nationalist resentment was just as strong. Proportional representation had been introduced by Westminster in 1920 to ensure fairness for the minority, and Craig's removal of this safeguard had baleful consequences for the future. Because of the divisions in Northern Ireland society and the geographical distribution of the two communities, the 1929 reversal drastically reduced local democratic activity: there had been only eight uncontested seats in 1925 but by 1933 there were thirty-three.

The determination of the catholic church to control its schools, even to the exclusion of lay members of its own flock, was in part responsible for catholic disadvantage in education. Nevertheless, the education act of 1923 breached the safeguarding terms of the government of Ireland act, and ensured that state schools were in effect protestant schools more generously funded than catholic ones; a situation only partly remedied by the 1930 act,[7] which made 'simple Bible instruction'—completely unacceptable to catholics—mandatory in state schools. Petty corruption and unfair influence was rife in local government appointments both north and south; in Northern Ireland, after the abolition of proportional representation, this worked to unionist advantage. The civil service enforced higher standards but no attempt was made there to ensure adequate catholic representation, especially in the higher grades. Taking a lead from Sir James Craig himself, other ministers, notably J. M. Andrews, Dawson Bates, and Sir E. M. Archdale, actively discouraged the appointment of catholics.

The government of Ireland act gave Westminster the authority to intervene, but that power was not exercised. Supervision of devolved administration in Northern Ireland from London was perfunctory, as successive Westminster governments attempted to cope with mass unemployment, the burden of the national debt, crises on the European mainland, and imperial difficulties in India, the middle east, and elsewhere. The view in Whitehall was that the Irish question had largely been solved. The economic ailments that afflicted established industrial regions in Britain from 1921 onwards had a similar impact on Belfast, Derry, and other towns dependent on producing linen, ships, and engineering products primarily for export. The first world war had drastically altered trading conditions, and Northern Ireland experienced mounting difficulties in attempting to sell goods in surplus abroad.

[5] 12 & 13 Geo. V, c. 15 (11 Sept. 1922).
[6] 19 Geo. V, c. 5 (16 Apr. 1929).
[7] 20 & 21 Geo. V, c. 14 (17 June 1930).

The fate of Belfast and Derry was similar to that of other industrial ports such as Glasgow, Liverpool, and Newcastle upon Tyne. The creation of a new frontier in 1921 and the violence accompanying the birth of Northern Ireland probably only had a marginal impact, in that the new light industries making electrical and white goods, and automobile manufacturing firms, preferred the midlands and south-east of England. The Belfast administration had meagre powers to give special assistance, though it seems likely that loans and guarantees voted in the Northern Ireland parliament saved Harland & Wolff from closure.

In a 1924 census of production 51.77 per cent of Northern Ireland's total labour force was employed in making linen. The grave problems facing this industry were not the result of inefficiency and poor marketing but arose from a long-term decline in world demand for this textile and a fall in cotton prices. Production levels remained high but margins were narrow and wages were wretchedly low. Wages were far higher in engineering and shipbuilding, but there the problem was reduced output. In the 1920s around one-fifth of all insured workers had no jobs. The impact of the depression following the Wall Street crash of 1929 was probably greater on Northern Ireland than on the Irish Free State. By 1933 the volume of international trade dropped to barely one-third of what it had been on the eve of the stock market collapse. Not a single ship was launched at Queen's Island between 10 December 1931 and 1 May 1934, and in 1935 Workman Clark, once one of the world's most productive yards, closed down. In the 1930s around 27 per cent of insured workers were unemployed in what had become the most economically disadvantaged region of the United Kingdom.

The Northern Ireland government made desperate attempts to keep 'step-by-step' with the rest of the United Kingdom in the provision of welfare services, but in the interwar years it was often unsuccessful. The poor law remained after it had been phased out in Britain, and the niggardly and humiliating relief given by the Belfast guardians precipitated outdoor-relief riots on a large scale in 1932, which briefly witnessed a measure of cooperation between protestants and catholics in the city. Prevailing poverty caused an increase in maternal mortality by one-fifth between 1922 and 1938 and, when compared with six British cities, Belfast had the highest infant mortality rate (it had the lowest in 1901). The mortality rate from tuberculosis was higher than in the Irish Free State and 20 per cent higher in Northern Ireland than in the rest of the United Kingdom. The steady deterioration in the region's housing stock, a consequence of the cautious approach to public housing by comparison with Britain, does much to explain the poor statistics on the health of Northern Ireland's citizens.

The shared experience of poverty did not lead to anything but the most ephemeral cooperation between protestants and catholics. Indeed, there was much evidence of deteriorating relationships in the 1930s. In part this was the consequence of Fianna Fáil's accession to power, the economic war, and the 1937 constitution. The border became a greater barrier to trade, and Dublin's anti-partitionist rhetoric prompted inflammatory speeches by unionist government ministers. Fierce though localised riots ensued in Belfast in 1935, resulting in thirteen deaths. Westminster turned down nationalist requests for an inquiry.

The outbreak of war in 1939 found the government of Northern Ireland very poorly prepared to cope with the world crisis. With an unassailable majority the administration had grown complacent. The average age of ministers was 62 in 1938, and by 1939 only twelve individuals had served in government. International conflict converted the border into a chasm, and the experience of those living to the north and south of it was to be profoundly different. Refusing to believe that Northern Ireland was exposed to real danger, little was done to protect citizens from attack, and after Craig had died in 1940 there was no increased sense of urgency. Belfast was the most unprotected major city in the United Kingdom, and as a consequence it lost more citizens in one night's air raid than any other city save London. Over one thousand people were killed or wounded in Belfast on the night of 15–16 April 1941, and on 4–5 May 1941 great damage was inflicted on the shipyards and aircraft factory. The direction of the war was altered by the invasion of Soviet Russia, and eventually Northern Ireland became a significant Allied arsenal and the United States' first base in western Europe. Southern neutrality ensured that Northern Ireland's harbours and aerodromes had a vital role to play in the battle of the Atlantic. The Westminster government was to show its gratitude after the war in a very practical way.

The German air raids exposed to public view the extent of deprivation and social neglect of the previous two decades. Even before the end of the war decisive remedial action was being taken, and the welfare legislation of the Labour government brought about the most striking improvement in the quality of life of citizens of Northern Ireland since its foundation. Such progress was made possible by the willingness of London to underwrite the cost, over and above that collected in taxation in the region. The shared experience of hardship during the war only temporarily damped down intercommunal rivalry, which reappeared with its former virulence following Taoiseach John Costello's announcement of his government's intention to declare a republic.

A great many who lived in Northern Ireland, and most of those beyond who bothered to take an interest in the region's affairs, assumed that steady progress was being made and that the inexorable advance of modernisation would ensure the marginalisation of sectarian and political bitterness. The I.R.A. campaign of 1956–62 mainly impacted on the border areas and was shattered by the eventual willingness of the Dublin government to intern suspect activists. There was no postwar economic slump, and while there

were grave difficulties as traditional industries ran down, the Northern Ireland government was imaginative and energetic in attracting external investment and multinational firms to the region. Captain Terence O'Neill, who
had replaced Lord Brookeborough in 1963 as prime minister, had been responsible for the more dynamic approach to economic regeneration and was
the first premier to state clearly that reconciliation was a central part of his
programme.

In retrospect, the conquests made by late twentieth-century modernisation
were strictly limited. O'Neill always faced serious criticism in the protestant
community, and eventually from within his own party. In the end he alarmed
many traditional supporters by seeming too eager to appease the minority,
and at the same time he created intense frustration among catholics by raising hopes of change but—in spite of frequent public displays of friendli-
ness—failing to deliver reforms of substance.

The huge increase in public expenditure after 1945 aggravated inequities
and petty injustices firmly in place since 1921. Local authorities augmented
the number of their employees and had responsibility for many services,
including council housing. The manipulation of local government boundaries
to unionist advantage put several councils, in particular west of the River
Bann, permanently in unionist control where catholics and nationalists were in
the majority. In a region where catholics were poorer on average than protestants, the refusal of postwar Stormont governments to follow Britain step-
by-step, when Westminster removed property restrictions on local government franchise, prevented any reduction of electoral disadvantage. The
blatant discrimination in favour of protestants in local appointments and in
the allocation of council houses was matched by poor representation of catholics in the senior and middle ranks of the civil service and on public bodies.
No legislation sought to ensure fairness in appointments in the private
sectors, where most leading employers were protestant. The impact of educational reforms was slowly felt, but by the end of the 1960s a significant
cohort of catholics from comparatively humble origins were receiving university education or had just graduated; these were to be in the van of the civil-
rights movement.

The adoption of direct but non-violent protest against discrimination and
unfairness can be dated back to the occupation of prefabricated dwellings by
seventeen catholic families in Dungannon in 1963. Developing from modest
beginnings, the civil-rights movement drew inspiration from the black civil-
rights movement in America, protests against the Vietnam war, and, later,
student direct action in Paris and the pacific defiance of Soviet military
power in Prague. O'Neill made many mould-breaking gestures, but local
government was not reformed and fair systems in making public appointments and in allocating council houses were not adopted. The prime minister's courage in inviting Taoiseach Seán Lemass to Stormont in 1965 at the

same time alienated key members of the Unionist party and gave fresh support for loyalist opposition led by the Rev. Ian Paisley.

Action by the civil-rights movement was projected suddenly on to the international stage by television coverage of a march in Derry on 5 October 1968: images of unrestrained police batoning unarmed demonstrators flashed across the world. Henceforth Northern Ireland was destabilised, as a bewildering succession of marches, protests, riots, and explosions led to O'Neill's resignation in April 1969, followed by intense conflict in the summer, culminating in the 'battle of the Bogside' in Derry and the violent deaths of ten people by the middle of August.

For more than forty years British governments had exercised the minimum of interference in the only region of the United Kingdom with a devolved administration. Now decisive action was imperative, and government ministers and civil servants alike had to acquaint themselves with the salient features of the situation at great speed. The 1920 government of Ireland act could have been invoked and direct rule from London reinstated. Harold Wilson's government preferred to limit itself to placing troops on active service in the streets and arranging for the implementation of a package of reforms. The original demands of the civil-rights movement had largely been met, but the hatreds of the past had welled up to the surface to sustain a bitter conflict. British soldiers were placed under the authority of Stormont, and this assisted the emergence of a new militant republican force, the Provisional I.R.A. The unionist government reacted to republican violence by imposing internment in August 1971: this signally failed in its objectives and provoked intense catholic alienation. The final nail in the coffin of the Stormont regime was delivered by the killings of 'Bloody Sunday' in Derry on 30 January 1972. Direct rule was imposed at the end of March 1972.

The devolved administration was suspended originally for a year as Edward Heath's Conservative government hoped that a new local body could be put in place during that time, capable of satisfying a substantial proportion of both catholics and protestants. In dealing with Northern Ireland successive Westminster governments sought to end—or at least curb—violence; to restore a devolved elected assembly in which representatives from the unionist and nationalist communities would share administrative power; and to improve relations between London and Dublin, principally by finding some way of recognising the all-Ireland aspirations of the catholic minority without alienating the protestant majority.

Britain was facing the longest-running conflict in western Europe since the end of the second world war. The year 1972 was the worst in terms of lives lost, people maimed, and property destroyed, but direct rule failed to stem the violence and year after year the population endured a cycle of bombings, assassinations, and shootings. Rejecting the full integration of Northern

Ireland into the rest of the United Kingdom, the Conservative government brokered a remarkable agreement at Sunningdale towards the end of 1973 which provided for a power-sharing administration and the revivification of the 'council of Ireland', provided for in the 1920 act, to promote greater formal collaboration between Dublin and Belfast. The power-sharing executive failed to win the support of a majority of protestants and fell apart during one of the most successful political strikes in Europe for decades. Attempts to make fresh arrangements for a local power-sharing body came to nothing thereafter.

In the absence of a political solution, successive British governments sought to curb republican and loyalist paramilitary violence, to promote economic regeneration, and to upgrade public services. In the overhauled local government structure, elected councillors found their responsibilities drastically reduced as the provision of public housing, social services, health care, and education and library services became the remit of largely appointed boards. The Housing Executive began its task as, in the words of a government minister, 'the largest slum landlord in Europe': in Northern Ireland as a whole 19.6 per cent of the total dwelling stock was statutorily unfit, compared with 7.3 per cent in England and Wales. The organisation established and maintained a reputation for impartiality, but the existence of thirteen 'peace lines' in Belfast was a visible sign that housing a divided community presented exceptional problems. It was not till the end of 1981 that the government agreed to make housing its first social priority in Northern Ireland. By the mid 1980s the Housing Executive was able to spend around £100 million a year on its capital programme, reducing the unfitness level for the region to 8.4 per cent by 1987.

The Ulster Workers Council strike in May 1974 coincided with a leap in world oil prices and the onset of a long period of economic difficulties in Northern Ireland. The synthetic fibre industry was severely affected, leading to the closure of Courtaulds in Carrickfergus in 1979 and British Enkalon in Antrim in 1981. Manufacturing declined by 5 per cent annually between 1973 and 1979, a period when jobs were being lost even faster in the multinationals than in the traditional export industries. The decline became a crisis after the return of a Conservative administration in 1979. Between 1979 and 1981 110 substantial firms in the region closed down. The De Lorean sports car factory failed in May 1982 and Goodyear closed its plant in July 1983. The business failure rate in 1989 was 22 per cent in Northern Ireland compared with 9.7 per cent in England and Wales.

The public sector gross domestic product in Northern Ireland rose from 33 per cent of the whole in 1974 to 44 per cent in 1986. This was made possible only by the British subvention—money transferred from Westminster over and above the sum raised in taxation in Northern Ireland—which increased from less than £100 million in 1972 to £1.6 billion in 1988–9. The bulk of the subvention was spent not on aid to industry, nor on security, but on the public services. A particular problem was that of equality of opportunity: in 1971 catholic males were 2.6 times as likely to be unemployed as protestant males, and this proportion had only fallen to 2.5 by 1985. Though protestants had lost jobs in manufacturing, the policy of 'Ulsterisation' ensured that nearly one in ten of all protestant men were in paid employment in the security forces in some capacity by the late 1980s. In 1989 the Fair Employment Agency was replaced by the Fair Employment Commission, with stronger powers, in a new attempt to address this issue.

Levels of violence continued to be extremely high till the end of 1976 and, in addition, republican militants took their campaigns to Britain in an attempt to make the withdrawal of British troops a major issue: the most horrific bombings were in 1974 on the M62 and in Guildford, Woolwich, and Birmingham. The events of Monday 27 August 1979, when eighteen soldiers were killed at Warrenpoint, and Earl Mountbatten, his grandson Nicholas, Paul Maxwell, and Dowager Lady Brabourne were killed at Mullaghmore, galvanised the new Conservative government into fresh attempts to work out solutions with Dublin. Early approaches seemed encouraging, but relations between the two capitals were damaged by the H-block hunger strike which began in March 1981.

The funeral that followed the death of Bobby Sands on the sixty-sixth day of refusing food in the Maze prison in May 1981 saw at least 100,000 people line the route to Milltown cemetery. The strike only ended in October 1981 after ten men had starved themselves to death. Electoral successes by Provisional Sinn Féin alarmed both London and Dublin. Taoiseach Garret FitzGerald organised a multi-party conference, the New Ireland Forum, which began in May 1983 and published a report in May 1984. Margaret Thatcher's public rejection of the three options offered in the report seemed to ruin any chance of accommodation. The bombing of the Conservative party conference at Brighton on 12 October 1984 by the Provisional I.R.A., however, made the prime minister determined to develop formal talks between the London and Dublin governments. The outcome was a historic settlement, the Anglo–Irish agreement signed at Hillsborough Castle on 15 November 1985.

The most striking characteristic of Northern Ireland in this period was the depth of its intercommunal division. The propensity of its inhabitants to look back to distant events pointed to another notable characteristic: conservatism. Like the rest of Ireland, though to a lesser extent, the six north-eastern counties had seen a fall in population due to emigration, in the second half of the nineteenth century, of the most energetic, radical, and discontented young adults, which helped to reinforce traditional attitudes.

The population of the six north-eastern counties had stabilised when Northern Ireland was being created, and thereafter it rose gently until the onset of violence in 1969 helped to create another plateau. The concentration of population in Belfast was reversed as people moved out to other areas east of the Bann. The 'troubles' discouraged inward migration by, for example, people from the Asian subcontinent. The result was that by the end of the period Northern Ireland had—if sectarian divisions are not included—the most homogeneous population in the United Kingdom. Conservatism was reinforced further by the tendency of the ablest of young adults to leave the region: in 1991 it was shown that emigrants were better qualified than the population at large.

Conservatism is illustrated by the tardy progress made by women in seeking greater equality with men in Northern Ireland. Only seventeen women stood as parliamentary candidates between 1921 and 1972, and no more than nine were ever elected, mostly for the Queen's University seats. It was only in 1953 that a woman was elected to Westminster. Marriage bars in the civil service, the teaching profession, and banking were not removed till the late 1960s. The women's movement took off properly only with the formation of the Northern Ireland Women's Rights Movement in 1975 and the lead given by women in the 'Peace people' the following year.

For most of the period the press was firmly in the hands of conservatives, whether unionist or nationalist, and it was left to a journal from another state, the *Irish Times*, to provide detailed analytical reports on the region's political affairs before the 'troubles' began. Broadcasting began in 1924, and until the 1960s the B.B.C. did not behave with the same political independence as in other regions in the United Kingdom. Dramatic liberalisation followed in the years after 1968.

The conservative architectural style of the parliament buildings at Stormont, opened in 1932, seemed to reflect the resistance of the inhabitants to the new. It was not till the 1970s that there was any sign that the vigour and imagination shown by Victorian and Edwardian architects in Belfast could be revived.

In the nineteenth century Ulster, and Belfast in particular, had apparently not been a centre for the creative arts; it was in the years of economic difficulty after the first world war that the north was to shake off its reputation for being a cultural wasteland. John Lavery was the first citizen of Belfast to win international fame as a painter, and others, such as Paul Henry, William Conor, and T. P. Flanagan, later achieved wide acclaim. The Belfast Museum and Art Gallery and the Belfast College of Art, along with linen firms, did much to promote local talent. Probably the finest sculptor was F. E. McWilliam, who created deeply moving images of the violence of the 1970s.

In the twentieth century Ulster, and subsequently Northern Ireland, produced a succession of outstanding writers who achieved large audiences far beyond Ireland's shores. They included Louis MacNeice, C. S. Lewis, John

Hewitt, and John Montague, and the list grows rapidly as the 1947 education act took effect to add the poets Seamus Heaney, Michael Longley, Medbh McGuckian, Derek Mahon, and many others; playwrights Stewart Parker and Brian Friel; and novelists Bernard McLaverty and Glenn Patterson. Whether or not the violence stimulated creativity is open to debate, but there is little doubt that Northern Ireland had become a flourishing centre of artistic activity by the end of the period.

THE Irish Free State was, in the eyes of Eamon de Valera and his supporters, born out of a process of revolution followed by a process of counter-revolution in which the signatories of the Anglo–Irish treaty on 6 December 1921 lacked the courage to press on to lay firm foundations for the ultimate establishment of an independent thirty-two-county republic.

For the chairman of the provisional government, William T. Cosgrave, an independent administration with dominion status had been secured through the revolution brought about during the Anglo–Irish war (1919–21), and the defeat of dissident militant elements, the anti-treatyites, during the civil war (1922–3). That war had claimed the life of (among others) Cosgrave's predecessor as chairman, Michael Collins, in the summer of 1922. However, a decisive victory was secured by the Free State government in spring 1923 in a war that was all too often characterised by a lack of chivalry on both sides and by the government's use of extra-judicial powers. For the revolutionary anti-treatyites the civil war was a war of liberation, fought against fellow Irishmen who were proxies for the British government. By contrast Cosgrave's government saw the anti-treatyite forces as insurrectionists, or 'Irregulars' in the language of the day, who had refused to obey the legitimate authority of the new state.

The lines of an Austin Clarke poem aptly capture the ambiguous sentiments of revolutionary anti-treatyites and of those liberal constitutionalists who viewed with disdain the extra-judicial actions of the Free State government:

> They are the spit of virtue now.
> Prating of law and honour,
> But we remember how they shot
> Rory O'Connor.[8]

The O'Connor in question was the leader of the Four Courts 'garrison' in Dublin which had surrendered on 30 June 1922. He was one of four anti-treatyite leaders imprisoned in Mountjoy prison who were executed on 8 December 1922 as a reprisal following the shooting, while on his way to

[8] 'Sentences: civil war 2', in Austin Clarke, *Selected poems*, ed. Thomas Kinsella (Dublin, 1976), p. 16.

Dáil Éireann, of a pro-treaty deputy, Seán Hales. (The *leas ceann comhairle* (deputy speaker), Pádraic Ó Máille, was wounded in the same attack on 7 December.) The executions had the desired effect: the anti-treatyites abandoned their tactics of shooting leading politicians. The government, however, continued the policy of executions: seventy-seven had taken place by the end of the civil war in May 1923. The precise number of those killed during the civil war, including partisans on both sides and innocent bystanders, is difficult to determine, but it is generally agreed that the figure was in excess of one thousand. Though the fatalities were small in number by the standards of civil wars in other countries, the conflict cast a long shadow and had a profound influence on the political culture of the Irish Free State.

During the remainder of the 1920s, and beyond, each side continued to celebrate its own carefully tailored martyrology and develop its own mythology. Yet, when Cosgrave died in 1965, President de Valera expressed his regret that political differences dating from the treaty should have marred their previous personal friendship. De Valera may never have realised it, but in the still unsettled times following the end of the civil war hostilities in May 1923 he perhaps owed his life to the decision by Cosgrave and the Free State authorities to place him in 'protective custody'. The arrest took place on 15 August of that year in Ennis, County Clare, in the middle of a speech to crowds of followers during a general election rally. De Valera accordingly remained in Arbour Hill and Kilmainham jails until his release on 16 July 1924, by which time the new state was in a stronger position to impose the rule of law.

De Valera and Cosgrave may never again have enjoyed the personal friendship of pre-civil-war years, but that did not mean a loss of mutual respect. The two men differed on political issues, but de Valera was to use the instruments of government established by the treaty and the Free State constitution to achieve ends not altogether dissimilar from those of Cosgrave: the building of a democracy bound by liberal constitutional principles.

After much deliberation and soul-searching, de Valera broke with the abstentionist wing of Sinn Féin on 11 March 1926, founded the Fianna Fáil party on 16 May, and entered Dáil Éireann a year later on 11 August 1927 with those deputies who supported him. They took the hitherto unacceptable oath of allegiance, describing it as 'merely an empty political formula', and then took their seats. Cosgrave's government has been praised for forcing that outcome, which turned out to be a decisive step on the road to securing and strengthening the fledgling democratic system in Ireland.

The civil war had a distorting influence on the development of the Irish party system. Political scientists have tried and failed to provide an adequate model to explain the development of what has been described as a 'two-and-a-half party system'—Cumann na nGaedheal (later Fine Gael), Fianna Fáil, and the 'half' an under-performing Irish Labour party. Models have been devised, models based on cleavages between treatyite enlightenment values and anti-treatyite romanticism, and also between nationalist pragmatism and republican moralism.[9] However suggestive and useful such models may be, they fail to convey the complexity of the reasons for the taking of sides in the wake of the treaty split and subsequent civil war. The use of an archivally based historical method reveals the fallaciousness of the thesis that the fault-line caused in Irish public life by the treaty split was a clean ideological, political, or social division. A survey of memoirs and relevant archives demonstrates that choice of sides could be affected by chance location and geography; patronage and recruitment to the Garda Síochána and national army; the views of a strong local commander; the influence of the local press; and the advice provided by the leaders of the churches and of the trade union movement. The stance of the Gaelic Athletic Association and other national organisations also affected the choice of sides.

Further local studies of the war of independence and the civil war will reveal the complex nature of the origins of the Irish party system. But for whatever reason, the Labour party remained politically subordinate to the two 'civil war' parties—Fianna Fáil and Cumann na nGaedheal. Led by Tom Johnson, Labour supported the treaty settlement and provided the main opposition to Cumann na nGaedheal in Dáil Éireann between 1922 and 1927. Labour was, for most of that time, little more than a one-man opposition, but Johnson, as this one-man opposition, nevertheless played a vital role in the development of the Irish democratic system.

The dissident and defeated Irish Republican Army (I.R.A.) maintained a political front: Sinn Féin. That party failed to attract mass support in the south after the mid 1920s. The I.R.A., based mainly in the south from the 1920s, remained an active enemy of the Irish Free State, intimidating and murdering witnesses and plotting quixotically to bring down the government in Dublin. The Free State government felt the deadly echoes of civil war directly, on 10 July 1927, when the minister for justice, Kevin O'Higgins, was assassinated on his way to mass in Booterstown church, County Dublin. De Valera immediately called his death murder, and said that it was 'inexcusable from any standpoint ...It is a crime that cuts at the root of representative government'.[10] Those words were uttered only a few weeks before Fianna Fáil entered Dáil Éireann.

THE treaty was, as Michael Collins had once fruitlessly pointed out to de Valera, a 'stepping stone' providing 'the freedom to achieve freedom'. But

---

[9] See Tom Garvin, *1922: the birth of Irish democracy* (Dublin, 1996), pp 139–51.
[10] Maurice Moynihan (ed.), *Speeches and statements by Eamon de Valera 1917–1973* (Dublin, 1980), p. 149.

Collins did not live to witness that evolution. He and Arthur Griffith, president of Dáil Éireann, died within ten days of each other in August 1922. This thrust Cosgrave into the foreground. Ever in the shadow of Collins, Cosgrave appeared to be a most unlikely successor to that soldier politician and to Griffith. In the 1920s, Cosgrave's photographs reveal him as being a model of middle-class respectability—low sized and of slight, spare physique, he sported a neat moustache and usually wore a starched white shirt with winged collar, a dark tie, rumpled suit under a black crombie, and bowler hat. Yet he and his ministerial colleagues were not without revolutionary pedigree. One of Cosgrave's forebears had been hanged for seditious activities during the 1798 rising. The family involvement in radical politics had obliged his grandfather to move from Wexford to Kildare. Born in James's Street, Dublin, in 1880, Cosgrave worked in his father's public house. At 18 he became involved in nationalist politics. He attended the inaugural convention of Arthur Griffith's Sinn Féin movement in 1905.

Cosgrave served as a radical nationalist member of Dublin corporation from 1909, joined B Company of the Irish Volunteers in 1913, fought in the garrison of the South Dublin Union in 1916, and was sentenced to death. The sentence was commuted and Cosgrave remained in jail till his release in January 1917. He became a treasurer of Sinn Féin, and an alderman on Dublin corporation. Elected in 1918 for the constituency of Carlow–Kilkenny, he was appointed minister for local government in the first Dáil Éireann. He took the pro-treaty side, and succeeded Michael Collins as chairman of the provisional government on 25 August 1922, becoming president of the executive council of the Irish Free State on 6 December 1922.

The above is hardly the profile of a conventional politician. Cosgrave was called on many times during the 1920s to display firmness and qualities of strong and decisive leadership. That strength was most in evidence on the numerous occasions when the government found it necessary to pilot emergency anti-subversion legislation through Dáil Éireann. Illness—the nature of which has not been fully explained—prevented Cosgrave from taking a dominant leadership position in 1924 during the 'army mutiny', or more accurately, 'army crisis'. Dissident elements in the army gave the government an ultimatum on 6 March to halt the process of demobilisation. (The plan was for the army to be reduced from over 50,000 to half that number.) The crisis, which was also rooted in other grievances, was quickly averted, but not before the resignation of two ministers and three of the army's highest-ranking officers. But the 'army crisis' never remotely reached Bonapartist proportions, threatening a *coup d'état*. It was a measure of the professionalism of the army that Ireland, unlike other new states, never underwent a phase of direct military rule in its formative years.

There has yet to be full recognition of the role played by Cosgrave and the Cumann na nGaedheal generation in the development of a democratic state. In the 1920s the apparently rudimentary and mundane task of state-building appeared far less exciting to many contemporaries than the revolutionary struggle. Yet Cosgrave and his colleagues gave the country a professional army, an unarmed police force, an efficient transport system, new coinage, and educational and social reform. Above all, perhaps, Cumann na nGaedheal managed to secure the functioning of a national court system under an independent judiciary. The writ of the government ran throughout the country, helping to establish the rule of law and return the country to a sense of normality.

An impecunious government, burdened by the debts incurred in reconstruction following the civil war, also tackled agricultural reform. The minister responsible, Patrick Hogan, brought in the land acts of 1923,[11] which reconstituted the land commission, abolishing the congested districts board and the estates commission. Hogan did much during his ten-year term in office to stimulate farming reform under difficult free-trade conditions. And all accounts of the Cumann na nGaedheal government celebrate the building of the successful Shannon hydro-electric scheme (1925-9) which helped initiate the mass electrification of the country. It was imaginatively conceived and showed real vision for the achievement of rapid industrialisation.

Post-revolutionary Ireland, living with expectations elevated unrealistically by the political rhetoric of 1919-21, did not provide the government with much opportunity to achieve rapid or radical social reform. Emigration continued, with over 220,000 people leaving for the United States between 1921 and 1930. Those numbers were reduced radically only when the country was affected by the international depression in the late 1920s. The minister for finance, Ernest Blythe, may have made many good decisions during his tenure of office, but he will be most remembered for his reduction of old-age pensions in 1924, and for cutting the pay of national teachers and gardaí in 1931—the year before a general election.

His colleague the minister for education (1922-5), Eoin MacNeill, was an effective and creative manager of a portfolio that established a highly centralised system of educational control. His progressive ideas, and those of his predecessor, J. J. O' Kelly, for the teaching of Irish are only beginning to be acknowledged, as are Cumann na nGaedheal's efforts to publish and provide books in Irish at an economical price. MacNeill's name tends to be associated with the failure of the boundary commission in 1925. Although he was not to blame for the fiasco when, contrary to nationalist expectations, some transfers of territory from as well as to the Free State were proposed, he subse-

---

[11] 1923/27 (24 July 1923); 1923/42 (9 Aug. 1923).

quently resigned from his role as Free State representative on the three-man committee. He left the cabinet when the Irish government signed an agreement with the British and Northern Ireland governments shelving the commission's findings. The 'failure' of the boundary commission was a propaganda victory for the republican opposition: the border remained unchanged and partition intact. But, given the complexities of the problem, 'failure' was not a fair reading of the outcome. However, Cumann na nGaedheal remained particularly poor at public relations. Caught up in the affairs of state, the government made no attempt to build Cumann na nGaedheal into a modern party organisation. Ministers regarded their responsibility to the nation as all-consuming.

Cosgrave's government secured greater recognition of Irish independence in the international arena. The government had been swift to join the League of Nations and register the Anglo–Irish treaty in Geneva as an international agreement. In respect of the British commonwealth, the constitutional creativity of Kevin O'Higgins helped give member states greater legislative independence from Westminster. Beginning with the Balfour declaration, the process concluded with the passage of the statute of Westminster in 1931. This gave dominion parliaments the right to repeal or amend any act of the United Kingdom parliament (in so far as it was part of dominion law), and also removed the possibility that dominion laws would be judged inoperative on the grounds of repugnancy to British law. In 1924 Ireland became the first among the members of the commonwealth to send an envoy, a professor of economics at University College, Cork, T. A. Smiddy, to Washington. There was already an Irish high commissioner in London, and in 1929 the Free State established diplomatic relations with France, Germany, and the holy see at ministerial level. Thus, despite Britain's desire to obfuscate the independence of commonwealth countries in international affairs, Cosgrave's government took full advantage of working on the international stage to demonstrate the country's sovereignty.

Perhaps, too, the Cumann na nGaedheal government of 1922–32 has been incorrectly characterised as being conservative. That description deserves to be strongly qualified. Reference is often made to the power of the catholic church and its influence over film (the Censorship of Films Act, 1923) and books (Censorship of Publications Act, 1929),[12] and over the prohibition of divorce. Yet James Joyce's *Ulysses* was not banned in Ireland when it was published in 1922, although the printers working on the *Dublin Review* refused to set a favourable review by Con Leventhal, who wrote the famous lines in revenge: 'a censoring God came out of the machine to allay the hellfire fears of the compositors' solidarity.' (Leventhal, not to be bested, pub-

---

[12] 1923/23 (16 July 1923); 1929/21 (16 July 1929).

lished his review in a single-issue magazine, which he called *The Klaxon*.)[13] That defiant streak was countered in the 1920s by a strong censorious spirit which found expression in the hearings of the committee of inquiry on evil literature in 1926. However, when the censorship act of 1929 was passed, its terms scarcely suggested the scale of the banning of works of literature of all kinds, including some by the best of international and Irish writers, that would come in the 1930s and 1940s.

Nevertheless, the Free State remained predominantly catholic and nationalist in ethos and in outlook. The government was active in the celebration of the catholic emancipation centenary in 1929, and throughout the 1920s the leaders of the state and the catholic church were prominent on public and state occasions. Yet the intimacy in the relationship between prelates and politicians did not result in the creation of a sectarian or confessional state.

Cosgrave's government sought to protect the rights of minority religious groups and fought against church attempts to institutionalise discrimination. That independent frame of mind was displayed in Cosgrave's letter to Cardinal Joseph MacRory on 28 March 1931: 'We feel confident that your eminence and their lordships the bishops appreciate the effective limits to the powers of government which exist in relation to certain matters if some of the fundamental principles on which our state is founded are not to be repudiated.'[14] Cosgrave and his ministerial colleagues had the strong desire to achieve a society characterised by tolerance south of the border.

Viewing the 1920s in the round, it is important to stress the success of Cumann na nGaedheal's democratic revolution—establishing a liberal democracy and upholding the institutions of the state, parliament, executive, and judiciary. That legacy was recognised in Dáil Éireann by a once archopponent, Seán Lemass, whose brother, Noel, had been killed by government forces in somewhat sinister circumstances during the civil war. Speaking as taoiseach, Lemass paid a generous tribute to Cosgrave after his death in 1965. He spoke of Cosgrave's generosity of spirit, the exemplary character of his long life, and the enduring work that he had done for Ireland. The same could also have been said for other Cumann na nGaedheal ministers who had been revolutionaries of the first wave. Their collective style in government during the 1920s was to eschew flamboyance for a sober patriotism and a self-effacing zeal designed to return the country to normality.

De Valera and his Fianna Fáil party confounded their critics at home and the colonial and commonwealth sceptics abroad by taking power peacefully on 9 March 1932 after a robust but relatively peaceful general election

---

[13] *The Klaxon* (Dublin, [1924]).
[14] Quoted in Dermot Keogh, *Twentieth-century Ireland: nation and state* (Dublin, 1994), p. 57.

campaign. Despite rumblings on the fringes of the army, the result of the election on 16 February was accepted by Cosgrave and the governing party. With the support of the Labour party, which remained outside the government, de Valera won the vote to become president of the executive council by 81 votes to 68. Thus began for Fianna Fáil, and for Eamon de Valera at the age of 50, a period of sixteen consecutive years in office.

Is it accurate to describe those years as 'the age of de Valera'? No other politician in twentieth-century Ireland has had such a profound impact on the development of the country. He came closer to being charismatic than any of his peers or successors. He appeared to lead Fianna Fáil in the style of a Parnell or an O'Connell. He used the old-fashioned props of bonfires and brass bands to give colour to his arrival as he rode into a country town astride a white horse during election time. But that was combined with the most careful attention to the detail of machine politics, to vote management, and to the influence of the U.S. Democratic party. De Valera may have feigned a lack of interest in the mundane and the ordinary. But that was a conceit; he and his cabinet colleagues paid the closest attention to the detail of party machine management. Thus, Fianna Fáil became the first essentially professional political party in the history of modern Ireland, winning under de Valera's leadership six consecutive general elections in 1932, 1933, 1937, 1938, 1943, and 1944. That was achieved without gerrymandering, but with the invaluable aid of Fianna Fáil's own national daily newspaper from 1931 to the end of our period and beyond, the *Irish Press*.

But de Valera also combined a radical political pragmatism with a stubborn economic and social conservatism. At one level he became in office more Michael Collins-like than Collins himself. He used the constitution of 1922 as a 'stepping stone', and in doing so he followed on the example of Cosgrave and Cumann na nGaedheal in the 1920s.

Originally opposed in 1923 to Irish membership of the League of Nations, de Valera became in office an enthusiastic supporter and a personal attender at Geneva whenever the occasion required his presence. He was viewed as a League reformer, and a consistent supporter of increasing the League's powers in the area of collective security and the capacity to intervene with force where necessary to impede the advances of imperial expansionism. Irish foreign policy in the 1930s was characterised by its strong adherence to the ideals of the League and, in the year preceding the outbreak of war, by a sense of pessimism and foreboding about its likelihood. Unlike Cosgrave, however, de Valera eschewed attendance at meetings of the commonwealth and sought to define Ireland's foreign policy in terms that were essentially independent of British colonial entanglements. He was in a position to do this because the previous government had laid the constitutional foundations for greater autonomy within the commonwealth. Thus, de Valera was able to amend the constitution of 1922 in order to abolish the oath of allegiance, downgrade the office of governor general, end Irish appeals to the privy council, and remove all reference to the crown from the constitution. That was being more Collins-like than Collins himself.

Such actions were also of great appeal to those who looked back to the economic ideas of Arthur Griffith, who as a polemicist and political thinker was at his most active when de Valera, born in 1882, was a young man. The policy of protectionism marked de Valera off from Cosgrave and his laissez-faire approach to the economy, but was very much in harmony with the current economic thinking in many countries. The decision in 1932 to with-hold land annuities, payable annually to the British exchequer, provoked a tariff war between Dublin and London. There is agreement among scholars that the 'economic war', so called, did much to disrupt national industrial development. But it also helped bring into being a weak form of economic autarky, and helped create a local business elite that was very much in keeping with Griffith's logic and vision. There was a cost—the substitution of economic nationalism for Cumann na nGaedheal internationalism—and this was not really reversed until the 1960s.

In his political actions, de Valera was to confound his most bitter critics by his display of support for liberal democracy. Although one of his first steps on taking office in 1932 was to authorise the release of a batch of political prisoners, during the 1930s and 1940s he did not shrink from clamping down on I.R.A. activists: in 1936 the I.R.A. was declared an illegal organisation. In that respect too he proved to be most Collins-like. He proved equally resili-ent in his opposition to the Blueshirts, who shared some of the tendencies of fascist movements on the European continent.

Besides the I.R.A. leadership, who mistakenly viewed de Valera as a Ker-ensky-like figure, there were others who were surprised by the religious and cultural policies of Fianna Fáil in power. The ethos of the country was profoundly catholic, as displayed by the manner in which church and state cooperated in the staging of the international eucharistic congress in the summer of 1932. Certain pieces of legislation have been singled out as under-pinning the 'confessionalism' of de Valera's state. The sale or importation of contraceptives was forbidden under an amendment to section 17 of the Criminal Law Amendment Act, 1935.[15] The Public Dance Halls Act of the same year made it necessary to acquire a licence from a local district court for the holding of all public dances.[16]

These pieces of legislation are often advanced (together with the very stringent interpretation and implementation of the law on censorship of books and periodicals that operated during the period) to support the view that de Valera's rule was 'Rome rule'. But there were other forces at work besides the influence of catholicism. The residual strength of Griffith's

[15] 1935/6 (28 Feb. 1935).   [16] 1935/2 (19 Feb. 1935).

legacy moved de Valera towards a policy of de-anglicisation and a filtering out of the 'foreign' from Irish civic culture, much to the disappointment of literary figures such as Sean O'Faolain and others in the 1930s.

Not content to continue a piecemeal process of constitutional reform, de Valera embarked on the drafting of a new constitution to replace what he considered to be the profoundly unsatisfactory constitution of 1922. By May 1937 he had brokered with difficulty a text that reflected his Ireland: democratic, with a new office of president, and influenced by catholic social and moral thinking. The catholic church was not given established status, but a 'special position', while the other churches in the country, including the Church of Ireland and the Jewish congregations, were also recognised. Articles 2 and 3 laid territorial claim to the six counties of Northern Ireland.

By offering the country an opportunity to accept the new constitution in a referendum, the Fianna Fáil government was highlighting the democratic credentials of the new formula at the expense of the 1922 constitution, supposed in some quarters to have been crafted by the British government and foisted on a supine Irish administration. The Irish electorate went to the polls on 1 July 1937 to vote in a general election and referendum on the new constitution. If de Valera had been anxious to secure a ringing endorsement for his government's policies he was disappointed. Fianna Fáil were returned to power with 69 seats. The constitution was accepted by 685,105 votes to 526,945.

The impact of the economic war had told in the relatively poor Fianna Fáil results secured in the general election. De Valera responded to positive soundings for reconciliation coming from London, and the 1938 Anglo–Irish agreement on finance and trade brought the unnecessary tariff conflict to an end. That placed Fianna Fáil in a commanding domestic political position. The return of the 'treaty ports' was another major step in de Valera's determination to remove all vestiges of the treaty settlement of 1921.

The government made much of the actual handing over of the ports by Britain. It was presented in the national press, particularly Fianna Fáil's *Irish Press*, as if it were the manifest and final departure of the 'foreigner' after 700 years. Striking while the iron was hot, de Valera called a snap election for 17 June 1938, which Fianna Fáil won with ease, raising its number of seats in Dáil Éireann to 77. The new position of president of Ireland was filled, unopposed, by the Gaelic scholar Douglas Hyde, who was inaugurated on 25 June. On the eve of world war, Fianna Fáil had good reason to praise the political skills of de Valera and many members of his cabinet. The country had gained in international stature since 1932, particularly because of de Valera's personal involvement in the League of Nations and his sure handling of Anglo–Irish affairs and foreign policy during the testing Ethiopian crisis and the Spanish civil war.

When Britain and France declared war on Germany on 3 September 1939, de Valera's Ireland was quite unprepared for the possible military challenge to its sovereignty. Neutrality was, in the circumstances, the preferred if not the only viable policy. Ireland was one of the very few countries in Europe to sustain that policy successfully till 1945. On receiving news of the death of Adolf Hitler in early May 1945, de Valera went to visit the German envoy in Dublin to express condolences. That misjudgement won for the Irish leader the opprobrium of the international press and media, the hostility of the Allied powers, and a wholly undeserved reputation that he (de Valera) was an unrepentant Axis supporter. That was to misrepresent completely Irish wartime policy and de Valera's personal position of support for the Allies. But the taoiseach was obliged to take full responsibility for such a diplomatic gaffe and humiliating personal débâcle.

The war years had in fact brought Dublin and London closer together than at any time since the establishment of the Irish state. That fact was not reflected in the personal relationship between de Valera and the British prime minister, Winston Churchill, who engaged in intermittent skirmishing and megaphone diplomacy. But that belied the healthy functional relationship that existed between the intelligence services and armed forces of the two countries, their combined counter-insurgency campaign against the I.R.A. and Axis spies, and their sharing of strategic information on weather, Axis flights, and Axis naval movements. The list of activities could be extended to include Dublin's permission for the overflight of Irish territory by Allied planes, return of Allied airmen, and the complete reliance by the Irish army on the rapid arrival of British troops in the event of a German invasion.

Life in wartime Ireland was largely free of the danger of Axis bombing raids, which had been visited on the docks of Belfast and Derry. But rationing, wage freezes, and stricter censorship than anything implemented in either neutral Sweden or Switzerland made life in the country dull and difficult. Ireland's dependence on Britain for many industrial products helped accentuate the economic difficulties experienced by the people. However, even in such adverse conditions, Fianna Fáil succeeded in winning a general election in 1943 and another in 1944. The misery of the war years was continued into 1945 and 1946 with the perpetuation of wage freezes and rationing. The government's difficulties were made even more acute by a sustained spell of unprecedentedly cold winter weather and wet summers, which destroyed the harvests. Growing social unrest gave rise to the founding in 1946 of Clann na Poblachta, with a former chief of staff of the I.R.A., Seán MacBride, as its leader. After the general election of 1948, this party joined forces with four other parties—Fine Gael, Labour, National Labour, and Clann na Talmhan—to form the first inter-party government with John A. Costello (Fine Gael) as taoiseach. For the first time in sixteen years Fianna Fáil was out of office.

The inter-party government was the first major experiment in the politics of consensus in government since the foundation of the state. The three years of its existence were marked by rancour and political division in cabinet and in domestic politics. In the area of foreign affairs, the country experienced a lack of consistency in policy, and a series of decisions were taken that tended to mystify even some of those who sat around the cabinet table. Seán MacBride, who became minister for external affairs, was a devout catholic who displayed an unparalleled sycophancy in his handling of church–state relations. Yet he contrived through his own ineptitude to find himself out of favour with the holy see because of the government's failure in 1948 to provide the *agrément* for the prelate nominated to replace the deceased papal nuncio, Paschal Robinson. The government had humilatingly to accede to the wishes of the holy see a year later.

While that particular débâcle was outside the purview of the Irish public, two other foreign policy decisions that created tensions within the inter-party cabinet received more publicity. The taoiseach, John A. Costello, leader of Fine Gael (a party whose subsidiary name was 'the commonwealth party'), made a major announcement on 7 September 1948 while on a visit to Canada: Ireland would repeal the external relations act (1936) and leave the commonwealth. On 18 April 1949 Ireland formally became a republic outside the commonwealth. The decision displayed all the signs of haste, the implications of which had not been properly thought through in relation either to Northern Ireland or to Britain.

The government made yet another decision that stupefied many of Ireland's friends in the United States. Early in 1949 Ireland was invited to join the emerging North Atlantic Treaty Organisation (N.A.T.O.). MacBride, hoping to trade off Irish membership in return for movement on partition, sought to set preconditions for Irish membership. When N.A.T.O. refused to countenance such a cheeky advance from a country that had been neutral during the second world war, a virulently anti-communist Ireland found herself outside the newly formed defence system.

Even with the assistance of the Irish News Agency, an official public relations company that was government-funded, the political fortunes of Costello and his cabinet were soon in sharp decline. In 1950 MacBride's Clann na Poblachta party colleague Noel Browne incurred the hostility of the catholic hierarchy and the opposition of a united medical profession to a 'mother-and-child' scheme pledging to provide free medical care without the use of a means test to all mothers and their children up to the age of 16. This political crisis absorbed most of the energies of government from late 1950 until its collapse in the spring of 1951.

It was an ignominious end to this first experiment in consensus politics, and the adverse circumstances in which the inter-party government collapsed virtually guaranteed the return of Fianna Fáil to power. De Valera was elected taoiseach in Dáil Éireann on 13 June by 74 votes to 69. He was now 69 and practically blind; his major political contribution to the country had already been made. But he insisted on remaining active in politics for another eight years, during three of which, between 1954 and 1957, Fianna Fáil was again replaced by an inter-party government led by John A. Costello.

The decade of the 1950s in Britain and on the European continent was a period of unprecedented economic expansion. The British welfare state gave many thousands of Irish emigrants their first experience of prosperity—an experience that those who remained at home sadly lacked. The Irish revolution had literally run out of reforming zeal, and it was time to develop along different lines. However, a limited experiment in state medicine had brought down one government and warned successors away from revisiting a policy area in which the catholic church proved to be such an implacable opponent. Dogmatism kept the country behind tariff walls, which fostered a lack of competitiveness in industry and agriculture. There was little alternative for tens of thousands but to take the boat to Britain or to the United States. It was a lost decade. Moreover, I.R.A. fundamentalism manifested itself in the later 1950s with the organisation of a quixotic cross-border campaign of raids on Royal Ulster Constabulary barracks. Internment was again introduced by the government in Dublin to contain the violence and halt the activities of the I.R.A.

But while political and social conservatism tended to characterise the decade, there were those in the civil service and in the policy-making elites who saw the need to break with the policy of protectionism. De Valera resigned as taoiseach in 1959 and was elected president. Seán Lemass became the leader of Fianna Fáil and taoiseach on 23 June. The changing of the guard coincided with, and helped precipitate, the 'modernisation' of Ireland. The new direction was signalled by the determination of the Lemass government to replace the policy of protectionism with free trade. Lemass's determination to pursue that new economic path was plain to see when in 1961 the Irish government unsuccessfully sought full membership of the European Economic Community. The country had to wait till 1973 to gain admission. But in the preceding years, Lemass—until his retirement in 1966—prepared the way for greater economic openness. Incentives were provided to attract foreign capital and to engage major multinationals in the setting up of Irish subsidiaries. It was a strategy that enjoyed some success. In order to prepare a skilled workforce, the decision was taken to introduce free education at secondary school level. Education was at last seen as being an investment in helping to better the country's economic future.

It is trite, however, to argue that the modernisation model satisfactorily explains the nature and extent of change in Irish society during the 1960s. Subsequent events in the 1970s and 1980s demonstrated very clearly the resilience and strength of conservatism in the country. Ireland was very much subject to push-pull factors in the period. Negotiations to enter the E.E.C. proved successful at the third attempt and membership helped galvanise social and economic change. Women's rights, very much a forgotten area for the revolutionary and post-revolutionary generations, were pushed to the fore as a result of the E.E.C. requirement to harmonise Irish and E.E.C. law. Membership also helped challenge the decision-making elites to Europeanise their social and political frame of intellectual reference. Irish foreign policy developed a more Eurocentric dimension under the guidance of Dr Garret FitzGerald—minister for foreign affairs in the Fine Gael–Labour coalition between 1973 and 1977. Irish farmers received major cash incentives and grant transfers in a country that had allowed its agricultural sector to stagnate in the 1950s and for much of the 1960s.

If the E.E.C. was a source of hope pushing the country towards prosperity, the violence that broke out in Northern Ireland in 1968 and escalated throughout the early 1970s damaged the path to progress in ways yet to be fully analysed. The opportunity cost of northern violence was very high for the Dublin government. It made Ireland less attractive for the location of multinationals; it lowered the country's capacity for the development of tourism; and it radically increased the cost of internal security to combat the activities of I.R.A. subversives and defend the country against loyalist attacks.

The impact of 'the troubles' on the capacity of the Irish government to act in a collective fashion is another subject that has yet to be fully assessed. Jack Lynch had taken over as leader of Fianna Fáil and as taoiseach on the retirement of Seán Lemass in 1966. His consistent opposition to the use of force to bring about a solution to the Northern Ireland problem provoked opposition inside his party. The extent to which his opponents in cabinet unilaterally adopted a different policy remains to be fully documented. But Lynch felt compelled on 6 May 1970 to sack the minister for finance, Charles Haughey, and the minister for agriculture, Neil Blaney. The minister for local government, Kevin Boland, resigned in protest at the taoiseach's action. Lynch had persuaded his minister for justice, Micheál Ó Moráin, to resign on health grounds days before. A political crisis of such gravity had not faced any government leader since the 1920s and it contributed to a popular loss of confidence in Lynch and Fianna Fáil. A Fine Gael–Labour coalition was returned to power in a general election on 28 February 1973.

Charles Haughey was acquitted on 23 October 1970 of a charge of conspiracy to import arms. He had to remain on the back benches for five years until he was appointed by Lynch in 1975 as opposition spokesman on health. Two years later Lynch led Fianna Fáil back to power in triumph with a substantial majority. He was 60 years old. In 1979 he resigned without much notice, and the surprise outcome of the election for the leadership of Fianna Fáil was a victory for Haughey. The historian is at a serious disadvantage in

trying to assess the early Haughey years. The printed sources provide insufficient evidence to explain the inconsistencies in domestic and foreign policy
between 1979 and 1982. Government tribunals and a Dáil Éireann committee
have brought forward a range of findings that raise serious questions about
government style and practice during the Haughey years. This contributed
to a growing sense of cynicism among the public towards politicians in the
closing years of the twentieth century. There were solid grounds for such
public disillusionment. The death of idealism was marked by planning scandals, bribery of local officals and local politicians, illegally-held offshore bank
accounts, passports-for-sale, and tax amnesties. The world of W. T. Cosgrave and Cumann na nGaedheal in the 1920s appeared to be on the far
horizon. De Valera's spartan republic of 'frugal comfort' was the object of
ridicule in the 1980s. The philosophy of Arthur Griffith's Sinn Féin had, in
the end, been supplanted by the vision of political technocracy and by radical
individualism.

CHAPTER I

From treaty to civil war, 1921–2

MICHAEL HOPKINSON

THE Anglo–Irish treaty of 1921 was designed to produce a settlement of Anglo–Irish differences over the issue of self government, differences which from 1919 onwards had taken the form of an armed conflict. A home rule measure, passed by the United Kingdom parliament in 1914,[1] but suspended for the duration of the first world war, had been vitiated in the eyes of Irish nationalists by the British government's concessions to the anti-home rule sentiments of unionists. Moreover, 'home rule' had been overtaken by events such as the Easter rising of 1916 and the later eclipse of constitutional nationalism by the growth of Sinn Féin ('ourselves alone'), a party committed to abstaining from the London parliament in order to pursue Irish interests at home. Sinn Féin's triumph was reflected in the results of the December 1918 general election, when the party won 73 of the 105 Irish seats. Following this victory, the newly elected Sinn Féin members decided to implement their abstentionist policy and assemble in Dublin. Although about half of those members were in prison, some twenty-seven Sinn Féin representatives met as the first Dáil Éireann (Irish assembly) on 21 January 1919 in Dublin's Mansion House. They unanimously adopted a provisional constitution, and, with the 1916 precedent in mind, a declaration of independence: 'We, the elected representatives of the ancient Irish people in national parliament assembled, do, in the name of the Irish nation, ratify the establishment of the Irish republic.'[2]

The dáil subsequently proceeded to set up what aspired to be an alternative government, with ministers, courts, and a defence force drawn from the

[1] Government of Ireland Act, 1914 (4 & 5 Geo. VI, c. 90) (18 Sept. 1914); operation suspended by 4 & 5 Geo. V, c. 88). In this chapter and ch. II, sources have been cited principally for quoted matter. Additional references may be found in Michael Hopkinson, *Green against green: the Irish civil war* (Dublin, 1988).

[2] Quoted in Dorothy Macardle, *The Irish republic* (London, 1968 ed.), p. 253. The most detailed treatment of the Sinn Féin party in this period is Michael Laffan, *The resurrection of Ireland: the Sinn Féin party, 1916–1923* (Cambridge, 1999).

Irish Volunteers, to bypass the official administration. By the summer of 1920 in all parts of Ireland outside the north-east (where there was a strong concentration of unionists) elements of this alternative administration had come into effect, particularly in the south and west. This represented a clear challenge to the authority of the British government, and in addition from January 1919 onwards there were sporadic attacks on policemen and police barracks. Such attacks, though not intended as the beginning of a war of independence, in fact turned out to be so. The British authorities responded in 1920 with the deployment of the so-called 'Black and Tans', and a cycle of violence resulted. By 1921 both sides were war-weary and anxious for a resolution to the conflict; in July that year a truce was arranged and serious negotiations subsequently got under way.[3]

In the meantime, the British government under David Lloyd George had attempted its own resolution of the Irish problem in the form of the government of Ireland act of 1920.[4] This took account of the desire for a measure of self-government on the part of nationalist Ireland, while also recognising the vehement opposition to home rule among unionists. The act provided for two (subordinate) Irish parliaments, north and south, together with a council of Ireland for consultation on matters of common interest. In the north the unionists were prepared to work the new local parliament, which was opened by King George V on 22 June 1921; in the south the elections held for the southern parliament in May 1921 were all uncontested, the seats being filled by 124 Sinn Féin members and just four others (Dublin University representatives). Sinn Féin boycotted the opening of the southern Irish parliament, which was consequently adjourned *sine die*. Instead, elected representatives from the whole of Ireland were summoned to meet as the second Dáil Éireann on 16 August 1921. Unionists stayed away, but among the Sinn Féin deputies who had been elected to 'the parliament of Southern Ireland' there were a handful of republicans who had also been elected to constituencies in Northern Ireland. The second dáil proceeded to reelect Eamon de Valera as president of the Irish republic. Thus on the eve of the negotiations that would lead to the Anglo–Irish treaty of December 1921 there were already two functioning parliaments in Ireland: 'the parliament of Northern Ireland' authorised by the government of Ireland act, and the second dáil, claiming to be the national assembly of all Ireland. There were also two executives: a Northern Ireland cabinet under Sir James Craig as prime minister, and a dáil cabinet under de Valera—the latter considerably hampered in its functions by the disturbed state of the country.

For all the controversial circumstances surrounding its signing on Tuesday 6 December 1921, the Anglo–Irish treaty represented, in most respects, the best possible compromise available at the time. Ireland was to have dominion

---

[3] Above, vi, ch. XI.   [4] 10 & 11 Geo. V, c. 67 (23 Dec. 1920).

status and to be known as 'the Irish Free State' (article 1); Northern Ireland was given the power to opt out of the new arrangement (article 12). For Lloyd George's coalition government, and particularly its tory members, constitutional symbols were as important as they were for hardline republicans. Recognition of the crown and Irish membership of the commonwealth, therefore, were to be insisted on; de Valera's suggested compromise of 'external association' had no hope of being accepted.[5] The British made important concessions on fiscal and economic issues at the very end of the negotiations, and amendments were made to the wording of the oath of allegiance to the crown. Despite an amount of verbal sparring in the early stages of the conference, there was little dispute about the British being granted defence safeguards. Only the constitutional and northern issues provided a threat to the achievement of a settlement.

If it was always evident that a republic could not result from the negotiations, it was also inconceivable that the other main stated aim of the Irish negotiators—'essential unity'—could be won. The northern question played a strange, shadowy role in the negotiations. Both sides saw it as the likely issue over which the conference could break up. The constitutional status of the six counties had been established in 1920. That could only be changed by physical coercion (firmly ruled out by the British and Irish negotiators) or by the consent of the Northern Ireland government, and that was out of the question. Craig, therefore, proved obdurate when during the conference Lloyd George put considerable pressure on him to accept some loose form of Irish unity, with strong safeguards for northern loyalist interests. That the negotiations did not founder on the north came through Lloyd George's suggestion that provision for a boundary commission could be made in the treaty. In private talks with Arthur Griffith (minister for foreign affairs in the dáil cabinet) the British premier suggested that if the northern government refused to take up its option to join the southern government, 'at some undefined time after a treaty was signed a boundary commission should meet to adjust the border in accordance with the wishes of the inhabitants, so far as may be compatible with economic and geographic conditions'.[6] Griffith's agreement not to stand in the way of such a compromise prevented him from making the northern question the decisive one at the end of the conference. The day before the treaty was signed Lloyd George gave Michael Collins (finance minister in the dáil cabinet) to believe, according to Collins's testimony, that the commission's finding would result in at least two and one-half

---

[5] 'External association' implied an association with Britain and the British dominions from the outside; recognition of the crown as the bond of association, but with the right to remain neutral in wartime. See Nicholas Mansergh, *The unresolved question: the Anglo–Irish settlement and its undoing 1912–72* (New Haven and London, 1991), pp 166, 182–5.

[6] Thomas Jones, diary, 8–9 Nov. 1921 (Jones, *Whitehall diary, iii: Ireland 1918–1925*, ed. Keith Middlemas (London, 1971), pp 155–7.

of the six counties being transferred to the Free State. Extremely devious means were used by Lloyd George to win Griffith's and Collins's acceptance of the commission, but the Irish leaders were themselves glad of the chance to postpone and sidestep the northern block in order to progress towards a settlement. Following the treaty they were able to argue that Irish unity had only been delayed.

What is surprising is that Griffith and Collins did not insist that article 12, providing for the commission, should be more clearly framed. What precisely was meant by 'economic and geographic conditions', and how they related to majority opinion, went undefined. It was not clear by what means opinion was to be measured, or which demographic or geographical units should be considered. No guidance was offered on what would happen if, as was extremely likely, the northern government refused to appoint a commissioner. There was no clarification on when the commission should sit. In sum, article 12 was the weakest part of the treaty.

Controversy over the treaty was to focus not only on its terms but also on the circumstances of its signing. Lloyd George had placed extreme pressure on the Irish delegation on the evening of 5 December by brandishing two letters, one of which was to be sent to Craig. One contained news of acceptance of the terms, the other rejection of them. They were given two hours to decide, under the threat of the resumption of war if the treaty was not signed by all the delegation. A stormy meeting followed at which Collins, Griffith, and Eamon Duggan made clear their intention to sign—Robert Barton, the only member of the delegation against the treaty who was a member of the dáil cabinet, reluctantly agreed to sign to avoid being personally responsible for war, and George Gavan Duffy followed his lead.

Griffith and Collins were widely accused of breaking Sinn Féin unity at a stroke by signing without first referring the document to the Dublin cabinet. The previous Sunday, Griffith had renewed his promise to do that. Both Griffith and Collins must have dreaded further complications with their colleagues in Dublin—a meeting with them in Dublin the weekend before had revealed profoundly different expectations and progressively worsening relations between Griffith and Collins on the one hand and Cathal Brugha (minister for defence) and Austin Stack (home affairs) on the other. The British negotiators knew of the divisions among the Irish delegates and of those between Griffith and Collins and the rest of the dáil cabinet. They were well aware, moreover, that Collins had refused to accompany the delegation to present external association terms to the British following the recent return from Dublin. That goes far to explain Lloyd George's tactics at the end of the conference.

British and international opinion eagerly welcomed the settlement. Press opinion in Britain widely hailed the removal of the Irish sore from British politics. The *Boston Globe* commented: 'The sanguine may even dare hail the birth of the Irish Free State as the most auspicious event since the gallant Lee passed over his sword to Grant at Appomattox.' When de Valera declared his opposition to the treaty, the *New York Times* declared: 'Mr de Valera is too late. The world's approval and supporting opinion for the agreement is now too strong to be overcome.' Opinion elsewhere, however, was greatly to underrate the problems the treaty was to face in Ireland.[7]

Public reaction to the treaty in the twenty-six counties was overwhelmingly favourable. The *Connachtman* was the only newspaper to express anti-treaty sentiments. The *Kilkenny People* rhapsodised on 10 December: 'One of the greatest and most heroic fights for freedom ever put up in ancient or modern history by any small nation has ended in a victory as complete and as striking as any nation, great or small, has ever achieved ... Freedom's battle has been won.' The unionist *Irish Times*, the day before, concluded: 'The whole nationalist press and, as we believe, the vast majority of southern Irishmen have accepted it with joy.' There was a solid chorus of support for the settlement from public bodies. General Sir Nevil Macready's report of 5 January to the British government stated that 101 statutory bodies had expressed a pro-treaty preference, with only those in Bantry and Cahirciveen against. Church leaders enthusiastically supported the prospect of a native government, the archbishop of Cashel concluding: 'The people of Ireland, by a vast majority, are in favour of the treaty, and in a democratic country the will of the people is the final court of appeal.'[8]

There can be little doubt also that there was a considerable pro-treaty majority in the population at large, as demonstrated by the 1922 and 1923 general elections. There was, however, no outward show of enthusiasm following the treaty's signing. Celia Shaw, a university student, recorded in her diary: 'We heard tonight Ireland is a Free State and every English soldier to be out of Ireland in 6 months ... Not a flag, not a bonfire, not a hurrah.'[9] It was to be difficult to express any passion for a Free State, and it was too early to sing the virtues of a strong central government; the republic had a more striking appeal.

The undemonstratively positive reception of the treaty owed much to a yearning for peace and prosperity and for an end to the dislocation of trade, communications, and civil order. That constitutional and political issues dominated the public debate over the treaty should not detract from the fact that, as J. J. Lee argues, 'popular support ... did reflect socio-economic differences'.[10] Economic considerations did not account for the split in the dáil but explained much in the country at large. Broadly speaking, where

[7] *Boston Globe*, 7 Dec. 1921; *New York Times*, 5 Jan. 1922.
[8] Macready report, P.R.O., CAB 24/131; archbishop of Cashel, quoted in *Cork Examiner*, 3 Jan. 1922.
[9] Celia Shaw diary, Dec. 1921 (N.L.I., MS 23409).
[10] J. J. Lee, *Ireland 1912–1985: politics and society*, p. 542.

prosperity was most apparent, where connections with the British economy were closest and communications most developed, treaty support was greatest. It dwindled the further west one travelled. Opposition to the treaty in the south and west was inextricably connected with economic grievances, particularly relating to the land, and with alienation from central government. Those areas that had most to gain from the establishment of a strong, centralised government contrasted strongly with regions such as Kerry, west Cork, and Mayo, which became republican bastions during the civil war. The treaty divisions hardly existed in parts of Leinster, where opinion was overwhelmingly favourable.

The decision on the treaty, however, was to be made by the dáil and the I.R.A., and they were unrepresentative of important sections of the population. Kevin O'Higgins (assistant to W. T. Cosgrave, minister for local government) reminded the dáil that de Valera had stated that they 'were only a section of the country...a selection from its left wing'.[11] At sundry times during the treaty and civil war period, pro- and anti-treaty sides acted without much consideration for public accountability. A small number of T.D.s changed their views to support the treaty during the Christmas adjournment following constituency pressure, but they were too few to prove decisive in the dáil's vote. After a much longer debate than had been expected, a majority of 64 to 57 decided in favour of the treaty. A separate vote for president of the dáil, with both Griffith and de Valera standing, resulted in an even narrower majority—60 to 58—for the former.

The character and historical development of Sinn Féin had made the movement ill equipped to respond in anything but a divided manner to the treaty. Sinn Féin represented an uneasy coalition of interests, and had deliberately postponed any decision on what character an independent government should assume. The policy that Sean O'Faolain described as 'freedom first, other things after' was to store up vast problems for the future.[12] The claim that the republic had been in existence since January 1919 could not be reconciled with the realities of negotiations with the British government. The potential, therefore, for conflict between republican purist and nationalist pragmatist was enormous and had long roots. In an organisational sense, also, Sinn Féin was in no position to control reaction to the treaty. The Irish Republican Army (formerly the Irish Volunteers) was largely responsible for bringing the British government to the negotiating table, but (despite de Valera's statement of March 1921)[13] was not in practice accountable to the dáil or its government. The Sinn Féin political organisation had virtually ceased to function during the Anglo–Irish war. Underlying these

[11] O'Higgins in *Dáil Éireann deb.*, ii, 906 (17 Jan. 1923).
[12] Sean O'Faolain, *Vive moi! an autobiography* (Boston, 1964), p. 146.
[13] Macardle, *Ir. republic*, pp 401–2.

problems was the lack of definition in the relationship of the various nationalist institutions to each other. Until 1919 the Irish Republican Brotherhood held that the president of its supreme council was also the president of the Irish republic;[14] though the organisation's constitution was amended during the Anglo–Irish war, it held on to its position as a revolutionary elite bearing an uneasy relationship to the political and military public organisations. The weakness of the various nationalist institutions and the speed and improvised character of their growth made for an increased importance for individuals and the divisions between them.

The circumstances of the treaty's signing, together with the nature of the document itself, brought to the surface all these long-implicit divisions within the nationalist coalition. De Valera felt personally affronted by the delegation's failure to honour the commitment to refer the treaty back to Dublin before signing. There was talk within the I.R.A. of arresting the delegates on their return. The treaty could hardly have been better framed to cause divisions within Sinn Féin and I.R.A. ranks. If less had been offered, something akin to the British government's July 'dominion status' terms or a small advance on that, it would have resulted in an agreed rejection. If the treaty terms had been more generous, in accordance, say, with 'external association', there might have been wide acceptance in Sinn Féin ranks, even though problems would have remained in reconciling much of the I.R.A. to a retreat from the full republican position.

DURING the dáil treaty debates only Arthur Griffith expressed anything that amounted to enthusiasm for the document. Even Kevin O'Higgins, who was to become the staunchest of Free Staters, admitted that the treaty fell a considerable way short of the ideal. Those supporting the treaty in the dáil did so from a largely defensive stance, arguing that nothing better could be won and that the settlement had potential for future development towards complete independence. Pro-treaty I.R.A. members of the dáil argued that renewal of war was not feasible. Thus, Richard Mulcahy (chief of staff of the I.R.A.) stressed how limited any military success in the Anglo–Irish war had been, and concluded that 'the Irish army at the present time does not hold in its possession the elements of a military decision, and short of a definite military decision the further purpose is not capable of fulfilment . . . In short, acceptance of the treaty is a quicker way to complete independence than rejection'. Seán McGrath quoted Collins as saying: 'If I had enough arms I wouldn't have signed the treaty, and you know that.' Such emphasis on political and military realities led to considerable disdain for what was regarded as anti-treaty obsession with constitutional symbols and abstractions. Piaras Béaslaí recalled John Mitchel saying: 'I do not care a fig for

[14] See Tim Pat Coogan, *The I.R.A.* (2nd ed., London, 1970), pp 43–4.

republicanism in the abstract', and Collins commented: 'The true devotion lies not in melodramatic defiance or self-sacrifice for something falsely said to exist, or for mere words and formalities, which are empty.'[15]

Collins was the crucial supporter of the treaty and hence consideration of his motivation is particularly important. Uppermost in Collins's mind was the fact that the treaty would lead to the rapid evacuation of British troops from the twenty-six counties. Study of Collins's policies in the period between the treaty and his death points to his signing the treaty for tactical reasons, not out of any positive commitment to the document. Collins's involvement in the planning of the joint I.R.A. northern offensive between February and June 1922,[16] and his persistent search in that period for a compromise with the military and political opposition, in a manner incompatible with adherence to the treaty, suggest strongly that he remained a physical-force nationalist who placed an especial emphasis on attacking partition. In the months following the treaty Collins told some anti-treatyites that for him prospects for republican unity were more important than the need to abide by the treaty: his only disagreement with them was over the means and strategy by which complete independence was to be won. Robert Barton commented: 'Brugha wanted to die for the republic, Michael Collins to live for it.'[17] Political leaders on the pro-treaty side—Griffith, O'Higgins, William Cosgrave, and Ernest Blythe—accepted the treaty in a far more literal manner than Collins, who during the next six months strove time and again to bend the meaning of the settlement in order to accommodate the republican opposition.

The philosophy behind the anti-treaty reaction was straightforward. Republican ideals could not be compromised, the dáil could not be overriden by any British-inspired document, and the majority in the dáil had no authority to end its existence. In the dáil treaty debates Mary MacSwiney (whose brother Terence had died on hunger strike in 1920) affirmed that it was a question of right and wrong, not peace and war; Austin Stack remembered his fenian forbears, while many, including widows and mothers, stressed that republican martyrs would not have accepted the treaty. Such unyielding republicans had no time for de Valera's compromise policy. De Valera's 'Document No. 2',[18] his alternative to the treaty, which was placed before an early secret session of the dáil, amounted to a restating of his 'external

[15] Griffith in *Dáil Éireann treaty deb.*, 21–2 (19 Dec. 1921), and O'Higgins, ibid., 174–5 (15 Dec. 1921); Mulcahy memo to army, undated (U.C.D., A.D., Mulcahy papers, MS P7/A/32); Seán McGrath in O'Malley notebooks (U.C.D., A.D., MS P17b/100); Béaslaí in *Dáil Éireann treaty deb.*, 178 (3 Jan. 1922); Michael Collins, *The path to freedom* (Dublin, 1922), p. 31.
[16] Below, pp 26–30.
[17] For examples of Collins's emphasis on republican unity rather than adherence to the treaty, see Liam Manahan recollections (O'Malley notebooks, MS P17b/117), and Robert Barton (ibid., P17b/99).
[18] See Mansergh, *Unresolved question*, pp 202–4.

association' idea. It had possessed some potential as a means of preserving nationalist unity during the negotiations, but once the treaty was signed it had no relevance to the increasingly intransigent stances being adopted. From early January onwards de Valera was forced to return to a firm republican line in order to retain his position at the head of anti-treaty ranks.

Much controversy has focused on de Valera's motivation in opposing the treaty. Judging by his long quest for amendment of the settlement, de Valera did sincerely believe in external association as a means of satisfying republican demands while restoring nationalist unity. He had been taken by surprise by the treaty's signing, and subsequently failed to impose his will on events. During the course of 1922 de Valera became a progressively marginal figure. His personal influence with the I.R.A. was of minimal significance and his attempts to bring the army under government control in the autumn of 1921 had proved stillborn. At a meeting of anti-treaty T.D.s during the dáil debates de Valera made it clear that he wished opposition to the treaty to take political rather than military form. He moved that 'should the army fall under the control of the provisional or Free State government the best course for members of it who refused to come under that control would be to leave the army and become members of republican clubs'.[19] While the Sinn Féin organisation first divided and then disintegrated in the early months of 1922, de Valera desperately sought to make it the basis of compromise and treaty revision—that, however, was ruled out by British refusal to make further concessions. The lack of scope for political compromise meant that military divisions and realities became crucial.

There was often a contrast between pro- and anti-treaty sides on grounds of personal character and temperament: the cautious outlook of Cosgrave and Blythe, for instance, on the one hand, and the romantic, self-sacrificial dispositions of Cathal Brugha, Liam Mellows, and Liam Lynch. A pragmatic outlook was often, but not always, related to experience of government and administration, appreciation of a national, as opposed to a local administration, and of a national, as opposed to a local perspective. Thus the Cork I.R.A.'s attitude to the truce and treaty appears to have been dictated by immediate and local considerations, in contrast with Collins's and Richard Mulcahy's stress on problems over arms and ammunition throughout the twenty-six counties.[20]

The display of Sinn Féin public unity between 1917 and 1921 had hidden ideological, personal, and temperamental divisions, which only became apparent once the treaty had been signed. The dáil treaty debates ended amid abuse and vituperation, most notably in Brugha's speech bitterly attacking

[19] For meeting of anti-treaty T.D.s, see 'Account of president's committee on policy', 8 Jan. 1922 (T.C.D., Childers papers, MS 7848).
[20] An important study of the I.R.A. in Cork is Peter Hart, *The I.R.A. and its enemies: violence and community in Cork, 1916–23* (Oxford, 1998).

Collins's reputation. Contemporaries unsurprisingly sought to explain their treaty stances in terms of straightforward ideological motivation—adherence on the pro-treaty side to democratic principle, on the anti-treaty side to republican purity. Choices, however, were often made on less lofty grounds. Many took a long time to decide; Brian O'Higgins related that Peadar O'Keefe changed his mind nine times, and Frank Aiken, commanding the crucial 4th Northern Division, did not commit himself to the republican side till over two months after the civil war had begun. In several instances decisions related to personal loyalties and ambitions. Many, for instance, said they supported the treaty because Michael Collins had signed it. The cry, 'What's good enough for Mick is good enough for us', was frequently heard. Senator Michael Hayes considered that 'the loyalty of the individual volunteers to Collins and Mulcahy I think was one of the greatest influences rather than what they thought about the treaty'.[21] The importance of Collins's influence was to be demonstrated by the fact that many of Collins's close entourage in the I.R.A. turned away from support of the government after their chief's death. On the anti-treaty side Harry Boland initially expressed approval of the document when hearing of it in the United States; his attitude abruptly changed when he read in the press of de Valera's renunciation of the settlement. The attitude of local I.R.A. men was frequently determined by their degree of loyalty to their local O.C. That the 2nd Battalion was the only one in the Dublin Brigade to support the treaty was ascribed to the personality and influence of Tom Ennis, the O.C. However, it took considerable courage for individual I.R.A. men to express a view contrary to the prevailing mood in their areas. When a maverick line was taken, it sometimes arose from special local considerations. Demotion from his position as brigade engineer of Kerry No. 2 Brigade may have explained why Tom 'Scarteen' O'Connor was one of the few I.R.A. officers in his area of Kerry to go pro-treaty, and the court martial of some of the I.R.A. in east Cork may have explained why some of the I.R.A. there made the same choice.

Broader considerations usually explained I.R.A. attitudes to the treaty. The character of an area's relationship with G.H.Q. during the Anglo–Irish war was often of considerable import. Strong fighting areas such as Cork and south Tipperary resented the lack of assistance with arms and ammunition they had received during the war, and the fact that they had not been consulted over the truce and treaty negotiations. Florrie O'Donoghue, appointed adjutant general of the I.R.A. in April 1922, was to document how few arms were sent by G.H.Q. to Cork brigades during the war. The nature of guerrilla warfare had reinforced local particularism within the Volunteers,

---

[21] Conversation with Mulcahy, 22 Oct. 1922 (Mulcahy papers, P7/D/78). See also Macardle, *Ir. republic*, pp 694–6.

who had always been dependent on local initiative for their strength. G.H.Q. could not provide central direction by means of discipline and pay. Antagonism to G.H.Q. was felt by weak as well as strong fighting areas during the Anglo–Irish war. For instance, the Mayo and Sligo I.R.A. had frequently been berated by Mulcahy and Collins for lack of organisation and action, and for trying to buy arms through their own channels in Britain. Mulcahy was to ascribe the anti-treaty line of such areas to a desire to compensate for their earlier shortcomings. Any degree of centralised control was more difficult to exert in remote areas, and distance from Dublin was an additional factor in explaining anti-treaty attitudes. Remoteness aided republican resistance during the civil war, but in the Anglo–Irish war hindered I.R.A. activity. Personal animosities often exacerbated these tensions. The leaders of the Cork No. 1 Brigade, notably Seán Hegarty, had tense relations with G.H.Q., and Richard Mulcahy was to ascribe much of the anti-treaty attitude of the majority of the Dublin Brigade to Oscar Traynor's taking over as O.C. after the death in November 1920 of Collins's and Mulcahy's close colleague Dick McKee.

Leading anti-treaty figures, notably de Valera and Mary MacSwiney, identified the Irish Republican Brotherhood as the key to winning acceptance for the treaty. According to them Collins used his I.R.B. position and contacts to influence several T.D.s, to an extent that swung the dáil vote on the treaty. It was also argued that the I.R.B. was responsible for key I.R.A. officers, together with a considerable majority of the army's G.H.Q., supporting the treaty. At the time de Valera wrote of Collins 'getting the I.R.B. machine working' and concluded: 'Curse secret societies!'[22] The majority of the I.R.B., however, were against the treaty, and, although there was a pro-treaty majority on the supreme council, no clear guidance was given by the organisation, so demonstrating that it was in no position to control opinion. Moreover, the I.R.B. and its organisation had been on the decline since 1916 and had been overshadowed by the growth of the I.R.A. The I.R.B. was one of the means by which Collins tried to win support for the treaty, but there were other influences at work, notably the personal loyalty so widely shown to Collins. It appears inconceivable that I.R.B. influences alone could have been decisive in the treaty vote.

The northern question had little relevance to the immediate split over the treaty. Only T.D.s with northern backgrounds, such as Seán MacEntee, Ernest Blythe, Seán Milroy, and Eoin O'Duffy, had much to say about the north during the treaty debates. The weakest part of the treaty, therefore, was little commented on, and de Valera's Document No. 2 had no alternative to the boundary commission to offer. This lack of emphasis on northern issues reflected Sinn Féin's belated recognition of their intractability.

22 De Valera to McGarrity, 27 Dec. 1921 (N.L.I., McGarrity papers, MS 17440).

Besides, J. J. Walsh conceded during the treaty debates that the war had been fought to achieve a republic for only three-quarters of Ireland.[23]

DIVISIONS over the treaty represented only one aspect of the critical situation that faced the twenty-six counties in the early months of 1922. Apart from personal and ideological differences there were certain to be major problems in establishing strong, centralised government and law and order. For much of the Anglo–Irish war the British government's writ had hardly functioned in large areas of the south and west, while the dáil government's claim to represent an effective replacement of it was more a matter of propaganda than of reality. Rates went uncollected, the bailiff had ceased to function in many areas, and by the time of the July 1921 truce the dáil courts, so often described as the major achievement of the republican government, operated, in as far as they could under increasingly dangerous conditions, largely outside the control of that government.[24]

The constitutional basis of the Irish government was unclear during the first six months of 1922, and the timetable by which the Free State was to come into being was vague. Following on the dáil's acceptance of the treaty, formal ratification required that 'the house of commons of Southern Ireland' (deriving from the 1920 government of Ireland act) should approve the treaty (article 18). Accordingly, this body, consisting of the pro-treaty T.D.s and the four Dublin University representatives, met on 14 January 1922, elected the new provisional government, and agreed to some powers being transferred from Westminster. 'The house of commons of Southern Ireland' was never to meet again. The second dáil continued to meet until June, and its government also continued in existence; the relationship between the two governments continued to be undefined. Collins, still minister for finance in the dáil cabinet, and still president of the supreme council of the I.R.B., became chairman of the provisional government, which some other members of the dáil cabinet (but not Griffith) also joined. The ambiguity could only be resolved by the adoption of a constitution and the holding of a general election. The latter was delayed till June, and the constitution (for procedural reasons) was delayed till December. Until then the fate of the new government and the treaty hung in the balance. In a famous comment Kevin O'Higgins looked back on the position of the government as: 'simply eight young men in the city hall standing amidst the ruins of one administration, with the foundations of another not yet laid, and wild men screaming through the keyhole. No police force was functioning through the country,

---

[23] *Dáil Éireann treaty deb.*, 188 (3 Jan. 1922).

[24] In Jan. 1922 as part of the treaty settlement the provisional government decided that the dáil courts would be discontinued; however, this proved unrealistic, and they were eventually adapted to the remodelled Irish Free State judiciary in 1924. See Mary Kotsonouris, *Retreat from revolution: the dáil courts, 1920–24* (Dublin, 1994), pp 13, 59–62.

no system of justice was operating, the wheels of administration hung idle, battered out of recognition by the clash of rival jurisdictions.'[25]

ONCE the provisional government had been formed, the viceroy, Viscount Fitzalan, formally handed over power at Dublin Castle on 16 January 1922. The provisional government's position was made the more insecure by the rapid evacuation of British troops from all but major centres. In most areas there were no reliable pro-treaty troops to replace them. Nothing demonstrated the provisional government's weakness so dramatically as their reluctant agreement to evacuated military barracks being taken over by local I.R.A. units, regardless of their attitude to the treaty. As a consequence of this and of the anti-treaty feelings of the majority of the I.R.A., by the spring barracks in almost all of Munster and much of the west were controlled by anti-treaty I.R.A. units. Just as worryingly, the new government failed in its first attempt to establish a police force after the R.I.C. was withdrawn. The twenty-six counties went unpoliced while post offices and banks were raided and commandeering and looting began again. A settled court and police system was not set up until well into the civil war. Meanwhile the army on both sides of the treaty split remained independent of and unaccountable to politicians. Nevertheless, by the summer of 1922 the pro-treaty forces were being described, in official sources, as 'the national army', and later, by a decree of the provisional government of 2 August, it was ruled that all commissions for officers 'in Oglaigh na hÉireann or other armed forces of Saorstát Éireann' were to be issued under the hands of the general commanding in chief and the minister of defence.[26] 'Oglaigh na hÉireann', it may be noted, was the name given to the Irish Volunteers and the I.R.A. in Irish. Likewise, 'Saorstát' (though later used in the 1922 constitution as the Irish version of 'Free State') was the name for the republic, hitherto preferred by republicans to 'poblacht', as in the first dáil's declaration of independence in 1919.[27] The use of such terms perhaps illustrates the persistence of an all-Ireland interpretation of the role of the provisional government in military and political affairs.

Given the prevailing climate of uncertainty, the southern unionist leadership had particular reason to be alarmed. Lord Midleton told George V of an 'extremely grave' situation, and continued: 'The hasty withdrawal of British troops, against which your majesty's government were repeatedly warned, has left the south of Ireland without any force to preserve order and even if

---

[25] O'Higgins's address of 1924, 'Three years' hard labour', quoted in Terence de Vere White, *Kevin O'Higgins* (London, 1948), pp 83–4.
[26] Decree no. 3, 1922, *Iris Oifigiúil* (*Dublin Gazette*), no. 72 (29 Sept. 1922).
[27] *Dáil Éireann, miontuarisc an chead dala, 1919–21; minutes of proceedings of the first parliament of the republic of Ireland 1919–21: official record* (Dublin, n.d.), p. 14; Macardle, *Ir. republic*, p. 439; Tom Garvin, *1922: the birth of Irish democracy* (Dublin, 1996), p. 138.

individuals were made amenable, there are no courts sitting effectively to deal with them...The mutiny of the I.R.A. is probably the least serious element in crime.'[28] In such a context it was not surprising that the pro-treaty leadership followed a policy of procrastination and delay over the various political and military crises that confronted their government, while they strove to build its resources, authority, and power. There was an unwill-ingness, particularly among the military leadership, to precipitate civil war with old colleagues. There was also a realisation that the provisional govern-ment lacked the means to make a firm stand. But the anti-treaty political and military leadership also had reservations about bringing matters to a final test. Some republicans argued that to strike early, and particularly in Dublin, represented the best hope of success, but their leaders continued to search for some form of unity based on a republican constitution and a coalition government. This meant that events could only come to a head after the publication in June of a constitution that the British government insisted was in accordance with the treaty terms, and after the June election, which gave the necessary democratic authority for any military actions that should follow. British pressure meant that by late June all members of the provi-sional government had to place adherence to the treaty ahead of any desire to conciliate former colleagues. For its part, up to June, the British government treated the southern government with what John McColgan has called 'kid gloves', turning a blind eye to sundry infringements of the treaty on both sides of the border, and complaining only in private about the pro-treaty leadership's failure to face up to the domestic opposition. Such indulgence, however, did not extend to the constitution or to any pro-treaty hesitation in asserting authority after the election.[29]

ATTEMPTS to restore Sinn Féin unity began during the dáil treaty debates. Various abortive initiatives were floated in an attempt to avoid a vote on the settlement being taken, and to enable de Valera to remain as president. Finally an apparently unplanned compromise emerged, by which the dáil and the dáil government remained in existence alongside, and sometimes overlapping with, the provisional government. At the end of the debates Richard Mulcahy, the new minister for defence, claimed that the I.R.A.'s position was unchanged. Such a desire to avoid acknowledging divisions was shown again when the Sinn Féin ard-fheis met on 22–3 February 1922. A vote on the treaty was then avoided by Mulcahy's resolution providing for a delay in the general election for three months, the constitution to be pub-lished before the election (implying that it should be republican in character).

---

[28] Midleton to George V, 30 Apr. 1922 (P.R.O., Midleton papers, 30/67/50).
[29] John McColgan, *British policy and the Irish administration, 1920–22* (London, 1983), p. 104.

This compromise was agreed to by the new government despite the fact that it appeared to have a majority for its own views at that assembly.

In the long run the republican opposition had most to lose by this delaying policy. De Valera was basing his hopes for a restoration of political unity on a revival of the Sinn Féin organisation. From February onwards, however, it was clear that Sinn Féin was a mere rump of the old movement. Accordingly de Valera founded a new political party, Cumann na Poblachta, which made so little impression that he was later unable to remember when it ceased to exist. Debates in the dáil, meanwhile, became little more than a replay of those over the treaty. The political split had served to define and nationalise the issues.

Following the Sinn Féin ard-fheis the British government quickly expressed alarm about the provisional government's delaying policy, but were reassured by Griffith's promise that the constitution would have to be given British approval before it could be published. Reporting from Dublin for Lloyd George's government, Andy Cope, assistant under-secretary at Dublin Castle, placed his usual optimistic interpretation on developments. He told Churchill:

An election at the present time would have given them a clear majority, but at too heavy a price. It would have permanently split the I.R.A. with the certainty of many conflicts and murders. The outrages since the treaty was signed are symptomatic of this tendency. So also are the revolts in south Tipperary, Limerick, and west Cork, where the provisional government is practically repudiated. The agreement will allow passions to cool and discipline to be restored in the I.R.A. An election now would also force de Valera into permanent opposition. The agreement gives the provisional government time to get on its feet. At the end of three months it should be a going concern and much of the opposition should have lapsed.[30]

FROM February 1922 onwards the most crucial developments were happening within the I.R.A. Military divisions over the treaty took more time to be defined than the political ones, but as early as January were threatening the settlement. For all de Valera's and Brugha's efforts prior to the treaty there was still no political control over the I.R.A., which remained a volunteer organisation. Anti-treaty I.R.A. members argued that allegiance to the dáil had been conditional on the continued existence of the republic. They held that after the treaty control of the army should revert to its executive convention, which had been unable to meet during the Anglo–Irish war. Already by early January the strongest I.R.A. areas outside Dublin were in the anti-treaty camp. On 10 December 1921 the 1st Southern Division had declared its opposition to the treaty, and feeling was even stronger in the 2nd Southern Division. Without Collins's support for the treaty it is difficult to conceive how the settlement could have stood any chance of implementation, but

---

[30] Cope to Churchill, 26 Feb. 1922 (P.R.O., C.O. 906/20).

even Collins could take only a strong minority of the I.R.A. with him—the majority of the G.H.Q. staff, a minority of the Dublin Brigade, and the crucial support of Seán McKeon in Longford and Michael Brennan in Clare, the only leading I.R.A. figures outside Dublin who supported the treaty. McKeon's and Brennan's commands prevented the linking up of southern and western anti-treaty areas. As already noted, whatever support there was in the I.R.A. for the settlement appears to have stemmed from personal loyalty, rather than from any ideological commitment to the treaty.

On 10 January a meeting of divisional and brigade O.C.s and of G.H.Q. members opposed to the treaty reaffirmed the independence of the army and demanded the meeting of an army convention on 5 February. They also established a military action committee, afterwards known as the army council. At a stormy meeting with anti-treaty officers on 18 January Mulcahy reluctantly agreed to the holding of a convention, but won acceptance for his demand that it should be delayed for two months. He did not consult either the provisional or dáil governments in making this commitment. The same meeting elected a 'watchdog committee' which was to ensure that there was no departure from the original character of the I.R.A. Key units of the army, however, notably the South Tipperary Brigade, were to pay no attention to this compromise, and the watchdog committee had little effect. As with the Sinn Féin compromise, all that had been achieved was postponement. Meanwhile the weakness of both pro- and anti-treaty leadership encouraged independent local I.R.A. activity. A whole series of infringements of the truce occurred, notably in south Tipperary, where the printing presses of the *Clonmel Nationalist* were wrecked for the refusal to publish I.R.A. proclamations, and a successful large-scale raid was made on Clonmel R.I.C. barracks. Cope relayed to Churchill Collins's view that 'for the provisional government to attempt forcible recovery at the present moment would be to invite disaster. The best thing to do was to let matters in south Tipperary work themselves out which would not be long.'[31]

It was in the period leading up to the tensely awaited convention that G.H.Q. began to build up loyal local units into an independent army. The provisional government, therefore, financed units that swore allegiance to it, before taking over barracks, most notably Beggars' Bush, where the first regular unit of the new army was installed by March. The new army was hastily recruited, and the loyalty of many of its recruits was questionable. It had no discipline code, and had particular problems in finding effective officers. Emmet Dalton, one of its few trained officers, described the new force as 'a rag-tail and bobble-tail one'. A later Free State memorandum

---

[31] Anti-treaty I.R.A. members to Mulcahy, 11 Jan. 1922, and statement by Mulcahy on 'genesis of army situation' (Mulcahy papers, MS P7/B/191); Cope to Churchill, 1 Mar. 1922 (P.R.O., C.O. 906/20).

commented: 'When the regular army started it was not possible to confine the number of officers to the proportion required for a regular army but any Volunteer officer who was pro-treaty and willing to join the army was appointed an officer.'[32] The British government supplied the new force with weapons and ammunition. A considerable period was to elapse before the provisional government would have any confidence in using such a force with which to establish its authority.

The speed of British troop evacuation had dangerous implications for the provisional government, whose embryonic and (until the March I.R.A. convention) undercover army was a weak and unreliable force to contest republican I.R.A. control of many areas of Ireland. Ironically Collins, the firmest of enemies of British military presence, was to urge the British authorities to slow down their evacuation of Limerick, and, later, Cork barracks.

When British troops left the city of Limerick in early March the pro-treaty leadership was no longer willing to tolerate local republican I.R.A. units taking over barracks. If the anti-treaty I.R.A. gained control in Limerick, the republican south would have been linked to the republican west; Brennan's and McKeon's commands would have been isolated. To prevent this outcome, Brennan was hastily summoned to cross the Shannon and take over barracks in the city with loyal men from the 1st Western Division. In retaliation republican units from all over Munster swarmed into the city. With different barracks occupied by rival forces, the conditions for the outbreak of civil war were in place. The fight for Limerick, however, was to be delayed until July. Old military and I.R.B. colleagues—Liam Lynch and Richard Mulcahy to the fore—hastily cobbled together an agreement by which outside forces vacated Limerick, and local units were to take over. Griffith had wanted a firm stand to be taken during this crisis and some of the pro-treaty forces, notably J. J. O'Connell, the deputy chief of staff, regarded the agreement as a sell-out. Mulcahy, however, stressed that the army was by no reckoning ready for large-scale confrontation. Gearóid O'Sullivan, the adjutant-general, commented: 'At that time we were in Beggars' Bush I did not know but the man in the next office would blow me up.'[33]

The next two months saw a succession of clashes over barrack occupation, particularly in the 'frontier' areas of the south and west. A crisis, similar to the Limerick one, at Kilkenny in early May saw another last-minute compromise. The most alarming of such developments resulted in a stoppage of British troop evacuation, and heightened British government fears that the arms they were giving over to the pro-treaty army were ending up in the wrong hands. The holding of pro-treaty political meetings in various parts of

---

[32] Dalton in R.T.É. television programme 'Emmet Dalton remembers' (first broadcast 7 Mar. 1978); 'Memo on officers' submitted to army inquiry (Mulcahy papers, MS P7/C/42).
[33] O'Sullivan at army inquiry (Mulcahy papers, MS P7/C/36).

Munster and the west also threatened to produce major military confrontations. Trains were prevented from conveying crowds going to hear Collins
speak in Cork, and Collins was stopped from visiting the republican graves in
the city's cemetery. Shots were fired while Collins addressed the crowd. The
most dramatic such event occurred when Griffith addressed a crowd on
Easter Sunday in Sligo town—the 3rd Western Division, which had earlier
proscribed the meeting, decided at the last moment not to disrupt it. Griffith
spoke surrounded by rival units of the I.R.A. In the spring much attention
was also focused on a succession of speeches given by de Valera in a speaking
tour of Munster. At Killarney de Valera told his audience that if the treaty
was accepted by the electorate, I.R.A. men 'will have to march over the dead
bodies of their own brothers. They will have to wade through Irish blood.' In
response to an outraged press reaction de Valera stressed that he had been
warning against the dangers of civil war rather than inciting his countrymen
to civil war. He had shown, however, considerable insensitivity towards the
inevitable reaction to his pronouncements. By that time, however, de Valera
was having little influence on events.[34]

The election of delegates for the March I.R.A. convention revealed a
considerable anti-treaty majority. As a result Griffith issued an order banning
it. The dáil cabinet meeting of 15 March asserted that the dáil should be 'the
sole body in supreme control of the army and that any effort to set up
another body in control would be tantamount to an attempt to establish a
military dictatorship'. While the G.H.Q. leadership made a desperate attempt to achieve a *rapprochement* with the 1st Southern Division, Rory
O'Connor, representing diehard republican resistance, held a press conference on 22 March at which he commented that 'there were times when
revolution was justified and the army had overthrown the government in
many countries in that way'. When asked whether he supported a military
dictatorship, O'Connor replied: 'You can take it that way if you like.'[35]

The meeting of the army convention, on 26 March, finally defined the
military split. While the convention reaffirmed the army's independence,
elected a new executive, and reimposed the boycott of Belfast goods, it was
to be criticised by many republicans for not ordering decisive military action.
Tom Maguire, O.C. 2nd Western Division, reminisced: 'We were undecided
... because the last thing we wanted to do was to start to shoot. We would
have done anything to avoid that.' A decision was deferred as to whether the
I.R.A. should prevent a general election being held.[36]

[34] *Irish Independent*, 17 Mar. 1922; de Valera to *Irish Independent*, 23 Mar. 1922.
[35] Griffith to minister for defence, n.d., probably mid-Mar. 1922 (Mulcahy papers, MS P7/
B/191); dáil cabinet minutes, 15, 21 Mar. 1922 (N.A.I., DE1/4, pp 85–100); O'Connor's
interview, *Irish Independent*, 23 Mar. 1922.
[36] Tom Maguire in Uinseann MacEoin (ed.), *Survivors* (Dublin, 1981), p. 291. For the
Belfast boycott, see below, p. 24.

The convention also saw the emergence of differences in executive I.R.A. ranks, which were to develop up to and beyond the beginning of the civil war. Revealing their old disdain for less strong areas, Cork I.R.A. men were dissatisfied with their representation on the new army executive and were opposed to talk of 'interference with the election' and 'an army dictatorship', issues over which Seán Hegarty and Florrie O'Donoghue, two of the leaders of the Cork No. 1 Brigade, resigned from the executive. Even at this early stage it was apparent that members of the executive I.R.A. were independent of any political control and direction. Consequently, they were all too easily depicted as mutineers and blamed for the prevailing disorder. The future Free State general M. J. Costello reflected: 'The anti-treaty forces beat themselves before a shot was fired by alienating the people in the spring of 1922 and because they rejected the dáil as the supreme authority.'[37]

On 14 April units of the Dublin Brigade took over the Four Courts and various other prominent buildings in Dublin, including the Kildare Street Club, exclusive bastion of the Anglo-Irish ascendancy, now to be used as a home for Belfast refugees. Within the Four Courts members of the army executive, Rory O'Connor and Liam Mellows to the fore, issued intransigent press releases and came to represent a kind of military vanguard. The leadership of the 1st Southern Division, however, continued to strive to find some basis for unity with their old colleagues.

Initially peace talks centred on the I.R.B. That organisation failed to produce any agreed formula, but some of its members, who had high rank in the I.R.A. and were mainly hostile to the treaty, issued the 'army officers' statement' on 1 May. This was presented to the dáil and began the official negotiations in the dáil and the army that culminated in the pact between Collins and de Valera of 20 May. The compromise terms suggested were essentially those accepted later by Collins and de Valera—that the treaty should be accepted as the basis for army unification, that a Sinn Féin panel of candidates be drawn up for the election (thus preventing the contest from appearing as a referendum on the treaty), and that a coalition government should be set up following the election.

For over two weeks prospects for achieving a successful compromise looked bleak. A committee, representing all sides of the dáil, failed to achieve any consensus and on the floor of the dáil Griffith and O'Higgins set themselves resolutely against any talk of appeasing the opposition. Eventually Collins and de Valera engaged in direct negotiations and surprised everyone by approving a pact on 20 May. A Sinn Féin panel was agreed on for the election, the proportion of pro- and anti-treaty candidates to be determined by their existing strengths in the dáil. A coalition executive after the election was also agreed to. Collins only proved adamant, it appears, on the clause

---

[37] M. J. Costello, 13 Sept. 1953 (N.L.I., Florence O'Donoghue papers, MS 31423 (5)).

that non-Sinn Féin candidates be allowed to stand at the polls. The pact greatly alarmed the British government, Churchill concluding that 'it left the [provisional] government in its present weak and helpless position'. Collins, it seemed, was preventing any clear verdict on the treaty and making provision for potential government ministers to avoid endorsing it. Ernest Blythe recorded that Griffith was so dismayed by the pact that he never again addressed Collins by his Christian name.[38] The pact showed how far Collins and de Valera were prepared to go to avoid civil war. While Collins appeared to have made far more concessions than de Valera, the fate of the agreement lay in Collins's hands: would he be able to win British approval for a republican constitution? The issues, in fact, had been no more than postponed.

The vital test for the provisional government, therefore, came not as a consequence of British alarm about the pact but rather from Lloyd George's insistence that the constitution abide by the treaty's terms. The treaty had envisaged (article 17) that within a year the provisional government would give way to a permanent government following the adoption of a new constitutional framework for the Free State. Accordingly a constitution committee was established following approval of the treaty by the dáil.[39] All the British government's worst fears were confirmed on receiving the draft constitution, whose framers had seized the opportunity to enhance Irish national aspirations by eliminating any role for the crown in Irish affairs. In late May Griffith and Collins were called over to London by Lloyd George to receive his ultimatum about the constitution. This was the first time that the prime minister had involved himself directly in Irish affairs since signing the treaty. In meetings with the two Irish leaders Lloyd George made clear in the strongest terms that they must abide by the treaty—if they did not, they would find themselves back in the position they had been in on the evening of 6 December. Lloyd George told a meeting of British signatories to the treaty: 'The one thing on which the British government could fight was allegiance to the king.'[40] Thomas Jones, the prime minister's private secretary, recorded Collins's determination to dwell on northern issues, partly as a means to avoid awkward constitutional questions. Eventually Lloyd George demanded satisfactory answers from the provisional government on six issues relating to the constitution,[41] including the demand that the crown retain genuine authority, and the insistence that a coalition government could not be tolerated. After Lloyd George made a final, melodramatic appeal to Grif-

---

[38] British cabinet minutes, 30 May 1922 (P.R.O., CAB 23/C/30); Blythe article and review of Calton Younger, *Ireland's civil war* (London, 1968), in Máire Comerford papers (U.C.D., A.D.).
[39] Leo Kohn, *The constitution of the Irish Free State* (London, 1932), pp 77–8.
[40] Lloyd George at British signatories' meeting, 26 May 1922 (P.R.O., CAB 43/1).
[41] Mansergh, *Unresolved question*, pp 211–12. For the 1922 constitution see also below, pp 87–90.

fith and Collins, Collins returned in a grumpy mood to Dublin, while Griffith left work on the constitution in the hands of Hugh Kennedy, the government's chief legal adviser, who hammered out amendments with Lord Hewart. To Lloyd George's pleasant surprise Griffith's reply on the six points satisfied him in every respect. The form of the published constitution was to be consistent with the treaty, and was to include the necessary symbols relating to the crown and privy council and the establishment of the office of governor general, but its spirit was that of an essentially independent country. Neither the national flag (the tricolour) nor military uniforms were to show any trace of royal symbols.

Meanwhile army unity talks had been given a considerable fillip by the pact between Collins and de Valera. A truce between pro- and anti-treaty forces was extended and agreement was virtually secured on the distribution of G.H.Q. appointments in a reunited army: a disproportionate share of the jobs was given to executive I.R.A. members. These conclusions, however, did not win the approval of the Four Courts executive. An I.R.A. convention on 18 June finally rejected the army unity proposals and a resolution of Tom Barry's giving British forces seventy-two hours to leave before being attacked was only narrowly defeated. Those who voted for the latter resolution staged a new split within the army by walking out at the meeting and electing their own executive, Liam Lynch being replaced by Joe McKelvey, O.C. 3rd Northern Division, as chief of staff.

The concessions made to the British by the provisional government over the constitution ended any hopes of the pact producing a restoration of Sinn Féin unity. Collins's speech in Cork city two days before the 16 June election, advising the electorate to vote for candidates of their choice regardless of the Sinn Féin panel, would appear, therefore, to be a symptom of the pact's collapse rather than its cause. The constitution was published on the day of the election itself, adding to the sense of republican grievance. The use of proportional representation for the first time, together with the publication in the press of candidates' positions on the treaty, made it all the more apparent that the election would amount to a referendum on the treaty.

The election results revealed a strong pro-treaty majority. Anti-treaty candidates received under 22 per cent of the first-preference votes, and won a majority only in Sligo and East Mayo. Out of the total of 620,283 votes cast, pro-treaty panel candidates won 239,193; anti-treaty candidates won 133,864 votes. Otherwise the poll was notable for the large non-Sinn Féin vote. The Labour party exceeded all expectations by winning 29.4 per cent of all votes cast, a result that would have been even better if they had put up more candidates. Farmer and independent candidates did well also. This not only indicates that Sinn Féin had not represented large elements of Irish opinion, but suggests also a widespread dissatisfaction with the way in which post-treaty developments had been handled. The election was not a vote of confidence in the provisional government, but rather an expression of a popular desire for stability. It did, however, serve greatly to strengthen the provisional government and the treaty settlement. Henceforth the pro-treaty side could claim that it was acting in accordance with a legitimate popular majority mandate. Meanwhile the British government could now stress the necessity for the provisional government's authority to be enforced in every respect.[42]

It was at that time also, on 22 June, that an event occurred that further precipitated the likelihood of civil war. Sir Henry Wilson, chief of the imperial general staff during the world war, had since his retirement from the army been security adviser to the Northern Ireland government and M.P. for North Down. Thanks to his diehard opinions he was a prime I.R.A. target. There had been several abortive plans to kill him since the truce. On 22 June Wilson was assassinated outside his London home by Reginald Dunne and Joseph O'Sullivan, two London I.R.B. members. Dunne, head of the I.R.A. in London, had gone pro-treaty, apparently out of loyalty to Collins. O'Sullivan had lost a leg while in the British army during the world war. Both of them were arrested in the chase and mayhem that followed the shooting.

There has been a long and virulent debate over whether Dunne and O'Sullivan acted on their own initiative in assassinating Wilson or on instructions from Dublin. Some evidence exists to link Collins with the assassination. It has been claimed that he had inadvertently failed to cancel instructions sent several months earlier; given Collins's meticulous methods of operating, this appears unlikely, and there is oral testimony that the orders were given the day before. Hard as the British government tried, no proof was found of republican I.R.A. involvement in the killing. Earlier in June Dunne had been in Dublin visiting both Collins and the men in the Four Courts. If Collins did issue the instructions he must have been aware of the calamitous results should his involvement become known to the British government; it would demonstrate how high a priority he placed on the need to reassure the northern I.R.A. of his support, and how little regard he had for the strict observance of the treaty. During the first few weeks of the civil war both pro- and anti-treaty sides were involved in abortive plans to free Dunne and O'Sullivan.

The British government's response to the assassination was immediate and extreme. On 23 June the provisional government was given a final warning to end republican I.R.A. occupation of the Four Courts. It was made clear that if positive action were not taken the British army would reoccupy Dublin. When an equivocal reply was received, the British government planned action. The only debate within the cabinet was whether, in view of religious

---

[42] For election results, see Michael Gallagher, 'The pact general election of 1922' in *I.H.S.*, xxi, no. 84 (Sept. 1979), pp 404–21.

susceptibilities, the attack should take place on the Sunday or the Monday. Orders were given for ships to be ready to collect prisoners, and a proclamation was drawn up to be published after British occupation of the Four Courts. At the eleventh hour, however, the instructions were rescinded after the military commanders in Dublin had pointed out the disastrous potential such an action had for dragging British forces back into a hopeless mire, and for bringing about reunification in republican ranks. Although Collins protested about Winston Churchill's speech in the commons of 26 June, demanding action from the provisional government, it is clear that he no longer had room for manoeuvre.

It appears that the provisional government decided to attack the Four Courts on 26 June, the day before another series of events occurred which have often been held responsible for the decision. Leo Henderson, the director of the Belfast boycott, was arrested by pro-treaty troops while raiding a garage in Lower Baggot Street in search of northern goods; this despite the fact that the I.R.A.'s united northern policy was still operative. In retaliation the Four Courts executive ordered the kidnapping of J. J. O'Connell, the pro-treaty army's assistant chief of staff. But while O'Connell's seizure helped, as Collins later argued, to consolidate support within the provisional government army for the Four Courts attack, it should not be seen as the cause of the decision to act.

The politicians in the provisional government, led by Griffith and O'Higgins, had long wanted a firm stand to be taken. Military action, however, needed Collins's and Mulcahy's agreement, and that was only to be given with extreme reluctance. The British government had left them with no choice between adherence to the treaty and the continued search for republican unity. Collins did not know of British plans to take over the Four Courts but must have been aware of the likelihood of direct British military action if his government did not act. He may well have hoped that the war would be over quickly and would be limited to Dublin, and was aware of the split in executive I.R.A. ranks, though not of a last-minute *rapprochement* between the two. Nonetheless Collins must have realised that an attack on the Four Courts would be likely to bring a concerted response from the executive I.R.A.

The outbreak of the civil war had not been willed by either side: it represented the failure of both Collins's and de Valera's strategies since the dáil treaty debates. Even those within the Four Courts had made no preparations for war; right up to the attack they appeared to believe that any action would be taken by British forces and not by fellow Irishmen. Given this background it is not surprising that the early stages of the civil war were half-hearted and confused.

THE Northern Ireland government was established against a background of violence and upheaval, which coincided with great economic problems: it was not recognised by the dáil government or by organisations representing the northern catholic minority.[43] A purge of catholic shipyard workers in the Belfast yards during the summer of 1920 had provoked the dáil to authorise a boycott of Belfast goods. While the Anglo–Irish war had little direct relationship to the north-east, the later stages of the conflict, and particularly the truce that followed it, saw a considerable increase of I.R.A. activity there.

From its beginning Craig's government placed an overwhelming stress on security, heavily conscious of external and internal threats to its survival. In April 1922 the first wide-ranging special powers act was passed. Initially it was to apply for one year only, but eventually it lasted as long as the northern government.[44] The northern loyalist position was made the more vulnerable by the winding-down during the treaty period of the R.I.C., which had been 400 below strength in early 1922, before its replacement, the R.U.C., was set up on 31 May. By midsummer of that year the R.U.C. was still nearly 2,000 below its authorised strength of 5,000. The limited British army presence of sixteen battalions could not compensate. This situation necessitated a considerable reliance on the three categories of special constabulary—the full-time 'A', part-time 'B', and reserve 'C'. The specials had evolved directly from the Ulster Volunteer Force and represented the northern government's acknowledgement of the need for a large-scale loyalist self-defence unit. The special constabulary's strength had reached 42,250 by midsummer 1922; it was widely criticised from the beginning for its sectarian practices and outlook, and for its lack of training and discipline. S. G. Tallents, the British government's representative in Belfast from June 1922, said of the special constabulary: 'The catholics regard it with a bitterness exceeding that which the Black and Tans inspired in the south, and several prominent unionist public men told me privately that this purely partisan and insufficiently disciplined force was sowing feuds in the countryside which would not be eradicated for generations.'[45] The new government was largely dependent on Whitehall financing and was open to scrutiny by the British government. The transfer of government services was not completed until 1922. It is not surprising that the circumstances of Northern Ireland's birth heightened the traditional loyalist siege mentality.

The six months following the treaty saw a vast increase in the level of violence and disorder in the north-east, and particularly on the border and in Belfast; the consequences of this appeared at times to threaten the stability and very existence of the northern government. Between 6 December 1921

[43] A study that takes a comparative approach to revolution and state formation in the two parts of Ireland is David Fitzpatrick, *The two Irelands, 1912–1939* (Oxford, 1998).
[44] 12 & 13 Geo. V, c. 5 [N.I.] (7 Apr. 1922), made permanent by 23 & 24 Geo. V, c. 12 [N.I.] (9 May 1933); repealed by 1973/53 [U.K.] (25 July 1973).
[45] Tallents to Masterton-Smith, 4 July 1922 (P.R.O., C.O. 739–16). For the establishment of the Northern Ireland government, see below, pp 161–70.

and 31 May 1922, 147 catholics and 73 protestants were killed in Belfast, and 22 catholics and 8 protestants elsewhere.[46]

The boundary commission, which appeared to threaten the territorial integrity of Northern Ireland, was one destabilising factor. In May Craig declared that it had been at the root of all evil since the treaty. The prospect of the commission greatly raised the expectations of the northern catholic minority, while it increased loyalist fears. The northern government found it impossible to accept Lloyd George's assurances that Northern Ireland might gain territory from the commission's conclusions. Craig wrote to the leader of the Conservative party, Austen Chamberlain:

So intense is local feeling at the moment that my colleagues and I may be swept off our feet, and contemporaneously with the functioning of the treaty, loyalists may declare independence, on their own behalf, seize the customs and other government departments, and set up an authority of their own. Many already believe that violence is the only language understood by Mr Lloyd George and his ministers.

The treaty period saw evidence of an increasing lack of sympathy on the part of the British coalition government and the civil service towards the northern government, and particularly its security forces. The treasury became restive at the costs involved in financing the specials, and there was increasing concern about many of their activities. In a British government memorandum two key government advisers, Thomas Jones and Lionel Curtis, wrote:

It is impossible to assume that the formidable forces now being organised under the guise of the police are directed solely against the danger of invasion from the south. The British government has armed and is paying for forces which, it is told by the government which controls them, will in certain eventualities be turned against itself... It is difficult to avoid the conclusion that the government of Northern Ireland has succeeded in assuming the military functions, specifically reserved to the British government, simply by calling their forces 'police'.[47]

The fact that the British government showed some flexibility on northern issues and was frequently critical of Craig's government in the first half of 1922 owed much to a desire to aid the southern provisional government's position and hence to preserve the treaty settlement. Looking back on the coalition government after Lloyd George's fall from office in October 1922, Craig told the new Conservative colonial secretary in November 1922 of his dissatisfaction with the support he had received from London, and concluded: 'There is no doubt that the late government was inspired by a desire to concentrate attention on the Irish treaty rather than on the act of 1920', and to avoid upsetting 'the susceptibilities of the Irish provisional

[46] Notes on situation in Ireland, casualty figures (P.R.O., C.O. 906/30).
[47] Craig to Churchill, 26 May 1922 (P.R.O., C.O. 739/14); Craig to Austen Chamberlain, 15 Dec. 1921 (P.R.O., C.O. 906/30); Lionel Curtis and Thomas Jones, memo for P.G.I. committee, 25 Mar. 1922 (P.R.O., C.O. 739/4).

government or... imperilling the passage of the treaty through the parliament in Dublin'. When Craig pressed for retaliatory action as a response to I.R.A. kidnappings of leading Fermanagh and Tyrone loyalists in February 1922, Churchill told him that 'violent measures would do more harm than good and might entail the resignation of the Irish provisional government, thus creating chaos and leaving the extremists in control'.[48]

For their part southern Irish nationalists, whether pro- or anti-treaty, were to become much more concerned with northern affairs than in the pre-treaty period. During the first six months of 1922 the provisional government acted as the guarantors and protectors of northern minority interests, and found favourable political circumstances in which to press northern demands on the British government.

The immediate cause of the crises on the border in January and February was the increased level of I.R.A. activity, which provoked a hysterical reaction by the northern authorities. On 14 January men from the 5th Northern Division of the I.R.A. were arrested in County Tyrone on their way to Derry for the Ulster final of the Gaelic Athletic Association championship. Documents were found on them relating to plans to bring about the escape of I.R.A. prisoners who were under sentence of death in Derry jail. The I.R.A. responded to this by kidnapping, in early February, forty-two prominent loyalists in Fermanagh and Tyrone. Shortly after that a body of special constabulary was involved in an armed skirmish at Clones station, in southern territory, while travelling by rail between Newtownards and Enniskillen. Four were killed and several kidnapped. The reaction of the northern government to this was predictably alarmist. Craig was even to ask Churchill if there was 'any legal obstacle to our sending a flying column of 5,000 constabulary to recover the kidnapped loyalists'. Churchill, as head of the new 'provisional government of Ireland committee', was left to remonstrate with both Irish governments and to complain to his wife: 'Ireland is sure to bring us every form of difficulty and embarrassment.'[49]

January 1922 had seen agreement on a combined I.R.A. policy to provide direct support to northern divisions. While claiming he was striving to bring about the release of kidnapped loyalists, Collins was personally involved in approving offensive actions. This policy had the double purpose of destabilising the northern government and providing a means by which a final I.R.A. split in the south could be avoided by concentrating on northern affairs. It was decidedly not in accord with the provisional government's public policy.

[48] Craig to Lord Devonshire, 6 Nov. 1922 (P.R.O., C.O. 739/1); Churchill to Craig (House of lords records dept, Lloyd George papers, MS F/102/45).
[49] Correspondence between Churchill, Cope, Craig, and Collins, 11–15 Feb. 1922 (P.R.O., C.O. 906/20, C.O. 739/4; P.R.O.N.I., C9B8x2/1); Churchill to Mrs Churchill, 4, 11 Feb. 1922 (quoted in Martin Gilbert, *Winston S. Churchill, iv: 1917–1922: companion, iii* (London, 1977), pp 1752, 1768).

The increasingly alarming security position, together with an unspoken acknowledgement that there were many northern issues left festering as a consequence of the treaty, led Churchill to call Craig and Collins to a meeting in London on 21 January. Surprisingly this resulted in an apparently wide-ranging agreement, which became known as the first Craig–Collins pact. One clause laid down that the boundary question would be settled by mutual agreement, and not by the boundary commission. Collins vouchsafed to bring to an immediate end the Sinn Féin boycott of Belfast goods, while Craig promised to facilitate (economic conditions allowing) the return of expelled catholic shipyard workers to their jobs. A large-scale system of relief was to be established. Finally the two leaders were to try to find 'a more suitable system than the council of Ireland [provision for which was made in the government of Ireland act and the Anglo–Irish treaty] for dealing with problems affecting all Ireland'.[50] The weaknesses, however, of this agreement soon became apparent. Representatives of the northern catholic minority quickly complained to Collins and Griffith of what had seemed to be the implicit recognition of Craig's government, and hence of the government of Ireland act; Craig was unable to make headway on the shipyard workers issue; and Collins failed to bring the economic boycott to an end, while little was achieved on prison releases. A second meeting between Craig and Collins in Dublin, on 2 February, revealed that the two leaders had completely different expectations concerning the extent of any border changes. The first pact, therefore, was stillborn.

There was a clear contradiction between Collins's public stance on the north and his secret support of an aggressive military policy. The plan to kidnap prominent loyalists had been postponed because of his meeting with Craig. Aggressive I.R.A. actions on the border continued through March, and Churchill's formation of a border commission, consisting of British, northern, and southern liaison officers, never functioned effectively. A combination of border tensions and outrages in Belfast led Churchill to bring representatives of the two Irish governments together in London on 30 March. Again, against expectations, a detailed agreement resulted.

The so-called second Craig–Collins pact, signed by representatives from all three governments, began with the exclamation: 'Peace is today declared.'[51] For its part the provisional government promised to try to end I.R.A. activity in the north, and to bring about the release of kidnapped loyalists. The northern government committed itself to try again on the catholic shipyard workers issue, and to free some political prisoners. Various committees were to be formed to defuse disputes, to consider the

[50] For terms of the agreement, see N.A.I., D.T., S1801A; P.G. minutes, 30 Jan., 2 Feb. 1922 (N.A.I., S.P.O., G1/1); *Irish Times*, 2, 3, 4 Feb. 1922.
[51] 'Heads of agreement between the provisional government and the government of Northern Ireland' (P.R.O., C.O. 906/30).

possibility of greater catholic involvement in the northern security forces (with the possibility of catholic specials to be discussed), and to administer a British-supplied relief fund. Despite the hopes aroused by a very favourable press reaction in Britain and southern Ireland, the agreement proved to be what Lord Hugh Cecil warned it would be—'a statue of snow'.[52] Little commitment to its implementation was shown by either the northern or the southern leadership. Craig, who received a stormy reception when he returned to Belfast, interpreted the security aspects of the pact extremely narrowly. Shortly after his return from London he told a meeting of northern businessmen that the southern government's commitment to end I.R.A. activity and to accept northern court decisions were the only two important elements in the agreement. Only the relief committee proved effective, primarily because all stood to gain and it was not concerned with sensitive issues. Collins demonstrated a progressively cynical attitude to the pact and used it as a means to forward northern grievances to Belfast and London. More fundamentally the agreement had failed to address the basic issues—the border, and the minority population's recognition (or otherwise) of the northern government. The British government never resolved to enforce the pact's provisions. Far from reducing tensions, the pact provided the immediate prelude to a considerable increase in sectarian violence.

When it became clear that little was to be gained for nationalists from the pact, plans were made for a joint I.R.A. northern offensive. Arms were to be sent north to enable general attacks to take place on 19 May. I.R.A. units in areas adjoining northern territory were to aid in the offensive, and volunteers from Cork and Kerry were sent north to stiffen northern units. The offensive, however, proved a dismal failure. It appears to have been called off at the last moment, but, despite that, isolated attacks and widespread burning and destruction of property took place. The response from the northern security forces was severe and effective. Internment was introduced: 350 I.R.A. and Sinn Féin men were captured, partly in consequence of a raid on the Belfast I.R.A.'s liaison office at St Mary's Hall, where a list containing the names of 'practically every officer in the division' was captured. Many of those who escaped internment left the six counties. By late May the prospects for the I.R.A. in the north were dismal. A memorandum from the 3rd Northern Division, of which Belfast was a part, concluded: 'the demoralisation has practically completed its work . . . The position in No. 2 and 3 Brigades today is that the military organisation is almost destroyed . . . [The enemy] now believe that they have beaten the I.R.A. completely in Antrim and Down.' General Macready, G.O.C.-in-C., concluded that police work since 22 May meant that 'the majority of the I.R.A. gunmen in the north

---

[52] Gilbert, *Churchill*, iv, 702.

were either wiped out of the six counties or are in hiding'.[53] In late May and early June clashes between I.R.A. units and specials, in and around the awkward border salient extending from Belleek to Pettigoe, resulted in British army occupation of much of the territory and the first direct clashes between British and I.R.A. arms since the treaty. For all Collins's protests over the crisis, it resulted in continued British army presence in the area and I.R.A. withdrawal.

The I.R.A.'s aggressive policy and the failure of the pact led to an increasing alienation of the northern minority from the southern government. Hugh A. McCarthy, who reported on opinion in south and east Down and Newry for the provisional government, concluded:

The people of all creeds and classes had got on well together until the attack on the barracks in May last...The only result of the affair [the I.R.A. offensive] was to embitter feeling and place the catholic population at the mercy of the specials. The aftermath of the I.R.A. offensive was to leave the minority population more exposed than ever to reprisal. Large numbers were arrested and many of the I.R.A. forced to cross the border.[54]

The northern catholic minority had all too little control over events from which they were to suffer the direct consequences. In the post-treaty period they were in a kind of limbo—not recognising the government under which they lived, expectantly waiting for the boundary commission, and heavily dependent on their southern co-religionists to provide political and military support. They were also divided among themselves into Sinn Féiners and old-style nationalists (supporters of organisations such as the Ancient Order of Hibernians and the United Irish League). Belfast nationalists, in particular, having less to hope for than border nationalists from the boundary commission, were keen to take their seats in the Northern Ireland parliament and work at implementing the council of Ireland.[55]

The negative results of both the aggressive and conciliatory southern policies towards the north produced a change of strategy. During June northern considerations came to be neglected while the provisional government and army were faced with military and constitutional crises at home and in London. The partition issue had to be postponed. Collins retreated, publicly at least, from an aggressive northern policy, giving the politicians within the government the opportunity to decide 'that a policy of peaceful obstruction should be adopted towards the Belfast government and that no troops from

[53] 3rd N. (I.R.A.) Div. memo from Séamus Woods, 27 July 1922 (Mulcahy papers, MS P7/B/1); Macready, report for week ending 8 July 1922 (P.R.O., CAB 24/138). See also Eamon Phoenix, *Northern nationalism: nationalist politics, partition and the catholic minority in Northern Ireland, 1890–1940* (Belfast, 1994), ch. 6.
[54] Hugh A. McCarthy's report for south and east Down and Newry (U.C.D., A.D., Kennedy papers, MS P4/V/2, P4/L1/6).
[55] See Phoenix, *Northern nationalism*, chs 4–5.

the twenty-six counties, either those under official control or attached to the executive, shall be permitted to invade the six-county area'. Collins himself told the *Daily Mail*: 'I think my attitude towards Ulster, which is the attitude of all of us in the government, is not understood. There can be no question of forcing Ulster into union with the twenty-six counties. I am absolutely against coercion of any kind. If Ulster is to join us it must be voluntarily. Union is our final goal, that is all.'[56]

For all the lack of success of the southern government's northern policy, the northern government's position was increasingly vulnerable. In British government circles, demands became increasingly frequent for a judicial inquiry into the Belfast disturbances since the treaty and for the establishment of martial law in the northern capital. During his negotiations with Lloyd George in late May and early June, Collins was able to use the northern situation as a diplomatic weapon. The possibility of direct British intervention in security affairs appeared imminent. Eventually a British civil servant, S. G. Tallents, was sent, with Craig's grudging acceptance, to Belfast to report on the reasons for the second pact's failure and whether there was need for an official inquiry to be held. By the time that Tallents reported, the outbreak of the civil war in the south had taken all southern attention away from the north. I.R.A. men in the north were garrisoned in the Curragh and told by Collins, in early August, that I.R.A. actions against the north had to be suspended. Civil war in the south made it possible for the northern government to stabilise its position and for the British government to show less interest in the affairs of the six counties.

[56] P.G. minutes, 3 June 1922 (N.A.I., S.P.O., G1/2); Collins in *Daily Mail*, quoted in *Belfast Newsletter*, 30 June 1922.

CHAPTER II

Civil war and aftermath, 1922–4

MICHAEL HOPKINSON

THE provisional government army's attack on the occupied Four Courts proved far from easy to accomplish successfully. It was delayed for a few hours because of doubts about the reliability of troops and when it did start, at 4.15 a.m. on 28 June, the use of 18-pounder guns, loaned from the British government, initially had little effect on the building's walls. Even the normally optimistic Alfred Cope feared that any further delay would result in the republican side winning sympathy. The new army had considerable difficulty in finding trained men to operate the artillery; Collins desperately sought men with British army experience to provide on-the-spot instruction. Emmet Dalton, who was in charge of the operations and one of the very few with any experience of such arms, at one stage had to take over operation of the artillery himself. While General Macready was scornful of the pro-treaty army's ability and counselled against supplying further aid, Churchill urged Collins to accept more offers of equipment, including 60-pounder guns which Collins thought completely impractical for his troops to use. Churchill told Cope on 28 June: 'Tell Collins to ask for any assistance he requires and report to me any difficulty that has been raised by the military.' At one stage during the siege Churchill considered that British troops might have to take over; he also suggested that British aircraft be loaned to the Irish government, painted in Irish colours to cover up British involvement.[1]

Within the Four Courts, however, the republican position soon became hopeless. Seán MacBride, who as a very young man was prominent during the siege, recollected: 'We were never a large enough garrison to have held such a building, nor did we expect to have to hold it.' There had been a lack of cooperation between those in the Four Courts and the Dublin Brigade, whose leaders had been opposed to the continued occupation of the building.

[1] Collins to Churchill, 24 June 1922; Churchill to Cope, 28 June 1922; Churchill to Cope for Macready, 28 June 1922; correspondence between Churchill, Cope, and Curtis, 28–9 June 1922 (P.R.O., C.O. 906/21).

Oscar Traynor, commandant of the Dublin Brigade, dreaded the prospect of a replay of the Easter rising and Tommy Merrigan, one of the men under him, commented that they were sitting in buildings when they should have been fighting. Buildings around the Four Courts had not been taken over— the neighbouring Four Courts Hotel had previously been handed back to Stephen O'Mara, its owner, because he was a leading Limerick republican. The possibility of organising an escape from the Courts apparently went unconsidered until the last moment. There was considerable confusion within the building as to who was in charge. While Liam Mellows and Rory O'Connor were the senior army executive men there, they yielded command to Paddy O'Brien, of the Dublin Brigade, on grounds of military experience, and then to Ernie O'Malley when O'Brien was wounded.[2]

Eventually the pro-treaty army's shelling culminated in an enormous explosion in the Public Record Office, which was being used by the republicans as a munitions centre. The roof was blown in and fire spread. By that time the debate within the Four Courts, among the desperate and the wounded, was about whether surrender could be justified, but that was terminated when Traynor issued orders to surrender in order to preserve the position of those outside. While O'Connor and Mellows gave in with troubled consciences, never to be free again, Ernie O'Malley and Seán Lemass, among others, escaped from a loosely organised pro-treaty guard in Jameson's distillery.[3]

Attention next switched to the east side of O'Connell Street, where the Dublin Brigade had established their H.Q. in four neighbouring hotels. They were soon joined there by prominent anti-treaty figures, notably de Valera, Brugha, and Seán T. O'Kelly, who had been caught unawares by the outbreak of fighting. De Valera quickly released a press bulletin expressing his support for republican arms, referring to 'men who are now being attacked by the forces of the provisional government' as 'the best and bravest of our nation', and rejoined his old Dublin I.R.A. battalion. Privately, however, de Valera was extremely depressed and showed considerable interest in the Labour party's peace initiative. Erskine Childers told his wife at the time: 'Dev says we should surrender while we are strong I believe.'[4] Republican-held buildings scattered around the fringes of the centre of Dublin were

[2] MacBride in MacEoin, *Survivors*, p. 117; Oscar Traynor in O'Malley notebooks (U.C.D., A.D., MS P17b/95, 98, 142); Tommy Merrigan (ibid., P17b/110); Ernie O'Malley, *The singing flame* (Dublin, 1978), pp 92–112; Peadar O'Donnell in MacEoin, *Survivors*, p. 25; Moss Twomey in O'Malley notebooks (MS P17b/95).

[3] For the fate of O'Connor and Mellows, see below, pp 47–8: for Lemass see below, p. 120, and John Horgan, *Seán Lemass: the enigmatic patriot* (Dublin, 1997); for O'Malley, see Richard English, *Ernie O'Malley: I.R.A. intellectual* (Oxford, 1998).

[4] *Poblacht na h-Éireann War News*, no. 3, 29 June 1922; *Irish Times*, 1 July 1922; earl of Longford and T. P. O'Neill, *Eamon de Valera* (Dublin, 1970), p. 196; Childers to Mrs Childers, 12 July 1922 (T.C.D., Childers papers, MS 7855).

quickly taken over by pro-treaty troops. On O'Connell Street an initially hesitant provisional government offensive was quickly reinforced by the use of artillery. During 5 July republican troops in the Hammam Hotel surrendered, but before that it had been decided to evacuate the centre of the city. While de Valera, in common with other political leaders, was smuggled across the Liffey to safety, Brugha staged his own blood-sacrifice by refusing to surrender and being shot while running out of his headquarters, arms at the ready. He died that evening. A letter de Valera sent to Brugha, while under the impression that he had survived the shooting, well revealed the differences in approach between them. De Valera wrote: 'The brigade has disengaged from the very foolish type of battle into which it has been drawn and will now be able to engage in operations more suited to its training and equipment.' He continued: 'I had no idea in view of the plan agreed on that you would attempt to hold the hotels as long as you did. We were all extremely anxious... You were scarcely justified... in taking the risk you ran—and we were all more than vexed with you—but all's well that ends well. And the opening of the campaign otherwise not to be dreamt of by us gave [sic] a definite beginning.'[5]

The republican evacuation was hastily improvised but accomplished with arms and men for the most part intact. During the Dublin fighting sixty-five were killed and twenty-eight wounded; the value of property destroyed was estimated as £3–4 million. The republican retreat abruptly ended the war's opening chapter. Never again was Dublin to be central to the republican strategy in the civil war. From April onwards the thinking of the Four Courts executive had been Dublin-centred, but with Liam Lynch back as chief of staff that policy was to be reversed. Lynch, along with Liam Deasy and Seán Culhane, had been given a safe-conduct from Dublin back to the south in the mistaken belief that they would oppose a continuation of hostilities. Lynch soon announced that all I.R.A. men should return to their own areas. Large areas of Ireland, however, had been unaware of the fighting in Dublin.

During the Dublin fighting Oscar Traynor had appealed for reinforcements. The only practical response came from a column of over 100 from south Tipperary, which stopped at Blessington, among the Wicklow hills, and was soon joined by units that had evacuated Dublin. Any hope of this force moving back on the capital soon ended in another scattered retreat after limited skirmishing with pro-treaty troops in the Blessington area. Following that, Ernie O'Malley led a force to Wexford, which took various towns there with little resistance. At the same time Seán Moylan took a contingent of Cork I.R.A. men to New Ross by train, only to return after a failure to link up with O'Malley for a possible move back on Dublin. Both O'Malley and

[5] De Valera to Brugha, 6 July 1922 (U.C.D., A.D., MacSwiney papers, MS P48a/255(1)).

Moylan saw little point in remaining in the area. The episode typified the desultory character of the war's early stages.

The civil war is easily depicted as a hopeless cause for republican arms. In the early part of the conflict, however, the republican side appeared to possess many advantages. The provisional government was totally dependent on its army but had little reason to be confident about the army's ability and potential performance. Seán MacMahon, the army's quartermaster and later chief of staff, related that it was only after the Dublin fighting that 'the realisation came to us that [we] were in for a long struggle and we began to look around for an army'.[6] A war council consisting of Collins, as commander-in-chief, Mulcahy, chief of staff, and Eoin O'Duffy, in charge of the new, crucial south-western command, was hastily formed. Collins and Mulcahy were among those excused their civil functions. The council was never to meet again after its formation. On 3 July the provisional government issued an appeal for a further 20,000 men to be enlisted in the army, and around 15,000 appear to have joined in the first half of July. Men were enlisted without training or medical tests and in many cases without a uniform. MacMahon estimated that of the 8,000 in the army at the start of the fighting only around 6,000 were well armed. The huge majority enlisted for the money, not from any commitment to the cause. Mulcahy admitted that many of the criminal class joined, and MacMahon commented: 'It was a case of accepting every man that came along and offered his service.' Many men had to be shown how to use a rifle on their way to the fighting areas. The supplies situation was just as worrying. Gearóid O'Sullivan, the adjutant-general, commented that having started the war they now had to look for supplies, and Mulcahy testified that men 'were absolutely thrown on their own resources and had to commandeer and take supplies' as 'the only way they could get them'.[7]

The paramount need in this desperate position was to place reliable men in key positions. O'Sullivan declared: 'You had to walk out and get men whom you could trust, not because they had any particular ability.'[8] There were frequent small-scale mutinies in the first months of the army's existence. Whatever alarm was to be felt about the performance of McKeon's Athlone and J. T. Prout's 3rd Southern commands could not result in changes in leadership. Particular concern was soon expressed about prison accommodation after a major riot in Mountjoy in July: in the first weeks of the war prisoners were released on a mere pledge not to take up arms again.

[6] MacMahon at 1924 army inquiry (Mulcahy papers, MS P7/C/14).

[7] P.G. minutes, 3 July 1922; conference at Portobello barracks, 17 July 1922 (Mulcahy papers, P7a/56); P.G. minutes, 26 Aug. 1922 (N.A.I., S.P.O., G1/3); MacMahon and Mulcahy at army inquiry (Mulcahy papers, P7/C/14, P7/C/7); O'Sullivan at army inquiry (ibid., P7/C/12); Mulcahy at army inquiry (ibid., P7/C/37).

[8] O'Sullivan at army inquiry (ibid., P7/C/12, 31).

As a consequence Collins soon placed some of his I.R.B. associates in control of prisons.

Against such a background it is scarcely surprising that the pro-treaty army proved a clumsy tool for restoring order. Testimony from all sides pointed to the army's limitations and its alienation from the population in many localities. O'Duffy grew to despair of his troops in the south-western command, saying 'we had to get work out of a disgruntled, undisciplined, and cowardly crowd.' Collins reserved his special venom for the standard of the Curragh command; General Diarmuid MacManus said that 80 per cent of the junior officers he had met were 'utterly unfitted for their rank and position'.[9] There was no discipline code until the end of the year. In the war's early stages there were strained relations between the leaders of various commands—notably between O'Duffy and Emmet Dalton. The troops' position was to be further hindered by their appearance as outsiders; the occupation of south Kerry by forces from Dublin and the north was to resemble, in this respect, that of the Black and Tans. Moreover, the troops could not be confined to their military role. The Civic Guard was only slowly established.[10] All armies are unsuited to police functions, and this was particularly true of the pro-treaty army.

The war quickly produced tensions between the political and military wings of the provisional government. Collins and Mulcahy had embarked on the conflict with considerably greater reluctance than their political colleagues, and had different war aims. The cabinet frequently pressed Collins and Mulcahy on the need to supply regular military reports. In correspondence with Cosgrave and Desmond FitzGerald, Collins opposed the tightening of press censorship and continued to hold out hope for negotiations with old military colleagues. With the dáil unable to meet till September, there must have been an awareness of the potential for military dictatorship, but Collins and Mulcahy, to their credit, never showed any desire for a military government to be formed. Meanwhile, in the war's early stages any criticism of the army within the government had to be bottled up. Again, the existence of two executives, the dáil government and the provisional government of Ireland, could have been a source of difficulty, despite the broadly similar membership of the two bodies. However, there was sufficient unity of purpose to make the system work.

[9] O'Duffy to Mulcahy, n. d., early Aug. 1922 (ibid., P7/B/71); MacManus to adj.-gen., 18 Sept. 1922, and undated memo by him (U.C.D., A.D., O'Malley papers, MS P17a/215).
[10] Enlistment for a police force of the provisional government ('Civic Guard') began in February 1922, but the Garda Síochána was not set up till 1923 (1923/37 [I.F.S.] (8 Aug. 1923)). Two recent studies of the Garda Síochána are Liam McNiffe, *A history of the Garda Síochána: a social history of the force 1922–57, with an overview for the years 1952–97* (Dublin, 1997), and Gregory Allen, *The Garda Síochána: policing independent Ireland 1922–82* (Dublin, 1999). They supplement the still valuable study by Conor Brady, *Guardians of the peace* (Dublin, 1974). See also below, p. 97, n. 23.

It was surprising that the consequences of the army's failings were not more disastrous. That they were not owed much to the ineffectiveness and indecisiveness of the republican military challenge. The Donegal republican Peadar O'Donnell was to reflect: 'We made soldiers of the Free State army by putting up a show of fight while retreating away from them... Early in 1922, republicans had the ball at their feet, the right objective situation, but the subjective aspect, namely the leadership, failed.'[11]

At the war's beginning the I.R.A. was much better armed than at any stage of the Anglo–Irish war. The seizure of arms in early April from H.M.S. *Upnor*—400 rifles and 700 revolvers were said to have been captured—was but the most notable of many such coups. The republican forces were led by the cream of the guerrilla warfare fighters of the Anglo–Irish war, and were to have the advantage of fighting in their own localities. The appeal of fighting for the revered ideal should have resulted in far more commitment than that shown by the pro-treaty mercenaries. Any such favourable auguries, however, were quickly dissipated by the failure to define aims and to adopt a coherent or aggressive policy in the early stages of the war. From his prominent position within the I.R.A. Moss Twomey wrote in late July: 'There is too much talk of our waging this latest war...as a "defensive" war, and only because we were, and are being, attacked.' He asked of the army executive: 'Have they any definite policy outlined beyond fighting it out? We say we are out (a) to maintain the republic (b) to get control of the army. These are very vague and ambiguous terms and should be defined beyond possibility of misunderstanding... The executive should some time define their objects, as it is generally believed they have no policy, and it is difficult to dispel or despise this view.'[12]

Ernie O'Malley and Tom Barry, among others, were to criticise the defensive strategy adopted by Liam Lynch, most notably in initiating a truce in Limerick in July. Both pro- and anti-treaty contemporaries talked of a fortified line protecting republican Munster and extending from Waterford to Limerick, although they were uncertain as to its exact course, whether along the Suir or the Blackwater; it was, however, to prove myth rather than reality. At no stage of the civil war did the republicans adopt an organised offensive policy; when their armies did have some success, as with the captures of Kenmare and Ballina in early September, there was no follow-up—the overall significance of such events being confined to propaganda, and indicative of the pro-treaty army's weaknesses rather than the I.R.A.'s strength. The continuation of the local particularism and resistance to central control of the Anglo–Irish war period was to plague the republican effort throughout the civil war. There was a great lack of strategic planning and of co-ordination between

[11] Peadar O'Donnell in MacEoin, *Survivors*, pp 23–34.
[12] Moss Twomey, 'Memo on present situation', 25 July 1922 (O'Malley papers, MS P17a/34).

areas. There was no question of strong areas helping weaker ones. Special services within the I.R.A. were poorly organised—even Liam Lynch had to admit the poverty of organisation and intelligence, so vital in guerrilla warfare. Ernie O'Malley complained to Lynch that the northern and western command he nominally led existed only on paper. All available accounts of republican military resistance testify to its improvised character. Throughout the conflict there was to be a chronic indecisiveness about republican policy and aims. Shortly after Lynch appointed him as his deputy, O'Malley asked: 'Could you give me an outline of your military and national policy as we are in the dark here with regard to both?'[13]

Many of the barriers to republican success, however, went beyond strategic considerations. There must have been a consciousness that military success would only result in the return of the British and that in time pro-treaty arms and resources would vastly outnumber those of the I.R.A. In areas of mixed pro- and anti-treaty strength, for instance Dublin city, local pro-treaty leaders had a knowledge of old Anglo–Irish war haunts and safe houses that made a resort to the former tactics more difficult. There was also a very natural disinclination to risk taking the life of old colleagues. This was particularly true in the early stages of the war, before the passage of the public safety bill. George Gilmore, of the Dublin Brigade, commented: 'I had a desire not to kill the enemy, all of our men had it to some extent, and the officers who were operating against us were our former friends. We never tried to kill.' Walter Mitchell, from Offaly, reminisced: 'No one wanted a civil war, and no one... liked fighting it when it came.'[14] Access to funds and other necessities was soon to prove a major concern, and (particularly after the retreat from towns) raids on villages and towns arose more often from material need than military strategy. Attempts to establish republican police and courts proved ineffective. It was to be impossible for the I.R.A. to hold their prisoners; it was problem enough to provide for themselves. Newspaper censorship meant that from early August, and the end of republican control of (most notably) the *Cork Examiner*, the republican point of view went almost entirely unheard. It was also to be of great significance that key anti-treaty men did not participate in the war. Seán Hegarty and Florence O'Donoghue, among the most important of Cork I.R.A. leaders, had declared their neutrality after the March executive convention. From the war's beginning the resistance of the Cork I.R.A. was half-hearted and the 4th Northern Division, the best armed of I.R.A. areas outside Munster and

[13] Lynch to O.C. 1st S. Div., 3 Sept. 1922 (ibid., P17a/17). See also two notes from Con Moloney (ibid., P17a/15); O'Malley, *Singing flame*, pp 148–50; O'Malley to Lynch, 21 July 1922 (Mulcahy papers, MS P7a/81).
[14] George Gilmore (O'Malley notebooks, MS P17b/100); Walter Mitchell in MacEoin, *Survivors*, p. 390; Hegarty to Liam Lynch, 11 July 1922 (U.C.D., A.D., FitzGerald papers).

Dublin, only joined the conflict in early September, by which time the republican military cause was looking hopeless.

The most vital consideration of all, however, in limiting republican prospects was the lack of popular support for any continuation of an armed struggle. Following the election it was easy for the provisional government to depict itself as defending majority rule and maintaining law and order. Meanwhile the tactics of the Four Courts executive since the March army convention had played into the hands of those depicting the republican opposition as little more than brigands. The necessary reliance on commandeering and on armed raids during the war further antagonised the populace. Harry Boland admitted in July: 'There is no doubt that the people in the main is [*sic*] against us at present, believing that we are to blame for the present state of affairs.' Joseph Connolly told Joe McGarrity: 'One thing occurs to me quite obvious...Republicanism is going to be made anathema to the people in this country for many generations to come. There seems no doubt that the will of the people is very definitely set on using the Free State.'[15] Where republican resistance was most successful during the war, notably in west Mayo and south Kerry, there was considerable popular support and a widespread resistance to the imposition of central government. Republican support was most manifest where it related to social and economic grievances. In more prosperous areas any hope of popular support was diminished still further by an overwhelmingly unfavourable reaction from press, clergy, and public bodies.

The fundamental weakness of the republican position was vividly depicted by Seán Moylan (O.C. Cork No. 3 Brigade) in a letter to Liam Lynch in September, strongly taking issue with Lynch's perennial optimism. Moylan wrote: 'The fact that we have more arms, more fighting men, and a more widespread war area than we had in our fight with the British is more than balanced by the people's attitude towards us and by several other facts.' Moylan went on to consider the attitudes of those who had given support during the Anglo–Irish war:

The republicans are still with us. Almost all the others are now hostile. The fact that we are fighting brother Irishmen, the further fact that our opponents represent to them peace, security, are altogether in favour of the Free Staters. Our principal weakness then is that we have lost by the opposition of the people, our cover, our sources and intelligence, our supplies, transport...We may therefore regard ourselves as an invading army in a hostile country and without a base.

Moylan concluded: 'The republican forces may have military successes, they cannot hope to beat the people. We cannot drive them, let us try to lead

---

[15] Boland to Luke Dillon, 27 July 1922 (FitzGerald papers); Connolly to McGarrity, 31 Aug. 1922 (N.L.I., McGarrity papers, MS 17654).

them.'[16] Such a pessimistic attitude was shared by several republican leaders, including Tom Barry and Dan Breen, and when Liam Deasy (assistant chief of staff of the I.R.A.) appealed for an end to republican resistance in February 1923 he came out with similar arguments.

The republican cause was not helped by the refusal of the military leadership to relate to political aims and social and economic grievances. Father Dominic O'Connor, a Dublin Capuchin friar, complained to Ernie O'Malley: 'We are without a government—nothing more in the eyes of the world than murderers and looters.' Liam Lynch rigidly held out against all pressure for the establishment of a republican government until the meeting of the army executive in October. He told O'Malley on 30 August 1922: 'Republican representatives must work under our officers ... We have been too soft in this respect in the past.' He concluded that the 'views and opinions of political people are not to be too seriously considered'. When in two memoranda from Mountjoy jail Liam Mellows pressed the need for a government and for a social policy, Lynch said of him: 'I fear his ideals prevent him from seeing the same military outlook as others at times.'[17] Throughout the war the voice of military resistance was completely to dominate the republican cause, with the consequence that the public remained confused about anti-treaty aims. Sinn Féin clubs all but disappeared during the war. Republican political leaders found little positive role for themselves. Erskine Childers wandered around remote areas of west Cork and east Kerry with a printing press placed on a pony and trap, desperately trying to continue to bring out *Poblacht na h-Éireann War News*. The British and provisional governments erroneously gave Childers credit for the republican military leadership. Harry Boland was killed as a result of a pro-treaty raid on a Skerries hotel in County Dublin in late July. During July de Valera strove to find a useful role for himself in south Tipperary and became increasingly criticised in military circles for his sympathy towards peace moves. While pro-treaty and British sources continued to attach the major blame for the conflict to him, de Valera complained with considerable justice: 'I am almost wishing I were deposed, for the present position places upon me the responsibility for carrying on a programme which was not mine.'[18]

Outside Dublin the war's first activity consisted in late June and early July of the republican takeover of isolated government-held barracks, for instance Skibbereen and Listowel in Munster, and Sligo town in the west. Attention then switched to areas yet to declare their allegiance, such as Wexford and Louth, and regions of mixed pro- and anti-treaty strength. For the only time

[16] Seán Moylan to Lynch, 14 Sept. 1922 (N.L.I., O'Donoghue papers, MS 31421 (15)).
[17] Fr Dominic to O'Malley, quoted in C. D. Greaves, *Liam Mellows and the Irish revolution* (London, 1971), p. 377; Lynch to O'Malley (Mulcahy papers, MS P7a/81); Mellows memos, late Aug. and early Sept. 1922 (ibid., P7/B/86); Lynch to O'Malley, 18 Sept. 1922 (ibid., P7a/81).
[18] De Valera to Joseph McGarrity, 10 Sept. 1922 (N.L.I., McGarrity papers, MS 17440).

in the conflict there was widespread military action in the midlands, where after minor confrontations republican units evacuated small towns such as Birr, Nenagh, and Templemore. In the 4th Northern Division Frank Aiken's persistent refusal to take sides was challenged by the pro-treaty takeover of Dundalk. On 14 August Aiken retook Dundalk barracks, releasing 240 republican prisoners and claiming to have taken 400 rifles. That success, however, was not built on, and three days later Dundalk was back in pro-treaty hands. By early September pro-treaty occupation of the area forced Aiken to declare allegiance to the republican military cause.

The first crucial events in the conflict, after the Dublin sieges, occurred in Limerick during July. Limerick city again became of crucial strategic importance. O'Duffy declared that 'we cannot afford a defeat in Limerick...we may have to fight the whole 1st Southern in Limerick', and Michael Brennan, who was in control of many of the pro-treaty troops there, agreed that 'the whole civil war really turned on Limerick'.[19] In early July key republican units from Cork and Kerry, aided by a truce in east Limerick with the pro-treaty Limerick leader Donnchadh O'Hannigan, marched to Limerick city, where much of the I.R.A. leadership, including Liam Lynch, Liam Deasy, and Seán Moylan, assembled. This was the only time in the war when there was a heavy concentration of republican units from many areas. The republican forces were in a clear majority, more experienced, and better armed, but in that promising situation the pro-treaty side was allowed to buy time. Aided by local priests, Brennan and Lynch agreed on a truce on 7 July. Before that Brennan's loyalty had apparently been questioned at G.H.Q. and Diarmuid MacManus was sent to investigate. Though MacManus was severely critical of what he found, it was soon apparent that, considering the shortage of arms and ammunition, the pro-treaty side had little choice other than to seek delay. Lynch, for his part, claimed that the truce aided the republican cause in other areas, but many were to criticise his failure to take the initiative. Frank Bumstead, one of the men from the Cork 1st Brigade in Limerick, commented that 'Liam Lynch and his bloody truce ruined us in the civil war', and Mick Leahy, the O.C. of that brigade, concluded that Limerick 'finished our fellows...the waiting there demoralised the men'.[20] When two arms consignments, including artillery, arrived to boost the pro-treaty forces, the truce was terminated. Republican-held positions in the city were attacked on 19 July, the Strand barracks by artillery. Little fighting ensued. By 21 July the republican retreat had begun. Again, barracks were evacuated with arms intact. Republican resistance, however, proved much more severe to the south of the city.

---

[19] O'Duffy memo, n.d., probably mid-July 1922 (Mulcahy papers, P7/B/69); Brennan quoted in Younger, *Civil war*, p. 370.

[20] Frank Bumstead (O'Malley notebooks, MS P17b/112); Leahy, ibid. (P17b/108).

During the Limerick city crisis the republicans had taken control of important garrisons in east Limerick, most notably Kilmallock, which became the centre of republican resistance after the retreat from the city. During the last week of July and the first week of August the Bruff–Bruree–Kilmallock triangle saw the heaviest fighting of the war. Initial pro-treaty advance on the area was repelled, and O'Duffy decided to wait for reinforcements. The fighting in County Limerick revealed all the provisional government army's weaknesses—posts were given up, and men deserted. O'Duffy told Mulcahy:

We had to get work out of a disgruntled, undisciplined, and cowardly crowd. Arms were handed over wholesale to the enemy, sentries were drunk at their posts, and when a whole garrison was put in clink owing to insubordination, etc., the garrison sent to replace them often turned out to be worse, and the divisional, brigade, battalion, and company officers were, in many cases, no better than the privates. To get value out of those the command staff had to work very hard—eighteen hours out of twenty-four—as there was always fear we might lose some of the posts through treachery, as actually happened on two occasions.[21]

When provisional government reinforcements arrived, however, Kilmallock and the area around it were hastily evacuated. While Cork and Kerry units had been engaged in the Kilmallock area, pro-treaty landings took place on the Munster coast. Tired men arrived back in their home counties too late to make any effective resistance to the landings.

The collapse of the resistance in Limerick effectively ended the war's first stage—direct military confrontation by the republicans after that was to be avoided. Any pretence that the republicans could defend Munster from pro-treaty invasion was destroyed. Seán MacSwiney was to tell Liam Deasy: 'After Limerick I personally did not believe that we could attain a complete military victory. Prior to Limerick I did think we could win in the field.' The republican retreat had an intensely damaging effect on morale. Tom Kelleher remembered the retreat to Buttevant as 'hopelessly disillusioned and disheartened'.[22] The poor position and performance of pro-treaty troops had not been exploited. The advance on Kerry and Cork could proceed by land as well as by sea.

Before the Limerick fighting the provisional government had decided on a risky policy of landing convoys of troops and arms at several points on the western and southern coasts. Before the sea landings a pro-treaty force occupied Waterford between 19 and 21 July. An expedition landed at Westport on 24 July, and the most important landing occurred at Passage West on 8/9 August, which provided the gateway to the taking of Cork city. Two separate pro-treaty forces at that time disembarked at Youghal and at Union Hall.

[21] O'Duffy to Mulcahy, n.d., early Aug. 1922 (Mulcahy papers, MS P7/B/71).
[22] MacSwiney to Deasy, 5 Feb. 1923 (N.A.I., D.T., S2210); Kelleher in MacEoin, *Survivors*, p. 245.

Further forces landed at Fenit on 2 August and Kenmare on 11 August. The intention in the south and west was that the overland forces should link up with those that had come in by sea to mop up the centres of republican resistance. Despite the improvised character of the landings—there were worries that the boat would be too large to land at Westport, and the ship's captain had to be forced to land at Passage West by a gun held to his head— the expeditions proved successful. In no case was there effective resistance, despite the fact that local republicans had been aware of the likelihood of such a strategy. There was some resistance to pro-treaty movement into Cork city, with limited fighting at Douglas and Rochestown. Those who should have been putting up a fight in Kerry and Cork were otherwise engaged in Limerick. Cork troops, meant to come to the aid of Waterford, arrived too late; and south Tipperary columns, which could have provided a major obstacle to Prout's force, showed a characteristic unwillingness to be concerned outside their own areas. Forced on to the defensive, the I.R.A. burned barracks and evacuated the towns. Prout hesitated before moving on to take the various republican centres in south Tipperary, but despite some small-scale resistance the republican evacuation of Carrick-on-Suir was followed by that of Cashel and Clonmel in the first nine days of August. By mid August pro-treaty control had been established in all places of any size in Munster. It seems clear that, even allowing for the excesses of the censored press, provisional government troops were enthusiastically received. Republican occupation of the Munster towns had involved forced levies and commandeering, and had proved unpopular with large sectors of an electorate that had endorsed the treaty in June. Despite a circular from the South Tipperary Brigade that warned against antagonising the local population, the burning of creameries created widespread hostility, and most unpopular of all was the destruction of key bridges, most notably the old bridge at Mallow. Republican occupation had meant destruction of communications and anxiety about economic prospects.

Evacuation of the towns prompted the republican military leaders to order the adoption of guerrilla tactics; in most cases, however, the need for this had long been recognised. Memoranda from Liam Deasy, the O.C. of 1st Southern Division, and Con Moloney, the adjutant-general, ordered the establishment of small columns, consisting of 'the very best and most experienced men', who were to concentrate on wrecking communications and attacking isolated pro-treaty posts with the aim of making government impossible. These instructions implicitly acknowledged the weakness of the republican position—many I.R.A. men were effectively discharged, although a high proportion had already taken that decision for themselves. On 5 August Collins reported that military resistance was confined to very few areas in the south and west, and talked optimistically of the forthcoming establishment of police and courts and of normal conditions. There was much press talk of the impending end of the war. O'Duffy admitted, however, on 22 August: 'Our forces have captured towns, but they have not captured Irregulars and arms on anything like a large scale.' The provisional government had failed to accomplish its major aim of preventing the republican resort to guerrilla warfare.[23]

It was during this key period that the government suffered a blow to both its military and political leadership. On 11 August Michael Collins embarked on an inspection tour of army units in Munster. His journey was soon interrupted by the need to return to Dublin following Griffith's death from a cerebral haemorrhage. While Griffith's importance in the government had progressively diminished, the British government feared that the treaty had lost its one true supporter in the Irish government. Collins recommenced his tour after the funeral, ill and depressed.

Collins had other reasons than those stated for his Munster visit. Arrangements were being made for him to meet old republican colleagues. Although he had no intention of compromising his government's position he did wish to arrive at some form of accommodation by which old colleagues could retain their principles while laying down their arms. On 22 August Collins's convoy travelled by a circuitous route through strong republican territory in west Cork, the area of Collins's own childhood. On its way west from Cork city the party passed through the valley of Bealnablath, where an I.R.A. brigade council meeting was being held. An ambush was set up for a possible return by that route. That evening, after the main ambush party had been broken up and the mines removed, the convoy returned and was attacked. Collins ordered it to stop and return fire. Near the end of what appears to have been a half-hour exchange of firing, Collins was shot and died shortly afterwards.

Controversy has run riot since on the question of who killed Collins. A multitude of conspiracy theories, seeking to link Collins's own side, or British intelligence, with the shooting, have produced only circumstantial evidence. Any mystery almost certainly owes more to an understandable Cork reticence on this most sensitive of subjects than to any elaborate official cover-ups. The most likely explanation, in conformity with recent investigations, is that Collins was shot by a bullet from one of the ambushing party.[24] Attention, however, should be allowed to turn to the significance of Collins's death. The event shocked Irishmen at home and abroad. Within weeks of each other the two chief signatories of the treaty were dead.

[23] Moloney memo, 14 Aug. 1922 (Mulcahy papers, MS P7/B/93); Deasy to O.C. Cork, 4, 12 Aug. 1922 (ibid., P7/B/71); Deasy to all O.C.s, 12 Aug. 1922 (O'Malley papers, MS P17a/87); Collins to acting chairman of provisional government (Cosgrave), 5 Aug. 1922 (Mulcahy papers, MS P7/B/29); O'Duffy, 22 Aug. 1922 (Mulcahy papers, MS P7/B/63).
[24] For debate concerning Collins's death, see T. P. Coogan, *Michael Collins* (London, 1990), pp 400–15.

Mulcahy moved swiftly into the breach, as commander-in-chief, to ensure the continued loyalty of the army and strove, for the most part successfully, to prevent reprisals. On 25 August Cosgrave was appointed chairman of the provisional government, a position he had held in a temporary capacity since the start of the war. The fledgling government had lost its one popular figure. Collins has been all too easily romanticised but his death left an enormous gap, never adequately filled. It is difficult to doubt that he, 31 at his death, would have played a continuing dominant role despite his impatience of politics and politicians. The British government was torn between concern about the future of the treaty settlement and relief that it no longer had to face Collins's double-dealing. Craig and his government had every reason to be grateful that the one minister who had made a major priority of challenging their position was gone. The immediate consequence of Collins's death was to make the war much harsher. Soon afterwards, unknown to his cabinet colleagues, Mulcahy made a secret, last, abortive effort to find a *rapprochement* with de Valera. Following that, Mulcahy supported the passage of a public safety bill by which military courts were to be given powers to inflict punishment, including death, for a range of offences.[25] If he had lived Collins would probably not have agreed to such policies: he had warned against 'steamrollering' the republicans.[26] Cosgrave and the rest of his government adopted a much more straightforward view of their role. Henceforth the treaty provisions were to be enforced without qualification and without limitations on the military means to be used.

Despite the widespread alarm following Collins's death the provisional government felt its position established enough to allow the new dáil, elected in June, to meet on 9 September. Lord Midleton was told by a fellow-unionist: 'I really believe that the assembling of the dáil and the progress already made with the constitution has done more to damage the republican forces than any action taken by the Free State army.'[27] Apart from the aged Laurence Ginnell, who was immediately expelled for asking repeated questions about the constitutional basis of the new assembly, the republicans abstained from attendance. This meant that controversial measures, most notably the public safety bill, were only opposed in the dáil by members of the Labour party, and a valuable opportunity for stating the republican case was lost. On the government's side, virtually complete dominance in the dáil meant that there seemed little need to court public opinion. The energy of ministers was entirely taken up by considerations of national security and the

---

[25] Emergency measures in the south of Ireland are discussed in Colm Campbell, *Emergency law in Ireland, 1918–1925* (Oxford, 1994), ch. 3; see also Eunan O'Halpin, *Defending Ireland: the Irish state and its enemies since 1922* (Oxford, 1999), ch. 1.

[26] For Collins's opposition to 'steamrollering', see Paddy O'Connor (O'Malley notebooks, MS P17b/100); for the public safety bill, see below, pp 52–3, n. 47.

[27] Andrew Belton to Midleton, 3 Oct. 1922 (P.R.O., Midleton papers, 30/67/51).

establishment of administrative authority, and not by day-to-day political demands. All ministers, with the exception of Mulcahy, were soon to be forced to live in their government offices for fear of assassination, and in that context there was little appreciation of any need to court popularity.

With the third dáil functioning, the republican leadership came under heavy pressure from within its own ranks, both political and military, to form its own government. Leading I.R.A. figures in Mountjoy jail and Ernie O'Malley were among those applying pressure on Liam Lynch. In correspondence intercepted by the pro-treaty side, de Valera expressed opposition to forming a government on pragmatic rather than ideological grounds. He also expressed his distaste for the military's dominance of republican counsels, writing: 'The position of the political party must be straightened out. If it is the policy of the party to leave it all to the army ... the obvious thing for members of the party to do is to resign their positions as public representatives. If I do not get the position made quite clear, I shall resign publicly.'[28] Despite Lynch's and de Valera's original opposition, the first army executive meeting since the opening of the war, on 16 and 17 October, agreed to the formation of a republican government with de Valera as 'president of the republic and chief executive of the state'.[29] There was no prospect of this government meeting, let alone functioning. De Valera appointed Seán Moylan to it, unaware that he had already left for the United States to serve as the I.R.A.'s representative there. Meanwhile the military voice was to remain dominant until the end of the war. If anything, de Valera's voice was to be even more constrained.

For all the press and pro-treaty optimism during August about the hopelessness of the republican military position, the adoption of guerrilla tactics in many ways proved successful. O'Duffy and Emmet Dalton, the pro-treaty military leaders in the south, both felt that a great opportunity to mop up republican resistance was lost in late August and early September. A major planned sweep of the strong republican area between Killarney and Macroom was postponed; McKeon's command, based inconveniently in Athlone, made faltering moves to clear up resistance in Mayo and Sligo. The Athlone command's intelligence officer commented: 'Last July when the national forces reached Castlebar, a force of 150 men would [have] defeat[ed] Kilroy's men in a week if they followed them up. Every day's delay since is adding strength to his force.' Pro-treaty troops in the various localities soon lost their early popularity, their position not helped by weaknesses in transport and supplies. Mulcahy complained that in the west 'if the troops had been kept busy and on alert the areas could have been cleared long before ... The

[28] De Valera to Charles Murphy, 12 Sept. (two letters), also 7 and 13 Sept, 1922 (Mulcahy papers, MS P7/B/86).
[29] I.R.A. executive meeting, 16–17 Oct. (ibid., P7a/81).

people of the area feel that no impression at all is being made on the situation, and that [sic] they are beginning to whisper to themselves that they have no confidence in "Sean McKeon".' Emmet Dalton blamed the performance of his own Cork command for what he saw as a worsening situation.[30]

A more efficient force than the pro-treaty army, however, would have had considerable problems in dealing with guerrilla tactics. Initially Dalton had been surprised by the lack of republican resistance when pro-treaty troops arrived in Cork, but in September reported that the republican side 'have now adopted a type of warfare, of which they have years of experience. They now operate over territory which they know. They are now better armed and better trained than they were against the British. In short, they have placed me and my troops in the same position as the British were a little over a year ago.' In November, shortly before he resigned his command, Dalton reported: 'In Cork, we are going to be beaten unless we wake up and at once. The state of things is very bad—it is my plain duty to say so.' The *Irish Times*'s special correspondent, Kingsmill Moore, feared that the war would be much prolonged unless there was a speedy improvement.[31]

The republican capture of Kenmare and Ballina in early September well illustrated the vulnerability of the pro-treaty army's position and proved major propaganda coups for the republican side. But light was also shed on the republican military limitations, and the tragi-comedy of much of the fighting. Despite a number of blunders Kenmare was taken on 9 September. Only one-half of the intended men from 1st Cork Brigade joined the attack and David Robinson's report complained of 'insufficient information... insufficient forces and... what appeared to me to be a lack of assistance or enthusiasm on the part of the brigade staff'.[32] Once the republicans arrived in the town they tunnelled through buildings only to find the Lansdowne Arms and the post office were not, as expected, occupied by pro-treaty troops. Having occupied the bank they tried to shoot their way into the safe, unaware that the money had been hidden in the garden. At the start of the attack republicans burst into a shop and shot dead Tom Scarteen O'Connor, the O.C. of pro-treaty troops there, and his brother; both were unarmed. For all the chaos and confusion of the attack Kenmare was taken—many of the pro-treaty troops were away on sweeping-up activity at the time and the

[30] Athlone I.O., 30 Oct. 1922 (Military Archives, Cathal Brugha barracks, Rathmines, Dublin); Mulcahy (?) to 2nd S. Div., n.d., probably mid Dec. 1922 (Mulcahy papers, MS P7/B/64); C.-in-C. (Mulcahy) to Mac Eoin, 22 Dec. 1922 (ibid., P7/B/75); Dalton to C.-in-C., 18 Nov. 1922 (ibid., P7/B/67).
[31] Dalton to C.-in-C., 12 Aug. 1922 (ibid., P7/B/20); Dalton to C.- in-C., 11 Sept. 1922 (Military Archives, CW/Ops/13); Dalton to C.G.S., 2, 5 Sept. 1922 (Mulcahy papers, MS P7/B/71); Dalton to C.-in-C., 18 Nov. 1922 (ibid., P7/B/67); *Irish Times*, 20 Sept. 1922.
[32] David Robinson's report, 13 Sept. 1922 (Mulcahy papers, MS P7/B/90); Robinson memoir (T.C.D., Childers papers, MS 7851).

remaining men precipitately surrendered. One hundred and ten rifles were captured and 120 prisoners taken, but the success did not lead, as was expected, to a major republican advance on the Iveragh peninsula. The aim of the attack appears to have been nothing more than a raid for provisions and arms. A similar, but bigger, attack on Killorglin, on the other side of the peninsula, on 27 September was as poorly planned and this time ended in failure. Three days after the Kenmare coup republican columns took Ballina, where again there was feeble resistance from pro-treaty troops. The plans that Michael Kilroy, the republican O.C. there, had for moving on to take other towns in Mayo had to be called off, with Kilroy dismayed by the heavy drinking of his men in Ballina. While the republicans controlled large areas of west Mayo and south Kerry and successfully interfered with communications, their successes were limited; there was no intention of moving on to challenge the pro-treaty army elsewhere. Meanwhile areas that were expected to provide the strongest republican resistance in the war saw little action. The Cork I.R.A. was active in peace moves throughout the conflict and showed little heart for armed action, while disunity within the I.R.A. leadership in south Tipperary greatly weakened the republican military effort there.

Limited as the republican military achievements were, there was increasing concern that the war was dragging on for an unacceptable period. The decision to execute some republican prisoners implied, as Eoin MacNeill was to point out, that the military campaign was not achieving the desired effect. Four Dublin men who had been captured carrying arms were the first to be executed, on 17 November. Kevin O'Higgins's remark in the dáil that the first batch did not include an I.R.A. leader or 'an Englishman' suggested that the first executions were, to quote de Valera's secretary, 'a forerunner for Childers's execution'.[33] Childers had been arrested on 10 November at the family home of his cousin Robert Barton and charged with possession of a small revolver, given him by Michael Collins. He had been journeying to Dublin with the intention of working for the republican government. His execution on 24 November took on the appearance of a vengeance killing. The first executions provoked Liam Lynch to issue death threats against all those who had voted for the public safety act. The only occasion on which these reprisal orders were acted upon came on 7 December 1922 when men from the Dublin Brigade killed Seán Hales, a West Cork T.D., and wounded Pádraic Ó Maille, the *leas-cheann comhairle* (deputy speaker of the dáil). The following morning, as a deliberate reprisal for these shootings, four of the original Four Courts executive held in Mountjoy prison, Rory O'Connor, Liam Mellows, Dick Barrett, and Joe McKelvey—one from each province

---

[33] O'Higgins in *Dáil Éireann deb.*, i, 2267 (17 Nov. 1922); for Childers's arrest and execution, see David Robinson's report (T.C.D., Childers papers, MS 7851).

and all I.R.B. men—were executed. There could be no argument that these executions had any legal basis. The leader of the Labour party, Thomas Johnson, commented in the dáil: 'I am almost forced to say you have killed the new state at its birth.'[34] The largest number of executions in any month was thirty-four in January, and the policy was then adopted of threatening to execute prisoners if their local areas saw further military activity.

The execution policy, unjustifiable in a democratic state, may have helped to shorten the war. Some I.R.A. men admitted that the executions damaged morale and helped to promote peace moves in the prisons. There was also much talk of assassination, but no action. The long-term effect of the Free State's ultimate deterrent policy was gravely to weaken the popularity of the pro-treaty cause. The executions had helped turn the war into something resembling a national vendetta. The republican cause had earlier come under attack in the catholic bishops' joint pastoral of 10 October, which depicted the republican resistance as lacking any legitimacy: 'it is only', it declared, 'a system of murder and assassination of the national forces.' While some (especially younger) priests continued to support the republican cause, many refused to give the sacraments to prisoners. The church had adopted its preferred role of supporting the established order, now that order was Irish, and the pastoral helped to ostracise the republicans socially.[35]

Meanwhile the dáil, now augmented by representatives of the Labour party and of Dublin University who had not participated in the previous dáils, was proceeding to consider a bill 'to enact a constitution for Saorstát Éireann for implementing the treaty between Great Britain and Ireland'. The bill was introduced on 18 September and passed, after much debate and some limited amendments, on 25 October. The British parliament—concerned exclusively with the question of whether the constitution was in conformity with the treaty—endorsed the constitution as approved by the dáil,[36] and the Irish Free State came into being on 6 December 1922. This coincided with the period of most alarm for the new government. Cosgrave admitted his own anxiety in February 1923. There was increasing concern within and without the government that the Free State was failing to function in large areas of the south and west. Since military resistance to the state was on such a small scale, doubts about the army and its leadership came to the surface. Within the government O'Higgins and his close friend, Patrick Hogan, the minister for agriculture, led the way in expressing such concern. Their opportunity came when Cosgrave asked in January that ministers circulate to their colleagues memoranda discussing methods to deal 'with the lawlessness prevailing throughout the country, with a view to bringing it to a

---

[34] Johnson in *Dáil Éireann deb.*, ii, 49–54 (8 Dec. 1922).
[35] For the pastoral, see Irish newspapers, 11 Oct. 1922.
[36] Leo Kohn, *The constitution of the Irish Free State* (London, 1932), pp 85–9. The 1922 constitution is considered in more detail below, pp 87–91.

speedy end'. O'Higgins and Hogan in their memoranda drew an alarming picture of lawlessness and anarchy. Hogan thought that 'the civilian population will surrender definitely before long if the Irregulars are able to continue their peculiar form of war... Two months more like the last two months will see the end of us and the Free State.' To deal with the crisis they urged more numerous executions, spread across the country, and substantial changes in the army's organisation.[37] Implicit in these views was a strong criticism of the army's performance and its leadership, and of Mulcahy's combining the posts of minister for defence and commander-in-chief, together with suspicion of I.R.B. influence. There was much to criticise in the army but O'Higgins showed insufficient sensitivity to Mulcahy's problems—the need, for instance, to preserve McKeon's and Brennan's support. Important elements within the army were increasingly concerned about the war's conduct and purpose. Many of those who supported the treaty out of support for Collins had little faith in the new leadership. Michael Brennan told Mulcahy: 'We all here have been very worried for some time past at the prospect of finding that the Free State was the end for which we fought, not the means to that end.'[38] Members of Collins's old 'squad', who had never found an effective role in the pro-treaty army, established in January a new organisation, known as either the 'Old I.R.A.' or the 'Irish Republican Organisation'. Such tensions were to become acute after the end of the war with the problem of army demobilisation.

Meanwhile, in the first months of 1923 there was some improvement in the army's performance: a new command structure and discipline code were set up; intelligence proved more effective, notably in the round-up of much of the republican military leadership in March and April. O'Higgins's pet scheme of the 'special infantry corps' to concentrate on local areas only began in March and appears to have had no time to be of any importance in bringing the war to an end. Attempts to achieve closer control of the military's actions by setting up a supreme war council provoked Mulcahy to resign, although he hastily changed his mind.

For all the pro-treaty disquiet, the republican military effort progressively disintegrated from the end of 1922. In much of the country the only activity possible was house-burning and the wrecking of communications. The aspect of republican policy that caused most alarm to the Free State government and to the population generally was the continued interference with the railways. Probably for fear of the effect on the general population, the Anglo-Irish war had seen little attempt to prevent the rail system functioning, but during the civil war a Free State politician commented: 'There never has been a case of any country in which such a fierce attack was made on its

[37] O'Higgins memo, 11 Jan. 1923 (Mulcahy papers, MS P7/C/21); Hogan memo, 11 Jan. 1923 (ibid., P7/B/321).
[38] Brennan to Mulcahy, 15 May 1923 (ibid., P7/C/10).

railway system.' Liam Lynch affirmed: 'A hundred bridges blown up was just as effective a blow...as a hundred barracks blown up.' In January a report from the Great Southern & Western Railway Company revealed that in the previous twelve months the line had been damaged in 375 places, 42 engines had been derailed and 51 over-bridges destroyed. For most of the civil war there was no direct rail transport between Dublin and Cork. West Cork and Kerry lost their rail communications till mid 1923 and Wexford and Tipperary saw particularly frequent interference with the system. The formation of the railroad protection and maintenance corps, made up of railroad workers and navvies who used a system of blockhouses, contributed to a diminution of republican attacks in many key areas during 1923.[39] While there was a marked slackening in the general republican military effort in the early months of 1923, that same period saw a considerable rise in the number of attacks on the property of southern unionists.[40] The houses of thirty-seven senators were destroyed in January and February, and Senators Bagwell and Oliver St John Gogarty were kidnapped. The Free State government, no doubt aware of the disastrous image this created for the independent country abroad, talked of the need for reprisals on republican property. The burning and wrecking had a deeply disturbing effect on the government's morale, but that could not detract from the disintegration of the I.R.A.

Even in south Kerry and west Mayo, the last bastions of any widespread republican military activity, any action was patchy and defensive in character. Nothing demonstrated the hopelessness of the I.R.A. position better than a meeting of the council of the 1st Southern Division on 26 February, where representatives from all the Munster brigades depicted a forlorn present and hopeless future for their efforts. The O.C. 1st Cork Brigade, Tom Crofts, concluded: 'The present state of the division is that we are fought to a standstill and at present we are flattened out.' In County Cork 'if five men are arrested in each area we are finished. The men are suffering great privations and their morale is going.' Even in the comparatively active Kerry 1st Brigade Humphrey Murphy, its O.C., admitted that 'the steamrollering of the south would soon finish us'. The republican resistance in Munster had been dealt a further blow by the decision in January of Liam Deasy, the assistant chief of staff and O.C. 1st Southern, to make an appeal for a ceasefire to republican units just before he was to be executed. Deasy thus avoided the death penalty. Considerable pressure had been exerted on Deasy

[39] Notes for speech, possibly by Mulcahy (ibid., P7/B/179); army intelligence report, 29 Aug. 1922 (ibid., P7/B/113); *Manchester Guardian*, 8 Jan. 1923; army report, 23 Jan. 1923 (Mulcahy papers, MS P7/B/123); Russell to C.G.S., 25 Oct., 3 Nov. 1922 (ibid., P7/B/110); *An t-Óglach*, 21 Apr. 1923; Padraig Yeates, 'The unsung war of the iron road' in *Sunday Press*, 1 May 1983.
[40] See R. B. McDowell, *Crisis and decline: the fate of the southern unionists* (Dublin, 1997), chs 6–7.

by the Free State authorities to get him to act thus, but he claimed that he had long intended to make such an appeal. The republican military leadership responded adversely to Deasy's communication, but his action had a disastrous effect on the morale of prisoners. Peace initiatives began at that period in Cork and Clonmel jails. Cork I.R.A. men commented that some of the men 'won't ever have the same confidence in any one of the leaders again'. Deasy's appeal, however, only confirmed what had long been apparent—the half-hearted character of the Cork resistance. A Cork I.R.A. man declared: 'We were beaten anyhow.'[41] In February the staunchest of south Tipperary column leaders, Dinny Lacey, was killed at a time when he was reportedly showing interest in peace terms, and Con Moloney, the adjutant-general, was captured on 7 March with some of his notes which concluded: 'Course of struggle run—not agree summer campaign if war lasts till then, we will be beaten or very nearly so.'[42]

Some of the war's nastiest events occurred as it spluttered to a close. In Kerry small-scale ambushes and raids continued until the end, and in the same county the Dublin guard (a special military unit, not to be confused with the civic guard) and troops from six-county units garrisoned there became increasingly unpopular. A republican ambush at Knocknagoshel on 6 March resulted in General Daly's order that henceforth mined obstructions should be cleared by republican prisoners. In the days following seventeen prisoners were killed clearing mines in three separate incidents—at Ballyseedy Cross, Countess Bridge, and Cahirciveen. A military inquiry soon denied that these were deliberate reprisals, but few were convinced. In April a siege of Timothy 'Aeroplane' Lyons's column at Clashmealcon Caves resulted in further charges of prisoners being deliberately killed. South Kerry has retained the bitterest memories of the war.

The war lasted so long because there appeared no means of achieving a compromise, nor a complete military victory. Liam Lynch's continuing never-say-die optimism was also a major factor. Until February Lynch was based in a hideaway at Ballymun in Dublin, unable to exercise any control of events but still able to place a veto on negotiations. He claimed on 9 February 1923 that the I.R.A. was 'in a stronger military position than at any period in its history...Victory is within our grasp if we stand unitedly and

[41] 1st S. Div. meeting, 26 Feb. 1923 (Mulcahy papers, MS P7/B/89). For the Deasy affair, Deasy (O'Malley notebooks, MS P17b/86); Deasy statement (O'Malley papers, MS 17a/22); Deasy to all battalions and O.C.s, 30 Jan. 1923 (ibid., P17a/99). For examples of response to Deasy, Seán MacSwiney to Deasy, 5 Feb. 1923 (N.A.I., D.T., S2210); Frank Carty to Deasy, 6 Feb. 1923 (ibid.). For prisoners' peace efforts, Denis Lacey to O.C., Clonmel, 12 Feb. 1923 (Mulcahy papers, MS P7/B/89); 1st S. Div. meeting, 26 Feb. 1923 (loc. cit.). Cork prisoner to Pa [Murray], 13 Feb. 1923 (Mulcahy papers, MS P7/B/89); letter from prisoner in 'hospital wing', 21 Feb. 1923 (N.A.I., D.T., S1859).
[42] 'History of Tipperary No. 3 Bde' by C. F. Colmcille (O'Malley notebooks, MS P17b/127); Moloney notes, 7 Mar. 1923 (ibid., P17a/24).

firmly.'[43] Key I.R.A. men, including Tom Barry and Dan Breen, responded positively to peace efforts led by the 'neutral I.R.A.'[44] and clerics sympathetic to republican aims. With great reluctance Lynch agreed to the holding of an army executive meeting, held over four days from 24 March in the Nier valley, County Waterford. At that meeting Lynch clung to the twin hopes of mountain artillery arriving from Germany, paid for by American money, and republican successes in the west. The arms deal never materialised and Lynch knew little of the situation in the west, where the limited republican resistance had little relevance to the situation east and south of the Shannon. After an inconclusive vote on bringing the war to a close, the army executive meeting decided to adjourn for three weeks, by which time it was hoped to have information on western developments and on de Valera's attempts to find a basis for negotiation. Within that period, however, important republicans, including Austin Stack and Dan Breen, were captured, and on 10 April Liam Lynch himself was shot dead in the Knockmealdown mountains. A large-scale Free State army sweep of relevant areas in south Tipperary and Waterford, based on accurate intelligence about the executive meetings, was responsible for these coups.

Lynch's death meant that the door to republican acceptance of a ceasefire was open. When the adjourned executive meeting met at Poulacapple, County Tipperary, on 20 April 1923, Frank Aiken was elected to replace Lynch as chief of staff. Aiken was much closer personally to de Valera than Lynch had been, and much more amenable to taking a pragmatic stand. The meeting empowered de Valera to undertake peace negotiations. When talks between de Valera and Senators Andrew Jameson and James Douglas,[45] who acted as intermediaries, produced no basis for compromise, a joint republican government and army meeting of 13–14 May instructed Aiken to issue a 'cease fire and dump arms' order, which was published on 24 May. De Valera's message to the army, issued on the same day, concluded: 'Military victory must be allowed to rest for the moment with those who have destroyed the republic.'[46]

The fact that the war ended without a compromise had extremely important short- and long-term consequences. The Free State remained on a war footing and around 12,000 republican prisoners remained in jail. Some leading I.R.A. men—Humphrey Murphy in Kerry and Liam Pilkington in Sligo, for instance—were rounded up long after the war ended. The government set its face against reconciliation. A tougher public order bill was put through the

[43] Lynch to all ranks of I.R.A., 9 Feb. 1923 (O'Malley papers, MS P17a/23).
[44] An association of those who had fought in the war of independence but had not taken part in the civil war (Macardle, *Ir. republic*, p. 760).
[45] Jameson was head of Jameson's distillers; Douglas, a quaker businessman, had served on the committee to draft the 1922 constitution.
[46] De Valera proclamation, 27 Apr. 1923 (Mulcahy papers, P7/B/90).

dáil, including a provision for flogging sentences and the power to detain without trial.[47] In the autumn no sympathy was shown towards a general hunger strike. The gradual release of political prisoners was not completed till the summer of 1924. O'Higgins talked of the paramount need to avoid a replay of the conflict and for strong executive authority.[48] Major problems remained concerning the army. A force of over 50,000 could not be justified once the ceasefire had been declared. Increasing criticism was heard of the employment of former British and northern officers in dominant positions at the expense, it was claimed, of veterans of the Anglo–Irish war. Such feelings came to a head when plans for the demobilisation of over 20,000 men were announced. Meanwhile elements within the government, notably O'Higgins, were to demand an end to the independence of G.O.C.s in the localities and of both the I.R.B. and its alleged control of G.H.Q. Only with demobilisation completed and the army no longer required to perform police duties could it become a disciplined, professional organisation suited to a small state, and only after the confused failure of the spring 1924 army mutiny, which resulted in the resignations of Mulcahy and much of G.H.Q., was the army placed firmly under political control.[49]

The circumstances of the war's end enabled the political leadership of the republican movement to recover some status. Agreement to the ceasefire meant an acknowledgement that guerrilla warfare tactics were impractical. There was little cause to think that once the Free State had become fully established the prospects for military opposition would be any brighter. Frank Aiken commented: 'If we have to fight another war with the Staters, it will have to be short and sweet, and our units will need to be trained in taking the offensive in large numbers.'[50] Soon the I.R.A. leaders were to be heavily divided on whether to concentrate on a northern or British offensive, or to relate republican aims to social and economic grievances, as Peadar O'Donnell was to advocate for so long. In the immediate aftermath of the war Aiken had no choice other than to advocate concentrating on political opposition, which, in turn, helped to restore de Valera's position. Despite the fact that it contravened republican orthodoxy concerning the continued exist- ence of the second dáil, de Valera won widespread backing for the decision to contest the general election of August 1923. His clumsy arrest by Free State forces while he was addressing his old constituents in Ennis town square, and the length of his imprisonment, further helped to raise de Valera's stock. The republicans did surprisingly well in the election—forty-four of their candidates were elected, compared with sixty-three pro-treaty candidates

---

[47] 1923/29 [I.F.S.] (1 Aug. 1923).
[48] *Dáil Éireann deb.*, iii, 356–7, 1984–6 (20 Apr., 15 June 1923).
[49] Below, pp 98–104.
[50] Aiken to Ernie O'Malley, 27 June 1923 (Military Archives, A/1120).

—and did best in small farming areas that had seen considerable resistance during the war: Mayo, Kerry, Wexford, and Clare. It was to take considerably longer, however, for the divisions between the republican political and military sides, and between hardliners and pragmatists in Sinn Féin, to come to a final test. The logic of de Valera's role had always been to form a constitutional opposition, bent on achieving reform of the treaty. His position, even after his release from prison in July 1924, was too weak for him to advocate republican entry into the dáil. Meanwhile the cause of intransigent republicanism was dealt a further blow by the collapse of the October–November prison hunger strike. The strike was intended as a general action in support of a protest against conditions in Mountjoy but was to demonstrate the impossibility of achieving coordinated action when so many prisoners were involved. While many of the republicans, including such prominent men as Con Moloney and Dan Breen, came off the strike and signed a pledge not to take up arms against the government again, two Cork men died.

By comparison with civil wars in other countries—Finland, for instance, let alone the United States—the Irish civil war was a small-scale affair.[51] It lasted for only around ten months. There were no major military confrontations and for most of its course the conflict hardly merited the term 'war'. The number of dead was relatively low, probably less than 4,000. Material damage probably amounted to more than £30 million; defence and compensation costs long continued to absorb an unacceptably high proportion of government expenditure; and trade and communications were disrupted; but the war did not prevent the effective establishment of the Free State government. None the less the war and its memory were to stamp Irish society and politics for the following half-a-century. The two major parties of the Free State and republic were to be divided by civil-war allegiances; old colleagues of the pre-treaty period refused for decades afterwards to socialise with those who had taken a different stance on the war. Mrs Wyse Power recorded during the war that a friend arrived with a message stating 'that all family relations must be severed with those who had married men who deserted the nation, and stained the family record'.[52] The impact is partly explained by the fact that the treaty issues failed to be resolved till long after the war: the *raison d'être* of republicanism—opposition to any British role in the new state's constitution and partition—remained. That in turn meant that political and constitutional questions dominated the politics of the new state, as illustrated by the general election of 1923 when the Labour party vote severely declined from that in June 1922. The root cause of the war's depressing effect, however, lay in its bitter, incestuous character. It was a question less of how many were killed, than of who was killed—so many of

---

[51] For comparative analysis, see Lee, *Ire. 1912–85*, pp 67–9.
[52] Wyse Power letter extracts, letter 24 (Mulcahy papers, MS D/3).

the leading figures in the twenty-six counties on both sides died during the war, and so many of them in extremely controversial circumstances. The debate over the deaths of Michael Collins, Brian MacNeill (son of Eoin MacNeill), killed in September 1922, and Harry Boland, together with controversy over responsibility for the executions, long continued to plague Irish society. Major figures in the conflict (de Valera being the obvious example) and their descendants in many cases continued to dominate Irish politics for decades to come and helped to ensure that civil-war animosities would survive. A small country could ill afford to lose so many of its leaders and to have so much of the remaining political elite so profoundly divided by historical and personal bitterness. Many republicans were effectively shut out of employment after the war and forced to emigrate, and the potential for full protestant involvement in the new state was immensely harmed by the attacks on unionist property during the conflict. The consequences of the war were greatly to enhance the conservatism of the new state. While socialist elements within the republican opposition had become progressively marginalised, Kevin O'Higgins was able to boast: 'We were probably the most conservative-minded revolutionaries that ever put through a successful revolution.'[53] The civil war had helped to turn Ireland in on itself and contributed to the long-term dominance of the conservative elements of the 'new nationalism'.

The war can best be understood as representing the end of the revolutionary period in Irish history. Even without the divisions over the treaty there would have been major problems in winning widespread acceptance of the need for a strong central government in a country traditionally loosely governed and in many areas hardly governed at all in recent years. The war had resulted in the establishment of such a government, and the pro-treaty side had that to its credit, as well as the achievement of a settled court system and unarmed police force. Moreover, the conflict enabled both the pro-treaty and republican political leaderships eventually to gain independence from their military wings—any threat of military dictatorship had disappeared. These achievements, however, had been purchased at a considerable cost.

THE six counties of Northern Ireland were almost completely unaffected by the civil-war fighting. There was small-scale republican I.R.A. activity on the Louth–Armagh and Donegal–Fermanagh borders but no considered attempt was made by anti-treaty forces to extend operations to Northern Ireland. Kevin O'Shiel, the leading adviser to the provisional government on northern matters, commented about the republicans: 'Although they are waging war against us in the south, they have tacitly agreed to leave the six counties alone until the findings of the [boundary] commission.' To a considerable

[53] *Dáil Éireann deb.*, ii, 1909 (1 Mar. 1923).

extent this was to be expected. Ernie O'Malley, who was for a time nominally in control of the I.R.A. in the north-east, despairingly reported of the 3rd Northern Division: 'They are absolutely snowed under. I met some of the senior officers and they said they could not do anything in the divisional area.' The outbreak of war in the south had abruptly ended any hope of the continuation of a united I.R.A. offensive policy, which led to charges of apostasy against the pro-treaty side. Arms originally intended for the united I.R.A. offensive were now used against republicans who had retreated to Donegal. One of them, Lt-comdt Conway, concluded: 'I can come to no other conclusion but that the orders about training columns to fight inside [the six counties] and the sending in of arms was only to hoodwink us.'[54] The Four Courts attack served to turn the British government's attention away from the situation in the north and lessened the need to take account of the interests there of the minority population and the southern government. In early August 1922 Churchill was able to report: 'In the area of the northern government the position had sensibly improved: murders and incendiarism had almost entirely ceased, and a state of quiescence established. This might be due to the fact that the gunmen were engaged in the south.' The British government saw no need to change this state of affairs by inquiring any further into the shortcomings of the northern government and its security system. Tallents's report produced some strong criticisms of the Belfast regime but by the time it was published there was little interest in the conclusions.[55]

The tactics adopted by the provisional government towards the north-east changed abruptly from June 1922 onwards. For all Collins's desire to make a priority issue of the north, he had been forced to concentrate on stabilising his government's position within the twenty-six counties. This reality he explicitly recognised when he addressed northern I.R.A. men at Portobello barracks on 2 August, and announced that northern volunteers were to train at the Curragh and be paid by the provisional government. Of the 524 northern I.R.A. men who went to the Curragh, 243 later joined the pro-treaty army. Mulcahy commented to Collins: 'Our officers seem to realise there is no other policy for the north but a peace policy of some kind, but the situation for peace or war has gone beyond them.' This concluded the depressing series of events for the I.R.A. in the north since April. Tom MacAnally, of the 3rd Northern Division, commented: 'The Ulster crowd had us completely disorganised—northern men could no longer stay in the north; the

[54] O'Shiel's memo to minister, n.d., probably end of Nov. 1923 (U.C.D., A.D., Blythe papers, MS P24/171); O'Malley to Lynch, 28 July 1922 (Mulcahy papers, MS P7a/81). See also O'Malley to Lynch, 28 July 1922 (ibid., P7a/81); Lt-comdt Conway to Mary MacSwiney, 11 Mar. 1923 (U.C.D., A.D., Mary MacSwiney papers, MS P48a/117(2)/4).

[55] Churchill to British cabinet, 3 Aug. 1922 (P.R.O., CAB 45/30); Tallents's report (P.R.O., C.O. 739/16).

I.R.A. there never recovered.' His O.C., Séamus Woods, declared in August 1922: 'The national spirit amongst the people is practically dead at the moment.' Many I.R.A. men who did not leave the north were interned during the civil war.[56]

Collins sought to reassure the northern men in the Curragh that his change of policy was only temporary. Woods reported of the Portobello meeting: 'The late C.-in-C. made it clear to us that the government in Ireland intended to deal with the Ulster situation in a very definite way, and as far as their division was concerned, every officer present felt greatly encouraged to carry on the work when we had a definite policy to pursue and an assurance that the government... would stand by us'.[57] Collins's death, however, meant the end of any hope of a return to an aggressive northern policy. A month later Woods was to ask the provisional government whether its northern policy had changed; the answer should have been in the affirmative. Early in the civil war the provisional government, while Collins's attention was elsewhere, appointed a committee to discuss northern policy, for which Ernest Blythe wrote a report implicitly critical of Collins's earlier strategy. Blythe concluded: 'There is no prospect of bringing about the unification of Ireland within any reasonable period of time by attacking the north-east... The belligerent policy has been shown to be useless for protecting the catholics or stopping the pogroms.' Blythe thought that to renew guerrilla warfare would result in the extermination of the catholic population in the north-east within two years, and he was also pessimistic about the effect of an economic boycott policy. For all Blythe's apparent realism, however, he was over-sanguine in his conclusions about prospects for Irish unity following the boundary commission's findings and a period of amicable relations between north and south. In another memorandum set before the government, Kevin O'Shiel drew similar conclusions on the need for a changed southern policy towards the north. He affirmed:

Without doing anything very definite for the present or showing any undue haste in going out of our way to oblige the north-eastern government we should, if I may say so, do nothing to obstruct the working of its government, which has been guaranteed by the treaty, or to add to the bitterness and hatreds of the last twelve months. Our policy should in its broad, general sense aim rather at attracting towards us these northern Irishmen than alienating them still further from us, with a view to shortening the period to the ultimate and inevitable union.[58]

[56] Mulcahy to Collins, 24 July 1922 (Mulcahy papers, MS P7/B/78); MacAnally (O'Malley notebooks, MS P17b/99); Woods's note of 3 Aug. 1922 (Mulcahy papers, MS P7/B/79).
[57] Woods's memo, 29 Sept. 1922 (N.A.I., D.T., S1801).
[58] Blythe's memo (Blythe papers, U.C.D., A.D., MS P24/70); O'Shiel to ministers, 2 Sept. 1922 (U.C.D., A.D., Kennedy papers, MS P4/V/1).

The northern policy of Cosgrave's government was in accordance with such views. Cosgrave denied claims made by prominent members of the Northern Ireland government that his administration was desirous of forcing portions of their territory into the Free State, affirming: 'Our northern policy, as [with] our policy in every other sphere, must be construed with respect to the signed articles [the treaty].' Cosgrave's government sought to defuse various crises in the north and was often forced to complain about the northern government's attitude, but not in a way to seriously embarrass either Belfast or London. While criticising the continued intransigence of the northern government Cosgrave declared: 'Since I have assumed office I have striven to bring about a better feeling between Northern Ireland and ourselves, especially along the inflammable border regions.' In addition the provisional government's civil obstruction policy faded away during the civil war. By the end of 1922 the government had stopped paying the salaries of catholic schoolteachers in the north,[59] allegedly on economic grounds. It was still too early for any Dublin government to be seen to cooperate with the northern regime, which would have been to commit political suicide, but Cosgrave's executive council did not advise northern catholics to do so. After all the aggressive interventionism of the months preceding the civil war, O'Shiel commented: 'Our position with regard to the nationalists of the north-east was that merely of friendly spectators. We let the local people decide what is best for them, and what was acceptable to them would be acceptable to us (always presupposing that it was not a decision against the national policy).'[60] Nevertheless, as between that section of northern nationalists (supporters of Joe Devlin and the Ancient Order of Hibernians) who were inclined to cooperate with the northern regime, and 'Sinn Féiners' (who were not), O'Shiel preferred to side with the latter, at least until the boundary commission had met and reached its conclusions, and his view was adopted by the Cosgrave government.[61]

The civil war, however, meant that it was necessary to postpone any call for the boundary commission to be established. O'Shiel affirmed: 'What a ridiculous position we would cut—both nationally and universally—were we to argue our claim at the commission for population and territory when, at our backs in our own jurisdiction, is the perpetual racket of war, the flames of our burning railway stations and property, and the never-failing daily lists of our murdered citizens.'[62] By the time, following the war, that Cos-

---

[59] Below, p. 195.

[60] Cosgrave in *Dáil Éireann deb.*, ii, 14 (6 Dec. 1922); Cosgrave to Devonshire, 10 Jan. 1923 (P.R.O., C.O. 739/17); O'Shiel to Free State ministers, 10 Oct. 1922 (U.C.D., A.D., Kennedy papers, MS P4/V/1).

[61] Phoenix, *Northern nationalism*, pp 256–8.

[62] O'Shiel report sent on by Cosgrave to Mulcahy, 25 Jan. 1923 (Mulcahy papers, MS P7/B/101).

grave requested that the commission sit, the prospects were far from encouraging for the south.

While circumstances had caused a reappraisal of attitudes in the south, that should not hide the fact that Cosgrave's government made no great priority of northern issues. Little attempt was made to reassure the northern minority on the boundary and other matters. The leading British civil servant Sir John Anderson commented that 'the belief is prevalent that the [Free State] government is abandoning all its claims.' Northern minority spokesmen grew increasingly alarmed. Joe Devlin thought that the delay in the boundary commission 'was seriously prejudicing the interests of the minority in the six counties by giving the Belfast parliament time to "dig themselves in" '. James O'Flynn, a member of the Downpatrick rural district council, while saying that the nationalist population of south and east Down wished to be in the Free State, pointed out: 'There was growing apathy and indifference on account of the delay in putting the boundary clause into operation and the feeling that the Free State was not troubling about the minority in the six counties.' It was at this time that an estrangement developed between southern nationalists and their coreligionists in the north. Peter Hughes declared in the dáil that the northern minority 'think that their interests have been neglected', and Cahir Healy, a Sinn Féin leader in the west of Northern Ireland, concluded: 'We have been abandoned to Craig's mercy.' Séamus Woods argued that the breaking-up of the northern I.R.A. 'is the first step to making partition permanent'.[63]

The fact that civil war in the south was of enormous benefit to the stability of Northern Ireland produced no change in that regime's attitude or policies. A siege mentality prevailed even after the siege had lifted. Initially there was scepticism among northern loyalists as to whether the southern government was in earnest about tackling the republican resistance, and there was much talk of it being a fake war. In the early months of the civil war Maj.-gen. Solly-Flood, the northern government's security adviser, was concerned about the threat that the southern government's air force, a few second-hand planes, posed for the north. The advent of the new Conservative U.K. government in October intensified Craig's demands that his government and security forces be properly supplied and trained. Any decision about reducing the size of the special constabulary was delayed and no concessions were made to the nationalist minority, or to British government pressure for more liberal policies. In fact Craig chose the first few weeks of the civil war to ask for the royal assent to ending proportional representation in local government

[63] Anderson to Tallents, 31 Oct. 1923 (P.R.O., C.O. 739/20); Devlin and O'Flynn, quoted in Hugh A. McCarthy report sent on by O'Shiel to executive council, 6 Nov. 1923 (U.C.D., A.D., Blythe papers, MS P24/203); Hughes, in *Dáil Éireann deb.*, iv, 1222–3 (20 July 1923); Healy letter, 30 Sept. 1922 (U.C.D., A.D., Kennedy papers, MS P4/V/1); Woods's memo, 29 Sept. 1922 (N.A.I., D.T., S1801).

elections in Northern Ireland; a bill for this purpose had passed through its stages by 5 July 1922. Irrespective of how much this could change voting patterns in the north, the request's timing demonstrated a supreme tactlessness. The southern government complained that the northern government was involved in gerrymandering, and thus trying to affect the findings of the boundary commission. Churchill told Cosgrave: 'I agree with you in thinking the bill most unfortunate and ill-timed.' Aware that the northern government was acting within its rights according to the 1920 act, the British government sought to hold off both the royal assent and the local government elections, to postpone the difficulty created by Craig and his colleagues. Lionel Curtis told Churchill: 'Our only object is to tide over the period of the boundary commission without putting the fat in the fire.' The legislation, however, could only be delayed.[64]

A similarly inflexible attitude was demonstrated by the northern government's insistence on carrying out flogging sentences on I.R.A. prisoners, while generally refusing to carry out such punishments on loyalist prisoners. The British government stressed that this might well result in a revival of violence on the border and argued that such methods could only be justified as a deterrent in a deteriorating security situation. Craig's government also insisted on bringing to trial southern I.R.A. officers who had been involved in incidents before the civil war. When Captain Heuston of the Monaghan I.R.A., who had been involved in the shoot-up of the special constables at Clones in February 1922, strayed across the border on his bicycle and was picked up by northern security forces, the British and Free State governments were reluctantly plunged into a minor crisis. Tallents—then acting as British government representative in Belfast—commented: 'No doubt it was a pity that he ever got caught—if police considerations only had come in, I think he would . . . possibly have been put over the border for the sake of peace; but once he was taken, all sorts of local political considerations came in, and these also it will be difficult to disregard.' Such an incident brought back all the old British impatience with the northern regime. Sir James Masterton-Smith, permanent under-secretary at the colonial office, told Lord Devonshire, his new secretary of state: 'The northern government is too ready to forget that something like two millions of British taxpayers' money are being provided this year for the maintenance of Ulster specials alone.' In such cases a somewhat flexible attitude by Craig and Lord Londonderry was pushed aside by the majority's insistence, in the northern cabinet, on the need to leave the judicial process to itself. Londonderry told the British home secretary that 'with every desire to assist Mr Cosgrave and

---

[64] Churchill to Cosgrave, 2 Sept. 1922 (P.R.O., C.O. 906/22); Curtis to Churchill, 2 Sept. 1922 (House of lords records dept, Lloyd George papers, F/10/3-2 42). The bill received the royal assent on 11 Sept. 1922 (12 & 13 Geo. V, c. 15).

his government in the difficult task which they have in restoring law and order in the south, we feel that we can best do so by insuring that law and order are enforced in the north.' In other words, internal northern considerations were paramount—wider issues relating to the south and to Northern Ireland's relations with the British government were secondary. British ministers sympathised with Cosgrave's protestations that by such attitudes Craig's government was endangering the new, peaceful atmosphere on the border, but even Bonar Law failed to get the northern government to change its mind. Cosgrave was left to speak 'very sadly about the unconciliatory and unbending attitude of the northern government and pointed to the fact that the pinpricks were all on the one side and the forbearance on the other'.[65]

The civil-war period, therefore, made it even less likely that the north would move even one inch towards accommodation with the south, let alone towards Irish unity. Soon Craig was to refuse to appoint the northern commissioner on the boundary commission. The northern catholics were the main long-term victims of the treaty and civil-war period. Southern nationalists had failed to make a priority of the northern question, or, for all their protestations on the subject, to defend northern nationalists' interests. Despite the rhetorical emphasis continually placed on Irish unity, southern considerations had been given priority. It appeared that the achievement and consolidation of Irish independence had become more important than any prospect of Irish unity. The northern minority was not to find a wide audience for its grievances again till the 1960s, and only then were some southern nationalists to examine the limitations of their traditional northern policy.

[65] Review of Heuston case and correspondence on it, 22–6 Dec. 1922 (P.R.O., C.O. 739/1); Tallents to Masterton-Smith, 6 Dec. 1922 (ibid.); Masterton-Smith to colonial secretary, 23 Dec. 1922 (ibid.). For Cosgrave reference, Londonderry to Bridgeman, 22 Dec. 1922 (ibid.).

CHAPTER III

Land and people, *c*.1926

DESMOND A. GILLMOR

HUMAN territoriality of various kinds has had a profound influence on the history and geography of Ireland, and the partitioning of the island in 1920–22 illustrates this well. The establishment of an international boundary between the newly independent Irish Free State and Northern Ireland, which remained part of the United Kingdom, was the most important territorial division in Ireland's history. The initial geographical impacts of partition were mainly political, but the repercussions on other aspects of human geography developed with time as policies and practices in the two territories diverged. These distinctions became superimposed on gradations that predated the border. Little of the new differentiation had emerged by the mid-1920s, but the existence of two states with different data sources necessitated the making of some distinctions between them in this geographical panorama, the reference date for which derives from the holding of the first separate census of population in both territories in the year 1926.

The nature of the border derived from the definition of Northern Ireland under the government of Ireland act, 1920,[1] as comprising the six counties of Antrim, Armagh, Down, Fermanagh, Londonderry, and Tyrone, together with the county boroughs of Belfast and Derry. The boundaries that constituted the perimeter of this group of counties became the lengthy and convoluted border. Thus it was not delimited initially as an international border: its origins lay mainly in the divisions between counties established in the sixteenth century, when the precise alignment of these boundaries had little significance. The border followed some natural features such as rivers, but it was generally not readily distinguishable in the landscape. It lay across some mountain districts, but also divided many densely settled areas. One effect that was felt immediately was the extent to which the border disrupted activity patterns and business by cutting across the trade areas of towns such as Derry and Clones. The treaty had allowed for a redrawing of the border in accordance with the wishes of the inhabitants in so far as might be compatible with economic and geographic conditions. The commission established

---

[1] 10 & 11 Geo. V, c. 67 (23 Dec. 1920).

for this purpose in 1925 endeavoured to effect a better separation of those of unionist and nationalist sentiment, but the extent of spatial intermixture rendered a satisfactory solution impossible.[2] Besides, the Irish Free State government found the proposed transfer of even a small part of its territory to Northern Ireland unacceptable, and the commission's report was accordingly suppressed.

Not only did county boundaries provide the basis for border delimitation, but the county's administrative status had been reinforced by the mid 1920s, largely as a result of the local government act of 1898.[3] County status was then granted to the six main cities through creation of the county boroughs of Dublin, Belfast, Cork, Derry, Limerick, and Waterford. County Tipperary was divided for administrative purposes into north and south ridings, and minor adjustments were made to county boundaries. Later extension of local government activity further strengthened the role of the county. The organisation of Gaelic sport contributed substantially to popular county consciousness. Confirmation of the administrative status of the county represented a degree of centralisation through some loss of function by smaller units. Towns and (in Northern Ireland) rural districts retained their roles, but baronies, poor-law unions, and (in 1925) rural districts in the Irish Free State had ceased to be a part of the hierarchical structure of public administration.

CHANGES in the rural landscape since pre-famine times had been largely a product of population decline, improved circumstances of rural dwellers, and alterations in land use, rather than a consequence of change in the more visually apparent pattern of field boundaries and roads. Field enclosure and the road network had been largely completed by the mid nineteenth century, so only in some western localities where the rundale layout of land was subsequently eradicated had the form of the cultural landscape altered significantly. The extent of improved land had reached a maximum in the 1870s, but some of the fields reclaimed on hill slopes and bog margins had reverted to the semi-natural state by the mid 1920s. Diminishing population had effects on farm size and rural settlement patterns. The subdivision of holdings that had been the accompaniment of population growth was replaced by amalgamation, especially among the smaller units. Many rural dwellings had been abandoned, but most had been built of mud and had consequently disappeared, so that the number of derelict houses gave no indication of the extent of population decline. Improved housing was one of the most distinctive features of rural landscape change. This applied both to farmsteads and also to the construction of labourers' cottages in recent decades as a result of a pioneer public housing programme for agricultural workers.

[2] Below, ix, map 98.   [3] 61 & 62 Vict., c. 37 (12 Aug. 1898).

TABLE 1. *Land use, 1926*

	Irish Free State		Northern Ireland		Ireland	
	(acres)	(%)	(acres)	(%)	(acres)	(%)
Tillage	1,551,447	9.1	574,626	17.2	2,126,073	10.4
Hay	2,287,849	13.5	484,090	14.4	2,171,939	13.6
Pasture	8,416,439	49.4	1,402,276	41.8	9,818,715	48.2
Woods and plantations	234,411	1.4	39,598	1.2	274,009	1.4
Other land	4,534,335	26.6	850,854	25.4	5,385,189	26.4
Total area	17,024,481	100.0	3,351,444	100.0	20,375,925	100.0

The pattern of Irish land use in 1926 is shown in table 1. Usage was predominantly pastoral, with pasture and hay together covering 62 per cent of the country, and tillage accounting for only 10 per cent. The decline in arable cropping that had been almost continuous during the second half of the nineteenth century was reversed at the time of the first world war but had quickly reasserted itself, so that by 1926 the arable acreage was the lowest since agricultural statistics were first recorded. The extent of pasture was in part an adaptation to physical circumstances that favoured grass growth rather than arable farming, in part a response to the market stimulus of relatively higher prices for livestock and livestock products, and in part related to the diminishing agricultural population as a labour force and as consumers of crop products. Other factors were the import of grain and increased use of conserved grass as fodder, the acreage of hay having expanded greatly. Irish forests were almost completely depleted following extensive cutting associated with the demise of the landlord system and with wartime conditions. State afforestation designed to rectify this situation had begun on a small scale, but its impact on the landscape was negligible. Much of the remainder of the 'other land' comprised bare rock, moorland, bog, and marsh. An unspecified amount of this land served useful purposes as rough grazing to supplement the limited area of improved land on many of the adjacent farms, and as a source of peat for fuel.

Ireland was still a country of predominantly small agricultural holdings, despite the trend towards larger units. More than 60 per cent of the holdings over 1 acre were less than 30 acres, and only about 20 per cent exceeded 50 acres. Large holdings were a more significant feature of the landscape than their numbers suggest: those of over 100 acres occupied over one-third of the agricultural land in the Irish Free State. Because of the nature and pattern of colonisation and land settlement, smallholdings tended to be more numerous, and the average size of holding smaller, on the poorer land and in the north and west. Only one-tenth of holdings in Connacht exceeded 50 acres. While the majority of farmers remained smallholders, their status had been transformed following the various land acts whereby security of tenure had been granted, and most either owned or were becoming owners of their holdings. This land reform had little direct impact on the landscape, but it was a social watershed, with the change in control over land having major economic implications for the development of Irish agriculture.

Irish agriculture was characterised by mixed farming, but major regional variations in enterprise structure had developed, and this was evident in arable cropping (map 1).[4] Tillage was most common in Ulster (except on the water-retentive soils of Fermanagh and Cavan) and in the south-east. Its spatial pattern was a complex one but related in part to the physical variables of relief, soil, and climate, and to farm size, cropping being more common on the smaller holdings. The historical role of landlords and settler tenants in initiating arable farming, and the established tradition of tillage, were important in some areas. The physical influences were most evident in the instances of wheat and barley, which tended to concentrate in areas of drier and sunnier climate and on well-drained soils. Barley was more localised, densities being highest in Laois, Wexford, Louth, and Offaly. Oats, being more tolerant of physical conditions, were grown throughout the country, with the counties Donegal, Londonderry, Tyrone, and Down being major producing areas. Oats occupied nearly half the total acreage of arable crops, with potatoes ranking second. Potatoes were the most uniformly distributed of crops, a function of the feasiblity of satisfactory growth under very varied conditions and the universal local demand for the product. Densities were highest in the north and west, where farms were small and rural population density high. Root and green fodder crops, of which turnips were most important, were especially favoured in the south-east. Flax was almost confined to Ulster, its market area, the major concentration being on the fertile, heavy, basaltic soils of the Lower Bann valley and Lough Neagh districts, where it was an important cash crop. Fruit was of relatively minor importance except in the apple-orchard area to the south of Lough Neagh, to which it may have been introduced by settlers from fruit-growing districts in England.

Commercial dairy farming was concentrated in Munster and in Ulster and north Connacht, as indicated by high cow densities (map 2).[5] These were traditional dairying areas, and cooperative creameries had been established there from the late 1880s onwards in order to manufacture a more uniform and better-quality product than home-made butter. Dairying was associated with heavy soils, and milk production was highly seasonal in response to land conditions and food supply; output was at a minimum in winter, when soils

[4] Below, p. 81.   [5] Below, p. 81.

were wet and soft and grass growth was retarded. The south-west had the advantage of a milder climate and longer growing season than other parts of the country. The separated milk returned from creameries was used in calf- and pig-rearing. Outside the dairying regions most milk was fed to livestock or consumed by the farm household. Urban supply to Dublin and Belfast was of significance, with output being concentrated in close proximity to the cities because of transport time and cost.

Cattle production was the most uniformly widespread farm enterprise. Some rearing was practised on almost all farms, but there was a general tendency for dairy farmers and smallholders to sell animals when young. Despite the large numbers of calves born in the dairying regions, densities of dry cattle aged 1 year and over were low there (map 3).[6] There was a well-established movement of young stock and store cattle towards the north central lowland for further feeding. Cattle production, with its low labour requirements, was favoured by large farmers. Other reasons for the concentration of advanced cattle in north Leinster were the suitability of the fertile grassland for fattening and proximity to the port outlets for export to Britain. Irish cattle production was largely off summer grass, with supplementary winter feeding being most common in tillage districts.

Unlike other livestock, some of the main concentrations of sheep were associated with upland areas (map 4).[7] Their ability to exist on rough herbage, to walk easily on steep slopes, and to withstand severe weather conditions, gave them a comparative advantage over other animals. Densities were higher on eastern mountains, notably the Leinster Chain and the Mournes, which were less exposed and provided more satisfactory grazing than western ranges. Many sheep were sent to lowland areas, especially in east Leinster and east Ulster, for fattening. Lowland sheep production was most important on the thin, dry limestone soils of east Galway and south Roscommon, where the dry conditions were favourable. Sheep densities were lowest in areas of heavy, wet soils, where susceptibility to disease was greatest and weight gains rendered difficult under the damp conditions, and where competition with dairying was strongest.

Pig production was important in some of the dairying areas, in south Munster and in Counties Cavan, Monaghan, and Antrim (map 5).[8] Many dairy farmers kept pigs, using the skim milk returned from the creameries as a feedstuff. The other major area of production was the arable south-east, where barley was the principal feedstuff. Densities were lowest in north Leinster, where the large farmers were not interested in pig production. Although pig-keeping was an intensive enterprise and was most common on smallholdings, there was little tendency to adopt it on a commercial scale in western districts.

[6] Below, p. 81.　　[7] Below, p. 81.　　[8] Below, p. 82.

There was a close spatial association between poultry production and smallholdings, with the industry concentrated in the north and north-west (map 6).[9] The sale of eggs and poultry provided a valuable source of income on many small farms, where there was adequate labour to grow the oats and potatoes for feeding and to tend the poultry.

Agricultural income was derived largely from the sale of livestock. About three-quarters of the crop production was fed to livestock or used as seed on the farm, and a substantial proportion of the remainder was consumed by the farm household. Livestock and livestock products accounted for 85 per cent of the total value of agricultural output, with cattle and dairy farming contributing 46 per cent, and pig and poultry production 32 per cent. The strong subsistence element in Irish agriculture and the importance of export markets were indicated by the disposal of Irish Free State output during the period 1921–7, 37 per cent being consumed by the farming community, 18 per cent by others in the state, and 45 per cent exported.

The livestock fair was the most distinctive feature of agricultural marketing in Ireland. Although the sale of cattle by auction had been introduced in Dublin towards the end of the nineteenth century, the traditional method of sale by private treaty at fairs was the normal practice throughout the country. Fairs were held in most towns and villages, though there had been a tendency for some time for the frequency of fairs and volume of sales to increase at some centres at the expense of others. Expansion occurred in towns where communications and other services were best developed, especially in places served by railway. The fair had varied functions in addition to the marketing of livestock. The opportunity to purchase goods from shops and travelling salespeople was availed of; the fair provided a break in the routine of rural life, a chance to mingle with people and to renew acquaintances; there was entertainment and a spirit of revelry, the fair being recognised as a time of special licence. The commercial function of the fair was uppermost, but social aspects were important, epitomising the fact that farming was not simply an economic activity but a way of life.

THE differing roles of agriculture and manufacturing comprised the main distinction between the economies of the Irish Free State and Northern Ireland. The two industries combined accounted for over 60 per cent of employment in both areas. The other categories of employment were quite similar, except for commercial activities being of greater importance in the more industrialised economy of Northern Ireland, and the presence of many more domestic servants in the Irish Free State (table 2). The tertiary sector had a predominantly urban distribution. Manufacturing accounted for 35 per cent of the labour force in Northern Ireland but only 10 per cent in the Irish

9 Below, p. 82.

TABLE 2. *Employment structure, 1926*

	Irish Free State		Northern Ireland		Ireland	
	Persons	Employment (% of total)	Persons	Employment (% of total)	Persons	Employment (% of total)
Agriculture	648,376	53.0	147,461	25.8	795,837	44.4
Forestry	199	0.0	53	0.0	252	0.0
Fishing	5,533	0.5	1,108	0.2	6,641	0.4
Mining	1,704	0.1	2,172	0.4	3,876	0.2
Manufacture	118,219	9.7	199,187	34.9	317,406	17.7
Construction	36,456	3.0	22,318	3.9	58,774	3.3
Utilities	2,462	0.2	2,754	0.5	5,216	0.3
Transport and communication	38,890	3.2	21,817	3.8	60,707	3.4
Commerce	105,320	8.6	64,151	11.2	169,471	9.4
Finance	8,917	0.7	5,535	1.0	14,452	0.8
Public administration and defence	59,713	4.9	29,726	5.2	89,439	5.0
Professions	55,356	4.5	19,210	3.4	74,566	4.1
Personal service	127,956	10.5	48,155	8.4	176,111	9.8
Entertainment and sport	4,786	0.4	2,197	0.4	6,983	0.4
Other industries	9,127	0.7	4,862	0.9	13,989	0.8
TOTAL	1,223,014	100.0	570,706	100.0	1,793,720	100.0

Free State. Northern Ireland had nearly two-thirds of the country's manu-facturing employment.

Linen textile manufacturing was Northern Ireland's main industry, employing one-third of the manufacturing labour force: 68,000 workers were employed, two-thirds of them female. The linen industry had been a domes-tic activity until mechanisation was introduced to spinning about 1830 and weaving from 1850. It then became highly concentrated in the Lagan valley and the Lough Neagh basin: half the mills were in Belfast, and other import-ant centres were Lurgan, Banbridge, Portadown, Ballymena, and Lisburn. The linen mill was a prominent and distinctive feature of the landscape of the north-east. Once the spinning of fine linen yarn had been mechanised, the industry soon outstripped its rivals in other textile industries, such as cotton. Streams flowing off the southern edge of the Antrim plateau pro-vided water power for many mills in west Belfast. When coal was used it was readily available through the expanding port, which also facilitated the export of linen goods. Other factors favouring the north-east were the industrial experience of the population and the availability of local capital. The Irish climate was suitable for the industry. Domestic flax contributed less than one-third of raw material requirements in the mid 1920s, Belgium, Latvia, and Estonia being the major supply areas. There was much industrial activity in Northern Ireland based on further fabrication of linen cloth, the shirtmak-ing industry of Derry and its vicinity being a notable example. Much of the output of linen yarn and manufactures was exported, principally to North America.

Northern Ireland's second manufacturing industry was the Belfast ship-building industry, employing 20,000, nearly one-fifth of the city's industrial labour force. The yards had expanded during the nineteenth century to the extent that Belfast had become one of the major world centres of shipbuilding. As the port developed, the need for ships increased and the harbour was easily dredged to provide a depth of water sufficient for large vessels. Reclaimed mud flats afforded suitable waterside sites, which were gradually extended. Raw materials were not available locally, but they could easily be imported: steel and coal from northern Britain and timber from Scandinavia and Canada. Thus Belfast had some natural advantages for shipbuilding, but these alone would not have ensured the success of the industry. Much must be attributed to the initiative and enterprise of Edward Harland and Gustav Wolff, who had developed the largest firm in partnership from 1861.[10] Other industries in Belfast had linkages with shipbuilding, including the associated ropeworks, which was the largest in the world, and varied engineering activities.

The processing of food, drink, and tobacco was the most important industrial category in the Irish Free State, employing 28 per cent of the

---

[10] Above, vi, ch. 12.

manufacturing labour force. This situation reflected the important role of agriculture in the state's economy and the limited extent of other industrial development. Individual industries, in order of employment content, were baking, brewing, grain milling, biscuit making, sweets and jam manufacture, dairy processing, tobacco manufacture, bacon curing, soft-drink manufacture, and malting and distilling. County Dublin accounted for 45 per cent of the employment in food, drink, and tobacco manufacturing. The most centralised activities were biscuit making, tobacco manufacture, brewing, sweets and jam manufacture, and distilling. Although there were establishments in provincial towns, large Dublin firms accounted for the bulk of output. The Guinness brewery was the largest in the world, and the Jacob firm ranked among the major manufacturers of biscuits. Location in Dublin afforded proximity to the major concentration of Irish population and ease of assembly of raw materials and distribution of products by rail from and to the remainder of the country. Access to the state's largest port and to Britain was of great importance to those firms using imported coal and raw materials or exporting some of their produce. The role of Dublin individuals and families was important in contributing to concentration in some industries. Although there was also a disproportionate share of baking and soft-drink manufacture in Dublin, these market-oriented industries were more widely dispersed. Because of the bulky nature and perishability of the product and because of the feasibility of operation in small units with relatively low capital input, bakeries were present in most medium and large towns. Transport considerations also favoured dispersion in the mineral-water manufacturing industry, the product consisting largely of the ubiquitous raw material, water. The major centres of grain milling were Cork, Limerick, and Dublin, the import of grain and coal favouring a port location. Milling had become more concentrated in a greatly reduced number of establishments, but there were mills in every county and especially in the cereal-growing districts. Malthouses were concentrated in the barley-producing areas of the south-east; however, because of association with the brewing industry, Dublin was the most important single centre of malting. Creameries and bacon factories were strongly raw-material-oriented, four-fifths of the employment in dairy processing and bacon curing being in Munster. The butter industry had been transformed through the establishment of creameries, which were dispersed throughout Munster except County Clare, and in County Kilkenny, with smaller numbers in the northern dairying belt from Sligo to Monaghan. The principal bacon-curing centres were Limerick, Cork, Waterford, Tralee, Dublin, and Enniscorthy. Although quite widely distributed, food and drink processing was most important in the east and south because of the better land and greater output of agricultural products there, and the easier access to markets.

Clothing manufacture was the second industrial category in the Irish Free State, employing 19 per cent of the manufacturing labour force. The principal employment counties were Dublin (28 per cent) and Cork (15 per cent) but the industry was widely dispersed, its distribution being related to market demand and labour supply. More than three-quarters of the employment was in tailoring and dressmaking, much of it on a handcraft basis. The manufacture of shirts, millinery, and poplin was highly concentrated in Dublin. The woollen textile industry was undergoing change as the factory product made inroads on the cottage industry of Donegal and other western seaboard counties, and it was important in the south. The principal footwear centres were Dublin, Cork, and Tralee.

Manufacturing as a whole was highly concentrated in the north-east of Ireland, with Belfast, the Lagan valley, and adjacent areas dominating the industrial scene (map 7).[11] In Belfast resided 54 per cent of Northern Ireland's industrial employees. County Dublin was the industrial centre of the Irish Free State, having 36 per cent of the manufacturing labour force; an additional 11 per cent lived in the cities of Cork, Limerick, and Waterford. The forces drawing factory industries towards the major ports were very strong. These were the largest cities and hence the main concentration of consumers, purchasing power, and labour supply. The orientation of transport routes towards them facilitated contact with the interior. Power and raw-material assembly costs also favoured port locations, as almost all industrial energy was derived from imported coal and many of the raw materials used by industry had to be imported.

COAL imported from Britain was Ireland's main source of energy. Most of the local coal resources had adverse structural and quality characteristics, but even their limited potential had not been developed to the full. Mining was mainly in the Castlecomer plateau and Slieve Ardagh districts of the Leinster coalfield, together with the Arigna area in the Connacht field and at Coalisland in Ulster. Of greater significance was the production of handcut turf, which was used largely as a domestic fuel and contributed about one-quarter of energy supply. It was cut mainly by the farming community and so did not figure in the employment data. Production was principally from western and midland counties, but cutting occurred wherever there were peat bogs.

Electricity had been generated in Ireland since the late nineteenth century but was still generally restricted to the cities and larger towns and was used mainly for lighting. Production was in independent private and local-authority plants, which were based mainly on imported coal. There were some small hydroelectric generators, and there had been proposals to harness some of the major rivers, including the Liffey. It was the Shannon, however, that was in the limelight in the 1920s, through the proposal, approval, and implementation of the scheme that involved the construction of the plant at

---

[11] Below, p. 83.

Ardnacrusha on the lower river. It was a very ambitious undertaking in the context of the limited electricity demand, financial resources, and technical capabilities of the time. The Shannon scheme had an importance extending beyond its energy role because it was the first major enterprise undertaken by the independent Irish Free State.

Apart from peat and coal production, mining comprised mainly the quarrying of stone, and to a lesser extent sand and gravel. Granite was quarried in the Wicklow and Dublin mountains and in the Mourne mountains. Other quarrying was carried on mainly in the vicinities of the cities to meet their construction requirements and on a small scale throughout the country for road and building purposes. Cement was manufactured from chalk and clay near Larne, but reliance was mainly on imported cement. Other mining in County Antrim included bauxite, iron ore, salt, and diatomite. Barytes was mined in west Cork. Most of the metalliferous mines that had operated in the nineteenth century lay abandoned, as world market price trends had rendered working uneconomic and the more easily accessible minerals had been depleted at some of the sites.

THE mid 1920s marked a distinctive phase in Irish transport development, heralding the decline of the railways after the rail network had attained its maximum extent. Canals retained only the shipment of some heavy bulk commodities. They had lost business to improved road transport and especially to the railways, which provided a faster and more widespread service. Railways had come to dominate the inland transport scene, with road traffic functioning mainly as feeder services for the railways and for short distances. Yet the profitability of Irish railways was always hampered by the relative scarcity of mineral and industrial traffic, by absence of the through traffic of Great Britain and mainland Europe, and by the short distances involved. The enthusiasm with which railway building was pursued in Britain in the mid-nineteenth century extended to Ireland, but implementation of some of the early plans was delayed by difficulties encountered in the raising of capital. Government loans were needed to supplement private enterprise, and from the early 1880s state planning and support of the railways as a regional development measure in areas of low traffic potential was the main incentive to further extension of the network.[12] No lines were added after 1920. Rail services were disrupted and property damaged during the political disturbances of the early 1920s, but by the middle of the decade the challenge of competition from motorised road transport, which was to have much more widespread and permanent repercussions on the railways, had become evident.

The railway system of the mid 1920s was a fairly open network focused on the two hubs of Dublin and Belfast.[13] The earliest routes radiated from

---

[12] Above, vi, 309–11, 312–14.   [13] Below, ix, map 99.

Dublin, the major city and port. As Belfast developed during the second half of the nineteenth century, it became the focus of railways in the northern part of the country. The simple radial pattern linking Dublin and Belfast with the principal provincial towns and ports developed into a network form as transverse railways were built to join the main arteries. Although the region served by Belfast was smaller than Dublin's hinterland, it was more highly urbanised and industrialised, and the mesh of its rail network was closer. The routes followed by railways were controlled by the positions of the towns that they were intended to serve and by the physical landscape. The physical influence was evident in the distortion of network symmetry by Lough Neagh and upland areas in the vicinity of Belfast, by the orientation of the Dublin–Cork line which curved around the Galtee mountains, and by the Dublin–Wexford route following the coast and then the valleys of the Avoca and Slaney. From the 1880s the rail network was extended with government support into parts of the country that were more rugged, remote, and poor, especially along the west coast. Many of these were light narrow-gauge railways because of topographical difficulties and cost considerations, as in Donegal and west Clare. Such lines greatly increased the accessibility of remote districts but were handicapped by the small amount of traffic generated, the short distances involved, the need for transshipment between standard and narrow-gauge lines, and speed restrictions. They thus became particularly vulnerable to competition from road transport. Yet the rail network remained almost intact in the mid 1920s; government support had ensured that the early demise of the Birr–Portumna line in 1878 was not the precursor of other closures. Accessibility to the railways, however, failed to halt population decline, which in turn impaired the railways' ability to generate business.

THE most remarkable feature of Ireland since the 1840s has been the extent of depopulation, giving it a unique position in demographic history. The number of people had halved over a period when the world population had doubled. This was largely a consequence of emigration, which was deeply ingrained and had pervasive effects on Irish society and the economy. Demographic trends and characteristics touched every aspect of Ireland's human geography in the 1920s.

Although there was still a net annual emigration of about 30,000 people, the general tendency had been for a diminishing rate of population loss since the famine. This trend had been reversed in the 1880s, largely because of the agricultural difficulties of the times, and in the 1911–26 intercensal period by war deaths and the exodus of British army and police personnel and their dependants in consequence of the independence of the Irish Free State. Differential trends in the total populations of the two political units had emerged from the turn of the century, with growth being recorded in the area that became Northern Ireland. Thus a decline of 3.4 per cent in the island's population in 1911–26 comprised an increase of 0.5 per cent in Northern Ireland and a decrease of 5.3 per cent in the Irish Free State. Their respective populations in 1926 were 1.26 million and 2.97 million, the Irish Free State containing 70 per cent of Ireland's population.

The pressure of population on the land had greatly diminished, so that the density of 133 per square mile in 1926 was low compared with the more industrialised and urbanised parts of western Europe. Population density in Northern Ireland was twice that in the Irish Free State. Within the two territories there was substantial variation in the distribution of population, related mainly to differences in the level of urbanisation, in the distribution of agricultural land and farm size, and in the rates of population change.

The impact of the relative trends in the numbers of rural and urban dwellers was reflected in the fact that the proportion of the population resident in cities, towns, and villages had increased from one-fifth in pre-famine times to nearly one-half. The process of urbanisation was most marked in the north-east, focusing on the Lagan valley and Belfast Lough, where it was associated with industrialisation. Belfast had grown so rapidly that its population of 415,000 in 1926 comprised one-third of the Northern Ireland total. The population of Dublin and its immediate environs was 400,000, but its position was less dominant as this accounted for less than one-eighth of the Irish Free State total. Development in the two main centres led to the growth of towns in their vicinities and affected adjacent urban areas. There had been substantial rural-to-urban migration, with the main cities drawing population principally from adjacent counties. One-quarter of the people resident in Dublin had been born elsewhere in the state. Much of the national loss of population came from rural areas, but even towns declined throughout much of the country, the rates of decrease being greater in the smaller settlements. The urban structure of the west was particularly weak, with one-tenth of the people of Connacht resident in towns (map 8),[14] and the population of these had diminished by one-half since 1851. Thus the increasing level of urbanisation of the population was attributable more to rural decline than to widespread urban growth. The largest Irish towns were on river estuaries accessible to Britain and adjacent to good agricultural land. The peripheral location of much of this urban development had a considerable influence on the distribution of the Irish population, so that almost two-thirds of the Irish Free State total lived within twenty miles of the coast.

The major gaps in the settlement pattern coincided with mountain ranges. This was most marked in western areas but was also evident in the Leinster Chain, the Mournes, the Sperrins, and other upland districts. Agriculture and human settlement were hindered by the steep and rugged topography,

---

[14] Below, p. 84.

the scanty and infertile soils, and the adverse climatic conditions. Yet population had spread up the lower slopes in the eighteenth and nineteenth centuries. The downslope retreat of the upper limit of improved land from the 1870s had been initiated by agrarian depression but continued with diminishing population pressure. In the lowlands there were gaps in the settlement pattern where peat bogs occurred, especially in the midlands. Population density on the agricultural land varied, being highest in the small-farm areas of the west and north and in more confined districts around the cities. In the Irish Free State, the density of the open country population on the agricultural land of Donegal was nearly three times greater than that in Meath.

The spatial pattern of population change altered over time. The area of highest loss in the post-famine period was in central Ireland, but by the early twentieth century the focus of decline had shifted northwestwards.[15] In the period 1911–26 there was population increase in Belfast and County Down, while Dublin was the only county in which growth was recorded in the Irish Free State. Decline exceeded 10 per cent in Kildare, Leitrim, Roscommon, and Mayo, but the high loss in Kildare was in part attributable to the departure of the British army. Of every five people leaving an Irish county, on average four emigrated and one migrated internally. The level of internal migration was proportionately greater in the east and the rate of natural increase was slightly lower there, so that the extent of population decline in western areas was almost entirely a result of their high rates of emigration. These were closely related to employment structure and the level of urbanisation. Much of the population decline was among the farming community, with losses being greatest in the areas of smallholdings and difficult environmental conditions. Towns, which would help to retain population through the employment opportunities in manufacturing and service industries that they afforded, were few and of only small size in the west. Emigration occurred everywhere, but the rate per 1,000 of population in 1911–26 was 12.8 in Connacht compared with 5.5 in Leinster.

One characteristic of the population that was strongly influenced nationally and regionally by emigration was its age structure. The number of people aged 65 years and over, per 100 aged 15–65, was 15 in the Irish Free State, the highest in Europe, and 13 in Northern Ireland. Most emigrants left as young adults, so that the comparatively aged nature of the Irish population was attributable mainly to emigration and only slightly to somewhat longer life expectation. The number aged 65 and over per 100 aged 15–65 was 17 in rural areas of the Irish Free State, compared with 10 in urban areas. Differential urbanisation and the inversely related levels of migration largely accounted for the pronounced spatial variation in the age structure of the population (map 9).[16] The percentage of the population aged 65 and over

[15] Below, ix, map 73.   [16] Below, p. 85.

ranged from 5 in Belfast to 13 in Leitrim. The older age structure of the population in western areas occurred despite a higher proportion of children there, arising from greater fertility of marriages. The proportions of old people and children in the Irish population contributed substantially to a comparatively high level of dependence on those at work, especially in rural areas and the west.

The gender structure of the Irish population was balanced, the numbers of males and females being almost equal. An excess of males at birth was compensated by the greater longevity of women. Females comprised 49.2 per cent of children under 5 years, but 55.8 per cent of people aged 75 and over. The gender structure was also influenced by differential rates of migration between males and females, which contributed to distinct trends and spatial patterns. With women becoming relatively more migratory, the number of females per 1,000 males in the population had declined from 1,050 in 1871 to 999 by 1926. The ratio of 973 in the Irish Free State was much lower than that of 1,066 in Northern Ireland, and its proportion of females was less than that of any other European country, reflecting the impact of emigration. Dublin was the only county in which females formed a majority, whereas in Northern Ireland there was an excess of males only in Tyrone and Fermanagh (map 10).[17] The number of females per 1,000 males was 1,202 in Irish urban areas but only 937 in rural areas. The characteristic rural industries, notably agriculture, were largely male-employing, so that women had to a greater extent to seek employment in the manufacturing and service industries of towns or to emigrate.

Another unique feature of Irish demography related to marital status, in that the proportions of people remaining single at all ages and the age of marriage were higher than those in any other European country. The percentages of men who were still single at ages 55–65 were 26 in the Irish Free State and 21 in Northern Ireland. The order was reversed for women, at 26 per cent in Northern Ireland and 24 per cent in the Irish Free State, which reflected the interrelated differences between the two areas in gender structure and urbanisation. The proportion of men who were single in every age group was higher in rural areas than in urban districts. This applied also to women under 35 because of the younger age of marriage in the towns, but in all older categories the proportion of single women was higher in urban areas. The likelihood of men being married increased with the size of the town. One major factor accounting for the differences between rural and urban areas was the different availability of marriageable males and females. Among Irish Free State people in their thirties, single males outnumbered single females by almost two to one in rural areas, but there was a small majority of females in the towns; clearly marriage prospects were higher for

[17] Below, p. 85.

men in urban areas and for women in the countryside. Despite the availability of men, however, one-fifth of rural women never married. One increasing influence on rural marriage rates was the late age at which many farmers' sons gained control of their holdings and house, so that marriage was postponed or did not occur. The higher rate of rural emigration had some effect, removing many of those who were most likely to marry. Even city marriage levels were low compared with those in other countries, so that the Irish marital uniqueness was not related only to the rural character of the country. The marriage rate had been declining since pre-famine times, when the proportions of people remaining single were less than half of those in 1926. This trend was related to some extent to emigration, but the precise reasons for it are not understood.

Diminishing population combined with house-building had led to substantial improvements in housing conditions, though considerable deficiencies and inequalities remained. If overcrowding were interpreted as densities of over two persons per room, the percentages of people living under these conditions were 27 in the Irish Free State and 18 in Northern Ireland. The latter was twice the level in England and Wales, but even the Irish Free State conditions were substantially better than those in Scotland. Overcrowding was most acute in the two contrasting areas of Dublin city centre and remote areas of the rural west (map 11).[18] Nearly one-half of the population of Dublin lived at more than two per room and one-third of city-centre residents lived at densities of twice this level. Conditions were markedly different and improving further in Belfast, where the proportions of people living at these levels of overcrowding were 14 and 1 per cent respectively. This more favourable situation occurred despite the landscape impression of congestion that the extent of small terraced houses in Belfast might suggest, and it was only in part attributable to the smaller proportions of large families in Northern Ireland. In Dublin the number of one-room tenements had increased and they contained over a quarter of the population, twice the proportion in overcrowded Glasgow. In contrast, one-room dwellings in rural areas were greatly depleted. Overcrowding in the countryside was highest in the western seaboard counties of small farms.

There were distinctive spatial patterns and trends in the religious adherence and linguistic attainments of the population. The distribution of protestants was closely related to the nature of colonisation and settlement, their proportion being highest in the areas of sixteenth- and seventeenth-century plantations, notably the Ulster plantation, and in districts where British influence historically had been strongest and where the highest proportions of foreign-born people currently resided.[19] Although this pattern was largely inherited and had considerable stability, some spatial change was occurring. The Roman

---

[18] Below, p. 85.   [19] Below, ix, map 81.

Catholic minority in what had become Northern Ireland had declined at each census from 41 per cent in 1861 to 33 per cent in 1926. The proportion of protestants in the declining population of the Irish Free State had been relatively stable but diminished from 10 per cent in 1911 to 7 per cent in 1926, the rates of decline being 32 per cent for protestants and 2 per cent for catholics.[20] Although the losses were greatest in urban areas and especially in the military towns, the exodus of British forces accounted for only a minor part of the decrease. This is indicated by the facts that the decline was five times greater than the total number of protestants who had been in the forces in 1911, and that the rates of decline among native and foreign-born protestants were similar. Comparative protestant decrease was least in the areas where the minority was strongest, notably in the counties of Donegal, Cavan, and Monaghan. Trends in the Irish Free State, combined with growth in Northern Ireland, meant that a process of greater concentration of protestants in the northern core had become established, resulting in an increasing level of spatial separation of religions.

A similar trend towards an increasing degree of concentration had characterised the Irish language, as the ability to speak it diminished throughout most of the country.[21] It remained strong only in some western refuge localities of difficult environmental conditions, which were relatively inaccessible to external influences and were designated as the Gaeltacht areas. A reversal of the locational shift emerged in the period 1911–26: of all people in the state who declared that they could speak Irish, the Gaeltacht's share declined from 57 per cent to 45 per cent. Within the Gaeltacht areas, the number of people who could speak Irish declined by one-fifth and their percentage of the Gaeltacht population decreased from 59 to 52. Elsewhere in the Irish Free State, the proportion who could speak Irish increased from 9 to 11 per cent, reversing the earlier trend. Growth was confined to those aged under 20, and resulted from the great increase in the teaching of Irish in the schools before, and especially after, independence.[22]

THE differing patterns of land use, economic activities, and social characteristics of the population, superimposed on and to some extent influenced by the varied physical landscape, resulted in great regional diversity within the small land area of Ireland. The regional characteristics were complex and exhibited considerable local variation. The clearest broad differentiation was between east and west, though in some respects an intricate gradation from one coast to the other might be considered more appropriate than recognition of two distinct regions. However it might be delimited and by whatever criteria its status might be assessed, the west was demonstrably disadvantaged compared with the rest of the country.

[20] Below, pp 806–7.   [21] Below, ix, maps 79, 80.
[22] Below, pp 542–4, 564–72, 726–32.

There were many physical, historical, economic, and social reasons why the west lagged behind the rest of the country. The physical difficulties included rugged relief, poor soils, inadequate drainage, and unfavourable climatic features. These conditions affected in particular agriculture, which was further handicapped by small farm size, fragmented holdings, low marketability of production, and in some areas inappropriate farming systems. Hindering other sections of the economy, as well as agriculture, were the limited amount of capital available or being invested within the west, and the distance from the major domestic and export markets and from sources of supplies. The perceived natural resource disadvantage of the west and its remoteness from the east- and south-coast entry points contributed to its being the area towards which displaced native inhabitants had been directed. It was also the area least affected by settlement, development, and other influences emanating from Britain and the major ports. This peripherality was in part responsible for, and in turn was accentuated by, the easterly orientation of manufacturing development, service industry location, and urban growth. Thus, despite the difficulties afflicting farming, there was a very high dependence on agriculture, which accounted directly for three-quarters of employment throughout most of the west (map 7).[23] The meagre returns from the land were supplemented to varying extents by fishing, collecting of seaweed, sale of turf, cottage industries, occasional or seasonal labouring locally or on a migratory basis, and remittances from emigrant relatives. The rural economy could not provide an adequate livelihood for the existing population or support its natural increase. There were few sizeable towns to provide alternative employment opportunities in service and manufacturing industries. Thus there was high outmigration, which lessened pressure on the land but had detrimental effects on demographic structure, social fabric, and personal attitudes. Although conditions had improved, deprivation was widespread in the west.

The government response to the conditions in the west, through establishment of the congested districts board in 1891, had been unique internationally, both as a quantitative delimitation of a disadvantaged region and as a pioneer effort in integrated rural development.[24] Although it had been handicapped by inadequate finance and wartime conditions, the board had substantial achievements by the time the Irish government dissolved it in 1923 and allocated its functions to various state bodies, notably the land commission.[25] Considerable agrarian restructuring had been achieved in its later work through an emphasis on the purchase, consolidation, improvement, and resale of land in order to provide larger and more viable farms and to create new holdings. Agricultural schemes had improved the breeds of livestock and

---

[23] Below, p. 83.   [24] Above, vi, 87–90, 283–7, 587–9; below, ix, map 85.
[25] 1923/27 [I.F.S.] (24 July 1923).

poultry and had provided training and better farming practices. Two major spheres of activity had led to the development of the fishing industry through aiding the catching, landing, and processing of fish, and to the promotion of home and small manufacturing, principally in textiles and clothing. Infrastructural improvement had been effected in relation to roads, bridges, ports, steamship services, housing, water supply, telegraph extension, and education services. Yet the extent to which the west remained deprived, and lagged behind even the rest of Ireland despite such improvements, indicated the magnitude of the problem of regional disparity.

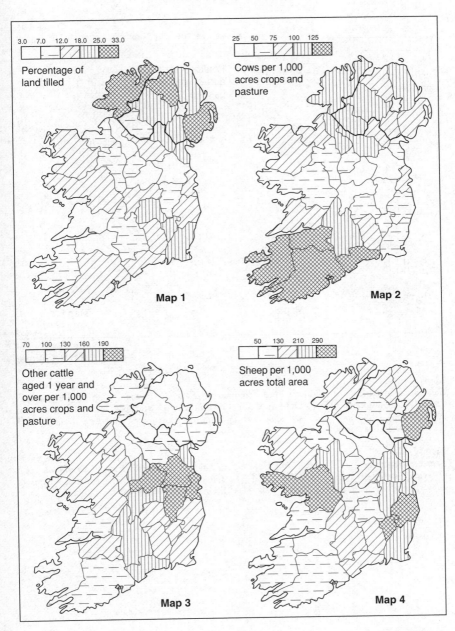

3.0   7.0   12.0 18.0 25.0 33.0

Percentage of
land tilled

Map 1

25   50   75   100   125

Cows per 1,000
acres crops and
pasture

Map 2

70   100   130   160   190

Other cattle
aged 1 year and
over per 1,000
acres crops and
pasture

Map 3

50   130   210   290

Sheep per 1,000
acres total area

Map 4

D.A. Gillmor

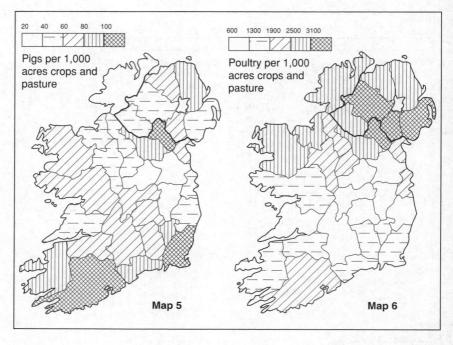

20   40   60   80   100

Pigs per 1,000
acres crops and
pasture

600   1300 1900 2500 3100

Poultry per 1,000
acres crops and
pasture

Map 5

Map 6

D.A. Gillmor

Maps 1–6:
Sources: Department of Industry and Commerce, *Saorstát Éireann. Agricultural statistics 1847–1926* (Stationery Office, Dublin, 1930); Government of Northern Ireland, Ministry of Agriculture, *Third annual report upon the agricultural statistics of Northern Ireland 1927* (H.M.S.O., Belfast, 1920).

Maps 7–11:
Sources: Department of Industry and Commerce, *Saorstát Éireann. Census of population 1926* (10 vols, Stationery Office, Dublin, 1928–34); Government of Northern Ireland, *Census of population of Northern Ireland 1926* (8 vols, H.M.S.O., Belfast, 1928–9).

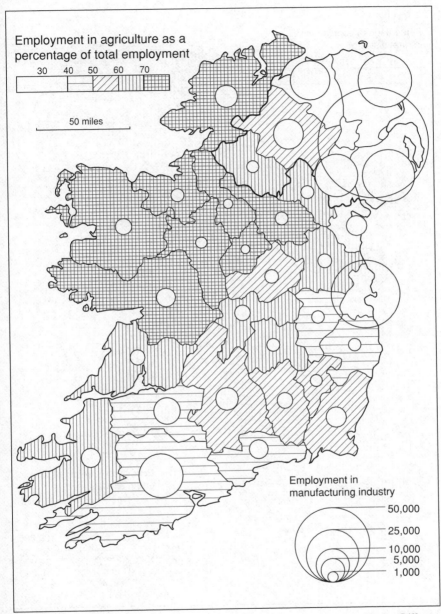

Employment in agriculture as a
percentage of total employment

30   40   50   60   70

50 miles

Employment in
manufacturing industry

50,000
25,000
10,000
5,000
1,000

Map 7   D.A. Gillmor

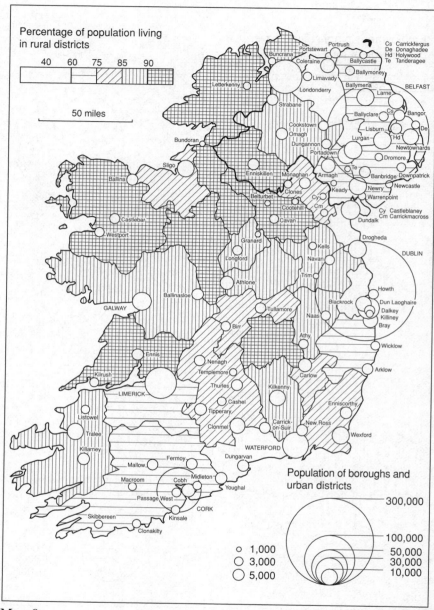

Percentage of population living
in rural districts

40   60   75   85   90

50 miles

Population of boroughs and
urban districts

300,000

100,000
50,000
30,000
10,000

o 1,000
O 3,000
O 5,000

Cs Carrickfergus
De Donaghadee
Hd Holywood
Te Tanderagee

Cy Castleblaney
Cm Carrickmacross

Map 8

D.A. Gillmor

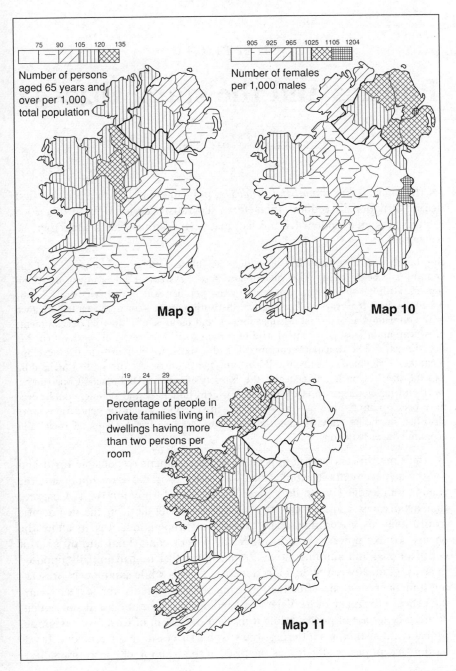

75   90   105   120   135

Number of persons
aged 65 years and
over per 1,000
total population

Map 9

905   925   965   1025   1105   1204

Number of females
per 1,000 males

Map 10

19   24   29

Percentage of people in
private families living in
dwellings having more
than two persons per
room

Map 11

D.A. Gillmor

CHAPTER IV

Politics and the state, 1922–32

EUNAN O'HALPIN

IN the *Saorstát Éireann official handbook*, published in 1932 to mark the 'first decade of national freedom', the veteran separatist Bulmer Hobson described the progress independent Ireland had made. Bypassing politics altogether, he wrote that

the foundations have been laid on which the future security and prosperity of the country are being built. The rule of law and a system of government based on universal adult suffrage and amenable to the popular will have been firmly established. A short ten years of free political institutions have shown substantial advance in the domain of agricultural organisation, of land tenures, of industrial development, of education, of local government, and of certain social services. The legal system has been recast, public transport reorganised, and a state-owned hydro-electric development has brought electricity to all parts of the country. At the same time public expenditure has been reduced and the burden of taxation lightened. Constructive work and development in every direction which, under the old regime, could never have been attempted are now possible, and the energies which for generations were absorbed in the struggle for political autonomy set free for the work of social and economic reconstruction.[1]

By the time this encomium appeared, the government responsible for it and for the achievements it extolled had lost office to its bitterest opponent, the Fianna Fáil leader Eamon de Valera. It was a cruel irony for W. T. Cosgrave that his greatest achievement, the vindication of his faith in the democratic institutions his government had brought into operation, was to allow the enemy to take power. Once in office, de Valera could luxuriate in a set of constitutional and administrative arrangements that he had initially opposed in arms, gradually removing objectionable symbols while assiduously preserving and operating the effective elements uninterruptedly for sixteen years. The sheer effrontery of de Valera's unapologetic assumption and subsequent effortless exercise of power, while it marked the extent of Cosgrave's triumph, probably intensified his bitterness towards his successor in government. It was hard to accept personal defeat as the price of the triumph of constitutionality.

[1] Bulmer Hobson, 'Introduction' in *Saorstát Éireann official handbook* (Dublin, 1932), p. 16.

Examined from different perspectives, Cosgrave's ten years in power from 1922 to 1932 can be seen as a vindication of constitutionality and liberal democracy; as a triumph for decency, for pragmatism, and for modest innovation; as a catalogue of lost economic, social, and political opportunities; as an era when Northern Ireland was forgotten, the quest for unity abandoned, and its champions repressed; as a time when laws embodying catholic moral and social precepts, from censorship to the 'holy hour',[2] were imposed wholesale on a supposedly pluralist and secular polity; and as a period when a system of government and a pattern of politics were established which were to endure, despite their apparent inability to come to grips with persistent economic malaise.[3]

It is, however, a mistake simply to look back. Irish politics in the 1920s have to be appraised in terms of the positive aims and actions of the principal figures, parties, and forces involved. To do this, we must first look at the framework of politics between 1922 and 1932. This is greatly complicated by the circumstances of division and civil war that followed the treaty.

THE formal framework of politics in the Irish Free State was determined by two instruments, the 1921 treaty and the 1922 constitution. The one provided for qualified independence for the twenty-six counties within an imperial framework, the other for a liberal-democratic system based on allowing the Irish people to elect their own parliament and thereby to choose their own government, with elaborate protection for individual rights. Despite some symbols of subordination to the British crown, notably an oath of allegiance, a governor general, and a right of appeal from the Irish courts to the privy council, the constitution was that of an effectively as well as a nominally Free State. Leo Kohn wrote of it in 1932 that while 'its structural design is that of a limited monarchy... its tenor is essentially republican'.[4] In operation, if not in conception, it defined patterns of politics and government that have endured in Ireland. Consequently, although superseded after only fifteen years by Bunreacht na hÉireann, de Valera's constitution, it merits some scrutiny.

The symbols of subordination in the constitution were a necessary part of the deal struck with Britain in 1921, as was made clear to the Irish side during the drafting process. The proclamation that brought the constitution into operation expressly subordinated it, and any subsequent amendments, to

---

[2] Below, n. 78.
[3] Donal O'Sullivan, *The Irish Free State and its senate: a study in contemporary politics* (London, 1940), and Macardle, *Ir. republic*, give useful early assessments from Free State and republican viewpoints.
[4] Leo Kohn, *The constitution of the Irish Free State* (London, 1932), p. 13. The historiography of the 1922 constitution is discussed in Charles Townshend, 'The meaning of Irish freedom: constitutionalism in the Free State' in *Transactions of the Royal Historical Society*, 6th ser., viii (1998), pp 45–70.

the treaty. The constitution itself provided a place for the king as the third element of the oireachtas (legislature) and head of state, though his role and that of his representative in Ireland was severely limited: in the exercise of his powers the governor general was the constitutional prisoner of domestic political institutions. In practice he was to be even more in thrall to the Irish government than the constitution suggested: Cosgrave treated Tim Healy and his successor James McNeill with a combination of courtesy and firmness, leaving them in comfortable isolation in the Phoenix Park except when needed for formal purposes.[5]

Even the oath prescribed for all members of the oireachtas in article 17, from 1923 till 1927 the main sticking point for de Valera in his refusal to take his seat, was equivocal. Those taking it swore 'true faith and allegiance to the constitution of the Irish Free State', and only secondarily and consequently pledged to 'be faithful to H. M. King George V, his heirs and successors by law in virtue of the common citizenship of Ireland with Great Britain and her adherence to and membership of the group of nations forming the British commonwealth of nations'.[6]

The constitution's democratic thrust began with article 2, which stated that 'all powers of government and all authority legislative, executive, and judicial in Ireland, are derived from the people of Ireland'. This declaration was given substantive support in a number of subsequent articles, the overall aim of which was undoubtedly to prevent the replication in the new state of constitutional norms in Britain, where cabinet government had reduced the role of parliament. The bicameral legislature or oireachtas broadly followed the Westminster model, with the dáil and the seanad taking the place of the house of commons and the house of lords, and with the king's assent required for all legislation. But article 26 prescribed a system of election 'upon principles of proportional representation'. This provision was required by the British government in order to safeguard minority rights, but it was also intended to promote a multi-party legislature far less amenable to cabinet domination than was Westminster. The electoral legislation that followed provided for a particularly pure form of proportional representation, based on the single transferable vote and multi-seat constituencies.[7]

The hand of the electorate was additionally strengthened through articles 47 and 48. Article 47 provided for the suspension for ninety days of any measure passed by both houses of the oireachtas on the written demand of two-fifths of the members of the dáil or a majority of the seanad. If, within that time, three-fifths of the seanad or one-twentieth of the electorate so

---

[5] See the detailed discussion of the post in Brendan Sexton, *Ireland and the crown, 1922–1936* (Dublin, 1989), and for a case study see Frank Callanan, *T. M. Healy* (Cork, 1996).
[6] Article 17 of *Constitution of the Free State of Ireland [English translation]* (Dublin, 1922).
[7] Cornelius O'Leary, *Irish elections, 1918–1977: voters, parties and proportional representation* (Dublin, 1979), pp 15–16.

asked, the measure would be submitted 'to the decision of the people' through a referendum. Article 48 went even further, granting a means by which the electorate could initiate proposals to amend the constitution or to introduce new legislation, by preparing a petition to the oireachtas signed by 50,000 voters. The oireachtas would then either accept the petition or reject it and submit the matter to a referendum. This radical departure from British constitutional practice, where government had come virtually to monopolise the legislative programme, had potentially momentous implications. Together with the fragmentation and volatility promised by the electoral system, it seemed a hostage to fortune for future Irish governments. Events were to bear this out.

The desire of the constitution's framers to avoid reproducing Westminster norms was also apparent in the details of the machinery of government. While national affairs would be in the hands of an executive council of not fewer than five and not more than seven ministers, collectively responsible to the dáil and nominated by the president, there was provision for up to five other 'extern' ministers, to be nominated by the dáil as a whole. These were not required to be members of the oireachtas, and they could be recommended to the dáil by 'functional or vocational councils representing branches of the social and economic life of the nation', should such be created under the constitution (articles 45 and 56). In theory, this meant that non-contentious areas of administration, always supposing there were any to be found, could be left to those with particular expertise, endorsed by the relevant interests. Such ministers would be answerable to the dáil only for their own departments and would not take part in or be responsible for the wider deliberations of the executive council. By the same token, the executive council would have no responsibility for the activities of such ministers. This provision rested on two proto-corporatist premises: first, that many areas of policy were best left to experts representing the main interests involved, free from party political pressures, and able to take a dispassionate, professional view of affairs; and secondly, that the political culture of independent Ireland would accommodate a severing of the link between political and administrative accountability. In practice the provision was unworkable: while extern ministers enjoyed lower status than members of the executive council, from the first all were members of the oireachtas and were considered part and parcel of the government. The extern minister concept was jettisoned through a constitutional amendment in 1927, when the membership of the executive council was increased to twelve.[8]

[8] Kohn, *Constitution*, pp 277–83. There were in fact at least three modern British precedents for ministers who were not members of either house of parliament. Sir Horace Plunkett remained vice-president of the department of agriculture and technical instruction till 1908 despite losing his seat in 1900; C. F. G. Masterman was a cabinet minister for almost a year in 1914–15 after losing his seat; and Neville Chamberlain was minister for national service in 1917–18 before he even stood for parliament.

Other provisions of the constitution also went against its broadly liberal-democratic grain. The National University of Ireland and the University of Dublin were each allocated three of the 153 dáil seats, a somewhat anomalous carry-over from British practice in a new, popularly elected assembly. Furthermore, the second chamber, the seanad, was an unhappy compromise between the need for a forum for religious and political minorities, an efficient revising chamber, a check upon majoritarian politics, and a democratically legitimate body. Its convoluted election system—half its sixty members were to be elected by the dáil and half nominated by the president of the executive council—and its unrepresentative character, combined with its important powers of delay and, in some circumstances, of forcing a referendum on measures passed by the dáil, invited the criticism that it was intended simply as a bastion of ascendancy privilege. It was particularly disliked by republicans, who saw it as nothing more than an Anglo-Irish club and an undemocratic impediment to the popular will. Despite some constructive work in its first decade, when the Cosgrave government afforded it a modest role in shaping legislation, the seanad continued to be regarded by republicans as an alien institution hostile to the aspirations of most Irish people. Ex-unionists, on the other hand, took comfort in its existence: its first chairman, Lord Glenavy, had been a diehard unionist M.P. and Irish law officer. Once Fianna Fáil came into office the seanad's days were numbered, although de Valera was ultimately persuaded of the virtues of a weakened second chamber once purged of an ascendancy ethos.[9]

Perhaps the greatest weakness of the constitution, however, lay in its provisional character. Under article 50, for eight years following its enactment it could be amended simply by way of ordinary legislation. Subsequently, changes would require ratification by referendum. The consequence of this provision was that it was all too simple for the executive council to alter or suspend elements of the constitution that appeared ineffective or that stood in the way of robust public-order policies, simply by having the oireachtas pass the necessary bill. The constitution, so far from being the fundamental, inalienable law of the state, was left at the mercy of the executive and the legislature it was designed to constrain. There was a strong case for an initial experimental period on technical grounds, as the chaos surrounding the first seanad elections was to show, but an eight-year period was inordinately long. Furthermore, there was nothing in the constitution to prevent that provision being renewed, as it eventually was in 1930, for a further eight years. This undoubtedly weakened the seanad's status in both legal and political terms.[10] It also left the way open for de Valera, once he gained

[9] O'Sullivan, *Ir. Free State & its senate*, *passim*; the earl of Longford and Thomas P. O'Neill, *Eamon de Valera* (London, 1970), p. 291; Thomas Garvin, *The Irish senate* (Dublin, 1969), pp 14–15.
[10] Kohn, *Constitution*, pp 254–9.

power in 1932 with an express mandate to revise the constitution, to do so simply by legislation under article 50. That could scarcely have been Cosgrave's intention.

IN parallel with the 1922 constitution and its institutions of government, there existed a rival authority, an irredentist republican assembly, together with a president and government of an Irish republic, and an Irish republican army, the I.R.A. These claimed to be the legitimate institutions of a thirty-two-county republic. They derived their authority variously from surviving republican members of the second dáil, elected in 1921, along with successful republican candidates elected to the Free State dáil on an abstentionist ticket; and from the republic's inalienable claim already to exist, as articulated in the fenian oath and set out in the 1916 proclamation. On his release from prison in July 1924 de Valera added to the confusion by proposing a further body, Comhairle na dTeachtaí, to consist of republican T.D.s elected after the second dáil came into being, and to which the second dáil would delegate the task of acting as the legitimate republican government. The intention was apparently to create a shadow cabinet to which the public could turn when the Free State administration collapsed. However, these institutions, the I.R.A. apart, were beset by chronic constitutional and political difficulties that made practical work impossible and exposed their members to ridicule. Although republican ministers attended the fitful proceedings of the republican assembly, their government's status, affairs, and purpose remained wreathed in confusion. It was unable to govern anything, least of all the I.R.A., which, in a curious inversion of conventional democratic practice, had initially appointed it during the civil war. The republican assembly itself had only a vestigial existence. De Valera laboured under the empty title of 'president of the Irish republic' until the spring of 1926, when he despaired of these make-believe arrangements and publicly split from the intransigent majority in the Sinn Féin leadership.[11]

The significance of the republican dáil and government between 1923 and 1926 lay not in their actions but in their very existence. The fact was that, in an election fought entirely on the Free State's terms in the immediate aftermath of the civil war (August 1923), a significant minority of the electorate voted for republican candidates. This lessened the legitimacy of the Free State constitution, while doing nothing to hinder its effective operation. The question both for Cosgrave and for de Valera thereafter was whether electoral support for republicans would wane as the practical authority of the Free State grew. Would people continue to vote for a party that was pledged to

---

[11] Longford & O'Neill, *De Valera*, pp 200–09; T. Ryle Dwyer, *De Valera's darkest hour, 1919–1932* (Dublin, 1982), pp 149–51. For a sympathetic exploration of the purist republican view, see Brian P. Murphy, *Patrick Pearse and the republican ideal* (Dublin, 1991).

boycott the existing constitutional arrangements, when those arrangements showed every sign of functioning effectively?

EXPERIENCE was to show that under the 1921 treaty and the 1922 constitution, the new state was in practice independent of Britain, coequal rather than subordinate. But that outcome resulted from the course of domestic politics, of Anglo–Irish relations, and of commonwealth developments down to 1932. These must now be examined.

The general election of August 1923 inaugurated an enduring system of electoral politics. The election was to some extent a plebiscite on the civil war and related issues. In its timing so soon after the ceasefire, the government had all the obvious advantages. It had won the civil war, and it had implemented the treaty endorsed by the second dáil and by the electorate in June 1922. By contrast, many of the leading republicans were in detention along with their most committed and enthusiastic followers; their campaign organisers were continually harassed by government forces; the national press and the catholic hierarchy were actively hostile; and the country was still counting the cost of the widespread destruction wrought during the fighting.

The outcome, therefore, came as a shock to the government. The turnout, at 60 per cent of an electorate in which women for the first time had the same voting rights as men, was disappointingly low, perhaps reflecting a combination of popular apathy and exhaustion. Cosgrave's Cumann na nGaedheal party, formed in April 1923 by pro-treaty T.D.s, won about 39 per cent of the vote, and sixty-three of the 153 seats. Other pro-treaty groups won about 35 per cent, distributed as follows: the Farmers' party 13 per cent, and fifteen seats; Labour 11 per cent, and fourteen seats; and others 11 per cent, and seven seats. Thus almost three-quarters of those who voted chose candidates who, whatever their other differences, accepted the treaty and the 1922 constitution. The republicans took 28 per cent of the votes cast and won forty-four seats despite their abstentionist policy, making Sinn Féin the second largest political party in the state.[12]

The results were profoundly important for the future pattern of Irish politics. First, they again demonstrated majority support if not unbridled enthusiasm for the treaty settlement. Secondly, they dealt a severe blow to the left, which, so far from capitalising on the discontent caused by political unrest and economic dislocation since 1921, saw its vote fragmented and its representation fall. Thirdly, the election saw modest success for a number of small parties and for independent candidates. Bolstered by the form of proportional representation adopted under the constitution, small parties and independent T.D.s were to persist in the Irish political system without,

---

[12] O'Leary, *Ir. elections*, pp 18–20; Michael Gallagher, *Political parties in the Republic of Ireland* (Dublin, 1985), p. 41.

however, limiting the dominance of the government over the dáil as some proponents of proportional representation had expected.[13] Lastly, the results showed republican politicians, marginalised by the military arm during the civil war, that there was still a future for them in electoral politics.

Popular acceptance of the treaty and the constitution, confirmed by the 1923 election, strengthened in subsequent years. Despite the trauma of the 1924 army mutiny, the fiasco of the boundary commission in 1925, and the limitations of national economic and social policies throughout the decade, the legitimacy of the new state, its laws, institutions, and boundaries, grew until only a tiny minority of militant republicans dissented. Within two years of the civil war, de Valera was clamouring to be admitted to conventional politics; within a decade, he assumed office as president of the executive council of the Irish Free State.

The dip in electoral support for the left in 1923 presaged decades of disappointment for those who sought the radical transformation of Irish society by conventional democratic means. Labour, the oldest Irish political party, had emerged as a political offshoot of the Irish trade union movement. However, after its success in the 'pact' election in June 1922, the party began to develop a separate identity. In the absence of republican deputies, Labour constituted the main parliamentary opposition to the government throughout the civil war period. Under Thomas Johnson the party played a notable part in the work of the third dáil. By and large its deputies were constructive critics of the government, though they protested vigorously at some of its excesses, notably the maltreatment, execution, or murder of republicans. While members of the parliamentary party showed themselves to be, like their British counterparts, eminently responsible and anything but godless revolutionaries, the broader labour movement from which they came was in turmoil. By the spring of 1923 labour unrest was rife in parts of the country, particularly the south-east. It was sometimes accompanied by the rhetoric of revolution, sometimes by more prosaic lists of economic grievances.[14] In addition, the trade union movement was convulsed by the split between the incandescent radical James Larkin, deported from the United States in 1923 after three years in prison for labour agitation, and the more conservative group of officials under William O'Brien of the transport union, who had taken over in Larkin's absence. In some respects, this was a dispute between two visions of labour organisation, one socialist and revolutionary and the other far more narrowly focused on economic issues. It was also a clash of personalities: the untameable, erratic, messianic firebrand Larkin against cautious dependables such as O'Brien and Thomas Johnson of the Labour party. Larkin actually won a dáil seat in 1927 while he was a self-proclaimed

---

[13] O'Leary, *Ir. elections*, p. 13.
[14] Emmet O'Connor, *Syndicalism in Ireland, 1917–1923* (Cork, 1988), pp 102–10.

communist, but as a bankrupt (the result of a dispute about his handling of union funds) he was unable to take the seat.[15] Such internecine warfare hampered the labour movement's organisational efforts and weakened the party just when it might have been exploiting the vacuum created by republican abstentions.

Despite the disappointment of the 1923 election the Labour party again found itself the main opposition party in the dáil, because the republicans continued to abstain and the Farmers' party generally supported the government. These parliamentary responsibilities may have inhibited the party in policy terms: certainly it became what it was to remain, essentially a moderately social-democratic party more concerned with decency and fair play than with social and economic transformation. Left-wing critics argued that the party had betrayed its working-class roots and reduced its electoral appeal. However, attempts by splinter groups to stir up enthusiasm for class war, whether through elections or through agitation inside and outside the trade union movement, proved singularly unsuccessful. Radicals such as Larkin and, in a lower key, Peadar O'Donnell, inspired by the Russian revolution and by the progress of socialism in the Soviet Union, had plenty of charisma but very few followers. The Labour party eschewed such utopianism, soldiering on along the unspectacular path of parliamentary democracy, winning considerable respect from the other parties while remaining a polite minority in dáil affairs. After 1926 Labour found itself in unequal electoral competition with Fianna Fáil, a party whose social and economic policies, combined with republican ideology, had considerable appeal for potential Labour voters in both town and country.

The 1923 election produced one avowedly sectional parliamentary party, the Farmers' party, an offshoot of the Irish Farmers' Union. It also produced a large number of independent T.D.s. On the face of it such a multiplicity of banners should have meant highly unstable government, or at the very least a coalition, since Cosgrave's Cumann na nGaedheal party held only sixty-three of the 153 seats. In practice Cosgrave had no trouble at all in dominating the business of the dáil to an extent that any British prime minister would have envied. This can be attributed to three factors. First, the sixteen independent T.D.s remained just that: they did not coalesce into a parliamentary group, and they avoided absorption into one or other of the existing parties. As individual representatives, uniquely accountable to the electorate and without a party machine, they were predisposed towards stability. What use was an election to an independent who already had a dáil seat? The second reason for Cosgrave's effortless exercise of power was that the Farmers' party sided with the government whenever needed, without exacting the obvious quid

[15] Arthur Mitchell, *Labour in Irish politics, 1890–1930* (Dublin, 1974), pp 171–91; Emmet Larkin, *James Larkin, Irish labour leader 1876–1947* (London, 1965), pp 271–3.

pro quo of representation in it. The price of its support—low taxes, the promotion of efficiency in agricultural production, and single-minded protection of the agricultural export trade to Britain—was one that the government was quite happy to pay. Although Cumann na nGaedheal suffered significant defections on three occasions—in 1924 when nine T.D.s led by Joseph McGrath left in protest at the handling of the army mutiny, and twice in 1926, when three T.D.s founded Clann Éireann and Captain William Redmond formed the National League—party fragmentation did not translate into government instability: Cosgrave knew that his government had no credible rival within the dáil.[16] This was owing to the continued absence of the republican T.D.s. That was the third, most crucial factor in his government's stability. While they stayed out, Cosgrave was safe.

For de Valera, in solitary confinement since the election campaign, the August 1923 results came as a pleasant surprise. But what lesson was to be drawn from them? Initially, the republican leadership was united in interpreting them as an endorsement of its entire policy, embracing not only abstention from the dáil but the operation of a rival set of institutions—army, dáil, and government—in parallel with those of the Free State. It was only gradually that de Valera came to view the results rather as an invitation from the electorate to consider participation in the public life of the Free State, an offer that voters might eventually withdraw if republican T.D.s continued to abstain. De Valera remained in prison till July 1924. This gave him time to ponder his political future, though it was also, undoubtedly, a period of intense frustration: the electorate had thrown republican politics an unexpected lifeline, and there was no one of any stature outside to grab it. All he could do was to attempt to reassert control over the republican movement through the very instrument in which he had least faith, the spectral republican government of which he remained president. But he was inside prison walls, reduced to communicating with his notional subordinates outside through querulous notes written in defective secret ink and signed 'Flynn', smuggled out through insecure channels under the eye of army intelligence.[17] Outside, the absolutist '"Mary MacSwiney" line' took root in republican political and military circles.[18] The republic could not be compromised, participation in Free State political institutions could not be countenanced, and the faithful would have to await the day when a thirty-two-county Irish republic would magically materialise. That was not a very practical political agenda.

In summary, the 1923 election produced a multi-party dáil, but not the weak executive and strong legislature some had expected. Furthermore, it

[16] O'Leary, *Ir. elections*, pp 22–3; Gallagher, *Political parties*, pp 98–9.
[17] The texts of messages smuggled to and from de Valera are in the Mulcahy papers (U.C.D., A.D., P7/B/138).
[18] Longford & O'Neill, *De Valera*, p. 235.

initiated a pattern of politics that persisted for decades, in which the majority of the electorate chose between two major parties primarily defined by the treaty split and overwhelmingly male. In these conditions alternative patterns of division, based on class, sectional, regional, or religious differences, played only a subordinate role in political conflict.

THE priorities of the Cosgrave administration in its nine years of office after the civil war were clear. Ministers were determined to show that the new state was sovereign, that it was legitimate, that it was resourceful, that it was solvent, that it was respectable, and that it was peaceful. In one sense they were, in Kevin O'Higgins' phrase, 'the most conservative revolutionaries that ever put through a successful revolution'—they had no desire to transform Irish society, no intention of restructuring the economy, no plans to embark on foreign adventures.[19] Their conservatism was reinforced by the aftermath of civil war.

It did not follow that they were a government without ambition or direction, content simply to hold power: on the contrary, under Cosgrave they set themselves a formidable agenda. Cosgrave had not been anyone's first choice to lead the country in 1922: he became chairman of the provisional government only because of the unexpected deaths of Griffith and Collins, and while the leading military men were fully occupied with the civil war. Driven by a sense of duty more than a love of power, by nature a consolidator not an innovator, he came to command the respect though never the adulation of his colleagues. But he had a head for administration: it was no coincidence that his local government department had been the most effective, if one of the least prestigious, of the dáil ministries before 1922. He also had a talent, sometimes sorely tested, for containing animosities and rivalries among his colleagues. Finally, he had a definite view of how relations with Britain should develop, on a basis of amicable equality rather than of respectful subordination.

The first task for Cosgrave's government once victory was secured was to get the country back on its feet. This necessitated the substitution of civil for military authority, and the construction of a consensus on public order.[20] The government faced an immediate dilemma, because at the war's end it held about 12,000 prisoners. While their release was politically desirable, and a necessary element in the establishment of a peaceful, law-bound polity, the I.R.A. still had its weapons hidden around the country and still proclaimed its defiance of the new state. A cautious policy of gradual releases was, accordingly, adopted. When republican prisoners responded by going on

[19] Quoted in Michael Laffan, '"Labour must wait": Ireland's conservative revolution' in Patrick J. Corish (ed.), *Radicals, rebels & establishments* (Belfast, 1985), p. 219.
[20] See Eunan O'Halpin, *Defending Ireland* (Oxford, 1999), ch. 2.

hunger strike *en masse* in October, the government simply suspended releases and waited for the strike to collapse. It attracted little public support, and soon began to crumble. After the deaths of two men in November, it was abandoned. This was a further blow to republican morale; its futility was compounded by the government's astute and speedy resumption of releases.[21] In addition to civil war prisoners, Eamon de Valera had been locked up in August 1923 during the general election campaign. This was plainly an act of selective detention, inspired by political rather than security reasons. While it may have generated some sympathy for republicans, it deprived them of their natural leader for a year. With him in jail the movement was left in less experienced, less able, and less dexterous hands, which was all to the good for the government.

In the aftermath of the civil war there was considerable disorder. It took many forms: land seizures, armed crime, freelance republican attacks, and violent labour disputes. All this reflected a number of problems: the decay of civil policing and central authority since 1919; a general demoralisation after years of conflict; the breakdown of the courts system in some parts of the country; an abundance of republican and ex-army guns and gunmen at large in the country; and genuine economic and agrarian grievances.

Within the government there were conflicting views both on the nature of the crisis and the appropriate way of addressing it. At one extreme Kevin O'Higgins, the minister for home affairs, argued that the state could not relax its repressive policies while any form of disorder, which he saw as forming a continuum from non-payment of debts and illicit distilling to arson, murder, and rebellion, remained. What confronted government was a 'whole revolt against all idea of morality, law, and social order'. 'No greater disaster', he thought, 'could happen to the country than that "peace" should overtake it, leaving conditions such as these to be dealt with by a new and unarmed police force and by legal processes.' It was the job of the army, acting under emergency laws, to restore order.[22] By contrast the defence minister, Richard Mulcahy, advised recourse to civilian law enforcement, arguing that the army was neither designed nor trained to act as a police force and that to use it as such would inhibit its military effectiveness, confuse its personnel, and perpetuate an atmosphere of abnormality and crisis. Furthermore, he felt that the Garda Síochána, by then rehabilitated after the force's early disasters in 1922,[23] should be able to cope with non-political crime. However, O'Higgins' view prevailed. While the police slowly established themselves in the community, it was left mainly to the army to

---

[21] C. S. Andrews, *Dublin made me* (Dublin, 1979), pp 301–2; J. Bowyer Bell, *The secret army: a history of the I.R.A., 1916–1970* (London, 1970), pp 44–5.

[22] O'Higgins to Cosgrave, 5 Apr. 1923 (N.A.I., D.T., S 582).

[23] These included a mutiny in Kildare barracks in April, which led the government to abondon the original plan for an armed force, analogous to the R.I.C. See Gregory Allen, *The Garda Síochána* (Dublin, 1999), ch. 3.

deal with lawlessness. Its performance was patchy and, in land and labour disputes, often partisan.[24] Early in 1924 O'Higgins acknowledged what the army had long argued, that soldiers 'make bad policemen. There is a fundamental difference of outlook.'[25] Furthermore, the army was frequently implicated in the crime it was supposed to combat. The army's director of intelligence reported in January 1924 that it would be 'unfair ... to say that all recent crimes can be attributed' to the army. In 'the south and west released prisoners and outlawed Irregulars are chiefly responsible ... although ex-soldiers have helped to swell the total. Besides, in counties like Clare and Waterford agrarian and labour disputes have led to a good deal of crime.' Nevertheless, 'from statistics in our possession it is clear that a high percentage of the crimes committed during the second half of 1923 have been definitely traced to members or ex-members of the army'.[26] In fact the wave of apolitical crime was limited and short-lived, and the grievances underlying agrarian unrest were addressed in the 1923 land act,[27] the legislative culmination of the process of Irish land reform begun in 1870.

Although O'Higgins continued to declaim against the cancer of lawlessness, by the autumn of 1924 the unarmed Garda Síochána had sufficient authority and public support to operate effectively, backed up by the revamped armed detective unit of the Dublin Metropolitan Police under David Neligan. In 1925 two important pieces of legislation improved the position further: police powers against political crime were considerably strengthened by the treasonable offences act, while the police forces amalgamation act merged the Dublin force with the Garda Síochána to create a unitary national police force. Under this legislation the new force was, like the old R.I.C., placed firmly under the government's thumb. The executive council controlled all promotions above the rank of inspector, and there was no insulating layer of authority between the commissioner and the minister for justice.[28] Time was to demonstrate that these arrangements facilitated not simply ministerial control but political interference in policing.

Under the guidance of its able if impetuous commissioner General Eoin O'Duffy the Garda Síochána quickly developed into a resilient and effective force. The practice of assigning the gardaí miscellaneous non-police functions, such as census enumeration and the enforcement of school attendance and weights-and-measures legislation, went against the canons of police pro-

---

[24] O'Connor, *Syndicalism in Ire.*, p. 163.
[25] Memorandum by O'Higgins, 7 Feb. 1924 (N.A.I., S 3435).
[26] Report by director of intelligence, 8 Jan. 1924 (Mulcahy papers, P7/B/140).
[27] 1923/42 (9 Aug. 1923).
[28] 1925/18 (6 June 1925); 1925/7 (2 Apr. 1925); Brady, *Guardians of the peace*, pp 102–5. In the autumn of 1925 the army was instructed to cease its extensive political intelligence activities and to transfer the relevant records to the Garda Síochána; see Eunan O'Halpin, 'Army, politics, and society in independent Ireland, 1923–1945' in T. G. Fraser and Keith Jeffery (ed.), *Men, women and war* (Dublin, 1993), pp 164–8.

fessionalism, but it increased the force's contact with the public and probably contributed to its rapid and enduring acceptance by the community. An R.I.C. veteran's description of relations between police and people before independence applied equally well after 1923: 'a sergeant of the police, they all went to him for everything, nearly, he was the chief adviser and all like.' On occasion both O'Higgins and O'Duffy wavered in their attachment to unarmed policing, but it is clear that the success of the uniformed branch owed a great deal to it, the principal characteristic distinguishing it from the old R.I.C.[29] While the special detective branch that dealt with the residue of militant republicanism was armed, its members acquired a reputation for rough methods rather than for killing. The I.R.A. and its offshoots were never completely crushed, but the extent and degree of political violence dropped dramatically after 1923: in 1931 the gardaí calculated that since the end of the civil war republicans had been responsible for just twenty-one deaths, including the killing of eight policemen and the assassination of O'Higgins in 1927. Some republican activists gravitated towards communism, but social and economic revolution remained far down the mainstream I.R.A.'s agenda. In the late 1920s it flirted uneasily with issues of social inequality, through involvement in land agitation, strikes, and attacks on moneylenders, but it retained its primary anti-Free-State and anti-British thrust through gestures ranging from the burning of the union flag and the disruption of boy-scout outings to attacks on jurymen and witnesses in political cases.[30] Militant republicanism was marginalised through a combination of vigorous policing, draconian laws, enforced emigration of activists, popular repudiation of political violence, and, perhaps above all, de Valera's creation of a strong constitutional republican party in 1926.

Except for its domestic intelligence functions (not transferred to the gardaí till 1926), from the middle of 1924 the army was left to concentrate on military duties and on its own internal difficulties. Since its establishment in 1922 these had been formidable, and in March 1924 they resulted in mutiny. The army's problems arose from its origins, its personnel, its tasks, and its size. It had been formed by Michael Collins in the midst of the political crisis preceding the outbreak of civil war. During the war the government's solution to military inefficiency was wholesale expansion: the priority was to defeat the republicans, not to nurture an effective, disciplined military machine. The army grew fivefold in less than a year. Once the civil war was over, drastic contraction was inevitable, in tandem with a drive to turn the army into a competent, permanent servant of the state. But almost all those who had

[29] Quoted in John D. Brewer, *The Royal Irish Constabulary: an oral history* (Belfast, 1990), p. 87; memorandum by O'Higgins, 7 Feb. 1924 (N.A.I., S 3435); O'Duffy to minister for justice, 6 Dec. 1926 (N.A.I., S 5260).
[30] Tim Pat Coogan, *The I.R.A.* (London, 1970), pp 70–72; interview with Maurice Twomey (I.R.A. chief of staff, 1927–35), July 1975.

served during the civil war expected some reward for their efforts, and many officers felt that this should take the form of senior positions. This feeling was particularly strong among the old guard of officers, led by Liam Tobin. They had operated directly under Collins during the war of independence, at his behest had joined the provisional government's army and confronted their former comrades in the I.R.A., and felt that their contribution had been insufficiently recognised after Collins's death. Their sense of grievance was increased by the army's recruitment of former British army officers with practical experience of military organisation, which stood in contrast to the techniques of clandestine warfare in which the Irish officers were expert. Dissatisfaction during the war matured into a more potent strain of conspiracy after it, as the officer corps faced the prospect of decimation through demobilisation. Who would be left, and who would get the plum jobs?

Ministers were well aware of the problem of unrest. They knew that the officer corps was splitting into factions. Of these the 'Tobinites', seeking to mobilise support through a new secret society, the 'Old I.R.A.', posed the greatest problem. In addition to its capacity to make mischief within the army, the Old I.R.A. also threatened to become a channel for clandestine reconciliation with republican elements. Both Cosgrave and Richard Mulcahy, the minister for defence, had uncomfortable meetings with the Tobinites, whose grievances could be boiled down to the simple complaint that the wrong people were getting the good jobs. Mulcahy adopted a dual approach. In making decisions about the army's peacetime officer corps, he tried to reconcile the desirability of recognising past service with the necessity of fostering military professionalism. He also encouraged the revival of the venerable republican society, the I.R.B., within the army as a counterweight to the conspirators' Old I.R.A. In conception this was a scheme worthy of Collins himself; in practice it was a mistake. It blurred or appeared to blur the basic issue of loyalty to the elected government, and it threatened to breathe new life into the traditional I.R.B. aspiration of a thirty-two-county republic. Events were to show that it was a hostage to fortune, because when the crisis came it allowed Mulcahy's civilian critics to portray him as at best naive, at worst an anti-democratic, even potentially a republican conspirator.[31]

After months of rumblings, the mutiny finally began on 6 March 1924, when the Old I.R.A. issued a written ultimatum to the executive council. This demanded the removal of the army council (a triumvirate of generals in overall command of the army), insisted on the immediate suspension of demobilisation and reorganisation, complained that the government had betrayed the ideal of eventual unity, and threatened 'to take such action that

[31] Maryann Gialanella Valiulis, *Almost a rebellion: the Irish army mutiny of 1924* (Cork, 1985), is the most detailed study of this episode.

[*sic*] will make clear to the Irish people that we are not renegades or traitors to the ideals that induced them to accept the treaty ... we can no longer be party to the treachery that threatens to destroy the aspirations of the nation'.[32] Simultaneously almost fifty officers tendered their resignations, and a number absconded with weapons. Initially the government stood firm, ordering the arrest of the signatories of the ultimatum, Liam Tobin and Charles Dalton, and refusing to be coerced. The minister for industry and commerce, Joseph McGrath, who had close associations with the Tobinites, resigned in protest at this inflexibility. Thereafter events took a strange turn. Cosgrave suddenly fell ill, leaving a void of authority at the centre of the government and facilitating the full play of personal animosities and rivalries between competing ministers. On 10 March the executive council, against Mulcahy's wishes, placed the Garda commissioner, General Eoin O'Duffy, in supreme command of the defence forces. Whether intentionally or not, the implication that the army's commanders had been found wanting put Mulcahy and the army council almost on a par with the mutineers. Two days later, after McGrath had spoken powerfully on the mutineers' behalf at a Cumann na nGaedheal party meeting, the executive council agreed to hold a full inquiry into army administration. Ministers also indicated that mutineers who returned stolen weapons and reported for duty would be treated leniently. This remarkable and apparently unnecessary volte-face gravely weakened Mulcahy and the army council, who had argued that a firm response to the mutiny was essential if military discipline was ever to be restored. In the event, the mutineers, buoyed up by these concessions and by McGrath's temporary ascendancy, continued to conspire. On 18 March army intelligence officers discovered through telephone taps that a crucial meeting of conspirators, to include the leaders Tobin and Dalton, was to take place in a public house in Parnell Street. It was believed they were planning the kidnap or assassination of key figures. After consulting with Mulcahy, but without the knowledge of O'Duffy or of the executive council, the adjutant general sent troops to raid the premises and arrest any officers found inside. When the raid was launched, the mutineers refused to surrender. After some hours they were arrested and their weapons seized, despite the intercession of McGrath, who turned up, allegedly intoxicated, outside the building and attempted to have the raid called off.[33]

The raid broke the mutiny. However, it also cost Mulcahy and the army council their jobs. It is difficult to establish the facts of the decision to make the raid. Mulcahy and the army council maintained that the action was

---

[32] Quoted ibid., p. 51.
[33] Maryann Gialanella Valiulis, *Portrait of a revolutionary: General Richard Mulcahy and the founding of the Irish Free State* (Dublin, 1992), pp 209–17; note by Maurice Moynihan (secretary to the government, 22 Dec. 1948) of a talk with Gen. M. J. Costello (army director of intelligence at the time of the mutiny), 12 Dec. 1948 (N.A.I., S 5478B).

legitimate, that O'Duffy was not supreme commander at the time in view of his earlier conditional resignation, and that the conspiracy had to be tackled decisively. McGrath complained that the mutineers—decent, brave, and honourable soldiers—had been insulted and betrayed by the army's commanders. The executive council had the best of both worlds. The mutineers were discredited as an assortment of gun-toting braggarts. Mulcahy resigned, and the three-man army council was dismissed for acting contrary to government policy. In the absence of the republican abstentionists, there was no group in the dáil capable of exploiting the discord in Cumann na nGaedheal ranks. Bitter charges and countercharges were levelled by executive council members in the chamber, yet the government carried on serenely. Politically, the victor was Kevin O'Higgins, who castigated his long-time adversary Mulcahy in what was probably the most venomous personal attack heard in the dáil since Cathal Brugha's notorious diatribe against Collins during the treaty debates. Opinion on O'Higgins's motives still differs. He can plausibly be portrayed as a sea-green incorruptible who only sought to uphold the constitutional principle that the government must control the army.[34] He can also be depicted as a devious, hysterical opportunist, a hedger who, once his political enemies showed the necessary resolve and sense of constitutionality to crush the mutiny, demanded their fall as the final vindication of the principle of civil supremacy.[35] The mutiny saw the departure of another of his enemies, Joseph McGrath, who after his resignation from the executive council left Cumann na nGaedheal with eight other T.D.s to form a new party, the 'National Group'. They resigned their seats *en masse* in October 1924, a curious move as only one of the group contested the resulting by-elections. Seven of the seats were won by Cumann na nGaedheal, and two by the republicans.[36] Despite this spectacular eclipse McGrath repaired relations with all the major political groupings in the state, from southern unionists to hardened republicans. A failure in electoral politics, he was to become one of the country's wealthiest men through his control of the hospitals sweepstake, a monopoly granted to him by his former colleagues.

The committee of inquiry into army administration broadly exonerated Mulcahy and the army council, while failing to cast much light on the central question of what the government's policy, as distinct from that of Mulcahy and his associates, had been before and during the crisis. Mulcahy himself was rehabilitated three years later, when he was reappointed to the executive council as minister for local government and public health after the June 1927 election. A few days later his former tormentor Kevin O'Higgins was murdered by gunmen in Booterstown. The assassination precipitated a fur-

[34] Terence de Vere White, *Kevin O'Higgins* (London, 1948; 2nd ed., Tralee, 1966), p. 168.
[35] Lee, *Ire. 1912–85*, pp 100–05; Valiulis, *Mulcahy*, pp 217–19.
[36] Gallagher, *Political parties*, p. 42.

ther election, the entry of Fianna Fáil into the dáil, and the redefinition of parliamentary politics in Ireland.

The army mutiny and its aftermath were a watershed for the new state. After much vacillation on the part of the government, the mutiny had been ultimately knocked on the head by the army's commanders. Those responsible for crushing it were rewarded by being singled out for punishment. The fact that they, who had been consistent, accepted this unfair treatment at the hands of a government that had been irresolute and duplicitous during the crisis, demonstrated the army's acceptance of the hard principle that, whatever mistakes were made, ultimately it was for the elected government to settle all matters of military policy. The victory of this principle was reflected in the executive council's subsequent ruthlessness towards the defence forces. Whatever fears there had been about the consequences of demobilisation were swept away. In the years that followed, so too was most of the army. So far from seeking to appease their generals, in the tradition of most new states, the government humiliated them, stripping them of men, equipment, and professional purpose. In the year to March 1924 defence spending was over £11 million; the next year it was reduced almost by two-thirds to £4 million; by 1931 it was £1.5 million, which was spent on fewer than 7,000 men with virtually no equipment—and not a dog had barked. These reductions were less the product of a serious assessment of defence priorities than of a desire to save money, though ministers may privately also have felt, in the wake of 1922 and 1924, that a severely emaciated military establishment was less likely to threaten civilian government again. An American military attaché reported in 1928 that the minister for defence had informed him that 'his idea is the biggest army possible for the least money', a suitably elastic formula under which the defence forces were allowed to shrink practically to nothing. The exception to this frugal policy was 'a very fine band . . . the authorities feel that a good band and snappy turnout is a good political argument for maintaining the army'.[37] Broader defence issues, including the possibility of cooperation with British forces, and the important question raised in the treaty of Ireland's assumption of partial responsibility for coastal and maritime defence, were deliberately left hanging. The government had no wish to spend money on such matters while the Royal Navy remained the guarantor of Ireland's coastal waters and trade routes, and while Britain shielded the country from continental Europe. Since the government had no desire to become embroiled in external quarrels, the defence implications of the ports and facilities provisions of the treaty were simply ignored. The systematic attenuation of the country's defence capacity was to have serious consequences in the late 1930s when such questions became

[37] G-2 report no. 6000, n.d., with Sterling (Dublin), to Marriner, department of state, Washington, 11 May 1928 (U.S. National Archives, RG75/841d 20/1).

central to national survival, and when it was belatedly recognised that the state had a positive obligation to prevent other countries using Ireland to harm Britain's defence and security interests.

PROBLEMS of defence were closely linked with those of external relations. Both were bound up with the 1921 settlement with Britain, with Ireland's membership of the commonwealth, and with the fact that Ireland shared a land border with the United Kingdom. Under Cosgrave the government pursued an external relations policy that to its opponents appeared a craven surrender to Britain, to the British government initially seemed a calculated assault on the conventions and assumptions underpinning the empire, and to its members was the logical embodiment of the treaty. While maintaining good and close relations with Britain, the government would take its own line on questions of external policy, reserving to itself the final decision on every issue.[38] The ports and defence provisions of the treaty notwithstanding, this included the vital matter of involvement in any war, where the government assumed that it would fight only if the country was being directly attacked.

Efforts to demonstrate the Free State's independence in external affairs took a number of forms. In September 1923 Ireland was admitted to the League of Nations.[39] With its dedication to the promotion of international amity, non-violent resolution of disputes, and worldwide disarmament, the league was and remained an important repository of the hopes for a peaceful future for the new European countries created by the Versailles settlement. Although the Free State had come to independence by a different path, its politicians shared the general European hope that the league would protect the weak against the strong, and would be the best guarantor of territorial integrity. Irish membership inevitably led to a 'family quarrel' with the British government, on the issue of Irish registration of the treaty as an international agreement, and on the broader question of the status of dominion states in an international assembly where Britain claimed to speak for the entire empire. In the same year the Irish representative in Washington was accorded full diplomatic status, again despite British misgivings. In succeeding years, with the fitful support of the other dominions, the government steadily chipped away at the concept of imperial subordination. The logic of the Irish approach was ultimately recognised in 1931 in the statute of Westminster,[40] which unequivocally recognised the coequal status of all the member nations of the commonwealth. Despite British reservations about its

---

[38] D. W. Harkness, *The restless dominion: the Irish Free State and the British commonwealth of nations, 1921–31* (London, 1969), p. 20.

[39] See Michael Kennedy, *Ireland and the League of Nations 1919–1946: international relations, diplomacy and politics* (Dublin, 1996).

[40] 22 Geo. V., c. 4 [U.K.] (11 Dec. 1931).

efforts to further the constitutional evolution of the commonwealth in the direction of coequality and independence, the 'restless dominion' won considerable respect for the diplomatic and legal skills of its representatives, particularly Kevin O'Higgins.[41] By contrast, de Valera's policies provoked ire after 1932. Yet the differences were largely matters of style. The Cosgrave government, while firm, was respectful of the institution of the commonwealth, but differed little from de Valera in its fundamental approach to external relations. It was the Cosgrave government that first demonstrated that Ireland would decide for and speak for itself in external as in internal matters, and so laid the groundwork for the more openly iconoclastic line later pursued by de Valera.

The vigour with which the Cosgrave government pursued the principle of independence within the commonwealth was balanced by the practicalities of relations between two countries situated side by side, sharing an open land border, and economically intertwined. Whatever the political and constitutional difficulties, there remained a high degree of interdependence between the Free State and Britain, and between the Free State and Northern Ireland. For example, under the treaty Britain retained the right to determine control of the transatlantic cable stations in Ireland. Furthermore, the Free State and the United Kingdom formed a common travel area. When, despite British misgivings, the department of external affairs began to issue its own passports in April 1924, British security officials concluded that it was 'essential to maintain close cooperation with the Irish government in passport matters and to arrange for the free exchange of information in regard to undesirables', as without Irish help 'there was no means of enforcing control of persons travelling between the two jurisdictions'.[42] Ireland benefited disproportionately from these arrangements, because Britain effectively carried out most of Ireland's immigration control at the channel ports. Very few prospective immigrants reached Ireland, and very few of those who did so were given rights of residence. Jews in particular were frowned on by the department of justice on the grounds that to admit them would exacerbate anti-Semitism, an argument that appears to support the conclusion that the relative rarity of virulent anti-Semitism in interwar Ireland was attributable mainly to the scarcity of Jews.[43] At the administrative level, there were understandings on cross-border passage of members of the R.U.C. and the Garda Síochána, and on Garda vetting of Irish applicants to the British

[41] Harkness, *Restless dominion*, ch. 6; Dermot Keogh, *Ireland and Europe, 1919–1948* (Dublin, 1988), p. 23. See the particularly fulsome letter of condolence to Cosgrave by Leo Amery, the dominions secretary, on the news of O'Higgins's death, 10 July 1927 (N.A.I., S 5478A).

[42] Quoted in Eunan O'Halpin, 'Intelligence and security in Ireland, 1922–1945' in *Intelligence and National Security*, v, no. 1 (Jan. 1990), p. 59.

[43] Department of justice memo, 'Question of admission of Jewish refugees', 28 Feb. 1953 (N.A.I., S 11007/B/2); Lee, *Ire. 1912–85*, p. 78.

army. The residual British naval and military presence in the treaty ports also necessitated some practical accommodation and transport arrangements. Even where interjurisdictional cooperation formally broke down, for example in relation to extradition to and from Northern Ireland, local understandings between the respective police forces sometimes emerged to circumvent the difficulties.[44] The macabre profession of public executioner remained a British monopoly—the state sending to England for a hangman whenever one was needed to carry out death sentences passed by the Irish civil courts.

THE Cosgrave government's considerable achievements in external relations were not of a kind to excite much popular interest. But its greatest disappointment, the perpetuation of the boundary with Northern Ireland established under the government of Ireland act, was quite a different matter. While recognising the fact of partition, the treaty had provided some hope for nationalists through the provision of the device of a boundary commission to 'determine in accordance with the wishes of the inhabitants, so far as may be compatible with economic and geographic conditions, the boundaries between Northern Ireland and the rest of Ireland', should Northern Ireland opt to stay outside the new Free State, as it duly did in December 1922.[45] At the time of the treaty in 1921, with the ink scarcely dry on the huge postwar territorial revisions produced by the Versailles settlement, such a commission seemed a credible revising instrument. However, the onset of civil war in the south, coupled with the untimely death of Michael Collins, the Irish leader most exercised by the northern problem, meant that Irish pressure for the appointment of such a commission was slow in coming. Cosgrave eventually asked the British government to set up a commission in June 1923, but action was delayed by Northern Ireland's hostility and by British reluctance to be seen to force either north or south into such a process. The commission was eventually established in the autumn of 1924, under the chairmanship of a South African judge, Richard Feetham. The Free State nominated as its representative the minister for education Eoin MacNeill, himself a northerner, while the British government nominated J. R. Fisher to represent Northern Ireland because the northern government refused to make a nomination.[46]

Southern expectations of the boundary commission were high when the treaty was signed—some treaty supporters saw the commission as the ultim-

[44] Instances of such arrangements can be seen in N.A.I., S 1978, S 4779, S 6091A; O'Halpin, 'Intelligence and security', p. 64; Gerald Hogan and Clive Walker, *Political violence in the Republic of Ireland* (Manchester, 1988), p. 28.

[45] Article 12 of the treaty, reproduced with *Constitution of the Free State of Ireland*.

[46] Michael Laffan, *The partition of Ireland, 1911–1925* (Dundalk, 1983), pp 98–105; David Harkness, *Northern Ireland since 1920* (Dublin, 1983), pp 38–41.

ate instrument of Northern Ireland's undoing, believing it would take away almost half its territory and population. Such optimism waned considerably in the intervening years. The northern government had taken vigorous steps to consolidate its 1920 borders, and had dealt harshly and decisively with republican activity. There was little hope, whatever the commission's recommendations, that the north would make territorial or population concessions on the scale considered by nationalists to be the minimum justified by geography and by political and religious allegiances. Conversely, although some northern unionists had seen the commission as a possible means of securing more or different territory, for example in east Donegal, Craig's government felt it had more to lose than to gain from the commission's activities. Northern nationalists saw the commission as the last chance to remedy what they believed were the most anomalous features of partition, notably the inclusion in Northern Ireland, despite their nationalist majorities, of Counties Tyrone and Fermanagh, and the severing of Derry from its Donegal hinterland.

The commission's activities were constrained by the ambiguity of its remit. Its chairman concluded that on balance its brief was to make adjustments to the existing border rather than to begin *a priori* with political demography, as the phrase 'in acccordance with the wishes of the inhabitants' seemed to imply. This meant that the commission was reduced to considering a series of minor frontier changes. It is difficult to believe that Cosgrave, who had shown himself exceptionally well versed in realpolitik since 1922, did not foresee this—indeed it may partly explain the nomination of Eoin MacNeill, a somewhat fatalistic figure already wearied of political life, as the Free State representative in preference to a more abrasive negotiator. There were other northerners in Cumann na nGaedheal such as Patrick McGilligan, Blythe, or Kevin O'Sheil, better equipped to argue about procedure, details, and technicalities, if Cosgrave had genuinely believed that substantive changes were possible. The reality was that the Free State had no worthwhile cards to play in the discussions, and could only hope for the best. For domestic reasons, nevertheless, the government had to hold out the expectation of a beneficial outcome. This made its position more difficult when, in November 1925, the outlines of the commission's report became known through a leak to a London newspaper. The report proposed no more than the removal through territorial transfers of a few of the most glaring local anomalies created by the existing border, involving transfers of territory on both sides representing a net reduction of 1.8 per cent in population and 3.7 per cent in the size of Northern Ireland. In nationalist and southern eyes this was disastrous. MacNeill resigned from the commission rather than sign the report, although he had been an unhappy party to it. It remains a matter for debate whether his resignation was intended as a repudiation of the report, or as an admission of personal misjudgement in tamely allowing matters to reach such a pass.[47] News of the report's recommendations provoked a crisis for the Cosgrave government. After hurried negotiations it was agreed with the British that the report would be shelved, the existing border retained, full civil rights restored to northern nationalists, and the 'council of Ireland' (provided for in the government of Ireland act) scrapped. The government of Northern Ireland readily concurred, although it offset the impact of the subsequent release of internees by forcing many to leave Northern Ireland. As a face-saving sop to Cosgrave, the British government agreed to waive some of Ireland's indeterminate financial obligations under the treaty. A tripartite agreement embodying these decisions was signed on 3 December 1925.[48]

On the face of it this should have been Cosgrave's darkest hour, the time when northern nationalists, hostages to fortune since 1921, were finally abandoned in return for somewhat ephemeral financial concessions, and when an Irish government explicitly accepted Northern Ireland as defined under the government of Ireland act. In practice, and despite its acute embarrassment, the government rode the storm with ease. Three Cumann na nGaedheal deputies broke away to found a new party, Clann Éireann, but Cosgrave's majority came under no threat. This was because the largest opposition party, being outside the dáil, was unable to make serious capital out of the débâcle. De Valera's biographers have noted that no more than twenty deputies voted against the government during the crisis, and have pointed out that the forty-seven abstentionist T.D.s would not have been sufficient to tip the balance. It could equally be said that, given his particular skills, de Valera's presence in the chamber would have produced a completely new political situation, and that therefore a great opportunity was missed of weakening the Cosgrave government. The evidence suggests that this was de Valera's view, although he had no magic formula for coaxing more concessions out of either Sir James Craig or the British government. Within weeks of the boundary commission crisis he signalled his unhappiness with out-and-out abstention, and within months he split decisively with the majority in Sinn Féin, arguing at a special party conference that once the oath was dropped abstention should be simply a tactical question, a matter of policy rather than of principle.[49] Less than half of the

[47] Geoffrey Hand, 'MacNeill and the boundary commission' in F. X. Martin and F. J. Byrne (ed.), *The scholar revolutionary: Eoin MacNeill, 1867–1945* (Shannon, 1973), pp 254–9. O'Sheil, a barrister, was involved in the process, as director of the north-eastern boundary bureau established to support the Free State case for a substantial revision of the border.

[48] Laffan, *Partition*, p. 104; Clare O'Halloran, *Partition and the limits of Irish nationalism* (Dublin, 1987), pp xiii, 20–21.

[49] Gallagher, *Political parties*, p. 99; Longford & O'Neill, *De Valera*, p. 241; John Bowman, *De Valera and the Ulster question, 1917–1973* (Oxford, 1982), pp 91–3; Owen Dudley Edwards, *Political portraits: Eamon de Valera* (Cardiff, 1987), p. 112. In his *Recollections of a rebel* (Tralee, 1944), p. 70, J. J. Walsh, then minister for posts and telegraphs, claimed

republican T.D.s departed from Sinn Féin with him. The split enabled de Valera to begin the work of founding a new republican party unencumbered by impolitic absolutes, a party of reality in place of a party of dreams, one in which aspirational rhetoric would complement rather than prevent participation in practical politics. The boundary commission fiasco thus hastened the creation of Fianna Fáil in May 1926, an unlikely but enduring monument to the abortive endeavours of Mr Justice Feetham and his commissioners.

THE Cosgrave government was economically and socially conservative throughout its decade in power. Its watchwords were low taxation, frugal administration, and the promotion of national efficiency. In 1923 ministers believed that the country was close to ruin, its infrastructure shattered, its towns scarred, and its people demoralised by years of turmoil culminating in civil war. What was needed was stability, not adventure. For Cumann na nGaedheal, sound government and sound finance were synonymous. While it understood and pressed the need for reform in the management of public business, in order to increase efficiency, prevent abuse, and tighten political control, in its ideology the government was profoundly non-interventionist in economic affairs—though practice did not invariably conform with principle. A combination of habit and expediency meant that the government looked mainly to Britain, for example in the management of economic affairs, but despite this respect for British ways the country's particular circumstances inspired some innovations in the system of justice and the machinery of government.

The new state faced major difficulties in the administration of justice. It was essential to maintain continuity between the workings of the law in the old jurisdiction and the new; at the same time, in addition to the necessary remodelling of the judicial system inherited from the British, the parallel and sometimes conflicting work of the dáil courts in civil law from 1919 to 1922 had to be accommodated. Furthermore, for sound political reasons the government wished to abolish the lowest tier of the old British system, the thousands of unpaid local magistrates, replacing them with full-time district justices less susceptible to local pressures in the administration of the law. All this had to be done swiftly in order to command public confidence in the fairness and efficiency of the new system. Despite many problems, and considerable friction between the two men primarily responsible, the minister for home affairs Kevin O'Higgins and the attorney general Hugh Kennedy, it was accomplished: in 1924 the courts of justice act set the seal on a

that some Cumann na nGaedheal colleagues had asked him 'to form a government, and meetings were held for this purpose'. However, he remained a minister under Cosgrave till quitting politics in the autumn of 1927 in protest at 'the abandonment of protection for native industries' (p. 71).

restructured judicial system, which, with minor changes, has continued ever since.[50]

The Irish administrative system before independence had been notorious for its complexity, its inefficiency, and its politicisation. During the last two years of British rule these weaknesses had belatedly been addressed by the treasury as part of its postwar reform of the British civil service. The result was that the new state inherited a central bureaucracy that had just been thoroughly overhauled.[51] Over 20,000 personnel, from heads of departments to typists, messengers, and postmen, exchanged the crown for the harp, and, joined by something under 200 officials of the dáil administration established in 1919, continued on working much as before.[52] In local government, the position was much the same. This continuity in personnel served somewhat to obscure important changes in both the structure and the practice of central and local administration in independent Ireland.

The first set of changes concerned the way in which public officials were selected. This involved not so much the continuation of British apolitical values in the civil service as their adoption. Before independence the senior ranks of the civil service in Dublin had been highly politicised: officials were routinely appointed and promoted on the basis of their religion and putative political beliefs. At lower levels, as the royal commission on the civil service had reported in 1914, 'temporary clerical employment', often obtained by 'personal influence', was 'an outstanding and demoralising feature' in Irish departments.[53] Similarly, local government was notorious for the favouritism and corruption surrounding appointments. The 'British' meritocratic virtues generally ascribed to the Irish public service, exemplified in the rapid establishment of a civil service commission in 1923 and the local appointments commission three years later, were insisted on by the government in the early years of the state to prevent the perpetuation, not the creation, of a system based on influence and patronage.[54] This is illustrated in Richard Mulcahy's dismissive comment to a nun who sought his help in fixing up a young man with a government job: 'Everything possible has been done to do away with patronage or favouritism throughout the . . . public service—governmental or

[50] 1924/10 (12 Apr. 1924); Paul C. Bartholomew, *The Irish judiciary* (Dublin, 1971), pp 4–11; V. T. H. Delany, *The administration of justice in Ireland* (Dublin, 1962; 4th ed., ed. Charles Lysaght, 1975), pp 32–42. For an illustration of the tensions, see the exchange of correspondence between Kennedy and O'Higgins in May and June 1923 (U.C.D., A.D., Kennedy papers, P4/760).
[51] John McColgan, *British policy and the Irish administration, 1920–22* (London, 1983), pp 134–7.
[52] Ronan Fanning, 'Britain's legacy: government and administration' in P. J. Drudy (ed.), *Ireland and Britain since 1922* (Irish Studies 5; Cambridge, 1986), p. 51.
[53] *Royal commission on the civil service, 1912–14: report and minutes of evidence* [Cd 7338], H.C.1914, xvi, 86–7.
[54] Eunan O'Halpin, 'The civil service and the political system' in *Administration*, xxxviii (1991), pp 287–9.

local.'[55] By and large that was so, as even republican critics later acknowledged, although the notorious Dunbar-Harrison case in 1930–31 suggested that there were limits to the government's resolution in the face of local pressures, reinforced by the weight of the catholic church.[56] This indicates the persistence among politicians of the Sinn Féin ethic of hard work, honesty, and frugality in administration, developed in reaction to the sometimes laxer political style of the Redmondite nationalist party. Additionally, ministers were so preoccupied with the political and financial consequences of the civil war and its aftermath that they left questions of public service management largely to the new department of finance, and specifically to its secretary Joseph Brennan and his mentor C. J. Gregg, a personal friend of Cosgrave on loan from the British board of inland revenue. Their priorities of reform, efficiency, economy, and increased central control of administration coincided with the executive council's concerns about the cost of the war and reconstruction.[57]

The same officials were also largely responsible for the ministers and secretaries act of 1924, the single most important piece of public service legislation passed in independent Ireland. In place of the assortment of over forty boards, commissions, and departments, many largely free from ministerial control, through which Ireland had been governed before independence, the act consolidated national administration under eleven departments of state, each the responsibility of a minister. The act also enunciated the principle that a minister was a corporation sole, in complete control of and with final responsibility for everything his department did.[58] It prescribed a highly centralised administrative system, the clear intention both of the officials who drafted it and the ministers who supported its enactment. They may not have been aware that in this the act echoed the plans made in 1915 by John Redmond and John Dillon for administration under home rule. The act also met the key criterion of direct control by ministers of the machinery of government.[59] It was, like the civil service commission and the local appointments commission, one of those centralist measures that de Valera loudly objected to in opposition, and then exploited to the full when in government.

The government displayed much the same penchant for standardisation and centralisation in its treatment of local government. Local government reform was a matter close to Cosgrave's heart: he had made his name as the

[55] Mulcahy to 'My dear Reverend Mother', 1 Dec. 1927 (Mulcahy papers, P76/68).
[56] Whyte, *Ch. & state* (1980), pp 44–7; Lee, *Ire. 1912–85*, pp 161–7.
[57] Ronan Fanning, *The Irish department of finance, 1922–58* (Dublin, 1978), pp 59–80.
[58] 1924/16 (21 Apr. 1924); Basil Chubb, *The government and politics of Ireland* (2nd ed., London, 1982), pp 248, 250–51.
[59] Fanning, *Department of finance*, pp 72–5; Eunan O'Halpin, *The decline of the union* (Dublin, 1987), pp 97–8.

local government minister in the dáil government from 1919, and he knew the defects of the system inherited from the British. These ranged from limitless opportunities for corruption, inefficiency, and waste to the subversive potential of local elected bodies. The radical changes introduced by his government in matters such as appointments, purchasing, and administrative control were inspired partly by the need to improve the deplorable performance of many local authorities, and partly by the desire to deny republicans a significant political platform. In December 1922 local government elections were postponed for three years, the first of numerous occasions when an Irish government has deferred potentially embarrassing local polls. A few months later the county councils of Kerry and Leitrim were dissolved under new legislation, essentially because of their republican sympathies; each body was replaced by a government-appointed commissioner. Over the next decade many other recalcitrant local authorities suffered the same fate, sometimes for political reasons, sometimes simply on grounds of inefficiency.

Republicans railed at Cumann na nGaedheal's negation of local democracy, but in 1934 Fianna Fáil was to use similar means to dissolve county councils supporting the Blueshirts' anti-rates campaign. On the eve of local elections in 1925, the minister for local government and public health told an American diplomat that republicans in local authorities had used 'exactly the same tactics as the old Irish movement had used against the British government'. While 'he could not hope that partisanship would be eliminated from the local government bodies altogether, he did have hopes that a distinct advance in that direction would be obtained'. His party set an example by putting forward no candidates, a policy Cumann na nGaedheal adhered to for some years.[60] The elimination of partisanship was never fully achieved, but in 1929 the government succeeded in driving a permanent wedge between local politics and local administration with the Cork city management act; a similar measure for Dublin was passed a year later.[61] Although Fianna Fáil opposed these innovations as reflecting an undemocratic, bureaucratic, and centralist attitude towards the problems of local government, after taking office the party gradually introduced the same system in all cities, counties, and county boroughs.[62] This illustrates a wider point: whatever his complaints about the treaty, the constitution, external relations, or economic policy, de Valera in power was content to operate the administrative system fashioned by his opponents.

---

[60] C. M. Hathaway, consul-general, to state department, 16 June 1925 (U.S. National Archives, state department, 841d00/776).
[61] 1929/1 (23 Feb. 1929); 1930/27 (17 July 1930).
[62] Eunan O'Halpin, 'The origins of city and county management' in *City and county management, 1929–1990: a retrospective* (Dublin, 1991), pp 1–19.

CUMANN na nGaedheal has frequently been criticised for adopting a react-ive, almost fatalistic approach to economic issues, and for lacking any positive conception of national development. In examining the Cosgrave govern-ment's performance, however, it is important to note that Keynesian ap-proaches to macroeconomic policy had yet to be invented, a point that critics of Irish economic performance in the 1920s sometimes seem inclined to overlook. Furthermore, given the volatility of world trading conditions, the country's geographic isolation, the structure of its economy, its traditional dependence on the British market and on British credit, and the fact that Ireland's handsomely designed national currency (adopted in 1928) was fixed at par with sterling, the range of economic options open to the administration was perhaps not all that wide.

Broadly speaking, Cumann na nGaedheal adopted the view that the Free State should, after making good the damage caused by the civil war, spend as little as possible. The lower the burden of national and local taxation, the better the prospects for economic activity. The government should build on the existing economic base, rather than attempt to restructure it. This strat-egy echoed not so much the heady mix of protection, state intervention, and social reform put forward by Sinn Féin before independence, as the policy of John Redmond and John Dillon, who in 1915 had planned just such a pro-gramme for a home rule administration.[63] In 1922 the economy was domin-ated by agriculture, which depended overwhelmingly on the British market. The thrust of policy throughout the decade under the dynamic and acerbic minister for agriculture, Patrick Hogan, was to develop agriculture further, by encouraging greater production, improved quality, and efficient organisa-tion. Hogan was conservative but not cautious. He saw agriculture as the only realistic source of economic growth, and his policies were aimed at maximising its export potential. He regarded Britain as Ireland's primary market, and the improvements in standards he sought were intended to protect Irish sales there in the face of competition from other producing countries whose relative efficiency threatened to offset Ireland's natural geo-graphic advantages. Ireland's best defence was high standards and low costs of agricultural production. A number of difficulties emerged with this strat-egy. By pinning hopes for national development mainly on agriculture, it lessened the possibility of significant growth in the country's industrial base. Tax and spending concessions to agriculture absorbed public funds that might otherwise have gone to stimulate manufacturing industry. Further-more, free trade, a sine qua non of Hogan's approach until he was forced by external circumstances to abandon it in 1931, made it difficult to stimulate growth in domestic manufacturing.

[63] O'Halpin, *Decline of the union*, p. 97.

Hogan was also constrained by unfinished business concerning land purchase. As far back as Balfour's land act of 1891 the British government had accepted that peasant proprietorship should be the basis of land tenure in Ireland, and arrangements for buying out the landlords, through low-cost annuity payments, had been widely taken up by the time of the first world war.[64] However, when the Irish convention of 1917 discussed proposals to complete the process, up to one-third of Irish agricultural land, subject to the land purchase code as established by the acts of 1891 and 1896, was still unsold or awaiting closure, and the situation was complicated by the plight of tenants who had been evicted during the land war. A bill to implement the convention's proposals on the matter failed in the Westminster parliament in 1920, and meanwhile agrarian disturbances were rife during the war of independence, particularly in the west of Ireland. The first dáil, keen to develop its own structures for land purchase, unaccountably failed to follow Northern Ireland's example and take advantage of a clause in the government of Ireland act of 1920 which allowed the annuity payments, instead of being paid to the British government (which had put up the stock to buy the landlords out), to be retained by the two parliaments set up under the act. In 1919 the dáil did, however, acknowledge the destabilising potential of the issue by setting up a land bank to allow tenants to obtain mortgages, and by establishing its own land settlement commission in 1921 to deal with land purchase claims.[65]

The 1921 treaty made no mention of land purchase, and Hogan (who was agriculture minister in both the provisional government and the dáil cabinet) appears to have accepted the obligation to pay the annuities to Britain; in February 1923 President Cosgrave signed an agreement to that effect (not made public till Fianna Fáil came to power in 1932). However, it was also agreed in 1923 that Britain would continue to provide the credit for future Irish land stock, in return for which the British government would have the right of prior approval of forthcoming land legislation. Again, for obvious reasons, this was not made public at the time. The old land commission, still operating under British authority and on an all-Ireland basis, continued to sign new purchase agreements till April 1923. Thereafter the Free State government introduced legislation[66] to reconstitute the land commission, which under new auspices was able to proceed with the completion of land purchase.[67]

[64] Above, vi, 274.

[65] See Joseph Sheehan, 'Land purchase policy in Ireland, 1917–23: from the Irish convention to the 1923 land act' (M.A. thesis, St Patrick's college, Maynooth, 1993), ch. 3. The land settlement commission was quietly wound up in December 1923.

[66] 1923/42 (9 Aug. 1923).

[67] Sheehan, 'Land purchase policy', ch. 4.

Apart from these concessions, Hogan's policies frequently went against the interests of the smaller, marginal farmers and of farm labourers, for whom maxims such as lower production costs meant in practice lower incomes and ultimately less employment. Finally, for all his local achievements Hogan's policy foundered on the rocks of world recession after 1929, as agricultural prices collapsed, world trade contracted, and countries turned *en masse* to wholesale protectionism. But it is hardly fair to castigate him for the failings of the world economy, while the benefits of his policy should not be over-looked. If nothing else, he familiarised farmers with the unwelcome message that they had to compete with other countries in terms of the quality of their produce; he succeeded (till 1930) in the immediate aim of increasing the volume and value of exports; and he provided the outlines of a development structure through the reorganisation of creameries and the establishment of the agricultural credit corporation and the first state-financed sugar beet factory.[68] Where he and his colleagues erred was in treating agriculture largely as an alternative to industrialisation rather than as a complement to it.

Cumann na nGaedheal's policy towards industry was governed by the assumption that business did best when the state stood back. In practice the state did intervene, but only in a haphazard and apologetic fashion. Concern for national solvency, instinctive frugality, and the government's commit-ment to free trade together ensured that action was limited to steps calculated not to alarm business and banking circles, an approach that precluded a systematic approach to industrial development. Cumann na nGaedheal was consequently somewhat diffident in its attitude towards its most celebrated industrial success, the Shannon hydro-electric scheme and the subsequent establishment of the electricity supply board, which was pushed through by Patrick McGilligan, the minister for industry and commerce, despite the bitter opposition of the department of finance. A more populist party would have proclaimed such a project as a triumph long before the first sod was turned. Equally, a government with grander economic ambitions would probably not have allowed one man to be responsible simultaneously for the departments of industry and commerce and of external affairs as McGilligan was from 1924, an arrangement that arguably impeded progress in industrial policy.[69]

THE Cosgrave government's approach to economic management had conse-quences for social policy. The government was far from callous: despite

[68] James Meenan, *The Irish economy since 1922* (Liverpool, 1970), pp 303–7, 312–13; see Brian Girvin, *Between two worlds: politics and economy in independent Ireland* (Dublin, 1989), pp 11–89, for an extensive discussion of the economic record of the Cosgrave governments.
[69] Maurice Manning and Moore McDowell, *Electricity supply in Ireland: the story of the E.S.B.* (Dublin, 1984), pp 21–69; Brian Farrell, *Seán Lemass* (Dublin, 1983), p. 33; Girvin, *Between two worlds*, p. 87.

McGilligan's chilling warning in 1924 that 'people may have to die in this country and may have to die from starvation' (a phrase that has earned a permanent place in Irish political memory) and its notorious decision to reduce the old age pension by 1s., it was composed of men who were in varying degrees Christian, humane, and pious, brought up with a strong sense of social responsibility and a firm belief in the virtue of charity.[70] Before independence Sinn Féin had made issues of poor housing, urban squalor, unemployment, low wages, disease, and privation, and the first dáil had accepted a 'democratic programme' largely focused on addressing these social ills.[71] But Cumann na nGaedheal's policies owed much to an older legacy, the constricted domestic ambitions of the Irish nationalist party. The 1920s saw a number of important legislative and administrative developments in aspects of welfare and health provision, and these laid the foundations for reform in the 1930s and 1940s under later administrations. As in other aspects of national affairs, the Cosgrave government was more interested in providing efficient machinery than in operating it to best effect. In the 1920s action on health and welfare problems usually involved spending on a scale that local authorities wished to avoid, and that central government would not countenance—although, three years after the death of the somewhat puritanical Kevin O'Higgins, who 'did not think it was possible to run sweepstakes without fraud', the government did permit the establishment of the Irish hospitals sweepstakes as a means of funding hospital-building, entrusting the profitable task of promoting and administering the scheme to the former minister Joe McGrath.[72] In the meantime unemployment and privation remained problems to which the government could offer no solution; bad housing, sickness, and disease were sad facts of life about which little could be done by the state without ruinous expense. There is no point in applying the yardstick of a welfare state to the social policies of the 1920s, when expectations were so much lower and when money was so scarce. But we may note the equanimity with which the Cosgrave government viewed social problems that it believed it lacked the money to address.

Primary education had been a responsibility of central government long before independence. Here the government had one distinctive aim, inherited from the old Sinn Féin agenda: to gaelicise the education system. This policy, applauded by all the major parties, was faithfully pursued, though the results were disappointing. Irish had ceased to be a living language in most parts of the country, and the pedagogic fixation with reviving it arguably impeded the development of a curriculum focused on the practical needs of

[70] Quoted in Lee, *Ire. 1912–85*, p. 127.
[71] Above, vi, 241–2.
[72] Joseph Robins, *Fools and mad: a history of the insane in Ireland* (Dublin, 1986), pp 184–90; Ruth Barrington, *Health, medicine and politics in Ireland, 1900–1970* (Dublin, 1987), pp 89–112.

pupils and society in town and country. Not all Cumann na nGaedheal ministers shared the private view of their colleague Patrick Hogan that the Irish language movement was one of the greatest 'rackets' that the country had had to endure, but there was a certain fatalism in the government's attempts to promote the use of Irish.[73] The new emphasis on Irish apart, the system continued much as it had done under the British, apart from a recasting of the history syllabus—if anything, the Cosgrave government was less inclined to experiment than the old regime. The establishment of the department of education in 1924 led to significant administrative improvements, but the management of the system remained overwhelmingly in the hands of the religious denominations, while, somewhat bizarrely, the police were also brought in as the enforcers of the school attendance act of 1926.[74] Despite the passage in 1930 of the vocational education act,[75] which empowered local authorities to provide non-denominational education, vocational and technical training languished for want of finance and initiative, in the face of official indifference, clerical hostility, and middle-class disdain. Secondary education remained a minority pursuit, and universities continued to serve mainly as finishing schools for the children of the privileged. On the whole, education was viewed as a public cost, not as an investment; as an unavoidable obligation of statehood, rather than as a means of social change and economic modernisation.[76]

HOWEVER limited its vision of social progress, the Cosgrave government was quite conscious of the moral pitfalls that lay in wait for the Irish nation. This led to some significant initiatives in areas of social policy and public morality. The most striking attempt to reform the Irish character came with the intoxicating liquor act of 1927.[77] This was introduced at the prompting of the minister for justice and vice-president of the executive council, Kevin O'Higgins, a man who took a distinctly pessimistic and censorious view of the proclivities of most Irishmen, including some of his colleagues. In the best traditions of their trades, the distillers, brewers, and licensed vintners succeeded in having the measure considerably watered down by the time that it reached the statute book; nevertheless it was a notable attempt at social engineering, designed to tackle the scourge of drunkenness by strict regulation of the sale of alcohol. Among its innovations was the 'holy hour' in Dublin and Cork, a device indelibly associated with O'Higgins's personal

---

[73] Interview with Mr John Joe Broderick, a former constituency worker for Patrick Hogan, Kilrickle, Co. Galway, July 1991.

[74] 1926/17 (27 May 1926).

[75] 1930/29 (21 July 1930).

[76] Séamas Ó Buachalla, *Education policy in twentieth-century Ireland* (Dublin, 1988), pp 60–64; John Coolahan, *Irish education: its history and structure* (Dublin, 1981), pp 41–2, 74–8, 96–8.

[77] 1927/15 (20 May 1927).

crusade against licentiousness.[78] The government, under pressure from organised catholic interests, also moved to protect the people from themselves through the banning of divorce in 1925 (a measure much at odds with Cosgrave's aim of assimilating protestants and unionists into the new state) and later through the censorship of publications act of 1929.[79]

Despite its later reputation as a symbol of the most narrow-minded and intolerant catholicism, the censorship of publications act marked the culmination of an extensive review process involving protestant as well as catholic authorities. In 1926 O'Higgins established a 'committee of inquiry on evil literature' composed of two university professors, two clergymen, and a representative of the Irish National Teachers Organisation, the Labour T. D. T. J. O'Connell. Three of the members were catholic and two protestant. The committee's report laid the basis for the bill eventually presented to the oireachtas in 1928. This was designed to thwart the publication and dissemination in Ireland of blasphemous or immoral material, including publications advocating birth control, which might offend or corrupt members of the public. The bill received extensive consideration during its passage, was treated as a cross-party matter—Patrick Hogan spoke strongly and presciently against it—and, most unusually for a government measure, was amended substantially despite the sponsoring minister's objections. The act has frequently been assailed as an unnecessary, prudish, and repressive law, which stifled free expression, increased Irish isolation from Europe, and retarded the country's intellectual and artistic maturation. Such criticism, however, applies more fairly to the manner in which the law was subsequently administered, and to the state's failure to review the censorship process in the light of social change.[80] At the time the act was passed, it reflected rather than created Ireland's pronounced public piety, general fear of sin, and suspicion of things foreign; in 1930 the secretary to the government initiated a police investigation of the Dublin Film Society, composed, it transpired, of thoroughly respectable government supporters. He remained, nevertheless, 'somewhat nervous of the "cinema as an art medium" in the hands of a Society such as the present'.[81] In the religious and political atmosphere of the 1920s, with uniformly pious political parties, with a powerful ultramontane catholic hierarchy in place, and with a eucharistic

---

[78] Lee, *Ire. 1912–85*, p. 153. The term 'holy hour' was satirically applied to the ban on the sale of intoxicating liquor in county boroughs, 2.30–3.30 p.m., imposed by the 1927 act. The ban was repealed (except for Sundays) in 1988 (1988/16 (22 June 1988)).

[79] 1929/21 (16 July 1929); below, pp 488–90, 680–81.

[80] Michael Adams, *Censorship: the Irish experience* (Dublin, 1968), pp 24–68; Lee, *Ire. 1912–85*, pp 158–60; Elizabeth Cullingford, *Yeats, Ireland, and fascism* (London, 1981), p. 193; Kurt Bowen, *Protestants in a catholic state* (Dublin, 1983), pp 55–64, 196–7.

[81] O'Hegarty (secretary to the executive council) to E. M. Coulson (secretary to the governor general), 19 Feb. 1930 (N.A.I., S 6002). Film censorship had been introduced without controversy in July 1923.

congress on the horizon, it is difficult to believe that the act had much immediate impact on public attitudes. We may, however, note here that the act underlined the conditional nature of the Cosgrave administration's adherence to the non-interventionist, secular, and pluralist approach to politics suggested by the Free State constitution. In the new state's first decade non-catholics were allowed to enjoy their property, to practise their religion, to hold public office, to run their own schools, and to carry on their businesses and professions unmolested. This applied not only to the various protestant denominations but to Jews, although as already noted the latter were actively discriminated against in immigration policy. Apart from freemasonry, which most catholics regarded as a deeply sinister movement, the government and its supporters found nothing to complain about in the activities and attitudes of most Irish protestants. In the new Ireland religious and political minorities were acceptable, as long as they did not challenge the hegemony of the catholic church; moral minorities were not, any more than they were in Britain.

IN May 1926, weeks after a dramatic but widely predicted rift at the Sinn Féin ard-fheis, in which, as in the second dáil in 1921, he found himself in a minority, de Valera unveiled a new political party, Fianna Fáil. Twenty-one of the forty-four abstentionist T.D.s joined it. His Cumann na nGaedheal and Sinn Féin opponents ridiculed this further split, but it was a decisive one for Irish politics. Fianna Fáil was the vehicle that was to bring de Valera decades of political supremacy in Ireland. It also became the cornerstone of the Irish party system, according the issue of the treaty 'a sufficient degree of salience to more or less obliterate . . . alternative dimensions' of political conflict on economic and social issues.[82]

In its first year of existence, Fianna Fáil laboured under the same handicap that de Valera had feared would asphyxiate Sinn Féin: it remained an abstentionist party, though only for so long as the oath of allegiance remained. Furthermore, it was now in competition with Sinn Féin for the republican vote. It differed sharply from its rival in key respects. First, however grudgingly, partially, and conditionally, the party recognised the practical legitimacy of the Free State and its institutions. Secondly, it forsook violence as a means of achieving political power in the state. Thirdly, in order to widen its electoral appeal it adopted the language of modest social amelioration and of thoroughgoing economic protectionism, whereas post-treaty Sinn Féin had been 'totally preoccupied with the question of political autonomy on the naive assumption that the solution of this issue would automatically resolve all other national problems'.[83] This gave Fianna Fáil some prospect of

[82] Peter Mair, *The changing Irish party system* (London, 1987), p. 16.
[83] C. S. Andrews, *Man of no property* (Dublin, 1982), p. 57; interview with Andrews, 8 May 1982.

attracting support from non-aligned voters as well as from fervent believers in the republic. Fourthly, the party included men such as Gerry Boland and Seán Lemass, who proved themselves outstanding national political organisers. In complete contrast to Cumann na nGaedheal, which relied on loose associations of prominent citizens to get out the vote in each constituency at election time, Fianna Fáil built a disciplined party machine, akin to Sinn Féin in 1918 but with a much broader social base, which enlisted and retained the unswerving support of ordinary people throughout the country. A sympathetic journalist once described the first generation of Fianna Fáil leaders as 'politicians by accident'; if so, it was an accident of birth, not of mere circumstances.[84]

The first electoral test for de Valera's new party came in June 1927. The election made Fianna Fáil the dominant party in republican politics. It took 26 per cent of the vote, while the sterile absolutists of Sinn Féin and other republicans between them won less than 5 per cent. Sinn Féin lost most of its seats, holding just five, while Fianna Fáil, soon to be joined by an independent republican T.D., won forty-four. Cosgrave's Cumann na nGaedheal won only forty-seven seats, a loss of sixteen, while the smaller parties and independents fared well, taking over 40 per cent of the vote and fifty-six of the 153 seats.[85] This inconclusive but disappointing result placed Cosgrave in a difficult position since, even with the support of the Farmers' party, he would be in a minority should Fianna Fáil reenter the dáil.

If Cosgrave's position was difficult, de Valera's was agonising. There was a real chance of unseating the government in a dáil vote, but not while Fianna Fáil remained outside. A preliminary foray to Leinster House ended, predictably enough, in a rebuff: de Valera was refused admission to the chamber as he had not taken the oath of allegiance. What was he to do? His party's success in the election, and the collapse in support for Sinn Féin, suggested strongly that the electorate wanted Fianna Fáil to participate in parliamentary politics. But de Valera had split with Griffith and Collins in 1921 over precisely such symbols as the oath, he had endorsed civil war as a preferable alternative to accepting the oath in 1922, and Fianna Fáil had campaigned on the basis that the party would not take it under any circumstances. How could he resolve the present impasse without reneging on that principle now—and without a fatal loss of political face?

De Valera's dilemma was resolved for him by opponents from opposite ends of the Irish political spectrum. On 10 July 1927 Kevin O'Higgins was fatally wounded by three gunmen near his home while on his way to mass. He died that night. The murderers, who were never caught, were probably

[84] Gallagher, *Political parties*, pp 44–5; Liam C. Skinner, *Politicians by accident* (Dublin, 1947); Farrell, *Lemass*, pp 18–19.
[85] O'Leary, *Ir. elections*, pp 23, 101.

maverick republicans, although there were rumours that the shooting was the work of disgruntled ex-army men or even the police.[86] The killing of O'Higgins deprived the government of its most striking member, courageous and decisive, with a sharp mind, an acid and embittered tongue—his father had been murdered during the civil war—and, as the 1924 army crisis had shown, considerable political finesse. The government's reaction to his death, whether the product of panic or of calculation, was as decisive as he would have wished. Cosgrave announced the introduction of three exceptional measures to restore stability. These were a draconian public safety bill, aimed at the I.R.A. and republican fringe groups; an electoral amendment bill under which all dáil candidates would have to swear on nomination to take their seats if elected; and a bill to alter the constitution by removing article 48, which enabled the electorate to initiate a referendum by petition.[87] The two latter measures were calculated to force de Valera to make up his mind about participation in the dáil once and for all, by whittling down the options to two: either to take the oath, with every chance of quickly ousting the Cosgrave government, or to be permanently excluded from electoral politics. His biographers comment that 'if ever a statesman was confronted with a moral dilemma or torn between rival principles it was de Valera at this time'. To less sympathetic eyes those conflicting principles included the overriding political imperative of never letting slip a chance of power. After much party and personal agonising, de Valera and his Fianna Fáil colleagues came up with a solution that was at once predictable and novel: they would fulfill the constitutional formalities required of them in taking their seats, but only because the offending oath was in fact 'an empty political formula'.[88] De Valera, supported by some obliging clerics, found genuine solace in this formulation; his opponents, and probably many of his supporters, saw it simply as a necessary piece of casuistry.[89] If the oath was only an empty, meaningless formula in 1927, why had the republicans engaged in a civil war rather than accept it and the other formal trappings of imperial subordination in 1922? De Valera had to choose between being consistent and being constitutional. The decision he made transformed the politics of independent Ireland.

Fianna Fáil's arrival in the dáil on 11 August posed a major challenge to the government. For a time it looked as though Cumann na nGaedheal, now in a minority despite the support of the Farmers' party, would lose office. On 16 August the Labour leader Thomas Johnson moved a motion of no confidence: the arithmetic suggested that this would be carried by a combination of Fianna

[86] De Vere White, O'Higgins, p. 232.
[87] The first two bills passed as 1927/31 (11 Aug. 1927) and 1927/33 (9 Nov. 1927); the third did not proceed beyond its second reading.
[88] Longford & O'Neill, De Valera, p. 254.
[89] Lee, Ire. 1912–85, p. 155.

Fáil, Labour, the National League, and independents. Johnson had reached an understanding with de Valera, whom he had pressed for years to abandon abstention, whereby Fianna Fáil would then support a Labour/National League coalition government. The plan, however, took insufficient account of human frailty: when the vote was called, one of the National League T.D.s, John Jinks of Sligo, was absent, having unwisely accepted the lunchtime hospitality of a pro-government T.D. and the editor of the *Irish Times*.[90] The motion was defeated on the casting vote of the ceann comhairle, and the dáil was dissolved a few days later. This manoeuvre was promptly condemned by de Valera, now firmly ensconced within the parliamentary fold, as constitutional 'sharp practice', an observation that did not prevent him adopting much the same tactics in 1933, 1938, and 1944 after elections had failed to yield the desired Fianna Fáil majority.[91] The September 1927 election saw the smaller parties and independents severely squeezed: Cumann na nGaedheal's share of the vote went up by 11 per cent and its number of seats by fifteen, and Fianna Fáil's by 9 per cent and thirteen seats respectively. Labour's representation fell from twenty-two seats to thirteen, the Farmers' party from eleven to six, and the National League from eight to two. In coalition with the Farmers' party, Cosgrave was able to muster a threadbare majority of four seats. This made the government 'to all appearances a "lame duck" administration', and on one occasion in 1930 Cosgrave resigned as president and was reelected after a dáil defeat.[92] However, the reality was that he continued to manage affairs much as before till 1932.

Fianna Fáil's entry into the dáil completely changed the tenor of parliamentary politics. The enormous bitterness between Fianna Fáil and Cumann na nGaedheal frequently found expression in debate. Furthermore, despite embracing constitutional politics Fianna Fáil ostentatiously paraded its continued sympathy for militant republicanism, an attitude that naturally enraged the government. Fianna Fáil was also the first credible dáil rival encountered by the Cosgrave administration. And it was the very heat of debate that proved the value of parliamentary participation: the two largest groups in the Irish political system had once more found an agreed forum in which to exchange insults. The main issues to divide the government from its principal opponents were, predictably, constitutional and political: the symbols of empire in the Free State constitution, Anglo–Irish relations, and state repression of republican organisations. Here de Valera was to the fore. Fianna Fáil also advocated

---

[90] Longford & O'Neill, *De Valera*, p. 260; Andrews, *Man of no property*, p. 83; J. Anthony Gaughan, *Thomas Johnson, 1872–1963* (Dublin, 1980), pp 317–18.

[91] O'Leary, *Ir. elections*, p. 25.

[92] Ibid. Cosgrave resigned on 28 Mar. after losing a vote on a private member's bill on old-age pensions. He was reelected on 2 Apr. after Fianna Fáil had failed to support the Labour party's nominee. De Valera was in the United States, and his party's room for manoeuvre was consequently very limited (*Dáil Éireann deb.*, xxxiv, 276–7, 281–468 (28 Mar., 2 Apr. 1930)).

greater protection for native industry and agriculture, more social spending, and state intervention to foster economic growth, although such matters were not de Valera's strong suit and were addressed more knowledgeably and coherently by Seán Lemass, a man whose dáil performances soon marked him out as an exceptional figure.[93] These developments allowed the party to differentiate itself from Cumann na nGaedheal on practical issues; they also broadened its electoral appeal, threatening the interests of the smaller parties and independents in the dáil. While Fianna Fáil was initially regarded with suspicion by most of the catholic hierarchy, its leaders said and did nothing to offend catholic susceptibilities, instead competing enthusiastically with Cumann na nGaedheal in public demonstrations of piety.

It was Cosgrave's threat of legislation that had forced de Valera to accept the oath and enter the dáil. Having achieved this, the government did not intend to let de Valera forget his apostasy. Early in 1928 Fianna Fáil collected the required number of signatures to a petition under article 48 of the constitution. This called on the oireachtas to establish the machinery envisaged for plebiscitary legislation, the 'initiative', which would then become the vehicle for a popular vote to abolish the oath of allegiance. The dáil considered this but, before a decision was taken, the government pre-empted any action by forcing through a constitutional amendment abolishing the initiative altogether. Such opportunism was within the letter of the constitution; it was, equally, flagrantly against its spirit to abolish an important provision just when it was being invoked for the first time.[94] The episode underlined the propensity of the government to regard the constitution simply as an enabling device. This was illustrated once more in 1930, when legislation was passed renewing the eight-year term during which constitutional amendments could be enacted by ordinary legislation, and again in 1931, when a very severe public safety bill was enacted as a constitutional amendment because it would otherwise infringe individual rights guaranteed by the constitution.[95] Underlying this apparent cynicism was the Cosgrave government's loathing of Fianna Fáil, and its fear of militant republicanism. Such sentiments were understandable: de Valera in his new guise as leader of the opposition seemed as incorrigibly devious, irresponsible, and inconsistent as ever, while his party made no secret of its sympathies for violent republicanism, and by extension for those who had murdered Kevin O'Higgins and continued to threaten the lives of ministers and their families.[96] Fianna Fáil

[93] Farrell, *Lemass*, pp 26–31.

[94] Kohn, *Constitution*, pp 242–4.

[95] 1931/52 (17 Oct. 1931).

[96] After the assassination of O'Higgins, protection for ministers was increased considerably and responsibility transferred from the gardaí to a special army unit (N.A.I., S 5511A); Ronan Fanning, 'De Valera and the I.R.A., 1932–40' in J. P. O'Carroll and John A. Murphy (ed.), *De Valera and his times* (Cork, 1983), p. 162; Edwards (*De Valera*, pp 112–13) records de Valera's earlier interventions to block assassination attempts against MacNeill, O'Higgins, and Blythe.

reciprocated this hostility and suspicion in full measure. In the circumstances, some doubted whether Cumann na nGaedheal would ever bring itself to relinquish power, even if fairly defeated in an election. Concern was also expressed in other quarters: in the summer of 1931 the catholic bishops, primed by the government with alarmist police reports, issued a dramatic pastoral warning of the links between communism and mainstream republican organisations. This was plainly calculated, *inter alia*, to damage Fianna Fáil. In the autumn, the Garda commissioner Eoin O'Duffy began taking soundings among senior police and army officers about the possibility of staging a *coup d'état* should Fianna Fáil win the next election.[97] It was in this venomous climate that Cosgrave eventually sought a dissolution of the dáil in January 1932.

The election campaign of February 1932 was predictably bitter. Cumann na nGaedheal emphasised its achievements in office, stressed the folly of Fianna Fáil's economic policies, made great play with supposed links between Fianna Fáil, the I.R.A., and communism, and warned of the armed chaos into which the country would descend should de Valera win power. Fianna Fáil, with the open support of most republicans, campaigned on the abolition of the oath, retention in Ireland of the land annuities payable to Britain, and economic regeneration through a policy of thoroughgoing self-sufficiency. With the political temperature at fever pitch, the smaller parties and independents found it hard to make a mark. Nevertheless, they were to play a key role after the poll, because the election result was indecisive. Fianna Fáil emerged as by far the largest single party, seeing its vote rise by 9 per cent and its number of seats to seventy-two; Cumann na nGaedheal's vote dropped by 3 per cent and its number of seats fell to fifty-seven, while its allies in the Farmers' party took only three seats. Labour won just seven seats, but these allowed it the decisive say as to whether de Valera or Cosgrave would run the country. It was obvious that Fianna Fáil had more to offer Labour in return for the party's support in the dáil.[98]

Republicans were jubilant at the outcome of the election, although some feared it might be the prelude to an anti-Fianna Fáil coup.[99] Their opponents were shattered and appalled but, apart from the incorrigible General O'Duffy, no significant figure contemplated action in order to save the people from the consequences of their electoral folly. There was, perhaps, some consolation in the fact that de Valera would be dependent on the support of the Labour party, which had shown itself to be by any standards a modest and responsible

[97] Dermot Keogh, 'De Valera, the catholic church and the "Red scare", 1931–1932' in O'Carroll & Murphy, *De Valera & his times*, pp 134–59; Brady, *Guardians of the peace*, pp 167–9; interview with Col. Dan Bryan (who spent most of his career from 1922 to 1952 in army intelligence), July 1983.

[98] O'Leary, *Ir. elections*, p. 26; Gaughan, *Thomas Johnson*, p. 339.

[99] Longford & O'Neill, *De Valera*, p. 275.

force in parliamentary politics since 1922. Cosgrave's government prepared to leave office with reasonable grace, and de Valera to assume power with as little fuss as possible. The British government was unhappy at the prospect of dealing with a man ministers dismissed as an impractical, erratic mystic, but it could only watch from the sidelines, and for a time clung to the hope that Cosgrave would soon regain power.[100]

On 9 March 1932 de Valera was elected president of the executive council, as head of a minority Fianna Fáil government. The transfer of power was smooth and uneventful, as befitted the outcome of a democratic process. Both Cosgrave and de Valera displayed notable maturity and calm, in spite of the pressures from their supporters and the mutual animosities between the parties. There was no bloodletting, no exodus of civil servants or influx of placemen, no clearing out of the army or the police: even O'Duffy was allowed to stay on for a year.[101] De Valera showed not the slightest interest in modifying, let alone replacing, the machinery of government developed by his predecessor. On the contrary, it was just what he needed to pursue the constitutional and economic goals that differentiated Fianna Fáil from Cumann na nGaedheal. As head of the second largest party in the dáil, Cosgrave became leader of the opposition. Any hopes he and his party had of a quick return to power were dashed in the general election held early in 1933, when Fianna Fáil consolidated its hold on government. Cosgrave was not an inspirational figure in opposition: ten years in power had left him too experienced and responsible, too much the elder statesman to play the parliamentary firebrand. When he resigned as party leader in 1944, he wrote that 'we appealed to strength—and the others to weakness...in the sphere that we considered the least important but which was the most important we failed viz to retain popular support'.[102] This, and the marked personal animosity with which he—and his principal associates—continued to regard de Valera, 'the man they could never forgive', may give the impression of a rather desiccated, embittered figure, out of touch with national aspirations.[103] But it was the achievements in office of Cosgrave and his colleagues—constitutional, political, administrative and diplomatic—that made possible the constitutional, economic, and foreign policy adventures of the next decade. On his death in 1965, the dáil was asked to accept a 'departure from parliamentary precedent' in order to mark its 'appreciation of the work and influence of the late Mr Cosgrave in the history of the state',

[100] Paul Canning, *British policy and Ireland 1921–1941* (Oxford, 1985), p. 125; Deirdre McMahon, *Republicans and imperialists: Anglo–Irish relations in the 1930s* (New Haven and London, 1984), pp 36–7.
[101] Fanning, *Department of finance*, pp 216–17; Brady, *Guardians of the peace*, p. 169.
[102] Cosgrave to Hayes, 3 Feb. 1944 (U.C.D., A.D., Hayes papers, P53/258).
[103] Andrews, *Man of no property*, p. 232; Maryann Gialanella Valiulis, '"The man they could never forgive"—the view of the opposition: Eamon de Valera and the civil war' in O'Carroll & Murphy, *De Valera & his times*, pp 92–100.

his part in the struggle for independence, his capacity in government, 'the grace with which he handed over responsibility when the people so willed', and 'the dignity with which he carried out his duties as leader of the opposition'. These were 'the elements of a legacy which we in Ireland, and indeed people who value freedom and democracy everywhere, will forever cherish'.[104] That sober tribute came not from an old party colleague or successor, or even a 'revisionist historian'. The speaker was Seán Lemass.

[104] *Dáil Éireann deb.*, ccxviii, 1838–9 (17 Nov. 1965). Since the completion of this chapter John M. Regan's *The Irish counter-revolution 1921–1936* (Dublin, 1999) has appeared. This offers a challenging reinterpretation both of Cumann na nGaedheal in office and of Cosgrave's achievements as president of the executive council from 1922 to 1932. For an innovative comparative study of the consolidation of democratic norms in the new state, see Bill Kissane, *Explaining Irish democracy* (Dublin, 2002).

CHAPTER V

The republicanisation of Irish society, 1932–48

BRIAN GIRVIN

THE 1932 Irish general election took place on 16 February and by any estimation was a remarkable event. It was the first election to occur under stable political conditions and it followed five years of competitive party politics, the first since the state was established. The election took place against a threatening background of potential violence. The Army Comrades Association (A.C.A.) had been formed on 9 February to protect members of Cumann na nGaedheal, the outgoing government, from the assaults of paramilitaries. Moreover, many members of that party feared that the election itself would be disrupted, and they demanded action by the police to prevent any such eventuality.[1] In addition, economic conditions in the Irish Free State had deteriorated as a consequence of the worldwide depression then disrupting both the political and social equilibrium of many European states. The election campaign itself was characterised by deep hostility between Cumann na nGaedheal and Fianna Fáil. The parties were divided on virtually every issue: foreign policy, domestic reform, and constitutional change.

Despite the omens, the election, though hard fought, produced little actual violence. The results provided Fianna Fáil with enough support for de Valera to form his first government. The outcome was a clear rejection of the outgoing government as well as a qualified mandate for Fianna Fáil. Although the new government commanded a minority of seats in the dáil, Fianna Fáil was the largest party and, most importantly, could depend on the support of the Labour party on most issues. This placed the government in a strong position to dictate policy, but its position was enhanced by the quality of its ministers. Seán Lemass was the most radical appointment.[2] As minister for industry and commerce he committed the government to the transformation of the Irish economy. By contrast, Seán MacEntee as minister for finance was a conservative appointment.

[1] 'General election 1932—precautions against disorder', 9 Feb. 1932 (N.A.I., D.T., S8878)
[2] The most substantial biography of Lemass is John Horgan, *Seán Lemass: the enigmatic patriot* (Dublin, 1997).

However, de Valera dominated the cabinet and the party in terms of influence and prestige. He commanded the loyalty of his ministers as well as the rank and file of the party, a position that allowed him to stamp his own authority on what otherwise might have been an unstable cabinet. De Valera's strength was further enhanced by the sense of unity in Fianna Fáil and by the belief that the election provided an opportunity to implement a radical programme of government: one that would change the contours of Irish political life and give society a republican ethos.

Fianna Fáil not only harnessed the traditional republican vote in 1932, but also attracted new support on the basis of its socio-economic programme.[3] Reflecting wider European trends as well as the values of its republican predecessor, Sinn Féin, the party stressed the importance of economic self-sufficiency. The outgoing government had pursued conservative policies that often reflected the interests of just one section of the agricultural community, whereas Fianna Fáil urged the necessity for a radical approach to the formulation of national economic goals. Consequently the party gained votes from the urban poor and other groups not previously attracted by republicanism; its appeal was wider and deeper than that of Sinn Féin.

Fianna Fáil also scored over Cumann na nGaedheal in the appeal of its foreign policy. Although Cumann na nGaedheal had achieved a considerable amount of diplomatic autonomy for the new state in its negotiations with Britain, Fianna Fáil insisted that there was a need to break decisively with the treaty settlement and with Ireland's perceived subordination to the United Kingdom.

Despite the attractiveness of Fianna Fáil's agenda there were clear limitations on the new government's freedom of action in 1932. The incoming government had received a mandate to implement some changes, but not for changes that would lead to instability. During the election campaign Fianna Fáil had been sensitive to the charge that, if elected, it would undermine the achievements of the previous administration. Of particular concern to critics was the attitude that the party would take to the constitution and the institutions of the state. In its election manifesto Fianna Fáil played down the importance of partition, but promised to remove the oath of allegiance as unnecessary and divisive. However, the manifesto also made an explicit commitment to protect basic civil rights, and more strategically maintained that 'we shall not in the field of international relations exceed the mandate here asked for without again consulting the people'. Although the party may still have been, in Seán Lemass's terms, 'a slightly constitutional party' in 1932, it was also one that was willing to work within the existing constitutional structures to achieve change. The party's objectives were radical by Cumann

---

[3] This theme is developed by Richard Dunphy, *The making of Fianna Fáil power in Ireland, 1923–1948* (Oxford, 1995).

na nGaedheal standards, but the means of achieving them were to be grad-ualist.[4]

The success of Fianna Fáil at the election generated the conditions for the full legitimisation of Irish political institutions in an independent state. Most republicans, no matter how reluctantly, now accepted the existing institu-tions and electoral politics.[5] The lack of a clear majority did not prevent Fianna Fáil from acting decisively once in government. Moreover, the events of the following twelve months were to provide the basis for securing that elusive majority. In the interim the government was dependent on the good-will of the Labour party, whose support was forthcoming on a wide range of issues. The major reason for suspicion between the Labour party and Fianna Fáil in the past had been the latter's refusal to accept the treaty and the will of the electorate. On economic and social policy the two parties were close and in urban areas were often in competition for working-class votes. Common opposition to the conservative policies pursued by the outgoing government allowed the two parties to cooperate closely, though not to enter a formal coalition, as this would have created serious divisions within each organisation. In fact, Fianna Fáil's minority position gave the Labour party a virtual veto over policy, and the government had to be sensitive to this. De Valera insisted to his own supporters that the government would not move beyond its own mandate: it would implement the election manifesto, and no more.

In practice the government followed the evolutionary direction that de Valera had outlined in 1926; that the oath of allegiance would be removed and then a republican government would seek 'internal sovereignty', which, once secured, would lay the basis for a resolution of the questions of partition and reunification.[6]

The incoming government had a more expansive view of sovereignty than Cumann na nGaedheal, though it is worth remembering that from the outset the latter had adopted several symbols, including the tricolour, the harp without a crown, and distinctive uniforms for the armed forces which bore no traces of the British connection. However, for Fianna Fáil the constitution itself remained a symbol of British rule in Ireland, and as such had to be transformed. But the party's understanding of sovereignty also included an alternative view of how the state and society should be organised, embracing foreign policy, the constitution, the economy, and national culture. Its aim in 1932 was what may be characterised as the republicanisation of Irish society.

---

[4] 'Election address, 1931' (U.C.D., A.D., FitzGerald papers, P80/1126); Fianna Fáil elec-tion manifesto, 9 Feb. 1932, in Maurice Moynihan (ed.), *Speeches and statements by Eamon de Valera, 1917–73* (Dublin, 1980), pp 189–91.

[5] Jeffrey Prager, *Building democracy in Ireland* (Cambridge, 1986), pp 185–92.

[6] Moynihan, op. cit., pp 134–5, for the 1926 speech; see also speech by de Valera, 8 Nov. 1932 (pp 223–30).

Freedom, it was believed, remained limited unless all aspects of policy were controlled by an Irish parliament answerable only to the Irish people. The 1922 constitution limited that sovereignty, as did the oath of allegiance and the role of the crown in Irish foreign policy. Ireland's overwhelming dependence on trade with Britain in addition was suspect because it cramped the freedom of action of Irish policy-makers; Irish welfare was subordinated to the dictates of foreign markets.[7] This last preoccupation was not unique to Ireland: a desire to avoid dependence on foreign markets was shared by many governments in the 1930s.

The policy package announced by de Valera after forming his government accordingly concentrated on enhancing Irish sovereignty. Some aspects were symbolic, such as diminishing the office of governor general by merging it with that of president of the executive council; more substantive was the decision to introduce a constitutional amendment to remove the oath of allegiance. The decision to withhold payment of the land annuities, implemented in June 1932, provoked the British government to impose a 20 per cent duty on Irish imports to make up the loss.[8] The Irish government retaliated with the emergency imposition of duties act,[9] and these exchanges marked the beginning of the economic war between the two states. The domestic economy was also tackled. Lemass quickly introduced a policy of industrial protection to generate the conditions for the rapid expansion of Irish-controlled industry. The control of manufactures act[10] was introduced to control foreign access to investment opportunities in Ireland. The department of industry and commerce quickly gained control of most sectors of the Irish economy and dictated the terms under which investment and expansion could take place. Agricultural policy was also quickly transformed. Traditionally, the cattle sector had dominated Irish agriculture; now, the government offered incentives for farmers to move into other areas, especially cereal production. The emphasis was on self-sufficiency and on diversification generally. The 1932 housing act[11] provided funds for house-building by local authorities in the belief that this would enhance both employment and welfare. These changes were supplemented by alterations in unemployment benefits and social welfare; in general permitting easier and more liberal access to state benefits.[12] These policies coincided with and reinforced a conviction within Fianna Fáil that a new age had begun: one in which a

---

[7] Brian Girvin, *Between two worlds* (Dublin, 1989), pp 88–101.

[8] The land annuities were paid by Irish farmers to the British government in respect of monies owed for the purchase by occupiers of their farms from the landlords under the later land legislation (above, vi, 275–6; see also above, pp 114, 124).

[9] 1932/16 (23 July 1932).

[10] 1932/21 (29 Oct. 1932).

[11] 1932/19 (3 Aug. 1932).

[12] Girvin, *Between two worlds*, pp 88–105; Mary E. Daly, *Industrial development and Irish national identity, 1922–1939* (Dublin, 1992), pp 59–102.

sovereign Ireland would finally break the historic connection with the United Kingdom and establish a specifically Irish dimension to social life and the economy.[13]

The break in continuity between Fianna Fáil and Cumann na nGaedheal was radical both in intent and practice. In virtually every field of policy the new government disowned the passive and conservative approach of its predecessor. The changes introduced in Ireland from 1932 have much in common with counter-cyclical policies introduced by democratic governments elsewhere. A radical response to the depression, job creation, enhanced welfare provision, and state intervention were all features of reformist governments in the United States and Scandinavia during the decade.[14] Ireland had in common with a number of these countries a commitment to the regulation of industrial development and the management of the economy that went well beyond what had been deemed acceptable during the 1920s. The 1930s, unlike the 1920s, were politically and economically unstable, and this instability affected both the left and the right, although in different ways depending on the prevailing circumstances. The National government in the United Kingdom, though elected on the basis of orthodox economic policy, moved towards more interventionist strategies under pressure of the recession, though not towards redistribution of wealth.

None of this would have necessarily assured the government of the majority it gained in the January 1933 election, called by de Valera in the hope of renewing his mandate and, if possible, securing a majority of seats in the dáil. The party increased its share of the vote by over 5 per cent to give it an overall majority which, with continuing support from the Labour party, assured de Valera of the means he required to move beyond his limited objectives of March 1932. This was an impressive achievement at a time when electoral turnout was increasing. At the September 1927 election 67.9 per cent of the eligible electorate voted: this figure increased to 75.3 per cent in 1932 and to 80.4 per cent in 1933. The vote for the opposition declined as a proportion of the total. Cumann na nGaedheal suffered most with a decline of 4 per cent, though this was in part compensated for by the success of the Centre party, in effect a farmers' party, which gained 7.2 per cent of the vote and 11 seats, some of which were gained from Cumann na nGaedheal.[15] In contrast to Cumann na nGaedheal it was a genuinely mass party, drawing support into a tightly knit organisation. Its strength rested on its ability to

---

[13] MacEntee to de Valera, 18 Mar. 1932 (U.C.D., A.D., MacEntee papers P67/94 (1)). See Deirdre McMahon, *Republicans and imperialists* (New Haven and London, 1984) for a balanced view of the economic war and of the realistic options available to the government at this time.

[14] See Peter Gourevitch, *Politics in hard times* (Ithaca, N.Y., 1986), for a comparative discussion.

[15] Calculated from Cornelius O'Leary, *Irish elections, 1918–1977* (Dublin, 1979), pp 100–02; Thomas T. Mackie and Richard Rose, *The international almanac of electoral history* (2nd ed., London, 1982), pp 196–9.

compete effectively within the national community. Previous mass organisations placed an extraordinarily high premium on the absence of competition
within the nation, whereas Fianna Fáil benefited from the divisions that
existed within the new state. Fianna Fáil can be treated as a party of mass
integration, a political form that distinguishes it from the cadre-style party of
its predecessors. As such, the party shares its organisational success with
other contemporary European parties, especially those on the left. The
reasons for Fianna Fáil's victory were various, but superior organisation and
attractive policies were crucial. The 1933 election was decisive and marked a
turning-point in modern Irish politics. It confirmed the entry of the poor
and those previously unrepresented into political life, and their electoral
importance.

THE weakness of the opposition was palpable after January 1933, but was
already in evidence during 1932. The Cumann na nGaedheal party was ill
suited for opposition, and, as Richard Mulcahy admitted, the party had been
unaware of the shift in public opinion and had not recognised the attractiveness of Fianna Fáil. Mulcahy conceded the political and organisational superiority of Fianna Fáil, adding regretfully that 'the politicians have beaten the
statesmen, and however unpalatable it may be, it was the fault of the statesmen'.[16] Cumann na nGaedheal was hostile to most of the policies pursued by
the government, especially those concerning the treaty settlement, with
which Cumann na nGaedheal was closely associated. It remained opposed
to the new social and economic policies on conservative grounds. In fact,
Cumann na nGaedheal was in a dilemma. Criticism of Fianna Fáil made it
all too easy for the government to portray the opposition as the upholder of
British interests in Ireland. The revelation in April 1932 that Cosgrave had
secretly agreed in 1923 to pay the annuities made the charge more plausible.
Cosgrave recognised the danger that Cumann na nGaedheal would develop a
pro-British image, and distanced himself from Desmond FitzGerald's view
that the British were right to impose duties while the annuities were not
being paid. It was, Cosgrave added, 'not for us to make the case'.[17] The
dilemma was not to be resolved for some years. The party continued to
pursue a negative and conservative approach to the government throughout
most of the 1930s.[18]

By the end of 1932, throughout much of 1933, and into 1934, as Irish
politics were transformed, Cumann na nGaedheal was a party without secure
moorings. This allowed the government to consolidate its political power.

---

[16] Undated memo in file marked Mar./May 1933 (Mulcahy papers, P7b/90 (31)).
[17] Cumann na nGaedheal party minutes 20 Apr., 2 June, 9 Nov. 1932 (U.C.D., A.D., P39MIN/1/3).
[18] Cosgrave to Michael Hayes, 21 Sept. 1932 (U.C.D., A.D., FitzGerald papers, P80/1111);
Cumann na nGaedheal policy on tariffs, 1932 (P80/1113).

The opposition's warnings about communism and the threat of anarchy failed to make a significant impact. Indeed, the government was well placed to criticise the opposition's association with the A.C.A. and the National Guard, while insisting on its own role as the guarantor of the parliamentary system. Cumann na nGaedheal continued to warn that the government and republican militants were conspiring to destroy parliamentary institutions; but in practice the government's conduct belied such charges and made it difficult for them to stick.[19]

These years were uncertain ones for both the government and the opposition. The threat of violence from militant republicans and other paramilitaries was at times real. This explained the formation of the A.C.A. to defend speakers during the 1932 and 1933 election campaigns, at a time when some openly denied Cumann na nGaedheal's right to free speech. In this the A.C.A. was successful, and by the time of the second Fianna Fáil administration the basic right of association was recognised by both government and opposition. Although this may not have been true of the I.R.A., the actions of the A.C.A. and of the government ensured the relatively peaceful organisation of elections and political activity.

The rapid changes taking place in the Irish political system were accelerated after Fianna Fáil's electoral triumph in January 1933. On the opposition side Eoin O'Duffy's dismissal as police commissioner was followed in July 1933 by the transformation of the A.C.A. into the National Guard, known as the 'Blueshirts'. The National Guard was declared illegal in August, and subsequently a new party, soon to be known as Fine Gael, was formed out of Cumann na nGaedheal, the Centre party, and the National Guard, with O'Duffy as leader, in September 1933. These developments were prompted, in part, by economic difficulties. By 1933 the economic conflict with the United Kingdom over the annuities had reached crisis point with the effective closing of British markets to Irish cattle. The wealthy farmers who formed the electoral backbone of the opposition parties attempted to use the A.C.A. to confront the government. It is difficult to know whether the threatened march on the dáil on 13 August, ostensibly to commemorate Griffith, Collins, and O'Higgins, was anything more than bluster on O'Duffy's part, but given the rise of fascism elsewhere in Europe the threat had to be taken seriously by the government, and the march was banned. O'Duffy backed down and cancelled it.[20]

---

[19] 'Notes for speakers', Nov. 1932 (FitzGerald papers, P80/1121); policy in this area can be followed in Mulcahy papers P7b/90 (43), 30 Mar. 1933; Cumann na nGaedheal party minutes (P39MIN1/3 (1932), P39MIN/1/4 (1933)).
[20] U.C.D., A.D., Blythe papers, P24/629; Eoin O'Duffy, *An outline of the political, social and economic policy of Fine Gael (United Ireland)* (Dublin, 1934) (opening address at first annual Fine Gael ard-fheis, 8 Feb. 1934); 'A.C.A. policy' (P24/649), a brief discussion of the early dynamic behind the movement.

The failure of the Blueshirt movement, and indeed of the Irish right generally during the 1930s, can be explained in several ways. It would be a mistake to consider fascism as inherently alien to Irish susceptibilities. Fascism in Europe had attracted its militants from the young and the disaffected, but its success was dependent on an alliance with traditional conservative elites. The Blueshirt movement failed on both counts. It was Fianna Fáil that succeeded in attracting the militants and the disaffected, besides which its brand of nationalism operated as a force for integration rather than destabilisation. Moreover, in Ireland the right was restrained by its own record in suppressing militant nationalism, though O'Duffy did attempt to develop a form of right-wing republicanism towards the end of 1934. It was, therefore, the governing party that mobilised the marginal elements in society and incorporated them into a political party that had some similarities with the mass fascist movements, yet operated on democratic rather than totalitarian lines. The political opportunities for fascism were thus quite limited, and to the extent that it generated any significant support this can be accounted for by the conflict over the annuities and the collapse in the living standards of the bigger farmers, who represented only one section of opposition supporters. In so far as there was violence and a rejection of the government and the rule of law, this tended to be concentrated in those areas most affected by the farming crisis; other sections of the rural community either supported the government or were indifferent to the plight of the prosperous farmers.[21]

But perhaps the most striking difference between Ireland and continental European countries was the extent to which the conservative elites remained committed to parliamentary methods and the rule of law. This was the result of a conscious decision on the part of the Fine Gael leadership. O'Duffy's anti-parliamentary antics proved increasingly unpopular and during August and September 1934, after a poor showing in the local elections, the party elite moved against him. Cosgrave admitted that the elections had been a setback for the new party, and he blamed the party itself: 'We have to teach the people to understand that if they vote wrong the opposition cannot pull the chestnuts out of the fire for them. Fianna Fáil is neither honest, nor democratic, nor national. But we have not succeeded in getting that over to the people.'[22] The choice for the party after this was either to accept Fianna Fáil's democratic right to govern or move towards some form of

---

[21] Andrew Orridge, 'The Blueshirts and the "economic war": a study of Ireland in the context of dependency theory' in *Political Studies*, xxxi, no. 3 (1983), pp 351–69. The dimensions of non-parliamentary right-wing politics during the interwar years are assessed by Stanley C. Payne, *Fascism: comparison and definition* (Madison, Wisc., 1980). Payne distinguishes between radical right-wing politics and traditional elites embracing authoritarian methods to combat the left (pp 7–17).

[22] Cosgrave, 'Notes of speech to national executive', 30 Aug. 1934 (U.C.D., A.D., Mulcahy papers P7b/92(4)).

extra-parliamentary confrontation. When O'Duffy suggested urging farmers to withhold the new, reduced annuities, Cosgrave delivered a formidable challenge: he warned the party executive that anti-democratic behaviour would play into the hands of the government and allow de Valera, 'the son of a Mexican', to bring in a 'Mexican state'. According to Cosgrave, 'there is a courage that is higher than physical courage and it is moral courage. We have to make up our minds "are we going to stand for law?"' He continued, asserting that the government was strong and the opposition was weak and what the demands would lead to was a dictatorship that would destroy the opposition. In conclusion he insisted that 'the people have the right to control the ballot boxes', and that this should not change.[23]

Towards the end of 1934, after government moves to curb the I.R.A., many of Fine Gael's worries about Fianna Fáil's commitment to constitutional methods had evaporated, and the differences between the other leaders and O'Duffy came to a head. O'Duffy resented his colleagues' criticism of his anti-parliamentary rhetoric, and he submitted his letter of resignation on 20 September, still insisting that Fianna Fáil was in decline. His behaviour had already prompted the resignation of Professor James Hogan as vice-president on the grounds that O'Duffy was not following party policy and was moving dangerously close to extra-parliamentary politics. This induced the party to act decisively against O'Duffy. At a special meeting of the party executive on 21 and 22 September the main issues were discussed and O'Duffy's resignation accepted, while the League of Youth was placed under the control of Commandant Edmund Cronin and reorganised.[24]

The Fine Gael party was not seriously affected by the O'Duffy resignation, but it did continue to encounter long-term problems that plagued it till the end of the 1940s. By refusing to move along O'Duffy's road the party had secured its allegiance to parliamentary democracy, but may also have restricted its electoral appeal. As a constitutional party its only role was that of a conservative party, albeit a conservative party that was often in agreement with much of what the government was doing. As early as November 1933 in a review of policy the party had moved much closer to the republicanisation of Ireland then associated with the government. Despite some reservations on industrial, welfare, and foreign policy, the difference between the two parties was slight. Fianna Fáil's arguments were largely accepted, though Fine Gael would have adopted a more cautious approach in

[23] 'Cosgrave's speech to national executive', 30 Aug. 1934 (P7b/92(4)), circulated to party branches.
[24] 'Special meeting of national executive', 21 Sept. 1934 (P7b/92 (21–2)); adoption of resolution on resignation, 22 Sept. 1934; Lee, *Ire. 1912–85*, pp 178–84. Paul Bew, Ellen Hazelkorn, and Henry Patterson, *The dynamics of Irish politics* (London, 1989), pp 48–72, assesses the fascist potential in the Blueshirt movement and its significance for Irish politics; see also Maurice Manning, *The Blueshirts* (Dublin, 1970), and most recently Mike Cronin, *The Blueshirts and Irish politics* (Dublin, 1997).

implementing the 'republicanisation' programme. Fine Gael continued to stress the importance of agriculture, though it was now admitted that there were other paths to development. And Fine Gael remained a national (and a nationalist) party, despite the gibes of the government. But with Fianna Fáil in power and helping to set the political agenda, the scope for a conservative party was limited. By 1936 Fine Gael T.D.s were reporting on the weakening of the party organisation, even in its electoral heartland; and the ard-fheis of that year gave the impression of an extremely conservative party on the defensive against a confident government.[25]

THE republicanisation of Ireland had three components: political, constitutional, and diplomatic. The political was the first to be asserted, though this was closely associated with the constitutional. The economic war provided the opportunity to reduce Ireland's dependence on the United Kingdom and to reorganise the economy along lines more congenial to Lemass's developmental nationalism. In industrial and agricultural policy there was a marked change in direction, with the emphasis now on import substitution. Whereas previously the government had played a passive role in economic policy, Fianna Fáil provided an interventionist framework within which Irish sovereignty could be asserted in economic and social policy. It may be that in terms of free-trade economics the policies followed were inefficient and irrational, but the government was more concerned with the fact that under existing circumstances any policy that depended on external markets for success was open to unpredictable influences. In a protected economy policy could be dictated by national concerns and implemented by national policy-makers.

Social policy was determined by the same concerns. A national policy that ignored the poor or the disadvantaged rested uneasily with a belief in the citizenship of all. Increased taxation could be justified on the grounds that it was in the national interest to have a welfare policy, and that the wealthy should share some of their advantages with the less well-off. This inevitably meant challenging the influence of the department of finance. This department was considered, with some justification, to be the most conservative agency in government, being strongly committed to the economic and trading links with the United Kingdom and to the attendant restrictive financial policy. Equally, the government's priorities meant that agriculture was no longer the main determining factor in government policy. Even within the agricultural sphere, the government's concerns were not necessar-

---

[25] 'Draft heads of policy', 9 Nov. 1933 (P39MIN/1/2); resolutions for Fine Gael ard-fheis, 1936 (P24/638); 16 Feb. 1935, 12 Mar. 1936, 16 July 1936, where the weakening of party organisation is detailed (P39MIN/1/2). Fine Gael's refusal to associate with the anti-constitutional right should be contrasted with the conduct of conservatives in many European states (Martin Blinkhorn (ed.), *Fascists and conservatives* (London, 1990)).

ily those of the hitherto dominant exporting sector of agriculture, and this
was reflected in such initiatives as the establishment of the Irish Sugar Company and the 1936 agricultural wages act, which set minimum rates for farm
workers.[26] In addition, the number of new companies opened, the number of
houses built with government aid, and the panoply of controls and inducements testified to the transformation of public policy and the agencies of
power within society and the state.[27] The Fianna Fáil government could
claim, with considerable justification, that it had republicanised domestic
policy and created an institutional framework where the requirements of the
Irish state and of its citizens would take priority over all other considerations.[28]

The government's success between 1932 and 1936 can be appreciated at a
number of levels. The first is clearly legislative: its activism in these terms
was unprecedented. The reform programme had far-reaching consequences
for the state, economy, and society. The government also succeeded in
defeating the challenge to parliamentary democracy from the Blueshirt movement, and after a number of high-profile murders orchestrated by the I.R.A.,
that organisation was proscribed in 1936. This was a significant step, given
the close ties that had existed between Fianna Fáil and radical republicans
while the party was in opposition. By that time too the crisis in Irish politics
had abated, partly as a result of government successes, but also because the
ongoing economic war fostered a sense of national unity. The alliance between the Labour party and Fianna Fáil continued through 1936, but the gap
between Fine Gael and the government also narrowed. Fine Gael continued
to criticise the government, but it was from within the consensus established
by Fianna Fáil. MacEntee also recognised the changes and acknowledged the
contribution of the Cosgrave government to the stabilisation of democratic
politics.[29]

Fianna Fáil was never fully united behind the radical economic and social
policies identified with Lemass. Though much of the legislation passed between 1932 and 1936 had his imprint, he was not politically dominant. The
department of finance fought a successful rearguard action against his most
ambitious plans and was often in a position to obstruct his department's
proposals. MacEntee became an enthusiastic exponent of his own finance
department's ethos of low taxation and the primacy of agricultural exports.

[26] 1936/53 (28 Nov. 1936).
[27] Girvin, *Between two worlds*, pp 105–20, for more detailed discussion. For the weakening
of the department of finance, see Ronan Fanning, *The Irish department of finance, 1922–58*
(Dublin, 1978), pp 216–64. See also Daniel Hoctor, *The department's story: a history of the
department of agriculture* (Dublin, 1971), pp 166–98; Raymond Crotty, *Irish agricultural production* (Cork, 1966), pp 133–57.
[28] See Daly, *Industrial development*, pp 75–153, for discussion.
[29] MacEntee to secretary of Fianna Fáil, 27 Jan. 1936 (U.C.D., A.D., MacEntee papers,
P67/453).

He was consistently sceptical about the effectiveness of protection, and embraced the conservative fiscal orthodoxy of the right and of his own department.[30] These differences became more important once stability had returned to the political system in 1936, but even so the critics of the new policies were not demanding a return to the pre-1932 position. The attacks on tariffs, for instance, were less a criticism of the principle of protection than of inefficiency and the burden of taxation. Moreover, as long as the conflict with Britain continued the government could not be attacked too strongly for fear of jeopardising negotiations with Britain.

Meanwhile, the republicanisation of Irish society went hand in hand with the cultivation of a more catholic and Gaelic identity. When Fianna Fáil came to power in 1932 MacEntee had boasted of the party's catholic nature, and while such claims were not made regularly, they were in keeping with the public's strong religious sentiments, so much in evidence at the time of the Eucharistic Congress later in 1932. No less than its predecessors, Fianna Fáil believed that 'Irish' was synonymous with 'catholic'. The contradiction between such a view and 'secular' republicanism was rarely noted, and Fianna Fáil did not recognise the fears that might be generated by the close association between the state and the catholic church. Though Fianna Fáil was not anti-democratic, it does not appear to have had a strong attachment to liberal values. Under the new government a growing and more systematic catholicisation of many aspects of the political culture was in evidence; nor was this taken to be in conflict with the government's commitment to republicanism. The *Irish Press*, controlled by the de Valera family, was an ideological arm of Fianna Fáil, overt in its catholicism, giving considerable space to catholic affairs, thought, and sentiment. The link between catholicism and nationalism was almost unconscious; it did not prevent the paper condemning as 'sectarian' the perceived connections between unionism and protestantism in Northern Ireland.[31]

Education in the Free State remained under denominational control, which in most cases meant catholic control. But catholic sentiment became more pervasive and influential in educational policy during the 1930s. Cumann na nGaedheal had given a written commitment to the catholic hierarchy that vocational education would not be permitted to encroach on the secondary school system, which was directly controlled by the church. Each successive government maintained this commitment, though it could be argued that

---

[30] Professor Seán Busteed (U.C.C.) to MacEntee, 28 Nov. 1932, criticising the latter's pessimistic views of the economy (U.C.D., A.D., MacEntee papers, P67/107); Fanning, *Department of finance*, pp 244–64. The MacEntee papers are replete with notes and memos reflecting this conservative pessimism.

[31] The comment on the *Irish Press* draws on non-editorial matter for the 1930s consulted on a random basis. See Whyte, *Ch. & state* (1971), pp 1–61, for a discussion of religious issues during the 1920s and 1930s.

such an arrangement worked to the disadvantage of successive generations of Irish people. Although the vocational schools were in theory secular, Fianna Fáil issued a memorandum in 1941 that religious instruction should be mandatory.[32]

This interpenetration of the religious with the institutional was a reflection of the strength of religious values in a homogeneous society. By 1936 the Roman Catholic population of the state comprised 93.4 per cent of the whole, while all others stood at 6.6 per cent. The equivalent figure for non-catholics in 1911 in the area that later comprised the Irish Free State had been 10.4 per cent; clearly southern protestantism was in decline, though it should be remembered that much of the decline stemmed from the exodus of army and other personnel who left Ireland after independence. In educational terms protestants were not penalised by the department of education (in some cases they actually received preferential treatment, and were no less firm than catholics in defending their own denominational control); nevertheless, the reality was that a significant number of non-catholics did not find the new state's catholic ethos congenial, and emigrated. This in turn increased the extent to which the culture reflected the dominant religion.[33] Public manifestations of anticlericalism were virtually absent (though anticlericalism was latent in some circles), while personal piety and mass participation in religious ritual demonstrated catholicism's popularity. For members of minority religious groups this popularity could be perceived as triumphalism, and they found themselves increasingly marginalised by the dominant ethos.

Fianna Fáil's comfortable relations with the church would not necessarily have been predicted in 1932, when there was a degree of suspicion on both sides. However, in a relatively short period of time each side satisfied the other of its credentials. On the major issues of concern to the hierarchy, the government proved willing to legislate where necessary in a fashion acceptable to the church. The criminal law amendment act of 1935[34] prohibited the sale and importation of contraceptives, while the government continued to apply the censorship act introduced in 1929.

THE 1922 constitution rested uneasily with Fianna Fáil's commitment to republicanism. Despite Cumann na nGaedheal's insistence that the treaty

[32] Donald Harman Akenson, *A mirror to Kathleen's face: education in independent Ireland. 1922–1960* (Montreal, 1975), pp 93–108, provides a general survey.

[33] Brian Girvin, 'Social change and moral politics: the Irish constitutional referendum 1983' in *Political Studies*, xxxiv, no. 1 (1986), pp 61–81, discusses the relationship between church and people and its impact on politicians. Religion was not the only issue that 'pushed' non-catholics out of the new state, but it was one of the most overt expressions of the new order. The causal relationships between religion, nationalism, and imperial sentiment are extremely complex and cannot be analysed in detail here.

[34] 1935/6 (28 Feb. 1935).

provided the means to achieve a fuller freedom and that the constitution was more than adequate to protect the individual and the state, Fianna Fáil was never reconciled to it. De Valera was committed to its gradual but thorough emasculation. The abolition of the oath of allegiance was followed at the end of 1933 by a number of constitutional amendments that further limited and restricted the crown in Irish affairs. More radical was the Irish nationality and citizenship act in 1935, which sought to define Irish citizenship more clearly, as well as the status of those born in Northern Ireland. The related aliens act (1935) stipulated that all persons other than citizens of the Free State were aliens (British subjects were exempted). Although this legislation fell short of declaring a republic, de Valera's claim that it brought that objective closer had considerable validity.[35]

The abdication crisis in Britain provided de Valera with the means to remove all references to the crown and the governor general from the constitution. Moreover, the introduction of the Executive Authority (External Relations) Bill and its immediate enactment confined the role of the crown to external matters, excluding the monarch from any influence over domestic Irish matters, thus laying the basis for more radical reform in the future. Although de Valera stretched the fabric of the constitution in 1936, the overall structure remained intact.[36]

The decision to introduce a new constitution was the logical extension of these moves. The original decision appears to have been made in 1935, and the cabinet agreed in June 1936 to communicate the outline of the constitution to Edward VIII.[37] The preliminary details of the document were established in early 1937, following which various revisions were made prior to the publication of the final draft on 1 May.[38] The evidence suggests that de Valera himself was responsible for drawing up the constitution, consulting individuals only on a bilateral basis, and, for certain key sections, consulting no one. Although often described as a liberal-democratic document, the new constitution did not compare well with its predecessors. In certain areas it was restrictive rather than permissive. Article 40, concerned with personal rights, did not fundamentally extend the rights contained in the 1922 constitution. The articles concerned with the family, education, private property,

---

[35] 1935/13, 14 (10 Apr. 1935); McMahon, *Republicans & imperialists*, pp 140–43; 'Irish Republic: motion re declaration . . . 1935' (N.A.I, D.T., S6584).

[36] 1936/58 (12 Dec. 1936); memo on abdication crisis (undated, but late 1936 from internal evidence) (U.C.D., A.D., MacEntee papers, P67/115); MacEntee to de Valera, 20 Jan. 1937 (P67/118).

[37] 'Progressive development of the constitution' (N.A.I., D.T., S9748) contains a copy of CAB 7/329 (5 June 1936) from S8946, which at the time of writing was not obtainable in N.A.I.

[38] The most detailed discussion of the constitution is Dermot Keogh, 'The Irish constitutional revolution: an analysis of the making of the constitution' in Frank Litton (ed.), *The constitution of Ireland, 1937–1987* (special issue of *Administration*, xxxv, no. 4 (1988)), pp 4–84; Lee, *Ire. 1912–85*, pp 201–11.

religion, and social policy (articles 41–5) reflected in large part the teaching and doctrine of the catholic church. The indirect influence of papal encyclicals was detectable in a number of these articles. The preamble, the prohibition on divorce, and the relationship between the church and the state in education were essentially catholic in character. Admittedly there were some, including Cardinal MacRory, who wished to see an even more decidedly catholic gloss on the document, but the fact that de Valera resisted this, and the demand for a concordat with the holy see, should not lead to the conclusion that the constitution was liberal in tone or objective. Indeed, it could be argued that while it was democratic in origin, the 1937 constitution possessed a theocratic intellectual framework, and may be more properly regarded as a democratic-republican document rather than a liberal one.

In later years it was articles 44.1.2 and 44.1.3, recognising the special position of the catholic church and also recognising other designated religions, that caused most controversy. At the time of publication public opinion was satisfied with these articles, although there had been considerable debate between de Valera and his clerical consultants over them. Cardinal MacRory, Fr John Charles McQuaid (the future archbishop of Dublin), and possibly also the pope, objected to the wording and particularly to the recognition of the non-catholic churches.[39] So concerned was de Valera with this controversy that he sent an emissary to the Vatican to obtain sanction for his version of the constitution. In the event the most that could be extracted was neutrality: the pope would neither approve nor condemn it. MacRory remained unhappy with the wording, though neither he nor the pope criticised the constitution openly.[40] The denominational nature of several of the articles provoked little criticism from the protestant churches in the Free State, and it is only fair to note that in devising the constitution de Valera did consult protestant as well as catholic churchmen on the same bilateral basis.

The other area of the constitution that departed radically from its predecessor was the section on the state and the nation (articles 1–3). Article 1 asserted that the Irish nation affirmed its inalienable right to choose its own form of government. Articles 2 and 3 made explicit claims concerning the national territory and citizenship. Article 2 stated the nationalist view that the national territory was the island of Ireland, and accordingly that all inhabitants of the island were part of the nation. Article 3 recognised the political reality of partition and affirmed that the constitution would apply only to the twenty-six counties till such time as the island was reunited. Article 9.2 supplemented articles 2 and 3 with the claim that 'fidelity to the nation and loyalty to the state are fundamental political duties of all citizens'. These articles provided the framework for a strongly nationalistic sense of

[39] For McQuaid and the constitution, see John Cooney, *John Charles McQuaid: ruler of catholic Ireland* (Dublin, 1999), ch. 8.
[40] Keogh, 'The Irish constitutional revolution', pp 43–53.

citizenship, one consonant with Fianna Fáil's conception of nationhood.[41] The 1937 constitution was thus a republican constitution, even though de Valera was reluctant to describe it as such while partition endured. But the articles in question also effectively, if not formally, broke the link with the empire. They left no room for compromise with unionists and they undermined the slow progress made by the Cumann na nGaedheal government, which had at least been seeking through negotiation to find grounds for accommodation with the northern unionists within the empire.[42]

Thus the 1937 constitution enshrined an illiberal form of nationalism, invoking indefeasible rights that left unionists no legitimate destiny outside the Irish nation. Other countries, especially in central and eastern Europe, were also making irredentist claims at this time. However, the Irish government, though refusing to yield on the principle of the matter, stopped short at resorting to violence to achieve its goals. In the event the articles provided a further obstacle to good relations with northern unionists, nor did they help the northern minority.

THE new constitution was also criticised for its treatment of women. In an abrasive article in the *Irish Independent* the journalist Gertrude Gaffney condemned articles 40 and 41 on the grounds that they would diminish the status of Irish women and place them in an inferior position. She compared de Valera to Hitler in his attitude to women, and highlighted the regressive intention behind the conditions of employment act of 1936,[43] which she believed had been framed to exclude women from the workforce. For her, and for other contemporary critics, the constitution was part of a systematic process whereby women would be forced to accept an inferior status in society, one that would explicitly restrict their role to that of wife and mother.[44] Gaffney compared the new constitution unfavourably with the

---

[41] The continuing influence of these articles was reflected in the supreme court decision in the McGimpsey v. Ireland case (1990), which determined that all those resident on the island of Ireland were Irish citizens under the meaning of article 9.2. This appears to have been de Valera's intention. As part of the implementation of the British–Irish agreement of Apr. 1998, articles 2 and 3 were revised to drop the territorial claim to N.I. in Dec. 1999.

[42] Clare O'Halloran, *Partition and the limits of Irish nationalism* (Dublin, 1987), pp 174–7, takes a different view of the intention of articles 2 and 3. But it is doubtful if de Valera thought that they were 'an aspiration rather than a realistic ambition' (p. 175). Indeed, in the circumstances of the period, the articles may be seen as embodying the key republican claim over N.I. and attempting to realise this gradually within a constitutional framework. De Valera and Fianna Fáil continued to take the claim seriously during the 1938 negotiations with the United Kingdom and later. In Oct. 1938 de Valera returned to the claim in an interview with the *Evening Standard* and insisted that his aim was to end partition, which remained the only major outstanding point of difference between the two states (reported in *Irish Press*, 18 Oct. 1938).

[43] 1936/2 (14 Feb. 1936). See also below, pp 873–4.

[44] *Irish Independent*, 7 May 1937, p. 5. The conditions of employment act gave power, *inter alia*, to the minister for industry and commerce to exclude women from any industry. However, the demand to exclude women from certain industries arose from some sections of the trade union movement, and was not the sole initiative of the minister or de Valera.

relevant sections of the 1922 constitution and with the 1916 declaration, claiming that these recognised the equal worth of women, whereas the constitution placed them in a special category. Nor was Gaffney an isolated or eccentric critic. Her criticism was echoed by the nationalist historian Mary Hayden, representing the women graduates of the N.U.I. This statement called for the deletion of articles 40, 41, and 45 from the draft constitution, and the reinsertion of article 9 of the existing constitution, on the grounds that it was more adequate to the needs of women. Similar criticism appeared in the newspapers from Mary Kettle, who chaired the Joint Committee of Women's Societies, and Louie Bennett of the Irish Women Workers Union. The *Irish Press* unleashed a vitriolic counter-attack, claiming that Kettle's accusations amounted to no more than 'gratuitous libel', sneering at the Joint Committee, and calling for affiliated organisations to acknowledge publicly whether Kettle spoke for them or not. With Louie Bennett and Mary Hayden the paper was more careful; after all, Bennett's union was sympathetic to Fianna Fáil and Hayden had long associations with the nationalist movement. Yet over none of these issues was the *Irish Press*, or indeed de Valera, prepared to give ground. When de Valera met delegations from the Joint Committee of Women's Societies and other women's organisations on 14 May he was careful to claim that he did not share their anxiety concerning the articles, insisting instead that his purpose was to ensure that there would be no discrimination against women in terms of citizenship or the franchise. In fact de Valera was probably quite justified in this claim, but that was beside the point; the articles in question were condemned for their social consequences, rather than for their effect on women's political rights. There is no evidence that de Valera wished to support any restrictions in this area.[45]

De Valera was a conservative on women's issues, but in this he was at one with most of his party. And having finalised the drafting process he was not inclined to change his mind. A revolt within the party or an attack by the church would have affected him, but he had already covered himself for this eventuality. In a personal letter to him, his biographer Dorothy Macardle associated herself with the views of Louie Bennett and criticised the existing draft. She went so far as to offer alternative wording for article 45.4.2, claiming that while the conditions of employment act could not be dismantled, an amendment along the lines she suggested would allay fears and 'leave the way open for advanced legislation'. Otherwise, Macardle concluded, 'as the constitution stands, I do not see how anyone holding advanced views on

[45] *Irish Press*, 11 May 1937, editorial 'A gratuitous libel'; correspondence over the names of Mary Hayden and Mary S. Kettle; letter from Louie Bennett, 12 May 1937; report of speech by de Valera on women's position and defence of the constitution. See also two editorials on the position of women, 13 May 1937. For de Valera's meeting with women's organisations see 'Women: position under constitution, 1937' (N.A.I., D.T., S9880).

the rights of women can support it, and that is a tragic dilemma for those who have been loyal and ardent workers in the national cause'.[46]

The key issue was the extent to which the constitution and social policy restricted women outside the home, and whether there was any discrimination against them in public life. Even on the question of citizenship there was less than full equality, as the department of justice pointed out. If an Irishman married a foreign woman she became a citizen, whereas a foreign man had to fulfil a two-year residency requirement. The reason given was that men would want to work in the state, while it was assumed that this would not be the case with women. Furthermore, for children born abroad Irish citizenship was transmitted through the father rather than the mother. The organisation Old Cumann na mBan, representing women who had participated in the war of independence, moreover complained that its members were discriminated against because of their sex in the matter of pension rights, pointing to the anomalies in the military service pensions act of 1934[47] introduced by a Fianna Fáil government. The conditions of employment act also reinforced the view that employment policy was essentially designed for men rather than women. When Mary Kettle returned to her criticisms in the *Irish Press* the bad-tempered response included the claim that 'the action taken by the minister for industry and commerce had for its object to protect the interests of the male workers who, without such restriction, might have been swamped by lower-paid women in the new industries'. This was somewhat disingenuous given the strength of trade unions in Ireland, and the potential control available to the minister, but it did highlight the extent to which Kettle's case had merit: the act was designed specifically to discriminate against women, and was more-over devised with the support of the Labour party and the trade unions.[48]

At a meeting with women's groups held in January 1937 to consider claims that women were discriminated against in a number of public areas and were treated less fairly than in Northern Ireland, de Valera implied that he was helpless to change the circumstances: 'The president pointed out that any inadequacy in the representation of women in the legislature and in public bodies was attributable to the state of public opinion. It would be difficult to do anything to give women a larger place in public life while public opinion remains as it is.'[49] This was disingenuous to say the least. At the time of this

---

[46] Macardle to de Valera, 21 May 1937 (S9880). The amendment reads: 'The state shall endeavour to secure that neither in opportunities for employment nor in conditions of employment shall women suffer unfair discrimination on the sole grounds of sex.' Macardle added that, while not ideal, this could provide the basis for a compromise.

[47] 1934/43 (13 Sept. 1934).

[48] Department of justice to department of taoiseach, 15 May 1937 (S9880); Old Cumann na mBan, statement dated 17 May 1937; *Irish Press*, 17 May 1937: letter from Mary S. Kettle, p. 2, followed by editorial reply on same page.

[49] 'Women: constitutional and economic position in Dáil Éireann', correspondence Sept. 1936–Jan. 1937; report of meeting with de Valera, 29 Jan. 1937 (N.A.I., D.T., S9278).

meeting de Valera was in the process of consulting a number of senior clergymen on the articles that would, it was later claimed, restrict the status of women. If he wished to educate public opinion on the issue, then he had the opportunity but failed to use it. There was also the question of political representation for women. As the National Council of Women was to complain in 1939, the electoral panel for the senate excluded most women's organisations from the nominating process. By this time the taoiseach appears to have been bored with the women's question, offering only a perfunctory reply. Attempts to raise issues of concern to these organisations met with a similar response.[50]

More palatable to de Valera was the advice given to him in 1937 by J. J. Walsh, a leading protectionist businessman and sympathiser with the European right, who urged him to ignore what he claimed were unrepresentative women: 'As one who has had some experience in sensing the mind of the ordinary man or woman, I can positively say that the most popular thing you could do, as well also as the very best thing nationally, would be to make it known that your desire was to send women back to the home where they belong.' Walsh then commended the Brazilian example as one to follow. There, he claimed, the restriction of women's work had led to full employment.[51]

Certain other reservations concerning the new constitution were expressed. Some opposition deputies were concerned that it marked the end of the link with the crown and the empire, but their criticisms were muted. In general the constitution was well received at home, especially by Fianna Fáil and Labour. The referendum, held in July, saw the electorate break along partisan lines. It may have been a mistake to hold the referendum and the general election on the same day, as this probably heightened the partisan nature of the response. Yet the vote itself (over 40 per cent of those who voted rejected the constitution) was deceptive. In a relatively short period of time the constitution won general acceptance. This can be attributed to its republican and catholic nature, which proved acceptable to the general population well beyond Fianna Fáil's supporters. De Valera's remarks on radio on the night of 29 December 1937, when the constitution came into effect, reflected his vision of its nature and status: 'The chief significance of the new constitution coming at the present time is that it is in complete accord with national convention and tradition in these matters, and that it bears upon its face, from the first words of its preamble to the dedication at the close, the character of the public law of a great Christian democracy.'[52]

[50] National Council of Women of Ireland to taoiseach, 11 Apr. 1939; reply, 12 Apr. 1939 (N.A.I., D.T., S9287, op. cit.; see also S16210 for correspondence on women's police force).
[51] Walsh to de Valera, 15 May 1937 (N.A.I., D.T., S9880, 'Women').
[52] Irish Independent, 30 Dec. 1937, reporting remarks made by de Valera the previous evening on radio.

THE British government viewed with growing concern the rapid changes taking place in Ireland. There was anxiety about the specific changes in the relationship between the two countries, and about the impact such changes would have on the other dominions. Furthermore, in view of the worsening European situation, the position of Ireland on the western seaboard seemed neither secure nor stable. While the constitution was considered to be a departure from the spirit of the treaty, the British concluded that no substantive alteration had occurred. This may have been wishful thinking on their part, as the Irish government explicitly insisted that its relationship to the commonwealth was now contingent.[53] The logic of the 1937 constitution was to weaken links with the commonwealth, though this was rarely spelled out. Once the constitution was in place de Valera believed that he was in a strong political position to negotiate a settlement of the outstanding disputes with Britain. Some relief had been achieved by the 'coal–cattle' pacts, originally negotiated in 1934–5 and renewed annually thereafter, but these agreements were limited in scope. What was required was a political settlement.[54]

Identifying the range of possible problems to resolve did not in itself establish the conditions for agreement. In a series of complex and at times acrimonious meetings, beginning in London in January 1938 and continuing into the spring, a set of agreements was worked out, which conceded much to the Irish side. In particular a satisfactory compromise emerged on the annuities issue, which had been the main sticking point, and to back it up the British agreed to return the ports to Irish sovereignty. Moreover a trade agreement was negotiated, which granted to Ireland considerable benefits compared to the other dominions or to competitors such as Denmark. Yet there was doubt from the very beginning whether an agreement would be reached. Despite the willingness of the British ministers, and especially Neville Chamberlain, to compromise on major issues, de Valera continued to insist that unless the ending of partition formed part of the agreement then nothing could be achieved. This obduracy on his part generated serious divisions within the cabinet. MacEntee was particularly pessimistic, expressing his fears in a letter to his wife: 'We shall not get the ports, and . . . if we do not reach agreement about trade and finance . . . it will be much less satisfactory than it would have been if we had been prepared to deal with obvious facts and not to go window-dressing now about partition.' Such was MacEntee's concern that he wrote to de Valera on 17 February expressing his dismay that an agreement was being delayed because of the taoiseach's preoccupation with partition. He argued that the terms available were the best on offer and that ending partition was not a realistic option in the present circumstances. He also contended that

---

[53] 'Constitution 1937: attitude of British government' (N.A.I., D.T., S10463).

[54] McMahon, *Republicans & imperialists*, gives a comprehensive discussion of the negotiations (pp 150–52, 168–70).

questions of national defence and the stabilisation of the economy made an agreement imperative. Speculation about the British forcing the northern unionists into a united Ireland was wishful thinking. He continued:

I feel that the partition problem cannot be solved except with the consent of the majority of the northern non-catholic population. It certainly cannot be solved by their coercion. Hitherto we as the government here have done nothing of ourselves to secure a solution, but on the contrary have done and are doing certain things which have made a solution more difficult. The demand which we make continuously that the British should compel the Craigavonites to come in with us, has only had the effect of stiffening them against us.

MacEntee went on to accuse de Valera of bad faith, insisting that 'the three objectives which six weeks ago we thought practicable appear to be within our grasp. The question is whether we shall secure them now, or abandon them because we cannot get immediately what we all, with maybe the exception of yourself, feel is at the moment unobtainable.' He also argued that the country wanted an agreement, and it would be bad for the country, for the government, and for the party if one was not achieved. Partition, he believed, was not an obstacle to public opinion accepting the agreement, but he suspected that certain ministers were using the issue to obstruct an end to the economic war. According to MacEntee, Gerry Boland and Oscar Traynor, respectively ministers for land and for posts and telegraphs, were publicly criticising government policy, and he could not understand how Boland had not resigned from the government. MacEntee followed the logic of his position and offered his own resignation to de Valera, adding that if the negotiations broke down because of intransigence over partition he would not stand for the dáil again.[55] De Valera soon came under different pressures. Northern nationalists, including Bishop Mageean of Down and Connor, sought to persuade him not to sign an agreement that did not involve an end to partition. They argued that anything less would involve a denial of their interests.[56]

---

[55] MacEntee to Margaret MacEntee ('Fri. morning', no date) (U.C.D., A.D., MacEntee papers P67/179); MacEntee to de Valera, 17 Feb. 1938 (P67/155). McMahon reports her interviews with MacEntee and Maurice Moynihan to the effect that there were no major divisions on partition during the negotiations (*Republicans & imperialists*, pp 242–7). It is puzzling that the only two individuals besides de Valera who would have known about MacEntee's letter, and its criticism, should have denied that there were any such difficulties. John Bowman's very careful analysis of the politics of partition in *De Valera and the Ulster question, 1917–1973* (Oxford, 1982), ch. 5, suggests that the discussion on partition may have been symbolic. There is also a contradiction between the evidence from the MacEntee papers cited above and that cited from a number of sources by Bowman. In particular, if MacEntee's personal correspondence is to be accepted, then it may be that de Valera deliberately misled the journalist Paddy Quinn on the question, or that Quinn may have been disposed to be misled on it.

[56] 'Negotiations with Britain 1938', 20, 24 Feb. 1938 (N.A.I., D.T., S10596). On 24 Feb. a delegation of northern nationalists met de Valera and MacEntee to press this case.

In the event the negotiations were resumed and an agreement along the lines acceptable to MacEntee was concluded and signed in April 1938. No concessions were made by Britain on partition. There can be little doubt that the Irish side gained the most from the agreement, although the British obviously believed that some benefit had been derived from an end to hostilities. Irish agriculture received privileged access to the British market, while British manufacturers would have privileged, though not unrestricted, access to the Irish market. Most significantly for the future, with the handing back by Britain of the treaty ports the state had obtained sovereignty over its coasts and waters.[57]

IN June 1938, shortly after the agreements with Britain, de Valera took the opportunity once again to call a general election. In contrast with the experience of the previous year, the 1938 poll returned the party with a comfortable overall majority. This fourth election in just over six years confirmed the dominance of Fianna Fáil in the political system and established it as the governing party. All other parties had become weaker, with Fine Gael apparently in terminal decline. The electorate had accepted the republicanisation of Irish politics and given Fianna Fáil a mandate to continue on similar lines. The period 1932–8 had been eventful; the country had experienced rapid change while retaining and strengthening its democratic foundations. Yet, while the optimism associated with the first six years of Fianna Fáil government had not evaporated, many of the early objectives of the government, with the exception of ending partition, had been achieved. The deteriorating international situation caused concern and undoubtedly had facilitated the agreements with Britain. The return of the ports to Irish sovereignty had been the triumph of the negotiations, helping to secure the Irish state in the event of war.

In other areas, too, the government was beginning to encounter difficulties. The economy, which had boomed for most of the 1930s, began to slow down early in 1937. There was a danger that the programme of industrial expansion promoted by import substitution would come to an end. The reopening of the British market to Irish cattle on favourable terms threatened to restore the traditional dominance of the cattle economy over other sectors. Conservative opinion certainly welcomed this prospect, and the department of finance used the opportunity to claw back some of its lost influence.[58] Nor had traditional problems disappeared; emigration had begun to increase again, fostered by

---

[57] 'Prices commission', memo by department of industry and commerce, 12 June 1939 (N.A.I., D.T., S10633), noting the benefits that Ireland derived from the agreement; see also Girvin, *Between two worlds*, p. 128.

[58] 'Dr Per Jacobson: letter on economic situation, 1938', Jacobson to de Valera, 25 Mar. 1938 (N.A.I., D.T., S10620); Fanning, *Department of finance*, pp 269–75; Lee, *Ire. 1912–85*, p. 216.

employment opportunities in Britain and by relatively slow growth at home. De Valera had insisted in 1937 that it was not the function of an Irish government to encourage people to emigrate, but to provide the means for everyone to remain in employment at home. The reality was somewhat different, and emigration to Britain, then the only realistic outlet, had crept up inexorably throughout the decade. Even before the 1938 agreements and the revival of the British economy, emigration was returning to the levels criticised by Fianna Fáil during the 1920s.[59]

There were also serious divisions within the government on fiscal policy. Revenue was dropping because exports had fallen by over 50 per cent since 1929, while imports had held up at around two-thirds of the 1929 figure. The department of finance calculated in late 1937 that the only way to expand the economy was to increase agricultural exports to Britain. But that would take time. By February 1938 the department considered that government finances were in crisis, and that the commitments arising from a possible agreement with Britain would make matters worse. Accordingly, it would be necessary to increase taxation.[60]

MacEntee was opposed to further taxation. He proposed that the 1939 budget should include substantial cuts in social expenditure. The cabinet disagreed with the minister's advice, and decided that while the budget should be balanced this aim should be achieved by increased taxation rather than through cuts in expenditure. Further meetings did not resolve the conflict, and MacEntee offered his resignation (which was not accepted).[61] He appears to have represented a section of the party that sought to stabilise the political and economic system along conservative lines. His opposition to family allowances, championed by Lemass and some members of the catholic hierarchy, appealed to small producers and taxpayers. MacEntee warned that order and the social hierarchy would be threatened if young people were able to establish a family independent of the ownership of property. In the end, the cabinet view prevailed and the 1939 budget was a stringent one, raising income tax and duties on tobacco and petrol.[62]

Leaving aside MacEntee's conservatism, he had identified a real problem for policy-makers. Ireland had advanced rapidly during the 1930s and had acquired an industrial base within a heavily protected environment. However, the next stage was not at all clear, nor were the alternatives. A return to

[59] 'Emigration: government policy, 1937' (N.A.I., D.T., S9627); statement in dáil by de Valera, 17 Feb. 1937 (emigration had increased from a low of 9,517 in the financial year 1933/4 to 23,711 in 1935/6); 'General election, 1937' (U.C.D., A.D., FitzGerald papers, P80/1123).
[60] 'Notes on economic situation', Nov. 1937, including minute by McElligott (U.C.D., A.D., MacEntee papers, P67/153); memo on budget situation, 28 Feb. 1938 (P67/169).
[61] Memo by minister for finance to de Valera, 20 Apr. 1939 (P67/132); MacEntee to de Valera, 30 Apr. 1939, for resignation offer (P67/133).
[62] Lee, Ire. 1912–85, pp 283–4, for detailed discussion on family allowances and MacEntee's attitude; Mulcahy notes on defence conference, 11 Mar. 1940 (Mulcahy papers, P7a/210).

a simple agricultural economy was not possible, but there was no guarantee that further economic development was possible either. In 1940 Lemass circulated a memorandum that drew on the recently published *Conditions of economic progress* by the developmental economist Colin Clark, to show that Irish living standards were high in a comparative context, and that Ireland was one of the world's major creditor states. It was also contended that, as a result of deliberate monitoring, standards of efficiency in industry by 1938 were close to those prevailing in Britain. In some cases competition was weak or non-existent, but in the case of over 70 per cent of new firms the level of competition was considered adequate. And the record was encouraging: industrial output had expanded quite rapidly between 1931 and 1939, as had the numbers employed, in addition to which some 100 new industries with 900 new factories had been established since 1932. However, the economy was estimated to have remained stable throughout the 1930s, which led the taoiseach's economic adviser to conclude that 'there are some fundamental forces at work which render agriculture...inelastic to both [*sic*] price, legislative, and educational influences'.[63] By 1939, therefore, the prospects for sustained expansion were uncertain.

THE second world war postponed some of the difficulties facing Ireland, but posed a number of other serious challenges. In the first place there was an implicit threat to the sovereignty of the state, though by late 1942 this danger was receding. Pressure came initially from the British government, particularly after Winston Churchill became prime minister, for Ireland to enter the war, or that some arrangement for the use of the ports or other facilities be made. Later on, American entry increased tensions between the United States and Ireland. There appears to have been little doubt that Ireland would remain neutral in the event of any European conflict. De Valera believed that only through a policy of strict neutrality could Ireland maintain its national integrity. He also seems to have considered that any departure from neutrality would have brought dire consequences for the country. MacEntee, for his part, had opposed increasing expenditure on the armed forces in January 1939, arguing that there was no real threat from Britain, and that if Ireland were attacked from any other quarter the British would give protection to Ireland.

There were a number of reasons why the Irish government, or more correctly de Valera, adopted and maintained the policy of neutrality, announced formally on 2 September 1939. It was more in tune with Irish policy than any of the alternatives. It was a logical step in the light of the 1937 constitution. It followed on from de Valera's determination (despite pressure

---

[63] Lemass memo, 12 Sept. 1940 (S12070); 'Irish industries: standard of efficiency', department of industry and commerce to department of taoiseach, 24 Nov. 1938 (S11018); 'National income', various memos, 1943/4 (S11563).

from clerical and opposition interests) not to intervene in the Spanish civil war. It also reflected Irish isolation from world affairs and a confidence in the moral superiority of what Ireland had achieved. There were grounds for congratulation on these counts, but the upshot was a narrow view of national interest. A most important contributory factor was the belief that any other course would lead to serious divisions within the party and indeed within the country as a whole. Leading officials in the department of external affairs showed a strong partiality for the German side in the early years of the war, and a number of senior Fianna Fáil members may have felt likewise. Even Fine Gael was divided over whether it should give full support to the neutrality position, though only one member, James Dillon, openly advocated entry into the war on the Allied side.[64] Richard Mulcahy believed in May 1940 that the I.R.A. was preparing for an uprising in support of the Germans, to be accompanied, perhaps, by an invasion. This was far-fetched but it helps to explain the consensus that emerged among the political parties for the government's policy. De Valera stressed that to enter the war under any circumstances would be divisive and that even if Fianna Fáil and Fine Gael were agreed on the issue they would not be able to carry the country with them, adding that 'the people were pro-German and . . . this would drive whatever instinct they had now the other way completely on to the German side'.[65] Mulcahy estimated that Fine Gael could carry two-thirds of its supporters for the war, but that de Valera could only carry about half of Fianna Fáil, and that consequently about one-third of the state would be opposed to entry.[66] This appears to have been a realistic assessment of the situation. It was significant that Cosgrave and Fine Gael were as opposed to British threats to Irish sovereignty as were Fianna Fáil, showing the extent to which the political climate had changed since 1932.[67] However, the British government continued to exercise pressure on the Irish government to modify its position. On specific issues de Valera's response reflected his certainty that Ireland must remain outside the conflict. Thus whether the British asked for transshipment facilities or for the Ford motor company in Cork to carry out work for Britain, he rejected the requests, though some of his ministers may have taken a different view.[68]

[64] See Maurice Manning, *James Dillon: a biography* (Dublin, 1999), chs 10–11.
[65] Note, 25, 27 May 1940; memo (Quinn) 5/6 July 1940, on de Valera interview with Patrick Herdman (Mulcahy papers, P7a/210).
[66] See Mulcahy papers, P7a/210, for Mulcahy's assessment (5 July 1940).
[67] Memo by Cosgrave, 15 Nov. 1940 (U.C.D., A.D., FitzGerald papers, P80/1119Ci); see also memo by Mulcahy, 14 Sept. 1939 (ibid.).
[68] N.A.I., D.T., S11846, for transshipment discussion; memo from department of finance, 16 Jan. 1939 (U.C.D., A.D., MacEntee papers, P67/195); MacEntee to de Valera on Ford's, 1 Feb. 1941 (P67/234). In reply to a pro-German letter in 1940, MacEntee claimed he was neither pro-German nor pro-British but pro-Irish, but added that he was under no illusion as to the consequences if Britain went down.

Perhaps the most serious challenge to neutrality came when Churchill offered an arrangement on Northern Ireland if the south joined in the war effort. It remains debatable whether this was a serious offer, and the hostile reaction of northern unionists highlighted the difficulties associated with any such scheme. Their response cast doubt on the Irish government's claim that all that was required to end partition was a decision by the British to withdraw support from the northern unionists. De Valera's rejection of the offer was realistic not because of his doubts about Churchill's good faith, but because of his recognition that the unionists could not be coerced into a united Ireland. In fact, partition was strengthened by the war. The animosity between nationalists and unionists in Northern Ireland increased, with a significant proportion of the northern nationalist population demonstrating pro-German sentiments.

At home, de Valera's government adopted a hard line against I.R.A. activists. An I.R.A. bombing campaign in Britain in 1939—which, had it continued, could have undermined Irish neutrality—prompted the introduction of internment without trial and the death penalty for treasonable acts.[69] During the war hundreds of I.R.A. members were interned, three died on hunger strike, and six were executed for murder. De Valera's defence of such measures, in answer to I.R.A. claims that recognition of the Free State (regardless of the oath) was treason to the republic, was to insist that the approval given by the people to the 1937 constitution had given a new legitimacy to the state. Meanwhile, neutrality, whatever its benefits, effectively excluded the Irish government from any influence it might have had with the Allies when the war ended.[70]

Despite the tension between the United Kingdom and Ireland the danger of British invasion in 1940 and 1941 was probably not high, whatever de Valera may have believed. The government also adroitly rebuffed American pressures to end neutrality after U.S. entry into the war in 1941.[71] Nevertheless the Irish state was lucky to avoid being dragged into the war. The rather spartan life imposed by isolation and wartime conditions was undoubtedly better than any that would have resulted from entering the war, on either side. In part British hostility was assuaged by the favourable treatment extended to military personnel detained in Ireland. Moreover, close cooperation existed between the Irish and British intelligence services.[72] In some

[69] Treason Act, 1939 (1939/10 (30 May 1939)); Offences against the State Act, 1939 (1939/13 (14 June 1939)). See also Eunan O'Halpin, *Defending Ireland* (Oxford, 1999), ch. 6.

[70] See Robert Fisk, *In time of war: Ireland, Ulster and the price of neutrality 1939–45* (London and Dingle, 1983), pp 236–70, for a thorough discussion of the war period; Lee, *Ire. 1912–85*, pp 223, 258–70, for a judicious assessment of neutrality.

[71] T. Ryle Dwyer, *Irish neutrality and the U.S.A., 1939–47* (Dublin, 1977); for the failure of the 'Aiken mission' in 1941, pp 107–21; for the deterioration of relations after American entry, pp 139–221; for the British and German pressure, see Fisk, *In time of war, passim*.

[72] Fisk, *In time of war*, pp 148–53. However, Fisk notes that while the cooperation was tangible there were real limits to its extent.

respects, too, partition may have allowed the Allies to be benign to Ireland; if a united Ireland had existed, then the cost for the British and Americans of Irish neutrality might have been too high. Close arrangements also developed between the Irish state and British government agencies to provide Irish labour for British war industries. The level of private collusion, which suited both sides, was extensive and worked to the advantage of the Irish in providing an outlet for surplus Irish labour at high wages at a time when Irish industry could not hope to keep output at pre-war levels.[73] When all this has been considered, however, it is apparent that once war had broken out, the options open to a small sovereign state were limited.[74]

Ireland stayed out of the war, but was not wholly unaffected by contemporary European social and political trends. In August 1944 the report of the vocational organisation commission was published, recommending the reorganising of Ireland's socio-economic structures along lines compatible with catholic social teaching. The thrust of the report involved the establishment of a form of corporatism, a series of vocational councils, designed to counteract the alleged defects of bureaucracy. However, there was considerable opposition to the proposals from within the government, particularly from Lemass. Civil servants, too, responded defensively, highlighting the alleged fascist tendencies and the danger to parliamentary institutions implicit in the proposals, which accordingly came to nothing.[75] In fact, most economic and social initiatives, during and after the war, tended to increase state intervention and bureaucracy. The establishment of the Central Bank in 1942 and of Córas Iompair Éireann in 1944 and the introduction of the children's allowance act, also in 1944,[76] were centralising measures. The war, or 'the emergency', as the period became known in Ireland,[77] had also prompted the department of supplies to establish quasi-governmental agencies that would have the capacity to intervene quickly and decisively to overcome wartime difficulties. Such initiatives bore the imprint of Lemass's dynamic personality and constituted a response to the full-employment and welfare policies adopted in Britain and elsewhere towards the end of the war.[78]

[73] Maureen E. Hartigan, 'Irish emigration, 1931–1961' (M.A. thesis, N.U.I. (U.C.C.), 1990).
[74] N.A.I., D.T., S13590; report of de Valera speech (*Irish Press*, 2 Nov. 1944).
[75] N.A.I., D.T., S13552, contains a number of departmental comments on the commission's report; all are scathing in their criticism, but most of the comments are not simply defensive reactions by threatened bureaucrats, but represent a defence of democratically elected government. See Joseph Lee, 'Aspects of corporatist thought in Ireland: the commission on vocational organisation, 1939–43' in Art Cosgrove and Donal McCartney (ed.), *Studies in Irish history* (Dublin, 1979), pp 324–46.
[76] 1942/22 (4 Nov. 1942); 1944/21 (8 Dec. 1944); 1944/2 (23 Feb. 1944). For the Central Bank, see also below, p. 466.
[77] The term was borrowed from official usage: see First Amendment of the Constitution Act, 1939 (2 Sept. 1939); Emergency Powers Act, 1939 (1939/28 (3 Sept. 1939)).
[78] See Girvin, *Between two worlds*, for a discussion of changes in policy after 1945 and the obstacles that Lemass faced.

Throughout the war competitive party politics retained their importance. Though Fine Gael had called for the formation of a national government to meet the crisis, this demand was dismissed as undemocratic by the government. Party leaders were invited to participate in the defence council, but this was a consultative rather than a decision-making body.[79] The 1943 and 1944 general elections highlighted the beginning of a period of instability in the Irish political system that was to last till the end of the 1950s. Indeed, 1944 was the only election between 1943 and 1957 in which a single party received a majority of seats (Fianna Fáil obtained fourteen more seats than the combined opposition parties). In fact the 1940s marked the beginning of a challenge from smaller parties, which lasted for a decade or more.

From 1943 onwards the election results showed that Fianna Fáil was becoming vulnerable to rivals from the left, from the right, and from republican dissidents. In any given election its success depended on winning ten or more seats over and above those won by all the other parties. The loss of these seats removed its majority, though not necessarily its ability to govern. Losing its majority in 1943 did not deprive the party of office, but in 1948 it did. There was no simple explanation for the outcome of the elections, but one factor was the growth of a number of parties that concentrated on a specific issue, or on a narrow range of issues. This damaged both Fianna Fáil and Fine Gael. The 1943 and 1944 elections were disastrous for Fine Gael. The loss of thirteen seats in 1943, and of a further two in 1944, indicated the growing disenchantment of the voters. Cosgrave resigned shortly after the 1943 election and was replaced as leader by Richard Mulcahy, who proved no more successful in improving the party's fortunes. Indeed in 1945 Mulcahy confessed to his party colleagues his feeling of helplessness. Such had been the party's decline that there was some doubt whether it could field a candidate at a forthcoming by-election. Mulcahy acknowledged that a crisis existed, but was sanguine that it would strengthen the party rather than weaken it.[80]

The Labour party had done remarkably well at the 1943 election, but its vote was to collapse in 1944 as a result of the split that led to the formation of the National Labour party. The latter was the creature of William O'Brien of the Irish Transport and General Workers Union; all the defecting T.D.s from the Labour party were members of the union. The new party's existence was dependent on the I.T.G.W.U. and after 1945 on the related split that occurred within the Irish Trade Union Congress. All these splits had been orchestrated by O'Brien, who was seeking to dominate the trade union

[79] *Irish Press* editorial, 28 Feb. 1944; report of de Valera's appeal to voters for a Fianna Fáil majority, *Irish Press*, 15 May 1944; 'National government proposals, 1943' (N.A.I., D.T., S13240a).

[80] Fine Gael general purposes committee: party meeting called by Mulcahy to discuss by-election strategy, 14 Nov. 1945 (U.C.D., A.D., P39MIN/1/2).

movement through the I.T.G.W.U. He skilfully invoked nationalism to divide the unions, and communism to divide the Labour party. The result was that the opportunity that opened in 1943 was quickly closed in 1944, and thereafter the political influence of the I.T.U.C. and the Labour party diminished during the postwar years.

It might have been expected that Fianna Fáil would benefit from these developments. After all, they appeared to reinforce the party's claim that only Fianna Fáil could rule on its own. As the number of new parties escalated, the possibility of stable government without Fianna Fáil diminished. Yet the multiplication of parties also posed a problem for Fianna Fáil. In Clann na Talmhan there emerged a threat to its traditional rural base. Fianna Fáil was heavily dependent on small farmers and the rural poor in the west, and it was to them that the new party appealed. Essentially an anti-system party, similar to agrarian parties on the Continent, Clann na Talmhan attracted votes from both Fianna Fáil and Fine Gael, but particularly from Fianna Fáil. Clann na Talmhan support was associated with high levels of emigration and a high percentage of people engaged in agriculture on their own account.[81] In urban areas Fianna Fáil was losing votes to the Labour party/National Labour and later to Clann na Poblachta. The latter party appealed for support on the basis that nothing had been done to end partition; it also highlighted economic and welfare issues. Electoral fragmentation between 1938 and 1948 consequently weakened Fianna Fáil rather than strengthened it. This was compounded by the party's refusal to countenance coalition under any circumstances, and also perhaps by weariness after sixteen years in office.

Fianna Fáil's problems were increased by internal difficulties that turned out to be difficult to resolve. During the war Lemass devised an ambitious developmental strategy, which built on his earlier industrial successes, and which sought to generate a fully integrated expansionary system to foster full employment. His proposals were, with the exception of the industrial relations act of 1946,[82] neutralised by conservative opposition both within the party and within the civil service. There were also strategic and policy divisions within the party. Although never made explicit, the aim of the Lemass strategy was to redirect the entire thrust of economic policy towards industry and the working class. This was too much for most of his colleagues, even some who had been traditionally close to him.[83]

[81] Michael Gallagher, *Electoral support for Irish political parties, 1927–1973* (London, 1976), pp 23–4, 53–5.
[82] 1946/26 (27 Aug. 1946).
[83] This was at the heart of the full employment debate during and immediately after the war. See Girvin, *Between two worlds*; Lee, *Ire. 1912–85*, pp 224–36. For a typical response, see the memo 'Observations of minister for agriculture on full employment', indicating why no action should be taken to interrupt the stability of the agricultural community (U.C.D., A.D., MacEntee papers, P67/264 (5)).

Lemass's policy would also have required some sort of accommodation with the Labour party, or at least with the labour movement. This was anathema to certain sections of the party, and after the 1943 election a serious rift emerged within the leadership. MacEntee had become engaged in a systematic campaign against the Labour party and particularly against its left wing, which he accused of being communist. In one speech he suggested that the state was in danger, and that the divisions between Fianna Fáil and Fine Gael, brought about by the civil war, should be relegated to the past. For Lemass, James Ryan, and Oscar Traynor, the attack on Labour was counter-productive. Lemass argued that Fianna Fáil would get the bulk of the labour vote if a more conciliatory approach were adopted. MacEntee's tactics were condemned by his fellow cabinet ministers, and this led him once again to offer his resignation to the taoiseach. At the same time he offered a spirited defence of his tactics during the election campaign and assessed each of the lost seats in considerable detail. He concluded that the accusations made against him by his colleagues were incorrect if not malicious, and repeated his intention to retire.[84] The results of this episode are difficult to assess. MacEntee remained at his post, but he fought the 1944 election in a less confrontational fashion. Indeed, he commended the children's allowance legislation that he had earlier systematically opposed, and his general approach reflected the welfarist strategy promoted by Lemass. But in 1944 the circumstances were different; the Labour party had split and the National Labour party was under the direction of William O'Brien, with whom MacEntee had cooperated on the trade union act in 1941.[85] It is difficult to establish whether MacEntee was close to O'Brien at this time, but what is clear is that the split in the Labour party suited both men. The outcome also proved to be satisfactory for the government, giving it once again a working majority.

THE immediate postwar years were fraught with difficulties for most European states. Many expected that severe economic downturns would occur, as had been the case after the first world war. However, the division of Europe and the subsequent political and economic polarisation on the Continent only indirectly affected Ireland. For most Irish people, Ireland's neutrality had been vindicated. The traditional relationship with the United Kingdom had been preserved relatively intact, and Dublin hoped that the election of a Labour government in 1945 would provide a favourable climate in which to raise the issue of partition. But the war had reinforced Northern Ireland's position in the United Kingdom and for a further generation, at least, Irish

---

[84] 'Benefits derived from a Fianna Fáil government' (undated but prepared for 1943 election) (U.C.D., A.D., MacEntee papers P67/362); copy of speech at Harold's Cross, 7 June 1943 (P67/364); Lemass to MacEntee, 10 June 1943 (P67/363); MacEntee to de Valera, 28 June 1943 (P67/366).
[85] 1941/22 (23 Sept. 1941).

demands on partition were to be ignored. The government responded with alacrity to the provisions of the British nationality bill[86] in 1947 by reasserting its claim over Northern Ireland. In an *aide-memoire* sent to the British government at the time this was posed in uncompromising terms: 'For the Irish people the national territory is the whole of Ireland, and citizens owe fidelity to the Irish nation and loyalty to the Irish state as fundamental political duties. The Irish can acknowledge no other nationality or allegiance.' The note made clear that the claim was being made for all the inhabitants of Northern Ireland and went on to state that the government was not prepared to 'recognise the moral validity of partition or accept as imposing upon Irish citizens of the partitioned area the duty of allegiance to any nation other than Ireland'.[87] However, the Labour government was not prepared to act against the northern unionists. If war had secured a consensus in Ireland on social, economic, and diplomatic matters, it had also provided the northern unionists with moral credit with the British government, which was not to be exhausted for some time. De Valera appears to have become exasperated by these difficulties, but quite unable to handle the subtle and complex environment developing in the postwar world.[88]

Despite the flurry of proposals that emerged at the end of the war, very little was achieved by the government between 1945 and 1948. There were a number of explanations for this. One was exhaustion. The government had performed well during the war and the 1944 election result was perhaps a recognition of this. But the continuous period in power was taking its toll. Another problem was the deep divisions within the party between left and right and between urban and rural supporters. Although Lemass became tánaiste (deputy prime minister) in 1945, he appears to have lacked the ascendancy to push through his radical reforms. This demonstrates the balance of power within the party, which had moved to the right. Perhaps it would be more accurate to say that the party, reflecting public opinion in general, favoured stability over risk-taking. Lemass remained a risk-taker up to 1948, but his colleagues may have been closer to the national mood. Yet even this may not be entirely accurate, for the political instability of the period 1943–8 possibly indicated that the electorate was looking for something innovative. As a radical republican party Clann na Poblachta, formed in 1946, appeared to fit that description. But even here there was little evidence to suggest that the new party was anything more than an updated version of Fianna Fáil, which had absorbed some of the social-democratic policies then becoming fashionable in Britain. More generally the immediate postwar years

---

[86] Enacted as 11 & 12 Geo. VI, c. 56 [U.K.] (30 July 1948).

[87] Minister for external affairs to British embassy (23 Jan. 1947), refers to cabinet meeting of 22 Jan., where the decision was taken; memo on above, 25 Oct. 1947, reiterates the same argument (N.A.I., D.T., S14002).

[88] Bowman, *De Valera & Ulster question*, pp 262–73.

were as austere as the wartime period itself. The trade unions were unhappy with the quasi-judicial nature of the labour court, set up in 1946, and threatened to boycott it. There was considerable disquiet over the failure of wages to keep pace with inflation during the war years and after. To compound these troubles, the crucial section of the 1941 trade union act, which provided the minister with the power to grant or deny negotiating licences to trade unions, was declared unconstitutional by the supreme court in 1946. Further difficulties were created for the government by Lemass's proposed legislation on prices and efficiency (1946–7) which was actively opposed by the business community. The precarious nature of the economic situation was highlighted in February 1947 by the closedown of much of Irish industry because of cold weather and a shortage of fuel. Once again Ireland's dependence on external support for economic survival had been demonstrated.

The political pressure on Fianna Fáil became palpable after the three by-elections held in October 1947, in which Clann na Poblachta won two out of the three contests. De Valera believed that this reflected a move to the left on the part of the electorate, and argued that only the end of partition would meet the challenge. Underlying his concern was the recognition that the British government was committed to building a welfare state and that Ireland tended to measure its well-being against United Kingdom standards. The extension of British welfare provisions to Northern Ireland meant that a welfare gap was opening up between the two parts of Ireland. Faced with these developments, one official strategy was to deny that the living standards of the two areas differed significantly. MacEntee explicitly denied that the standard of living had risen appreciably in Britain since 1938; on the contrary, he argued, it was lower. De Valera suggested that any extra welfare benefits available in the north had been provided at the cost of higher taxation. However, as one northern journalist was quick to retort, higher taxation was a sign of prosperity, high exports, and high consumption; low taxation, he implied, was a consequence of low income and poverty in the south.[89] A memorandum prepared for the taoiseach in August 1947 alerted the government to the attractions that Britain offered Irish emigrants: high wages, employment opportunities, and welfare services. The expenditure on welfare services in Britain increased the pressure on Irish policy-makers to follow suit. A note prepared for the new taoiseach in 1948 suggested that some of the unionist claims were justified, that the south would not come well out of a comparison with the north, and that such comparisons would lead to demands for the introduction of similar services in the south.[90]

[89] P.R.O., Do35/3924; U.C.D., A.D., MacEntee papers, P67/289, 8 Sept. 1947; statistics on tax levels in 'Budget 1947' (P67/290); 'Twenty-six counties and Northern Ireland: contrast of conditions, 1947' for details of exchanges (N.A.I., D.T., S14186).

[90] 'British financial crisis 1947', memo, minister for finance to taoiseach, 27 Aug. 1947; memo, minister for industry and commerce to taoiseach, 27 Aug. 1947 (N.A.I., D.T., S14134a); memo note to taoiseach, 13 Nov. 1948 (S14186).

All this reflected the beginning of a process that was to continue into the 1960s. Whereas the difference between the two parts of Ireland in wages, welfare, and employment opportunities were not significant before 1939, thereafter the gap grew rapidly. Already in 1947 the government and the opposition were sensing this and attempting to respond to it. By 1947, and the announcement of the Marshall plan, Ireland had restored much of its prewar economic structure; but, unlike certain other small European countries, the state appeared reluctant to seize the opportunities offered by Marshall Aid.[91]

Nor did the electorate take a different view. Some voters may have wanted more welfare, but not at the expense of giving up neutrality, protectionism, or the state's specifically catholic ethos. The new political parties failed to take up the challenge; they all continued to reflect the consensus that had been established during the 1930s by Fianna Fáil. Clann na Talmhan's success in winning seats in the west in 1943 simply demonstrated the political effectiveness of small and medium farmers in organising to protect their land and community. By the time of the 1948 election all the political parties were agreed on the major issues of policy, with differences only of detail.

Accordingly, the 1948 election did not mark a significant break with the past. Fianna Fáil lost its overall majority for several reasons. There was widespread, if diffuse, dissatisfaction with the government. The economy was in a bad way. Fianna Fáil's appeal to the voters lacked vision. Erskine Childers complained that many deputies did no more than praise de Valera and condemn the principle of coalition; this, he argued, was not the way to appeal to waverers. He also identified a number of short-term problems such as the hostility of vested interests and the weakness of budgetary policy. He added that there was a feeling that Fianna Fáil had 'ceased to be the poor man's government', and that it would be necessary to have a 'Lemass for agriculture'. All this, he maintained, together with bad organisation and a certain despondency within the party, explained the result. Moreover, he believed that the party had overestimated Clann na Poblachta and underestimated Fine Gael.[92]

The most surprising aspect of the 1948 election was not the decline in Fianna Fáil's vote—the party lost eight seats—but the capacity of the opposition to form a government from the various alternative parties. That an inter-party government composed of such disparate elements as Fine Gael

[91] The extent to which the Irish economy lagged behind most of western Europe has been discussed in Brian Girvin, 'The political economy of failure: Ireland's experience of postwar recovery, 1945–60' (paper delivered at the European Consortium for Political Research Annual Workshops, Apr. 1993); Lars Mjøset, *The Irish economy in a comparative institutional perspective* (Dublin, 1992), pp 262–70.

[92] Childers to MacEntee, undated, but written after the 1948 election; Childers to Tom Mullins, 10 Feb. 1948 (U.C.D., A.D., MacEntee papers, P67/299).

and Clann na Poblachta could be formed reflected the depth of disillusionment with sixteen years of Fianna Fáil government. What was not entirely clear in 1948 was whether the new government would prove to be any different from its predecessor. The fact that the inter-party government is best remembered for its declaration of an Irish republic in 1949 testifies to the continuity in values between the old and new governments, and reflects the enduring preoccupation with republicanisation. This further attests to the ascendancy that Fianna Fáil had established over Irish political culture as a consequence of its sixteen years in government.

CHAPTER VI

Northern Ireland, 1920–25

BRIAN BARTON

SOON after its emergence in the mid 1880s, the Ulster unionist movement established itself as the most significant counter-revolutionary force in Irish political life. Its members were motivated by a desire to maintain the union and a yet deeper determination to resist the authority of any future Dublin parliament. During the years immediately before the first world war, they responded energetically and effectively to their first substantial challenge—the third home rule bill. Subsequently, despite their apparent wartime quiescence, there was no abatement in the intensity of their opposition to all-Ireland institutions. Indeed during the course of the conflict unionists succeeded in defending and, arguably, consolidating their negotiating position.

Meanwhile, between 1915 and 1919, a convergence of opinion concerning the Irish question emerged at the highest level in British political life. It found expression in the government of Ireland act, 1920.[1] This provided for the formation of devolved governments in both southern and a six-county northern Ireland, each to be responsible for 'peace, order, and good government' within their respective jurisdictions. Ireland was to remain an integral part of the United Kingdom and the sovereignty of the Westminster parliament was to be undiminished. In the south, the Sinn Féin leaders used the procedures laid down by the measure as an opportunity to renew their electoral mandate; in the north, its terms were implemented more faithfully. In due course, an executive, composed of seven departments, was formed, and also a bicameral parliament, with procedures broadly replicating those of the Westminster parliament.

The decision to establish a regional government in Belfast arose from the anxiety of British ministers to legislate in a way that would redeem former pledges to unionists and yet be relatively acceptable to nationalists. Thus, in an attempt to minimise the gravity of partition, direct rule was terminated; it was considered that no one could therefore legitimately claim Britain was ruling the northern minority against its will or actively supporting unionists in their refusal to unite with the south. Westminster's underlying objective,

[1] 10 & 11 Geo. V, c. 67 (23 Dec. 1920). For a comprehensive account of the formation of Northen Ireland see Brian Follis, *A state under siege: the establishment of Northern Ireland, 1920–1925* (Oxford, 1995).

reflected in the government of Ireland act, was the creation of a united Ireland, formed with Ulster's consent, governed by a single, separate parliament, and bound closely to Britain. The category of 'reserved' powers was devised to provide an inducement towards this goal; they were to be transferred once unity had been achieved.[2] It was also hoped that the council of Ireland might serve as the dynamic institutional framework through which the two devolved governments might ultimately coalesce. These policy assumptions were mistaken and the expectations were to remain unfulfilled. Regional institutions merely strengthened and confirmed the sense of separate identity shared by Ulster unionists, while direct rule would have been more acceptable to northern nationalists than devolved government under unionist control.

The unionist movement succeeded in determining the fact but not the form of partition. Its members would really have preferred another Cromwell, but unlike their supporters among the Conservative party diehards, they did not vote against the measure during commons divisions. Their leaders' protestations that acceptance of a Belfast parliament represented a supreme sacrifice on their part were made largely for tactical reasons during the Anglo–Irish talks in 1921; they were responding to pressure from Lloyd George to make concessions. Meanwhile Sir James Craig and his colleagues publicly acknowledged the additional security that resulted from devolution. They had earlier, with some success, striven to amend the government of Ireland bill, so ensuring that the incipient institutions were more amenable to unionist control. They helped define the boundary of the excluded area, a majority of the Ulster Unionist Council preferring six counties—an area more likely to be amenable to unionist control—to the nine initially proposed by British ministers. They supported an amendment to ensure that the composition of the northern senate would precisely reflect the relative strength of the political parties in the lower house. They attempted but failed to weaken the proposed council of Ireland and to eliminate proportional representation from local parliamentary elections. None the less, Northern Ireland's first election, on 24 May 1921, was a unionist party triumph. It won forty of the fifty-two commons seats; all its candidates were successful.

There were some grounds for optimism when on 22 June 1921 George V formally opened the new parliament in Belfast. His speech presaged the Anglo–Irish truce. Moreover, early in the subsequent negotiations, de Valera indicated that Sinn Féin would not attempt to coerce the six counties into a united Ireland. Meanwhile, Craig expressed his belief that the devolved institutions were regarded as sacrosanct in London. In such circumstances, it seemed possible that a secure, unionist government might prove willing to

---

[2] Hence the powers transferred to the two parliaments under the 1920 act fell far short of dominion powers. For discussion of this point, see Mansergh, *Unresolved question*, ch. 5.

broaden its programme rather than act merely as an instrument for the maintenance of the protestant ascendancy. Contemporary speeches by party leaders were optimistic in tone and suggested both an awareness of responsibilities and consciousness of opportunities. Craig himself stated: 'God grant that our footsteps may never be diverted from the path of honour'; he promised 'to look to the people as a whole', and to be 'absolutely fair in administering the law', and he appealed for friendship with the south.[3] It was reasonable to expect that these generous impulses would be reinforced and guided by Westminster and also by the cadre of competent, high-ranking civil servants who transferred to Belfast from Whitehall and Dublin Castle.[4]

In general, it seemed possible that class issues might eventually transcend the traditionally sectarian basis of local politics. There were some indications that this process had already begun. In June 1918 the Unionist party had formed the Ulster Unionist Labour Association, mainly as a means of counteracting the appeal of socialism and the Labour party to its erstwhile working-class supporters. Nevertheless, the success of Labour party candidates in municipal elections two years later was considerable; they polled 10,000 protestant votes in Belfast alone and were supported by one-fifth of the catholic electorate in the west of the city. If these trends were sustained, unionist ministers might be constrained to reconsider their policies, and nationalist M.P.s also might feel obliged to respond, possibly by abandoning recent electoral pledges to abstain from the Belfast parliament.

Hopes of a stable province, led by an effective, even-handed, regional government, living in harmony with its southern neighbours, proved to be both illusory and short-lived. In part, this failure was rooted in the content of the 1920 act. Arguably, its gravest defect lay not in its institutionalisation of partition, but rather in the type of government it provided for Northern Ireland. Ministers found their political options nullified by the 'excepted' and 'reserved' powers retained at Westminster. Public affairs and services under the exclusive control of the British parliament included (besides the crown and foreign relations) trade, navigation, the post office, radio, coinage, and weights and measures. The Northern Ireland parliament also had only very limited taxing powers; the bulk of taxation, including income tax and customs and excise, was imposed by the British chancellor of the exchequer. Some 90 per cent of total revenue from taxes in Northern Ireland was paid direct to the British exchequer. Under the 1920 act the first call on the

---

[3] *Belfast Telegraph*, 24 Dec. 1920; *Hansard N.I. (commons)*, i, 36–7 (23 June 1921).

[4] For the background to the formation of N.I. see above, vi, 247–8, 251–2; Patrick Buckland, *Irish unionism: two—Ulster unionism and the origins of Northern Ireland* (Dublin and New York, 1973); Peter Gibbon, *The origins of Ulster unionism: the formation of popular protestant politics and ideology in nineteenth-century Ireland* (Manchester, 1975); Nicholas Mansergh, 'The government of Ireland act, 1920, its origins and purposes: the working of the "official mind"' in *Hist. Studies*, ix (1974), pp 19–48; A. S. Queckett, *The constitution of Northern Ireland* (3 vols, Belfast, 1928–46).

revenue so raised was the 'imperial contribution', Northern Ireland's share of the cost of imperial services such as the armed forces and the national debt, a contribution that was initially fixed (by a joint exchequer board set up for the purpose) at a level well above the province's ability to pay. The cost of Northern Ireland services had to be met out of the limited taxes paid directly into the Belfast exchequer, plus whatever was transferred from London after the imperial contribution and other costs had been deducted. The result was that ministers lacked the freedom of action necessary to initiate distinctive and relevant regional programmes. In addition, no consideration had been given to the distribution of powers within Northern Ireland. The new government was particularly constricted by being forced to share responsibility for services with the seventy-five local authorities that formed part of its inheritance; non-unionist representation on these bodies had substantially increased since the introduction of proportional representation into local government elections in 1919.

From the outset, Craig and his colleagues were confronted by awesome political problems. Inevitably Northern Ireland became the focus of Irish irredentism; in 1921 Dáil Éireann refused to recognise its existence. Thereafter, southern attitudes and policies reduced the likelihood that devolution would succeed. They reinforced the unionist sense of siege, largely determined security policy within the six counties, and exacerbated northern nationalist hostility towards the new government. In any case, these nationalists felt vulnerable and resentful after the passing of the 1920 act; they had somewhat over-optimistically assumed that Sinn Féin would overcome unionist demands for separate treatment.

However, the nationalist minority was weakened in its response to the new government because of deep internal divisions over partition, which did not even begin to be overcome till after the outcome of the boundary commission. The divisions had been present since 1916, between followers of Belfast M.P. Joseph Devlin, leader in Ulster of the more pragmatic nationalist party, and the strongly anti-partitionist Sinn Féin supporters in border areas.[5] Despite these divisions the minority shared a derisive contempt for partition. Both elements fought the 1921 general election on an uncompromising policy of abstention from the house of commons and non-recognition of the Belfast government. The catholic church's endorsement of this strategy sprang above all from fears concerning education: the spectre of a department of education in Belfast dominated by hard-line protestants filled the clergy with dread.[6] The church's stand was highlighted by Cardinal Logue's refusal to attend the state opening of parliament.

[5] On the background to this split, see Phoenix, *Northern nationalism*, ch. 1.
[6] Ibid., pp 26–7, 189.

Over the previous twelve months, the prolonged political uncertainty and an upsurge in I.R.A. activity in the north had sharpened sectarian feeling. Serious eruptions of violence resulted, especially in Belfast, Lisburn, and Derry. In July 1920 the R.I.C. reported the rounding up and expulsion of catholic workers from Belfast's two shipyards. This prompted a retaliatory dáil boycott of northern goods. Earlier, unionist doubts as to the will and the ability of Dublin Castle to preserve law and order had contributed to a revival of the Ulster Volunteer Force in June 1920; its function remained to preserve unionist discipline, protect property, and ultimately defend the union. In early September 1920, Westminster reluctantly agreed officially to recognise this force by recruiting its members into a legally constituted special constabulary; details of the scheme were published in October.[7] There were to be three classes: class A, full-time, temporary constables, armed, equipped and paid on terms similar to the permanent R.I.C.; class B, part-timers, serving locally; and class C, unpaid emergency reservists. The decision to proceed was taken (against a background of sustained pressure from unionists) in order to eliminate the risk of a clash between crown forces and paramilitary elements, and to relieve the already over-stretched local military presence. Though the specials were to have been raised from loyal citizens throughout Ireland, in practice they were organised exclusively in Northern Ireland, by the newly appointed assistant under-secretary in Belfast, Sir Ernest Clark.[8]

The formation of the new force helped assuage protestant anxieties but it exacerbated feelings of alienation among nationalists, as much for its success against the I.R.A. as for its excesses. Joseph Devlin accused Britain of arming 'pogromists to murder catholics'. In January 1921 the I.R.A. launched an offensive against members of the new force, whom it had described as 'traitors to the Republic'.[9] This campaign provoked further sectarian violence— both spontaneous outbursts and more calculated revenge killings. Thus levels of violence remained high; on some estimates twenty-six died and 140 were wounded in Belfast alone during July 1921.[10]

These deep-rooted and volatile problems required sensitivity and clear thinking on the part of politicians; but this was not forthcoming in the years 1921–2. During this crucial, formative period, the attitude of the imperial authorities towards Northern Ireland was determined by an overriding desire to arrive at and maintain a settlement with the south. When, in mid October

---

[7] Above, p. 24.
[8] These and other difficulties facing the Northern Ireland government in 1920–22 are discussed in Patrick Buckland, *The factory of grievances: devolved government in Northern Ireland, 1921–39* (Dublin, 1979), pp 1–6, 9–77, 181–2.
[9] *Hansard 5 (commons)*, cxxxiii, 1504 (25 Oct. 1920); *Northern Whig*, 6 Dec. 1920.
[10] G. B. Kenna [Rev. John Hassan], *Facts and figures of the Belfast pogrom, 1920–22* (Dublin, 1922), p. 63.

1921, the Anglo–Irish negotiations began in earnest, the Sinn Féin delegates pressed British ministers on partition, but the delegates lacked a coherent strategy on the issue, and independence remained their priority throughout. For their part, British ministers were concerned that the discussions should not founder on the Ulster question, and hoped that Craig could be cajoled into playing a conciliatory role. Thus, in early November 1921, Lloyd George pressed Craig to concede 'essential unity'. Residual sympathy in the Conservative party helped stiffen the resistance of unionist leaders and confirmed their refusal to capitulate. Bonar Law commented: 'What is asked of them is not concession but the surrender of everything for which they have been fighting for thirty-five years.'[11]

The negotiations had other repercussions. They raised nationalist hopes to new heights, and appeared to vindicate the refusal to recognise the new parliament. However, initial hopes were shaken in July by publication of the British government's proposals for a settlement. Later, de Valera's statements that no coercion would be used against the north, and that individual counties might opt out of a future self-governing Ireland, also caused deep unease. Both developments helped precipitate a spate of deputations by nationalists to Dublin and the passing of political resolutions by nationalist-controlled bodies in Northern Ireland. The aim was to reaffirm Sinn Féin's opposition to partition and, as far as possible, to strengthen its bargaining position. The actions taken by the Tyrone and Fermanagh county councils were particularly effective; they impressed Lloyd George and alarmed and embarrassed northern unionists.[12]

In the meantime, nationalists derived some reassurance from Westminster's apparent reluctance to implement fully the terms of the 1920 act. For more than five months after the truce no significant powers were transferred to the new government. British ministers were concerned not to prejudice or predetermine the outcome of the negotiations; while these were in progress, they claimed that the legal difficulties involved in devolving any responsibilities were insuperable.[13] The delay had particularly grave repercussions for security policy. Northern Ireland ministers faced the problem of preventing outbreaks of sectarian conflict, as well as countering violence directed at overthrowing or immobilising the new government. It was clearly a matter of the utmost urgency to establish quickly a system of law enforcement and justice that would have the confidence of both communities.

---

[11] Buckland, *Ir. unionism 2*, p. 149.
[12] They sent delegations to meet de Valera in order to strengthen his bargaining position and stiffen his resolve, they passed resolutions refusing to recognise the Northern Ireland parliament, and finally they pledged allegiance to Dáil Éireann; see records of Fermanagh and Tyrone county councils, July–Dec. 1921 (P.R.O.N.I., LA4, 6).
[13] E.g. remarks by Sir Hamar Greenwood, chief secretary, in cabinet conclusions, 31 Aug. 1921 (P.R.O.N.I., CAB4/17).

In late June 1921 the northern cabinet was encouraged to believe that the transfer of policing powers was imminent and that swingeing measures were being prepared to break the I.R.A. campaign. Neither materialised. Until 22 November law and order matters remained exclusively a Westminster responsibility. Meanwhile, unionist distrust of the security forces was confirmed by a decision, taken at Dublin Castle, to apply the terms of the truce to the six counties. This was done in order to facilitate the Anglo–Irish negotiations; the Northern Ireland ministers were not consulted. Thus, with no prior warning, the 20,000 members of the special constabulary were immobilised, raising protestant fears for the future of the force. Troops stationed in the province were relegated to a peace-keeping role. Police raids and searches ceased. Most galling, from the unionist government's perspective, was the official recognition simultaneously accorded to the I.R.A. In consequence, I.R.A. liaison officers negotiated with representatives of crown forces on equal terms and the leaders were provided with an opportunity to regroup and reorganise. Instantly I.R.A. activities increased, the G.H.Q. in Dublin providing arms, training, and finance. In Northern Ireland the I.R.A. exploited fully its enhanced status and rapidly expanded its support in catholic areas, thus (in Craig's phrase) 'gravely imperilling the position of Ulster'.[14] The I.R.A., together with the Sinn Féin party, was the chief beneficiary of the truce. Constitutional organisations, such as the United Irish League and the Ancient Order of Hibernians, seemed increasingly irrelevant to their erstwhile supporters. Only in west Belfast did constitutional nationalism, under Joseph Devlin's leadership, survive as a credible force.

The unsatisfactory security implications of these developments were immediately evident from the confused response by crown forces to three severe outbreaks of rioting in Belfast, between July and September 1921. During the first of these, in mid July, the northern cabinet requested General Sir Nevil Macready, the G.O.C.-in-C. Ireland, to restore the peace preservation measures in operation prior to the truce. Subsequently, additional troops were dispatched, but their actions were still to be guided by the spirit of the agreement. Ministers were, however, assured that sufficient forces and powers were available to deal with any situation that might arise.

Further severe rioting occurred in late August; on this occasion casualty figures might well have been lower had troops been dispatched promptly after being requested by J. F. Gelston, the city's police commissioner. Once again, though more vigorously than before, the Northern Ireland government pressed for firm security measures. It was conscious of mounting criticisms of its apparent impotence from its supporters, and stressed the danger of the

---

[14] Cabinet conclusions, 16 Aug. 1921 (P.R.O.N.I., CAB4/14); Buckland, *Factory of grievances*, pp 179–85; Phoenix, *Northern nationalism*, pp 139–43.

loyalist element getting out of hand. Ministers demanded the mobilisation of the special constabulary, full use by crown forces of their emergency powers 'on the advice of the Northern Ireland cabinet', and a display of military force to restore public confidence. Ministers claimed that laxity in security matters had provided Sinn Féin with the opportunity to bring additional men and arms into Belfast.[15]

During the following weeks efforts were made to devise a coherent law-and-order policy for Northern Ireland. There were many difficulties. The authorities in Dublin Castle often disagreed with the views of army officers, police, and politicians in Belfast, and also disagreed among themselves. There was disagreement as to whether the violence was political or sectarian in character. There was no consensus, either, over the appropriate security response—whether troop reinforcements were required, emergency powers could be applied, the special constabulary mobilised, or the regular police force placed under army command. One positive decision resulted from these deliberations; the military commander in charge of Belfast, Colonel George Carter-Campbell, assured the cabinet that he would dispatch troops more quickly in future and maintain fixed military posts and patrols in affected areas after peace was restored. Other issues, however, remained unresolved. Police authorities in Belfast forcefully resisted any suggestion that they should be placed under military control. A. W. Cope (assistant under-secretary for Ireland) indicated that, despite the truce, authority could and would be given to hold suspects without trial, but stipulated that both sides would have to be interned, as both sides were involved in acts of violence. However, a promised written assurance from him, which would have enabled arrests to proceed, had not been received by 12 September. On that day, increasingly demoralised Northern Ireland ministers discussed the impact on public confidence of the continuing drift in security policy.

None the less, when further serious disorders occurred in Belfast in late September, crown forces responded promptly and with vigour. Acting on representations from local politicians and security advisers, Dublin Castle agreed to a partial mobilisation of the special constabulary, on condition that the patrolling of catholic areas be entrusted solely to the army and regular police. Where violence persisted, Carter-Campbell assumed control of all constabulary personnel in the city. Troops acting under the Restoration of Order in Ireland Act made a number of arrests, and assemblies of three or more persons in affected areas were proscribed.[16] In nationalist communities

---

[15] See P.R.O.N.I., CAB4/17, which contains the conclusions for two cabinet meetings on 31 Aug. and one on 1 Sept. 1921, and also an unsigned typescript headed 'History of attempts to get peace-keeping forces on satisfactory footing'.
[16] 10 & 11 Geo. V, c. 31 (9 Aug. 1920); Buckland, *Factory of grievances*, pp 187–92; cabinet conclusions, 1, 12 Sept. 1921 (P.R.O.N.I., CAB4/17, 19).

these measures reinforced a tendency to look to the I.R.A. rather than crown
forces for protection. At the same time, unionists regarded the measures
as inadequate, even inappropriate. They criticised the continuing failure to
remobilise the special constabulary at full strength, complete with arms.
They resented the recurring imputation in military communiqués that the
disorder was sectarian rather than political in character, and they resented
the arrest of protestants as well as catholics under the emergency powers
provisions. Progressively, feelings of optimism and expectation in June 1921
had been replaced by a deepening sense of betrayal and disillusion. Northern
Ireland ministers were castigated for their unwillingness or inability to take
effective security measures and for their alleged over-confidence in the British government. Special constables complained bitterly that the I.R.A.'s 'organisation for attack' was being perfected without hindrance. These anxieties
were rendered more volatile by the context of economic recession, trade
boycott, and political uncertainty. Consequently the period from July onwards witnessed the proliferation of loyalist paramilitary organisations, and
later a revival of the U.V.F. throughout much of the province; the cabinet
hoped that the latter, with its traditions and discipline, might contain the
discontent. By mid November 1921 total membership of these unofficial
forces was estimated at 21,000.[17]

Later that month, orders in council were issued, fixing appointed days for
the formal handing-over of powers to the Northern Ireland government
under the terms of the 1920 act. On 21 November responsibility for maintaining law and order was handed over, and on 1 December control of local
government services was transferred. Craig and his supporters viewed these
developments with profound relief. To northern nationalists, they were cause
for trepidation. The extension of executive powers generated the sudden
realisation that the long-derided unionist administration might emerge from
the negotiations in London with its position substantially intact. In response,
by 7 December, nine local authorities with Sinn Féin–nationalist party majorities had repudiated the Northern Ireland government's jurisdiction and
defiantly pledged allegiance to Dáil Éireann.

At first it seemed possible that the transfer of power might at least ease
the local security problem by enabling a more prompt and considered response to such disorders as might arise. However, though the Belfast government had at last been granted formal responsibility for law and order, it still
lacked the financial, legal, and physical resources to develop a response,
independent of Westminster. Also the experience of the previous five months
further restricted its freedom of manoeuvre. Unionists demanded that the

---

[17] Philip McVicker, 'Law and order in Northern Ireland, 1920–36' (Ph.D. thesis, University
of Ulster, 1985), pp 44–8; Buckland, *Factory of grievances*, pp 192–4; Arthur Hezlet, *The B
Specials: a history of the Ulster Special Constabulary* (London, 1972), pp 53, 54–85; diary of
Frederick Crawford, 27 Oct. 1921 (Crawford papers, P.R.O.N.I., D640/11A).

government 'deal seriously with the Sinn Féiners in Ulster' and end the perceived policy of drift in relation both to law and order and to local government.[18]

Unionist distrust of Britain was strengthened, in early December, by publication of the Anglo–Irish treaty. Its terms formally recognised partition, but none the less clearly envisaged Ireland as a single entity, even if 'the assertion of the principle was accompanied by no prospect of a practical realisation'.[19] The Sinn Féin delegates were firmly convinced that as a consequence of the agreement 'essential unity' had been achieved; at the time this view was broadly shared by the imperial delegation. Article 12 was the main source of these expectations; it stated that if Northern Ireland excluded itself from the Free State (by passing a special address through both houses of its legislature) its frontiers were to be revised by a boundary commission. This provision prolonged the political uncertainty surrounding the future of Northern Ireland; Craig later described it as the 'predominant danger' facing his government and a surrender to Sinn Féin.[20] Unionists, especially west of the Bann, feared that it would result in the transfer of substantial portions of the six counties to the Free State.

Meanwhile, the boundary commission became the focal point of nationalist hopes and almost seemed designed to perpetuate their divisions. Article 12 was greeted with particular enthusiasm by border nationalists, among whom the Sinn Féin party was strongest and who believed that at the very least the greater part of Fermanagh and Tyrone would ultimately be included in the Free State. In contrast, Devlinite nationalists to the east of the province strongly opposed repartition. They hoped rather for a revised settlement that would enhance the prospects of national unity and provide, in the interim, guarantees for northern catholics in the areas of policing, education, and equitable representation. All nationalists, especially those in the west, favoured continuing the policy of non-recognition towards the unionist government.[21] For all the treaty's obvious limitations, neither border nor east Ulster nationalists considered that there was any practical alternative to it. Division over the issue of sovereignty, which preoccupied southerners, was a luxury that the half-million northern nationalists could not afford; opposition could place the boundary commission in jeopardy and perpetuate partition.

It was therefore in exceptionally difficult circumstances that the Northern Ireland government first sought to exercise its authority in December 1921.

---

[18] Crawford diary, 15 Nov. 1921.
[19] Nicholas Mansergh, *The government of Northern Ireland* (London, 1936), pp 119–20.
[20] *Hansard N.I. (commons)*, ii, 9 (14 Mar. 1922); Patrick Buckland, *James Craig* (Dublin, 1980), p. 70.
[21] This policy was actively encouraged by the Sinn Féin leadership in Dublin (Phoenix, *Northern nationalism*, pp 167–9; see pp 152–66 for analysis of northern nationalist attitudes to the treaty and boundary commission).

Within its borders—which could not yet be regarded as fixed—a substantial and embittered minority refused to recognise its authority and had reason to hope that the new institutions would not survive. Across the border, the hostile Sinn Féin leaders took a similar view.[22] More extreme nationalists, north and south, were also prepared to back a physical force campaign aimed at achieving unity. As a consequence of the truce, the I.R.A. had become better prepared and organised; by early 1922 its membership in the north numbered 8,500. And to compound these difficulties, support from the British government remained uncertain; its attitude was still determined by the exigencies of its larger Irish policy. Conditions in Northern Ireland required generous, sustained, and imaginative measures, directed towards winning over the nationalist community and assuaging its legitimate suspicions and fears. No such strategy was adopted. Rather, the traditional unionist siege mentality was accentuated by the context of actual siege. The circumstances of Northern Ireland's birth permanently distorted its political structures. The process had begun before powers were transferred.

On 1 December 1921 the cabinet considered how best to respond to the recalcitrant nationalist-controlled councils whose activities had caused embarrassment virtually from the outset of the Anglo–Irish negotiations. It was decided that any councils that persisted in rejecting the government's authority would be dissolved and replaced with paid commissioners. Emergency legislation giving the necessary powers was introduced into the commons on the following day and within two weeks had received the royal assent; the measure was regarded as more urgent once the terms of the treaty had become known.[23] Meanwhile, in order not to exacerbate the situation, 'flamboyant [verbal] effusions' by anti-unionists on local councils were ignored.[24] Some authorities staged a strategic retreat. On 7 December, Tyrone county council resolved that it would loyally carry out the terms of the treaty, so, in effect, giving *de jure* recognition to the northern government. Most of its members were anxious to avoid dissolution so that they would be in a position to articulate nationalist claims for inclusion in the south when article 12 was implemented. A number of other local elected bodies, however, continued to defy the 'partition parliament'; by March 1922 over twenty of these, including Fermanagh county council, had been suspended—initially, for a period of one year. Craig may have hoped that in the longer term border adjustments would ease his local government difficulties; in early

[22] One of the few studies to consider the formation of Northern Ireland in the light of the establishment of the Free State is David Fitzpatrick, *The two Irelands 1912–1939* (Oxford, 1998), ch. 5.
[23] 12 Geo. V, c. 5 (14 Dec. 1921).
[24] *Report of the ministry of home affairs on local government services* (Belfast, 1923), p. 9; also cabinet conclusions, 1 Dec. 1921 (P.R.O.N.I., CAB4/28).

January, the cabinet considered appointing Sir Edward Carson as the Northern Ireland representative on the boundary commission.[25]

During the following months, ministerial unease at the prospect of boundary revision was overshadowed by security matters; these became the overriding concern. Policy priorities bore the clear imprint of experience since the truce. Distrust of Westminster was reflected in the urgent efforts to achieve independence from the British military establishment in all circumstances short of an invasion of the six counties or cross-border raids in force: the cabinet unanimously agreed that 'the safety of Ulster must come first'. This was balanced by a fixed desire to 'bring the British government along with us'; Britain after all was the irreplaceable source of troops and finance and the font of sovereign power. At the same time, ministers were concerned that they should 'maintain the confidence of our [i.e. the unionist] people'.[26] This was to be achieved through the energetic adoption of policies thought necessary to restore law and order; liaison arrangements between crown forces and the I.R.A. were terminated as soon as security powers were transferred. The pace and intensity of the measures taken subsequently were largely determined by the unpredictable flow of events in early 1922; in particular, the progressive deterioration in relations with the south.

Craig met Michael Collins in London on 21 January 1922; he had earlier informed colleagues of his anxiety to ascertain whether the provisional government 'intended to declare peace or war with [*sic*] Northern Ireland'.[27] The meeting was arranged by Winston Churchill, secretary of state for the colonies, partly out of concern at recent rioting in Belfast after the release of 130 northern republican prisoners by the British authorities. Discussions between the two leaders were cordial and wide-ranging, leading to the first so-called Craig–Collins pact. In return for guarantees to catholics, Collins agreed to end the Sinn Féin boycott of Belfast goods. Afterwards, Craig expressed satisfaction. Collins had appeared to accept that Ulster could not be coerced into a United Ireland; his attendance in itself implied recognition of the northern government. However, when they met again on 2 February,

---

[25] Cabinet conclusions, 10 Jan. 1922 (P.R.O.N.I., CAB4/29). During discussions, ministers agreed that though refusal to take part would be popular with unionists, it contained the risk that a representative might be appointed to act on Northern Ireland's behalf, and thus a larger area might be lost. Such a course might also jeopardise residual Conservative party sympathy, and the unionist government might seem ridiculous if it did not cooperate in implementing a settlement agreed to by Westminster. Thus ministers considered nominating Carson: better terms might thereby result, and in Craig's view some boundary change might be advantageous.

[26] The most detailed cabinet consideration of priorities is in cabinet conclusions, 12 May 1922 (P.R.O.N.I., CAB4/41).

[27] Cabinet conclusions, 26 Jan. 1922 (P.R.O.N.I., CAB4/30); also, on 11 Jan. 1922 Craig indicated to Churchill that he was willing to meet Collins 'to ascertain clearly whether the policy of Southern Ireland is to be one of peace or whether the present method of pressure on Northern Ireland is to be continued' (Martin Gilbert, *Winston Churchill*, iv: *1916–22* (London, 1975), p. 684.

it was evident that they held incompatible views on the release of political prisoners, and above all, on boundary changes. Craig would only consider minor boundary adjustments. In contrast Collins sought substantial transfers of territory; he argued that 'majorities must rule', in the expectation that if this principle were applied the viability of Northern Ireland might be undermined.[28] He was dismayed when, days later, during a commons debate at Westminster, Churchill dismissed such an interpretation of article 12 as absurd.[29]

None the less, Britain's acute concern that the treaty should be implemented, and that the provisional government should establish its authority, enabled southern ministers to exercise a degree of influence over Northern Ireland affairs. As the split within the Sinn Féin movement deepened, partition emerged as an obvious issue on which to attack supporters of the recent settlement. It was also tempting to seek to preserve unity and perhaps avoid civil war by diverting attention towards the six counties. Collins took a keen personal interest in the plight of the northern minority, much more so than his cabinet colleagues. He quickly emerged as the minority's spokesman, acted as its protector, and successfully exploited the favourable circumstances in which to press his views and demands on Westminster. While negotiating with Craig in apparent good faith, he consistently supported the minority's refusal to recognise the regime, and he himself 'initiated policies of obstruction with every single government agency through which the north dealt with the south'.[30] From January, he also covertly provided the I.R.A.'s northern divisions with rifles and revolvers called in from Liam Lynch's Irregulars, and he personally authorised cross-border raids and kidnappings. His intention was not only to protect the interests of northern nationalists but to destabilise the province, to provide evidence that large areas were disaffected and ungovernable—in short, to achieve unity using any and every means. Nevertheless, Collins's concern for Irish unity was ultimately subordinated to his primary political tasks and responsibilities in Dublin.

A succession of border incidents in the early months of 1922 contributed to an alarming deterioration in north–south relations and heightened sectarian bitterness in the province. On 8 February an I.R.A. column, based in County Monaghan and acting on Collins's covert authority, kidnapped forty-two leading unionists and special constables in Fermanagh and Tyrone. The probable objective of this, and at least one earlier operation, was to effect the release of three republican prisoners, arrested before the truce and held under imminent death sentence in Derry. Next day the viceroy intervened and issued a reprieve, only hours before the time of execution. On 12

[28] Phoenix, *Northern nationalism*, p. 181.
[29] Ibid., p. 186.
[30] T. P. Coogan, *Michael Collins* (Reading, 1991), p. 339; also pp 333–43 for discussion of Collins's approach to Northern Ireland.

February 'A' special reinforcements dispatched by rail to Enniskillen clashed with an I.R.A. unit at Clones station; several deaths occurred. This was followed by outbreaks of shooting in Belfast, apparently inspired by the I.R.A.[31]

The northern government regarded border incidents as part of a concerted campaign to destabilise the province. Complicity and bad faith on the part of the Dublin leadership were taken for granted.[32] The British authorities were also denounced for the reprieve of the three Derry prisoners, which had incensed unionist opinion, and Craig himself had considered resignation. He and his colleagues proceeded to introduce far-reaching security measures. 'A' and 'B' specials were fully mobilised for the first time in almost eight months; Craig claimed in concurrent negotiations with the treasury that they had justified their existence.[33] The constabulary establishment was increased, partly as a means of absorbing and disciplining protestant paramilitary organisations. Also with this in mind, a new 'C1' class was planned to augment the 'C' category of special constables, in effect a territorial army; it had been under consideration for some time prior to powers being transferred. In March Craig invited Field-marshal Sir Henry Wilson, the former C.I.G.S., to advise on security matters. At his suggestion a military adviser, Major-general Sir Arthur Solly-Flood, was appointed; on 7 April he assumed overall responsibility for maintaining law and order in Northern Ireland, supported by officers seconded from the war office. In London these appointments may have been regarded as a means of bringing the special constabulary under a measure of military discipline. Meanwhile, the Civil Authorities (Special Powers) Bill was drafted. Its terms were less far-reaching than those contained in the restoration of order in Ireland act, but it still equipped the ministry of home affairs with extensive emergency powers. These the minister was authorised to delegate to his parliamentary secretary or even to a police officer. It provided for the death penalty or flogging to be applied in a range of political offences, and it specifically allowed for the introduction of internment.[34]

Although these initiatives were intended to provide a greater measure of regional self-reliance, Craig remained conscious of Northern Ireland's ultimate dependence on Britain in security matters. He himself noted that the north could not survive in a 'campaign of atrocity' with the south. In order to increase moral and financial support for Ulster, he therefore launched an

[31] Cabinet conclusions, 14 Feb. 1922 (P.R.O.N.I., CAB4/32); Churchill remarked that Belfast had an 'underworld ... with deadly forces of its own' (Gilbert, *Churchill*, iv, 696).

[32] Buckland, *Craig*, pp 57, 76.

[33] For Craig's meeting with treasury officials, 9 Feb. 1922, see P.R.O.N.I., CAB9A/4/1; McVicker, 'Law & order', pp 65–6.

[34] Bill enacted as 12 & 13 Geo. V, c. 5 (7 Apr. 1922); McVicker, 'Law & order', pp 68–70; Brian Barton, 'The development of Northern Ireland government policy in relation to law and order and local government, 1921–2' (M.A. thesis, University of Ulster, 1975), pp 25–9; Colin Campbell, *Emergency law in Ireland, 1918–1925* (Oxford, 1994), ch. 4.

energetic propaganda campaign both in the United Kingdom and the colonies. He also consistently rejected appeals for the introduction of martial law mainly because he feared that, if imposed, it would seem in England that 'one side [was] as bad as the other'.[35] His frequent absences in London, where he went to explain his policies, had the unfortunate consequence of allowing sensitive issues to be determined by uncompromising and partisan colleagues.

The British cabinet was largely uninterested in Northern Ireland's problems, but it was responsive to southern claims and criticisms and therefore wary of taking any action that could be interpreted as a breach of the spirit of the treaty. British ministers therefore felt especially uneasy at the expansion of the special constabulary. It was widely regarded as unnecessary and dangerous to the peace. Moreover, there was concern that the force would, in certain circumstances, be turned against the imperial government.[36] Nevertheless, ministers in general left responsibility for developing a satisfactory system of law enforcement to the Northern Ireland government; for his part, Craig suspected that they would have welcomed an opportunity to 'wash their hands of the whole affair'.[37] In order to avoid parliamentary controversy, grants towards the upkeep of the special constabulary were concealed in a general subsidy to Northern Ireland. Though additional troops were despatched, they maintained a peripheral role. From February 1922 onwards border defence became the exclusive responsibility of the special constabulary. British army involvement was avoided, as it would have increased the danger of a confrontation with the I.R.A., even a revival of the Anglo–Irish war. Churchill's response to the I.R.A. border offensive, the deepening north–south hostility, and continuing sectarian atrocities in Belfast, was to organise a further meeting between Collins and Craig. Representatives of the British and both Irish governments met on 30 March for the first time, and, after discussions, signed the second Craig–Collins pact. It contained a number of specific commitments: I.R.A. activity in the six counties was to cease, certain political prisoners in Northern Ireland to be released, and expelled catholic shipyard workers in Belfast to be returned to their former employment. Other provisions were intended to promote catholic confidence in the northern government and to elicit their cooperation in security matters. 'No-jury' courts were to be established for cases of serious crime; an inter-community conciliation committee was to be formed to investigate

[35] Cabinet conclusions, 14 Feb. 1922 (P.R.O.N.I., CAB4/32); *Hansard N.I. (commons)*, ii, 15 (14 Mar. 1922).

[36] Comment by Otto Ernst Niemeyer, deputy controller at the treasury, 23 Jan. 1922 (McVicker, 'Law & order', p. 65); memo by Tom Jones and Lionel Curtis, 18 Mar. 1922 (P.R.O., S. G. Tallents papers, CO 906/30).

[37] Cabinet conclusions, 14 Feb. 1922 (P.R.O.N.I., CAB4/32); discussion of British policy towards Northern Ireland in Buckland, *Factory of grievances*, pp 197–201.

reports of outrages and complaints of intimidation, and an all-catholic advisory body was to be appointed to select suitable recruits from among its co-religionists for service in the special constabulary. In addition, police personnel were to display official identification numbers when on patrol and to hand in their arms before going off duty.[38]

Implementation of these terms was rendered more difficult by the context of political uncertainty in both parts of Ireland and the persistence of violence, especially in Belfast, where 21 per cent of the labour force was unemployed. Given the depth of the slump throughout the north and an acute housing shortage, any suggestion that those expelled from their workplaces or homes would be speedily returned merely raised expectations that could not be realised. In any case, the Northern Ireland government showed neither imagination nor urgency regarding its obligations under the pact; had it done so, it would have undermined its credibility with most members of the unionist movement. To the party rank and file, the agreement seemed designed to tarnish the reputation of the province's legal system and of its special constabulary, to facilitate the assassination of policemen both on and off duty, and generally to weaken the forces of law and order in the hope of making Northern Ireland ungovernable.

Northern Ireland ministers, officials, and the military adviser sympathised with such views. Under pressure from colleagues, Craig interpreted the security clauses narrowly. Thus, he released only a small number of political prisoners, and exclusively those charged with technical offences; he himself had always regarded convicted republicans as a 'trump card to be played' in negotiations with the south.[39] Characteristically, Sir Richard Dawson Bates, minister for home affairs, took advantage of his leader's frequent absences to subvert the implementation of other provisions. In particular he delayed convening the intercommunal investigative committee; its activities had lapsed completely by mid May.[40] The advisory body to select catholic recruits for the special constabulary was similarly unproductive owing to ministerial indifference, I.R.A. intimidation, and catholic alienation; the attitude of border nationalists was governed mainly by the assumption that they would be transferred to the Free State by the boundary commission.

For his part, Collins appeared to be committed to conciliation and anxious to fulfil the terms of the agreement. Behind the scenes, however, he partici-

[38] Text in Macardle, *Ir. republic*, pp 894–6; detailed analysis in Michael Farrell, *Arming the protestants: the formation of the Ulster Special Constabulary and Royal Ulster Constabulary, 1920–27* (London, 1983), pp 104–24.

[39] Cabinet conclusions, 18 Apr. 1922 (P.R.O.N.I., CAB4/40).

[40] Dawson Bates regarded the committee as a 'voluntary' body and therefore refused it funding, denied it access to government reports on disturbances, and responded dilatorily to its requests. It met twice (12, 19 Apr.); by early May its catholic membership had withdrawn and it quietly lapsed. See editorial in *Irish News*, 20 Apr. 1922, and Eamon Phoenix, 'The nationalist movement in Northern Ireland, 1914–28' (Ph. D. thesis, Q.U.B., 1984), pp 505–7.

pated in preparations for a new northern offensive by joint I.R.A. forces, timed for mid May.[41] This was to appear as 'a defensive operation, a reaction against the activities of the specials';[42] its purpose was to wreak such havoc and destruction in the province that the unionist leadership would be compelled to seek an accommodation with the south. In fact, Collins had little influence with the Irregulars unless it was exercised towards war; during late March, they successfully revived the Belfast boycott without his approval. Meanwhile, the British government's tacit recognition of Collins as the custodian of the interests of northern nationalists exasperated unionists. Furthermore, within Northern Ireland the successive inter-governmental agreements tended to confer credibility and prestige on Sinn Féin and the I.R.A. As a consequence, the Devlinites, who favoured recognition of the northern parliament and the formation of a broadly based nationalist–Labour coalition, found their position repeatedly undermined.

An abrupt exchange of letters between Collins and Craig in late April effectively signalled the demise of the March pact;[43] subsequently, as Churchill noted ruefully, the two sides drifted even further apart. The level of violence in Northern Ireland rose as a result of the mounting I.R.A. campaign, sectarian clashes, and disillusion stemming from the repeated failure of negotiations. In response, the special constabulary was maintained at full strength and its size further increased. In addition, legislation was prepared to provide for the formation of the Royal Ulster Constabulary (despite Craig's protests, the British government had refused to halt the disbandment of the R.I.C.; the R.U.C. was established to take its place on 31 May, and the old force would be disbanded by 31 August 1922).[44] In the disturbed conditions then obtaining, the government's initial intention to ensure that one-third of recruits to the new force were catholics was jettisoned.[45]

None the less, when considering the measures to be taken, the Northern Ireland cabinet remained alert to the sensibilities of British ministers and was therefore reluctant either to maximise its latent powers or even to make optimum use of those it already possessed. Accordingly, although forewarned

---

[41] Above, pp 26–30.

[42] Coogan, *Collins*, p. 362.

[43] Craig to Collins and Collins's reply, 25, 28 Apr. 1922, in Phoenix, *Northern nationalism*, pp 216–17.

[44] 12 & 13 Geo. V, c. 8 (31 May 1922); 12 & 13 Geo. V, c. 55 [U.K.] (4 Aug. 1922).

[45] Hezlet, *B Specials*, pp 62, 73. The report of the departmental committee on police reorganisation in Northern Ireland (1922, Cmd 1, p. 5) recommended (though not unanimously) that one-third of R.U.C. places be reserved for catholics; Hezlet suggests that this went beyond the terms of the 1920 act. The stipulation was not included in the bill (*Hansard N.I. (commons)*, ii, 654 (24 May 1922)). Despite initial good intentions and fair selection procedures, the government did little to attract catholics: their recruitment peaked in early 1924 at 552, 19.2% of R.U.C. strength (Farrell, *Arming the protestants*, p. 191; Buckland, *Factory of grievances*, pp 21–2). Between June and Dec. 1922 81.7% of R.U.C. recruits were ex-R.I.C. or ex-U.S.C. (McVicker, 'Law & order', p. 101).

by local police authorities that a major terrorist offensive was being planned, ministers rejected the recommendation that suspects should be interned. Instead, they merely authorised lists of those of 'evil designs' so that they could be dealt with 'instantly if the crisis arises'.[46] Similarly, ministers rejected the suggestion that special courts should be established for those charged with serious political crimes, for fear that such an initiative would not be understood in England. The conspicuous security measures recommended by Solly-Flood were likewise ignored; he had advised equipping the special constabulary with aircraft, tanks, and bombs.[47]

The level of violence reached a peak in May 1922. In that month alone, an estimated seventy-five murders took place in Belfast, forty-two of the victims being catholics. Between 10 and 25 May, coinciding with the main thrust of the I.R.A. offensive, forty-one fires occurred, the latter mainly at protestant-owned business premises in catholic districts.[48] Such operations were conducted chiefly by indigenous, pro-treaty units, acting under authority from the southern I.R.A. headquarters. Although the campaign did not progress exactly as planned, it provoked a severe sectarian backlash. Unionist alarm was heightened by the signing of the de Valera–Collins electoral pact on 20 May. Ministers regarded this pact as an ominous portent, which would probably presage a concerted attack on the six counties. The agreement had in part been prompted by a delegation of northern nationalists to Dublin, two days earlier. Its members had warned the Sinn Féin leadership that civil conflict in the south might well render partition permanent and would certainly leave northern nationalists exposed and unprotected. At the Sinn Féin ard-fheis some days later, Collins stated that the agreement would enable him to concentrate on the affairs of the north.

The escalating violence in the north and news of the pact in Dublin prompted Craig and his colleagues to take full advantage of their emergency powers. On 22 May, a number of extreme nationalist movements were proscribed, including the I.R.A., I.R.B., and Cumann na mBan. Also on that day internment was introduced and enforced against those 'endeavouring to subvert our parliament'.[49] During the following weeks, over 500 I.R.A. suspects and sympathisers were arrested and held on the *Argenta*, a ship moored off Larne. Lord Fitzalan, the lord lieutenant, who had initially been reluctant to

---

[46] Cabinet conclusions, 19 Apr. 1922 (P.R.O.N.I. CAB4/40).

[47] Cabinet conclusions, 13 Mar., 19 June 1922 (P.R.O.N.I., CAB4/35, 48; Hezlet, *B Specials*, pp 66–7, 82–8).

[48] G. B. Kenna, *Facts and figures of the Belfast pogrom, 1920–22* (Dublin, 1922), p. 94; Buckland, *Ir. unionism 2*, p. 169; Buckland, *Factory of grievances*, pp 195–6, 320.

[49] Craig told the house of internment and the proclamation order on the afternoon of 23 May 1922 (*Hansard N.I. (commons)*, ii, 599). By then, there were 202 internees. The decision that certain nationalist movements should be 'immediately proclaimed' was taken by cabinet on 20 May 1922 (P.R.O.N.I., CAB4/43); Bates issued the relevant orders on 22 May (Phoenix, 'Nationalist movement', pp 542–9).

give his approval to internment, did so unhesitatingly after the assassination of a unionist M.P., William Twaddell, and the burning of Shane's Castle, County Antrim; its proprietor, Lord O'Neill, was father of the speaker of the Northern Ireland house of commons. In early June the imposition of a curfew covering the entire six counties, and the application of exclusion orders, effectively curtailed large-scale I.R.A. operations in rural areas. The cabinet underlined its commitment to the restoration of order by agreeing 'to stand over [i.e. indemnify] any action' taken by crown forces. In addition, the cabinet fully endorsed a suggestion made by the military adviser that the 'time [had] arrived when shooting from across the border should be replied to'.[50]

The increasing turmoil in the province and the government's extensive countermeasures coincided with delicate discussions between London and Dublin over the draft Irish constitution; these had begun on 27 May. From the outset, British ministers were concerned that the provisional government might exploit recent developments in Northern Ireland to justify non-compliance with the treaty, and perhaps even to break off the negotiations. On 30 May Collins raised the political situation in the north, alleging that members of the special constabulary were involved in the killing of northern catholics. He claimed that such outrages were the ultimate responsibility of the British government, which had authorised and financed the specials. He suggested that martial law be imposed and an impartial inquiry held into the actions taken by the Northern Ireland government.

By late May the British government had itself become acutely uneasy about the measures being adopted in Northern Ireland and also its own role in the region's affairs, particularly in relation to the special constabulary. In Lloyd George's opinion, 'the Ulster difficulty... was the weakest part of the British case'. He observed that 'the first murders were of catholics', yet 'no one had been punished. We had made no inquiry, we had armed 48,000 protestants.'[51] The consensus reached by British ministers was that an initiative should be taken to eliminate the Ulster question from the discussions with the south and so clarify the essential issue of 'republic versus empire'. The imposition of martial law was rejected on the grounds that it was unlikely to be effective, could lead to confrontation with republican forces, and was in any case unacceptable to Craig. Most ministers favoured holding a judicial inquiry into Northern Ireland; Lloyd George himself considered that it might at least create a lull in the violence and so facilitate a satisfactory resolution of the negotiations with the provisional government.

[50] Cabinet conclusions, 23 May 1922 (P.R.O.N.I., CAB4/44); *Hansard N.I. (commons)*, ii, 603-4 (23 May 1922).
[51] Calton Younger, *Ireland's civil war* (London, 1982), pp 288-9; Thomas Jones, *Whitehall diary, iii: Ireland 1918-1925*, ed. Keith Middlemas (London, 1971), p. 204.

Before Craig could be summoned to discuss these matters a new security crisis arose suddenly along the Fermanagh border. On 27 May pro-treaty I.R.A. forces occupied the Belleek–Pettigo salient, a remote triangular area, north of Lower Lough Erne, cut off by the lake from the rest of Northern Ireland. The motivation for the incursion was unclear; possibly it was a final, desperate bid to avoid civil war in the south by provoking a renewal of the Anglo–Irish war, or a protest against the security measures being implemented in the north; alternatively it may have been caused by the arrival in this volatile region of a new and more forceful regular commandant. On 30 May Craig telegrammed Churchill to request that British troops recapture the two villages; he claimed that Strabane and Derry were also at risk from a southern invasion. He was not hopeful of a favourable outcome. In fact, the colonial secretary responded promptly and sympathetically. He was anxious to reassure border unionists and convinced that military intervention would have a salutary effect on the provisional government. After seeking assurances from Collins that his forces were not responsible for the attack, and having obtained the agreement of reluctant cabinet colleagues, he instructed local army units to clear the occupied area and 'to inflict the greatest loss on the enemy'.[52] It was the first direct confrontation between British troops and the I.R.A. since the truce, which was still nominally operative. By 8 June the action had been successfully completed with only minor casualties. While Collins protested that southern territory had been violated, Lloyd George celebrated, with genuine relief, the 'great bloodless battle of Belleek'.[53]

Meanwhile, during talks with British ministers five days earlier, Craig had vigorously defended his government's record; he protested that the I.R.A., covertly supported by the authorities in Dublin, was seeking to destroy Ulster. He reiterated his opposition to martial law but stated that he would accept a judicial inquiry, if the request for it was presented to the public as coming from him. However, his colleagues strongly deprecated the suggestion.[54] During a second and decisive meeting at Westminster on 16 June, Craig therefore argued that this proposal was inopportune. He suggested as an alternative the sending of a 'trustworthy agent to Belfast who would be given every facility by the Northern Ireland government and who could furnish an unbiased report'.[55] British ministers themselves recognised that a judicial inquiry might weaken the authority of the unionist administration, and that, if attempted, it could cause Craig and his colleagues to resign. Finally, and with reluctance, they agreed to an official investigation, which was to be conducted by Colonel Stephen Tallents, private secretary to Lord Fitzalan. His brief was to report on whether a full public inquiry should be

---

[52] McVicker, 'Law & order', p. 87.
[53] Jones, *Whitehall diary*, iii, 212.
[54] Quoted in McVicker, 'Law & order', p. 91; also Jones, *Whitehall diary*, iii, 207.
[55] McVicker, 'Law & order', p. 91.

held to ascertain the reasons for the collapse of the latest Collins–Craig pact
and the subsequent eruption of violence.

Tallents visited the province in late June 1922. Though his subsequent
report did contain criticisms of the Northern Ireland government, especially
the ministry of home affairs, its overall conclusions were broadly favourable.[56] The recent disorders in Belfast were attributed partly to the climate
of political uncertainty and economic recession, but mostly to an organised
conspiracy by the I.R.A., conducted with southern support. There is evidence that references to Collins's covert involvement were suppressed, so as
not to provide diehards in the Conservative party with ammunition with
which to attack the treaty.[57] Tallents recommended that a permanent representative of the British government should be appointed to Belfast to liaise
between the two administrations; he himself took up this office in October
1922. He concluded that any additional inquiry would be unhelpful as 'inadvertently it would encourage . . . catholics in their refusal to recognise' the
Northern Ireland government and inevitably revive nationalist propaganda
about past events now 'best forgotten'. He also observed that if such an
inquiry forced Craig to resign, he would be replaced not by a moderate but
by an extremist.[58]

Armed with Tallents's recommendations and with levels of violence in the
north on the decline, the British government was spared from taking further
action. During June, I.R.A. ambushes and arson attacks gradually petered out,
and the number of deaths in Belfast attributable to the 'troubles' dropped to
twenty-five. Extreme loyalist organisations bent on the extermination of catholics became the main focus of the Northern Ireland government's concern.
The overall improvement in security was persistent and province-wide, and
arose in part from the sweeping measures taken by ministers over previous
weeks. By mid 1922 the special constabulary had an establishment of 42,000
and an actual strength of 32,000. In June 1922 the R.U.C. numbered 1,100,
roughly one-third of its recruitment target. Its upper ranks were experienced
men drawn from the R.I.C. The combined total of regular and part-time
police officers then stood at a ratio of one for every six families in Northern
Ireland.[59]

In addition, the government had exercised its emergency powers with
considerable effect: republican organisations had been proclaimed, a county
curfew imposed, most border roads closed, exclusion orders issued and,
above all, internment applied. Between May 1922 and December 1924, 728

[56] Tallents papers, June–July 1922 (P.R.O., CO 906/23–30).
[57] Coogan, *Collins*, p. 371, suggesting that if the extent of Collins's involvement had been
revealed it would have brought down the British government.
[58] Tallents to Masterton-Smith, 4 July 1922; Tallents's report, 6 July 1922 (P.R.O., CO
906/30); Tallents's diary (P.R.O., CO 906/24).
[59] Kenna, *Belfast pogrom*, pp 98, 117–18; Buckland, *Factory of grievances*, p. 197.

suspects were arrested; the disruptive impact of this action was enhanced by the discovery of lists of names of republican activists during a security force raid on St Mary's Hall, the I.R.A. liaison office in Belfast, on 18 March 1922.[60] The persistent haemorrhage of key personnel dealt a crippling blow to the Sinn Féin organisation. Its impact on the I.R.A. was more limited but still severe; acknowledging the cumulative effect of the various measures adopted and of the outbreaks of sectarian violence, Séamus Woods (officer commanding the northern divisions) noted: 'Our position is hopeless.'[61] Simultaneously, the deepening split in the Free State and the outbreak of civil war undermined the I.R.A.'s northern campaign and eliminated any prospect of a concerted assault on Ulster. Collins was compelled to concentrate on stabilising his own government and therefore to pursue, at least temporarily, a 'peace policy' towards the province. It was not, he observed, the time 'to take on war' with Great Britain and Northern Ireland.[62] In advance of the attack on the Four Courts, he was reassured by Churchill that it would 'have a tremendous effect on Craig and put me in a position to require from him action of the utmost vigour against the murder of Roman Catholics in the north'.[63] On 3 June, the provisional government had already decided that for the foreseeable future no regular troops would be permitted to cross the border. In due course, all units involved in the six counties campaign were instructed to suspend their activities; their officers were encouraged to believe that they would start again when circumstances were more favourable. In early August some leading Sinn Féin politicians expressed support for a more comprehensive change in strategy towards Northern Ireland; they proposed that the partition government should be granted official recognition, in the belief that unification would be accelerated by fostering harmonious relations between Dublin and Belfast.[64]

In part, the shifting emphasis in Collins's policy was prompted by reports he had received from northern I.R.A. commanders. From early June, they had progressively and unilaterally reduced the scale of their operations. Increasingly, they themselves favoured calling off the campaign, at least for the time being. Their numbers were being depleted by the constant drift of volunteers south to join the regulars and by internment. They were dispirited by the deepening split in Sinn Féin and by the imminence of civil war. Their supplies of arms and equipment were inadequate. Also, crucially, they were aware of the diminishing support for the campaign among north-

[60] Buckland, *Factory of grievances*, p. 210 n.; Phoenix, 'Nationalist movement', p. 456.
[61] Phoenix, 'Nationalist movement', p. 623; the comment was made on 2 Aug. 1923.
[62] Quoted in *Irish News*, 10 June 1922.
[63] McVicker, 'Law & order', p. 97. Churchill added: 'You are fighting not only for the freedom but for the unity of Ireland.'
[64] See description of memo 'Policy in regard to the north-east', dated 9 Aug. 1922, by Ernest Blythe, acting minister of home affairs, in Phoenix, *Northern nationalism*, pp 247–8.

ern nationalists; one local commander conceded that the national spirit was practically dead.[65] As a consequence, information was being passed on to the special constabulary, arms dumps were being discovered, and men forced to go on the run.

This changing mood was shared and articulated by members of the catholic hierarchy: Bishop Joseph MacRory personally appealed to de Valera to 'call away his gunmen'.[66] Devlinites had consistently opposed the I.R.A. campaign and favoured recognition of the northern parliament. By mid 1922, the use of force was widely perceived among nationalists as having been both ineffective and counterproductive. The Northern Ireland government had after all survived, while the minority had suffered from the resulting sectarian backlash. The incipient civil war in the south lowered morale yet further. The death of Collins, in August, reinforced the sentiments of despair, isolation, and abandonment. It accentuated the changed direction of provisional government policy; this in turn was reflected in Westminster's dwindling interest in the administration of justice in Northern Ireland. In the Free State, under W. T. Cosgrave's leadership, partition ceased to be a political priority. He consciously strove to improve north–south relations and publicly forswore the use of non-constitutional methods to achieve unity. The Dublin administration progressively abandoned its obstruction of the Northern Ireland government, and the minority was for the first time encouraged to recognise the Belfast government. One peculiar legacy from Collins's involvement in the earlier physical-force campaign remained. In December 1922 over 500 members of northern I.R.A. divisions were undergoing training at the Curragh; facilities at the camp had been provided after an approach to Dublin from the volunteers.[67] It is unclear whether the Dublin government under its new leader valued their presence more as a safeguard against their defection to the Irregulars or as an investment in the eventual resumption of the armed struggle in the six counties.

By mid 1922, the political siege was lifting. Northern Ireland had weathered the crisis, but at considerable cost. Before proceeding it will be worth taking stock of some of these costs. The most obvious were reflected in the deaths and damage to property. Between 21 June 1920 and 18 June 1922, 428 people were killed and 1,766 injured in the six counties as a result of the political turmoil. During 1922 alone, damage amounting to £3 million had been caused to property.[68] Moreover, patterns established during these years were to cast a long shadow over the subsequent history of the province. Out of the conflicting pressures acting on the Northern Ireland government there had emerged a system of policing that differed in several respects from

[65] Ibid., p. 245.
[66] MacRory interview with Tallents (P.R.O., C.O. 906/26).
[67] Phoenix, *Northern nationalism*, p. 247.
[68] Patrick Buckland, *A history of Northern Ireland* (Dublin, 1981), p. 46.

its British counterpart and lacked the confidence of a significant section of the local community. Both regular and part-time police forces were armed, and recruitment to both was almost entirely protestant. The special constables were poorly paid and inadequately supervised; even unionists were alarmed at their easy resort to the tactics of reprisals and death lists. Their use in border defence had helped to blur and distort their function as a police force. Overall, prevailing political uncertainty and sectarian tension rendered it extremely difficult to preserve the essential police virtue of impartiality.

These circumstances also conditioned the denominational composition of the regular and special constabularies. Potential catholic recruits, especially in Belfast, might be attracted by the prospect of helping to protect their communities, and by the proposition that their enlistment would 'displease the Orangemen more than anything we could do'.[69] But they were deterred by justifiable fears of I.R.A. retribution and social ostracism. In addition, recruits were obliged to make a declaration of allegiance, thereby effectively recognising Northern Ireland. Some, especially in border areas, considered that participation in the security forces would compromise the minority's case when the boundary commission began its work. The generally negative response from catholics relieved government fears that the law-and-order machinery would be infiltrated by republicans; but the overall result was that northern catholics felt alienated from the state.

The sense of alienation was reinforced by a somewhat selective system of law enforcement. It was widely held among unionists, for instance, that special powers legislation should only be enforced against those considered 'disloyal'. Although some members, including Craig, tried to take a broader view, others, together with the police authorities, were inclined to the popular side. This helps explain the laxity in dealing with loyalist paramilitary organisations such as the Ulster Protestant Association. Originally a respectable defence association, by mid 1922 it had degenerated into a gang of hooligans dedicated to the extermination of catholics. In June 1922 the government attempted to discipline its members by enrolling them into the special constabulary; but this only met with limited success. It was only later, after a small number of members had been interned, that the organisation collapsed. This outcome might have been achieved sooner and lives saved had ministers been willing earlier on to use their powers as fully against loyalist as against nationalist paramilitaries.

It was the catholic population that suffered disproportionately as a consequence of the 'troubles' in the province. In the years 1920 to 1922, an estimated 8,750 catholics were expelled from their employment and 23,000 driven from their homes, while possibly 50,000 left the six counties al-

[69] The views expressed in this paragraph were put forward by members of Collins's northern advisory committee, 11 Apr. 1922 (Phoenix, 'Nationalist movement', pp 488–9).

together. Almost all those interned were catholics. In particular, approximately two-thirds of those who died in the violence were members of the minority. In Belfast, where catholics comprised a quarter of the population, between 6 December 1921 and 21 May 1922, 236 persons were killed, of whom sixteen were policemen and military personnel, seventy-three were protestants, and 147 catholics. Of the 346 wounded, thirty-seven belonged to the crown forces, 143 were protestants and 166 catholics. Elsewhere in Northern Ireland, twenty-two catholics and eight protestants were killed.[70]

The degree of violence in Belfast and its disproportionate effects on catholics led to accusations from nationalists, north and south, of a deliberate attempt by official as well as unofficial protestant forces to purge the city of catholics. Such claims were taken up in certain British newspapers: one reported that 'protestant attacks on catholics have all the appearance of organised pogroms, and catholic attacks on protestants of unorganised reprisals.'[71] No evidence of such a policy has come to light; in any case, such claims take too little account of the impact of I.R.A. activity and of those who died as a consequence of indiscriminate firing by I.R.A. members inside their areas. Certainly I.R.A. activities played a central role in polarising communities, provoking sectarian retaliation and generating hostility between nationalists and the authorities in Northern Ireland. After the 1922 I.R.A. campaign had been abandoned, tensions eased. In July 1922, shortly after the campaign ended, Séamus Woods, an I.R.A. divisional commander in east Ulster, expressed concern at the improvement in relations between the northern minority and the security forces. This he attributed, in part, to the apparent 'policy of placation' being adopted by the special constabulary. Woods expressed particular unease at the increasing willingness of catholics to provide the police with information concerning I.R.A. volunteers.

He predicted that soon the entire nationalist community throughout the six counties would recognise the Northern Ireland government. He therefore concluded that if his organisation decided on a war policy, 'we would be compelled to mete out capital punishment among the civilian population'.[72]

By the autumn of 1922, it seemed to Craig that the 'land of promise, peace, and happiness'[73] was beckoning. Certainly by then the conditions of siege had receded; however, the policies of the Northern Ireland government remained characteristically defensive and unresponsive to their changing context. There was an inevitable relaxation of some of the law-and-order measures adopted earlier: the six-county curfew was lifted, trenched border roads were progressively reopened, and by 1924 all internees had been released.

---

[70] Buckland, *Factory of grievances*, p. 196; Macardle, *Ir. republic*, p. 664; Phoenix, 'Nationalist movement', p. 638.
[71] *Daily News*, quoted in *Irish Independent*, 9 Mar. 1922.
[72] Phoenix, 'Nationalist movement', pp 620–21.
[73] *Hansard N.I. (commons)*, ii, 1144 (27 Oct. 1922).

More substantial change was hampered by uncertainty, inertia, or simply because it was inconvenient. The application of narrow security criteria led to the retention of the special powers act, although (despite nationalist allegations to the contrary) it was used sparingly.

Following the resignation of Solly-Flood, the military adviser, in December 1922, C. G. Wickham, inspector-general of the R.U.C., resumed control of the full-time and part-time constabulary. Meanwhile, largely in response to treasury pressure, the frequency and size of patrols by specials were reduced. The cabinet also agreed to disband both 'A' and 'C' classes on 1 April 1923, if circumstances permitted. However, this aspiration was quickly abandoned; after the formation of Bonar Law's Conservative government in October 1922, Craig intensified his demands for the requisite financial support for the force. His commitment to it stemmed in part from factors other than security. The force's continued existence helped reduce unemployment; its disbandment would be unpopular within the unionist party, might well be resisted by the specials themselves, and could lead to a resurgence in the activities of undisciplined loyalist paramilitaries.

With British ministers, Craig argued that the force was cost-effective and necessary, given the persistence of civil war in the south. He continued to justify its retention, even after the Irregulars initiated a ceasefire in May 1923. He alleged that the Free State was still politically unstable, that a republican government might yet emerge, and that the I.R.A. could renew its campaign against the north at any time. Such arguments acquired additional force in view of the war office's concurrent anxiety to reduce further the number of battalions based in the six counties. Northern Ireland ministers also strongly resisted suggestions by the imperial authorities that the specials should be replaced by a territorial force under British military control. In mid 1924 combined membership of the 'A', 'B', and 'C' specials still stood at over 32,000; between 1923 and 1926 the Northern Ireland government was to receive almost £4 million in exchequer grants to defray local security costs. But support from Westminster on such a scale was made available with ever-increasing reluctance; in 1924, the first Labour administration threatened to withhold finance from the specials in order to press Craig into adopting a more accommodating stance towards the boundary commission. Craig claimed that the imminence of border revision made the force more necessary, and that if it was not preserved he could not continue to act as prime minister.

During 1922 Northern Ireland ministers had become increasingly optimistic about the probable outcome of the boundary commission. They were initially reassured by the comments of leading British politicians and later by the Conservative party's return to office. Collins's reticence about fulfilling the terms of the treaty, and his attempts to destabilise the province, diminished sympathy at Westminster for the south's territorial claims: Craig was later to assert that he was defending not only the boundary of Ulster but the boundary of the British empire.[74] The postponement of the commission's deliberations as a result of the civil war reduced further the likelihood of substantial border change or of any softening in the position of the Belfast cabinet. On 6 December 1922 the Irish Free State formally came into existence. Next day, Northern Ireland opted out of the jurisdiction of the Dublin government, thereby making some review of its boundaries, under the loosely phrased article 12 of the treaty, inevitable. Subsequently, despite the progressively more relaxed political atmosphere, unionist opposition to territorial modification did not diminish. During the months before the boundary commission first met (in November 1924), the Ulster Unionist Council organised province-wide demonstrations to protest against any prospective change. The northern government, heartened by expressions of support from influential opinion in England, refused to nominate a representative to the commission. Craig made public his threat to resign if its conclusions were unacceptable. Meanwhile he and his colleagues prepared for possible disorder in border areas, evaluated the prospects of an invasion from the south, and stressed to Ramsay MacDonald, the Labour prime minister, the potential for violence if boundary changes were proposed. British ministers were in any case fully aware of the danger of armed protestant resistance if the province sustained any significant loss.[75] The unionist leadership used the Westminster election (29 October 1924) to affirm its determination to preserve the six counties intact. Six months later, in the spring of 1925, Craig dissolved the Northern Ireland parliament in order once again 'to seek approval of the attitude I have adopted regarding the boundary question'.[76] During the campaign, he toured border areas promising not to relinquish one single inch. Nationalists gained three seats, all in Belfast.

The commission's eventual report[77] recommended minor transfers of territory and was never acted on. Instead, on 3 December 1925 representatives of the London, Dublin, and Belfast governments entered into a tripartite agreement. It was regarded as highly satisfactory by Craig and his colleagues; one authority has observed that, since each of those who signed did so on an apparently equal basis, 'the oft-repeated claims that Northern Ireland was subordinate [to Westminster] seemed empty indeed'.[78] The settlement

---

[74] Ibid., iv, 1206–7 (7 Oct. 1924).
[75] Memo by Lionel Curtis (colonial office), 9 May 1924 (P.R.O., CAB21/281); cabinet conclusions, 4, 6 Aug. 1924 (P.R.O., CAB23/46, 47). Northern Ireland government preparations for disturbances are considered in Dawson Bates's memo, 9 Aug. 1924 (P.R.O.N.I., CAB9A/4/3). Craig spoke of resignation in parliament (*Hansard N.I. (commons)*, iv, 1206–7 (7 Oct. 1924)) and also in the party manifesto (*Belfast Telegraph*, 16 Mar. 1925).
[76] *Belfast Telegraph*, 16 Mar. 1925. Unionist representation fell from 40 to 32 seats, an outcome described in the *Irish News* as a 'débâcle' (6 Apr. 1925).
[77] Above, pp 106–9. See also Thomas Hennessy, *A history of Northern Ireland 1920–1996* (Dublin, 1997), pp 38–40.
[78] Ronan Fanning, *Independent Ireland* (Dublin, 1983), p. 92.

removed the fear of territorial loss from the six counties. It resolved a number of important legal and financial matters: these included provision for the transfer to the northern cabinet of those powers that were to have been exercised by the council of Ireland. It also confirmed partition; in appending his signature W. T. Cosgrave was giving *de facto* recognition to his northern neighbour. This was a bitter pill for northern nationalists to swallow and accentuated their feelings of isolation. It served to alienate them from the pro-treaty government in Dublin and paved the way for their *rapprochement* with de Valera and the Fianna Fáil party. The latter was to lay particular emphasis on reunification.[79]

After the resolution of the boundary issue, the unionist leadership had no option but to implement the substantial cuts in security expenditure long urged by the treasury. Accordingly, on 9 December 1925, after a conference with British ministers, Craig informed parliament that both the 'A' and 'C' class special constabulary would be disbanded. Wickham, in particular, ex-pressed acute concern at the prospect; he considered that the south remained a potential threat to the preservation of order in the six counties, and warned that those specials in question would deeply resent being disbanded. In fact, the only hostile response was a localised, brief, and half-hearted revolt by 'A' specials; it lacked public sympathy and was effectively dealt with by a tactful but obdurate government. The 'B' specials alone survived; in March 1926 the class still contained 17,000 men.[80]

Although the threat of boundary change had not materialised, the prospect of the commission's inquiry had meanwhile helped to prompt legislation that permanently distorted Northern Ireland's representative institutions. On 12 May 1922 the northern cabinet decided in principle to abolish proportional representation and revert to single-member constituencies for the conduct of future local government elections. The initiative for change had come from unionist constituency branches; most sought not only the restoration of the simple majority system of voting but also an extensive revision of electoral boundaries. The objective, to increase their party's representation, was sup-ported most fervently by those from border areas to the west of the province. There, unionists were convinced that continued nationalist control of many local bodies would inevitably result in substantial territorial transfers to the south by the boundary commission.[81] In any case, unionist supporters be-lieved that they had a powerful case for increased council membership. This

---

[79] Phoenix, *Northern nationalism*, pp 332-4; David Harkness, *Northern Ireland since 1920* (Dublin, 1983), p. 40.

[80] A detailed analysis of the Northern Ireland government's security policy in this period is in McVicker, 'Law & order', pp 105-52, 162-4.

[81] Cabinet conclusions, 12 May 1922 (P.R.O.N.I., CAB4/41); Buckland, *Factory of griev-ances*, chs 10, 12 *passim*; Hugh de Fellenberg Montgomery to Craig, 5 Sept. 1922 (P.R.O.N.I., CAB 9A/40/1).

was based on the high proportion of rates they claimed to pay, even where
they were a minority. In addition, they alleged that political opponents had
discriminated against them in exercising the expanding executive powers
conferred on local government.

The party's leaders were responsive to grass-roots pressure; they had
themselves consistently opposed proportional representation (P.R.). They
had resisted its introduction into Irish local government in 1919 and, later,
into commons elections for the proposed devolved parliaments under the
government of Ireland act. They were critical of its alleged defects as a voting
system, contending that it was expensive to operate, caused instability, and
was unacceptably complex. They also argued that it weakened the link between elector and councillor, and that this would result in low polls and local
authorities of poor quality. Few of their assertions were justified on the basis
of Northern Ireland's limited experience to 1922, though P.R. did undoubtedly tend to lower unionist representation. Under P.R., the labour movement
had emerged as a serious threat to traditional voting patterns in Belfast and
larger towns. At parliamentary elections, independent unionists significantly
eroded support for official candidates, particularly in the capital. The most
striking advance made by the nationalist and Sinn Féin parties was in the
1920 local government contests, the only set of council elections held under
P.R. in Northern Ireland till May 1973. In the west of the province they
increased their majority on Fermanagh county council, captured Tyrone
county council, and also dislodged their political opponents from control of
Derry corporation for the first time since the Williamite revolution.[82]

In fact, results under the P.R. system were a fairer reflection than before
of votes cast. Owing to its success in broadening the field of political representation and debate, it quickly came to be regarded as a valued safeguard by
minority interests. By contrast, unionist leaders observed its impact with
acute unease. They considered disunity among their traditional supporters
to be a potential threat to the political stability of Northern Ireland, and
to their own monopoly of power. Craig and his colleagues wanted an electoral system that would provide strong government, encourage a stable two-
party system in which smaller groupings were eliminated, and thus permit
the traditional issues of unionism against nationalism to be placed clearly
before the electorate.

Legislation to abolish proportional representation was introduced into the
Northern Ireland house of commons on 31 May 1922 and had completed its
passage through parliament, virtually unopposed, by 5 July. Throughout its

[82] Urban elections were held on 15 Jan. and county and rural districts in June 1920. See
Buckland, *Factory of grievances*, pp 223–4; Alec Wilson, *PR urban elections in Ulster, 1920*
(London, 1972); Sydney Elliott, 'The electoral system in Northern Ireland since 1920' (Ph.D.
thesis, Q.U.B., 1971), pp 123–52. In urban districts and towns, Elliott concludes, 'Sinn Féin
gained most from the new method of election' (p. 132).

progress ministers were concerned to give effect to the views of their supporters and to safeguard loyalist interests; they were apparently unaware of the
wider implications of the measure. In some respects their short-sightedness
was understandable. During the bill's preliminary stages the government was
struggling for survival and ministers were absorbed by their departmental
responsibilities. Moreover, since many opposition-controlled councils had
previously been suspended, and nationalist M.P.s were continuing to boycott
parliament, the minority's views went largely by default, though Labour
M.P.s did protest against the bill. None the less, the proceedings indicated a
lack of political vision.

The measure also provided the southern government with an additional
opportunity to involve itself in Northern Ireland affairs. In correspondence
with British ministers Collins contended that abolition of P.R. was a malicious attack on the civil rights of northern catholics because it removed one
of their vital safeguards under the local government act. He predicted that it
would eradicate minority representation in the west of the province—in his
phrase, 'paint . . . Fermanagh and Tyrone with a deep orange tint'. Moreover,
he asserted that the measure was not, as Churchill claimed, solely of domestic
concern to the six counties. On the contrary, he claimed that it violated and
therefore jeopardised the treaty, as its object was to defraud nationalists of
their rights before the boundary commission met, and its tendency was away
from a policy of Irish reunion. It was, he suggested, the 'duty of his majesty's
government to preserve the *status quo*' until after the border inquiry had been
completed. Finally, he indicated that the bill would further complicate his
own efforts to have the treaty implemented in the south. Griffith's pledges to
southern unionists would be more difficult to honour; the risk of reprisals
against them would increase, and hence the danger of a confrontation between London and Dublin.[83]

British ministers were responsive to these criticisms. They were extremely
anxious that the provisional government should adhere to the treaty, determined that they themselves should fulfil its terms, and anxious to foster good
relations between north and south. Accordingly, on 8 July Craig was
informed by the lord lieutenant that the royal assent would be withheld from
the bill. This decision raised a number of complex issues. In the first place,
there were grave doubts as to both the legality and the propriety of such an
action. The bill seemed clearly to lie within the transferred powers of the
unionist government, under clause 4 of the 1920 act. Sir Francis Greer,
parliamentary draughtsman at the Irish office, advised that the law-making
powers of the Northern Ireland parliament were equivalent to those of a
dominion legislature, despite significant constitutional differences in other

---

[83] Collins to Churchill, 28 June, 9 Aug. 1922, and Cope to Curtis, 31 Aug. 1922 (P.R.O.,
HO45/13371/463565/1); Gilbert, *Churchill*, iv, 740–41.

respects. Nor was he convinced that the measure impaired southern rights under the treaty; it did not affect the composition of the Belfast parliament, and local authorities had no status either in the procedures laid down for the six counties opting out of the Free State or in the determination of the boundary. None the less, it was arguable that the measure was not merely a Northern Ireland domestic concern. To prevent, or at any rate delay, the measure would facilitate a settlement between the British and Irish governments. Also, as British taxpayers were meeting the cost of restoring order in Northern Ireland during the transition period, ministers acting on their behalf had a legitimate interest in preventing legislation that would imperil the prospects for peace by intensifying distrust among northern nationalists.[84]

Against all these considerations, however, the real obstacle to Westminster exercising the veto power was the hostile reaction of Craig and his colleagues. They responded with anger and incredulity, their indignation sharpened by the presumption that British intervention had been prompted by Collins. Regarding Northern Ireland as having the status of a dominion, they considered that the British government would be exceeding its powers in withholding assent.[85] A veto would be all the more indefensible at a time when their own efforts to reestablish order in the province were achieving some success. They protested that if the royal assent were not granted they would lose all confidence and authority, and that no government could carry on. Accordingly, on 27 July the cabinet decided that unless British ministers reversed their decision it would have no choice but to resign.[86]

During these deliberations Craig was confident that Westminster would yield rather than risk uproar in Northern Ireland, and his expectations turned out to be fully justified. British ministers recognised that a general election held on the veto issue would endorse Craig's leadership. In such circumstances they would have either to suffer the indignity of capitulation or accept responsibility for governing Northern Ireland themselves. Craig's cooperative stance helped to avert a constitutional crisis; he remained anxious to work in harmony with Britain, not least because of his continuous dependence on treasury funding for the special constabulary. Therefore, much to the annoyance of his own supporters, he consented willingly to a token delay in the granting of the royal assent; this was represented publicly by Westminster as a concession to the sensibilities of border nationalists.

---

[84] Note by Greer, 11 Aug. 1922 (P.R.O., HO45/13371/463565/1); Buckland, *Factory of grievances*, pp 270–71.

[85] Mansergh, *Unresolved question*, p. 254.

[86] Ministers believed that resignation 'would prove the most effective course of action'; see cabinet conclusions, 27 July 1922 (P.R.O.N.I., CAB4/50), and minute by R. D. Megaw, junior minister of home affairs, 13 July 1922, and Craig to Masterton-Smith (P.R.O.N.I., CAB9B/40/1).

Meanwhile, the British government sought to relieve southern suspicions of the measure. Though his remonstrances lacked Collins's anger and invective, Cosgrave too had complained that it 'loads the dice against the Free State before the boundary commission',[87] and he requested that the royal assent be withheld till after the border inquiry had been completed. Churchill responded by arguing that the bill could not be relevant to the work of the commissioners as their grounds of decision were already enshrined in the terms of the treaty. However, Westminster applied further pressure to Craig and he agreed to postpone the county council and rural district elections for one year or, if they were held earlier, to conduct them under the existing system (they were in fact held under the simple majority voting system one year later, but before the commission had begun its investigation). In return, the royal assent was granted on 11 September 1922.[88]

This episode illustrates the limited nature of British government control over the north's ministers, even though Northern Ireland remained part of the United Kingdom and the supreme authority of Westminster remained intact. It was the only occasion of real significance during the interwar years when an attempt was made to thwart major legislation and correct the myopia of the unionist administration. A possibly 'crucial instrument of Westminster control thus subsequently lapsed into disuse'; though Westminster retained the constitutional right to veto Northern Ireland legislation, a 'precedent of non-interference ... [had] been established'.[89] The British government exercised little supervision, partly out of respect for parliamentary sovereignty and partly on account of a deep-seated reluctance to become embroiled in Irish politics again. This passive role was also a realistic one. There was no alternative leadership to call on if Craig and his colleagues resigned. Hence they were permitted to administer their transferred services with minimal restraint.

Collins had protested that Craig's bill repealed the 1919 act in its effects both on P.R. and on the constituencies.[90] Although this aspect had been virtually ignored during its passage through parliament, it was the redrawing of electoral boundaries that in the longer term made the measure so controversial. The act required either a reversion to the old local electoral areas (those in operation before P.R. was introduced in 1919) or the redrawing of new ones. Where it was decided that boundaries should be redrawn, this was to be done primarily on the basis of population, but (as a result of a commit-

[87] Cosgrave, 30 Aug. 1922, quoted in Phoenix, 'Nationalist movement', p. 636.
[88] 12 & 13 Geo. V, c. 15 (11 Sept. 1922). Churchill to Cosgrave, 9, 11 Sept. 1922 (P.R.O.N.I., CAB9B/40/1); the county and rural district elections were postponed from June 1923 to May–June 1924.
[89] Derek Birrell and Alan Murie, *Policy and government in Northern Ireland: lessons of devolution* (Dublin, 1980), pp 9, 12.
[90] Collins to Churchill, 9 Aug. 1922 (P.R.O., H.O. 45/13371/463565/1).

tee-stage amendment) valuation also had to be taken into account. Border unionists, ever conscious of the prospective boundary commission, were particularly anxious for this work to proceed; they considered that the 1919 boundaries were likely to perpetuate nationalist control of many councils.[91]

On 9 August 1922 the cabinet decided to return as far as possible to the pre-1919 electoral areas for urban elections.[92] But it favoured a more comprehensive redistribution of rural districts, not just to appease party members but also because glaring anomalies existed under the old system. The pre-1919 rural divisions had been based on the original poor law unions, devised in the 1840s, and therefore long out of date in terms of population distribution and valuation. The ministers' object was to achieve a redrawing of boundaries that would favour their own party but would, at the same time, withstand reasonable scrutiny.

The one-year delay (stipulated by the Westminster government) before polling for county councils and rural districts provided the government with its opportunity to implement a wholesale recasting of electoral divisions. It decided against making these alterations on its own initiative. Instead, in areas where the matter was likely to be uncontentious, boundaries were to be determined on the basis of information available to the ministry of home affairs after consultation with the appropriate local authorities. A commission, under Judge John Leech, deputy recorder of Belfast, was appointed to conduct inquiries where new boundaries were likely to be controversial. In such cases, well-publicised public meetings were to be held, and local ratepayers and interested parties invited to make submissions. In an attempt to reassure members of the minority, Leech explained that the government had no blueprint of its own, so all submissions would be given equal consideration.[93] Though this course of action had much to commend it, its studied openness could only bear limited fruit in conditions where most nationalists were persisting in their strategy of non-cooperation with the northern government. They mainly boycotted the procedures, protesting that the home affairs ministry should have produced its own plan, and then asked for amendments from those affected. They were apt to dismiss the public inquiries as a farce, laid on to legitimise their own disfranchisement. However, the underlying reason for their negative response was the fear that participation would jeopardise their case at the boundary commission.

Only at Irvinestown, County Fermanagh, and Ballycastle, County Antrim, did catholics participate fully, and there new and uncontroversial divisions were agreed. Elsewhere, local unionists exploited nationalist reticence,

---

[91] Brian Barton, *Brookeborough: the making of a prime minister* (Belfast, 1988), pp 63–4; James Cooper (Unionist M.P. for Fermanagh) to Craig, 9 Aug. 1922 (P.R.O.N.I., CAB9B/40/1). Local unionist associations were preparing schemes from Jan. 1922, and possibly earlier.
[92] Cabinet conclusions, 9 Aug. 1922 (P.R.O.N.I., CAB4/51).
[93] Buckland, *Factory of grievances*, pp 237–8.

Westminster's apparent indifference, and the sympathy of their own government. They attended the inquiries, equipped with detailed submissions that maximised their party's advantage. Leech habitually commended their industry and, in most instances, accepted their proposals with only minor alterations; he was anxious to rectify the anomalies of the 1919 electoral areas, and was not in a position to grasp fully the implications of the new proposals. His recommendations were in turn endorsed by the ministry of home affairs. Though the reorganisation was virtually dictated by unionist activists, the authorities could make a plausible case against later allegations of gerrymandering. The refusal by nationalists to participate diminished the force of their subsequent protests that they had been treated unfairly.[94]

The postponed local government elections held in 1924 proved to be a fiasco. They were boycotted by nationalists in Tyrone, Fermanagh, south Armagh, and south Down, in protest against both the new rural districts and the oath of allegiance required under the 1922 act from members of local authorities. As a result, unionists regained control of Fermanagh and Tyrone county councils (no contest took place in either county) and eight rural district councils, including Dungannon, Cookstown, Newry, and Omagh. In Belfast, unionists seized the opportunity to channel their efforts into wards likely to fall to Labour. Overall, nationalist, Sinn Féin, and Labour party representation collapsed after the abolition of P.R. After the council elections in 1920 they had controlled twenty-four (32 per cent) of the seventy-five local bodies in Northern Ireland; by 1927, this had dropped to twelve (16 per cent).[95] They sustained their greatest losses in the west of the province and only retained their dominance in areas where they had held substantial majorities. Meanwhile, undeterred by the prospect of further protest, the cabinet made preparation to abolish P.R. in parliamentary elections also. Craig, in particular, was anxious to press on with this before the 1925 general election, but in the event refrained from carrying it through (till 1929), for fear of prejudicing the unionist case before the boundary commission.

The pressures on the administration to abolish P.R. and maximise unionist control of local government were undoubtedly strong, particularly in view of the looming threat of the boundary commission. None the less, it was a grave act of misgovernment. Ministers failed to place wider considerations of state above the narrow interests of the unionist movement. The abolition of P.R. served to polarise local politics and prevent alliances. During the 1920s, the

---

[94] Ibid., pp 238–43.

[95] Ibid., p. 226; Elliott, 'Electoral system', pp 271–2. Elliott notes that 'in the county councils there were only twelve contests out of a total of 131 seats' in 1924. The full list of rural district councils that the nationalists lost through 'wilful neglect' was Cookstown, Dungannon, Kilkeel, Lisnaskea, Newry No. 1, Newry No. 2, Omagh, and Strabane (ibid., p. 272). 'The Unionist and Nationalist parties consistently benefited from the simple majority system of election', whereas Sinn Féin, Northern Ireland Labour, and splinter unionist candidates suffered because of its restoration (pp 141–6 and *passim*).

number of uncontested seats in all elections rose rapidly and enthusiasm for smaller parties, such as Labour, declined. P.R. might have reduced communal hostility by providing opportunities for finding common ground on issues that did not concern partition.[96]

MEANWHILE a system of state education was emerging that was tailored to the requirements of the protestant community. From the outset catholics threw away any chance they might have had of influencing local state educational provision. The bishops refused to nominate representatives to the Lynn committee, appointed in September 1921, to consider education reform. When control of education services was transferred to the Northern Ireland government in January 1922, local catholic school managers were offered financial support by the provisional government if they refused to recognise the authority of the Belfast ministry of education; for Collins this offer was a part of his strategy against partition. As a consequence a number of headmasters of catholic intermediate schools who were 'ready to acquiesce in the inevitable... and... put their schools under the northern parliament'[97] decided not to do so. Armed with Collins's assurances, twenty-three secondary schools, and in addition 270 (roughly one-third) of the elementary schools under catholic management, refused to recognise the northern ministry, rejected payments from the local administration, and were reimbursed by the Dublin government. This policy persisted for nine months (February–October 1922); it was eventually abandoned by Cosgrave as a consequence of his government's adoption of a 'peace policy' towards Northern Ireland and also the difficulty of finding the money, estimated at £18,000 a month.[98] The gesture of non-recognition was 'political rather than religious in motivation';[99] it sprang from an awareness of 'the serious consequences resulting from a recognition of partition in the most important sphere of education'.[100] Bishop MacRory acknowledged that it was 'a political rather than a religious issue'; in February 1922 the northern bishops agreed that 'catholic interests [with regard to education] were not threatened... [as] the northern government undertook to conduct the schools under the rules at present in force by the national board'.[101]

For his part the minister for education, Lord Londonderry, sought in the 1923 education act[102] to transform Northern Ireland education by establishing

---

[96] Mansergh (*Government of N.I.*, p. 143) describes abolition as 'at the worst...a party manoeuvre, at the best a psychological mistake'.

[97] Rev. James Clenaghan, secretary of the Association of Catholic Headmasters in Northern Ireland, to Collins, quoted in Phoenix, 'Nationalist movement', p. 440. See also below, p. 712.

[98] Phoenix, 'Nationalist movement', pp 441–2, 633–4.

[99] Ibid., p. 443.

[100] Ibid., p. 438.

[101] The views of a meeting of catholic bishops, Feb. 1922 (ibid., p. 443); also extract from MacRory's lenten pastoral, 26 Feb. 1922 (pp 443–4).

[102] 13 & 14 Geo. V, c. 21 (22 June 1923).

a non-denominational system, combining efficiency with popular responsibility. Voluntary bodies were encouraged to transfer their schools to local education committees; the level of financial support offered to them by the government was increased with the degree of control relinquished by their management committees. Under the terms of the bill, religious instruction was permitted in the public elementary sector; but children were not compelled to attend, and instruction was to be given only by clergymen or other persons approved by those parents who wanted such provision for their children.

These terms were finally unacceptable to protestant clergy, who refused to transfer schools without assurances that 'Bible instruction' and 'protestant teachers for protestant pupils' would be provided. The campaign they conducted till 1929 revealed their political strength and sophistication; most importantly, by winning over the Orange order they were able to demonstrate that they had widespread lay support. Craig was responsive to the campaign, partly because of the prospective boundary commission, and partly because he was anxious to present a united front to the London and Dublin governments. Amending legislation was introduced in 1925. In effect it increased local control of appointments and repealed the proviso that forbade education authorities to take cognizance of the religion of a candidate for a teaching post. Authorities were also empowered to require a programme of simple Bible instruction (tacitly understood to be protestant in nature) to be given in provided or transferred schools. This arrangement involved an endowment of protestantism, as teachers paid by the state could be required to give in publicly financed schools a form of instruction that was acceptable to protestants but not to catholics. The settlement was therefore 'contrary to the 1920 act'.[103]

IN his 1920 Christmas message, which coincided with the passing of the government of Ireland act, Craig had expressed the hope that future generations would bless those about to lay the foundations of a separate administration in Northern Ireland.[104] During the years immediately following, the tenor of unionist rule was set; but its performance in government quickly drew bitter accusations rather than praise. In 1925 Kevin O'Higgins told Craig that northern nationalists were 'living in conditions of catholics prior to catholic emancipation'.[105] There is ample evidence of discrimination against the minority: a large, armed, almost exclusively protestant police force; emergency powers applied selectively; a judicial system with a reputation for bias; rural electoral districts gerrymandered; and P.R. extinguished

---

[103] Buckland, *Factory of grievances*, p. 256.
[104] *Belfast Telegraph*, 24 Dec. 1920.
[105] Conversation between O'Higgins, Free State minister of home affairs, and Craig, 29 Nov. 1925 (Jones, *Whitehall diary*, iii, 241).

in local elections. After the 'troubles' had flared up again in the late 1960s, Westminster progressively dismantled the institutional structures built fifty years earlier: the special constabulary, the special powers act, and the simple majority voting system were among the first to go.

In retrospect, much of what happened was probably predictable. The chief priority of the Northern Ireland government was to maintain unionist loyalty and unity. Progressive tendencies were stifled. Communal divisions were confirmed and deepened. One authority has stated: 'Craig's cabinet was neither vindictive nor deliberately oppressive, and it was often well intentioned, but it was too responsive to the claims of its supporters.'[106] The narrow, defensive policies it adopted were undoubtedly expressive of unionism's traditional siege mentality; but they also owed much to the actual conditions of siege, which all but overwhelmed the fledgling government. The violence, constitutional uncertainty, and acute insecurity of these formative years reinforced the negative instincts of local ministers, aggravated sectarian feeling, and lowered the level of political debate. Given the overall circumstances of its establishment, discrimination in Northern Ireland was perhaps an inevitable consequence of parliamentary devolution.

It is of course arguable that northern catholics were, in part at least, architects of their own misfortune, and that Collins's interventionist role also aggravated their position. The policy of non-recognition, which he encouraged, inflamed their internal divisions and proved counterproductive. His pacts with Craig raised unrealisable expectations and achieved little, while they inhibited more constructive responses by local leaders, such as Devlin. The I.R.A. campaign, in which Collins was directly implicated, not only unleashed a violent, sectarian backlash but also provoked far-reaching security measures, such as internment, which were enforced almost exclusively against the catholic population. Demoralisation was accentuated by the outbreak of civil war in the south and by Collins's death.

The provisional government's decision to adopt a peace policy towards the north, and to withdraw support from the I.R.A. divisions active there, was not followed by a change of attitude among northern catholics. Border catholics continued to hope for transfer to the Free State by means of the boundary commission; and the southern government, also with an eye to the commission, continued to encourage the minority not to participate in the Belfast parliament. These attitudes, combined with the insensitive policies adopted by Craig and his colleagues, helped frustrate Devlin's attempts to persuade the minority to participate fully in political life.

The result of all this was that vital decisions were taken on central aspects of public life in Northern Ireland (including representation, policing, and education) without nationalists' views being fully expressed or their interests

---

[106] Buckland, *Factory of grievances*, p. 222.

adequately defended. Almost certainly, political participation would have improved their position within the framework of the six counties. The tripartite boundary agreement of December 1925 ended a decade of uncertainty and forced the minority belatedly to confront the reality of partition and unionist control for the foreseeable future. It brought home the need for a constitutional movement to seek to redress the grievances of the nationalist minority.[107]

[107] Phoenix, *Northern nationalism*, ch. 9.

CHAPTER VII

Northern Ireland, 1925–39

BRIAN BARTON

By the mid 1920s there seemed reason to hope for a 'new departure' in Northern Ireland politics, for peaceful cooperation between north and south, and internal divisions healed. The tripartite agreement on the boundary question, which was endorsed by the dáil by 55 votes to 14, was projected by both Irish governments as a basis for lasting peace; northern ministers appeared willing to act in a conciliatory manner. The catholic workers expelled from the shipyards in 1920 had returned to their workplaces by 1924, and those who had resisted their return had been dismissed. By early 1926 all internees and political prisoners had been released, the 'A' specials had been disbanded, and P.R. had been preserved (for the time being) in parliamentary elections. In the 1925 Northern Ireland general election three Labour party candidates and four independent unionists were returned for constituencies in the east of the province. This suggested that, outside border areas, voters could look beyond constitutional and religious issues. A further encouraging feature of the poll for the northern government was the relative failure of the Sinn Féin party. It attracted just 20,615 first-preference votes, as against the 91,452 cast for the nationalist party. The contrast suggested that the minority broadly supported constitutional politics.

During the years that followed, however, no new spirit arose. North–south relations were characterised by a pervasive cold war. Internally, Northern Ireland became the most economically and socially disadvantaged region in the United Kingdom and it remained the most politically divided. As a British civil servant (who did not expect partition to be permanent) noted in 1938, 'the bias of the Northern Ireland authorities is bound to be in favour of those who are supporters of the present regime'.[1] The constitutional aspirations of the two communities were mutually exclusive: a traumatised and embittered nationalist community sought Irish unity, while the majority, feeling insecure and under siege, wished to preserve the union. Both traditions, from their conflicting perspectives, could make a convincing case, based on the right to self-determination.

[1] Sir Harry Batterbee (below, n. 92), quoted in Harkness, *N.I. since 1920*, p. 80.

Moreover, the economic and political context in the late 1920s and 1930s was not conducive to increased tolerance and mutual understanding. Persistent recession not only accentuated sectarian conflict, it lessened the government's chance of winning over a section at least of the nationalist community. Recession also encouraged ministers to discriminate as a means of appeasing their own supporters. Meanwhile, the Free State retained and pursued its irredentist claims. Westminster's commitment to and influence in Northern Ireland remained uncertain, restrained as always within the confines of imperial self-interest. Above all, the 1920 act provided the northern cabinet with responsibility, but not the power to initiate effective policies. The British model of democracy was superimposed on local political conditions, to which it was unsuited; crucially, it did not safeguard the interests of the minority.

Given these circumstances, it is hardly surprising that the Northern Ireland administration proved unable to resolve the internal problems and create a prosperous and genuinely democratic society. The cabinet was generally competent and acquired a level of expertise. It was predominantly drawn from the upper economic and social strata; none the less, it identified with and was perceived to represent the interests of the protestant population as a whole. Despite occasionally heated disputes over policy, its members shared a commitment to the union, a prejudice in favour of private enterprise, a tendency towards economic fatalism, and an associated aversion to deficit spending. Their general attitudes towards government largely conformed to those of the British Conservative party and reflected the innate conservatism of Northern Ireland itself. Advancing years and ill-health sapped their energy: just twelve ministers were appointed between 1921 and 1939, and their average age between 1921 and 1938 rose from 54 to 62. They became less active and less open to new ideas. In any case, their limited experience and background contributed to a narrowness of vision and a generally defensive political posture.

The rapidly expanding civil service was unable to compensate for the government's deficiencies. Officials had ample scope and opportunity for administration, but ultimate authority for policy concerning sensitive issues rested with their political masters, whose attitudes reflected their closeness to their own community. Shortly before he fell from power in 1943, J. M. Andrews observed bitterly that Northern Ireland was 'too small for its own government ... People go to the prime minister over trifles'.[2] Cabinet ministers were sensitive to criticism and responsive to pressure groups, character-

---

[2] Spender diary, 30 Mar. 1943 (Wilfrid B. Spender papers, P.R.O.N.I., D715). For the background to N.I. between the wars see Sydney Elliott (ed.), *Northern Ireland parliamentary election results, 1921–1972* (Chichester, 1973), ch. 4; Buckland, *Factory of grievances*, pp 1–6, 9–77; Sabine Wichert, *Northern Ireland since 1945* (Harlow, 1991), introduction and pp 1–6, 11–35.

istics that impeded the formulation of a balanced regional policy and compromised an intention to apply the law, or indeed to govern, impartially.

The influence of the Orange order (whose membership included two-thirds of Northern Ireland's protestant males) and of constituency branches combined to ensure that the Unionist party remained exclusively protestant. Likewise, political weakness, distrust of state action and expenditure, and a reaction against perceived over-centralisation by Dublin Castle before 1921, prevented the Northern Ireland government from compelling local authorities to fulfil their administrative responsibilities. Lax supervision by the ministry of home affairs resulted in the neglect of vital services, waste, and delay. Councils were conducted on party lines. They were defiant and mendacious towards ministers, and considered their main priority was to keep rates down. Parochialism and lack of resources diminished their capacity for enterprise; the existence of a devolved government may also have reduced the incentives.

Notwithstanding its imposing new buildings at Stormont, near Belfast (opened by the prince of Wales in November 1932), the Northern Ireland parliament failed to become an effective part of the decision-making or policy-making process, or to exploit its limited powers under the 1920 act; it largely endorsed arrangements and settlements reached elsewhere. Most M.P.s were middle-aged, amateurish, ill informed, socially unrepresentative, and no more willing to depart from the principle of free enterprise than ministers. They had a limited perception of their role and were enmeshed in localised interests and issues. The most profound division across all parties, leaving aside the question of partition, was between members returned for Belfast and those representing other areas.

The virtual irrelevance of the house of commons was in part a consequence of its domination by a single party. The Unionist majority was never less than twelve out of a total of fifty-two seats during the interwar years, and was usually inflated by opposition abstentionism and walkouts. This political predominance contributed throughout to the timidity of the chamber. Cahir Healy, nationalist M.P. for Fermanagh South, calculated that sixteen out of thirty-seven Unionist M.P.s in the late 1920s had cabinet posts or were parliamentary secretaries. Northern Ireland was therefore, he suggested, 'a bureaucracy rather than a democracy'.[3] The unity of the unionist movement was largely preserved by the distribution of rewards, governmental discrimination, effective party organisation, and a programme that stressed the defence of protestantism and the union.[4] The prevalence of the constitutional issue was to a degree caused by the continuing sense of a nationalist threat to

---

[3] See copy of newsletter issued by Healy in 1929 (P.R.O.N.I., Healy papers, D2991/A/9C).
[4] Patrick Buckland, 'The history of Ulster unionism, 1886–1939' in *History*, lx (1975), pp 211–23.

the political *status quo*, both from across the border and internally. It was also perpetuated through legislation—in particular, the abolition of proportional representation—that helped stereotype and polarise local politics. The necessity for ministers to make nakedly sectarian appeals was reduced by their provision of major cash social services.

Despite these stratagems and policies, during the 1930s the Unionist monolith showed increasing signs of strain; rank-and-file party members, backbenchers, and even junior ministers became more fractious. To a growing number, the leadership seemed ineffective, incompetent, and vacillating, although, as a British official observed, 'no attempt at revolt would survive Lord Craigavon's frown'.[5] The prime minister—who was to retain his post till his sudden death in 1940—had been at his best during the first few troubled years, when he had shown courage, energy, and confidence, and had been capable of a broader, more tolerant perspective than his colleagues. Thereafter, he progressively failed to assert himself or to develop long-term plans, and became a source of weakness. He increasingly adopted an informal, whimsical style of leadership. He made important decisions in a casual, hasty manner, without adequately consulting ministers. He held cabinet meetings less frequently, and randomly interfered in the administration of departments. His ready accessibility to protestant deputations served to reinforce an impression of partiality, and he became more intolerant of criticism. Rather than respond constructively, he offered concessions that were politically expedient, or alternatively he sought to divert attention from economic and social problems by more overt appeals to protestantism and loyalty. However, given the intractable nature of the problems he faced during these decades, it is far from certain that different leadership would have produced substantially different results.

A major part of the government's difficulties continued to flow from the nature of the devolved structures themselves. Apart from the need to share responsibility with local councils, government actions were constricted most by the extensive powers retained by Westminster under the terms of the 1920 act. The sovereign authority of the imperial parliament was undiminished: Northern Ireland bills had routinely to be submitted to the home office, and they all required the royal assent. Differences between London and Belfast arose most frequently over matters such as finance, aspects of social and economic reform, and Britain's policy towards the Free State. Inter-governmental relations, which were largely determined by a small group of ministers and civil servants, were generally harmonious, and easiest when the Conservative party was in office. Successive British governments strove anxiously to avoid commons controversy and debate about Northern Ireland;

[5] Comment by Herbert Shaw, a British official, in a report to the foreign office, 1 Jan. 1941 (P.R.O., FO371/29108).

owing to speakers' rulings, members could not discuss, let alone legislate on, areas of responsibility transferred to the devolved parliament. Most in any case were not interested in its problems, and those who were, particularly among the Labour and Liberal M.P.s, tended to be hostile to unionism.

In general, Westminster failed to influence Unionist policy decisively on the key sensitive issues, though awareness of British opinion did have some ameliorative effect. Early experience had illustrated that if British ministers attempted to block controversial legislation that had the full support of the Northern Ireland government and a significant body of unionists, they would jeopardise the 1920 settlement. Since ministers remained anxious to avoid direct involvement in Irish affairs, the result was that the veto power lapsed. After the boundary settlement in December 1925, the imperial authorities ceased to concern themselves officially with the administration of justice in Northern Ireland. From time to time, Stormont's powers were extended, or the home office permitted it to proceed with bills that clearly transgressed the 1920 act, both in order to facilitate the Northern Ireland government and to prevent controversial issues being raised at Westminster.

Throughout the interwar years, however, financial constraints effectively reduced the devolved administration to a state of virtual impotence. Its resulting dependence on London was the key to what real influence Westminster was able to exert over the province's affairs. The relevant provisions of the 1920 act were never fully implemented; they had envisaged separate British and Irish budgets, and an 'imperial contribution' raised from the whole of Ireland. Those sections that were applied did not guarantee Northern Ireland sufficient revenue, as they were based on the erroneous estimates contained in the May 1920 white paper, which had been produced against the background of the postwar restocking boom. The prolonged depression and tax cuts that followed considerably reduced the government's actual income: in 1925 it was little more than half the predicted figure. In addition, transferred revenue amounted to just 10 per cent of the total, and as with other aspects of imperial policy the level and nature of reserved taxation were determined by the needs and capacity of Great Britain.

Public expenditure rose considerably during the interwar years because of persistent economic difficulties. The pace and direction of the regional government's spending were largely decided at Westminster, where the response to economic hardship in Britain was to expand the provision of social services. Unionist ministers felt unable to deny their supporters the benefits that other British citizens enjoyed. Their adoption of a 'step by step' policy with Britain from 1922, the unexpectedly high cost of maintaining law and order, and the provision of some vital services by grants in aid, resulted in financial commitments far in excess of earlier projections in white papers. As insufficient income could be raised in Northern Ireland to pay for its transferred services, Craig and his colleagues had no option but to seek exchequer support. Their preferred solution was a revision of the 1920 act, in order to provide the region with sufficient revenue to meet its expenditure without increasing local taxation. The full amalgamation of the Northern Ireland and British unemployment funds was considered to be an acceptable, though less desirable, alternative.

Westminster's response was largely determined by treasury officials, for whom imperial budgeting needs were paramount—in particular, the priority of servicing the massive national debt generated by the first world war. They were therefore reluctant to undertake any fundamental review of Britain's financial relations with Northern Ireland. A joint exchequer board had been formed under the 1920 act, representing both the treasury and the ministry of finance, to determine the allocation of funds between the two governments. The most far-reaching subsequent British initiative was the setting up in 1923 of an arbitration committee, under the chairmanship of Lord Colwyn, which devised a formula to determine the required imperial contribution in future years. It recommended that expenditure on necessary services should rank as the first charge on Northern Ireland's revenue, and that its per capita expenditure should rise at the same rate as that in Great Britain. Consequently, the imperial contribution became a residual payment. It dwindled in size during the 1920s and had become a token sum by the early 1930s. The British government did not accept, even in principle, a negative contribution till 1938.[6]

Consequently, in the inter-governmental agreements of 1926 and 1936, the treasury would only accede to the partial amalgamation of unemployment funds; complete integration might necessitate an increase in contributions in Britain. The treasury's preferred response to Northern Ireland's fiscal difficulties was through *ad hoc* arrangements, such as grants, or the reassessment of the province's provisional residuary share; these it characteristically agreed to after hard and protracted secret negotiations. This approach was favoured because it limited the extent of the exchequer's commitments while providing it with the opportunity to express views on and supervise the finances of the devolved administration. Its overriding concern throughout was to ensure that Northern Ireland did not equip itself at Britain's expense with services superior to those found elsewhere in the United Kingdom. In practice, Northern Ireland was treated with greater parsimony than regions in Great Britain, even though it was, in virtually all respects, the most disadvantaged. On the whole it was Westminster that benefited from devolution, in that it was thus relieved of direct responsibility for Northern Ireland's acute social problems. The willingness of Northern Ireland's ministers broadly to accept

---

[6] See R. J. Lawrence, *The government of Northern Ireland: public finance and public service 1921–1964* (Oxford, 1965), pp 37–62, and Buckland, *Factory of grievances*, pp 81–104, for detailed analysis of financial relations between Belfast and London.

subordination to and scrutiny by the treasury is a reflection of the nature of unionism itself; it was centripetal in constitutional outlook, and was largely content with a settlement that provided protection, security, and financial support.

None the less, pressure from the exchequer did result in strains and divisions within the Northern Ireland cabinet and civil service. For example, Hugh M. Pollock, minister for finance, and his department firmly believed that the north should live off its own resources, and sternly opposed those ministers and officials who favoured a negative contribution. Budgetary matters also caused friction between central and local government, prompting a heated debate over the proper allocation of financial responsibility between taxpayer and ratepayer. Treasury officials claimed that Northern Ireland was not entitled to equality of services with Great Britain because its citizens paid lower taxes. Such claims had substance, as Northern Ireland's schedule A income tax was assessed on outdated valuations; its rate-borne disbursements were also substantially lower than in other parts of the United Kingdom, because its police and education costs were met almost entirely by the relevant government departments. Northern Ireland ministers responded by attempting to bring the financial system they had inherited into closer conformity with British practice. In order to raise rates as a proportion of total public domestic expenditure, they introduced in 1934 an educational levy; two years earlier, parliament had passed legislation providing for quinquennial general revaluations. An unfortunate consequence of these measures was a marked slowing down in the development of those social services dependent on local initiative, including education, housing, and health. Councils (Belfast corporation, in particular) refused to take advantage of their expanding powers without additional aid from the government. But the cabinet could only afford to offer words of exhortation.[7]

Behind these sterile clashes and accusations lay serious issues. The inadequate financial resources and powers of Northern Ireland ministers crucially curtailed their independence, restricted their policy options, and diminished their capacity for comprehensive, long-term planning. During discussion of budgetary matters, the question that transcended all others was not what was in the best interests of Northern Ireland, but rather what would prove most acceptable to the imperial treasury. The resulting inability of Craig's government to provide more comprehensive social services, or seriously to attempt the regeneration of the local economy, encouraged discrimination and further reduced the prospects of winning over nationalists.

A distinct system of social services, modelled on that in Britain, gradually emerged in Northern Ireland during the interwar years. Its impact was

[7] Harkness, *N.I. since 1920*, p. 67; Buckland, *Factory of grievances*, pp 102–4; Lawrence, *Govt of N.I.*, pp 48–9, 57–62.

diluted by the still limited perception of state responsibility held by Northern Ireland ministers. Their innate conservatism was reinforced by the acute financial constraints under which they governed, and the inertia and impecuniousness of the local authorities with whom they shared power. The services that resulted were, in consequence, imitative in content, piecemeal in provision, and variable in performance. They were probably poorer in quality than if Northern Ireland had been governed direct from Westminster, but higher than if it had been left to itself or had become an autonomous part of a united Ireland.

In March 1922 Craig announced his 'step by step' policy of keeping pace with British welfare benefits. Although this was to become the cornerstone of Northern Ireland's financial relations with Britain, the initial commitment was made after little preliminary consideration. Its implementation proved divisive: apart from the prime minister, it was enthusiastically supported by Dawson Bates and the minister for labour, John M. Andrews, whereas Pollock and officials at the ministry of finance fought strenuously to restrict the government's financial obligations. Those in favour of 'step by step' based their case partly on notions of equity. It was argued that since Northern Ireland citizens made the same taxation payments as in Britain, they were entitled to equivalent benefits and ought not to be disadvantaged through having a parliament of their own. Moreover, some unionists were concerned that if equal standards were not maintained, sections of the workforce might become so disaffected that they would vote socialist, or perhaps even emigrate. These arguments acquired additional force on social and humanitarian grounds, as traditional support agencies, such as the Belfast board of guardians, provided derisory levels of relief. For ministers, other financial considerations intensified the inducements to replicate at least some of Britain's welfare legislation. In pressing for a revision of the 1920 act, a key supposition made by ministers had been that expenditure on transferred services should be the first charge on Northern Ireland's resources and that the region should enjoy social services equal to Britain's. As these premises became more acceptable to Westminster, the 'step by step' policy became self-perpetuating; to abandon it seemed short-sighted, even irresponsible.

Opponents of the 'step by step' principle could, none the less, advance powerful arguments against its adoption. The ministry of finance was concerned that the high costs involved would not only accentuate its difficulties in balancing the budget, but could result in a negative imperial contribution and thus undermine its generally harmonious relationship with the treasury. Reservations were also expressed over the desirability of state intervention in social matters; there was a widely held conviction that expenditure on welfare services not only was economically unproductive but demoralised and pauperised the recipients.

In addition, there were those who considered it inappropriate for the Northern Ireland government slavishly to reproduce Westminster legislation of this nature. *Per capita* earnings, living costs, and taxable capacity were all substantially lower in Northern Ireland than in Great Britain. Some regarded these differences as sufficient to justify at least a scaling-down of both contributions and benefits. Thus, apart from their concern at the additional tax burden likely to be caused by social reform, employers also warned of substantial voluntary unemployment unless the scheme was adjusted so as to reflect the substantially lower average wages available locally. The relatively high level of distress and deprivation in the north, as well as the government's overall lack of financial resources, might in themselves suggest that the 'step by step' principle was more fundamentally flawed. Certainly, as a result of its adoption, there was never any attempt to identify social priorities better suited to the province or to devise a coherent plan tailored to meet its needs.[8]

The policy was first applied to the major cash social services. Consequently, the Northern Ireland government introduced and maintained its national insurance scheme on the same basis as in other parts of the United Kingdom and did the same with national assistance in the 1930s. Contributory widows', orphans', and old-age pensions were brought into conformity with British standards in 1925, and thereafter moved in tandem with them. Health insurance, a politically less sensitive area, was eventually made to comply with the British scheme in May 1930, after pressure from local trade unions and other interested bodies. Meanwhile the decision to follow Westminster's lead on derating in 1929 further reduced the imperial contribution and also crippled the spending capacity of the administration in its other areas of responsibility.

Collectively these measures absorbed most of the budget of Northern Ireland; expenditure on other vital services suffered accordingly. In 1921 housing, health, and education provision already lagged significantly behind that in Britain; and though there was evidence of improvement in all these areas, the gap had generally widened further by 1939. Interwar housing policy was mainly determined by limited finances and the desire to placate treasury opinion. Both from preference and necessity, legislation was directed towards the building of inexpensive, small, working-class dwellings by private enterprise. This strategy conformed to mainstream Conservative party thinking in Britain. Moreover, the cabinet shied away from the use of compulsion against lethargic and negligent local authorities. Most councils were reluctant to assume any direct liability for building homes, and inclined as always to justify their own inaction by casting responsibility on to ministers. To stimulate construction, contractors were offered single lump-sum

---

[8] Buckland, *Factory of grievances*, pp 150–56.

subsidies, as opposed to the Westminster approach of annual payments over a fixed period. On the whole, the terms available in Northern Ireland were less generous and more frequently changed than in Britain.

The measures taken represented a minimum level of response to the housing problem. A total of 34,312 dwellings were constructed under the housing acts of 1923–36: 32,146 of them by private enterprise. The local authorities were responsible for a mere 2,166; with justification, Cahir Healy described the lamentable performance of Fermanagh county council in this field as a 'liquidating policy'.[9] Throughout the 1930s rents remained at relatively high levels; they were virtually unregulated, and affordable only by skilled artisans or the lower middle classes. When the north's first comprehensive survey was conducted in 1944, it estimated that 100,000 new houses were urgently required, and 230,000 of the existing stock were in need of repair.[10] In retrospect, senior officials recognised the shortcomings in government performance during the interwar years, noting that construction had been 'allowed to lag very materially behind England' and that the aggregate housing subsidy had been 'half what it should be'. They also regretted the fact that no slum clearance 'of any kind, sort, or description' had been attempted.[11]

However, when compared with the British Isles as a whole, Northern Ireland does not appear to have been uniquely disadvantaged in the area of housing. Roughly one-sixth of its housing stock was renewed between the wars, and there was significantly less overcrowding than in the Irish Free State. Although proportionately fewer dwellings were built than in other regions of the United Kingdom during these years, local demand was lower. There was a relatively slow rate of population growth, the marriage rate was also low, and there was comparatively little internal migration. In Belfast itself, the housing stock in 1919 was much younger than in most British cities, reflecting its more recent industrialisation and expansion. In 1936–7 Belfast had on average 0.88 persons per room; in 1931 the equivalent figure for Glasgow was 1.57, for Edinburgh 1.15, and for Scotland as a whole 1.27. In Northern Ireland, census data indicate that, contrary to British trends,

---

[9] Retrospective comments by Healy, Aug. 1948 (P.R.O.N.I., D2991/A/169). *The interim report of the planning advisory committee* [Cmd. 224] (Belfast, 1944) concluded that 30 per cent of all houses in Northern Ireland were in urgent need of replacement. In Co. Fermanagh the figure was 43.7 per cent for Enniskillen and over 50 per cent for most of the rural districts. 'No houses at all were built [1921–45] by any of the three Fermanagh rural councils' (Michael Farrell, *Northern Ireland: the Orange state* (London, 1976), p. 87; 'Catholic businessmen [in local government]... did not exert themselves in the interest of housing. They had no great desire to see the rates being raised' (Peadar Livingstone, *The Fermanagh story* (Enniskillen, 1969), pp 322–3). In the inter-war years, not a single labourer's cottage was built in Fermanagh (J. M. Mogey, *Rural life in Northern Ireland* (London, 1947), p. 34).

[10] *Interim report of planning advisory committee, passim.*

[11] Brian Barton, *The blitz: Belfast in the war years* (Belfast, 1989), p. 8.

housing conditions were least satisfactory in the countryside. A contributory factor was a higher level of marital fertility in rural than in urban areas.[12]

Public health statistics provide more certain evidence of deprivation during these years. Although life expectancy was rising faster than in the Free State, suggesting a relative improvement in performance, there was much preventable illness and death, and the standards of local medical care lagged further behind those in Britain. During the interwar years maternal and infant mortality was consistently 50 to 60 per cent higher in Northern Ireland than in Great Britain. Childbirth actually carried increasing rather than diminishing risks for Ulster women: maternal death rates rose by one-fifth between 1922 and 1938. In 1944 a Unionist backbencher alleged that in the 'slaughter of innocents' the Stormont government had 'out-Heroded Herod', and he appealed for the immediate establishment of a ministry of health.[13] The mortality rate for tuberculosis fell by 40 per cent in the same period, but it likewise remained 20 per cent above the levels of the rest of the United Kingdom. An official investigation into municipal health provision in Belfast (December 1941) concluded that it fell far short of what ought reasonably to be expected in a city of its size and importance.[14] In the late 1930s infectious diseases accounted for 51 per cent of all mortality there, a figure 25 per cent higher than in English county boroughs.

The relatively high death rate in Northern Ireland was mainly caused by inferior medical services, lack of hygiene, poor housing, and low standards of nutrition; average incomes were at least one-third below British levels. Responsibility for public health care lay with the local authorities, but despite departmental pressure they were largely inactive. They were restrained by lack of funds and a presumption that such provision was properly a function of either central government or the extended family. Budgetary considerations discouraged ministers from investing more heavily themselves; yet successive inquiries indicated that even a minor increase in spending on health services and rudimentary health education would have significantly reduced mortality and morbidity.[15] The educational system in general provided low-income families with little opportunity for self-improvement. In 1938 only 5 per cent of pupils in secondary schools held scholarships, and

[12] Ulster Unionist Council, *Annual reports* (Belfast, 1939–45), *passim*; D. J. Johnson, *The interwar economy in Ireland* (Dundalk, 1985), *passim*; Arthur Beacham, *Report of a survey of living conditions made in a representative working class area in Belfast, Nov. 1938–Feb. 1939* (Belfast, 1939), *passim*.

[13] *Hansard N.I. (commons)*, xxv, 2902–6 (28 Oct. 1942), 3120–32 (15 Dec. 1942).

[14] Dr T. Carnwath, *Report to the special committee of the Belfast corporation on the municipal health services of the city* (Belfast, 1941), *passim*.

[15] In Carnwath's opinion, the high maternal death rate stemmed from the inadequate provision of personal medical services. He attributed the high infant mortality to mothers' lacking a rudimentary knowledge of child care and hygiene, as shown in the prevalence of unclean milk, hands, teats, bottles, clothes, floors, yards, and houses.

the local authorities awarded just twenty-eight university scholarships. The funding of the service was inadequate, and religious divisions made a rational application of the available resources more difficult. Despite measurable progress in key sectors, here too the gap between Northern Ireland standards and those in Great Britain widened appreciably.

Financial constraints influenced all aspects of government policy. Even after the disbandment of the 'A' and 'C' specials in December 1925, cabinet consideration of further retrenchment in the security forces was unavoidable and inevitably divisive. Pollock and Spender favoured additional reductions both in the interest of economy and in response to treasury opinion. Bates and his ministry, for whom law-and-order matters took priority over their other wide-ranging functions, generally resisted. They consistently alleged that real internal and external threats to Northern Ireland continued to exist. Moreover, they attached supreme political and ideological importance to maintaining strong security forces as a means of preserving unionist unity.

The increasing budgetary difficulties enhanced Pollock's influence. Between 1926 and 1928 slight reductions were made in the number and remuneration of special constables, in the strength of the R.U.C., and in the pace of its barrack-building programme. The salaries of regular police were not affected; Sir Charles Wickham, the inspector-general, had argued that they had proved their loyalty during the general strike of 1926.[16] For political reasons, these modest, penny-pinching trends were temporarily relaxed in the late 1920s. The Unionist leadership considered that party members needed reassurance after the formation of the National League of the North (May 1928) and discoveries of republican arms (June 1928).[17] Ministers were particularly sensitive to popular anxieties in view of the election held in May 1929.

Thereafter, Pollock's influence on government policy rose, culminating in an economy drive on security spending, launched in March 1931. Cabinet opposition was overcome partly because of a strong prevailing desire among its members to avoid confrontation with the Labour administration formed at Westminster in June 1929. Craig (created Viscount Craigavon in 1927) described this development as 'what governs everything'.[18] The chancellor of the exchequer, Philip Snowden, especially, was identified with a commitment to strict financial rectitude; he was also believed to harbour a 'bitterness towards Ulster'.[19] These considerations were reinforced by the international economic depression, severe structural unemployment, and an associated

[16] Memo by Wickham, 8 Dec. 1926 (P.R.O.N.I., CAB9A/4/4); for detailed analysis of the N.I. government's security policy see McVicker, 'Law & order', pp 162–221.
[17] Below, pp 218–20.
[18] Cabinet conclusions, 19 Nov. 1930 (P.R.O.N.I., CAB4/273).
[19] Ibid. Craigavon remarked that Snowden had 'always indicated that we should have thrown in our lot with the south'.

sharp deterioration in Northern Ireland's budgetary position. For the moment, at least, violence remained at a low level, making cuts in law-and-order expenditure more palatable. In November 1930 the lord chief justice, James Andrews, described the province as 'one of the most law-abiding areas in the empire'.[20]

By late 1931, however, the ministry of finance's predominance in security matters had begun to wane; Colonel Spender, head of the civil service, complained that the old state of affairs had returned. The change was related in part to the fall of the Labour government in August 1931. More significant was de Valera's 1932 electoral victory in the south, which heightened fears of a renewed I.R.A. offensive. Unionist apprehension was fuelled during June 1932 by the eucharistic congress held in Dublin. Bates observed that it generated 'excitement, amounting almost to frenzy'.[21] Craigavon later advised colleagues to 'avoid provocative action', and it was agreed that he should contact the press 'to calm their comments'.[22] In public speeches he and other ministers alike sought to calm their volatile supporters by reaffirming the protestant nature of the state.

As the economic crisis worsened, the potential for violence increased further: already several outbreaks of sectarian disorder had occurred, notably in August 1931. An additional cause for concern was reflected in the warning given by the minister for home affairs that 'a large body of the population... [would be] driven to desperation by poverty and hunger', and that the distress would be such as to exceed the capacity of the boards of guardians to provide relief.[23] By September 1932, 78,000 workers were unemployed in Belfast, 28 per cent of the insured population of the city. Over 20,000 of these had by then exhausted their claims to state benefit; they had therefore no alternative but to look to the city's poor law guardians for support.

These circumstances precipitated the renewal of an ongoing dispute between local authorities and the government over their respective roles. From the late 1920s the Belfast board of guardians had objected to providing outdoor relief on any scale to the able-bodied, as it considered that its proper function was to support those in chronic distress among the old, the ill, and the orphaned. Its attitude reflected a profound distrust of welfare expenditure. It did not of course escape the attention of the guardians, who were almost exclusively protestant, that a majority of their claimants were catholics. The grants that they did provide were heavily means-tested and were approximately half the value of those offered in comparable cities elsewhere in the United Kingdom (though it should be remembered that Northern

[20] *Belfast News Letter*, 3 Dec. 1930.
[21] Cabinet conclusions, 22 June 1932 (P.R.O.N.I., CAB4/303).
[22] Ibid., 8 July 1932 (P.R.O.N.I., CAB4/304); also Barton, *Brookeborough*, pp 32–3.
[23] Cabinet conclusions, 8 July 1932 (P.R.O.N.I., CAB4/304); McVicker, 'Law & order', pp 194, 228.

Ireland incomes were lower). Trouble might have been avoided had the government acted more quickly and assumed the board's responsibilities. But it hesitated to do so, aware that if such matters were transferred to parliament this would afford increased opportunities for opponents to attack its own record on relieving distress and reducing unemployment.

Meanwhile popular protest gathered momentum, reaching its climax in a rare, though brief, outburst of proletarian solidarity. On 3 October 1932, 60,000 people attended a torchlight meeting at the Customs House in Belfast to protest at relief levels.[24] Afterwards, against a background of sporadic looting and rioting, a further mass demonstration was arranged for 11 October, but it was banned twenty-four hours beforehand by Dawson Bates, using his emergency powers. Undeterred, crowds gathered as arranged next day, in defiant mood; an eruption of non-sectarian violence followed, in which two people were shot dead by police and thirty-four injured. The disorder was rooted in widespread distress and in passions inflamed by demonstrations and oratory. It represented the fleeting peak of Orange–Green cooperation. Under pressure from the government and the corporation, the guardians raised their levels of support; ministers made promises of orders for the shipyards, and belatedly legislation was introduced to transfer responsibility for maintaining most able-bodied poor to the state.[25]

The gradual escalation in street protests and disorder, together with allegations of Moscow's involvement (purportedly directed towards establishing an Irish republic), helped strengthen Bates's influence in cabinet. He refused to apply to the regular police the full extent of the salary reductions imposed by Westminster on the police forces in Britain. Despite the financial implications, the R.U.C. mobile reserve and special constabulary were mobilised from late 1931. The prime minister, backed by Bates, also sought the transfer of additional troops, with armoured cars, to the province, on the grounds that the 3,200 'B' specials posted on border patrol would be unable to cope with an I.R.A. incursion from the south. This request was raised with Viscount Hailsham, secretary of state for war, and Sir Herbert Samuel, the home secretary, in July 1932, but was rejected by both British ministers as they considered the three battalions already based in Northern Ireland to be sufficient. Craigavon had three months earlier, however, been able to reassure his supporters concerning the prospects for Irish unity. He stated publicly in April that he had seen J. H. Thomas, secretary of state for the dominions, who had informed him that unity would not occur 'except with the full consent of Northern Ireland'.[26]

---

[24] See Paddy Devlin, *Yes, we have no bananas: outdoor relief in Belfast, 1920–39* (Belfast, 1981), pp 116–36.

[25] Buckland, *Factory of grievances*, pp 156–9.

[26] Craigavon met Thomas on 13 Apr. 1932 and subsequently issued a press statement (*Belfast News Letter*, 14 Apr. 1932); see also McVicker, 'Law & order', pp 191–3.

As a further means of calming atavistic unionist fears, the special powers act was made permanent in 1933. This seemed more necessary given the strong criticism from within the party of government policy on matters such as the licensing laws.[27] Also, the republican threat to Northern Ireland appeared to be palpable; it had recently been underlined by aggressive speeches made by sections of the Fianna Fáil leadership, and the discovery of I.R.A. arms caches. In addition, since 1925, when nationalist M.P.s had begun to take their seats in the commons, debates on the renewal of the act had become the occasion for much mutual recrimination. Though the powers it conferred had been invoked less frequently than the opposition alleged, the ministry of home affairs still valued them, as they permitted a prompt response to any prospective danger. Moreover, if abandoned, they might well prove difficult to recover. But despite Bates's disclaimers that the special powers would be abused,[28] his use of them proved to be a continuing source of controversy; nationalist alienation was confirmed, and there were angry denunciations from some of the government's own supporters.

Intercommunal cooperation during the outdoor relief protests in Belfast proved to be abortive; as Patrick Shea, a civil servant, observed, 'inherited religious prejudices and fostered fears were too strong for the bonds created by immediate and real grievances'.[29] In the late spring and early summer of 1935 persistent and violent, though relatively minor, sectarian clashes were again occurring, mainly in the York Street and docks area of Belfast. Bates reacted boldly but controversially by banning all processions and assemblies in public places, including the annual 12 July demonstrations. His action outraged influential sections of unionist opinion. Sir Joseph Davison, the grand master of the county grand Orange lodge of Belfast, challenged the minister's order by holding meetings and demanding exemption for the traditional Orange celebrations, indicating that they would proceed as usual whatever the government's response. On 26 June 1935 Bates capitulated, not only lifting the ban on the Orangemen but doing so without the permission of the acting prime minister, Hugh Pollock.[30]

[27] N.I. government reform of the licensing laws in the 1920s contained provision for Sunday closing and ended the granting of licences to spirit grocers. But most temperance organisations favoured 'local option', which would have permitted citizens within a particular local authority area to vote in favour of preventing the sale of drink altogether. Activists therefore formed the Local Option Party, which launched a major temperance campaign and contested three seats in the 1929 elections; its candidates polled 28.5% of the votes cast. Its existence was obviously cause for government concern; see J. F. Harbinson, *The Ulster Unionist Party 1882–1973: its development and organisation* (Belfast, 1973), pp 216–19. Craigavon opposed local option, believing that legislation could not make a country sober; rather it was a matter for the individual (*Belfast News Letter*, 3 May 1929).

[28] Cabinet conclusions, 25 Jan. 1933 (P.R.O.N.I., CAB4/308).

[29] Patrick Shea, *Voices and the sound of drums: an Irish autobiography* (Belfast, 1981), p. 109.

[30] Pollock habitually deputised for Craigavon during the latter's increasingly frequent illnesses and expanding holidays. In 1935 Craigavon went with his wife on a three-month tour of South America (Buckland, *Craig*, pp 118–19). Pollock was himself 83 in 1935; he died in Apr. 1937.

Later police accounts indicate that the 12 July 1935 marches in Belfast contributed measurably to an escalation in the levels of violence; the city coroner also blamed inflammatory speeches made by men in positions of influence. Rioting, sniping, and arson, concentrated mainly in the Falls and Shankill districts, persisted over the following three weeks. Eleven people were killed, most of them protestant, and 574 injured. There were 367 cases of malicious damage and 173 of arson. An estimated 300 persons, mainly catholic, were driven from their homes. It was the most ferocious eruption of civil unrest to occur in Northern Ireland since 1922. The presence of additional police, special constables, and troops in sensitive areas, the imposition of a localised curfew, and the introduction of a 'peace line' helped restore order.

Demands from nationalists for a governmental inquiry into the causes and course of the disturbances were supported by 100 M.P.s at Westminster, but rejected by Stanley Baldwin, the prime minister, on the now familiar grounds that the maintenance of law and order was a transferred responsibility. The National Council for Civil Liberties did, however, hold an investigation and produced its own report, which broadly confirmed the findings of a northern catholic committee that had conducted a private inquiry. The N.C.C.L. report was a scathing indictment of Craigavon and his colleagues. It attributed the recent violence to provocative anti-catholic speeches by unionist leaders, and it also condemned alleged government bias in the administration of law and order. The report, however, lacked objectivity; it overstated the faults of Northern Ireland ministers and underestimated their difficulties, in a calculated attempt to discredit them and hasten Irish unity.

None the less, the judicial system did undoubtedly continue to discriminate in favour of the majority; the vigour with which the law was enforced against catholics and nationalists would suggest that at times the government's main concern was to reassure its own supporters. The emergency powers were characteristically invoked to ban republican rallies and demonstrations, or to detain suspected I.R.A. members and sympathisers. A typical instance was the 1933 order issued by Dawson Bates, prohibiting any display of the tricolour within Northern Ireland. By contrast, political considerations and discretion were likely to influence ministers when dealing with cases involving protestants and unionists. Thus, at the behest of the minister of home affairs, the attorney general and crown solicitor applied discreet pressure on magistrates trying the cases of protestants who attacked catholic pilgrims travelling south to the eucharistic congress in 1932. Bates advised Craigavon that bail would in most cases be preferable to prison sentences, as he did 'not want when the new parliament house [at Stormont, was] opened, or when we [were] engaged in very violent disturbances in connection with the Free State, to have the government handicapped by having 70 or so young fellows in jail'.[31] A similar pattern of sectarian bias was evident in the sentences passed on those charged after the July 1935 riots.

There remained a widespread presumption among members of the unionist party that emergency powers should not be used against unionists and protestants; all measures taken to preserve law and order were closely scrutinised. During the May 1935 disturbances, allegations were made that protestants in the York Street area were the victims of excessive force by the R.U.C. and of discrimination in subsequent court cases; these helped raise political tensions, led to demands for the resignation of the inspector-general, and prompted a home affairs investigation into the religious composition of the entire police membership.[32] Likewise, when later that year the government introduced legislation to replace the province's 1,500 unpaid J.P.s with salaried resident magistrates, it was accused of 'Hitlerism' in quarters normally uncritical of ministers; the measure also resulted in an appeal to the privy council and strident calls for cabinet change.[33]

Taken as a whole, the extent of the deterioration in community relations during the early and mid 1930s can easily be overstated. Certainly the years 1932 and 1935 were exceptional, and to focus exclusively on them is to give a distorted impression of normal levels of violence in Belfast. On 7 October 1937 T. C. Davison, the newly appointed parliamentary secretary to the ministry of home affairs, informed the commons that over the previous six years just eighteen murders had occurred in the city for which no one had been found guilty and convicted. Eleven of these had occurred during the 1935 riots, and in seven of these cases there was no evidence to show that there was any actual intention to assassinate the particular victim.[34] In Northern Ireland as a whole, 147 people were murdered between 1922 and 1955. Ninety-seven of the murders were politically motivated, and almost all took place during 1922 or 1935. In most years, no more than two or three murders were committed, a level that compares favourably with British

[31] Bates to Craigavon 26 July 1932 (P.R.O.N.I., CAB9B/200); McVicker, 'Law & order', pp 198–200.

[32] McVicker, 'Law & order', pp 217–19, 232, 241–2. The investigation was dated 31 July 1935. It revealed that at York Street R.U.C. station there were 24 catholics (including the head constable) and 60 protestants. The figures for the force as a whole were 2,344 protestants (82.7%) and 489 catholics (17.3%). There is no evidence of any government action as a result of the survey; controversy among protestants over the behaviour of the R.U.C. was to continue (ibid., pp 232–3).

[33] The measure was taken in the interests of greater efficiency and strong government; the attorney general, A. B. Babington, claimed that before long the bill would be copied in Britain. G. McElroy, a retired magistrate, described it as an attempt to turn 'democratic Ulster into a Prussianised province'. This view was supported by Sir William Moore, lord chief justice of N.I., members of the Magistrates' Association, and some Unionist backbenchers, many of whom used similar language (ibid., pp 203–10).

[34] Barton, Blitz, pp 21–2; David Johnson, 'The economic history of Ireland between the wars' in Ir. Econ. & Soc. Hist., i (1974), pp 49–61.

experience: in England and Wales, for example, with a population thirty times larger, the figure was 150 a year.[35]

Within the context of the United Kingdom, therefore, Northern Ireland society was far from being exceptionally violent during the interwar years, but it was still afflicted by unique and deepening sectarian divisions. The increasing protestant domination of power and public employment was a profoundly felt nationalist grievance, both a cause and a symptom of alienation. In the R.U.C., for example, the proportion of catholics never approached the one-third level originally intended to be reserved for them. In July 1936 there were 488 catholics in the entire force, 17.1 per cent of the total; and they occupied 16.3 per cent of the higher ranks. This represented a decline from 535 in June 1924, a figure that was related to the high proportion (approximately one-half) of the force that was admitted from the disbanded R.I.C.[36]

There was also a steady decline in the percentage of catholics in the civil service, despite initial hopes that its composition would be broadly representative. According to Spender, catholics comprised just 10 per cent of the lower ranks in November 1934. He observed, a little over a year later, that there had been a substantial diminution of their number in the senior ranks since 1925. By 1943 they made up a mere 5.8 per cent of administrative staff and analogous grades, and there were none among the fifty-five permanent and assistant secretaries. Yet apart from a small number of political appointments, selection procedures in the province followed British practice; they were strictly based on merit, and devoid of overt religious discrimination. Any employment safeguards adopted locally were directed against Free State residents rather than northern nationalists. However, there can be little doubt that political pressures operated to maintain the protestant character of the senior grades.[37] With the exception of J. M. Barbour and Pollock, ministers could not bring themselves to trust catholics in responsible posts. This was especially true of Dawson Bates; out of 140 employees at his ministry in November 1935, only two were catholics.[38] Rumours of 'disloyalty' in public office were taken up by protestant organisations and often taken seriously by Craigavon and his colleagues. The civil service did not, therefore, deliberately set out to be a protestant administration, but in essence that was what it turned out to be.

---

[35] Barton, *Blitz*, pp 21–2.
[36] Buckland, *Factory of grievances*, pp 20–21; Farrell, *Arming the protestants*, p. 191.
[37] See McMahon, *Republicans & imperialists*, pp 267–8; Phoenix, *Northern nationalism*, pp 368–9.
[38] J. Milne Barbour was minister for commerce, Apr. 1925–Jan. 1941; H. M. Pollock minister for finance May 1921–May 1937; and R. Dawson Bates minister for home affairs May 1921–May 1943. For statistics of the religious composition of Bates's ministry, see investigation, 31 July 1935 (P.R.O.N.I., CAB9B/236).

Other factors contributing to catholic under-representation included a lower level of educational attainment. While commenting that 'no Roman Catholic [had] entered the administrative ranks', Spender added that 'had one succeeded in passing the examinations, he would have been accepted'.[39] Disproportionately low catholic–nationalist recruitment also reflected the continuing unwillingness of many to accept the legitimacy of Northern Ireland. Patrick Shea noted, soon after joining the civil service in the 1930s, that 'the [catholic] bishop [in Belfast] had advised ... against seeking government employment'; he added that, to some of his co-religionists, 'we had joined the enemy; we were lost souls'.[40] In 1922 the nationalist *Irish News* contrasted unfavourably the attitude of southern unionists, who allegedly had quickly 'settled into their place in the Free State',[41] with the bitter and divided response of the northern minority to changed political circumstances. Over a decade later, one of the newspaper's reporters recorded a visit to the west of the province. He 'expressed great surprise that the partition issue was as much alive in Fermanagh today as if it had happened only a few weeks ago'.[42] Within the minority community the mentality of boycott and non-recognition was never fully abandoned in the interwar years; the community retreated in on itself and refused to play a full role in public life.

This is further evidenced by the minority's relationship with the Northern Ireland parliament. From April 1925 onwards, a growing number of nationalist M.P.s took their seats in the commons; their entry appeared to herald the emergence of a healthy political pragmatism and was certainly a precondition for the formation of a stable democracy in the province. Recognition of Northern Ireland and the creation of a cohesive six-county nationalist organisation had long been supported and encouraged by the *Irish News*. In editorials it had argued that these steps would enable northern catholics to recover 'the rights they chose to sacrifice'; it concluded that they had been 'victims of [their] own ineptitude'.[43]

Preparation of the nationalist case for the boundary commissioners (1924–5) and the need for organisation during the general election that Craig had called on this issue (3 April 1925) provided a vital initial spur to greater unity among the fissiparous nationalist groups. The tripartite agreement of

[39] Buckland, *Factory of grievances*, p. 19.

[40] Shea, *Voices and the sound of drums*, p. 113; he does not identify the bishop, but it was possibly Daniel Mageean of Down and Connor. Shea was born in Co. Westmeath, the son of a member of the R.I.C. He was one of just two catholics to reach the rank of permanent secretary in the N.I. civil service (Bonaparte Wyse in the 1920s, Shea in the 1970s); he describes himself as a 'cuckoo in the nest ... between the two communities' (ibid., p. 113).

[41] *Irish News*, 19 Dec. 1922.

[42] Rev. J. McShane to F. J. Nugent, 10 Dec. 1937 (Healy papers, P.R.O.N.I., D2991/A/58B).

[43] *Irish News*, 4, 7 Dec. 1925. In Lawrence, *Govt of N.I.*, p. 36, these sentiments are echoed: 'The measures provoked by their [the minority's] own intransigence gave them ample ground for complaint.'

3 December 1925 finally removed the divisive influence of possible border change. It was universally regarded by the minority with bitterness and as a betrayal: partition had been reinforced without either boundary rectification or the inclusion of any additional safeguards for catholics within Northern Ireland. In addition, prospects for the council of Ireland, which Healy had described as 'the last hope of unity in our time', had lapsed.[44] The settlement marked the irrevocable alienation of northern catholics from Cosgrave and Cumann na nGaedheal, and the beginning of their rapprochement with de Valera and his supporters.[45]

The agreement inevitably increased the pressures on nationalist M.P.s to recognise the Belfast parliament and test Craigavon's protestations of good-will; as early as 1923 even the normally irreconcilable Cardinal MacRory had observed that the Northern Ireland government was 'moving heaven and earth to bring the nationalists in'.[46] By 1925 it was clear that the abstentionist strategy had failed. However, grave damage had by then been done to the minority's interests; earlier entry would almost certainly have improved its position within the six counties. The sensitive nature of the reforms being considered by the northern commons in the late 1920s highlighted the need to end abstention. These included the imminent abolition of P.R. in parliamentary elections; legislation to prolong the special powers act for a further five years; and the prospect of further amendments to the 1923 education act. The final and decisive stimulus to recognition came from the Free State, where de Valera had concluded that abstention from the dáil was fruitless. As a consequence, in May 1926 he launched the Fianna Fáil party; by the summer of 1927 its members had contested an election and taken the oath of allegiance, which they declared to be an empty formula.

Meanwhile Joseph Devlin, nationalist M.P. for Belfast West, had already entered the northern parliament along with a colleague on 28 April 1925; he had delayed because of the boundary commission issue and fear of assassination by republican extremists. By March 1926 a total of five nationalist M.P.s had taken their seats, and this had risen to ten by November 1927. Devlin quickly became convinced of the need to form a political organisation outside the house; his intention was to enhance the effectiveness of the small nationalist group in parliament by mobilising popular support in Belfast and beyond. Illness prevented him from playing a significant part in laying the foundation of the new party. Instead, in December 1927 Cahir Healy drafted

---

[44] Phoenix, *Northern nationalism*, p. 333.

[45] Ibid., pp 333–4. Cosgrave's description of the tripartite agreement as a 'damned good bargain' offended northern nationalist sensibilities; see Bowman, *De Valera & Ulster question*, p. 92.

[46] Report of an interview between MacRory and H. A. MacCurtain, 16 Mar. 1923 (Phoenix, *Northern nationalism*, p. 280). MacCurtain was an agent working for the north-east boundary bureau, carrying out a review of northern nationalist opinion.

its manifesto. This contained commitments to Irish unity and independence, justice and equality for the minority, and the promotion of Gaelic ideals. It was approved by the sitting M.P.s and the catholic hierarchy. Soon afterwards, with the endorsement of Fianna Fáil, the 'National League of the North' was publicly launched on 28 May 1928; Devlin was its president and Healy its secretary.

The party never fulfilled the high hopes and expectations of its founders. In part this was because it failed to rouse northern catholics from the disappointment and apathy generated by the flow of political events since 1918. Its leadership was sectional: almost exclusively Devlinite and drawn from the ranks of the Ancient Order of Hibernians.[47] Republicans denounced the whole initiative and persisted in their refusal to take their seats. Likewise, pro-treaty Sinn Féin supporters, apart from Healy, remained aloof from the new movement; they never lost their suspicion of Devlin, which dated back to mid 1916, when he had supported Redmond and temporary partition during the Lloyd George negotiations. Among other nationalists also there were those who continued to oppose entry into the northern house of commons, because of their unwillingness to take the oath of allegiance or in the belief that without an opposition the unionist party would disintegrate. Thus, even after the boundary issue had been resolved, the minority retained deep internal divisions. Despite the efforts of Devlin and others, no organisational equivalent of the Ulster Unionist Council was ever formed by its political opponents. The National League was a loose alliance of elements within the catholic community, and it proved incapable of mobilising and sustaining an effective political opposition outside parliament. It expired shortly after the 1929 election; its successor, the Irish Union Association, formed in 1936, was equally ephemeral.[48]

Devlin also quickly became disillusioned with the exclusivist catholic character of the league; he was embarrassed, from the outset, that it was being forced to play a sectarian role. Though it adopted a socialist rhetoric and an expansive programme, including a commitment to foster the cooperation of all creeds and classes, its actions and composition belied its words.[49] It made no real effort to reach beyond the minority community by espousing a blend of social and economic reforms with cross-sectional appeal. Despite its policy

[47] Sometimes described as the catholic counterpart of the Orange order, the A.O.H. had acquired its name in the 1830s. In the early twentieth century Joseph Devlin was its leading personality (above, v, 705; vi, 115).

[48] See Phoenix, *Northern nationalism*, pp 359–71, for detailed analysis of the formation and development of the National League of the North; also Buckland, *Factory of grievances*, pp 29, 33–5.

[49] See David Kennedy, 'Catholics in Northern Ireland, 1926–1939' in Francis MacManus (ed.), *The years of the great test, 1926–39* (Cork, 1967), pp 138–49. The League's 1929 election manifesto contained a demand for an end to unemployment, the raising of the school-leaving age, and increased (and earlier) old-age pensions (Buckland, *Factory of grievances*, pp 33–4).

documents, it was not in essence socialist or radical but a catholic party, acting in defence of catholic interests. It claimed to represent the population without social or political distinction; in practice, it represented the catholic middle classes who led and organised it. In failing health, Devlin (who died in 1934) was unable to attempt the league's transformation into a broader political alliance that might ultimately have mounted an effective challenge to unionism. A Belfast Labour newspaper wrote of the emerging organisation that it was 'as politically bankrupt as the older group so ponderously led by the prime minister. They are both capitalist parties, and their entire legislative outlook is determined by big business.'[50] Indeed, despite the deep divisions between them over constitutional and religious issues, both the major parliamentary parties generally shared a profound distrust of state activity and expenditure, and displayed comparable zeal in defending local parochial interests.

None the less, nationalist M.P.s soon despaired at the dismissive nature of their treatment by members of the Northern Ireland government. Some had initially favoured making their recognition of parliament conditional on Craigavon's introduction of further electoral, educational, and security legislation to assuage minority grievances. Such proposals were rejected by ministers; Craigavon and Pollock claimed that the catholic community was being treated well, and argued that it was the failure of its elected representatives to take their seats that had deprived them of legitimate influence over earlier reforms. In response, Devlin bitterly criticised the prime minister for welcoming the opposition into the commons and then proceeding to ignore and insult it. He told Craigavon in March 1932: 'We were willing to help. But you rejected all friendly offers. You refused to accept cooperation.'[51]

The nationalist leader characteristically overstated his case by exaggerating his party's potential contribution, and also the extent of the offence by ministers. Arguably he and his colleagues had little of a positive nature to offer to Northern Ireland parliamentary institutions; their participation seemed conditional only. Their focus was on a united and independent Ireland, not on the development and improvement of Northern Ireland. They therefore failed to exploit the opportunity of properly representing and defending catholic interests. They refused to act as an official opposition when Labour members suggested this in November 1927. In parliament, most contented themselves with ritual denunciations of the government and its measures or with wrecking amendments. Devlin himself railed against Craigavon's apparent indifference to unemployment and the imposition on the province of

---

[50] Joe Keenan (ed.), '*The Labour opposition of Northern Ireland*': *complete reprint of the first Labour newspaper in Northern Ireland, 1925–26* (Belfast, 1992), p. 45. See also Farrell, *Orange state*, p. 116.

[51] Buckland, *Factory of grievances*, p. 34.

taxation from Westminster; he seemed unable to grasp either the very limited nature of the powers transferred to Northern Ireland or the extent of the treasury's grip on fiscal policy. To his opponents, he appeared to be merely attention-seeking, indulging in gesture politics.

It is of course the case that while some ministers treated the nationalist members with courtesy and openness, the government collectively made little or no concession to the repeated accusations of discrimination and injustice. Despite bitter nationalist protests, the special powers act was eventually made permanent.[52] Also, through amending legislation in 1925 and 1930, Lord Londonderry's vision of a non-denominational educational system, without compulsory religious instruction and under popular local control, was diluted.[53] The catholic hierarchy had regarded reform from the outset as a pretext for an attack on their schools. The changes were made, however, in response to a powerful campaign orchestrated by protestant clergymen and the Orange order. The effect was to make the state primary schools generally acceptable to protestants but not to the catholic hierarchy.[54] However, the possibility that the concessions to protestants might be challenged under the terms of the government of Ireland act made the government amenable to concessions to the voluntary (catholic) sector. The 1930 education act accordingly allowed state funds to be used to finance up to half the capital cost of voluntary schools. Their resulting funding was therefore higher than it would have been in Great Britain.[55] Meanwhile, real progress was made throughout the educational system during the interwar years, especially in primary school provision, in pupil numbers attending secondary schools, and in teacher training. However, this did nothing to alleviate the acute sense of injustice felt by northern nationalists.

Meanwhile, in 1929, amid fervent opposition from all minority groups, P.R. was abolished in parliamentary elections. In contrast to the course adopted in respect of local government electoral reform, on this occasion the government produced its own scheme. In doing so, it was concerned to preserve the same number of constituencies as before. It also paid due regard to population distribution, while striving to cause minimal disturbance to existing electoral areas and administrative boundaries. Craigavon's stated intention was to maintain 'the balance of power which exists today', and not to diminish nationalist representation unduly.[56] The government was most

[52] 23 & 24 Geo. V, c. 12 (9 May 1933).
[53] Below, pp 714–17.
[54] Cardinal Logue, the catholic primate, described the Lynn committee as a 'foundation and pretext' for an attack on catholic schools; see cabinet conclusions, 2 Sept. 1921 (P.R.O.N.I., CAB4/18).
[55] Buckland, *Factory of grievances*, p. 263. See also Harkness, *N.I. since 1920*, p. 64, and below, pp 716–17.
[56] *Hansard N.I. (commons)*, x, 429 (5 Mar. 1929). Craigavon claimed that the bill was 'absolutely fair to all parties in Ulster' (ibid.).

open to informed criticism in its complete failure to consult the opposition. The only opportunity provided for comment was during the passage of the bill. Yet throughout its progress requests for consultation, suggestions, and amendments were rejected, although it was suspected that local unionist politicians, who had easy access to government, were able to give their views.

The minority's suspicion of ministerial bias was reinforced by subsequent electoral results. In the 1929 general election nationalist candidates took eleven seats; one fewer than under P.R. in 1920 and 1925, and significantly below the sixteen or seventeen that they should in theory have won.[57] Although the difficulties in devising an equitable scheme were considerable, it was an observable feature of the reform process that doubtful matters were consistently resolved in favour of government supporters. The principle that the redistributed boundaries should conform to existing administrative divisions was selectively applied. More blatant partisanship was displayed several years later, in response to the increasingly insecure unionist majority on Derry city council. The ministry of home affairs scheme, implemented by order in December 1936, guaranteed the party a majority of four in the chamber even though its members then clearly represented a minority of the electorate; Craigavon described the outcome as being 'in the interests of the province'.[58]

The government's main motive in returning to the former voting system in parliamentary elections was not to crush the nationalist minority or to bring local electoral practices into line with Britain. Rather it was symptomatic of the siege mentality and the myopia that persisted within the unionist leadership. Craigavon feared that the proliferation and success of candidates from smaller parties and groups, which P.R. facilitated, would cause political instability and ultimately imperil the union. Herbert Dixon, the Unionist chief whip, tersely expressed the view of ministers and officials: 'There is no room in Ulster for diversities of opinion, and the people have got to learn

---

[57] Concerning the abolition of P.R., Devlin stated: 'I think he [Craigavon] wants to weaken us [nationalists], but . . . it is to wipe out what are called the Labour and independent members' (ibid., 449–50). In contested seats (excluding the university), proportionately Labour should have won 1.88 in 1925, but won 3; in 1929 it should have won 2.02, but won only 1. In 1929 independent unionists should similarly have won 3.64: they won 2; nationalists, who should have won 3.05, won 5; the Unionist party, which should have won 13.22, won 18 (Elliott, *N.I. election results*, p. 354; see also Buckland, *Factory of grievances*, pp 239–43).

[58] Cabinet conclusions, 15 Dec. 1936 (P.R.O.N.I., CAB4/369). The ministry scheme arranged the electorate into three wards, taking account of population, valuation, and existing parliamentary constituency boundaries. In two of the three wards there were safe unionist majorities, while the third was overwhelmingly nationalist; as a result, 9,961 nationalist voters returned eight councillors and 7,444 unionist voters returned twelve (Buckland, *Factory of grievances*, pp 243–6). The government had also recently endorsed a gerrymandering scheme to ensure protestant control of the mainly nationalist Omagh urban district (Phoenix, *Northern nationalism*, p. 380).

that sooner or later.'[59] The immediate context for the reform was the success of Labour and independent candidates in the 1925 election, followed by deepening economic depression, and internal party strains as education and temperance reformers attacked the Unionist leadership.

Although the abolition of P.R. exacerbated the minority problem in the north, Westminster was unable or unwilling to intervene, even to delay its implementation. Joynson-Hicks, the home secretary, responded to the protests of a local Labour party delegation by affirming merely that the measure lay within the powers transferred to the Northern Ireland parliament. Abolition effectively dashed the hopes of Devlin and Healy for a major political realignment in the north, and for a less frozen political system, which might be conducive to reform and hasten unity. During the 1927 parliamentary session Labour and nationalist M.P.s had formed a fairly strong alliance, opposing P.R. abolition and the trade disputes act[60] and cooperating on motions of censure. With the return of the former voting system they were both forced to compete for the same votes, and party divisions sharpened along traditional sectarian lines. The proportion of uncontested seats rose steadily. In the 1929 election nationalist and unionist candidates opposed each other in just two constituencies; in 1933 there was no contest in thirty-three of the province's forty-eight parliamentary divisions.[61]

As early as May 1932 the nationalist party had withdrawn from the commons for a period that was to last for eighteen months. Although it continued generally to do well in election clashes with republican candidates, the party was dispirited by five years of barren opposition and the unwillingness of unionists to share power. Its decision to withdraw was taken in response to a speaker's ruling that forbade discussion of the post office during a debate on the Northern Ireland budget. Such judgements consistently interpreted the constitutional position narrowly, so precluding parliamentary discussion of 'accepted' and 'reserved' powers and enabling the government to evade unwelcome criticism. Ministers in any event never regarded the commons highly in the making of decisions and policy. However, nationalist withdrawal was not determined solely by the attitudes and stratagems of Craigavon and his colleagues but also by broader changes in Irish politics. De Valera's coming to power in February 1932 raised sharply once again the issue of the future of the border. Thereafter, nationalist M.P.s increasingly opted to enlist his support and that of other outside agencies when seeking to draw the attention of British ministers to the position of the minority in Northern Ireland.

[59] Dixon to Spender, 23 Aug. 1924 (P.R.O.N. I., CAB9B/101/1). For detailed consideration of the impact of the abolition of P.R. on parliamentary elections, see Elliott, *N.I. election results*, pp 283–369.
[60] 17 & 18 Geo. V, c. 20 (21 Dec. 1927).
[61] Elliott, *N.I. election results*, chs 4, 6.

After Devlin's death in 1934 nationalist politics entered a new phase. T. J. Campbell, a former *Irish News* editor and an able lawyer, was Devlin's successor, but he lacked the powers of leadership that the situation required. The parliamentary party adopted a policy of 'creeping abstention' from the house. Hopes that de Valera would give northern nationalists a lead were disappointed, although in 1936 he did encourage the formation in the north of a new (short-lived) nationalist organisation, the Irish Union Association. In general, de Valera made it clear that while his government would do what it could to end partition, it would not be drawn into the differences between northern nationalists. De Valera also failed to press partition at the League of Nations. At home, northern nationalists were unsuccessful in obtaining an inquiry into the 1935 riots, and this reinforced the case for abstention from Stormont. By 1937 only two nationalist M.P.s, both from Belfast (Campbell and Richard Byrne), attended regularly. The boycott was less a political tactic than an expression of apathy, despair, and impotence. No attempt was made to establish an alternative assembly or to organise a popular campaign outside Stormont on issues such as unemployment or poor housing. Abstention itself was a divisive issue; Anthony Mulvey, Westminster M.P. for Fermanagh–Tyrone, was leader of a hard-line abstentionist faction, drawing support from the western counties, while Cahir Healy and the Ancient Order of Hibernians continued to regard outright abstention—the failure even to take the oaths—as likely to result in the forfeiting of seats and playing into the hands of unionists.[62]

The new southern constitution of 1937 prompted the establishment of a strongly anti-partitionist organisation, the Northern Council of Unity, which received the backing of several senior clergy. There was talk of acting on the 'all-Ireland' scope of the new constitution by introducing northern M.P.s to the dáil; however, de Valera opposed any such move. During 1938 de Valera did take the opportunity of trade talks with the British government to raise the issue of partition, urged on by Cahir Healy. The British government agreed to investigate charges of ill-treatment of catholics, but the inquiry produced only a 'predictably bland' defence of the unionist regime. Northern nationalists were still divided over strategy when in October 1938 de Valera launched an anti-partition campaign with a view to influencing British public opinion. An Anti-Partition League was formed, which drew support from the different nationalist factions in the north, and from Fianna Fáil; meetings were held in Britain and Ireland, and continued into 1939.[63]

In 1938 Daniel Mageean, bishop of Down and Connor, claimed that the history of the northern parliament was 'one long record of partisan and

[62] Phoenix, *Northern nationalism*, pp 373–4, 377, 380–83; Farrell, *Orange state*, pp 144–5; Buckland, *Factory of grievances*, pp 34–5.
[63] Phoenix, *Northern nationalism*, pp 382–7.

bigoted discrimination in matters of representation, legislation, and administration'.[64] To many catholics, such a judgement must have seemed justified;
certainly attendance by nationalist M.P.s at Stormont had brought no redress
of their grievances. In these adverse circumstances the catholic church itself
flourished, especially in the diocese of Down and Connor. It provided its
members with increased confidence and security, and also with an all-Ireland
social, intellectual, and political focus. It thus served to reinforce an attitude
of non-cooperation towards the northern government. According to one observer, the church's activities 'tended to develop a spirit of mutual admiration and complacency... [and] emphasised the apartheid mentality which is
the curse of Northern Ireland.'[65] Religious differences were stressed: in 1931
Cardinal MacRory, archbishop of Armagh, declared that the protestant
Church of Ireland was 'not even part of the Church of Christ'.[66] Such
attitudes confirmed protestants in their negative view of the catholic church,
and offered a justification for discrimination. The monolithic strength and
ubiquity of the catholic church not only appeared to protestants as a political
threat but also suggested to them the enslavement of the individual both to
the priest and to the church.[67]

The course of events leading to the formation of the National League
seemed to provide graphic evidence of the pervasive political power of the
catholic clergy. In 1923 the northern bishops had issued a protest against the
mistreatment of the minority in Northern Ireland, and called on the minority
to organise politically for its own defence, though without suggesting that the
northern state should be recognised. Eighteen months later, the hierarchy
played a seminal role in the formation of a united nationalist front before the
1925 elections to the Northern Ireland parliament. The resulting conference
was broadly representative of catholic opinion and arguably the most significant development in minority politics since 1921; it laid the basis for eventual
reconciliation between the two competing nationalist groupings during 1927–
8. When setting up the National League, Cahir Healy was fully aware that 'to
make the organisation a success, the assistance of the clergy is quite essential'.[68] Thus, before it was launched, its draft policy was placed before the
northern bishops, who gave it their approval; Archdeacon John Tierney of
Enniskillen subsequently became vice-president of the League. Mounting
sympathy among the clergy for the recognition of northern institutions was
by then evident from their more widespread encouragement of electoral

---

[64] Kennedy, 'Catholics in Northern Ireland, 1926–39', p. 146.
[65] Ibid., p. 149. See also Conor Cruise O'Brien, States of Ireland (2nd ed., St Albans, 1974),
p. 290, which suggests that the church inculcated a sense of moral superiority and 'systematically fostered... avoidance of social contact with protestants'.
[66] Buckland, Factory of grievances, p. 265.
[67] Wichert, N.I. since 1945, p. 27; Patrick Buckland, A history of Northern Ireland (Dublin,
1981), pp 3–5.
[68] Phoenix, 'Nationalist movement', p. 908.

registration and increasing involvement in local constituency conventions. It was also indicated, less directly, by the growing number of nationalist councillors in the rural divisions of Fermanagh, Tyrone, and south Armagh who took their seats in council chambers.

But behind the monolithic appearance of the church in this period lay deep divisions and tensions, often unobserved by its detractors, which severely tested the bonds between the northern clergy and between priests and people. After partition there had been at first no consensus, least of all within the hierarchy, on how best to achieve Irish unity or to protect church interests within the six counties. From the outset, throughout Northern Ireland, a number of senior clergy who had been closely identified with the old Irish party were sympathetic to Devlin and his strategy. They had remained loyal to him despite the divisive impact of his support for temporary partition in 1916. Their attitude was moulded by a fixed hostility to Sinn Féin (whether pro- or anti-treaty), and by a deep concern as to the long-term effects of abstention from the Belfast parliament on catholic interests, especially with regard to education; they therefore favoured recognition.

However, a number of northern bishops, fully backed by the influential Cardinal MacRory, fervently opposed Devlin's approach and his associated efforts to persuade border nationalists to support entry into the northern parliament. In August 1922 John Dillon wrote: 'The bishops are blocking it [recognition and entry], and a section of the Sinn Féin priests are furious at any sign of reconciliation between the Orange party and the catholics.'[69] These ecclesiastics, of course, shared Devlinite apprehension at the content of the 1923 education act. But they believed that catholic educational interests could be effectively safeguarded only under an all-Ireland parliament, the prospects of which would be fatally jeopardised if catholics were to recognise the northern parliament. According to Stephen Tallents, secretary to the viceroy, Devlin's supporters had 'hoped that the church would insist on their going in [to parliament] to work against the education bill'; they found instead that the hierarchy was content to observe the protestant churches do 'whatever was necessary for them'.[70]

By 1926–7 an increased proportion of influential catholic clergy had reached the conclusion that the 'interests of catholic education must take precedence to [sic] political considerations',[71] and that the nationalist M.P.s should therefore take their seats. Even then, however, on the eve of the National League being launched, a significant number of parish priests still supported abstention; many were young, with strong Sinn Féin sympathies,

---

[69] Ibid., p. 632.
[70] Phoenix, *Northern nationalism*, p. 286. The hierarchy was aware of the hostility of protestant churches to the original bill, on account of its 'religiously neutral nature' (below, pp 714–15).
[71] Phoenix, 'Nationalist movement', p. 892.

and they were mainly, though not exclusively, drawn from the west of the province. MacRory's own support for the new party was regarded by its founders as by no means certain; hence their relief that, when consulted, he 'approved [it] without qualification'.[72] None the less, continuing divisions and apathy among catholics, both clerical and lay, were seriously to impede and frustrate the party's future development.

FOR smaller political minorities also, the interwar period was one of frustration and disillusionment. A significant socialist challenge to unionism might reasonably have been expected during these years, in both central and local government. Northern Ireland contained a substantial working class, which had undergone a high degree of unionisation, particularly within its skilled sectors. From 1920 onwards, the region's staple industries experienced sustained and pervasive recession. When the Northern Ireland Labour party was formed in 1924, building on the foundations of a labour movement active locally since the 1880s, it could respond to the patent current need for a far-reaching programme of social reform.[73]

In fact, the Unionist party contained the socialist threat at successive elections with relative ease. From the early 1920s onwards, its control of Belfast corporation remained unshaken, almost unchallenged. It consistently held over fifty of the sixty seats in the council chamber; the remainder were virtually monopolised by nationalist representatives. In 1932, the trough of the great depression, just three of the city's fifteen wards were contested, falling to two in 1934. Labour candidates actually experienced their greatest success before partition: in 1920, the year in which the postwar boom ended, they won thirteen seats. Labour never again approached this level of success but instead struggled to survive as a credible force even in its heartland, the central areas of Belfast and the docks. The N.I.L.P.'s performance in parliamentary elections was similarly unimpressive. Though it won all of the three constituencies it contested in 1925, it was successful in just one out of five in 1929, two out of three in 1933, and one out of seven in 1939. Its inability to construct a single safe seat anywhere in the north was a measure of its failure. Much of even its limited success was achieved by manipulating the sectarian balance in certain divisions or by tailoring its principles to suit local circumstances.

Many factors contributed to the N.I.L.P.'s record of impotence and ineffectiveness. In part this reflected the inadequacy of its leaders; the more gifted members too often quarrelled and left the party, and in some instances emigrated. In any case, the party faced formidable difficulties. Its electoral

[72] Ibid., p. 909.
[73] For detailed analysis of the performance of the Labour party in these years see J. F. Harbinson, 'A history of the Northern Ireland Labour party, 1891–1949' (M.Sc. (Econ.) thesis, Q.U.B., 1966), pp 38–104, 236–81.

prospects never recovered from the abolition of proportional representation. Subsequent efforts to attract cross-sectional support were constantly thwarted by the divisiveness of sectarianism and the ambiguity of the party's position on partition.[74] As with all non-sectarian parties in Northern Ireland, the N.I.L.P.'s support wilted in times of apparent political crisis. Its commitment to socialism was not necessarily a vote-winner even in the context of high unemployment and social deprivation. The catholic hierarchy condemned its policies as incompatible with the church's teaching, and the appeal of its candidates in staunchly nationalist areas was diminished by their invariably protestant and trade unionist background.[75] They therefore needed to exercise discretion: in the 1938 election the N.I.L.P. candidate Harry Midgley needed a police escort in the Belfast Dock constituency, after having denied in a pamphlet that the Republicans in Spain were conducting anti-catholic pogroms. The party's difficulties were exacerbated by the tendency of the Unionist cabinet to preempt its demands through the adoption of 'step by step' policies with Westminster; as a consequence, the fruits of British Labour victories were transmitted to Northern Ireland. The relevance of the local labour movement was thus reduced, but its continued existence at least provided the government with an additional incentive for responding to the needs of the industrial working class.

The presence of independent unionists may also have helped focus ministerial attention on urban needs; six were returned to the commons between 1921 and 1938. Along with Labour candidates they achieved their best result in the 1925 parliamentary elections, when four were successful. Thereafter their fortunes were similarly impaired by the abolition of P.R. Typically, their candidates were individualists, Orangemen and Unionist party dissidents, devoid of either party organisation or distinctive policies. In Belfast they generally competed for votes in the same divisions as the official Unionist party and N.I.L.P. The spontaneity of their appeal is emphasised by the lack of continuity in the seats they contested.

The strongest unionist challenge to the government was mounted in the late 1930s with the formation of the Progressive Unionist party. Its campaign centred on such issues as housing and unemployment, and it sought, though with little success, to attract the unpolled nationalist vote. It did not survive the February 1938 general election. That election was ostensibly called as a

---

[74] Until 1949 the N.I.L.P. sought to avoid adopting any clear position on the partition question. The issue was evaded in its first constitution, and its members were at liberty to advocate whatever views they liked. On 8 Apr. 1949, however, at a special delegate conference, a motion was carried: 'The N.I.L.P. will maintain unbroken the connection between Great Britain and Northern Ireland.' This was adopted in the context of Ireland's secession from the commonwealth (ibid., ch. 8).

[75] All five N.I.L.P. M.P.s who sat in the N.I. parliament during the interwar years were protestants and trade unionists; these qualities rendered the party particularly suspect in catholic eyes (Buckland, *History of N.I.*, p. 69).

riposte to the irredentist claims contained in the new Irish constitution and the prospect of imminent negotiations to be held between de Valera and British ministers, at which partition would be raised. Craigavon claimed that voters were being empowered to 'put the question of Ulster beyond doubt'.[76] In Andrews's view this 'was not quite fair to the electorate',[77] as he and his colleagues had received private assurances from Westminster that they would be consulted and that Northern Ireland's interests would be safeguarded. The contest was, in fact, a calculated attempt by the prime minister to crush the 'wreckers', and it proved to be a strategic triumph. The revolt by the independents was suppressed; they failed to win a single seat, and the Union-ist party won its highest share of the popular vote since 1921.

The episode illustrated Craigavon's willingness to exploit the border and sectarian issues shamelessly in order to mobilise his grass-roots supporters and maintain unionist cohesion. However, southern claims, policies, and attitudes continued to make devolved government in Northern Ireland less likely to break out of the pattern established in the early 1920s. The tripartite agreement in 1925 had appeared to offer the prospect of a new era of peace-ful coexistence in Ireland, with the Dublin government abandoning its boundary claims based on the treaty.[78] Though the outcome was disappoint-ing for Dublin, unity remained the ultimate goal and the government hoped to generate mutual goodwill through the settlement and so accelerate the unification process. At the time of the agreement, both governments spoke optimistically of more cordial relations in the future and of their hopes for lasting peace. Echoing the terms of his pacts with Collins, the northern prime minister agreed to meet Cosgrave when necessary to discuss issues of common interest. This vague prospect was all that remained of the council of Ireland projected in the government of Ireland act. In fact, there was no personal contact between the respective heads of the two neighbouring ad-ministrations until the historic O'Neill–Lemass encounter forty years later, and no joint session of the two Irish cabinets ever occurred.

From the outset unionists had viewed the southern government with pro-found wariness, though a working relationship had gradually evolved. Cross-border involvement in attempts to destabilise the north during and after the Anglo–Irish war had confirmed unionist feelings of dislike and suspicion, and these endured notwithstanding the apparent cordiality of the boundary agreement. Mutual relations were strained by the continued unwillingness of Free State leaders to renounce all territorial claims to Northern Ireland and by their oft-repeated demands for unity. Moreover, Free State leaders from time to time raised the issue of partition at Westminster and elsewhere,

[76] Quoted in *Irish News*, 14 Jan. 1938.

[77] Spender diary, retrospection note dated 2 Nov. 1940; see also entry for 13 Jan. 1938. For background see Robert Fisk, *In time of war* (London, 1983), pp 46–8.

[78] Phoenix, *Northern nationalism*, pp 334–6.

endorsing the minority's claims of misgovernment. The resulting awareness among unionists 'that they were not, after all, masters of their own fate was a key factor in the evolution of internal politics' in Northern Ireland.[79] The persistence of southern pressures and claims helped to perpetuate the endemic siege mentality of northern ministers, whose constant need was for reassurance that the London government would not succumb to Dublin pressure.

Unionist defensiveness was reinforced by a perceived ambivalence in the attitude of southern leaders towards the use of force to achieve unity. For the most part, after 1922, Free State pronouncements on the north relied heavily on nationalist rhetoric (which served as a substitute for any major policy initiative), although there was a preoccupation with Dublin's legal rights under the treaty. Still, there were always—especially within the Fianna Fáil party—some extremists who advocated physical force and leaders who threatened to use it. Thus in 1927 Frank Aiken, who became minister of defence five years later, suggested that armed force might be used in addition to negotiation and bargaining. In 1934 Seán T. O'Kelly, minister for local government, stated that a united Irish republic was 'our aim, and if the gun [was] necessary, the people have the government to direct the army and they have the volunteer force behind them'; the Fianna Fáil leadership, he contended, did not deny Ireland the right to use force.[80] De Valera's own position was not that of a pacifist; rather, if he was convinced that force could unite the island, he was prepared to give it his support. Though the more extreme comments of his colleagues may have been uttered merely to reassure militant republicans in the south, they were widely interpreted among northern unionists as a straightforward endorsement of armed action. This perspective gained additional credibility from the context of the Fianna Fáil government's other policies.

North–south relations enjoyed a period of relative quiescence between 1925 and 1932, when Free State irredentism was pursued least aggressively. Even then, however, the assassination of Kevin O'Higgins, the occasional Fianna Fáil threats of using force to achieve unity, and the discovery of I.R.A. arms caches, all caused concern among unionists. Their unease in-

---

[79] Dennis Kennedy, *The widening gulf: northern attitudes to the independent Irish state, 1919–49* (Belfast, 1988), p. 228, and Buckland, *Factory of grievances*, p. 5; for the overall impact of Dublin's policy on N.I. between the wars, see ibid., pp 68–77. Cf. Clare O'Halloran, who writes of the Free State government's 'rejection of all responsibility for the northern minority by December 1925' (*Partition and the limits of Irish nationalism* (Dublin, 1987), p. 131).

[80] For the O'Kelly and Aiken speeches, see Kennedy, *Widening gulf*, pp 141, 198–200; for Fianna Fáil attitudes to the use of force, see Bowman, *De Valera & Ulster question*, pp 305–6. O'Halloran describes the attitude of southern political parties to N.I. as 'irredentism-in-theory and partitionism-in-practice' (*Partition*, p. 157); she also observes of the use of 'propaganda . . . as a "safety valve" for nationalists' that 'however successful [it was] within Fianna Fáil, it did not deter the I.R.A. from their 1939 bombing campaign' (ibid., p. 182).

creased in 1932 with de Valera's electoral victory, which they perceived as a triumph over the Anglo–Irish treaty. They noted with alarm his anti-partitionist, republican, catholic rhetoric, and also his policies: the lifting of the ban on the I.R.A.; the release of I.R.A. prisoners; the dismantling of military courts; and the abolition of the oath of allegiance, permitting the most irreconcilable nationalists to enter public office. All this combined with the eucharistic congress in 1932 to convey a powerful impression that catholic and republican Ireland was on the march. Craigavon and his colleagues associated later outbreaks of violence in the north with developments in the south. They attributed the mid 1935 riots in part to cross-border nationalist provocation. Later, they considered that articles 2 and 3 of the 1937 constitution helped to stimulate and legitimise the renewed I.R.A. campaign of 1939–40. The inclusion of these articles was certainly a calculated attempt by de Valera to attract extremist support, and as such has been described by T. P. Coogan as the 'I.R.A. component' in the document.[81]

The negotiations preceding the Anglo–Irish trade agreement in 1938[82] added to the unionists' worries. They feared that the settlement would presage a renewed southern campaign against partition as the only outstanding national issue complicating Dublin–Westminster relations. Sir Basil Brooke professed himself to be 'puzzled' by the 'persistent pressure on us to give up our position'. He continued: 'I imagine that the Austrians and Czechs must have felt . . . the same way when they read in German newspapers that their "unreasonable stubbornness" was preventing the realisation of the pan-German Reich.'[83] However, despite the rhetoric of its leaders, the extent to which the Free State in practice accepted the existence of Northern Ireland was underlined by the increasing marginalisation of militant republicanism there. During the 1930s, thanks partly to de Valera's successful attraction of support for Fianna Fáil, the I.R.A. had contracted to a rump, largely devoid of popular support. It took no part in politics and posed no real threat to the northern state.

None the less, the content of much government policy and politics in the north was determined by the sense of persistent pressure from the south. This largely dictated the nature and scope of the security measures adopted by the northern cabinet against an enemy still powerful in menace if not in deed. It served to constrict and debase the level of political debate, as was exemplified in 1938 when Craigavon's opportunistic general election diverted attention from the real social and economic issues. It ensured that a continuing premium was placed on unionist unity, thus helping to account for, and

[81] T. P. Coogan, De Valera: Long Fellow, long shadow (London, 1993), p. 493. Coogan describes articles 2 and 3 as 'an act of coat-trailing provocation' (ibid.). Conor Cruise O'Brien suggests that the 1937 constitution 'repudiated the boundary agreement' and helped mark 'a more or less open renewal of the siege' (States of Ire., p. 132). For the constitution, see above, pp 140–42.
[82] Above, pp 146–8.
[83] Barton, Brookeborough, p. 127.

serving to justify, the abolition of proportional representation. Fear of 'peaceful penetration' from the Free State prompted the imposition of residence qualifications for major cash social services, and parallel restrictions on the local government franchise. In 1936, while there were 809,562 registered parliamentary electors, there were just 534,519 electors for Northern Ireland's local councils. Ministers also debated whether voters should be required to affirm their loyalty to the crown.[84]

The political attitudes of northern nationalists were also profoundly influenced by those of the south. In general, until 1925 the Dublin authorities continued to foster and encourage non-recognition of the unionist administration. Their influence delayed the formation of a coherent political strategy among northern nationalists, accentuated their disunity, and stifled the emergence of a moderate and constructive local leadership during a seminal stage in the history of Northern Ireland. De Valera's decision to abandon his abstentionist policy (itself caused partly by the 1925 settlement) contributed to the decision of most nationalist M.P.s to enter the Belfast parliament and try to create a united, popular, political movement. Likewise, his electoral victory in 1932 helped precipitate their withdrawal and subsequent adoption of a 'creeping abstentionism' strategy.

Meanwhile, though the Free State's claim to the north was maintained and from 1937 was enshrined in the constitution, in practice the gulf between north and south widened. In utilising its greater powers under the treaty, the Dublin government caused considerable economic disruption in the north. During the 1930s the Free State became one of the most highly protected countries in the world. Its tariff policy roused unionist resentment for overpricing or excluding Northern Ireland produce, while farmers in the province suffered from the cross-border dumping of surpluses. Devlin's warning, that such policies would merely reinforce the existing boundary, went unheeded. Southern protectionism also generated internal criticisms of Craigavon and his colleagues, prompted by the unflattering contrasts drawn between the latter's ineffective measures and the trenchant actions being taken by Fianna Fáil. This further impeded the formation of a cohesive and effective regional policy. Stormont ministers had no choice but to attempt to conceal their relative impotence and to seek either retaliation or compensation by influencing Westminster policy, or to mollify their own supporters by yielding to populist, illiberal demands.[85]

The political and cultural development of Northern Ireland and the Free State also increasingly diverged during the interwar years. In the north, the

---

[84] For cabinet discussion of the 'affirmation of loyalty' proposal, see cabinet conclusions, 11, 25 Apr., 22 May 1934; 16 Jan. 1935 (P.R.O.N.I., CAB4/320, 321, 324, 333); Harkness, *N.I. since 1920*, p. 66.

[85] Buckland (*Factory of grievances*, pp 73–7) assesses the impact of the southern government's economic policy on the northern government.

power and privileges of the protestant majority became ever more deeply entrenched. Moreover, Ulster unionists never lost their centripetal constitutional outlook, as was evidenced by their continuing desire to cooperate with Westminster, their instinctive loyalty to the monarchy, and their genuine pride in membership of the empire. The Free State, on the other hand, became a more overtly catholic state, acquired a Gaelic veneer, and progressively divested itself of its links with Britain. This process reached its zenith after the 1932 election. While supporting close cooperation between the minority and Fianna Fáil in the mid 1920s, Cahir Healy had also urged the leadership of the new party to make the south more attractive to unionists. A decade later, one of his correspondents reflected on the 'mad policy' that de Valera was then adopting. It had 'estranged' the north, he claimed, and he warned: 'What is a border today will be a frontier tomorrow.'[86] The new taoiseach, however, refused to dilute his emphasis on Gaelic, catholic, and republican values in order to accelerate the creation of a unitary state. As he informed the senate in 1939, he would not 'for the sake of a united Ireland give up the policy of trying to make this a really Irish Ireland—not by any means'.[87]

Certainly the northern majority was unlikely to be attracted by the 'special position' accorded to the catholic church under the provisions of the 1937 constitution, which in its draft form had secretly been shown to the pope. The church already enjoyed more control over education than in any other country in the world. Its pervasive influence was also evident in the repression of birth control and of literature on contraception; the outlawing of divorce; and the censorship of books and films. Similarly, the government's attempts to promote the Irish language—for example, by making it compulsory in schools and a requirement for public appointments—held little appeal for unionists; they regarded such policies as obscurantist and draconian.[88] Furthermore, they attributed the sharp and persistent decline in the southern protestant population, in both absolute and relative terms, to cultural oppression and the implementation of narrow, fanatical, and intolerant policies by successive Free State governments. In 1934 Craigavon sought to defend his notorious claim that 'we are a protestant parliament and a protestant state' on the grounds 'that in the south they boasted of a catholic state'.[89] Such speeches, selectively quoted, did much to discredit northern ministers in the eyes of catholics, north and south.

[86] D. F. Curran to Healy, 1 Dec. 1934 (P.R.O.N.I., D2991/A/22).
[87] Bowman, *De Valera & Ulster question*, p. 311. During his final election campaign (1957) de Valera stated that if 'we make sure that this five-sixths is made really Irish we will have the preservation of the Irish nation in our hands. Time will settle the other thing' (ibid., p. 312).
[88] Above, pp 116–17; below, pp 540–44, 726–31.
[89] *Hansard N.I. (commons)*, xvi, 1031–5 (24 Apr. 1934). O'Brien writes of southern protestantism being 'conquered more effectively by catholic marriage regulations than by any material force' (*States of Ire.*, p. 161).

During these years the Dublin authorities also progressively dismantled the remaining vestiges of the union; after 1922 the Free State may have been part of the empire constitutionally, but never psychologically. This was reflected in the adoption of a separate coinage, and, in effect, a national flag and anthem from the mid 1920s. It was expressed constitutionally in the removal of any right of appeal to the privy council, the diminishing role accorded to the governor general, and the passing of the external relations act.[90] Simultaneously, the southern government developed an independent foreign policy, evidenced by the acquisition of a seat on the council of the League of Nations, and the appointment of a minister for external affairs. Given this context, the adoption of neutrality in 1939 was regarded by unionists not just as a predictable assertion of Irish sovereignty but also as a rejection of a British identity and consequently of the northern majority itself.

The Northern Ireland administration was not as vindictive or as repressive as contemporary regimes elsewhere with compact and substantial irredentist minorities. Probably the internal and external difficulties were intractable anyway, particularly given the framework of restricted powers and inappropriate political structures. However, the administration did govern in the interests of its unionist supporters with too little concern for the sensibilities of the minority, and made insufficient effort to achieve consensus. Its performance in these years leaves the case for parliamentary devolution unproven.[91] In constitutional terms it succeeded in preserving the union but failed to achieve a more fundamental unity through the replication of British standards of justice and political behaviour. Though Craigavon's role was vital in enabling Northern Ireland to emerge, he was unable to create the conditions that would promote its long-term survival.

In 1938 an experienced official of the dominions office observed with acuity and even-handedness: 'If the government of Northern Ireland wish partition to continue, they must make greater efforts than they have made at present to win over the catholic minority, just as on his side Mr de Valera if he wishes to end partition can only do so by winning over the northern protestants. At present both sides are showing a lamentable lack of statesmanship and foresight.'[92] Arguably, however, this critique was too objective, or at least too disinterested. Westminster, eager to extract itself from Irish affairs, had failed to fulfil its own responsibilities, certainly with regard to Northern Ireland. British ministers had preferred to rationalise passivity, rather than assert their authority in the interests of greater justice, and ultimately of political stability.

---

[90] Above, pp 139–40.
[91] Buckland (*Factory of grievances*, pp 278–9) concludes that N.I.'s experience of devolved government between the wars 'provides a cogent argument in favour of administrative devolution', but that in some respects it 'is a poor advertisement for parliamentary devolution and a conclusive argument against the form of devolution adopted in 1920'.
[92] Observation by Sir Harry Batterbee, assistant under-secretary at the dominions office, quoted in Harkness, *N.I. since 1920*, p. 80.

CHAPTER VIII

Northern Ireland, 1939–45

BRIAN BARTON

ON 4 September 1939, the day following Britain's entry into war, Lord Craigavon promised a tense and expectant commons at Stormont that there would be 'no slackening in [Ulster's] loyalty. There is no falling off in our determination to place the whole of our resources at the command of the [imperial] government...Anything we can do here to facilitate them, they have only just got to let us know.'[1] In fact, however, from the earliest stages of the conflict a stark and, for some ministers, embarrassing contrast emerged between the province's wartime experience and that found elsewhere in the United Kingdom. In Northern Ireland attitudes, patterns of behaviour, and the overall pace of life remained uniquely static and unchanging.

Of course, a measure of disruption could not entirely be avoided. Within the first six months of war, rationing in certain supplies had forced some modification in public consumption; travel restrictions and censorship had resulted in a progressive narrowing of cultural life, and parts of the province were already struggling to absorb the burgeoning military camps set up to accommodate British troops. Nevertheless, during the spring of 1940, a Belfast diarist was justified in describing Northern Ireland as 'probably the pleasantest place in Europe'. She added: 'We are unbombed, we have no conscription, there is plenty to eat, and life is reasonably normal.'[2] The perpetuation of 'normality' extended to other, less desirable, peacetime characteristics. Northern Ireland's industrial capacity was being seriously under-utilised. Thus, in December 1940, after fifteen months of hostilities, not a single new factory had yet been constructed; the shipyards in Belfast alone had benefited from substantial munitions contracts, and the overall level of unemployment was similar to that experienced by Great Britain in 1932, the trough of the great depression. An official report to this effect prompted Churchill to initiate an immediate, full-scale, governmental investigation.[3]

[1] *Hansard N.I. (commons)*, xxiii, 1902 (4 Sept. 1939).
[2] Tom Harrisson mass observation archive (University of Sussex), diary MO 5462, entry for 7 Mar. 1940; also Barton, *Blitz*, pp 43–4.
[3] Churchill to Ernest Bevin, 23 Jan. 1941 (P.R.O.N.I., COM61/440); also Barton, *Brooke-borough*, pp 172–3.

In addition, informed British visitors were shocked by the entirely different atmosphere that they detected in Northern Ireland, in comparison with other regions of the United Kingdom. The entire absence of any real sense of urgency regarding the war effort and the general slackness in public attitudes prompted one experienced observer to speculate that if anyone were to behave in London or Liverpool as they were continuing to do in Belfast, they would at once be noticeable and might even cause a riot.[4] There is no lack of evidence to corroborate these impressions, including the persistently low level of military enlistment, the recurrence of disruptive labour disputes in several of the north's main industries, the inferior output and productivity of its largest munitions factories compared with similar firms in Great Britain, and the pervasive apathy towards, and consequential inadequacy of, its civil defence provision. These features may be related to such factors as Northern Ireland's relative remoteness both from the theatre of conflict and from Westminster, its internal sectional divisions, and the absence of conscription. A further vital consideration was the complacency and ineffectiveness of the Stormont government.

A year before the outbreak of war, Sir Wilfrid Spender, head of the Northern Ireland civil service, had recorded in his diary a devastating indictment of the collective incompetence of Craigavon and his colleagues. He itemised their serious 'mistakes' and expressed deep concern at the resulting decline in popular support and respect for their leadership. He reflected on the prime minister's alarming tendency to make important decisions in a casual, hasty manner, and noted with apprehension that owing to the deterioration in Craigavon's health he was unable to perform more than one hour's work daily. He concluded that Craigavon was too unwell to carry on, though informed medical opinion warned that any drastic or enforced change in his lifestyle might prove fatal. Spender also considered that at least two other senior ministers ought to retire immediately, as they too were suffering from prolonged and incapacitating illness. He observed of a third that though he was the main focus of public criticism, he had none the less gone off on holiday abroad, and his officials could not count on his decisions. As a consequence of these failings, the main burden of government fell on the willing, though ageing, shoulders of the minister for finance, J. M. Andrews. Spender concluded dejectedly that if the present loose conduct of affairs continued, it would do irreparable harm to the unionist cause and might even pose a threat to the survival of democracy in Northern Ireland.[5]

When war began twelve months later, the composition of the Stormont cabinet was unchanged. Against his own inclination Craigavon had been persuaded by his wife to remain in office, mainly for reasons of financial necessity

---

[4] Tom Harrisson mass observation archive, report FF1309, 12 June 1942.
[5] Personal memorandum, in Spender diary, 2 Aug. 1938 (P.R.O.N.I., D715).

and social ambition; she was apparently unaware of the extent to which the progressive deterioration in his health had impaired his capacity for leadership. He led his colleagues in increasingly dictatorial and whimsical fashion, in the process straining the proper functioning of the cabinet system to breaking point. He habitually reached important decisions without prior discussions with the ministers most concerned; on occasion, he encouraged colleagues to act on their own responsibility or after consultation with himself; he brought his chief whip, Lord Glentoran, more into his confidence than the members of his cabinet. Craigavon characteristically responded to the increasing gravity and volume of attacks on his government by making grossly extravagant claims regarding the success of its policies, or by trying to silence critics through politically expedient concessions. These ranged from grants and subsidies to the creation of a new department with responsibility for civil defence, the ministry of public security. But such measures fell short of what was most stridently sought—a change in the composition of the cabinet itself. Edmund Warnock, one of two junior ministers to resign on this issue, protested with justification that 'death, old age, or promotion' were the only cause of changes in cabinet membership and that no one had ever been replaced 'because of incapacity or failure'.[6]

Criticism of the government focused mainly on its failure to reduce unemployment or make adequate provision for civil defence, and on its persistent equivocation over such matters as education, electricity, and transport. The marked deterioration in the strategic position of the western allies by mid 1940 and the formation of a more dynamic administration at Westminster made the fumbling ineptitude of Craigavon and his colleagues seem even more indefensible. These considerations and, more particularly, the entirely unsatisfactory relationship between the home affairs ministry and the British military authorities based in Northern Ireland, prompted Spender to predict that the imperial government would before long impose martial law. In December 1939, he had observed ruefully: 'there is one factory in which we could probably claim that we or the Free State are the largest manufacturers—namely the factory of grievances.'[7]

Apart from Sir Basil Brooke's success in raising tillage output on Ulster's farms, decisive government measures were restricted almost exclusively to security matters, where ministers displayed their customary zeal. The major steps taken were of course initiated by Westminster (particularly from the spring of 1940) and were common to regions throughout the United Kingdom. These included the introduction of an identity-card system, restrictions on travel, the censorship of mail and of trunk telephone calls, controls on the press, the imprisonment of male enemy aliens, the formation of a local home

---

[6] *Hansard N.I. (commons)*, xxiii, 2155 (25 Sept. 1940).
[7] Spender diary, Nov. 1939–4 May 1940, p. 84; 16 Dec. 1940.

guard and auxiliary territorial services, and the devising of administrative arrangements in case of 'emergency', specifically German invasion or the breakdown of communications with London.

However, some of the actions taken were distinctive. As the official war history of Northern Ireland states: 'The British in their extremity could... take no risks... in Northern Ireland the dangers confronting them were all the greater because of the "open" frontier with Éire and the existence of a potential "fifth column" in the form of the Irish Republican Army.' (The I.R.A. had launched a bombing campaign in Britain in January 1939 which continued into 1940.)[8] Thus on the first night of the war, internment was introduced and directed against I.R.A. suspects. Subsequently, special constabulary patrols were increased and the movement of persons across the Irish border closely monitored. Such measures were vindicated by the virtual absence of internal civil disorder during the war years; I.R.A. activities had died down by late 1940. Meanwhile, in May, the imperial government had permitted Stormont ministers to copy the protection arrangements being made in Britain by raising a force of Local Defence Volunteers (later called the Home Guard). But given the political divisions within Northern Ireland, the force was not raised on the same basis as elsewhere in the United Kingdom. Despite strong representations from opposition M.P.s, Craigavon insisted that the 'B' specials should form its nucleus. Soon afterwards, in view of Westminster's unwillingness to apply conscription to the north and embarrassed by persistently low levels of voluntary enlistment, Craigavon asked Brooke to organise a military recruiting drive. The resulting eight-week campaign, held in July–August, proved to be largely ineffective; reliance throughout on the Unionist party machine must have discouraged recruitment among catholics.

During the spring of 1940 such concerns had been eclipsed by another one, infinitely more grave and potentially more divisive. From April onwards, Stormont ministers and officials watched the current Anglo–Irish trade talks with growing apprehension. They feared that constitutional issues would be raised, with de Valera possibly offering, or being asked, to trade Irish neutrality for an end to partition. From late May, against the background of the Dunkirk evacuation and the fall of France, Craigavon came under more intense pressure from Westminster than at any time since 1921. Initially he was asked to make constructive suggestions as to how the taoiseach might be drawn into meaningful discussions about the defence of Ireland; later, more ominously, he was invited to attend open-ended negotiations with de Valera in London. His response was as inflexible as it had been twenty years before; his priority remained the preservation of Northern Ireland within the United Kingdom. He adamantly refused to participate in an inter-governmental

---

[8] J. W. Blake, *Northern Ireland in the second world war* (Belfast, 1956), p. 171.

conference before the south had abandoned its neutrality, or in any circumstances in which constitutional matters were to be considered.

By mid June, however, there were indications that a split was emerging
inside the Stormont cabinet. Both Brooke and John MacDermott (minister
for public security) were apparently prepared to accept a change in Northern
Ireland's constitutional status if, in response, the south proved willing to
enter the war on the allied side. For them, loyalty to king and empire and
the defeat of the axis powers transcended commitment to the maintenance of
the union. To their immense relief the crisis passed without the issue being
put to the test, as de Valera flatly refused to abandon Irish neutrality, fearing
irreparable divisions in the south if he altered his policy. At this time too
he may have expected, though did not desire, that the Allies would be
defeated.[9]

How did members of the nationalist minority respond to these events?
Encouraged by de Valera, northern nationalists had backed the Anti-Partition
League of 1938, designed to highlight the need to resolve partition if any
Anglo–Irish agreement on defence matters was to be reached. After a series
of public meetings in Britain and Ireland addressed by nationalists from both
sides of the border, the campaign was undermined by the I.R.A. offensive
in Britain of 1939–40.[10] However, de Valera continued to press British ministers on partition. Craigavon responded to the challenge in April 1939 by
calling for Northern Ireland to be included in the plan to introduce conscription in Britain. The raising of this issue succeeded as no other in recent years
had done in uniting the Mulveyite and Healyite factions in the north, as well
as the catholic church, and in May 1939 the British prime minister, Neville
Chamberlain, announced that Northern Ireland would not be included in the
conscription programme. But divisions reappeared once conscription had
receded (for the time being), and it became apparent that the Anti-Partition
League was doomed by the effects of the I.R.A. campaign on British public
opinion.

Early in 1940 another northern nationalist deputation approached de
Valera, appealing to him as having 'a moral right to speak for all Ireland',
and urging him to give a lead to northern nationalists. However, de Valera
was not encouraging, indicating that his own priority was the integrity of the
south against any invader, and that this must not be risked in any attempt to
reunite the country. This position was confirmed when he made it clear to
British ministers that he was not prepared to give up Irish neutrality. This
came as a severe blow to northern nationalists.[11]

---

[9] See Bowman, *De Valera & Ulster question*, pp 220–38; J. T. Carroll, *Ireland and the war years 1939–45* (Newton Abbot, 1975), pp 49–59.
[10] Tim Pat Coogan, *The I.R.A.* (London, 1970), ch. 5. Dozens of bombs exploded in towns and cities, and there were several deaths.
[11] Phoenix, *Northern nationalism*, pp 387–9, 398.

On 29 October 1940, Craigavon made his last major speech in parliament—a typically impassioned assault on an opposition motion in favour of Irish unity. Four weeks later, on 24 November, he died peacefully at his home; Spender noted that he had finally 'thrown off all the weight of illness and cares that had hung so heavily upon him during the last few years of his life'.[12] Next day, after taking private soundings, the governor, Lord Abercorn, asked John Andrews to form a government. He accepted but only on condition that he was selected leader of the Unionist party. Some informed opinion regarded this condition as procedurally wrong and politically inept, as it was likely to prejudice his authority during the initial weeks of his premiership.

Andrews's succession was widely regarded as inevitable and deserved on grounds of his seniority and experience. It was, none the less, greeted with resignation rather than enthusiasm and it has been suggested that Craigavon himself might have preferred Brooke. Craigavon, however, had resolutely refused to nominate a successor, and at the time Brooke betrayed no expectation of preferment or trace of disappointment. Rather he backed the new premier 'for all he is worth',[13] and along with Spender urged upon him on several occasions the political necessity of making far-reaching changes. Unwisely, Andrews rejected this advice. He appointed just one new minister: Glentoran, the chief whip, became minister of agriculture. From the outset it seemed unlikely that a 'new' government composed of the 'old guard' would be capable of responding adequately to the frustration and disillusionment evident among junior ministers, Unionist backbenchers, and even within the party beyond Stormont. Hitherto, Craigavon's authority had been enough to check revolt.[14]

Andrews was unfortunate to have become prime minister in almost his seventieth year, when his health had begun to fail, and in the context of total war. In family background, personality, and experience he was ill-equipped to provide the leadership necessary in the supreme crisis. Inevitably, his personal appeal was lessened by his long and close identification with Craigavon's increasingly unpopular administration; in his choice of cabinet he did nothing to reduce the negative force of this inheritance. The fall of his government was arguably the most dramatic episode in Northern Ireland's early political history. But from the start it appeared ineffective and vulnerable. In March 1941 it lost its first by-election, in Craigavon's old seat, while in the commons Unionist members were described as 'not inclined to give any support... whenever they can find an excuse for abstaining'.[15] Over the course of the

---

[12] Spender diary, 26 Nov. 1940.
[13] Brooke diary, 27 Nov. 1940 (Brooke papers, P.R.O.N.I., D3004/D/31–46).
[14] H. Shaw, report to the foreign office, 1 Jan. 1941 (P.R.O., F.O. 371/29108).
[15] Spender diary, 1 Mar. 1941.

next two years, backbench criticism tended to rise and the cabinet suffered from diminishing morale and growing fractiousness.

Andrews's premiership began inauspiciously; neither its confidence nor its prestige were enhanced by the German air raids of April–May 1941. Owing mainly to earlier ministerial neglect and prevarication, Northern Ireland's active and passive defences were hopelessly inadequate and the public psychologically unprepared for severe aerial bombardment. In the course of four attacks on Belfast at least 1,100 people died and many were injured, 56,000 houses were damaged, and extensive damage was caused to property. Fear and panic reached epidemic proportions; perhaps as many as 220,000 fled from the city. The collapse in civilian morale led MacDermott to predict attacks on the parliament buildings at Stormont by an irate and frightened populace.[16]

The blitz exacerbated the government's problems and confirmed its directionless, hesitant posture. The shocking experience of the raids helped focus interest once again on conscription. During the aftermath of the assault, MacDermott advocated conscription as an essential means of restoring communal discipline and achieving equality of sacrifice. Others, notably Lord Abercorn, also advised it, encouraging Andrews to 'strike when people's feelings are hot'.[17] Meanwhile, quite independently, on 12 May 1941, Ernest Bevin suggested to the imperial war cabinet that the application of conscription to Northern Ireland should be given further consideration in view of Britain's deteriorating strategic position.[18] During the resulting negotiations, held at Westminster on 24 May, the response of Stormont ministers was unequivocally enthusiastic. None the less, three days later, on 27 May, British ministers decided against extension. This was in response to accumulating evidence of opposition from the Dublin government, the United States, and Canada, and, crucially, from within Northern Ireland itself. Nationalist M.P.s and senators had orchestrated a province-wide anti-conscription campaign, with catholic church support, culminating in a mass rally on Sunday 25 May 1941. This had impressed Andrews in particular. On his own initiative he immediately contacted the home office and indicated that the level of resistance would be greater than expected. He advised that the 'real test... must be whether it [conscription] would be for the good of the empire'.[19] Almost immediately the British government issued a statement that concluded that its application

[16] For MacDermott's fears see Spender, ibid., 15, 31 May 1941. See also Barton, *Blitz*, pp 233–40. In addition to those leaving the city altogether, thousands of others trekked into the suburbs and beyond nightly, returning shortly before dawn when there was little danger of a raid.

[17] O. Henderson (governor's secretary) to R. Gransden (cabinet secretary), 13 May 1941 (P.R.O.N.I., CAB (CD/217)).

[18] Cabinet conclusions, 12, 19 May 1941 (P.R.O., CAB 65/49, 51). It was estimated that had conscription been applied, 48,000–53,000 men could have been raised (Blake, *N.I. in second world war*, p. 196).

[19] Cabinet conclusions, 26 May 1941 (P.R.O., CAB 65/53).

would be 'more trouble than it was worth'.[20] The Stormont government's about-turn can only have served to reduce its credibility at Westminster and to raise serious doubts about the quality of its leadership. Within Northern Ireland, this outcome was no doubt in the best interests of public order. However, the government had failed to implement its publicly stated policy, and its political opponents might reasonably claim a victory.

By the autumn of 1941, Andrews was convinced that his political position had become stronger, but a second by-election defeat in November dispelled this assumption. Soon afterwards, he expressed his fear that in a general election his government would lose its majority; a number of senior colleagues shared this anxiety. Consciousness of their vulnerability reinforced their cautious instincts. Further by-elections were delayed and more determined efforts were made to avoid contentious policies or unpopular legislation. However, some politically hazardous issues required attention; among these were the much-publicised activities of Belfast corporation. A home affairs inquiry in June 1941 indicated that the corporation had been guilty of wide-ranging corruption and abuse of patronage, and as a result many local ratepayers were calling for its dissolution. The cabinet's position was a delicate one as the councillors were predominantly Unionist and had considerable influence both within the Belfast associations and inside the broader party organisation. Dawson Bates, the minister for home affairs, therefore recommended that as a compromise measure city administrators should be appointed who would act as an executive, but guided by the elected council. If he were to take more punitive action, he believed that the government would find it 'impossible to hold office'.[21]

Even this modest proposal was adopted by some ministers with extreme reluctance. Andrews, especially, was anxious 'not to have any trouble with the corporation', or as he explained to colleagues, not to 'detract from the unity of effort...needed to win the war'.[22] Under strong pressure both from Belfast corporation and the city's Unionist branches, a cabinet majority accordingly agreed to dilute still further the punitive element in the legislative terms that Bates had proposed. However, one of the two agreed amendments was criticised by opposition M.P.s with such devastating effect that it was hurriedly withdrawn. Overall, the legislation deepened divisions within the government and alienated those who had opposed the measure, while failing to satisfy others who had favoured firmer action.[23]

[20] Ibid., 27 May 1941 (P.R.O., CAB 65/54).
[21] Cabinet conclusions, 20 Apr. 1942 (P.R.O.N.I., CAB4/505); also Barton, *Brookeborough*, pp 201–2.
[22] Cabinet conclusions, 8 June 1942 (P.R.O.N.I., CAB4/512); also Spender diary, 18 Oct. 1941.
[23] The cabinet had agreed, though not unanimously, to support two amendments that significantly weakened the Belfast county borough administration bill by specifying the period for which city administrators would be appointed, and restoring to the council some of its

The government's handling of industrial unrest was an unavoidable aspect of its wartime responsibilities, which also provoked adverse comment and aroused serious doubts about its competence. In part public censure was directed at the official machinery for resolving trade disputes, which even John MacDermott, then attorney general, described as clumsy and slow. A much more damaging criticism, expressed strongly by sections of local management, some senior civil servants, and the British ministry of labour and national service, was that the Northern Ireland cabinet was weak and complacent in its attitude towards labour, and that this had contributed to a deterioration in industrial discipline. Thus W. P. Kemp, director at Short & Harland's aircraft factory, complained in September 1942 that refractory workers knew their actions would be 'winked at by those in authority'.[24] Next month, the worst strike of Andrews's premiership originated at a Short's dispersal unit. Within two weeks, it had spread to affect 10,000 men in Belfast's major strategic industries, prompting Churchill to state that he was 'shocked at what [was] happening'.[25] The strike had arisen directly out of an attempt by management to implement an instruction from the ministry of production regarding Sunday work. Its root causes were complex, but inevitably much blame attached to the role of the government. Westminster officials considered that it had shown 'deplorable weakness' during the strike, while locally it was castigated for the general policy of drift.

By November 1942, MacDermott had become extremely despondent over the government's whole approach to labour relations. Accordingly, he suggested to Andrews that the order making it an offence to strike should be repealed as it clearly did not deter mass industrial action and consequently threatened to bring the rule of law into contempt. Once more he strongly advocated conscription. Soon afterwards Churchill likewise reopened this issue and similarly justified its introduction on the grounds of Ulster's poor output and productivity and disappointing level of voluntary recruitment.[26] Andrews again rejected conscription, stating that it did not fall within the realm of practical politics. Meanwhile, the government's method of dealing

powers of appointment. The latter was hurriedly withdrawn; the measure finally adopted provided for the appointment of three city administrators for a $3\frac{1}{2}$-year period, who would 'make all appointments, purchases, contracts and rates and municipal taxes' (Ian Budge & Cornelius O'Leary, *Belfast; approach to crisis: a study of Belfast politics, 1603–1970* (London, 1973), pp 153–4).

[24] W. P. Kemp to Andrews, 23 Sept. 1941 (P.R.O.N.I., CAB9C/22/1); see also MacDermott to Andrews, 2 Nov. 1942, ibid. Spender's diary (24 Jan. 1942) assesses, and considers perceptions of, the N.I. government's handling of labour.
[25] Churchill to Andrews, 15 Oct. 1942 (P.R.O.N.I., CAB9C/22/1); also Barton, *Brookeborough*, pp 202–4.
[26] See Churchill to Roosevelt, 11 Apr. 1943 (cabinet conclusions, P.R.O., CAB 66/36), where he refers to 'young fellows of the locality...[who] loaf about with their hands in their pockets', impeding 'not only recruiting but the work of...Belfast shipyard, which is less active than other British shipyards'.

with labour disputes, including its judicial machinery for their resolution, remained unchanged; so too did the tensions within the cabinet and the wider dissatisfaction with government.

There was, however, a more positive aspect to the policies of Andrews and his cabinet. Immediately after taking office, the new premier became noticeably more enthusiastic about raising public expenditure on social services, setting aside more resources for postwar reconstruction, and asserting more forcefully his government's independence of treasury control. He expressed these opinions all the more stridently as he became more aware both of the political weakness of his administration and of the changing aspirations of the Northern Ireland electorate. As elsewhere, war stimulated expectations of social improvement, a development associated with increased levels of taxation, the north's huge imperial contribution, the publication of the Beveridge report, and greater popular awareness of the inadequacy of local welfare provision compared with that in Great Britain, as well as of the extent of poverty in Belfast, so starkly brought to light by the recent German air raids. By mid 1942, influential elements within the unionist movement were urging on the prime minister the need to react positively by formulating plans for the postwar years; they described this as being essential for the future of the province as well as of the party. Andrews's favourable response was, however, based on conviction as well as expediency. He fully shared public concern at the extent to which housing, health, education, and poor relief in Northern Ireland lagged behind standards in Britain; was convinced that over the years the imperial government had not treated the region equitably; and felt increasingly frustrated by Westminster's restraints on his proposed expenditure.[27]

The tangible result of these sentiments was both meagre and contentious. On 30 July 1942, the prime minister made a detailed statement at Stormont on postwar policy, containing a strong commitment to improvements in a wide range of social services and referring to future plans for transport, local government, and industry. The statement immediately prompted an angry response from Kingsley Wood, the British chancellor of the exchequer, and from treasury officials. They were baffled by its timing, concerned by the specific nature of its content, and irritated by the total absence of any preliminary consultation, more especially because they regarded parity of service as

---

[27] Cabinet conclusions, 2, 19 June 1942 (P.R.O.N.I., CAB4/510, 513); Spender diary, 6 June 1942. Spender and Gransden were surprised by Andrews's sudden enthusiasm for greater government spending and struck by the contrast between his views as premier and those he had earlier held as minister for finance. Spender suspected that Andrews sought better terms for the north than were available in Britain, and regarded this as unjustifiable and damaging to N.I.'s reputation. This view was shared by Brooke and influential junior ministers, such as Maynard Sinclair, and contributed to their overall uneasiness at the unpredictable nature of Andrews's leadership. See Barton, *Brookeborough*, pp 204–11.

the sheet anchor of inter-governmental financial relations. In subsequent correspondence, Wood recognised that the major responsibility for postwar planning in Northern Ireland lay with the regional government. But he also stressed that though it might legitimately exercise the right to make up 'leeway' with Britain in its social services, it could not claim preferential treatment. Andrews deduced from this that he had gained 'extended financial powers'.[28] This interpretation was not shared either by treasury or by ministry of finance officials. Spender presciently observed that the chancellor's letter merely confirmed existing arrangements. In the meantime, the governmental machinery for postwar reconstruction, established at Stormont by the prime minister, had degenerated into a hopeless muddle of competing committees, duplicating the tasks of planning and preparing policy recommendations. Not surprisingly, when the question was eventually debated in the commons a number of backbenchers expressed strongly their reservations regarding Andrews's ability to fulfill the promises made in his earlier statement; his claim that he would apply foresight, energy, and courage to resolve future problems lacked credibility.

Overall, there seemed no shortage of evidence to confirm the collective incompetence of the 'old guard', whether in the lack of preparation for the blitz, the level of unemployment, the persistent industrial unrest, the failure to apply conscription, or the confusion over postwar planning. There was obvious validity in MacDermott's comment that Northern Ireland appeared to be 'only half in the war';[29] it was an impression that struck informed British observers even more forcefully. Though the ultimate responsibility for some of the province's unenviable features lay at Westminster rather than at Stormont, a growing and influential sector of local opinion attributed them to the failings of Andrews and his colleagues. In Spender's view they had encouraged complacency, and, unlike Carson in 1914, had failed to offer leadership and sacrifice. By January 1943 Spender was convinced of the need for cabinet change. Brooke, the deputy premier, also considered that there was a great deal in what the critics were saying and that the prime minister 'must come in with a declaration that he is out to win the war and nothing else matters'.[30] Neither he nor his leader, however, appreciated just how tenuous the political position of the government had become, particularly in parliament.

At the time, any revolt at Stormont that might seriously threaten the survival of Andrews's administration seemed highly improbable. Out of thirty-eight government supporters in the house sixteen held offices of profit under the crown, while the number of private members was depleted by

[28] Spender diary, 24 Sept. 1942; see also Lawrence, op. cit, pp 68–73.
[29] Cabinet conclusions, 15 May 1941 (P.R.O.N.I., CAB4/473).
[30] Brooke diary, 4 Dec. 1941.

military service. Moreover, there was a dearth of decisive leadership among Unionist backbenchers that might be capable of articulating their unease or mobilising effectively their voting strength. None the less, there are clear indications that dissension within their ranks was growing. Parliamentary party meetings had gradually become more tense, with, on occasion, even routine business leading to acrimonious debate. As a result, ministers were more reluctant to meet members; their reticence was used by critics to justify bringing forward private motions on the grounds that there was no alternative means of ventilating grievances. There is also evidence of a deterioration in party discipline during commons divisions. Moreover the arrival at Stormont of newly elected, independent members helped sharpen debate and focus the attack more effectively on familiar targets such as the inadequacy of the war effort, unemployment, the shortcomings of postwar planning, and the incompetence of the cabinet.

The extent of parliamentary disaffection was starkly revealed on 9–10 January 1943 when Unionist backbenchers held a secret meeting at which they formulated demands later forwarded to the chief whip. They called for a change of leadership and the immediate appointment of younger ministers. Their action was as much a symptom as a cause of political crisis. There was at the time a widespread recognition among senior party members and civil servants that the public had lost confidence in the government. A number of junior ministers already favoured not just a reshuffling of the cabinet but the removal of Andrews himself. They had come to regard him as the source of the administration's ineffectiveness, and his continuation in office as a threat to the preservation of law and order, to party unity, and even to the union.

After hearing of the backbenchers' proposals, Brooke noted privately that Andrews ought to 'retire at once', adding that it was 'difficult for any of us to remain'.[31] Somewhat surprisingly, given his government's consistently conciliatory record, Andrews's own response was to resist the malcontents and to defend himself and his ministers. However, at a party meeting held to discuss the crisis, on 19 January, eight speakers called for a 'new team' and a 'change of leadership' if electoral disaster was to be avoided. A resolution followed, which was passed unanimously; it stated that the 'subject requires careful . . . consideration' and that the premier would make a further statement at a future meeting convened for the purpose.[32]

Though it was now generally assumed that Andrews would at least make changes in his cabinet, informed sources reported that his attitude was in fact stiffening. This was soon evident from his efforts to rouse support through a series of speeches delivered to audiences throughout the north and from the

[31] Ibid., 11, 12 Jan. 1943.
[32] Ulster Unionist parliamentary party, minute book of meetings, 19 Jan. 1943 (P.R.O.N.I., D1327/10/1).

expansive content of the king's speech. On 23 February he instructed the parliamentary party, just returned for a new session of the commons, that no decision regarding ministerial changes would be made before Easter. This prevarication served to confirm doubts about his leadership, which were re-inforced by a further by-election defeat (in west Belfast), a labour dispute that paralysed the docks, and large-scale I.R.A. breakouts from prisons in Belfast and Derry. Newspapers meanwhile reported rumours that three ministers had resigned and that the cabinet was 'split from top to bottom'.[33] At a further party meeting held on 19 March, Andrews stated categorically that he would not tolerate interference in his selection of ministers, and reaffirmed his opin-ion that his government colleagues were the best available. A vote of confi-dence in the premier was then moved, challenged, and reluctantly withdrawn. A second resolution passed unanimously; it requested that the prime minister 'reconsider the question of changes in the cabinet'.[34] Clearly Andrews had seriously miscalculated the mood of the M.P.s; however, he again sought to rally support by addressing local Unionist associations and preparing an appeal to the annual meeting of the Ulster Unionist Council. It seemed likely that he would then proceed to purge his front-bench critics and probably replace them with older men. Senior civil servants privately expressed fears that this would precipitate a terminal split in the party.

When the U.U.C. met on 16 April, it passed by acclamation a resolution of unabated confidence in the prime minister; he later informed Churchill that out of 750 delegates, just two or three had dissented. Possibly Andrews now believed that the crisis would pass, given this success, the expressions of support received from local associations, and the assumed backing of a majority of the party at Stormont. In his statement to the council, however, he had again implied that he would make no cabinet changes. As a result, at least three junior ministers were 'eager to push in their resignations right away'.[35] On reflection, they decided to delay till the next party meeting; it had been reluctantly arranged for 28 April. Meanwhile, Brooke placed his resignation in Andrews's hands so that he would 'have an opportunity to speak'.[36] When the thirty-three Unionist M.P.s assembled at the party head-quarters in Glengall Street, Andrews defiantly repeated his defence of his colleagues and insisted that he must be free to appoint his own ministers. Over the next three-and-a-half hours, most of those present spoke. No

[33] *Sunday Dispatch*, 28 Feb. 1943. The article was written by the marquis of Donegall, for whom Dawson Bates acted as solicitor. This prompted speculation that Bates was the source of his information. The matter was discussed by cabinet; see cabinet conclusions, 2 Mar. 1943 (P.R.O.N.I., CAB4/533).
[34] Ulster Unionist parliamentary party, minute book, 19 Mar. 1943 (P.R.O.N.I., D1327/10/1).
[35] The three junior ministers were Brian Maginess, Maynard Sinclair, and Dehra Parker (Brooke diary, 19–21 Apr. 1943).
[36] Ibid., 21 Apr. 1943.

formal vote was taken, but it was far from certain that the prime minister enjoyed the support of a majority of those present. It was evident that if he continued as leader six junior ministers would leave the government; and the party, in parliament and beyond, would be irretrievably divided. Clearly shocked and saddened, he reluctantly decided to resign, and accordingly next day reported to the governor.

Andrews's unwillingness to make the required cabinet changes stemmed not only from loyalty to long-serving colleagues and reluctance to rock the boat in wartime, but also from political weakness; he refused to replace ministers whose inadequacies he recognised. His uncharacteristic obduracy also owed something to the confrontational manner in which the matter had first been raised by the Unionist backbenchers. In any case, he regarded cabinet appointments as the prerogative of the prime minister. His overall response to the crisis suggests as well a considerable measure of political miscalculation; specifically, his assumption that he could silence his critics by a resolute, inflexible stand, and his apparent inability to appreciate the true nature of the pressures that ultimately forced his resignation.

Amid confusion over correct procedure, Lord Abercorn took soundings from representative opinion and, on 1 May, asked Brooke to form a government; it is doubtful whether any other member would have commanded a majority in the house. However, it is unlikely that he had the backing of Andrews, who was firmly convinced that Brooke had conspired against him. Brooke dismissed the charge. Certainly his career was not marked by overriding personal ambition, and he had entirely failed to anticipate either the timing or the scale of the party revolt in January 1943. His role during the crucial weeks that followed was a passive one; he made no attempt to contact or instruct disaffected Unionist backbenchers, and those junior ministers who sought his advice made the first move. Ultimately, the province's administration collapsed through the weight of its own incompetence.[37]

Brooke had much to offer the unionist movement, including his relative youth, a distinguished record of ministerial service, military experience, useful contacts in Britain, and a genial, affable personality. As premier, he displayed more courage, energy, and tact than either Andrews or Craigavon in his later life. Arguably, however, like his predecessors, he failed to rise to that higher level of leadership that does not simply pander to its supporters but dares to chip away at their prejudices. His ministers were little known and, by Stormont standards, also young.[38] Most had proven administrative experience and probably all had been convinced for some time of the need for a change

[37] See Barton, *Brookeborough*, pp 221–9.
[38] Of the new cabinet, Harry Midgley, Robert Corkey, and Robert Moore had never before held ministerial office. Brooke, William Grant, J. M. Sinclair, and William Lowry had served in the previous governments as minister for commerce, minister for public security, parliamentary secretary at finance, and parliamentary secretary at home affairs respectively.

of leadership. The Labour M.P. Harry Midgley became minister for public security in order to broaden the government's representation in Northern Ireland and to create a favourable impression at Westminster; officials there had long been advocating that the Stormont cabinet should be composed on a more national basis. Brooke appointed no deputy and he advised his colleagues not to regard their appointments as permanent. Their agreed policy priorities were to maintain the present constitution, bring greater drive to the war effort, and devise plans for the postwar years.

The change of government, and more particularly the manner in which it had occurred, caused deep and enduring tensions inside the party. There was considerable residual sympathy for the 'old guard' in the influential but increasingly unrepresentative committees of the U.U.C. and within sections of the unionist press. Most of the ex-ministers felt embittered by recent events. Andrews himself was also disappointed by his own exclusion from Brooke's cabinet and, as a backbencher, was acutely sensitive to any perceived criticism of his government. He invariably attacked, with Lord Glentoran's support, less popular aspects of Brooke's policy, and on occasion briefed disaffected M.P.s with ammunition that might be used in debate. He continued to assert that as prime minister he had gained spending concessions from the British chancellor, thus tending to belittle Brooke's achievements. In March 1944 his querulous behaviour attracted a strongly worded, though ineffective, public rebuke from Lord Londonderry.[39]

Among backbenchers, old loyalties and frustrated ambitions helped ensure that the new administration's control over the house would be at best uncertain. During its first months in office one measure had to be withdrawn in view of imminent defeat, and another was substantially amended for lack of backbench support.[40] Soon afterwards, a commons select committee report on parliamentary salaries was shelved because some M.P.s strongly criticised the payment of expenses to ministers; Brooke conceded that the practice amounted to an evasion of income tax. These difficulties called in question Brooke's own prospects as prime minister. In December 1943 Spender recorded rumours, then current in local business circles, that Glentoran would replace him inside three months. Four weeks later, a newspaper reported that Andrews and Glentoran could, if they wished, defeat the government on the forthcoming king's speech.[41] As late as November 1944 Brooke stated privately that he would not continue if these critics remained 'part of the machine and are not supporting me'.[42]

---

[39] Minutes of annual meeting of U.U.C., 2 Mar. 1944 (P.R.O.N.I., D1327/8/10).

[40] The local government officers' bill was withdrawn on 16 June 1943 (*Hansard N.I. (commons)*, xxvi, 1149; its purpose was to standardise employment practices among local authority employees. The Planning (Interim Development) Bill was substantially amended. It was devised to extend and strengthen planning controls throughout Northern Ireland; see Spender diary, 25 Nov. 1943.

[41] Spender diary, 23 Dec. 1943, 31 Jan. 1944.

[42] Brooke diary, 19 Nov. 1944.

Like his predecessors, Brooke sought to avoid making controversial decisions in wartime. However, he showed greater enterprise and activity than they had done. One important issue was education, on the agenda because a general system of secondary education was about to be introduced for England by the education act of 1944. In February of that year Brooke decided to ask his minister for education, the Rev. Professor Robert Corkey, to resign. The prime minister was satisfied that in spite of repeated warnings Corkey had consistently neglected his duties; he had attended his department in Portrush just three times during the previous six months. In a statement, however, Corkey protested that his dismissal had been precipitated by disagreements on matters of principle relating to education reform. Specifically, he alleged that Brooke was not committed to the compulsory provision of religious instruction in state schools. He also claimed that there was an anti-presbyterian bias in his own ministry, connived at by Brooke, though emanating mainly from its permanent secretary and parliamentary secretary. The effect of Corkey's allegations was to impose a severe additional strain on party loyalty; he received strong support, particularly from members of his own denomination, having in Spender's opinion introduced a 'sectarian' point of view.[43] However, when the cabinet first fully discussed the education question three months later, the principle of compulsory religious instruction was unanimously and unhesitatingly endorsed. Instead, debate centred on whether Stormont would require enabling powers from Westminster in order to bring Northern Ireland into line with the English reforms, and how to protect teachers' freedom of conscience. The far-reaching nature of the proposed legislation did, of course, raise a number of sensitive and complex issues—that these required three more years to resolve was due in part to the bitterness aroused by Corkey's dismissal.

From the outset, the government was obliged to respond to another, similarly delicate, matter, which was for several years a source of tension within the unionist movement. There was persistent pressure from councillors, high-ranking party officials, and a number of local associations to restore to the formerly discredited Belfast corporation those powers transferred to administrators in 1942. The government was sympathetic, anxious to remove a long-standing source of contention, but also concerned to prevent a recurrence of the corruption and nepotism that had previously been rife in the borough. In 1943 a measure was agreed on that, while returning some functions to the council, restricted its powers of patronage and conferred exclusive authority to place contracts on the town clerk and town solicitor. This proposal was so severely criticised by dissatisfied councillors, who in Spender's view had learnt nothing from past experience, that the cabinet decided to abandon it.

[43] Spender diary, 17, 25 Feb. 1944; Brooke diary, 8, 11, 17 Feb. 1944.

The issue was finally resolved when, in the spring of 1945, the government relented and introduced legislation that in essence restored to the corporation its original functions. It passed through the commons quickly, with little debate and without controversy. There was by then a widespread feeling that the council had been sufficiently punished for past, almost forgotten, misdeeds, while the restrictions prepared earlier by the cabinet had been consistently denigrated as undemocratic. Government members themselves hoped that their action would assuage internal party divisions, particularly at a time when they were conducting complex negotiations over future arrangements for electricity and transport.[44]

But the most widespread criticism of the government's performance concerned housing. By 1943 the housing shortage had become the main focus of public interest, surpassing unemployment; and the government decided that even in wartime it was politically necessary to do something. Northern Ireland's first official housing inquiry, which was initiated by Brooke soon after becoming premier, estimated that 100,000 new houses were required to meet immediate needs. Experience suggested that there would be many obstacles in the way of an effective response: local authorities were usually dilatory in fulfilling their housing obligations, through caution, inertia, and financial constraints; and, in some cases, because the housing shortage was perceived to be a catholic issue. There was also a shortage of building materials, of appropriate sites, and of labour. These problems were compounded by avoidable confusion over departmental responsibility between the ministers for finance and home affairs (Sinclair and Lowry) and the difficulty of attracting treasury approval and funding for schemes at a time when housing construction in Britain had been virtually abandoned, in response to the priorities of war.

However, in late 1943 representations were made to London, appealing for financial support for a local housing programme. When Westminster agreed to the immediate construction of 250 houses with generous subsidies, Lowry greeted the offer with derision, stating that 'people would reply that they had asked for bread and been offered a stone'.[45] For its part, Belfast corporation declared that there were no suitable sites for these houses within the city boundary; later, in November 1944, the corporation indicated that it would take no action till building costs had fallen. In order to expedite progress in the city and elsewhere, the cabinet meanwhile (in July 1944) decided to establish a housing trust, a corporate body empowered to secure in coordination

---

[44] Brooke diary, 19 Apr. 1945; also 3 Oct. 1944. See minutes of meetings of the parliamentary Unionist party, 19 Sept., 10 Oct. 1944, 2 May 1945, in Ulster Unionist Council papers (P.R.O.N.I., D1327/22); cabinet conclusions, 15 Sept. 1944, 19 Apr. 1945 (P.R.O.N.I., CAB4/597, 622).

[45] Quoted in Spender diary, 27 Sept. 1943; cabinet conclusions, 27 Sept. 1943 (P.R.O.N.I., CAB4/556).

with local authorities the provision of housing accommodation for workers. The associated legislation elicited a predictably hostile response from Unionist backbenchers, who claimed that such centralisation was unprecedented and unwarranted, and expressed concern about the respective roles of private enterprise and of local government in meeting future housing needs.[46]

During late 1944 Brooke's considerable political difficulties were exacerbated by a succession of domestic tribulations. On 2 October Henry Brooke, the older of his surviving sons, was wounded by shrapnel when serving with the 10th Hussars in North Africa. On 13 October, his wife Cynthia was diagnosed as suffering from a serious spinal disorder, which severely incapacitated her for the next two years. One week later he himself was forced by a duodenal ulcer to relinquish his prime-ministerial duties till late January 1945, evidence perhaps of the growing demands of his public and private life. Brooke responded to these political and personal strains with ability and confidence. He had foreseen strong initial opposition to his cabinet; throughout his premiership he was constantly aware of and sensitive to the fissiparous tendencies within the unionist movement. He always regarded unity as, at best, tenuous and ultimately dependent on the 'border question', without which, he believed, 'various opinions would make themselves felt'.[47] He fully recognised the necessity of boosting party morale. Hence, he was concerned to ensure that his government won its first by-election, and from the outset invited leading British politicians to address public meetings in the province. Unlike Andrews he regarded publicity as a priority. Soon after becoming prime minister he set up a cabinet publicity committee and appointed both a public relations officer in London and a government publicity officer in Belfast. He himself constantly briefed and sought advice from journalists, and at his first cabinet exhorted his colleagues to do likewise.[48]

Shortly before Andrews's government collapsed, Brooke had strongly advised him that the parliamentary party was 'the only thing that mattered';[49] as prime minister he employed a variety of tactics to win and maintain its support. He sought to improve consultative procedures between ministers and backbenchers on proposed legislation. Thus meetings were held more regularly so that cabinet policy could be explained and defended, alternative

[46] See *Interim report of the planning advisory committee* [Cmd 224] (Belfast, 1944), *passim*; cabinet conclusions, 10 Aug., 19 Oct. 1944 (P.R.O.N.I., CAB4/595, 602); Lawrence, op. cit., pp 146–57; Housing Act (Northern Ireland), 1945 (8 & 9 Geo. VI, c. 2) (6 Feb. 1945).

[47] Brooke diary, 9, 10 Oct. 1943.

[48] Cabinet conclusions, 6 May 1943 (P.R.O.N.I., CAB4/541). The list of British ministers to visit N.I. (1943–5) included Stafford Cripps (production), Herbert Morrison (home affairs), Oliver Lyttleton (production), Hugh Dalton (board of trade), and J. J. Llewellin (food). For Brooke, however, the real coup was the visit of George VI and his family, 17–19 July 1945.

[49] Brooke diary, 25 Mar. 1943. For the internal structural changes within the Unionist party discussed here, see Ulster Unionist Council papers, 1943–5 (P.R.O.N.I., D1327/8, 9), *passim*.

measures considered, and grievances aired. Brooke also made frequent appeals for unity in the interests of the war effort and the preservation of the union. Reflecting by implication on recent experience, he suggested that constant criticism would induce among ministers a defensive hesitancy that would result in political stagnation. On occasion he indicated his own willingness to resign, but stressed that the alternative to his continued leadership was a general election. In addition, he set in motion a process of party reorganisation, mainly in response to demands from the U.U.C., which had originated during the final months of Andrews's premiership. The British Conservative party was the model that the membership wished to emulate; the holding of an annual Unionist conference and appointment of a paid party chairman were among the earliest innovations that resulted.

Brooke also strove continuously to reduce the level of personal bitterness between himself and the politically active remnants of the 'old guard'. In March 1944 he proposed as a conciliatory gesture that Andrews be reelected president of the U.U.C.; it was a post that he himself aspired to, but which the incumbent showed no apparent inclination to vacate. Moreover, from July 1944, acting on a suggestion from his chief whip, Brooke deliberately chose to bring Glentoran more into discussion, and helped ensure that he was appointed party treasurer and a trustee. These carefully calculated steps reflected Brooke's mounting confidence in his own authority; he noted privately that he was 'quite prepared' to take them now, whereas he was not 'going to appear as an appeaser before'.[50] No doubt partly in reciprocation, Andrews proposed and Glentoran seconded Brooke's nomination as party leader at a specially convened standing committee meeting held in March 1945. This was certainly a gesture that Brooke valued. He had earlier complained that he had 'no status' and had become leader merely by virtue of being prime minister.[51] None the less, for the moment, the presidency of the U.U.C. remained beyond his grasp. When eventually Andrews did resign, in 1947, Glentoran succeeded him, even though Brooke had indicated his willingness to accept if he were offered the position. At the time he reflected despondently on how residual sympathy for the 'old guard' could still influence Unionist voting behaviour.

Meanwhile, Brooke and his colleagues began to devise plans for the postwar years in response to the pressures from within the party that had earlier helped precipitate Andrews's fall. Andrews's response to Britain's Beveridge report (1942), which called for an extension of social services, as the report put it, 'from the cradle to the grave', had been guarded; there was a risk of arousing unrealisable expectations. For his part, Brooke stated his firm intention to keep pace with the rest of the United Kingdom in health and social services, including the Beveridge scheme of social security, and he

[50] Brooke diary, 19 July 1944.   [51] Ibid., 23 Mar. 1945; also 29 July 1943.

immediately initiated a series of investigations aimed at quantifying more precisely the comparative backwardness of Northern Ireland's welfare services. The necessary substantial increase in government spending required a reexamination of the financial relationship between Stormont and Westminster. During the winter of 1943 Northern Ireland officials decided the time was right to initiate preliminary negotiations, aimed at ensuring that their departments had sufficient funds to maintain parity in social services and to recover any proven leeway relative to British standards. Spender observed that there had been a general loosening in the recent budgetary policy of the British government, relations with treasury officials were friendly, and the chancellor was sympathetic; he also noted with obvious gratification that the socialist members of the coalition were appreciative of Ulster's war effort.[52] By early 1944, the basis for a future reinsurance agreement had been laid which guaranteed adequate financial support from the exchequer to meet all Ulster's reasonable expenditure. Over the next twelve months the Northern Ireland cabinet prepared an unemployment insurance scheme and a system of family allowances, both based on the British model, and agreed to establish a ministry of health.

The substantial expansion of government responsibility envisaged in these wartime decisions helped precipitate a major reallocation of functions between the Stormont departments. This had first been contemplated during the spring of 1943 when Andrews was premier. It had arisen then partly because of the foreseeable closure of the ministry of public security and also because it was considered that the duties of the ministry of home affairs were too unwieldy to be conducive to administrative efficiency. Brooke's eventual implementation of the necessary changes, in 1944–5, was complicated by the political situation. Ministers were reluctant to relinquish functions that they had quite recently acquired, fearing that the electorate would conclude that they were 'unable to cope' with the work done by their predecessors.[53] Also during the consequent cabinet reshuffle, Unionist backbenchers blocked the prime minister's choice of Midgley as minister for health, considering that he might 'do harm' there at a time when major legislation for a national health service was imminent. Brooke was obliged to revoke the appointment and eventually persuaded his reluctant minister to accept the ministry of labour portfolio instead.

The economy represented the government's other major area of attempted postwar planning. As at Westminster, Northern Ireland ministers were committed to a policy of full employment after hostilities had ended. As the flow of military contracts diminished from 1943 onwards, however, they shared a

---

[52] Spender diary, 17 Aug., 2 Dec. 1943, 28 Apr. 1944; Lawrence, op. cit., pp 71–3; John Ditch, *Social policy in Northern Ireland between 1939–50* (Aldershot, 1988), pp 86–8.
[53] This is discussed in Spender to E. Clark, 4 Aug. 1943, included in Spender diary, op. cit.

deepening apprehension at the approaching spectre of severe peacetime recession. When the ministry of labour estimated the likely cost of applying the Beveridge report to the province it assumed an unemployment level of 12 per cent, a figure 4 per cent above the projection for Great Britain. Maynard Sinclair expressed the conviction that no government could survive if the percentage of jobless locally remained 'substantially above' that of other regions of the United Kingdom.[54]

In response to these anxieties, a postwar reconstruction committee was established in September 1943. Six months later, Sir Roland Nugent (then minister without portfolio and soon to become minister for commerce) was given overall responsibility for the development and coordination of planning.[55] In addition, further legislation was prepared at Stormont with the objective of attracting new industry to Northern Ireland in the postwar period. Both ministers and established local firms regarded the dismantling of the pervasive wartime controls, imposed by Westminster, as a peacetime priority. Meanwhile, Brooke and his colleagues constantly pressed British departments for further orders and investment; attempted to clarify more precisely with them their respective areas of responsibility in generating employment; sought better liaison regarding postwar planning and future legislation that might affect the region; and urged, in particular, that Northern Ireland be officially designated a development area by the British board of trade.

Brooke's commitment to parity of social services with Great Britain and his growing anxiety about postwar prospects for the local economy contributed to his continuing enthusiasm for the introduction of conscription. In early 1945 he became aware of the British government's intention to extend compulsory military service beyond the period of hostilities, and he immediately requested that Northern Ireland be included in these plans. He justified this partly on grounds of principle: it would be a potent affirmation of Northern Ireland's constitutional status. He anticipated Westminster's probable response that it would be 'more trouble than it was worth' by stressing that, after the war, larger numbers would be available for military service than in 1941 or 1943 and that any disruption that might result would have much less grave consequences in peacetime. However, he also particularly emphasised that if conscription was not applied it would be difficult for Britain to help either by contributing to the cost of the north's social services or by assisting it to achieve full employment. He noted, too, that military service would ease the difficulties of demobilised personnel returning to civilian life. Such was Brooke's enthusiasm that he favoured establishing

[54] Cabinet conclusions, 6 Feb. 1945 (P.R.O.N.I., CAB4/614); also Brooke diary, 21 Mar., 2 May 1944.
[55] Cabinet conclusions, 16, 27 Sept. 1943, 23 Mar. 1944 (P.R.O.N.I., CAB4/555, 556, 576).

contact with the catholic hierarchy in order to explore whether more generous grants to voluntary schools would lessen hostility to the idea.[56]

To British ministers and officials these arguments amounted to 'no case at all'. They considered that to extend conscription to Northern Ireland for economic reasons would be 'indefensible' and that to apply it after hostilities had ended would be to invite universal condemnation. Moreover, they believed that Brooke and his colleagues would be exposed to ridicule if they were to introduce military service at a time when it involved no risk to the conscripts. Underlying Westminster's response was the conviction that Brooke's request was not in the best interests either of Ulster or of the preservation of the union. Some officials had clearly come to value the latter more highly, no doubt influenced by the experience of war. Thus one official observed: 'The important thing is that the affairs of Northern Ireland be so conducted that the unionist ascendancy be maintained. Nothing should be done to provoke rebellion . . . by a large minority who can always look for support from across the border.'[57]

Relations between Westminster and Stormont certainly became closer and warmer in wartime, irrespective of the conscription issue. This did not stem from any outstanding commitment shown, or sacrifice made, by the people of the province in the course of the conflict. Voluntary recruitment levels remained a source of disappointment, even embarrassment, to Northern Ireland ministers, and local munitions industries performed only moderately well throughout.[58] It was Ulster's strategic position that was crucial, in view of Germany's military domination of Europe and the south's undeviating policy of neutrality. As V.E. day approached, Brooke expressed the 'hope that you [Britain] now realise that we are necessary to you'.[59] His wish was fully vindicated; the imperial government's warmer attitude was to find tangible expression in the declaratory clause of the Ireland act of 1949.

---

[56] Ibid., 19 Apr. 1945 (P.R.O.N.I., CAB4/622). Brooke suggested that initially contact should be made with local catholic leaders, who he hoped could establish whether increased expenditure on voluntary schools would win the hierarchy's acceptance of conscription; he was aware of the risk that this strategy might provoke protestant anger. No more formal lines of communication appear to have existed between the government and the catholic community.

[57] See minute by C. Markbreiter, 9 May 1945, also note by Herbert Morrison, 29 Oct. 1946, in 'Conscription 1945–6' (P.R.O., H.O. 45/24213). No one was more concerned to preserve the union than Brooke. But he believed that if conscription was not applied, it would cause 'ill-feeling' in Britain. Above all, he was convinced that if N.I. expected to be treated by Britain as a development area after the war (in which special measures would be applied to reduce unemployment) then it must accept the 'obligations of common citizenship' (P.R.O.N.I., CAB4/622).

[58] After an initial spurt in October 1939, average monthly enlistment dropped below 1,000. The rate was influenced by several factors including seasonal unemployment, the growing absorption of people in war work, the needs of the services themselves, and the war situation. There was a surge of volunteers after Dunkirk, and again between June and Sept. 1943. During the war years *c*.38,000 men and women from Northern Ireland are known to have enlisted. See Blake, *N.I. in second world war*, pp 199–200.

[59] Fisk, *In time of war*, p. 470.

Meanwhile, within Northern Ireland itself there was little sign of any shift in traditional political perspectives. Unionists remained sensitive to any criticism of the treatment of the minority. On 7 November 1944, remarks by Bernard Griffin, catholic archbishop of Westminster, caused outrage among Stormont ministers and their supporters. Referring to catholics being 'persecuted in Germany and Poland', he added: 'I need hardly mention the persecution going on even at the present time in Northern Ireland.'[60] Certainly it is clear that unionist suspicion of the minority did not diminish in wartime. A recurring theme of resolutions discussed by the party's standing committee was concern at catholics 'getting in all over the province', purchasing houses or farms, or finding employment in the civil service, post office, or local industry.[61] In 1943, when he was struggling for his political survival, Andrews stated privately that the appointment of a single catholic permanent secretary or assistant secretary would be sufficient to 'end the government';[62] his confidant, Spender, noted that the highest echelons of the civil service were still exclusively protestant.

The war itself could be used to justify illiberal policies and practices. During its final stages Spender received representations that houses should be erected 'in certain places on political grounds' (i.e. that houses should be built for protestants in those areas, so as to enhance their electoral strength). Though he had in the past forthrightly condemned sectarian discrimination, he considered that there was now 'some justification' for it, because 'protestants have been more willing to join the forces and volunteer for work in England than catholics and are therefore entitled to preferential treatment'. Occasionally, he reflected disparagingly on the 'lack of any contribution' made by the minority to the war effort.[63] No doubt many northern catholics regarded the outcome of the conflict with at best indifference. Unionists certainly tended to regard them as a sort of fifth column—pro-German and anti-British by instinct and tradition, ever willing to aid and abet the enemy; a community whose grievances were not as great as they made out.

In fact, considerable numbers of catholics had given voluntary service during the war, but this was not without difficulties. The case of the national fire service serves as an example. When it was set up in April 1942, former auxiliary workers, including catholics, became full-time state employees, which under existing regulations required the taking of an oath of allegiance. For a few, this was completely unacceptable; others indicated to the civil

---

[60] Griffin's speech was discussed by cabinet, 9 Nov. 1944 (P.R.O.N.I., CAB4/605); ministers agreed to send a letter of protest to Morrison at the home office, and pressed him to see the archbishop.

[61] Minutes of Ulster Unionist party standing committee, 11 Apr., 10 Nov. 1944, 9 Feb. 1945 (P.R.O.N.I., D1327/7).

[62] Spender diary, 30 Mar. 1943.

[63] Ibid., 16 Mar., 11 Sept. 1944. See also Barton, *Blitz*, pp 265–83.

servant who administered the oath that they took it 'with varying degrees of "mental reservation" '.[64] As noted above, catholic participation in the Ulster 'home guard' formed from the Local Defence Volunteers in 1941 was not encouraged; not only had the force been originally raised as a wing of the 'B' specials, but in March 1942 members were required to indicate their willingness to accept full military service in the event of any emergency being declared.[65]

The war years also witnessed considerable pressure being put on the I.R.A. in Northern Ireland. It became more difficult to maintain communications between the leaders in Dublin and Belfast, and this encouraged the idea of a self-contained northern unit. In 1939 a 'northern command' was formed, covering seven counties, under Hugh McAteer of Derry. In March 1942 it was decided to begin a campaign in Northern Ireland, which resulted in the deaths of several members of the R.U.C., as well as three I.R.A. men. The execution in Belfast in September 1942 of Thomas Williams for the murder of a policeman led to disturbances in nationalist areas, which continued into October and were only brought under control by the imposition of a curfew in west Belfast. Despite these activities, I.R.A. numbers in the north (as in the south) remained very small.[66]

Although the I.R.A. received little support for its campaign from northern nationalists, there was little sign of any rapprochement between northern catholics and the state. The political representatives of the minority community for the most part remained aloof from the parliamentary process. The two Belfast M.P.s Campbell and Byrne attending Stormont in 1939 continued to do so, being joined in 1941 by Michael McGurk, who was returned at a by-election for mid Tyrone. But on Byrne's death in 1942 the vacant seat was taken by an abstentionist, Eamon Donnelly. As the historian of the northern nationalists has noted, the minority, forming one-third of the population, 'had virtually opted out of the state'. Equipped with its own social infrastructure of 'church, schools, hospitals, sporting activities, newspapers, businesses and sectarian Ancient Order of Hibernians', it formed something like 'a state within a state'.[67]

For the government's part, not all its policies reflected old prejudices. On occasion, ministers led by example and attempted positively to counteract local discriminatory forces. Thus, for instance, the housing trust, from its inception in 1945, had a statutory obligation to allocate houses fairly. Sir Lucius O'Brien, first chairman, stated with apparent confidence that there was never any opportunity for undue influence to be used; mainly, he explained, because tenants were selected on the basis of an objective though

[64] Quoted in Harkness, *N.I. since 1920*, p. 103.
[65] Ibid., pp 83–4.
[66] Coogan, *I.R.A.*, pp 226–37.
[67] Harkness, *N.I. since 1920*, p. 104; Phoenix, *Northern nationalism*, p. 399.

undisclosed points system.[68] The trust was of course inevitably exposed to powerful political pressures; however, objective research has generally 'exonerated [it] of all conscious desire to discriminate'.[69] Similarly, when the cabinet began in late 1944 to consider the scale of future government grants to voluntary schools, Brooke spoke strongly in favour of generous treatment, advising colleagues that the children must be the 'first consideration'. Lt-col. Hall-Thompson, the new minister of education, likewise argued that as catholic pupils comprised about 40 per cent of the school population they 'must be dealt with on a statesmanlike basis' and be accorded 'just treatment'. Furthermore, when Stormont ministers decided to introduce family allowances on the same basis as at Westminster, they were fully cognisant of the fact that the minority would benefit disproportionately from their proposed scheme.[70]

The introduction of family allowances touched a highly sensitive unionist nerve. Stormont ministers had hopes, if not expectations, that social welfare measures, combined with economic growth, might in the long term deflect the minority from its aspiration to Irish unity. Indeed, in Brooke's opinion, expressed in 1944, the 'only chance for the political future of Ulster' was if it became 'so prosperous that the traditional political alliances [were] broken down'. In the meantime he and his cabinet regarded the relatively high catholic birth rate with great concern. Brooke recorded a wartime discussion with John MacDermott on this issue; both reached the depressing conclusion that there was no immediate 'solution' to the problem of what Brooke called the 'increasing disloyal population'.[71]

The government did, however, respond indirectly to the perceived threat by regulating more closely the flow of southern labour into Northern Ireland. Brooke, of course, fully appreciated that 'even if we stopped all entries from

[68] Statements at a meeting of the Ulster Unionist Council executive committee, 23 May 1950 (P.R.O.N.I., D1327/6). O'Brien explained that besides a points system, housing allocation involved a visit to the applicant's existing accommodation to see 'what kind of housekeepers the women were'. He defended the failure to publish details of the points system, despite the opportunities for discrimination, because disclosure 'would leave no choice to the Trust in the selection of candidates'.

[69] See J. H. Whyte, 'How much discrimination was there under the unionist regime, 1921–68?' in Tom Gallagher and James O'Connell (ed.), Contemporary Irish studies (Manchester, 1983), p. 19; also Thomas Wilson, Ulster: conflict and consent (Oxford, 1989), pp 126–7. Wilson writes: 'No suggestion was ever made that [the trust] operated in a sectarian manner ... Admittedly the houses it built were of a slightly higher standard than those provided ... by the local authorities and were, to this extent, less suitable for lower-income catholics.' It selected candidates on the basis not just of need but of ability to pay. Thus, it did less for catholics than protestants (D. P. Barritt and C. F. Carter, The Northern Ireland problem: a study in group relations (London, 1962), p. 112.

[70] For cabinet discussion of family allowances see cabinet conclusions, 28 June, 15 Oct. 1945 (P.R.O.N.I., CAB4/628, 650); education was considered on 25 July, 12 Oct. 1944 (P.R.O.N.I., CAB4/594, 601). The local family allowance scheme differed from the Westminster provision only in its inclusion of a residence qualification. For the 1947 education act, see below, pp 718–20.

[71] Brooke diary, 11 July, 5 Sept. 1944.

Éire it would only scratch the difficulty'.[72] A system of residence permits was strictly administered by Stormont departments, acting under powers derived from a British government order. Much thought was given to the possibility of differentiating southern 'loyalists' (those who accepted partition) from the rest and facilitating their permanent settlement in the province, but no practicable scheme could be devised. Mounting anxiety that Westminster might refuse to sanction the continued monitoring of migration from the south after the war prompted the Unionist leadership to consider whether the 1920 act ought to be amended. Some favoured reform in order to provide Northern Ireland with dominion status, thus transferring to Stormont the necessary regulatory powers.[73]

This internal party debate on the merits of constitutional change was given added impetus by political events in the summer of 1945. As hostilities in Europe drew to a close, Brooke noted privately: 'I find I have no feelings of elation, only thankfulness that others will not have to endure the losses that we have suffered. One realises also the vast and difficult problems which lie ahead.' No doubt with these thoughts in mind he consulted his cabinet colleagues, as well as Glentoran and Andrews, during the euphoria of V.E. day (8 May), and 'decided to go to the country at once'.[74] When the results of the general election were declared in June, the Unionist party emerged with just over 50 per cent of the votes cast, thirty-three seats, and an overall majority of only fourteen in the new parliament. This was the worst result for the party since 1925.[75]

[72] Ibid., 11 July 1944.
[73] See cabinet discussions of southern migration in cabinet conclusions, 10 July, 16 Nov. 1944; 6, 15 Feb. 1945 (P.R.O.N.I., CAB4/592, 606, 614, 615); also Brooke diary, 2 May, 14 July 1944.
[74] Brooke diary, 7, 8 May 1945.
[75] The result was particularly disappointing, because the party had won 39 seats in the previous election (9 Feb. 1938). Only in one of the contests held between 24 May 1921 and 24 Feb. 1969 was it to win fewer seats (32 in 3 Apr. 1925). Labour, rather than nationalist or republican parties, gained most, winning almost one-third of the votes cast. See Elliott, *N.I. election results*; Brendan Lynn, *Holding the ground: the nationalist party in Northern Ireland 1945–72* (Aldershot, 1997), ch. 1.

CHAPTER IX

To the declaration of the Republic and the Ireland act, 1945–9

J. H. WHYTE*

ANYONE writing the history of Ireland in the period 1945–72 has to marry together two themes that at first sight do not fit well with each other. On the one hand, this was a period, in Ireland as in the world as a whole, of unprecedented social and psychological change. Television, the growth of foreign travel, and emigration on an unprecedented scale to England were making Irish men and women more aware of the outside world and of other value-systems than their own. Economic growth, punctuated by economic difficulties, were making them more aware of the possibilities of affluence and of the problems that lay in the way of achieving it. The explosion in higher education meant that more and more people were being educated to a level where they were no longer satisfied with old clichés. The churches, and particularly the Roman Catholic church, were experiencing a turmoil, which was particularly important in a country where a uniquely high proportion of the population was actively connected with one denomination or another. Even world changes that did not primarily affect Ireland, such as the crumbling of colonial empires, indirectly influenced the Irish situation; they altered, for instance, British attitudes towards maintaining the position of Northern

---

*REVISOR'S NOTE: John Whyte's death in 1990 robbed Ireland of one of its most talented and respected scholars. His books include *Church and state in modern Ireland, 1923–1979* (1971), *Catholics in western democracies: a study in political behaviour* (1981), and *Interpreting Northern Ireland* (1990). In these works, as in his other writings, he was scrupulously fair and meticulously thorough. The same qualities are evident in the drafts that he wrote for this history, covering the period 1945–72. Were he alive, he would certainly have sought to incorporate into these chapters material unavailable at the time of their drafting. In revising his chapters I have therefore sought to amplify certain points through reference to the more recent literature, while leaving the essential text as its author had written it. For the most part new material has been added by way of footnotes.

Richard English
The Queen's University of Belfast

Ireland, and they led to troops from the Republic of Ireland being sent to such far-flung places as the Congo and Cyprus. The historian of these years has to bring out the multifarious and increasing pace of change. At the same time, the historian has to note the permanence and intractability of political problems. The politics of these years seemed to revolve interminably around the same issues. Most salient of all was the relationship between north and south: how to reconcile the deep feeling among most southern Irish people that partition was unnatural and an injustice with the equally immovable fear among northern protestants of being absorbed in a Roman Catholic republic. Linked with this was the abiding tension between the two communities in the north. Linked with it also were contrasting attitudes to Great Britain, with one side emphasising its Britishness and the other its distinctiveness from the British way of life.

However, these two themes—the rapidity of change in the social field and the apparent absence of it in the political field—are not so contrasting as they appear at first sight. For though the political problems appeared so immutable, the attitudes displayed towards them altered very considerably in the course of this period. These changes in attitude did not, on the surface at least, occur steadily, but rather in a series of jumps, as some fresh event occurred to educate public opinion both north and south of the border. Five such 'jumps' in attitudes to the north–south problem can be detected in the years under review. The first occurred in 1948–9, with the announcement of the decision to declare the twenty-six counties a republic, and the consequent passage by the Westminster parliament of the Ireland act, entrenching the constitutional status of Northern Ireland. The second occurred in 1956–7, when border raids by the I.R.A. and other organisations were at their height. The third occurred in 1963, with the accession of Terence O'Neill to power in Northern Ireland. The fourth occurred in 1968–70, with the long-drawn-out northern disturbances. The fifth occurred in 1972, with the introduction of direct rule in Northern Ireland.

The existence of these 'jumps' facilitates the organisation of this unit of narrative. It will be divided into five chapters, each ending with one of these 'jumps'. The dividing lines for the unit, then, are 1949, 1957, 1963, 1968, and 1972. Each of the chapters will deal with internal developments in the twenty-six counties, with internal developments in Northern Ireland, and with events involving both parts of Ireland and also their relations with Britain.

THE end of the war in Europe found the Fianna Fáil government, then in its fourteenth year of office, in an apparently unchallenged position. Electorally, it had held the lead in six general elections running, and the return of its candidate, Seán T. O'Kelly, at the presidential election held in June 1945 indicated that its lead was still secure. True, at the local elections held on the same day Fianna Fáil lost ground, but the gainers were independents rather than any of the opposition parties. The opposition parties, in fact, were in utter disarray. The largest of them, Fine Gael, was in full decline. Its share both of seats and of first-preference votes had declined at each of the four general elections since 1937, and at the last of these, in 1944, it had retained only just over 20 per cent of the first-preference votes, and thirty seats out of 137. At four out of five by-elections in 1945 it put up no candidates. The reason given at the time was that it did not wish to 'divide the nation'. This was not convincing, and the real reason appears to have been that the party simply could not find candidates prepared to stand on its behalf.

If Fine Gael was in decline, the Labour party was in open schism. In the early 1940s it had appeared to be gaining as Fine Gael lost ground. In the local elections of 1942 it had won as many seats as Fine Gael, and in the general election of 1943, while not doing quite as well as that, it had none the less gained its highest proportion of first-preference votes at any general election so far: 15.7 per cent. But at the beginning of 1944 had come the split between it and National Labour which was to endure till 1950. Both sections of the party suffered from the split: in the general election of 1944 they together won only 11.1 per cent of the vote, and in 1948 they won 11.3 per cent.[1] The only other party with any parliamentary strength in 1945, Clann na Talmhan, was a sectional group representing only small western farmers. It was no threat to the government and seemed in any case to have lost some of the impetus from its foundation in 1938.[2]

The political history of 'Éire'[3] during the years covered by this chapter is the history of the decline and fall of this Fianna Fáil hegemony. The troubles of the government appear under two headings: economic, and those more strictly political. The economic troubles were perhaps the more galling for the government, because it might reasonably have expected that with the end of the war, and the reopening of international trade, things would have begun to get better. Financially, the country appeared extremely strong. It had built up enormous sterling balances during the war; now that the war was over, it could hope that in due course goods would appear on which money could usefully be spent. The government certainly seemed to begin the post-war period in a mood of optimism. A £5 million building programme was

---

[1] For a discussion of Labour's fortunes in this period, see Emmet O'Connor, *A labour history of Ireland, 1824–1960* (Dublin, 1992), pp 150–67.

[2] For Clann na Talmhan, see John Coakley, 'Minor parties in Irish political life, 1922–1989' in *Econ. & Soc. Rev.*, xxi, no. 3 (Apr. 1990), pp 282–3.

[3] The 1937 constitution (above, pp 140–42) stated 'the name of the state is Éire, or, in the English language, Ireland' (article 4). However, 'Éire' cannot properly be used to designate what had formerly been the Irish Free State (Saorstát Éireann) because it referred to the whole island. Article 3 contained clarification: 'pending the reintegration of the national territory' the laws enacted by the Irish parliament would only apply to the area covered by the former Free State.

begun. Three huge tuberculosis hospitals were planned. Rural electrification was planned in detail. New departments of health and of social welfare were established. In January 1946 a ten-year scheme for the development of turf production was announced. Meanwhile, the government found it possible simultaneously to cut taxes and to make £3 million available for the relief of distress on the European continent. During 1946 a further cause for optimism became apparent: Ireland was enjoying an unprecedented boom as a tourist centre. English people, deterred from holidaying on the Continent by the currency restrictions of their own government and by the shortages and restrictions in potential host countries, were turning in their thousands to Ireland. Ireland had the advantage of being in the sterling area and therefore not subject to British currency restrictions; it also had the advantage of having plenty of food, and in particular of meat, so that visitors weary of six years of rationing could once again eat in a way that had become only a memory for them.

But by the middle of 1946 it was clear that the postwar era was going to be much more difficult economically than had been hoped. The first major postwar strike had broken out; in March, members of the Irish National Teachers' Organisation in Dublin struck in support of their claim for higher pay. But in spite of the sympathy of the catholic bishops, the newspapers, and a considerable section of the public, the government was adamant that their claim could not be met without opening the door to a host of other claims, which the economy could not afford. The strike dragged on till October before the teachers unconditionally surrendered. Meanwhile, it became clear that the 1946 harvest was going to be very bad, as a result of continual rain. In January 1947 it became necessary to introduce bread rationing, a measure that had never been necessary during the war. The worst privations were yet to come, however. In February 1947, in the middle of the coldest winter in living memory, the British coal supply—on which Ireland also depended—proved inadequate to the demands made upon it. As part of a frenzy of cuts, all supplies to the twenty-six counties were cut off, and the Irish government in its turn had to make draconian economies. Long-distance trains were cancelled; factories were closed down; power stations worked at half capacity; on 20 March even firewood was put on the ration list. Finally, in April, the British government was prevailed upon to allocate some coal once more to the twenty-six counties, and gradually things reverted to normal. But fuel remained scarce till the Anglo–Irish trade agreement of November 1947 gave promise of a better supply. Meanwhile there had been another bad harvest in the summer of 1947. Wheat was still short and bread still rationed, and it also became necessary for a time to halve the butter ration.

What caused most discontent, however, was the rise in the cost of living. Prices continued to rise after the war as they had done during it. Ireland's economy was so dependent on others that when inflation was a world trend it was impossible to avoid it at home. But for eighteen months after the end of the war the government enforced its wage standstill order, and thus, by keeping money income stable at a time when costs were rising, ensured that real incomes actually declined. Without this policy, inflation would doubtless have been even greater; but it was understandably unpopular. The teachers' strike of 1946 was the harbinger of a wave of industrial unrest, which mounted higher in 1947. In 1946 the government abrogated the wage standstill order, and henceforward relied on a newly established institution, the labour court, to act as a buffer for wage claims.[4] The labour court, however, could only mediate: it had no compulsory powers, and although it was extremely busy in its first few months and its recommendations were accepted by both employers and workers in many cases, in some of the most important areas they were not. There was a serious bus strike in 1947: there was also the first of a series of industrial disputes for which Ireland was to become notorious—namely, between the bank managements and their employees. Finally, by the autumn of 1947, the government found it necessary to take drastic measures. On 15 October, de Valera announced that, in order to reduce the cost of living, the subsidies on flour, bread, tea, and sugar would be increased. But the extra money had to be found somewhere, and the only way to do it was to increase taxes. This was done partly by raising income tax, partly by putting fresh duties on a range of goods including beer, spirits, and tobacco. To many Irishmen, beer and tobacco were hardly less staples than bread, tea, or sugar; and to increase the price of the former in order to lower the price of the latter was giving them no advantage. Two weeks later, on 29 October 1947, de Valera's government experienced two serious by-election defeats.

Before we examine these, however, it is necessary to retrace our steps and examine the political developments of 1945–7. It would not have been surprising if long years of power had made the Fianna Fáil government overbearing, and this was the burden of opposition criticisms in the years just after the war. Ministers were attacked for the brusqueness with which they dismissed the Dignan national insurance plan and the vocational organisation report.[5] They were accused of taking unnecessarily sweeping powers under the public health bill of 1945 and the county management acts.[6] There was

---

[4] Established by the Industrial Relations Act, 1946 (1946/26) (27 Aug. 1946).

[5] In 1944 John Dignan, bishop of Clonfert, who chaired the National Health Insurance Society, had published a pamphlet, *Social security: outlines of a scheme of national health insurance*, calling for a contributory national insurance scheme. It was bitterly attacked by Seán MacEntee, then minister for local government. For a detailed discussion of ministers' reactions to this plan and the vocational organisation report (above, p. 153), see Whyte, *Ch. & state* (1971), ch. 4.

[6] County management acts, 1940/12 (13 June 1940); 1942/13 (25 June 1942). The public health bill was a casualty of the resignation of the parliamentary secretary dealing with the legislation, Dr Conn Ward, T.D. for Co. Monaghan.

indeed some truth in this. The prevailing administrative style at the time could be aptly condemned as bureaucratic: ministers and departments displayed an impatience with interest groups, a confidence in their superior wisdom, that could easily lead to overbearing behaviour. It is significant perhaps that when, in 1948, the Irish Association of Civil Liberties was founded, its main purpose was stated to be the curbing of bureaucratic power. To the young and liberal-minded people who founded the association, this was where the greatest danger seemed to lie: not with the church, not with oppressive social structures in the Irish countryside, but with the governmental machine.[7]

The government suffered greater damage, probably, from rumours of corruption in high places. Hitherto, this was a complaint from which the de Valera government had been largely free; but in 1946–7 allegations were made with such specificity that on three separate occasions the government was obliged to set up tribunals of inquiry. In June 1946 a tribunal was set up to investigate charges of fraud made against a parliamentary secretary, Dr Conn Ward, in the operation of a bacon factory he owned in Monaghan. The tribunal found the grosser charges against him unfounded, but it did decide that he had made incorrect returns for tax purposes, and he was obliged to resign. About the same time it was alleged that friends of government ministers appeared to have had advance warning of a government plan to nationalise the railways, and that they had been able to make pickings on the stock exchange by buying shares. A tribunal of inquiry exempted ministers from all blame. In 1947 a more sensational rumour of corruption surrounded the sale of a moribund firm, Locke's distillery, in County Westmeath. It was alleged that the foreigners who bought it had suborned officials of the department of industry and commerce into giving them the necessary authorisation, and that the minister himself, Seán Lemass, was not unaware of these goings-on.[8] A tribunal of inquiry found the charges irresponsible and malicious, and rebuked the deputy responsible for publicising them, Oliver Flanagan, an independent from Leix–Offaly. But though the government may have been cleared by these tribunals, it was unlikely that public opinion would exonerate it so completely. There was a natural feeling that where there is smoke there is also fire, and there can be little doubt that these episodes contributed to the government's unpopularity. In Leix–Offaly, for instance, during the general election of 1948, Oliver Flanagan, unabashed by the rebuke received from the tribunal on the Locke case, made his

[7] Cf. Whyte's observation that 'by the mid-1940s a rift had emerged in Ireland between two philosophies of government. One could be labelled "vocationalist", and called for the diffusion of responsibility among vocational groups. The other could be called "bureaucratic", and defended the centralisation of authority in government departments' (Whyte, *Ch. & state* (1980), p. 117 and ch. 4, *passim*).

[8] John Horgan, *Seán Lemass: the enigmatic patriot* (Dublin, 1997), pp 130–31.

'unmasking' of the government a principal plank in his campaign, and received the highest number of first-preference votes won by any candidate anywhere in the twenty-six counties.

However, these troubles endured by the government would not have been sufficient to unseat it unless there was an opposition active enough to attract the votes that the government was alienating. In the immediate post-war period this did not appear to be so. The decaying Fine Gael party, the divided Labour party, and the sectional Clann na Talmhan appeared to be no threat to the government. Fianna Fáil won four of the six by-elections in 1945–6. In July 1946, however, a new party, Clann na Poblachta, was founded, which appeared for a short time to transform the situation. The new party was founded largely by republicans who had become disenchanted with the policy of physical force. Its leader was Seán MacBride, son of Major John MacBride, the executed 1916 leader, and of the famous patriot Maud Gonne MacBride. Seán MacBride was an able barrister and senior counsel. He had also been active in the I.R.A. during the 1920s and 1930s and (according to some sources) even later.[9] The event that led him to embark on constitutional politics was the agitation for the release of political prisoners early in 1946. In May, an I.R.A. leader, Seán McCaughey, died on hunger strike at Portlaoise prison. The inquest, at which MacBride appeared on behalf of McCaughey's relatives, revealed the harrowing conditions in which McCaughey had been kept—in solitary confinement, naked in an unheated cell, because he refused to wear prison clothes. The episode aroused indignation among others as well as militant republicans: it was raised in the dáil, for instance, by a member of Clann na Talmhan. To those members of the republican movement who felt that the physical-force policy was sterile and should be abandoned, the agitation offered an opportunity. It enabled them to switch to a constitutional policy without losing face.

The new party was accordingly launched in July 1946 at a press conference in Dublin. It had a left-wing social policy, with special emphasis on the elimination of tuberculosis. It quickly won the support of many idealists who had never been connected with the republican movement but who felt dissatisfied with all existing parties. In October 1947 it had its first opportunity to test its electoral strength. By-elections took place in three constituencies simultaneously: Dublin county, Tipperary, and Waterford. The results were a sensational success for the new party. MacBride was elected in Dublin county, and a colleague in Tipperary. Only in Waterford did Fianna Fáil retain the seat, and even there the government vote showed a serious decline.

---

[9] Indeed, in conversation with de Valera during the early 1930s, MacBride had expressed his doubts about the viability of majority rule, arguing that 'it had been found that progress towards national freedom could not be made through majority rule' (MacBride to McGarrity, 19 Oct. 1933; N.L.I., McGarrity papers, MS 17456). For MacBride and republicanism in the 1940s see Dermot Keogh, *Twentieth-century Ireland* (Dublin, 1994), pp 173–4.

The mounting unrest at economic difficulties and rising prices, the distaste aroused by the Ward and Locke investigations, finally the announcement of increased taxation only a fortnight before the by-elections: all these had helped to damage the government. Simultaneously the rise of Clann na Poblachta had given the voters an alternative. The result was the most serious by-election defeat that any Irish government had yet suffered.

De Valera responded by announcing that the dáil would be dissolved, and a general election ensue, as soon as essential financial business could be completed. The dáil was dissolved on 12 January 1948, and polling took place on 4 February. De Valera's calculation presumably was that by fighting an election at once he would lose less ground than if he allowed the new party to perfect its organisation. If this was his calculation, it proved not far off the mark. Clann na Poblachta put up ninety-three candidates at the general election, but they were a scratch group, hastily got together from many different backgrounds, and few of them proved to have much electoral drawing power. Only ten of them secured election. The other opposition parties gained some ground, and Fianna Fáil returned with only sixty-eight seats out of 147, as compared with seventy-six seats out of 137 at the previous general election in 1944. But it remained by far the largest party in the dáil, and only if all the opposition groups, including most of the twelve independents, could be persuaded to unite, would it be turned out of office.

Immediately after the general election it was by no means certain that this would happen. Four of the five opposition parties—Fine Gael, Labour, Clann na Talmhan, and Clann na Poblachta—met and agreed to form a coalition. But together they mustered only sixty-two deputies, fewer than Fianna Fáil, and even if they received the support of eleven out of the twelve independents—which was more than they were likely to get—they would still not have a majority of the dáil. All turned on the attitude of the remaining party in the dáil, National Labour. This exiguous group, with only five deputies, held the fate of the government in its hands. At first sight it seemed likely to support de Valera. It had fought the campaign on a basis of independent support for Fianna Fáil, and its members were under instruction from the I.C.T.U. to continue this policy. There was also the natural spirit of rivalry between the competing Labour parties. However, as soon as the election results had been declared, individuals on the opposition side realised the potential importance of National Labour and set to work to win it over. General Seán Mac Eoin of Fine Gael was one such ambassador; there were others. The result of their work was seen on the day that the dáil convened, when the five National Labour deputies announced that they would vote against de Valera. Despite a blast of disapproval from the I.C.T.U., they stood firm in their decision, and the fate of the Fianna Fáil government was sealed. In February 1948, after almost exactly sixteen years in office, de Valera was defeated on renomination for the post of taoiseach, by 70 votes to 75.

The new coalition was not out of its difficulties yet. It was one thing to overthrow the existing government; another, to form a new one in its place. Agreement was quickly reached on the division of ministries between parties; it was decided that each should be represented according to its parliamentary strength. The question of leadership took a little longer to solve. It was agreed that Fine Gael, which with thirty-one seats was by far the largest partner in the coalition, should provide the taoiseach. But the party's leader, General Richard Mulcahy, was unacceptable to the republicans in Clann na Poblachta because of the prominent part he had taken, twenty-five years earlier, in the civil war, and, with creditable self-abnegation, he withdrew all claim to the premiership.[10] The choice thus narrowed itself to some member of Fine Gael who had not been too identified with the Free State side in the civil war. Two names quickly suggested themselves: Sir John Esmonde and John A. Costello. Sir John Esmonde was an active and radical-minded deputy who in many ways would have been acceptable to the more left-wing elements in the coalition, but he suffered from one defect which might be embarrassing: he was the holder of a British baronetcy. The party leaders accordingly settled on Costello. John A. Costello was in many ways well qualified. He had been attorney general under the Cosgrave regime, and so had experience of high office, but he had not been personally involved in the civil war and so was acceptable to Clann na Poblachta. He was a highly successful lawyer with a large young family: the main doubt was whether he would feel able to accept the cut in income that acceptance of the taoiseach-ship would involve. However, he was persuaded to do so, and so the coalition found its leader.

Early impressions made by the inter-party government, as it was known, were favourable. After sixteen years of office the Fianna Fáil government appeared to have lost its dynamism, and some of the newcomers were like a breath of fresh air. James Dillon proved a flamboyant minister for agricul-ture, propagating his 'parish plan' for the improvement of agriculture by a local advisory service and establishing a land rehabilitation project which channelled Marshall Aid funds towards reclamation of land.[11] Michael Keyes was, as minister for local government, energetic in building houses. William Norton, as minister for social welfare, prepared a unified social insurance scheme to replace the patchwork of independently administered schemes that had hitherto existed. Seán MacBride, as minister for external affairs and cultural relations, was a tireless attender of international conferences and

[10] For a scholarly treatment of Mulcahy, concentrating on the period to 1924, see M. G. Valiulis, *Portrait of a revolutionary: General Richard Mulcahy*...(Blackrock, 1992).
[11] 1949/25 (30 July 1949). See also Maurice Manning, *James Dillon* (Dublin, 1999), ch. 14.

used his command of French to make Ireland better known on the European continent than it had been since the days when de Valera was president of the League of Nations. Patrick McGilligan, as minister for finance, was an astringent critic of high-flown schemes, whether his colleagues' or the opposition's. Probably the greatest impact was made by the youngest member of the government, Dr Noel Browne, who, at the time of his appointment as minister for health, was 32. Browne made it his first task to tackle the problem of tuberculosis, and he showed a restless, tearing energy that soon began to show results. The greatest shortage was of sanatorium beds. The preceding government had planned three large regional sanatoria, which would in the long run solve the problem; but they had not yet even completed the planning stage, and it would be five years before they were all ready. In the meantime literally thousands of lives might be lost. Browne met the problem by improvising temporary accommodation in every possible way: by taking over barracks and training colleges, by adding to existing hospitals, by converting other kinds of hospital to tuberculosis use. After two years in office he was able to claim that the backlog of 3,000 beds had been made up, and that no tuberculosis patient need be denied treatment.

The total achievement of the inter-party government was more chequered than this brief survey might indicate. During its three years of office it was responsible for two decisions that have had far-reaching effects: the declaration of the Republic of Ireland and withdrawal from the commonwealth in 1949, and the abandonment of Browne's mother-and-child welfare scheme in 1951. It can be argued that these episodes were mishandled by the government: but a fuller discussion of both comes more appropriately at a later point in this narrative.

IN Northern Ireland the post-war era began with a spate of electioneering. During the war general elections both for the Stormont and the Westminster parliaments had been postponed and were heavily overdue. There had been none since 1938 for Stormont, none since 1935 for Westminster. The contests produced none of the surprising upsets that occurred across the water. In the Westminster elections, the Unionists lost the highly marginal seat of West Belfast to an Independent Labour candidate, Jack Beattie. In the Stormont elections, they lost two seats in Belfast to Labour and two of the four Queen's University seats to independents. But in general, the notable feature of the 1945 election was the lack of change. The Unionists still held thirty-three out of the fifty-two seats at Stormont, and ten out of the thirteen seats at Westminster. Sir Basil Brooke's government continued in unchallenged power.

The Northern Ireland government, like that of the south, had serious economic troubles to face in the early post-war years. Indeed a comparison of privations gives some idea of the relative advantages of staying out of, and being inside, the United Kingdom at that time. On the whole, advantages and disadvantages probably broke even. On the one hand, Northern Ireland got a somewhat less raw deal during the fuel crisis of 1947 than the south. On the other hand, as part of a food-importing state, Northern Ireland had to accept food rations that were in some ways more spartan than those in the south. The bread ration was only three-quarters of that of the south, and potatoes were rationed for a time. Home-produced foodstuffs such as eggs and meat were much more plentiful in the south, and customs examinations for cross-border travellers were often a rigorous affair. On the other hand, the south seems to have suffered more from strikes during these years.

The years 1945–9 are, however, notable in the internal history of Northern Ireland above all for the spate of legislation they produced. To some extent this legislation was simply the application to Northern Ireland of the welfare state being fashioned by the Labour government in Britain. To some extent it was the result of an internal momentum for reform: there was much dissatisfaction in Northern Ireland with the existing public services, and a wave of reform measures was likely as soon as the return of peace made it possible. To some extent also, the measures were defensive reactions by the Unionist government to the dangers, real or imagined, of a nationalist take-over. Under the last heading can be put two measures that caused bitter controversy at the time: the Safeguarding of Employment Act, 1947, and the Elections and Franchise Act, 1946.[12] The first continued the practice, introduced under wartime regulations in 1942, of refusing employment to non-Northern Ireland residents in most categories of employment unless it could be shown that no Northern Ireland resident was available. Although the measure applied to immigrants from other parts of the United Kingdom, such as England and Scotland, its primary purpose was taken to be the prevention of a flood of immigrants from the south who might use their vote to overthrow the constitution. It was on this ground that it was both defended and attacked. The elections and franchise act, while being primarily a consolidation measure, introduced one or two changes in the electoral law, which, it was reckoned, would further increase the unionist advantage. For instance, it increased the possible number of business votes that any one occupier might wield in a local election to six. As most businessmen probably were unionists, this increased the government party's voting strength.

These measures, however, despite the acrimony they provoked, made no great change in the status quo. Much more important were the social reforms that crowded these years. First in time, and by no means the least important in its effects, was the establishment in 1945 of the Northern Ireland Housing Trust. This body, established to supplement the work of local authorities, many of whom had extremely poor records for house-building, greatly

[12] 1947, c. 24 (23 Dec. 1947); 1946, c. 6 (28 Feb. 1946).

helped to reduce the housing shortage in Northern Ireland. Moreover, in contrast to some local authorities, it was never accused of discrimination in its house-letting policies. Other important measures followed: the National Insurance Act (N.I.), 1946, and the Health Services Act (N.I.), 1948.[13] These applied to Northern Ireland the main provisions of the welfare state as it had been developed by the Labour government in Britain. The first provided for a comprehensive scheme of social insurance whereby the entire population received protection from all the major hazards of life—sickness, unemployment, bereavement, industrial injuries. Benefits and contributions were at the same level as in Great Britain, and an equalisation agreement with Westminster ensured that if either the Northern Ireland or the British fund were in deficit, it would be supplemented by the other. In practice, this meant that Northern Ireland social welfare benefits would be subsidised by the British taxpayer. The second measure virtually replicated the British national health service for Northern Ireland. Again, agreements with Westminster ensured that Stormont would receive sufficient finance to maintain health services at the British level. In detail the measure caused controversy as it moved through the Northern Ireland parliament. The clauses providing for the taking over of voluntary hospitals by a new Northern Ireland Hospitals Authority caused much controversy, and a Roman Catholic voluntary hospital, the Mater Hospital in Belfast, refused altogether to come into the scheme. But on the whole, the new comprehensive health service was welcomed on all sides. It meant that free medical treatment was guaranteed to every resident of Northern Ireland who wished to take advantage of it.

The most controversial piece of legislation put through during these years was the Education Act (N.I.), 1947.[14] This was the Northern Ireland equivalent of the British education act that R. A. Butler had put through in 1944. Like that measure it provided for secondary education for all from the age of 11. As in the British measure also, secondary education was to be provided in three kinds of school—grammar schools for the academically minded, technical schools for the technically gifted, and intermediate schools (the Northern Ireland equivalent of what in England were christened secondary modern schools) for the rest. The school-leaving age was to be raised to 15, and local authorities were obliged to provide facilities even beyond that age for those who were able to profit by them. The measure was designed, therefore, to raise very considerably both the quantity and the quality of the education that young people received. Its principle received wide acceptance, but there were two features in particular that aroused controversy. The first was the provision that state aid for the building and maintenance of voluntary schools was to be increased from 50 to 65 per cent. This was justified on

---

[13] 1946, c. 3 (19 Feb. 1946); 1948, c. 3 (4 Feb. 1949).
[14] 1947, c. 3 (27 Mar. 1947).

the ground that the education act would put a very considerable extra burden on the owners of voluntary schools, if they were to bring their establishments up to the standards required by the act, and that they therefore required additional financial help. But the scale of help offered was higher than that then provided in England, where it remained at 50 per cent, and, as most voluntary schools were Roman Catholic, it was attacked by some protestants for being unreasonably generous. The other controversial feature was the one providing for greater state control of the existing grammar schools, mostly protestant. This was fought tooth and nail, and considerable modifications were eventually achieved. The education act of 1947 was to be of the highest importance in the development of Northern Ireland. The facilities it offered greatly increased the proportion of children going on for further education. The effect was particularly noticeable among the catholic population, who, being generally poorer, had more need of assistance. In the long run, as later chapters will show, the impact of educational change had the most important consequences not just for the economic, but for the political development of Northern Ireland.

The legal relationship between Dublin and the United Kingdom was still, in 1945, in the state of vagueness in which de Valera had deliberately left it when he carried the external relations act in 1936 and the constitution of 1937. In other words, no official document explicitly stated whether the state was a republic or not, or whether it was a member of the commonwealth or not. This ambiguity had been justified by de Valera as being the furthest that a southern government could go towards meeting the views of northern unionists while still getting agreement in the south. But it had its inconveniences. On the one hand it did not go far enough for convinced republicans, and one of the planks in the programme of Clann na Poblachta was the repeal of the external relations act. On the other hand, it was open to probing by skilful opposition speakers in the dáil, and this was a pastime which several of them, notably James Dillon (then an independent deputy), indulged in during the immediate post-war period. In 1945, for instance, de Valera, in reply to a taunt from Dillon that nobody knew whether the state was a republic or not, felt obliged to resort to the curious exercise of reading out dictionary definitions of a republic, ending with the conclusion that that in fact was the country's status. The probing of opposition deputies then shifted to the question of what was precisely the nature of the relation with the commonwealth. In 1946 Dillon read out in the dáil the standard letter of credence presented by Irish diplomatic representatives, signed as it was by King George VI, and asked de Valera to explain away this intervention by a monarch in what he (de Valera) claimed was a republic. In this baiting of the taoiseach, Dillon was joined by one or two leaders of Fine Gael. Patrick McGilligan, for instance, said he would rather see the present arrangement ended than 'perpetuate a lie'. This was a significant statement, coming from a leader of the party that was supposed to favour the maintenance of the commonwealth link. It meant that de Valera's compromise of 1936–7 was coming increasingly under attack from all sides. Even had there been no change of government in 1948, it is unlikely that it could have lasted indefinitely.

The change of government, however, almost certainly hastened the process. Indeed only five months after its formation—in July 1948—the government decided in principle on the repeal of the external relations act.[15] The occasion for this decision appears to have been the fear that Captain Peadar Cowan, a maverick independent deputy who had been elected as a member of Clann na Poblachta but had already been expelled by that party, might introduce a private member's bill to repeal the act. This would put members of the government on the spot. Several of them—notably Seán MacBride, leader of Clann na Poblachta, and William Norton, leader of the Labour party, were known to be personally in favour of repeal; even some of the Fine Gael ministers had shown themselves, when in opposition, lukewarm about its retention. It was hardly possible for ministers to argue in favour of an act about which their feelings were so tepid; the only alternative was to get rid of it themselves.

Ministers' next move appears to have been to prepare the public for the change. Speeches by MacBride in July and by Norton in August, and notably by Costello himself when on a visit to Canada in September, all foreshadowed the repeal or at least the amendment of the external relations act. Ministers in fact were preparing the ground rather too well. On 5 September 1948 the *Sunday Independent* carried as its leading news story an article under the headline 'External relations act to go'. The story did no more than gather together extracts from the speeches by ministers just mentioned, and make the obvious deduction from them. But the result was that an official announcement had to be made more quickly than ministers had intended. On 7 September Costello, who was still in Canada, was asked at a press conference whether the government did in fact intend to repeal the external relations act, and he answered frankly that it did.

It should be noted that, in all this, there was no hint that Irish ministers were seeking to irritate the British. On the contrary, they were careful to proclaim their anxiety for good relations with Britain, and they argued that the repeal of the act would help foster such relations, by removing what had in Irish circumstances been an irritant—namely, the link with the crown. British ministers, for their part, seem to have mastered any disappointment they may have felt, and accepted the decision graciously. At a meeting of

[15] In a study of the circumstances leading up to the repeal of the external relations act, Ian McCabe confirms that there was no formal cabinet decision on the matter before the announcement of Sept. 1948 (Ian McCabe, *A diplomatic history of Ireland, 1948–49* ([Blackrock, 1991]), p. 149). See also Manning, *Dillon*, p. 244.

Irish and British ministers in October, it was agreed that reciprocal citizenship rights and trade preferences should continue, and that neither country would treat the other as a foreign country.

Indeed, a general feature of the years 1945–8 was the cordiality of relations between the south and Great Britain. The Labour government in London showed ample goodwill. It negotiated trade agreements in 1947 and 1948. By an act of 1948,[16] it made changes in British citizenship law which, while not fully meeting the wishes of the Irish government, went a very long way to eliminate features in the existing law that had for long been irritants. Meanwhile, many British ministers were getting to know Ireland at first hand. The number who came on holiday was remarkable. In the summer of 1948 the lord chancellor, Lord Jowitt, the minister of supply, G. R. Strauss, the secretary of state for commonwealth relations, P. J. Noel-Baker, and the prime minister himself, Clement Attlee, all took their holidays in Ireland. In doing so, they were probably doing no more than thousands of other Britons who found Ireland a tourist mecca of red steaks and green fields at this time. But it all helped to strengthen the appearance of cordiality between the two governments.

If there were any bad relations during these years, they existed not between Dublin and Westminster but between Stormont and Westminster. The Unionists were allied with the Conservative party, which was now in opposition at Westminster; there was a certain strain in having to cooperate with a government composed of political opponents. The Stormont government appears to have accepted readily enough the main lines of the welfare state, as is shown by its sponsoring of the national insurance and health services acts. But it did not imitate all items of legislation at Westminster: it did not, for instance, alter the legislation on trades disputes; nor did it concede universal suffrage in local government elections (adopted in Britain in 1948). Westminster, for its part, annoyed Stormont by its actions or omissions. An air agreement of 1946, with its galling concession of flying rights from Belfast to a Dublin-based airline, appears to have been negotiated without reference to the Northern Ireland government. In July 1948 Costello in Dublin made an alarming claim to the effect that his government had some hope of ending partition, adding 'I make that assertion with all the confidence I have within me. To say any more would be to damage the advances that already have been made.'[17] This statement drew an angry rejoinder from Sir Basil Brooke to the effect that Ulster was not for sale. It drew no such rejoinder from Westminster.

If relations between the Northern Ireland and British governments were less than cordial, relations between some of their respective followers were

---

[16] 11 & 12 Geo. VI, c. 56 (30 July 1948); above, p. 157.
[17] Cited in McCabe, *Diplomatic hist. Ire.*, p. 36.

positively frigid. On the one hand, the Unionist government had to contend with a noisy section of the party, headed by the M.P. for South Tyrone, W. P. McCoy, K.C., who wanted to cut the links with a socialist Britain and obtain dominion status for Northern Ireland. On the other hand the Labour government at Westminster had to deal with a group of several dozen backbenchers, of whom the most prominent was an English M.P. of Ulster provenance, Geoffrey Bing, who considered the regime at Stormont to be hopelessly reactionary and corrupt. These critics made themselves most felt during the passage of the Northern Ireland Act, 1947,[18] which extended the power of the Northern Ireland parliament to legislate on the social services, transport, and several other matters. Bing and his friends strongly objected to this increase in the powers of an institution that (they claimed) had used its existing powers in a dictatorial and discriminatory way. By the end of 1948, Unionist leaders in the north were feeling distinctly insecure. When, in January 1949, Sir Basil Brooke called a general election, it was interpreted at the time as being a demonstration to Westminster quite as much as to Dublin of the strength of Unionist determination to maintain the status quo intact. In this it was undoubtedly successful. Unionists won thirty-seven seats, with independent unionists winning two more. The anti-partition opposition was confined to its usual safe eleven seats (nationalist 9, Independent Labour 1, Socialist Republican 1). Most significant of all, the Labour party, which had always tried to sit on the fence with regard to the partition issue, was wiped out. Ulstermen were in no mood for trimmers. Those who supported the union would vote only for candidates whose own support for the union was equally firm.

Fortified by this display of support, in the early months of 1949 Sir Basil Brooke engaged in some tough negotiations with Westminster. The British government was preparing legislation to cover the consequences of the south's secession from the commonwealth—for instance, to declare that Irish citizens would not be treated as foreigners—and the Stormont government wanted certain safeguards for Northern Ireland included. One was a restriction on the franchise for Irish citizens living in Northern Ireland. Here, it obtained less than it had hoped: all that the British government conceded was a three-months residence qualification for all voters—British subjects as well as Irish citizens—in Northern Ireland, a qualification that was not required in the rest of the United Kingdom. The other item that Stormont asked for was a guarantee that the constitutional status of Northern Ireland should not be altered without its consent. Here, it obtained what it sought. The Ireland bill (1949), when published, was found to include a clause stating that 'in no event will Northern Ireland or any part thereof cease to be part of his majesty's dominions and of the United Kingdom without the consent of the parliament of Northern Ireland.'

---

[18] 10 & 11 Geo. VI, c. 37 [U.K.] (31 July 1947).

The publication of this bill raised a storm of indignation in the twenty-six counties. A special session of the dáil passed unanimously a resolution protesting against the introduction in the British parliament of legislation 'purporting to endorse and continue the existing partition of Ireland'. The bill, however, went through the Westminster parliament notwithstanding.[19] Attlee pointed out that the Irish government had only itself to blame: there would have been no need for Westminster to pass legislation on Ireland at all, had not the Dublin government decided to declare a republic. But, if legislation were introduced, then it was inevitable that some guarantee of the status quo in Northern Ireland should be included. To omit such a guarantee would itself be an alteration of the status quo; it would suggest that the position of Northern Ireland had become bargainable. It is hard not to feel, in short, that the inter-party government had bungled the negotiations. It had decided to repeal the external relations act without consulting the British government.[20] This was within its rights; but it could not then complain if the British government decided to draft its constitutional legislation without consulting the Irish government. The period 1945–9 ended, then, with an abrupt reversal of alliances. For most of the time the Labour government in Britain had appeared on cordial terms with the two successive Irish governments, and it had been the unionist government at Stormont that appeared to be out in the cold. But the period ended with the Stormont regime winning the strongest guarantee that it had yet secured from a British government, and with the Irish government feeling indignant and humiliated.[21] The scene was set for the ensuing period, in which relations between Dublin and Westminster, and between Dublin and Stormont, reached their most glacial level.

[19] 12, 13, & 14 Geo. VI, c. 41 [U.K.] (2 June 1949).
[20] The Republic of Ireland Act, 1948 (1948/22; 21 Dec. 1948) repealed the external relations act, and provided for the declaration of a republic, which came into force on 18 Apr. 1949, when Ireland left the commonwealth.
[21] Attlee believed that cutting the last ties with the commonwealth was more important to southern ministers than ending partition. In fact, they probably hoped to achieve both, though (failing to grasp Britain's commitment to those who had stood by her during the war) in the short term their actions made the attainment of Irish unity more remote (Brian Barton, 'Relations between Westminster and Stormont during the Attlee premiership' in *Irish Political Studies*, vii (1992), p. 19).

CHAPTER X

Economic crisis and political cold war, 1949–57

J. H. WHYTE

In the Republic of Ireland, the years covered by this chapter were, by Irish standards, ones of exceptional political instability. There were three changes of government, and three general elections, in eight years. The inter-party government lasted only till 1951, when it lost ground at a general election and was replaced by Fianna Fáil. The incoming government was in its turn defeated in 1954 and replaced by the second inter-party government. The second inter-party government survived till 1957 when it was once again defeated by Fianna Fáil. A feature of all these governments down to the general election of 1957 was that they relied on independents and had no safe majority in the dáil. A fuller account and explanation is necessary of this long period of instability.

The inter-party government appeared unshaken by the events surrounding the declaration of the Republic in 1949. Irish public opinion does not appear to have blamed it for the Ireland act at Westminster, and—apart from a snap defeat on a minor issue early in 1950—it remained parliamentarily secure for eighteen months. By the end of 1950, however, clouds were beginning to gather. The cost of living was rising rapidly. Two independent deputies representing rural areas withdrew their support from the government on the grounds that it was not doing enough for farmers. The government's reputation was damaged by what came to be known as the 'battle of Baltinglass', an affair sparked off by the appointment by the minister for posts and telegraphs of a political supporter as postmaster of Baltinglass, over the head of a well qualified and popular local candidate. The minister eventually backed down, but only after pickets had forcibly prevented telephone engineers removing the local switchboard to the new postmaster's house, and a great deal of feeling against political jobbery had been whipped up. But the most serious difficulty with which the government had to deal was what has gone down in history as 'the mother-and-child scheme crisis'.

The origins of this crisis went back to the final days of the previous government, which in 1947 had passed a health act providing, among other things, for a free mother-and-child welfare scheme to be extended to the entire population. The act had given sweeping powers of inspection to the dispensary doctors who were to administer the scheme, and unlike similar schemes in other countries it made no provision for free choice of doctor. One would not be entirely unreasonable in detecting in it a hint of totalitarianism, and at the time it had been the subject of protests from doctors, from the Fine Gael party in parliament, and (privately) from the catholic bishops. Significantly, this was the first time since the foundation of the state that an Irish government had received a formal protest from the hierarchy against a specific piece of legislation. The government, however, had ignored these protests and the act was on the statute book when the inter-party administration took over in February 1948. The new government decided to implement the act, while introducing modifications to make it less objectionable. The task fell to the energetic young minister for health, Dr Noel Browne, and in June 1950 he circulated a draft mother-and-child welfare scheme to the Irish Medical Association for discussion.

The scheme was designed to meet many of the criticisms of the parent act. For instance, it included provision for choice of doctor. However, it was fiercely attacked by the Irish Medical Association, objecting particularly to its free-for-all nature, which would, the association believed, strike a crippling blow at private medical practice and tend in the long run to convert all doctors into salaried state servants. This objection, along with others, was also taken up by the catholic hierarchy, and in October 1950 a committee of bishops conveyed the hierarchy's objections to Browne.

During the following months, however, Browne pressed ahead with his scheme. He believed that in his conversation with the bishops in October 1950 he had satisfied their objections, and that he had nothing further to worry about from that quarter. He concentrated on his antagonists in the Irish Medical Association and finally, in March 1951, announced that they were indulging in delaying tactics and that he would implement the scheme despite their opposition. He believed that he had enough support in the junior ranks of the profession to enable him to defy the I.M.A. At this point, however, the archbishop of Dublin, John Charles McQuaid, repeated his objections to the scheme.[1] Browne, believing that he had satisfied the bulk of the bishops and that this was McQuaid's personal view, appealed to the hierarchy for a ruling. The hierarchy unanimously condemned the mother-and-child scheme, but with one small modification. Browne had asked for a ruling on whether the scheme was contrary to catholic moral teaching; the hierarchy replied that it was contrary to catholic *social* teaching. Browne, claiming that this was an important distinction, asked the cabinet to back him in persevering with his scheme. The cabinet refused, and on 11 April 1951 Browne resigned.

[1] John Cooney, *John Charles McQuaid: ruler of catholic Ireland* (Dublin, 1999), ch. 17.

There are many more ramifications to the mother-and-child controversy than this bald summary might suggest. An important factor was that Browne's relations with his colleagues had already deteriorated even before his resignation. Some of them found him personally uncongenial. Others doubted whether his scheme could be implemented against the opposition of the I.M.A. With his party leader, Seán MacBride, he was engaged in a fierce dispute, originating not in the mother-and-child scheme but in different interpretations of party strategy. Normally, in a coalition government, a minister might expect to obtain his strongest support from those ministers who were his party colleagues; but in Browne's case, thanks to this quarrel, his party colleague in the cabinet, MacBride, was not his warmest ally but his bitterest opponent.

None the less, when all this is said, the inter-party government did not come well out of the episode. Two interpretations were possible. Either it could be said that they cravenly abandoned a scheme as soon as the catholic bishops objected; or else it could be said that, though they never really liked Browne's scheme, they were too frightened of the electoral risks of standing up to him until the hierarchy, by its intervention, let them off the hook. Either way, they looked like men who did not have the courage of their convictions.[2]

The crisis raised wider questions about church–state relations in the post-war republic. Some have argued that it proved Ireland to be a theocratic state, where the power of the catholic hierarchy was decisive in any matter in which it chose to intervene. Others have rejected this, seeing the bishops as stooges used by lay politicians to get rid of Browne. Neither side is wholly convincing. Clearly the intervention of the hierarchy had a decisive effect; on the other hand, the bishops' opposition was only one of the forces that Browne had aroused against himself. Whether the hierarchy's intervention would have been so decisive without these other factors seems uncertain. The episode shows that the hierarchy enjoyed great influence, but it would be unreasonable to deduce the exact nature and scope of that influence from

---

[2] John Whyte's detailed discussion of the mother-and-child controversy in *Ch. & state* (1980 ed.) has been widely praised as a model piece of historiography. A number of subsequent works now complement that treatment; notably Ruth Barrington, *Health, medicine and politics in Ireland, 1900–1970* (Dublin, 1987), and Eamonn McKee, 'Church–state relations and the development of Irish health policy: the mother-and-child scheme, 1944–53' in *I.H.S.*, xxv, no. 98 (Nov. 1986), pp 159–94. McKee plays down the importance of a clash between a 'vocational' and a 'bureaucratic' understanding of government and argues instead that the hierarchy's intervention was prompted largely by concern voiced by conductors of convent schools and by the medical profession. J. J. Lee has argued that Browne was his own worst enemy, and notes that he neglected to obtain cabinet approval before embarking on the scheme. Lee also points out that in addition to its principal objections, the medical profession feared the scheme would reduce doctors' incomes (*Ire. 1912–85*, pp 315–16, 318). Browne published his own account of the episode in *Against the tide* (Dublin, 1986), in which he presented it as a straightforward clash between church and state.

this episode alone. More broadly, anyone seeking to determine how the church–state relationship worked would need to take into account the catholic church's hold on the loyalty of the people; a tradition of independence from clerical guidance on certain issues; a tradition of church–state aloofness; the uniquely strong church grip on education; and the authoritarian strain in Irish culture. Accordingly, it is impossible to give a simple answer to the question of the extent of the hierarchy's influence on Irish politics in this period: the answer would always depend on the circumstances.[3]

The mother-and-child scheme crisis virtually brought the first inter-party government to an end. It meant the defection from the government benches not only of Browne himself (who now sat as an independent) but of two other deputies who joined with him in deploring the government's decision. This made the ministerial majority extremely narrow; when, three weeks later, three rural deputies announced their intention of voting against the government, its majority disappeared altogether. Costello, without waiting for a defeat in the dáil, called a general election. The results showed a net gain for Fianna Fáil of only one seat, and at first it seemed possible that the inter-party government would survive. But on the reassembly of the dáil, the proposal that Costello be renominated as taoiseach was defeated by 72 votes to 74. Among those voting against Costello were Noel Browne and two of his allies among the independent deputies. De Valera thereupon resumed office with a team of Fianna Fáil ministers, but obliged to rely for a majority on independents.

It is not surprising that so precarious an administration produced little in the way of adventurous legislation. Probably the most important measure was the health act of 1953,[4] which, among other things, settled the question of mother-and-child services. After further negotiations with the hierarchy, it provided that the free mother-and-child service should be available, not to the entire population as originally planned, but to 85 per cent of it. The retention of a modest means test could be considered a token concession, and the substance of the government's plans remained.[5]

But the main reason why this government did not have more of a legislative record was that it faced a serious and intractable economic crisis. Everything seemed to be going wrong at once. The cost of living was rapidly rising, largely due to factors quite outside Irish control, such as the inflation caused by the Korean war. There was a wave of strikes, with a hotel-workers' strike in 1951–2 and a newspaper strike in 1952 being the most prominent.

---

[3] See Whyte, *Ch. & state* (1980), ch. 1, pp 231–8; and id., *Interpreting Northern Ireland* (Oxford, 1990), pp 155–8.

[4] 1953/26 (29 Oct. 1953).

[5] The ease with which the contentious issues were settled lends substance to McKee's claim that the mother-and-child crisis had not involved any fundamental clash of interests between church and state (McKee, 'Church–state relations', pp 193–4).

Public expenditure was rising, largely due to public demand for welfare measures such as the health act, and in 1953 reached the point where ministers declared that it must be kept from rising higher at all costs, even if this meant cutting existing services. Worst of all, perhaps, the country faced a continuous balance of payments deficit. It had ended the war with vast sterling balances, but these had now largely been dissipated with little to show for them; the time was coming when the country would have used up all its savings and, if something drastic were not done first, a savage cut in the standard of living would impose itself.

The government decided that it would do something drastic. An extremely stiff budget in 1952 raised taxes and cut subsidies, and the budget of 1953 continued this policy. These measures, it could be claimed, served their purpose. Government expenditure was kept under control and the balance of payments deficit was for a brief period almost wiped out. But unfortunately they had other effects which were less palatable and more obvious to the public. The cut in food subsidies raised the cost of living. The rise in taxes and in living costs had a severely deflationary effect; employment dropped and emigration rose. The government's popularity suffered severely in consequence, and in March 1954 by-elections in two widely separated constituencies, Cork city and Louth, produced a heavy swing against Fianna Fáil. De Valera announced that as soon as financial provision had been made for the ensuing financial year, a general election would be held.

In the general election of May 1954 Fianna Fáil, helped perhaps by tax concessions in the pre-election budget, did less badly than the by-elections of two months previously might have led one to expect. None the less, the party suffered a net loss of three seats, while the opposition parties gained ground. When the dáil met, Costello was elected taoiseach for the second time, and formed the second inter-party government. It consisted of Fine Gael, Labour, and Clann na Talmhan ministers. These three parties between them mustered seventy-three deputies—almost exactly half the membership of a dáil of 147. With the aid of Clann na Poblachta, whose three deputies supported the government while refusing to accept office, and of some of the five independents, they had a safe majority.

The path of the inter-party government of 1954–7 proved, however, to be no easier than that of the Fianna Fáil government of 1951–4. Like its predecessor, it faced economic problems of daunting severity. The balance of payments deficit—which Fianna Fáil seemed momentarily to have eliminated—reappeared, widened rapidly, and reached proportions of unprecedented severity by the early part of 1956. This was due to various causes. On the one hand, bad weather and changes in British agricultural policy reduced Irish agricultural exports to the British market—by far the most important section of the Irish export trade. On the other hand, a round of wage increases in 1955 increased consumption at home and therefore raised imports. It was politically difficult for a coalition of which the Labour party was an important component to resist such wage increases, but before long the government was paying for its failure to do so. In 1956, the minister for finance was obliged to announce unprecedented measures to rectify the balance of payments deficit. A series of import levies, introduced in March and extended in July, placed additional duties on almost the whole range of Irish imports, in the hope of reducing their volume. In this, the import levies were successful: 1957 was to produce the first balance of payments surplus since 1946. But, like the deflationary measures of the previous government, they had disagreeable short-term consequences. Unemployment rose still higher, and emigration rose to cataclysmic proportions. After six years of virtual stagnation at a time when every other country in Europe was enjoying rapid economic growth, the Irish people seemed overwhelmed by a panic loss of self-confidence. As one writer, T. P. Coogan, has put it: 'I remember only too vividly the depressing experience of saying goodbye seemingly every week to yet another bank clerk, lawyer, student, carpenter, or whatever—all of them emigrating. "This bloody country is finished" was a phrase heard with dirgelike regularity.'[6] In 1957, net emigration almost equalled the total number of births for the year. If this continued, there would soon be no country left.

It can be said in favour of the inter-party government that it initiated some of the policies that appear to have lifted the Republic out of the rut in the years since 1957. It sought to improve agricultural productivity by increasing investment and extending educational services. As far as industrial expansion was concerned, it began the policy of attracting foreign investors and of giving special incentives to export leaders. William Norton, who held the portfolio of industry and commerce in the second inter-party government, visited Germany and the United States in search of foreign investment. Tax remissions were granted to profits made from exports, and grants offered for factory buildings. Last but not necessarily least, it was the minister for finance in this government, Gerard Sweetman, who selected as secretary of his department T. K. Whitaker, then a young and relatively junior civil servant, to whose plans many attribute a great share of the credit for the economic recovery that set in after 1957.

At the time, however, it was too soon for the public to detect the possible long-term benefits of the government's economic policy. All it knew was that taxation was high, unemployment rife, and emigration worse than it had ever been. Simultaneously—although this will be dealt with in a later section of this chapter—the government dissatisfied many by its shilly-shallying with regard to the I.R.A. By-elections began to go against the government, and in January 1957 Clann na Poblachta announced that it could no longer give the

---

[6] T. P. Coogan, *Ireland since the rising* (London, 1966), p. 107.

government its support. This meant that the administration was no longer sure of a majority, and Costello decided to go to the polls. At the general election of March 1957, the parties supporting the inter-party government suffered a serious defeat. Fianna Fáil returned with seventy-eight seats out of a total of 147, and for the first time in nine years a single party had a safe majority in Dáil Éireann.

Along with the political instability and the recurring economic crises, another phenomenon was noticeable during these years in the Republic. It was the growth of what might be labelled as 'clericalism'—a tendency for the influence of the catholic church to be, if not objectively greater than in previous years, at any rate more visible. This was shown in all sorts of different ways. An early example was the rise of Maria Duce, an organisation formed after the war whose specific platform was the complaint that article 44 of the constitution did not pay sufficient honour to the catholic church. The article recognised the 'special position' of the catholic church as 'the guardian of the faith professed by the great majority of the citizens', but Maria Duce wanted it to go further and acknowledge the catholic church as the one true church. The influence of Maria Duce was limited, and it had no success with a campaign launched in 1949 to persuade local authorities to pass resolutions calling for the amendment of article 44; but it cannot be written off as entirely insignificant. It could attract crowds of thousands to some of its demonstrations, and it and its successor organisation, Firinne, remained active throughout the 1950s. At the very least, it was significant that the movement should have flourished at that moment in Irish history, and not earlier or later.

Another sign of the times was the tendency of certain judges, notably the president of the high court, George Gavan Duffy, to give a more catholic cast to judicial decisions. The most famous instance was the Tilson judgement of 1950, when first the high court, and then on appeal the supreme court, ruled that the courts would, in some circumstances at least, enforce the pre-nuptial undertaking required by the catholic church in mixed marriages, whereby the parents agreed that all the children of the marriage should be brought up as catholics. The previous common-law rule was that these pre-nuptial promises had no legal force.[7]

Nor was the 'clericalism' of these years simply manifested by zealous laymen. Some of the bishops took a share in it, and showed a willingness to pronounce on public affairs which their predecessors had on the whole avoided since the civil war. The mother-and-child scheme crisis is the best-known instance, but it was not the only one. There was also the negotiation between the hierarchy and the Fianna Fáil government on the terms of the

---

[7] For the Tilson case and a wider discussion of the question of mixed marriages, see Kurt Bowen, *Protestants in a catholic state* (Dublin, 1983), pp 40–46.

health act of 1953. Again, in 1955 the archbishop of Dublin, Dr McQuaid, aroused controversy by calling for the cancellation of a football match with a visiting team from communist Yugoslavia. The match was not cancelled, but the government withdrew facilities such as the use of an army band and the provision of a radio commentary, which had previously been promised.[8] Earlier in the same year, the bishop of Cork, Cornelius Lucey, aroused controversy when, in a speech to a religious congress at Killarney, he defended the actions of the bishops in the health-service controversies of 1951 and 1953 in remarkably absolute terms. He said that the bishops 'were the final arbiters of right and wrong even in political matters. In other spheres the state might for its own good reasons ignore the advice of the experts, but in faith and morals it might not.'[9]

By extending the period covered by this chapter for a few weeks after the change of government in 1957, a further striking instance of the 'clericalism' of this period can be brought in. This was the Fethard-on-Sea boycott. Fethard-on-Sea is a tiny village in County Wexford where, in May 1957, the catholic inhabitants began a boycott of the protestant minority. The reason given was that the protestants had aided one of their community, a woman married to a catholic farmer, to desert her husband and abscond to Belfast with their children, with the intention of bringing them up as protestants. Incidents like this do not arise out of a clear sky, and there was undoubtedly a record of tension in Fethard, but the episode did no good for the reputation of Irish catholics. De Valera, now taoiseach for the third time, deplored it, but the local clergy supported it and the bishop of Galway, Michael Browne, publicly defended the boycott as 'a peaceful and moderate protest'.[10]

The impression so far given in this chapter is that the years 1949–57 in the Republic were marked by political instability, economic crisis, and an oppressive clericalism. Lest the reader be left with too gloomy an impression, all three of these conclusions must be qualified. The political instability was only relative: it was the worst that the twenty-six counties had known, but even so the governments of this period averaged three years in office, a record that would have seemed stable indeed in France, Italy, or Belgium at this time. The economic crisis, though certainly real, did not hit everyone with the same force. Social services were improving during this period and there was a creditable record in house-building. It was in the early 1950s that barefoot children ceased to be a common sight in the centre of Dublin. The Republic's real shame was not that it was not growing economically, but that it was growing so much more slowly than its neighbours. Similarly with the growth of 'clericalism': the incidents mentioned to illustrate the extent of

[8] Keogh, *Twentieth-century Ire.*, pp 228–9.
[9] Quoted in Whyte, *Ch. & state*, p. 312.
[10] The incident is discussed more fully in Whyte, *Ch. & state*, pp 322–5.

clericalism could also be used to illustrate its limitations and the resistance it was liable to arouse. After all, Maria Duce, noisy and active though it was, did fail to secure the support from public representatives for which it campaigned. Noel Browne did resist the hierarchy over the mother-and-child scheme, and received considerable public sympathy. The Yugoslav football match did take place despite the archbishop's opposition. The Fethard-on-Sea boycott was denounced by many catholics, from the taoiseach down. As far as the church was concerned, this was a period of what the French call *contestation* rather than of dominance, in which the views of church leaders were providing more controversy than they had since the early 1920s.

None the less, when all these provisos are made, it is probably fair to say that the years 1949–57 were the gloomiest in the history of the twenty-six-county state. Its people were confused, leaderless, unable to see a way out of their difficulties. They saw themselves falling progressively behind their neighbours, and in increasing proportion were simply giving up the effort to make a living at home. By the end of the period there seemed to be a crisis of the national morale.

NORTHERN Ireland during this period was comparatively free of such troubles. Politically, the province displayed an even greater than usual stability. It went without saying that the Unionist party remained permanently in power: in fact there was not even a change of prime minister during these years. Sir Basil Brooke (Lord Brookeborough as he became in 1952)[11] maintained an unshaken dominance as head of the government. There were a number of ministerial changes, but these were normally due to the death or retirement of older ministers and their replacement by younger men. There was only one instance during these years of an officeholder being dismissed or resigning because of a policy difference. This was the attorney general, Edmond Warnock, who was required to resign in 1956 after he had criticised a housing bill. The only general election during the period, in 1953, produced but trifling changes.

Ecclesiastically, too, the 'clericalism' we have observed among catholics in the Republic had no comparable importance in the north. In Northern Ireland catholics were in a minority, and no parallel phenomenon was to be seen among the protestant denominations that constituted the majority. Indeed, so far as the north was concerned, the main importance of 'clericalist' tendencies in these years was to provide staple fare for unionist propaganda. Every fresh illustration of clerical influence in the Republic was seized on as further justification of the unionist stand. This was particularly true of those episodes that occurred early enough in the year to be referred to at the Orange celebrations on 12 July. The mother-and-child crisis, for instance,

[11] For a detailed treatment of Brooke, see Barton, *Brookeborough*.

was mentioned on practically every platform in July 1951. Dr Lucey's Killarney speech provided ammunition for the Orange day celebrations in 1955, and the Fethard-on-Sea boycott occurred in time to be used at the speech-making in 1957.

Economically, the province was far from trouble-free. Linen, once its staple industry, was in inexorable decline. The acreage under flax was rapidly dropping and has since disappeared altogether; such linen factories as still operate are dependent on imported raw material. The shipbuilding industry, once Ulster's second staple industry, faced recurrent anxieties over whether there would be a sufficiently continuous stream of orders to maintain its capacity. The aircraft industry faced anxieties similar to those of shipbuilding. Emigration, while running at nothing like the level reached in the south, was persistent and substantial. Above all, the unemployment rate remained obstinately high.[12]

None the less, the north had considerably more success in grappling with its economic problems during these years than had the south. The decisive factor was the availability of aid from Westminster. This was provided, grudgingly at first, and then with increasing lavishness as Britain's own economic problems appeared to be diminishing. In 1954, for instance, when changes in British agricultural policy put farmers in both parts of Ireland under a disadvantage, those in the north received a special grant as compensation, which those in the south did not. In 1956, when there was a credit squeeze in Britain, the chancellor of the exchequer specifically exempted Northern Ireland from some of its effects. Throughout the period, the British government placed a proportion of its defence contracts with the Belfast shipbuilding and aircraft industries, and, while the size of these contracts never fully satisfied northern wishes, they none the less made a considerable contribution to the northern economy.

Above all, the Stormont regime's efforts to attract foreign investment both began earlier than in the south and were pursued with more determination and success. Already by 1953, measures such as the Industries Development Acts (N.I.), 1945 to 1953, and the Reequipment of Industry Acts (N.I.), 1951 to 1953,[13] offered substantial incentives to businessmen wishing to set up new industries or expand existing ones. By the end of this period, major new factories had been built for such firms as Dupont at Derry.

It was in this period that Northern Ireland was most obviously drawing away from the Republic economically. Though unemployment was worse than in the south, on every other index the north's performance was better.

---

[12] In N.I. employment in textiles alone fell from a peak of 76,000 in 1951 to 51,000 in 1958 (Liam Kennedy, *The modern industrialisation of Ireland, 1940–1988* (Dublin, 1989), p. 11).

[13] The industries development acts comprised 1945, c. 12 (29 Aug. 1945), 1950, c. 27 (21 Dec. 1950), and 1953, c. 17 (19 May 1953); the reequipment of industry acts comprised 1951, c. 2 (23 Jan. 1951), and 1953, c. 8 (17 Feb. 1953).

Capital investment was higher, *per capita* income was higher, social welfare benefits were superior. Northern Ireland had a television service from 1953, whereas the Republic did not obtain one till December 1961. Indeed even the unemployment rate paradoxically reflected this. If it was higher than in the south, part of the reason may have been that unemployment benefit was higher and so the unemployed could survive on it. In the Republic, they had little choice but to emigrate.

The relative prosperity of Northern Ireland in these years did not, however, mean that the province just sank into apathy. One further feature of northern life in this period is worth commenting on: it is the vigour of controversy within the ruling Unionist party. The Unionist party had always been a coalition of divergent interests, and had always therefore experienced a considerable measure of intra-party disagreement. But these disagreements seemed more varied in their subject-matter, and more frequent in their incidence, in the years 1949–57 than they had been in any previous period.[14]

Sometimes the disagreement was on a regional basis, as when the County Down members objected to closures on the Belfast & County Down Railway in 1949, or when, in the same year, Belfast members managed to prevent the absorption of the city's fire service by the Northern Ireland Fire Authority. Sometimes the cleavage on an economic issue was between a right and a left of the party, such as when, in 1950, the more radical members objected to the introduction of health service charges, or when in the following year the more conservative members secured a reduction in estate duty, which would, they claimed, benefit local family businesses. A particularly sharp disagreement on an economic issue occurred in 1956, when a bill to decontrol rents was ferociously opposed by Unionists sitting for working-class constituencies, and was only passed after extensive concessions had been made.

Another crop of disagreements arose over attitudes to the anti-unionist (or, which was practically the same thing, the catholic) minority. At the outset of this period, the immediate issue was education. Many unionists, and particularly the Orange order, objected to what they considered was the undue generosity shown to voluntary schools by the Education Act (N.I.), 1947, and made persistent efforts to get its terms revised. On the whole the government stood firm, and the only modification secured was a minor one; by an act of 1951[15] it was arranged that henceforth the state would pay only 65 per cent of the employer's contribution to the national insurance scheme for teachers in voluntary schools, as against 100 per cent, which it had been paying till then. But in the meantime, the minister responsible for the 1947

[14] For a provocative discussion of intra-unionist tensions, see Paul Bew, Peter Gibbon, and Henry Patterson, *The state in Northern Ireland, 1921–72: political forces and social classes* (Manchester, 1979), pp 129–45. A revised edition of this work appeared under the title *Northern Ireland 1921–1994: political forces and social classes* (London, 1994).
[15] 1951, c. 10 (29 Mar. 1951), s. 8.

act, Lt.-col. Samuel Hall-Thompson, had been forced to resign, and in the general election of 1953 he was unseated by an independent unionist, Norman Porter, who campaigned against him on the ground that he was too soft towards catholics.

Hardly had the education controversy died away than another arose, this time on the question of flag-flying. The question of what flag should be allowed to fly in what area had always been a tense one in Northern Ireland. A set of conventions had grown up whereby, in practice, the union flag was not normally flown in areas where unionists were a minority and no one tried to fly a tricolour in areas where nationalists were a minority. But 1953, being the year of the coronation of Queen Elizabeth II, was a vintage one for flag-flying, and in some areas enthusiastic loyalists started putting out union flags where this had not previously been usual. In several places this led to incidents, and the police, under the direction of the then minister for home affairs, Brian Maginess, directed the flags to be taken down. Maginess then came under criticism from many of his fellow unionists. The episode was settled the following year, when Maginess was promoted to be minister for finance, and a new minister for home affairs, G. B. Hanna, carried the Flags and Emblems (Display) Act, 1954,[16] which made it illegal to prevent the flying of a union flag anywhere in the province.

Another controversy suddenly erupted in 1956, this time on a question of social services. Northern Ireland policy hitherto had been to maintain strict parity with Britain, extending benefits and raising contributions *pari passu* with Westminster. In May 1956, however, the minister for labour and national insurance, Ivan Neill, seized the occasion of an announcement by Westminster of a rise in family allowances to propose a modification in the scheme as it affected Northern Ireland. Instead of granting a flat-rate increase in the allowances for all children, Neill proposed that there should be a large increase in the allowance for second and third children, and no increase at all for children after the third. The measure was obviously designed to discourage large families, and was defended on the grounds that the economy of the province would suffer if population growth were not checked. However, it did not escape attention that the majority of large families were catholic, and that the measure therefore would, whatever its intention, discriminate against catholics. Neill obtained the support of the Unionist parliamentary party for his scheme; but some backbenchers remained doubtful and, from outside parliament, the general assembly of the presbyterian church denounced it as unjust. What finally persuaded the government to abandon the scheme was the advice of Unionist M.P.s at Westminster that it would damage the north's image in Westminster's eyes. Coming as it did immediately after

---

[16] 1954, c. 10 (6 Apr. 1954).

the row over rent decontrol, this episode made the year 1956 an unusually disturbed one in Unionist party history.

Too much should not be made of these disputes within the Unionist party. Brookeborough's supremacy was never in doubt. Whatever he had said in the 1930s, he was not now an extremist, and he led the party from a position near its centre, able to balance liberals like Hall-Thompson or Maginess against intransigents like Harry Midgley[17] or Hanna. But these controversies are worth recalling because they make intelligible what occurred later. When in the 1960s the Unionist party almost collapsed from internecine war, this did not occur out of a clear sky. The strife of the 1960s was only an accentuation of divisions that had been quite visible in the 1950s.

Relations between the Dublin government on the one hand, and the Stormont and Westminster regimes on the other, at the beginning of the period 1949–57 were frigid. The government of the Republic was wounded by the entrenching of partition in the Ireland act of 1949, and riposted by intensifying an anti-partition campaign that was already under way. The intention, it appears, was to mobilise world opinion against the British government for maintaining an unjust arrangement. In Britain itself demonstrations were held and questionnaires sent to parliamentary candidates seeking their views on a united Ireland. It was hoped that the size of the Irish vote in some English constituencies might induce sympathy for the Irish position, though in the case of major-party candidates party discipline proved a sufficient bulwark against these blandishments. In the United States, Irish-American influence in the house of representatives was strong enough for a motion to be passed in March 1950, calling for the withdrawal of economic aid to Britain so long as Ireland remained divided, although administration lobbying caused the vote to be reversed two days later. At international conferences Irish delegates adopted what was known as the 'sore thumb' policy, raising the partition question at every opportunity. This occurred, for instance, at meetings of the Council of Europe, of the Interparliamentary Union, and of the commonwealth parliamentary conference, which Irish delegates continued, rather surprisingly, to attend. The 'sore thumb' policy was continued by the incoming Fianna Fáil government in 1951, and it was only towards the end of 1953 that it appears to have been quietly dropped, having proved totally unproductive. The truth was that it was an unpropitious time to mobilise international sentiment against Britain. Most of the countries represented at international conferences had been Britain's allies during the war, and memories were still fresh enough for them to feel some resentment, perhaps, at the south's neutrality. More important, most of these conferences were concerned with matters which, to the other participants, seemed a good

[17] For an excellent discussion of Midgley, former Labour M.P., see G. S. Walker, *The politics of frustration: Harry Midgley and the failure of Labour in Northern Ireland* (Manchester, 1985).

deal more urgent than the woes of Ireland. The Council of Europe, for instance, was concerned with building unity in a continent that had suffered horribly from its divisions in the past. The peccadilloes of the Stormont regime appeared trivial by comparison.

The deterioration of relationships between Dublin on the one hand and Stormont and Westminster on the other should not be pressed too far. The first inter-party government, at the very time that it was intensifying the anti-partition campaign, was at the same time pursuing a policy of cooperation with Northern Ireland on matters of common interest.[18] The Northern Ireland government, for its part, was ready to reciprocate: Brookeborough's repeatedly stated policy was that he was anxious to live as a good neighbour to the south. The result was shown in agreements during 1950 on the control of the River Foyle fisheries and on hydro-electric development on the River Erne. A more ambitious proposal was that the two governments should take over the Great Northern Railway, which was bankrupt, and operate it jointly. Here a mutually acceptable solution proved harder to reach, and did not survive: the railway was operated as a joint enterprise only from 1953 to 1958. However, the scheme was a proof that neither government had any objection on principle to cooperation.

None the less, the 'sore thumb' policy had important consequences. In one field they are still with us. In 1949 the North Atlantic Treaty Organisation was in process of formation as an alliance of non-communist states that felt themselves threatened by Russian expansion. The Republic of Ireland was invited to join, but refused, and still remains outside N.A.T.O. Much of the motivation for this refusal, which seems to have been generally accepted by Irish public opinion, may lie in a feeling that Ireland's best interests are served by a policy of neutrality. Such a feeling is found among Swiss and Swedes and has nothing necessarily to do with partition.[19] This, however, was not the reason officially given for the refusal to join. The argument used was that the treaty obliged all its signatories to recognise the territorial boundaries of the others, and this was something in which the Republic could never acquiesce.

Although by 1954 Irish ministers were no longer stressing the partition issue, this did not mean that it disappeared from view. What happened was that, as the politicians lost interest, so the tradition of physical-force republicanism revived. The I.R.A. survived the hammering it received from the de Valera government during the war, and in the late 1940s it began to revive. About 1950 it took a crucial policy decision that future action should

[18] See Michael Kennedy, 'Towards co-operation: Seán Lemass and north–south economic relations, 1956–65' in *Ir. Econ. & Soc. Hist.*, xxiv (1997), 42–61.
[19] The question whether post-war Ireland enjoyed the freedom of action and independence necessary to real neutrality is discussed in T. C. Salmon, *Unneutral Ireland: an ambivalent and unique security policy* (Oxford, 1989), esp. pp 286–7, 311.

be directed exclusively against the 'British forces of occupation in the six counties', and that twenty-six-county forces should be left alone. Between then and the launching of its main offensive on 12 December 1956, it was responsible for two raids on targets in England and four in Northern Ireland. Of these the best-known were an attack on Gough Barracks, Armagh, in June 1954, in which the raiders got away with over 400 weapons of various kinds, and an attack on Omagh barracks the following October, which was beaten off. Meanwhile splinter groups, tired of waiting for the I.R.A. to launch its main offensive, started operations on their own account. A group known as 'Saor Uladh' (Free Ulster) made an unsuccessful attack on Rosslea police barracks in November 1955, and another, headed by Liam Kelly and Joseph Christie, burned down a number of customs huts and other targets in November 1956. The I.R.A.'s own offensive, at the end of 1956, began with attacks on ten different targets ranging from a B.B.C. transmitter to bridges and a courthouse. Its best-known exploit was an attack on the police barracks at Brookeborough, County Fermanagh, on New Year's day 1957, which led to the death of two young I.R.A. men, Seán South and Fergal O'Hanlon.

It is hard to assess how much influence these incidents had. In the north, perhaps the most important effect was to bring the warring elements of the Unionist party closer together, and so to delay the dissolution of traditional political patterns that eventually took place in the 1960s. Otherwise, it made surprisingly little difference to the tenor of life. There were no outbursts of sectarian feeling, as there easily might have been; the casual visitor, driving through the province, was reminded only by the sandbag emplacements round police stations that anything unusual was happening.

Probably the raids had more importance in the south. There the second inter-party government, under which they came to a head, was caught in a dilemma. On the one hand, Costello himself, and most if not all of his ministers, sincerely believed that force was not the right way to undo partition. On the other hand, they were aware that there was a good deal of emotional sympathy with the raiders among the public: the funeral cortege of Seán South, for instance, from the border to his native Limerick was followed by immense crowds, and many local authorities passed resolutions of sympathy with him and his fellow victim. The Labour members of the government, in particular, were not prepared to take any serious measures against the raiders. The result was that the government followed an apparently ambivalent policy: on the one hand ministers, or some of them, denounced the raids; on the other hand they did nothing effective to stop them. Some of the raiders coming back from the attack on Gough Barracks, for instance, were picked up by gardaí but subsequently released. In several parts of the country, I.R.A. men openly drilled with the knowledge of the public and the local police. It was only after the Brookeborough raid on 1 January 1957 that the inter-party government began to take stronger measures, and known activists were arrested. Even then, they were liable to receive court sentences of three or six months for offences such as illegal possession of arms, which did not seem a very powerful deterrent.

The general election of May 1957 proved in this, as in other matters, to be a turning-point. For one thing, it demonstrated the limits of public sympathy for the illegal organisations. Sinn Féin, the political ally of the I.R.A., put up candidates in nineteen constituencies, but only four of them were elected. For another thing, the general election resulted in the return of de Valera to power. De Valera, as he had shown in the 1940s, was quite uninhibited by his own revolutionary past from taking strong measures against other revolutionaries.[20] He considered that he had a mandate from the people to govern and that the I.R.A. had not. Soon after returning to power, the government brought into force the Offences Against the State Act, 1939,[21] which contained the power to intern without trial, and between July 1957 and March 1958 130 men suspected of I.R.A. activities were interned. Although the I.R.A. did not formally abandon its campaign till 1962, from now on it was crippled.

The I.R.A. campaign of 1956–7 was perhaps of symbolic rather than practical significance. Though it took few lives and did limited damage to property, it marked the low-water mark of relations between the two parts of Ireland. The fact that the raiders could launch their attacks with impunity from republican soil aroused resentment in the north; the fact that the attacks could take place at all showed the depth of resentment that partition engendered in the south. But they got nowhere: it was obvious within a few weeks that the northern state was not going to be toppled so easily. This accordingly forced a reappraisal, a swing back to realism. The course of this swing back will be charted in the next chapter.

[20] Eunan O'Halpin, *Defending Ireland* (Oxford, 1999), chs 6–7.
[21] 1939/13 (14 June 1939).

CHAPTER XI

Economic progress and political pragmatism, 1957–63

J. H. WHYTE

FOR the Republic of Ireland, a watershed occurred in the years covered by this chapter. This was apparent to many historians and other observers in the 1960s. F. S. L. Lyons wrote of the situation being 'transformed' in the years 1957–61. T. P. Coogan, writing in 1966, described 'the new air of confidence in the future which began to blow through Ireland at the end of the 'fifties'. Garret FitzGerald identified 'a transformation of the economy of the Republic and, most important of all perhaps, a transformation of the outlook of the Irish people' in the years 1958–63. Charles McCarthy, writing in 1968, stated that 'there has been a remarkable change in our society in recent years'. Moreover there was a general consensus among these writers on the nature of the transformation. They agreed that the Republic became a more open, questioning, self-confident society. The years 1916–21 might seem the most important watershed in modern Irish history: but though they transformed the country politically, they did remarkably little to remould the social, cultural, and psychological features of the country. In all spheres except the strictly political, the years under consideration in this chapter were of more critical importance in the development of the twenty-six counties.[1]

Many causes converged to produce this revival in the Republic. One of the most important was the economic transformation of the state.[2] During the nine years 1949–57, the Republic's annual growth rate was only 1 per cent—easily the lowest in western Europe. During the next six years, 1958–64, it shot forward to 4 per cent—a respectable figure by European standards, and better than that achieved by Britain. This sudden injection of wealth exhibited itself in many different ways. Wages went up; so did social welfare benefits. A new breed of Irish entrepreneurs—such as Tony O'Reilly and

---

[1] F. S. L. Lyons, *Ireland since the famine* (London, 1973 ed.), p. 582; Coogan, *Ire. since rising*, p. 330; Garret FitzGerald, *Planning in Ireland* (Dublin and London, 1968), p. 41; Charles McCarthy, *The distasteful challenge* (Dublin, 1968), p. 112.

[2] Below, pp 460, 475–6.

Tony Ryan—came to the fore. New office blocks arose in Dublin, posing challenges for those who wished to preserve the capital's Georgian architecture. New kinds of retail outlet, the supermarket and the self-service shop, reached Ireland from abroad. The number of cars on the road leapt upwards: so much so that the Republic had to break with its easy-going tradition and introduce driving tests for new drivers. The new wealth was, of course, unevenly spread, with the east benefiting more than the west, and townspeople gaining more than farmers. Furthermore, the pace of change fell off after 1964, and the years 1964–6 saw an exceptional amount of industrial unrest. But by then the watershed had been decisively crossed; and even though the national growth rate fell in 1965 and 1966 to 2 per cent, this was still comparable with the British performance in the same years. Irish people at least had the consolation of knowing that, in terms of economic growth, they were no longer at the bottom of the European league.

Economic growth not only had a psychological effect on the people, it also helped to bring them into greater contact with foreign influences. Northern Ireland had already shown what could be done to improve the economy through attracting foreign enterprises by means of grants and loans. The same policy had been initiated in the south in a small way by the first inter-party government, which in 1949 set up the Industrial Development Authority, partly with the object of bringing in foreign capital. The I.D.A., however, was hampered by the Control of Manufactures Act, 1932,[3] which placed narrow restrictions on the employment of foreign capital in Ireland. The act could be got round, but, as James Meenan has pointed out, 'it was not easy...to explain to inquiring foreigners why their first move in Ireland must be to engage legal advisers skilled in the arts of evading the law'.[4] The obstacle was removed by the Industrial Development (Encouragement of External Investment) Act, 1958.[5] This exempted from the control of manufactures act foreign-owned industries that appeared likely to make an important contribution to Irish exports. Simultaneously a major base for such industries was provided by the establishment of the Shannon Free Airport industrial estate in County Clare. With the aid of these measures, foreign investment in the Republic increased considerably, and a number of British, American, German, French, Dutch, and even Japanese firms started production. Not all of the new firms were a success, but, for better or worse, the irruption of such firms into Irish country towns was one of the factors transforming Irish society.

More important, probably, in bringing new influences to bear was the growth of the tourist industry. Ireland's scenic variety, uncluttered roads,

---

[3] 1932/21 (29 Oct. 1932).
[4] James Meenan, *The Irish economy since 1922* (Liverpool, 1970), p. 152.
[5] 1958/16 (2 July 1958).

and quiet pace of life proved attractive to many from more industrialised countries. For British and American visitors, many of them with Irish roots, the absence of a language barrier was particularly appealing. A state-sponsored body, Bord Fáilte, was established in 1952 to organise this trade,[6] and from about 1957 it carried on an energetic campaign to expand it. Grants were made available for the reconstruction and improvement of hotels, training courses were run, a grading scheme introduced, and in 1965 a boost was given to motoring visitors by the introduction of the first car ferries across the Irish Sea. All this had its effect: between 1958 and 1964 income from tourism rose at the rate of 4 per cent a year. Many of the visitors were Irish people who had settled in Britain during the peak years of emigration in the 1950s, and who, when they returned on holiday, inevitably disseminated some of the ideas and values they had absorbed in their adopted country.

One aspect of foreign influence aroused controversy in the early 1960s. This was the buying of land by foreign nationals. 'Germans' became a general term for continental buyers of Irish land, many but not all of whom were Germans. To such buyers, Irish land was cheap, and they were prepared to offer prices that seemed highly attractive to Irish farmers with land to sell. They were sometimes insensitive to local feeling and custom, and caused resentment by closing off access to beaches. Eventually the problem was met by legal measures: in 1961, an additional stamp duty was introduced for non-nationals; from 1965, purchases by non-nationals were controlled by the land commission. But the fact that such a problem could have arisen was evidence of the unprecedented extent to which the Republic was being opened to foreign influence.

There was another way in which the Republic was increasing its foreign involvements. This was through participation in international organisations. A request to join the United Nations had been made in 1946, soon after that body had been formed, but applications had to meet the unanimous approval of the five great powers on the security council before they were accepted, and the Irish application was vetoed by the Soviet Union. This was explicable in the international situation of the time: the cold war between the communist powers and the western powers was then under way, and the Soviet Union presumably saw Ireland as a potential recruit to the western camp. Ten years later, however, the international climate had improved sufficiently for the question to be reopened, and the Republic of Ireland was allowed into the United Nations as part of a package deal whereby a number of countries on both sides of the east–west divide, whose applications had hitherto been blocked by one side or the other, were admitted

---

[6] 1952/15 (3 July 1952); the new body replaced Bord Cuartaíochta, established by the previous tourist traffic act, 1939/24 (27 July 1939).

simultaneously.[7] The Irish delegation took its place at the end of 1956, only a few months before the fall of the second inter-party government. It fell to the incoming Fianna Fáil administration and in particular its minister for external affairs, Frank Aiken, to mould the Republic's policy in this new forum. The Irish delegation was talented and articulate and soon made its mark. Aiken's policy was one of non-alignment. On the one hand the Republic, as a catholic and democratic country, had no sympathy for communism; but on the other hand, as a country that had only recently gained its independence, it could be critical of the colonial powers of the west. The Irish delegation won considerable respect for its independence of view. The Republic's permanent representative, Frederick Boland, served a term as chairman of the general assembly (1960–61), and from 1962 to 1964 the Republic held one of the non-permanent seats on the security council.

Irish participation in the United Nations brought with it the task of sharing in that body's peace-keeping role. In 1958, at the beginning of a protracted presence in that country, Irish officers acted as observers in the Lebanon. In the early 1960s Irish officers were sent to help police the ceasefire line in Kashmir, and from 1964 Irish troops were to form part of the United Nations peace-keeping force in Cyprus. But the greatest challenge occurred when in July 1960 the Belgian Congo was granted its independence and promptly lapsed into anarchy. The United Nations hurriedly organised a peace-keeping force, and the Republic of Ireland was one of the countries that provided a contingent. It was the first time that Irish troops had served away from home, and they acquitted themselves respectably. Twenty-six died on active service. Their commander, General Seán Mac Eoin, became commander of the entire United Nations force in the Congo. One Irish diplomat, Conor Cruise O'Brien, who was on secondment to the United Nations secretariat, played a spectacular part in preventing the secession of the province of Katanga. Internationally, the Republic never played a more generally esteemed role than at the time of the Congo intervention of 1960–62. There was only a limited number of countries that could play such a role successfully. Among the qualities required were a foreign policy not too overwhelmingly aligned with any of the great powers; an army sufficiently trained and disciplined to sustain a peace-keeping operation; and a political system at home of sufficient efficiency and integrity to earn world respect. Those that seemed most conspicuously to attain such standards were the Scandinavian countries. For a moment in the early 1960s, the Republic seemed to have found an international vocation for itself as a kind of honorary Scandinavian country—as a state widely respected for the efficiency with

[7] See Joseph M. Skelly, *Irish diplomacy at the United Nations, 1945–1965: national interests and the international order* (Dublin, 1997).

which it ran its own affairs and for the public spirit it showed on the world stage.[8]

The country's 'Scandinavian' moment soon passed. The growing movement for economic integration in Europe produced new pressures to which Irish foreign policy was obliged to react. Between 1958 and 1961 it looked as if these pressures might be avoided: during those years most European countries belonged either to the tightly knit European Economic Community (founded 1957) or to the more loosely structured European Free Trade Area (founded 1959), and there was no compelling reason for the Republic to belong to either. But the situation was transformed when in 1961 Britain (already a member of E.F.T.A.) decided to apply for entry to the E.E.C. As Britain was the Republic's principal trading partner, there would be great difficulties for the latter in remaining outside, and so the Irish government decided that it too would apply to join the E.E.C. This entailed a shift in foreign policy. All the existing members of the E.E.C., and all the other applicants (Britain, Norway, and Denmark) were members of a military alliance, the North Atlantic Treaty Organisation. If the Republic of Ireland were to join the Common Market, it was at least possible that she would be expected to join the alliance as well. Seán Lemass, who succeeded de Valera as taoiseach in 1959, appreciated this point, and in a number of speeches during 1962 signalised his readiness to do this if necessary. The French veto on British entry into the Common Market in January 1963 led automatically to the Irish application being put in abeyance, and no further attempt was made to enter the Common Market till 1967. However, the hope of one day entering a united Europe remained. While the Labour party, after some hesitation, came to oppose entry, Fianna Fáil and Fine Gael were united in favour. An active European movement sprang up in the country, and, in the period covered by this chapter, there were no corresponding pressure groups on the other side. The Republic was developing a new destiny, not as a good neutralist but as a good European. The direction was different, but the effect was the same: the country was becoming more involved internationally, and more open to foreign influences, than it had been before.

One further external influence on the Republic must be mentioned. It is a commonplace that the pontificate of John XXIII (1958–63) and the second Vatican council (1962–5) led to a transformation in the Roman Catholic church. This transformation had particularly important effects in so deeply catholic a country as the Republic of Ireland. For the average catholic, the most obvious changes were liturgical and devotional—the use of English or Irish instead of Latin in the mass and other services, the abandonment in

---

[8] In his massive, trenchant essay on twentieth-century Ireland, Joseph Lee draws frequent comparisons between Irish and Scandinavian experience; he often finds Irish performance wanting (see, for example, Lee, *Ire. 1912–85*, pp 597–601, 663–4).

1970 of Friday abstinence. But the change was also important in helping to make the Republic a more open society. One instance of this was the development of the ecumenical movement. For historical reasons the Roman Catholic church had for long been even more wary of contacts with other Christian bodies in Ireland than in most countries. For instance, the rule against *communicatio in sacris*—against joining in religious services of other denominations—was for years interpreted even more strictly in Ireland than elsewhere. In other countries, catholics might at least attend the marriages and funerals of their friends in other denominations; in Ireland this right was effectively denied. However, the mid 1960s saw something of a thaw in this attitude. A glance through the chronicle section of the *Irish Catholic Directory* shows a great increase in the number of ecumenical meetings and events from 1964 onwards. An example was the series of talks given by Patrick Cremin, professor of theology at Maynooth, in Trinity College, Dublin, during the Church Unity octave of 1965.

A second way in which the new climate in world catholicism helped to alter the psychological climate in Ireland can be seen in the growing freedom of discussion in the catholic church. The second Vatican council encouraged catholics to speak their minds; the process was carried to lengths that even the more liberal of the council fathers must have found disconcerting. In Ireland, the turning-point can be precisely dated: it occurred at the very end of 1963 and the beginning of 1964. Down to that time, the church had enjoyed a remarkable degree of immunity from criticism in public. But then two events happened, independently and almost simultaneously, to crack the mould. The first was that the archbishop of Dublin, John Charles McQuaid, forbade two well-known theologians of liberal inclinations, the American Fr John Courtney Murray and the Canadian Fr Gregory Baum, to speak publicly in the diocese of Dublin.[9] The fact became known, and a public controversy boiled up in the press. The second event was the publication in an English newspaper, the *Guardian*, of a series of articles highly critical of the Irish church by an expatriate journalist, Peter Lennon. These articles also provoked a public controversy in Ireland. Subsequently the church came in for far more public discussion and criticism.

However, it would be misleading to imply that the psychological changes that Ireland underwent during these years were simply the product of outside influences. Internal changes also played their part. One phenomenon of these years was the growth of scholarly, objective study of Irish society. To some extent, the instruments through which this was achieved had been forged before this period began: the Irish Management Institute was founded in 1952, the periodical *Christus Rex* in 1947, the quarterly *Administration* in 1953. Others appeared subsequently: the Institute of Public Administration

9 Cooney, *John Charles McQuaid*, p. 365.

was opened in 1957, and the Economic Research Institute (now the Economic and Social Research Institute) was established in 1960. The universities began expanding their social science departments. Serious factual research began to appear in sociology and political science. The advent of economic programming after 1958 generated a great volume of enquiry into the economy: the committee on industrial organisation, for instance, produced a series of reports on twenty-six different Irish industries. In education, a landmark in research was provided by the report of a survey team sponsored by the Organisation for European Economic Cooperation and Development into Irish educational needs. This flow of research made a significant impact. If Irish society appeared more compassionate than it used to—if there was more concern about disadvantaged groups such as the aged, the mentally ill, the itinerants—it was partly because more factual information about such groups was now available.

Not only was more research being done on Irish society, but the means for disseminating conclusions were improving. There was a visible improvement in the level of Irish journalism. New periodicals were established, such as *Business and Finance* (1964), and older ones, such as *Hibernia*, were improved. The *Irish Times*, which, after surmounting a financial crisis in the early 1960s, began to rise in circulation, brought together a distinguished team of writers. Two may be singled out for the impact they made in these years: Garret FitzGerald, who subsequently made a notable career in politics but was then known as an economic journalist, and who did much to prepare the Republic for entry into the E.E.C.; and John Healy, whose 'Backbencher' column in the *Irish Times* provided incisive comment on political and social affairs. Irish publishers, too, were improving. The Mercier Press of Cork made a special impact during this period. Founded in 1944, it had through the 1950s specialised in English translations of continental religious works; but in the 1960s it turned its attention to Irish authors publishing works about Ireland, and has since built up a notable list of attractively produced books. Radio Éireann, too, made its contribution. The Thomas Davis lectures that it began to sponsor in 1953 provided a popular treatment, for the general listener, of many aspects of Irish scholarship, and are usually published later in book form.

One cause, or at least symptom, of the growing openness of Irish society in these years was the decline of censorship. During the 1940s and 1950s the censorship of publications board had come under increasing criticism for the stringency with which it interpreted its brief.[10] The number of books banned, which had averaged a little over a hundred a year during the 1930s, reached a peak of over six hundred a year in the period 1950–55. Many of them were books considered as classics in other countries; among them were

[10] Below, pp 504–5.

titles by André Gide, Jean-Paul Sartre, Ernest Hemingway, John Steinbeck, Tennessee Williams, and Graham Greene. The board seemed particularly hostile to Irish writers, and among those who had titles banned were Frank O'Connor, Sean O'Faolain, Edna O'Brien, Liam O'Flaherty, Austin Clarke, and Brendan Behan. However, in 1956–7 the policy of the board was transformed. This was done, not by legislation, but by replacing the existing members of the board by a more liberal-minded team, a process in which two successive ministers for justice—James Everett of the second inter-party government, and Oscar Traynor of Fianna Fáil—shared. The board was not entirely free from subsequent criticism—witness the controversy over the banning of John McGahern's *The dark* in 1965—but it did generate far less controversy than in the past. Subsequently the film censorship, which had come under criticism similar to that directed at the literary censorship, was also liberalised. In 1964 the minister for justice, Brian Lenihan, appointed a new appeal board, which reversed some of the more stringent decisions of the film censor, and so opened a wider range of films to the viewing public.

The most potent new influence within the Republic, however, was without doubt television. To some extent its influence began even before the period covered by this chapter. From the early 1950s it was possible to pick up the signals of the B.B.C. and I.T.V. transmitters in areas near enough to Wales or Northern Ireland, and hence developed one of the most characteristic features of the Dublin skyline in this period—the forest of tall aerials erected to pick up the distant signals of British transmitters. But the real impact began with the inauguration of a domestic service, Telefís Éireann, on 31 December 1961. Telefís Éireann, unlike the British stations, covered the whole of the Republic; and its programmes catered directly for an Irish audience. Before long, Telefís Éireann was provoking an examination of established Irish institutions and values on a scale hitherto unknown. The nature of the medium dictated this. Whereas a newspaper can get away with a single, slanted, presentation of news for years on end, the only effective way for a television station to handle current issues is by way of discussion; and once discussion is allowed, then rival views are called for. It took Telefís Éireann some years to work its way through to a full appreciation of the possibilities of the medium, and its greatest impact did not come until the late 1960s. But already in the period covered by this chapter its influence was growing. In programmes such as 'The late late show', compèred by Gay Byrne, there was increasingly frank discussion of topics that hitherto had rarely been discussed in public, ranging from the role of the clergy to sexual mores.

One final cause of the transformation of Irish society that took place in these years must be mentioned: the change in political leadership. All three political parties changed their leaders in these years. In Fine Gael Richard Mulcahy gave way to James Dillon in 1959, and the latter in his turn was succeeded by Liam Cosgrave in 1965.[11] In the Labour party William Norton, who had been leader since 1932, retired in 1960 and was replaced by Brendan Corish. However, it is fair to say that the new leadership in the opposition parties was not, at least in the years covered by this chapter, associated with any sharp change in style or policy. The really important changes took place in Fianna Fáil, which was in office throughout this period. Eamon de Valera retired from active politics in 1959, on being elected president of the Republic. He was succeeded as taoiseach and as leader of the party by Seán Lemass, who remained in office till 1966. Lemass was, like de Valera, a 1916 veteran; but he was seventeen years younger, and in many ways seemed to belong to a different generation. Where de Valera's greatest passion, apart from the ending of partition, was the restoration of the Irish language, Lemass never mastered Irish. His main interests lay in economics and administration. He had been an energetic and successful minister for industry and commerce, and he had a restless, questing mind, always seeking better ways of doing things. Under him a generation of vigorous new ministers came to the fore. A start had already been made by de Valera before he retired from politics: on the formation of his last government in 1957 he brought three new men into the cabinet: Jack Lynch, Neil Blaney, and Kevin Boland, then aged 40, 35, and 40 respectively. Under Lemass, these three found promotion, and were soon joined by others with equal or greater drive and ambition: Patrick Hillery in 1959, Charles Haughey in 1961, Brian Lenihan in 1964, Donogh O'Malley and George Colley in 1965, to name the best-known. Simultaneously, the old guard of ministers who had served with de Valera was being steadily reduced. After 1965 the only survivor of the original 1932 team, apart from Lemass himself, was Frank Aiken, the minister for external affairs. These years, then, saw a generational change in Irish politics. A new team came to the fore, whose technocratic, managerial interests fitted in well with the new mood in the country.[12]

Despite the dramatic psychological changes that swept over the Republic in this period, in internal politics these years were the most uneventful since the foundation of the twenty-six-county state. Only a few episodes need be singled out for mention. In 1959 occurred the first attempt since 1940 to amend the constitution. De Valera's government proposed that proportional representation be replaced by a British-type electoral system, with single-member seats filled by simple majority. This change was likely to produce governments with larger majorities, and so to reduce governmental instability. But on the other hand the party most likely to benefit by it was Fianna

[11] For Cosgrave see Stephen Collins, *The Cosgrave legacy* (Dublin, 1996).
[12] Lemass has been the subject of extensive scholarly treatment. For widely differing perspectives, see Paul Bew and Henry Patterson, *Seán Lemass and the making of modern Ireland, 1945–66* (Dublin, 1982); Brian Farrell, *Seán Lemass* (Dublin, 1983); Lee, *Ire. 1912–85*, pp 371–408, and most recently Horgan, *Lemass*.

Fáil, so it is not surprising that opinion split along party lines, with Fianna Fáil supporting the change, and all the other parties opposing it. A long-drawn-out parliamentary battle followed, which was noteworthy for producing the first occasion since the 1937 constitution was adopted in which the senate rejected a government bill. The powers of the senate, however, were so limited that it could do no more than delay the measure for ninety days, and it passed through the oireachtas by May. In June it was put to the people in a referendum, and rejected by a margin of 34,000 votes. However, the poll was not without consolation for Fianna Fáil. In the presidential election held simultaneously, de Valera was victorious over Fine Gael's General Seán Mac Eoin by a majority of 120,000. These contrasting results were a comment on the political sophistication of the Irish voter.

Another event of 1959 was the reunification of the trade union movement. The Irish Trade Union Congress and the Congress of Irish Unions came together in a new organisation, the Irish Congress of Trade Unions. The original causes of the split of 1945 had disappeared or diminished. In so far as they were personal, they were removed by the retirement of William O'Brien in 1946 and the death of James Larkin in 1947. The division of the labour movement into two factions obviously weakened each of them, and there was no good reason why it should be allowed to continue.

The next event of interest was the general election of October 1961. The Fianna Fáil majority in the general election of 1957 had been exceptionally large, so it was only to be expected that the party should lose some ground. In the event it returned with 70 seats out of 144, and had to rely on the support of independents for a majority. For most of the parliament of 1961–5 this did not matter, and Lemass's government displayed just as much energy and adventurousness as if it had a safe majority. The one critical moment occurred in 1963, when the government, faced with rising expenditure, felt obliged to introduce a new form of taxation, the turnover tax. This was an indirect tax, of $2\frac{1}{2}$ per cent, on a wide range of goods. It was bound to raise the cost of living and was therefore intensely unpopular. In the dáil, the government's majority dropped to one in the crucial division in April; the following month, a by-election in Dublin north-east showed a massive swing against Fianna Fáil. However, by the time the next by-elections occurred, in February 1964, the government's place in public esteem had improved. That month employers and trade unions, cashing in on the economic boom, negotiated a remarkably generous wage-settlement—it was agreed in principle that wages should be allowed to rise 12 per cent over the next two years. Though the government had not engineered this settlement, and indeed seems to have thought the figure too high, it benefited from the popularity, and in the Kildare and Cork city by-elections of 1964 it gained appreciably in votes, retaining one seat and gaining the other.

One event of 1963 should not be passed without mention. This was the state visit in June of the president of the United States, John F. Kennedy. President Kennedy was the great-grandson of famine emigrants, and he was the first person of Irish catholic descent to win the American presidency. His success gave vicarious pleasure to many Irish people and he received a warm welcome when he visited the Republic. One writer (Tony Gray) has written that his visit 'probably did more than any other single factor to boost Irish morale and destroy the last vestige of national self-consciousness'. Another (Donald Connery) has written that 'the essential business of creating and sustaining Irish self-confidence was given an historic boost' by the visit.[13] Such statements cannot possibly be proved, but there is no doubt that the president's movements (efficiently covered by the infant Telefís Éireann) aroused great public interest, and the visit seemed to symbolise the boom atmosphere of the early 1960s.

ANGLO–Irish relations started the period 1957–65 on a slightly uneasy footing. The I.R.A. campaign that began in 1956 was still going on, and, though the de Valera government introduced internment in July 1957, there were occasional complaints from Belfast and Westminster that Dublin was not doing all it could to prevent the I.R.A. operating. In 1959, after two years of relative quiet, the southern government released its internees. This drew a protest from the British government, and there were reports that the British government was procrastinating over trade negotiations as a means of bringing pressure. In 1961, following an I.R.A. ambush in south Armagh, there was a further protest from the British government and military tribunals were reintroduced in the Republic. Finally, on 26 February 1962 the I.R.A., complaining of lack of public support, announced the end of its campaign.[14]

However, relations between Dublin and Westminster were on the whole cordial. An earnest was the settlement in 1959 of an issue, trivial in itself, that had stirred up resentment for years—the matter of the Lane bequest. This was the name given to a valuable collection of pictures owned by Sir Hugh Lane, who had been drowned when the *Lusitania* was sunk in 1915. Lane was an Irishman who had proclaimed his intention of bequeathing his pictures to Dublin. Shortly before his death, however, in a moment of irritation, he had altered his will and left the pictures to the Tate Gallery in London. Later still, however, he had changed his mind again, and added a

---

[13] Tony Gray, *The Irish answer: an anatomy of modern Ireland* (London, 1966), p. 361; Donald S. Connery, *The Irish* (London, 1968), p. 31; Keogh, *Twentieth-century Ire.*, pp 250–52.

[14] J. Bowyer Bell, *The secret army: the I.R.A. 1916–1979* (4th ed., Swords, 1989), p. 334. During the 1960s, certain republican leaders sought to draw the republican movement to the left, to concentrate more on social, radical issues than on military struggle; see Henry Patterson, *The politics of illusion: a political history of the I.R.A.* (London, 1997) (originally published as *The politics of illusion: republicanism and socialism in modern Ireland* (London, 1989)).

codicil leaving the pictures, after all, to Dublin. The codicil was unwitnessed, and so had no legal effect. But morally it could be considered binding, and many had resented over the years the insistence of the Tate Gallery in claiming its legal rights and retaining the pictures. Under the settlement of 1959, the collection was divided in two halves, and each was to be shown alternately in Dublin and London. It was a satisfactory ending to a long-standing source of discord.[15]

Meanwhile, the Anglo–Irish trade treaty of 1948 had come up for revision. Voices had already been heard in Ireland suggesting economic integration between Ireland and Britain. Dr Juan Greene, president of the National Farmers' Association, had proposed it in 1957, and an influential economist, Patrick Lynch of University College, Dublin, also recommended it in 1958. When Lemass met the British ministers for talks in 1959, he startled them by proposing that there should be complete integration between the two economies. The Irish market would be opened completely to British industrial goods; in return, Irish agriculture would receive British subsidies and be sold in British markets under the same conditions as British produce. The proposal was rejected by the British, on the ground that the balance of advantage was weighted too much on the Irish side. A more limited agreement was then negotiated in 1960, providing in the main for the continuance of the arrangements made in 1948.[16]

COMPARED with the Republic, the years 1957–65 proved less of a watershed epoch for Northern Ireland. This was partly because some of the factors that made such an impact in the south during these years were already operating in the north—for instance, the influence of foreign investment and of television. It was partly that other changes had slighter impact in the north. Economic progress was less dramatic because the north had been doing better earlier. Foreign involvements mattered less, because the north was not a sovereign state. The changes in the Roman Catholic church brought about by Pope John XXIII and the second Vatican council affected only a minority in what remained a predominantly protestant population.

None the less these years were of considerable importance in the political history of Northern Ireland. There were signs on both sides of the community divide of an increasing readiness to break away from entrenched attitudes. On the catholic side the first faint sign of the change, perhaps, was a letter to the press by a group of catholic laymen on the eve of the Twelfth of July celebrations of 1957, disavowing the intolerant attitude of the catholic bishop of Galway over the Fethard-on-Sea boycott,[17] and calling for mutual trust. This

[15] Above, vi, 480–84; below, pp 593–4.
[16] For these agreements see Meenan, *Irish economy since 1922*, p. 79.
[17] Above, p. 285.

was followed in 1958 by a conference held by a catholic organisation, the Social Study Conference, at Garron Tower in County Antrim. Several of the papers at this conference—most notably one by G. B. Newe, secretary of the Northern Ireland Council of Social Services—urged catholics to participate more in the affairs of the province, and stressed that they might themselves, by their own attitudes, be partly responsible for the injustices of which they complained.

In the absence of public-opinion polling, which did not begin in Northern Ireland till 1967, it is hard to estimate how far attitudes such as these found echoes in the catholic community as a whole. Certainly the Garron Tower resolutions produced as much public criticism from catholics as they did public approval. Election results, however, provide a pointer to public opinion, and they suggest some movement of catholic attitudes in the late 1950s. The trend was first visible in the Stormont general election of 1958. At that election, the Northern Ireland Labour party made a breakthrough, gaining four Belfast seats. All four constituencies had protestant majorities, but two of the four had sizeable catholic minorities, and, from a comparison of voting figures, it seems that catholic voters who in previous elections had supported anti-partitionist candidates on this occasion supported Northern Ireland Labour. This was significant because the Northern Ireland Labour party supported the constitutional link with Britain. It would be a mistake to deduce from this that catholics were becoming converted to support for the union. All that can fairly be concluded is that, when faced with a choice of two candidates supporting the union, catholics would support the one who on other issues was more congenial to them. But even this was a change from previous attitudes. The same trend was seen in two other constituencies, Clifton and Iveagh, where Unionist candidates faced, both in 1953 and 1958, independent unionists of an extreme kind. In both constituencies the Unionist party poll went up, and this was attributed at the time to catholic support. Indeed in Clifton the swing was sufficient to recapture the seat for the Unionist party.

The Westminster general election of 1959 also revealed new voting trends in the catholic population. In both this election and the previous one, in 1955, Sinn Féin, the political wing of the I.R.A., put up candidates in all twelve Northern Ireland constituencies. In 1955 they gained 26 per cent of the popular vote—and therefore, presumably, a substantial majority of the catholic vote—and two parliamentary seats (Fermanagh and South Tyrone, and Mid Ulster). In 1959 they gained only 14 per cent of the vote and no seats. The difference appears to have arisen from catholic abstentions—turn-out merely dropped, and there was no sign of an actual swing to the unionists—so it certainly cannot be interpreted as meaning increased catholic support for the border. But it does suggest growing catholic disenchantment with the I.R.A. campaign of violence.

Among constitutional nationalists the early 1960s were years of ferment. First, a group of younger nationalists, tired of the internecine divisions on the anti-partitionist side, between abstentionist and non-abstentionist, republican and constitutionalist, labour and non-labour, formed in 1960 an organisation called National Unity, with the object of securing a united front of the anti-partition forces. The attempt was not successful, and ultimately some of the organisers founded a new party of their own, the National Democratic party, thus increasing instead of reducing the confusion on the anti-partitionist side. However, their attempt was a symptom of the increasing dissatisfaction among the younger nationalists with the combination of rhetoric and lack of hard work they perceived among too many of their seniors.

On the protestant side, too, there were some signs of greater flexibility. Election results showed increasing support for political parties that sought to appeal to catholics as well as protestants. One such was the Northern Ireland Labour party. This had some lean years following its débâcle in 1949, and it won no seats in the Stormont general election of 1953. In the general election of 1958, however, as already mentioned, it gained four seats. In the general election of 1962 it held these seats, and increased its poll in many constituencies. The Northern Ireland Labour party upheld the constitutional connection with Britain, but it had no sectarian affiliations such as the Unionist party had with the Orange order, and it had substantial catholic support. Another party of the same type was the Ulster Liberal party, refounded in 1957, with a minister of the non-subscribing presbyterian church, the Rev. Albert McElroy, as its leader. The Liberals, a much smaller party than Northern Ireland Labour, had a membership that never went beyond the hundreds, but they too managed to appeal across denominational divisions. They had one interesting electoral success. In 1961, at a by-election for one of the four Queen's University seats, the Liberal candidate, Sheelagh Murnaghan (who was a catholic) defeated the Unionist. The poll was low, and Queen's University was an exceptional constituency. But the contest was significant as being the first time that an electorate with a protestant majority had returned a catholic to Stormont. Murnaghan retained her seat in the general elections of 1962 and 1965.

Too much can be made of these episodes. The great majority of protestant constituencies continued to return unionist M.P.s. Many unionists continued to look with suspicion on any attempt at rapprochement, either from the catholic side or their own. A stock reaction to the Garron Tower resolutions was that of the young minister for home affairs, Brian Faulkner, who was emerging as the leading spokesman for right-wing unionism. He dismissed the Garron Tower speeches as an attempt by the catholics at peaceful penetration from within. When the lord mayor of Belfast ordered the flag on the city hall to be flown at half-mast for the death of a pope (Pius XII) in 1958, and again in 1963 (on the death of John XXIII), this provoked protests from extremist protestant organisations.

These suspicions within the protestant majority were highlighted in the winter of 1959–60, when a controversy suddenly blew up about the recruitment of catholics into the Unionist party. The controversy began when, at a Young Unionist political school at Portstewart, County Londonderry, Sir Clarence Graham, chairman of the standing committee of the Ulster Unionist Council, said he saw no reason why a catholic should not be selected as a Unionist parliamentary candidate. A few days later, the grand master of the Grand Orange Lodge of Ireland, Sir George Clark, made a speech asserting that in no circumstances could the Orange order accept that catholics could be admitted even to membership of the Unionist party. This was an astonishingly intransigent line to take; and yet Clark was by no means on the extreme edge of the Orange order. Indeed, ten years later he was deposed from the grand mastership for being too moderate.

In 1962 and 1963, in an attempt to improve community relations, a series of talks were arranged between Clark and the nationalist senator Gerry Lennon. It is not surprising that they were abandoned after several meetings, without any conclusion being reached.

CHAPTER XII

Reconciliation, rights, and protests, 1963–8

J. H. WHYTE

I t was in this climate, of ancient rigidities and the timid signs of new flexibility, that a leadership crisis broke in the Unionist party. At the beginning of 1963, the situation in the party resembled that of twenty years earlier, with an ageing leader being faced by mounting criticism from within the parliamentary party. The main difference was that, whereas in 1943 the principal critic of the leader was Sir Basil Brooke, in 1963 the latter (now Lord Brookeborough) was the incumbent on the defensive. The issue, however, was substantially the same, with the government on each occasion being accused of lack of drive in tackling the main problem facing Northern Ireland—the war effort in 1943, economic difficulties in 1963. What brought matters to a head in 1963 was the emergence of a fresh issue—a case of apparent impropriety by a government minister. A backbencher, Dr Robert Simpson, discovered that a member of the cabinet, Lord Glentoran, had allowed a company of which he was a director to insure government-built factories. Lord Brookeborough tried at first to brazen things out, stating that he had complete confidence in Lord Glentoran's objectivity, but there were some acrimonious meetings of the parliamentary party, ten backbenchers were reported to be in revolt, and finally, on 1 March, it was announced that Lord Glentoran had resigned his directorship.

Lord Brookeborough might have weathered the storm had he not been obliged to go into hospital for an operation on the same day, 1 March. While in hospital he came to the conclusion that he was too ill to carry on, and on 25 March he unexpectedly announced his resignation. There was at that time no machinery in the Unionist parliamentary party for electing a successor, and the governor, Lord Wakehurst, was faced with the task of selecting the new prime minister. He appears to have asked the chief whip of the Unionist party, William Craig, for an appraisal of party feelings, and Craig replied that the minister for finance, Captain Terence O'Neill, was the man who would be most acceptable to the party. O'Neill was acting prime minister in Lord Brookeborough's absence, but his selection was not a foregone conclusion.

Other possibilities canvassed at the time were the energetic minister for home affairs, Brian Faulkner, and the minister for commerce, J. L. O. Andrews, an older and widely liked man who was son of the former prime minister J. M. Andrews. Craig's intervention tipped the scale in favour of O'Neill—oddly enough, in view of their subsequent relations.

O'Neill was 48, and thus a full generation younger than his predecessor, who was then 74. It was to be expected that he would introduce a new style of government, and changes were soon visible in the structures of adminis- tration, parliament, and party. He replaced the secretary to the cabinet and built up a team of young and liberal-minded civil servants as his personal advisers, the best-known being James Malley and Kenneth Bloomfield.[1] He issued a code of practice for cabinet ministers in matters of business, so as to prevent a repetition of the Glentoran affair. He altered the standing orders of the house of commons so as to allow more time for private members' busi- ness, and he imitated Westminster practice by arranging for the leader of the opposition (Tom Boyd of Northern Ireland Labour) to be paid a salary. On the structure of the Unionist party he made less impact. A shy man, O'Neill did not have a personality suited for stumping the country, rallying grass- roots unionists to his policies. However, he did replace the long-serving secretary of the Unionist party, William Douglas, by a new man more con- genial to himself.

It was particularly in matters of economic policy that O'Neill proved an innovator. When he became head of government, Northern Ireland was still reeling from the impact of the Hall report, published in 1962. This was the report of a working party of Stormont and Westminster civil servants appointed to look into the economic prospects of Northern Ireland. It was a gloomy document: the implicit conclusion was that Northern Ireland's prob- lems were intractable and that no government policy would make much difference. O'Neill refused to accept this as final. He appointed his own team of consultants, headed by an expatriate Ulsterman, Professor Thomas Wilson of Glasgow University, to work out alternative recommendations, and it produced a more optimistic report in 1965. Meanwhile, in 1963, the first major investigation into problems of physical planning in Northern Ireland —the Matthew report—appeared. It was an imaginative document, propos- ing a limit to the growth of Belfast and the establishment of alternative growth areas, including a new town in the Lurgan–Portadown area. Its rec- ommendations were accepted by the government, and in 1964 a ministry of development was established to implement the consequential changes. In his technocratic style and economic interests, O'Neill was in many ways the counterpart of Seán Lemass in the south.

[1] Bloomfield's memoirs of his time as a civil servant appeared as *Stormont in crisis: a memoir* (Belfast, 1994).

Another development of these years was the founding of the Campaign for Social Justice, by Dr Conn McCluskey of Dungannon and his wife Patricia, a local councillor, in January 1964. The object of this campaign was to collect information about, and then to expose, discrimination. Its foundation was in one sense a sign of the new militancy on the opposition side, but in another sense it could be taken as showing a new moderation or realism among the minority community. Whatever the personal aspirations of its members might be, the Campaign for Social Justice was not concerned with the removal of the border: its concern was to remove injustices within the existing framework of Northern Ireland.

In the thorny fields of community relations, O'Neill moved much more cautiously. In 1964 he paid an official visit to a catholic school—the first unionist prime minister to do so. But he also made a speech complaining of the self-segregation pursued by catholics. In 1964 also, his government introduced legislation to facilitate the entry of the Mater Hospital into relationship with the national health service—but negotiations hung fire, and in the event it was not till 1971 that an agreement was reached. When sectarian riots broke out in west Belfast during the Westminster general election of 1964, the government, mindful of electoral realities in an evenly balanced constituency, in effect conceded the demands of protestant rioters and forced the removal of the tricolour from a republican office in an exclusively catholic area. In 1964, again, O'Neill made a speech claiming that his principal aims were to make Northern Ireland prosperous and to build bridges between the two traditions in Northern Ireland.[2] But correspondence published in the same year cast doubts on the vigour with which the latter aim was being pursued. Two catholic professional men, Brian McGuigan and J. J. Campbell, wrote to the prime minister deploring the small proportion of catholics appointed to statutory bodies. The prime minister replied that it was difficult to find qualified catholics willing to serve. McGuigan and Campbell denied this, and provided a list of qualified catholics who would be prepared to serve on such bodies. To this there was no reply, and after two new boards had been established without catholic representation, they published the correspondence. Thus O'Neill's advance towards better community relations followed a more than Leninesque pace, with every two steps forward being followed by very nearly two steps back.

The best illustration of O'Neill's difficulties is provided by his relationship with the Irish Congress of Trade Unions. This was an all-Ireland body, representing trade unions both north and south of the border; to offset this, of course, many of the trade unions included in it had originated before the 1920s and had their headquarters in London. However, as an all-Ireland

---

[2] Speech to Queen's University Unionist Association, 13 Feb. 1964, in Terence O'Neill, *Ulster at the crossroads* (London, 1969), pp 46–9.

body it was regarded with suspicion by many unionists, and the Brookeborough government had refused to recognise it. This mattered little so long as contacts between government and trade unions were infrequent. But O'Neill, with his interest in economic planning, could not afford to leave things like that. He hoped to set up an economic council, on which all interests would be represented, to advise the government on its economic policy, and trade union representation was essential if the economic council were to be taken seriously. O'Neill himself realised this, and favoured recognition of the I.C.T.U., but he showed extreme caution in approaching the issue. He left most of the running to be made by outside interest groups, and did not move until he felt that backbench opinion had been sufficiently softened up to acquiesce in a change. Negotiations were delayed by the fact that the I.C.T.U. had its own intransigents, who felt as strongly about recognising Stormont as some unionists felt about recognising an all-Ireland body, and it was not till the autumn of 1964 that a compromise was hammered out. The I.C.T.U. granted a greater degree of autonomy to its Northern Ireland committee and the latter was then recognised by the Northern Ireland government, its representatives being appointed to the economic council.

The year 1965 continued with this counterpoint of conciliation and rebuff. On 14 January O'Neill met Lemass at Stormont. It was the first time since 1925 that the premiers of the two parts of Ireland had met, and it seemed to herald an improvement of relations. This promise was strengthened when in February the nationalist party at Stormont agreed to accept the role of official opposition, thus displacing the numerically smaller Labour party, which had held the role for seven years only because the nationalists had refused it.[3] But in the same month, the Lockwood committee on higher education in Northern Ireland recommended that the proposed new university should be sited at Coleraine, and the government accepted its recommendation. This surprise selection was looked on as a blow to Derry, which was Northern Ireland's second largest city, already possessed a small university institution in Magee College, and therefore seemed the most likely choice. But Derry had a catholic and anti-unionist majority, and there were suspicions that this weighted the scales against it.[4] Also in the same month, it was announced that the new city recommended by the Matthew report for the Lurgan–Portadown area would be named 'Craigavon', after Northern Ireland's first prime minister. This was at once attacked as a divisive decision: Craigavon's name might be held in respect by one section of Northern Ireland's population, but it evoked the opposite feeling in the other.

---

[3] Nationalist politics in this period are discussed in Brendan Lynn, *Holding the ground* (Aldershot, 1997).
[4] Bloomfield, *Stormont in crisis*, pp 78–9.

Despite the caution that O'Neill displayed, his policy was too liberal for some of his supporters. The meeting with Lemass produced criticism from some parliamentary backbenchers, and also from outsiders such as the Rev. Ian Paisley, who was rapidly becoming known as the spokesman of extreme protestantism.[5] However, the complaints were as much at the manner in which the visit had been arranged—O'Neill had acted in his characteristic presidential style, not even consulting his cabinet—as at the substance of what had happened, and O'Neill secured retrospective approval from both the Grand Orange Lodge of Ireland and the Ulster Unionist Council. The general popularity of his policy seemed proved by the results of the Stormont general election of October 1965. These were gratifying for the Unionist party: two of the four seats lost to Labour in 1958 were recaptured, and there was a swing to the Unionists of 6 per cent in Belfast and 10 per cent in the country.

Indeed, there was a general feeling among both communities in Northern Ireland during this period that relations were improving. The atmosphere of these years was well recaptured in an article by Denis Tuohy, who was a student at Queen's University in the late 1950s, and a television producer in Belfast in the 1960s. He wrote:

The sectarian violence of the twenties and thirties was not part of my generation's thinking. Such bigotry was buried in the past, to be resurrected solely for satirical purposes.

All this is not to say that we were unaware of the faults in Northern Ireland's social structure, of the continuing tension between catholic grievance and protestant privilege. The jeremiads of seasoned politicians, unionist and nationalist alike, and their annual parades, made it impossible to forget, as did the continuing I.R.A. border campaign, however haphazard and however lacking in widespread catholic support. The mainstream attitude, however, among the brightest and most alert minds with whom I associated, among protestants and catholics, among men who have since become teachers and lawyers, technologists and businessmen, and politicians on both sides of the fence, was that reasonable men (and of course we were reasonable, were we not?) could break the fetters of the past, that progress through compromise (although the precise nature of that compromise was debatable) was not only possible but probable.

Even in my immediate postgraduate years there was little to suggest that we had been victims of delusion. As Belfast entered the sixties a play called 'Over the bridge', written by Sam Thompson, an ex-shipyard worker, which dealt with sectarian strife in the yard, was played to packed houses. True, the state-supported theatre, to which the play was originally offered, had refused to stage it for fear of creating a disturbance, but as it turned out the only disturbance was the clamour for tickets. The shipyard workers themselves placed block bookings night after night and watched with fascination a fiction which surely could never again become terrifying

[5] See Steve Bruce, *God save Ulster! The religion and politics of Paisleyism* (Oxford, 1986).

fact. The success of the Northern Ireland Labour party in Belfast in the 1962 Stormont election seemed to emphasise that new political aspirations were supplanting the old and that new alignments were forming to embody them. As late as 1964 I myself was introducing on B.B.C. television in Belfast a provincial 'TW3' called 'The 64 group' which set out to mock the rigid thinking of our parents. Press reviews and public reaction seemed to prove beyond doubt that our views were welcome, that the tide was turning.[6]

Within the Republic, an important political development had affected the principal opposition party, Fine Gael. A young front-bencher, Declan Costello, son of the taoiseach of 1948–51 and 1954–7, felt concerned at the right-wing image of Fine Gael, which seemed doomed to relegate the party permanently to the position of runner-up. In May 1964 he put to the parliamentary party an outline programme known as 'The just society'. This committed Fine Gael to a higher level of social expenditure, and to tighter government control of the economy. It was a surprising document for a party hitherto so conservative to accept, and it was approved by only a narrow majority. However it did the party no electoral damage, for the next two by-elections (Roscommon, July 1964, and Galway East, December 1964) both showed a swing in favour of Fine Gael. Fine Gael's new stance also had the advantage that it would make easier a coalition with Labour should Fianna Fáil lose its overall majority at the next general election.

The next general election took place in April 1965. It was a measure of the improvements of the last few years that both opposition parties concentrated their attack on the government's social policy. Its economic policy had so obviously produced results that it could not easily be faulted; the only chink in the government's armour was the claim that it had not used the additional wealth that the country had earned so as to benefit those most in need. The results made little difference to party strengths. Fine Gael remained the same as in 1961, with 47 seats. Fianna Fáil gained slightly, with 72 seats, and Labour more substantially, rising to 22 seats—the highest proportion of the dáil it had ever had. Lemass's government was able to remain in office, its position marginally improved. But though the election caused little change in the relative position of the main parties, it generated some shifts of greater importance. It produced some rejuvenation of the dáil: there were thirty-seven deputies under 40 years of age in 1965, as opposed to twenty-eight in 1961. Several veteran deputies retired or were unseated—for instance, Patrick McGilligan and Seán Mac Eoin of Fine Gael, James Ryan of Fianna Fáil. The educational level of the dáil rose: the proportion of deputies with university or professional education reached 30 per cent, the highest yet. The

---

[6] *Listener*, 9 Sept. 1971. 'TW3' stood for 'That was the week that was', a satirical programme produced in London by B.B.C. television. On Sam Thompson's work and Ulster writing of this period, see below, pp 521–7.

Labour party not only made overall gains, but showed an interesting territorial shift in the basis of its support. Whereas hitherto it had been strongest in a belt of rural constituencies in the south and east and had been weak in Dublin, it now made substantial gains in the metropolitan area: six of its deputies now came from Dublin city and county, as against one in 1961. The election also marked the lowest point yet reached by independents and minor parties: only three of their representatives were returned. Clann na Talmhan no longer fought elections, and Clann na Poblachta disbanded itself as a political party later in 1965. For the first time since the 1930s, the Irish electorate was faced with only three parties: Fianna Fáil, Fine Gael, and Labour. Television, too, played a part in the election for the first time. In a number of ways, then, the general election of 1965 appeared to mark the beginning of a new era in Irish politics: a transition from the old, intensely locally oriented politics, to a new, more sophisticated, and more nationalised type.

RELATIONS between Northern Ireland and the Republic were distant in the early years of this period. On becoming taoiseach in 1959, Lemass had tried to improve communications. In a series of speeches, he urged that the two Irish governments should cooperate in matters of common concern.[7] However, first Brookeborough and then O'Neill always insisted that before they would do so, the Dublin government must recognise the constitutional position of Northern Ireland. This Lemass always refused unequivocally to do, and so talks hung fire for years.

Accordingly, there was general surprise when on 14 January 1965 it was announced that Lemass had visited O'Neill at Stormont. Statements on both sides made clear that attitudes to partition had not changed, but there was agreement to work for the common good in tourism, industrial development, electricity, and other fields. On 9 February O'Neill paid a return visit to Lemass in Dublin, and thereafter a number of meetings occurred between cabinet ministers in the two governments.

The origin of these meetings appears to have lain in a friendship that grew up between O'Neill, then minister for finance for Northern Ireland, and T. K. Whitaker, then secretary of the department of finance in Dublin, who had met each other at conferences of the World Bank. Recollections differ as to who first suggested the meeting: O'Neill felt obliged to insist that the first meeting must be at Stormont, so that he could not be accused by his own extremists of abandoning his stand on the constitutional issue.

In the north, as we have seen, the talks, despite this precaution, encountered some criticism. In the south, however, they met with almost universal approval. Though few southerners had abandoned their hopes for the ultimate reunification of the island, there was a growing acceptance of the fact that

---

[7] Above, p. 291. See also O'Neill, *Ulster at the crossroads*, ch. 7.

Northern Ireland existed and had to be lived with. North–south relations appeared to be moving to a new footing of mutual respect.

Before the end of 1965 relations between the Republic and Great Britain also reached a new level of closeness. On 14 December a further Anglo–Irish trade agreement was signed. A revision of the 1960 agreement had been asked for by the Irish government, following the failure of the British and Irish attempts to enter the Common Market in 1963. Lemass's government still hoped that membership of the Common Market would be possible at some future date, and in the meantime a freeing of trade with Britain seemed a good way of accustoming Irish producers to the rigour of competition. By the agreement, Britain undertook to remove almost all restrictions on Irish goods by July 1966, and the Republic agreed to remove its restrictions on British goods over a period of ten years. Britain was to allow in larger quantities of Irish bacon, butter, live animals, and meat products. Furthermore, Irish farmers secured for the first time a limited share in British agricultural subsidies. The bargain was favourable for the Republic in the short run; in the long run, if other things did not change, the balance of advantage was likely to be with the British. The Irish government gambled on the chance that in the long run things would change—and that in particular both Ireland and Britain would find themselves in the Common Market. As a member of the Common Market, the Republic would concede no more to Britain than it was doing by the free trade agreement, while in return it would receive other important benefits, particularly the hope of a fresh market on the Continent for its agricultural produce.

This period ends, then, on a note of unwonted harmony. Relations between the two communities in Northern Ireland, between the two parts of Ireland, and between the Republic of Ireland and Britain, were all more cordial than they had ever been before. The only exception was the sign of some tension between extreme and moderate protestants in Northern Ireland.

CHAPTER XIII

The north erupts, and Ireland enters Europe, 1968–72

J. H. WHYTE

IN the Republic, the best word to describe the years 1968–72 is 'chequered'. If there were no longer the intractable difficulties of the years 1949–57, neither was there the boom atmosphere of the succeeding period: elements of gloom and optimism coexisted. Under Jack Lynch, who succeeded to the leadership on Lemass's retirement as taoiseach in 1966, the Fianna Fáil government survived throughout the period, but triumph and near-disaster succeeded each other with startling rapidity. The period began with a defeat. On 16 October 1968 the government put two constitutional amendments to the people in a referendum. One amendment was a repeat of that narrowly defeated in 1959—to abolish the single transferable vote. The other was to permit greater variations in the proportion of deputies to population in different parts of the country. Both proposals were opposed by Fine Gael and Labour, and both were defeated by a margin of 61 per cent to 39 per cent. This was a far more serious rebuff than in 1959, and left an atmosphere of recrimination in Fianna Fáil.

As evidence of this, one can point to the exceptional number of intra-party controversies that beset Fianna Fáil during the winter of 1968–9. On the question of relations with Northern Ireland, the minister for agriculture, Neil Blaney, made a speech openly describing as futile the policy of discussions between the two Irish governments that the taoiseach was pursuing: for this he received a rebuke from the taoiseach. The criminal justice amendment bill, sponsored by the minister for justice, Micheál Ó Moráin, gave the gardaí such unprecedented powers to regulate the right of public meeting that it roused protests inside as well as outside Fianna Fáil, and at the party's ard-fheis in January 1969 Ó Moráin was obliged to promise amendments to the most controversial sections. Most acrimonious of all was the controversy over Taca, a fund-raising organisation for the Fianna Fáil party. Taca was reputed to bring the party £7,000 a year—a sizeable figure by the modest standards of Irish party budgets. But its minimum subscription of £100 was so large that membership was virtually confined to affluent businessmen, and rumours flourished, whether well or ill founded, of the favours that these businessmen obtained from government in return for their subscriptions. Members of the party had apparently found these rumours electorally damaging during the referendum campaign, and their discontent was voiced at party meetings in the following weeks. In December 1968 Lynch announced that Taca would be reconstructed: henceforward £100 would be the maximum subscription instead of the minimum, and the minimum would be only £5.[1]

Yet within a few months of this phase of defeat and mutual recrimination, Lynch led his party to electoral victory. When he called a general election for June 1969, almost all commentators extrapolated from the referendum results and predicted another defeat for Fianna Fáil. Instead, it increased its total to 75 seats, thus obtaining its best result since the general election of 1957, and an absolute majority. Fine Gael improved its position as compared with 1965, and gained 50 seats, but Labour dropped back to 18. Independents were further eroded, and only one was returned.

Two reasons can be suggested for this unexpected success. One was the miscalculation of the Labour party. From 1967 Labour sought to offer an alternative more clearly distinct from the other two parties by moving to the left. It adopted a number of fresh policies, more decidedly socialist than anything to which it had been committed before. These changes seemed to tap a reservoir of latent enthusiasm, for membership rose by 68 per cent in the four years 1966–9, and attendance at party conferences was higher than ever before. However, as Clann na Poblachta had discovered in 1948, and as Alliance was to discover in Northern Ireland in 1973, a surge of enthusiasm among party activists is not necessarily matched in the electorate as a whole. At the general election of 1969 Labour did well in the Dublin area, gaining ten seats as against six in 1965. But in the conservative and property-conscious countryside, the party dropped back sharply, from sixteen seats in 1965 to only eight in 1969. It seems likely that Labour had swung too far to the left for its electoral advantage.

More important, however, than Labour's miscalculation was the skill shown in electoral boundary-drawing by the Fianna Fáil government. Its instrument was the Electoral (Amendment) Act, 1969,[2] piloted through the oireachtas by the minister for local government, Kevin Boland. This act was designed so that it maximised Fianna Fáil votes in terms of seats. In areas where Fianna Fáil was relatively strong, three-seat constituencies were preferred, for in these, with 50 per cent of the first-preference votes or even less, Fianna Fáil could hope to secure two seats out of three. In areas where

---

[1] For a discussion of Taca, see Paul Bew, Ellen Hazelkorn, and Henry Patterson, *The dynamics of Irish politics* (London, 1989), pp 91–3.
[2] 1969/3 (26 Mar. 1969).

the party was weaker—notably round Dublin—four-seat constituencies were preferred, for here Fianna Fáil could, with only 40 per cent of the first-preference votes, secure two quotas and thus half the seats. Five-seat constituencies were less efficient than either three- or four-seat constituencies in maximising seats, and only two were retained. The care shown in constituency delimitation had its reward: at the general election of 1969 Fianna Fáil dropped 2 per cent in first-preference votes as compared with the previous general election, but it made a net gain of three seats.

Only a few weeks, however, after Fianna Fáil's triumph at the general election, there was another turn of fortune's wheel. The troubles in Northern Ireland, which had been going on since October 1968, reached a horrifying climax, as will be explained later in this chapter, in the deaths and burnings of August 1969. These events caused divisions in the government between those who wanted energetic intervention on behalf of the northern nationalists, and those who preferred a more restrained approach. Among the former were the minister for agriculture, Neil Blaney, the minister for local government, Kevin Boland, and, less vocally, the minister for finance, Charles Haughey. Among the latter were the minister for external affairs, Patrick Hillery, the tánaiste, Erskine Childers, and the taoiseach himself, Jack Lynch. In August 1969 the cracks between the two wings of the government were papered over: the taoiseach broadcast a speech, drafted at a cabinet meeting, which did not fully express the views of either section. But during the remaining months of 1969 it became clear that the rift remained. While Lynch and Hillery made increasingly pacific speeches, Blaney made belligerent ones, and in December 1969 he was again publicly rebuked by the taoiseach. The crux came in the spring of 1970. In April Lynch learned that Blaney and Haughey were involved in a plan to import arms from the Continent, so as to have them available to northern nationalists should civil war erupt in Northern Ireland. This did not square with the taoiseach's policy, but he was in a difficult position. His parliamentary majority was small, Blaney and Haughey were among his ablest and most influential ministers, and to act strongly against them might destroy his government. To add to the complications, at the crucial moment Haughey was seriously hurt by a fall from his horse, and could not be interviewed for a fortnight. On the other hand, the leader of the opposition, Liam Cosgrave, was informed of developments by the special branch of the gardaí, and was prepared to expose the whole matter if the taoiseach did not take action. Finally, on 6 May 1970, Lynch resolved his dilemma. He dismissed Haughey and Blaney.

By his action Lynch endangered his government. Kevin Boland resigned in sympathy with the dismissed ministers, as did a parliamentary secretary, Paudge Brennan. Several backbenchers were believed to sympathise with the departing ministers. In October Haughey gained a moral victory when a Dublin jury threw out a charge against him of conspiracy to import arms;

Blaney had already had a similar charge against him thrown out by a district justice. The main outline of events was revealed in the court proceedings and is not in dispute. Northern republicans asked southern ministers for arms. An Irish army intelligence officer, Captain James Kelly, went to the Continent to make the purchases. Blaney found him an interpreter, Albert Luykx, an Irish businessman of Belgian origin. Haughey was prepared, as minister for finance, to authorise the import of arms without the normal customs clearance. The case turned on whether these proceedings were legal. The importation of arms would be legal if the minister for defence, James Gibbons, approved—his approval did not have to be in writing. Kelly insisted that his arms-buying trip to the Continent was made with Gibbons's approval. Gibbons denied this, and implied that Kelly was acting off his own bat. The jury preferred to believe Kelly. Despite this setback, Lynch had the advantage of a central position. While Blaney and Boland attacked him for not being hawkish enough on the north, the opposition parties were inclined to criticise him for not being more dovelike. This made it difficult for his opponents to coalesce. Furthermore, Lynch could rely on the traditionally strong party loyalty of Fianna Fáil. When it came to the point, very few of those who criticised his policy were prepared to leave the party. Boland left in June 1970, to found a new party, Aontacht Éireann; the following year Blaney was expelled from the parliamentary party in November 1971; and three other deputies (Seán Sherwin, Paudge Brennan, and Des Foley) either resigned or were expelled during 1971. But the great bulk of the parliamentary party, whatever their personal feelings might have been, were prepared to vote as the whips required. An example was Haughey, who refused to join Boland and Blaney in public criticism of the taoiseach, and spent the two years following his dismissal as a loyal backbencher. Thanks to these advantages, Lynch was able to weather all the critical votes in Dáil Éireann for the remainder of this period.[3]

In the religious field also, 'chequered' is an appropriate word for this period. The catholic church maintained its hold on the allegiance of the great majority in the Republic. A survey carried out in February and March 1971, on behalf of the Catholic Communications Institute, showed that 96 per cent of the catholic population claimed to have attended mass the previous Sunday. The sharp decline in vocations that had marked the 1960s showed signs of coming to an end: the number of clerical students at Irish seminaries in 1971–2 showed, for the first time in ten years, a slight rise as compared with the year before.[4] Relations between denominations continued to im-

---

[3] The 'arms trial' episode is discussed in Keogh, *Twentieth-century Ire.*, pp 300–14, Eunan O'Halpin, *Defending Ireland* (Oxford, 1999), ch. 8, and Justin O'Brien, *The arms trial* (Dublin, 2000).

[4] Liam Ryan, 'A case study in social change' in *Social Studies*, ii, no. 3 (June–July 1973), p. 260.

prove, a milestone being the establishment in 1970 of the Irish School of Ecumenics at Milltown, with Father Michael Hurley, S.J., as director, and an interdenominational staff. On the other hand, religious issues aroused some major controversies.

One of these concerned the anti-contraception laws. In the 1920s and 1930s laws had been passed forbidding the import or sale of contraceptive devices and the dissemination of literature advocating contraception. These laws reflected the traditional teaching of the catholic church, and in an over-whelmingly catholic state they for long aroused little resistance. But during the 1960s, as noted in a previous chapter, catholics came increasingly to question the teaching of their church in this matter; and sooner or later this questioning was bound to be applied to the legislation that teaching had inspired. Moreover there was a political reason for changing the law. Most people in the Republic hoped to persuade northern protestants some day to join in a united Ireland. The chances of success were clearly reduced if laws in the Republic were framed on a sectarian basis. By the early 1970s, it appeared that time might be ripe for a change. The taoiseach seemed to be hinting at this when he told the Fianna Fáil ard-fheis in February 1971 that there must be no hint of sectarianism in a united Ireland. A family-planning clinic was operating openly in Dublin from 1969, but it went unprosecuted. In March 1971 three independent senators, Mary Robinson, John Horgan, and Trevor West, sought leave to introduce a private member's bill amending the contraception laws. Leaders of the principal protestant denom-inations in the Republic expressed their support for a liberalisation of the law. At this point, however, counter-pressures began to emerge. The catholic hierarchy issued a statement opposing any change in the law. Archbishop McQuaid of Dublin went further, and in a strongly worded pastoral letter declared that any such change would be 'a curse upon our country'. There were signs that public opinion was not keen for a change. An opinion poll published in June found that 63 per cent of those questioned were against legalising the sale of contraceptives, and only 34 per cent were in favour. Fianna Fáil backbenchers, traditionally respected for their knowledge of local opinion, were reported to be against change. Faced with this conflict of pressures, the government decided on the more prudent course. It secured the rejection of the private member's bill in the senate, and of a similar private member's bill, introduced a few months later by two Labour dep-uties, in the dáil. The episode provided a revealing measure of the strength of conservative forces in the country.

Another church-related controversy in this period concerned the question of community schools. Since 1967 the department of education had been committed to securing equality of opportunity in post-primary education. A serious obstacle in achieving this aim was the difficulty of securing cooper-ation in areas where the existing secondary and vocational schools were too small individually to provide a full range of courses, and too jealous of their independence to develop a joint programme. In 1970 the minister for education, Pádraig Faulkner, proposed that a new type of school, the community school, should be established in such areas to replace both the secondary and vocational schools and take over post-primary education. The proposal affected the catholic church, because most secondary schools were run by religious orders. However, by May 1971 it became known that the catholic hierarchy would accept the new schools, provided that on each board of management the church authorities nominated four out of the six members, the other two being appointed by the local vocational education committee. These proportions were justified on the ground that many more pupils attended church-run secondary schools than attended the non-denominational local-authority-run vocational schools. At this point, however, the plan came under fire from the vocational school authorities, and from opposition spokesmen such as Garret FitzGerald.[5] They argued that the minister's scheme gave the church too much. The vocational schools formed the one sector of the education system that was not under church control. Hitherto, therefore, parents had had a choice between denominational and non-denominational education. But now, in the areas where community schools were to be set up, the choice would disappear, and a single school would be established in which church influence would be predominant. Faced with such arguments, Faulkner modified his proposals. A clause providing for a check on the 'faith and morals' of teachers in community schools was dropped. The trustees in whom the school property was vested were to be appointed by the minister and not by the bishop. Most important of all, the composition of the six-member board of management was to be altered. It would now consist for most schools of two members selected by the church authorities, two by the vocational education committee, and two by the parents of children in the school. In this area, then, the church authorities proved more flexible than on the issue of contraception. The outcome was a reduction rather than an extension of church influence.

Socially, this was also a chequered period in the history of the Republic. It was remarkable for a wave of demonstrations and protests generated by a most varied range of issues. Most of these were simply the Irish manifestation of movements found in many western countries. The demonstrations against a South African rugby football team in 1970 were counterparts to similar demonstrations organised in Britain, Australia, and elsewhere, by opponents of the South African policy of apartheid. The women's liberation movement, established in the Republic in 1970, was an outcrop of a movement already strong in the United States and Britain. In Ireland, its most publicised exploit was a mass excursion to Belfast in May 1971, to buy the

[5] Garret FitzGerald, *All in a life: an autobiography* (London, 1992 ed.), pp 87–8.

contraceptives forbidden in the south. The student sit-ins that occurred at University College, Dublin, and at the college of art in 1969 were part of an international wave of student unrest that affected many parts of America and Europe in the late 1960s—although there were specific local grievances, such as poor library facilities, to focus discontent in Ireland. The movement to prevent Georgian Dublin from being torn down by developers, which reached its climax with the forcible eviction of protesters from a property in Hume Street by a demolition squad in June 1970,[6] may have been not unconnected with the fact that 1970 was European Conservation Year.

Events in Northern Ireland, too, influenced forms of protest in the south. A Gaeltacht Civil Rights Association was set up to publicise the underdevelopment of Irish-speaking areas; in April 1971 a demonstration it mounted in Dublin was broken up by gardaí, and complaints ensued of police brutality in a manner reminiscent of Derry two years before. The idea of a rent strike, as a form of protest by tenants of local-authority houses, was also imported— although with different objects; for whereas in Northern Ireland it was a protest against internment, in the Republic it was simply a protest at the allegedly high level of rents. But by the end of 1971 large numbers of tenants in Cork, Dublin, and elsewhere were withholding their rents.

Some forms of protest were organised by elements in the republican movement. As explained in the previous chapter, republicans turned after the failure of the military campaign of 1956–62 to the infiltration of social movements, and they had increasing success in this period. At Oughterard, County Galway, businessmen involved in the development of a golf-course, on land that local farmers were said to need, were threatened. In several places, fish-ins were organised to draw attention to the monopoly rights often held by individual proprietors over long stretches of river bank. Most important of all the republican front activities was the development of the Dublin Housing Action Committee. The housing shortage in Dublin was an increasing source of discontent. During the 1960s the population of the city was rising rapidly, and housing for working-class families fell increasingly short of needs, at a time when office-block developers seemed to have no difficulty in securing funds. The D.H.A.C. highlighted the problem by organising the squatting of homeless families in unoccupied property. The government riposted with the Prohibition of Forcible Entry and Occupation Act, 1971, a controversial measure that gave the gardaí sweeping powers of arrest in such circumstances.[7] Meanwhile a republican splinter group, Saor Éire, was engaged in more violent activities. Between 1967 and 1970 there were thirteen armed robberies in the Republic, for which responsibility was attributed to Saor Éire. At the last of them, in April 1970, an unarmed policeman, Garda Richard Fallon, was shot dead as he courageously tackled the raiders.

---

[6] Below, p. 589.   [7] 1971/25 (1 Sept. 1971).

Other protests and demonstrations, however, arose more spontaneously from specific problems. Economic conditions, as already noted, led to an exceptionally severe wave of strikes in 1970–71. The National Farmers Association, while not quite so militant as in 1966–7, organised a number of protests against the widening gap between the farmers' standard of living and that of the rest of the country. Educational changes caused a number of local protests, as the department of education's plans for amalgamating small schools gathered momentum. These plans, though they generally made sense educationally, often meant disturbing local loyalties, and were not always as carefully explained as they should have been. Of the many school disputes reported in the newspapers during these years, two may be singled out for mention. At Montpellier, County Limerick, the department and clergy agreed, without consulting the parents, to close the local school and have the children taken elsewhere by bus. The parents objected, and kept the school open for nearly two years from their own resources before finally giving in.[8] Another widely publicised dispute occurred at Dún Chaoin, in the Kerry Gaeltacht, where a one-teacher school was closed down and the children sent to a larger school at Ballyferriter, some miles away. The department claimed that the move was in the educational interests of the children, but the protesters argued that to close the school was to strike a blow at Dún Chaoin as a community. The school was for a time kept open by voluntary effort; finally, it was reopened officially in 1973. The itinerant problem was another cause of bitterness in these years. Attempts to settle itinerant families in council housing estates aroused tensions among families already living there. In July 1971 the allocation of a house at Mervue Park, Galway, to an itinerant woman was forcibly prevented by the settled people of the area. In December 1971 trouble between itinerant and other families at Athlone led to troops being called out in aid of the civil power, for the first time in many years.

All these troubles occurred at a time when the Garda Síochána was facing special difficulties. A government commission, set up under the chairmanship of Judge John C. Conroy to investigate pay and conditions, reported in 1970, but although its recommendations were implemented by the government, discontent did not come to an end.[9] Complaints persisted of poor equipment, faulty liaison between ordinary police and the special branch, and trying conditions of work. Crime was on the increase, with a concomitant increase in the burden on the gardaí. In 1971 the crime rate was 26 per cent higher than in 1970, and the highest in the history of the state. The judges aroused resentment among the police by being far too ready, in the

---

[8] *Irish Times*, 25 Sept. 1971. For the beginnings of the dispute see *Nusight* (Nov. 1969), pp 3–7.
[9] Gregory Allen, *The Garda Síochána* (Dublin, 1999), pp 187–90.

view of the latter, to let dangerous prisoners out on bail. When, at Christmas 1971, Cardinal Conway warned that 'the crust of civilisation' was dangerously thin, and that the troubles then convulsing the north could easily spread to the Republic, the harassed state of the Garda helped to make his warning credible.

However, in this field as in others, there was light as well as shade. Although the Republic saw what by its own standards was an exceptional number of protests during these years, by the standards of many countries it remained profoundly peaceful. While crime might be rising, it remained low in comparison with Britain, let alone the United States. The gardaí, in contrast to most European police forces, remained unarmed. Problems such as drug abuse, while not unknown in Ireland, reached nowhere near the same level of seriousness as in the United States or some European countries. Nor had the country lost its capacity for peaceful change. As illustrations, one can point to two reversals of seemingly entrenched attitudes that took place during this period. The first was the rescinding by the catholic hierarchy of the ban on catholic students attending Trinity College, Dublin, without special permission. The hierarchy had a long-standing distrust of Trinity College with its protestant traditions and continuing links with the Church of Ireland.[10] In recent times this distrust had seemed to be hardening: the regulations of the national council of 1956 on the subject of entry into Trinity by catholic students were more stringent than those of any preceding council. But in 1970 the prohibition was quite suddenly repealed. The bishops, in explaining their decision, stated that the proposals (then under consideration but subsequently abandoned) for merging Trinity College with University College, Dublin, had created a new situation; but the growth of the ecumenical movement, and changes in the personnel of the episcopal bench, probably had as much to do with it. The following year, the Gaelic Athletic Association dropped its prohibition on members playing 'foreign games' such as rugby and association football. This ban had long been criticised, both inside and outside the association, for fomenting needless divisions; but criticism had always been met by the claim that the ban was essential if the G.A.A. was to retain its purity of national purpose. Then, quite suddenly, and for reasons that to an outsider are not clear, the atmosphere changed, and what had hitherto been regarded as essential was quietly abandoned.[11]

IF the years 1968–72 are described as 'chequered' in the Republic, some gloomier epithet might seem appropriate to Northern Ireland. The province

[10] Above, vi, 544, 558, 565–6; below, pp 764–5.
[11] Marcus de Burca, *The G.A.A.: a history* (Dublin, 1980), pp 65, 91–3, 168–70, 207–13, 232; W. F. Mandle, *The Gaelic Athletic Association and Irish nationalist politics, 1884–1924* (London and Dublin, 1987).

experienced in these years its worst period of civil disorder since the 1790s. However, even in the north, the word 'chequered' can still be adopted as the key to the period, for, although gloom dominated over light to a much greater extent than in the Republic, not everything was uniformly bleak. There were forces making for conciliation in the province, as well as forces making for conflict, and they were not unevenly matched. Indeed there were several occasions during these years in which it looked as if the forces of conciliation were going to prevail after all, and the most interesting problem for a historian to discuss is why, by a narrow margin, they came to be defeated. This is best done by subdividing the political history of these years into three periods: a period of generally deepening crisis, June 1968 to October 1969; a plateau period, October 1969 to July 1971, in which the forces making for conflict and those making for conciliation were in almost even balance; and another period of deepening crisis, from July 1971 until the introduction of direct rule from Westminster in March 1972.

The first of these periods starts with the eviction on 20 June 1968 of Austin Currie, nationalist M.P. for Tyrone East, from a council house he had illegally occupied in the village of Caledon. This is generally taken as the first in a chain of civil rights protests which was to build up within a few months to a horrifying climax. Currie did not foresee such dramatic consequences from his action. His purpose was simply to draw attention to the discrimination he detected in the allocation of houses by Dungannon Rural District Council. The last straw came when a house was allocated in Caledon to a 19-year-old unmarried protestant girl, at a time when, according to Currie, there were catholic families in the neighbourhood whose need was much more acute. Currie's first reaction was to try to settle the question through established channels. This was at a time when O'Neill as unionist leader and Edward McAteer as nationalist leader were both speaking the language of conciliation,[12] and Currie had no desire to break the harmony. It was only after he had approached the district council, the relevant ministry, and the prime minister's office, had put down a parliamentary question, and had raised the matter in an adjournment debate, all without result, that he finally took direct action and occupied the house himself. His eviction, however, in front of the newsmen's cameras, seems to have awakened him to the usefulness of such demonstrations in attracting publicity to a grievance.

Emboldened by this success, Currie decided to mount a general protest against housing discrimination in the Dungannon area. He persuaded the locally based Campaign for Social Justice to organise it, and the Northern Ireland Civil Rights Association—which had not hitherto been thinking

---

[12] For O'Neill, see *Ulster at the crossroads*, ch. 5; for nationalists, see Brendan Lynn, *Holding the ground* (Aldershot, 1997), ch. 5.

along such lines—to endorse it.[13] The demonstration took the form of a march from Coalisland to Dungannon on 24 August 1968. This, the first of the civil rights marches, displayed a pattern that was to persist. No tricolours or other symbols of anti-partition sentiment were displayed: it was made clear that this was a protest against grievances within Northern Ireland, not against the existence of the state as such.[14] As a corollary, the right was demanded to march not just in nationalist but also in unionist areas. This presented the police with an unfamiliar difficulty: hitherto, nearly all parades in Northern Ireland, apart from the trades unions' May Day parade, could be identified as unionist or nationalist, and a body of custom had developed regulating what routes might or might not be considered provocative for a parade of one colour or the other. But here was a march that claimed not to fit into the familiar categories. Local unionists insisted that it be treated like a nationalist march, and kept out of protestant areas; the police thereupon excluded it from a protestant part of Dungannon, and the 2,500 people on the march were stopped, short of their objective, by police barriers. They accepted the ban, and there was controversy afterwards on whether the march had been a success or a failure. But enough people thought it had achieved something for the formula to be tried again elsewhere.

The next march was called for Derry, on Saturday 5 October 1968. Derry was an obvious site for such a demonstration. No city in Northern Ireland had such an accumulation of grievances. Gerrymandering was at its most acute there—a Unionist minority of less than 40 per cent held 60 per cent of the council seats. The council refused to allocate houses to catholics except in one ward, so as not to upset the electoral balance, and when every building site in that ward was full, it had refused to seek an extension of the city boundary. Economic and unemployment problems, too, abounded, and a considerable blow was dealt to morale when the government decided not to site the new university in the city.

Yet despite these circumstances, it was by no means certain that the march would be a success. The organisers were left-wingers who were regarded with suspicion by many local nationalists. The timing of the march coincided with a popular local football fixture. There is a great weight of opinion that if the minister for home affairs, William Craig, had not banned the march it would have been a fiasco. Craig, however, regarded the march—as he made clear at a press conference the day after it took place—as republican-inspired,

[13] For an assessment of the extent of discrimination under the unionist regime, see John Whyte, 'How much discrimination was there under the unionist regime, 1921–68?' in Tom Gallagher and James O'Connell (ed.), *Contemporary Irish studies* (Manchester, 1983), pp 1–35.
[14] It should, perhaps, be noted that republicans did play an influential role in establishing and supporting the civil rights movement, and that republican groups were prominent in supporting the Coalisland–Dungannon march; see Bob Purdie, *Politics in the streets: the origins of the civil rights movement in Northern Ireland* (Belfast, 1990), pp 127–30, 135.

and he accordingly banned it from entering unionist parts of the city. This ban had important effects. It probably increased the number of people attending. It ensured extensive press and television coverage. And it saddled the police with the task of enforcing the ban should the marchers try to break it. The marchers did try to break it, and were beaten back with considerable police brutality. Even this might not have been too serious if there had been plenty of other news that weekend to occupy the television screens. But there was not—and the result was that the behaviour of the police in Derry was publicised on television screens all over Ireland, Britain, and beyond.

During the next two months the momentum was kept up. Further demonstrations were held in Belfast, Armagh, Dungannon, and repeatedly in Derry. At some of them—notably at Armagh—protestant extremists staged counter-demonstrations, and, by their belligerence in face of the civil rights demonstrators' restraint, increased the moral advantage of the latter. The interest of the British government was attracted, and the prime minister, Harold Wilson, saw O'Neill and pressed for reforms.[15] On 22 November, after repeated cabinet meetings, the Northern Ireland government announced a five-point programme of reforms. They were: (i) local authorities would be required to allocate houses on some readily understood and published system; (ii) consideration would be given to machinery for the remedy of the citizens' grievances, and in the sphere of central government an ombudsman would be appointed; (iii) in Derry the city and rural district councils would be abolished and replaced by a development commission; (iv) local government franchise would be reviewed and the company vote abolished; (v) as soon as it could be done 'without undue hazard', those sections of the special powers acts that were in conflict with the United Kingdom's international obligations would be withdrawn.

The programme was an incomplete response to the civil rights demands. 'One man one vote' was still not conceded; while an ombudsman was granted for central government, nothing definite was promised in the much thornier area of local government grievances. But it did mark a step forward, and was soon followed by an impressive rallying of the more moderate elements of the community. On 9 December, following a speech by Craig that seemed a deliberate defiance of his policy of reconciliation, O'Neill made his 'Ulster at the crossroads' broadcast to the people of Northern Ireland. The message, somewhat histrionically delivered but effective when read in print, was an appeal to both sides of the community to collaborate in a policy of moderate reform.[16] It evoked a massive wave of support, more than 100,000 messages being received. Fortified by this response, on 11 December he dismissed

---

[15] Recent biographies of Wilson (prime minister 1964–70, 1974–6) have offered brief consideration of his relations with N.I. See Austen Morgan, *Harold Wilson* (London, 1992); Ben Pimlott, *Harold Wilson* (London, 1992).

[16] For the text, see O'Neill, *Ulster at the crossroads*, pp 140–46.

Craig. This action evoked a corresponding gesture on the other side: the Derry Citizens' Action Committee, which had taken charge of civil rights activities in the Derry area, announced that it was suspending marches for a month. It looked as if a consensus of moderate unionists and moderate civil rights supporters was reemerging: the former acknowledged that further reforms were still required; the latter recognised that O'Neill must have time to deliver them.

The consensus was broken by a tiny minority on the extreme left of the civil rights movement.[17] Following the 5 October march in Derry, a group of civil rights supporters had been formed at Queen's University, Belfast, under the title of 'People's Democracy'. The group had no constitution, no executive, and no recorded membership. Decisions were taken at full meetings of the body, and could be rescinded by any subsequent meeting. This arrangement gave the advantage to those with most staying power, and those with most staying power tend to be those with the most extreme views. A group of left-wing members, of whom a Queen's graduate, Michael Farrell, was the most prominent, proposed that a march from Belfast to Derry be held at the beginning of January. This would have been the longest civil rights march yet, and when first put to a People's Democracy meeting it was turned down. But the proposal was reintroduced at a second and more poorly attended meeting, after the end of the university term, and adopted. The project was received with almost universal disapproval. Not only unionists, but also many civil rights supporters, opposed it. Eddie McAteer, the nationalist leader, remarked that it was bad marching weather in more senses than one. When the marchers left Belfast on 1 January 1969 they were only sixty strong.

The marchers were saved from failure by the folly of protestant extremists. On their way they were repeatedly harried as they passed through unionist areas. The worst incident happened when they reached Burntollet bridge, a few miles from Derry, on 4 January. Here they were ambushed by a crowd armed with stones, sticks, crowbars, and lead piping, and many of the marchers were badly hurt. The police escort seemed to do little to restrain the attack. That night there was serious rioting in Derry. Police in pursuit of the rioters made irruptions into the catholic Bogside area, and, in the words of an official report, 'a number of policemen were guilty of misconduct which involved assault and battery, malicious damage to property ... and the

---

[17] For the influence of left-wing ideas on the civil rights movement, see Purdie, *Politics in the streets*. The Dublin Wolfe Tone Society is credited with suggesting a civil rights campaign. Its republican and/or radical members were influenced by James Connolly's vision of uniting working-class Irish people, north and south, catholic and protestant, in a workers' republic. See also Anthony Coughlan, *C. Desmond Greaves, 1913–1988: an obituary essay* (Dublin, 1991), and Richard English, *Radicals and the republic: socialist republicanism in the Irish Free State, 1925–1937* (Oxford, 1994).

use of provocative sectarian and political slogans'.[18] Once again the civil rights movement had been given the moral victory by its opponents.

The government was forced to respond with a further concession. On 15 January it announced that a commission of inquiry (subsequently known, after its chairman, as the Cameron commission) would be set up to examine the causes of the disturbances. This concession eroded O'Neill's support. On 24 January the minister for commerce, Brian Faulkner, resigned from the government, and was followed two days later by the minister for health and social services, William Morgan. The grounds on which Faulkner resigned caused surprise. He had hitherto been reputed to be on the right of O'Neill; he now resigned on grounds that put him on the prime minister's left. He argued that the mere appointment of a commission did not go far enough, and that if further reforms were needed the government should introduce them on its own responsibility, without sheltering behind any recommendations that the commission might make. This did not, however, make O'Neill any more popular with his right wing. On 30 January it became known that twelve Unionist backbenchers, known for their right-wing views, were demanding a change in the Unionist leadership. O'Neill could see only one way to strengthen his position. Believing that he was stronger in the country than in the Unionist parliamentary party, he called a general election.

The election campaign, which lasted from 3 February to 24 February 1969, was the most confusing in the history of Northern Ireland. The principal contest took place between different kinds of unionist. It was fought out first in the constituency associations. The Unionist party had always been extraordinarily decentralised, with party headquarters exercising no control over the selection of candidates by constituency associations. O'Neill, therefore, could not count on the associations selecting candidates who would support his policy, and in the event only thirty-one of the forty-four official Unionist candidates could be classified as pro-O'Neill. This, however, did not end the matter, for where the constituency associations had selected anti-O'Neill candidates, unofficial pro-O'Neill Unionist candidates came forward. On the other hand, in some cases where the constituency associations selected pro-O'Neill candidates, they were opposed at the election either by unofficial anti-O'Neill Unionists or by members of Ian Paisley's Protestant Unionist party. Anti-unionist constituencies also saw unwonted activity. Traditionally, these had, outside Belfast, been held by the nationalist party, but on this occasion three of the incumbent nationalists were challenged— successfully, as it turned out—by young men who had become prominent in the civil rights movement, John Hume, Ivan Cooper, and Patrick O'Hanlon.

---

[18] *Disturbances in Northern Ireland: report of the commission appointed by the governor of Northern Ireland* [Cmd 532] (H.M.S.O., Belfast, 1969), p. 73; this is the report of the Cameron commission, mentioned below.

The Northern Ireland Labour party put up candidates in both protestant and catholic areas, as did, less successfully, the People's Democracy.

	at dissolution	after election
Official pro-O'Neill Unionists	22	23
Independent pro-O'Neill Unionists	—	3
Official anti-O'Neill Unionists	15	13
Northern Ireland Labour	2	2
Nationalists	9	6
National Democratic Party	1	—
Republican Labour	2	2
Independent	—	3
Liberal	1	—
People's Democracy	—	—
TOTAL	52	52

Thus, pro-O'Neill Unionists appeared to have made a net gain of four seats. Moreover, they had only narrowly missed winning several more. In Larne, Craig held his seat against an unofficial pro-O'Neill Unionist by only 653 votes. In Londonderry North another anti-O'Neill Unionist, Joseph Burns, held his seat by a majority of only 115. Three other anti-O'Neill Unionists— Desmond Boal, Harry West, and Commander Albert Anderson—held their seats by minority votes in three-cornered contests.

However, the gain was not decisive enough. However narrow the margin whereby some of the prime minister's opponents had held their seats, the important fact was that they had held them. And O'Neill himself suffered a moral defeat when he retained his own constituency of Bannside only by a minority vote, in a three-cornered contest against Ian Paisley of the Protestant Unionists and Michael Farrell of People's Democracy. Moreover, some of the Unionists classified as 'pro-O'Neill' were uncertain in their support, and could be detached under pressure from their constituents or provocation from their opponents.

That pressure and provocation was soon provided. March and April 1969 were disturbed months in Northern Ireland. During April there was a particularly severe riot in Derry, during which the R.U.C. again entered the Bogside and individual policemen disgraced themselves. In March and April a number of explosions occurred, at an electricity transformer, an electricity pylon, and at several points on the water mains leading to Belfast. At the time many blamed the I.R.A., but subsequent court cases made it clear that a protestant extremist organisation had been responsible—presumably with the purpose of raising tension and thus helping to bring down O'Neill. Meanwhile the prime minister used his enhanced majority to push through one further reform—the acceptance of 'one man one vote' in local government elections. On 22 April a meeting of the Unionist parliamentary party (M.P.s and senators) accepted the reform by a vote of 28 to 22. But the decision produced yet another defection from the government.

Major James Chichester-Clark, M.P. for Londonderry South and minister for agriculture, was not himself a hard-liner but he represented a hard-line constituency. He came to the conclusion that, though he had no objection in principle to 'one man one vote', the reform was not one that could be sold to the unionist rank and file at that time, and he forthwith resigned. O'Neill felt that the time had come for him to resign as well. He now believed that he had a majority of only three among official Unionist M.P.s: if one more supporter changed sides, he would have a majority of one. He announced his intention on 28 April.

The Unionist parliamentary party had formalised its rules about selecting a leader since the last vacancy in the premiership. The rule now was that the leader should be selected by the official Unionist M.P.s. The election took place on 1 May. Two candidates went forward: Brian Faulkner and James Chichester-Clark. Despite the fact that when Faulkner resigned in January, he appeared to have criticised O'Neill from the left, and that, when Chichester-Clark resigned in April, he appeared to criticise him from the right, it is probable that the latter did better among the O'Neillites, and that the former did better among the anti-O'Neillites. By the narrowest of margins, 17 to 16, Chichester-Clark was victorious. He was forthwith appointed prime minister.

Chichester-Clark's government was substantially the same as O'Neill's, although three anti-O'Neill Unionists, John Dobson, John Taylor, and John Brooke, received junior office, and Faulkner reentered the government as minister for development. The new administration got off to a reasonable start. On 6 May the prime minister announced an amnesty for all offences connected with the demonstrations since 5 October 1968, and while this entailed the dropping of charges against some policemen and protestant extremists, it also lifted a threat over many civil rights activists. The civil rights association announced the temporary suspension of its campaign, and the next two months were relatively free from demonstrations. On 18 June the prime minister met the thirteen opposition M.P.s, and they pronounced themselves satisfied with his timetable for implementing the reforms already promised. During June and July there was a good deal of sporadic violence in many places, especially in Derry and west Belfast, and the first reports came in of a phenomenon that was to become more widespread in the next two years—that of people being intimidated into leaving their homes. But there was room for cautious hope. After nine months of incessant agitation, it was remarkable how little damage Northern Ireland had yet suffered. With two doubtful exceptions, no deaths had yet been caused by the civil disturbances.[19] There had been little damage to property. A consensus between government and civil rights supporters did seem to be reemerging, and if the summer marching season—traditionally the most dangerous time for disturbances—could be got through, there seemed a real hope that harmony might be reestablished.

The hope was soon smashed. Once again, the scene of the trouble was Derry. The Apprentice Boys organisation existed to commemorate the closing of the city gates by protestant apprentices against a catholic army in December 1688.[20] On 12 August its main annual parade, to celebrate the lifting of the siege, was due to take place. This ceremony brought business and colour to Derry and usually passed off without serious incident. But in August 1969 the circumstances were different from previous years. In January and again in April the R.U.C. had entered catholic areas of the city and caused bitter resentment by their conduct; on several occasions militant protestants had massed in the town. Now there was to be a protestant parade protected by armed police, and a further invasion of the Bogside seemed a probable consequence. Chichester-Clark's government seriously considered banning the procession, but a number of considerations deterred it, of which the most cogent was the fear that if the procession was banned protestant extremists would march anyway, and might cause worse trouble than in a properly marshalled procession. But everyone realised how dangerous the situation was. The journalists and television cameras descended on Derry, and awaited the outcome.

It proved worse than almost anyone had dreamt. On this occasion the violence, it seems generally accepted, was started by catholics. A mob of Bogside youths systematically stoned the procession and its protecting police at the one point where it came within range. The police stood their ground for two-and-a-half hours before they charged into the Bogside. But when they did so, the Bogsiders saw it as a repetition of the invasions in January and April; previously prepared barricades went up, and the stoning became much more intense. The R.U.C. was so hard pressed to maintain its position that it asked for, and received, permission to use CS gas. The use of this painful, choking, and irritating gas, specially developed for riot control, gave them the advantage for a short time; but the Bogsiders proved resourceful in finding ways to counter it, and the next day they were able to bring as much

[19] In Derry Samuel Devenny died three months after being beaten up by police. Devenny was a cardiac patient, and it is not possible to say how far his death was brought on by his injuries. In Dungiven Francis McCloskey was found dead from a head injury after a police baton charge. It is not certain whether he was hit by police, or fell. See David McKittrick, Seamus Kelters, Brian Feeney, and Chris Thornton, *Lost lives: the stories of the men, women and children who died as a result of the Northern Ireland troubles* (Edinburgh and London, 1999), pp 32–3.
[20] The changing significance of the siege of Derry over time is discussed in Ian McBride, *The siege of Derry in Ulster protestant mythology* (Dublin, 1997).

pressure as ever on the police. The latter, whose strength in the whole of Northern Ireland was only 3,000, and who had only a few hundred in Derry, were too few to sustain the conflict. The Northern Ireland government had only one other force under its control—the 8,000-strong part-time Ulster Special Constabulary, known as the 'B Specials'.[21] On 13 August, all special constables were called out for duty by appeal over the radio. But though this increased the manpower available to the police, in other ways it made the situation worse. Firstly, the U.S.C. had no training in riot control and might well mishandle riot situations; secondly, it was an entirely protestant force and bitterly unpopular among catholics. This was appreciated by officers of the R.U.C., and in fact the B Specials were used only in small numbers and on the fringe of the main confrontations in Derry the following day. But the broadcast calling them out was heard in catholic areas as well as protestant, and served to heighten fears and resentments.

That evening an event occurred that correspondingly heightened tensions on the protestant side. The part played by the government of the Republic in the Northern Ireland troubles had hitherto been muted. True, Lynch had on several occasions between October 1968 and August 1969 declared that partition was the fundamental source of the disorder, and that there would never be final peace until Ireland was united. But this had been so predictable that it had aroused no more than a ritual reaction from unionists; indeed criticism had been stronger from some civil rights supporters, who felt that their efforts to detach their cause from the partition question were being damaged. On the evening of 13 August, however, Lynch broadcast a statement that went beyond the usual depreciation of partition. He stated that 'the Irish government can no longer stand by and see innocent people injured and perhaps worse',[22] and added that Irish army hospitals were being established along the border. The implication was that the Irish army itself might be moved across the border, and there is evidence that it was taken in this sense by many in Northern Ireland—with hope by nationalists, with fury by unionists. From revelations since, it appears that the speech was the product of a compromise between the different elements in his cabinet, and that its ambiguity was the result of trying to straddle different views, rather than a deliberate attempt to imply threats. But that did not lessen its impact at the time.

---

[21] For the origins of the Ulster Special Constabulary, see above, p. 165.

[22] Cf. Conor Cruise O'Brien's observation that 'videotape records [Lynch's] words as "stand idly by"'(C. C. O'Brien, *States of Ireland* (2nd ed., St Albans, 1974), p. 171). On the subject of southern Irish political responses to N.I., see D. G. Boyce's excellent survey, '"Can anyone here imagine...?": southern Irish political parties and the Northern Ireland problem' in P. J. Roche and Brian Barton (ed.), *The Northern Ireland question: myth and reality* (Aldershot, 1991), pp 173–88.

Meanwhile, sensational events were taking place elsewhere. On the evening of 12 August a call went out from the Bogside for diversionary demonstrations elsewhere in Northern Ireland, so as to take police pressure off the Derry catholics. The following day, demonstrations and violence were reported in Dungiven, Lurgan, Strabane, Omagh, Enniskillen, Newry, Coalisland, and Armagh (where a group of special constables panicked when faced with a hostile mob and shot one man dead). But much the most serious events took place in Belfast. On the evening of 13 August there were sporadic riots and demonstrations in two catholic areas of Belfast—Lower Falls and Ardoyne. The combination of these incidents and Lynch's broadcast heightened tensions on the protestant side. On 14 August, when catholic crowds assembled in the same areas, protestant crowds gathered too. The police interposed a cordon. The catholics threw stones and petrol bombs at the police. The police baton-charged the catholics. The protestant crowds, without invitation, surged out along with the police. To the catholics, who saw a huge mob of protestants headed by police descending upon them, this was the final proof of police partiality. Some among the catholics opened fire. To the police and the protestants, this was the final proof of what *they* had all along suspected—that they were faced with a republican uprising. The police fired back, much more heavily, while behind them protestant crowds systematically burnt scores of catholic houses. By the end of four days of rioting in Belfast, seven people had been killed, five of them catholic, and 179 premises had been damaged beyond repair, 83 per cent of them catholic-occupied.

Long before the crisis was over, however, a vital new factor had entered into the situation. The police had called on the British army for aid. Any police force in the United Kingdom has the right to call in the aid of troops to suppress disturbances if its own resources are exhausted. In Derry, the police decided that this moment had come on 14 August; in the Falls, on 15 August; in Ardoyne, on 16 August. Accordingly, troops moved into each of these areas on these dates and took up positions dividing the factions. Everywhere, they were welcomed by the catholics with relief.[23]

The intervention of the British army was so important because it brought with it the intervention of the British government. For although the army had come to the aid of the Northern Ireland police force, it was maintained and controlled by the British government, and the latter could not be expected to let it be used in effect for supporting the policies of the Northern Ireland government without ensuring that those policies were ones that it

[23] The account in the last five paragraphs is largely derived from the report of the Scarman tribunal, an exhaustive and impartial inquiry, which heard evidence from 428 witnesses of all shades of opinion (*Violence and civil disturbances in Northern Ireland in 1969: report of tribunal of inquiry* [Cmd 566] (2 vols, H.M.S.O., Belfast, 1972)). For the army, see Desmond Hamill, *Pig in the middle: the army in Northern Ireland 1969–1984* (London, 1985).

could approve. Over the next few weeks, the pressure on the British government was palpable. On 19 August, Chichester-Clark was summoned to London to meet Wilson. On 27–9 August James Callaghan, who as home secretary was the minister directly responsible for Northern Ireland, visited Northern Ireland and met representatives of all shades of opinion. On 8–13 October he returned. At each of these contacts between British and Northern Ireland ministers, a fresh crop of reforms was announced.[24]

The reforms of August–October 1969 made a formidable list. A tribunal, the Scarman tribunal, was set up to inquire into the causes of the violence of the preceding months. A senior officer of the British foreign service was appointed as British government representative in Northern Ireland, to ensure that Whitehall had a channel of information independent of the Northern Ireland government. A ministry of community relations was announced, together with an independent community relations commission. A joint Whitehall–Stormont working party recommended ways of preventing discrimination in central and local government service. Alongside the parliamentary commissioner (already appointed in June) who dealt with complaints against central government departments, a commissioner for complaints was promised who would deal with the much more numerous grievances provoked by local authorities.

In the field of local government reform, progress was also made. The Northern Ireland government had already, before the riots began, produced a white paper proposing reorganisation into a single tier of seventeen local authorities, controlling all local government functions including housing. Callaghan, however, evidently decided that housing was so contentious an area that it could not be left in local government hands. At the end of his second visit, therefore, it was announced that housing would be taken out of local authority hands altogether, and placed in charge of a unified housing authority, based on the Northern Ireland Housing Trust. This had consequential effects for other local authority services, such as drainage and planning, and thus threw local government reform back into the melting pot. In December 1969 a committee was set up, containing both protestants and catholics, under the chairmanship of Patrick Macrory, to make recommendations on the new shape of local government in the light of the decision that housing should be centralised.

The most sweeping reforms were made in the police. On 26 August a committee was set up, consisting of two British police officers under the chairmanship of the famous mountaineer, Lord Hunt, to consider the reorganisation of the Royal Ulster Constabulary and the Ulster Special Constabulary. Its report, published on 10 October, was drastic. It recommended

---

[24] For Callaghan's reflections, see James Callaghan, *A house divided: the dilemma of Northern Ireland* (London, 1973).

that the R.U.C. be disarmed, civilianised, and relieved of its paramilitary functions. More daring still, it proposed that the U.S.C. be abolished and replaced by two forces: an R.U.C. reserve to aid the R.U.C. in its civilian policing functions, and an armed force to operate under the control of the British army. It hoped that all sections of the community would be represented in both these forces. These proposals, and particularly the abolition of the U.S.C., filled many unionists with dismay. They had looked on the special constabulary as their surest bulwark—an armed force, composed exclusively of reliable men, and under the control of Stormont, it was their surest safeguard against a sell-out by Westminster. But the Northern Ireland government, with Callaghan waiting discreetly in a neighbouring room, felt obliged to accept the Hunt committee's recommendations in full. Callaghan thereupon imposed a new inspector-general of the R.U.C., a distinguished English policeman, Sir Arthur Young, to preside over the reorganisation.

The acceptance of the Hunt report produced a vicious response among protestant extremists. On 11 and 12 October the Shankill Road area, one of the most militantly loyalist parts of Belfast, burst into riot. One policeman was shot dead, and many soldiers wounded. The soldiers for their part killed two protestants, and beat many of those whom they arrested. One journalist who had covered most Belfast riots wrote that 'in its incredible intensity, the battle of the Shankill had surpassed anything that had taken place in August.'[25] Among catholics, on the other hand, the reforms were welcomed. Almost the whole of the original demands of the civil rights movement had now been met, or were in process of being met. The only gap was that the special powers act remained, but even here the promise made in November 1968 still stood, of withdrawing its provisions as soon as this could be done 'without undue hazard'. The British army remained popular in catholic areas. Its only difficulty had been in persuading the people to dismantle the barricades erected after the August riots to keep out the protestants. This was finally achieved, after much diplomacy and profuse assurances of protection, during September.

The publication of the Hunt report marked the end of the first phase of the Northern Ireland troubles. During it, the civil rights movement had consistently held the upper hand in the propaganda war. Police and protestants had repeatedly put themselves in the wrong by over-reacting to civil rights demonstrations, and as a result the Northern Ireland government had been forced to concede almost the whole of the civil rights demands. A second phase now opened, lasting from October 1969 till July 1971. During this period the problem was: could a consensus be achieved? Would it be

[25] Max Hastings, *Ulster 1969: the fight for civil rights in Northern Ireland* (London, 1970), p. 186.

possible to develop a new order going far enough to satisfy most catholics, but not so far as to be intolerable to most protestants?

There were certainly factors working against such a consensus. One of the most serious was the distrust between catholics and the British army that developed during this period. That such a distrust should emerge might at first sight seem surprising, for the army had come to protect the catholics. But there were deeper psychological forces that worked the other way. Most catholics were nationalists; they had been brought up to believe that partition was a wrong inflicted on their country by the British, and that if the British would only go away they could easily make up their differences with the unionists. To look upon British troops as their protectors, then, went against ingrained habits of thought, and it is not surprising if in the long run the more deeply rooted attitudes prevailed.

The first confrontation between catholics and the army occurred at Bally-murphy on 1 and 2 April 1970. Ballymurphy is a housing estate on the western edge of Belfast, high up on the slopes of Divis Mountain. It had not been involved in the troubles of 1969, but it was lacking in amenities, had an appalling unemployment rate, and was famous among social workers for the number of its problem families. It was a natural breeding-ground for riot; it was also solidly catholic. On 1 April an Orange parade moving past the edge of the estate was stoned by youths; British troops interposed between the factions and were themselves stoned; they retaliated by using tear gas which drifted through the streets, infuriating many who had had nothing to do with the riot so far.

During the next three months there were a number of other three-cornered riots in Belfast, in which the troops acted quite as vigorously against protestants as against catholics, and in which their reputation among cath-olics seems at least to have grown no worse. But early in July, catholic–army relations took a further downward plunge. On 3 July, acting on a tip-off, troops raided a house in Balkan Street, in the heart of Lower Falls, and found arms. If the task of loading the arms on to trucks and taking them away had taken thirty minutes instead of forty, the incident might have passed off quietly; but the longer the troops stayed, the more restive the watching crowd became. Stones began to be thrown; the troops responded with tear gas; the crowd became more angry and began to throw up barri-cades. The British commander, Lt-gen. Sir Ian Freeland, decided to sur-round the area with troops to prevent aid arriving from other parts of Belfast. The area was then placed under curfew for thirty-six hours. By the time this confrontation ended, six civilians had been killed, and a house-to-house search conducted in which some soldiers caused needless damage. The final insult occurred when two ministers in the Stormont government, Captains William Long and John Brooke, led a group of journalists through the curfewed area in army lorries. This was taken as meaning that the army was becoming more closely identified with the Stormont regime than it had been hitherto. There had just been a change of government at Westminster, where Edward Heath and the Conservatives took over from Harold Wilson and the Labour party on 19 June, and many catholics believed that the new severity against them was connected with the change of government. The best evidence available indicates that this was unfounded;[26] but the belief was sincerely held, and embittered relations.

From then on, relations between Belfast catholics and the British army deteriorated. On 31 July rioting spread to a fresh catholic area, the New Lodge Road. Sporadic riots continued in catholic areas through 1970 and into the early weeks of 1971. Meanwhile, fresh grounds for grievances were emerging. There were complaints that the army searched for illegal arms only in catholic, never in protestant areas. There were allegations that particular regiments, especially Scottish ones, were anti-catholic.

Early in 1971, the deteriorating situation took an important new turn for the worse. The I.R.A. went on to the offensive. To explain how this came about, we must retrace our steps and examine the progress of the I.R.A. from 1969. In the disturbances of August 1969, the I.R.A. played very little part. The policy of abandoning military in favour of political action, favoured since 1962 by the Dublin leadership, ensured this. According to one source, the leadership had sold their arms in 1968 to the Free Wales Army.[27] According to another, an appeal from the Belfast I.R.A. to headquarters in May 1969 to make defensive preparations a priority was met with the reply that 'they would put it up to the official forces, the British army and the R.U.C., to defend the people'.[28] So when the August disorders broke out, the I.R.A. was almost without equipment. A handful of members helped fight off the protestant incursion into Lower Falls on 14 August, and that was the extent of their involvement. Indeed, there was a good deal of bitterness in catholic areas that the I.R.A. had done so little.

There was also bitterness within the ranks of the northern I.R.A. itself. Many of its older members had disliked the left-wing approach of the Dublin radicals, and had drifted away from the movement. Their drift is said to have been accelerated by offers, made through intermediaries by leading members of Fianna Fáil, of substantial sums of money for arms, provided that an independent northern command was set up and that I.R.A. activities in the republic ceased.[29] The Dublin leadership, on the other hand, continued

[26] Richard Rose, *Governing without consensus: an Irish perspective* (London, 1971), p. 175; the *Sunday Times* 'Insight' team, *Ulster* (Harmondsworth, 1972) (hereafter cited as 'Insight', *Ulster*), pp 214–21.
[27] 'Insight', *Ulster*, p. 89.
[28] Ruairí Ó Brádaigh, review of Bowyer Bell, *Secret army* (1st ed., London, 1970), in *Irish Press*, 30 Jan. 1971.
[29] For an illuminating discussion of this episode, see Patterson, *Politics of illusion* (1997 ed.), pp 121–4.

along its path of exchanging military for political activity. At an army convention in December 1969 a momentous change of principle was proposed: that the I.R.A. should recognise *de facto* the existing regimes in Belfast and Dublin. It was carried, by 39 votes to 12 according to one report,[30] by 28 to 12 according to another.[31] At this point the dissidents broke away and, under the generally accepted label of 'Provisional I.R.A.', proceeded to organise their own force; while the majority, under the name of 'Official I.R.A.', maintained their emphasis on radical social action.[32] The break was mirrored in Sinn Féin, the political counterpart of the I.R.A.

This did not mean that an I.R.A. offensive was about to begin. The Provisionals were weak, both in numbers and equipment. It is not even clear what their objective was in the early stages. Though bitterly anti-British, they also looked on themselves as a kind of home guard to defend the catholic areas of Belfast against protestant incursion, and this aim would not be furthered by antagonising the British army as well. The *Sunday Times* 'Insight' team depicts the Provisional leadership as being in negotiation with the British army as late as January 1971. Certainly any military action they took up to that date seems to have been sporadic and generally defensive, the most celebrated being the defence of St Matthew's church in east Belfast against protestant assailants at the end of June 1970.

By February 1971, however, the Provisionals appear to have been ready to go over to the offensive. On 6 February the first British soldier was killed; several others were killed or injured in the following weeks. In March, the Provisionals made clear their aims in interviews with journalists. They intended to induce a 'bring the troops home' campaign in Britain and then, by stages, conquer Northern Ireland.[33] The Official I.R.A., too, was drawn into the attack. Although its Marxist ideology led it to doubt whether an atmosphere of sectarian war would further the social revolution at which it aimed, it had to appear as militant as the Provisionals, or it would lose support. The main weapon of assault was the bomb—generally planted in some office, shop, club, or factory, with a warning being given. The object seems to have been to do economic damage, to raise the cost of British involvement in Northern Ireland, and to harass the army and police. As 1971 continued, the number of explosions went inexorably upwards: January, 12; February, 28; March, 33; April, 37; May, 47; June, 50; July, 91.

It should not be thought that, as nationalists grew more militant, unionists therefore grew more docile. On the contrary, another discouraging feature of these eighteen months was the strength and persistence of unionist extremism. It was shown firstly in the internal affairs of the Unionist party.

[30] 'Insight', *Ulster*, p. 194.   [31] Ó Brádaigh, loc. cit.
[32] See Patrick Bishop and Eamon Mallie, *The Provisional I.R.A.* (London, 1987); Patterson, *Politics of illusion* (1997 ed.), ch. 6.
[33] *This Week*, 12 Mar. 1971, pp 7–10; cf. *Sunday Press*, 14 Mar. 1971.

Throughout these months the battle ebbed and flowed between moderates and hard-liners in the unionist associations. If the moderates sometimes had successes, as when they won back Clifton Unionist Association from the hard-liners in May 1970, they also had setbacks, as when Carrick Unionist Association censured its moderate M.P., Anne Dickson, in July 1970. In January 1970, a number of right-wing constituencies in the three western counties founded the West Ulster Unionist Council, under the chairmanship of Harry West. It acted as a focus for hard-line sentiment, and before the end of the year right-wing associations in the eastern part of the province, such as Shankill, had affiliated with it. In parliament, right-wing unionists consistently sniped at reform legislation, and in March 1970 five of them—Harry West, William Craig, Desmond Boal, John McQuade, and Dr Norman Laird—were deprived of the whip for refusing to support the government on a vote of confidence.

Electorally, results showed that right-wing sentiment was at least as strong in the protestant part of the electorate as it had been in 1969. In April 1970, the Protestant Unionist party gained two seats from official Unionists at by-elections, Ian Paisley being elected in Bannside and the Rev. William Beattie in Antrim South. True, in both cases they were returned on a minority vote, but none the less their party's share of the poll increased as compared with the general election. The results of the Westminster general election of June 1970 indicated the same trend. In Antrim North Ian Paisley defeated a moderate Unionist, Henry Clark, and in several other constituencies the Unionists bought off Protestant Unionist opposition only by shifting their own position to the right. The only ray of hope for moderates lay in the Belfast North result, where the Unionist sitting M.P., Stratton Mills, a moderate, faced up to a Protestant Unionist opponent and successfully held his seat.

Most of all, the protestant right wing made itself felt in the streets. Rioting was not confined to catholics. In June 1970 and again in April 1971 Orange marchers attacked troops for showing what they regarded as partiality to catholics. A recurring problem of Saturday afternoons throughout the period was the behaviour of Linfield Football Club supporters as they returned to their homes in the Shankill past the catholic-tenanted Unity Flats. A large force of police and troops had regularly to be stationed there to move them past as they shouted taunts at the catholics. Explosions, too, during this period were by no means always the work of the I.R.A. Particularly in the early part of 1970 they seem, to judge by the targets, to have been generally the work of militant protestants.[34] The homes and offices of well-known moderate individuals and organisations, such as Richard Ferguson, Sheelagh

---

[34] Steve Bruce, *The red hand: protestant paramilitaries in Northern Ireland* (Oxford, 1992), ch. 2.

Murnaghan, and the New Ulster Movement, were bombed. So were several catholic churches. One of the most alarming explosions took place in a Belfast courthouse in February, during the trial of some protestants for causing the explosions of March–April 1969.[35] As the jury acquitted the defendants, it seems to have taken the hint.

Yet it would be unfair to picture the period October 1970–July 1971 as simply one of mounting violence from both extremes. Throughout the period there were countervailing forces. Not all catholics in the disturbed areas were rioters: a recurring feature of the riots of 1970 was the efforts of many local residents to disperse the stone-throwers. On several occasions the women of the neighbourhood emerged and, with linked arms, interposed themselves between the rioters and the troops. Not all catholics refused the opportunities to cooperate that were offered in this period. The reorganised security forces gained considerable catholic support in the early stages. The new Ulster Defence Regiment was reported in July 1970 to be 21.4 per cent catholic in membership: a figure that, while it fell short of the catholic proportion in the total population of 34.9 per cent (according to the 1961 census), was none the less a great advance on the proportion of 0 per cent in the old B Specials. In April 1970 it was reported that 40 per cent of applicants to the newly remodelled R.U.C. were catholics.[36]

Politically, an important development on the anti-unionist side occurred with the formation of the Social Democratic and Labour party in August 1970.[37] Six M.P.s launched this party—three independent civil rights supporters, John Hume, Ivan Cooper, and Patrick O'Hanlon; one nationalist, Austin Currie; one Northern Ireland Labour member, Patrick Devlin; and one Republican Labour M.P., Gerry Fitt, who became the leader—as well as Patrick Wilson, Republican Labour senator. Their programme was moderate and constructive, stressing the need for social justice and economic development within Northern Ireland. On partition, it stated that its aim was 'to promote cooperation, friendship, and understanding between north and south with a view to eventual reunification of Ireland through the consent of the majority of the people in the north and south'. The S.D.L.P. contained several men of great energy and ability, and the party worked hard at its parliamentary duties. In December 1970 the political correspondent of the moderate unionist *Belfast Telegraph* remarked that 'the opposition is possibly more constructive now than it has ever been.' When the Provisional I.R.A.

[35] See above, p. 331.

[36] Following the Hunt recommendations and the passing of a Stormont police act (1970, c. 9 (26 Mar. 1970)), the R.U.C. lost much of its paramilitary character and was remodelled on the lines of police forces in Britain. The U.D.R. was the part-time force under army control established in Dec. 1969 (1969, c. 65 [U.K.] (18 Dec. 1969)), also in line with the Hunt recommendations.

[37] Ian McAllister, *The Northern Ireland Social Democratic and Labour party: political opposition in a divided society* (London, 1977).

campaign developed in the following spring, the S.D.L.P. displayed no sympathy for it.

Another encouraging feature of this period was the growth of organisations bridging the sectarian divide. Such organisations were not new; the Northern Ireland Labour party, and the Ulster Liberal party, as well as such non-political bodies as the Irish Association and the Corrymeela Community, had succeeded in attracting support from both protestant and catholic. In February 1969 they were joined by a new body which, though not itself a political party, performed many of the functions of a political party. This was the New Ulster Movement, founded by moderates of all parties and of none to support O'Neill. From it there sprang in April 1970 the Alliance party, designed to attract both catholic and protestant by its policy of reconciliation. Community groups developed too. P.A.C.E.—Protestant and Catholic Encounter—was formed in 1968 as a forum where protestants and catholics could frankly face their differences. In many disturbed areas of Belfast, peace committees composed of catholics and protestants were formed to organise vigilante patrols and act as mediators in local conflicts. 'Women Together' was founded in November 1970 to mobilise women with the same object. The Community Relations Commission, under the imaginative chairmanship of Dr Maurice Hayes, sponsored research into the sources of community tension, and built up a team of community development officers.

The interested governments outside Northern Ireland also lent their weight to the forces of reconciliation. As already mentioned,[38] the Dublin government was notably dove-like in this period, particularly after Lynch dismissed his hard-liners in May 1970. The same was generally true of the British government. The change from a Labour to a Conservative administration in June 1970 made little difference. In August 1970 the new home secretary, Reginald Maudling, warned the unionist right wing that 'to go back on what has been done—or depart from the ideals of impartiality and reconciliation—would endanger the present constitutional arrangements under which Northern Ireland governs its own affairs'.[39] In other words, a swing to the right would bring direct rule from Westminster. The most striking illustration of Westminster's reluctance to be pushed from a middle-of-the-road position occurred in March 1971. The Provisional I.R.A. offensive had already begun. On 10 March three young Scottish soldiers were found gruesomely murdered on the outskirts of Belfast. On 12 March 6,000 shipyard workers left their workplace and marched through Belfast demanding the internment of known I.R.A. men. Faced with such pressure from his right wing, on 15 March Chichester-Clark flew to London to say that he would resign if tougher measures were not taken. But all he could

---

[38] Above, pp 319–20.   [39] *Irish Times*, 11 Aug. 1970.

extract from Whitehall was a promise of 1,500 more soldiers. It was not enough, and on 20 March 1971 he resigned. The British government was at that stage prepared to let a Northern Ireland prime minister fall rather than intensify its measures against the I.R.A.

The Unionist government, for its part, stuck gamely to its reform promises. By the end of 1969 it had appointed its first ombudsman and its first commissioner for complaints, and had set up the ministry of community relations and the community relations commission. During 1970 the B Specials were disbanded, and the R.U.C. reserve and the Ulster Defence Regiment were launched. Electoral law was brought into line with Great Britain's, and both central and local government franchise were now based on universal suffrage for all men and women over 18. The slowest task, because the most complicated, was local government reorganisation, but even here substantial progress was made. The new housing executive was established by an act of February 1971.[40] The Macrory review body submitted its recommendations in May 1970; they were generally endorsed by both government and opposition during a debate in January 1971, and much parliamentary time in the ensuing months went in carrying the consequential legislation. Serious criticisms were subsequently made of the effectiveness of this reform programme. It was claimed that the terms of reference of the ombudsman and of the commissioner for complaints were too narrow for them really to root out discrimination. It was pointed out that, despite all the paper changes in the R.U.C., the constables who disgraced themselves in the Bogside in January and April 1970 were not dismissed. All these complaints had substance; but it is also true that the reform programme marked a substantial advance on the situation existing in 1968, and was a genuine contribution to reconciliation.

Not only did the Northern Ireland government implement the reforms already promised; it even began, in a tentative way, to watch out for fresh grievances and to meet them before they festered. During 1970, the main demand from opposition spokesmen switched from 'civil rights' to 'participation'; they came to realise that, even when the full reform programme was granted, they would still be no nearer to exercising power in Northern Ireland, and they came to demand a share in power as well. Instead of rejecting this demand out of hand, as might have been expected from the past record of unionist governments, Chichester-Clark received it sympathetically, and was still considering methods of implementing it when he fell from office.

The momentum was continued by Chichester-Clark's successor, Brian Faulkner. Faulkner had been minister for development in the Chichester-Clark administration, and as such had been responsible for a large proportion of the reform legislation. He had shed his right-wing image, and had served

[40] 1971, c. 5 (25 Feb. 1971).

Chichester-Clark with a loyalty that he had never shown to O'Neill. When the election for leader of the party took place, he had no difficulty in winning it by 26 votes to 4 for William Craig. His government included two known moderates: Robin Bailie and a former Northern Ireland Labour M.P., David Bleakley, who was appointed under a hitherto unused section of the government of Ireland act that enabled non-members of parliament to be ministers provided they did not stay longer than six months. True, Faulkner also strengthened his right wing by bringing Harry West back into the government—but by doing so he also decapitated the West Ulster Unionist Council.

With this team, Faulkner pursued the theme of participation. In June 1971 he put to the Northern Ireland house of commons some concrete proposals for ensuring it. He suggested that the house establish (alongside its already existing public accounts committee) three functional committees to cover social services, environmental services, and industrial services, with powers to initiate policy and to review executive performance. Through these committees, non-ministerial members of parliament would have much more substantial influence over policy than they had had hitherto, and opposition members could thus fill a larger role; he also suggested that two of the four committees be chaired by the opposition. The speech was welcomed by the opposition; Patrick Devlin even called it Faulkner's 'finest hour'. While it is clear that the proposals did not fully meet the demand for power-sharing— the executive would still be in unionist hands—they were none the less a considerable step forward, enough to ease evolution to some more permanent settlement.

At the end of June 1971, then, the situation did not seem hopeless. At Stormont, government and opposition were edging towards a more cordial relationship. Though the I.R.A. campaign was growing in strength, it had failed to do any serious damage to the Northern Ireland economy, and was abhorred by many of the catholics on whom it hoped to rely. It was, also, almost confined to Belfast. Optimists hoped that if the I.R.A. campaign could be contained for just a bit longer, until the reforms had begun to 'bite' and the catholic population could feel for itself that the bad old days were indeed gone, Northern Ireland might yet move into a period of harmony. In support of such hopes they could point to the one area in the province where the reforms had already 'bitten'. This was Derry, where the Derry commission had been operating since the beginning of 1969, and was making remarkable changes. It had broken with the discriminatory practices of the old corporation. It had practically ended the city's housing shortage, and had made perceptible advances even in dealing with the far more difficult unemployment problem. These achievements, it seemed, had paid off. Though Derry was not yet trouble-free, it had far less disorder than Belfast. Except for one protestant killed in a riot in September 1969, and one soldier killed by a petrol-bomb attack in March 1971, there had been no deaths attributable to the civil disturbances since that of Samuel Devenny. Derry was the bright spot, which seemed to show that progress by evolution was possible.

These hopes were not fulfilled. Indeed it was in Derry that the events occurred that opened our third period, lasting from July 1971 to March 1972, in which Northern Ireland plunged rapidly to further depths of turmoil.

From 4 to 8 July 1971, Derry witnessed its worst wave of rioting since August 1969. There was much throwing of stones and petrol bombs and—a sinister new development—for the first time a good deal of shooting at troops. There was no obvious reason for this outbreak, and the most likely explanation is that it was a deliberate attempt by the Provisional I.R.A. to provoke British troops into creating an incident. If this was the object, its perpetrators, after four days of hard work, succeeded. For on 8 July soldiers shot dead two men, Séamus Cusack and Desmond Beattie, believing them to be armed. Although the soldiers had been under great provocation, it seems clear that they had shot the wrong men.[41] There was an immediate reaction from even the more moderate Derry catholics. The S.D.L.P. M.P.s met, demanded a public inquiry, and threatened to withdraw from Stormont if the demand were not met. The leader of the party, Gerry Fitt, was not present at the meeting at which this decision was taken, did not approve of it, and tried frantically to negotiate some compromise with the British home secretary, Maudling. But his efforts were disowned by the Derry members of the party. The British government refused the inquiry demanded, and on 16 July the S.D.L.P. M.P.s announced their withdrawal from the Northern Ireland parliament. They were followed by nationalist and Republican Labour members.

There were puzzling features about the S.D.L.P.'s decision. It seemed inconsistent with the strong line that the party had hitherto taken against violence from the catholic side. It seemed illogical to punish Faulkner by withdrawing from his parliament, for an action by the British army over which he had no control. By playing their most powerful card at this time, the party lessened its capacity to retaliate against other, and yet more unpalatable, actions that the Stormont or Westminster governments might subsequently take. The decision seems to have been initiated by the Derry members of the party, John Hume and Ivan Cooper, and it may have been an attempt to win back influence from the Provisional I.R.A., whose supporters staged a well attended meeting in Derry on 11 July. Or it may have been simply an emotional expression of their outrage. But whatever the causes, the decision marked a turning-point in the history of Northern Ireland. It rendered progress by evolution almost impossible.

[41] For the most objective appraisal of this incident, see *Fortnight*, 6–31 Aug. 1971, pp 7–8.

A few weeks later, the Stormont and Westminster governments struck their own, and much more serious, blow at the chances of such progress. Faulkner was under increasing pressure from the unionist right wing to take more drastic action against the I.R.A. The obvious weapon was internment of suspected members of the I.R.A. Because of intimidation of witnesses, and sympathy among sections of the catholic population, the police found it difficult to bring home a charge of membership in the I.R.A., and yet they often had a shrewd idea of who the members were. In the 1920s, 1940s, and 1950s such people had been interned without trial, and the measure had helped to defeat the I.R.A. campaigns of those years. On this occasion, the British army commanders appear to have been sceptical of its efficacy; they knew it would cause bitterness in the catholic population, and feared that it might help rather than damage the I.R.A. But as the weeks went by, and existing measures failed to prevent a rise in violence, their arguments had decreasing force. There was another pressure operating on Faulkner during the summer: the annual parade of the Apprentice Boys was due in Derry on 12 August. It would certainly cause trouble if it were allowed to take place, but he was unable to persuade the organisation to abandon it voluntarily, and faced great difficulties from his right wing if he banned it without offering some quid pro quo. Such a quid pro quo could be provided by internment. By early August Faulkner had persuaded the British government that it must be tried.

Internment was introduced on 9 August 1971. In the early hours of that morning, British troops arrested 342 men. Simultaneously, Faulkner announced that all public parades were banned for the next six months. It very soon became clear that the move was a failure. Police intelligence seems to have been much worse than on previous occasions when internment had been employed, for it is clear that many of the most active I.R.A. men escaped, while many of those arrested had little or nothing to do with the I.R.A. campaign. The I.R.A., far from fading out, stepped up its activities. During the first three days after internment, twenty-three people were killed; much the highest death rate that the province had yet seen. Explosions increased: from 164 incidents in July to 207 in August, 242 in September, and a peak of 279 in October. In the autumn, the shooting campaign took a new turn in savagery, with the killing in their own homes of policemen and members of the U.D.R. Violence bred counter-violence, and massive displacements of population occurred as catholics were driven from protestant areas and vice versa: the community relations commission estimated that about 2,100 households moved in the three weeks following internment, 40 per cent of them protestant and 60 per cent catholic.[42] The army commander, Lt-gen.

---

[42] Northern Ireland Community Relations Commission Research Unit, *Flight: a report on population movement in Belfast during August 1971* ([Belfast, 1971]), p. 6.

Sir Harry Tuzo, subsequently admitted that while polarisation of the communities had been foreseen, its intensity had not.[43]

The non-violent protest was as ominous as the violent. In mid-August, following a meeting of nine opposition M.P.s in Belfast, a civil disobedience campaign was launched. Its main weapon was the withholding of rates and, in the case of council tenants, of rents. By the middle of September it was reported that 26,000 households—about half the catholic households in council housing—were on rent strike. Another weapon was the withdrawal of opposition councillors in local authorities: by January 1972 enough had withdrawn for four councils—those of Strabane, Newry, Keady, and Warrenpoint urban districts—to be suspended because not enough councillors were attending to provide a quorum for necessary business. Many catholics serving on statutory bodies also ceased to attend. The Ulster Defence Regiment was hit by a similar movement: by October the proportion of catholics serving in it had dropped to 11 per cent, and by January 1972 to 6 per cent.

In their intransigence, northern catholics received moral support from the Republic. Lynch denounced internment as soon as it was introduced, and called for the suspension of Stormont and for the appointment of a commission to rule the north on the basis of parity between the two communities—a much more extreme demand than any he had hitherto made. This was followed by an acrimonious exchange of telegrams between himself and the British prime minister, Heath. In September attempts were made to repair relations by a meeting between Lynch and Heath, and then between Lynch, Heath, and Faulkner, but nothing concrete emerged from them. In December, the Dublin government added to the British government's embarrassments by laying a complaint before the European Commission on Human Rights, charging the army and police in Northern Ireland with brutality. Meanwhile I.R.A. men attacked British troops and policemen repeatedly from across the border, and I.R.A. spokesmen held press conferences in Dublin. The Irish government, while not condoning such activities on the part of an organisation which, after all, was illegal in the Republic as well as in the north, did not pursue the I.R.A. with as much rigour as it had done on occasions in the past, and was to do in the future.

Nevertheless, by the beginning of 1972 there were signs that Northern Ireland was beginning to grope back towards normality. After its peak in October 1971, violence was beginning to fall away. The British army was claiming the arrest of an increasing number of I.R.A. men. About the beginning of the year, a switch in I.R.A. policy was observable. From leaving bombs inside buildings, it was coming to leave them in cars parked in the streets. This was a much less efficient method of attack: a far larger amount

[43] See report of his lecture to the Institute of Strategic Studies, London, in *Irish Times*, 20 Oct. 1971.

of explosives was required to do the same amount of damage to buildings, and there was more risk of injury to passers-by. It was made necessary by the increasing efficiency of military patrols in the centre of Belfast.[44] The non-violent resistance campaign seemed also to be flagging slightly: the numbers on rent strike, for instance, dropped from 26,000 in September to 22,000 in December. Meanwhile British politicians were making important concessions to the anti-unionist point of view. In November, the leader of the opposition, Wilson, proposed a fifteen-point plan for a Northern Ireland settlement, including provision for an eventual united Ireland. Shortly afterwards the home secretary, Maudling, while not going so far as this, stated that if north and south could agree on a united Ireland, the British people would warmly welcome it. These statements brought a less violent reaction from unionist leaders than might have been expected. Even Paisley, in interviews on television and in the press following Wilson's statement, seemed to imply that, if the sectarian features of southern society were eliminated, a united Ireland might not be totally unacceptable. The situation remained a great deal more intractable than it had been before August: internment continued to cause great bitterness among catholics,[45] just as the rent and rate strike did among protestants. But a little hope was again visible.

It is worth painting a picture of life in Northern Ireland at this time. In the catholic areas of Belfast and Derry, street-lights were often not working, traffic-lights were broken and roads unrepaired, the buses stopped running as soon as trouble broke out, and many post offices and banks had been closed following repeated robberies. The army generally appeared in the catholic areas of Belfast driving at speed in armoured vehicles; in the catholic areas of Derry it did not appear at all. The police were not present in either. In some border areas, notably south Armagh, conditions were similar. Elsewhere in the province ramps had been built on the roads outside police stations and military posts to slow down traffic and make attacks by tip-and-run raiders more difficult. In the spring, after the introduction of car bombs by the I.R.A., parking regulations were introduced that made it illegal to leave an unoccupied car in the centre of almost any town. But despite these inconveniences, to a surprising extent life went on as normal. Schools still opened, social welfare officers did their work, shops served goods, milk floats and bread vans went on their rounds, even in the most disturbed districts. Even in Belfast, the centre of most disturbances, most of the inhabitants experienced the troubles as something they saw on their television screens, rather than as part of their personal life. For most people in Northern Ireland the worst discomforts of this period were caused by two events,

---

[44] Maria McGuire, *To take arms: a year in the Provisional I.R.A.* (London, 1973), p. 102.
[45] Over 1,500 arrests had been made by the end of 1971, though nearly two-thirds of those detained had been released.

one natural and one industrial, unconnected with the political disorder. In October, water rationing was introduced in Belfast and neighbouring areas, following an unusually dry summer. In December an electricity strike meant that whole districts in turn had their electricity supply cut off, at the coldest and darkest time of the year. Road accidents still caused more casualties than the I.R.A. and the British army combined: during 1971 302 people were killed in road accidents, as against 173 killed in civil disturbances.

Once again, however, the hope that Northern Ireland had passed the worst point of its troubles was to be shattered. The occasion was a move by the Northern Ireland government that seemed directed more against its own extremists than against the catholic population. In mid January 1972 Faulkner announced that the existing ban on processions would be continued for a further year. The most obvious victims were the Orange order, the Black Institution, and the Apprentice Boys, all of which would have to abandon their summer parades. The announcement caused great annoyance among the unionist right wing. At Stormont the government had to face a vote of censure from a section of its own followers. As a result of the vote two more Unionist M.P.s, John Laird and Captain Robert Mitchell, were deprived of the party whip for voting against the government. But though the move was seen by protestants as directed primarily against them, it was with catholics that the fatal clash came.

On Sunday 30 January 1972 the Northern Ireland Civil Rights Association held a march in Derry to protest against internment. The march was, of course, illegal, and the decision was taken to prevent it spilling from the Bogside into the centre of the city, by erecting barriers. A further and more fateful decision was also taken. The army in Derry had long been harassed by what it described as the hooligan element—largely teenagers throwing stones and petrol bombs. It anticipated that these would be attracted in strength by the procession and that this might be a good moment to scoop them up. An arrest operation was consequently planned to take place after the procession had passed the barriers. It was to be carried out by 1 Battalion of the Parachute Regiment, which was reputed to be the toughest of all the British units then stationed in Northern Ireland.

Events developed as the army anticipated. The procession's organisers did not attempt a confrontation with the army but led the procession away from the barriers. The hooligan element made its appearance, and stoned troops guarding the barriers with great severity. The paratroopers advanced through the barriers and started to make arrests. At this point things went wrong. There is an irreconcileable conflict of evidence as to what happened. The soldiers said that they came under fire, and fired back at particular individuals who appeared to be armed with guns, nail bombs, or acid bombs. Civilians claimed that the soldiers fired without warning and shot indiscriminately at unarmed people. But whatever the precise circumstances, the fact remained that after a few minutes' firing thirteen civilian men lay dead and thirteen others had been wounded. No soldiers were hurt.

This was not quite the worst single episode for loss of life in Northern Ireland. Six weeks earlier, McGurk's bar in a catholic part of Belfast had been blown up without warning, killing fifteen people. But on that occasion indignation had a less clear-cut target: it was uncertain whether the bomb had been planted by loyalist extremists, or was an I.R.A. bomb that had gone off prematurely while awaiting collection from the building. At Derry on 30 January there could be no doubt about the responsibility: it was British soldiers who had fired the fatal shots.[46]

The episode plunged community tensions within Northern Ireland to even greater depths than before. Catholic areas of the province held demonstrations of mourning. In Derry John Hume was reported as saying that 'it is a united Ireland or nothing'. On the protestant side there was a widespread feeling that catholics were making an unreasonable fuss about something for which they themselves were to blame, by going ahead with an illegal march. The worst outrages yet soon occurred in the weeks following 'Bloody Sunday', as the episode in Derry came to be called. On 22 February a bomb placed at the officers' mess of the Parachute Regiment headquarters in Aldershot killed seven people—five charwomen, a gardener, and a catholic army chaplain. The Official I.R.A. claimed responsibility. On 20 March a bomb exploded in Donegall Street, Belfast, killing six people, most of them corporation binmen. The Provisional I.R.A., while claiming that its telephoned warning had been distorted, admitted responsibility. What is generally considered the most horrifying of all the explosions occurred on 4 March in the Abercorn restaurant, Belfast, when it was crowded with afternoon shoppers. The Abercorn explosion is remembered not for the number it killed—'only' two died—but for what it did to some of the 136 injured. One girl lost both legs, an arm and an eye; her sister lost both legs; several others lost limbs. No organisation has admitted responsibility for this deed.[47] Meanwhile a new form of terror began in the province—the sectarian murder.

If Bloody Sunday worsened relations in the north, its effect was dramatic in the Republic. A wave of anti-British feeling swept the country. British-owned

[46] Despite the inquiry (completed by April 1972) by Lord Widgery, controversy still surrounds the events of Bloody Sunday. As Bew and Gillespie observe, 'It has never been established who fired the first shot' (Paul Bew and Gordon Gillespie, *Northern Ireland: a chronology of the troubles* (Dublin, 1993), p. 44; cf. 'The issue of who opened fire remains extremely controversial' (*Sunday Times Magazine*, 26 Jan. 1992)). The episode is still deployed to propagandist effect. See, for example, an account written in connection with the Bloody Sunday Initiative, a group aiming 'to work for British withdrawal and to build an independent, pluralist, democratic, and non-sectarian Ireland' (Eamonn McCann, Maureen Shiels, and Bridie Hannigan, *Bloody Sunday in Derry: what really happened* (Dingle, 1992), p. vii). The McGurk's bar bombing has been attributed to the Ulster Volunteer Force (Bew & Gillespie, *N. Ireland*, p. 43). Bloody Sunday became the subject of a new official inquiry in 2000.
[47] It is attributed to the I.R.A. in Bew & Gillespie, *N. Ireland*, p. 47.

businesses were attacked; British people living in Dublin felt real fear. Lynch recalled his ambassador from London and—probably to channel public emotion rather than to inflame it—proclaimed 2 February 1972, the day when the Derry victims were being buried, as a national day of mourning. That evening, an immense crowd gathered in front of the British embassy in Merrion Square; it was repeatedly attacked, and finally completely burnt out.[48]

The mood in the Republic provoked a reaction in Britain. Ground staff at various airports refused to handle Aer Lingus planes. The Scottish and Welsh rugby football associations cancelled their fixtures in Dublin. The tourist industry, which depended so heavily on the British market, reported a catastrophic fall in the number of bookings. The minister for transport and power told the dáil on 7 March that eighteen conferences, involving an estimated 12,000 delegates, had been cancelled for that year. On the same day the managing director of the Industrial Development Authority stated that nine industrial projects, which would employ a thousand people, had been postponed as a result of damage to British industry. The weeks following Bloody Sunday brought Anglo–Irish relations to the lowest point they had reached, probably, in fifty years.

A turning-point, however, was only a short distance away. There is evidence that for some months the British government had been growing disenchanted with the Faulkner regime. Faulkner had pressed the policy of internment; it had not paid the dividends he had promised, and had done great damage to Britain's reputation abroad. As early as October 1971, James Downey of the *Irish Times*, attending the Conservative party's annual conference at Blackpool, reported that the government was contemplating direct rule in Northern Ireland.[49] The following month confirmation of the story came from an unexpected quarter—Ian Paisley, who had evidently heard it from some of the contacts he had made since he became an M.P. at Westminster. Other more pressing problems—such as negotiating entry into the European Community, and dealing with industrial trouble in England—may for a time have distracted the government's attention. But the Derry events must have forcefully recalled it and also highlighted the dangers of relying on Faulkner. Although British troops had been responsible for the deaths, they were executing a ban that Faulkner had instituted. The first move to undo the damage was made almost at once. On 1 February, only two days after the shooting, Heath, the British prime minister, announced that a judicial tribunal would be set up to inquire into the shootings, under the lord chief justice of England, Lord Widgery. Soon after that, reports started appearing in various newspapers about the British government's plans for creating a new structure in Northern Ireland. Though the details varied between one report

[48] See below, p. 358.   [49] Henry Kelly, *How Stormont fell* (Dublin, 1972), pp 112, 132.

and another, they were so numerous and so consistent in tone that there can be hardly any doubt that they were orchestrated by the British government so as to prepare public opinion for a drastic change.

Meanwhile, Heath was in contact with the Northern Ireland government. On 4 February he met Faulkner in London, and asked his views on a number of possible elements in a political solution. The Northern Ireland cabinet sent its replies to these points in letters of 16 February and 1 March. On Wednesday 22 March Faulkner flew to London again, accompanied by his deputy prime minister, Senator John Andrews. They imagined that the subject of discussion would be the proposals of their government. To their consternation, they found that these played little part: instead Heath was asking that Stormont surrender all its powers in the judicial field, including not only control over the police and the power of internment but such matters as prosecutions and judicial appointments. This would leave Stormont with a greatly reduced role, and on 23 March the Northern Ireland government informed Heath that it would resign rather than accept such terms. On 24 March Heath announced in the house of commons that the Northern Ireland government and parliament would be suspended for one year, and that a secretary of state for Northern Ireland would be appointed. On 28 March 1972 the relevant legislation passed through Westminster with Labour and Liberal support, and the Stormont parliament met for the last time. After nearly fifty-one years of existence, the autonomous regime in Northern Ireland had come to an end.[50]

The importance of this event can easily be exaggerated. It did not put an end to violence; it did not reduce antagonisms between the two communities. But it did mark the end of a phase: of the attempt to settle Northern Ireland's problems by evolution from existing institutions. It showed that the British government accepted that a clean break with the past was needed. If it did not offer a solution, it at least altered the terms of the problem.

Anglo–Irish relations during the years 1968–72 were dominated by the Northern Ireland crisis. Beneath the tensions, however, in many respects ties between the Republic and Britain remained as strong as ever, or even became stronger, during these years. When Britain experimented in 1968 with having 'summer time' all the year round, the Republic followed suit. When Britain abandoned the experiment in 1971, the Republic did likewise. When Britain introduced decimal coinage in February 1971, the Republic did the same. Some people would have liked even closer integration between the two countries in certain fields. There was pressure for the courses of the Open

---

[50] This paragraph is largely derived from Edmund Curran, 'The last days of Stormont', an article based on interviews with former Northern Ireland ministers, in *Belfast Telegraph*, 25 Apr. 1972.

University, which opened in Britain in 1971, and which carried out much of its instruction through radio and television programmes, to be made available in the Republic. There was agitation also, particularly in Cork city, for British television channels to be made available to those parts of the country where they could not be received.

THE degree to which Britain and Ireland remained a unit, however, was best demonstrated by the negotiations for entry into the European Community. In 1963 and again in 1967, the French veto on British entry had automatically brought with it a failure of the Irish application. In 1970, with the accession to power of a British prime minister (Edward Heath) much more committed to European unity than his predecessor (Harold Wilson) was, the British government reactivated its application—and the Irish government, along with those of Denmark and Norway, followed suit. Serious negotiations began in September 1970, but the fear remained that the French would once again block the way. The doubts were not lifted until Heath had a cordial meeting with President Pompidou in Paris in May 1971, which signalled to the world that this time the French meant to allow the applicants to join. Negotiations thereafter continued smoothly. Each applicant sought modifications in detail to the Community treaties, to meet particular economic problems of its own. The Republic obtained concessions on fisheries, the car assembly industry, and the tax incentive scheme for industrial development. On behalf of Northern Ireland, British negotiators obtained a continuation of the safeguarding of employment act, which infringed Community regulations about free mobility of labour, till 1978. The treaty of accession was signed by the United Kingdom, the Republic of Ireland, Denmark, and Norway (although Norway subsequently withdrew) on 22 January 1972.

Accession was not assured yet. Enabling legislation had to be passed through the national parliaments, and its fate was not certain. In Britain particularly, whose accession brought with it that of Northern Ireland, the decision of parliament lay in the balance. The Conservative parliamentary majority was only thirty, and included up to forty M.P.s who were unfriendly to entry. The Labour opposition was officially opposed to entry on the terms negotiated, and although a minority of Labour M.P.s felt so strongly in favour of entry that they would defy the party whip, it was uncertain whether they would be sufficiently numerous to offset Conservative defections. In these circumstances every vote counted, and Ulster unionists—the majority of whom were unsympathetic to entry—found themselves being taken more seriously than was usually their lot. It may not be an accident that direct rule was not introduced in Northern Ireland till after the European communities bill had passed its second reading (by a majority of eight votes) on 17 February 1972. However, in the end, and by only narrow margins on several divisions, the bill successfully made its way through parliament.[51]

In the Republic passage through parliament of the enabling bill was smoother. With Fine Gael joining the government in support, and only the Labour party opposing, there were large majorities at every stage. In the Republic, however, there was a further hurdle to be jumped. Accession to the European Community required an amendment to the constitution, which would have to be put to the people in a referendum. Opponents of entry had become more articulate since the previous attempts at accession. Not only the Labour party but the two wings of Sinn Féin campaigned against entry. So did the Common Market Study Group, an association that produced a number of seriously argued pamphlets. It was thought that nationalist emotions might have been heightened by events in the north and might swell the vote against entry. Though few people expected the proposal to be defeated, expectations about the size of the margin varied widely. In the event the referendum, on 10 May 1972, showed a majority for entry of 83 per cent—larger than the most optimistic supporters of entry had dared to hope for. Accession to the Community did not take place till 1 January 1973, but on 10 May the people of the Republic made their choice. However dramatic events in the north might seem, this was the more fundamental decision of the spring of 1972. It meant that the two parts of Ireland, and Britain, were all moving together into a new relationship. No one could foresee how that relationship would develop, but it seemed likely to prove a more important turning-point in Anglo–Irish relations than any since the treaty of 1921.

[51] European Communities Act, 1972 (1972, c. 68 (17 Oct. 1972)).

CHAPTER XIV

Ireland, 1972–84

DERMOT KEOGH

THE early 1970s witnessed the retirement and death of the two primary symbols of the power and influence of both church and state in modern Ireland. Eamon de Valera ended his second term of the presidency in June 1973, completing over sixty years in Irish public life. He died on 29 August 1975. Dr John Charles McQuaid was replaced in February 1972 after thirty-two years as archbishop of Dublin. He died on 7 April 1973. The two men had been friends since the late 1920s when de Valera's children first went to Blackrock College, Dublin, where McQuaid was dean and then president between 1931 and 1939. That friendship had survived the skirmishes, the conflicts, and the confrontations of church and state during the 1940s and 1950s. Both men had, in their respective ways, shaped modern Ireland in the mould of catholic nationalism.[1]

According to the late Nicholas Mansergh, de Valera's life had been 'interwoven with the pattern of Irish history for half a century'. His official biographers, the earl of Longford and Thomas P. O'Neill, have underlined his devotion to principle, the supreme importance to him of his religious faith, his attachment to democracy, his role as a constitutionalist, his belief in republicanism, and his sense of nationality. Dr Conor Cruise O'Brien wrote in the early 1980s that paradoxically de Valera's greatest achievement was 'the consolidation of the Irish Free State ... into a stable, working democracy'.[2]

McQuaid, who had taken *Testimonium perhibere veritati* ('to bear witness to the truth') as his motto when he became archbishop in December 1940, was a vigorous upholder of the authority and place of the catholic church in the public sphere. During his time as archbishop, he expanded church influence in education, in the social services, and in the area of the voluntary hospitals. In the early 1950s, he successfully fought to prevent the application of

---

[1] Dermot Keogh, *Ireland and the Vatican: the politics and diplomacy of church–state relations 1922–1960* (Cork, 1995), pp 160–371.
[2] See Diana Mansergh (ed.), *Nationalism and independence* (Cork, 1997), pp 223, 227–8, quoting from a review of the earl of Longford and T. P. O'Neill, *Eamon de Valera* (London, 1970); Conor Cruise O'Brien, 'Mystique, politique and de Valera' in *Observer*, 17 Oct. 1982.

welfare state ideas in Ireland.[3] He built new churches and greatly strengthened the institutional church. He left behind a social services structure which, although partly funded by the exchequer, operated beyond its control. However, his concept of church engagement in society was predicated on the continuation of the high numbers of those presenting themselves for the priesthood and the religious life that was characteristic of his own generation. That presupposition did not conform to patterns of development in other parts of western Europe. Wrestling with the challenge of change in the wake of the second Vatican council, McQuaid loyally sought to implement the council's reforms.[4] If the McQuaid model of the church could not be sustained, then the leaders of the Irish hierarchy in the last three decades of the twentieth century were fatally slow to recognise the obvious need for renewal and structural reform.

McQuaid and de Valera, therefore, lived long enough to witness a changing society over which neither could exercise any further guidance or control. Both the Irish state and the catholic church were unprepared for the pace of the change that characterised the 1960s and 1970s. McQuaid and de Valera were very much products of more innocent and naive times. The 'system' of informal consensus between church and state, which had operated as an agent for stability since 1922, was to show signs first of strain in the 1970s and then of breakdown in the 1980s and 1990s as Irish society struggled with the implementation of the principles of pluralism and parity of esteem.

Rapid economic 'modernisation', based on the principles of the free market, was the primary goal of a political elite that had abandoned the social objectives of the early de Valera period. That elite, too, had replaced de facto the traditional objectives of Fianna Fáil nationalism, restoration of the language and reunification, as the prized goals of the party. Only the rhetoric remained. Industrialisation brought in its wake greater urbanisation and the mass relocation of the Irish population to centres such as Dublin.

In 1972 Fianna Fáil had been in power for fifteen consecutive years. Jack Lynch had become taoiseach in 1966 only to witness the radical deterioration of the situation in Northern Ireland. That, in turn, contributed to the outbreak of virtual 'civil war' within Fianna Fáil in 1969–70 leading to the removal/resignation from the cabinet of the minister for finance, Charles J. Haughey, and others. The 'arms trial' followed, the outcome of which had significant long-term consequences for the leadership of Jack Lynch and for his wing of Fianna Fáil. Lynch, wrongly perceived as a weak leader, had the

[3] Whyte, Ch. & state (1980 ed.), pp 156–272.
[4] For overviews of McQuaid's life and times see Roland Burke Savage, 'The church in Ireland: 1940–1965' in Studies, liv, no. 216 (1965), pp 297–338; Sean P. Farragher, Blackrock College 1860–1995 (Blackrock, 1995), pp 193–243; anon., 'Dr John Charles McQuaid' in Blackrock College Annual 1973, pp 262–73.

firmness in 1970 to impose unity on the party from above with manageable losses of personnel—even if those losses involved the scions of two of the most important republican families, Kevin Boland and Neil Blaney.[5] Charles Haughey, condemned to the back benches, never deemed that to be a permanent state bestowed upon him by providence. His 'rightful place'—and that of his wing of the party—was in the vanguard of Fianna Fáil and he shocked many by replacing Lynch as leader in 1979.

SIR John Peck, the British ambassador in Dublin between 1970 and 1973, wrote of Lynch in his memoirs that 'all those concerned with, and committed to, peace with justice in the North owe a very great deal to his courage and tenacity in pursuing what he believed to be the right policy'. The ambassador added: 'I do not think that I ever succeeded in convincing British politicians of how much we owed him at that stage, or what the consequences would have been if he had lost his head.'[6]

Peck also acknowledged that the British government's 'law-and-order' obsession in 1971 made Lynch's task all the more difficult.[7] On 30 January 1972, thirteen people were shot dead in Derry by soldiers of 1 Battalion, the Parachute Regiment, during a march organised by the Derry Civil Rights Association. The Irish Republican Army (I.R.A.) hijacked a large demonstration on 2 February outside the British embassy on Merrion Square and burned the building.[8] However, Lynch responded to the domestic challenge from the rival branches of the I.R.A. and other subversive groups with determination and firmness. The threat to the stability of the state from self-styled revolutionary 'republican' groups during the early 1970s has been seriously understated.[9]

Against a backdrop of conflict in Northern Ireland, the Lynch government succeeded at last in bringing Ireland into the European Economic Community (E.E.C.). This had been made possible indirectly by the departure from power in 1969 of General Charles de Gaulle,[10] who had blocked British entry in the 1960s. His retirement from public life opened the way for

---

[5] See Dermot Keogh, 'Jack Lynch' in Seán Dunne (ed.), *A Cork anthology* (Cork, 1993), pp 334–42; above, p. 319.

[6] John Peck, *Dublin from Downing Street* (Dublin, 1978), p. 142.

[7] In his memoirs Peck endorsed the view of those who thought that the introduction of internment in the north on 9 Aug. 1971 was 'an appalling error' (ibid., p. 128).

[8] The author was a member of the National Union of Journalists delegation that marched to the British embassy that day and witnessed I.R.A. men in uniform take over and 'police' proceedings outside the embassy.

[9] Although this chapter is being written without the benefit of access to official archives of the relevant government departments, the author believes that files of the department of justice will bear out these observations.

[10] De Gaulle and de Valera both shared doubts about a 'United States of Europe'. See Pierre Joannon, 'Charles de Gaulle and Ireland: a return to the sources' in Pierre Joannon (ed.), *De Gaulle and Ireland* (Dublin, 1991), pp 1–22: 19.

Britain, Ireland, Denmark, and Norway to reactivate their applications for membership.[11] The minister for external (later changed to foreign) affairs, Dr Patrick Hillery, opened negotiations on 30 June 1970 on behalf of the Irish government, affirming 'our full acceptance of the treaties of Rome and Paris, their political finality and the decisions taken to implement them'.[12] He further expressed the view that Ireland looked forward to participating in the strengthening of the E.E.C. and in its future development.

Discussions followed at ministerial and civil service level. The taoiseach, Jack Lynch, toured the capitals of the member states in order to reinforce the efforts of the official negotiators. The treaty of accession was signed on 22 January 1972 by Jack Lynch and Patrick Hillery. Ireland successfully negotiated to have a four-year transition period in order to adjust to the removal of industrial tariffs and the imposition of a common external tariff.[13]

A white paper on Irish membership was laid before Dáil Éireann in January 1972.[14] The government, supported by Fine Gael, defeated the motion tabled by the Labour party opposing full membership. The government found that major economic interest groups—with reservations from certain sectors—were supportive of full membership. These included the Irish Farmers' Association as well as representatives of the industrial sector. The leadership of the trade union movement was hostile to the idea of membership, fearing that indigenous Irish industry would be swamped by multinationals and international capitalism. The Labour party feared that E.E.C. membership would lead inevitably to a loss of sovereignty, the abandonment of neutrality, and possible entry into a military alliance such as N.A.T.O. The two Sinn Féins both opposed entry, as did a variety of small pressure groups.[15]

The white paper provided the framework for public debate. It covered the constitutional and legal implications of membership. This included the proposed constitutional amendment and the likely effects of entry on the economy. The possible alternatives for Ireland to an E.E.C. that included Britain were outlined. The political implications with regard to national sovereignty were also presented. However, the government recommended that the national interest would best be served by joining an enlarged community.

The white paper argued that the E.E.C. had passed from 'its transitional to its definitive phase'. It had already achieved an essential part of the

---

[11] See Jean Lacouture, *De Gaulle, the ruler: 1945–1970* (London, 1991), pp 577–82; Stephen George, *An awkward partner: Britain in the European Community* (Oxford, 1990), pp 38–43.

[12] *The accession of Ireland to the European communities* (Prl 2064) (Dublin, 1972), p. 8.

[13] D. J. Maher, *The tortuous path: the course of Ireland's entry into the E.E.C. 1948–1973* (Dublin, 1986), pp 334–5; John Cooney and Ruth Barrington, *Inside the E.E.C.: an Irish guide* (Dublin, 1984), p. 15.

[14] *Accession of Ireland.* For the dáil debate, see Maher, *The tortuous path*, pp 342–7.

[15] For the Labour party's views, see Raymond Crotty, *A radical's response* (Dublin, 1988), pp 72 ff. For the two 'Sinn Féins' see above, p. 340.

objectives of the treaty—the establishment of a customs union; common policies in the field of trade and agriculture; the abolition of obstacles to the free movement of capital, persons, and services; and, finally, the taking of important decisions concerning internal development. For the authors of the white paper such achievements represented 'major progress' in the E.E.C.'s advancement towards its ultimate political goal as envisioned by the founder members. Anticipating difficulties over the question of ultimate political union, the white paper argued that 'the political evolution of the community is still at a very early stage'. It referred to the debate that had taken place within the community since its foundation, between those who sought to bring about union on federal, confederal, or unitary state lines. There was no question of Ireland having to become involved in any military or defence commitments.[16]

The white paper did not neglect to address the question of national sovereignty, which became a central issue in the subsequent referendum campaign: 'We must contrast this with our present position as a very small country, independent but with little or no capacity to influence events abroad that significantly affect us. One of the major problems facing small countries such as Ireland is how to exercise their national sovereignty as fully as possible in today's highly complex and interdependent world.' It was pointed out that small countries found their actions circumscribed to a great extent by the complex nature of international economic and trading relationships. That was very much the position for Ireland in 1972, argued the white paper.[17]

Irish membership was debated in Dáil Éireann between 21 and 23 March. Fine Gael again sided with the government. The taoiseach, Jack Lynch, told the house: 'Today we stand at a most important crossroads in our history.' The Labour party, arguing for associate rather than full membership, based its opposition on both political and economic grounds, and Brendan Corish, the party leader, wanted to know whether membership would entail military commitments. The minister for external affairs, Patrick Hillery, announcing that a referendum would be held on 10 May, spoke about the origins of a new Europe:

The construction of a Europe, this new Europe, in which war would be impossible, has yet to be completed, but what has been achieved so far by the Community is the framework of a broader and deeper community between countries which have long been opposed to each other in conflict and this, the true basis of lasting peace in Europe, is being made by the creation and enlargement of the European Communities.

---

[16] Maher, *The tortuous path*, p. 336; *Accession of Ireland*, p. 57.
[17] *Accession of Ireland*, pp 58–60.

Lynch, speaking in his native Cork on 5 May, put the choice before the Irish people in the following terms: '[It was between taking part]...in the great new renaissance of Europe, or opting for economic, social, and cultural sterility. It is like that faced by Robinson Crusoe when the ship came to bring him back into the world again.' He argued also that true independence was frequently undermined by dependence on the decisions of a larger, more powerful state: 'What we seek is an end to domination or dependence and the freedom to act as a full partner while taking full account of the interests and wishes of fellow partners. We do not seek total freedom of action—for freedom without constraint means anarchy. We seek the independence necessary to advocate and pursue our interests.'[18]

In the referendum campaign, the Labour party continued to articulate the fear that after membership the country's industrial sector would be swamped by multinationals and international capitalism. The two wings of Sinn Féin, the political fronts for the rival I.R.A.s, continued to campaign against membership. One anti-E.E.C. campaigner, Anthony Coughlan, saw the choice as follows:

[It]...is not between staying as we are or moving to join the E.E.C. It is between opting for membership of a system where control of our economic and ultimately our political life will pass largely into the hands of others, or seeking to maintain and use the powers of an Irish state in the interests of the Irish people, adapting with imagination and courage to the challenges of following an independent course.[19]

The case for E.E.C. membership was eloquently expressed in the eve-of-referendum editorial in the *Irish Times* entitled: 'We should join.' The editorial argued:

The E.E.C. is not a capitalist clique, nor a mutual assistance society, nor a rich man's club, nor a poor man's paradise. It is not the answer to all Ireland's problems nor is it the end of the world... Far from seeing our country submerged in a conglomerate of nations, entry to Brussels may be one of the final steps in the establishment of Ireland as a nation, a further approach to the day when Emmet's epitaph may at last be written.[20]

WHEN the votes were counted on 11 May, the outcome surpassed even the most optimistic projections of the 'yes' side. The majority was five to one in favour of entry. In a 71 per cent turn out, 83 per cent or 1,041,890 voted in favour and 211,891 against. Every one of the forty-two

[18] *Irish Times*, 6 May 1972.
[19] Ibid., 9 May 1972; Anthony Coughlan, *Ireland and the common market: the alternatives to membership* (Dublin, 1972), p. 16.
[20] Quoted in Dermot Keogh, *Ireland and Europe 1919–1989: a diplomatic and political history* (Cork and Dublin, 1990), pp 253–5.

constituencies had voted 'yes'.[21] It had been a resounding defeat for the 'no' side.

Entry to the E.E.C. yielded many benefits to different sectors of the country in the decades that followed. First, between 1973—the year of membership—and 1995, the total net transfers amounted to IR£18.45 billion, the bulk coming from the common agricultural policy and the structural funds.[22] E.E.C. membership, therefore, gave Ireland her first real opportunity since independence to diversify her exports and find new markets among the nine member states. Secondly, great as the economic benefits might have been, E.E.C. membership gave the country a new international status as an equal member of one of the most important political blocs in the world. The impact of membership on the development of Irish society was much greater than that of its membership of any other multilateral organisation, the British commonwealth, the League of Nations, or the United Nations. Thirdly, E.E.C. membership opened the country more directly to the ideological, religious, social, and cultural pluralism of that historically diverse community of nation states in western Europe. That reinforced the movement for change within Irish society which had become so marked in the 1960s.

Dr Patrick Hillery, nominated by the Irish government for the position of commissioner, was appointed on 6 January 1973 to the portfolio for social affairs. Replaced by Brian Lenihan as minister for foreign affairs, the future president of Ireland was a major success in his new position.

Paradoxically, Ireland appeared to be changing only very slowly. For example, the number describing themselves as catholics in 1961 was 94.9 per cent; ten years later the figure was 93.9 per cent. Surveys showed that over 90 per cent of catholics claimed to have attended mass the previous Sunday. In a country where over 50 per cent of the population was aged under 25, mass attendance in the age group between 18 and 30 was reportedly very high—over 80 per cent, according to certain surveys. The pastoral fears of an earlier generation of clergy about the moral welfare of Irish emigrants in British cities were transferred to urban Ireland, where traditional standards of sexual morality seemed to be changing. Illegitimacy rates grew from 2.4 per cent in 1969 to 4.5 per cent in 1977 and declined to 4.2 per cent in 1979. The number of women having abortions in British clinics who gave addresses in the Republic of Ireland rose from 122 in 1969 to 2,183 in 1977. The figure was 4,064 in 1990.[23]

The women's movement, which had developed in Ireland from the late 1960s, provided further proof of a growing tension in Irish society between

---

[21] Ibid.
[22] *Challenges and opportunities abroad: white paper on foreign policy* (Pn 2133) (Dublin, 1996), p. 59.
[23] Whyte, *Ch. & state*, pp 381–4; Keogh, *Twentieth-century Ire.*, p. 371.

traditional roles and values and the rights of women to play a greater role in the workplace and in society in general. Many of those objectives—such as equal pay for equal work—would be achieved through E.E.C. directives rather than a willingness on the part of the Irish state to implement change voluntarily.

The conflict in Northern Ireland was another impetus for change. Barriers to greater understanding between churches were more readily identified. Consensus had been reached in 1972 between the main leaders of the churches and the Lynch government to advocate the removal of a section of article 44 from the constitution, which spoke of 'the special position' of the catholic church. A second referendum was held in 1972 on 7 December, and 84 per cent (in a poll of only 51 per cent) voted for the change. In Cork, Lynch's home city, Bishop Cornelius Lucey encouraged a 'no' vote, but his intervention appeared to make no significant impact on the outcome. The 'yes' vote was over 70 per cent in each of the three constituencies that corresponded with the diocese of Cork. Change had been achieved through consent and, according to John Whyte, consent was to characterise the methodology of the adjustment of church–state relations in the 1970s.[24] That approach broke down in the 1980s.

The principles of tolerance, pluralism, and consent did not hold any particular appeal for the two wings of the I.R.A.[25] Lynch responded to the threat of subversion with decisiveness. The minister for justice, Desmond O'Malley, established the special criminal court on 26 May 1972. On 6 October the gardaí closed down the main office of Provisional Sinn Féin at Kevin Street, Dublin. The R.T.É. authority was replaced by the government after a radio interview with the chief of staff of the Provisional I.R.A., Seán Mac Stiofáin. This was considered to be in breach of section 31 of the broadcasting act.[26] Mac Stiofáin was arrested and went on hunger strike. Sentenced on 25 November, he continued to refuse food and water. As the international press gathered to cover the story, the retired archbishop of Dublin, Dr McQuaid, and his successor, Dr Dermot Ryan, visited him in hospital. After a foiled I.R.A. escape plan, he was moved to the Curragh, County Kildare, where he came off his fifty-eight-day hunger strike in January 1973.

On 22 November 1972 Lynch introduced the Offences against the State (Amendment) Bill in Dáil Éireann. This permitted the conviction of a suspect on the testimony of a senior police officer that he believed that the accused was a member of an illegal organisation. The opposition, Fine Gael and Labour, strongly opposed the measure, and on 1 December the

---

[24] Whyte, *Ch. & state*, pp 384, 388–9.
[25] See Paul Bew and Gordon Gillespie (ed.), *Northern Ireland* (Dublin, 1993), p. 47.
[26] The distinguished R.T.É. journalist Kevin O'Kelly was sentenced to three months imprisonment for contempt for refusing to identify Mac Stiofáin as his interviewee. He was released within a few days.

government appeared to be on the point of losing the vote in Dáil Éireann, when two bombs exploded in central Dublin, killing two people and injuring 127. Within an hour of the two blasts, Fine Gael announced that it had withdrawn its amendment and agreed to abstain in the vote, which the government won by 69 to 22.[27] It was signed into law by the president on 3 December.[28] The taoiseach, however, refused to listen to Brian Lenihan's advice to call a snap general election. Nevertheless, Lynch took many of his most senior party colleagues completely by surprise when, on 5 February 1973, he announced without any warning the holding of a winter election on 28 February.[29]

The Labour party formed a coalition pact with Fine Gael as early as 7 February. It was agreed that the Fine Gael leader, Liam Cosgrave, would be taoiseach and the Labour leader, Brendan Corish, would be tánaiste. The two parties signed a fourteen-point programme to transform Ireland into a 'modern progressive society based on social justice'.[30] It pledged strict price control and voluntary wage control, removal of V.A.T. (value-added tax) from food, the abolition of rates, and the removal of the differential rents system. On the defensive, Fianna Fáil changed its strategy on 22 February, promising to increase social welfare and children's allowances and the abolition of rates on domestic dwellings by 1 April 1974. That was portrayed as a bribe to the electorate by a party in despair. An editorial in the *Irish Times* commented that the Fianna Fáil campaign seemed 'to be going to pieces'.[31] The paper was right.

Fianna Fáil was defeated, with three former ministers losing their seats.[32] Neil Blaney and Charles Haughey, who had both been sacked by Lynch in 1970, headed the poll in their constituencies, with 8,368 and 12,901 first-preference votes respectively. (Jack Lynch himself polled 12,427 votes in Cork city.) Political disgrace had not weakened Haughey's electoral hold: he had polled 11,677 votes in 1969. Many in Fianna Fáil may have discounted any chance of his return to the front benches, but he continued to rebuild his

---

[27] For a Fine Gael account of the background to the debate on the bill, see Thomas F. O'Higgins, *A double life* (Dublin, 1996), pp 240–54.

[28] 1972/26 (3 Dec. 1972). More car bombs were to follow: one in Belturbet, Co. Cavan, on 28 Dec. killed two and injured nine, and another in Dublin on 20 Jan. 1973 killed one person and injured thirteen. A systematic crackdown on subversion followed the passage of the act; the president of Provisional Sinn Féin, Ruairí Ó Brádaigh, was arrested and imprisoned for six months on 11 Jan. 1973 under the act.

[29] Author's interview with Brian Lenihan, 1989; Lenihan commented that after sixteen years 'the people were tired of us'.

[30] *Irish Times*, 6, 7 Feb. 1973; Michael Gallagher, *The Irish Labour party in transition 1957–82* (Manchester, 1982), p. 118.

[31] Michael McInerney, 'Fine Gael, Labour endorse manifesto pledging widespread social reform' in *Irish Times*, 8 Feb. 1973; *Irish Times*, 23 Feb. 1973.

[32] The ministers were Micheál Ó Moráin, Michael Hilliard, and Kevin Boland. See also *Irish Times*, 2 Mar. 1973.

base within the party. In 1979, he was to become the leader of Fianna Fáil in what the R.T.É. commentator Seán Duignan termed 'the greatest comeback since Lazarus'.

THE state of the parties after the election was Fianna Fáil 69, Fine Gael 54, Labour 19, and two independents. That gave the Fine Gael–Labour coalition 73 seats, a majority of four over Fianna Fáil. The latter party was out of office for the first time since 1957. Liam Cosgrave of Fine Gael was the leader of the new government announced on 14 March. The leader of the Labour party, Brendan Corish, was tánaiste. Declan Costello was made attorney general. Dr Garret FitzGerald, who had been shadow spokesman on finance, was made minister for foreign affairs.[33]

The political parties had to fight a presidential election on 30 May 1973. Fianna Fáil had a good candidate in Erskine Hamilton Childers, a man who had been unwavering in his support for Lynch's position on Northern Ireland. Childers, indeed, had never failed to conceal his contempt for those in the party who remained equivocal on the question of violence. Fine Gael put up the veteran Tom O'Higgins who had been beaten by de Valera in the 1966 election by only 10,700 votes. On his second attempt, O'Higgins lost by 48,584 votes in an election which 'many had felt I was certain to win'. He had no regrets as he left public life after twenty-five years in Dáil Éireann. Childers, he said, had 'behaved with honour and dignity'.[34] Sworn in as the fourth president of Ireland on 25 June 1973, Childers was, like the first holder of that office, Douglas Hyde, a member of the Church of Ireland. Taking up residence in Áras an Uachtaráin, he sought immediately to make the presidency more open to the Irish people. As part of that plan he had promised during the course of his campaign to set up a think-tank to plan the future of the country. Cosgrave gave a short answer to that request, and Childers told Garret FitzGerald that he had no alternative but to resign. He was talked out of doing so, but FitzGerald felt that Childers continued to chafe at the restrictions on his actions imposed by his role as non-executive president. The new president threw himself into a round of visits, speechmaking, and travelling. He imposed a punishing schedule on himself and his health suffered in consequence. On 17 November 1974, he suffered a heart attack and died shortly after delivering a lecture on drug abuse—a subject he had chosen to highlight throughout his short presidency—to the Royal College of Physicians. FitzGerald states that 'while he was always very correct in the way he accepted the advice tendered to him as to what he might not do

---

[33] Richard Ryan became minister for finance; Patrick Cooney, justice; Richard Burke, education; and Paddy Donegan, defence. The Labour ministers were Brendan Corish, tánaiste and minister for health and social welfare; James Tully, local government; Michael O'Leary, labour; Justin Keating, industry and commerce; and Conor Cruise O'Brien, posts and telegraphs.
[34] O'Higgins, *A double life*, p. 262.

or say, his frustration was intense, and I believe almost certainly contributed to his sudden tragic death...'. FitzGerald argues further that 'tragically, he was temperamentally unsuited to the constraints of the position to which he had been elected'.[35] There is another interpretation: Childers was ahead of the government of the day. Seeking to develop the role of the president within the constraints of the constitution, he was prevented from doing so by the conservatism of the coalition government—a conservatism also evident during the tenure of his successor.

Neither government nor opposition had the appetite to fight a new presidential election. The distinguished jurist Cearbhall Ó Dálaigh was the agreed successor and he was inaugurated as the fifth president of Ireland on 19 December 1974. He made history by becoming the first Irish president to attend a service at the Adelaide Road synagogue, in Dublin, on the day of his inauguration.[36] His resignation two years later, in controversial circumstances (discussed below), helped seal the fate of the coalition in the 1977 election.

The coalition had come to power in 1973 at a time of growing economic optimism. Although he did not have the finance portfolio, Garret FitzGerald played a leading role in Irish–E.E.C. relations at the council of foreign ministers. Irish membership of the E.E.C. had added a significant economic dimension to the portfolio of Iveagh House (headquarters of his department). In response to the new challenges, he expanded the diplomatic service, extending the number of missions; in 1974, FitzGerald negotiated the opening of diplomatic relations with the Soviet Union, and Moscow set up an embassy in Dublin. The new minister also increased the intake of diplomats into his department. It is understood that during FitzGerald's time in Iveagh House the number of third secretaries (the usual entry grade) from Northern Ireland increased. Ireland assumed the presidency of the E.E.C. for a six-month term in January 1975, and the various administrative and political tasks were considered after the end of the six months to have been successfully executed.[37]

The E.E.C.'s common agricultural policy gave the new government an opportunity to invest in an unprecedented manner in the improvement of farm production. The government's first budget was described as the 'greatest social welfare budget of all time'.[38] But the optimism did not last the year. The economic policies of the coalition were determined by inter-

---

[35] Garret FitzGerald, 'Presidential candidates should be aware of the realities of office' in *Irish Times*, 20 Sept. 1997.

[36] Aidan Carl Mathews (ed.), *Immediate man: cuimhní ar Chearbhall Ó Dálaigh* (Portlaoise, 1983).

[37] *Irish Times*, 14, 15 Mar. 1973; Raymond Smith, *Garret the enigma: Dr Garret FitzGerald* (Dublin, 1985), pp 209–13; Garret FitzGerald, *All in a life* (Dublin, 1991), pp 146 ff.

[38] *Irish Times*, 12 Mar. 1973, quoted in Gallagher, *Ir. Labour party*, p. 197. Local authority rates were cut, death duties abolished, and social welfare benefits and services were extended. V.A.T. was removed from food.

national factors. Ireland imported over 70 per cent of its primary energy requirements, and the price of domestic oil rose to ten times the 1972 rate following the Yom Kippur war. Inflation rose to 20 per cent in 1974.[39] The minister for industry and commerce, Justin Keating, described the impact of the crisis as like 'falling over a cliff'.[40] Forced to respond to the deterioration, the government in 1975 introduced subsidies on basic foodstuffs and increased spending on social welfare.[41] Unemployment rose from 71,435 in March 1973 to 115,942 shortly before the coalition left office in 1977. A wealth tax was introduced, giving the following yield: £3,672,411 in 1975, £6,488,613 in 1976, and £5,806,067 in 1977. Fianna Fáil abolished the tax in 1978. However, arrears were paid up to 1984, netting over £4 million for the revenue commissioners. Under direction from Brussels, equal pay legislation was passed. The government lost much credibility after it failed in a move to gain an exemption for public service pay in 1975. That general policy of high spending continued until the minister for finance, Richard Ryan, felt compelled to cut back severely in the years 1976 and 1977.[42]

The quest for pluralism was not embraced equally by all ministers during the coalition's term of office. Following a supreme court ruling in the Mrs Mary McGee case of 1973, which found the ban on the import of contraceptives to be unconstitutional, the minister for justice, Patrick Cooney, introduced a bill that would have permitted the importation and sale of contraceptives under very restrictive circumstances.[43]

That initiative is best set in the context of the prevailing teaching of the catholic church on birth control. Archbishop McQuaid argued in 1971 that to speak of a right to contraception on the part of the individual, 'be he Christian or non-Christian or atheist, or on the part of a minority or of a majority, is to speak of a right that cannot even exist'. The archbishop remarked that the public consequences of immorality that must follow upon legalisation of contraception 'are only too clearly seen in other countries'[44] and said that such legislation would be 'a curse upon our country'. Referring to the linking of the reunification of Ireland with the enactment of contraceptive laws in the Republic, he said: 'One must know little of the Northern

---

[39] Kieran Kennedy, Thomas Giblin, and Deirdre McHugh (ed.), *The economic development of Ireland in the twentieth century* (London, 1988), pp 75–6; Gallagher, *Ir. Labour party*, p. 198.

[40] Interviewed in Aug. 1990.

[41] Keating brought in legislation to protect state interests in the area of mining and off-shore gas and oil exploration; e.g., the gas act, 1976/30 (19 July 1976). See Gallagher, *Ir. Labour party*, p. 198.

[42] Smith, *Garret the enigma*, p. 252, Lee, *Ire. 1912–85*, p. 471.

[43] At this time it was still illegal, under the criminal law amendment act of 1935 (1935/6, 28 Feb. 1935), to import or sell contraceptives. Yet the 'pill' was available on prescription and it was estimated in 1978 that 48,000 Irish women were using it. Moreover, in 1979 there were five family-planning clinics in Dublin, and one each in Cork, Limerick, Galway, Bray, and Navan. See Whyte, *Ch. & state*, pp 403–4; Keogh, *Twentieth-century Ire.*, pp 325–6.

[44] Quoted in Whyte, *Ch. & state*, pp 405–6, 414.

people if one can fail to realise the indignant ridicule with which good Northern people would treat such an argument.'[45]

Cardinal William Conway followed suit, arguing in December 1973 that the legalisation of the sale of contraceptives in the Republic would bring about a change for the worse in the quality of life, just as it had done in Northern Ireland. Neither did he think that it would be possible to restrict the use of contraceptives to married couples. Their use would spread, he said, to young people; marital fidelity would be affected, and there would be a general extension of promiscuity. Like McQuaid, Conway considered that 'it would be utterly unrealistic to think that the attitudes of the average unionist towards a united Ireland would be changed in the slightest degree if the law in the Republic were changed'.[46]

However, an official statement on contraception from the catholic hierarchy in 1973 noted: 'There are many things which the catholic church holds to be morally wrong and no one has ever suggested, least of all the church herself, that they should be prohibited by the state.'[47] Fine Gael permitted a free vote on Cooney's bill when it came before the dáil in 1974. Fianna Fáil opposed the bill. The measure was defeated by 75 to 61 votes on 16 July 1974. The taoiseach, Liam Cosgrave, the minister for education, Richard Burke, and five other Fine Gael T.D.s helped defeat their own government's bill.

Garret FitzGerald, who voted in favour, continued to work for social and political change. In office, he continued to develop his model of pluralism for the 'new' Ireland which would have greater appeal to the protestant/unionist tradition in Northern Ireland. A year before the defeat of the contraception bill, in July 1973, FitzGerald had met Cardinal Secretary of State Agostino Casaroli in Helsinki. In a bilateral meeting, he explained the concern of the Irish government to establish 'a positive relationship' with both unionists and nationalists in Northern Ireland. He argued that it was his belief that the process might be assisted if certain features of the Republic's constitution and laws which they found unattractive were modified. The ban on contraception and divorce were cited as examples.

Concerning Northern Ireland, FitzGerald referred to the contentious question of mixed marriages and the absence of integrated education. He found that Casaroli was interested, and on returning to Dublin FitzGerald prepared a memorandum which he submitted to the taoiseach. Cosgrave did not show any 'negative reaction' and after incorporating a number of comments submitted by the Irish ambassador to the holy see the memorandum was sent to Rome on 14 August 1973. When FitzGerald was next in Rome he again met Casaroli who told him that the document had been referred to the

[45] *Irish Catholic Directory, 1972*, quoting McQuaid, 28 Mar. 1971, p. 730.
[46] *Irish Catholic Directory, 1975*, quoting Conway, 3 Dec. 1973, p. 658.
[47] See statement of the hierarchy in national press, 26 Nov. 1973; also Whyte, *Ch. & state*, p. 407.

Congregation for the Doctrine of the Faith for comment. The cardinal discussed with FitzGerald the comments of the nuncio in Dublin, Gaetano Alibrandi, on the document. Alibrandi suggested that since unity was not imminent there could be little reason to upset people by making such changes. FitzGerald went on to speak about unionist fears and the question of mixed marriages. At that point, according to FitzGerald, Casaroli suggested 'discussions with the nuncio, Cardinal Conway, and some of the bishops'.[48] It is not known whether those follow-up discussions ever took place.

Pope Paul VI intervened personally in 1977 to express his opposition to FitzGerald's blueprint for the new Ireland. It was arranged for a papal audience to coincide with the minister's attendance at a meeting of the European Council in Rome on 25–6 March. Paul VI, reading from a script, told FitzGerald uncompromisingly that Ireland was a catholic country—perhaps the only one left—and should stay that way. Laws should not be changed in any way that would make the country less catholic. FitzGerald's memoirs record: 'The tone and content of his remarks suggested that he had been told I was a dangerous liberal bent on destroying catholicism in Ireland: someone who had to be admonished in no uncertain terms, and whose expressed concerns about the Northern Ireland tragedy should not be taken seriously.'[49] After seeing Paul VI, FitzGerald had discussions with Casaroli and others. Casaroli asked whether the Irish government wanted a united Ireland. FitzGerald replied that the Irish government had such an aspiration, but that the form of unity might be federal or confederal. 'But in a federal state you could have divorce in one part and not in another', Casaroli said 'quick as a flash'. FitzGerald wrote that he found the meeting with the pope to be a 'depressing experience' and that he had left 'somewhat shell-shocked'.[50]

Did FitzGerald alert the leaders of the Irish hierarchy to his intended informal discussion at the holy see on the question of pluralism? Cardinal Conway, who died on 17 April 1977, would not have welcomed such an initiative. Neither would his successor, Cardinal Tomás Ó Fiaich, who was consecrated in October 1977. Neither would his former colleague from University College, Dublin, Archbishop Dermot Ryan. It was a fundamental departure from the manner in which church–state relations had been conducted since the foundation of the state, and likely to anger the taoiseach as much as the hierarchy. It had been the custom for church–state matters to be discussed at the highest levels when necessary, without alerting the holy see to the content of those deliberations. That episode contributed to the mistrust that grew up later between the catholic bishops and FitzGerald.[51]

[48] FitzGerald records that Casaroli was persuaded by his arguments to the extent that the cardinal felt that the nuncio had given him the 'wrong slant' (*All in a life*, pp 184–5).
[49] Ibid., p. 186.
[50] Ibid.
[51] Keogh, *Ire. & the Vatican*, pp 357–69.

Northern Ireland, however, overshadowed the work of the government and required the investment of considerable resources to protect the state against loyalist bomb attacks and the armed activities of the I.R.A.[52] The taoiseach, Liam Cosgrave, showed Cumann na nGaedheal-like resolve in the teeth of such attacks on the democratic institutions of the state. Threats to the lives of ministers, intimidation of the families of those in public life, and attacks on the homes of politicians had historical resonances for the son of the man who had been president of the executive council from 1922 to 1932. The minister for justice, Patrick Cooney, and the Labour minister for posts and telegraphs, Dr Conor Cruise O'Brien, also took the lead in the fight against terrorism. The latter will be best remembered for the broadcasting amendment act in 1976 which, according to Lee, curbed I.R.A. 'opportunities for propaganda, while nevertheless providing some safeguards for serious comment'. Cruise O'Brien remained an outspoken critic of the I.R.A. and the unrelenting exposer of ambivalence towards physical-force nationalism.[53]

On 21 July 1976 the British ambassador, Christopher Ewart-Biggs, and a British civil servant, Judith Cooke, were murdered by the I.R.A. in a land-mine explosion near the ambassador's official residence at Sandyford on the outskirts of Dublin.[54] In the aftermath of the murder, the government declared on 1 September 1976 that 'a national emergency' existed, affecting 'the vital interests of the state', and introduced a criminal justice bill, which increased the powers of the security forces, and an emergency powers bill. On 24 September President Ó Dálaigh signed the first but referred the second to the supreme court. The latter bill permitted the detention for seven days of people suspected of offences under the offences against the state act. The president's action was prudent, correct, and proper. Anyone familiar with his earlier career on the bench would not have been surprised at his action on that occasion.[55] In 1965, he had delivered the following judgment: 'It was not the intention of the constitution in guaranteeing the fundamental rights of the citizen that these rights should be set at naught or circumvented. The intention was that rights of substance were being assured to the individ-

---

[52] These incidents included the interception and seizure of arms from the Cypriot M.V. *Claudia* by Irish naval vessels on 28 Mar. 1973, and the subsequent arrest of six persons including the leading Provisional I.R.A. member Joe Cahill, who was sentenced to three years penal servitude. A year later, on 17 May 1974, loyalists planted bombs in Monaghan and Dublin: 25 died in Dublin and over 100 were injured, while 6 were killed in Monaghan.

[53] Gallagher, *Ir. Labour party*, pp 209–10; Lee, *Ire. 1912–85*, p. 477. On the broadcasting issue see also below, p. 705.

[54] Bruce Arnold, *What kind of country: modern Irish politics, 1968–1983* (London, 1984), p. 121; J. Bowyer Bell, *The secret army* (revised ed., Dublin, 1979), p. 427.

[55] Criminal law act, 1976/32 (24 Sept. 1976). On 10 Mar. 1976 Ó Dálaigh had referred the Criminal Law (Jurisdiction) Bill (which empowered the courts to try certain offences committed in Northern Ireland) to the supreme court to test its constitutionality. It was found to be constitutional and was signed by the president on 6 May (1976/14). See also Rory O'Hanlon, 'A court in session' in Mathews, *Immediate man*, pp 23–36.

ual and that the courts were the custodians of these rights.'[56] In the fight against subversive organisations, the state had to maintain a balance between personal liberty and the use of special powers. It was not always evident that the 1973–7 coalition successfully maintained such equilibrium.[57]

On 15 October 1976 the supreme court found the bill to be constitutional. The president signed it at midnight the same day. The following day, an editorial in the *Irish Times* noted that the ruling had explicitly preserved the detained person's right to communicate and to have legal and medical advice present. According to Mr Justice Hugh O'Flaherty, writing over twenty years later, President Ó Dálaigh's action 'delivered a landmark judgment which is the cornerstone of our law of civil liberties'.[58] But within a week Ó Dálaigh felt compelled to resign in circumstances that did not reflect well on the Cosgrave government.

His resignation must be set against a background of tension and misunderstanding which existed between the president and the taoiseach's department for most of his time in office. Ó Dálaigh was extremely scrupulous in the discharging of his official duties, and quite uncomprehending of low standards. Did some members of the coalition regard the president as being a little too pedantic? Garret FitzGerald, writing in 1997, found him to have been erudite and charming but lacking in 'political experience' and sometimes 'difficult and even eccentric'.[59] Was that view widely held within the coalition?

A number of episodes occurred during the lifetime of that coalition which wounded Ó Dálaigh personally. He was a president who always behaved with admirable correctness and high-mindedness in keeping with his appreciation of his office. For example, catholic church authorities had invited him to Rome to attend the canonisation of Blessed Oliver Plunkett on 12 October 1975. He wrote to the government for permission to be present on that historic occasion. It is understood that he never received a reply to his letter. There were also occasions when he was upset by breaches of protocol. For example, he was leaving a church where he had attended a service in his capacity as president when he was beckoned to one side in the porch by a cabinet minister. As he felt that such a gesture did not reflect an understanding of how to conduct business with the president, he simply said something like

[56] Mr Justice Hugh O'Flaherty, 'Single greatest champion the constitution ever had' in *Irish Times*, 29 Sept. 1997, written in reply to FitzGerald's 'Presidential candidates', ibid., 20 Sept. 1997.
[57] There had been persistent rumours that elements within the gardaí were guilty of treating suspects in an unduly heavy-handed manner. See Joe Joyce and Peter Murtagh, *Blind justice* (Dublin, 1984); Derek Dunne and Gene Kerrigan, *Round up the usual suspects: Nicky Kelly and the Cosgrave coalition* (Dublin, 1984).
[58] Emergency powers act, 1976/33 (16 Oct. 1976); *Irish Times*, 16 Oct. 1976; O'Flaherty, 'Single greatest champion'.
[59] FitzGerald, 'Presidential candidates'. FitzGerald's view was strongly contested by O'Flaherty, 'Single greatest champion'.

'now is not the time', and returned directly to the official car to be driven to Áras an Uachtaráin.[60]

Returning to 1976 and the referral of the emergency powers bill, the minister for defence, Patrick Donegan, made critical remarks about the president while addressing a function on 18 October at Columb Barracks, Mullingar. He was reported as describing the president, who was the commander-in-chief of the armed forces, as 'a thundering disgrace'. There was surprise, shock, and outrage at such a remark, even as it had been reported. An *Irish Times* editorial felt that Donegan had gone too far and that he would have to resign. The question was asked whether his views were shared by other members of the government: in particular, were they shared by the taoiseach?[61] Donegan offered his resignation to the taoiseach, who refused to accept it.

The offending minister sought a meeting with the president to tender an apology. Ó Dálaigh was not available to receive him. FitzGerald records in his memoirs that the cabinet was sent a letter, in which Ó Dálaigh did not explicitly state that he would resign. But he did refer to the fact that he considered the relationship between the president and Donegan to have been 'irreparably breached', and that the minister's remarks could only be construed as an insinuation that the president did not stand behind the state. In the dáil, on 21 October, Cosgrave made it clear that a written apology had been sent to the president. The taoiseach said: 'He [Donegan] made what I regard and what he himself regards as a serious comment on what the president did in a personally disrespectful way and he immediately announced his intention to apologise for it.' The Fine Gael T.D. and constitutional lawyer John Kelly felt that it was a 'bottomless absurdity' to claim that the Donegan comment was an attack on a state institution.[62] A majority of five votes decided that Donegan should not resign.

Ó Dálaigh resigned as president of Ireland the following day. From his home in County Wicklow, he issued a statement stating that it was the only way to assert publicly his personal integrity and to protect the dignity and independence of the presidency as an institution. He did not lack political experience. The government simply did not know how to treat the incumbent in Áras an Uachtaráin.

---

[60] This was not the first time that Ó Dálaigh felt his office had not been treated with respect: on first becoming president, he had been supplied with a Mercedes-Benz from the ministerial car pool which had seen better days. He sought instead to have the use of a Citroën, a make he knew from his time at the European court of justice in Luxembourg. He was supplied with a second-hand Citroën. (Details concerning the presidencies of Childers and Ó Dálaigh were supplied to the author from several different sources.)

[61] *Irish Times*, 19 Oct. 1976. The minister's exact phrase was 'thundering bollix'.

[62] FitzGerald, *All in a life*, p. 315; *Irish Times*, 22 Oct. 1976.

Finding a successor was more easily achieved than overcoming the wide-spread public revulsion at the government's brazen disrespect for the presidential incumbent. The taoiseach spoke immediately to Jack Lynch about the possibility of finding an agreed candidate. Patrick Hillery, who had just come to the end of his term as E.E.C. commissioner, was approached by Jack Lynch and asked whether he would take the position. Hillery did not particularly want to become president, but he felt that he could not turn it down once he had the honour of being asked. At 53, he was a possible future leader of Fianna Fáil. Inaugurated president on 3 December 1976, he held that position for fourteen years.

The Donegan affair marked a low point in the term of a coalition that had struggled to make economic progress at a time of an international energy crisis, growing conflict in Northern Ireland, and increased activity by I.R.A. and loyalist subversives in the south. Against all the predictions by political commentators, a well-organised but profligate Fianna Fáil was returned to power at the general election of 1977.[63] 'Coalition set to take election', read the headline in the *Irish Times* on 16 June. Fianna Fáil won a historic victory, but Lynch must have been very surprised at the convincing margin, which gave his party an absolute majority of twenty seats in the dáil.[64] Among the defeated candidates was Mary Robinson, a future president of Ireland, who narrowly missed taking a seat for Labour in Dublin.

JACK Lynch returned to power having won a very large majority—a feat unequalled by his predecessors or by the Fianna Fáil taoisigh who followed him in the 1980s and 1990s. Lynch had received 20,079 first-preference votes and Charles Haughey 11,041. George Colley, Lynch's loyal supporter and strong opponent of Haughey, was made tánaiste and minister for finance and the public service. Jim Gibbons, Haughey's main antagonist during the arms trial in 1970, returned to the department of agriculture.[65] To the surprise of many people in public life, Lynch brought Haughey back into the cabinet as minister for health and social welfare. He was quick to demonstrate his political ability as a minister, becoming one of the most often photographed and talked about members of the cabinet. While his critics may have felt that he was permanently discredited, he thrived on such complacency. Within

[63] Fianna Fáil promised the abolition of domestic rates and motor taxation. The coalition failed to benefit from the radical redrawing of constituency boundaries by the Labour minister for local government, Jim Tully. Known popularly as the 'Tullymander', it worked against the electoral interests of two Labour ministers, who lost their seats (Lee, *Ire. 1912–85*, p. 481).

[64] Compared with the 1973 general election, Fine Gael dropped from 54 to 42 seats, Labour from 19 to 17 (Brian M. Walker, *Parliamentary election results in Ireland, 1918–92* (Dublin, 1992)).

[65] Michael O'Kennedy became minister for foreign affairs; Gerard Collins, justice; Brian Lenihan, fisheries; Desmond O'Malley, industry, commerce and energy; and John Wilson, education. Anthony Hederman became attorney general.

two and a half years of his return to government office, Haughey was taoiseach and leader of the Fianna Fáil party.

Lynch, with his large majority, was determined to put the country back to
work. There were 116,000 people unemployed in 1977, falling to 90,000 two
years later. Dr Martin O'Donoghue, an economist from Trinity College, had
been made minister for economic planning and development. The Fianna Fáil
strategy was profligate and prodigal. The national debt was £4,220 million in
1977; the following year it rose to £5,167 million, and to £6,540 million
in 1979. In 1980 the figure was £7,896 million, and £10,196 million in 1981.[66]
The white paper *National development 1977–1980* proved to be a case, as J. J.
Lee has termed it, of the Hibernian miracle that never was.[67] The new government's economic strategy assumed rapid growth. A second oil crisis ended
any such prospects.

Nevertheless, Lynch's last administration took many decisions that had a
beneficial impact on the development of the Irish economy.[68] Ireland joined
the European Monetary System when it was first set up in 1979. Since the
British did not join the system, the link with sterling was broken.[69] Ireland
held the presidency of the E.E.C. in 1979 and discharged the duties with
efficiency and tact.

The return of Fianna Fáil marked the eventual decline of the power of
local government. The promise to remove domestic rates had proved very
attractive to middle-class householders; but rates were the main source of
revenue for local government. By the early 1980s, a depleted national exchequer was unable to live up to its original commitment to fund local
government from Dublin. That enforced centralism was further strengthened
by the government practice of routeing all contact with the E.E.C. through
the capital.[70]

The Irish hierarchy privately welcomed the return of Lynch and Fianna
Fáil to power.[71] Suspicious of FitzGerald's project for pluralism, the hierarchy was now led by Tomás Ó Fiaich, who became archbishop of Armagh
on 2 October 1977 and cardinal on 30 June 1979. There were, however,
certain moral issues which the Fianna Fáil government could not evade

---

[66] Figures kindly supplied by the department of finance.
[67] Lee, *Ire. 1912–85*, p. 491.
[68] R.T.É's second radio and television channels opened; the Moneypoint E.S.B. coal-fired
power station was given the go-ahead; and Údarás na Gaeltachta was established in 1979. The
consumer information act (1978/1 (21 Feb. 1978)) provided for the appointment of a director
of consumer affairs. A new social welfare system was announced in Apr. 1978 based on a
simple pay-related contribution (P.R.S.I.).
[69] Below, p. 484.
[70] Desmond Roche, *Local government in Ireland* (Dublin, 1982), pp 148–50; Keogh, *Twentieth-century Ire.*, p. 330; Joseph Lee, 'Centralisation and community' in Joseph Lee (ed.),
Ireland: towards a sense of place (Cork, 1985), pp 84–102.
[71] Interviews with church sources, 1979.

or postpone. One of these was the legalisation of contraception—a matter that had been in need of resolution since the ruling in the Mary McGee case in December 1973.[72]

Quite apart from its possible impact on unionist opinion in Northern Ireland, there was growing discontent in the south over the failure to legislate on this issue. Of the main churches in Ireland, only the Roman Catholic church considered contraception to be morally wrong. Many catholics, however, had chosen to reject the teaching of their church on that question. Opinion polls showed that attitudes had changed during the 1970s. A 1971 poll had found that 63 per cent of respondents were opposed to the sale of contraceptives; only 34 per cent were in favour. A 1977 poll found that 43 per cent favoured the legalisation of contraceptives for married couples, 21 per cent favoured legalisation for all adults, and only 23 per cent were opposed to any legalisation.[73] While there had been no substantial change in the attitude of the hierarchy in the intervening years, the Lynch government found it impossible to postpone action any further. Ironically, it fell to Charles Haughey as minister for health to pilot the legislation through the oireachtas. Taking extensive soundings from the catholic hierarchy, the Church of Ireland, other churches, and seventeen interested bodies, he acted with great caution. On the one side, the Church of Ireland favoured the sale of contraceptives.[74] The catholic church stood resolutely against that innovation.

Haughey published the Health (Family Planning) Bill toward the end of 1978. Only the very naive expected a liberal bill. It was, however, much more restrictive than expected; contraceptives were to be sold through chemists' shops on presentation of a doctor's prescription. That could only be given if the doctor was satisfied that the person was seeking the contraceptives, bona fide, for family planning purposes or for adequate medical reasons and in appropriate circumstances.[75]

The bill provoked an acrimonious debate in Dáil Éireann. A Fine Gael deputy for South West Cork, Jim O'Keeffe, told the house that contraception was a question of private morality and that couples should be guided by their own consciences. The distinguished jurist John Kelly simply argued that the removal of section 17 of the criminal law amendment act of 1935 would render the legislation superfluous. Generally the arguments, for and against the legislation, developed along predictable lines. Haughey explained that he had been faced with the necessity to make 'artificial contraceptives' available 'to married persons or for family planning purposes'. On the other

---

[72] Above, p. 367.
[73] Whyte, Ch. & state, pp 404–5.
[74] Irish Times, 5 Apr. 1978.
[75] Ireland was to become the only country in western Europe where condoms were a prescription item. See Whyte, Ch. & state, p. 415.

hand, he did not and could not accept 'the situation where artificial contraceptives would be made freely available to everybody without any limitation of any kind'. The minister offered his legislation as a 'sensible, middle-of-the-road type of solution to a serious and complex situation'.[76] Fine Gael allowed a free vote to its members in the dáil and seanad. Labour opposed the measure. The bill was voted through on 17 July 1979.[77]

Haughey's success was one piece of good news for a government that appeared to be in crisis throughout 1979. A world oil crisis had radically reduced the availability of petrol to the public. Rationing might have been introduced, had it not been for the fact that the country had experienced a postal strike for five months. The introduction of rationing was postponed till the autumn. Fianna Fáil faced two sets of elections on 7 June 1979—the first direct elections to the European parliament, and Irish local elections. Charles Haughey, showing his open disregard for government policy, revealed shortly before the elections that he was having clandestine talks with one of the postal-strike union leaders. His action should have merited the sack at a time when Lynch was trying to maintain a firm line on pay increases, but he kept his ministry. The continuation of the postal strike angered voters and there was outrage in the farming community over the imposition of a 2 per cent levy on their turnover. Striking workers, out of work for months, attacked Lynch's car in his native Cork while he was on the campaign trail.[78] Party predictions, meanwhile, had rashly boasted that Fianna Fáil would return eight out of fifteen M.E.P.s. The outcome was a humiliation for Fianna Fáil, the party's share of the vote dropping by 16 per cent from the record level of the previous general election. Fianna Fáil won just five seats in the European parliament.[79]

Garret FitzGerald, who had taken over the leadership of Fine Gael in 1977, seized the opportunity to challenge the beleaguered Lynch, accusing him of a 'weak-kneed' approach to the business of government.[80] Indirectly, Lynch's style stood in marked contrast to that of Margaret Thatcher, who had been returned to power at the head of a Conservative government in Britain on 3 May 1979. Within Fianna Fáil there were growing signs of frustration with Lynch's leadership. By July 1979, a small group of T.D.s

[76] Martin Mansergh (ed.), *The spirit of the nation: the speeches and statements of Charles J. Haughey (1957–1985)* (Cork, 1986), p. 261; *Dáil Éireann deb.*, cccxiii, 774, 1283–6 (5 Apr. 1979), 1477–90 (25 Apr. 1979); cccxv, 1088–90 (26 June 1979).

[77] Health (Family Planning) Act, 1979/20 (23 July 1979).

[78] *Irish Times*, 1, 2 June 1979; Joe Joyce and Peter Murtagh, *The boss: Charles Haughey in government* (Dublin, 1983), p. 91; Arnold, *What kind of country*, p. 135.

[79] The party received 34.68 per cent of the vote compared with 50.63 per cent in 1977, and lost a seat in Munster to the farmers' candidate, T. J. Maher. The dissident Fianna Fáiler Neil Blaney was elected in Connacht–Ulster. Labour and Fine Gael both won four seats (*Irish Times*, 12 June 1979).

[80] *Irish Times*, 2 June 1979.

were actively campaigning to replace him as leader.[81] About twenty of the main anti-Lynch people met in Dublin on 5 July to discuss a strategy for takeover. The Kildare T.D. Charles McCreevy and the Mayo T.D. Pádraig Flynn attended. Efforts were made to recruit further support in the parliamentary party in the late summer. Lynch was aware of the moves against him. A T.D. who attended the meeting had given him a full report of the proceedings and the names of those who were present.[82] Lynch felt confident enough to leave for holidays in Portugal, where he learned on 27 August that the Provisional I.R.A. had blown up Earl Mountbatten's boat off Mullaghmore in County Sligo, killing the earl, his grandson, and a boat-boy. A few hours after those murders, the Provisional I.R.A. killed eighteen British soldiers in two bomb blasts at Narrow Water Castle, between Newry and Warrenpoint in County Down.[83]

Lynch attended the funeral of Mountbatten in London on 5 September where he later had discussions with Prime Minister Thatcher. Against a background of increasing sectarian murders of catholics in Northern Ireland, the taoiseach and the prime minister agreed to undertake a radical security review involving greater cross-border cooperation. Permission was given for a five-mile overflight of the border by British helicopters. This decision was to be used against Lynch some weeks later as the challenge to his leadership grew. There was further evidence of dissent inside Fianna Fáil when, four days after the funeral of Mountbatten, a granddaughter of the 'chief', Síle de Valera, used the occasion of the commemoration ceremony for the military leader of the anti-treatyites, Liam Lynch, to launch a public challenge to Lynch's leadership.[84]

The visit by Pope John Paul II to Ireland from 29 September to 1 October was a welcome intermission for the taoiseach. The timing, from the perspective of the holy see, was not arbitrary. The movement towards pluralism had to be arrested. The visit was an outstanding popular success. Over 2.5 million people attended the seven main venues. Advised against going to Northern Ireland, the pope nevertheless said mass in the archdiocese of Armagh, near Drogheda.[85] He appealed to all men and women engaged in violence to renounce it. The I.R.A. failed to respond.

[81] They were Albert Reynolds, Thomas McEllistrim, Jack Fahey, Seán Doherty, and Mark Killilea. A junior minister in the department of finance, Ray MacSharry, later joined the group, as did Senators Flor Crowley and Bernard McGlinchey (Arnold, *What kind of country*, p. 137; interviews with former *Irish Press* political correspondent Michael Mills, and other journalists).
[82] Joyce & Murtagh, *The boss*, p. 91; Arnold, *What kind of country*, p. 138; interview with Jack Lynch.
[83] The dowager Lady Brabourne, another passenger in the boat, died later of her injuries (Patrick Bishop and Eamonn Mallie, *The Provisional I.R.A.* (London, 1987), pp 248–50).
[84] Lee, *Ire. 1912–85*, p. 495.
[85] The visit was originally intended to include Northern Ireland, with an ecumenical service of reconciliation at St Patrick's cathedral, Armagh, but increased violence in Northern Ireland forced a change of plan (interviews with officials at the holy see, 1979).

Speaking at Limerick to a very large crowd before departing for the United States, John Paul II replied indirectly to FitzGerald's pluralist project for a 'new Ireland'. His sermon addressed traditional family values. It would be demonstrated within two years that the popular success of the papal visit helped accentuate resistance among more traditional catholics to ideas about making Irish identity more inclusive.

That would be somebody else's battle, for in October 1979 Jack Lynch took the decision to resign as taoiseach. By this time he was 62; his wife's health had not been good and he needed more time to be with her. He had also been disheartened by the murkiness of Irish politics as reflected in the rumours rife in Dublin that autumn, concerning President Patrick Hillery, who was said to be about to resign. In an effort to protect the president, Lynch arranged for a press conference between Hillery and the editors and political correspondents of the national newspapers. That only added to the confusion.[86] The entire episode outraged the taoiseach.

There was further bad news for Lynch on 7 November 1979 when Fianna Fáil lost two by-elections to Fine Gael in the taoiseach's native Cork. A dispirited Lynch had left with his wife on an official trip to the United States on polling day. In Washington, his fortunes took a further downturn. He found himself embroiled in a row within the party over his decision to allow border overflights by British helicopters. That security arrangement with the British—a practice continued by his successors—was confirmed by Lynch at a press conference in Washington.[87] In Ireland, one Fianna Fáil T.D. went so far as to call Lynch a liar. On his return, Lynch was visited by George Colley. Allowing himself to be persuaded that Colley could win an election for the leadership of Fianna Fáil, Lynch announced his retirement on 5 December. He had been assured that the sums had been done and that Colley had the necessary forty-two votes to win.[88] Charles Haughey emerged as Colley's opponent and as the winner. When the votes were counted on 7 December Colley had thirty-eight and his arch-rival forty-four.

DURING an extended debate in the dáil on 11 December 1979, leading members of the opposition questioned Haughey's suitability for the job of taoiseach. Fine Gael's John Kelly declared him totally unfit for that office; what he disliked most about Haughey was his relentless publicity and remorseless self-advertising. He objected to Haughey's concern with his image.

---

[86] A question by one of the journalists (about an alleged trip supposed to have been made by the president to the Isle of Wight without government permission) was the source of speculation that it might have been planted by a hostile source in the cabinet (interview with Michael Mills; interview with Dr Hillery, who described the rumours as 'structured').

[87] It seems unlikely that the arrangement had received cabinet approval (interview with Michael Mills, who was among the journalists who travelled with the taoiseach).

[88] Interview with Brian Lenihan and other members of Fianna Fáil.

De Valera, in his view, did not have that, nor did Lemass. Kelly hated the back-slapping, the currying favour, and the polished veneer. When it slipped, he said, something very ugly appeared in view. Garret FitzGerald, who had been at U.C.D. with Haughey, said that an overweening ambition was attributed to him which was not so much a desire to serve but rather a wish to dominate, indeed to own the state. Despite Haughey's recognised political skills, he came, according to FitzGerald, 'with a flawed pedigree'.[89]

The Labour leader, Frank Cluskey, contended that Haughey had helped to bring about an unjust society: as taoiseach he would only reinforce injustice, since he belonged to a breed of people who believed that the end justified the means. Cluskey claimed that such people set out to acquire personal wealth, influence, and political power. They were the ambitious, ruthless young men of the middle and late 1960s who were responsible for land speculation and jerry-built houses. Dr Noel Browne said that Haughey was 'one of two politicians in Irish life of whom I have always been afraid in his use of power': a dreadful cross between Richard Nixon and António de Oliviera Salazar.[90] Browne questioned whether Haughey would hand over power if defeated in the house. Despite the attacks, 'the boss', as Haughey was to become known, was elected taoiseach by 82 votes to 62.

However, he was a taoiseach with strong opposition from within his own party. In a speech on 20 December 1979, George Colley indicated that he would not promise loyalty to the taoiseach. After being called in for a reprimand, he made the scholastic distinction between giving loyalty to Haughey as taoiseach, which he was prepared to do, and giving loyalty to him as leader of Fianna Fáil. Colley's critical views of the new leader were shared by remnants of the old Fianna Fáil, Seán MacEntee and Frank Aiken.[91] Haughey was part of the Irish nouveaux riches, expensively dressed, with a taste for fine wines, modern Irish art, and life in the fast lane. Taoisigh from William T. Cosgrave to Lynch—including Haughey's own father-in-law, Seán Lemass—were a class apart. Lee has depicted Haughey as having much in common with David Lloyd George.[92] The comparison is appropriate and apt at many levels. But it may be too flattering. Richard Nixon offers greater possibilities as a historical parallel—years shut out from the White House by the U.S. electorate. Suspicious, mistrustful, authoritarian, secretive, contemptuous of his subordinates, Haughey, like Nixon, was nevertheless a politician of imagination and great ability. Haughey, like the disgraced former president of the United States, built around himself in the 1970s a

[89] Donal Foley, 'New taoiseach bitterly criticised in dáil debate', *Irish Times*, 12 Dec. 1979. In his memoirs, FitzGerald set the speech in context (*All in a life*, pp 341–2).

[90] *Irish Times*, 12 Dec. 1979.

[91] *Irish Press*, 20 Dec. 1979; Michael McInerney, 'Seán MacEntee: "All my sins are public"', *Irish Times*, 13 Dec. 1979.

[92] Lee, *Ire. 1912–85*, p. 499.

loyal entourage of T.D.s, business people, members of the professions, and leading lights in the visual and performing arts. He prized loyalty above ability in the selection of his cabinets and paid the price.

Once in office, Haughey kept Colley as tánaiste but sacked Jim Gibbons (agriculture), Martin O'Donoghue (economic planning and development), Denis Gallagher (Gaeltacht), and Bobby Molloy (defence). Those promoted to cabinet included a woman, Máire Geoghegan-Quinn (Gaeltacht), as well as Michael Woods (health and social welfare), Patrick Power (fisheries and forestry), Ray MacSharry (agriculture), and Albert Reynolds (posts and telegraphs). Michael O'Kennedy, who had provided one of Haughey's crucial votes, was given the department of finance, and was nominated E.E.C. commissioner in January 1980. (Gene Fitzgerald then moved from labour and public service to finance.) Colley went from finance to tourism and transport. He was expected to move shortly to the new department of energy. Desmond O'Malley retained industry, commerce, and energy. Gerry Collins remained in justice and Brian Lenihan moved to foreign affairs.[93]

Haughey's first period as taoiseach lasted till 21 May 1981. It was not an easy time to be in office. The international and national economic situations were deteriorating. Yet he surprised many of his critics by following broadly Lynch's policies on Northern Ireland and he attempted to grapple with a runaway economy. Haughey went on television on 9 January 1980 to argue that: 'In our present economic situation, it is madness to think that we can keep on looking for more money for less work . . .' He asked for a commitment to industrial peace.[94] Inflation had reached about 20 per cent by the middle of May. His government's first budget was framed against a background of pay-as-you-earn (P.A.Y.E.) marches and demands for radical reform of the taxation system. In a bid to defuse the discontent, cabinet ministers declined a pay increase due to them, and the building societies were subsidised to prevent a jump in interest rates. But ameliorative actions did not buy industrial peace. A strike by Aer Lingus craft workers ended on 3 July only after a month of chaos in air travel. Haughey demonstrated his interventionist style of government. He played a direct personal role in the resolution of industrial disputes, as in the cases of a teachers' pay dispute, and the Talbot car workers who were based in his own constituency. A new national wage agreement was signed in the autumn of 1980.

Yet Haughey's leadership had already attracted criticism. His authoritarian and interventionist style was resented by ministers and senior civil servants. His propensity to make policy 'on the hoof' provoked serious disquiet in government departments, finance in particular. On a visit to the proposed site of Knock airport, for example, he decided to fund the airport (which was

[93] *Irish Times*, 12 Dec. 1979.
[94] Mansergh, *Spirit of the nation*, p. 325; Keogh, *Twentieth-century Ire.*, pp 347–8.

near the Marian shrine) at an eventual cost of £13 million to the taxpayer. That was done against the express recommendations of the departments of finance and transport.[95] The Knock decision was illustrative of Haughey's volatile and arbitrary administrative style—a style that he occasionally carried into his handling of Northern Ireland affairs.

On 21 May 1980, the taoiseach held discussions with the British prime minister, Margaret Thatcher, in Downing Street, an occasion on which he gave her a present of an Irish Georgian silver teapot. The communiqué spoke of the two leaders' mutual desire to 'develop new and closer political cooperation between their governments'. It was agreed to hold regular summit meetings at which other ministers would be present when appropriate. While agreeing with Thatcher that any change in the constitutional status of Northern Ireland would come about only with the consent of a majority of the people of Northern Ireland, Haughey reaffirmed that it 'is the wish of the Irish government to secure the unity of Ireland by agreement and in peace'. Finally, the communiqué stated that both leaders agreed on 'the importance they attached to the unique relationship between the peoples of the United Kingdom of Great Britain and Northern Ireland and of the Republic and on the need to further this relationship in the interest of peace and reconciliation'. Reference was made to the satisfaction of both leaders at the efforts being made, separately and jointly, in the field of security.[96]

The human cost in the Republic of violence linked to the Northern Ireland troubles was illustrated again on 7 July 1980 when Detective Garda John Morley and Garda Henry Byrne were shot dead near Ballaghaderreen, County Roscommon, while trying to apprehend bank robbers. In a midnight sitting of the special criminal court a man was charged on 9 July with the murder of one of the gardaí after the £35,000 raid. On 27 July Haughey condemned Noraid, the U.S.-based fund-raising committee believed to be channelling funds to the Provisional I.R.A., for providing 'support for the campaign of violence' in Northern Ireland.

The Fianna Fáil leader's political fate became intertwined with the campaign to restore 'special-category status' for prisoners in Northern Ireland: this had been conceded in 1972 and withdrawn for new prisoners after March 1976. The campaign ultimately resulted in the 'dirty protest', during which prisoners smeared their cells with excrement and refused to wash or wear prison clothes. After a visit to the H-blocks (the Maze prison cell blocks, so-called because of their ground plan) Cardinal Ó Fiaich commented: 'One would hardly allow an animal to remain in such conditions, let alone a human being.'[97] The protest had been going on for four years. It

95 Arnold, *What kind of country*, p. 167.
96 Mansergh, *Spirit of the nation*, p. 362; Keogh, *Twentieth-century Ire.*, p. 350.
97 Bishop & Mallie, *Provisional I.R.A.*, p. 281.

moved into a new phase when seven republican prisoners refused breakfast on 27 October 1980. On 25 November, Haughey told the dáil that a solution would be possible if some adjustment could be made in the prison rules.

The government conveyed its concern to the British authorities. In mid December the hunger strike was suspended in the expectation of concessions, but negotiations broke down in January 1981 and some prisoners decided to go back on hunger strike. Staggering the starts, Bobby Sands, a 27-year-old from Belfast, began on 1 March. He was joined by Francis Hughes on 15 March, and others followed. By the time the campaign was called off in October 1981 ten of the prisoners had died.

Sinn Féin decided to put Sands forward as a candidate to fill the Westminster seat for Fermanagh–South Tyrone left vacant by the death of Frank Maguire, an Independent Republican M.P. The Social Democratic and Labour party declined to put up any candidate, and on 9 April Sands won the seat by 1,447 votes from the official Unionist, Harry West. Various efforts were made to obtain concessions in order to save the lives of the hunger-strikers. John Paul II sent his secretary, John Magee (later bishop of Cloyne), to Northern Ireland. Sands was presented with a silver crucifix. In April, Charles Haughey met members of Sands's family. But Sands died on 5 May on the sixty-sixth day of his hunger strike. Thousands attended the funeral, which attracted international media attention. A guard of honour, clad in black, flanked the coffin and was led by a pipe-and-drum band. This death brought ugly scenes to the streets of Dublin, Belfast, and Derry. Francis Hughes died on 12 May after fifty-nine days on hunger strike. There were further demonstrations in Dublin. Haughey met the sister of another hunger-striker, Patsy O'Hara, on 19 May. O'Hara died two days later, as did Raymond McCreesh.[98]

The deterioration in Anglo–Irish relations, from the first summit meeting in December 1980 to the succession of hunger strikes, must be seen against the background of an impending general election in the Republic. Haughey had hoped to obtain a new mandate soon after the Fianna Fáil ard-fheis due to be held on 15 February 1981. But the ard-fheis was postponed because of a fire on 14 February in the Stardust ballroom, Artane (which happened to be in the taoiseach's constituency). The fire claimed the lives of forty-eight young people and left 128 seriously injured. Visiting the scene of the disaster, the taoiseach declared a special day of mourning, and adjourned the dáil on 17 February as a mark of respect. A tribunal of inquiry was set up.[99]

An election was eventually announced on 21 May, with polling day fixed for 11 June—the shortest campaign period permitted under the constitution. Fine Gael and Labour again formed an electoral pact. When the votes were

[98] Mansergh, *Spirit of the nation*, p. 405; Padraig O'Malley, *Biting at the grave: the hunger strikes and the politics of despair* (Belfast, 1990), pp xi–xiv.
[99] Keogh, *Twentieth-century Ire.*, pp 353–4.

counted Fianna Fáil had won 78 seats out of 166, compared with 84 out of 148 in 1977. Fine Gael took 65 and Labour 15 seats. There had been eight H-block candidates, and two were elected at the expense of Fianna Fáil.

Garret FitzGerald formed his first government on 26 June 1981. Frank Cluskey, the Labour leader, had lost his seat and was replaced by Michael O'Leary, who became tánaiste. The coalition held power with the support of several independents, including the Limerick socialist deputy, Jim Kemmy. After receiving the seals of office from the president, FitzGerald told the dáil: 'In the couple of hours since I was appointed taoiseach... even in that brief time I have learned something of the scale of the damage done.' The new minister for finance, John Bruton, introduced a supplementary budget on 21 July 1981. It imposed an embargo on public-service recruitment and on new special pay increases. The V.A.T. rate was raised from 10 to 15 per cent. Haughey attacked the new economic strategy as 'a harsh, uncaring policy', which put 'bookkeeping before people'.[100]

However, the continuation of the hunger strikes soon took precedence over concerns about the economy. On 18 July 1981 an H-block demonstration in Dublin ended in violence at a cost of about £1 million in riot damage and injuries. A tenth hunger-striker, Michael Devine, died on 20 August. The hunger-strike campaign was called off on 3 October 1981.

Anxious to reconcile the different traditions on the island, FitzGerald sought to address the problems that he believed were most divisive. Returning to the pluralist issues he had raised with officials of the holy see during the 1970s, he indicated in an interview on 27 September 1981:

I want to lead a crusade, a republican crusade to make this a genuine republic... If I were a northern protestant today, I cannot see how I could be attracted to getting involved with a state that is itself sectarian—not in the acutely sectarian way that Northern Ireland was... [but] the fact is our laws and our constitution, our practices, our attitudes, reflect those of a majority ethos and are not acceptable to protestants in Northern Ireland.[101]

In his memoirs, FitzGerald admitted that his constitutional crusade was 'stillborn', but warned that the matter was 'a time-bomb ticking away at the heart of the narrow and exclusive form of catholic nationalism to which Fianna Fáil traditionally ties its fortunes'. Haughey did not share that view. 'I cannot see our state as sectarian', Haughey said on 7 January 1982. He criticised the constitutional crusade as a 'goldmine of propaganda' for the enemies of unity, who would use it 'relentlessly and remorselessly from here on in'.[102]

[100] Mansergh, *Spirit of the nation*, pp 508, 511.
[101] FitzGerald, *All in a life*, p. 378.
[102] Ibid., p. 380; Mansergh, *Spirit of the nation*, pp 522, 572.

The coalition government fell unexpectedly on 27 January 1982 when the budget was defeated by the vote of Jim Kemmy, who objected to the imposition of V.A.T. on children's shoes. As the result of the vote in the dáil became clear, FitzGerald experienced a moment of total exhilaration. 'This was it. We were going into battle on a budget that we could defend with conviction and enthusiasm.'[103] But Haughey had other ideas. After a meeting of the Fianna Fáil front bench immediately after the government had lost the vote, Haughey issued a statement: 'It is a matter for the president to consider the situation which has arisen now that the taoiseach has ceased to retain the support of the majority in Dáil Éireann. I am available for consultation by the president should he so wish.'[104] It is alleged that several phone calls were made to Áras an Uachtaráin by Fianna Fáil front benchers in an effort to get President Hillery on the line. FitzGerald was delayed in going to Áras an Uachtaráin because the president's secretary, who was required to be present, was at the theatre. FitzGerald was with the president for three-quarters of an hour, and he recorded that Hillery vigorously propounded to him the inappropriateness of exercising the presidential prerogative not to grant a dissolution in the circumstances.[105] The number of calls made to Áras an Uachtaráin that night, and the names of the callers, were carefully logged by the military officer on duty. It is probable that the president also kept detailed notes of those developments. Those records, it is to be hoped, will eventually be released under the thirty-year rule.

A general election was held on 18 February 1982. Fianna Fáil won 81 seats, Fine Gael 63, Labour 15, the Workers' party 3, and independents 4. The electorate had denied an overall majority to Haughey. Two of his strongest critics inside the party, George Colley and Desmond O'Malley, met to discuss tactics, and it was decided that O'Malley would challenge Haughey's nomination for taoiseach at the parliamentary party meeting. Jack Lynch issued a statement supporting O'Malley's decision. With both camps canvassing strongly, Haughey brought the meeting forward to 25 February. It was a particularly tense time in Fianna Fáil, as rumours began to circulate of Haughey's impending resignation. A young reporter in the *Irish Press*, Stephen Collins, recalls going, on the instructions of his news editor, to the dáil on 24 February to ask Haughey one question: did he intend to resign? The response was as unexpected as it was explosive. Collins was told 'Would you fuck off', as Haughey made a run at him, and shouted in his face: 'That's F.U.C.K. O.F.F.' Regaining his composure, Haughey asked Collins to repeat his question, and on Collins complying, Haughey replied calmly, 'That's complete nonsense. I have no intention of resigning', and walked out. The Fianna Fáil parliamentary party met the following day, during which

[103] FitzGerald, *All in a life*, p. 397. [104] Smith, *Garret the enigma*, p. 24.
[105] FitzGerald, *All in a life*, p. 398.

support for O'Malley buckled. Without any need for a vote, Haughey emerged the victor, backed by several T.D.s believed to have been in O'Malley's camp.[106]

Both Haughey and FitzGerald still hoped to become the next taoiseach. The courtship of the independents had already begun. Charles McCreevy, an independent-minded ex-member of Fianna Fáil's parliamentary party from Kildare, had agreed to support Haughey. The crucial vote to form the next government was held by Tony Gregory, an independent T.D. from Dublin's inner city. He met both sides, but agreed to support Haughey after securing a £50 million deal for what was effectively his own constituency. Whether it was for Moscow or Marx, the three Workers' party T.D.s, Joe Sherlock, Proinsias de Rossa, and Paddy Gallagher, also agreed to support Haughey. But when the division bell went for the crucial vote on 9 March 1982 the three were locked outside the chamber. Led by a Fianna Fáil senator, they burst into the press gallery, jumped across to the distinguished visitors' gallery, and reached the floor of the chamber in time to vote for Haughey and put Fianna Fáil back into power.

The second Haughey administration which followed lasted till 4 November 1982. Born in controversy, its short life was marked by a series of scandals which were to reverberate into the 1990s. The new cabinet included new as well as old faces. Ray MacSharry was made tánaiste and minister for finance. Paddy Power from Kildare was appointed to defence, and his name became internationally known during the Falklands crisis. Seán Doherty from Roscommon was given the justice department. Desmond O'Malley was given industry, commerce, and tourism. Gerard Collins became minister for foreign affairs. Martin O'Donoghue took the education portfolio, and Raphael Burke went to the department of the environment. Michael Woods was appointed to health and social welfare; Padraig Flynn to the Gaeltacht; Albert Reynolds, industry and energy; Gene Fitzgerald, labour and the public service; and John Wilson, transport, posts, and telegraphs. Given the rivalries within Fianna Fáil, this administration was as much a coalition as the previous government had been.

The decision by Michael O'Kennedy to return from Brussels, where he had not been happy as commissioner, provided an opening for Haughey to gain another vital vote. Contrary to the tradition of keeping such patronage inside one's own party, Haughey decided to offer the post to Richard Burke, a former commissioner who since his return from Brussels had been left by FitzGerald on the Fine Gael back benches. Burke took the job, and as he set out for Brussels, MacSharry brought in the budget on 5 May 1982 which included provisions to cover the Gregory deal. Among these provisions were

[106] Stephen Collins, *The Haughey file: the unprecedented career and last years of the boss* (Dublin, 1992), pp 56–8; Arnold, *What kind of country*, pp 181–2.

the nationalisation of a twenty-seven-acre site in Dublin port, the nationalisation of the Clondalkin paper mills, and the creation of nearly 4,000 new jobs in inner Dublin over three years. FitzGerald described the budget as an 'unstable edifice', and in his memoirs claimed that it had largely collapsed during the course of the year.[107]

The same month as the budget was introduced, Haughey found himself involved in the worst Anglo–Irish stand-off since the economic war of the 1930s. On 2 April the Argentinian military junta invaded the Falkland Islands in the south Atlantic. Haughey withdrew support for an international boycott against Argentina in early May, after the sinking by a British submarine of the _Belgrano_, an Argentinian warship that was outside the exclusion zone around the islands. The crisis deepened when Ireland's signal to withdraw sanctions at a meeting of E.E.C. senior foreign-ministry officials left a reluctant Italian government (itself under considerable pressure from Italian-Argentinians) with no choice but to comply. To compound matters, Haughey called for an immediate meeting of the U.N. security council to review the crisis, at a juncture in the war when such a move would have threatened the fragile unity of the anti-Argentinian international consensus that the British had so painstakingly built up.[108]

As the British tabloids used phrases such as 'stab in the back' to describe the Irish government's reaction, relations between London and Dublin deteriorated, and well-known branded Irish exports to England in particular experienced a fall in sales. To add to Haughey's problems, his gamble to snatch a Fine Gael seat in the Dublin West by-election on 25 May failed. Haughey also faced acute personal embarrassment when his election agent, a close friend, was charged and tried for personation in the general election. Although there was no conviction, the incident was ridiculed publicly, and it set the tone for the new administration.[109] Worse was to follow.

In August, one Malcolm Edward McArthur was arrested in the flat of the attorney general, Patrick Connolly,[110] and charged with the murder of a nurse, Bridie Gargan, in the Phoenix Park three weeks earlier. Speaking in place of the minister for justice, who was on holiday, Haughey described the episode as 'grotesque, unbelievable, bizarre, and unprecedented'. Conor Cruise O'Brien devised the acronym 'G.U.B.U.', which passed into the lexicon of Irish politics. It encapsulated for the taoiseach's critics the style of his short-lived administration. Haughey's run of bad luck, if that is how those events may be described, did not end there. In late September the minister

---

[107] FitzGerald, _All in a life_, pp 406–7; Mansergh, _Spirit of the nation_, p. 616; Collins, _Haughey file_, p. 58.

[108] See Keogh, _Twentieth-century Ire._, pp 360–61.

[109] Joyce & Murtagh, _The boss_, p. 127.

[110] The attorney general, who had merely loaned his flat, returned from holiday in New York and resigned.

for justice, Seán Doherty, was involved in a controversy (which became known as the 'Dowra affair') over a case in which his brother-in-law, who was a garda, was cleared of an assault charge. It was revealed that a leading prosecution witness from Northern Ireland had been unable to attend court at Dowra, County Cavan, because he had been detained by the R.U.C.[111]

Doherty, unquestionably the most controversial minister for justice in the history of the state, continued to make unwelcome headlines. As minister, he authorised a tap on the phones of two prominent journalists, Bruce Arnold of the *Irish Independent* and Geraldine Kennedy of the *Sunday Tribune*, as part of an effort to prevent information being leaked to the press after cabinet meetings. Almost ten years later Doherty confirmed that he had been authorised by cabinet to stop the leaks. Doherty further claimed that he had actually handed the transcripts of the phone taps to Charles Haughey in his office. The taoiseach, allegedly, took them without comment. Three other members of that cabinet disputed Doherty's recollections. They were Ray MacSharry, John Wilson, and Desmond O'Malley. Wilson, who was minister for posts and telegraphs, denied that he had ever authorised the phone-tapping of either of the two journalists.[112]

Disquiet within Fianna Fáil about Haughey's leadership, which had been present since the day of his election, manifested itself again in autumn 1982. Desmond O'Malley and Martin O'Donoghue expressed their reservations on the subject at a cabinet meeting on 5 October, and resigned. Charles McCreevy (a future minister for finance), now back in the parliamentary party, put down a no-confidence motion in Haughey's leadership on 6 October, and called for the party to reach its decision by secret ballot. McCreevy indicated that he wanted an end to political strokes, deals, and 'convulsion politics'.[113] Haughey replied on radio that he would meet the challenge head on. Although he depicted the dissidents as a small minority, he expressed a preference for a roll-call vote over a secret ballot. The dissidents would have to 'stand up and be counted'. The party meeting on 6 October lasted twelve hours. Haughey won by 58 votes to 22.

But the death of a Clare T.D., Bill Loughnane, on 18 October, and the heart attack suffered shortly afterwards by Jim Gibbons, T.D. for Carlow–Kilkenny, seriously weakened the survival chances of the Haughey government. Fianna Fáil launched its policy document *The way forward* on 21 October, and later that day the minister for finance, Ray MacSharry, had a meeting in his office with the former minister for education, Martin O'Donoghue. The former recorded the discussion with equipment supplied

[111] Shane Kenny, *Go dance on somebody else's grave* (Dublin, 1990), p. 12.
[112] *Irish Times*, 16 Jan. 1992; *Cork Examiner*, 16 Jan. 1992; Joyce & Murtagh, *The boss*, pp 127 ff. For a sympathetic profile of Doherty, see John Waters, *Jiving at the crossroads* (Belfast, 1991), p. 157.
[113] Kenny, *Go dance*, p. 13.

(at the request of the minister for justice) by the assistant commissioner of the gardaí, Joe Ainsworth.[114] That information was leaked to the press in 1983, and prompted yet another attempt to remove Haughey as leader of the party.

Fine Gael put down a motion of no confidence in Haughey, and after a two-day debate in the dáil the three Workers' party deputies changed sides and helped defeat the government by 82 votes to 80. There was to be a third general election within eighteen months on 24 November. Fianna Fáil entered the campaign with the opinion polls recording a 7 per cent drop in support for the party. FitzGerald was preferred as taoiseach by 51 per cent, to 31 per cent for Haughey. This was a challenging campaign for the Kerry North T.D. Dick Spring, who had become leader of the Labour party on 1 November 1982 after the defection of Michael O'Leary to Fine Gael. There was no prior agreement on a programme for government between Fine Gael and Labour. Both parties were modest in their electoral promises. But an issue that was to grow in importance insinuated its way into the campaign. An anti-abortion lobby calling itself the Pro-Life Amendment Campaign (P.L.A.C.) attempted to play one side off against the other. Fearing the emergence of a bloc of orthodox catholic votes, both Fianna Fáil and Fine Gael proved receptive to such overtures. In his memoirs FitzGerald recorded that there was a whispering campaign against him, alleging that he was soft on abortion. In September 1982 he had met that challenge head on, stating his conviction that abortion was wrong and should not be legalised. But he was also conscious of not wanting to introduce an amendment to the constitution that might have been perceived as sectarian. As he told the Fine Gael ard-fheis in October, he preferred to see an amendment as an integral part of a general constitutional review. According to FitzGerald, 'Charles Haughey went one better by promising an amendment during 1982'.[115] Two days before the election Fianna Fáil produced a text for a constitutional amendment which read: 'The state acknowledges the right to life of the unborn and, with due regard to the equal right to life of the mother, guarantees in its laws to respect, and as far as practicable, by its laws to defend and vindicate that right.'[116] Although that wording was acceptable to FitzGerald at the time, he changed his mind shortly after returning to power.

The abortion question formed one of the underlying issues of the election campaign, and so did a certain paranoia about British interference in Irish politics. A lunch between FitzGerald and the catholic duke of Norfolk was converted into a conspiracy when it was alleged that the duke had been a former head of British military intelligence.[117] It was an inglorious end to a campaign that had provided numerous illustrations of just how vitriolic and negative Irish politics had become—power being an end in itself.

---

[114] Ibid., pp 14–15.   [115] FitzGerald, *All in a life*, pp 416–18.   [116] Ibid., p. 417.
[117] Mansergh, *Spirit of the nation*, pp 709, 713.

The election resulted in a loss of six seats for Fianna Fáil, while Fine Gael gained seven and Labour one. A Fine Gael–Labour coalition came into office on 14 December 1982. FitzGerald was taoiseach, a position he was to hold till March 1987. Dick Spring was tánaiste. The early weeks of the new coalition's tenure of office were dominated by the scandal concerning the phone-tapping of the two journalists Arnold and Kennedy. The new minister for justice, Michael Noonan, revealed the evidence on 20 January 1983 in a thirteen-page document. He stated that his predecessor had requested the tapping of the phones in order to end the leaks from the cabinet to the media. He explained that it was usual for the garda commissioner to request permission for a phone-tap, but that in this case the procedure had been reversed. Noonan announced that the commissioner, Patrick McLaughlin, and his deputy Joe Ainsworth, would retire on 1 February. Seán Doherty and Ray MacSharry both defended their own actions, while Haughey denied any intention of resigning. Confident that Haughey was in fact about to resign, the de Valera family daily, the *Irish Press*, published his political obituary on 27 January. A more prudent *Irish Times* carried the headline 'Haughey resignation thought imminent as support crumbles', while the *Irish Independent* conjectured 'Haughey may quit'.[118] Even his loyal supporters had begun shifting ground, so sure were they that Haughey was about to step down. The Fianna Fáil deputy from Donegal, Clem Coughlan, who had always supported Haughey, told R.T.É. radio at the end of January that it was time for a change of leadership.

On 31 January Haughey's supporters rallied outside the party's headquarters in Mount Street, Dublin, days before a critical meeting of the parliamentary party. When the party met on 7 February, after some delays occasioned in part by Coughlan's death in a road accident, Haughey had been cleared of all blame in the phone-tapping episodes by an internal party inquiry. A motion calling on him to resign as leader was defeated by forty votes to thirty-three. From 1983 to his return to power in 1987, Haughey purged the party of his opponents. Desmond O'Malley was expelled on 26 February 1985 for defying the party whip again. Subsequently a Dublin T.D., Mary Harney, was expelled for supporting the signing of the Anglo–Irish agreement. These deputies formed the Progressive Democrat party in December 1985, and they were joined by the Fianna Fáil Galway West T.D. Bobby Molloy in February 1986.[119]

[118] Kenny, *Go dance*, pp 15–17. The political correspondent of the *Irish Press* at that time, Michael Mills, revealed in an interview that the 'obituary' (prepared to follow the expected resignation announcement) had been published by mistake. A decade later, revelations about the phone-tapping affair (n. 112, above) were substantially responsible for Haughey's sudden retirement in Feb. 1992.

[119] The P.D.s were to win fourteen seats in the general election of 1987. Denying Haughey an overall majority, they failed to keep him out of power, but obliged him to rely on the casting vote of the ceann comhairle (speaker of the house) to cling on to office. In 1989 Haughey

Returning to the events of 1982, shortly before leaving office, Haughey had taken up the anti-abortion cause, and had produced the wording of the constitutional amendment which has been quoted above. That placed Fitz-Gerald seriously on the defensive. An anti-abortion campaign had gathered speed from 1980 onwards, and it had been turned into an election issue. The reasons for the emergence of the Society for the Protection of Unborn Children (S.P.U.C.) and the launching of the P.L.A.C. are unclear. Both organisations were led by members of the laity. It is not possible to ascertain, on the basis of the available evidence, the degree of authority that the Irish bishops exercised over these bodies. But the probability is that the hierarchy as a body was not directly influential in respect of either their policies or their tactics.

Under some pressure FitzGerald accepted the Fianna Fáil formula. The dáil was the scene of many bitter exchanges, during which FitzGerald was accused of being pro-abortion.[120] Had he been stronger in his stance—based on the evidence he had received from the attorney general, Peter Sutherland—the outcome might have been different.[121] Belatedly FitzGerald argued against the original Fianna Fáil wording. He warned on 3 September 1983: 'If, therefore, we adopt this amendment we could be opening up the possibility that we are all trying to close off: the introduction of abortion.' The catholic archbishop of Dublin, Dermot Ryan, advised his church members: 'A "yes" vote . . . will . . . prevent any attempt to legalise abortion in the country.'[122]

Nearly a decade later, FitzGerald revealed that in 1983 he had been critical of the catholic hierarchy's refusal to allow the taoiseach the opportunity to explain to the bishops face to face the legal defects that had emerged, and of their insistence 'on discussing the proposed change in the amendment with us through an intermediary, with all the dangers of confusion inherent in such indirect contact'. He felt that the bishops were also wrong to have 'set

gambled on calling a general election in order to secure an overall majority. The gamble failed, and for the first time in the history of the party Fianna Fáil was obliged to enter into coalition, and with the Progressive Democrats. Kenny, *Go dance*, pp 21–2; T. Ryle Dwyer, *Haughey's thirty years of controversy* (Cork, 1992), p. 134.

[120] See Tom Hesketh, *The second partitioning of Ireland: the abortion referendum of 1983* (Dun Laoghaire, 1990).

[121] Sutherland wrote a long memorandum outlining his reservations about the Fianna Fáil wording, predicting with some accuracy the difficulties that emerged during the 'X' case of 1992 (Keogh, *Twentieth-century Ire.*, p. 370). The case involved a pregnant 14-year-old alleged statutory-rape victim. The high court granted an injunction to prevent the victim's family from taking her to England, but the supreme court overturned the decision and accepted that abortion was legal in limited cases where there was a real danger that the pregnant woman was liable to commit suicide. It might have been expected that legislation would follow this ruling, but towards the end of the 1990s the matter continued to remain 'bare of legislative direction' (Keogh, *Twentieth-century Ire.*, pp 370–71; *Irish Times*, 6, 7, 9–13 Mar. 1992).

[122] Quoted in Gerald Barry, 'A constitutional nightmare' in *Sunday Tribune*, 8 Mar. 1982.

themselves up as authorities on constitutional law superior to the government's constitutional advisers, as they did in their pro-amendment statement [22 August 1983]'.[123]

The referendum was held on 7 September 1983 and the Fianna Fáil wording duly became article 40.3 of the constitution. The eighth amendment to the constitution was passed by 66.9 per cent (841,233 votes) to 33.1 per cent (416,136). The turnout was 53.7 per cent. Writing in 1992, FitzGerald expressed regret about what had happened at that time:

For my part I was seriously at fault in accepting without adequate consideration or legal advice—however much in good faith—the proposed wording when it was put forward by Fianna Fáil in early November 1982. The fact that, given the scale of the Fine Gael and Labour defections in the eventual dáil division on the issue, the amendment would clearly have been put through the dáil by Fianna Fáil in opposition, even if I had rejected it from the outset, is a poor excuse for my error of judgment.[124]

FitzGerald's plans to promote greater pluralism in Ireland had thus met strong resistance from the still formidable traditional or conservative forces in society. He had devised a blueprint for the development of a pluralist society, but found it very difficult to convert important sections of the population to his point of view. A referendum to remove the constitutional ban on divorce was to be defeated in 1986. Despite these setbacks, FitzGerald was responsible during his time as taoiseach (1982–7) for organising the most comprehensive review of Irish identity conducted since the drafting of the 1937 constitution. Together with the leader of the S.D.L.P., John Hume, FitzGerald co-sponsored the idea of establishing a 'New Ireland Forum'.[125] The first session of the forum was held in Dublin Castle on 30 May 1983. The president of University College, Galway, Colm Ó hEocha, was in the chair. All the major constitutional nationalist parties sent representatives. The unionist parties did not join the deliberations, although some individual unionists did participate. There were twenty-eight private sessions, thirteen public sessions, and fifty-six meetings of the steering group. A total of 317 written submissions were received from Ireland and abroad. A forum delegation visited Northern Ireland on 26 and 27 September 1983 and held discussions in London on 23 and 24 January 1984 with groups from all the major parties. Several important reports were commissioned by

[123] Garret FitzGerald, 'Damage of 1983 amendment will not be easily undone' in *Irish Times*, 22 Feb. 1992.
[124] Joe Lee, 'Dynamics of social and political change in the Irish Republic' in Dermot Keogh and Michael Haltzel (ed.), *Northern Ireland and the politics of reconciliation* (Cambridge, Mass., 1993), p. 124; Garret FitzGerald, 'Damage of 1983 amendment will not be easily undone' in *Irish Times*, 22 Feb. 1992.
[125] Interviews with Garret FitzGerald and John Hume on the origins of the New Ireland Forum.

the forum,[126] and the final report was published in May 1984. Among the findings of the forum was the following: 'It is clear that a new Ireland will require a new constitution which will ensure that the needs of all traditions are fully met. Society in Ireland as a whole comprises a wider diversity of cultural and political traditions than exists in the south, and the constitution and laws of a new Ireland must accommodate these social and political realities.'[127]

The minister for foreign affairs, Peter Barry, gave expression to those views at a lunch in Iveagh House in September 1985 in honour of the cardinal secretary of state, Agostino Casaroli, with whom FitzGerald had held informal discussions in the mid 1970s. Barry told his audience of the intimate relationship between the catholic church and government since the foundation of the state: 'Nevertheless, in retrospect, it has been argued— most notably by the catholic bishops at the public session of the New Ireland Forum on 9 February 1984—that the alliance of church and state was harmful for both parties.' The minister conceded the right of all church leaders to alert the consciences of their followers to what they perceived to be the moral consequences of any proposed legislation, but he also affirmed the right of the oireachtas to legislate in accordance with what members considered to be in the best interests of the Irish people.[128]

The New Ireland Forum was notable for its acknowledgement of the legitimacy of unionist identity. However, a united Ireland remained the ultimate aspiration for most participants: the final report concluded that 'a united Ireland in the form of a sovereign independent Irish state to be achieved peacefully and by consent' was 'the best and most durable basis for peace and stability'. Charles Haughey was among those who endorsed a unitary state option; for him this would 'embrace the whole island of Ireland governed as a single unit under one government and one parliament elected by all the people of the island'. Other participants stressed the two other options explored in the report, a federal or confederal state and a system of joint authority.[129]

The openness of the forum approach contributed directly to the signing of the Anglo–Irish agreement on 15 November 1985 at Hillsborough Castle, County Down, by Garret FitzGerald and Margaret Thatcher.[130] Although

---

[126] These included *The cost of violence arising from the Northern Ireland crisis since 1969* (Dublin, [1984]); *The economic consequences of the division of Ireland since 1920* (Dublin, [1984]); *A comparative description of the economic structure and situation, north and south* (Dublin, [1983]).
[127] *New Ireland Forum report (2 May 1984)* (Dublin, 1984), p. 23. For a personal account see FitzGerald, *All in a life*, pp 460 ff; see also Lee, *Ire. 1912–85*, pp 675–82; Clare O'Halloran, *Partition and the limits of Irish nationalism* (Dublin, 1987), pp 195 ff.
[128] Quoted in Keogh, *Twentieth-century Ire.*, p. 369.
[129] See Tom Hadden and Kevin Boyle, *The Anglo–Irish agreement: commentary, text and official review* (London, 1989), pp 6–7; see also Arwel Ellis Owen, *The Anglo–Irish agreement: first three years* (Cardiff, 1994).

detailed examination of the agreement lies beyond the scope of this chapter, it provided the framework in which Dublin and London were to address both the long-term and the day-to-day problems of Northern Ireland. A permanent secretariat was set up at Maryfield, near Belfast, staffed by British and Irish civil servants. Despite difficulties, the Anglo–Irish process had been established, and during the 1990s it would help to bring about several ceasefires and all-party talks in Northern Ireland.

BETWEEN 1972 and 1984, the Irish state was obliged to function against a background of subversive violence, north and south of the border. That conflict had profound direct and indirect consequences for economic growth on the entire island. Two international oil crises in the 1970s further damaged the prospects for expansion in key sectors of the economy, such as service industries. Irish and British membership of the E.E.C. helped bring significant net transfers of funding to both sides of the border. But the healthy cash flow—particularly to the agricultural sector and for infrastructural investment—was only one benefit of membership. E.E.C. membership transmitted and reinforced greater national self-confidence at a time of great tension over Northern Ireland.

Part of a club of nine in western Europe, E.E.C. membership provided a new context in which the country could operate at an international level. It also offered a new framework in which to explore questions of identity and diversity at home. Taoisigh from Jack Lynch to Garret FitzGerald were committed to the task of responding to the challenge of legislating for that diversity. Lynch secured the deletion of the special position of the catholic church from article 44 of the constitution in 1972. However, so much of the time and energy of successive Irish leaders was taken up with the 'spill-over' effects of conflict in Northern Ireland that very often it was not possible to develop a strategy for social reform. Lynch's time in office illustrated very dramatically the domestic political consequences of 'the troubles' for Fianna Fáil in government. He kept his nerve. His successor, Liam Cosgrave, also acted with great determination to suppress the activities of political subversives. But between 1972 and 1984 the state paid a very high economic price for having to deal with the activities of the I.R.A. and other paramilitaries.

The emergence of Charles Haughey as leader of Fianna Fáil in 1979 did not materially influence the general bipartisan approach in Dáil Éireann to Northern Ireland and Anglo–Irish affairs. There were moments of great difficulty with London, as in 1982, but Haughey did not diverge from the Lynch approach on Northern Ireland. However, his legacy on the development of the Fianna Fáil party and domestic politics is more difficult to

[130] See Anthony Kenny, *The road to Hillsborough: the shaping of the Anglo–Irish agreement* (Oxford, 1986), Hadden & Boyle, *Anglo–Irish agreement*, and FitzGerald, *All in a life*, pp 494 ff.

assess. His leadership style was radically different from that of his predecessors. Haughey was a *fear ann féin* (his own man). The opening of the state archives under the thirty-year rule will provide a more comprehensive view of his time in office.

Garret FitzGerald, who was taoiseach for not quite five years in the 1980s, made the more enduring strategic contribution to the development of Irish society. The establishment of the New Ireland Forum set in train a process of political self-reflection which was to have tangible results in the peace process of the 1990s. Drawing a road-map to set people on the way to a 'new Ireland' was a challenging intellectual exercise. The reaching of the chosen destination proved very difficult in a country where the impulses towards 'modernisation' and 'secularisation' were challenged by social forces that were often underestimated by those who advocated a 'liberal crusade'.

CHAPTER XV

Northern Ireland, 1972–84

PAUL ARTHUR

THE period is best characterised as a time of drift and of helplessness, the collapse of old certainties and the beginnings of a new siege. The political landscape changed utterly and, while there were some bright lights on the horizon, intransigence rather than illumination was the order of the day. The new regime of direct rule was like a tidal wave, affecting one community before the other appreciated its impact and intent. It was the unionist community that felt the greatest sense of loss. It seemed to them that, overnight, untrammelled one-party rule had been replaced by a form of bureaucratic dictatorship from afar. The intimacies of the old Stormont system gave way to a fundamental debate about identity and a profound pessimism for the future. Unionists felt betrayed by their 'guarantor', the government and parliament of the United Kingdom. For much of the period they were to engage in a form of intra-ethnic debate between those who called themselves unionists and those who were more comfortable with the term 'loyalism'. In time, that discussion centred on what method of government best suited Northern Ireland: whether it should be fully integrated into the United Kingdom or ruled through a revised version of devolution.

The nationalist community welcomed direct rule from the outset, if only because it discomfited unionists. For a period of about eighteen months nationalists were uplifted. They believed that their sense of justice and equity was being addressed under the system of direct rule. Optimism disappeared with the collapse of the experiment in power-sharing in May 1974. In the following years they perceived themselves to be engaged in a struggle for survival, not dissimilar to that of the unionists. With the onset of the hunger strikes in 1980 and the decision of Sinn Féin to contest elections, the catholic community was drawn into the internal debate between nationalist and republican, a debate concerned not with the ends of Irish unity but with the means to attain that end.

Three features of the period suggest themselves. The first is that it can be divided into three phases. Initially the new secretary of state and his team at the Northern Ireland office (N.I.O.) indulged in constitutional innovation culminating in the creation of a power-sharing executive in January 1974. Its collapse in May led to the end of optimism among the policy-makers and some of the politicians. The second phase lasted for the life of the Labour government, from 1974 to 1979. It was characterised by one desultory attempt at an internal settlement, with more emphasis being placed on security and economic policies. During this period the population began to grasp that the machinery of direct rule was nominally temporary but that in certain circumstances it could be made permanent. The beginning of the third phase coincided with Margaret Thatcher's accession to office in 1979. The Conservative government was to be more interventionist in terms of constitutional experiment and it was to broaden the base of the problem by analysing it on a British–Irish, rather than a purely United Kingdom, level.

The second feature is the disintegration of political life within Northern Ireland. This took many forms. The introduction of the single transferable vote system of proportional representation allowed initially for the efflorescence of minor parties, especially within the unionist community. Much of the period was characterised by a struggle for dominance of that community. By 1984 the best that could be said was that unionism was no longer a monolith and that it was controlled by an uneasy alliance of two parties, the Ulster Unionist party (U.U.P.) and the Democratic Unionist party (D.U.P.). The pervasiveness of paramilitarism in the catholic community produced a similar outcome, although this was not apparent till the 1980s. By the end of the period neither community had produced a political leadership that could speak unequivocally on behalf of their respective constituents. The resulting vacuum created problems for those who were trying to fashion a political solution.

A third feature concerns the lack of an internal political forum where issues could be debated and politicians could engage in dialogue. Just as importantly, very few politicians were in receipt of a parliamentary salary. The outcome was twofold. The parties were dominated by the same personalities with the same fixed views; and a younger generation were eschewing politics by involving themselves in other activities, including paramilitarism, or were emigrating in search of a more secure future. 'Alienation' may have been a term introduced to explain the catholic community's sense of powerlessness; in fact it related to virtually everyone in Northern Ireland. When the leader of the S.D.L.P., John Hume, told his party's annual conference in 1980 that 'not only are we not in government, we are not even in opposition',[1] unwittingly he was speaking for all the political parties and he was enunciating their essential powerlessness.

WHEN Stormont was prorogued in March 1972 and direct rule introduced, the assumption was that it was for a period of one year only, during which

---

[1] *Irish Times*, 10 Nov. 1980.

the indigenous politicians would be given some breathing space to sort out their problems. There can be no doubt that the British government saw it as a last desperate remedy. Direct rule had been mooted as early as August 1969; but, as James Callaghan recalls in his memoirs, the government was only too aware of its lack of knowledge of Northern Ireland and was uncertain as to how the police and Northern Ireland civil service would react to direct rule's introduction.[2] Greater familiarity with the problem created greater trepidation about becoming too closely involved. In November 1971 the leader of the opposition, Harold Wilson, warned that direct rule 'cannot be ruled out as a last resort, as a council of despair, where the existing process of law and order and government has failed. But as an act of policy, as something to be worked for, direct rule must be totally rejected.'[3] Its introduction was indeed a last resort, and reaction to it was largely predictable. The Dublin government welcomed direct rule, following which there was a marked improvement in Anglo–Irish relations.[4] The nationalist response inside Northern Ireland was such that before the end of May the S.D.L.P. had called on those catholics who had withdrawn from participation in public affairs, as a protest against internment, to return and, in effect, cooperate with the new administration, which now came under a secretary of state for Northern Ireland, William Whitelaw. Unionist condemnation of the move was universal. The deposed prime minister, Brian Faulkner, supported a two-day loyalist strike on 27–8 March, which paralysed industry in many areas; and he set up a sort of government-in-exile, which used every opportunity to attack the direct rule administration while preparing for the day when it would be recalled to office. One Unionist association (Londonderry and Foyle) invoked a sense of history when it described the fall of Stormont as 'the most complete betrayal since Lundy'.[5] Outside the political arena the government committee of the presbyterian church issued a statement that 'deplored' the decision to prorogue the Northern Ireland parliament.[6] It was this sort of reaction that the authorities feared. They were conscious that the creation of a democratic deficit would make their task more difficult and that they would have to move quickly to impose the conditions for stability. One well-informed commentator wrote that when 'the Heath government took over direct rule of Northern Ireland on 28 March, private estimates in Whitehall of the amount of time that had been "bought" for a peaceful

---

[2] James Callaghan, *A house divided: the dilemma of Northern Ireland* (London, 1973), *passim.*
[3] Cited in *Irish Times*, 26 Nov. 1971.
[4] Adrian Guelke, *Northern Ireland: the international perspective* (Dublin and New York, 1988), pp 113–14.
[5] *Belfast News Letter*, 25 Mar. 1972. Robert Lundy, commander of the garrison during the siege of Derry in 1689, acquired the reputation of a traitor and is annually burned in effigy; see above, iii, 491–2; v, plate 9 (a).
[6] The statement is given in full in Eric Gallagher and Stanley Worrall, *Christians in Ulster, 1968–1980* (Oxford, 1982), p. 68.

settlement ranged from three to six months'.[7] In an attempt to overcome the problem of lack of accountability, the secretary of state for Northern Ireland (who governed through three junior ministers and the newly created N.I.O.) told the commons on 25 May that he had appointed an advisory commission of eleven Ulster 'notables', seven of whom were protestants and four catholics. But it made little difference to prevailing attitudes in the wider community.

If the 'history of the N.I.O. is the history of the secretary of state for Northern Ireland',[8] then the authorities were blessed in their first secretary of state, William Whitelaw. He faced massive administrative and political problems. Administration was partly a question of structure: two locations, Belfast and London; two sets of departments; and two civil services coexisting within the one ministry. The office had to be built up incrementally, and it needed to be sensitive to inherited animosities. The memoirs of two former Northern Ireland civil servants uncover tensions within the indigenous service in the period following direct rule; as for relations with the home office in the period prior to the establishment of direct rule, this had been 'a time of great difficulty'.[9] However, when Whitelaw first arrived on 25 March he won the confidence of the civil servants at once. A second problem concerned the intimacy of the political culture in Northern Ireland. Successive direct rule ministers have commented on the easy access of interest groups to centres of power, which 'encouraged a style of instant politics that concentrates attention on the immediate without adequate concern for the future'.[10] Indeed, after Merlyn Rees became secretary of state in February 1974 he issued an instruction to prevent elected representatives going direct to the civil servants.

Politically the new administration faced massive problems. The ancient quarrel had become more intense because of the sense of betrayal among many protestants and the feeling inside the I.R.A. that the tide of history was on its side. Extreme loyalists flocked to join the Ulster Defence Association (U.D.A.), founded in September 1971 as a paramilitary organisation with the ostensible aim of defending its territory from the I.R.A. With the imposition of direct rule the U.D.A. entered a hyperactive phase, with activities ranging from illegal marches by masked and becudgelled men to the creation of loyalist 'no-go' areas. The immediate aftermath of direct rule saw, too, a rapid increase in what the authorities called 'motiveless murders':

[7] David Watt in *Financial Times*, 19 May 1972.
[8] P. N. Bell, 'Direct rule in Northern Ireland' in P. Madgwick and R. Rose (ed.), *The territorial dimension in United Kingdom politics* (London, 1982), p. 193.
[9] J. A. Oliver, *Working at Stormont* (Dublin, 1978), p. 99; Patrick Shea, *Voices and the sound of drums: an Irish autobiography* (Belfast, 1981), pp 190–91.
[10] Lord Windlesham, 'Ministers in Ulster: the machinery of direct rule' in *Public Administration*, li (1973), p. 270.

eighty catholics and thirty-eight protestants were murdered before the end of
the year. And, for the first time since the reintroduction of internment in
1971, early in 1973 the first loyalists began to be interned. They retaliated
with a one-day strike in February in which five people were killed, most of
them in the course of a two-hour gun battle with the army. Similarly the
I.R.A. rejected the prorogation of Stormont as a placebo, not a remedy. On
the day it was announced, the S.D.L.P. sent two of its senior members to
persuade the Provisional I.R.A. chief of staff, Seán Mac Stiofáin, to call off
its campaign of violence, but to no avail. Given all these circumstances the
establishment of the N.I.O. was a triumph over adversity. It was conceived as
a temporary phenomenon; it was an exercise in crisis management; and it was
constantly reminded of the impact of political violence and the ensuing political uncertainty. Administrative evolution had to follow the more pressing
security and political problems, although there was one instant bonus in
efficiency: security policy was now the sole responsibility of the U.K. government. Direct rule came into force on 30 March 1972 following the enactment of the Northern Ireland (Temporary Provisions) Act, 1972.[11] The new
N.I.O. was staffed by officers mainly on loan from the home office, ministry
of defence, and foreign and commonwealth office (F.C.O.) and was paid for
out of the home office budget. This caused some problems for existing officials in Belfast.

The secretary of state's Northern Ireland office in Belfast was understandably staffed
for the greater part with officials from London and was quite separate from our
Northern Ireland departments... Bill Neild [permanent secretary to the secretary of
state, Whitelaw] recognised the danger at once... We therefore advised ministers and
the secretary of state direct; and the N.I. office concentrated rather on security,
parliamentary matters, and preparations for the constitutional settlement that was to
come.[12]

That quotation indicates that despite the tensions the transition to direct rule
was reasonably smooth. The business of government went on as normal; it
was political control that had changed. The 15,100 members of the Northern
Ireland civil service went on with their usual work, and the cabinet office at
Stormont remained. The real change was the replacement of the Northern
Ireland cabinet structure with meetings chaired by the secretary of state and
attended by his ministers, by the principal civil advisers, and usually by the
heads of the security forces. Over time the two civil services were to become
more integrated. Through more frequent contacts with their colleagues in
London, Northern Ireland officials learned to live with the more daunting
Whitehall machine; and in January 1974 the N.I.O. took on the executive
responsibilities of the former N.I. ministry of home affairs, together with the

---

[11] 1972, c. 22 [U.K.] (30 Mar. 1972).   [12] Oliver, *Working at Stormont*, p. 104.

civil servant staff of the old ministry. Although a number of senior posts in the N.I.O. were filled through secondment from other U.K. departments, a corps of permanent home civil service officials was to develop within the N.I.O.

The major difficulty was not so much with the machinery of government as with the nature of the problem. It was emotionally draining for those who came to the issue for the first time, and it was incredibly time-consuming. Douglas Hurd, who served in Edward Heath's private office between 1970 and 1974, describes the effect it had on the prime minister: '... the subject had a very high emotional content. To those who dealt with it, including the prime minister, it was clearly the most important matter of the moment.'[13] Heath was not slow to express his exasperation with certain loyalist behaviour: he told a television interviewer in March 1973 'how much offence it gives to the rest of the United Kingdom to hear people who are prepared to say they will not work the institutions, they will not abide by the law which was passed by Westminster, that they will wreck this or wreck that. To describe them as "loyalists" is completely untrue ... they are in fact disloyalists.'[14]

The Irish problem interfered in Heath's conduct of European business and his handling of a very serious coal-miners' strike. It led him to postpone a vital cabinet reshuffle till November 1973, and to question whether he should call a general election in February 1974. It put the hastily assembled N.I.O. into fourth place in the house of commons league table of hours consumed in parliamentary business in the first fourteen months of its existence, ahead of such giants as the home office and the F.C.O. With the prorogation of Stormont the remainder of the legislative programme for the 1971–2 session was transferred to Westminster. In addition much new legislation was needed, including a new constitutional architecture; but because direct rule was considered to be temporary it was decided to proceed by way of order in council. This allowed for pre-legislative discussion but curtailed parliamentary discussion and ensured that draft orders could not be amended, only approved or rejected. That was to remain a source of discontent among M.P.s from Northern Ireland, especially unionists who had been used to the easygoing ways of Stormont.

It was left to William Whitelaw to feel his way through this political minefield. He did so assiduously by keeping open the lines between the government and the two communities. He pursued a policy of steady release of I.R.A. internees—but not at such a rate as would offend protestant opinion absolutely. As a quid pro quo he stressed the economic advantages of the

---

[13] Douglas Hurd, *An end to promises: sketch of a government, 1970–74* (London, 1979), p. 102.
[14] *Irish Times*, 30 Mar. 1973.

union: for example, in May 1972 he announced a £35 million expansion plan for the ailing Belfast shipyard, which would provide 4,000 extra jobs. All these efforts won him the (not entirely hostile) loyalist epithet of 'Willy Whitewash'. He made one serious effort to coax republicans in the direction of political discourse. In June 1972 he introduced 'special category status' at a time when one of the I.R.A. leaders, Billy McKee, was close to death on a hunger strike in prison. Special category status distinguished such prisoners from ordinary criminals and allowed them certain freedoms inside the prisons. The Provisionals took this as a sign that the government was prepared to parley with them, even against the advice of the Irish authorities. On 26 June they called a ceasefire, and early in July secret talks were held in London between Mr Whitelaw and a Provisional team that included the I.R.A. chief of staff Seán Mac Stiofáin, Gerry Adams, and Martin McGuinness. They demanded, inter alia, that the British government should declare its intention 'to withdraw all forces from Irish soil' by 1 January 1975.

Sinn Féin released information at a later date about this meeting. By that stage the N.I.O. team were disabused of any fond hopes they may have had that they could negotiate with the Provisionals. There was growing concern in government about the outgrowth of 'no-go' areas where the rule of law no longer prevailed. Matters came to a head after 21 July—'Bloody Friday'—when the Provisionals set off a series of bombs in Belfast, causing eleven deaths and many injuries. Ten days later Operation Motorman was implemented. At the cost of two civilian lives in Derry the army moved into all no-go areas, removing barricades and restoring the semblance of normality.

The whole operation was conducted as a large-scale military exercise. It was but one indication of how entrenched Provisionalism had become in working-class communities. Its genesis went back to the defencelessness of catholics, particularly in Belfast, in August 1969. An intense sense of communal solidarity had arisen (on both sides of the community divide) based on kin, class, religion, and territory,[15] a solidarity that allowed for communal memory of perceived misdemeanours by the 'other side' and of a heroic past encapsulated in 1916 by the Easter rising or the slaughter on the Somme. It belonged to a culture of intimidation that had existed long before the 'troubles'[16]—one that encouraged a territorial sense and the need for vigilance to resist encroachment. One of the social skills employed in this resistance is the concept of 'telling':

the pattern of signs and cues by which religious ascription is arrived at in the everyday interaction of protestants and catholics... Telling is based on the social

---

[15] See Frank Burton, The politics of legitimacy: struggles in a Belfast community (London, 1978), passim.
[16] John Darby, Intimidation and the control of conflict in Northern Ireland (Dublin, 1986), pp viii–x, 10, 30.

significance attached to name, face, and dress, area of residence, school attended, linguistic and possibly phonetic use, colour, and symbolism. It is not based on undisputed fact but as an ideological representation is a mixture of 'myth' and 'reality'.[17]

Telling is part of the warp and woof of everyday social life in Northern Ireland. The community has developed its own highly sensitive antennae whereby 'one of the other side' or a 'stranger' can be identified immediately. It is considered to be part of the survival package, particularly for those at the communal interface, and forms part of a wider aural and visual culture, emphasising the community divide. The territorial boundaries become marked by distinctive symbols, the Union Jack or the Irish tricolour or Connolly's Starry Plough; wall murals celebrating William III or Mother Ireland or conveying warning symbols to the other side; graffiti and kerbstones depicting party colours. This was not a culture that had to be invented by the troubles. The wall murals, for example, were part of a tradition that went back to the turn of the century in the loyalist community and was visible in party banners for as long as the Orange order and the Ancient Order of Hibernians marched in their traditional parades. They were part of a folk tradition, a 'people's art', brought up to date to allow for present realities. They were seen as a defensive celebration of one's heritage rather than an offensive symbol of hatred.[18]

All of this should be borne in mind when we examine the increase in violence since 1972. The figures for loss of life from violence in Northern Ireland had risen from fifteen in 1969 to twenty-five in 1970 and to 173 in 1971. Disturbing as this increase was, the figure leapt to a horrendous 474 in 1972—the year that was to record the highest level of violence-related deaths. Republican paramilitaries were responsible for 255 of those deaths in 1972; loyalist groups, such as the Ulster Freedom Fighters, a breakaway group from the U.D.A., were responsible for 103 and the security forces for 74; 42 deaths were non-classified.[19] In addition to the deaths there were nearly 1,400 explosions, and the army neutralised another 500 bombs in that year alone.

An ambiguity about the use of violence, widespread fear, and communal solidarity manifested in activities like 'telling', all assist in explaining the intensity of violence. One source calculates that the U.D.A. had as many as 26,000 dues-paying members by the end of 1972 and that it 'had changed its structure to take on a deliberately military shape'.[20] All of this meant that security was to become a more dominant issue on the political agenda, with a

---

[17] Burton, *Politics of legitimacy*, p. 37.

[18] Belinda Loftus, *Mirrors: William III and Mother Ireland* (Dundrum, 1990), *passim*.

[19] New Ireland Forum, *The cost of violence arising from the Northern Ireland crisis since 1969* (Dublin, [1984]), pp 6–7; appendix 1, tables 1 and 2, pp 27–8.

[20] Steve Bruce, *The red hand: protestant paramilitaries in Northern Ireland* (Oxford, 1992), p. 59.

rising expectation that the best that could be achieved was 'an acceptable level of violence'.[21] The insensitivity of the security forces was another major irritant. O'Malley has calculated that there were 36,000 house searches in 1972, double that again in 1973 and 1974, 30,000 in 1975, 34,000 in 1976, 20,000 in 1977, and 15,000 in 1978, 'and in every household searched there was left behind a sense of alienation, of estrangement, of the anger felt when one's privacy is rudely and brutally invaded'.[22] Burton's observer-participation in one self-contained catholic ghetto in Belfast confirms the sense of anomie. Dozens of people had been killed and many more seriously wounded within its streets: 'The area has been saturated by troops and is under constant surveillance. Hundreds of the district's inhabitants had been interned or detained or sentenced to prison.'[23] Figures for deaths, injuries, and explosions suggest that the period 1971–6 was particularly active, with 'normalisation' setting in afterwards. O'Duffy and O'Leary assert that the 'years 1976–7 were turning-points in the scale of all violence—not simply deaths—for three main reasons'. The first was improvements in security capability (including intelligence) with, particularly after the ending of internment in 1975, a reduction in republican militancy. Secondly, loyalist activity diminished because loyalists grew more self-confident after the success of the U.W.C. strike in 1974, and because increased residential segregation meant that fewer easy targets were available. Finally, I.R.A. reorganisation in 1976–7 around a new cell structure led to a reduction in the scale of their activities.[24]

It would be a mistake to concentrate solely on the security question, particularly in the period immediately after the imposition of direct rule, when British policy-making entered its most creative phase since the 1920s. The first major indication of policy intentions appeared in a discussion paper, *The future of Northern Ireland*, published in October 1972.[25] That paper moved outside the Westminster model of government in search of a constitutional solution by looking at the experience of other 'divided communities [that] have made special constitutional provision to ensure participation by all' (paragraph 58); and it also acknowledged the significance of what it called 'the Irish dimension' (paragraphs 76–8). While these reflections were to raise deep misgivings within the unionist community, perhaps more serious fears were aroused by an implied lack on the part of the British government of any positive commitment to the union: 'No United Kingdom government for many years has had any

[21] The phrase was coined by Reginald Maudling (W. D. Flackes, *Northern Ireland: a political directory 1968–83* (London, 1983), p. 147).
[22] Padraig O'Malley, *The uncivil wars: Ireland today* (Belfast, 1983), p. 259.
[23] Burton, *Politics of legitimacy*, p. 9.
[24] Brendan O'Duffy and Brendan O'Leary, 'Violence in Northern Ireland, 1969–June 1989' in John McGarry and Brendan O'Leary (ed.), *The future of Northern Ireland* (Oxford, 1990), pp 318–41: 331.
[25] *The future of Northern Ireland: a paper for discussion* (H.M.S.O., London, 1972).

wish to impede the realisation of Irish unity, if it were to come about by genuine and freely given mutual agreement and on conditions acceptable to the distinctive communities' (paragraph 77). Unionist fears were compounded by the guarded welcome given to the discussion paper by the taoiseach, Jack Lynch, when he said that the paper's opportunities imposed a duty and a responsibility on his government to respond in a constructive way.[26]

The next stage, after widespread dissemination of the discussion paper, was the publication on 20 March 1973 of a white paper, *Northern Ireland: constitutional proposals*.[27] Power-sharing was now government policy; the secretary of state was to have ultimate power in the selection of the executive; and the government announced that it favoured 'and is prepared to facilitate the formation of' a council of Ireland (paragraph 110). In May legislation was passed establishing a seventy-eight-seat assembly to be elected by proportional representation.[28] Assembly elections based on the single transferable vote were held on 28 June; and negotiations to form a power-sharing government culminated in the creation of an executive-designate on 22 November. The final stage was a meeting between the putative executive and representatives of the two governments at Sunningdale in Berkshire on 6–9 December 1973. In the meantime the Northern Ireland constitution act was passed.[29] The key issues in all of these documents were 'the status of Northern Ireland, the nature of its internal institutions of government, the degree of participation by different sections of the community in those institutions, and the relationships between Northern Ireland and the Irish Republic'.[30]

Whereas those who had fashioned this experiment in power-sharing had some cause for short-term satisfaction, they were to learn that the accretions of historical prejudice could not be removed in a matter of a few months. Although the executive had received the blessing of both governments, there was sufficient ambiguity about its support inside Northern Ireland. Power-sharing was anathema to virtually all shades of unionism/loyalism—as was to become evident during the U.W.C. strike. Apart from anything else, it was felt to be un-British. The Provisional Republican movement rejected any such panacea as early as March 1973 when it suggested that the white paper proposals highlighted 'the artificiality of the Northern Ireland state'; and that '"power-sharing" [required] the acceptance of an English politician as a virtual dictator'. In short, the white paper was not 'a basis for a lasting and just solution for the conflict in occupied Ireland'. That would not come about until 'Britain recognises that the Irish people, and the Irish people

---

[26] Lynch's leadership during the critical period in N.I., 1969–72, is discussed in Lee, *Ire. 1912–85*, pp 458–61, and above, pp 317–20, 357–8.
[27] *Northern Ireland: constitutional proposals* [Cmnd 5259], H.C. 1972–3, xxvi, 1081–20.
[28] 1973, c. 17 (3 May 1973).
[29] 1973, c. 36 (18 July 1973).
[30] Ken Bloomfield, *Stormont in crisis* (Belfast, 1994), p. 24.

alone, have the right to rule Ireland ... '.[31] That was a message that brooked no compromise.

Earlier that month the people of Northern Ireland, in accordance with the Northern Ireland (Border Poll) Act, 1972,[32] voted overwhelmingly in favour of remaining part of the United Kingdom in a percentage poll of 58.5 by 591,820 to 6,463. In fact this was no more than a religio-political census, because nationalists boycotted it and unionists used it to demonstrate their distance from the Republic. Nevertheless the parties to the Sunningdale agreement cobbled together a settlement that produced a power-sharing executive and recognised an Irish dimension. The former was based on the 1973 constitution act, which stated: 'that a Northern Ireland executive can be formed which, having regard to the support it commands in the assembly and to the electorate on which that support is based, is likely to be widely acceptable throughout the community, and that ... there is a reasonable basis for the establishment in Northern Ireland of government by consent.'[33] The key words in that passage were 'executive' and 'assembly', because both called in question the pretensions to parliamentary sovereignty of the system that had operated till 1972, with their insistence on the notion of the government and parliament of Northern Ireland. And the concept that motivated the 1973 act was based on 'support [which] is likely to be widely acceptable throughout the community'. Both the terms and the concept challenged the old certainties on which unionism had been nourished. And so it was on 1 January 1974 that, for the first time since Northern Ireland was established, an executive representative of the two communities was installed in Belfast.

It was to collapse within five months, after the Ulster Workers' Council (U.W.C.) strike, notoriously organised as a demonstration of unionist hostility to 'the Irish dimension'. There is no doubt that this dimension was generally reviled in unionist circles, although the reaction was based on emotion and on symbolism rather than on reasoned judgement. Kenneth Bloomfield, who was permanent secretary to the executive, commented almost two decades later that if 'you read today that part of the paper [that refers to the Irish dimension] you will see, I think, that these passages of the document represent in large measure a recognition of reality rather than a declaration of policy'.[34] Bloomfield may have been adverting to the fact that in its discussion of the Irish dimension the white paper recognised the constitutional guarantee: that subsequent change in Northern Ireland's status could be achieved only through consent. Secondly, in keeping with both states' accession to the E.E.C. on 1 January 1973, emphasis was placed on functional cooperation. And thirdly, the Irish dimension also assumed closer security cooperation. Nevertheless, the white paper did give its blessing to the

[31] *Irish Times*, 24 Mar. 1973.   [32] 1972, c. 77 (7 Dec. 1972).   [33] Sect. 2.
[34] Bloomfield, *Stormont in crisis*, p. 30.

future establishment of a council of Ireland (a principle accepted at Sunningdale); and others placed a less benign construction on the Irish dimension. One M.P. is quoted as saying:

...It was more likely to put their children into a united Ireland in twenty-five or thirty years time. I said that the Sunningdale agreement was designed not to kick us out of the United Kingdom but to change our attitudes, to swing our gaze slowly from...London towards Dublin and by slow process to change the attitude of the loyalist people so that one day they might believe the myth of Irish unity which so bedevils many people in Northern Ireland.[35]

There are more complex reasons for the executive's collapse. There is one body of opinion which claims that nationalists had been too successful in the negotiations before 1974. They won too much, and left Brian Faulkner, the leader of divided unionism, with too little to sell to his own supporters. A decade later the leader of the Alliance party at Sunningdale, Oliver Napier, stated that the 'two people I blame—and both were superb at Sunningdale— are Garret FitzGerald and John Hume. They were going out to negotiate the best possible deal they could get from Faulkner for the nationalist tradition and to hell with everything else, and they did it very well.'[36] He contended that he would have traded the council of Ireland (which institutionalised the Irish dimension) for recognition by the Dublin government of Northern Ireland and extradition. There was the view, too, that the British negotiators at Sunningdale were exhausted by more pressing domestic and foreign affairs and came to the negotiations unprepared.[37]

It is conceivable that had the coalition government been given a fair wind it might have earned popular acceptance, though the early signs were not encouraging. It started life with twenty-seven anti-power-sharing unionists holding more seats than the Unionist party led by the chief executive, Brian Faulkner. When he led twenty-two of his own supporters into a three-party executive along with nineteen S.D.L.P. and eight Alliance party members, the Ulster Unionist Council rejected by 427 to 374 the Sunningdale agreement, which provided the basis of the executive. Such was the animosity towards the executive that in some of its first sittings the police had to be called into the assembly to prevent obstructive opposition. But in any case the announcement of a British general election (for reasons external to Northern Ireland) to be held on 28 February had enormous repercussions on the political process. Anti-Sunningdale unionists used the opportunity to form the United Ulster Unionist Coalition (U.U.U.C.) and to contest the general election on a slogan of 'Dublin is just a Sunningdale away'. It was

[35] Harold McCusker, quoted in Keith Kyle, 'Sunningdale and after: Britain, Ireland, and Ulster' in *The World Today*, xxxi, no. 11 (Nov. 1975), pp 439–40: 443.
[36] *Sunday Tribune*, 7 Oct. 1984.
[37] Stephen Fay and Hugo Young in *Sunday Times*, 29 Feb. 1976.

highly emotive and highly effective and was combined with a campaign directed against the principle of partnership with the S.D.L.P. and the idea of a council of Ireland. With 50.8 per cent of the total poll and eleven of the twelve Westminster seats, the U.U.U.C. claimed a tremendous victory.

With hindsight we can place the demise of the Sunningdale agreement with the February 1974 general election. The Conservative architects of Sunningdale had been replaced by a Labour government in Britain, and the Northern Ireland results had given the U.U.U.C. huge self-confidence. Its more militant supporters decided to increase the pressure and move on to extra-parliamentary opposition. They formed the U.W.C. and called a 'strike'—at the time Lord Hailsham called it 'a conspiracy against the state . . . because it's an attempt to overthrow the authority of the queen in parliament'[38]—in May against Sunningdale (without the support of most of their political leaders). It soon became clear that there was to be little interference from the security authorities.

There was one discussion at Stormont, of a particularly heated nature, in which [Merlyn] Rees [secretary of state for Northern Ireland] was told in blunt terms that the army could not perform the kind of miracles that the authorities expected of it and could not destroy the U.W.C. It was a profoundly important moment for it was the first time in two decades that a British minister had been told by the army that it could not cope with large-scale non-violent civil disturbance.[39]

The U.W.C. adopted a masterly strategy, turning off the power supplies for industry (gas and electricity) with sewerage to follow, if necessary, one at a time.

It is conceivable that the executive would have collapsed of itself. It had taken up office with much contentious unfinished business in the areas of law and order and the administration of justice; and it was composed of parties with different economic philosophies. But it is likely that the change in government in February had made an important impact. Sunningdale was not Labour's creation. The new secretary of state's diary entry for 27 September 1973 read: 'We would have to face up to the fact that the new constitution could not work.'[40] That suggests that he was temperamentally unsuited for the task of facing down the strikers. The previous government, he subsequently argued, should not have imposed Sunningdale on the loyalists; too many members of the executive did not behave sensibly; and the R.U.C. 'was not organised in a way that would have enabled it to respond quickly in the first days of the strike'. Although he allows that there may

[38] Robert Fisk, *The point of no return: the strike which broke the British in Ulster* (London, 1975), p. 203.
[39] Ibid., p. 153.
[40] Merlyn Rees, *Northern Ireland: a personal perspective* (London, 1985), p. 31.

have been 'marginal mistakes' in the handling of the strike, the fact was that it was not possible to put down an 'industrial/political dispute supported by a majority in the community'.[41] That begs too many questions. The dispute was industrial only in the sense that the strikers used the withdrawal of their labour from key industries as their most potent weapon. Violence, or the threat of violence, was part of their strategy, particularly in the early days of the strike. It ignores, too, the role of the army, which was out of sympathy with the secretary of state. And it ignores the disastrous handling of the strike by the government, including Wilson's inept and insensitive broadcast on 25 May 1974 complaining about Ulster people 'who ... spend their lives sponging on Westminster and British democracy'.[42] In the opinion of one of the Sunningdale strategists the greatest factor in explaining U.W.C. success 'was the lack of will on the part of the British government, particularly its prime minister, to face up to the loyalists and instead to adopt a policy of inaction and delay which could only lead to the collapse of the executive, while absolving itself from any apparent responsibility'.[43]

Whatever the reason for the collapse of the 1974 experiment, it had to be set against the record of the Labour party in the province. Northern Ireland was governed between March 1974 and May 1979 by two secretaries of state, Merlyn Rees and Roy Mason. One interesting aspect of the period 1972–84 is that any sustained constitutional initiative came from the Conservatives rather than from Labour. Rees's immediate problem was how to stifle loyalist euphoria and inject some hope into constitutional nationalism. In an effort to prevent loyalist paramilitaries moving into the vacuum created by the collapse of the executive, the government published a white paper, *The Northern Ireland constitution*,[44] and carried the Northern Ireland act, 1974, which provided for a constitutional convention 'for the purpose of considering what provision for the government of Northern Ireland is likely to command the most widespread acceptance throughout the community'.[45] Elections for the seventy-eight-seat constitutional convention were held on 1 May 1975, with the U.U.U.C. winning forty-six seats as against thirty-two for those in favour of some form of partnership. The result reflected changing fortunes inside the unionist 'family'—Brian Faulkner had to wait until the ninth count before he was elected in South Down, and his newly formed Unionist Party of Northern Ireland (U.P.N.I.) won only five seats. It suggested as well that there were going to be difficulties in arriving at widespread acceptance, because the white paper had insisted that there 'must be some form of power-sharing and partnership', and that 'any political arrangements must

[41] Ibid., p. 90.
[42] Paul Bew and Gordon Gillespie, *Northern Ireland* (Dublin, 1993), p. 86.
[43] John Hume in *Irish Times*, 15 Nov. 1975.
[44] *The Northern Ireland constitution* [Cmnd 5675], H.C. 1974, xiii, 595–618.
[45] 1974, c. 28 (17 July 1974), sect. 2.

recognise and provide for this special relationship [with the Republic]. There is an Irish dimension.'[46]

The convention met under the chairmanship of Sir Robert Lowry, Northern Ireland's lord chief justice, and issued a report in 1975; but Rees did not consider that it commanded 'sufficiently widespread acceptance throughout the community ... to provide stable and effective government'.[47] It was reconvened briefly in 1976 but failed to make further progress. Perhaps the convention's only real contribution was that it helped 'to dissipate loyalist euphoria which was being swiftly translated into uncompromising demands for a return to the Stormont system of government'. It served, then, as a 'distraction' and acted as 'a buffer between the U.W.C. strike and indefinite direct rule'.[48] Thus ended Rees's one foray into constitutional tinkering. He was to devote most of his time to the security question, which he considered his greatest triumph.

Before we consider that, we should look at the state of the indigenous political parties in the post-Sunningdale period. The imposition of direct rule had heralded a sea change in unionist politics. The Ulster Unionist Party (U.U.P.) no longer appeared to be monolithic. It was being challenged by parties that claimed to be more loyalist, such as the Democratic Unionist Party, and by parties, such as Alliance, that claimed to be both centrist and unionist. In the 1973 assembly election, candidates stood under a dozen different unionist banners; and as a result of Brian Faulkner's decision to enter into partnership with the S.D.L.P. in 1974, the U.U.P. split into two factions, one led by Faulkner and the other by Harry West. The latter was to join with Ian Paisley's D.U.P. and William Craig's Vanguard Unionist Progressive Party (V.U.P.P.) to form the U.U.U.C. in January 1974 in opposition to Sunningdale. Its success in the two 1974 general elections and the 1975 convention election was indicative of the growing self-esteem within the loyalist community after the U.W.C. strike. But its very existence represented an innovation in unionist politics—the emergence of a coalition. And that signalled the disarray of the protestant community: for the first time since 1921 no single party dominated that community.[49]

Ian Paisley's D.U.P. (founded in 1971) sought that domination—a position he believed he had attained after a massive personal victory following the first direct elections to the European parliament in 1979. His rise symbolised the personalisation of unionist politics and the disappearance of old certainties institutionalised inside one party.[50] The U.U.U.C. was meant to restore

---

[46] N.I. constitution, para. 45, p. 16.

[47] Rees, N.I., p. 280.

[48] Ian McAllister, The Northern Ireland Social Democratic and Labour party (London, 1977), p. 159.

[49] The weakening of the protestant position in N.I. in the 1970s, partly through the abolition of Stormont, and partly because of economic change, is discussed in Joseph Ruane and Jennifer Todd, The dynamics of conflict in Northern Ireland (Cambridge, 1996), chs 5–6.

[50] Ed Moloney and Andy Pollak, Paisley (Swords, 1986), pp 336–8.

certainty, but it lacked a common leader and contained the seeds of its own destruction. For example, during the convention William Craig, a respected (because hardline) loyalist leader, suggested an emergency coalition government, including the S.D.L.P., on the basis of British wartime precedents. This would have permitted the S.D.L.P. to share in power but, equally, its members would have had to carry their share of responsibility for a security policy with which they might not always have been in agreement. They were not put to that embarrassing test, because Craig's plans were sabotaged by his coalition partners, and his party split into two wings.

It was tensions such as these that led to the collapse of the U.U.U.C. in 1977 after a 'constitutional stoppage' led by the D.U.P. and the U.D.A. in an effort to persuade the authorities to restore Stormont and to take the offensive against the I.R.A. The D.U.P.'s overt alliance with the U.D.A. proved too much for the majority of the U.U.U.C., who refused to support the stoppage. In any case there were those who felt that Paisley had become too domineering. The outcome of all of this internal squabbling was that by the late 1970s the unionist community was represented by two political parties, the (revamped) U.U.P. and the D.U.P. Stalemate ensued. Neither was powerful enough to overwhelm the other, and both realised that they could not live without each other. It was like a bad marriage. The loyalists' self-respect, recovered after the U.W.C. strike, was based on community strength through the exercise of their veto. But it was a negative power. Loyalists may have stopped the encroachments of constitutional nationalism, but they had nothing positive to offer the British government; and the Provisional movement considered the collapse of Sunningdale had done them a favour, because they feared the establishment of a common area of law enforcement throughout Ireland, which would have been geared against the I.R.A.

It may be that the British authorities had been attracted to the Sunningdale formula because it held out the prospect of much closer security cooperation. In the aftermath of the U.W.C. strike the secretary of state had to explore new methods of restoring normality. His record suggests that he had little faith in the political process in Northern Ireland. Indeed, he had little confidence in the very constitutional convention that he had proposed: 'Although it was idle to pretend that the convention had a strong chance of succeeding—indeed there was a high likelihood of failure—this time the politicians could not blame the British for the outcome. The ball was in their court.'[51] In other words, policy seemed to consist of ensuring that his government was not held responsible, a policy that, Mary Holland wrote, 'appears to be one of stultifying indifference',[52] and that did little to help the hapless Craig when he proposed his emergency coalition.

---

[51] Rees, *N.I.*, p. 135; see also p. 107.   [52] *New Statesman*, 5 Dec. 1975.

It was not that Rees lacked a plan, but his plan was based on a security initiative: 'The primacy of the police was my long-term aim and in my first major speech as Northern Ireland secretary on 4 April, I had told the house of commons that the cornerstone of my security policy was "a progressive increase in the role of the civilian law enforcement agencies in Northern Ireland".'[53] He was to be the architect of what became known as 'Ulsterisation' and its corollary, 'criminalisation'. Essentially what these policies entailed was placing the police in the front line at the expense of the army, and criminalising the paramilitaries by removing their special-category status inside the prisons. In adopting this line Rees was convinced that he had helped to drive a substantial wedge between the Provisional I.R.A. and the catholic population as a whole. That is a large claim.

'Ulsterisation' grew out of an official reassessment of security policy in the mid 1970s. It is as well to remember that the authorities already possessed a battery of legislation to deal with the threat of violence: the prevention of terrorism act,[54] introduced after the Birmingham bombing of 21 November 1974; various emergency provisions, consolidated in the emergency provisions act of 1978;[55] and (since 1973) provision for terrorist (or 'scheduled') offences to be dealt with in special non-jury courts, popularly known as 'Diplock' courts (so called after the British judge Lord Diplock, who recommended such a system because of the intimidation of jurors and witnesses).[56] But the authorities remained concerned that the paramilitary campaign had been given greater legitimacy as a result of internment and the special-category status enjoyed by the volunteers inside the prisons—and, it should be said, the damage they also feared that Britain's international reputation had suffered as a result. The vast bulk of the internees were housed in the Maze prison[57]—the army ruefully called it the 'I.R.A. Sandhurst'. Internment had begun on 9 August 1971, when over 300 were detained, and it came to an end on 5 December 1975, by which time 2,158 'graduates' had passed through the camps. Special-category status was abolished in March 1976 because the N.I.O. considered it mistaken. In effect the prisoners had run their own regime, strengthening their organisations within the prisons and their respectability without. In its place the authorities introduced 'criminalisation' in an effort to erode the officially recognised distinction between 'political' and 'ordinary' crime.

Another aspect of this wider policy was the attempt made at restoring the status and credibility of the R.U.C. This received official backing with the production of a document called *The way ahead* in 1975. It arose out of a committee of senior army, R.U.C., and intelligence officers, chaired by an

---

[53] Rees, *N.I.*, p. 109.
[54] 1974, c. 56 (29 Nov. 1974).
[55] 1978, c. 5 (23 Mar. 1978).
[56] 1973, c. 53 (25 July 1973).
[57] The later official name for the prison camp set up at Long Kesh, Co. Antrim.

N.I.O. civil servant. It was to lead to the policy of police primacy and was the most important security initiative of the late 1970s. 'Under this plan, the role of the regular army was to be reduced and overall direction of the security effort given to the R.U.C. in 1976, thus requiring an expansion of locally recruited forces.'[58] As a result, from January 1977 the day-to-day direction of policy was in the hands of a security coordinating committee, chaired by the chief constable, who, in consultation with the G.O.C., reported to the secretary of state. The policy also led to a reorganisation of the police to permit more flexible deployment. But we shall see that differences of opinion between the army and the police did not disappear altogether.

A more immediate concern had been the police's relationship with the local catholic community since the outbreak of the troubles in 1969. Then, they had been seen by the catholic community as the armed wing of unionism. In so far as a more tentative respect was to grow out of police primacy, three reasons can be adduced. The first was somewhat fortuitous. In the most sustained years of violence, 1970–76, the police maintained a lower profile as they set about reorganising and reforming after the Hunt report.[59] It was the army that bore the brunt of nationalist wrath. Secondly, a greater awareness of 'professionalism' and public relations was inculcated inside the R.U.C.—this, indeed, may have been the real benefit of the shift towards police primacy. Finally, the police were to demonstrate a capability to deal evenhandedly with political thuggery. The R.U.C. got its opportunity in May 1977 in the so-called 'constitutional stoppage' led by the D.U.P. and the U.D.A. Decisive political and security leadership defeated the attempt.

Ulsterisation had certain advantages for the British authorities: the use of locally recruited security forces allowed the problem to be presented to international observers as an internal one between conflicting Irish groups, and therefore downplayed the role of Britain and the British army as part of the equation. This was reinforced by the use of the legal process rather than detention, which emphasised the 'criminal' nature of the violence rather than the political element.[60] Britain had adopted what one official described as a 'cottonwool' policy of blurring and defusing potentially explosive situations.[61] But it was one that entailed high risks, because essentially it was concerned with managing, rather than resolving, conflicts.

One aspect of this policy concerned relationships with the republican movement. During Rees's tenure of office the Maze prison was burned down by republicans (15 October 1974); subsequently a ceasefire negotiated be-

[58] Mark Urban, *Big boys' rules: the secret struggle against the I.R.A.* (London, 1992), p. 17.
[59] Above, pp 336–7.
[60] Michael J. Cunningham, *British government policy in Northern Ireland, 1969–89* (Manchester and New York, 1991), p. 104.
[61] Quoted by Conor O'Clery in *Irish Times*, 15 Nov. 1975.

tween the Provisionals and the N.I.O. lasted from February to November
1975 (and yet, despite that, more died from conflict-related incidents than
in the previous year). In order to ensure that the ceasefire would hold, a
number of incident centres manned by civil servants on a twenty-four-hour
basis were established in various parts of the province, and talks were held
between the N.I.O. and Sinn Féin. This led to a number of allegations,
including one that 'cottonwool was given to the Provisionals in the early days
of the ceasefire in the form of ambiguous statements about Britain's intentions';[62] and that the incident centres gave Sinn Féin (and the I.R.A.) a
spurious legitimacy. In any case it appeared to make redundant the role of
the S.D.L.P., and added to that party's unhappiness with the secretary of
state over his handling of the U.W.C. strike. Relations between the government and the S.D.L.P. (and between the British and Irish governments)
were not good.[63]

In September 1976 Rees became home secretary and was replaced in
Northern Ireland by Roy Mason. Those politicians who had been in the
1974 executive were happy to see him go. His performance in Northern
Ireland had been overshadowed by his handling of the U.W.C. strike. His
relationship with the S.D.L.P. and the Irish government continued to deteriorate, largely because he was seen as being unsympathetic to the latter and as
being too closely involved in giving legitimacy to Sinn Féin. His one effort at
constitution-making had the merit of defusing loyalist euphoria but was
considered to be a retreat from Sunningdale. In the longer term, it may be
that Rees's real contribution to the Northern Ireland problem lay in the
security area. Criminalisation did not have the desired effect, in that it
failed to drive a sufficient wedge between the Provisionals and the catholic
community—as the hunger strikes were to demonstrate in the 1980s. But
he does deserve credit for laying the groundwork for the reform of the
R.U.C.

With the exception of a round of desultory talks with the local politicians,
Roy Mason concentrated on placing greater emphasis on the local economy
and on security policy: 'A key security adviser recalls that Mason seemed
uninterested in political initiatives, believing simply that Ulster needed substantial economic help and that the pressure on the I.R.A. should be
stepped up. He had no hesitation about escalating operations against them,
and said publicly that he intended to squeeze the I.R.A. "like a tube of
toothpaste".'[64] He had limited success in that direction, because the I.R.A.
was to follow the security authorities' initiative and reform itself. That
reform led to the abandonment of the I.R.A.'s leaky neighbourhood structure in 1977 in favour of a much tighter cellular system, which continued to

[62] Ibid.   [63] For Rees's account, see Rees, *N.I.*, pp 149–81, 217–19.
[64] Urban, *Big boys' rules*, p. 11.

rely on communal support. While that restructuring was going on, there was something of a lull in violence; meanwhile, the closing months of 1976 had witnessed the formation of the movement known as the 'Peace people', which for a time gave hope that community pressure would lead to a permanent end to violence. During that period, Mason made the mistake of assuming that the I.R.A. was a spent force. In October 1977 he announced that it was his view that 'their strength has waned to the point where they cannot sustain a campaign'.[65] And yet in 1979 a secret report for the army written by Brigadier Glover—'Northern Ireland: future terrorist trends'— alluded to the 'calibre of the rank-and-file terrorists [which] does not support the view that they are merely mindless hooligans drawn from the unemployed and unemployable. P.I.R.A. now trains and uses its members with some care. The active service units (A.S.U.s) are for the most part manned by terrorists with up to ten years of operational experience...' They were assisted by 'a substantial pool of young Fianna (junior I.R.A.) aspirants, nurtured in a climate of violence, eagerly seeking promotion to full gun-carrying terrorist status, and there is a steady release from the prisons of embittered and dedicated terrorists'. Glover concluded gloomily that he saw no prospect in the political or military terrain of defeat of the I.R.A. over the next five years.[66]

Mason's strong security initiative may have come from his previous incarnation as secretary of state for defence between 1974 and 1976. He was to enjoy a good relationship with Lt-gen. Timothy Creasey, the General Officer Commanding (G.O.C.), and Maj.-gen. Dick Trant, Commander Land Forces (C.L.F.), both appointed in 1977. They believed in intensifying undercover operations and in increasing the success rate of court prosecutions by obtaining more detailed intelligence about suspects. Hence between 1976 and 1978 the S.A.S. were responsible for ten deaths in ambush operations: seven were of I.R.A. members but three were of innocent bystanders. The ambushes stopped in December 1978 and the S.A.S. did not kill anyone again till December 1983.[67] Controversy was stirred also by police interrogation procedures, and after a highly critical Amnesty International report in 1978 the government asked Harry Bennett, Q.C., to look at these allegations. His report[68] was published on 16 March 1979 and was critical of some aspects of interrogation methods, and noted the fact that the government had shown little determination to punish the perpetrators of past offences. Plainclothes interrogation teams had become an essential plank of security policy: '90 per cent of cases coming before the special non-jury Diplock courts result

[65] Cited by David McKittrick in *Irish Times*, 16 May 1979.
[66] Cited in O'Malley, *Uncivil wars*, pp 262–3.
[67] Urban, *Big boys' rules*, pp 12, 81.
[68] *Report of the committee of inquiry into police interrogation procedures in Northern Ireland* [Cmnd 7497] (H.M.S.O., London, 1979) (Bennett report).

in conviction and 80 per cent of these convictions rest solely on confessions of guilt made during police interrogation.'[69]

If security policy appeared to be a mirage, it had at least the semblance of some activity about it. The same could not be said about moving towards political progress. When he arrived as secretary of state Mason announced that he would not 'enter the whirlpool' of local politics; but he was to make some attempts at a form of interim devolution. More importantly he was forced to take sides in the political debate in Northern Ireland after March 1977 because the Labour government at Westminster had to rely on unionist support to stay in power. Despite Rees's earlier pledge that he did not see 'any circumstances in which extra representation of Northern Ireland with its history would be a means of bringing the peace that we all want',[70] the prime minister, James Callaghan, made a firm commitment in March 1977 to increase the number of Northern Ireland seats at Westminster by about five. That was to antagonise the S.D.L.P., an antagonism compounded by Mason's statement to the house on 12 January 1978 that he had

never used the expression 'power sharing'; I have always insisted that it should be a case of partnership and participation in the administration in Northern Ireland. The house will remember that my predecessor, more than fifteen months ago, had also dropped the use of that emotive term. It is right to inform the house that the term 'power sharing' tends to be taken in Northern Ireland as meaning the system laid down in the 1973 act. The government are in no way committed to this system or, indeed, to any other system.[71]

And, finally, when Mason described the S.D.L.P. as an extremist party the gap between the government and constitutional nationalism became unbridgeable. When the government lost a vote of confidence in the house on 28 March 1979 by 311 to 310, the two Irish nationalist M.P.s, Gerry Fitt and Frank Maguire, abstained.

On the day when Mason effectively left office (30 April 1979) he announced that a contract had been signed with the American Hyster company to build a £30 million factory in Craigavon to manufacture fork-lift trucks. This was the seventh such U.S. plant agreed to in an eighteen-month period, bringing total American investment in the province to £550 million. After a sustained period of failure to encourage inward investment, all of this was very welcome news, yet it could not hide the fact that the policy of economic regeneration had not succeeded. Despite the secretary of state's success in wheedling extra money out of the treasury, the record shows that unemployment continued to increase even though something like £140 million a year had been spent in maintaining jobs.

[69] Peter Taylor in *New Statesman*, 16 June 1978.
[70] Quoted by Patrick Wintour in *New Statesman*, 9 Mar. 1979.
[71] *Hansard 5 (commons)*, cmxli, 1834 (12 Jan. 1978).

If Roy Mason will be remembered for any one enterprise, it will be the De Lorean project, involving a deal to construct a purpose-built car factory on a green-field site in west Belfast to manufacture a revolutionary sports car. Negotiations with John De Lorean had been rushed through in an extraordinary forty-eight days before the deal was announced in Belfast in August 1978. The government was committed to investing £88 million, whereas the manufacturer offered only $4 million (£2.15 million). It was recognised that this was high-risk investment and that the taxpayer was paying £23,000 for each job created. Despite warnings from such bodies as the U.S. securities and exchange commission, which had noted seventeen high-risk factors in the De Lorean project, the contract was signed and the project prospered for two years. But a collapse in the U.S. market, and a more hardheaded approach by the government's Conservative successors, saw the end of the De Lorean gamble and the return of pessimism to west Belfast. De Lorean was to be another mirage that had held out hope only in the short term.

That was to be the message of the Mason tenure of office. The I.R.A. was not on the run by the time he returned to Britain; the economy remained in serious difficulties; and the government had bought unionist support in a bid to stay in power at Westminster. But the cost was considerable. The S.D.L.P. and the Irish government had been alienated and had begun looking elsewhere for allies. Unionists remained suspicious of British intentions, and many problems remained unsolved for the Labour government's successors.

WHEN the Conservative party won the 1979 general election there was little indication that a radical initiative on Northern Ireland would be undertaken. The manifesto had barely touched on such matters, save to stress the traditional policy of defeating terrorism and of maintaining the union 'in accordance with the wish of the majority in the province'. A cryptic reference to future reforms stated that in 'the absence of devolved government, we will seek to establish one or more elected regional councils with a wide range of powers over local services'.[72] This policy bore the stamp of Airey Neave, who had been opposition spokesman on Northern Ireland and close confidant of Margaret Thatcher (the new prime minister) until his murder by the Irish National Liberation Army (I.N.L.A.)[73] in London on 30 March 1979. His policy remained, and the Conservatives, with a comfortable majority, could count on the enthusiastic support of the Ulster Unionists, led by James Molyneaux. Nor was there any reason to expect major opposition from the Labour party. Both parties seemed to be engaged on a retreat from Sunning-

---

[72] Quoted in Cunningham, *British government policy*, p. 141.
[73] The military wing of the Irish Republican Socialist party, formed in Dec. 1974 as a breakaway group from Official Sinn Féin. See Jack Holland and Henry McDonald, *I.N.L.A.: deadly divisions* (London, 1994).

dale; it was accepted that while Whitelaw had made a valiant effort to set up a power-sharing executive, and while the principle of coalition government was still correct, the time was not yet ripe for bold experiments. The appointment of Humphrey Atkins—a man without any previous cabinet experience or knowledge of Ulster—seemed to confirm that a period of consolidation was under way. Moreover the new government inherited Labour's legacy. It did not worry unduly about the economic situation. The Thatcherite policy of non-intervention was to wreak its damage over time. Security was another matter. It came to a head on 27 August 1979 when eighteen soldiers were killed in a carefully constructed I.R.A. ambush in County Down. On the same day a member of the royal family, Earl Mount-batten, and three other people were killed by a bomb concealed in their pleasure boat in the Republic. According to a senior security forces official these 'spectaculars'—greater in their impact even than the Birmingham bombs of 21 November 1974 when twenty-one civilians were killed— 'brought to a head a crisis which had been brewing between the police and the army'.[74] The prime minister had to become involved, and so she flew to Northern Ireland where she was confronted with the army's desire to roll back police primacy and with the R.U.C.'s concern about the effect of offensive operations by army special forces. Her solution was the appointment on 2 October of a security coordinator, the former head of MI6, Sir Maurice Oldfield, and the expansion of the R.U.C. by 1,000 officers. Oldfield's appointment coincided with the departure, which had been expected, of the two senior security officers. Their successors, Jack Hermon as chief constable of the R.U.C.[75] and Lt-gen. Richard Lawson as G.O.C., established a close rapport and left the resolution of operational matters to their respective deputies. The whole business demonstrated just how sensitive were security issues and how near the surface the question lay.

The prime minister was stung into action on a second front as well. Notwithstanding the modesty of the manifesto proposals it was not long before the government embarked on an ambitious political project that recognised the wider dimensions of the Northern Ireland problem. In many respects it was a response to an attempt made by some politicians—in particular John Hume, the deputy leader of the S.D.L.P.—who despaired of arriving at a solution internal to Northern Ireland, and who sought to shift the problem on to an international plane. They invoked the assistance of Irish-America through a threefold strategy designed to discourage Irish-Americans from contributing to I.R.A. funds; to link substantial United States aid to Northern Ireland economic development if an acceptable political solution could be found; and to use the presidency's good offices in

[74] Urban, *Big boys' rules*, p. 85.
[75] John C. Hermon, *Holding the line: an autobiography* (Dublin, 1997), ch. 11.

search of a solution. Hume won the support of prominent Irish-American politicians such as 'Tip' O'Neill, speaker of the U.S. house of representatives, and Senators Edward Kennedy and Daniel Moynihan. They persuaded President Carter to issue a statement in August 1977 promising economic aid for Northern Ireland if peace and stability could be established—although he was to insist that 'there are no solutions which outsiders can impose'.[76] However, his intervention had established that Northern Ireland was a legitimate subject for concern in American foreign policy, so that no longer would it be regarded as solely a British domestic issue. Pressure was maintained, culminating in a speech made by 'Tip' O'Neill at the height of the 1979 general election, when he said: 'Britain bears a heavy responsibility for the failure of recent years on the political front'; so he demanded 'an early, realistic and major initiative on the part of the incoming British government, so as to get negotiations moving quickly'.[77]

Despite N.I.O. resistance the government produced a discussion paper, *The government of Northern Ireland: a working paper for a conference*,[78] in November 1979. It sought no more than 'the highest level of agreement... which will best meet the immediate needs of Northern Ireland'. Although the areas for discussion were narrowly circumscribed—debate on Irish unity, confederation, independence, and the constitutional status of the province were ruled out of order—the paper moved well beyond the integrationist thrust of the manifesto. And it carried the stamp of the prime minister: in her first major newspaper interview (significantly, with the *New York Times*) she expressed her impatience: 'We will listen for a while. We hope we will get agreement. But then the government will have to make some decisions and say "having listened to everyone, we are going ahead to try this or that", whichever we get most support for.'[79] To underline her personal investment she appointed a high-powered cabinet committee to oversee the process.

The plan for a conference ran into trouble from the outset. Only the Alliance party endorsed it immediately. Molyneaux's Ulster Unionists were unhappy at the departure from the manifesto and refused to attend; whereas the D.U.P. (after initial reservations) saw it as an opportunity to upstage their Unionist rivals in the battle for electoral supremacy. The D.U.P. had made substantial gains in the 1977 local council elections, and their Westminster representation had increased from one to three seats in the general election in May. But it was the direct elections to the European parliament

---

[76] Jack Holland, *The American connection: U.S. guns, money, and influence in Northern Ireland* (New York, 1987), p. 127.

[77] Quoted in Bernard Crick, 'The pale green internationalists' in *New Statesman*, 7 Dec. 1979, p. 888.

[78] *The government of Northern Ireland: a working paper for a conference* [Cmnd 7763] (H.M.S.O., London, 1979).

[79] *New York Times*, 12 Nov. 1979.

on 7 June 1979 that confirmed Ian Paisley's personal popularity: 'I believe at this election that I became the elected leader of the Ulster people and especially of the protestant people and unionist people in the province.'[80] D.U.P. participation, therefore, represented an effort to establish the party as the primary voice of unionism. The S.D.L.P.'s difficulties were of a different magnitude. Their leader, Gerry Fitt, pronounced himself happy with the document, but his party baulked at the omission of an Irish dimension and refused to attend. Fitt resigned as leader and was succeeded by Hume, who negotiated an agreement whereby Atkins would be ready on request to have separate meetings with the parties represented at the conference on wider issues.[81] So the idea of parallel talks was established, enabling the S.D.L.P. to invoke the Irish dimension. It was also accepted that parties not represented at the conference could submit papers to the secretary of state.

With the absence of the largest single party (the U.U.P.) the Atkins conference was unlikely to succeed. It opened on 7 January 1980 and adjourned on 24 March while the government prepared proposals for further discussion in the form of another paper, *The government of Northern Ireland: proposals for further discussion*, published in July 1980.[82] It narrowed the options to either a form of power-sharing or a system of majority rule with an in-built blocking mechanism to protect the minority. But the gap between the parties was too wide, and Atkins's conference went the way of the constitutional convention and other attempts at a purely internal settlement.

In the meantime other matters were exercising the attention of the government. The most urgent was the prisons issue. On 27 October 1980 republican prisoners went on hunger strike in the Maze prison in protest at their conditions and status. It was the continuation of a battle that had been waged between the prisoners and the government over the question of political status. Republicans resented criminalisation. The Sinn Féin president, Gerry Adams, later cited the Glover report and a study by lawyers of defendants appearing before the Diplock courts on 'scheduled' offences, to justify the claim that the republican prisoners 'do not fit the stereotypes of criminality which the authorities have from time to time attempted to attach to them'. He insisted that it 'has nothing to do with any contempt for the "ordinary criminals", who are so often the victims of social inequality and injustice. From Thomas Ashe to Bobby Sands the concern has always been to assert the political nature of the struggle in which the I.R.A. has been engaged.'[83] Generally the wider nationalist community shared Adams's belief that the

---

[80] *Irish Times*, 12 June 1979.
[81] Cunningham, *British government policy*, p. 144.
[82] *The government of Northern Ireland: proposals for further discussion* [Cmnd 7950] (H.M.S.O., London, 1980).
[83] Gerry Adams, *The politics of Irish freedom* (Dingle, 1986), pp 67–8, 71.

profile of the prisoners was not that of a criminal class.[84] And they were aware of a tradition of hunger-striking, which had already claimed twelve republican lives earlier in the twentieth century. We have seen that Whitelaw had conceded special-category status in 1972 but that it had been removed by Rees in 1976. The prisoners reacted by refusing to wear prison clothing or to clean out their cells. It was only when all of that failed that they resorted to the ultimate protest—the hunger strike. They were supported by 'relatives' action committees' (R.A.C.s) which were often independent of the republican leadership. There is evidence of republican incomprehension at this nuisance, which was distracting attention from the war. It was at this point that Sinn Féin began to engage in the electoral process proper. They had no candidates in the May 1979 local council elections, but four independent republicans were elected in Belfast. They realised that there was a constituency to be nourished and that they needed to reconsider their policy of abstentionism.

The first hunger strike began on 27 October 1980 and the second on 1 March 1981; seven prisoners volunteered on each occasion. The timing and the numbers were significant. The first was to culminate at Christmas (but was called off on 18 December when the strikers believed, wrongly, that they had extracted sufficient concessions from the authorities) and the second at Easter—both great Christian celebrations. The seven corresponded to the number of signatories to the 1916 proclamation. Their self-image was one of a revolutionary vanguard; they were the sacred keepers of the nation's history. Bobby Sands, who was the first volunteer and the Provisionals' O.C. in the Maze, could expect to be dead by Easter—a secular celebration of destruction and renewal as well as a holy beginning—if their demands were not met. From the outset the imagery and the symbolism of the hunger strike was politico-religious in character: 'A man can have no greater love than to lay down his life for his friends.' They were engaged in the 'theology of mystical republicanism, the philosophy of non-violence, of physical-force separatism, the embodiment of the warrior without weapons, the fighting man as the apostle of passive resistance'.[85] Bobby Sands died on 5 May 1981. Whereas 4,000 had marched in support of his decision to go on hunger strike, 70,000 turned out for his funeral procession. Nine others (six members of the P.I.R.A. and three of the I.N.L.A.) were dead by 20 August and the remainder ended their protest on 3 October. The whole episode created deep emotional scars inside Northern Ireland and polarised the community as never before. It also threatened to make constitutional nationalism

---

[84] See Edward Moxon-Browne, *Nation, class and creed in Northern Ireland* (Aldershot, 1983), p. 72; E. E. Davis and R. Sinnott, *Attitudes in the Republic of Ireland relevant to the Northern Ireland problem*, i (Economic and Social Research Institute, Dublin, 1979), pp 97–100.
[85] John 15: 13 (*The Jerusalem Bible* (London, 1966)); Padraig O'Malley, *Biting at the grave* (Belfast, 1990), pp 26–7.

redundant inside Northern Ireland; created tremendous tension between the British and Irish governments; and aroused an inordinate amount of international attention, much of it embarrassing to Britain. In short, it was a disaster.

That is not to say that lessons were not learned. The I.R.A. (in the name of the people and the dead generations) sought the high moral ground: 'In 1976 the British government tried to criminalise the republican prisoners. In 1981 the republican prisoners criminalised the British government.' Republicanism underwent a transformation with the fusion of military and political tactics. An example of the metamorphosis was the decision to contest elections with 'an Armalite in one hand and a ballot box in the other';[86] 'the essence of republican struggle must be in armed resistance coupled with popular opposition to the British presence. So while not everyone can plant a bomb, everyone can plant a vote.'[87] Before his death Bobby Sands had been elected M.P. for Fermanagh–South Tyrone in a by-election on 9 April under the highly effective slogan of 'Your vote can save this man's life'. It did not, and his election agent, Owen Carron, succeeded Sands at a further by-election on 20 August. In the meantime nine prisoners stood in the Irish general election in June 1981 and two were elected. That was enough to deprive Charles Haughey and the Fianna Fáil party of power. Contesting elections was becoming addictive, and was playing 'a major role in changing the nature of Sinn Féin'.[88] Adams himself became M.P. for West Belfast at the 1983 general election, by which time Sinn Féin had become the largest nationalist party in Belfast. The gap between Sinn Féin and the S.D.L.P. had narrowed; each held one Westminster seat, and the S.D.L.P. had 17.9 per cent of the vote to Sinn Féin's 13.4. It was as a result of this upsurge in Sinn Féin support that the word 'alienation' came into vogue, and both governments began to recognise that they needed to act in concert to prevent any further republican gains.

DESPITE her rigid public stance, the lessons of the hunger strikes and the failure of yet another internal initiative had not been lost on Margaret Thatcher. When during the 1979 general election 'Tip' O'Neill called for a British initiative, he incurred the wrath of U.K. politicians and leader-writers, but his message was not lost altogether. At the same time as the Atkins initiative was getting under way, the British and Irish governments began a reassessment of their separate approaches to the Northern Ireland problem. They were returning to a consideration of the Irish dimension. Its meaning had been expressed most cogently by the taoiseach, Liam Cosgrave, as early as 1973.

[86] This phrase was launched by Danny Morrison at the Sinn Féin ard-fheis, 31 Oct. 1981 (Bew & Gillespie, *Northern Ireland*, p. 157, citing *Republican News*, 5 Nov. 1981).
[87] *Republican News*, 16 Sept. 1982.
[88] Adams, *Politics of Ir. freedom*, p. 151.

The full measure of the problem of Northern Ireland is that reconciliation between its communities cannot be brought about successfully in isolation from the larger issue of reconciliation within the island as a whole. The two issues are inseparable... This...is the real meaning of the 'Irish dimension'...—an essential, and not a secondary, aspect of the problem. This means that it must be faced if the problem is to be solved. It is primarily as an institution which could respond to this need, and not simply as a means of smoothing out minor overlapping problems deriving from a common border, that a council of Ireland seems to me to be called for.[89]

The whole matter went into abeyance during Labour's tenure of office, but after the failure of his initiative Atkins spoke in the commons of the 'geographical and historical facts of life [that] oblige us to recognise the special relationship that exists between the component parts of the British Isles...we improve our chances of success by recognising that the Republic is deeply interested in what happens in Northern Ireland...there will continue to be a practical "Irish dimension".'[90]

One reason for a growing interest in the Irish dimension was increasing security cooperation. When Charles Haughey succeeded Jack Lynch as leader of Fianna Fáil and taoiseach in December 1979, there was some apprehension in London that he might be soft on the I.R.A. In fact he demonstrated his anti-terrorism credentials, and political cooperation followed security cooperation with an Anglo–Irish summit meeting in London on 21 May 1980. The communiqué released after the meeting referred to the 'unique relationship' between the two islands and promised to engage in much closer functional cooperation. A second summit was held in Dublin on 8 December 1980, when it was agreed that substantial progress had been made since May in matters of energy, transport, communications, cross-border economic developments, and security. Additionally, senior officials agreed on joint studies covering possible new institutional structures, citizenship rights, security matters, economic cooperation, and measures to encourage mutual understanding.

At this point relationships became strained. The December communiqué had been wrapped in deliberate ambiguity and contained the fateful phrase 'the totality of relationships within these islands'. In a dáil address three days later the taoiseach interpreted these words to mean 'that the special consideration to which our next meeting will be devoted does not exclude *anything* that can contribute to achieve peace, reconciliation, and stability, and to the improvement of relationships within these islands' (italics added). Such rhetoric—and further remarks made by the minister for foreign affairs, Brian Lenihan—raised the temperature in Northern Ireland, already high because the first hunger strike was reaching its climax. The hunger-strike campaign

---

[89] *Dáil Éireann deb.*, cclxv, 578–9 (8 May 1973).
[90] *Hansard 5 (commons)*, cmlxxxviii, 557 (9 July 1980).

dominated events during 1981, doing untold damage to the political process—although that was not immediately apparent in the sphere of Anglo–Irish relations. Indeed, when Garret FitzGerald, leader of the Fine Gael party, became taoiseach at the head of a coalition government in June 1981, expectations were that the process would be improved. And so it appeared when at a third summit (November 1981) an Anglo–Irish inter-governmental council was established. That met on seven occasions during 1982, but meanwhile the relationship between the two governments had become damaged.

Three factors undermined the process of reconciliation. The first concerned different perceptions of the hunger-strike campaign. The Irish government accepted that while there could be no concession on the strikers' demand for political status, compromise on humanitarian grounds should be sought if only to avoid polarisation within Northern Ireland. But Margaret Thatcher conducted the debate in terms of a battle between good and evil. Secondly, Ireland's stance during the Falklands/Malvinas war (after the sinking of the *Belgrano*) in opposition to E.E.C. trade sanctions against Argentina had a catastrophic effect during a period when jingoistic feelings were running high in Britain.[91]

Finally, Anglo–Irish relations had been upset at yet another attempt to find an internal settlement to the Northern Ireland problem. In September 1981 Humphrey Atkins had been replaced as secretary of state by James Prior. Prior came to Northern Ireland as a cabinet heavyweight and one who was not anxious to be out of the public eye. He was seen as a rival to Mrs Thatcher and had come to the province reluctantly. He launched yet another blueprint in April 1982, *Northern Ireland: a framework for devolution*,[92] a managerial and minimalist plan for devolution, based on 'acceptance' rather than 'reconciliation'. The first stage was to be an election in October 1982 for an assembly that was to be invested with a scrutinising and consultative role to make direct rule more amenable. If and when the assembly could demonstrate that there was cross-community agreement on, say, agricultural policy, devolution of powers would be granted to the assembly committee concerned with agriculture; and if it could be proven in other areas that there was cross-community agreement then those powers too would be devolved—hence 'rolling devolution'.

But it was never to happen, because neither Sinn Féin (with five out of seventy-eight seats) nor the S.D.L.P. (fourteen seats) supported the proceedings; the former opposed them on grounds of principle and the latter on the grounds that there was no longer any purely internal solution to the problem. Instead the S.D.L.P. turned its back on the narrow ground of Northern

[91] 'When British territory is invaded it is not just an invasion of our land, but of our whole spirit' (*The Times*, 5 Apr. 1982).
[92] *Northern Ireland: a framework for devolution* [Cmnd 8541] (H.M.S.O., London, 1982).

Ireland and looked to the larger Anglo–Irish canvas. Both Fianna Fáil and (eventually) Fine Gael expressed their reservations about the 'rolling devolution' initiative; and when Prior persisted with his plan the Republic's main constitutional parties embraced the S.D.L.P. manifesto proposal of 'A council for a new Ireland'. Thus was the New Ireland Forum born, established (in the words of its final report) 'for consultations on the manner in which lasting peace and stability could be achieved in a new Ireland through the democratic process and to report on possible new structures and processes through which this objective might be achieved'.[93] Four political parties took part: Fianna Fáil, Fine Gael, and Labour from the Republic, and the S.D.L.P. from Northern Ireland. The first public session of the forum was held on 30 May 1983, and after twenty-eight private sessions and thirteen public sessions the final report appeared on 2 May 1984. It had established, wittingly or not, a parallel process to the Northern Ireland assembly.

If we examine its potential to influence the Anglo–Irish debate, several factors suggest themselves. The first is that the report was but one section of the forum process. All of the published documents were relevant: Oliver MacDonagh noted that the forum 'published several support papers on special subjects, these last being, generally, of marked and lasting value'.[94] In addition, many of the public sessions, especially those involving the economists Sir Charles Carter and Professor Louden Ryan, the Irish episcopal conference, and the evidence presented by two U.U.P. members, Christopher and Michael McGimpsey, may have had an educative effect on the Republic's electorate. Secondly, constitutional nationalists now recognised that Irish unity was not a simple matter of manifest destiny. Despite a rather superficial reading of Irish history, the final report recognised 'that one essential presupposition of traditional Irish nationalism was erroneous... the identification of Irish national identity with the values of the oldest and largest component of the island's population, what we might loosely term the catholic–Gaelic culture'. Moreover, 'the very acknowledgement of Ulster unionist parity represented a striking change'.[95] Thirdly, the forum was concerned with more than the three preferred options of a unitary state, federalism/confederalism, and joint authority. 'The most important aspect of the report is not the three options', John Hume told the commons on 2 July 1984, 'but the views of Irish nationalists about the ways in which realities must be faced if there is to be a solution'.[96] In other words, the forum process did not end with the publication of the report, but was intended to open up a fundamental debate within these islands.

[93] *New Ireland Forum: report, 2 May 1984* ([Dublin, 1984]), p. 1.
[94] 'What was new in the New Ireland Forum' in *The Crane Bag*, ix, no. 2 (1985), pp 166–70: 166.
[95] Ibid., p. 167.
[96] *Hansard 6 (commons)*, lxiii, 57 (2 July 1984).

The Anglo–Irish process that began in 1980 had been the tentative opening of that debate. We have seen that with the hunger strikes and the Falklands/Malvinas imbroglio it was a faltering process. But with the reelection of a Conservative government at the general election on 9 June 1983, continuity seemed to be preserved and a further Anglo–Irish summit was held in November 1983. It was against that backcloth that the Irish government entered another summit in November 1984 with some confidence. The forum report had been published and the Irish authorities expected some acknowledgement of their labours. They received it in terms of a carefully worded communiqué; but its meaning was lost in the subsequent press conference when the British prime minister so peremptorily dismissed the three preferred forum options. It seemed as if the period had ended as it had begun—with a sense of bewilderment and loss of direction.

CHAPTER XVI

Land and people, *c*.1983

DESMOND A. GILLMOR

IRISH land was put to predominantly pastoral use in the early 1980s, as it had been, except under abnormal circumstances, since clearance of the natural forests. Improved pasture and grass conserved for winter feeding covered 60 per cent of the island in 1980 but tillage accounted for only 8 per cent of the total (table 1). Arable crops were generally not a significant element in the landscape outside counties adjacent to the northern, eastern, and southern coasts, where climatic and soil factors were most favourable. Although the spread of state afforestation had made a considerable impact on the landscape of many areas, only 5 per cent of the country was under forest and woodland. Much of the unimproved land comprised moorland, bog, marsh, and bare rock, but over half of it served agricultural use as rough grazing. This land also had recreational, water catchment, and fuel supply functions. Between 1926 and 1980 the net loss of agricultural land had been 400,000 hectares (*c*.1,550 square miles), a decline of 7 per cent. This was because the reclamation effected by some farmers, especially in recent decades, had been much more than offset by retreat from marginal land elsewhere, but changes in the recording of statistics had some effect on the

TABLE 1. *Land use, 1980*

	Republic of Ireland		Northern Ireland		Ireland	
	hectares	%	hectares	%	hectares	%
Tillage	553,900	8.0	80,400	5.9	634,300	7.7
Hay and silage	1,212,800	17.6	264,100	19.5	1,476,900	17.9
Pasture	2,929,000	42.5	510,200	37.6	3,439,200	41.7
Woods and plantations	318,200	4.6	67,000	5.0	385,200	4.7
Rough grazing	1,008,700	14.7	214,800	15.8	1,223,500	14.8
Other land	866,600	12.6	219,800	16.2	1,086,400	13.2
Total area	6,889,200	100.0	1,356,300	100.0	8,245,500	100.0

data. Loss of farmland through urbanisation was on a small scale except in the environs of the principal towns, notably Dublin and Belfast. Urban areas covered less than 2 per cent of Irish land.

The agrarian landscape of the early 1980s clearly bore the imprint of past conditions and influences. The greatest regional contrast continued to be that between west and east, western areas having smaller fields and farms, less substantial farmsteads, and a greater density of rural population. Yet the landscape was not static. The work of the Irish land commission was responsible for some of the changes that had been taking place in earlier decades, though by no means for all the development. The enlargement of uneconomic holdings and the reduction of farm fragmentation had become the principal functions of the land commission, special emphasis being laid on the relief of congestion in western areas. Many fragmented holdings there were rearranged and consolidated into more compact, workable units. Such rationalisation sometimes involved the movement of people out of the congested area and their settlement on new farms elsewhere, usually in the east and especially in Counties Meath and Kildare. Throughout the country, large estates and land not being worked properly had been acquired through purchase by the land commission. The land was either divided among smallholders in the locality or laid out in new farms for former workers on the estate, landless people, or migrants. The average size of farm created in the 1920s and 1930s had been 10 hectares (25 acres), but even the later target of double this size was too small for modern commercial farming. Land commission activity had transformed the appearance of some rural areas through farm and field rearrangement, the building of dwelling and farmyard houses, road construction, land drainage, fencing, and other improvements.

Despite the decline of the estate, demesnes still constituted a distinctive feature of the landscape in many areas in the early 1980s. They could readily be recognised by their varied deciduous trees and often retained their high perimeter walls. Many of the large houses associated with former estates had been destroyed or had fallen to ruin; others were adopted for institutional use, housing religious orders, schools, research organisations, government agencies, hotels, and commercial companies; others continued to serve private residential functions, and some had become important tourist resources through being opened to the public.

Changes other than those effected by the land commission were occurring in the density and distribution of rural settlement and in the number, design, and building materials of rural dwellings and farmyard buildings. The ruins of deserted houses were melancholic landscape expressions of the decline in rural population, especially during earlier decades. They were most common in western districts, in remote areas, and near the margins of the agricultural land. The rural landscape reflected a general improvement in housing conditions, either through the modification of existing structures or the construction of new ones. Some were provided by local authorities, but new private housing, either individually or in ribbon form along rural roads, had become the most obvious form of change in the landscape of the countryside. This was much less evident in Northern Ireland, where there was stricter planning control on open country development because of its landscape effect and servicing cost. The new houses, among which bungalows constructed of concrete with tiled roofs predominated, did not harmonise as well with the landscape as did the traditional buildings, which were a diminishing feature of the countryside. Much of the new housing was occupied by people who were not engaged in farming, reflecting the increased occupational diversification of rural dwellers. Development was greatest in the vicinities of towns, to which many of the occupants commuted.

Although the urban landscape still constituted a comparatively small element in the Irish scene, it was there that the extent and pace of change were greatest. Transformation was most pronounced along the rural–urban fringe, principally around the cities but to some extent at all towns. It was effected largely through the outward extension of residential building, both private and public. Much of the expansion of the cities and adjacent settlements was in the form of housing estates, most of which had a monotonous appearance initially but improved as they matured. Much of the new manufacturing development was also located on the urban fringe where land was most readily available, with many factories concentrated into industrial estates around the larger centres. New retail facilities were built in response to increasing consumer demand, and planned suburban shopping centres with extensive car-parking areas became a feature of the landscape, following the first developments at Newtownbreda in south Belfast in 1964 and at Stillorgan in County Dublin in 1966.

Urban change and development were not confined to the outer suburbs. Urban renewal schemes initially comprised new local authority housing designed to alleviate the poor and overcrowded living conditions of certain areas near central Dublin and Belfast. Early on, provision was mainly in the form of flats; later, some individual houses were built. Private apartment development in the form of purpose-built blocks began from the 1960s, principally in inner suburban areas of high socio-economic status, especially in Dublin. An even more conspicuous new feature of the urban landscape were modern office blocks, reflecting the growth in this sector of the economy. Development was greatest in Dublin, where expansion led to a shift in the focus of office-based activity south-eastwards in the most affluent sector of the city, which was most attractive to developers. Shopping arcades and some other new retail provision had begun in inner city areas, including Dublin, Cork, and Ballymena, partly in an attempt to counteract the increasing suburbanisation of trade. Some of the commercial development and modern housing replaced high-density residential land use and thus contributed to the decline of inner city living and greater suburbanisation of the population. Another impact was the effect on the urban fabric, for among the old buildings demolished were some of considerable historical and architectural value, notably in Georgian Dublin. There were also many vacant and derelict sites, particularly in those parts of towns that were least commercially attractive. Yet many city buildings and most of those in country towns experienced no change of use, so that the intrusion of new shop fronts was often the principal novelty. A welcome tendency towards rehabilitation of old buildings had begun and held out the hope that there might be greater concern for the conservation of landscapes, both urban and rural.

THE combined population of both parts of Ireland was 5.01 million in 1981, the first time that it had exceeded 5 million since the mid 1880s. The post-famine decline had continued until the population numbered only 4.2 million in the 1930s. Subsequently, apart from the 1950s, there had been an upward trend, at first slight but accelerating from the 1960s. Ireland's uniquely high rate of emigration declined to the extent that it became lower than the rate of natural increase and then diminished further. Over the decade 1971–81 there were 469,000 more births than deaths and a net emigration of just 8,000, so that the population of Ireland increased by 461,000, representing a growth of 10.2 per cent.

The populations in 1981 as compared with 1926 were greater by 22 per cent in Northern Ireland (1,532,157) and 16 per cent in the Republic of Ireland (3,443,405), but there had been considerable divergence in trends between the two areas. The tendencies established before partition were accentuated in the period 1926–61, when growth of 13 per cent occurred in Northern Ireland and a decline of 5 per cent in the Republic. The Republic's trend was reversed in the 1960s but its rate of growth was still exceeded by that in Northern Ireland. A major change occurred in the decade 1971–81, when a slight decrease of 0.3 per cent in Northern Ireland contrasted with an increase of 16 per cent in the population of the Republic. There was no simple cause of this difference but contributory influences were likely to have included the following: employment increased by 8 per cent in the Republic, while it decreased by 7 per cent in Northern Ireland; the employment trend in Northern Ireland was in part related to the internal troubles, which in themselves must have contributed to the decision by many people to migrate, so that the net emigration of 110,000 was greater by three-quarters than in the preceding decade; considerable advances had been made in social welfare provision and in the levels of income and living standards in the Republic, so that they improved relative to those in Northern Ireland; the rate of natural increase was greater in the Republic, mainly because of a higher birth rate, which was 21 per thousand population in 1981 compared with 17 per thousand in Northern Ireland. The reduction in emigration from the Republic was in part related to difficulties in procuring employment elsewhere and in gaining admission to the United States of America, Canada, and Australia. There was net immigration in the years 1972–6 but emigration increased subsequently and was regaining high levels by the early 1980s. This, combined with a sudden drop in the birth rate, began to lessen the rate of population increase. The high rate of growth, the high birth rate, and the young age structure of the population, with 30 per cent aged under 15 years, had made the Republic demographically unique among western European countries.

The most striking feature of the spatial pattern of population change within the Republic and Northern Ireland during the twentieth century had been an eastward shift in the distribution of people. During the period 1926–61 growth was largely confined to eastern and northern parts of Northern Ireland and to east Leinster.[1] The east–west contrast was greater in the Republic, where the population of County Dublin increased by 42 per cent but that of the western counties declined by 25 per cent. The loss was 40 per cent in County Leitrim, and the north-west in general suffered most. With the upturn in the state's total population from the early 1960s, growth extended progressively from Dublin and surrounding counties and from the larger urban centres. It diffused westwards, down the urban hierarchy and into many rural areas.[2] Despite this, the role of the eastern region, which comprised Dublin and contiguous counties, continued to grow; by the early 1980s its population was twice that of 1926 and its share of the state's total had increased from 23 to 38 per cent.

The pattern of population change was the result of spatial variations in the interrelated rates of migration, natural increase, and urbanisation. Emigration was highest in those areas most reliant on low-income farming but it lessened as the agricultural population became depleted and as alternative employment and social welfare benefits improved locally. Because of the older age structure of the relict population and its predominantly rural character, the rate of natural increase in western areas became only half that of the eastern region. Urban growth came about more through natural increase than by migration from rural areas, yet the predominantly eastward movement of people in response to the distribution of cities and large towns was a significant component in the pattern of population change. The open country population of the Republic increased in the 1970s for the first time since the famine, but this was greatest close to the towns and the rate of urban growth was much higher. Data difficulties prevent precise comparison of the levels of urbanisation, but by the early 1980s about 80 per cent of the population in Northern Ireland and 65 per cent in the Republic lived in towns of all sizes. Despite increasing urbanisation, decline was occurring in inner city areas,

[1] Below, ix, map 103.   [2] Ibid., and below, p. 450, map 12.

most notably in Belfast and Dublin, as populations became more suburban-ised. This was reflected in the population of Belfast county borough, which fell by over one-fifth in the period 1961–81 as growth spilled over into adjoining areas.

THE 1.66 million people in employment in Ireland in 1981 represented a 7 per cent fall compared with 1926, a slight increase in Northern Ireland having been more than offset by decline in the Republic. That the number at work should have decreased, over a period when births exceeded deaths by more than 2 million, indicated the extent of the failure to provide em-ployment for the natural increase in the population. The decline in male employment was even greater, for there had been substantial growth in female participation in the workforce. This was related principally to the greatly increased tendency for married women to work outside the home, and to expansion in service occupations. Female participation rates were higher in Northern Ireland, but only one-third of the people in both parts of Ireland were in employment. This low level of participation resulted in a high dependency ratio compared with other developed countries. Another unfavourable feature was the level of unemployment, at 21 per cent in Northern Ireland and 16 per cent in the Republic in 1983, which had escal-ated with economic recession in the 1970s and early 1980s.

The proportions of people employed in the different sectors of the econ-omy in 1981 were as follows: primary (agriculture, forestry, fishing, mining) 14 per cent; secondary (manufacturing, construction, utilities) 31 per cent, tertiary (service industries) 55 per cent. The relative size of the secondary sector was the same in both political units but this had been arrived at from different positions, in that manufacturing had been much more important in Northern Ireland but substantial deindustrialisation had occurred, whereas industrial expansion had been a feature of the Republic's economy albeit with setbacks in the recent recession. Both areas, in common with trends in other developed economies, had experienced declines in the primary sector and expansion of tertiary activity. They were at different stages in these processes, as primary activity provided 6 per cent of employment in North-ern Ireland and 18 per cent in the Republic, with the respective roles of the tertiary sector being 63 per cent and 51 per cent. Employment in the con-stituent industries may be compared by area and with 1926 in the accom-panying tables,[3] in which the census classification, particularly for Northern Ireland, has been modified to enable such comparison. The trends involved major relative and absolute growth in white-collar occupations and especially in office work, so that office occupations increased to one-quarter of all employment.

<hr>

[3] Above, p. 68; below, p. 443.

EMPLOYMENT in agriculture in the early 1980s was only a quarter of that of the 1920s and its importance compared with other industries had diminished greatly, yet farming retained a key role in the Irish economy. Combined with food processing and other ancillary activities, it accounted for more than one-fifth of total employment. Half of agricultural output was exported and production had a low import content, so that it made a critical contribution to the international balance of payments. Reliance on farming remained highest in western areas, where more than one-quarter of the workforce was engaged directly in agriculture.

Ireland remained a country of medium and small holdings, as farm size had not increased to the extent that the decrease in the agricultural population would suggest. This was because decline had been much greater among agricultural labourers and relatives assisting on farms than among farmers, and because there was an increasing proportion of holdings owned by people recorded as being in other employment and who worked the land part-time or let it to others. Features of agriculture other than land ownership had changed more rapidly, enabling farm output to expand greatly despite the depleted labour force. This was achieved through farm mechanisation, modernisation of farm buildings, use of fertilisers, chemicals, and purchased feedstuffs, improved livestock and crop varieties, and much better farm management. State support for agriculture and accession to the common agricultural policy of the European Community had provided an important impetus to development, and led to substantial growth in the farm sector in the 1970s. By the early 1980s, however, the problems of surplus production and financial restrictions had begun to cast a shadow over the future prospects for farming. Also there was a substantial number of farmers who had benefited much less from the modernisation of Irish agriculture because of small farm size, age, family circumstances, or other constraints.

One feature that characterised agricultural development was a trend towards greater specialisation in production. At the national level, it involved especially increased concentration on beef and milk production, which by 1983 together contributed 70 per cent of Irish farm output. This response to relative price trends reflected market demand and state support, accentuated by accession to the E.C. At the level of the individual farm, the traditionally mixed character of Irish farming lessened considerably as farmers concentrated their resources on a diminished number of enterprises in order to achieve greater efficiency. They had become increasingly commercially oriented as the subsistence element in agriculture diminished.

The distinct regional pattern of agriculture was largely inherited, but some recent change had occurred. Beef cattle production was important to farmers everywhere, with the densities of stock being highest in the midlands and east Ulster, and the traditional tendency persisting for more rearing in the west and fattening in the east. The two major dairying regions were those of

Munster and Ulster, though milk production had spread into other areas. Contraction of arable farming had led to an increased level of crop concentration in eastern areas where conditions were most favourable. Sheep production had concentrated in upland districts where competition from other enterprises was least, but recently had begun to expand in the lowlands also. The structure of poultry and pig production had altered radically, as output became increasingly dominated by large specialised units and the role as subsidiary farmyard enterprises diminished. Pigs and poultry contributed almost one-quarter of agricultural output in Northern Ireland but only one-tenth in the Republic, where Cavan and Monaghan were the leading areas. The overall tendency in locational change had been for the various farm enterprises to become more concentrated and distinct from one another.

PARTIAL renewal of the depleted forest resources was largely attributable to government planting, which had led to 315,000 ha (780,000 acres) of forest in the Republic and 55,000 ha (136,000 acres) in Northern Ireland, covering 4.5 per cent of the island's land area. Policy was always to minimise conflict with farming through use of land that was considered less suited for agriculture. Thus, apart from the use of former estate woodland, planting was mainly in upland areas and on peat bogs. Early afforestation took place principally in the east and on lower slopes, but the use of hardy North American species of trees, mechanical ploughing, and fertilisers facilitated planting under more difficult conditions, so that forests moved up slope and westwards. In contrast with the former natural woodland, the new forests were predominantly coniferous. Conifers grew much better than hardwoods on poor-quality land, they matured more rapidly, and the major market demand was for softwoods. Output of timber was still quite small because much of the afforestation was recent.

The principal objectives of forestry were to provide a domestic supply of timber and exports, to promote industrial development, to make profitable use of land, and to afford employment. There had been rapid growth in the recreational use of forests in recent decades. Twenty forest parks had been created and there were 400 other sites with less developed facilities open to the public.

The considerable marine resources had been under-utilised until major expansion of the Irish sea fishing industry occurred from the 1950s. Bord Iascaigh Mhara, a state-sponsored company, played a vital role in promoting development in the Republic. Provision of government grants and credit facilities for the purchase of craft and gear did much to encourage expansion and modernisation of the fleet. Although much of the fleet still engaged in inshore fishing, there was a pronounced trend towards bigger and more powerful vessels, which were better equipped and could undertake longer fishing voyages. There was major harbour and industrial development to improve landing and processing of the catch and servicing of the fleet. Investment in the Republic was principally at Killybegs, Rossaveel, Castletownbere, Dunmore East, and Howth. In Northern Ireland it was concentrated at the three County Down ports of Ardglass, Kilkeel, and Portavogie, which dominated the industry there. Training schemes were provided for practising fishermen and new recruits in order to improve skills and counteract a certain reluctance to adopt fishing as a livelihood. There were 3,200 full-time and 5,400 part-time fishermen. The former were concentrated in the major ports; many of the latter owned small farms along the western seaboard. Substantial improvements in the transport and marketing of fish were effected, with cooperative societies playing an important role. The major handicap of low domestic consumption diminished as fish gained acceptance as a food, but about three-quarters of the catch was exported.

The expansion of Irish fish landings, combined with the even greater effect of increased takings by the fleets of other countries off the Irish coast, led to resource-supply problems and reduced catches. Landings of the main species were subsequently controlled by the European Community and national quotas were fixed under the common fisheries policy initiated in 1983. In that year 200,000 tonnes were landed at Irish ports, four-fifths in the Republic, and a further 20,000 tonnes were landed by Irish vessels at other ports, principally in Britain. The most valuable species in the Republic were mackerel, herring, prawns, and cod, while prawns had for long been the leading variety in Northern Ireland.

THE most productive phase in Irish mining history had begun in the 1960s, leading to Ireland becoming a metalliferous producer of international status. There was intense exploration and development of five mines. This phase resulted from changes in mineral legislation and tax incentives, from technological developments in exploration, mining, and processing, from the realisation that there was a favourable mining environment in Ireland, and from the participation of foreign mining companies. Mining began or recommenced at Tynagh, County Galway, Gortdrum and Silvermines in County Tipperary, and Avoca, County Wicklow. These mines had ceased working by 1983. The remaining mine was by far the most important, being at Navan, County Meath, where production had begun in 1977 on one of the largest zinc–lead deposits in the world, employing 800 people. The ore concentrates from all the mines were exported to European smelters.

Production of non-metallic minerals other than fuels employed 4,000 people. This sector was dominated by the output of materials for the construction industry. Quarrying of stone, sand, and gravel as aggregate was widespread, but especially near the main centres of construction in the Dublin and Belfast regions. Limestone was quarried for cement manufacture near Drogheda and Limerick and was ground as a soil improver in many places. Gypsum was mined at Kingscourt, County Cavan, for the production of plaster, plasterboard, and cement. Barytes was produced mainly at Bally-noe, County Tipperary, for oil drilling.

Ireland's world role was greatest in peat production, in which it ranked second to the U.S.S.R. This was achieved mainly by mechanised strip ex-traction, carried out by the semi-state company Bord na Móna, which had an annual output of 5 million tonnes and employed 6,000 people. Because of the desirability of using large tracts of level bog with substantial depths of peat, extraction was concentrated on the raised bogs of the midlands. Power stations were the main consumers of peat and supplied nearly one-fifth of the Republic's electricity needs. They were built in the period 1950–65 and because of transport costs most were located close to the main producing bogs.[4] With the prospect of the major peat resources being depleted over the next few decades, there was increasing concern about the implications for the economy and society of the midlands. The traditional cutting of turf by hand as a domestic fuel had diminished greatly, but some renewal of interest in private peat production was stimulated by rising costs of energy and the development of small cutting machines. Four small electricity stations on the western coast used privately produced turf. Coal was mined mainly at Arigna in County Roscommon and much of the output went to an adjacent power station on Lough Allen. Reopening of a mine at Ballingarry, County Tipper-ary, indicated renewed interest in coal production.

By the early 1980s water power accounted for less than one-tenth of the electricity generated in the Republic. Development of the hydroelectric po-tential of the Shannon in the 1920s had been followed in the 1940s and 1950s by schemes for the rivers Liffey, Erne, Lee, and Clady.[5] This was considered to be near to the practical limit for river development. A large pumped storage plant began production in 1975 at Turlough Hill in the Wicklow mountains, where favourable physical conditions occurred near to the Dublin market for electricity.

Some drilling for petroleum occurred on land in the 1960s but, prompted by developments in the North Sea and beginning in 1970, attention focused largely on the offshore potential. The Marathon company achieved a very quick return on its exploration effort in the discovery of the Kinsale gasfield off the coast of south Cork. The natural gas was brought ashore in 1978 for electricity generation, urban gas supply, and fertiliser manufacture. It was confined to Cork at first but was extended to Dublin through construction of a pipeline in 1981–2. Natural gas was providing one-half of the Republic's electricity by 1983. The Kinsale discovery and energy price increases stimu-lated further exploration: over seventy wells were drilled in the sedimentary basins of the Irish offshore area. Attention focused mainly on the North

---

[4] Below, ix, map 114.   [5] Ibid.

Celtic Sea Basin off the south coast and the more distant and exposed Porcupine Basin off the west coast. Significant finds of oil and gas were made in both areas but they lacked commercial viability at that time.

Energy policy in the Republic was to maximise the use of indigenous resources. They contributed about 40 per cent of energy supply till the early 1960s. As limits to domestic resources were reached and as energy demand began to rise steeply from 1960 with economic and social development, increasing reliance had to be placed on imported supplies. Coal had been the traditional standby, but oil assumed increasing importance, so that three-quarters of total energy was derived from imported oil by the mid 1970s. Electricity was generated from oil in large coastal power stations in Dublin, Cork, south Wexford, and the Shannon estuary. High inflation in oil prices and instability in supplies prompted efforts to reduce dependence. This was achieved in part by greater use of other existing energy sources, but especially by the development of natural gas. The percentage contributions of the different sources to energy supply in the Republic in 1983 were oil 50, natural gas 20, peat 15, coal 12, and hydroelectricity 3. Energy consumption had reached a peak in 1979 at nearly three times the level of the 1950s.

Energy in Northern Ireland was derived almost entirely from imported oil and coal, with oil accounting for 69 per cent of the total. Oil-fired power stations near Carrickfergus, Larne, and Derry generated four-fifths of the electricity and the remainder came from a coal-fired plant in Belfast. Coal was imported mainly from Britain and supplied three-quarters of domestic heating fuel.

Energy and transport were the two basic infrastructural services on which the economic and social life of the country had become dependent. The demand for both had risen steeply with development; yet their cost in Ireland was comparatively high. This resulted from the peripheral island location, dependence on imported energy, the small and dispersed population, and high taxation levels. There were 92,000 people recorded as employed in transport and communications, including 15,000 in the Republic's semi-state transport authority Córas Iompair Éireann. These data underestimated the sector's true importance, however, as they related to employment in transport and communication companies, whereas private passenger traffic and own account haulage predominated. The postal and telecommunication services were responsible for 40 per cent of the recorded employment in this sector.

Although the transport system of the early 1980s had to provide for the modern needs of the country, it was the product of an evolution spread over centuries and bore the imprint of past conditions. Yet the system developed and changed in conjunction with the development of the economy and with changing means of transport. The major features of evolution since partition had been contraction of inland waterway and rail transport, huge growth in motorised road transport, development of telecommunications and air transport, and technological changes, which included the great impact of containerisation on freight movement in recent decades.

Commercial traffic on the canals had ceased but there was a revival in the use of inland waterways for recreational purposes, especially on the Shannon and Lough Erne. As the coming of rail transport had heralded the decline of inland navigation, so the railways in turn had lost traffic to the roads. Rail was used mainly for longer journeys, with the exception of the increasingly important city commuter services. Most freight movement comprised bulk commodities and container traffic. The major responses to the deteriorating position of the railways had been increasing control and subvention by the state and a contraction of the network of railway lines and stations. The most uneconomic branch lines had been closed first, leaving a network consisting essentially of trunk line and commuter services.[6] By 1983 the length of rail routeway had declined by more than half, to 2,300 km (1,400 miles).

The roads dominated inland transport, carrying over nine-tenths of traffic, much of it by private motor vehicle. There was more road relative to population than in other European countries, mainly because the network had been designed to serve a denser population and the settlement pattern was dispersed. There were 116,000 km (72,000 miles) of roads of varied grades but with an unusually high proportion metalled. Extension of the network in the twentieth century had been largely confined to construction of new roads in expanding urban areas, some town bypasses, and in Northern Ireland 110 km (68 miles) of motorway. The road system and in particular the main routes had been modified through widening and straightening, in order to adapt to the growing volume of traffic and the increasing speed and size of vehicles. The number of motor vehicles using the roads had risen to 1.4 million, giving rise to considerable problems of traffic congestion in and around the major urban centres, and revealing the inadequacy of some of the main inter-urban routes.

External sea and air links were vital to Ireland because of its island location. Almost all the goods traffic and over half the passenger movement went by sea. Trade was conducted predominantly through east-coast and to a lesser extent southern ports, despite the fine natural harbours along the west coast. This reflected the mainly eastward orientation of Irish links and trade towards Britain and Europe and the internal distribution of manufacturing output, agricultural production, urban population, and consumption. Traffic had become more concentrated at the larger ports, where better facilities and land connections were available and more frequent shipping services operated, but provision for container and vehicle handling led also to growth at some smaller places. The major cargo ports were Belfast, Dublin, Larne, and

[6] Below, ix, map 100.

Cork, followed by the Shannon estuary, Waterford, Rosslare, and Warren-point. Passenger services by car ferry to Britain operated from Larne, Belfast, Dublin, Dun Laoghaire, Rosslare, and Cork, with sailings from the latter two ports also to France.

Air traffic had grown to the extent that 5.5 million passengers used Ireland's international airports annually. There were scheduled services to the principal British cities, to eight mainland European countries, mainly from Dublin, and to the United States direct from Shannon. Charter flights operated principally to the Mediterranean region and to North America. Nearly half the traffic was through Dublin airport, which served the widest range of destinations. Belfast International Airport at Aldergrove had connections with twenty British cities, and Belfast Harbour Airport at Sydenham was reopened to scheduled traffic in 1983. The role of Shannon was principally to service transatlantic traffic, and Cork was the other international airport. A number of small aerodromes had been developed in other parts of the country. Aer Lingus, the national airline, carried 2.2 million passengers annually.

THE pattern of manufacturing in Ireland in the early 1980s was in striking contrast to that of a half-century earlier. Over the period 1926–81, manufacturing employment had declined by 40 per cent in Northern Ireland and doubled in the Republic. Although the proportion of the workforce engaged in manufacturing in Northern Ireland was slightly higher still than in the Republic, its share of the island's industrial employment had declined from 63 per cent in 1926 to 33 per cent in 1981, having been surpassed by that of the Republic about 1960. The trends in the amount, nature, and distribution of manufacturing industry in the two parts of Ireland were markedly different.

The major industrial problem in Northern Ireland had been that its substantial manufacturing economy was too narrowly based on a few export industries, which were being affected by changing market demand and by company closures, rationalisation, and reduced labour forces. These were shipbuilding and marine engineering, and the textile industries dominated by linen. Harland & Wolff in Belfast, together with other U.K. shipyards, lost business because of price and delivery-time considerations. The company was affected also by diminished demand for the types of ship that it had produced and by labour difficulties. Employment diminished from 25,000 in the 1950s to 7,000. The process of adjustment in the linen industry was even harder. The industry had employed 60,000 people in the early 1950s; by 1983 there were only 11,000 textile workers of all kinds. The major reason for the difficulties in the linen industry was the loss of market to other textiles, especially cotton and synthetic fibres. Lesser factors included changes in fashion, trade restrictions, slowness to adapt to new circumstances, and competition from other industries for workers.

Major state loans and grants were given for the maintenance and readjustment of the shipbuilding and aircraft industries, and military contracts were allocated to Belfast. Assisted modernisation of the linen industry occurred to a much lesser extent. The major objective of Northern Ireland manufacturing policy, however, was to broaden the industrial structure. Development of existing industries that were not in decline was encouraged and there was substantial expansion in the 1950s. The main focus was on the promotion of new industry through grants, factory provision, and other assistance. Incentives were slightly higher than in other regions of the United Kingdom and the pool of unemployed skilled and young labour was a further attraction for industrialists. Much new industry was established, especially in the 1960s, so that by the end of the decade one-third of all manufacturing employment was in new projects. Most of the new development took the form of British branch plants, with some American participation. The new light industry, which included synthetic fibres, electronics, and engineering, greatly diversified the industrial structure. Despite greater incentives in the areas of highest unemployment, the new projects located mainly in the east, which offered the advantages of external accessibility, market potential, developed infrastructure, and skilled labour. The new industry was mainly capital-intensive, and increasingly its labour content was inadequate to compensate for redundancies, especially in respect of male employment. The situation deteriorated rapidly in the 1970s, when the violence and political uncertainty were major locational disincentives which accentuated the scarcity of international mobile investment, so that there was little new development. Existing industry, including the important synthetic fibres sector, was adversely affected by competition and the international manufacturing recession. Decline in the core area reduced the level of industrial concentration.

The industrial problem in the Republic was different in that there was comparatively little manufacturing at the time of independence, so that the establishment of a substantial industrial base was required in order to afford badly needed employment and counteract emigration. Policies designed to achieve this aim fell into two main phases, before and after about 1960. Manufacturing in the early 1980s reflected the differing impacts of these two phases.

A strong policy of economic nationalism and protectionism was adopted in the Irish Free State in the early 1930s with the aim of developing a manufacturing sector under Irish control to supply the home market. High tariffs and other trade restrictions were imposed on a very wide range of imported goods. Firms involved in the new industrial development could incorporate only a minority share of foreign ownership. During the thirty years of protectionist policy, manufacturing employment increased by one-half and a significant industrial sector on a factory basis was established. The government objective was that the new manufacturing development should be dispersed throughout the state and in particular outside Dublin, in order to reduce the level of industrial concentration and counteract emigration which was occurring everywhere. Yet trends over the period 1926–61 were at variance with this objective: County Dublin's share of manufacturing employment increased from 36 to 47 per cent; industrialists discouraged from locating there showed a strong preference for the counties adjacent to Dublin and for the major ports; and the employment created in new factories in the less urbanised areas was insufficient to compensate for the decline in handcraft industries that occurred everywhere. Achievements fell farthest behind needs in the west, so that in the 1950s state grants payable to industries establishing there were used as a new incentive and produced some results.

Major change occurred with the adoption of a vigorous programme of open industrial development. Protection was reduced in phases and the movement towards free trade culminated in accession to the European Community in 1973. Export orientation was especially encouraged. Capital grants, major tax concessions, and a variety of other incentives were used to promote manufacturing, mainly through the agency of the Industrial Development Authority. The restrictions on foreign ownership were lifted and a major campaign to attract such industry was commenced. Much of the new development took the form of branch plants of multinational corporations, which were principally American, British, and German. Small industries had a larger Irish participation. Development consisted predominantly of varied light industries, among which engineering was the leading category and electronics constituted a major growth sector. Employment in manufacturing increased from 178,000 in 1961 to a peak of 248,000 in 1980. There was a setback in 1974–5 and greatly increased redundancies occurred in the early 1980s, so that employment had declined to 222,000 by 1983. Older industry was affected by the advent of free trade and technological change, but all sectors suffered the impact of recession. With increasing productivity, however, the volume of output had trebled since 1960 and the contribution of manufacturing to total exports had increased from one-fifth to almost two-thirds in 1983.

A striking reversal of the earlier locational trend in manufacturing industry in the Republic occurred in the period 1961–83. The share of employment in County Dublin declined from 47 to 30 per cent, whereas that in Connacht and the three counties of Ulster increased from 9 to 17 per cent. Decentralisation resulted from official policy, company preferences, and the distribution of redundancies. State policy was to promote proportionately greater rates of growth in the least industrialised regions, principally in the west and midlands. This was implemented through allocation of higher grants to industries in designated areas,[7] provision of advance factories, and encourage-

---

[7] Below, ix, map 108.

ment to firms to locate in such places. Industrial estates were developed at Shannon, Galway, and Waterford. Irrespective of state incentives, the modern branch plants in light manufacturing showed a strong tendency towards dispersion, with many preferring not to locate in the main industrial centres. Thus factories were established in all sizes of towns throughout the state. Comparative decline of the major centres stemmed chiefly from their lower rates of employment creation, but there were also higher job losses in the older industries. Manufacturing decline was greatest in County Dublin, which lost over one-quarter of its industrial labour force in the decade to 1983, but it affected also County Louth and Cork city.

By the early 1980s tourism had become one of Ireland's most important industries. It was a major earner of foreign exchange, though increasingly this was counterbalanced by the numbers of Irish people holidaying abroad. The employment and other effects of tourism were widely spread through the community and interpenetrated with other economic activities, making precise assessment of its impact difficult. An important regional effect was that the parts of the country that had the greatest attraction for tourists tended to be those that were most in need of the employment and income benefits.

Much of the Irish tourist industry had developed since the second world war. It was actively promoted and organised by Bord Fáilte Éireann and the Northern Ireland Tourist Board. Access to the island had been facilitated by the introduction of air and car ferry services. Other factors contributing to growth included greater affluence, more leisure time, better education, and the increase of urban populations. Yet there was a severe setback to tourism in 1969–72 associated with the violence in Northern Ireland; the number of visitors there declined by more than one-half and in the Republic by a quarter. Subsequently a gradual recovery took place, but tourists showed continued reluctance to visit Ireland. Other hindrances included price inflation, economic recession, and competition from other destinations. The numbers of visitors in 1983 were 2.27 million to the Republic and 0.86 million to Northern Ireland, with four-fifths of the revenue being earned in the Republic. The principal sources of visitors were Britain, North America, and continental Europe, which had been the major growth market. The home holiday market was also of major importance to Irish tourism.

The main reasons why people visited Ireland were its scenic and cultural attractions, the relaxed and friendly atmosphere, and ethnic links with the country. The variety of scenery encountered within short distances and the pleasant greenness of the countryside, as well as the grandeur of some areas, contributed to the reputation for scenic attractiveness. Much of the tourism was oriented towards the maritime counties because of the combination of seaside attractions and coastal scenery with the peripheral distribution of the principal uplands and urban areas. Dublin was the single most important focus for tourists, being the main gateway to the country and having the attractions of a capital city. Otherwise the west had the greatest appeal, because of the combination of its physical assets, a long attractive coastline and extensive upland scenery, plus the character of its people, culture, and human landscape. Historic and literary associations and the large number of antiquities and buildings that could be visited had major appeal throughout the country. The opportunities to participate in activities such as angling, equestrian sports, golf, boating, and festivals were an increasingly important attraction for many people. Irish tourism had a major ethnic element, with emigrants returning home on holiday and people of Irish descent visiting relatives and places with ancestral ties. Many visitors from Britain fell into this category and such connections were also important in North American traffic.

The provision of greatly increased amounts and variety of accommodation had been a prerequisite to tourism development. This was facilitated by state incentive grants. The range of accommodation included hotels of different grades, guesthouses, town and country homes, farmhouses, youth hostels, self-catering houses, caravans, and camp sites. Coastal caravan sites were a conspicuous feature in Northern Ireland. Recent expansion was greatest in self-catering accommodation, for reasons of cost and independence, and farmhouse holidays were popular. Growth of second-home ownership, although small compared with many developed countries, reflected increased affluence and mobility. With the greater mobility of tourists, through use of the motor car and also coach tours, accommodation and other facilities had become dispersed more widely throughout the country. Growth of touring holidays, combined with travel to the Mediterranean and other foreign destinations and changing lifestyles, had served to undermine the traditional seaside holiday that had dominated tourism in the past. The marked seasonality of tourism, with half the annual business concentrated in the months of July and August, remained a major operational problem in the provision of accommodation and other sectors of the industry.

Other services were of major economic and social importance and of varied character (table 2). Employment had increased by one-half since 1926, despite the decline in total employment over that period. Huge growth occurred in financial services, principally banking and insurance, and in the professions, chiefly education and medicine. There was substantial expansion in leisure services, public administration, and commerce. Personal service was the exceptional category in which there was major decline; this was attributable mainly to the virtual demise of private domestic service, which more than offset increased employment in hotels, restaurants, and hairdressing. The number in religion had been increasing until the 1950s but subsequently fell as vocations began to decline. The expansion and change in the service

TABLE 2. *Employment structure, 1981*

	Republic of Ireland		Northern Ireland		Ireland	
	Persons	% of total employment	Persons	% of total employment	Persons	% of total employment
Agriculture	182,436	16.0	27,071	5.2	209,507	12.6
Forestry	3,667	0.3	605	0.1	4,272	0.3
Fishing	2,452	0.2	781	0.1	3,233	0.2
Mining	11,120	1.0	1,555	0.3	12,675	0.8
Manufacture	238,144	20.9	117,148	22.3	355,292	21.4
Construction	102,190	9.0	39,322	7.5	141,512	8.5
Utilities	14,434	1.3	9,279	1.8	23,713	1.4
Transport and communication	69,286	6.1	22,941	4.4	92,227	5.5
Commerce	166,143	14.6	72,261	13.8	238,404	14.3
Finance	49,532	4.3	29,201	5.6	78,733	4.7
Public administration and defence	69,393	6.1	65,681	12.5	135,074	8.1
Professions	154,719	13.6	87,223	16.6	241,942	14.6
Personal service	53,146	4.7	18,400	3.5	71,546	4.3
Entertainment and sport	11,301	1.0	6,637	1.3	17,938	1.1
Other industries	9,864	0.9	26,189	5.0	36,053	2.2
Total employment	1,137,827	100.0	524,294	100.0	1,662,121	100.0

industries involved complex processes but resulted mainly from the absolute growth and greater complexity and specialisation in the economy, the social advancement, personal affluence, and changing lifestyles of the population, and the growth in government administration and the public sector in general.

Despite the heterogeneity of the other services, they were essentially urban activities and their spatial pattern was closely related to the distribution of the urban population.[8] The propensity to concentrate in towns was affected by the tendency to choose locations accessible to consumers, and by inter-relationships between the services, which favoured close proximity. There was a distinct hierarchical ordering of centres. The smaller towns were quite closely spaced and provided limited services for the surrounding areas. The larger towns had higher-order services and provided a greater range of functions. They were widely spaced, serving substantial hinterlands. The hierarchical ordering of educational services, for example, meant that the 4,400 primary schools occurred in towns of all sizes and even in the open countryside; the 1,000 second-level schools were located predominantly in towns of medium and larger size; and the smaller number of institutions of further and higher education were concentrated in the larger towns and especially the cities. Specialist medical services required large populations and hinterlands to support them and thus were located in the cities, whereas general practitioners were much more dispersed to serve local needs. In some services there were highly centralised headquarter functions while contact with consumers was maintained through a network of local executive units. Thus in financial services the banking, building society, and insurance headquarters were highly concentrated in Dublin and Belfast, but the many branch offices were located in the medium and larger towns and in city centres and suburbs. Central government administration was concentrated in Dublin and Belfast, but local officers in certain public services such as police and social services were dispersed in relation to the population.

The organisation and spatial distribution of many individual services were affected by the processes of rationalisation and centralisation. Larger and more complex organisations developed in response to the growing demand for services, the economies of large-scale operation, and the improvements in technology and administration. Spatial concentration was facilitated greatly by the technological development and availability of modern means of transport and communication, so that distance became progressively less of a hindrance to contact between supplier and customer. Examples of rationalisation and centralisation of services included merging of commercial banks in the 1960s, closure of small primary schools in rural areas, and replacement of some individual doctors by group practices and health centres. An opposing

---

[8] Below, ix, map 102.

trend towards greater dispersion occurred in some services in response to growth in demand meriting provision in smaller communities, as had occurred recently in accountancy, building societies, and fast food outlets. The overall tendency towards centralisation, however, combined with the greater concentration of population, had led to an increased share of service provision in the larger urban centres and to domination of the service sector by Dublin and Belfast in particular. This dominance of the two leading cities was evident in their complex networks of interrelated office activities.

Some of the locational patterns and processes in service provision were illustrated by the distributive trades or commerce, comprising mainly retailing and wholesaling. This industry was essential to the functioning of the economy and society, and its share of total employment had increased to one-seventh, ranking next only to manufacturing as an economic activity. Hierarchical arrangement dictated that grocery shops and pubs were the most ubiquitous outlets, occurring in all sizes of settlement, while the sale of household durables, clothing, and other high-order goods, varied specialist shops, and wholesaling were more concentrated in the larger towns. People living in smaller communities might get convenience goods locally and travel to the larger centres for other purchases. A notable feature of provincial towns was the extent to which increased volume and range of consumer demand had led to improvement in shopping facilities. With increasing incomes, a diminishing proportion of expenditure was on food, so that growth was proportionately greater in other sectors. Grocery was the form of business most affected by structural and technological change, including greater size of store, greater concentration of ownership under the control of multiple-outlet companies which operated chains of supermarkets and department stores, and growth of self-service retailing and cash-and-carry wholesaling. Self-service had developed first in Belfast and Dublin and then diffused down the urban hierarchy to smaller places and westwards across the country. Because of these trends and their greater impact in the larger centres, many grocery shops closed altogether and those that remained in rural areas were often significantly smaller than their urban counterparts.

THE outstanding feature of territorial organisation in the early 1980s was clearly the existence in Ireland of two separate states, the independent Republic of Ireland, and Northern Ireland forming part of the United Kingdom. One phenomenon generated by the existence of the border was smuggling, the amount and form of which varied with changing price differentials, subsidies, taxes, and controls on individual products; but its extent diminished with accession to the European Community. The operation of the separate policies of two political and administrative systems for sixty years was certain to have had a profound impact on the attitudes and lives of the people. The divergence of institutions and of economic and social policies and measures, whereby the Republic followed an independent course while practices in Northern Ireland were more closely integrated with those of Great Britain, had considerable repercussions on the human geography of the two areas. The differential impact was lessened by the administrative similarities and many strong links between the Republic and Britain which continued after political independence, and by the fact that for several decades the rate of change was slow. Some of the differing policies, such as those relating to agriculture, manufacturing, amenities, and physical planning, found expression in the respective landscapes; others, including those concerned with education, health, welfare, and legal affairs, were less evident visually. Dissimilarities that coincided with the border and were obvious to even the most casual observer included road signposting, public-transport vehicles, telephone kiosks, mail boxes, and police uniforms. Variation in some features, such as in local-authority housing and in road construction, occurred within as well as between the two parts of the island. Some differences, as in the greater tidiness of the cultural landscape of the north-east, were a continuation and sometimes a reinforcement of earlier trends and did not have a precise coincidence with the border. The overall landscape expression of political division was not great, sixty years representing only a short period in the evolution of the Irish landscape.

Developments from the early 1970s served both to accentuate and to reduce differences. Violence had detrimental effects on attitudes, relationships, and social activities within Northern Ireland, but also left marks on the landscape that distinguished Northern Ireland further from the Republic. It led to fortified police stations and other security installations and to much dereliction of property and need for rebuilding. Spatial segregation of residence and activity patterns, based on religion and political loyalty, was further accentuated, and this was reflected visibly in dividing barriers and in the street decorations that marked the territories dominated by each community. The effect of violence on the physical and social fabric was most evident in Belfast. People living along both sides of the political boundary were severely affected by restrictions on cross-border movement, particularly through closure of many unapproved roads. The extent to which the existence of the border increased isolation, retarded development, and separated areas with common problems became the subject of several cross-border studies under the auspices of the European Community. It was the accession of both the United Kingdom and the Republic to the E.C. in 1973 that helped to reduce some differences. Transfer of certain administrative roles from Dublin, Belfast, and London to Brussels resulted in increased alignment of policies and measures. This affected many aspects of the two economies and societies but was most evident in relation to agriculture.

Reform of local government in Northern Ireland in the early 1970s constituted the only major change in Irish regional public administration since the mid 1920s. A single tier of twenty-six local authority areas, known as local government districts, was created to replace the counties, towns, and rural districts. The districts were delimited so that each contained a main population centre (map 13).[9] They varied considerably in area and the populations ranged from 14,000 to 323,000. Following this change, census data were not made available on a county basis.

In the Republic, the organisation of local government remained essentially the same as in the mid 1920s, apart from marginal adjustments in the areas controlled by some authorities. Suggestions had been made that the structures should be reorganised so as to achieve greater efficiency in operation and to effect closer relationships with current population distribution and socio-economic geography. Some new systems of regional organisation had been established by different bodies. These had the common characteristics of being based on functional regions larger than individual counties, and of a conservatism of approach in the general correspondence of their boundaries with existing county boundaries: most of the new regions were in effect groups of counties. Western parts of the country which had been defined as 'congested' by the congested districts board were selected for special incentives towards manufacturing development under the Undeveloped Areas Act, 1952.[10] Extended and renamed the 'designated areas',[11] the former congested districts constituted a region that was also used for other administrative purposes. In 1964 the state was divided into nine planning regions, and although regional development organisations were established later, these were not given any executive functions. The planning regions were adopted for industrial development purposes; other systems of territorial organisation were selected for tourism, health, agriculture, forestry, electricity, transport, courts, police, civil defence, public works, and taxation. Although many of these regional systems were devised by state authorities, there was a lack of coherence between them, hindering the processes of overall regional coordination, planning, and development.

There was great regional diversity within Ireland: imposed on the varied physical landscape there were differing patterns of land use, economic activities, and social characteristics of the people. Yet, apart from the dissimilarities that developed between the Republic and Northern Ireland, the general trend was towards an increasing homogeneity in the landscape. This was a consequence of the introduction and diffusion of modern building and farming techniques, the mass production of standardised goods, greater ease of transport, and the unifying influence of the mass media. One diminishing feature was the regional pattern of traditional house types, many having been abandoned because of emigration or in favour of new dwellings as urbanised housing spread through the countryside.

[9] Below, p. 451.   [10] 1952/1 (22 Jan. 1952).   [11] Below, ix, map 108.

Different parts of the country and different sections of the population had shared unequally in the benefits of increased affluence and modern living. Although conditions in general had improved greatly, geographic imbalance had been inherent in the growth process. The main general regional disparity continued to be that between the eastern and western parts of the country, as was indicated by the correspondence of criteria relating to population change, employment, income, and social conditions. In the Republic, per capita income levels in the northwest, midlands, and western regions were only two-thirds to three-quarters those in the eastern region. Similarly, in Northern Ireland unemployment rates in the urban travel-to-work areas ranged from 17 per cent in Belfast to 40 per cent in Strabane. Yet the regional evidence available for the Republic suggested that by the early 1980s the overall trend was towards greater uniformity in regional economic structure and in the levels of well-being. This must have been related to the diminishing role of agriculture, the spread of manufacturing and its decline in the older centres, and the growth of some service industries and social welfare payments. Superimposed upon the general regional pattern there were considerable local variations in the levels of socio-economic development. This could be seen in the relative rural deprivation of some isolated upland districts in the east and bog margins in the midlands, and within the west the comparative urban affluence of certain places such as Galway, Shannon, and Sligo. Urban growth had associated disadvantages, however, including traffic congestion, housing shortages, crime, pollution, and damage to adjacent rural areas. It was within the cities, and in particular Dublin and Belfast, that the most striking local contrasts existed, relating in particular to economic and social deprivation in the inner city areas. The inner-city problem had been accentuated and brought to greater public attention by industrial decline and population loss. Features of inner-city deprivation included low incomes, high unemployment, poor housing, property dereliction, environmental pollution, and problems of drugs and crime.

A growing awareness of the problems arising from regional disparities and from the detrimental effects on landscape and life of uncontrolled economic development had emerged in both parts of Ireland, together with appreciation of the need for corrective state intervention. After some earlier sporadic development measures, the 1960s saw a higher priority being given to regional planning and development and related physical planning, and in the 1970s to environmental conservation and resource management. Regional policy in Northern Ireland sought to restrict the expansion of Belfast. The specification of a stop line around Belfast was used to restrict urban sprawl and to protect the natural setting of the city. Growth was directed towards towns around Belfast, and development elsewhere was promoted through the designation of key centres. The number of centres for development was increased to twenty-six, comprising the main town in each local government area, under the district towns strategy formulated in 1977. The new town of Craigavon had been developed in the Lurgan–Portadown area as a counter-magnet to Belfast but its growth had fallen short of expectations. In the Republic a new town had arisen at Shannon, associated with the airport and industrial estate there. Virtually new towns developed through the huge expansion of settlements to the west of Dublin, most notably at Tallaght. A comprehensive growth-centre policy, however, was not adopted in the Republic: the emphasis was on a more even and dispersed form of development, and in particular on promoting growth in the west. Western areas were especially favoured in government measures relating to manufacturing and agriculture but also in the development of tourism, fisheries, and forestry. Although there was no coordinated policy, commitment to regional development was more evident in the Republic than in Northern Ireland. Conversely, there was more effective implementation of environmental conservation in Northern Ireland. Concern with the national economic and political difficulties of the 1970s and early 1980s unfortunately distracted attention from the regional dimension. A beneficial by-product of this was to foster self-help and community development. A new concern was with inner-city revitalisation. Although there had been considerable achievements in regional development and control, the need remained for greater integration of development and control measures and for formulation and implementation of coordinated spatial planning, in order to shape more effectively the future geography of Ireland.

Land and people, c.*1983*

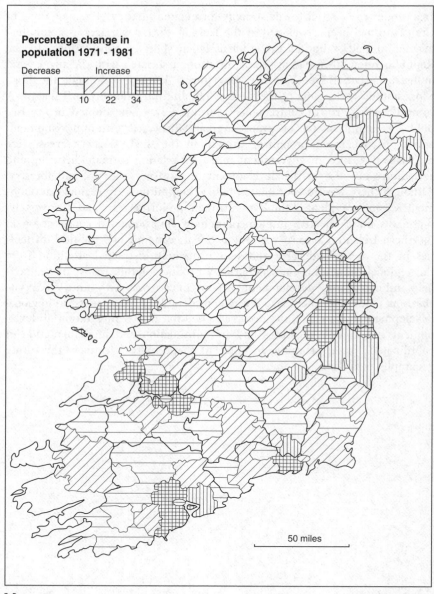

Percentage change in
population 1971 - 1981

Decrease   Increase

                    10   22   34

50 miles

Map 12

D.A. Gillmor

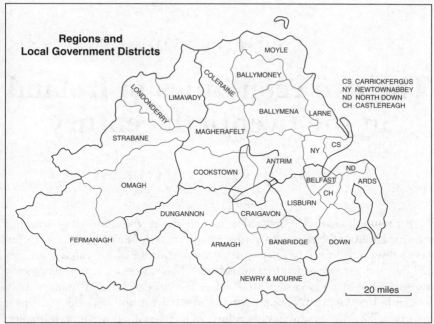

Regions and Local Government Districts

MOYLE

BALLYMONEY

COLERAINE

LIMAVADY

LONDONDERRY

STRABANE

MAGHERAFELT

BALLYMENA

LARNE

CS CARRICKFERGUS
NY NEWTOWNABBEY
ND NORTH DOWN
CH CASTLEREAGH

NY CS

ANTRIM

COOKSTOWN

OMAGH

BELFAST

ND

ARDS

CH

LISBURN

DUNGANNON

CRAIGAVON

FERMANAGH

ARMAGH

BANBRIDGE

DOWN

NEWRY & MOURNE

20 miles

Map 13   D.A. Gillmor

Map 12:
Source: Central Statistics Office, Ireland, *Statistical abstract 1982–1985* (Stationery Office, Dublin, 1986).

Map 13:
Source: Ordnance Survey of Northern Ireland, Belfast, 1983.

CHAPTER XVII

The two economies in Ireland in the twentieth century

D. S. JOHNSON AND LIAM KENNEDY

THE twentieth century witnessed a marked rise in the standard of living of the inhabitants of Ireland. In terms of material comforts, people were between three and four times better off at the beginning of the 1990s than they had been on the eve of the first world war. This sustained rise in incomes is unequalled in the island's history and is the primary fact of modern Irish economic development. The nations of western Europe also enjoyed major increases. The question arises, therefore, as to Ireland's relative performance. Generally, this is thought to have been poor in comparison with other countries of the developed world. Kieran Kennedy, for example, considered the performance of the Republic's economy to have been no more than 'mediocre', arguing that the growth of gross national product (G.N.P.) per capita was 'below that of every European country apart from the U.K.'.[1] Joseph Lee was more dismissive still: 'Irish economic performance has been the least impressive in western Europe, perhaps in all Europe, in the twentieth century.'[2] Some writers take the post-independence Irish economy out of Europe altogether, transplanting it to the Third World. Thus, it is argued, while the appearances may be those of a First World country there are close parallels between Ireland and the evolution of Third World post-colonial societies.[3] For some, the case for Northern Ireland is much the

---

[1] Kieran A. Kennedy, Thomas Giblin, and Deirdre McHugh, *The economic development of Ireland in the twentieth century* (London, 1988), pp 121–2. G.N.P. can be defined as gross domestic product (G.D.P.) together with net property income from abroad. G.D.P. is defined as the total output of goods and services produced within a given country in a particular time period. Both G.N.P. and G.D.P. are indirect measures of economic welfare. Though useful and widely used indicators, they have several shortcomings: in particular, they give no idea of the distribution of income in a society or how this changes through time.

[2] Lee, *Ire. 1912–85*, p. 521.

[3] Frederik Jameson, *Nationalism, colonialism and literature: modernism and imperialism* (Field Day Pamphlet, Derry, 1988). For a critique of such arguments see Liam Kennedy, 'Modern Ireland: post-colonial society or post-colonial pretensions?' in *The Irish Review* (winter 1992–3), pp 107–21.

same; its position has been derided as little better than a Victorian 'work-house economy'.[4]

We dissent from these various interpretations, and their dismal antecedents. In relation to the Irish Free State, later the Republic of Ireland, the general conclusion reached in this chapter may be briefly stated: assessed relative to Europe, which seems the appropriate comparative framework, Ireland's economic performance during the twentieth century was a modal rather than a mediocre experience. Over the whole period 1913–91 the Irish growth rate for gross domestic product (G.D.P.) per capita was only marginally below the average for all the states that in 1991 comprised the European Community. In most subperiods it would seem that Irish growth was actually above the European average. In one decade alone—the 1950s—was Irish growth markedly lower than in western Europe, something that distorts the picture for the century as a whole. Only with respect to demographic change, and emigration in particular, does Ireland differ greatly from its European neighbours.

Before advancing these arguments in detail, we need to refer briefly to the condition of Ireland before the first world war. Contemporary critics, and not only Irish nationalists, argued that Ireland was economically backward, possessed of little industry, and heavily dependent on agriculture and the export of primary products. While there was great unrealised potential—among the people, in the bogs, in the undrained farmlands, in the industries that might have been—the self-evident truth was that 'a nation governed by another nation never does succeed'.[5] Irish underdevelopment, therefore, was in large measure the product of British colonialism. This ideological construct had a wide currency in Irish nationalist circles, where ambivalence towards Ulster, and its apparently deviant economic performance, was most pronounced. 'Ireland failed to industrialise outside of the north-east' was the stock wisdom, which summed up the inevitable record of failure and also disposed of the awkward historical reality of the industrialisation of the Lagan valley.

How valid is this representation? Ireland, was, admittedly, underdeveloped relative to England. But how relevant is such a comparison? England had been the world's first industrial nation. In terms of living standards it had been a world leader throughout the nineteenth century. By this standard, most of Europe, and virtually all of the world, was underdeveloped.

Is it fair to say that Ireland had not industrialised? One has only to note the presence of such internationally successful firms as Harland & Wolff and Workman Clark in shipbuilding, Guinness and Jacob's in the food-and-drink sector, Barbour in linen manufacture, and Mackie's and Sirocco in engineering, to begin to entertain some doubts. Still, these may be the exceptional cases. However, a broader view of the industrial structures reveals that a

---

[4] Bob Rowthorn and Naomi Wayne, *Northern Ireland: the political economy of conflict* (Cambridge, 1988), pp 95–6.
[5] C. S. Parnell in *Hansard 3*, cclxi, 896 (19 May 1881).

good quarter of the Irish workforce in 1911 was engaged in industry. This puts Ireland on the same footing as Sweden, Norway, Portugal, Italy, and the Netherlands, and ahead of Spain, Austria, and all the countries of eastern Europe.[6] Perhaps failure resided in the fact that modern industry had not spread evenly across the island, being concentrated in one region of Ireland? But then, as we know from European economic history, uneven industrial development was a feature of most societies. Far from being anomalous, Ireland conformed to the regional pattern that accompanied the process of industrialisation in Britain and continental Europe.[7]

What of relative living standards? In 1913, with an income per head of 55–60 per cent of the British level, Ireland was very much in the middle rank of the countries of Europe.[8] This is confirmed by an array of indicators that are easier to grasp, perhaps, than figures for national income. Life expectancy at 54 years was slightly above the average for the countries of north-western Europe, and much higher than the levels to be found in southern and eastern Europe. Infant mortality in Ireland was lower than the European average. The proportion of the population in agriculture, at 43 per cent, was the same as the European average. With respect to education, the proportion of the population aged 5 to 14 years and still at school was around 80 per cent, which was one of the highest participation rates in the world.[9] An adequate physical infrastructure is suggested by the fact that the railway mileage, at 1.26 km per inhabitant, exceeded the European norm. There is little doubt, therefore, that Ireland in 1913 lay within rather than outside the European mainstream.

During the first world war Ireland improved its economic position relative to many of the countries of Europe. Technically Ireland was a belligerent country. But as a semi-detached part of the United Kingdom, with no conscription and unenforced wartime economic controls, it received most of the benefits of war without many of the hardships felt by combatant nations elsewhere. The period 1914–20 was one of very considerable prosperity for Irish agriculture. After some initial problems, both linen and shipbuilding prospered under the stimulus of war and postwar demands. True, the second half of 1920 and the year 1921 saw a decline in prosperity from peak levels. None the less, when the political union between Britain and Ireland was being forcibly broken between 1919 and 1921, the Irish economy was prob-

---

[6] Calculated from data in B. R. Mitchell, *European historical statistics, 1750–1970* (London, 1975).

[7] Sidney Pollard, *Peaceful conquest: the industrialization of Europe 1760–1970* (Oxford, 1981); Philip Ollerenshaw, 'Industry' in Liam Kennedy and Philip Ollerenshaw (ed.), *An economic history of Ulster 1820–1939* (Manchester, 1985), pp 62–108.

[8] See D. S. Johnson, 'The economic performance of the independent Irish state' in *Ir. Econ. & Soc. Hist.*, xviii (1991), pp 48–53, and Kennedy, Giblin, & McHugh, *Economic development of Ire.*, pp 14–15.

[9] Peter Flora, Franz Kraus, and Winifred Pfennig, *State, economy and society in western Europe, 1815–1975* (2 vols, Frankfurt and London, 1983–7), ii, ch. 10.

ably better off relative to most European countries than it had been at the outbreak of the war.[10]

Images of the grossly unfulfilled economic potential of Ireland, espoused by nationalist ideologues of late Victorian and Edwardian Ireland, are clearly at variance with the realities of life on the island before and at the time of partition. Indeed modern nationalist scholarship has tended to shift the temporal locus of economic failure from the nineteenth to the twentieth century. A process of modernisation and rapid increases in income per capita during the second half of the nineteenth century, it is argued, resulted in an Ireland in 1900 or 1911 that experienced living standards in advance of many of its European neighbours. Despite starting off with so many advantages, the Irish Free State, followed by the Republic, emerged only to disappoint. With pleasing symmetry, God's chosen race on the Lagan, the Ulster protestants, also lapsed into mediocrity.[11] The conclusion therefore is that Ireland failed, not so much in the nineteenth as in the twentieth century.

Substantial progress in living standards and economic growth between the twin mortality peaks of the famine and the first world war must be acknowledged. But it is important not to overstate the case. The more inflated the view taken of Ireland's economic status on the eve of independence, the better is post-partition Ireland set up for the polemical kill. On the basis of work in progress, we are inclined to revise downwards accepted estimates of annual change in G.D.P. per head from 1.6 per cent to perhaps 1.4 per cent per annum for the period 1841–1913.[12] This is very similar to the growth rates of other western European societies, though it must be admitted at once that any such estimates, and the comparisons based on them, are little better than intelligent conjectures. A slower rate of growth for post-famine Ireland is consistent with the view that the country had a per capita income in 1913, relative to Britain, not of 60 per cent or more as is sometimes suggested, but of 57 per cent or thereabouts.

Let us look now, first in outline terms and then in more detail, at Irish economic performance during the course of the twentieth century. Worldwide, two decades stand out in terms of rapid economic advance. These were the super-growth decades of the 1950s and the 1960s. The Republic, for a variety of reasons, missed out on the first of these, a failure that exerted an enduring influence on its long-term growth performance, whether considered in terms of the twentieth century as a whole or the second half of that century. But, if we consider Irish economic growth with reference to the constituent time periods of the twentieth century, it becomes apparent that the Republic did just about as well as most of its European neighbours in all

[10] Above, vi, 342–51.

[11] Lee, *Ire. 1912–85*, p. 522.

[12] D. S. Johnson and Liam Kennedy, 'Economic growth at the European periphery: Ireland in the 19th and 20th centuries: a modal experience?' (unpublished paper, Q.U.B., 1993).

TABLE 1.   *Average annual rates of growth of G.D.P. per head of population in the countries of the European Community, 1913–91 (%)*

	1913–50	1950–60	1960–91	1913–91
Belgium	1.15	2.02	2.89	1.87
Denmark	1.09	2.62	2.32	2.11
France	1.23	3.58	2.75	2.28
West Germany	0.68	6.05	2.59	2.24
Greece	0.55	4.47	3.68	1.75
Republic of Ireland	0.85	2.09	3.12	1.84
Italy	0.75	5.08	3.24	2.50
Netherlands	1.11	2.94	2.23	2.03
Portugal	0.74	2.26	3.77	1.39
Spain	0.20	4.06	3.04	2.05
United Kingdom	0.73	2.14	2.03	1.46
European Community	0.78	3.92	2.61	2.03

Sources: Paul Bairoch, 'The main trends in national economic disparities since the industrial revolution' in Paul Bairoch and Maurice Levy-Leboyer (ed.), *Disparities in economic development since the industrial revolution* (New York and London, 1981), p. 10; United States Department of Commerce, *Statistical abstract of the United States, 1990* (Washington, D.C., 1990); O.E.C.D., *National accounts: main aggregates, 1, 1960–89* (Paris, 1991), pp 19–20; O.E.C.D., *Main economic indicators* (Paris, 1992), pp 174, 180.

time periods, save one. Thus, between 1913 and 1950 growth in G.D.P. per head in Ireland was little different from that of western Europe as a whole (table 1).[13] In the subperiod 1929–50 the comparative story is much the same. It should be borne in mind of course that most estimates of G.D.P. for most countries prior to the second world war are suspect. Comparative growth rates for the first half of the century or, for that matter, for the century as a whole should be treated with caution. There are grounds, however, for allowing greater credibility to the postwar comparisons. Taking the three decades that followed the mid century crisis, we find that Irish growth performance compared more than favourably with that of most of its European neighbours.[14] It is true that the G.D.P. measure gives an exaggerated view of economic progress during the 1980s, as it does not make allowance for either the large outflow of profits from multinational companies or for interest payments to

[13] An alternative set of growth rates for European countries for the period 1913–50 may be found in Angus Maddison, *The world economy in the twentieth century* (Paris, 1989). While the figures for certain countries depart somewhat from those of Bairoch (used in table 1), the overall picture for western Europe is little affected by the choice of data set.
[14] Growth rates for the period 1960–91 are based on the linear trend in the logarithms of the original G.D.P. data, thereby taking into account the values for all years (rather than simply those of the base year and the terminal date).

foreign creditors. Both sets of outflows were unusually large in this subperiod, accounting for at least 10 per cent of G.D.P. at the end of the 1980s. As against this, as we argue in a moment, the high dependency ratio in Irish society had an opposite effect: serving to depress G.D.P. per capita and bias international comparisons against the Irish Republic and countries like it.

On the basis of G.D.P. growth indicators, the Irish performance after 1960 comes close to the top of the European league—well ahead of the older industrialised countries such as Germany, France, and Britain, and comparable to the faster-growing economies of the European periphery. Northern Ireland, it will be noted, is not included in the table, but broadly similar points would apply for much of the century. Taking the long view (1913–91), therefore, the Irish growth rate appears to have been about 10 per cent below the European average. Bearing in mind the uncertainty that attaches to national income estimates for the base year of 1913 and the problem of linking data from different sources and time periods, as well as the crudity of exchange rate conversions, the safest conclusion to draw is that Ireland was at, or close to, the modal experience of the countries of the European Community during the twentieth century.

As well as looking at growth in G.D.P. over time, it is instructive to view G.D.P. per capita at distinct moments in time. Table 2 does this in comparative form for Ireland, north and south, relative to the average for the countries that came to make up the twelve-member European Community. This suggests that the Republic enhanced its position during the first half of the century but slipped behind badly during the 1950s. There was little change in its relative position during the 1960s. After the Republic's entry into the E.C. in 1973, a process of catching-up ensued, with particularly strong gains being made during the late 1980s and early 1990s. In the case of Northern Ireland the long-run decline relative to the European norm appears to have been greater, though interestingly the two economies in Ireland seemed to hold the same relative positions in 1992.

Measuring economic welfare by reference to G.D.P., for reasons mentioned earlier, inflates the Irish performance. However, an alternative and more precise indicator of living standards—net disposable per capita income—also suggests some catching-up. The economic gap between Ireland (north and south) and the neighbouring island of Britain narrowed during the course of the century, the convergence being particularly rapid in the period since 1960. This may seem less than impressive in view of the secular decline of the British economy. But when compared with neighbouring European countries there is also evidence of convergence: net disposable income per capita in the Republic grew from 62 per cent of the E.C. level in 1960 to 70 per cent in 1991.[15] The

---

[15] Eurostat, *National accounts, 1960–85* (Luxembourg, 1987), pp 102–3; *National accounts, 1970–91* (1993), pp 50–51.

case of Northern Ireland is more difficult to interpret, both because of transfer payments from the British exchequer and because it has been a society at war for a quarter of a century. In terms of the material living standards experienced by the people of the province, however, there is no doubt that these moved closer to British standards. But compared to west European norms, there was some slippage over time.

The evidence of table 2, if taken at face value, suggests a significant but hardly catastrophic decline in living standards in Ireland, north and south, relative to E.C. countries during the century. The issue of economic performance can be approached from another angle, however, building on the data presented in table 2. Dependency ratios and participation rates vary widely between countries and over time. We can form a sharper, though by no means wholly satisfactory, impression of the relative productive performance of the western European economies by controlling for these factors. In

TABLE 2. *Comparative G.D.P. per head of population in selected years*

	R.I./E.C. (ec = 100)		N.I./E.C. (ec = 100)	
1913	84		92	
1950	86		102	
1960	72	62	84	79
1973		60		77
1992		76		76

Sources: G.D.P. figures (column 1) for the Irish Republic and the European Community for the years 1913, 1950, and 1960 are from Bairoch, 'Main trends in national economic disparities', p. 10. O.E.C.D. data are used for the later period and are not directly comparable with Bairoch's values (see column 2). The sources for these data are O.E.C.D., *National accounts: main aggregates 1, 1960–89*, p. 130, and O.E.C.D., *Main economic indicators*, pp 196, 202. In the interests of geographical, and hence economic, consistency through time, East Germany is excluded from the E.C. calculations for 1992. The Northern Ireland values are calculated on the assumption that G.D.P. per capita was 60% of the U.K. level in 1913, 67.6% in 1950 and 1960, and 77.6% in 1992. See Bairoch, p. 10 (cited above), Kennedy, Giblin, & McHugh, *Economic development of Ire.*, p. 124, and Graham Gudgin and Geraldine O'Shea, *Unemployment forever? the Northern Ireland economy in recession and beyond* (Belfast, 1993), p. 128.

other words, from the view point of productivity comparisons, it is helpful to recalculate the data in table 2 by reference to the workforce rather than the population as a whole. This is easier said than done. Because there were extreme inconsistencies in the inclusion or exclusion of women in agriculture (and to a lesser extent in services) across the European censuses, and also within individual country censuses over time, the relationship between the size of the workforce and the size of the population presents a problem. This is especially important for countries with large agrarian sectors, such as Ireland, Spain, or Greece. There is also the problem of unemployment and underemployment, for which no reliable comparative data exist for the first half of the century. So, for the years 1913 and 1950, we have simply weighted G.D.P. per capita by the share of the population aged 15–64 (using information from the censuses of 1911 and 1951 respectively). The approach is a little rough but sufficient for the task. For 1960, 1973, and 1991, we have used employment rates as the appropriate weights. There was substantial growth in part-time working in Europe after 1973, and because its incidence varied greatly between European countries we have, in addition, adjusted the 1991 employment data to take this factor into account.[16] (The assumption used here and elsewhere in the chapter is that two part-time jobs were the equivalent of one full-time job.) The perspective offered by table 3 yields

TABLE 3. *Comparative G.D.P. per capita of population, adjusted for differences in employment rates: selected years*

	R.I./E.C. (ec = 100)		N.I./E.C. (ec = 100)	
1913	87		99	
1950	95		107	
1960	75	64	90	84
1973		64		81
1992		87		77

Sources: G.D.P. per capita values: as in table 2. The weights for age structure and employment rates are calculated from Mitchell, *European hist. statistics*, and O.E.C.D., *Historical statistics, 1960–90* (Paris, 1992). The weights for Northern Ireland are derived from the censuses of population, the *Northern Ireland digest of statistics* (H.M.S.O., Belfast, various dates), and the *Northern Ireland annual abstract of statistics* (Belfast, 1991).

[16] The breakdown of full-time and part-time jobs is from Eurostat, *Labour force survey: results 1989* (Luxembourg, 1991), pp 112–13. See also Northern Ireland Economic Council, *Part-time employment in Northern Ireland* (Belfast, 1992).

findings that, at first sight, may appear surprising: not only supporting but extending the conclusions emerging from table 1 above. To summarise drastically, table 3 indicates that the Republic's relative position in Europe was maintained up to mid century, and that there were then dramatic gains in productivity during the period 1960–91. The Irish propensity to demand children as well as conventional economic goods also served to obscure the relative strength of Northern Ireland's productive performance, though this is less true of the period since 1973. In 1992 Northern Ireland was not only lagging behind Europe but also behind the Republic. On a more general point, it could be said that one of the unintended consequences of the natalist streak in Irish culture has been to bias international comparisons of Irish productive performance in a downward direction, at least when conventional measures such as G.D.P. per capita are used. But, it may be objected, if Hibernia could not find a living for all the children of the nation, is this not in itself a measure of the country's failure? Some hold it is the greatest indictment of all.[17]

There is no doubt that there was a problem of surplus labour throughout the century. Unemployment and underemployment were high during the interwar years, with statistics on unemployment almost certainly underestimating the scale of the problem. During the 1950s the rate of unemployment climbed higher. Despite high levels of economic growth between 1960 and 1992, the unemployment rate more than doubled. Thus by the winter of 1992 some 300,000 people in the Republic were out of work. This fourth sector of the economy—the reserve army of the unemployed—greatly exceeded the numbers engaged in agriculture and was virtually the same size as the country's industrial workforce. Arising from the same problems of surplus labour, emigration was a persistent feature of Irish life: moderate for the 1920s, low during the 1930s as emigration outlets contracted in North America and in Britain, and massive during the 1940s and especially the 1950s (table 4). Only during the exceptional decade of the 1970s was there a net inflow of people, the first sustained immigration since 1700. The 1980s witnessed a fresh surge of emigration. The census of 1991 confirmed what was apparent to contemporaries and was set to music by the Saw Doctors, an internationally acclaimed rock band from the west of Ireland. A new generation of young people was leaving, travelling on the N17 and other roadways out of rural and small-town Ireland.[18] The destinations were Britain,

---

[17] Raymond Crotty, *Ireland in crisis: a study in capitalist colonial undevelopment* (Dingle, 1986), pp 1–2.

[18] The allusion is to the lyric 'N17', written and performed by the Saw Doctors. This work conveys both the pain and the sense of adventure of leaving the west of Ireland, to live on 'foreign soil'. Indicative of changing times, the means of emigration is by air, not sea, and the title of the album, released in 1991, suggests the changing cultural influences on the postwar generation of Irish youth (*If this is rock'n'roll, I want my old job back*).

TABLE 4. *The components of population change (births, deaths, and net migration) for each decade, 1911–91*

(*a*) Republic of Ireland (rates per 1,000 population)

	Births	Deaths	Net migration	Population change
1911–21	20.8	16.2	−6.0	−1.4
1921–31	20.1	14.5	−10.9	−5.3
1931–41	19.3	14.2	−3.1	+2.0
1941–51	22.1	13.9	−9.3	−1.1
1951–61	21.2	12.0	−14.1	−4.9
1961–71	21.8	11.6	−4.5	+5.7
1971–81	21.6	10.5	+4.5	+15.6
1981–91	17.0	9.1	−5.6	+2.3

(*b*) Northern Ireland (rates per 1,000 population)

	Births	Deaths	Net migration	Population change
1911–21	23.0	17.6	−4.8	+0.6
1921–31	21.8	15.0	−8.0	−1.2
1931–41	19.9	14.4	−1.9	+3.6
1941–51	22.4	12.4	−3.6	+6.4
1951–61	21.4	10.9	−6.6	+3.9
1961–71	22.3	10.7	−3.8	+7.8
1971–81	17.8	10.8	−6.7	+0.3
1981–91	17.4	9.9	−4.8	+2.7

Source: Liam Kennedy, *People and population change: a comparative study of population change in Northern Ireland and the Republic of Ireland* (Dublin and Belfast, 1994), p. 23.

continental Europe, and North America. Back home, an earlier historic pattern, that of population implosion, was being re-created from a combination of the 'new emigration' and (an altogether novel development) a rapidly falling birth rate.

It is helpful to place these economic-demographic problems in a European comparative setting. Table 5 reveals, somewhat surprisingly perhaps, that growth in employment has been generally muted in western Europe in recent decades. Moreover, the divergence, oft-remarked in the Irish case, between growth in real product and growth in employment holds true for other countries also. Thus, among the countries of the E.C., while real G.D.P. more than doubled between 1960 and 1991, the corresponding increase in employment was a mere 5 per cent. In fact, seven out of the eleven countries

TABLE 5.   *Total employed population of the countries of the European Community, 1960–90*

	1960	1990	% increase
	(1000s)		
Belgium	3,359	3,539	5.0
Denmark	2,006	2,328	16.0
France	18,595	20,417	10.0
West Germany	25,954	26,073	0.0
Greece	3,386	3,596	6.0
Republic of Ireland	1,046	1,071	2.0
Italy	20,269	20,489	1.0
Netherlands	4,162	5,271	27.0
Portugal	3,290	4,342	32.0
Spain	11,353	12,276	8.0
United Kingdom	23,660	23,693	0.0
European Community	117,080	123,095	5.0

The full-time equivalents for 1990 are calculated using weights derived from data on full-time and part-time employment contained in Eurostat, *Labour force survey: results 1989* (Luxembourg, 1991).
Sources: O.E.C.D., *Labour force statistics, 1962–82* (Paris, 1984); O.E.C.D., *Historical statistics, 1960–90* (Paris, 1992).

shown above registered a net addition to employment of under 10 per cent over the three decades. Ireland was less of a special case than is sometimes imagined.

The point is all the stronger if we concentrate attention on employment change in the non-agricultural sectors. Obviously, given the natural orientation of Irish agriculture towards low-intensity farming in terms of labour inputs, there was no hope of stabilising, still less creating new jobs in the primary sector. During the second quarter of the century, as table 6 shows, the Irish Free State compared, more or less, with other European countries. What is most striking perhaps is that for the later period the Republic's experience of creating jobs outside agriculture corresponded to the mean for the Community as a whole. The performance was better in fact than that of most of the European partners. The decade of the 1950s, as mentioned earlier, was a deviation from the longer-term experience of Irish society during the course of the century.

What then of the abnormally high unemployment and emigration rates so characteristic of Ireland? These appear anomalous only if increases in population are expected to translate naturally into increases in employment. But

TABLE 6. *Percentage increase in employment in the non-agricultural sectors (industry and services) among countries of the European Community*

	c.1925–51	1951–61	1960–90
Belgium	7	15	12
Denmark	63	13	34
France	6	11	34
West Germany	6*	32	13
Greece	38	20	88
Republic of Ireland	28	−7	39
Italy	32	22	37
Netherlands	35	15	34
Portugal	2	12	95
Spain	6	41	56
United Kingdom	15	7	2
European Community	16	19	38

* refers to all Germany.
Sources: For the 1920s to the 1950s, Mitchell, *European hist. statistics*, pp 153–63; for 1960, O.E.C.D., *Labour force statistics, 1962–82*; for 1990, O.E.C.D, *Hist. statistics, 1960–90*; Eurostat, *Labour force survey: results 1989.*

there is no reason to expect that an increase in population will lead to the provision of sufficient jobs to absorb the resulting increase in the labour force. This happened to be the case in western Europe during the era of super-growth, but it was not true of the interwar period or of the nineteenth century. It was never true in Ireland's case. As in earlier periods, growing labour forces in the 1970s and 1980s were accommodated through mounting unemployment, underemployment, and migration. Spain and Ireland exemplify these responses. In Spain and Ireland, two countries that had both experienced rapid population increase, there was mass unemployment and large-scale emigration during the 1980s.

The popular notion that a link existed between high population growth in Ireland and subsequent unemployment and out-migration has been questioned.[19] However, some simple correlations, based on the recent experience of E.C. countries (see table 7) would suggest that common-sense reasoning on these issues has something to commend it. There is also some suggestion in the table that unemployment and emigration acted as substitutes for each other, which would also seem to fit the Irish and the Northern Ireland experiences, during the 1930s and the 1980s in particular. What appears to have been happening in the case of the two economies in Ireland, and the Community countries more generally during the later twentieth century, was

[19] Lee, *Ire. 1912–85*, p. 517.

TABLE 7. *Demographic change and the surplus labour problem within the European Community: some simple correlations*

Population change 1960–90 and unemployment rate in 1990:	R = 0.62
Fertility in 1970 and unemployment rate in 1991:	R = 0.50
Migration rate in 1988 and unemployment rate in 1993	R = −0.19

Luxembourg, because of its tiny size, was excluded from the analysis.
Source: O.E.C.D., *Hist. statistics, 1960–90*; O.E.C.D., *Economic outlook* (1991); O.E.C.D., *Main economic indicators* (1992); Eurostat, *Demographic statistics* (Brussels, 1990); *Eurostatistics* (1992).

that expanding labour forces were being accommodated, not through an equivalent expansion of employment, but through increasing unemployment. In 1991 unemployment in the E.C. stood at four times the 1971 level.

So far, our exercise in reinterpretation has been conducted with broad brushstrokes. To explore these ideas further, to introduce more light and shade into the picture, it is necessary to pursue a detailed or disaggregated approach. We use the conventional classification of the economy into three sectors—agriculture, industry, and services—as our organising principle. This is partly a matter of convenience: social scientists would accept immediately that the boundaries between these economic categories are far from watertight and that the tripartite division captures only roughly the complexity of economic activity as it unfolds in time. The analysis of the agricultural, industrial, and service sectors is preceded by an exploration of the economic role of the state. Though most government employment is concentrated in the services sector, the effects of government activity ramify through the economy and the society as a whole.

The period 1920–22 saw the fracturing of the United Kingdom and the partition of Ireland, with separate governments being set up north and south of the newly created border. The economic effects of partition were probably slight.[20] Certainly they were less significant than the other economic forces, national and international, that were operating on the two parts of the island throughout the twentieth century. In some ways partition enabled the two new governments to pursue more easily their differing economic policies, free from worries about how these might be received in the other part of the island. In the case of Northern Ireland this meant following policies determined by Westminster. Even had the province's government wished to adopt

[20] D. S. Johnson, *The interwar economy of Ireland* (Dundalk, 1985), pp 6–7.

policies that were radically different from those in Britain—which it did not—
its powers were severely circumscribed by the government of Ireland act of
1920.[21] In particular, it had no control over the major sources of revenue,
customs and excise, and income tax. Its room for manoeuvre was further
limited by the decision to maintain parity with Britain in important areas of
social service provision—old-age pensions, unemployment pay, and sickness
benefits in particular. These fixed commitments, coupled with revenues for
the province's government that were lower than expected owing to the postwar depression, inevitably curtailed expenditure on such things as aid to
industry or investment in the economic and social infrastructure. Only with
increased subventions from Westminster, which was largely a post-1945 phenomenon, was the Stormont government able to pursue a more active role in
economic development.

The Irish Free State, on the other hand, had plenary fiscal powers. In so
far as the new government had any economic, as distinct from political,
ideology it was that expressed in Arthur Griffith's 'The Sinn Féin policy'.
Griffith had one essential policy idea: that an Irish state should protect its
native industries. 'If an Irish manufacturer cannot produce an article as
cheaply as an English or other foreigner, only because his foreign competitor
has larger resources at his disposal, then it is the first duty of the Irish nation
to accord protection to that Irish manufacturer.'[22] Griffith went on to warn
Irish manufacturers against excessive profits under such sheltered conditions.
But this was simply a pious hope. This policy of import substitution was
the one pursued during the first forty or so years of independence—faint-
heartedly at first, with much vigour after 1932, and with waning confidence
during the 1950s.

Despite its fiscal powers, the new Irish Free State was slow to develop
anything like an independent monetary policy. This reflected the realities of
the period. Ireland was a net exporter of capital as well as labour to the
United Kingdom; moreover, in the 1920s it was still the norm for smaller
states to use the currencies of larger ones (which in turn used gold as backing
for their own currencies). Accordingly, the banking commission of 1926
recommended that Irish legal tender should continue to be linked to sterling.
The currency act of 1927[23] established a separate Irish currency backed by
gold and sterling, and ruled that the Irish pound should be equal to the
pound sterling. Control of the legal tender money supply was placed in the
hands of a currency commission.

A second banking commission established in 1934 endorsed the link with
sterling, but in a bid to exercise control over the commercial banks (whose

[21] Above, pp 163–4, 203–5.
[22] Arthur Griffith, 'The Sinn Féin policy' published as an appendix to *The resurrection of Hungary* (Dublin, 1918), p. 146.
[23] 1927/32 (20 Aug. 1927).

assets were for the most part held in the United Kingdom) recommended the creation of a central bank in place of the currency commission. This was acted on in 1942, with a new central bank becoming responsible for legal-tender issue. The bank could also take deposits from the commercial banks and act as a clearing agency for them, although it did not act as a banker for the government itself. However, the central bank was slow to exercise its powers either in respect of interest rates or the reserves of the commercial banks. It was only in the later 1950s when the latter had begun to experience liquidity problems that the central bank began to offer informal advice concerning the desirable ratio between net external assets and domestic deposit liabilities; the advice became more formal from the mid 1960s.[24]

It is important to note that both the Irish Free State and Northern Ireland inherited from the British an apparatus of government and state institutions that were highly developed. A social insurance scheme covering health, unemployment, and old-age pensions was already in existence and could be built on, if desired. There was an efficient, centrally controlled educational system. The institutions and traditions for a police force were deeply laid. Two popular state agencies, the congested districts board and the department of agriculture and technical instruction, were in place with powers to intervene in rural development.[25] From the viewpoint of public finances in the Irish Free State, this institutional inheritance was a mixed blessing. While it represented continuity as well as socially beneficial forms of intervention, it also meant that the fledgling state had to assume burdensome financial commitments. Not the least of these was a host of relatively expensive civil servants and other public employees whose salaries had been fixed at British levels. In the years before 1914, though popular opinion would have been reluctant to acknowledge the fact, government expenditure in Ireland had been financed in part by subventions from the British treasury.[26] After independence, this was no longer an option for the Irish Free State. Even in the case of Northern Ireland, the subsidies were niggardly and given only grudgingly.

One result of the British inheritance, and the object of adverse criticism from contemporaries,[27] was that government taxation and spending, and therefore the role of the state in society, was relatively large in both parts of Ireland from the beginning. Thus, in 1926 in the Irish Free State, central government revenue and expenditure accounted for around 18 per cent of

---

[24] See M. O'Donoghue, 'Monetary policy' in J. A. Bristow and A. A. Tait (ed.), *Economic policy in Ireland* (Dublin, 1968), pp 86–101; Kieran Kennedy and Brendan Dowling, *Economic growth in Ireland: the experience since 1947* (Dublin, 1975), pp 192, 224.

[25] Above, vi, 87–91, 282–7, 531–2.

[26] *Final report by her majesty's commissioners appointed to inquire into the financial relations between Great Britain and Ireland* [C 8262], H.C. 1896, xxxiii; see also above, vi, 482–8.

[27] Darrell Figgis, *The economic case for Irish independence* (Dublin, 1920), pp 14–17, for example.

G.N.P., a ratio exceeded only in Belgium and the United Kingdom. It is difficult to compute comparable figures for Northern Ireland in this period but there is little doubt that public expenditure levels were high there too.

The role of the state in Irish society continued to expand during the course of the twentieth century, driven by a variety of social changes—the shift from rural to urban living, the increasing visibility of unemployment and other social ills, the mobilisation of interest groups such as trade unions and farmers' associations—and above all, perhaps, by social developments on the neighbouring island. An enlarged role meant that public sector expenditure and employment rose over time, both in the north and the south. The social and economic programmes of the Fianna Fáil administrations of the 1930s enlarged further the role of the state. By the end of the 'economic war' in 1938, total public expenditure was equal to 30 per cent of G.N.P. in the Irish Free State, as compared to 24 per cent in 1926; and the public debt, which was zero at independence, had grown significantly.[28]

Public expenditure shifted on to a higher plane in the aftermath of the second world war and showed steady, if moderate, expansion over the following two decades. Thus expressed as a percentage of G.N.P., public expenditure rose from a level of 32 per cent in 1949/50 to 43 per cent in 1972/3. In the wake of the oil crisis of 1973–4 and worldwide deflationary pressures, the proportion jumped to 51 per cent in 1974. The following decade witnessed explosive growth, with public expenditure reaching the equivalent of 70 per cent of G.N.P. by 1983.[29]

During the 1950s and the 1960s budgetary deficits on current account in the Republic were normally the equivalent of less than 1 per cent of G.N.P. But an almost Gladstonian commitment to good national housekeeping evaporated during the 1970s. In the recessionary year of 1974 the ratio of budget deficit to G.N.P. climbed to 3 per cent. This almost trebled during the next ten years, reaching 8 per cent in 1985.[30] The gap between the expenditure of the Irish state and its receipts from taxation and other sources had to be met from borrowing, which was inevitably reflected in rising public debt. Government debt rose appreciably during the 1950s and was fairly stable—fluctuating around a level of 65 per cent of G.N.P. between 1960 and 1973. Thereafter, the debt burden grew alarmingly rapidly, and had assumed Third World proportions by 1985 when it measured the equivalent of 137 per cent of Irish G.N.P.[31] With more than 40 per cent of the debt in the hands of foreign investors during the early 1980s, interest payments abroad

---

[28] J. W. O'Hagan, 'An analysis of the relative size of the government sector: Ireland 1926–52' in *Econ. & Soc. Rev.*, xii (1980), pp 17–35.

[29] Ibid., pp 17–35; Central Statistics Office (C.S.O.), *National income and expenditure* (Dublin, relevant years).

[30] Calculated from budget statements and Central Bank of Ireland reports.

[31] Calculated from Central Bank of Ireland reports.

represented a major drain on the economy. Further borrowing became necessary, to pay the service charges on earlier borrowings. The future welfare of
the Irish people could not be mortgaged indefinitely, of course. Control of
government expenditure was tightened, albeit belatedly, after 1987. Luckily,
an improving international economic environment, with lower interest rates
and stronger economic growth, took some of the sting out of an otherwise
painful adjustment. By 1992 the major crisis facing the public sector was not
the size of the budget deficit—now reduced to (the equivalent of) 2.5 per
cent of G.N.P. Nor was it the cost of servicing past borrowings. Both were
still significant problems. But the economic and political skyline was dominated by a singular sight: mass unemployment on a scale hitherto unparalleled
in the history of the Irish state. When on 1 January 1993, the Republic was
inducted into the single European market, it brought with it an endowment
of 300,000 unemployed Irish men and women who were dependent on the
state for a livelihood.[32]

There are points of contrast as well as similarity between the evolution
of the public sector in Northern Ireland and the Irish Free State/Irish Republic. The government of Northern Ireland aspired to maintain parity with
the Westminster parliament in major areas of social welfare provision. The
rationale for this step-by-step emulation of Westminster policies was primarily political: the Ulster unionist population saw no reason why it should
accept lower standards of social benefits than its compatriots in Britain. The
difficulty was that Northern Ireland's expenditure needs were high relative
to its income and, in any case, income per capita was low by comparison with
other British regions. During the economically depressed interwar years the
dilemma was especially acute. What the Northern Ireland government
sought, therefore, was subsidies from the British exchequer that would allow
Stormont not only to maintain British levels of social expenditure but also to
bring health and welfare services in the province up to national standards. In
1942, in recognition of Northern Ireland's contribution to the war effort, this
principle was effectively conceded.[33] This formed the basis of the increased
public expenditure in the province after the war.

The reforms embodied in the postwar British welfare state, encompassing
health, education, and income support, were quickly extended to Northern
Ireland. In 1950 spending by the Stormont government was the equivalent of
21 per cent of the area's G.D.P.[34] This, however, is an underestimate as it

---

[32] Some 300,000, in round figures, were *registered* as being out of work. The live register
tends to give a higher total than that revealed by the periodic labour force surveys conducted
across the European Union. Thus a minority of those registered as unemployed may not have
been genuinely seeking work.

[33] R. J. Lawrence, *The government of Northern Ireland: public finance and public services,
1921–1964* (Oxford, 1965), pp 69–70.

[34] Calculated from K. S. Isles and Norman Cuthbert, *An economic survey of Northern Ireland*
(Belfast, 1957), pp 454–5, and *Ulster Year Book 1953* (Belfast, 1953).

does not reflect adequately the extent to which Northern Ireland benefited from transfer payments and services provided by central government in Britain. (This means, incidentally, that direct comparisons with public expenditure ratios in the Republic can be misleading.) These financial supports expanded further during the 1950s and 1960s. The really spectacular growth in public expenditure, and hence in the role of the state in northern society, came about in the two decades after the prorogation of Stormont and the imposition of direct rule in 1972.

Any remaining notions of a relationship between public revenue and spending were abandoned. Central government expenditure surged forward. It rose to just over half (52 per cent) of the size of Northern Ireland's G.D.P. in 1977, peaking at 61 per cent in 1984, in the aftermath of the depression of the early 1980s. It was still slightly above 50 per cent at the end of the decade. Bearing in mind that the ratio does not include capital expenditure by the state—in 1984, for example, the inclusion of capital expenditure would have produced a ratio in excess of 70 per cent of G.D.P.—we gain some idea of the pervasive role of the state in Northern Ireland life.[35] But unlike the case of the Irish Republic, where it was necessary to resort to heavy borrowing to meet budget deficits, Northern Ireland could rely on free transfers from the British exchequer—the equivalent of 25 per cent of the north's G.D.P. in the early 1980s—to finance the massive increases in public expenditure programmes.

It is possible, despite the obvious immediate benefits conferred by these subsidies and income transfers, that the emergence of a disproportionately large public sector at the regional level, whose size was independent of Northern Ireland's tax base, may have had some adverse consequences. It has been argued, for instance, that the public sector siphoned off potential entrepreneurs, that it cushioned Northern Ireland industry against market disciplines, thereby inhibiting innovation and adaptation, and more generally that it contributed to the creation of a dependency culture. Whether this was so or not, one thing seems clear: given the degree of deindustrialisation during the 1970s and 1980s, the expansion of the public sector was essential to the shoring up of employment and living standards. By 1990, four out of every ten jobs in Northern Ireland were located in the public sector, a higher proportion than in the Republic or Britain.

WHILE state policies and institutions affected the evolution of all sectors of the economy, their performance was moulded primarily by market forces. To consider the agricultural sector first, the prices of Irish produce were determined on the highly competitive British market. The quarter-century before

---

[35] Calculated from Northern Ireland, *Annual abstract of statistics* and *Ulster Year Book*, relevant years. See also Victor Hewitt, 'The public sector' in R. I. D. Harris, C. W. Jefferson, and J. E. Spencer (ed.), *The Northern Ireland economy* (London, 1990), pp 353–77.

1920 was something of a golden age for commercial farmers in Ireland, with prices rising gently but cumulatively from the late 1890s and showing explosive growth during the years of the first world war. Farm incomes expanded; rents and land annuity payments fell in real terms, though for cottiers and smallholders limited marketed surpluses meant only weak gains from rising prices. Agricultural prices fell sharply from their inflated scarcity levels in 1920 as the European and North American economies adjusted to peacetime conditions. By 1923 prices were only half the level of three years earlier.[36] Apart from brief rallies in 1924 and between 1927 and 1929, the trend was downwards during the whole interwar period. In response to falling prices, the volume of net agricultural output in the Irish Free State fell, so that by 1929—on the eve of the world depression—output was 4 per cent below the level of 1913.[37] Still, over the same period, the permanent farm labour force had fallen by 10 per cent, thus indicating a small gain in labour productivity. During the 1920s the Free State's export performance on the British market compared well with its main European competitor, Denmark. In egg production, for example, the Irish share of the British market fell from 21.7 per cent to 18.5 per cent between 1924 and 1929, but in the case of Denmark the fall was even greater, from 35.5 per cent to 25.5 per cent. In the butter trade, over the same period, the Irish share of the British market showed a marginal gain from 8.2 per cent to 8.5 per cent, while that of Denmark slipped a little from 36.5 per cent to 35.4 per cent.[38]

The decade of the 1930s was a period of crisis in agriculture. Worldwide economic depression, exacerbated in the case of the Irish Free State by the economic war with Britain, caused a fall in agricultural prices of more than a third between 1929/30 and 1934/5. While there was some recovery thereafter, as late as 1938/9 prices were still 14 per cent below the levels of a decade earlier. Irish exports, particularly of cattle, fell catastrophically. The decline was remarkable for its swiftness and depth: in 1934 the value of cattle exports was one-third that of 1931. Despite collapsing prices and exports, policy changes that involved fostering domestic production of cereals, sugar, and other tillage crops had the effect of keeping up the volume of net agricultural output. This fell by only 4 per cent during the 1930s, roughly in line with the contraction in the farm labour force.[39]

As in the case of the Irish Free State, the prices facing Northern Ireland farmers during the 1920s were determined by conditions on the British and

[36] Calculated from Northern Ireland, *Statistical abstract 1931* (1931).
[37] Calculated from R. O'Connor and C. Guiomard, 'Agricultural output in the Free State area before and after independence' in *Ir. Econ. & Soc. Hist.*, xii (1985), pp 89–97; Department of Industry and Commerce, Saorstát Éireann, *Agricultural statistics, 1847–1926: reports and tables* (Dublin, 1928); and the *Statistical abstract* for Ireland, 1931–40.
[38] Calculated from the *Annual statement of the trade of the United Kingdom* (years 1924–30).
[39] Calculated from O'Connor & Guiomard, 'Agricultural output', pp 89–97, and the *Statistical abstract* for Ireland, 1931–40.

world markets. Against an unpromising background of falling prices, Northern Ireland farmers increased output, in the process improving their productivity relative to British farmers generally. Over the period 1924/5 to 1930/31 output per farm worker in the province rose from 46 per cent to 48 per cent of the British level.[40] After 1931, in a major break with free-trade traditions, the British government granted protective tariffs and subsidies to farmers. As a constituent part of the United Kingdom, Northern Ireland farmers benefited. State-financed marketing schemes stimulated the production of milk, cattle, and, above all, pig production in the province. Farmers in Northern Ireland responded with greater alacrity than in many regions of the U.K. Moreover, it seems likely that farmers also benefited from the tariff war waged by Britain and the Irish Free State, as northern farmers were in competition with their counterparts in the Free State for a place in the British market. The outcome, in terms of productivity, was that by the end of the 1930s agricultural output per farm worker in Northern Ireland had risen to 52 per cent of the British level, which was a creditable performance in the circumstances.[41]

The outbreak of war changed the demand conditions facing Irish agriculture, though not to the extent expected in the south. Prices rose, though much more moderately than during the first world war. Agricultural production in the Irish Free State was well maintained during the period 1939–45. The largely unchanging level of output was a tribute to low dependence on imported farm inputs, itself a symptom of the underdeveloped state of Irish agriculture.[42] In Northern Ireland farm output expanded under the impetus of inflated wartime demand, and aided by greater access to tractors and other farm inputs.

Market prospects seemed bright in the aftermath of war. The output of European agriculture was at least one-third lower in 1945 than in 1938–9, with near-starvation prevailing in parts of the Continent.[43] Irish farmers found themselves in a sellers' market. Food prices rose more rapidly than prices generally. But these artificial conditions were not to last. Against all expectations, European agriculture had recovered its prewar level of production as early as 1950. During the 1950s the postwar world of scarcity gave way to an era of incipient agricultural surpluses. Few countries in Europe were prepared to accept the political and social costs of free trade in agricultural goods. There was, therefore, widespread resort to agricultural tariffs and quotas, so as to protect domestic producers.

[40] D. S. Johnson, 'The Northern Ireland economy, 1914–39' in Kennedy & Ollerenshaw, *Economic history of Ulster*, p. 198.
[41] Ibid., p. 198.
[42] R. D. Crotty, *Irish agricultural production: its volume and structure* (Cork, 1966).
[43] D. H. Aldcroft, *The European economy, 1914–1980* (London, 1980).

The closure of markets and low world prices for foodstuffs affected farmers in the Republic particularly badly. In fact, Irish agricultural prices, as measured in real terms, fell almost continuously between 1950 and 1971.[44] This was the continuation of a secular decline that, apart from the exceptional decade of the 1940s, had set in after 1920. It was at least fortunate for the Republic that the British market remained partially open. But it was fiercely competitive, with Irish farm exports pitted against New Zealand butter and lamb, Danish ham and bacon, and English eggs and poultry.

Northern Ireland farmers fared better. Because of their membership of the United Kingdom, they benefited from secure access to the British market and the guaranteed prices and subsidies this implied. During the 1940s and 1950s the price level facing them was, on average, at least 10 per cent higher than in the south.[45] This differential advantage was reduced during the 1960s, partly because of the more favourable treatment accorded by the U.K. to imports from the Republic and also because of heavier subsidies by the Irish state to the farming community. Despite differences in support systems, the growth of agricultural output was roughly comparable, north and south, between 1950 and joint entry into the E.E.C. in 1973.

Entry into the E.E.C. seemed to solve some of the major problems facing southern Irish farmers, including that of low and unstable product prices. There were indeed windfall gains in farm prices and incomes during the first six years of membership. But after 1978 prices (in real terms) resumed their downward trend, despite substantial subsidies from the common agricultural policy (C.A.P.). The halcyon days of high and rising prices proved to be shortlived. The problem that E.E.C. entry mitigated in very large measure was that of income support to the agricultural community. During the 1960s the burden of transfers from the non-agricultural to the farming sector had become acute. In 1957 financial aid from the Irish state amounted to 4 per cent of agricultural income; by 1972 this had trebled to 12 per cent.[46] Under the C.A.P., this proportion rose to a monstrous 59 per cent in 1980. The new national pastime of farming Brussels proved highly congenial to politicians and people. Faced with an exploding farm budget and massive surpluses of butter, skim-milk powder, and other commodities, the European Commission moved slowly but steadily to contain the problem. During the 1980s quotas on milk production and moderate farm price increases (generally below the level of inflation) were enforced, thereby restoring some balance between the supply of and the demand for agricultural produce.

---

[44] Alan Matthews, 'The state and Irish agriculture, 1950–1980' in P. J. Drudy (ed.), *Ireland: land, politics and people* (Cambridge, 1982), pp 254–5.

[45] Kennedy, Giblin, & McHugh, *Economic development*, pp 104, 115.

[46] Matthews, 'The state and Irish agriculture', pp 254–66.

Despite the generally downward trend in prices, farmers' incomes rose. The winds of technical change blew strongly across the countryside during the 1950s and the 1960s, resulting in expanded output per acre and per farm. Moreover, there were declining numbers seeking a livelihood from farming. The flight from the land was a particularly striking feature of Irish, and indeed European, agriculture. In the Republic the 1950s stood out as the decade of mass exodus. The number of males in agriculture, for instance, fell by 92,000 (or 21 per cent of the total) between 1951 and 1961. 'Rural Ireland', according to one pessimistic commentator, 'is stricken and dying and the will to marry on the land is almost gone.'[47] The rate of decline was even higher in Northern Ireland, but given the smaller weight of the agricultural sector in the north's economy, the economic and social impact was less intense. Looking at the whole postwar period, the size of the agricultural sector, north and south, continued to decline in both absolute and relative terms. Predictions of the imminent death of rural Ireland[48] were confounded, however, by demographic vitality during the 1960s and 1970s and the emergence of non-farming jobs in rural areas.[49] A new rural exodus, primarily from the Irish Republic, took hold in the 1980s. The exceptionally large numbers of people coming on to the labour market owing to earlier population growth, and the fall in employment in the Republic's economy between 1980 and the advent of economic recovery in 1987, combined to produce heavy unemployment and emigration.

AFTER the secession of the Irish Free State from the United Kingdom, the newly created state found itself with a shrunken industrial sector. The first census of population in 1926 recorded only 121,000 out of a total working population of 1.3 million as being employed in industry, with a further 36,500 in building. By 1936, largely as a result of the protectionist policies of Fianna Fáil, the numbers had risen to 143,000, with an additional 56,000 in building.[50] The largest increases in industrial employment took place in textiles and clothing, two subsectors that were particularly suitable for import substitution. Thus in terms of job creation protectionism had some success. It is sometimes suggested, however, that these gains were offset by a decline in labour productivity. This conclusion is reached on the basis of information drawn from the censuses of production. But by 1936 these censuses covered a

[47] Cornelius Lucey, bishop of Cork, quoted in John A. O'Brien (ed.), *The vanishing Irish* (London, 1954), p. 41.
[48] See e.g. Hugh Brody, *Inishkillane: change and decline in the west of Ireland* (London, 1973); Nancy Scheper-Hughes, *Saints, scholars and schizophrenics: mental illness in rural Ireland* (Berkeley, Cal., and London, 1979).
[49] Barry Brunt, *The Republic of Ireland* (London, 1988).
[50] See M. E. Daly, 'The employment gains from industrial protection in the Irish Free State during the 1930s: a note' and D. S. Johnson, 'Reply' in *Ir. Econ. & Soc. Hist.*, xv (1988), pp 71–5, 76–80.

larger proportion of the labour force than had hitherto been the case. The presumption must be that some of the smaller firms, which by 1936 now came within the scope of the census, were those where productivity was low. Their inclusion served to drag down the average productivity level.

While the pace of industrialisation quickened during the 1930s, this did not result in increased self-sufficiency—one of the goals of the Fianna Fáil party—because industrial production needed imported fuel, raw materials, and semi-manufactured goods. This dependence on imported inputs became an acute problem during the second world war. Because of Britain's own needs, and because of heavy pressure on shipping space, there was a squeeze on supplies to the Free State economy. Consequently, by 1943 industrial output had fallen by over a quarter from the level of 1938.[51] This was the low point and was followed by some mild expansion, which laid the basis for the rapid recovery once the war ended.

More so than in the Irish Free State, the interwar years were characterised by severe difficulties for the industrial sector in Northern Ireland. The prosperity experienced during the opening two decades of the century were never regained. From 1920 onwards the twin pillars of the north's industrial structure—the linen industry and shipbuilding—were faced with severe, long-run falls in demand. The reduction in output of these staple industries could not be offset by expansion in other areas of manufacture, and there was an overall decline in manufacturing output during the interwar period. The extent is difficult to evaluate. Much of the fall in production had occurred before the first census of production was taken in 1924. By that time the shipping tonnage launched was only 60 per cent or so of the prewar level, while the proportionate fall in linen exports was in excess of 40 per cent.[52]

After 1924 the decline in industrial production was arrested and it is possible that there was a very modest increase. The continuing decline in linen and shipbuilding was offset by increases in the output of smaller industries, notably food, drink, and tobacco, engineering, building, and public utilities. The censuses of production indicate a fall of 14.2 per cent in the value of industrial output between 1924 and 1935, as measured in current prices. This was a period of falling prices, however, so the degree of change, when measured in real terms, was slight. The cost of living fell by 18 per cent during the years 1924–35, while industrial prices in the U.K. as a whole fell by more than one-fifth. The choice of either of these price deflators would suggest a mild increase in the value of industrial output.[53]

---

[51] Department of Industry and Commerce, *Ireland: statistical abstract, 1951* (Dublin, 1952).

[52] Based on *Annual statement of the trade of the United Kingdom, 1913–29*; Workman Clark (1925) Ltd, *Shipbuilding in Belfast* (Belfast, n.d.); Michael Moss and John Hume, *Shipbuilders to the world: 125 years of Harland and Wolff, Belfast 1861–1986* (Belfast, 1986); *Ulster Year Book* for 1924 and 1929.

[53] Isles & Cuthbert, *Economic survey of N.I.*, p. 267.

War brought prosperity. Under the pressure of wartime demands, the traditional sectors of the Northern Ireland economy were revitalised. Unemployed and underemployed resources were brought back into production. Net industrial production expanded by 62 per cent between 1935 and 1949, ahead of the United Kingdom as a whole, which enjoyed a rise of 39 per cent. Over the same period the industrial workforce rose by 46 per cent, while labour productivity advanced by 11 per cent.[54] With industry as the engine of growth and nearly full employment, there were major gains in income, thereby opening up a significant gap in living standards between north and south.

Industry recovered its prewar level in the Republic sooner than in most European countries. Indeed by 1947 the volume of industrial output was well above the 1938 level, having suffered a severe but not catastrophic decline during the war years. This momentum was maintained over the next few years on the basis of gains in farm incomes, a generally favourable trend in the Irish terms of trade, and a surge in government capital expenditure in the late 1940s.[55] The major expansion was exhausted by 1950, however. During the decade 1950–59 industrial output grew at the painfully slow rate of 1.3 per cent per annum, compared with 5.6 per cent in France, 4.1 per cent in Denmark, and 9.3 per cent in West Germany. Less developed countries, such as Spain and Greece, were engaged in a process of catching up with the advanced nations during this decade, enjoying annual rates of industrial expansion of 8 per cent and 9 per cent respectively.[56] Independent Ireland was not catching up; in relative terms it was retrogressing. This failure was all the more surprising when related to developments in the world economy. The 1950s, indeed the long period 1950–73, were a time of rapid technical change and productivity gains. Tariff barriers were coming down in industrial (though not agricultural) markets; and international trade was buoyant. Why the Republic missed the first phase of this long expansionary wave is not easily explained.

In part the problem derived from unfavourable interactions between domestic and external conditions. Steep fluctuations in the Irish terms of trade, and consequent balance of payments difficulties, precipitated a series of deflationary budgets that served to depress economic activity. Moreover, the British economy, with which the Irish economy was inextricably linked, was among the slowest-growing in the western world. In terms of industrial structure and policy, the limits of industrialisation based on import substitution had been reached and overreached. High protective duties subsidised

---

[54] This is based on data in Isles & Cuthbert and the price index implicit in Charles Feinstein, *National income, expenditure and output of the United Kingdom 1855–1965* (Cambridge, 1972), table 25.
[55] Kennedy, Giblin, & McHugh, *Economic development*, pp 57–8.
[56] Liam Kennedy, *The modern industrialization of Ireland 1940–88* (Dublin, 1989), p. 9.

inefficiency and created a bias against exporting. Most of the 'infant industries' proved incapable of growing beyond the small, protected home market. Moreover, this market showed little buoyancy. Incomes were growing slowly. Perhaps most importantly of all, the young adult population was falling dramatically as employment in industry as well as agriculture contracted. Thus, while the population as a whole dipped by 5 per cent between 1951 and 1961, the numbers in the age category 20–34 years fell away by almost a quarter (23 per cent). This was unlike any other country in western Europe, and must surely have exerted a depressive effect, not only on consumption but on production and investment activity. Doubts regarding the efficacy of the policy of import substitution had been sharpening during the 1950s. In 1958 the secretary of the department of finance, T. K. Whitaker, completed his famous report *Economic development*, which inaugurated a form of light economic planning. *Economic development* signalled a gradual retreat from protectionism, an enlarged role for foreign capital and enterprise in the Irish economy, and a new emphasis on exports and export-led growth.[57] In the eyes of some, this report launched the modern industrialisation of Ireland. If so, it must rank as the most influential document in Irish history since George Nicholls's plan in 1836 for a poor law system for the country.[58]

There is no doubt that during the 1960s, in terms of industrial and overall economic performance, the Irish Republic reentered the European mainstream. The most significant change was the inflow of foreign capital, as multinational companies established satellite manufacturing plants in greenfield sites north and south of the border. These flows were not of course unique to Ireland, being part of an internationalisation of capital that marked the postwar era.[59] The strong contribution to industrial exports of these firms ensured that in the space of a decade—the 1960s—the Republic moved from being an exporter of primary commodities to being an industrial exporter. Domestic firms also benefited from an expanding home market, but significantly most failed to transcend its limits by breaking into foreign markets.

The problems of the Northern Ireland economy during the 1950s were different from those in the Republic, though the increase in net industrial output, at 2.1 per cent a year, was little better. The narrowness of its industrial base—shipbuilding and engineering, linen textiles and clothing—meant that it was vulnerable to shifts in demand and to new competitive pressures. In the case of linen, the long-run decline in demand noted earlier reasserted itself following the acute international recession in textiles of 1951–2. In areas

---

[57] Department of Finance, *Economic development* (Dublin, 1958).

[58] More sceptical views may be found in Paul Bew and Henry Patterson, *Seán Lemass and the making of modern Ireland 1945–66* (Dublin, 1982), pp 112–17, and in Kennedy, *Modern industrialization*, pp 14–15.

[59] Lars Mjøset, *The Irish economy in a comparative institutional perspective* (Dublin, 1992); Northern Ireland Economic Council, *Inward investment in Northern Ireland* (Belfast, 1992).

such as north and west Belfast, and in the provincial towns and the few surviving mill villages, the linen industry collapsed, leaving behind the red-brick shells of a previous industrial age. Within two decades, Ulster's oldest, most distinctive, and internationally renowned industry had virtually disappeared.[60]

Massive redundancies did not hit shipbuilding till the beginning of the 1960s. Thereafter, Harland & Wolff shed workers continuously, with the firm escaping the fate of most British yards only by receiving heavy public subsidies. Other forms of traditional engineering withered in the face of outside competition. But alongside the decline of traditional industry came the emergence of new firms and new products. Beginning in the 1950s, but gathering momentum in the following decade, externally owned firms set up branch plants in Northern Ireland. As in the Republic, these were attracted by the ready availability of labour and government financial inducements. Symbolic of the new era was the synthetic fibre industry, which seemed a natural replacement for linen textiles. It manufactured modern products, using advanced technologies, and created extensive employment in east Antrim and Derry. By 1973 just over half the manufacturing labour force in Northern Ireland, as compared to one-third in the Republic, was employed by externally owned firms.[61]

THE period between Ireland's entry into the E.E.C. and ratification of the Maastricht treaty on European unity in 1992 was one of considerable turbulence in the international economic environment. Yet, in terms of industrial output and exports, the Republic continued to forge ahead. Direct foreign investment continued to play a vital role during the last quarter of the twentieth century. Duty-free access to the huge European Community market made Ireland attractive as a site for internationally mobile capital. Industrial output and exports continued to grow. The census of industrial production for 1988 recorded that externally owned firms were responsible for 44 per cent of employment in manufacturing industry and a remarkable 68 per cent of net industrial output in that year. They accounted for an even larger share of exports. The downside of this success was that indigenous industry fared badly, once exposed to the more competitive trading conditions of the Community. Sectors such as textiles, clothing, and footwear, for example, lost heavily in terms of employment and sales, as imports penetrated the formerly protected home market.[62] However, a small number of

[60] J. W. Black, 'Industrial development and regional policy' in N. J. Gibson and J. E. Spencer (ed.), *Economic activity in Ireland: a study of two open economies* (Dublin, 1977), pp 40–78.

[61] Graham Gudgin, Mark Hart, John Fagg, Eamonn D'Arcy, and Ron Keegan, *Job generation in manufacturing industry 1973–1986* (Belfast, 1989).

[62] Eoin O'Malley, *Industry and economic development: the challenge for the latecomer* (Dublin, 1989).

Irish firms—Jefferson Smurfit, Guinness Peat Aviation, Allied Irish Banks, Glen Dimplex, Avonmore Foods, Dairygold, Waterford Glass—succeeded in making the transition to international corporate status, becoming what might be termed green, baby multinationals. Some of the 'infants' of the era of protectionism grew up; but, from a national viewpoint, all too few. Even among the firms listed above, only a minority owed much to the stimulus of protection.

One of the most striking aspects of Irish industrialisation was the growing divergence between growth in output and growth in employment. Thus, while net industrial output doubled between 1973 and 1990, the numbers employed actually fell. The decline in industrial workers was from 243,000 to 214,000, or a proportionate drop of 12 per cent.[63] This divorce between employment and output growth was not, however, unique to Ireland, being a feature of industrial economies generally in the postwar era. There are reasons, though, why this phenomenon, which stems from rapid productivity gains, might be particularly evident in the Irish case. As Ireland was a late-industrialising country, the type of industry established was likely to be technologically advanced and capital-intensive. The large electronics, chemical, and pharmaceutical sectors that emerged during the 1970s confirm this. With permanent technological change built into the manufacturing system, and with new layers of industry added cumulatively through time, the growth paths for labour and non-labour inputs inevitably parted. These tendencies were reinforced by the fact that externally owned firms—the principal users of advanced technologies—assumed increasing dominance during the final quarter of the century. Transfer pricing among the subsidiaries of multinational companies may also have some limited explanatory value. Reverting to the main theme, in view of the severe declines in manufacturing employment experienced by neighbouring economies, such as the United Kingdom during the 1970s and 1980s, perhaps the surprising point is how well net employment in Irish industry held up during that period.

By contrast with the industrial fortunes of the Republic, Northern Ireland encountered an economic and political blizzard during the 1970s. During the decade 1973–83 the industrial machine was driven into reverse, with net industrial output falling by a quarter, and manufacturing output by one-third.[64] Inevitably, this translated into massive job losses. The manufacturing labour force was 40 per cent smaller at the end of the decade. Three factors help to account for this dismal performance. There was the continuing run-down of traditional industry. There were also significant job losses among the externally owned firms that had come to the province in the postwar

---

[63] Central Statistics Office, *Statistical abstract 1991* (Pl 8085) (Dublin, 1991); *Irish statistical bulletin 1992* (Dublin, 1992).
[64] Calculated from reports of the N.I. census of production.

decades. Both sets of problems, it is worth remarking, were common to other regions, especially peripheral regions of the U.K. economy. Both were exacerbated by two severe recessions in the British economy, coming in quick succession in 1973–5 and 1979–82. What was unique in this British story of industrial decline, however, was the role of political violence in deterring further inward investment. As compared to the Republic, few manufacturing projects materialised. In effect, the main thrust of industrial policy in Northern Ireland—renewing the industrial structure through outside investment—was rendered inoperative.[65]

At the beginning of the twentieth century the Northern Ireland region constituted the industrial heartland of the island. By the 1990s it had experienced severe deindustrialisation, and the major concentration of industry had shifted to the south.[66] Most remarkable of all, most of this decline was concentrated in a short period, the decade 1973–83. The mild recovery of the later 1980s was followed by another recession throughout the U.K. in 1991–3. Though the north was less severely affected than Britain—'if such a thing can be said, Northern Ireland had a good recession'[67]—the underlying picture was one of a weakened industrial sector and continuing political crisis.

Those who rail against the iniquities of foreign investment in peripheral regions may find a salutary warning in the experience of Northern Ireland, where outside investment was compulsorily choked off. Still, dependence on outside capital does raise serious questions about the nature of industry in the Republic and the durability of its industrial structures. The modern industrialisation of Ireland was conducted largely on the basis of foreign capital and enterprise, with the aid of substantial subsidies from the Irish state. The result was the emergence of a dual industrial structure: a modern sector characterised by technologically advanced products and production techniques, generating large profits, geared to export markets but only weakly integrated into the Irish economy (in terms of purchases of inputs from local firms); and a traditional sector using more labour-intensive methods of production, with stronger linkages to the Irish economy but with much lower profits and productivity, and a low export orientation.[68] By and large the modern sector was externally owned while the sluggish sector was in the hands of indigenous capitalists.

[65] Gudgin and others, *Job generation in manufacturing industry*, pp 33–5.
[66] Kennedy, *Industrialization of Ire.*, p. 4.
[67] Graham Gudgin and Geraldine O'Shea (ed.), *Unemployment forever? the Northern Ireland economy in recession and beyond* (Northern Ireland Economic Research Centre, Belfast, 1993).
[68] Telesis Consultancy Group, *A review of industrial policy* (Dublin, 1982); National Economic & Social Council, *Ireland in the European Community: performance, prospects and strategy* (Dublin, 1989).

In a kinder world, or one in which there was a greater supply of indigenous entrepreneurship, far more of the modern sector would have been under Irish control. This would have ensured that more of the higher value-added areas of production, such as industrial research and marketing, were located in Ireland. It might also have enhanced the durability of jobs in the modern sector, though this is far from certain. (While employment in manufacturing in the Republic declined by 11 per cent overall between 1973 and 1990, there was no contraction in the externally owned subsector, where the number of jobs actually expanded by 27 per cent.) The likelihood is that Irish-owned firms would have sourced more of their inputs from other Irish firms, thereby producing a better-integrated Irish economy. But it is also important to point out that greater external ownership was a trend in industrial societies generally, and not just in late-industrialising countries like the Republic, during the last quarter of the century. In the powerful German economy, for instance, one-fifth of manufacturing output was accounted for by externally owned firms in 1987, and the proportion must have been considerably higher in some of its constituent regions.

Any balanced view of the industrialisation process in the Republic and in Northern Ireland must recognise the limitations as well as the benefits of multinational investment. It must also acknowledge the problems facing two small, open economies in their quest for industrial expansion. Whether there existed a feasible, alternative set of policies that would have produced deeper industrialisation and a better balance between indigenous and externally owned plants after E.C. entry, is hard to say. What can be discounted, however, are anachronistic notions of a largely Irish or Ulster industrialisation drive in an era of global competition and the internationalisation of capital and enterprise.

MORE so than industry or agriculture, the services sector spans a great diversity of activities and occupations. Bank clerks, brothel keepers, priests, lighthousemen, nurses, and teachers mingle indiscriminately in this hold-all category. The boundaries, with industry in particular, are somewhat arbitrary and subject to shifts over time. Problems of definition notwithstanding, there is no doubt that the size of the services sectors, north and south, expanded markedly during the course of the century. In 1926 services accounted for 34 per cent of employment in Northern Ireland; by 1951 this share had risen to 38 per cent.[69] The direction of change was the same in the south, with the services sector expanding its share of the workforce from 31 per cent to 35 per cent over the period 1926–51. The postwar era, however, witnessed the really dramatic shift towards service-type employment. The sector became in fact the major source of jobs. Thus, in 1990 two out of every three positions in the northern economy were in services, and more than half of these were

---

[69] Mitchell, *European hist. statistics, 1750–1970*, p. 158.

to be found in the public sector. While the trends, north and south, were in the same direction, it is interesting to note that dependence on services was much less pronounced in the case of the Republic (see table 8).

The evolutionary pathway traced by the service sector, and indeed by the agricultural and industrial sectors in Ireland, was broadly similar to that of other western societies. Typically, in industrialising economies the numbers engaged in agriculture fall, at first relatively and then absolutely, as industry assumes a greater weight within the overall economy. But, at an advanced stage of development, the industrial sector experiences the fate of agriculture, that is, a relative and perhaps an absolute fall in the extent of industrial employment. The services sector, in fact, becomes the dominant employer, with the state providing a substantial share of these jobs. Such structural shifts arise from a combination of the high income elasticity of demand for modern services and a slower rate of productivity change than in the economy generally. The nuances of these sectoral changes varied as between different societies, but the long-run contraction of agriculture and the rise to dominance of the services sector are features of all the western European countries shown in table 8. Among the more mature economies, as distinct from late-industrialising nations such as Greece and Ireland, it is also apparent that the share of employment accounted for by industry went into decline in the years after 1960.

TABLE 8. *Percentage share of employment by sector among E.C. countries, 1960 and 1990*

	Agriculture		Industry		Services	
	1960	1990	1960	1990	1960	1990
Belgium	9	3	45	29	46	68
Denmark	18	6	37	29	45	65
France	22	6	38	31	40	63
West Germany	14	3	47	41	39	55
Greece	57	24	17	28	26	48
Republic of Ireland	37	15	24	29	39	55
Italy	33	9	34	33	33	59
Netherlands	10	5	41	29	50	66
Portugal	44	17	31	35	25	47
Spain	39	12	30	34	31	54
United Kingdom	5	2	48	31	56	66
European Community	21	7	40	34	39	60

Employment data for 1990 are in the form of full-time job equivalents.

Sources: O.E.C.D., *Hist. statistics, 1960–90*, pp 22, 40–41; Eurostat, *Labour force survey: results 1989*, pp 112–13.

In view of the heterogeneity of the services sector, it is not perhaps surprising that its composition changed radically through time. At the beginning of the century domestic service accounted for a large proportion of female employment, though dependence on such traditional and low-paid work was much less pronounced in east Ulster than in the rest of the island. Even at mid century, one in every three women employed in services in the Republic was a domestic servant. More often than not, she lived in, under the continuous scrutiny and authority of the household. In Northern Ireland, with its more developed economic and industrial structure, the share of female service employment accounted for by domestic service was only half that for the Republic (16 per cent as against 31 per cent in 1951). By the 1960s, however, this form of service—in some cases servitude—had largely disappeared, thereby completing one of the quietest social revolutions in Irish life.

HAVING completed this overview of the main sectors of the economies of Northern Ireland and the Republic, it is now appropriate to return to the question of economic performance broached in the introduction. There are three significant benchmarks for any assessment of the island's progress in the period since partition. One is relative to its own performance in the past. The other is relative to other comparable societies during the course of the twentieth century. The third is relative to some hypothetical notion of its potential in that period. This can be attempted for the Republic but it is doubtful if such an exercise has the same meaning in the case of Northern Ireland, where we are dealing with a region rather than an independent state, and where the upsurge of violence from the late 1960s deeply distorted the economic record. Suffice it to say that the growth in output and incomes in Northern Ireland and the Republic between 1913 and 1973 seem to have been broadly similar.

While the estimate is somewhat conjectural, national product in the twenty-six counties seems to have expanded at an annual rate of less than 1 per cent during the period 1841–1913. This compares with an average annual growth rate of just under 2 per cent over the period 1913–93.[70] On this criterion, at any rate, independent Ireland outperformed Victorian Ireland. This impression is reinforced if the focus switches to Ireland's relative performance before and after 1911. Thus, between 1841 and 1913, if currently available estimates can be believed, Ireland had the slowest annual growth rate—0.7 per cent—of any European country.[71] This was less than half the mean value for some eighteen other European countries. Over the period 1913–85 the growth in total product in the twenty-six counties was two-thirds that of the European average.

[70] Johnson & Kennedy, 'Economic growth at the European periphery' (1993).
[71] Kennedy, Giblin, & McHugh, *Economic development*, p. 18.

In the twentieth century, therefore, Ireland performed well relative to its own past. The second benchmark involves contemporaneous comparisons between Ireland and its neighbours. As argued earlier, income per head grew during the course of the century at a rate that was little below that of the European average. Still, adherents of the convergence school of economic growth would surely object that a poorer country would be expected to grow more rapidly than a richer country. Barro and Sala-i-Martin, for instance, wonder if there are not 'automatic forces that lead to convergence over time in the levels of per capita income'.[72] Some catching-up is certainly true of the Irish Republic within a European context between 1960 and the 1990s (though historians would shudder at the thought of automatic forces in history). More fundamentally, though, it needs to be recognised that the international debate on long-run tendencies towards the equalisation of income per head across different countries is far from resolved. Convergence, particularly unconditional convergence, has been apparent for some groupings of countries but not for others. In view of the mixed empirical evidence, it is far from clear why convergence should be presumed to be the norm.[73]

What of independent Ireland's performance relative to its potential? As the latter has never been observed, the quest is a somewhat elusive one, but no less important for that. Like the indifferent schoolgirl, the assumption usually is that Kathleen could have done better. It is unnecessary to rehearse the various advantages with which the Irish Free State embarked upon nationhood.[74] But in forming a judgement it is important to remember also the various constraints that had a bearing on the progress of the economy and society.

The two economies, north and south, were small. Relative to Britain in 1951, for example, the labour forces were the equivalent of only 3 per cent and 6 per cent respectively. Neither had significant natural resources of an industrial kind, which were so important to the industrialisation of other small countries such as Norway or Sweden.[75] Taken together, these two features meant that both economies were necessarily open, with long-term growth prospects heavily dependent on conditions in international markets. Openness, in a trading sense, also meant that the scope for fiscal stimuli to the local economies was limited, as the bitter experience of expansionary action by the Republic's government in the late 1970s demonstrated.

---

[72] Robert J. Barro and Xavier Sala-i-Martin, 'Convergence' in *Journal of Political Economy*, c (1992), p. 223; eidem, 'Convergence across states and regions' in *Brookings Papers on Economic Activity*, i (1991), pp 107–57.

[73] Danny Quah, 'Regional convergence clusters across Europe' (Centre for Economic Policy Research, London; later published as Discussion Paper 1286 (1996).

[74] Above, p. 466.

[75] Mjøset, *Ir. economy in comparative institutional perspective*, pp 97–8.

In terms of geographical location, both economies may be considered peripheral, being situated behind the island of Britain and on the western edge of Europe. While transport costs may not have had a particularly important bearing on Irish competitiveness, there may have been other, more significant costs associated with location (what are usually referred to as 'distance costs').[76] There was also the issue of economic location. Both Irish economies have shown a striking trade dependence on the neighbouring island. This would be unexceptional but for the fact that Britain was the slowcoach among western economies during the course of the century. It was only after entry into the European Community in 1973 that the Republic succeeded in diversifying its exports towards faster-growing continental European markets. This shift was reinforced by the decision to join the European Monetary System (E.M.S.), which took effect in March 1979. The fact that Britain decided not to enter meant breaking the currency link with sterling, for the first time since 1826. Although the value of the Irish pound against sterling subsequently fell, in general the break with sterling had beneficial effects on exports to Britain. However, the ending of the link with sterling, if anything, reinforced partition. Henceforth cross-border travellers had to make special arrangements to acquire the local currency.

The Irish Free State started life with huge numbers of its workforce still engaged in low-productivity agriculture. The natural orientation of Irish agriculture was towards low-input and low-output livestock farming. Coupled with rising material expectations, and off-farm job opportunities (though mostly outside Ireland), a massive decline in agricultural employment was inevitable. Problems of access to European markets for Irish farm exports were compounded by unfavourable trends in relative agricultural prices. Though more apparent after the second world war, there was a slower growth in demand for temperate foodstuffs than for the sun-drenched produce of the Mediterranean.[77] In the case of Northern Ireland's largest industrial sector, linen manufacture, the relative price structure of textiles also moved in an adverse direction. Again the source of these price changes, in favour of cotton and artificial fibres, lay beyond the control of the local economy.[78]

In the later twentieth century, the free good of sunshine underpinned much of the tourist activity that added substantially to the income of the countries of the European periphery—Spain, Portugal, and Greece. In

---

[76] David Keeble, 'Core–periphery. Disparities, recession and new regional dynamisms in the European Community' in *Geography*, lxxiv, no. 1 (1989), pp 1–11; David Keeble, John Offord, and Sheila Walker, *Peripheral regions in a community of twelve member states* (Luxembourg, 1988).

[77] S. A. Sigma, *Los cítricos en España* (Madrid, 1974), pp 19–31; Commonwealth Economic Committee, *Fruit: a review, 1953* (London, 1954), p. 5.

[78] Isles & Cuthbert, *Economic survey*, pp 74, 555–7.

Ireland the climate changed little, but the 'free bad' of terrorism and, in particular, the 'economic war' of the I.R.A. imposed island-wide costs on the Irish peoples. More significantly, as a late-industrialising country, the Republic could not hope for the gains in employment that accompanied heavy investment in industry in earlier periods.

It is important to emphasise that these were constraints, not immutable limits to economic development. No doubt other parts of Europe experienced their own particular problems. Moreover, constraints can be broken, thereby opening up creative business opportunities, as the shipbuilders Harland & Wolff showed in the nineteenth century. But, at the very least, it has to be conceded that the twenty-six-county state entered on to a world stage not of its own making, with an inheritance of agriculture and industry that posed problems for the future. When business conditions, with respect to the supply of capital and enterprise to peripheral regions of the world economy, changed radically during the 1960s, both Northern Ireland and the Republic were well positioned in terms of policy to take advantage of these flows of internationally mobile capital.

Policy-making might have been better; it might have been worse. Ireland avoided the dire consequences of government-fuelled inflation that affected many European countries during the early 1920s. True, the economic war of the 1930s, while not as onerous as was once imagined in circles hostile to Fianna Fáil, might have been avoided with benefit all round.[79] Similarly, the state overreached itself in its drive for comparative self-sufficiency and the development of a largely or exclusively Irish capitalist class (an 'Irish Ireland for business'). Fiscal policy during the 1950s might have been less reactive to temporary fluctuations in the world economy, and hence less deflationary. That the lesson was well learned was demonstrated by fiscal policy during the 1960s. New lessons had to be learned after the irresponsible splurge in government borrowing and spending after 1977—lessons that for reasons of political instability and international recession were not implemented until almost a decade later. The shift to outward-oriented economic policies after 1960, the successful negotiation of improved access to British and later continental European markets, and the achievements of the Industrial Development Authority, are cases of positive and enduring state intervention. Taking the long view, the contribution of government has been a mixed one, but seems on balance to have favoured economic development. There is no unambiguous case for arguing that Ireland, north or south, underperformed grossly relative to its own intrinsic potential. While it is quite possible to daydream about any number of alternative pathways, the comparison with

[79] Mary E. Daly, *Industrial development and Irish national identity, 1922–1939* (Dublin, 1992); Cormac Ó Gráda, *Did tariffs matter that much? Ireland since the 1920s* (Centre for Economic Policy Research, discussion paper, London, 1988).

mainstream European experience (which is one way of getting a hold on a feasible alternative past) does not suggest lost worlds of wondrous but missed opportunity.

Postscript: This account of the two economies in Ireland, which was completed in 1993, was unfashionably buoyant in its assessment. The growth performance of the two economies in subsequent years serves as some kind of check on the validity of the interpretation. The economic momentum was maintained and even intensified, with the Irish Republic in particular emerging as the 'Celtic tiger' of the 1990s (though the uneven distribution of the gains from growth continued to give cause for concern). Northern Ireland, meanwhile, outperformed most other regions of the United Kingdom during much of the decade, turning in a creditable performance during the closing years of the millennium.

CHAPTER XVIII

Literature in English, 1921–84

VIVIAN MERCIER

THE length of the period to be covered in this chapter suggests that it may best be approached by breaking it down into three subperiods, 1921–39, 1940–68, and 1969–84. The first of these covers the formative years of both parts of post-partition Ireland, and it is appropriate to ask what cultural institutions were set up. Unhappily, Northern Ireland set up none before the second world war, while the Irish Free State did not do much better. Though in theory all the resources of the United Kingdom were at her disposal, Northern Ireland actually incurred some cultural deprivation as a result of partition. The National Library of Ireland, the National Museum, the National Gallery, the Royal Irish Academy (scholarship), and the Royal Hibernian Academy (fine arts) were all in Dublin. The library of Trinity College, Dublin, in spite of protests by some British publishers, continued to be one of the five libraries of deposit for copyright purposes, and the only one in Ireland. Dublin retained her advantage over Belfast as a publishing and printing centre for books and periodicals at least till 1939, although most books by Irish authors were still published in London and/or New York.

The introduction of compulsory Irish in Free State schools had important cultural consequences, discussed elsewhere;[1] but let us remember here that virtually all books and periodicals in Irish were printed and published in Dublin or Cork, giving an indirect subsidy to the industries concerned. The literary consequences of a more widely diffused teaching of Irish did not have time to make themselves felt before 1939, but most Irish writers of English after that date possessed some knowledge of Irish, even if they chose not to make use of it. Government encouragement of the language took a variety of forms. Original works and translations into Irish were issued by An Gúm (later Oifig an tSoláthair, the Stationery Office); the Irish Manuscripts Commission and Irish Folklore Commission were founded; and Royal Irish Academy publications were subsidised.

Successive Free State governments remained largely indifferent to cultural needs where the Irish language was not an issue. Yeats and Lady Gregory

[1] Below, ch. XIX.

thought that the state would be happy to take over the Abbey as a truly national theatre, but when they offered it unconditionally in 1924, it was refused. Instead, they were given a small annual subsidy—originally £850, but gradually increased later—on condition that two government nominees should join the board of directors of what was already called the National Theatre Society Ltd. On the whole, these appointees did not act as unofficial censors, nor, for some years at least, was the Abbey pressed to offer plays in Irish.

The Dublin Gate Theatre opened in 1930 at the Rotunda; generously supported by the sixth earl of Longford, it owes its fame primarily to the acting, designing, and directing talents of Mícheál Mac Liammóir and Hilton Edwards, whose company had played for two seasons (1928–9) at the Abbey's smaller annexe, the Peacock. The programme of international contemporary drama and English classics presented there—along with a number of works by Irish playwrights, often experimental plays unsuited to the Abbey style of production—complemented the Abbey's offering, but no government assistance was given to the Gate in 1922–39.

Some of the legislation pertaining to the arts that was introduced by the Free State aimed at regulation and restriction rather than encouragement. Censorship of films was probably inevitable; the necessary act was passed in 1923.[2] Its operation often resulted in the banning or mutilation of genuinely artistic films, and even the more routine activities of the film censor sometimes seemed unnecessarily absurd: for example, the film version of Thurber's *The male animal* was inexplicably retitled 'The female wins'. One branch of the performing arts, however, was left unhampered. It had been demonstrated when the Abbey put on Shaw's 'The shewing-up of Blanco Posnet' in 1909 that the lord chamberlain could not make his writ run in Ireland; no attempt was made to replace him with a Free State official, so that the Dublin theatre was, except for brief paroxysms of unofficial pressure, free from censorship, as the London theatre was not. Another type of censorship, in the shape of rioting and picketing, was attempted against Sean O'Casey's 'The plough and the stars' (1926), but, as with 'The playboy of the western world',[3] the Abbey Theatre directors called in the police and thwarted the rioters.

The restrictive legislation that most affected literature in the Free State was of course the Censorship of Publications Act, 1929.[4] Aimed in the first instance at the *News of the World*, it eventually struck down *The land of spices*, Kate O'Brien's tender spiritual novel about a mother superior. The organisations pressing for new legislation had directed most of their fire against cheap English newspapers; Irish literature received little notice. Books were included

---

[2] 1923/23 (16 July 1923).
[3] Above, vi, 119–20, 174, 372–3.
[4] 1929/21 (16 July 1929).

in the legislation, it appears, primarily under the mistaken impression that 'hard-core' pornography and birth-control manuals could more effectively be excluded in this way than through existing customs laws.

The Irish catholic bishops' lenten pastorals in 1924 and the vigorous, though unorganised, press campaign that followed led to the appointment of a committee of inquiry on 'evil literature' early in 1926. The committee members were laymen, including several protestants; their report was published early in 1927, but a censorship of publications bill was not introduced in the dáil till July 1928. The act that became law in 1929, though offering a rather broad definition of 'indecent', insisted that the literary merit of the book ought to be taken into account: it should not be banned unless it was 'in its general tendency indecent or obscene'. All publications advocating contraception or abortion were forbidden by the act, as was the sale of indecent pictures.

The operation of the act during the first ten years of its existence was questioned only as it applied to books. The Free State customs authorities made use of their powers under the Customs Laws Consolidation Act, 1876,[5] to draw the attention of the censorship board to far more books than were cited by private individuals. As a result, some 120 books a year were banned, of which too many possessed literary merit and an unfairly high percentage were by Irish authors: Samuel Beckett, Joyce Cary, Austin Clarke, St John Ervine, Ethel Mannin, George Moore, Kate O'Brien, Sean O'Casey, Frank O'Connor, Sean O'Faolain, and Liam O'Flaherty all had one or more titles banned in the first ten years. Bernard Shaw's *The adventures of the black girl in her search for God* was thought to have been banned because of John Farleigh's brilliant woodcuts of the nude heroine. A volume of Freud's *Collected papers* and novels by such writers as Faulkner, Hemingway, and Aldous Huxley were also banned.

Public criticism of the board's blunders did not reach the pitch it was to attain after 1945, but there was a lively correspondence in the *Irish Times* about the banning of O'Faolain's low-keyed novel *Bird alone* (1936). 'Lynn Doyle' (Leslie A. Montgomery), after serving a few weeks on the board in 1937, resigned in protest against the practice of judging books on the basis of passages marked by civil servants, which violated the 'in general tendency' proviso.[6]

The effect on an Irish author of having a book banned varied considerably. After the prohibition of *More pricks than kicks* (1934), Beckett wrote *Murphy* (1938) with such circumspection that he was able to defy the censors to make 'their filthy synecdoche'. O'Flaherty, on the other hand, sometimes gave the

[5] 39 & 40 Vict., c. 36 (24 July 1876).
[6] The above account of the censorship of publications act, its origins, and its consequences draws heavily on Michael Adams, *Censorship: the Irish experience* (Dublin, 1968).

impression of trying to make his next book more offensive than his last. On two occasions Kate O'Brien followed up a fine book that was banned with one that was innocuous, certainly, but also weak and hastily written.[7] At least one writer, Margaret O'Leary, lost a teaching post after her novel *Lightning flash* was banned.

Irish intellectuals, and creative writers especially, were not very well served by native periodicals during the years 1922–39. The Jesuit quarterly *Studies* continued its honourable career, but the only literary material it published was either scholarly or critical. The *Dublin Magazine* published poems, short stories, and even an occasional play (by George Fitzmaurice or Austin Clarke), as well as critical articles and book reviews, but, being a quarterly, it could not accommodate much creative writing in any one year. The would-be *avant-garde* periodical *Tomorrow* (1924) perished in a public outcry after two issues. Undoubtedly the most important Irish intellectual journal during its lamentably brief existence was A E (George Russell)'s *Irish Statesman* (1919–20 and 1923–30). This weekly, as its name implied, was modelled to some extent on the *New Statesman*. It commented on politics and literature in Ireland and elsewhere, also publishing poems and an occasional short story. After the demise of the *Irish Statesman*, no comparable new periodical appeared till *Ireland Today* (1936–8). This monthly published poems and short stories as well as articles and reviews. It in turn was without a successor until the first issue of *The Bell* in October 1940.

One monthly that made its debut almost simultaneously with the Irish Free State deserves special mention here, though very little of its content could ever be described as literary. *Dublin Opinion*, 'the national humorous journal of Ireland' as it called itself, strove to reconcile both sides in the civil war and indeed all parties, north and south. Such a policy inhibited the traditional Irish gift for satire, but it fostered a vein of humour best exemplified by the joke illustrations and political caricatures of C.E.K. (C. E. Kelly, one of its founders). Two generations of Irish readers were taught humour and humanity by *Dublin Opinion*.

THE rubric 'literature and society', which seems irrelevant to much of the literary work produced in the period 1891–1921, comes into its own from 1922 onwards. Whereas the plays of Yeats, J. M. Synge, Lady Gregory, and George Fitzmaurice—compounded of myth, folklore, and fantasy—had formerly dominated the Irish theatre, the prose realism that had certainly also been a part of the Abbey tradition in the works of William Boyle, Padraic Colum, T. C. Murray, Seumas O'Kelly, and Lennox Robinson now began to drive fantasy and verse from the Abbey stage. Irish drama became a more

---

[7] *Pray for the wanderer*, which followed the banning of *Mary Lavelle*; and *The last of summer*, following the banning of *The land of spices*.

faithful reflection of contemporary Irish society; the process that Yeats called in 1919 'the making articulate of all the dumb classes' continued with few interruptions. Some of the new writers preferred the novel, a genre that is traditionally preoccupied with the individual and society, or they wrote a type of short story, perfected in Moore's *The untilled field* and Joyce's *Dubliners*, full of keen sociological observation and often hinging on a social problem.

Fostering this swing towards realism, and also fostered by it, was a surprising wave of disillusionment. It is apparent that the literary revival had never been prone to illusion about the struggle for independence; the playwrights in particular were frequently accused of being anti-nationalist and indeed anti-Irish. But many of those who began to write in the 1920s and 1930s had necessarily been adolescents in or about 1916, when it was natural for them to expect a quick solution to all Ireland's problems; later, they took the anti-treaty side in the civil war. The defeat of their cause and the internment of some by the Free State government gave a very personal intensity to their feeling that the national revolution had gone seriously astray. No wonder they were sharply critical of the new state. Frank O'Connor, Francis Stuart, and Peadar O'Donnell all suffered imprisonment, the last being in danger of death for some weeks. Liam O'Flaherty, after making a futile revolutionary gesture, thought he had escaped imprisonment only by leaving the country. Sean O'Faolain, as deeply involved as any of these, could feel very lucky not to have been imprisoned.

O'Flaherty, the first of the younger writers to make a reputation, published his first novel in 1923 and won world fame with his third, *The informer* (1925). Meanwhile, Sean O'Casey, who had lost faith in nationalism even before 1916, began to strike a series of hammer blows at the romantic image of three different phases of the revolutionary movement. Although O'Casey left the Citizen Army in 1914 in protest against elaborate uniforms and other irrelevancies, his first book was *The story of the Irish Citizen Army* (1919). 'The shadow of a gunman' (1923) displays the cowardice of several presumably representative Irishmen in the face of Black-and-Tan harassment. At the same time, the courage unto death of Minnie and Maguire is made to seem futile. Maguire, the one genuine revolutionary, speaks a few insouciant lines early in the play and then disappears from the stage, so that the case in his favour, in a sense, is never put to the audience—though it is implicit in what we see and hear of the behaviour of the Black-and-Tans. Donal, the protagonist, reproaches himself for being a 'poltroon', but his real sin is not so much cowardice as the advantage he takes of the other tenement dwellers who mistake him for a gunman on the run.

'Juno and the paycock' (1924) is set at the very end of the civil war, when open fighting is over but murderous revenge persists. The play opens with the finding of the dead Tancred boy, killed without trial by the Free Staters.

Later, Johnny Boyle, who informed on him, is taken away and similarly 'executed' by the I.R.A. Juno, his mother, reproaches herself for not mourning Tancred's death 'because he was a diehard'. Now that Johnny too is dead, she sees that it does not matter which side a dead boy is on: the loss is the same. Johnny in fact had been a diehard too until he lost his arm fighting in the Free State army; he is the victim of both sides of the civil war. When he tells his mother that a man has to fight for his principles, she retorts: 'You lost your best principle when you lost your arm.' A manual worker cannot afford idealism. Indeed, the whole system is seen as hostile to the poor. When the Boyle family think they have inherited a small fortune, a flaw in the will deprives them of it.

It was not until 'The plough and the stars' (1926) that O'Casey dared to attack what was already revered as Ireland's Calvary and resurrection, the 1916 rising. But the attack, when it came, was a savage one. Bloodthirsty quotations from actual speeches by Patrick Pearse boom into the bar where Rosie the prostitute and Fluther the drunkard are carrying on. The very presence of Rosie among the characters provoked wrath, as did the bringing of the tricolour into a public house, but these were really minor irritations compared with the overall belittlement of the 1916 men. Jack Clitheroe is represented as joining the Citizen Army mainly in order to swagger in a fancy uniform. After the fighting starts, he and his fellows are only slightly less afraid of the enemy than they are of being accused of cowardice. Most of the slum dwellers pay lip service to the ideals of the rising, while joyfully seizing the opportunity it affords for looting. The Covey, the only character who, like O'Casey himself, denounces nationalism while advocating international socialism, remains a figure of fun throughout the play. The two characters who behave best under stress are the alcoholic Fluther Good and the Ulster protestant Bessie Burgess. Despite the outcry against 'The plough and the stars', all three of O'Casey's plays created a new popular audience for the Abbey, which began to operate at a profit. O'Casey, however, left Ireland in 1927, never to return.

In these early plays O'Casey made no attacks on the catholic clergy. Liam O'Flaherty, himself a former seminary student, was not so careful. The theme of the priest in love goes back a long way in Anglo-Irish literature, to *The Nowlans* (1826) by the Banim brothers, though it was not taken up again in literature—as opposed to sectarian propaganda—till George Moore's *The lake* (1905).[8] O'Flaherty chose it for his first novel, *Thy neighbour's wife* (1923), but left the reader convinced of the priest's fundamental innocence; far more offensive to Irish sensibilities was the drunken priest who tries to rape the heroine of *The house of gold* (1929) and later murders her. This was

---

[8] Above, v, 489; vi, 379–80.

perhaps the first book by an Irish author to be banned by the censorship board (30 October 1930).

Before O'Flaherty's debut, and even before 1921, another young writer, 'Brinsley MacNamara' (John Weldon), had depicted a clerical student in love in *The valley of the squinting windows* (1918), an indictment of small-town narrowness. In another novel, *The clanking of chains* (1920), too much of which reads like a political tract, he anticipated O'Casey by portraying a village that was singularly reluctant to take part in the struggle against the British, though it achieved unanimity in its opposition to conscription. Mac-Namara afterwards became best known as an author of Abbey comedies.

O'Flaherty was without question the outstanding new Irish novelist and storyteller of the 1920s. In certain episodes of his novels and a number of virtually plotless short stories, he presents familiar incidents and phases of life on the Aran Islands, where he grew up. Many of these stories and passages are genuine works of art, but they also—like much of the early work of William Carleton or Gerald Griffin a century before—have the interest of an anthropologist's field notes. Their sober 'documentary' realism reminds us of Synge's journal *The Aran Islands*. On the other hand, when O'Flaherty chooses a theme for a novel, another meaning of 'realism' comes into play, that which makes it an antonym of 'idealism'. O'Flaherty's fictional Ireland, especially his Dublin, seems to contain more than its fair share of religious maniacs, political fanatics, military sadists, chaste prostitutes, and lustful priests.

O'Flaherty's most famous novel, *The informer* (1925), is only vaguely related to the political situation in Ireland. *The assassin* (1928) is much more explicitly based on the murder of Kevin O'Higgins in 1927, and *The martyr* (1934) deals unequivocally with the civil war. In this last novel a ruthlessly efficient and materialist Free State leader crucifies his Christlike republican opponent, sets fire to the cross, and hurls cross and victim into a lake. O'Flaherty withholds his sympathy from both the executioner and his narrowly puritanical, somewhat cowardly victim. A communist who fights on the republican side is the most sympathetic figure in the book. In a typically provocative O'Flaherty scene, a jovial Free State killer leaps naked into bed with a girl, his holy medals jingling. The novel was banned, as O'Flaherty probably intended. In *The puritan* (1932), the protagonist is a Dostoevskian religious maniac, who passionately belives in burning 'evil books'; his obsession culminates in the murder of a prostitute.

Only where O'Flaherty succeeded in marrying the two types of realism, setting his novels within the farming and fishing life that he knew best, did he produce masterpieces. *Skerrett* (1932) records an archetypal struggle between a primary schoolmaster and the parish priest who is the school manager—all the more poignant because Skerrett himself is no beacon of enlightenment. *Famine* (1937) brings to life the 'great hunger' of the 1840s in the manner of

Zola's *Germinal*, focusing on the sufferings of a single peasant family but also presenting members of other classes who come in contact with them; it is one of the greatest Irish novels.

A mood of disillusionment might seem an excellent forcing-house for satire, but in fact our period contains only one even partially successful satirist, Eimar O'Duffy. His novel *The wasted island* (1919; revised ed., 1929) bitterly criticised the way the 1916 rising had been secretly imposed on the Irish Volunteers by a small faction led by Pearse. His three satires—*King Goshawk and the birds* (1926), *The spacious adventures of the man in the street* (1928), and *Asses in clover* (1933)—are, however, less local in scope. Their main attack is directed against international monopolistic capitalism: King Goshawk, for instance, 'corners' the birds of the world, unopposed at first by anyone but an impoverished Dublin philosopher. The pettiness, hypocrisy, and physical squalor of much of Dublin life in the 1920s are sharply rebuked *en passant*. Cuchulain (Cú Chulainn), the Irish folk hero, is summoned from the other world to set things right, but both he and his son Cuanduine find the task beyond their powers. In *The spacious adventures*, the spirit of a Dublin grocer's assistant named O'Kennedy, whose body Cuchulain has borrowed, travels to the planet Rathe and, borrowing a body, compares the customs there with those in Ireland. By invoking Cuchulain and his pagan ethic, O'Duffy judges the entire modern world, including Ireland, and finds it wanting. Cuanduine cannot even teach modern man to fight chivalrously in the old epic manner.

WE have already noted in O'Flaherty's fiction a vein of realism akin to that of the documentary film or an anthropologist's field notes. He may show us the last hours at home of a boy or girl who are going to America ('Going into exile') or even something as brief as the landing of a currach from a stormy sea ('The landing'); there is no plot, nothing but observation.

Whatever the explanation, the best examples of this documentary realism undoubtedly come from the islands off Ireland's coasts, as did Robert Flaherty's famous documentary film *Man of Aran*. The list includes several autobiographies in Irish, afterwards translated, from the Blaskets; all O'Flaherty's writing about the Aran Islands in Irish and English; Michael McLaverty's first novel, *Call my brother back* (1939), and several short stories of his, from Rathlin; and Peadar O'Donnell's novels about Aranmore and the neighbouring Donegal coast.

O'Donnell grew up on that coast himself in a family of eleven children, was a schoolmaster on the islands of Inishfree and Aranmore, and then became a union organiser of the migrant workers from Donegal who went all over Ulster and to Scotland because there was no living for them at home. He fought against the British, became a member of the republican executive in the civil war, was captured at the taking of the Four Courts, took part in a hunger strike, and eventually escaped from an internment camp.[9] His later activities included leading resistance to the payment of land annuities in 1926-7 and helping to found the Republican Congress, a socialist-oriented branch of the republican movement, in 1934. He was often accused of communism in the 1930s but remained a practising catholic.

In spite of his deep political commitment, O'Donnell's novels are documentary rather than doctrinaire. *Islanders* (1928), the second of them, is a good example. It begins with a cow calving and continues with incidents that are hardly more dramatic. O'Donnell is content to describe the fight against starvation of one large impoverished family, the Doogans. *Adrigoole* (1929) is based on an actual incident of 1928 in the remote townland of Adrigole near the Cork–Kerry border. O'Donnell transferred the locale to Donegal and showed how members of a family unluckier than the Doogans, though no less industrious, could starve to death, having become estranged from their neighbours because of the civil war. *The knife* (1930) gives a rather rose-tinted picture of how a catholic family manage to establish themselves on a farm in the heart of Orange territory in east Donegal. Like *Storm* (1925), *The knife* narrates incidents of the Anglo–Irish war; it also deals with the civil war.

O'Donnell gave his political convictions their freest rein in *On the edge of the stream* (1934), a fictional account of the establishment of a cooperative store in a Donegal townland against the opposition of the parish priest and the gombeen man. In *Salud: an Irishman in Spain* (1937), the passages in which O'Donnell describes his feelings of shock at the burning and looting of churches, while trying to understand the motives of those who committed the sacrilege, are deeply moving. The potentially divisive effect of the Spanish civil war on Irish politics made few other appearances in literature.

A fictional map of Ireland during this period would be a peculiar one, rather like a jigsaw puzzle abandoned by an impatient child. The islands off the western and northern coasts are filled in, as we have seen, along with bits of the adjacent mainland. Joyce's *Ulysses*[10] mapped Dublin fairly thoroughly, but O'Flaherty shows us almost nothing of it but the slums. Belfast, pending the arrival of Michael McLaverty, offers us only a glimpse of its suburbs as background to the psychological subleties of Forrest Reid. The rest of Ireland—with the exception of the cities of Cork and Limerick, as we shall see—offers us a farm here, a country house there,[11] and no villages or towns at all except those of Brinsley MacNamara. Realism goes hand-in-hand with regionalism, but only certain regions seem to have appeal for the novelist or storyteller. Fortunately the dramatist, whether as sophisticated as Lennox

---

[9] See his reminiscences of this period in *The gates flew open* (London, 1932).

[10] Above, vi, 381–4.

[11] E.g. in Elizabeth Bowen, *The last September* (1929); Joyce Cary, *Castle Corner* (1938); 'M. J. Farrell' (Molly Keane), *The rising tide* (1937).

Robinson or as naive as George Shiels, finds villages and towns highly appealing.

One of the most interesting developments of this regional tendency in the novel is the early work of Kate O'Brien. *Without my cloak* (1931) and *The anteroom* (1934) are set in 'Mellick' (Limerick) during the second half of the nineteenth century. Most of the characters are drawn from a group of inter-related families of the merchant class. *Without my cloak* bears signs of a wish to do for the Considine family what Galsworthy did for the Forsytes. *The anteroom*, which deals with the Mulqueen family, relatives of the Considines, is a tightly knit tragedy quite unlike its sprawling predecessor; the conflict between love and catholic teaching on chastity sets up a tension that is not released even by the suicide on the last page. *Mary Lavelle* (1936) shows us a girl from the same social class in Limerick who goes to Spain as a governess in 1922. Before or after Kate O'Brien, Irish novels of upper-middle-class catholic life are few indeed.

The city that bulks largest in Irish literature of the 1930s is Cork, which had a population of about 70,000 at that time. Daniel Corkery had already caught some of its atmosphere in the stories and sketches of *A Munster twilight* (1916) and his only novel, *The threshold of quiet* (1917). Cork and its people are so closely in touch with the rural hinterland that all the Cork writers deal with both city and county, as Corkery did in his book of stories *The stormy hills* (1929). Corkery taught both O'Connor and O'Faolain, influencing their earlier writing. According to him, the 'three great forces which, working for long in the Irish national being, have made it so different from the English national being' are the religious consciousness of the people, Irish nationalism, and the land.[12] Essentially O'Connor and O'Faolain agreed with him, but they were a little sceptical about the permanent validity of these forces. Whereas Corkery's second collection of stories, *The hounds of Banba* (1920), idealises the Irish Volunteers, the stories of O'Connor and O'Faolain about the Anglo–Irish war and the civil war present the Irishmen who fought in them as something other than single-minded heroes. The title story of O'Connor's *Guests of the nation* (1931) records the reluctance of an Irish squad to execute two Tommies with whom they have become friends in the course of guarding them. The long title story of O'Faolain's *Midsummer night madness* (1932) shows an I.R.A. leader taking advantage of the anarchic state of the country to satisfy his taste for easy living and easy women. However, a nostalgic feeling of

> Bliss was it in that dawn to be alive
> But to be young was very heaven...[13]

modifies the disillusioned tone of these and similar stories.

[12] Daniel Corkery, *Synge and Anglo-Irish literature* (Cork, 1931), p. 19.
[13] Wordsworth, 'The prelude', xi, lines 108–9.

Corkery prefaced *The threshold of quiet* with Thoreau's famous aphorism: 'Most men lead lives of quiet desperation.' The hero of this novel becomes resigned to his lot, thanks to his religious faith, but the heroes of O'Faolain's *Bird alone* and *A nest of simple folk* (1934) and of O'Connor's *Dutch interior* (1940) experience similar personal defeats without finding similar consolation. This note of quiet—though often comic—desperation is struck over and over again in the novels and stories of O'Connor and O'Faolain. If their work is truly symptomatic of the Irish mood in the 1930s, then its gentle hopelessness is more frightening than the savagely mocking response of O'Flaherty and O'Casey in the previous decade. O'Donnell, as we have seen, put his faith in socialism to lift Ireland out of the slough of despond. Francis Stuart—more concerned to purge Ireland of materialism than to raise her spirits—wavered between mystical Christian self-sacrifice and xenophobic Irish fascism in such disturbing, faintly absurd novels as *The coloured dome* (1932) and *Pigeon Irish* (1932).

Austin Clarke, in two works that are romances rather than novels, evoked an older Ireland to solve the problems of the new. In *The bright temptation* (1932), two young lovers escape from various restraints into a half-legendary, half-medieval Ireland where they discover the facts of love for themselves in the manner of Daphnis and Chloe. As Clarke says in one of his poems:

> Burn Ovid with the rest. Lovers will find
> A hedge-school for themselves...[14]

This belief may have comforted him when *The bright temptation* was banned. Its successor, *The singing-men at Cashel* (1936), also banned, is a work of much greater complexity, based on the life of the historical queen Gormlai (Gormlaith). Not till her third marriage does she find a relationship that satisfies both body and spirit. These essentially optimistic prose works contrast sharply with Clarke's lyric poetry of the same period, especially that found in *Night and morning* (1938), the small volume that followed his *Collected poems* (1936). In the poems, sexual passion is usually frustrated or made ashamed of itself by catholic teaching on chastity. 'Hell lies about us in our infancy' was a critic's comment that pleased and amused Clarke.[15]

THE Irish theatre after O'Casey shows a greater variety of attitudes to the new Ireland than does the novel. The dramatist is much more influenced by the audience than the novelist by the readers, so it is probable that the Irish people were of more than one mind also. Perhaps the keenest expression of disillusionment after O'Casey's three plays was 'The old lady says no' (1929),

[14] From 'Penal law' in Austin Clarke, *Collected poems*, ed. Liam Miller (Dublin and Oxford, 1974), p. 189.
[15] Personal knowledge, from one of many conversations with the poet.

in which Denis Johnston shows us Robert Emmet returning to Dublin in the 1920s and being disgusted by what is happening now that his country has taken 'her place among the nations of the earth'. In 'The moon in the yellow river' (1931), Johnston offers a wry look at the movement towards industrialisation in Ireland but seems to conclude that the values of the past must make way for a more materialistic society. Commandant Lanigan deliberately kills Darrell Blake, who wished to destroy the power house: it seems as though the audience is asked to approve this murder. Ironically, the power house is then destroyed by accident, suggesting that Ireland is too inefficient to enter the twentieth century even if she wants to. Here, Johnston reveals his lifelong Anglo-Irish prejudices. Rutherford Mayne's 'Bridgehead' (1934) also expresses regret that material progress, though desirable, inevitably injures or destroys some traditional values. It contains a type of hero unusual in Irish drama: to quote Curtis Canfield, 'Stephen Moore is a patriot of the new order who gives his life in the drudgery of peacetime service to his country'.[16]

The growth of industrialisation in the Free State, especially during the 1930s, was a theme taken up by several writers. Many saw a dilemma facing the country, the horns being the clergy—of all denominations—and the industrialists. Both of these were to some extent the artist's natural enemies: the clergy took literature seriously enough to try to ban it, whereas the industrialists would treat it with indifference.

In an important play, 'Shadow and substance' (1937), Paul Vincent Carroll showed the conflict between materialism and idealism occurring within the catholic church itself. The canon represents an aristocratic tradition in the church, whereas his curates are a pair of vulgarians. The local schoolmaster has written a book that shocks many parishioners; the vigilance committee, supported by the curates, wants to burn copies of the book and find another master for the school. The canon, however, feels that the church is too old, wise, and secure to be threatened by a hotheaded young man. On the other hand, he dismisses as symptoms of hysteria the visions of St Brigid of Kildare that are seen by his innocent young servant, Brigid. She is later killed by a stone aimed at the schoolmaster, whom she is trying to protect against the angry parishioners. Is she perhaps a saint? The canon, by comparison with his curates, is certainly an idealist, but his failure to take Brigid seriously suggests that he possesses the letter rather than the spirit. Brigid and the schoolmaster, one supposes, are in Carroll's view more truly spiritual.

Lennox Robinson was at the height of his powers as a dramatist at this time. 'The big house' (1926) and 'Killycreggs in twilight' (1937) deal with a theme that touched him deeply, the fate of the Anglo-Irish gentry. In the

---

[16] Curtis Canfield (ed.), *Plays of changing Ireland* (New York, 1936), p. 199; this is a valuable survey of the drama of this period.

first of these plays, the burning of Ballydonal House by the I.R.A. might seem to end both the play and the role of the Anglo-Irish, but the curtain rises again the next morning: young Kate Alcock decides to rebuild the 'big house' and live out her life in Ireland. Conversely, the heroine of 'Killycreggs in twilight' says in the 1930s: 'There's no room in Ireland now for places like Killycreggs... I wish we'd been burnt out in the troubles.' Robert Hogan comments shrewdly: 'In this play the businessman beats the aristocrat, a theme quite acceptable at the new Abbey.'[17]

The hero of Robinson's 'Church Street' (1934) is a young would-be dramatist who complains that nothing ever happens in his little Irish town. His aunt undertakes to open his eyes to its hidden dramas. A series of short expressionistic scenes act out for him and for the audience the substance of her narrative: he sees, for instance, the unmarried girl who has had to go to London for an abortion. Nothing nearly so outré happens in the small-town plays of George Shiels, but whatever does happen is implicitly judged by the standards of a lower-middle-class society that is Christian without being specifically catholic or protestant. The fact that Shiels was from County Antrim may have made him shun sectarian reference. Characteristic of Shiels's more serious vein is 'Give him a house' (1939), in which a man who has been at odds with society becomes reconciled to it after acquiring property. The conflicts in Shiels's plays, whether serious or comic, are always resolved on some such level. For instance, 'The new gossoon' (1930), in which the title character, a representative of the new generation, dashes off to dances on his motorcycle, ends in the traditional way with the hero 'settling down' in marriage.

That Shiels was one of the most popular as well as prolific of Abbey dramatists during this period suggests that many of the Abbey audience— and their counterparts at the countless performances of Shiels's plays given by amateur companies—were quite content with Irish life as they found it and with the methods of resolving conflict that were traditional within it. But what of the conflicts that cannot be resolved? T. C. Murray, a genuine tragic dramatist, who came from a small town (Macroom, in County Cork) as Shiels did, preferred to deal with these, but in his later plays he draws back from any ending that involves breaking society's laws. When in 'Autumn fire' (1924) a young wife falls in love with her husband's son by his first marriage, no resolution—not even suicide—is possible. Like Kate O'Brien's unhappy heroines, she must go on suffering. Teresa Deevy, a playwright whose work belongs almost entirely to the 1930s, showed that some sort of frustration, resigned or not, was a likely fate for women in Ireland. Her heroines—Katie in 'Katie Roche' (1936), for example—would like to be

---

[17] Robert Hogan, *After the Irish renaissance* (London, 1963), p. 24.

saints or femmes fatales, but Irish society offers them only a rather humdrum married life, which they accept not so much stoically as heroically.

THE years 1921–39 roughly coincide with the third and last phase of Yeats's poetic development, which began in 1917. Soon afterwards, he achieved international status, without ceasing to be the national poet. The history of the Nobel prize for literature suggests that its award to Yeats in 1923 was in part a gesture of recognition to the new Irish state. Only after the publication of *The tower* (1928), his next volume of lyric poetry, was he hailed, through-out the English-speaking world at least, as a great twentieth-century poet rather than an interesting survivor from the nineteenth. His thought, in spite of its involvement with the occult system expounded in *A vision* (first version 1925), was felt to be significant for the modern world as a whole.

The period under consideration coincides even more precisely with the gestation (1922–38) of *Finnegans wake*. After the publication of *Ulysses* Joyce, who now lived in Paris, found himself viewed as the spearhead of the inter-national avant-garde and thus felt free to experiment with language even more daringly than before. Yeats was given similar self-confidence by several events: his marriage in 1917, and the simultaneous discovery of what appeared to be mediumistic gifts in his young wife; his appointment as a senator of the Irish Free State in 1922;[18] and the Nobel award in 1923. His first reaction to the news of this honour was to think: 'Now perhaps they will listen to me in Dublin.' While Ireland, north and south, was turning in on herself to seek national or even parochial goals, two of her greatest writers, one protestant, the other catholic, steadily grew in international reputation.

Joyce maintained a lively interest in Irish events. 'Andrew Cass' (John Garvin) has suggested that Eamon de Valera (b. 1882) served as one of the models for Shaun in *Finnegans wake*, just as Joyce himself, born in the same year, was a model for Shem.[19] Shem the Penman typifies the Irish writer, while Shaun the Post—an amalgam of civil servant, politician, and priest—typifies Irish society. Much of the time they are at loggerheads, but some-times they coalesce or exchange roles.

By becoming a senator (1922–8) Yeats was to some extent exchanging the role of Shem for that of Shaun, though his longest and most famous speech in the senate pitted him against most of the population of the Free State. On 11 June 1925 he spoke against a resolution that would in effect make divorce impossible within the state. Ranging himself uncompromisingly with the protestants, he insisted: 'You will not get the north if you impose on the minority what the minority consider to be oppressive legislation.' Later in

[18] It should be noted that the seat was first offered to George Russell (A E), who refused it.
[19] John Garvin, *James Joyce's disunited kingdom and the Irish dimension* (Dublin, 1976), pp 6–7, 136–51.

his speech he invoked the names of Burke, Grattan, Swift, Emmet, Parnell, saying: 'We are one of the great stocks of Europe...We have created the most of the modern literature of this country. We have created the best of its political intelligence.'[20] Perhaps the most satisfactory accomplishment of his years in the senate was his guidance of the committee that organised a competition to obtain the designs for the state's handsome new coinage. Work on another senate committee dealing with education prompted one of his most famous philosophic poems, 'Among schoolchildren'. Yeats did not stand for election at the end of his appointive term.[21]

Although the ageing Yeats made more use of classical mythology than he had previously done, he never abandoned Irish myths and themes. His last play was 'The death of Cuchulain' (1939), while 'The herne's egg' (1938) adapts the same Irish legend as did Sir Samuel Ferguson's 'Congal'. 'Purgatory', the last new play of his to be performed during his lifetime (1938), aroused controversy because of its heretical, aristocratic views on sin and purgatory, but passed off without the interruptions that attended 'The Countess Cathleen', his first play, in 1899.[22]

The tower and its winding stair, two of the most pervasive symbols in Yeats's later poetry, had of course physical equivalents. The Norman keep at Ballylee that Yeats bought in 1916 and later restored is very carefully linked with local legend and scenery in part II of 'The tower'. 'Nineteen hundred and nineteen' and 'Meditations in time of civil war' are essentially two series of philosophic poems on traditional, aristocratic life and the forces that threaten it from within as well as without. Nevertheless, they contain explicit references to events that occurred near Ballylee during the Black-and-Tan period and the civil war.[23]

A number of shorter poems, however, are devoted to political commentary, though not usually dealing with immediately contemporary events. Apart from the divorce speech already quoted and his article 'The Irish censorship' (*Spectator*, 29 September 1928), Yeats's stoutest blow against censorship and the prohibition of divorce was 'The three monuments', in which he referred to the statues in O'Connell Street, Dublin, of the known adulterers Parnell and Nelson and of Daniel O'Connell, a reputed adulterer in Irish folklore.

Yeats admired the ruthlessness of Kevin O'Higgins ('A soul incapable of remorse or rest') and wrote a short philosophical poem, 'Death', after his

[20] Compare part III of the poem 'The tower' (W. B. Yeats, *Collected poems* (2nd ed., London, 1950), pp 222–5). The germ of 'The three monuments' will be found earlier in the speech.
[21] This account of Yeats's senate career is based on Donald R. Pearce, *The senate speeches of W. B. Yeats* (Bloomington, Ind., 1960).
[22] Above, vi, 107–8, 372.
[23] See parts V and VI of 'Meditations' and the reference to 'a drunken soldiery' in part I of the other poem (Yeats, *Collected poems*, pp 225–37).

murder. Indeed Yeats was far too prone to admire dictators and demagogues who professed to uphold traditional order. He admired Mussolini and the theory, if not the practice, of his 'corporate state'. There was a moment in the early 1930s when he expected great things from O'Duffy's Blueshirts, writing for them 'Three songs to the same tune'. He also mentions O'Duffy in a more philosophic poem, 'Parnell's funeral'.

Nobody can fail to be impressed by the optimism of Yeats's *Last poems* (1936–9). He was convinced that his own death and a new world war were imminent, but thanks to his beliefs in reincarnation and in the cycles of history—both enunciated in *A vision*—he was convinced of his own immortality and the eventual resurgence of civilisation.[24] He reiterated these views in 'Lapis lazuli' and his poetical testament 'Under Ben Bulben', among other poems. Looking back at the 1916 rising, he seemed more confident than ever that it had been worthwhile, writing ballads in defence of Roger Casement and in praise of The O'Rahilly. The third of 'Three songs to the one burden' begins:

> Come gather round me, players all
> Come praise Nineteen-sixteen...

It ends more ominously, even though Yeats, because of his beliefs, seems little disturbed.

> And yet who knows what's yet to come?
> For Patrick Pearse had said
> That in every generation
> Must Ireland's blood be shed.
> *From mountain to mountain ride the fierce horsemen.*[25]

1939 is for Ireland a more significant date in literary than in political history. Much came to an end that year: Yeats died in January; in February Joyce received the first bound copy of his last book, *Finnegans wake*; he died in 1941 without having begun another. Sean O'Casey was still to write many plays, but the publication in 1939 of *I knock at the door*, the first volume of his autobiography, seemed an admission that his creative powers were waning.

Finnegans wake, Joyce had informed the world, dealt with man's sleeping hours rather than his waking ones. It is all a huge Freudian dream recorded in appropriate language, even if scholars have not yet agreed who is or are the dreamer or dreamers. One can reasonably argue that it is dreamed by the whole Irish people—past, present, and to come.

In 1938 Samuel Beckett had published his first novel, *Murphy*. The title character feels happiest in a state of trance induced by tying himself naked to a rocking-chair and rocking to and fro: 'for it was not until his body was

---

[24] W. B. Yeats, *A vision, and selected writings*, ed. A. N. Jeffares (London, 1990).
[25] Yeats, *Collected poems*, pp 373–4.

appeased that he could come alive in his mind . . .'.[26] More and more, Murphy comes to envy the escape into an inner world of the schizophrenic and wishes he could become one himself.

The narrator of Flann O'Brien (Brian O'Nolan)'s *At Swim-two-birds* (1939) spends a good deal of his time in bed; he has imagined an author named Dermot Trellis who spends even more of his time in a drugged sleep. The characters in Trellis's latest novel have found that they can do what they like while he is asleep; they therefore conspire to keep him in that state as much as possible.

These literary works proved strangely prophetic, since, during the war and for some years after, southern Ireland, willingly or not, passed into a state of suspended animation resembling dream, hibernation, or trance.

WE turn now to the second of our chosen subperiods, 1940–68. After 1940, for reasons both psychological and economic, Irish writers became less exile-prone than they used to be. Yeats, and Synge when he was well, tried to spend half the year outside Ireland; Moore lasted ten years in Dublin, then left for good. Two somewhat younger men, Joyce and O'Casey, could not stomach the rejection of their work: after the destruction of the sheets of *Dubliners* in 1912 and the rejection of 'The silver tassie' by the Abbey Theatre in 1928, there was no serious likelihood that either would ever settle in Ireland again. The banning of Beckett's first book in 1934 was probably equally decisive: when the outbreak of war in 1939 found him on holiday in Dublin, he hurried back to Paris. The much-banned Liam O'Flaherty remained in America throughout the 1939–45 war, though he later returned permanently to Ireland.[27]

On the other hand, Austin Clarke and Sean O'Faolain, who had also suffered from censorship, were already settled in Ireland when war broke out. Patrick Kavanagh had returned in 1937 after only five months in London. Frank O'Connor spent much of the war period in Ireland. Though censorship and philistinism tended to wax rather than wane, the writers who remained at home during the war did feel a sense of gratitude to their country for shelter-ing them and providing them with alternative sources of income, now that the British and American markets for their work were disappearing. Radio Éir-eann, the *Irish Times*, and other Dublin papers helped prose writers—and sometimes poets too.[28] The Abbey Theatre devoted itself almost entirely to the production of new Irish plays, while the Gate, Gaiety, and Olympia theatres all produced more Irish work than before.

[26] Samuel Beckett, *Murphy* (London, 1977), p. 6.
[27] For a longer list of expatriates, see Daniel Corkery, *Synge and Anglo-Irish literature* (Cork, 1931), p. 4 and fn.
[28] See *Poems from Ireland*, ed. Donagh MacDonagh (Dublin, 1944), a selection of poems published in the *Irish Times*, most of them during the war.

During the second world war, and for some years thereafter, many writers not in exile shared the turning inward of life in Ireland. It was hard to see that any western nation's culture was superior to that of Ireland; Germany, Russia, Italy, and Spain had all succumbed to different forms of totalitarianism. France had become too corrupt, it seemed, to defend her traditional liberties. No Irishman had ever doubted that Englishmen would fight fiercely for their own freedom; the real question was whether India, Africa, or Ireland would be any more free if Britain won the war than if she lost. One of the minor themes of Irish literary history since the war has been the gradual rediscovery of continental Europe. During the war, however, surprisingly few writers hankered for what lay outside Ireland's boundaries.

This wartime easing of tension between the writer and society—it should not be exaggerated, for conflicts were still frequent—disappeared almost entirely during the grim decade after the war. All the psychological irritants that had driven Joyce, O'Casey, and Beckett into exile seemed to increase in virulence, while the economic situation deteriorated for writers as for their fellows. Among periodicals, the 1950s saw the end of *Irish Writing*, which had seemed to inaugurate a post-war rebirth in 1946, of *Envoy* (founded 1949), of *The Bell*, and of the much older *Dublin Magazine*.

The beginning of a new cultural *détente* in the Republic was roughly coeval (1957–9) with the beginning of economic planning. The replacement of all the members of the censorship of publications board, as the result of two appointments in 1956 and three in 1957, produced a body whose 'attitude of mind...seemed to be quite new', according to the standard authority.[29] Nevertheless, there was a brief flare-up of the older attitudes at this time, though the reconstituted censorship board was not always attacked.[30]

The first Dublin international theatre festival, held in the spring of 1957, was sadly marred by the arrest of Alan Simpson on 23 May; he was charged in court next day with having 'produced for gain an indecent and profane performance' at the Pike Theatre—Tennessee Williams's 'The rose tattoo'. Simpson was not acquitted until thirteen months later, and had to bear the heavy costs of legal proceedings. Meanwhile, early in 1958, Archbishop McQuaid refused to permit the opening of the Dublin Tóstal celebrations with any religious ceremony, on the ground that they would include a dramatisation of Joyce's *Ulysses* and a play specially written by O'Casey, 'The drums of Father Ned'. Others backed the archbishop's stand, and the festival had to be postponed and then cancelled. Since 1959, however, when a stage version of J. P. Donleavy's *The ginger man* was halted by clerical

---

[29] Adams, *Censorship*, p. 122.   [30] Ibid., pp 165–6.

opposition, there seems to have been no attempt to impose an unofficial censorship on the Dublin theatre.[31]

Prior to 1957, the censorship of publications board had been the chief point of friction between literature and society in the Republic. *The Bell*, a monthly founded by Sean O'Faolain in 1940, constantly criticised not the existence of censorship but the way in which the 1929 and 1946 acts were applied. During the war, liberal opinion was particularly offended by the banning of three books: Frank O'Connor's translation of Brian Merriman's famous poem in Irish, *The midnight court* (1945), the only Irish-published book ever to be banned; Kate O'Brien's novel *The land of spices* (1941); and *The tailor and Ansty* (1942), Eric Cross's record of the conversation of an old County Cork tailor and his wife. In 1942 the banning of *The tailor and Ansty* prompted Senator Sir John Keane to introduce a motion in the senate critical of the censorship board. Although the motion was lost, the debate provided an opportunity for criticisms of censorship to be aired. In 1945 the Fianna Fáil government belatedly responded with its own bill to amend the 1929 act; the main new feature of this was the establishment of a five-member appeals board.[32] Though the appeal procedure was costly for the author or publisher, in the period 1946–64 there were 432 appeals, 314 of which led to the revocation of prohibition orders. Meanwhile, the annual number of bannings rose steadily, reaching 1,034 in 1954 out of a total of 1,217 titles submitted for examination, chiefly by the customs authorities.

Any judgement on what constitutes 'indecent or obscene' literature is likely to be subjective, and the pre-1957 literary holocausts—only possible on the basis of reading marked passages instead of whole books—included both the romantic over-simplifications of Walter Macken and the obscure austerities of Beckett's *Molloy* (1951) and *Watt* (1953). Not that the censorship board became infallible after 1957; banned works included Brian Moore's objective study of an alcoholic, *Judith Hearn* (1955), later reissued as *The lonely passion of Judith Hearne*, and almost the entire *oeuvre* of Edna O'Brien. Following an uproar over the banning of John McGahern's *The dark* in 1965, a new censorship of publications act was passed in 1967. While preserving the principle of censorship by a board, this act limited the effect of a prohibition order to twelve years, although the order could be renewed thereafter. Since this procedure was retrospective, it released over 5,000 titles automatically.[33]

---

[31] David Krause, *Sean O'Casey: the man and his work* (paperback ed., New York, 1962), pp 272–81. For the 1959 incident, see 'What they did in Dublin with *The ginger man*' in *The plays of J. P. Donleavy* (New York, 1972), pp 17–42.

[32] 1946/1 (3 Feb. 1946).

[33] 1967/15 (11 July 1967). Again, I am deeply indebted to Michael Adams for the facts of this narrative, though not necessarily for the emphasis.

A more positive aspect of the relationship between literature and society—namely, the subsidising of that art, among others, by the state—became evident in the years after 1940. By 1943 Northern Ireland had its own Council for the Encouragement of Music and the Arts (C.E.M.A.), renamed 'The Arts Council of Northern Ireland' in 1962. The Free State had accepted the principle of support for the Abbey Theatre and drama in the Irish language as early as 1924; it was not till 1951, however, that the arts act established An Chomhairle Ealaíon (the Arts Council) in the Republic to foster 'painting, sculpture, architecture, music, the drama, literature, design in industry and the fine arts, and applied arts generally'.[34]

In 1951 the original Abbey Theatre and its smaller annexe, the Peacock Theatre, were put out of action by a fire that destroyed all of the back-stage premises. Performances by the Abbey company continued in the Queen's Theatre till 1966, when a new building was opened on an enlarged site; it houses both the Abbey and the Peacock. The rebuilding was aided by a 1959 act of the oireachtas, authorising a contribution of £250,000.[35] New directors and new shareholders were added to the National Theatre Society by the Irish government in 1964.

The sociology and economics of postwar literary life in Ireland were most sharply affected, however, by three relatively new factors: the growth of radio broadcasting, the establishment of local television channels (1955 and 1959 in Northern Ireland, 1961 and 1978 in the Republic), and the expansion of the universities. A number of plays by Irish authors—some written for the stage, others specially written for radio—were broadcast; indeed, the most unmistakably Irish of Beckett's plays, 'All that fall' (1957), was given its first performance by the B.B.C. Feature programmes and serials also offered opportunities to writers: while encouraging much ephemeral work, in Northern Ireland they provided Sam Thompson, for example, with his apprenticeship, and elicited the documentary talents of W. R. Rodgers. Austin Clarke's poetry programmes on Radio Éireann and Frank O'Connor's readings of his own short stories on the air exemplified another of radio's potentialities. Television, when it arrived, put almost every dramatist and potential dramatist to work—revealing, for instance, Hugh Leonard's and later William Trevor's skills as adapters of fiction. Brendan Behan, for better or worse, became known around the world for his appearances, and non-appearances, on television talk shows.

The Irish universities, north and south, have now learned to imitate their American counterparts by giving temporary or permanent employment as lecturers or writers-in-residence to authors old and young; furthermore, sev-

---

[34] 1951/9 (8 May 1951); An Chomhairle Ealaíon, *Twentieth annual report and accounts* (1971/2), p. 3.

[35] 1959/32 (24 Nov. 1959).

eral poets and playwrights are by profession teachers of English literature in the expanded university systems. The prestige of Irish writers and their opportunities for academic employment have been greatly enhanced by the strong interest in this literature shown by a number of universities and cultural organisations in North America. Great Britain, France, Sweden, the Lebanon, and Japan, among other countries, have followed the American example, so that year-round 'summer schools' for Anglo-Irish studies now exist in Ireland, both within and outside the universities.

Among the periodicals in the Republic that provided intellectual leadership as well as publishing poems, short stories, and book reviews, preeminence in this period must be given to the monthly *The Bell* (1940–48, 1950–54), especially under its first editor, Sean O'Faolain, who played a far more active part than its second, Peadar O'Donnell. O'Faolain was not content to solicit contributions with flair and persistence, he sometimes rewrote them. *Irish Writing* (1946–57) and its supplement, *Poetry Ireland* (1948–52), were purely literary publications, as was *Envoy* (1949–51) for the most part. The leading poetry magazine in the Republic is now *Cyphers*, founded in 1975, while the *Irish University Review*, founded in 1970, combines literature with scholarship.

In some cultural areas that are of importance to literature, Dublin lost the commanding position she held in the 1920s. The National Library, National Museum, and Public Record Office suffered greatly from governmental parsimony. Fortunately, Trinity College showed a proper sense of its responsibilities in the 1960s, obtaining funds from government, business, and the Ford Foundation to build and operate its new library. In literary publishing Belfast came to rival Dublin, the pace-setter being the Blackstaff Press. In the Republic the Dolmen Press, founded by Liam Miller in 1951, must however still be recognised as without peer in the postwar period. Among Miller's numerous finely printed editions of contemporary Irish poets, the crowning achievement is undoubtedly *The Táin* (1969), a vigorous modern translation in prose and verse by Thomas Kinsella of the 'Táin Bó Cuailnge', with black-and-white illustrations by Louis le Brocquy that seem to put the reader into direct contact with the archaic violence of the original saga.

One feature of the postwar period was that during much of that time the Irish writer and society were growing closer together. It was by no means a smooth, continuous process; the two parties attracted and repelled each other in turn. By now, though, as in a marriage of long standing, each had come to expect a good deal less of the other. The writer had ceased to demand that the Irish nation-state be the earthly paradise; the state and its people, for their part, had ceased to demand that the writer be, in word and deed, the fit inhabitant of that paradise. Society grew more patient with the impatience of the writer, with the hankering after freedom, with the need for a moral chaos on which to impose an aesthetic order. Irish writers became more at ease, both materially and morally, in their society than at any time since the heyday of the bards.

YEATS and Joyce died in 1939 and 1941 respectively. Who, then, enacted the difficult role of 'the Irish writer' before their countrymen in the three decades preceding the new troubles in the north? Who best typified the relationship between the writer and society during that period?

In general, the exiles could be ruled out, since those who lived entirely abroad could not feel the full weight of Irish society. O'Casey, however, continued to press his breast to the thorn: interviews, articles, letters to newspapers, even his plays and the successive volumes of his autobiography, were long-range missiles in his 'lover's war' with Ireland. There was, however, a widespread feeling that both O'Casey's art and his marksmanship had suffered by his too long absence. While most Irish writers and journalists naturally sided with O'Casey against those who tried to stop the Dublin production of 'The bishop's bonfire' in 1955, they plaintively wished that the old man had written a better play.

Let us therefore choose as representative of their profession seven writers, born and reared in Ireland, who spent most of their adult years at home also: Brendan Behan (1923–64), Austin Clarke (1896–1974), Conor Cruise O'Brien (1917–   ), Patrick Kavanagh (1904–67), Frank O'Connor (1903–66), Sean O'Faolain (1900–91), and Brian O'Nolan (1911–66). These names, arranged in alphabetical order, are not necessarily those of the seven best Irish writers of the period, though most of them would have to be seriously considered for such a selective list; all, however, chose or had thrust upon them a public role that other writers never felt impelled to play. Peadar O'Donnell (1893–1986) might have been included in this list, but somehow his intellectual position and his artistic achievements did not make a strong impression once the 1930s were over. Before 1968 no Northern Ireland writer, however revered at home, had great impact on the island as a whole. No woman writer, either, was accepted as the voice of her peers: Edna O'Brien might conceivably have been if she had stayed in Ireland, but like Elizabeth Bowen and Kate O'Brien she became an exile; Maura Laverty died young; Mary Lavin and Eilís Dillon had little time to spare from their work and their families.

The public commentary of these seven male writers could take the most diverse forms. Clarke would publish a verse epigram or a longer satiric poem, often in the *Irish Times*. Kavanagh too might comment in verse, or write what was less an article than a series of *obiter dicta*; some of this material is reprinted in his *Collected prose* (1967). As 'Myles na Gopaleen', O'Nolan might fill his column 'Cruiskeen lawn' for days or even weeks with some fantastic *reductio ad absurdum* of a trend he deplored; in the later years of the column, which ran in the *Irish Times* from 1940 to 1966, he was all too prone to substitute mere invective for irony and humour.

O'Faolain wrote editorials on a wide range of subjects, national and international, while in charge of *The Bell* (October 1940–April 1946). He was also a co-founder or member of various organisations—notably the Irish Association of Civil Liberty (1948) and the Writers, Actors, Artists, and Musicians Association (W.A.A.M.A.) (1941) which could apply pressure in matters that affected the quality of Irish life as a whole.[36] Both he and Frank O'Connor commented on Irish life in much of their non-fiction, whether travel books or biographies of Irish leaders.

Behan sometimes made up a ballad to a traditional tune, but usually favoured oral comment with a microphone, a tape-recorder, or a reporter's notebook handy. During his years as a dáil deputy and minister, Cruise O'Brien was able to comment orally at frequent intervals, but his most valuable insights into Irish life will be found in *Parnell and his party* (1957) and *States of Ireland* (1972), which are essentially works of history. During his twenty years as a civil servant and diplomat, he wrote critical articles on politics and literature under a number of pseudonyms, the first being 'Donat O'Donnell', adopted for *The Bell* in 1945.

All of these writers had a deep commitment to Ireland, if only in the sense that they were loath to live anywhere else; at least four of them (Behan, Cruise O'Brien, O'Connor, O'Faolain) risked their lives for their personal convictions, and two (O'Connor and Behan) suffered imprisonment. Lifted out of their Irish context, however, they could be arranged politically in a fairly wide arc to right and left of centre. O'Nolan was deeply conservative, as satirists tend to be; in Britain he would have been a tory. So would O'Connor, who found Yeats's aristocratic prejudices congenial. Kavanagh, like O'Connor, knew what poverty was; he felt that it hampered the mind even more than the body; but he supported no programme for changing the status quo. Clarke and O'Faolain were liberals in the American sense, deeply concerned about the liberty of the individual but willing to work for change within the existing system. Probably only Cruise O'Brien and Behan were ever convinced socialists, though Behan was by instinct an anarchist.

The burden of these writers' criticism of their society was much what one would expect: Ireland was priest-ridden, puritanical, philistine, hypocritical, snobbish, money-grubbing, provincial (Kavanagh stressed that to be parochial was good for a writer, while to be provincial, in the sense of taking one's standards from abroad, deprived one of originality). Provoked by similar developments in twentieth-century Ireland, they often echoed charges brought by Carlyle and Matthew Arnold against the English bourgeoisie of their day.

[36] For the Irish Association of Civil Liberty (subsequently the Irish Council for Civil Liberties) see Adams, *Censorship*, pp 148, 228 (n. 10); for the W.A.A.M.A. (subsequently the Irish Actors Equity Association) see Sarah Ward-Perkins (ed.), *Select guide to trade union records in Dublin* (Dublin, 1996), pp 185–6.

The fiercest opponents of clerical dominance in both the intellectual and the moral sphere were Clarke and O'Connor: its bitterest consequence, they felt, was sexual repression, with all the private anguish that entailed. O'Faolain agreed with them on this point, but felt that freedom of expression was equally fundamental; he resisted all forms of censorship and fought for freedom of speech in the broadest sense. Too many Irish people say one thing in public and the opposite in private; O'Faolain wished the private and the public voice to be truer to each other.

Kavanagh in his later years felt that it was a poet's duty to celebrate rather than criticise, but his essential charge against Irish rural society, conveyed so powerfully in *The great hunger* (1942), so humorously in his one novel, *Tarry Flynn* (1948), was that it thwarted too many of life's potentialities: poetry, love, generosity, magnanimity—even, in the end, true religious faith. He shared O'Nolan's contempt for middle-class Dublin's social and cultural snobbery. 'Myles na Gopaleen' brilliantly ridiculed the sort of person who likes to own a fine library without reading the books, or to talk impressively about the arts without real knowledge, though sometimes this ridicule went over the edge into vituperation. Nothing aroused his scorn more than politicians who traded on their national record or made a shibboleth of the Irish language—especially if they spoke it badly.[37] Behan too, in his play 'The hostage' (1958), directed harsh criticism against those who lived in the past, hoarding the old enmities between Ireland and England, republican and Free Stater. Paradoxically, in view of his own earlier violent record, he spoke too against cruelty, conscious and unconscious, in a society that took many forms of mental and physical cruelty for granted; his play 'The quare fellow' emphasised the barbarity of both imprisonment and hanging.

Cruise O'Brien escaped much of the pettiness of Irish society. Among his parents, cousins, uncles, and aunts was to be found virtually every shade of political and religious belief and unbelief; more important, his family tolerated each other's views and defended each other against society at large. As a result of his upbringing, he was able to see Ireland as part of a wider world, and helped her to play an important part during her first years in the U.N. Then and later, he reminded the Irish that their struggle against colonialism formed part of a worldwide movement. On the other hand, from the early 1970s he insisted that if the people of the Republic genuinely desired the unity of the whole island, they must abandon narrow tribalism for a broader concept of Irish nationality.

The social and economic backgrounds and educational attainments of these seven writers were at least as diverse as their political outlooks, though none was a protestant or closely connected with the landed gentry. It is worth noting that most of their families belied one Irish stereotype: O'Con-

---

[37] See *The best of Myles*, ed. Kevin O'Nolan (London, 1968).

nor and Cruise O'Brien had no brothers or sisters, while most of the others came from small families. Behan's family was fairly large because his mother married twice, but only O'Nolan came from a really large family, being the third child of twelve. In contrast with any comparable group of writers from earlier periods, a majority of them began life at the lower end of the social scale. Behan (son of a Dublin house-painter), O'Connor (son of a Cork manual labourer and former private soldier), and Kavanagh (son of a County Monaghan shoemaker and small farmer) all had only a primary education, leaving school no later than 14. O'Faolain, however, the son of an R.I.C. constable in Cork, won M.A.s from U.C.C. and Harvard. Clarke, whose family had been Dublin middle-class for generations, obtained a B.A. and M.A. from U.C.D. O'Nolan, born in Strabane but reared chiefly in Dublin, also earned an M.A. from U.C.D., although he had no formal schooling till nearly 12; his father was a revenue commissioner who died relatively young. Cruise O'Brien, whose father, a journalist, also died young, had two T.C.D. graduates for parents; his mother taught at a technical school; in due course he obtained a Ph.D. from Trinity. All of the seven except Kavanagh had some fluency in the Irish language, though not one was a native speaker. More remarkable still, all of them except Behan and Kavanagh achieved some scholarly knowledge of Old and Middle Irish. All except O'Nolan and Cruise O'Brien had at least one book banned by the censorship board.

There was one heartening sign about this generation of Irish writers. Although so many Irish novels have ended—like Moore's *The lake* and Joyce's *A portrait of the artist*—with the hero's departure from Ireland, many pre-1968 autobiographies—Kavanagh's *The green fool* (1938), Behan's *Borstal boy* (1958), Clarke's *A penny in the clouds* (1968), O'Faolain's *Vive moi!* (1964)—ended with the author's thankful return. When as many autobiographies end with an equally heartfelt return to Northern Ireland, we shall have reached a new phase of Irish literary and social history.

THE literary works most likely to have an impact on Irish society, especially after the introduction of television, were plays. In 1959 it was estimated that the maximum sale of any cloth-bound book in the Republic was 4,000 copies, while the typical sale of a cloth-bound Irish novel was about 750 copies.[38] Paper-bound sales would of course reach a higher figure. A playwright who captured the imagination of the Irish people, however, might reach not merely the theatre audience in the cities and the broadcast audience, but also a remarkable number of people who attended performances by the amateur dramatic companies, over 300 of which competed each year in fourteen regional festivals and the national finals. The audience for amateur drama was estimated at a quarter of a million people, only a fraction of whom,

---

[38] Adams, *Censorship*, p. 225, n. 52.

naturally, would see any one play, even the winning production, in a given year.[39] A really popular play, though, would go the round of a number of the competing groups over the years, besides being performed by others too modest or too unskilled to enter any competition.[40] In this way a playwright might reach, through a combination of live and broadcast performances, an Irish audience numbered in hundreds of thousands, as against tens of thousands for even the most successful novelist.

In 1959 John B. Keane, a publican in the small town of Listowel, County Kerry, had his first play, 'Sive', chosen by the local amateur group as their entry in the annual competition. This was a daring step, but the Listowel acting and production made 'Sive' a winner for the best production at the all-Ireland festival in Athlone. Performances at the Abbey and in Cork followed; 'Sive' was then broadcast twice on Radio Éireann and booked for a performance on British television—all before the end of 1959.[41] 'Sive' dealt with themes and character types often seen before in Abbey plays; the novelty was that the play's success began in the 'grass roots' and travelled to the capital, thus reversing the usual process.

It is sometimes difficult to understand why certain 'kitchen comedies'—or, more often, kitchen melodramas—captured the Irish imagination while others of similar formula did not. Still, by looking at some of the most successful new plays of a given period, one can gain insight into how the Irish people saw or would have liked to see themselves.

At the beginning of the second world war the Abbey Theatre management decided to let each new play run for as long as possible, instead of replacing it after two or three weeks with a work from the repertory. As it happened, the first play to have a long run by Dublin standards was George Shiels's 'The rugged path', which drew audiences for twelve weeks in 1940. It was a strong plea for law and order; indeed, the secret of Shiels's lifelong success was that he generally supported the rural and small-town status quo. The play ends, however, with the apparent victory of the lawless Dolis family over the law-abiding Tanseys. A sequel, 'The summit' (1941), showed other farmers siding with Michael Tansey to take the law into their own hands and drive Peter Dolis out of the district—rather contradicting the moral of the earlier play. At any rate, whereas a tramp or outlaw had been the true hero of many a play by Yeats, Synge, and other writers of the literary revival, Irish rural values were now reasserting themselves on the stage.[42]

---

[39] Mícheál Ó hAodha, *Plays and places* (Dublin, 1961), pp 123–8.

[40] In 1973, according to information supplied by Mervyn Wall, there were about 820 amateur dramatic societies in all Ireland.

[41] Mícheál Ó hAodha, foreword to John B. Keane, *Sive* (Dublin, 1964), pp 5–6.

[42] Much of my information about the Irish theatre at this period comes from Robert Hogan, *After the Irish renaissance* (Minneapolis, 1967).

Few Irish plays produced in Dublin dealt directly with the war, and none of those that did was very popular. Lennox Robinson adapted Maupassant's story 'Boule de suif' for the stage, updating it from 1870 to 1940, but the Vichy French legation in Dublin objected to its being performed. Hilton Edwards and Mícheál Mac Liammóir reluctantly withdrew the play after a few nights. Paul Vincent Carroll's 'The strings, my lord, are false' (1942), set in Glasgow during the heavy air raids, was put on at the Olympia Theatre but made few people feel that they had gained any deeper insight. O'Casey's 'Oak leaves and lavender' (1946) was apparently never performed in Ireland. Its glorification of the war, attributable to O'Casey's communist sympathies, comes very strangely from the author of 'The silver tassie' (1928), which is almost a tract against war.

The continuing depopulation of Ireland through emigration and late marriages inevitably inspired a number of plays during the 1940s, 1950s, and 1960s, as it had ever since Colum's 'The land' (1905). Michael J. Molloy's first play, 'Old road' (1943), dealt with those who took the old road out of their difficulties into exile. His evocatively titled 'The wood of the whispering' (1953) recalled 'the courting couples that used to be in it [the wood] some years ago before all the lads and the girls went foreign'. To prevent further emigration, people must marry younger, so the wise fool Sanbatch sets out to arrange marriages. John B. Keane's 'Many young men of twenty' (1961) reminds us that the playwright himself emigrated at the age of 24 in 1952, spending three years in England. But the classic play about emigration remains Brian Friel's 'Philadelphia, here I come!' (1964).

One section of the Republic's population that continued to shrink—through emigration, low birth rate, and intermarriage with catholics—was the subject of W. J. White's 'The last eleven' (1968), concerned with the remaining members of a Church of Ireland congregation, who generously present their empty church to the overcrowded catholic parish. Other plays took note of immigration as wealthy English people and other foreigners moved into Ireland to escape taxation or the pace of urban life: Sean O'Casey's extravaganza 'Purple dust' (1940), for example, and Louis D'Alton's 'This other Eden' (1953), a sort of poor man's 'John Bull's other island'.

Inevitably, many Abbey plays examined the relationship of the Irish priest with his flock. The two most popular such plays between 1940 and 1955 treated the clergy more tenderly than Paul Vincent Carroll's work of the 1930s had done. Frank Carney's 'The righteous are bold' (1946) invites interpretation as symbolic of Irish attitudes to the outside world during and after the war; the heroine returns from England a victim of demonic possession. The demon is exorcised by a priest at the cost of his own life. Joseph Tomelty of Belfast had an Abbey run of 112 performances in 1954–5 with 'Is the priest at home?' This problem play demonstrated that the Irish priest was in many ways dominated by his parishioners rather than lording it over them.[43]

Paul Vincent Carroll softened towards the clergy in his later years, especially in 'The wayward saint' (1955); O'Casey, on the contrary, who had been circumspect in his early plays, grew steadily more hostile. 'Cock-a-doodle dandy' (1949), a fantasy in praise of 'natural' sexuality, contained the aptly named Father Domineer, who kills an adulterous member of his flock with a blow of his fist, showing no remorse. 'The bishop's bonfire' (1955) dealt with the preparation for the visit of a newly consecrated bishop to his native place; the bonfire would consist of evil literature.

Plays about politics became harder to write after O'Casey destroyed the old patriotic melodrama once and for all with 'The plough and the stars' and its two predecessors. In doing away with all the old platitudes, O'Casey seemed also to have spoken most of the new disillusioned truths, leaving nothing else for anyone to say about revolution and civil war. One sympathises with Brian Friel, John Boyd, and others who have tried to write of the later northern troubles under O'Casey's shadow. Nevertheless, the most successful Abbey play of 1948, M. J. Molloy's 'The king of Friday's men', greatly resembled a Victorian patriotic melodrama. Molloy's play is in fact a good deal more subtle than at first appears, but it is extraordinary to think that only one other Irish play—Gerard Healy's 'The black stranger' (1945)—had previously made use of the sexual exploitation of Irish women by the foreign colonist. Only a few novels, including John Banim's *The Nowlans* (1826) and Liam O'Flaherty's *Famine* (1937), had ever touched on the subject. The very word 'tallywoman', the standard euphemism for a concubine, had been forgotten by all but a handful of Irish people.

Séamus Byrne's 'Design for a headstone' (1950), the last play to provoke an organised protest in the old Abbey Theatre before the fire of 1951, showed that O'Casey had not after all exhausted the subject of underground warfare. The paranoid suspicions and self-righteousness of the I.R.A. largely motivate the plot, but the prisoners in the jail where the play is set constantly discuss the ethics of hunger strike. Is it suicide, as the chaplain insists? And is he justified in denying absolution to members of an illegal, oath-bound organisation? In contrast to the multiple issues raised by Byrne's play, Behan's 'The quare fellow' (1954), also set in Mountjoy prison and also based on personal experience, raised a single issue, the morality of capital punishment. Joan Littlewood's London production of 1956 came at the height of the campaign against capital punishment in Britain. Without ever presenting the 'quare fellow' (the condemned man, admittedly in this case a brutal murderer) directly to the audience, Behan built up through naturalistic dialogue among governor, hangman, convicts, and warders a picture of

[43] Mathew J. O'Mahony, *Progress guide to Anglo-Irish plays* (Dublin, 1960), p. 65.

the cold-blooded cruelty of hanging. The play may have helped to create the climate in which capital punishment in Ireland eventually became unacceptable.[44]

Behan's 'The hostage' (1958) treated both politics and sex with gaiety and irreverence. In the years that followed, however, a number of Irish plays treated sex very seriously indeed. John B. Keane's 'Sive' was a standard Abbey melodrama about the 'made match', in which Sive, the heroine, kills herself rather than marry the ugly old man her grasping family has chosen for her. 'The highest house on the mountain', Keane's third play, had the longest run of the 1961 theatre festival. The basic situation here—a son returning with his wife to a house inhabited by his widowed father, his bachelor uncle, and his bachelor brother—anticipated that of Harold Pinter's 'The homecoming' (1965). All the men in the house desire the lone woman in both plays, but Keane's has the more wholesome ending, though a most unexpected one for a popular Irish play: the union of an ex-rapist and an ex-prostitute.

Homosexuality, however tolerantly and unsensationally treated, was the essential subject of Thomas Kilroy's 'The death and resurrection of Mr Roche', first performed at the 1968 festival. Subsidiary themes of Kilroy's play include the prolonged adolescence of many Irishmen, their use of alcohol as a surrogate for sex, and the rootlessness of country boys when they take jobs in the city. John B. Keane also dramatised these themes; but perhaps the most powerful of all such plays was Thomas Murphy's 'A whistle in the dark' (1961), set in a council house in Coventry. Michael Carney is torn between two loyalties: one to his English wife, Betty, the other to his three drunken brawling Irish brothers, who share his home. (This too is a one-woman play.) It ends tragically, for the gentle Michael kills his favourite youngest brother in a drunken fight, egged on by their feckless, bullying father.

For Robert Hogan, writing at the end of this period (and before the Northern Ireland troubles had made a significant impact on Irish writing), Irish drama was becoming extinct, in the sense that it was losing its Irishness. 'And the reason, quite simply, is that the Irishness of Ireland itself is every day being rapidly dissipated.' It is tempting to agree with Hogan's summary of the development of Anglo-Irish drama from 1899 to the late 1960s: 'There is first the attempt to recapture the disintegrating past. There is next the attempt to show the past in its losing battle with the present. And there is finally the surrender to the present by writing a play which can be labelled

---

[44] The last persons to receive capital sentences in Ireland were Noel and Marie Murray in 1976 (for the capital murder of Garda Michael Reynolds). However, the supreme court quashed the convictions for capital murder and sentenced them to life imprisonment for murder. The death penalty was abolished in N.I. in 1973 (1973, c. 53) (25 July 1973) and in the Republic in 1990 (1990/16) (11 July 1990).

Irish mainly because its author was an Irishman.'[45] One might add to this summing-up a further reflection: the tensions generated by the time-honoured subjects of religion, nationality, and the land had begun to slacken, and could no longer be relied on to give automatic coherence to a dramatic work—or, we shall find, to a novel.

IN the 1940s and 1950s the short story was the typical Irish narrative form. O'Connor and O'Faolain had abandoned the novel entirely. Among somewhat younger writers, Mary Lavin regretted ever having written her two novels; Bryan MacMahon, too, built his reputation chiefly on his short stories. Subsequently, however, the market for short fiction in the English-speaking world began to shrink. Simultaneously, the growth of the paperback industry encouraged the writing of novels, so that a new writer, instead of building a reputation slowly with a short story here and there, might emerge suddenly with the publication of a first novel. Besides this external pressure against the short story, the form was in danger of being cut off from its roots within Ireland. Because of radio and television, the custom of oral story-telling in both Irish and English became almost extinct; even the Irish habit of leisurely, anecdotal conversation was on the wane.[46] Nevertheless, short stories as well as novels were still broadcast regularly on Irish radio.

Nationalism lost some of its significance for writers in the south when it became clear that the United Kingdom would respect their country's neutrality during the war. The Irish who enlisted in the British forces or found employment in wartime England were usually either unable or unwilling to express their very mixed feelings. Leslie Daiken's *They go, the Irish* (1944), a miscellany of wartime writing from England, and Bryan MacMahon's delightful 'The plain people of England' in *The Bell* were perhaps the best contemporary testimonies. Later, Denis Johnston published his deeply ironic war memoirs, *Nine rivers from Jordan* (1953); he wanted to see Hitler defeated but much of the 'war effort' seemed a comic waste of energy. Later still, Anthony C. West published a long autobiographical novel, *As towns with fire* (1968), in which the hero tries to explain to himself, at great length, why he—an Irishman, a poet, and a pacifist—has become a combatant. Paradoxically, his accounts of taking part in R.A.F. bombing raids are the most fully realised scenes in the novel.

The subject of the land might have remained a burning one, but it seemed to hold little interest for those who began to write after 1940. Michael McLaverty, a northern writer, devoted his first two novels, *Call my brother*

---

[45] Robert Hogan, 'Where have all the shamrocks gone?' in Patrick Rafroidi (ed.), *Aspects of the Irish theatre* (Lille, 1972), p. 267.

[46] See Vivian Mercier, 'The Irish short story and oral tradition' in Ray B. Browne (ed.), *The celtic cross* (Lafayette, Ind., 1964), pp 98–116.

back (1939) and *Lost fields* (1941), to the plight of families who regretted leaving the land for the city. Usually, though, the land seemed a good place to escape from, as in Patrick Kavanagh's *Tarry Flynn* (1948)—though every page of that autobiographical novel breathes nostalgia for country smells, sights, and sounds. The related subject of emigration seemed not to tempt the novelist either.

Some Irish writers who had books banned for their alleged undue emphasis on sex were actually more concerned with one or all of Corkery's three forces. Frank O'Connor, though often banned, rarely confronted sexuality: his great theme was social control. Take his *The common chord* (1947), for instance, a volume of stories devoted to the theme of love *á l'irlandaise*. The book was duly banned, yet its whole burden was that in Ireland Cupid was never given a chance. The moment two people of opposite sex, young or old, showed the slightest interest in each other, their families, the priest, the neighbours, all began to meddle. O'Connor once ended a story with the words 'And that is why there are no Irish detective stories'; he might have written as epigraph to *The common chord* 'And that is why there are no Irish love stories'.

O'Faolain, on the other hand, was fascinated by the way sexuality manifested itself in the most unlikely places and found sustenance in the very steps taken to thwart it. 'Lovers of the lake' shows us a man and his married mistress on pilgrimage at Lough Derg; she may be sincerely penitent, but he finds a good deal of piquancy in the idea that she is submitting to all these austerities because of him; in the long run the shared ordeal may have strengthened their emotional ties to each other. Mary Lavin's 'The nun's mother' explored ambivalent feelings in a long interior monologue: while acknowledging that her daughter has escaped much that is sordid, the mother wonders whether the young nun realises all that she may be missing. Often, though, in a Mary Lavin story it was not a sexual problem but something apparently much more trivial that caused lifelong friction between a husband and wife.

In the novels and stories of Edna O'Brien—beginning with *The country girls* (1960) and its sequels, *Girl with green eyes* (1962) and *Girls in their married bliss* (1963)—we encounter a phenomenon previously unknown in novels by Irishwomen: a heroine who is determined to attain sexual experience and, if possible, sexual gratification. The French heroine of a very different kind of novel, Kate O'Brien's *The land of spices* (1941), took the veil in disgust with male sexuality: she had seen her father and a young man 'in the embrace of love' (those being the words that led to the banning of the novel). As a mother superior, head of an Irish convent school, she became a surrogate mother for an orphaned girl of 6, watching over her growing-up, and eventually learning to forgive, if not to understand, her dead father. In a later novel, *As music and splendour* (1958), O'Brien portrayed a lesbian attachment between two opera singers, one Irish, in Italy.

Oversimplifying, one might describe John Broderick's *The waking of Willie Ryan* (1965) as a novel of male homosexuality; in fact, Willie's passion for Roger lies twenty-five years in the past when the story opens. The crux of the novel is in Willie's refusal to repent, his family's anxiety lest it might seem that he died in a state of sin, and Willie's and Father Mannix's connivance in the final deception. Willie dies feeling that in his own weak yet stubborn way he has defeated the church. Among male novelists only Brian Moore in *I am Mary Dunne* (1968) seemed to have penetrated the secret of feminine sexuality, but at least Irishmen could no longer be accused of taking women for granted; in this, as in so many other areas, Joyce and George Moore were pioneers whose lead was ignored for many years.

Aidan Higgins, in *Langrishe go down* (1966), focused on the familiar Irish theme of decaying gentry, catholics in this case; Jennifer Johnston and Terence de Vere White, more traditionally, concentrated on the decline or perilous buoyancy of the Anglo-Irish. What was missing in most Irish fiction of the 1960s was an awareness that since 1922, and especially since 1958, more Irish people had been rising in the world than falling. O'Flaherty and O'Donnell set the fashion of viewing the wealthy and successful through the eyes of the underdog, whereas earlier Irish novelists tended to look at the underdog through the eyes of the well-to-do. In only a few novels, chiefly those of John Broderick, did one see the new wealth and power from the viewpoint of those who possessed it.

In a society so criss-crossed by family and community ties and social controls, novels of existential confrontation with such ultimates as pain, solitude, and death were rare indeed. John McGahern's *The barracks* (1963) is one such; it describes a young wife's year-long struggle with terminal cancer. She finds that religion holds little comfort for her as she searches for the meaning of her own life. Although she is surrounded by family, neighbours, the clergy, all the life of an Irish village, at her death, she is as much alone as the protagonist of Samuel Beckett's *Malone dies* (1951; English translation 1956).

Beckett's sense of the isolation of each individual human being could already be seen in *Murphy* (1938), but it must have been intensified by his experiences during the war: his share in the French resistance, escape from the Gestapo, and virtually penniless existence in hiding in the south of France. It would be idle to search in his later novels—written originally in French—for many reflections of Irish society, though it is possible to argue that his feeling of alienation began in awareness of the isolation of the protestant minority and became acute when he found no congenial place for someone of his artistic temperament within that minority.

Francis Stuart too had wartime experiences that deepened his awareness: *Black list, Section H* (1971), more autobiography than novel, tells of his years in Germany, during part of which he broadcast German propaganda to

Ireland, and of his postwar imprisonment by the French occupying forces, although he was never convicted of any crime. His novel *Redemption* (1949) contrasts the state of a German city after the Russians enter it with the smugly static condition of a postwar Irish village—where, however, lust, murder, and a false miracle soon shatter the apparent peace. Stuart's one flawless novel is *The pillar of cloud* (1948), set in postwar Germany: it tells of the healing love that grows between an Irish exile and a Polish girl refugee, and of the girl's forgiveness of a Nazi who had tortured her. Stuart, like Joyce and Beckett, reached his full stature as a writer in exile; unlike them, he returned to Ireland permanently, finding that he could live there comfortably enough in the changed intellectual and emotional climate of the 1960s.

THE poets of Ireland from 1922 onwards could be forgiven for looking back nostalgically at those heroic years 1913–21, when history seemed to be made not only for poets but by poets. After the death of Yeats in 1939, however, the poets often cast a cold eye upon contemporary life, recording what they saw with compassion, irony, or indignation. Patrick Kavanagh's *The great hunger* (1942), though he spoke slightingly of it in the author's note to his *Collected poems* (1964), was an important work: a long, serious poem, full of compassion. Patrick Maguire, its protagonist, is a typical Irish small farmer who postpones marriage while his mother is alive and finds himself too old for it when she dies. He has made the land fertile but remains infertile himself. The world looks on, envying the peasant his idyllic happiness, his simplicity, his purity, but Patrick Maguire's life has had few moments of joy, few of any intense feeling. His death will not be too different from his life:

> If he stretches out a hand—a wet clod,
> If he opens his nostrils—a dungy smell ...

Kavanagh wrote a number of satirical poems, often directed against the Dublin intelligentsia or the tendency to glorify dead poets while live ones starved. His most comprehensive satire, embracing politics as well as literature and the arts, was 'The Christmas mummers', patterned on a familiar type of folk play. His final poems, consciously unintellectual ('my purpose in life was to have no purpose'), were much admired by his younger contemporaries. These poems may not prove durable, but they do show that Kavanagh felt more at peace with his country during his last years.

The same could be said of Austin Clarke. For a number of years after *Night and morning* (1938) he published little except an occasional verse play written for stage or radio. Then came *Ancient lights* (1955) and *Too great a vine* (1957), whose contents were described as 'poems and satires'. Any intrusion of church and state upon the liberty of the individual, any callousness towards the helpless—be they children, the poor, or animals—provoked his epigrammatic satire. Soon afterwards, Dolmen Press editions of his *Later poems* (1961) and *Collected plays* (1963) reminded not only his countrymen but the English-speaking world of his stature as a poet. He was by then the author of eleven plays, chiefly about medieval Ireland, portraying what he called 'the drama of conscience'; though temptation, in truth, usually gets the better of conscience. Each play was a skirmish in Clarke's private war with the catholic church, but propaganda was concealed by art. Clarke in his sixties and seventies became mellower and more prolific. The growing ecumenism of the church prompted a sly, half-approving kind of satire, while the affluent society was taken to task for its vulgarity. From denouncing the thwarting of the sexual urge, he turned more and more to celebration of its fulfilment. He even found the courage to write a long poem, 'Mnemosyne lay in dust' (1966), about his experience in youth as a psychiatric patient. The title poem of *A sermon on Swift* (1968) celebrated the improbable occasion in 1967 when, during the Swift tercentenary celebrations, he mounted the pulpit of St Patrick's cathedral, Dublin, to deliver a lecture on Swift's frequently scatological verse.

Whereas Kavanagh and Clarke had to endure the hostility or indifference of their society for a longish period, younger poets such as Thomas Kinsella and Richard Murphy found less to quarrel with. Their northern contemporary John Montague wrote a poem in the early 1960s with the refrain:

> Puritan Ireland's dead and gone,
> A myth of O'Connor and O'Faolain.[47]

As they matured, however, these three poets began to comprehend their involvement with Irish history. In the words of Maurice Harmon, 'the typical movement in their work was an initial outward trend and then the return to Ireland'.[48]

Murphy's return was documented in *Sailing to an island* (1963). Besides the County Galway fishermen and their boats, he celebrated his maternal grandmother in his elegy 'The woman of the house'. With *The battle of Aughrim* (1968), a long poem, he plunged deeper into history, striving to reconcile the English and Irish elements in his heritage: his maternal and paternal ancestors had fought on opposite sides in that battle.

Kinsella's chief homage to the past of Ireland was paid in his translations from early Irish, notably *The Táin*. Two meditative poems—'A country walk' from *Downstream* (1962) and the long title poem from *Nightwalker* (1968)—contained passages sharply critical of contemporary Ireland. In the second poem, the whole generation who fought the civil war—especially those who were still government ministers when the poem was written, 'dragon old

[47] John Montague, *The rough field* (Dublin, 1972), pp 68–9.
[48] Maurice Harmon, 'New voices in the fifties' in Seán Lucy (ed.), *Irish poets in English* (Cork, 1973), p. 205.

men'—seem to be harshly condemned; but, as we read on, the new generation following them into power are seen to be successors 'worthy' of
them. Later, the satire becomes more gentle as 'Brother Burke' tells his
pupils

> Today there are Christian Brothers boys
> Everywhere in the government...

THE second world war, which isolated the south both politically and culturally, had an opposite effect on Northern Ireland. Sam Hanna Bell described
the feeling there as 'perhaps...a sudden sense of interrupted isolation'.[49]
The conviction that an artistic revival had begun during the war and was still
under way was given lively expression in *The arts in Ulster: a symposium*
(1951).

Unlike Sam Hanna Bell, John Hewitt felt that the war isolated Northern
Ireland and encouraged regionalism. Be that as it may, a regional consciousness had existed in east Ulster long before the establishment of Northern
Ireland. The Ulster Literary Theatre, so named from 1904 until it became
the Ulster Theatre in 1915, called itself the Ulster branch of the Irish Literary Theatre at its first performance (1902). The change of name and the
publication of the first number of *Uladh* in 1904 suggest a shift from provin-
cialism to true regionalism—foreshadowed by Bulmer Hobson's cry 'Damn
Yeats, we'll write our own plays!'[50] Unfortunately, this literary theatre discovered few dramatists: 'Gerald Macnamara' (Harry Morrow) wrote some
farcical satires on the Orange order and other local institutions, the best-
known being 'Thompson in Tir-na-nÓg' (1912). 'Rutherford Mayne'
(Samuel Waddell) set his comedies and an occasional tragedy in rural Ulster;
his most popular play was 'The drone' (1908), about a farmer who managed
to escape work in the fields by pretending to be an inventor. George Shiels,
whose Abbey Theatre career has been noted earlier,[51] made his debut with
two plays for the Ulster Theatre in 1918–19.

Despite this rather unpromising yield of writers from over thirty years
of amateur performances, the Ulster Theatre proved once and for all that
Ulster plays performed by Ulster players before Ulster audiences could create
a unique effect. During the 1930s a more professional group, the Belfast
Repertory Theatre Company, played at the Empire Theatre. They discovered
Thomas Carnduff, a shipyard worker, who wrote three plays based on his own
experience: 'Workers', 'Machinery', and 'Traitors' (1932–4).

---

[49] Sam Hanna Bell, Nesca A. Robb, and John Hewitt (ed.), *The arts in Ulster: a symposium*
(London, 1951), p. 19.
[50] Quoted in Sam Hanna Bell, *The theatre in Ulster: a survey...from 1902 until the present
day* (Dublin, 1972), p. 1.
[51] Above, p. 512.

This brief backward glance helps to explain why the theatre provided the first signs of a more vigorous mood in wartime Northern Ireland. The Ulster Group Theatre gave its first public performance on 11 March 1940; although it ranged over the international dramatic repertoire, some of its most successful productions were the work of Ulster playwrights, old and new. It took the air raid of 15/16 April 1941 to halt the revival of St John Ervine's 'Boyd's shop' (1936), a rose-tinted view of the presbyterian lower middle class. Three of Ervine's later plays were given first productions by the Group Theatre, and 'Friends and relations', a satirical view of upper-middle-class Belfast, was successfully revived. Three of George Shiels's later plays were first performed by the Group Theatre, and a number of others by him won the approval of its audience. Among the dramatists discovered by the Group Theatre was Patricia O'Connor; her 'Highly efficient' (1942) was the first Irish play ever to be, in the author's own words, 'concerned solely with the subject of public elementary education'.[52]

Joseph Tomelty (1911–95), however, was the younger dramatist most closely linked in the public mind with the fortunes of the Group Theatre, six of his plays receiving their first production there. His 'Poor errand' (1943), like Jack Loudan's earlier 'Story for today' (1941), showed some of the effects of the air raids on Belfast life. Tomelty's chief importance lay in the fact that no other Ulster dramatist, with the possible exception of Brian Friel, had succeeded in presenting a specifically catholic way of life to Belfast audiences. The success of 'Is the priest at home?' has already been mentioned,[53] but it was first produced at the Group Theatre, as was his tragedy of life in a fishing village, 'All souls' night' (1949). A second play about Father Malan, 'Year at Marlfield' (1965), was produced elsewhere in Belfast. Ironically, 'The end house' (1944), a tragedy about a poor Belfast catholic family with a son in the I.R.A., was performed at the Abbey but not at the Group.

The Group Theatre did, however, produce one play about sectarian hostility, Gerard McLarnon's 'The bonefire' (1958). It is strange, therefore, that they should have withdrawn from rehearsal a few months earlier Sam Thompson's 'Over the bridge', a tragedy of sectarian conflict in the shipyards. The board of directors issued a public statement in which they refused 'to mount any play which would offend or affront the religious or political beliefs or sensibilities of the man in the street of any denomination or class in the community'.[54] As a result, three of the directors and most of the actors resigned from the Group Theatre, virtually ending its history as a cultural force.

[52] Quoted in Bell, *Theatre in Ulster*, p. 89.
[53] Above, pp 513–14.
[54] Quoted in Bell, *Theatre in Ulster*, p. 92.

Meanwhile, 'Over the bridge' was produced in 1960 at the Empire Theatre, Belfast, having a long run by local standards, of six weeks to packed houses. Thompson, a protestant, was himself a former shipyard worker and union organiser, active in the Northern Ireland Labour party till his death, aged 49, in 1965. Stewart Parker has said that Thompson's three plays 'contain his complete diagnosis of Ulster's disease. "Over the bridge" shows sectarianism worming its way through people's working lives, "The evangelist" uncovers the fanaticism and hypocrisy deforming their religion, and "Cemented with love" the appalling corruption of their political parties, unionist and nationalist.'[55]

Side by side with Thompson's edifying plays of working-class life there appeared some by Stewart Love that showed sympathy for a younger, less conventional breed of working or non-working man. Love's 'The randy dandy' (1960) at the Group Theatre presented a Belfast shipyard version of the 'angry young man', as did 'The big donkey' (1964). 'The big long bender' (1962) concerns a hedonistic group of young people antedating the 'hippies'.

The true successor of the Ulster Group Theatre, the Lyric Players Theatre, was founded in 1951, under Austin Clarke's influence, by Mary O'Malley. Its sole original aim was to perform poetic drama—especially the work of W. B. Yeats—but later it broadened its scope to become, in a way, the national theatre of Northern Ireland. Its magazine, *Threshold*, appeared somewhat spasmodically from 1957 to 1987. In 1965 the company obtained its own permanent theatre building. While the Group Theatre staged Brian Friel's first play, 'This doubtful paradise' (1959), his early career is more closely associated with the Lyric; 'The enemy within', also produced at the Abbey (1962), presented an early missionary from Ulster, St Columba (Colmcille), while 'The blind mice' (1963) centred on a present-day missionary just released from prison in China. Friel was to return to this theme of exile for the faith in 'Aristocrats' (Abbey, 1979).

From the perspective of the late 1960s, much of the Ulster drama of the previous three decades seemed to reflect an obsolescent society. Plays set in the shipyards once made southerners feel that Belfast knew more about the twentieth century than they, but heavy industry of that type and the labour–management relations it engendered had come to be seen as survivals from the nineteenth century. The sophisticated technology of urban guerrilla warfare reached the stage only slowly, while the doubtless archaic attitudes of the combatants were still viewed through the eyes of O'Casey. It was also apparent that Brian Friel, for all his brilliance, had written two of his most popular plays, 'Philadelphia, here I come!' and 'Lovers' (1967),

---

[55] Introduction to *Over the bridge* (Dublin, 1970), p. 14.

about two of the weariest clichés in Irish drama: emigration and late marriage.[56]

The appearance in the London magazine *Horizon*, early in the second world war, of the first poems by W. R. Rodgers (1909–69), then a presbyterian clergyman in County Armagh, created a minor sensation. When his first volume, *Awake! and other poems* (1940), was published soon afterwards, it seemed as if the war had awakened not only the sleeping province but a major poet. Darcy O'Brien's remarkable study[57] relates how Rodgers's personal tensions prompted his poetry yet thwarted his full development as an artist. Although many of his poems had an Irish setting and he wrote one, entitled simply 'Ireland', that is a hymn of praise to the Mourne landscape, he was never able to confront directly in his verse the inner conflict that earned him the nickname of 'the catholic presbyterian'. He found a literary heritage in the Irish writers later commemorated by his famous B.B.C. radio programmes—Joyce, Synge, Gogarty, A E, George Moore, F. R. Higgins, Shaw—much of the oral documentation for which was obtained during visits to Dublin. Dan Davin's introductory memoir to Rodgers's *Collected poems* (1971) tells the tragicomic story of the long poem about Ireland that, from 1949 till 1969, the poet was always about to write: all that ever got written is contained in 'Epilogue', a three-page appendix to the volume.

Louis MacNeice (1907–63) wrote many more poems about Ireland than did Rodgers, but after his first departure to school in England at the age of 10, his native country was chiefly a place in which to spend holidays. Few of MacNeice's poems were expressions of Ulster, for he learned from his parents a love of their native Connacht, celebrated in, for instance, 'Western landscape'. His most thoroughly Ulster poem was 'Carrickfergus':

> The Scotch quarter was a line of residential houses
> But the Irish quarter was a slum for the blind and halt.

In the sixteenth section of *Autumn journal* (1939) he gave a rather stereotyped picture of the two Irelands, north and south, and finally dismissed the whole country as 'both a bore and a bitch'.[58] This was by no means his last word on the subject, but by and large Ireland was a relaxation or a distraction for him rather than an inspiration.

The true voice of at least one variety of Ulster protestant in this period was John Hewitt (1907–87). Though not as gifted as MacNeice or even Rodgers, he tenaciously cultivated the soil of Ulster like his planter forebears; *Collected poems 1932–1967* was published in 1968. A regionalist from the beginning, he wrote his M.A. thesis at Queen's University, Belfast, on nine-

---

[56] The preceding narrative is deeply indebted to Bell, *Theatre in Ulster.*
[57] Darcy O'Brien, *W. R. Rodgers* (Lewisburg, Pa., 1970).
[58] *The collected poems of Louis MacNeice*, ed. E. R. Dodds (London and Boston, 1979), p. 134.

teenth-century Ulster poets. Though he grew up in Belfast, a methodist by birth and education, one favourite poetic subject-matter of his was the rural life and landscape of the glens of Antrim, whose people he thought of as predominantly catholic. A longish poem, 'Conacre', offered an apologia for thus writing about the country rather than the city, though he was already three generations from the land. In 'Once alien here' he dedicated himself to finding a voice for Ulster, 'a native mode', for he was 'as native in my thought as any here'. In 'The green shoot' he described how he learned harsh sectarianism when young but also more tender feelings. From the effort to reconcile such opposites—city/country, protestant/catholic, English/Irish, violence/sentiment—his poetry was born.[59]

The fullest expression of his attitude, however, is to be found in 'The colony', written in 1950. The history of Northern Ireland since the plantation is thinly disguised as that of a fictitious Roman colony, of which the speaker is a member. He describes the original invasion, the counter-attack corresponding to 1641 ('that terror dogs us'), the penal laws. He tells how the colonists 'took the kindlier soils', and complains that the dispossessed inhabitants nevertheless 'breed like flies'. Some colonists, 'beguiled by their sad music, / make common cause with the natives'. As for the speaker, he hopes that

> by patient words I may convince
> my people and this people we are changed
> from the raw levies which usurped the land...
> for we have rights drawn from the soil and sky...
> we would be strangers in the Capitol;
> this is our country also, nowhere else;
> and we shall not be outcast on the world.[60]

This might be described as the 'No surrender!' of a northern moderate.

The writers of fiction through whose eyes the Republic and the United States viewed Northern Ireland were for a time predominantly catholic: one thinks of the novels of Michael McLaverty, Benedict Kiely, and Brian Moore, as well as of *New Yorker* stories by Kiely and Brian Friel.[61] Northern Ireland, on the other hand, sought its own image chiefly in the work of protestant writers, usually published in London: for example, Sam Hanna Bell, Stephen Gilbert, George Buchanan, Maurice Leitch, Janet McNeill, Anthony C. West. The second world war apparently did not give the

---

[59] See John Hewitt, 'No rootless colonist' in *Aquarius*, no. 5 (Benburb, 1972), p. 92. Hewitt's *Rhyming weavers* (Belfast, 1974) grew out of his M.A. thesis.

[60] John Hewitt, *Collected poems 1932–1967* (London, 1968), pp 75–9.

[61] Some of these stories are reprinted in Friel's *The saucer of larks* (London, 1962) and *The gold in the sea* (London, 1966) and in Kiely's *A journey to the seven streams* (London, 1963) and *A ball of malt and Madam Butterfly* (London, 1973).

impetus to fiction in Ireland that it did to the theatre and to poetry—though Stephen Gilbert wrote one war novel, *Bombardier* (1944).

The great theme of Michael McLaverty's later books was Christian charity—not almsgiving but love. Whether set in the city like *The three brothers* (1948) or in country villages like *In this thy day* (1945) or *The choice* (1958), they confront the sheer difficulty of loving one's neighbour, of cultivating understanding and patience. McLaverty rarely touched on religious or political tolerance; his point was that it is hard work being fair even to someone of one's own religion or one's own family. An earnest, almost humourless writer, McLaverty often seemed to be advocating an eleventh commandment, 'Thou shalt not gossip': gossip is more dangerous than false witness in, for example, *The brightening day* (1965).

Benedict Kiely's characters, on the other hand, in novels from this period such as *In a harbour green* (1949) or *Dogs enjoy the morning* (1968), would sooner die than not gossip. Kiely's Ulster novels and stories—he has written about other parts of Ireland too—were set in or near the town of Omagh. When writing about his home ground Kiely indulged in humour, sentiment, and an easygoing piety very different from the austere scrupulous catholicism of McLaverty; one finds it hard to believe that Kiely and not McLaverty was the ex-Jesuit.[62] Protestants scarcely appeared at all in Kiely's version of Ulster, though in his first novel, *Land without stars* (1946), the hero's brother, an I.R.A. man, is killed by the R.U.C. Early in his career Kiely wrote a biography of that other Tyrone storyteller, William Carleton; bearing this in mind, we should not be surprised that so many of his short stories were based on folklore and that his novel *The cards of the gambler* (1953) took its structure from a folktale.

Brian Moore emigrated to Canada in 1948 at the age of 27 and made his home there or in the U.S.A. until his death in 1999; as a result, his picture of Belfast catholic life preserved the traits of the 1940s, or even the late 1920s and the 1930s. Perhaps inevitably, the catholic community there was much more constricted and constricting than that of Dublin at the same period; Moore's protagonists in his early novels make vain efforts to escape. The title character in *The lonely passion of Judith Hearne* (1956) takes refuge in alcoholism when marriage eludes her; she loses her faith, yet must continue to conform. Her male counterpart, a timid 37-year-old bachelor schoolmaster, appears in *The feast of Lupercal* (1957), ironically named after a Roman fertility rite; he tries to escape by loving a protestant girl but achieves only scandal and humiliation. In *An answer from Limbo* (1962) and *Fergus* (1970), however, the values of pre-1940 Belfast were contrasted with those of the United States at the time of writing, to the detriment of the latter. *I am Mary Dunne* (1968), on the other hand, seemed to vindicate the North American attitude

---

[62] See Kiely's novel about a noviciate, *There was an ancient house* (London, 1955).

to divorce. Moore had not made up his mind about his heritage: if *The emperor of ice-cream* (1965) mocked the anti-British stance of Belfast catholics in wartime, *The revolution script* (1971)—a documentary rather than a novel—sympathised with their French-Canadian counterparts who were fighting the protestant Anglo-Canadian establishment.

Anthony C. West, a protestant writer brought up in Ulster on both sides of the border, had not made up his mind about his heritage either. In *River's end, and other stories* (1960), *The ferret fancier* (1963), and some early pages of *As towns with fire* (1968) he described with extraordinary vividness and passion life on a small, poor farm as seen through the eyes of a sensitive boy. This aspect of Irish life had become all too familiar in the work of catholic novelists and storytellers, but West's puritanical protestant upbringing gave it a new dimension. His typical protestant adolescent was envious of the emotional warmth and supposed sexual freedom of his catholic neighbours, and was both fascinated and repelled by the idea of seducing—or being seduced by—a catholic girl.

Sam Hanna Bell's *December bride* (1951), banned in the Republic, offered an unexpectedly passionate view of the presbyterian farming community: a woman lives with two brothers in a *ménage à trois*. Maurice Leitch's first novel, *The liberty lad* (1965), dealt with the sexual pitfalls of Belfast life: a young man is tempted to turn the homosexual tastes of an influential older man to his own advantage. A less lurid view of Belfast professional men and women was given by the novels of Janet McNeill. The title character of *The maiden dinosaur* (1964) is a 'large, plain, and intelligent' spinster schoolteacher of 52 who faces her loneliness with more dignity and humour than Moore's Judith Hearne. *As strangers here* (1960) had for its main character an underpaid presbyterian minister, with an invalid wife, who refused to pander to the religious and social prejudices of his congregation.[63] Such was the state of fiction in Northern Ireland when writers were faced with a new challenge: to explore the eruption associated with the troubles, beginning in 1968.

THE last of our subperiods, 1969–84, was one in which funding for the arts, from both public and private sources, became more substantial. By the early 1970s the arts council of Northern Ireland, set up in 1962, was disbursing annually hundreds of thousands of pounds. Drama and music made up the largest items in its budget,[64] with an allocation of over £70,000 for drama alone in 1973/4. Art, meaning the fine arts generally, took third place, while non-dramatic literature came a poor fourth. The most remarkable cultural achievement of the Northern Ireland government, however, lay in the area

---

[63] The preceding account of Ulster fiction owes much to John Wilson Foster, *Forces and themes in Ulster fiction* (Totowa, N.J., 1974) and to John Cronin's essay 'Prose' in Michael Longley (ed.), *Causeway: the arts in Ulster* (Belfast and Dublin, 1971).

[64] Below, pp 663–70.

of museum expansion: the Belfast Museum and Art Gallery had finally become a province-wide institution in 1962, while a series of legislative acts (1958–67)[65] established the Ulster Folk Museum (opened 1964) on a scale unparalleled by any similar institution in these islands.

In the Republic a government subsidy was offered in 1969 to Hilton Edwards and Mícheál Mac Liammóir of Dublin's Gate Theatre Productions to facilitate the redecoration and improvement of their theatre, which was reopened in 1971. Government allocations to non-dramatic literature in the early 1970s were small indeed, both north and south, amounting in all to about £10,000 in a normal year.

There has been a growing tendency in Ireland, north and south, for the arts to receive assistance from business and finance. Literature benefits through prizes offered for drama, fiction, and poetry; summer schools and international conferences often receive subsidies. Ireland's cultural heritage is viewed as something of a tourist attraction, so that local festivals of literature, not to mention the other arts, may receive subsidies from An Bord Fáilte and the Northern Ireland tourist board.

If Northern Ireland has in some respects overtaken the Republic in the area of government assistance to the arts, there is nothing in the north to compare with the provisions of the finance act of 1969, which exempt artists, writers, and composers resident in the Republic—regardless of nationality—from the payment of income tax on the earnings of their creative work.[66] Among the first 338 applicants, 71 per cent were writers.

In 1973 An Chomhairle Ealaíon initiated a bursary scheme to aid individual writers; this was later expanded to include composers and practitioners in the visual arts. The Arts Council then began consideration of an honours scheme for artists. With the assistance of Anthony Cronin, cultural adviser to the taoiseach Charles Haughey, the council worked out in detail the plan of an organisation, Aosdána ('Artists'), which was established in March 1981. It is described as 'an affiliation of artists engaged in literature, music, and visual arts', which 'honours those artists whose work has made an outstanding contribution to the arts in Ireland' and 'encourages and assists members in devoting their energies fully to their art'. In May 1986 Aosdána included fifty-one writers, as well as fifty-seven visual artists and fifteen composers, a number of whom were in receipt of bursaries.[67]

From the perspective of the mid 1980s, what writers seemed the acknowledged leaders of the generation that was reaching adulthood in or around 1969? Internationally, Seamus Heaney was by far the best known, but in Ireland itself Brian Friel, ten years his senior, might have won the prefer-

---

[65] 1958, c. 7 (10 June 1958); 1964, c. 17 (30 June 1964); 1967, c. 13 (17 June 1967).
[66] 1969/21 (29 June 1969).
[67] Information from Aosdána press releases.

ence. One thing at least seemed certain: any writer who aspired to speak for the new generation must articulate some deep, half-conscious feelings about events in Northern Ireland. The true exiles of the time were northerners—whether catholic or protestant—who had moved either to the Republic or to London.

IN the first decade of the troubles (1968–78) it was understandable that a number of novelists with established or growing reputations felt the need to set all or part of a novel in contemporary Ulster. In 1977 at least four such novels appeared: Kevin Casey's *Dreams of revenge*, Francis Stuart's *A hole in the head*, Jennifer Johnston's *Shadows on our skin*, and Benedict Kiely's *Prox-opera*. The last and best of these, by the author with the deepest knowledge of Ulster, describes a peculiarly nasty form of terrorism, the 'proxy operation', in which an innocent man is forced to transport a time bomb to its target in order to save his captive family. Kiely shirks the grim logic of the situation, in that his hero aborts the mission but his family luckily survive.

Tauter than any of the above-mentioned is the short novel *Victims: a tale of Fermanagh* (1976) by Eugene McCabe, from the border county of Monaghan. Six upper-class protestants are held hostage in Inver House by five members of the I.R.A., one a woman. After the killing of one hostage, a deal is made to save the lives of the others. Three I.R.A. leaders are released from the Maze prison in exchange for two men and the girl in the hostage-taking group. One of the terrorists, an epileptic, seems to fit the stereotype of insane blood-lust, but the other four are credible though not amiable. McCabe is less sure of himself with the hostages, but all are credible except Canon Plumm: a Church of Ireland clergyman might well be a bigot, but in a crisis he would never read words of comfort from any book but the Bible. McCabe's short story 'Cancer', which uses terrorism as a background for permanent evils such as disease and envy, is more fully convincing than *Victims*.

The troubles were also reflected in the work of the established generation of Irish poets. Kinsella was not in the habit of commenting immediately on current events, but he made an exception in his poem 'Butcher's dozen' (1972), published as a pamphlet three months after the killing of thirteen unarmed civilians in Derry on 'Bloody Sunday' (30 January 1972). John Hewitt's poem 'The colony' (1950) had already marked him out as a political moderate.[68] The events of 1968–9 prompted him to write several poems, which he published in magazines and then in a privately issued booklet, *An Ulster reckoning* (1971). He blamed Ian Paisley severely, but he also reproached less militant protestant politicians and those who simply accepted the status quo.

[68] Above, p. 525.

It was a brilliant idea on the part of the arts council of Northern Ireland to send Hewitt and one of the leading Ulster catholic poets, John Montague, on a poetry-reading tour of Northern Ireland in 1970. The resulting anthology of their contrasting yet complementary poems, *The planter and the Gael*, is one of the handsomest, least expensive, and most moving volumes of poetry ever published in Ireland. Montague, though born in the United States, spent his boyhood on a farm in the townland of Garvaghy, County Tyrone. From 1961 onwards he devoted a number of poems either to personal reminiscences of his home area or to evocations of the mainly unhappy history of Tyrone and Ulster. As time went on, these various poems took their places as parts of a projected longer poem entitled 'The rough field'—a literal translation of 'Garvaghy'. The only part of *The rough field* (1972) that deals explicitly with the Ulster crisis was 'A new siege', in which the resistance of the catholic Bogside in 1969 was paralleled with the protestant resistance during the siege of Derry in 1689. The bitterest lines of *The rough field* came in an earlier poem, 'The sound of a wound'.

> I assert
> a civilisation died here;
> it trembles
> underfoot where I walk these
> small, sad hills:
> it rears in my bloodstream
> when I hear
> a bleat of Saxon condescension,
> Westminster
> to hell, it is less than these
> strangely carved
> five thousand year resisting stones,
> that lonely cross.

Whether destruction of the past has occurred through enmity or through the drive for modernisation, as in 'Hymn to the new Omagh road', the poet cannot help lamenting it. Like its predecessor, Kavanagh's *The great hunger*, *The rough field* is part elegy, part satire; both poems are in the long run descendants of Goldsmith's 'The deserted village'.

Seamus Heaney, another catholic poet, younger than Montague by a decade, has drawn even more of his poetic sustenance from the land, in this case a small farm in County Londonderry. Poem after poem in his first three books—*Death of a naturalist* (1966), *Door into the dark* (1969), *Wintering out* (1972)—describes with loving accuracy the tasks and tackle of farming; one might almost mistake him for a pupil of E. Estyn Evans till one realises that everything so described becomes a metaphor, that Heaney like every good poet reaches the abstract by way of the concrete. He is not, after all, writing a handbook for the Ulster Folk Museum but exploring his own mind. Oddly, there are few individualised people in his poems, whereas Montague's contain a whole rustic gallery of grotesque or tender portraits. *North* (1975) confronts the violence in Ulster less obliquely than the earlier volumes but tries to set it in context: human history has always been violent. Satire and denunciation, even when of protestant by protestant or catholic by catholic, lead nowhere. One wishes that there were more Ulster writing in the vein of Heaney's poem 'The other side' from *Wintering out*, which mirrors a mutual tolerance between rural neighbours. A presbyterian farmer who can quote scripture to his purpose—to the secret amusement of his catholic neighbours—remarks tactfully in time-honoured phrases

> Your side of the house, I believe,
> Hardly rule by the book at all.

No reproach, just the quiet recognition of a difference.

Urban Ulster has its poets too, chiefly protestant—Roy McFadden, Derek Mahon, and James Simmons, for example—but they are more concerned with private than with public themes. By and large, the Ulster poets who grew up in the 1940s—Heaney, Michael Longley, Derek Mahon—avoided direct comment on the crisis that began in 1969, except for some cryptic elegies by Seamus Deane in *Gradual wars* (1972). Simmons, in a characteristic poem entitled 'Ulster today', wonders that 'nothing that troubles the TV news / moves me to write', and goes on to present some of the television images:

> an exploded pub, boys throwing stones
> that must hurt, running towards the camera,
> grinning. I have nothing to add;
> the stones hurt, the smiling boys are boys,
> the farcical and painful history of Ireland
> is with us, unchanged. If the next bomb
> kills *me* it will still be irrelevant.[69]

'I have nothing to add', he says, but in selecting from what he saw on television he in fact adds a great deal of implicit comment about the effect of the fighting on the psyches of children. Perhaps the function of poets in such times is to record what their unique sensibility perceives—not to comment, however judiciously, but not to turn away.

A new generation of Ulster poets, who were in their teens or early twenties in 1969, have received an eager welcome both at home and in Great Britain. Their names will be found in *Poets from the north of Ireland* (1979), edited by Frank Ormsby, except for that of Medbh McGuckian, winner of the British national poetry competition in 1979; her first major volume, *The flower master*, appeared only in 1982. None of these poets has exploited the topicality of

---

[69] James Simmons, *The long summer still to come* (Belfast, 1973), p. 22.

the northern situation in verse, except Tom Paulin in *Liberty tree* (1983), which discreetly contrasts Ian Paisley with the presbyterian jacobins of 1798.

It is in the theatre that Ulster writers of that generation have explored religious and tribal hostility most intimately. Their unblinking perception of reality finds room for compassion but not for sentimentality; a good example is Graham Reid's tragicomedy of love across the sectarian divide, 'Remembrance' (1984). Reid's 'The hidden curriculum' (1982) shows how that liberal panacea, non-sectarian education, can still produce terrorists. The Belfast-born Stewart Parker (1941–88) in 'Spokesong' (1976) made macabre fun of the troubles. Frank McGuinness, a catholic born in County Donegal, dramatises an extreme form of Orange loyalty in 'Observe the sons of Ulster marching towards the Somme' (1985), leaving the audience to find the implicit ironies for themselves. Parker's 'Northern star' (1984) is an experimental historical play about Henry Joy McCracken.

The troubles were also reflected in the work of the older generation of Irish playwrights. In 1973 the Abbey Theatre staged Friel's 'The freedom of the city', written before yet prophetic of Derry's 'Bloody Sunday'. Friel imagines that two men and a woman, catholics from a civil rights march, have taken refuge in the Derry guildhall, where they discuss at length their past lives and their motives for protesting; when they 'surrender' to the British army they are all shot down. A judge, a ballad singer, a television commentator, a priest, a sociologist, and others comment on their predicaments while alive and the justice or injustice of their deaths. Friel portrays three very human individuals victimised by forces too big for them to understand, but he oversimplifies the northern situation. A foreigner could read or see the play without, perhaps, ever realising that protestant Irishmen exist and belong to every class from the highest to the lowest.

A less one-sided play, 'The flats', by John Boyd, presbyterian by birth and socialist by conviction, was given a record total of forty-two performances at the Lyric during 1972. The Donnellans, a catholic family, are threatened by militant protestant mobs in the autumn of 1969. The mother wants to rely on the British army for protection, but the father and son are determined to fight back. In the firing it is a young protestant girl, a good friend of the Donnellans, who dies; a British private, who has fallen in love with her, is left with the last words, 'Who's to blame?' It is hard to escape the conclusion that those who aroused the protestant mobs are to blame, but they remain no more than 'voices off'. Whereas Friel ignores the militant protestant side of the triangle entirely, Boyd gives it no spokesman worthy of respect.

Subsequently, however, the older generation of Irish dramatists has turned away from the surface glitter of contemporary events to deeper, more permanent themes. Although Brian Friel's 'Translations' (1980), the first production of his Field Day Theatre Company, might be construed as merely transposing present-day conflict in terms of 1833, its real theme is language—Greek, Latin, Irish, English—and the intimate relations between language and culture. Set in an Irish-speaking hedge school at the time of Larcom's great ordnance survey of Ireland, it foreshadows the abandonment of Irish for English, symbolised in the anglicising or hybridising of Gaelic place-names by the mapmakers.[70] 'Faith healer' (1979) is an in-depth study of a single character; it consists of four monologues, two by the faith healer, one by his wife, and one by his manager. A tour de force, it oddly reminds one of Beckett's skeletal 'Play' (1964). Hugh Leonard is best known as a skilful adapter of Irish fiction for the stage, the films, and television, and the author of at least one brilliant satirical farce, 'The Patrick Pearse motel' (1971). Nevertheless, in 'Da' (1973) and 'A life' (1979) he presented character studies of a gardener (based on his foster-father) and a civil servant (based on his mentor in early life), which reveal universal human nature embodied in two recognisably Irish types.

Thomas Murphy, younger than both Leonard and Friel, has never been as topical or as popular as they, but his unremitting exploration of a tragicomic vision of life has made him possibly the greatest Irish dramatist since Beckett. All his leading characters are thwarted by circumstances, but they never become resigned to their fate. In registering a protest, they sometimes attain a comic catharsis, symbolised by the laughing contest in 'Bailegangáire' (1985), but the full humour of the situation is more apparent to the audience than to the protagonists. Murphy's first play, 'On the outside' (1959), a one-act written in collaboration with Noel O'Donoghue, shows us two young men trying to get into a dancehall without the price of admission. In a sense, all his plays focus on the price to be paid for having one's will. 'Famine' (1968), the most tragic, shows us an evicted farmer who clings to 'his' land in the great famine of 1845–7; the price he pays is the death or alienation of his wife and family. The small frustrations of Irish small-town life motivate some of the lighter plays such as 'Conversations on a homecoming' (1985), but the finer ones—'The morning after optimism' (1971), 'The sanctuary lamp' (1975), and 'The Gigli concert' (1983)—show that romantic love, the comfort of religion, and art itself demand a higher price than most people are prepared to pay. 'The Blue Macushla' (1980, rev. 1983), Murphy's most topical satire, presents modern Ireland, symbolised by the tatty nightclub of the title, in terms of a 1930s Hollywood gangster movie.[71]

[70] The Field Day company, set up by Friel and others, produces and tours plays mainly by Irish and Third World authors. It also acts as a cultural focus for the Derry–Donegal area—'a fifth province of the mind'—issuing pamphlets, publishing poetry, and generally promoting the arts.
[71] Murphy, born in Tuam in 1935, has written and directed plays for the talented Druid theatre company of Galway, a further example of the decentralisation of culture represented by Field Day.

The poets of Friel's generation have matured as artists and thinkers also. Richard Murphy's sonnet sequence *The price of stone* (1985) and Seamus Heaney's *Station Island* (1984)—especially the long title poem about St Patrick's purgatory—contain their best work to date; they have learned how to quarry their respective traditions more deeply and less self-consciously than in their youth. The Gaelic tradition has not been neglected by English-speaking poets either: witness Thomas Kinsella's translations in *An duanaire 1600–1900: poems of the dispossessed* (1981) and Heaney's *Sweeney astray* (1983). Eilís Dillon's definitive translation of Eileen O'Connell's 'Lament for Arthur O'Leary' has appeared in several anthologies.

Familiarity with Irish—even to the point of writing poetry in it—links several of the post-Kavanagh generation of poets in the Republic. Michael Hartnett published *A farewell to English* in 1975, and wrote mainly in Irish till the mid 1980s; Pearse Hutchinson's Irish poems were collected in *Faoistin bhacach* (1968); Brendan Kennelly in *A drinking cup* (1970) and Desmond O'Grady have translated felicitously from the Irish. Eiléan Ni Chuilleanáin chose not to write in Irish; of her five volumes of poetry, *Cork* (1977), with drawings by Brian Lalor, contains almost all of her work that reflects Irish life directly. Peter Fallon, himself a poet, has published in Gallery Books most of the recent poets, all more or less disciples of Kavanagh. Paul Durcan, whose confessional style recalls much contemporary American poetry, has taken up Kavanagh's role as commentator on Irish events: see *The selected Paul Durcan* (1982). Eavan Boland, usually regarded as a feminist poet—mistakenly, she insists—since *In her own image* (1980), writes confessional poetry also, but its tone provides a foil for Durcan's stridency.

The theme of women's sexual experience and gratification, pioneered in the fiction of Edna O'Brien, was continued by Julia O'Faolain. The heroine of *Godded and codded* (1970) is as headstrong as any of O'Brien's, rushing into a love affair with an Arab in Paris and then into an abortion, without any common prudence, let alone any moral scruples. One catches in these heroines an echo of the amoral hero of *The ginger man* (1955) by J. P. Donleavy, an Irish-American who based his first novel on experience of bohemian life in postwar Dublin—well described in Ulick O'Connor's life of Brendan Behan (1970) and in Anthony Cronin's *Dead as doornails* (1976). Behaviour that seemed normal enough in an ex-G.I. became shocking in an inexperienced girl. By the end of our period there had been a surge of consciously feminist fiction and non-fiction, and some established women novelists were writing with an authority missing from their earlier work. Val Mulkerns's *The summerhouse* (1984) is essentially a family chronicle, but one pruned and shaped with the skill of a bonsai gardener. In *Citizen Burke* (1984) Eilís Dillon portrays a renegade Irish priest during the French revolution, as complex and sophisticated as any of Graham Greene's Spanish-speaking clerics. Julia O'Faolain in *The obedient wife* (1982) presents the natural catastrophes and situation ethics of southern California with a light satirical touch often contrasting sharply with Brian Moore's handling of similar material.

Molly Keane (1905–96) may have been encouraged to abandon the ambiguous pseudonym 'M. J. Farrell' by the new feminist wave; her first novel under her own name, *Good behaviour* (1981), was recognised as a masterpiece of irony. As its title suggests, *Good behaviour* describes the kind of aristocratic upbringing that makes it possible to ignore vital elements in the life around one, not to mention obvious defects in one's own humanity. Aroon St Charles, narrator and anti-heroine of this novel, unwittingly reveals herself as a monster of egotism. *Time after time* (1983), perhaps because of its greater complexity, was not received with the same enthusiasm; a second reading, however, reveals depths and subtleties missing from its predecessor. In *Time after time* the horse-loving ascendancy stereotype is challenged by the Swift family. Its members are frightened of horses, and so poor that there is only one horse left to be afraid of, the appropriately named Wild Man: conclusive proof of their financial, moral, and physical decline. Long years after Hitler's war, which completed the destruction of their fortunes begun in 1914 and furthered by the Irish revolution, the family barely manage to defeat the treacherous invasion of Durraghglass by Cousin Leda, half-Jewish but at heart a Nazi. This somewhat grisly novel is enlivened by humorous glimpses of contemporary Irish gentility such as May Swift's lecture on flower-arranging to 'the milk-in-firsts', among whom 'almost every lady was on Weight Watchers (refusing sandwiches or milk in tea, first or last)'. Light reflected from these late novels illuminates earlier works, especially *The rising tide* (1937, repr. 1984) and *Two days in Aragon* (1941, repr. 1985). Far from being 'light' novels or glib imitations of Somerville and Ross, the M. J. Farrell books contain much harsh realism and grotesque humour. We are sometimes reminded of Faulkner, though the author may never have read him.

Regionalism in fiction has apparently been waning, except in Northern Ireland: not only the regionalism of place that made island life bulk so large in the fiction of the decades following independence but also descriptions of lives locked within narrow boundaries of trade and class. Daniel Corkery's 'three great forces'—the religious consciousness of the people, Irish nationalism, and the land—are still present in Irish fiction, but less oppressively so. Priests in novels are more likely to be treated as human beings, their virtues not making them saints, nor their vices turning them into monsters of depravity or despair. Two good examples are John Broderick's novels *An apology for roses* (1973) and *The trial of Father Dillingham* (1982). Until the onset of the troubles in Northern Ireland, the national struggle had ceased to be of interest except to the historical novelist: Eilís Dillon's *Across the bitter sea* (1973), running from fenian days to 1916, is perhaps the most enduring such work of its time.

Despite their dwindling numbers, protestants from the Republic still showed unexpected literary vitality. Samuel Beckett's *Complete dramatic works*, published in 1986 to mark his eightieth birthday, included eight short works written since 1976, among them the poetic 'Rockaby'. Outstanding among his brief prose fictions of the same decade are *Company* and *Ill seen ill said*. Nearly a quarter-century younger than Beckett and Molly Keane, William Trevor (1928–   ) was educated at St Columba's and Trinity College, Dublin; after a very tentative first novel, *A standard of behaviour* (1958), set in postwar Dublin, he made a solid reputation with a number of novels and short stories about life in contemporary England, winning several literary awards and a C.B.E. *Mrs Eckdorf in O'Neill's hotel* (1969) is set mainly in Dublin, but it could be argued that the city, rather than being presented for its own sake, merely provides a background for one of Trevor's studies of eccentric aliens. The same criticism cannot be made of *Fools of fortune* (1983), set chiefly in his native County Cork and dedicated to the memory of his father (surnamed Cox). The Quinton family, though middle-class, own a 'big house' named Kilneagh, supported by their hereditary flour mill. They have been protestant home rulers, and Willie's father knows Michael Collins. In revenge for the murder of a mill employee who had given information to the Black-and-Tans, Kilneagh is burned without warning by a detachment led by a Sergeant Rudkin; Willie's father and two sisters, the gardener, and the yard-boy are killed. Life at Kilneagh before the disaster shows protestants and catholics living contentedly together: 'everyone in Kilneagh had fish on Fridays, that being the simplest arrangement'; an unfrocked priest lodges at Kilneagh and teaches Willie Latin. After Willie grows up and takes revenge on Rudkin, Trevor abandons the realistic mode in favour of the romantic, but Willie's protestant education is a depressing affair. Stephen Dedalus's clerical mentors inspire religious conviction; Willie's do not.

Well before *Fools of fortune*, Trevor had been writing a steadily growing proportion of his short stories about Ireland. 'The Ballroom of Romance', which gave its title to a volume of stories published in 1972, made one hope that at last Ireland has produced a writer of fiction who can portray both religious communities with equal compassion and insight. Bridie, aged 36, is paying what she decides must be her last visit to the quaintly named dance-hall that provides the one spark of romance in her life. On this particular Saturday night she realises that the only neighbour she cares for will marry his landlady: 'She would wait now and in time Bowser Egan would seek her out because his mother would have died. Her father would probably have died also by then. She would marry Bowser Egan because it would be lonesome being by herself in the farmhouse.' It is no accident that this story was made into a convincing realistic film with an all-Irish cast.

Much of Trevor's recent writing about Ireland dwells on the idea of historical guilt: the initial violence by which the English possessed themselves of Ireland has made it impossible for their Anglo-Irish heirs to escape violence in generation after generation, no matter how gentle and well intentioned these descendants may be. His Abbey play 'Scenes from an album' (1981) developed this theme much more explicitly than does *Fools of fortune*; it appears again in the title story of *The news from Ireland and other stories* (1986). Perhaps events in Northern Ireland have set Trevor reading Irish history too hastily, like Cynthia in his own brilliant story 'Beyond the Pale', which gives its name to his 1981 volume. It is the story 'The distant past' (1979), which may have been the earliest statement of the guilt theme, that impresses me most, not only as art but as truth. The Middletons, brother and sister, members of the Church of Ireland, have remained loyal at heart to the British crown, though they live sixty miles south of the border. Nevertheless, the people in the neighbouring town, even those who once held them up at gunpoint, treat them with respect and friendship till the new troubles begin in Northern Ireland. After that, relations steadily deteriorate; guessing at the future, Miss Middleton thinks: 'Because of the distant past they would die friendless. It was worse than being murdered in their beds.'[72] Such bleak forecasts were made at the time, especially by protestants who had been adults in 1916–23, but they have rarely been fulfilled in the Republic. This story, like others by Trevor, is not exempt from historical errors. The essential point about it is that few catholics can have read it without feeling sympathy for the Middletons. Similarly, few protestants will read a recent story, 'The wedding in the garden',[73] about a catholic girl who goes to work in a protestant household, without feeling sympathy for Dervla. 'Poetry makes nothing happen', according to W. H. Auden—a daunting thought for those who write on the relationship of literature and society—but writers like William Trevor may civilise our emotions even though they fail to influence our actions.

[72] *The stories of William Trevor* (Harmondsworth, 1983), p. 351.
[73] William Trevor, *The collected stories* (Harmondsworth, 1993), pp 922–37 (originally published in the *New Yorker*).

CHAPTER XIX

Irish language and literature, 1921–84

NEIL BUTTIMER and MÁIRE NÍ ANNRACHÁIN

Language, by Neil Buttimer

A number of factors distinguish the story of the Irish language in the twentieth century from that of preceding centuries. Chief among these was the creation in 1922 of a largely independent, self-governing state in the south, which promptly adopted a policy of strong support for the language. The present chapter outlines the foundation, implementation, and modification of public policy during the decades in question, and offers some assessment of the achievement. The state's approach differed markedly from that of its forerunner. Certain measures by the British authorities had benefited Gaelic culture during the nineteenth century, and particularly in the final decades of British rule. For example, there was path-breaking work on early Irish history and law which appeared in publicly funded research series, and from the 1870s some limited admission of the Irish language into the state education system.[1] However, the status of the language under British rule was at best marginal, and the last century before independence had witnessed the marked decline of Irish as a widespread community language. This was already under way before 1800, but it accelerated dramatically during and after the great famine of 1845–9; fear of the prospective death of the language helped to inspire the Gaelic revival and 'Irish-Ireland' movements which were such a feature of the thirty years or so before independence. During that period the Gaelic League and similar agencies had conducted a vigorous campaign to revive the Irish language and culture. Tens of thousands of people had been mobilised. To what extent this involved a real intention to learn and use the language (as opposed to conferring on it a symbolic importance) is open to question, but the fact was that during these years the language became entrenched as one of the hallmarks of Irish nationalism. Building on these pioneering efforts, in the 1920s the new state committed itself to what

[1] Above, vi, 396–7.

amounted to a cultural revolution, in which the revival of the language was
expected to play a central part. Referring to the struggle for independence,
Michael Collins made the point: 'We only succeeded after we had begun to
get back our Irish ways; after we had made a serious effort to speak our own
language; after we had striven again to govern ourselves. We can only keep
out the enemy and all other enemies by completing that task ... The biggest
task will be the restoration of the language.'[2] However (and this is the second
major consideration of this chapter), translating such aspirations into reality
proved much more difficult than many had expected, and although there
were some successes, the process of decline of Irish as a community language
was not halted.

A third strand concerns the position of the Irish language in Northern
Ireland. While the attitude of government in Northern Ireland towards Irish
was not necessarily one of inveterate hostility, it was certainly less well
disposed than its southern counterpart. This was despite the fact that many
northerners of various political persuasions had taken part in the late nine-
teenth- and early twentieth-century movement that brought Gaelic culture
onto a broader stage. The Irish language continued to be spoken in a handful
of locations in what would become Northern Ireland during the opening
decades of the century, although these were admittedly small in scale and
isolated from each other, but the state-sponsored attempt to foster a language
revival was lacking there. Attitudes among northern protestants to the language were affected by the politicisation of the language issue in the years
before independence; in this respect the fate of the language raised wider
issues of nationhood, appreciation of the past and vision of the future, issues
that transcended narrow linguistic considerations. As the twentieth century
progressed, the language issue also took on an international dimension,
notably through Ireland's membership of the European Economic Community (later the European Union).

Despite the intrinsic importance of the subject, scholars have been slow to
attempt systematic evaluations of the history of Irish language and culture in
the twentieth century. Such attempts might have been expected from at least
two major perspectives. The first is from within the Irish-language interest
itself, because of the latter's inherent concern with the topic, and its credentials to deal with it. There have been valuable outlines of particular aspects,
for instance accounts of language and literature, as well as some treatment of
the state's role. However excellent in their own right, such works are sometimes rather narrowly focused, while objectivity can be a problem. Among
historians in general, wider cultural and educational issues are attracting
attention, but many historians lack expertise in Irish and familiarity with

[2] Quoted in Tomás Ó Fiaich, 'The language and political history' in Brian Ó Cuív (ed.), *A view of the Irish language* (Dublin, 1969), pp 101–11: 111.

Irish-language issues. A few are indifferent, if not actually hostile, to the Gaelic tradition. This unobjective approach curiously mirrors the lack of detachment often seen within the ranks of the Irish-language fraternity itself. But the failure to write the history of Irish in the twentieth century may simply reflect an uncertainty as to how best to proceed. For reasons of space, the present chapter can only seek to establish a possible framework, drawing particularly on the records of central government (legislature and executive). Fields such as education, which naturally intersect with the history of Irish, will be examined. In evaluating the history of Irish, due consideration will be given to the adequacy or otherwise of state structures to support the language, and the experimental nature of the attempt at language revival. Since the main initiatives towards language revival and gaelicisation took place in the first quarter-century after independence, the bulk of attention in this overview will be devoted to the years 1922–45. That era was followed by a period of reassessment (1946–72), and (particularly from the early 1970s) a period of gradual retreat from the idea of a state-imposed language revival, accompanied by a rise in voluntary efforts, especially among the middle classes.

THAT the enhanced public position of Irish preceded the establishment of the Irish Free State may be noted in the workings of Ireland's revolutionary government of 1919–22. Indeed, it is essential to bear in mind that many of the participants in government at this time 'had been brought up on Irish-Ireland ideals'.[3] The proceedings of the first dáil in January 1919 were conducted largely in Irish, and the programme for government was presented in Irish as well as English. Measures adopted included a ministry for the national language, with responsibility for education and the Irish-speaking districts. Implementation of these policies was interrupted by the troubled condition of the country and the civil war that followed the Anglo–Irish treaty of 1921, but many strands of the first dáil's activities were subsequently resumed when conditions allowed, for the commitment to the language largely cut across divisions over the treaty, and the language was one area in which the pro-treaty side could hope to demonstrate its unimpeachable national credentials. The 1922 provisional government was proclaimed in Irish, and its various ministries retained Irish names. An oireachtas translation service was formed to render statutes and other official documentation into Irish. The translation staff, whose numbers were small, faced an unprecedented challenge in attempting to express aspects of contemporary life in a vernacular little employed for such purposes for centuries. This branch of

---

[3] Margaret O'Callaghan, 'Language, nationality and cultural identity in the Irish Free State, 1922–7: the *Irish Statesman* and the *Catholic Bulletin* reappraised' in *I.H.S.*, xxiv, no. 94 (Nov. 1984), pp 226–45: 229.

the parliamentary secretariat thus gained a form of experience at the purely linguistic level which would see it play a more central part in language planning during later decades.

Irish formally owed its strengthened place in the new southern dispensation to article 4 of the Irish Free State (Constitution) Act, 1922,[4] according to which it was recognised as the state's national language, with English also declared an official language. This was a new departure: Canada and South Africa, for instance, had admitted the use of French and Dutch respectively but without implying derogation from the preponderant status of English. The recognition of Irish in the 1922 constitution and in the state deriving therefrom was continued, and in many respects augmented, in *Bunreacht na hÉireann*, the constitution of Ireland ratified in 1937, which (subject to amendments) remains in force in the Republic of Ireland. The 1937 constitution is characterised by a more explicit emphasis on the imagery of nationhood and statehood, from its preamble's rhetorical evocation of an ancient and resurgent people, to the identification of the national territory (articles 2 and 3)[5] and the adoption of a national flag (article 7). Following on from the first two articles on nation and state, article 8 explicitly reaffirmed the status of Irish as the national language and the state's first official language, with English as the second official language. Two further provisions showed an evolution in the 1937 position compared with that of 1922. Henceforth, in case of conflict between the texts of laws enrolled in both the official languages, the text in the national language was to prevail (article 25.4.6). More significantly, in case of conflict between the texts of any copy of the 1937 constitution incorporating any subsequent amendments, the text in Irish would also prevail (article 25.5.4).

Despite the important new status accorded to it in these constitutions, in practice those who attempted to act on such provisions faced many difficulties. From the early years of independence onwards, the right of plaintiffs, witnesses, or defendants as to choice of language in court proceedings had to be established; and following on from that, members of the legal profession had also to be competent in the language. An act of 1929 stipulated that no barrister was to be admitted to practise unless the chief justice was satisfied that the candidate possessed a competent knowledge of the language.[6] The means by which proficiency was to be tested was left to the profession, and the test itself seems to have had a certain informality. Solicitors, by contrast, appear to have been less compliant, with the result that they were required to sit written examinations approved by the minister for education.[7] For

[4] 13 Geo. V, c. 1 [U.K.] (5 Dec. 1922).
[5] In December 1999 articles 2 and 3 were amended to remove the territorial claim by the Republic to the whole island, and to state that a united Ireland can only come about by consent.
[6] Legal Practitioners (Qualification) Act, 1929 (1929/16) (17 Dec. 1929).
[7] Ibid.

members of the armed forces and the gardaí, as well as the civil service, some knowledge of Irish was made compulsory (in the civil service there were different requirements for different grades). While few challenged the underlying aim of the policy, concerns were expressed from time to time about its implications for those who (for instance) had been appointed to the civil service before the Irish-language requirement was made a necessary qualification: did promotional opportunities exist for them?[8] The commissioners of inquiry into the civil service in the mid 1930s had another concern. They feared that the preference shown to Irish in the examinations for the junior administrative grades was militating against an adequate supply of good candidates. Since 200 of the 900 marks for the entire examination were assigned to oral Irish, this was said to favour those candidates who had studied Irish as part of their university degree. The commissioners recommended that while Irish of a certain standard should be a necessary qualification for such posts, the strictly competitive part of the examination should not contain a compulsory Irish element. They also revealed that of the twenty-nine civil servants between 1 April 1924 and 31 December 1934 who had failed to survive their two-year probationary period, six had failed the special test for proficiency in Irish administered towards the end of the probationary period.[9]

It was the schools, however, that were allocated a crucial role in the revival of Irish. A fuller discussion of the place of Irish in the educational system will be found below,[10] but the main provisions can be outlined. The dáil cabinet from 1919 to 1922, in cooperation with the Gaelic League, took a number of initiatives, including the establishment of scholarship schemes and appointing two commissions to devise curricula for primary and secondary schools. The provisional government carried on the work, indicating that it would strive to give 'the language, history, music and traditions of Ireland their national place in the life of Irish schools'.[11] To this end an order was issued on 1 February 1922 setting out that as from 17 March 1922 Irish should be taught for at least one hour per day in primary schools where there was a teacher competent to teach it. Following the first programme conference of 1921–2 and a dáil commission on secondary education, further elements were added by 1924. The entire teaching in infant classes was to be carried out through Irish as soon as possible, with other primary school classes following in due course. In secondary schools the importance of teaching Irish was emphasised, on the understanding that it would soon become a compul-

[8] See *Dáil Éireann deb.*, lxxiii, 380–81 (9 Nov. 1938).
[9] *Coimisiún fiosrúcháin i dtaobh na stát-sheirbíse. Commission of inquiry into the civil service, 1932–1935*, i; final report with appendices (P 1844) (Dublin, n.d.), pp 46, 69, 112, 118.
[10] Below, pp 726–31.
[11] Pádraig Ó Brolcháin, chief executive officer for national education, quoted in Séamas Ó Buachalla, *Education policy in twentieth century Ireland* (Dublin, 1988), pp 344–5.

sory subject, as it did in 1927. Irish was a required subject for the intermediate examination from 1928 and for the leaving certificate from 1934.[12] Schools were to be encouraged to use Irish by a complex system of special grants, and bonus marks in examinations were to be given for schools that used Irish as a general mode of instruction. Awards were also devised for fluency in speaking Irish.

Clearly one of the foundations of such an ambitious programme would be the supply of suitably qualified teachers, and the government made available grants for summer courses and visits to Irish-speaking areas, with the effect that whereas in 1922 fewer than 10 per cent of primary school teachers were able to teach bilingually, by 1926 the proportion had risen to almost half. In addition, higher salary payments were offered to teachers who were qualified to teach through Irish. Second-level preparatory colleges for native Irish-speakers were established with a view to providing a ready-made pool of suitably qualified candidates for the civil service, the gardaí, and the professions, and this included the setting up of a Church of Ireland preparatory college, Coláiste Moibhí. Thanks to the earlier efforts of the Irish Guild of the Church, founded in 1914 to provide 'a bond of union for all members of the Church of Ireland inspired with Irish ideals', there were adequate numbers of Irish-speaking protestant teachers to staff the college, and to assist with teaching at the Church of Ireland training college in Kildare Place.[13] Although teachers were among the most enthusiastic supporters of the language revival, the new policies did not find support in all quarters, and in the early 1920s national teacher representatives opposed the exclusion of English from infant classes as impractical and premature.[14] Officials in the department of finance also expressed reservations, on grounds of cost.

It is apparent that the main planks of the educational policy of the new state for the revival of Irish were already in place well before the advent of Fianna Fáil governments in the 1930s, and a good deal had been achieved. By 1932 three-quarters of serving national school teachers were qualified to teach the language, and only thirty-two of the 5,401 national schools were failing to teach Irish. When Fianna Fáil came into power, the new minister for education, Thomas Derrig, enthusiastically pursued the language policy, and expressed renewed optimism about the prospects for revival: 'it is only a matter of years and more training in the schools until Gaelic again becomes the national language of the Free State.'[15] The number of Irish-medium

[12] Ibid., pp 347–8.
[13] David Greene, 'The Irish language movement' in Michael Hurley (ed.), *Irish anglicanism 1869–1969* (Dublin, 1970), pp 110–19: 117–18. See also F. S. L. Lyons, *Ireland since the famine* (London, 1973 ed.), pp 635–40.
[14] Ó Buachalla, *Education policy*, p. 346; but see Seán Ó Catháin, 'Education in the new Ireland' in Francis MacManus (ed.), *The years of the great test 1926–39* (Cork, 1967), pp 104–14: 109.
[15] Quoted by Ó Buachalla, *Education policy*, p. 354.

secondary schools increased rapidly in the decade after 1925, coinciding with the various incentive and other schemes and with the renewed vigour injected by Fianna Fáil's arrival in office. However, teachers were now becoming more vociferous in their criticisms of certain aspects of the system, and in 1937 they carried out a national survey, published in 1941, which showed that a majority of respondents disagreed with the policy of instruction through Irish where English was the home language. There is some evidence that by the early 1940s ministers themselves, including Eamon de Valera, were beginning to question the methods, if not the goal, of language revival; but there was no official change in policy.[16]

At university level (at least in the National University of Ireland) the place of Irish was already assured. Even before independence, in 1910 the Gaelic League had succeeded in obtaining government approval for Irish to be made compulsory for matriculation in the N.U.I. colleges, and this was introduced in 1913. During the 1920s links were fostered between new Irish-medium primary schools in the capital and University College Dublin; funds were provided to University College Cork to encourage gaelicisation of some of its activities; and in 1929 University College Galway was given a special role in the promotion of the language. Extra money was provided for the teaching of Irish, and when making appointments the college was required to give preference to those who were competent to discharge their duties through the medium of Irish, provided that they were competent and suitable in other respects.[17]

THE Irish authorities in the Free State were to gain their experience in cultural management principally through policies concerning education and the Gaeltacht. The Irish-speaking districts represented the living embodiment of the unbroken continuity of Irish as a spoken language. As a result, the Gaeltacht was of particular symbolic significance, and the need to enhance its endangered position seen as a national priority. It still remains one of the central spheres of state activity in matters Irish. Furthermore, a number of measures in education policy were adopted either to benefit Irish-speaking areas, or to facilitate educational objectives by drawing on Gaeltacht-based strengths. The interrelationship between these two domains persists to the present.

THE person credited with giving a major impetus to government thinking in relation to the Gaeltacht (and indeed to other policies for promoting Irish) was the Antrim-born presbyterian and minister for local government in the first Free State administration, Ernest Blythe. Working on the assumption that 'Irish cannot be revived in the Galltacht [English-speaking area] if the Gaeltacht disappears',[18] in late 1924 this Gaelic League veteran and lover of

[16] Ibid., pp 349–53.
[17] University College Galway Act, 1929 (1929/35) (17 Dec. 1929).
[18] Quoted by Ó Buachalla, *Education policy*, p. 345.

the arts recommended to the executive council that it investigate the preservation of the region, and take steps to ensure its future well-being. The situation was acute. In 1893 only 1 per cent of the population could speak Irish only, whereas 85 per cent could speak no Irish. By 1911 87 per cent could speak no Irish.[19] A commission was formally established in January 1925 and given its terms of reference by President W. T. Cosgrave. This followed the widespread contemporary practice of delegating to such bodies the task of advising on policy in matters requiring fresh initiatives such as railway management, the post office, and, most notably, the border issues examined by the boundary commission. The twelve-man Gaeltacht group included prominent figures in the language movement, academics, and public administrators. It worked under the chairmanship of Richard Mulcahy, who had recently relinquished his portfolio as minister for defence after the controversial army mutiny of 1924. It was probably as a result of this particular involvement with Gaeltacht affairs that Mulcahy would keep a watchful eye on Irish-language matters for the remainder of his lengthy parliamentary career.

The commission invited submissions from interested parties, held meetings in Dublin between April and July, and visited Donegal, Galway, Mayo, Clare, Kerry, Cork, and Waterford between August and October. Because the last national census to have included questions on the use of Irish was that of 1911, the commission arranged for local research by teachers and clergy to establish the extent of the Irish-speaking population in certain districts, as well as a special general enumeration for the same purpose by police engaged in collecting agricultural statistics during July and August 1925. In addition to the information relative to language, the Gaeltacht commission probably produced the most thorough inquiry into any part of Ireland, especially rural Ireland, during the early phase of independence.

A report was presented to the executive council in July 1926 and published the following August. On the basis of data at its disposal, the commission suggested that where 80 per cent or more of a region's population were Irish-speaking the area be regarded as what was subsequently termed a Fíor-Ghaeltacht (Irish-speaking area). Any district with not fewer than 25 per cent and not more than 79 per cent Irish-speakers should become a Breac-Ghaeltacht (partly Irish-speaking area). It was estimated that the total population of both types of Gaeltacht was in the order of 200,000 persons. Some eighty further recommendations were made, the majority coming under the three headings of educational facilities (twenty-seven proposals), the use of Irish in administration (twenty-four), and economic policy (twenty-five).[20]

[19] Brian Ó Cuív, 'Ireland in the modern world' in Ó Cuív, *View of Ir. language*, pp 122–32: 128.
[20] *Coimisiún na Gaeltachta report* (R. 23/27) (Dublin [1927]). The recommendations are summarised at pp 59–65.

Key proposals receive fuller treatment below, but an impression of the general reaction to the report may be given here. The seanad discussed it during early 1927. Responses varied, with some senators calling for government to implement the recommendations in full, and others, such as Dr Oliver St John Gogarty, expressing trenchant scepticism concerning virtually the whole Gaelic promotion enterprise.[21] The executive council considered the report for over twelve months. During December 1927, its conclusions, placed before both houses of the oireachtas in the form of a white paper, steered something of a middle course between the various positions adopted in the seanad.[22] The need to assist the Gaeltacht was acknowledged, as was the proposal to divide the region into areas of greater and lesser language use. Ten recommendations were rejected, especially the more obviously draconian or objectionable, such as proposals to remove from Gaeltacht areas within three years all teachers not properly trained to offer instruction in Irish (no. 5), or a similar directive relating to all non-Irish-speaking civil servants (no. 31). The white paper concurred in principle with about fifty recommendations, highlighted those where work was already in progress or about to commence, and suspended judgement on the remainder. It was debated in the dáil during 1928. The discussion is of interest both in its own right and as an early example of the contribution to the parliamentary process of the new opposition party Fianna Fáil. The party emphasised its own commitment to a strengthened Gaeltacht, spoke of the need to provide much greater resources for the region, claimed that government pledges of support were in many cases not being acted on, and commented on the failure to establish the administrative machinery needed to realise the commission report's objectives.[23]

The divergence of views could, perhaps, reflect the nature of an adversarial parliamentary system in which each party must seek to distinguish itself from others even where broad general agreement exists. However, the beginnings of rather more genuine differences of emphasis between the government and the new party may also be detected. After Fianna Fáil took power in 1932, Cumann na nGaedheal would in turn closely question the new cabinet on its Gaeltacht measures, monitor its expenditure, and enquire why a second Gaeltacht commission, rumoured to be imminent, was thought necessary. By that time all parties had become sensitive to the impact of public policy on elections, particularly in the light of proportional representation, a process subject to almost imperceptible local influences. A personal statement by one Gaeltacht commission member, Fr Seaghan Mac Cuinnigeáin, appended to the 1926 report, recommended the formation of a per-

---

[21] *Seanad Éireann deb.*, viii, 488–94 (10 Mar. 1927).
[22] *Coimisiún na Gaeltachta: statement of government policy on recommendations of the commission* (R. 23/28) (Dublin, 1927).
[23] See, e.g., contribution of Frank Fahy in *Dáil Éireann deb.*, xxiii, 695–718 (2 May 1928).

manent commission or board for the Gaeltacht.[24] The executive council rejected this proposition in its white paper, suggesting that such a body would lack proper authority and cause friction with those departments of state with an interest in Gaeltacht-related issues. Instead, the council proposed to create a ministry of state for the Gaeltacht, and to foster collaboration between departments with Gaeltacht-related responsibilities. Another commission member, L. C. Moriarty, furnished an addendum to the 1926 report not unlike Mac Cuinnigeáin's. He appears to have regretted the dissolution in 1923 of the congested districts board, regarding it as a virtual prototype of the Gaeltacht board his colleague had in mind.[25] In many respects it can be said that in its day the congested districts board did offer a relatively integrated approach to the development of those western counties that were to constitute the core of the Gaeltacht region. But the board had been criticised in the 1926 report, and the government was not disposed to re-create such a body.

The Gaeltacht commission report, and the ensuing debate, added considerable momentum to measures taken on behalf of the region. Land was one of the main issues in the report, which emphasised reclamation (no. 59) and arterial drainage (no. 62) as among the more desirable steps needed to increase and improve smallholdings in the Irish-speaking west and south, and encourage economically viable farming there. The government was in broad agreement with such proposals, and the work became the responsibility of the land commission, which in 1923 had taken over the functions of the congested districts board. By 1928 special reclamation schemes were in progress in the Cloosh, Oorid, and Maam Valley districts of Connemara, where the commission had earlier instituted proceedings for the acquisition of 23,121 acres of land.[26] Similar projects were also under way in the Ballycroy and Erris districts of County Mayo and the Rosses in Donegal. By 1929 the commission, in collaboration with other agencies, had begun road construction, fencing, and drainage schemes, costing some £8,000 in Connemara alone, where a road was opened between Oughterard and Cashla.[27] Southern counties, notably Kerry, benefited from similar ventures as the decade came to a close. In 1931 a small experimental scheme of pasture reclamation in the Cloosh area, modelled on the Isle of Lewis peat farm trials in Scotland, was among a number of innovations attempted in the commission's Gaeltacht activities, together with projects to grow special grasses in districts affected by coastal erosion.[28] In 1934 the land commission revealed that more than

---

[24] *Coimisiún na Gaeltachta report*, pp 66–7.

[25] Ibid., p. 68.

[26] *An roinn tailte agus iascaigh: Coimisiún Talmhan na hÉireann. Report of the Irish land commissioners... 1928–9* (P 55) (Dublin, n.d.), p. 7.

[27] Ibid., pp 7–8.

[28] *An roinn tailte agus iascaigh... Report of the Irish land commissioners... 1931–32* (P 764) (Dublin, n.d.), p. 30.

half the total funds available for land improvements and relief works were spent in the Gaeltacht counties of Donegal, Mayo, Galway, Clare, and Kerry. In the period since 1923 the commission had divided over 270,000 acres of untenanted land in Irish-speaking areas.[29]

The Gaeltacht commission report had suggested that Irish-speakers be encouraged to migrate from areas of 'hopeless congestion', particularly in western Donegal, Erris, and west Galway, to available lands elsewhere (no. 61). The white paper's response to this and similar proposals was cautious, initally concentrating on localised resettlement within Connemara. However, in the mid 1930s it was decided to extend the scheme to estates obtained by the land commission in County Meath. A compact area of 776 acres was acquired in the Rathcarran (Ráth Cairn) district of Meath. Of this, 588 acres were divided into twenty-seven holdings of just over twenty-one acres each and made available to Gaeltacht migrants, who surrendered their existing properties.[30] On each new holding a four-roomed dwelling house and out-offices comprising stable, piggery, poultry-house, and dairy were built. To assist the settlers a portion of each property was sown with wheat, oats, potatoes, and barley, and turf and provisions were supplied. A school and playing field for the district were also provided. A second 'colony' consisting of fifty holdings was soon developed at Gibstown, about six miles north of Rathcarran, and a third and smaller one at Kilbride, comprising thirteen holdings.[31] Families initially came from County Galway, but Kerry, West Cork, Mayo, and Donegal were subsequently represented.[32] The land commission sought to establish cordial relations between natives and newcomers by attending to land shortages among the local population before introducing the new settlers. A number of the early migrants returned to their home counties, but over time the new communities would remain relatively intact and perpetuate their linguistic and cultural heritage.

Many of these measures were intended to improve conditions in the original Gaeltacht areas while also assisting those who settled in recently founded Irish-speaking communities. Assessing their impact on agriculture awaits a thorough analysis of the industry in the early years of the new state. A full evaluation would also have to take into account a range of other initiatives sponsored by the department of agriculture in Irish-speaking districts, which can be briefly outlined here. In policy and planning statements

[29] *An roinn tailte agus iascaigh…Report of the Irish land commissioners…1933–34* (P 1471) (Dublin, n.d.), p. 29.

[30] *An roinn tailte agus iascaigh…Report of the Irish land commissioners…1935–36* (P 2518) (Dublin, n.d.), pp 6–7.

[31] *An roinn tailte agus iascaigh…Report of the Irish land commissioners…1936–37* (P 2934) (Dublin, n.d.), pp 6–7.

[32] One of these migrants was Mícheál Ó Conaire from An Máimín, west Connemara. See *Stairsheanchas Mhicil Chonraí: ón Máimín go Ráth Chairn*, ed. Conchúr Ó Giollagáin (Indreabhán, Co. Galway, 1999).

issued towards the end of the 1920s, the department expressly took cognisance of the Gaeltacht commission report's recommendations on agricultural development. Since 1923, the department had taken over many of the functions of the congested districts board in relation to rural advancement. In fact the department would, in its publications, continue to use the term 'congested district' throughout the 1930s and 1940s. Sometimes the term denoted the Gaeltacht as it came officially to be defined; sometimes it denoted both the disadvantaged regions of the pre-independence era and recently redefined Irish-speaking areas. The department reaffirmed its commitment to the work inherited from the congested districts board, while bearing in mind the special requirements of the newly designated Gaeltacht regions.[33]

The department furnished three general forms of assistance: the improvement of livestock and crops, the provision of equipment and hardware, and the supply of specialist personnel. Under the first heading, it offered loans and supplementary allocations for the acquisition of bulls, boars, sows, rams, and other livestock. Such loans increased noticeably after the publication in 1927 of the Gaeltacht report, resulting in a marked rise in the number of bulls and boars in congested districts. Loans for agricultural implements increased from 582 in 1925–6 to over one thousand in 1929–30.[34] The latter may be an interesting barometer of farming fortunes during this period, for they dropped dramatically throughout the mid 1930s (to 632 in 1933–4) as the Anglo–Irish economic war intensified. Veterinary surgeons were paid additional subsidies to attend dispensaries or travel to smallholdings in Gaeltacht and congested areas.

The Gaeltacht commission report attached particular importance to the role of agricultural advisers in strengthening farming practices in the region, and the department duly acknowledged this point. In 1927–8 the number of assistant agricultural overseers in congested districts went up from forty-five to fifty-two, with five new temporary assistants being also appointed.[35] The department noted that of a total of fifty-seven such staff in 1927–8, twenty-seven worked exclusively in the Gaeltacht. Additional advisors were recruited from the graduating classes of the department's training college at Athenry, County Galway. This college's curriculum was similar to that of the other agricultural colleges except that instruction was offered in Irish.[36] Special attention was devoted to providing advice most often sought in Gaeltacht and other congested districts: the building and improvement of farm outoffices, the reclamation and improvement of land, the prevention and

---

[33] *An roinn talmhaíochta—department of agriculture. First annual report of the minister for agriculture 1931–32* (P 802) (Dublin, n.d.), pp 16–20.

[34] Ibid., p. 91.

[35] *An roinn talmhaíochta—department of agriculture. Twenty-sixth general report... 1927–28* (Dublin, n.d.), p. 152.

[36] Ibid., *First ann. rep. 1931–2*, pp 16–17.

treatment of animal and crop diseases, and the development of the poultry and pig industries. Such services, together with the stock and equipment improvement schemes mentioned earlier, remained at the core of the department's input into the Gaeltacht down to the end of the period in question, but there were other forms of intervention from time to time, including experimental tomato-growing projects and poultry schemes in the mid 1930s.[37]

In pursuit of its economic objectives, the Gaeltacht commission report had recommended the consolidation of manufacturing and processing activities in the region (nos 70–76). The white paper reacted favourably to these proposals. However, the obstacles were considerable, and remained so for many decades to come. Local difficulties included the existing and continuing weakness of the Gaeltacht's industrial base, especially in the areas of skill formation, management controls, and marketing. Government supervision may have been inadequate, and the international terms of trade were frequently unfavourable. The history of industry in the Gaeltacht forms an interesting case-study in the state's initial involvement with the development of the country's peripheral economies.

The promotion of local industry in the less advantaged parts of Ireland had been entrusted in the first instance to the congested districts board. This body concentrated its attention mainly on the development of textile and clothing production. However, it appears to have received fewer funds for this purpose than for its other major undertakings, land management and infrastructural improvement, and those funds that were allocated to industry appear to have gone in large part to marine-related rather than manufacturing activity (the marine element is discussed below). In this connection, when the congested districts board was dissolved in 1923, its rural industries section was transferred en bloc to the emergent ministry for fisheries rather than to the department of industry and commerce. In its new departmental berthing, the rural industries head-office staff in the mid 1920s consisted of one junior executive officer, one clerical officer, two clerical assistants, and one technical officer. The work of this modest establishment was rendered highly demanding by virtue of the isolation and extent of the geographical areas within its remit.

The presence of a training-based objective inherited from pre-independence days further complicated the industrialisation mission. The congested districts board had attached more importance to providing workers with an elementary formation in particular industries than to running self-sustaining enterprises. Moreover, the board's industries were not expected to be competitive. These tendencies bequeathed a problematic legacy to rural industry

---

[37] Ibid., *Fourth ann. rep. 1934–5* (P 1943) (Dublin, n.d.), pp 99–100; *Sixth ann. rep. 1936–7* (P 2733) (Dublin, n.d.), pp 97–8.

in the Free State. Financial data may be considered once more to highlight the underlying difficulties. In 1925–6 government assigned some £30,700 for the equipment, personnel, and other requirements of rural industries, but only £21,000 was actually spent. A similar pattern was repeated in the next twelve months, when the estimate was £31,000, although the total of approximately £18,000 taken up proved smaller again.[38] The exchequer did hope to recoup some revenue from the profits of such enterprises, but receipts proved disappointing. Inquiries were made, revealing that government supported about forty industrial centres throughout congested or Gaeltacht areas.[39] The definition of a centre was itself quite loose. It might denote a factory in the accepted sense of the term, particularly in Donegal, the region with the most substantial manufacturing sector. Centres could equally denote more fluid arrangements. A substantial number comprised classes in which local women assembled to take lessons in particular crafts. Such women might also form teams of outworkers, such as the group of about forty young girls and older women engaged in embroidery in their homes at Ardara, County Donegal. The classes were frequently linked to convents, where instruction concentrated on lacemaking, crochet work, and knitting, as in Achill Sound, Louisburg, Benada, and Carna. Even as the system began slowly to be transformed in the early 1930s, one manageress was still conducting her knitting, training, and manufacturing business in the chapel vestry at Termon, County Donegal. In such cases record-keeping was often rudimentary or non-existent.

From the mid 1920s onwards, it emerged that the existing accounting systems were failing to reveal the real costs of running centres. They often gave a misleading impression of accumulated stores or the value of the stock in hand. Other defects were also apparent. From time to time the department of finance was forced to write off the debts of traders who had received goods from industrial centres, but who had subsequently gone bankrupt. Certain centres seem to have persisted with activities for which there was no longer a demand, as the case of artificial silk indicates. Substantial stocks of this material continued to accumulate even after 1925, when a British tariff on Irish silks adversely affected trade.[40] The publication of the 1926 Gaeltacht commission report thus coincided with a growing awareness of the need to reform this section of the state-supported economy. Some remedial measures had long been thought desirable. It had been observed that manageresses (they were usually women) of rural manufacturing centres were too far removed from their markets and too ill-circumstanced to attract buyers for their products. The Gaeltacht report recommended that a central depot be

---

[38] *Appropriation accounts 1925–26* (Dublin, 1927), p. 147; ibid., *1926–7* (Dublin, 1928), p. 160.
[39] *Report of department of fisheries* (Dublin, 1927), p. 45.
[40] Ibid., p. 44.

set up for the purposes of marketing the output of Gaeltacht rural industries (no. 74), and the white paper lent its backing to the recommendation. Approval was finally sanctioned by the department of finance in 1930. The old military barracks at Beggar's Bush in Dublin was chosen for the purpose, and after some time the premises were adapted for this new task, under the title 'Gaeltacht industries depot'.[41] The staffing initially consisted of a manager, a book-keeper, and a stock-keeper, as well as secretarial and other general operatives. Building and staffing costs were met by the fisheries and Gaeltacht Services department. The depot also drew on the assistance of the board of works and the stationery office. A clear working relationship between the depot and its parent Gaeltacht Services department was to emerge, although some time elapsed before the depot's own monitoring procedures were in order. By the early 1930s, five commercial travellers covering different parts of the country were promoting its products. The industries in turn would be responsible for paying 5 per cent of their turnover to the depot for marketing purposes, and 5 per cent to its selling agents. Henceforth, therefore, all activities were to be placed on as sound a commercial footing as possible, with the hope of making the enterprises in question competitive and viable.

In the Gaeltacht itself some reorientation took place to match this change in marketing policy. New products such as cheap cardigans and mass-produced men's pullovers would supplement earlier products such as socks and gloves, which still continued to be made. Higher-quality goods were also envisaged. The Gaeltacht authorities were set to invest substantially in home-produced tweeds, which gave employment to a mainly male workforce. Preliminary steps were taken to establish tweed manufacture in Rosmuc (Connemara) and other places. By 1930 centres had been set up in Donegal, including Kilcar and Ardara, while other schemes were getting under way.[42] Interest in the products was shown by major Irish retail stores such as Clerys of Dublin, and by retailers in London and subsequently New York. The brand-name Gaeltarra Éireann was later devised to promote the items, while a designated advertising budget facilitated greater representation at domestic and international fairs and exhibitions. Accompanying the change in direction was a substantial increase in funding in the early 1930s.

The higher turnover targets implied by the increases in funding were somewhat slow to be realised. The venture into tweed, for instance, was a new departure for Gaeltacht Services. Training weavers to the requisite standard could not be achieved overnight, and the output was subject to rigorous quality control, which meant that some work had to be rejected.

---

[41] *Report on the sea and inland fisheries and Gaeltacht Services for... 1929 and 1930* (P 915) (Dublin, n.d.), p. 10.
[42] Ibid., p. 11.

Adequate monitoring systems took some time to establish. In the late 1920s Gaeltacht Services had hoped to institute widely acceptable accounting procedures, but these were still not properly in place by 1935. The department of finance expected that accounts would be drawn up according to commercial norms, while Gaeltacht Services argued that the training element in its work meant that its industries could not be judged on strictly commercial lines. The view of Finance prevailed, and when estimates and later appropriation accounts were generated according to its prescriptions a more stringent regime came into force. Government funds for rural industries declined in the mid 1930s, though this may have reflected the depressed trading conditions of the time. However, there was also a more positive side to the story. A far greater balance was now achieved between departmental estimates and actual expenditure, suggesting better direction within the system. That the industries in question had indeed been placed on a sound fiscal and market-led basis is suggested by an upturn in their fortunes towards the end of the 1930s, when both anecdotal evidence and fiscal information confirm the acceptability of Gaeltarra Éireann products.[43] There was further improvement in the early 1940s, when the problems arising from interruptions to world trade arising from the second world war may have been offset by greater home sales.

Down to 1923 the congested districts board had supported various marine commercial activities. One of these was the gathering and sale of the purplish-red North Atlantic seaweed (*Chondrus crispus*) known as carrageen, and the more general varieties of large brown seaweed which could be made into kelp. Carrageen was used principally as a food additive or an ingredient in paint and distemper manufacture. Kelp, when burned, is a source of iodine and soda, and can be used in the manufacture of fertilisers. Harvesting these seaweeds provided seasonal labour and supplementary income for women and particularly for men. The state's participation in the trade had lapsed during the 1920s, but resumed in the early 1930s.[44] In respect of kelp, the aim was to break the near-monopoly British purchasers enjoyed in certain seaboard regions of the west. As in the case of industrial goods, the central depot was to play an important role in marketing these products, and state funds were provided, the bulk of which went to the kelp industry. The expectation that these industries could prosper turned out to be excessively optimistic during the 1930s. Indeed, a particularly sharp decline appears to have been experienced towards the end of the decade, and government funding declined.[45] However, as in the case of rural manufacturing industry,

---

[43] See *Appropriation accounts 1938–39* (P 3842) (Dublin, 1940); ibid, *1939–40* (P 4386) (Dublin, 1941), p. 183.
[44] *Report on the sea and inland fisheries... for 1929 and 1930*, pp 11–12.
[45] *Appropriation accounts 1938–39*, p. 180; ibid., *1939–40*, pp 184–6.

output and funding increased significantly when international supplies of fertilisers were disrupted during the second world war.

One further aspect of marine commercial activities, fisheries, can only be mentioned in passing. This was an industry in which most of the Gaeltacht counties were involved to some extent, and certain of the more salient features of the trade as it affected Irish-speaking areas may be traced. The industry had flourished throughout the first world war, during which demand for fish was steady, and fishermen were in a position to meet repayments of arrears on boats and equipment. There then followed a period of decline throughout the 1920s, a downturn from which the industry arguably never fully recovered. Stiff competition was encountered from foreign vessels, notably English, Scottish, French, and Belgian, which took the chance to return to Irish waters after the end of the war.[46] As these countries' demands were increasingly supplied by their own fleets, Irish fishermen lost market share and consequently experienced mounting financial difficulties. A series of poor fishing seasons during the first decade of independence greatly worsened the situation. In better times, the congested districts board had advanced loans for rural industry and fishing for periods of from five to twenty years, and continued the practice down to its dissolution in 1923, with fisheries accounting for 90 per cent of the outlay. Unpaid arrears from congested areas totalled some £50,000 in 1923.[47] As repayments of both principal and accumulating interest were delayed or did not take place at all, indebtedness had risen significantly by the end of the decade.

A new start seemed possible with the passage of the Fisheries (Revision of Loans) Act, 1931.[48] This measure, long contemplated, enabled the government to write off its losses on maritime loans advanced by the congested districts board down to the end of the first world war. A Sea Fisheries Association, comprising representatives of government and the fishermen, was established to regulate the purchase and building of new vessels. However, orders proved somewhat fitful, construction time was correspondingly tardy, and interest charges were high. Despite the 1931 act, a substantial proportion of old debt still burdened the system. The administrative context was also subject to change. At first an autonomous department of fisheries had been established, but this (along with Gaeltacht Services) was soon amalgamated with the department of lands, and then, in the mid 1930s, transferred to the department of agriculture, being severed completely from Gaeltacht Services.[49] Among other reasons, this may account for the fact that certain recommendations of the Gaeltacht commission report for marine development, such as no. 64 (the establishment of a training school for young fishermen in an Irish-speaking area), would not be realised.

---

[46] *Report of department of fisheries*, p. 6.   [47] Ibid.   [48] 1931/33 (31 July 1931).
[49] *Roinn talmhaiochta (brainse iascaigh). Report on the sea and inland fisheries for the year 1935* (Dublin, n.d.), p. 3.

IN its review of economic conditions, the Gaeltacht commission report had recommended (no. 55) that a special scheme of loans and grants be introduced for the improvement of the region's residential stock, a proposal to which the white paper readily assented. Agreement was probably facilitated by the substantial programme of building reform embarked on in the early years of the Free State in an attempt to improve the impoverished living conditions of inner-city Dublin, Cork, and other major centres.[50] This would duly result in one of the largest bodies of legislation relating to any single area of state activity. The first such measure was the Housing (Gaeltacht) Act, 1929.[51] This act sanctioned the erection of new houses in place of existing dwellings deemed unsuitable on health grounds (to a maximum grant of £80), and allowed for the refurbishing of partially suitable residences in order to make sanitary or other services available (maximum grant £40). It also provided for the erection or modification of farm buildings such as piggeries and poultry houses (grants ranging up to £5). The impact on country areas of the buildings eventually constructed would scarcely be as great as the alteration to the urban landscape wrought by city-based housing projects. Nonetheless, these new dwellings continued the gradual transformation in the appearance of the built environment in the Gaeltacht which the congested districts board had earlier set in train.

Not the least interesting aspect of the 1929 legislation was its definition of the Gaeltacht's extent. The basic territorial unit recognised by the act was the small-scale District Electoral Division (D.E.D.). Most of the D.E.D.s identified as Irish-speaking in the act were in a small number of core counties (listed alphabetically here): Clare (79), Cork (97), Donegal (58), Galway (103), Kerry (83), Mayo (94), and Waterford (53). There were also somewhat less obvious inclusions, such as those in Cavan (3), Leitrim (2), Louth (1), Roscommon (7), Sligo (11), and Tipperary South Riding (2). Both the number of counties and D.E.D.s involved make the 1929 act's schedule the most extensive delimitation then or since of the districts constituting either a Fíor-Ghaeltacht or a Breac-Ghaeltacht.[52] However, the act's inclusive approach incurred criticism. Objections were made that directing resources towards lesser Irish-speaking areas could prejudice the support given to regions in which the language was more widely used; and in the day-to-day running of the scheme, a more limited understanding of what constituted the Gaeltacht soon became the norm.

The 1929 act permitted expenditure on its programme to an upper limit of £250,000. Amending legislation increased the amount available by £100,000

[50] Below, pp 599–600.
[51] 1929/41 (20 Dec. 1929).
[52] For earlier attempts to define the Gaeltacht's extent using D.E.D.s, see above, vi, 390, n. 4.

in 1931,[53] and further increases followed in 1934 and 1939. The orderliness of this progression tends to disguise difficulties in implementing the scheme, especially during the early years. Although the act was passed in late 1929, a financial estimate was not ready till the following November. In 1930–31, less than £5,500 had been expended out of a block Gaeltacht housing grant of £60,000, administered by the land commission. From the 1931–2 estimate of £80,000 only some £46,000 would be drawn down, disbursed this time by the department of lands, fisheries, and Gaeltacht Services.[54] There was no lack of interest in the programme; in 1931–2 some 12,000 applications for assistance were submitted. But the need to ensure, by means of inspection, that prospective recipients and their households were indeed habitual Irish-speakers appears to have caused delays, and eventually applicants from more marginal Irish-speaking areas, such as those in the Breac-Ghaeltacht, would be encouraged to apply instead to other state housing schemes.

The operation of the programme became smoother in the mid 1930s, when the gap between estimates and expenditure was reduced, the cost per year being about £40,000. By the late 1930s about 400 houses a year were being completed under the terms of the various acts. Adverse economic and other conditions during the second world war were probably responsible for the programme's curtailment in the early 1940s: by 1944–5 the financial estimate had shrunk to £4,000.[55] One additional aspect of the programme should be mentioned. When financial support was first arranged, some £6,000 was set aside to provide teachers' residences in the Gaeltacht, in the hope of attracting well-qualified instructors to live there. Disputes involving the departments of finance and education concerning the rent to be charged, the location of the housing, and the establishment of title to properties, meant there were scarcely any applications or completions under this heading. The tiny amounts—mostly only a few hundred pounds per year—set aside for this purpose revealed that in practice, only the improvement of existing dwellings, not the erection of new homes for teachers, was contemplated.[56]

THE compulsory teaching of Irish in the Free State produced an immediate requirement for textbooks. Publishing in Irish had been greatly boosted by the establishment of the Gaelic League in 1893, and Eugene O'Growney's 'Easy lessons in Irish' had been available in collected form since 1902. Hundreds of thousands of copies of his grammar had been printed, but O'Growney was self-taught, and his work did not entirely meet the standards of the

---

[53] Housing (Gaeltacht) (Amendment) Act, 1931 (1931/53) (22 Dec. 1931).
[54] *Appropriation accounts 1930–31* (P 568) (Dublin, 1932), p. 147; ibid., *1931–2* (P 890) (Dublin, 1933), p. 148.
[55] Ibid., *1937–8* (P 3384) (Dublin, 1939), p. 174; ibid, *1944–5* (P 7297) (Dublin, 1946), p. 175.
[56] See, e.g., ibid, *1931–2*, pp 149–50.

new generation.[57] It was decided that the department of education would set up its own publishing venture which, from the word for 'scheme', would become known by the otherwise unfamiliar term 'An Gúm'. The department would solicit material mainly for post-primary schools, but could also consider texts suitable for other learners of Irish. Aspiring authors would have to agree to any changes required by the department. Grants not to exceed £50 would be provided, half to be paid in advance, the remainder following receipt from the author of corrected final proofs. The scheme was overseen by Coiste na Leabhar, whose membership and operations are noteworthy in their own right.[58] This committee had a full-time secretary, together with representation from the department of education's inspectorate and the holders of chairs in departments of Irish at the state's universities. In the early days the latter included Professor Tadhg Ó Donnchadha of U.C.C. and Professor Tomás Ó Máille of U.C.G.; later on, Professor Douglas Hyde of U.C.D. was a member. Amateur or part-time scholars also served on the committee, including Enrí Ó Muirgheasa, 'Fiachra Eilgeach' (the pseudonym of Risteárd Ó Foghludha), and Pádraig Ó Siochfhradha, better known by his nom de plume 'An Seabhac'. With the chief exception of Louise Gavan Duffy, who served for some years, membership was overwhelmingly male.

At meetings of the committee new submissions were noted and reports made on manuscripts under consideration for publication. Among the early submissions was a *cuntas cinn lae* (diary) by Tomás Ó Criomhthain, subsequently published as *Allagar na h-inise* (*Island cross-talk*) (1928). The same author's autobiographical *An t-oileánach* (1929) (translated by Robin Flower as *The islandman* in 1934) was also published by An Gúm. It is noteworthy that the committee's brief, the scrutiny of suitable manuscripts for publication, came at a time when the more general issue of censorship was under consideration, and legislation for censorship was to be enacted in 1929.[59] The inauguration of the department of education's publication scheme thus coincided with the drive to tighten control of publications during the 1920s.

By 1928 the publishing initiative had generated work under several major headings, the bulk of them of relevance to second-level education, as intended. Such material included textbooks of essays (*aistí*), arithmetic (*uimhríocht*), and geometry (*céimseata*) as well as some religious works, particularly hagiographical (*naoimh-sheanchas*). Some literature, too, was published, also with educational purposes in mind, including short stories (*gearr-sgéalta*), novels (*úirsgéalta*), and poetry (*filíocht*). There were some interesting innovations (building on Gaelic League precedents)[60] in those publications

---

[57] Eugene O'Growney, *Simple lessons in Irish* (Dublin, 1902). See also above, vi, 427.

[58] *An roinn oideachais tuarasgabháil: report of the department of education for the school year 1924–25 and the financial and administrative years 1924–25–26* (Dublin, 1926), pp 93–4, 115. Coiste na Leabhar's activities are outlined in the department of education's annual reports.

[59] Above, pp 118–19, 488–90.   [60] Above, vi, 427.

intended for the general public (*I gcóir an phobail*), such as translations, particularly from French, German, and also English. The publication of autobiographical works, such as those by Ó Criomhthain and Peig Sayers, marked a new departure in twentieth-century Irish publishing. They would give direct expression to the experience of everyday life and collective memory in rural and seaboard Ireland. By the mid 1930s over 400 works had been published, the bulk under the standard categories of the novel (127, of which 84 were translations), drama (100), and poetry (24). Biographies were also beginning to appear, together with travelogues and specialist titles for a younger readership (*leabhra don aos óg*).[61]

As in the case of the Gaeltacht, treated above, in practice the take-up of government grants for publishing was slow. The production of secondary-school textbooks was a case in point. Some £4,000 was allocated for expenditure on such books during 1926–7, but less than £300 was used. Matters had improved by 1930–31, but still less than half the allowance of £4,000 in that year was expended.[62] Problems in the early years included the slow processing of manuscripts at both the assessment and printing stages, and shortages of editorial staff. The formal establishment of a full-time publishing secretariat in the department of education in the mid 1930s may have helped expedite matters, for subsequently there was a better balance between allowances and expenditure. During the second world war ('the emergency') it is possible that constraints in other publishing fields encouraged some printers to speed up completion of school manuals, for in 1940–41 the estimate (of £2,250) was actually exceeded for the first time since the scheme's inception. Other factors making for wartime buoyancy included the reestablishment in 1938 of the national cultural festival known as An tOireachtas, which had flourished in the pre-independence days of the Gaelic League.[63] It included a broadly based literary competition which provided a spur to publication.

The war years in fact witnessed an unexpected upsurge in Gaelic creative writing. A university-based journal, *Comhar* ('Cooperation'), appeared in 1942. This would in time provide an outlet for authors uncomfortable with the restrictive outlook of the state printing enterprise. Such writing was not unknown in the 1930s, as the appearance of the largely socialist periodical *Misneach* ('Courage') indicated, but the war years saw a consolidation of this tendency. There emerged a handful of authors whose work ranks with the best of the century's writing in Irish. Such authors showed the continuing resourcefulness of the language, even if they remained unsure either of their own proficiency in it or its long-term future.

---

[61] *An roinn oideachais tuarasgabháil: report of the department of education 1928–29* (P 207) (Dublin, n.d.), pp 132–3; *Report of the department of education 1935–36* (P 2656) (Dublin, n.d.), pp 269–79.
[62] *Appropriation accounts 1926–7*, pp 125–6; ibid., *1930–31*, pp 119–20.
[63] Ibid., *1940–41* (P 5052) (Dublin, 1942), p. 157; above, vi, 417.

Much of the work of the young Cork poet Seán Ó Ríordáin appeared in *Comhar*. Tuberculosis contracted in the late 1930s brought him close to death and troubled him for the rest of his life. His verse explores the capacity of various world views, including organised religion and particularly catholicism, to account for the human predicament. He seems to have found as much consolation in wonder at the extraordinariness of the natural environment or the quirkiness of his fellow human beings as in any higher contemplation. His own indifferent health helped him to empathise with those less fortunate than himself, his writings on the mentally ill being particularly evocative. Galway-born Máirtín Ó Cadhain also came to maturity as an author around the same time. A prose-writer, he had completed translations for An Gúm in the mid 1930s, and subsequently likened the organisation to a 'Soviet monolith' (*gallán sóivéadach*). Ó Cadhain was interned during the emergency for his republican activism. Many of his political concerns are mirrored in his short stories and novels, particularly the devastating effect of isolation, marginalisation, and introspection on individuals, especially women, and communities in his native county's Irish-speaking heartlands. This was in marked contrast to the idealisation of the Gaeltacht that had been fostered by the Gaelic League, and underlined by the state itself through its Gaeltacht policies. From the mid 1940s the publishing house Sairséal agus Dill produced most of Ó Cadhain's writing. This firm's principals included Seán Ó hEigeartaigh, who had previously participated in the establishment of *Comhar*.

The state's support for Irish-language publishing was not confined to materials for use in schools. Other ventures supported in this period included An Comhar Drámaíochta's publications in the late 1920s, Lambert McKenna's English–Irish dictionary in the early 1930s, a history of Irish art by the director of the National Gallery of Ireland, and an updated and translated version of Rudolf Thurneysen's *Handbuch des Alt-Irischen*.[64]

The early years of the new state also witnessed the start of a range of other activities designed to support conservation of and research into the country's cultural heritage. One of the campaigners for this was Senator W. B. Yeats. Recalling his own indebtedness to the inspirational nature of Gaelic tradition, he argued in 1923 for adequate, long-term financial support for research into the linguistic, literary, and documentary record of the Irish past. Support for his motion came from fellow senators Edward MacLysaght and Alice Stopford Green, and a committee was established to see how it might be implemented. The committee made a preliminary report in autumn 1923, and presented its final proposals the following summer.[65] Seven activities would

---

[64] Lambert McKenna, *Foclóir béarla agus gaedhilge. English–Irish dictionary* (Dublin, 1935); Thomas Bodkin, *Tuarascáil ar na h-ealaíona in Éirinn* [report on the arts in Ireland] (Dublin, 1949); Rudolf Thurneysen, *A grammar of Old Irish* (Dublin, 1946).

[65] *Seanad Éireann deb.*, i, 992–6 (19 Apr. 1923); iii, 161–71 (4 June 1924).

be targeted: editing and publishing of texts, facsimiles of medieval manuscripts, the completion of a dictionary of Old Irish, the compilation of catalogues, the investigation of living dialects, the collection of folklore, and an archaeological survey of the whole of Ireland. The earlier interim report had also stressed the need to produce an inventory of modern written sources from the sixteenth century onwards.

The Royal Irish Academy was the obvious institution to organise and direct these activities. Founded in 1785, the R.I.A. had its own archival repository, was nationwide in its membership, and conducted and published research in most of the relevant areas. It was already fulfilling some of the functions that the senators had recommended. Government grants to the R.I.A of £1,600 a year in the period 1923–6 were designed, amongst other things, to facilitate the publication of Gaelic manuscripts, and 1926 saw the publication of the first fascicule of the catalogue of the R.I.A.'s own Gaelic manuscripts. This collection, at over 1,400, is the largest of its kind in the world, constituting not far short of one-third of the 5,000 such manuscripts to have survived from early medieval times down to the late nineteenth century. T. F. O'Rahilly, one of the foremost authorities of his day on the written and spoken language, inaugurated the published catalogue series.[66]

The R.I.A.'s Irish studies expertise was also drawn on for the completion of another long-term undertaking, the work now known as the *Dictionary of the Irish language* (based mainly on medieval sources). This project had been set on foot by the School of Irish Learning, an informal Celtic studies group founded in 1904 and subsequently absorbed into the R.I.A. Publication under the school's auspices had begun in 1913, but even after it had come under the R.I.A.'s aegis, shortage of staff and financial constraints caused delays. From the late 1930s onwards the government gave annual grants to support the project. The entire undertaking was completed in 1976, and the *Dictionary* has now become the standard reference work in its field.[67]

In the light of its long-established role in the field of Irish studies, it may seem surprising that the R.I.A. was not chosen from the outset to oversee the projects recommended by the senate. Assumptions about its 'ascendancy' overtones and the 'royal' component of its title may have militated against this. Even though the R.I.A. had launched the various manuscript projects outlined above, the government established a new body to oversee Ireland's documentary heritage. The Irish Manuscripts Commission (Coimisiún na Lámhscríbhinní) was set up in 1928, and given specific instructions to concern itself with written materials in the Irish language as well as other records. One of the senate report's proposals, the creation of facsimiles of

---

[66] T. F. O'Rahilly, *Catalogue of Irish manuscripts in the Royal Irish Academy*, fasc. i (Dublin, 1926).

[67] *Dictionary of the Irish language and contributions to a dictionary* (Dublin, 1913–76).

medieval codices, was placed high among its priorities. However, problems arose almost at once. Making reproductions was a specialist task for which the recently founded body lacked either facilities or technical expertise. The work was accordingly entrusted to the ordnance survey, which had been upgraded in the mid 1920s with the acquisition of lithographic machines and photographic and printing equipment. In 1929–30 the government granted the ordnance survey £1,000 expressly for machinery to copy the I.M.C.'s materials,[68] and recurrent grants were made through the 1930s and early 1940s, the amounts dropping in the wartime years.

Despite such funding, the number of facsimiles actually produced was small. During the 1930s these included the law tract *Senchas Már* (1931), the late medieval Connacht manuscript *The Book of Lecan* (1937), and *The Book of Armagh: Patrician documents* (also 1937). Facsimile reproduction of printed books, principally from the seventeenth century, was also carried out in the 1930s and 1940s, but even here few involved material in Irish. The picture was not much better in respect of new editions. The I.M.C. published over forty such editions between 1928 and the end of the 1940s, of which only six were based on material in Irish, four in the 1930s and two in the 1940s. The profile of Irish-language material in the I.M.C.'s in-house journal *Analecta Hibernica*, founded in 1930, was similar. Eighteen numbers of this journal appeared between 1930 and 1951, of which merely a handful contained Irish-language material, including Friar Ó Mealláin's diary concerning the wars of the 1640s and the Ó Clery book of genealogies, also from the seventeenth century.[69]

One of the difficulties that contributed to the slow pace of production was the realisation that the manuscripts themselves were more complex than had been hitherto recognised. Certain medieval documents, including the famous twelfth-century eastern manuscripts 'Lebor na hUidre' and the so-called 'Book of Leinster', had been copied out centuries later by the last of the traditional scribes in such a way as to disguise the various handwriting styles in the originals. Direct study of such sources and the introduction of photographic reproduction revealed their palaeographical complexities. The diplomatic edition of Lebor na hUidre produced by R. I. Best and Osborn Bergin, and published by the R.I.A. in 1929, marked a watershed in the handling of medieval sources by distinguishing the presence of various hands and hence different stages in their compilation.[70] All those involved in the completion of manuscript facsimiles might henceforth be expected to emulate this high standard. Inevitably this put greater pressure on those scholars who because

---

[68] *Appropriation accounts 1929–30* (P 353) (Dublin, 1931), p. 71.

[69] 'Cín lae ó Mealláin' in *Anal. Hib.*, no. 3 (1931), pp 1–49; 'The O'Clery book of genealogies', ibid., no. 18 (1951), pp ix–xxxiii, 1–194.

[70] See Kim McCone, 'Prehistory, Old and Middle Irish' in Kim McCone and Katharine Simms (ed.), *Progress in medieval Irish studies* (Maynooth, 1996), pp 7–53: 27.

of other commitments could only give part-time attention to the work. They included Kathleen Mulchrone, who worked on the 'Book of Lecan', and who held the chair of early Irish at U.C.G., and Professor Tadhg Ó Donnchadha of U.C.C., who was a member of Coiste na Leabhar and a contributor to *Analecta Hibernica*.

Soon, however, the I.M.C.'s obligations in respect of Irish-language publishing were diluted by a new institutional development. During the 1930s the taoiseach, Eamon de Valera, championed the idea of a specialised scholarly centre for Celtic studies, and he was largely responsible for designating its constituent schools of theoretical physics and Celtic studies. On the physics side, de Valera had a personal interest in mathematics, and was aware of the impending sale of Dunsink Observatory. In respect of Celtic studies, he also wished to provide career opportunities for young scholars. Consultative papers were prepared and the Institute for Advanced Studies bill was presented to the oireachtas in 1939. Both in the dáil and the seanad the bill generated one of the most extensive debates on an Irish studies issue for the period under review. It was objected that such an institute would weaken other centres of higher education by drawing away senior figures. Above all, it would be excessively costly at a time when the international scene was dangerously unstable, and economies might be called for.[71] Nevertheless, subject to certain amendments, the bill became law.[72] Its provisions for Celtic studies included work on textual editions, scientific study of the remnants of the spoken language, place-name analysis, and manuscript studies. The institute got off to a troubled start when two senior members resigned after disagreement with a third. There were delays in appointing junior staff, and throughout the war years the institute never managed to spend more than about three-quarters of its budget.

Despite such difficulties, the impact of the Celtic school in its first five years or so of operations was considerable, as reflected in its publishing profile. By 1946 monographs had been published in all of the core areas. Influential series in dialect description, bardic poetry, and annalistics were inaugurated, while an in-house journal, *Celtica*, began publication in 1946. Staff who were then relatively junior in years and experience worked on many of these projects and would subsequently go on to become academic leaders in their various fields, such as Brian Ó Cuív, James Carney, David Greene, Tomás de Bhaldraithe, and Nessa Ní Shéaghdha.

The 1924 senate report had recommended state support for research in the area of folklore. This came about gradually. In 1927 the Folklore of Ireland Society (An Cumann le Béaloideas Éireann) was founded. This voluntary

---

[71] See e.g., *Dáil Éireann deb.*, lxxix, 1077–1112 (10 Apr. 1940); *Seanad Éireann deb.*, xxiv, 1297–1408 (15 May 1940).
[72] Institute for Advanced Studies Act, 1940 (1940/13) (19 June 1940).

body sought to record and preserve the country's oral tradition in a systematic way, building on the efforts of the Gaelic League at the turn of the century and drawing on the experience of Douglas Hyde and others. Guidelines were drawn up for collectors, and the journal *Béaloideas* was founded. In 1927 the government collaborated with the society in setting up the Irish Folklore Institute, nominating one member to its administrative board, which also included three representatives from the society itself and three appointed by the Irish studies committee of the Royal Irish Academy. The state subvention to the institute amounted to some £500 a year in the early 1930s. Government support was to increase substantially with the formation in 1935 of the Irish Folklore Commission. This body was to draw its membership from the Folklore of Ireland Society, with some representation from the departments of finance and education. The I.F.C.'s role was to continue the work already in progress, particularly the attempt to gather as much as possible of Irish oral tradition while the older native Irish-speakers in the Gaeltacht were still alive. £3,000 per year would be granted over five years for this purpose, and a smaller publication grant was also made.[73] James Hamilton Delargy, who had an established record in the field, was put in charge of the work of collection, with power to hire assistants. This facilitated the compilation of a major world repository of such material in the later 1930s and well into the 1940s. Guidance came from *A handbook of Irish folklore* (Dublin, 1942) by I.F.C. archivist Seán Ó Súilleabháin. Over 2 million pages of text would be assembled in some thousands of notebooks. A schools project supplemented the main work. The material sheds valuable light on the culture and on the language. Collectors' notebooks are in effect records of social history for much of Irish-speaking rural Ireland in the first half of the twentieth century.

IN Northern Ireland the Irish language enjoyed a much more tenuous position than in the south. Irish had still been widely spoken in Counties Antrim and Down in the early nineteenth century, but a century later there were few Irish-speakers and even fewer native Irish-speakers. Not only was the commitment to the revival of Irish lacking on the part of the post-partition governments, but the language cause itself was widely perceived to be an instrument of catholic nationalism. This had not always been the case. There was a history of support for the language that stretched back into the eighteenth century, when the first printed periodical in Irish, *Bolg an tSolair*, appeared in Belfast in 1795. During the period of the 'Irish-Ireland' movement in the early decades of the twentieth century, nationalists and even some unionists in what would become Northern Ireland had backed the revival of Irish. Indeed, historians have pointed to the prominence of

---

[73] *Appropriation accounts 1937–8*, p. 137.

protestants, north and south, in the gaelicisation campaigns of the period before independence. However, as the cultural crusade became increasingly politicised, a cause that had been envisaged as bringing protestant and catholic together tended rather to drive them apart; and in Northern Ireland the surge of support did not survive the upheavals of the 1920s.[74] Divisions were reinforced by the sporting wing of the Gaelic movement. The Gaelic Athletic Association had been set up in 1884 by catholics, and its membership remained overwhelmingly catholic. Gaelic games (hurling, gaelic football, and handball) became the games of the catholic country people, while the urban working classes, catholic and protestant, played soccer. The G.A.A.'s ban on playing or watching 'foreign' games such as soccer and rugby, although not sectarian in intention, ensured that protestants would effectively be excluded. There was a further dimension to the ban that after 1922 had significant repercussions only in Northern Ireland: from 1919 onwards, the G.A.A. excluded anyone who had taken an oath of allegiance to the crown.[75] This meant that (for instance) members of the Royal Ulster Constabulary were ineligible to become members.

In the educational field, the Northern Ireland government retreated from even the limited provision for the teaching of Irish that was in place in 1920. The subject is considered in more detail below, but it may be noted here that notwithstanding the efforts of Comhaltas Uladh, the northern branch of the Gaelic League, by the mid 1920s the bilingual programme had been dropped, and the position of Irish relegated to the status of other foreign languages. In the 1930s special grants for teaching Irish were abolished. Despite these setbacks, Irish continued to be taught in many of the schools under catholic management. On the wider cultural front, suspicion about the political overtones of Irish ensured that the B.B.C., which opened a station in Belfast in 1924, did not transmit Irish-language programmes. However, traditional Irish music was sometimes broadcast.[76]

AFTER the end of 'the emergency', the next twenty-five years marked a period of reassessment in respect of Irish-language policy. Although there was no official retreat from the policy of language revival, there was growing concern about its methods, and the easy optimism of the 1920s and 1930s was replaced by a more uncertain climate. Whereas some of the early language enthusiasts had looked forward to the complete eclipse of English in the new

[74] See, e.g., Oliver MacDonagh, *States of mind: a study of Anglo–Irish conflict 1780–1980* (London, 1983), pp 108–13; R. V. Comerford, 'Nation, nationalism, and the Irish language' in Thomas E. Hachey and L. J. McCaffrey (ed.), *Perspectives on Irish nationalism* (Lexington, Ky., 1989), pp 20–41.

[75] Marcus de Búrca, *The G.A.A.: a history of the Gaelic Athletic Association* (Dublin, 1980), p. 145.

[76] Below, pp 659–60.

state, there was now a more realistic interest in the possibilities of bilingualism. Since the number of native Irish-speakers continued to shrink, doubts were again expressed about the capacity of the Gaeltacht to survive.[77]

In the field of education the most important development was a greater appreciation of the magnitude of the task that had been undertaken in the programme for language revival. Criticisms by teachers about the effect of placing infants from English-speaking homes in an all-Irish environment gained more weight as a result of studies on child psychology, and it became increasingly apparent that the department of education's attachment to testing language ability chiefly by written examinations, as opposed to oral competence, was inhibiting the speaking of Irish. The capacity of the schools to engender revival in the absence of a willingness to use the language outside the home was also questioned. In 1952 de Valera indicated to the Fianna Fáil ard-fheis that the time had come for a dispassionate review of 'our standards and methods'.[78]

The proportion of national schools teaching all subjects through Irish had never exceeded 12 per cent of the total, and by the early 1940s the number of primary and secondary schools using Irish as a medium of instruction had peaked. During the 1950s and 1960s the decline in their numbers gathered pace. Outside the Gaeltacht, by 1960–61 there were only 183 schools in the whole of the Republic where all teaching was given through Irish, and most of them bordered the Gaeltacht. Despite de Valera's own doubts about existing methods, it was Fine Gael that took the lead in reassessing official policies: in 1948 Richard Mulcahy, minister for education in the first coalition government, relaxed the requirement for Irish in the infant classes, and set up the council of education (1950) to review the national schools' curriculum. As early as the 1920s the preparatory colleges, which had been established to prepare Irish-speakers for a teaching career, had come in for criticism from the department of finance on account of their cost, and in 1961, under a Fianna Fáil government, it was decided to phase them out. This made further inroads into the supply of qualified teachers, and, of course, the numbers of students for third-level courses through Irish. New pedagogic methods were adopted for the teaching of Irish in the 1960s, but by the mid 1970s most teachers had received no training in the new methods.[79]

Meanwhile, in the civil service the policy of requiring a knowledge of Irish for certain grades had had disappointing results. By 1959 only some 14 per cent of civil servants were described as fluent in Irish, though some 50 per

[77] Ó Cuív, 'Ireland in the modern world', pp 129–32.
[78] Ó Catháin, 'Education in the new Ireland', pp 109–11; Ó Buachalla, *Education policy*, p. 351.
[79] See Lyons, *Ire. since famine*, p. 639; Ó Buachalla, *Education policy*, pp 347–54.

cent of the whole possessed a reading and writing knowledge. In 1951 even in the Gaeltacht itself only about half of the public officials had a competent knowledge of the language. At this period it emerged that with the exception of those departments that had a particular need to use the language, very little official business, perhaps 2 per cent of the total, was transacted in Irish. In semi-state bodies such as Aer Lingus and Bord Fáilte the language was very little used, and this was the case even in the houses of the oireachtas, where knowledge of Irish was well above average.[80]

However, it was the state of the language in the Gaeltacht that gave most cause for alarm. By the 1960s the Gaeltacht had only some 50,000 inhabitants, and monoglot adult Irish-speakers had virtually disappeared.[81] At least by that time an agreed geographical definition (covering 1,860 square miles and some 78,000 inhabitants) of the Gaeltacht had been formulated (in 1956), though the area lacked cohesion, scattered as it was along the western and south-western seaboard, and also including Ring in County Waterford and the two small outposts in County Meath. It was in 1956 too that a special government department was set up to look after the interests of the Gaeltacht. The various initiatives concerning housing, employment, and other services that had been introduced following the Gaeltacht commission report had proved insufficient to stem the tide of emigration, which had continued at high levels during the period since independence, peaking in the 1950s. In 1958 the state-sponsored body Gaeltarra Éireann was set up with responsibility for social and economic development in the area, and to coordinate government assistance to local industries, with a budget of £100,000 a year. The legacy of earlier government funding meant that the new body took over assets worth £700,000, mainly concerned with the production and marketing of textiles, embroidery, and toys. By the early 1960s there were some 1,700 full- and part-time employees. However, only the tweed industry was making a profit. Other subsidies, ranging from higher grants for houses to road-building, drainage, and water supply, were all provided.[82]

In 1969 a new council, Comhairle na Gaeilge, was established to advise government on language policy and implementation. This followed the report in 1964 of a commission on the restoration of the Irish language, which recommended the increased use of Irish in administration, church, and media. A government white paper in 1965 set out a ten-year plan for the restoration of Irish as a general medium of communication.[83] However, it has

---

[80] Lyons, *Ire. since famine*, p. 637; Gearóid Ó Tuathaigh, 'Language, literature and culture in Ireland since the war' in J. J. Lee (ed.), *Ireland 1945–70* (Dublin, 1979), pp 111–23: 114–15.

[81] Ó Cuív, 'Ireland in the modern world', p. 131.

[82] Lyons, *Ire. since famine*, pp 640–41; Ó Tuathaigh, 'Language, literature and culture', p. 112.

[83] *Athbheochan na Gaeilge. The restoration of the Irish language* (Pr 8061) (Dublin, n.d.).

been noted that despite the continuing official commitment to the revival of Irish, the implementation of official policy was less than wholehearted.[84] Nevertheless, certain useful steps were taken. Following a pirate radio experiment that gained much community support, in 1970 the state agreed to create a fully fledged station, and in 1972 a special Gaeltacht radio service, which had been talked of since the 1930s, was set up. Its headquarters were at Casla in the heart of the Connemara Gaeltacht, and other branches were set up in Donegal and Kerry. The radio thus provided the first daily linkage between native speakers of the language since the linguistic fragmentation of the late nineteenth century. Moreover, voluntary organisations continued to flourish, and new ones sprang up, including, notably Gael-Linn, which sought to enlist the help of the mass media to promote the language. During the 1950s and 1960s it made newsreels, documentaries, and records in Irish. One particular success in the revival of traditional Irish music has been the fleadh: these music festivals have been organised by Comhaltas Ceoltóirí Éireann (Traditional Music Society of Ireland) since the 1950s.[85] Cumann na Sagart ('Association of priests'), which helped to encourage the use of Irish in catholic church circles, also dated from this period. The Church of Ireland brought out a hymnbook in Irish in 1961, and An Gúm published a revised edition of the *Book of Common Prayer* in 1965.[86]

One of the problems inherent in the project to revive Irish concerned the written form of the language. It is not always appreciated that at the beginning of the twentieth century there were only a handful of native speakers who could read and write in Irish. This was not new; for two centuries or more before the revival movement of the late nineteenth century there had been little writing in Irish apart from devotional literature and traditional prose tales. Accordingly, it was open to the new state to devise its own standards for the written language. There were three main issues to be determined: spelling, grammar, and script. In practice, the example set by the learned Irish societies of the nineteenth century carried a good deal of weight. They had tended to favour the use of 'Gaelic' script, which had been used in most manuscripts written in Irish from the ninth to the sixteenth centuries, and this was carried over into the new state, at least for educational purposes, with the drawback that schoolchildren were obliged to learn to read and write in two scripts rather than one. However, for the state's own official purposes, such as the records of the oireachtas, the tendency was rather to use Roman type. There was something of a precedent for this in the records of the first dáil (1919–21), although that body had not used

---

[84] Lyons, *Ire. since famine*, p. 643; Ó Tuathaigh, 'Language, literature and culture', pp 113–14; Ó Buachalla, *Education policy*, p. 353.

[85] Lyons, *Ire. since famine*, p. 644; see also below, pp 623–4.

[86] Greene, 'The Irish language movement', p. 118; Ó Tuathaigh, 'Language, literature and culture', p. 114.

Roman type exclusively. In the absence of a general regulation on the subject, policy and practice vacillated till the 1950s and 1960s, when a consensus emerged in publishing and educational circles that Roman type should be preferred, except for antiquarian or decorative purposes.[87]

In respect of spelling, the position was complicated both by discrepancies between orthography and the spoken language, and by dialectal variations. The former had arisen as a result of the fact that after the twelfth century, when a standard literary language was devised, the classical Irish poets had simply ignored changes in spoken Irish. This meant that even by the seventeenth century, when the bardic schools broke up, the spelling could be considered antiquated. However, it was this spelling that was adopted by the learned societies and the revivalists of the nineteenth century, and embodied in Fr Dinneen's *Foclóir Gaedhilge agus Béarla* (Irish–English dictionary) (Dublin, 1904). Thus the old spelling was legitimised at the very time when agreement was emerging in favour of the still living language of the Gaeltacht, rather than the classical literary language, as the medium for future literary activity. Efforts to reform and simplify spelling encountered much opposition, which lasted well beyond independence. The new constitution, for instance, was published in 1937 in Gaelic type and the traditional spelling. Only in 1945 did the oireachtas translation staff produce a first draft of a new standardised and simplified spelling, and the publication of *An caighdeán oifigiúil* ('the official standard') followed in 1958. Despite resistance in some quarters, this was widely adopted for government publications, schoolbooks, periodicals, and newspapers.

As for grammar, the task of standardisation, also undertaken by the oireachtas translation staff, was even more challenging. One of the difficulties resulting from the adoption of spoken Irish for the literary language in the twentieth century was the very considerable variation in word-form and grammar arising from dialectal differences. Moreover, the quality of the spoken language was deteriorating as a consequence of the ever-increasing penetration of English into Gaeltacht areas. In these circumstances it was unrealistic to contemplate incorporating all the possible dialectal variants into a standard form of grammar, so the translation staff attempted to produce a standard based on the most commonly used forms of the spoken language in Gaeltacht areas. Designed primarily for those in the civil service whose duties included writing in Irish, an official standard grammar, *Gramadach na Gaeilge*, was published in 1953.[88]

One casualty of the lack of standardisation for the written language has been the 1937 constitution. As noted above, in cases of conflict between the

[87] Brian Ó Cuív, 'The changing form of the language' in Ó Cuív, *View of Ir. language*, pp 22–34: 24–6.
[88] Ibid., pp 27–33.

texts of any enrolled copy of the constitution, the text in the national language is to prevail (article 25.5.4). However, and leaving aside the issue of subsequent amendments, it has been pointed out that the draft constitution approved by Dáil Éireann, the Irish-language texts enrolled in the office of the registrar of the supreme court, and the edition published by the Stationery Office display significant textual variations. In addition to uncorrected copy errors, these include different typography, spelling, and grammar. The most inaccurate version appears to be that made available for general circulation by the Stationery Office, to which a degree of language standardisation was applied in the interests of greater accessibility, but at the cost of inaccurate rendition of the fundamental law.[89]

BY the early 1970s the weakening of the state's commitment to the revival of the language was becoming more obvious. In 1973 under a coalition government the requirement that Irish be an essential subject in state examinations was dropped, and it was also abandoned as an entry requirement for the civil service. The N.U.I. maintained its requirement for a pass in Irish in order to matriculate; but for this, there might have been a complete collapse in the subject in secondary schools. Fine Gael took the lead in advocating a retreat from compulsion. Among other reasons, it was argued in the early 1970s that in view of the desirability of a united Ireland, compulsory Irish was off-putting to northern unionists and showed the Republic in an illiberal light.[90] The desire to avoid the appearance of compulsion was reflected in the report of the New Ireland Forum of 1984, which indicated that in the context of any future 'unitary state' in Ireland, 'the Irish language and culture would continue to be fostered by the state, and would be made more accessible to everyone in Ireland without any compulsion or imposition on any section'.[91] In this period too, Ireland became a member of the European Economic Community. On joining in 1973, Ireland was one of the few countries in which the first official language was a minority language, and Irish was not accorded official-language status by the E.E.C. Although treaties of accession, and all subsequent agreements whereby the E.E.C. became the European Community and later the European Union, were promulgated in Irish as well as in the major European languages, and a small translation service for such purposes is maintained in Brussels, Irish was not made an official working language.

[89] Richard F. Humphreys, 'The constitution of Ireland: the forgotten textual quagmire' in *Irish Jurist*, xxii, pt 2 (winter 1987), pp 169–78. An all-party oireachtas committee on the constitution has recently examined the history, status, and divergent forms of the Irish text. See Micheál Ó Cearúil, *Bunreacht na hÉireann: a study of the Irish text* (Pn 7899) (Dublin, 1999).
[90] Garret FitzGerald, *Towards a new Ireland* (Dublin and London, 1972), pp 154–5.
[91] Quoted in Lee, *Ire. 1912–85*, p. 676.

Meanwhile, the decline of Irish as a language of everyday speech in Gaeltacht areas continued inexorably. Regardless of official figures about the Gaeltacht's extent, it was calculated that by the late 1970s only some 32,000, less than 10 per cent of the number in 1922, used the language habitually.[92] Yet even as its imminent disappearance as a community language was being forecast, by the 1980s there were signs in certain urban middle-class families of a determination to use Irish, to bring up their children to be bilingual, and to educate them through Irish.

There were other positive developments. One of the first recommendations from Comhairle na Gaeltachta had been for a more decentralised approach to the Gaeltacht, with the establishment of area committees in each county containing a Gaeltacht region. The business of such committees should be conducted in Irish, and certain powers of the county councils should be transferred to them. In addition, Gaeltarra Éireann and the Shannon Free Airport Development Company should be asked to inquire and report on the objectives and implications of development in the Gaeltacht areas.[93] The coalition government, under the energetic guidance of Tom O'Donnell, agreed in 1973 to implement several of these proposals, and this commitment eventually bore fruit in the form of the Údarás na Gaeltachta Act, 1979.[94] This established an authority of thirteen members, six to be chosen by the minister for the Gaeltacht and seven elected periodically from the three main Gaeltacht areas in the north, west, and south. The preponderance of Gaeltacht representatives gave Irish-speakers the decisive vote in case of a dispute. The authority was to subsume the functions of Gaeltarra Éireann, and its brief was to promote the linguistic, social, and economic welfare of the Gaeltacht regions, with state funding available for particular projects. At first the main undertakings included manufacturing industry, food processing, and training schemes; more recently there has been diversification into service and high-technology industries.

Another statutory agency, Bord na Gaeilge, was set up in 1978. Its primary task was to promote the use of Irish as a living language and means of communication. To this end it provides grants, for instance to Glór na nGael, the annual all-Ireland competition to find the community that has done most to promote Irish in everyday life, by such means as erecting Irish-language signage in towns and shop fronts. Bord na Gaeilge has been particularly active in the promotion of Irish in the arts, acting as the language's arts council. Among other enterprises it assists the Merriman summer and winter schools, the book-distribution company Áis, and the Irish-language theatre (here it may be noted that the Galway Gaelic Theatre, later called the Taibhdhearc theatre, has been staging Irish-medium theatre in Galway since

---

[92] Ibid, p. 673.   [93] Lyons, *Ire. since famine*, p. 642.
[94] Údarás na Gaeltachta Act, 1979 (1979/5) (19 Mar. 1979).

1928). In addition, Bord na Gaeilge's support played an important part in the growth of the Irish language pre-school movement in the early to mid 1980s.

In the field of broadcasting, Raidió na Gaeltachta at first put out only a few hours of programmes each day, but over the years it has been built up both in extent and variety. The sound archive has accumulated material covering storytelling, traditional lore, and everyday speech, as well as traditional music and other forms of expression. This constitutes the most important cultural resource of its kind since the Irish Folklore Commission's repository was built up in the 1930s and 1940s. By common consent, since its foundation the station has represented the best window on attitudes and experiences in rural west-coast Ireland during a period of great change in the lives of the agricultural and seaboard communities that it serves. It naturally gave rise to calls for a television service in the Irish language, although this was only achieved in the mid 1990s.

MEANWHILE in Northern Ireland government policy towards the language continued to veer between suspicion and neglect. Not that the authorities in general took explicit steps to prohibit the use of Irish. One exception was the introduction of an amendment to the Public Health and Local Government Bill (1949),[95] which stipulated that street signs must be in English. This followed a move by nationalist councils in Newry and Omagh in 1948 to erect Irish-language signs in parts of the towns. In fact, the ban apparently had the unintended effect of encouraging the use of street signs in Irish, especially in the late 1970s and 1980s. Although hundreds of signs sprang up illegally, the law was not enforced. Nor, however, was it repealed, despite many calls for its removal from the statute book. Repeal only came about in 1995, after which street signs were permitted to be erected in both Irish and English.[96]

The language revival movement in Northern Ireland had a patchy history, with interest waning after the 1920s. Irish continued, however, to be taught in many catholic schools, and it continued to be prized as a badge of national identity, particularly by catholics. Among republicans, it could serve additional purposes: there is evidence to suggest that for some members of the I.R.A., learning or perfecting Irish provided a means of occupation during spells of internment or imprisonment.[97] A limited renewal of revival efforts began again in Belfast during the 1950s and early 1960s, and this was to bear fruit later in the century. About a dozen couples who were involved in

[95] Public Health and Local Government (Miscellaneous Provisions) Act (Northern Ireland), 1949 (1949, c. 21) (13 Dec. 1949).
[96] Camille O'Reilly, *The Irish language in Northern Ireland: the politics of culture and identity* (London, 1999), p. 139.
[97] See Tim Pat Coogan, *The I.R.A.* (London, 1970), pp 216, 255; Padraig O'Malley, *Biting at the grave* (Belfast, 1990), p. 24.

language activities at that time set up homes on the outskirts of west Belfast, where they formed the first urban neo-Gaeltacht in Ireland. In 1971 they set up Northern Ireland's first Irish-medium primary school, Bunscoil Phobal Feirste. This was originally intended to cater for their own Irish-speaking children, but in 1978 it was opened to children from English-speaking families, on condition that such children first attended two years of Irish-speaking nursery school. By the mid 1980s the demand for places at the Bunscoil had outstripped supply, and subsequently five other primary schools opened in Belfast alone, most of them during the 1990s; by that time some were also appearing in other towns. The first Irish-medium secondary school opened in Belfast in 1991. At first such schools depended on voluntary donations, but after a long campaign by parents government funding was finally obtained in 1984.[98]

During the 1980s there were further signs of growing support for language revival. In 1982 the west Belfast committee of Glór na nGael was set up as an umbrella group to coordinate and encourage entry into the competition. Glór na nGael also organised Irish-language classes, making particular efforts to provide a neutral political climate that might attract protestants, and it provided grants and teachers for Irish-medium nursery schools. In a controversial move, its funding was withdrawn without notice by the Northern Ireland Office in 1990, but restored in 1992.[99] The Ulster counties also gained a higher profile in Gaelic games, with Armagh reaching the all-Ireland football finals on several occasions from 1980 onwards. The G.A.A.'s ban on watching or playing 'foreign games' was lifted in 1971; however, this did not extend to the ban on admitting those who had taken an oath of allegiance to the crown.[100]

WITH the benefit of hindsight it is clear that the revivalists of the 1920s were unduly optimistic in their expectations of what was likely to be achieved by way of restoring Irish to the language of everyday speech. Not only did they not succeed in that goal, but even the apparently more realistic aim of preserving the language in those areas where it was still habitually spoken turned out to be too ambitious. Several commentators have made the point that better results might have been achieved if the early enthusiasts had been content to put their efforts into promoting bilingualism.[101] The foregoing discussion has also highlighted the perhaps excessive centralisation in the efforts made by government on behalf of the language, and has also drawn attention to the bewildering changes in departmental reponsibility for the Gaeltacht regions during the 1920s and 1930s. Penny-pinching by the

[98] O'Reilly, *Irish language in Northern Ireland*, pp 20, 123–5.
[99] Ibid., pp 114–15, 122.   [100] De Burca, *G.A.A.*, pp 65, 233–4.
[101] Ó Cuív, 'Ireland in the modern world', p. 131; Lee, *Ire. 1912–85*, pp 670–74.

department of finance did not help; but on the other hand it has been shown that large state grants were made available for the Gaeltacht and that not all of the available funding was taken up. Better planning might have had good results. It also seems clear that while there was (and remains) much goodwill among members of the public towards the Irish language, and a sense that it continues to be important to Irish identity, in the population at large down to the present this attachment has not and does not extend to actually using the language.[102] That said, there have been many significant achievements, particularly in the field of literature (discussed below), music, and archives, which will provide solid foundations for any future developments. Moreover, cultural revival must be seen under a number of headings, including music (also discussed below) and sport. Under these headings it can be argued that the revival achieved very striking successes. It is difficult to think of another European country in which indigenous folk games have not only survived but prospered, and where folk music in its many forms has proved so popular.

Literature in Irish, by Máire Ní Annracháin

THE revival of the Irish language, conventionally believed to have been placed on a firm footing with the founding of the Gaelic League in 1893, brought with it the challenge of breathing new life into a literature that had allegedly suffered the best part of 300 years of decline. The decline was generally held to have reduced it from the intense voice of a confident establishment to a frail whisper from a spent peasant culture.

Whether or not this recently challenged pessimistic analysis[103] is accepted, it is certainly the case that early revivalists conducted a robust debate around the literary requirements and possibilities of the new Ireland. How to reconcile the demands of modernity and tradition? How to be faithfully indigenous while authentically modern? Would there be a single tradition or would there be two: the one modern, innovative, artistically self-conscious, urban, learner-driven, written; the other traditional, rural, conservative, produced for and by native speakers, and predominantly oral? Not all writers have found the same balance, but there has been general agreement, in practice if not always in theory, that finding some version of the balance had to be part of the communal project.

---

[102] Ó Buachalla, *Education policy*, pp 355–6.
[103] See Breandán Ó Buachalla, 'Canóin na creille: an file ar leaba a bháis' in Máirín Ní Dhonnchada (ed.), *Nua-léamha: gnéithe de chultúr, stair agus polaitíocht na hÉireann c.1600–1900* (Dublin, 1996), pp 149–69.

The initial preoccupation centered on questions of language, content, and form,[104] particularly in relation to prose literature. There was a conservative view on these matters, which was propounded most vocally by Risteard de Hindeberg (Richard Henebry) in the *Leader* at the end of the first decade of the century. Holders of this view favoured remaining close to the last viable written standard, namely *Gaeilge Chéitinn*, the Irish of Keating, which was internally consistent, if untouched by oral developments in the language over the intervening 250 years. They also advocated indigenous forms, most notably the folk-tale, and desired to eschew imported forms such as the novel and the short story. For content, 'modern' themes, including love, were to be shunned as incompatible with the genius of the Irish language. De Hindeberg did not often spare the feelings of his opponents. Of Pearse's story 'Íosagán' he said: 'This is the frivolous petulancy of latter-day English genre scribblers, and their utterance is as the mincing of the under-assistant floor-walker of a millinery shop.'[105]

The modernising approach preferred *cainnt na ndaoine*, the spoken language, with all its dialectal diversity, inconsistency, and lack of experience in dealing with higher registers. In terms of form and content there was a firm rejection of the conservatives' suspicion of the modern. Largely learners of Irish, and reared on literature in English, the modernisers willingly embraced the modern world, without losing sight of the native tradition. According to Patrick Pearse, they advocated that Irish literature should get 'into contact on the one hand with its own past and on the other with the mind of contemporary Europe'.[106]

Pearse was the prime mover and most innovative literary theorist for Irish during the early days of the revival, though Pádraic Ó Conaire, its most important fiction writer, was also an influential, modernising force in his theoretical writings.[107] The 'Gothic revival' that Pearse feared, and by which he described the refusal to modernise, was largely averted. However, the concept of the modern that had currency during the first decades of the revival was still, in literary terms, associated with realism. This had two main effects on Irish prose writing. First, in fiction, it directed a half-century of writers in the direction of the flat plains of the realist project, and gave little or no impetus to adapting indigenous literary forms to modern requirements and concerns. Second, the favouring of a relentless realism, combined both with romantic, anti-industrialist attachment to the supposedly pre-industrial life, and with the demands of cultural nationalism, together meant that in so

---

[104] For a description of these debates, see Cathal Ó Háinle (ed.), *Gearrscéalta an Phiarsaigh* (Dublin, 1979), and Philip O'Leary, *The prose literature of the Gaelic revival, 1881–1921: ideology and innovation* (University Park, Pa., 1994).
[105] Quoted in Ó Háinle, *Gearrscéalta an Phiarsaigh*, p. 21.
[106] *An Claidheamh Soluis*, 26 May 1906.
[107] See Gearóid Denvir (ed.), *Aistí Phádraic Uí Chonaire* (Galway, 1978).

far as literary interest continued in traditional Gaeltacht life, that interest found expression in a steady stream of regional, Gaeltacht, autobiography. The most celebrated of these was *An t-oileánach* by Tomás Ó Criomhthain,[108] which chronicles life on the Blasket Islands during the early years of the century. The most widely read, however, must surely be another of the Blasket Islands school: *Peig*,[109] the edition of Peig Sayers's autobiography abridged for use in schools.

In all, up to perhaps a hundred regional autobiographies have been produced, mainly from Munster and Ulster, usually through oral narration subsequently transcribed and edited. Although they purported to offer a transparent faithful reproduction of the lives of their narrators and their communities, they were in fact on the boundary of fiction, as is the case with orally transmitted memory in general, being subject to powerful personal editorialising forces. It could be argued that such works were guilty, to a degree, of the same dishonesty as realist fiction in general. Just as realist fiction dissimulates by giving the impression of following no rules other than the mimetic representation of reality, so too the Gaeltacht autobiography dissimulates by giving the impression of actual, rather than imagined, Gaeltacht life.

The regional autobiography flowed freely for much of the century and was testimony to a nostalgia for a lost, pre-industrial, rural idyll turned idol. Tomás Ó Criomhthain's words are immediately recognised in Irish-language circles: 'Scríobhas go mionchruinn ar a lán dár gcúrsaí d'fhonn go mbeadh cuimhne i bpoll éigin orthu agus thugas iarracht ar mheon na ndaoine a bhí i mo thimpeall a chur síos chun go mbeadh a dtuairisc inár ndiaidh, mar ná beidh ár leithéidí arís ann.'[110] ('I have written minutely of much that we did, for it was my wish that somewhere there should be a memorial of it all, and I have done my best to set down the character of the people about me so that some record of us might live after us, for the like of us will never be again.')[111] At its best, this form of autobiography represented a willingness to stand alone and delve into the specificity of Irish experiences, and, at its worst, a romanticisation, even a trivialisation, of poverty and deprivation. It could also be read as another example of the naive realism that took hold of the revival movement in its infancy, at the expense of a serious encounter with the core elements of the folk tradition. The respect accorded the Gaeltacht autobiography, and its dominance in Irish-language writing—notwithstanding the sharp satire it suffered at the hands of Brian Ó Nualláin (Brian O'Nolan, Myles na gCopaleen) in *An béal bocht*[112]—meant that there

---

[108] Tomás Ó Criomhthain, *An t-oileánach* (1929; new ed., Dublin, 1973).

[109] Peig Sayers, *Peig: tuairisc do scríobh Peig Sayers ar imeachta a beatha féin* (Dublin, 1954).

[110] Ó Criomhthain, *An t-oileánach* (1973 ed.), p. 256.

[111] Ó Criomhthain, *The islandman*, translated by Robin Flower (London, 1934), pp 322–3.

[112] Myles na gCopaleen, *An béal bocht* (1941): translated by P. C. Power as *The poor mouth: a bad story about the hard life* (London, 1973).

was little imaginative experimentation with the traditional element in modern literature until the second half of the century.[113]

As the reign of realism gradually eased, the path was cleared for literature in Irish to find ways of responding to what might loosely be called the spirit of modernism. This coincided with a change in the terms in which the relationship between contemporary literature and the tradition was negotiated. At the risk of simplification, the best of the response might be summarised as taking the form of fresh investigation of the imaginative potential of the traditional repertoire. That investigation showed that the older tradition had much that was very compatible with a modernist and, more recently, a post-modern, linguistically grounded sensibility, which is often anti-rationalist, ludic, allusive, and impatient of the concept of the centered, unified subject. The modern impulse is largely language-driven; it encounters, escapes from, and subverts the quotidian through the body's unconscious, repressed pleasure, which is accessed mainly in and through language. The traditional impulse is otherworldly and transcendental; it escapes from and subverts the quotidian through magic and wonder, and keeps uncertainty contained within reassuring boundaries. Contemporary literature draws on both for inspiration.

It would be inaccurate to suggest that the dominance of realism precluded any fruitful experimentation with material from the earlier, largely pre-modern, literature in Irish in the first half of the twentieth century. The encounter did take place. On occasion this was artistically crude, but more subtle interweaving did take place and has more recently gathered momentum. This has occurred both formally and at the level of subject-matter.

In terms of form, it has been demonstrated that both in theory and practice the supposed twin tracks of written and oral narrative are in fact inseparable, and that writers such as Pádraic Ó Conaire, Liam Ó Flaithearta, and Máirtín Ó Cadhain were greatly influenced by oral narrative technique. In terms of subject-matter, the magical otherworldliness of the folk tradition can be read, and then rewritten, or reinterpreted, in various ways by modern readers. The most important of these in the Irish context has been the metaphorisation of various breaches of the rules of time, space, and subjectivity. Thus, for example, Ó Cadhain's masterpiece *Cré na cille*[114] places language that is immaculately faithful to Connemara Irish in the mouths of the dead members of a small community, who continue their internecine feuds with unabated energy on the other side of the grave.

Ó Cadhain deserves special mention (along with Alan Titley, whose work is discussed below). He was highly influential as a critic. It is instructive to read his fiction against the backdrop of his critical works, notably his literary

---

[113] Máirín Nic Eoin, *An litríocht réigiúnach* (Dublin, 1982).
[114] Máirtín Ó Cadhain, *Cré na cille* (Dublin, 1949).

manifesto, *'Páipéir bhána agus páipéir bhreaca'*, in which he deplored the lack of psychology in the Irish novel.[115] While it might now be suggested that (leaving aside the early novels) there was no shortage of psychology in the earlier literature if read with the correct tools, the reader must also marvel at the breadth of Ó Cadhain's own experimentation in this respect. His whole literary career can be seen as an example of the progression from realism to a more modernist style. He wrote some excellent short stories and novellas in fairly strict realist mode, in which he developed a sure style of characterisation, and to that extent he practised the psychology he preached. He ventured farther than that, however. He rewrote folk motifs and motifs from the older literature, interpreting them metaphorically and modernising their contexts. In some of this work, it is true, he remained in realist mode, but by the late 1960s he had bravely turned his back, at least some of the time, on the tenets of realism and had begun to take steps towards a more modern type of writing. This sprang, in the view of the present writer, precisely from his willingness to return to an older, pre-modern submission to the rhythms of the language. It should be noted that this earlier sensitivity to the powers of the language had been adversely interpreted by some critics as lack of linguistic control on his part.

Two brothers, Seosamh Mac Grianna and Séamus Ó Grianna ('Máire'), must also be considered giants presiding over the middle years of the twentieth century. Seosamh's autobiographical novel *Mo bhealach féin*[116] demonstrates that bracing formal alternatives to the more pedestrian type of regional autobiography were possible. Séamus's more steadfastly realist prose provided Irish readers with works of great beauty and, on occasion, of considerable bite. His *Bean ruadh de Dhálach*, for instance, is a strongly feminist statement about the possibility of the social and economic emancipation of women. Published in 1966, it foreshadowed, perhaps unexpectedly, the concerns of the international women's movement of the 1970s.

In spite of the statistics that tell of a tiny linguistic population and of an even tinier literary subset, the twentieth century sends a message of vigorous life in the face of daunting adversity. That life is visible in both the quantity and the quality of the work produced. The publication of Alan Titley's study *An t-úrscéal Gaeilge*,[117] the first and, to date, the only serious survey of the novel in Irish, surprised many readers with the sheer volume of novels published. Titley lists about 160 in the ninety years up to 1990, which is an impressive number, regardless of quibbles concerning the inclusion of a small number of works under the heading of 'the novel'. The number is even more impressive when it is recalled that only a tiny fraction of their authors were full-time writers.

[115] Id., *'Páipéir bhána agus páipéir bhreaca'* (Dublin, 1969).
[116] Seosamh Mac Grianna, *Mo bhealach féin* (Dublin, 1965).
[117] Alan Titley, *An t-úrscéal Gaeilge* (Dublin, 1991).

Qualitatively, too, the situation is heartening. The current generation of mid-life (or slightly older) writers have dramatically deepened their understanding of the imaginative resources available to them in the tradition since they set out on their literary careers a quarter of a century ago. The work, for example, of Alan Titley, Breandán Ó Doibhlin, Liam Mac Cóil, Liam Prút, Liam Ó Muirthile, and several others shows all the signs of linguistic confidence, fruitful appropriation of traditional elements, and, in the case of many of these writers, a keen understanding of the implications of the abandonment of realism.[118] The rise in the level of formal education has been crucial. Few writers in the final third of the twentieth century have been without university-level education. This is somewhat akin to the levels of educational attainment enjoyed by the bardic order. Such opportunities have been lacking, on the whole, since the eighteenth century, and their arrival has facilitated the ability to harness the intellectual demands of modern writing to the imaginative depths of the older literature.

One of the debates around the novel during the period when, as a genre, it was conceived in terms of English or French realist discourse was its capacity to deal with the modern, and specifically urban, English-language Ireland through the Irish language. This remained an issue as long as a correspondence theory of representation went unchallenged: that is, as long as it was held that a fictional text could and should be read as a more or less transparent, faithful account of life, approximating to history, and creating the illusion that the format is chosen for no other reason than that it is a vehicle for representing as closely as possible the experience being described. This debate has become less urgent as the novel form has become less historical, less realist, and as the novelist's gaze has shifted back to the potential of the mythological and folk traditions. To take just a few examples, Alan Titley's *An fear dána*, Séamas Mac Annaidh's celebrated *Cuaifeach mo londubh buí* (1983), and some of the short stories of Dara Ó Conaola, all dispense with various requirements of the traditional realist text. It is often, though not always, the grounded, centered subject who is given the *coup de grâce*. Indeed, much of the complex novelty of many such texts derives from an intriguing combination of motifs from the older literature and a post-modern subversion of the unified subject.

Not only a writer of fiction, Alan Titley has been to the fore of critical thought, trenchantly advocating the rejection of literary theory in favour of an unmediated experience of the text by the reader. His own remarkable fiction, however, has progressed far beyond the type of controlled realism that purports to lend itself to transparent reading. His ludic subversions of

[118] See, e.g., Alan Titley, *An fear dána* (Dublin, 1993); Breandán Ó Doibhlin, *An branar gan cur* (Dublin, 1979); Liam Mac Cóil, *An Dochtúir Áthas* (Indreabhán, Co. Galway, 1994); Liam Prút, *Desirée* (Dublin, 1989); Liam Ó Muirthile, *Ar bhruach na Laoi* (Dublin, 1995); Robert Schumann (pseud.), *Kinderszenen* (Dublin, 1987).

most of the conventions of realism, and his superb coupling of folk conventions with an exuberant, playful, use of language, make him one of the most innovative and important writers of the final quarter of the twentieth century, comparable to Máirtín Ó Cadhain's domination of its middle years. In his *An fear dána*, the conventions of the historical novel, and indeed of the literary canon itself, are subverted when, placing the story in the mouth of one of the most famous of Irish bardic poets, the thirteenth-century Muireadheach Albanach Ó Dálaigh, Titley ascribes anachronistic language to him which is well known to Irish-language readers from a whole swathe of later canonical texts.

In the case of Mac Annaidh's *Cuaifeach mo londubh buí*, the Gilgamesh story with its tale of transformation is used as one strand of a richly layered plot in which it is impossible to establish whether there is a single directing voice. In Dara Ó Conaola's story, 'An neach', the eponymous shadow or alter ego of the folk tradition is presented as a bewildering range of options, from a manifestation of paranoia, to an eruption of the otherworld, to a subversion of the idea of a rational subject with defined boundaries.[119]

A similar shift may be discernible in drama,[120] away from naturalistic and towards more experimental ideas, often incorporating folklore elements. It is more difficult to gauge this because so few plays in Irish are actually produced on stage. This has the result that the only element of the play available is the script, and it is precisely in the other elements of a play that the script's potential for non-naturalistic drama finds expression. Drama in general has not developed with the vigour that might have been expected, given its obvious suitability as a medium that could draw heavily on the spoken language and the oral literary tradition. Hampered by commercial constraints, inadequate political support, and by the dispersed nature of its potential audience, writers of drama have been frustrated by how few of their plays have ever come to production. There have been several writers of distinction, including Mairéad Ní Ghráda, Críostóir Ó Floinn, and, most notably, Eoghan Ó Tuairisc.[121] The latter's passion and commitment were matched by his rigorous intellectual honesty as he grappled with the development of dramatic form from naturalistic to experimental and modern. His career can indeed be considered a microcosm of the general development already referred to.

The collective investigation of the earlier literary tradition mirrors various modern developments in major world languages, some—magic realism, for

---

[119] Dara Ó Conaola, *Mo chathair ghríobháin* (Dublin, 1981).
[120] For the history of drama in Irish see Pádraig Ó Siadhail, *Stair dhrámaíocht na Gaeilge: 1900–1970* (Indreabhán, Co. Galway, 1993).
[121] See, e.g., Mairéad Ní Ghráda, *An triail* (2nd ed., Dublin, 1975); Críostóir Ó Floinn, *Aggiornamento* (Dublin, 1969), *Is é a dúirt Polonius* (Dublin, 1973); Eoghan Ó Tuairisc, *Lá Fhéile Mhichíl* (Dublin, 1967), *Aisling Mhic Artáin* (Dublin, 1978).

instance—more clearly than others. This investigation has a particular depth and richness in the case of Irish because the pre-modern tradition remained so vibrant, so close to the surface, and therefore allows contemporary Irish literature privileged access to its treasures. This, in turn, it can be argued, is largely owing to the fact that the whole intellectual heritage of the enlightenment, including realism, individualism, the rise of the bourgeoisie, the centered subject, and rationalism, had never really become deeply rooted in Irish. Its main literary manifestation, the realist novel, had not developed in Irish in tandem with its English or French neighbours, though certain attempts were made throughout the eighteenth and nineteenth centuries.[122] It was grafted on to the tradition during the early days of the revival, but it never had time seriously to take root. In fact it came to hold sway unchallenged for scarcely more than the first fifty years of the twentieth century.

Because of the similarities between the traditional and the modern, they are prone to be confused, and the literature is currently being subjected to contesting interpretations. This has created a particular challenge for both writers and interpreters of twentieth-century literature in Irish. Much can be achieved by a fruitful liaison between the two impulses described above, the traditional and the modernist. This depends, however, on establishing the boundaries—which are sometimes almost imperceptible—between the two.

An example of the blurred boundaries is the poetry of Nuala Ní Dhomhnaill, which has been analysed in terms of post-structuralist French feminism, as *écriture féminine*,[123] but also in terms of a pre-modern gnosticism.[124] These approaches are not interchangeable, but do have certain similarities. It may well be the case that Ní Dhomhnaill's poetry is exhausted by neither analysis, and may need both. Likewise, the floating, imprecise subject of many pieces of twentieth-century fiction can be read as faithful to traditional Irish magical transformations, and also as part of current modernist and post-modern investigations into the nature of the subject.[125] Yet another example is the 'death of the author', which usually refers to his or her effacement as origin and guarantor of a text's meaning and stability. This, coupled with the current crisis of confidence in the reliable narrator, dovetails with earlier pre-individualist conceptions of authorship and the inherent instability of a manuscript tradition.[126]

[122] Cathal Ó Háinle, 'An t-úrscéal nár tháinig' in *Promhadh pinn* (Maynooth, 1978).

[123] Bríona Nic Dhiarmada, 'An bhean is an bhaineann: gnéithe den chritic fheimineach' in Máire Ní Annracháin and Bríona Nic Dhiarmada (ed.), *Téacs agus comhthéacs: gnéithe de chritic na Gaeilge* (Cork, 1998), pp 152–82. See also ead., 'Téacs baineann, téacs mná: gnéithe d'fhilíocht Nuala Ní Dhomhnaill' (Ph. D. thesis, N.U.I. (U.C.D.), 1995).

[124] Pádraig de Paor, *Tionscnamh filíochta Nuala Ní Dhomhnaill* (Dublin, 1997).

[125] This is as yet a relatively unresearched area. See Máire Ní Annracháin, 'An tsuibiacht abú, an tsuibiacht amú' in *Oghma*, vi (1994), pp 11–22.

[126] For a discussion of some aspects of these issues, see Louis de Paor, 'An scéalaíocht', and Máirín Nic Eoin, 'An t-údar, an téacs agus an criticeoir' in Ní Annracháin & Nic Dhiarmada, *Téacs agus comhthéacs*, pp 8–33, 64–93.

Moving now to poetry, it should be remembered that a Gaeltacht tradition of oral poetry had not only continued throughout the post-bardic period and right through the twentieth century, in a way unparalleled in oral storytelling, but had also developed considerably, particularly in keeping abreast of contemporary subject-matter. Therefore the challenge presented to the poets of modernity was in some, though not all, respects different from that faced by prose writers. The same question of transposing and interiorising elements of the older tradition arose, certainly. Thus, for instance, Biddy Jenkinson has reworked the ancient relationship of the king with the sovereignty goddess in terms of modern gender relations,[127] and Nuala Ní Dhomhnaill's encounters with the fairy woman, *bean an leasa*, or her personifications of the mermaid, can be fruitfully read as reflections on various liminal mental states such as depression, though these readings do not exhaust the literary richness of the poems.[128]

On the other hand, some of the earlier poets adopted external models almost without qualm. The two dominant figures of what is held to be the first wave of serious poets, in the middle of the century, namely Seán Ó Ríordáin and Máirtín Ó Direáin, were not obviously vexed by the question of the integration of their work into the tradition. However, it is interesting to note that their poetry contains an elegiac note which is conspicuously absent in the work of later generations of poets who repolished the traditional jewels for the final third of the century. Ó Direáin and Ó Ríordáin are, with good reason, held to be the fathers of modern poetry in Irish, being the first poets who, in the early 1940s, had both the necessary linguistic competence and artistic impulse to write poetry as art rather than as a pedagogical tool. The elegiac note can be read, in retrospect, as a response just as much to their own artistic exile from the Irish-language poetic tradition as to the abandonment by the Irish people of older ways of life. Thus a certain irony can be read back into the first-person plural pronoun in, for example, Ó Direáin's great lament for the modern world, 'Ár ré dhearóil' ('Our dismal age'). If Ireland had foolishly turned its back on the land and the shore as he claimed, his generation of poets did something similar in their poetry. They spent considerable energy investigating the spirit of English modernism and found it a more wearisome task than might have been the case had they directed their attention more to a reassessment of the native poetic tradition. In so doing they left a good deal of the work of rediscovery of the poetic

---

[127] Biddy Jenkinson's selected poems are published in *Rogha Dánta* (Cork, 2000). The individual volumes are *Baisteadh gintlí* (Dublin, 1986), *Uiscí beatha* (Dublin, 1988), *Dán na huidhre* (Dublin, 1991), and *Amhras neimhe* (Dublin, 1997).
[128] See several poems in Nuala Ní Dhomhnaill, *Feis* (Maynooth, 1991) and *Cead aighnis* (Daingean, 1998). Two other volumes of poems in Irish are *An dealg droighin* (Dublin, 1981) and *Féar suaithinseach* (Maynooth, 1984). Ní Dhomhnaill's poetry is extensively translated into English; see, e.g., *Pharaoh's daughter* (Oldcastle, Co. Meath, 1990).

potential of the land and the shore to a later generation of poets, and much of their own poetry was imbued with a sense of near-despair:

> Tá cime romham
> Tá cime i mo dhiaidh,
> Is mé féin ina lár
> I mo chime mar chách,
> Ó d'fhágamar slán
> Ag talamh, ag trá,
> Gur thit orainn
> Crann an éigin.[129]

(There is a prisoner in front of me, / a prisoner behind me, / and I am between them / a prisoner like all others, / since we abandoned / the land, the strand, / since the yoke of compulsion / fell on us.)

The same sense of imprisonment is expressed in Ó Ríordáin's poem 'Saoirse' ('Freedom'), an anthem to the alienated spirit of the early post-war period:

> Raghaidh mé síos i measc na ndaoine
> De shiúl mo chos,
> Is raghaidh mé síos anocht.
>
> Raghaidh mé síos ag lorg daoirse
> Ó mbinibshaoirse
> Tá ag liú anseo...[130]

(I will go down among the people / walking / And I will go down tonight. / I will go down in search of captivity / Release from the piercing freedom / Which howls here...)

Many boundaries between traditional 'folk' poetry and modern 'art' poetry have dissolved. Neither type is exclusively written or oral, stabilised in text nor performance-based, personal nor private, complex nor simple, urban nor rural, neither establishment-oriented nor anti-establishment. Nor is there a clear formal distinction between them. Given this convergence, it is appropriate to imagine the poetic spectrum as passing without a jolt from the traditional folksong to the intellectual masterpieces of Biddy Jenkinson, Mícheál Ó Hairtnéide, or Tomás Mac Síomóin.[131]

Notwithstanding the foreboding of Máirtín Ó Cadhain, who in *Páipéir bhána agus páipéir bhreaca* had expressed anxiety about the health of any literature that concentrated on poetry at the expense of prose fiction, poetry

---

[129] Máirtín Ó Direáin, *Dánta* (Dublin, 1980), p. 80.
[130] Seán Ó Ríordáin, *Eireaball spideoige* (2nd ed., Dublin, 1970), p. 100.
[131] See, e.g., Michael Hartnett/Mícheál Ó Hairtnéide, *Adharca broic* (Dublin, 1978); Tomás Mac Síomóin, *Cré agus cláirseach* (Dublin, 1983).

has been composed during the twentieth century which defies the despairing analysis that Irish literature is a spent force. In fact, in the case of many late-century poets, it is hard to imagine that art of a higher calibre, of greater complexity or linguistic richness could be produced in Irish whether or not the lamented decline of centuries took place.

Examples abound, and space allows no justice to be done. It may be more fruitful to examine a single short poem in some detail rather than to offer a listing of numerous titles. A poem by Pádraig Mac Fhearghusa may give a flavour. Note the integration of native and European elements—in particular through the common medieval motif of the struggle between the lily and the rose in the woman's cheek. Note the metaphorisation of the earlier belief in the redemptive power of baptism, and the implications for the whole religious efficacy of the Granacci painting, now that the religious function has been transferred to the woman. Note also the rewriting of the conventions of the *dánta grá*, or courtly love poems, in such a way as to allow the modern woman to transcend her traditional role as adored and absent object of both love and art. This is achieved in no small measure by linguistic nuance, such as the clear inclusion of both the speaker and the woman in the first-person plural pronoun 'sinn', which, in the *dánta grá*, usually referred simply to the poet himself. The poem evokes some of the most salient features of the *dánta grá*, but shifts the focus, and so not only gathers up powerful elements from the older literary tradition, both native and European, but also creates an unapologetically contemporary poem.

'An Teaghlach Naofa agus Naomh Eoin i dTírdhreach'
Curtha i leith Granacci, 1477–1543

Lá dár sheasamar anseo os comhair an *Granacci*,
Lá a baisteadh sinn in uiscí cumhra an cheana
Faoi ghúna craorag sin na Maighdine a bhí
I gcoimheascar beannaithe le deirge do ghrua,
Ba chumhra do chuidse dual
Ná cluas áilleáin ar bith de chuid an *quattrocento*.
Trím thost a bhínn ad' adhradh; b'urnaí ár dtost araon
I measc na c'leachtan beannaithe: Eoin, is an Críost
Ar ghlúin na Maighdine, Iósaf ag faire an róid ó dheas
'dtí an Éigipt, trí Apulia nach maireann,
Is an bhéist ainghiallta ag faire go foighneach ar a mháistir.
Ná múinfeá dom athuair a bheith im' shás molta agus foighne,
A fhionnachruth, is fada fada i ndobhrón do mhúchta mé—
Ba ghile tú ná an luan ar chúl na Máthar,
Ba mhíne ná lámh Eoin i lámh an tSlánaitheora.[132]

---

[132] Pádraig Mac Fhearghusa, *Mearcair* (Dublin, 1996), p. 11.

('Landscape with the Holy Family and St John', *Ascribed to Granacci, 1477–1543*.
On a day when we stood here before the *Granacci* / The day we were baptised in the fragrant waters of affection / Under the blood-red dress of the Virgin which was / in holy conflict with the red of your cheek, / Your curling hair was more fragrant / Than the hair of any *Quattrocento* beauty. / I adored you through my silence; our mutual silence was a prayer / Among the holy company: John, and the Christ / On the Virgin's knee, Joseph observing the road south / to Egypt, and Apulia which is no more, / And the dumb beast patiently watching his master. / Would you not teach me once again to be content to praise and be patient / Oh fairest one, I have for long been plunged in grief, obliterated—/ You were brighter than the halo behind the Mother, / You were gentler than the hand of John in the hand of the Saviour.)

The second half of the twentieth century has seen a number of major shifts in the profile of Irish-language writers. Reference has already been made to the change in levels of educational attainment. Women have burst into view, particularly in poetry, with subtle and challenging reworkings of the tradition from the double vantage-point of modernity and gender. Biddy Jenkinson and Nuala Ní Dhomhnaill have already been mentioned and in the present writer's estimation outrank all other twentieth-century Irish-language poets, male or female. Much of their work involves the appropriation of marginalised voices from the tradition. This often involves dealing with traditional female characters or types in such a way as to modernise them if their concerns had originally been countercultural, or subvert them if they had been passive victims of patriarchy. One of Jenkinson's many strengths is her reinterpretation of the voice of the ancient sovereignty goddess in ways that offer not only an arresting critique of gender relations, but also a radical ethical statement about relations between humanity and the natural world. In, for example, 'Eanair 1991' ('January 1991'), the pathetic fallacy, one of the main bulwarks of the patriarchal heroic code, with its appropriation of the sovereignty goddess, is reworked by a female voice to register protest at the first Gulf war:

> Ná póg in aon chor mé an Eanair seo.
> Ní éireodh aon fhuiseog ar do bhéalbhéim.
> Thitfeadh
> dreoilíní coscartha Stiofáin
> go talamh eadrainn...[133]

(Do not kiss me at all this January. / No lark would rise from your mouth's touch. / The mangled, melted wrens of St Stephen's Day / would fall / to the ground between us...)

In Nuala Ní Dhomhnaill's 'Cailleach', translated as 'Hag' by fellow-poet John Montague, the tradition of the land goddess offers raw material to

---

[133] Biddy Jenkinson, *Dán na huidhre*, p. 87.

modern poetry with an ease and a confidence that Máirtín Ó Direáin or Seán Ó Ríordáin might have envied:

> Taibhríodh dom gur mé an talamh
> gur mé paróiste Fionntrá
> ar a fhaid is ar a leithead
> soir, siar, faoi mar a shíneann sí...[134]

(Once I dreamt I was the earth, / the parish of Ventry its length and breadth, / east and west, as far as it runs...)

Other women poets have broadened the scope of subject-matter in Irish poetry and, collectively, have broken the silence of women across a range of topics. Some, most notably Máire Mhac a' tSaoi, have produced exquisite lyrics.[135] These, admittedly, can hardly be considered politically radical in terms of gender, except in so far as they point, by their very presence, to the absence of a women's perspective in much Irish literature hitherto.

The broadening by women of the scope of literature to include much material that would have been shunned by previous generations is to be celebrated as an innovation. Worthy of celebration, too, is the move to acknowledge once more the importance of certain types of material that would indeed have merited the title of literature in earlier centuries, although denied that title throughout the twentieth century (largely owing to the dominance of critical thinking by the belles-lettres model of English and French literature). This exclusivity has often been denounced at informal gatherings, and recently a trenchant plea has been made in print for the reassessment of various forms of non-fictional prose texts, such as journalistic material, diaries, biographies, literary criticism, and others.[136] Much of this type of material, or its equivalent, had been an intrinsic part of the bardic remit, and was an integral part of Irish public discourse. It was at a considerable remove from the kind of personal, emotional writing that came to dominate the European canon following the romantic age. This call to reinstate a kind of writing that is closer to an older, indigenous practice is yet another striking example of the coalescence of pre-modern tendencies in Irish and current modern trends. In this case what is at issue is the practice of collapsing the previous rigid categories such as 'literature', 'criticism', 'cultural products', into the more general category of 'text'. The present overview has confined itself largely to prose fiction and poetry, not entirely out of a desire to highlight these as exceptional expressions of the human imagination, but also because so much basic research remains to be done, in many cases even to be started, on so many other genres.

[134] Nuala Ní Dhomhnaill, *Feis*, p. 31.
[135] Selected poems are in Máire Mhac a' tSaoi, *An cion go dtí seo* (Dublin, 1987).
[136] Caoilfhinn Nic Pháidín, *Fáinne an Lae agus an athbheochan: 1898–1900* (Dublin, 1998).

As the 1990s give way to the 2000s, the demands of communication and the market-place have created two new pressures. Translation of Irish-language literature into English, if not lucrative, dramatically increases the readership and thus is an affirming experience for those whose work is translated. It is also fraught with danger. The requirement that a minority culture render an account of itself to any outside group, let alone a dominant neighbouring culture, has the potential, paradoxically, to make the minority culture invisible or at least undifferentiated from the target culture.

The growth of television, and the challenge it brings of producing imaginative, indigenous text, offers, at least at first sight, the opportunity for the Irish-language community to interpret itself to itself, and to do so in a medium that is closer to the oral tradition than the written word ever could be. However, there is a need for sustained, close, and detailed reflection and debate on the specific needs of Irish-language television. Otherwise there is a risk that the debate that took place at the turn of the century, which saw the new literature adopt debilitating and non-indigenous conventions to an excessive degree, would reproduce itself, and see Irish-language television writing bow to the conventions of the mass market.

One hundred years after the early efforts at revival, Irish literature shows signs of life worthy of wholehearted celebration. This claim is made not in a spirit of antiquarianism or nostalgia, but in recognition of the liberating and enhancing potential of the Irish language as an evocative, complex alternative to the mass culture of the western world. In this respect, while there is little overt social protest in the subject-matter of twentieth-century Gaelic literature, none the less it has functioned as an important, if small-scale, exercise in resilience and renewal on the part of an ancient and rich culture. This has been mirrored in the definite shift from the heritage model of Gaelic culture, which was associated with cultural nationalism, to a model imbued with a human-rights sensibility. If the best of the later modern subject can be most clearly glimpsed in 'places where the lust for life merges with real protest',[137] then contemporary literature in Irish is a testimony to that modern subject, alive and very well.

[137] Alain Touraine, *Critique of modernity* (Oxford, 1995), p. 323.

CHAPTER XX

The visual arts and society, 1921–84

CYRIL BARRETT

As far as the visual arts were concerned, it might have been thought that the provisional government began well when it appointed Count Plunkett (George Noble) minister for the fine arts. But when the Free State government was formed in 1922 there was no ministry of fine arts. Indeed, the first thirty years after independence has often been regarded as a particularly poor period for the visual arts in Ireland. Government neglect seemed almost total; sales of works of art and attendance at galleries and exhibitions were poor. Architecture, to judge by new church buildings, was insular and backward-looking. Art education at all levels was in a poor state.[1] As Sean O'Faolain (a future director of the arts council) put it, 'our sails sagged for a generation'.[2]

Certainly, political and economic circumstances were not propitious. The effects of the war of independence and the civil war had to be overcome before resources were available for the arts; there were more pressing needs. Then came the economic depression, the economic war, and the second world war. Recent work, however, indicates that even in the decades immediately after independence there was more vitality and innovation, greater openness to international ideas and models, especially in architecture, than this picture suggests. As early as 1922 Darrell Figgis, an independent T.D., commended 'simplicity and truth' as against 'antique manners' in a speech to the Architectural Association of Ireland that 'could have been an extract from an Internationalist manifesto'.[3] In 1925 the government recommended that continental housing styles be consulted in advance of slum clearance and municipal rehousing, and in the same year it was the German firm of

[1] Muriel Emanuel (ed.), *Contemporary architects* (3rd ed., London, 1994), p. 865; Terence Brown, *Ireland: a social and cultural history 1922–79* (London, 1981), pp 17–18, 34, 232–3.
[2] Sean O'Faolain, *The Irish* (Harmondsworth, 1947; revised ed., 1969), p. 162.
[3] Seán Rothery, 'Ireland and the new architecture 1900–1940' in Annette Becker, John Olley, and Wilfred Wang (ed.), *20th-century architecture: Ireland* (Munich and New York, 1997), pp 17–22: 18.

Siemens–Schuckert that was commissioned to undertake the massive Shannon hydro-electric scheme. This project, with its concrete weirs, dams, and bridges, and the utilitarian forms of several of the buildings (if not those of the power station itself) had a progressive, modern flavour and attracted visitors from all over the country. The Fianna Fáil governments of the 1930s were equally anxious to promote a modern image for Ireland, to judge by the Irish pavilion at the New York world's fair in 1939, commissioned by the government in 1937. Designed by Michael Scott, the pavilion had an undulating all-glass façade.[4]

The importance of promoting good design, because of its commercial potential, took some time to be recognised: it was little appreciated in the 1920s. In 1937 a committee was set up to advise the minister for industry and commerce (then Seán Lemass) 'on matters affecting the design and decoration of articles manufactured in Saorstát Éireann'.[5] It met forty-two times between 1937 and 1939 and finally recommended a major exhibition on the lines of the great exhibitions of the nineteenth and early twentieth centuries. However, the war intervened. It was not till 1955 that an exhibition was held in Dublin and Cork under the auspices of the Design Research Unit of Ireland and sponsored by the arts council, and even then it was not on the scale of the great exhibitions.

The inter-party government of 1948–51 took involvement in the arts a step further. In 1949 Seán MacBride, minister for external affairs, set up the Irish Cultural Relations Committee, a body resembling the British Council, which had been established in 1934. Each was responsible for making the culture of its country better known abroad. However, whereas the British Council had funds at its disposal, the Irish Cultural Relations Committee merely advised the minister for external affairs, who could ignore its recommendations.

Meanwhile, in 1948 a cabinet committee had been set up, and Professor Thomas Bodkin was commissioned to report on the state of the arts in Ireland. The Bodkin report (completed and published in 1949) was not complimentary, nor was it well received by politicians or bureaucrats. Among other things it favoured the setting up of an arts council. The taoiseach, John A. Costello, supported the idea and included it in his statements of government arts policy in 1950 (the first such statement, made on the occasion of the donation of a collection of paintings to the National Gallery by Alfred Chester Beatty). An arts council (An Chomhairle Ealaíon) was established in 1951.[6] Like its British counterpart (established in 1946) it was an autonomous body, supporting the visual arts either directly, by organising exhibitions, giving

[4] Ibid., pp 19–21.
[5] Thomas Bodkin, *Report on the arts in Ireland* (Dublin, 1949), p. 47.
[6] 1951/9 (8 May 1951).

grants, and purchasing pictures, or indirectly, as by supporting exhibitions, assisting purchases, and dispensing bursaries.

Though the major part of its funds are devoted to drama, the arts council has done much to further the visual arts. In 1954 it began to grant scholarships in painting, sculpture, and design. These were extended to architecture in 1958. Its offer of aid in purchasing works of art (50 per cent of the price) was not availed of greatly by public bodies, but was well received by schools, hotels, and institutions. In 1966 a scheme for helping artists in distress, 'Ciste Colmcille', was introduced. In 1980 the taoiseach, Charles Haughey, suggested that fixed-term grants should be given to established artists. This scheme, 'Aosdána' (described as 'an affiliation of artists . . . established by the arts council to honour those artists whose work has made an outstanding contribution to the arts in Ireland'),[7] was launched in 1981.

In 1957 the arts council, under the directorship of Sean O'Faolain, moved beyond an administrative role to launch campaigns and support causes. It began with a campaign against advertising hoardings in places of natural beauty. Next, and more far-reaching, was one for the protection of buildings of architectural and historical importance—a cause pioneered by An Taisce (the National Trust for Ireland, founded in 1948). Parts of Ireland's architectural heritage, such as Dublin's Georgian buildings, had survived, although many had degenerated into tenements. In 1963 the Electricity Supply Board decided to demolish a row of sixteen houses in Lower Fitzwilliam Street, and a Georgian vista over half a mile in length was compromised. Subsequently, in 1966 the Dublin Civic Group was set up by Professor Kevin B. Nowlan, Sheila Carden, F. H. Walker, and others to examine planning applications coming before the Dublin corporation and, where necessary, to lodge objections in order to preserve interiors, streetscapes, and skylines. Not everything went the developers' way. In the summer of 1970 buildings under threat of demolition in Hume Street were occupied by Deirdre Kelly of the Living City Group, and others; this became the centre of a formative controversy. Although the buildings were ultimately demolished, the developers were obliged to erect replicas on the site. This did something to curb the destruction of historic buildings in the name of progress, though in the interests of commerce. However, the direct action of thousands of citizens who marched in protest at the destruction of a viking site on Wood Quay failed to prevent the building there of new Dublin civic offices, the first two towers of which (1976, Sam Stephenson) were particularly stark examples of modernist architecture.

The arts council was reorganised in 1973. One outcome of this was to make official the collaboration that had existed in practice for years with the arts council of Northern Ireland. And a further outcome was the setting up

---

[7] *Aosdána* (Dublin, 1996), p. 5; see also above, p. 528.

of a joint venture at Annaghmakerrig, County Monaghan (a house donated by Tyrone Guthrie), where artists of all kinds may go to work and meet each other. In 1976 the council (in association with the Gulbenkian foundation) commissioned the Richards report on provision for the arts, which made far-reaching recommendations that were implemented. In the thirty years of its existence up to 1980 the council did remarkably well on a budget that in most other countries would have been regarded as derisory: £1,000 in 1951/2, rising to £80,000 in 1971/2. In the 1970s it was more generous, rising to £3 million in 1980/81. But by then inflation was eating into it.

In 1958 the arts council introduced a scheme by which grants were given to firms that employed professional designers, if their designs were approved. In 1960 industrial design was entrusted to An Córas Tráchtála, a body that had been incorporated in 1951 to encourage exports. An Córas Tráchtála immediately commissioned a group of Scandinavian industrial designers to report on the state of industrial design in Ireland, and in 1961 set up a design section of its own. The report of the Scandinavian group, *Design in Ireland* (1962), proposed the establishment of an institute of visual arts with departments of design, craft, architecture, and 'free arts'—painting, sculpture, and graphics—and also a design centre. However, neither proposal was taken up.

The design section of An Córas Tráchtála acquired premises in Kilkenny in 1963, and founded the Kilkenny Design Workshops. In 1966 the workshops became a wholly owned subsidiary of An Córas Tráchtála to provide design services for certain sections of Irish industry. The design section organised exhibitions, awarded grants, and kept a register of designers.

Indeed, by the 1970s design in Ireland ran the risk of suffocation by over-attention. In 1963 the minister for education had set up a council of design to review and coordinate the training under An Córas Tráchtála and the National College of Art. In 1969 a further body, the design advisory committee, was appointed by An Córas Tráchtála to inquire into education in design. And in 1971 the word 'Design' was added to the title of the National College of Art.[8] Thus the educational objectives of the previous century were restored.

Outside the state sphere, the promotion of Irish crafts owed a great deal to such organisations as the Irish Countrywomen's Association (1935; formerly the United Irishwomen), and its associated college, An Grianán. A particularly outstanding contribution to the support of rural crafts was made by Muriel Gahan (1897–1995), who was involved with both these bodies. It was her initiative that led to the opening of 'The Country Shop' in St Stephen's Green, Dublin, which for over forty years provided an outlet for the products of rural craftworkers.[9]

[8] 1971/28 (1 Dec. 1971).
[9] See Geraldine Mitchell, *Deeds not words: the life and work of Muriel Gahan* (Dublin, 1997); below, p. 848n. On arts and crafts down to the 1920s, see also above, vi, 488–93.

The government also had responsibility for art education. Since the beginning of the century there had been dissatisfaction about the running of the Metropolitan School of Art, Dublin, and successive committees had been set up to advise on its improvement. In 1924 this school, and other educational establishments, were transferred from the care of the department of agriculture and technical instruction to that of the department of education. Entries to the London board of education examinations ceased, which had an adverse effect on design studies. In 1927 yet another 'committee of experts' was set up. It consisted of two Irish (Thomas Bodkin and Dermod O'Brien) and three French experts. The French proposed far-reaching reforms that would have meant introducing a whole range of new subjects, including lace-making, ceramics, metalwork, and lithography. The Irish members, who had been instructed to bear economy in mind, considered that the proposals were too ambitious 'for the needs and opportunities of the time'. The proposals were not implemented.[10]

The name of the school was changed to 'National College of Art' (Coláiste Náisiúnta Ealaíne na hÉireann) in 1936, and it was divided into schools of painting, sculpture, and design. There were to be no entrance tests. Modest scholarships and bursaries, and some free places, were made available. But by the 1960s the college was coming under criticism. The most forthright was delivered by the Scandinavian group, which found that the methods of education were 'completely out of date and it is our opinion that the National College of Art as presently constituted cannot be the starting point for the education of people in the different crafts or indeed for the education of painters, sculptors, or designers'.[11] The commission on higher education questioned the notion of an academic institution under the direct control of a government department. The council of design questioned the suitability of the premises in Kildare Street. In 1968 a wave of student unrest swept Europe and America, and the students of the college carried their protests to the streets. In 1969 an advisory council, appointed by the minister for education, recommended changes in the structure, staffing, appointments, and teaching methods. However, nothing was done, and the unrest continued, with repeated closings, reopenings, and dismissals. In 1971 a board of governors was appointed and the college renamed. Eventually things settled down under a new management and a new structure. After wandering in the city for some years—in 1979 it was occupying four separate sites—the

[10] Bodkin, *Report on the arts*, pp 25–6. Some years later, however, Bodkin stated his own view that government should give greater encouragement to such Irish industries as china, carpet-making, furniture, and glass (Thomas Bodkin, *The importance of art to Ireland* (Dublin, 1935), pp v–vi, 7–11).

[11] *Design in Ireland* (Córas Tráchtála, Dublin, 1962), p. 45; John Turpin, *A school of art in Dublin since the eighteenth century: a history of the National College of Art and Design* (Dublin, 1995), ch. 24.

college settled in Thomas Street in 1980.[12] Its counterparts in Cork and Limerick, under local-authority control, were not beset with the same problems.

The problems in the National College of Art can be partly traced to the state of art education in primary and secondary schools. Under the 'first national programme' of 1921 (adopted in 1922 and confirmed in 1926)[13] the status of the Irish language was raised from that of an optional to a compulsory subject and one consequence was that drawing was demoted to the status of an 'additional' subject. In due course this demotion had an adverse effect on art education. As Bodkin remarked in 1949, 'owing to the lack of instruction in drawing in the primary and secondary schools, candidates for admission to the college have had no preliminary training, and are poor material for development into professional artists'.[14] In 1954 the council of education (an advisory body set up by government in 1950) recommended that art education, in the form of illustrative drawing, colour-matching, precision drawing, and art appreciation, should become compulsory in primary schools once more. The time taken from Irish (two periods a week) would, it was said, be compensated for by the gain to geometry, mensuration, handwriting, nature study, geography, and history. The recommendations were implemented. Matters were little better at secondary level. 'Art' (replacing 'drawing') had been introduced into secondary schools in 1924, but it was not regarded as an important subject and still consisted simply of drawing—from objects, nature, or memory, or to a theme. In its report on secondary schools in 1962 the council of education recommended that imaginative composition and the history and appreciation of art be included in the curriculum.[15] This was duly done.

Teaching at the Royal Hibernian Academy was discontinued when its premises were burned down in 1916. It occupied temporary premises in Ely Place, Dublin, but these had no teaching facilities. Many academicians found teaching posts in the National College of Art. This became a bone of contention during the upheavals there in the 1960s. The academy's annual exhibition continued to be held either in the National College or the National Gallery. In 1969 (thanks to funding from the building contractor Matthew Gallagher) a new gallery in Ely Place was planned for the academy, with studios as well as exhibition space, and in 1989 it was officially opened as the R.H.A. Gallagher gallery.

Public interest in the visual arts began to flourish in the 1960s, partly as a result of government sponsorship through the arts council, partly through improvements in art education. But it is instructive to compare the attendance at the National Gallery in 1960—39,524—with the lowest figure for the

---

[12] Turpin, *A school of art*, p. 608.
[13] Below, pp 727–8.
[14] Bodkin, *Report on the arts*, p. 27.
[15] *Report of the council of education* (Pr 2583) (Dublin, 1954); *Report of the council of education* (Pr 5996) (Dublin, 1962).

nineteenth century: 64,342 in 1895. It was not till 1964 that that figure was exceeded (68,137); and it was not till 1968 that the highest, that for 1867 (128,680) was exceeded, with an attendance of 199,102. Since then the figures have continued to rise.[16] This was largely due to the flair of James White, who became director in 1964. He had some of the financial resources of the Shaw bequest at his disposal, though this does not take from his achievement. The gallery had been underfunded up to the 1950s. Having been the first national gallery to introduce gas lighting, it was the last to introduce electricity, in 1930. Bodkin resigned as director in 1935 because there were no funds for publications, not even cheap reproductions and postcards. Up to 1950, when Thomas MacGreevy was appointed, the director's appointment was only part-time. By the time White was appointed, improvements were already under way.

In an earlier volume an account of the controversy surrounding Sir Hugh Lane's collection up to 1920 has been given.[17] Despairing of a suitable place being found in Dublin to display his remarkable collection of French paintings, Lane had bequeathed the collection to the National Gallery in London. However, shortly before his death in 1915, he had added a codicil (unfortunately unwitnessed) leaving the collection to Dublin, provided that a suitable building had been found for them within five years of his death. By 1933, through the efforts of Sarah Purser and the Society of Friends of the National Collections (founded in 1924), such a building had been found: Charlemont House, Parnell Square. It had been handed over by government to the Dublin corporation in 1929 and adapted as a gallery. Designated the Municipal Gallery of Modern Art, it was intended to house the municipal collection (mostly of Irish artists) as well as the Lane collection. However, when the gallery was opened in 1933, the Lane collection was not in it (though a room for it was kept vacant). The paintings had been in London at the time of Lane's death, and despite a campaign to regain them for Ireland, the British authorities were reluctant to hand them back. They became the subject of legal wranglings.

In 1923 the dáil and senate passed resolutions affirming that Lane believed that he had effectively carried out his testamentary obligations in stating his intention to leave his collection to Dublin under certain conditions. The following year a British parliamentary committee was set up to investigate the matter. It reported in 1926 that, though Lane had made a legal disposition (in a signed codicil) that it was his final intention to leave his collection to Dublin, it had not been witnessed. The defect could easily have been remedied by legislation, but the committee failed to recommend such action. The reasons for this illogicality are both curious and outrageous.

[16] Above, vi, 438–9; attendance in 1991 was nearly five times the figure for 1968.
[17] Above, vi, 480–84.

The committee found that for ten years the Dublin corporation had done nothing to implement Lane's conditions; that, were his will to be legalised, it would constitute a breach of faith to Lord Duveen who had added a wing on to the Tate Gallery in London to house the collection; and that had Lane lived to see the new Tate Gallery 'no doubt could be entertained' but that he would have destroyed the codicil![18] The corporation had not acted, in fact, because that would have been imprudent while the legality of the will remained in dispute. But in 1924 the Dublin civic commissioners (who took the place of the corporation between 1924 and 1930) had resolved that if the will were legalised they would provide a gallery within five years. If Lord Duveen intended his gallery for the Lane collection (which Lord Curzon, chairman of the Tate trustees, denied) he would have been guilty of the very same imprudence that the Dublin corporation wished to avoid. Comment on the third reason is superfluous. W. B. Yeats, speaking in the senate, summed it all up when he said that it was as if Ali Baba's forty thieves claimed their treasure because of the expenses they had incurred in digging a cavern to house it.[19]

But matters did not end there. The issue was repeatedly raised in both houses of the British parliament. Finally in 1959 the prime minister Harold Macmillan arranged a compromise with the Irish government, whereby it was agreed that the collection should be divided in two, and that each half should reside for five years alternately in each country.[20] This continued till 1979, when it was altered, giving Dublin the major share of the paintings with special arrangements for Renoir's 'Les parapluies'. Meanwhile, on the death in 1968 of Sir Alfred Chester Beatty, Dublin had acquired a priceless collection of oriental and near-eastern manuscripts, prints, paintings, and objets d'art, which was housed in the Chester Beatty library, Ballsbridge, and accessible to scholars and to the public.[21]

ALTHOUGH lacking the aristocratic and viceregal patronage available in the capital city with its noble tradition of Georgian elegance, Belfast had not only the first provincial museum in Ireland but the first public museum in the country to be built entirely by voluntary subscription. In a chaste Hellenic style, the Belfast museum of 1831 by Thomas Jackson still stands. It housed the collections of the Belfast Natural History and Philosophical Society, transferred in 1910 to the Belfast corporation, which since 1890 had been assembling significant collections in the upper floors of the Belfast central library. In 1912 the city council resolved to erect a new building on the edge of the botanic gardens. This building, though only partly completed, opened

[18] Thomas Bodkin, *Hugh Lane and his pictures* (2nd ed., Dublin, 1934), pp 55–6.
[19] Ibid., pp 47–8, 51–2.
[20] S. B. Kennedy, *Irish art and modernism 1880–1950* (Belfast, 1991), p. 11.
[21] The collection (which was opened to the public in 1953) was transferred to Dublin Castle in 2000.

in 1929 as the Belfast Museum and Art Gallery. In 1962 responsibility for the museum was transferred to the government of Northern Ireland as a national institution, thus facilitating the major extension that was completed in 1972.

Of the various art collections that moved to the new building in 1929, two were of special significance. In 1906 Sir Robert Lloyd Patterson died, having bequeathed his collection to the city, subject to the life interest of Lady Patterson, who handed over the collection in 1919. However, the perceptive curator, Arthur Deane, suspected that the bequest contained little of quality and arranged for the art critic Frank Rutter to advise. It was his view that the items in the bequest were 'of a kind undesirable for any art gallery that wished to maintain a high standard'. After appropriate arrangements, all but a few of the pictures were sold, and the Contemporary Arts Society was entrusted with building up a new collection of contemporary paintings with the proceeds. Thanks to this sensible strategy, the Ulster Museum possesses an important and representative collection of British and French paintings from the first four decades of the twentieth century, including works by both Spencers, both the Nash brothers, Sickert, Matthew Smith, Roberts, Lucien Pissarro, Augustus John, Wilson Steer, and other leading artists of the period. The other significant bequest (thirty-four of his own works) was made in 1929 by the Belfast-born artist Sir John Lavery.

The first curator at the Belfast Museum and Art Gallery was John Hewitt, poet, critic, lecturer, and broadcaster, who between 1930 and 1957 extended the collections by judicious acquisitions, mainly (though not exclusively) of works by contemporary Irish artists. John Hewitt was succeeded by Anne Crookshank, later to become the first professor of art history at Trinity College, Dublin, who, after the transfer from civic control, took full advantage of the increased resources available to the new national institution to buy adventurously and to build up a collection of international contemporary painting and sculpture that is one of the best of its kind in these islands.

In Northern Ireland, state support for the arts followed the pattern established in Great Britain by the Council for the Encouragement of Music and the Arts (C.E.M.A.). However, it did not follow automatically, and some tenacity and skilful negotiation were needed to persuade the Northern Ireland government of the need for provision along similar lines to that available in Great Britain. C.E.M.A. (N.I.) was founded in 1943 and was redesignated the Arts Council of Northern Ireland in 1962. The council remains independent of the Arts Council of Great Britain—the Welsh and Scottish councils are formally linked—and has practical if informal relations with its southern counterpart, with which it collaborates in artistic enterprises of common concern. The two Irish councils differ from each other in structure, the southern body having all its members appointed by government, while the constitution of the northern council provides for half its membership to be nominated by statutory bodies and institutions of higher education, the other half being appointed by the minister for education. Under Kenneth Jamison as director, good relations with the Republic were maintained and are now formalised. The arts council also maintained its activities and standards in spite of the troubled times after 1969.

Art education in Northern Ireland fared rather better than in the south. In 1920 the college of art came under Belfast city council, rather than the department of education, as in the south. Northern Ireland also continued to stress the importance of design, particularly in the linen industry, as it had done under the department of agriculture and technical education. Support for art education increased in the 1950s, when generous grants were given for primary and secondary education in fine art and crafts. Northern Ireland was thus a decade ahead of the Republic in this field. This applies to primary and secondary art education, but even more to higher-level education. In the 1960s, when its Dublin counterpart was experiencing various difficulties, the Belfast college of art was stable and developing rapidly. In 1968 the college of art became the faculty of art in the new Ulster College (since 1984 part of the University of Ulster), with power to grant academic degrees.

Thus from the 1960s, both north and south of the border, the arts began to prosper. This, no doubt, reflected increasing prosperity, just as did the interest in art in the latter part of the nineteenth century.

TURNING to the individual arts, Irish independence coincided with the sudden emergence in Europe in the early 1920s of the 'International style' in architecture associated (by those who coined the name) with the work of Le Corbusier, Walter Gropius, Mies van der Rohe, and the Dutch architect J. J. P. Oud. Modern materials such as reinforced concrete had already come into use before the first world war: some Irish examples were noted in an earlier volume.[22] But what was radical about the new architecture in the 1920s was the exploitation of materials such as steel, glass, and reinforced concrete to produce spatial and compositional effects that were associated with contemporary avant-garde painting. It was inspired often by a wish to reject the legacy of tradition and history, and to address contemporary problems in society, among which were mechanisation and mass-housing.

The *Irish Builder* alerted its readers to the new style by an article on Le Corbusier in 1928, and another entitled 'New architecture', devoted mainly to Erich Mendelsohn's Expressionist design for the Einstein tower for Berlin, in 1929. Walter Gropius visited Ireland in 1936 and Mendelsohn in 1937. The great (and satirical) advocate of the new architecture in Ireland was John O'Gorman, who from 1935 wrote for the *Irish Builder* under the nom de plume 'Wisbech' (his home town). Another devoted propagandist was J. V.

[22] Above, vi, 497.

Downes, who travelled widely, lectured, and built up a superb collection of photographs, books, and periodicals on modernist architecture.

In 1930 the London architect Harold Greenwood completed an ambitious house in the new style: 'Wendon', St Mobhi Avenue, Glasnevin. Superficial characteristics of this architecture included box-like structures, unencumbered by ornamentation and usually finished in white; flat roofs; large windows and steel casements; and an overall impression of cleanliness and austerity. There are clear parallels between 'Wendon' and pioneering houses in Britain of a few years earlier such as Peter Behrens's 'New Ways', Northamptonshire; the Silver End houses of Thomas Tait and Frederick MacManus; and in particular Amyas Connell's 'High and Over' in Amersham, Buckinghamshire.[23] The first indigenous examples are in Dublin, at Kincora Road, Clontarf (Downes, 1930–31), and in Dollymount (Robinson, Keefe), built in 1931.

These 'new' houses soon began to appear around Dublin and in the provinces. In 1938 Michael Scott built a house, 'Geragh', in the style of the bridge of an ocean liner, overlooking the Forty Foot swimming area at Sandycove, County Dublin, and in 1937–8 T. P. Kennedy built a 'new' shooting lodge at Lake Inchiquin, County Clare. They were called 'sunshine houses', but they were also known as 'German houses' and by less complimentary names. They were generally regarded as either eccentric or pretentious in those early days. Ludwig Wittgenstein, the philosopher, who spent much of his time in Ireland towards the end of his life, summed up this attitude: 'Southey was right. Concerning these houses: "Time will not mellow them; nature will neither clothe nor conceal them; and they will remain always as offensive to the eye as to the mind." '[24] This was rich, coming from someone who himself had built a house in Vienna in this very same style, and who was a friend of Adolf Loos, to whom 'ornament is a crime'.

The new style was not readily accepted for domestic architecture, and the 1920s and 1930s still showed much evidence of older architectural influences. One of the main preoccupations at the time of independence was the refurbishment of Dublin city centre. The city had earlier been the venue for a civic exhibition organised in 1914 by the Civics Institute of Ireland,[25] focusing on urban development and especially housing needs. It was attended by eighty mayors from all over Ireland, and by the chief secretary. The lord

[23] Seán Rothery, *Ireland and the new architecture, 1900–1940* (Dublin, 1991), pp 113, 199.

[24] *Recollections of Wittgenstein*, ed. Rush Rees (Oxford, 1984), p. 162.

[25] The Civics Institute of Ireland (C.I.I.) was established following a housing and health conference sponsored by the Women's National Health Association. Its brief was to study 'all problems affecting Irish citizens' and specifically to organise a civic exhibition in Dublin in 1914. After the first world war the C.I.I. was instrumental in organising the Dublin civic survey of 1925. See John C. Gordon and Ishbel M. Gordon, *'We twa': reminiscences of Lord and Lady Aberdeen* (2 vols, London, 1925), ii, ch. 14; Jacinta Prunty, *Dublin slums 1800–1925* (Dublin, 1999), pp 187–94.

lieutenant, Lord Aberdeen, offered a prize of £500 for the best town plan for Dublin, which was won in 1916 by Patrick Abercrombie and associates. The winning design was an ambitious one, and somewhat impractical (it was not implemented, though the plan was published in 1922), but the exhibition helped to raise awareness in Ireland of the ideals of town planning, and shows that the drive to improve urban housing in Ireland pre-dated the era of independence.[26]

The devastation of much of the lower end of Sackville Street as a result of the 1916 rising prompted a debate about the principles of reconstruction, with some calling for a coordinated approach, and others (especially the traders whose premises were affected) anxious to defend individual rights. The *Irish Builder* called for a special board to oversee the rebuilding plans, with a 'committee of taste' to give advice. By the end of 1916 the Dublin corporation had established an expert committee. Its report recommended reconstruction along traditional classical lines, with unity as to heights and materials, though allowing considerable freedom to architects.[27]

Wartime shortages threatened the rebuilding programme, but it was largely complete when the civil war began in 1922. The north-eastern side of Sackville Street (now coming to be known as O'Connell Street) was left in ruins, along with surrounding streets and buildings along the Liffey, including the Four Courts. This prompted another spell of rebuilding and restoration. Concerning O'Connell Street, there was some dissatisfaction at the overall results. An article in the *Irish Builder* criticised the lack of architectural unity, and the missed opportunity to place a terminating feature at the north end of the street. Nor were there any new public buildings as envisaged by the Abercrombie plan, such as a catholic cathedral or national theatre. Despite these strictures, and accepting that the new buildings were for the most part individual expressions, Maura Shaffrey has pointed out that the reconstruction of the capital's chief thoroughfare did incorporate a degree of unity, through uniformity of heights, cornice lines, and materials (a blend of brick and stone).[28]

Meanwhile, the Free State government had been faced with the problem of finding a suitable parliament building. Three suggestions had been put forward: the Bank of Ireland, College Green (the pre-union parliament building); the Royal Hospital, Kilmainham (which would have to be restored and drastically altered); and Leinster House, which the dáil temporarily occupied, the Royal Dublin Society (its former occupier) having moved out

---

[26] Gordon & Gordon, '*We twa*', ii, ch. 14; Patrick Abercrombie, Sydney Kelly, and Arthur Kelly, *Dublin of the future. The new town plan* (Liverpool and London, 1922); Rothery, *Ire. & the new architecture*, p. 82.
[27] Maura Shaffrey, 'Sackville Street/O'Connell Street' in *The GPA Irish Arts Review Yearbook 1988* (Belfast, 1988), pp 144–56: 150–53.
[28] Ibid., p. 154.

to Ballsbridge. The problem was solved when the Royal Dublin Society was induced to part with Leinster House in 1924 for £68,000.[29]

In Northern Ireland there were two new public buildings from this period that should be mentioned: the parliament building on Stormont Hill, and the Royal Law Courts in the centre of Belfast. The first, an arid, classical building designed by Arnold Thornely of Liverpool and completed in 1932, was said to be a gift to the province from the British nation. The second, a dull and ponderous building designed by James G. West of London, was opened in 1933.

Georgian traditions remained important in the Free State. The careful (if not exact) restoration of the Four Courts, the Custom House, and the G.P.O. were major undertakings of government in the 1920s. And in new building, the national maternity hospital, Holles Street (1933, Ralph Byrne), was in a competent neo-Georgian style. It is said to blend with the buildings in Merrion Square. One building that, in spite of its classical style (presumably to harmonise with the rest of the street), showed some influence of modernist architecture was the department of industry and commerce building, Kildare Street (1942, J. R. Boyd Barrett). This is not surprising: its architect was associated with the revolutionary Church of Christ the King, Cork (1927–31), designed by Barry Byrne of Chicago in 1927.[30] The new city hall in Cork (1924–35, Jones, Kelly), well sited on the Lee's bank, owes a heavy debt to the Georgian classicism of the Custom House, Dublin. A particularly important public project from the interwar period was Sir Edwin Lutyens's war memorial and gardens at Inchicore in Dublin, largely completed by 1939, commemorating the Irish who had died in the first world war. Although the memorial gardens subsequently fell into neglect for several decades, from the mid 1980s they underwent restoration and have been opened as a public park.

The interwar period marked the beginning of new and extensive housing programmes throughout the country. Between 1923 and 1931 nearly 5,000 municipal dwellings were built in the Dublin area alone, an average of 550 a year. In the next six years (1932–8) the Dublin corporation acquired over 1,000 acres of land for housing. In the previous forty-five years, from 1887, only 432 acres had been acquired. Housing was a major priority for the newly formed Irish state. In 1939 2,336 dwellings, with gardens, were built, bringing the average for almost two decades to over 1,000 per year. Quality was not ignored in the drive for quantity. At an early stage it became a matter of policy to introduce hot-water systems and baths, even though critics alleged that the latter were put to uses for which they were not intended.

[29] Terence de Vere White, *The story of the Royal Dublin Society* (Tralee, 1955), p. 191.
[30] Below, p. 603.

Here again there were signs that Ireland was open to continental influences. The *Irish Builder* had noted Amsterdam's international housing congress held in 1913, and twelve years later President Cosgrave himself suggested that the new Dublin housing architect, Herbert Simms, and others, should visit Dutch cities to inspect the different systems of domestic construction there (the Dutch were very progressive at this time in housing design). Subsequently, when the first four-storey blocks of flats to replace the Georgian slum tenements were built in Dublin, they showed strong traces of Dutch influence, particularly in such matters as balconies and entrances. Good examples are the Watling Street and Poplar Row flats of 1938.[31] Simms also introduced the system known as 'decanting', whereby tenants were temporarily evacuated from slum tenements, the tenements demolished, blocks of new flats built, and the evacuated tenants rehoused in the new flats.

THE new style was considered particularly appropriate for building types that did not enjoy a long tradition of architectural style. In the nineteenth century, buildings such as railway terminals had posed this problem. It was solved elegantly by making them look like Italianate *loggie*, renaissance palaces, or Egyptian temples (as exemplified in three Dublin stations, Harcourt Street, Kingsbridge, and Broadstone). The same approach was made in the twentieth century to theatres and cinemas down to the 1930s. It was then found that the new style, with its air of functional efficiency and cleanliness, its simplicity and unpretentiousness, and above all its modernity, was more appropriate to those types of buildings that aspired to modernity: factories, offices, cinemas, stations (whether train or bus), and even hospitals. The most important example of the new style was the Dublin airport terminal, designed in 1937 by a team under the direction of Desmond FitzGerald, and completed in 1940: the design has been called 'a mature and elegant exercise, in the same league as the best of contemporary European architecture'.[32] Another success was Michael Scott's bus terminal in Dublin, Áras Mhic Diarmada (Busárus), designed in the 1940s and completed in 1953. (Scott went on to win the queen's award at the Royal Institute of British Architects.)

The hospital-building programme of the 1930s exhibited the constructional energy of the new state and its openness to advanced European ideas. In an address in 1933 to the Royal Institute of the Architects of Ireland the then minister for local government and public health, Seán T. O'Kelly, praised Alvar Aalto's Paimio sanitorium in Finland; and Vincent Kelly, the architect in charge of the hospital programme, was sent to study hospital buildings in Europe. In under four months he visited sixty-five hospitals in eight coun-

---

[31] Rothery, *Ire. & the new architecture*, p. 19.   [32] Ibid., p. 21.

tries.[33] Meanwhile, in 1930, the Irish Hospitals Sweepstake was inaugurated.[34] A third of its profits—a considerable sum in those days—was set aside to fund the building of hospitals. Mullingar (opened April 1936) was the first hospital opened since 1904, and was followed by twelve new county hospitals in the next five years.[35] By this means the new style became familiar across the country.

The first factory in the modern idiom was the alcohol factory at Carrickmacross, County Monaghan (1938, J. D. Postma). After the second world war a prize-winning factory for the Aspro company at Inchicore, Dublin (designed by a British architect, Alan Hope), was built (1949). By then factories in the new style were not only efficient and bright, with extensive use of glass and steel: they were aesthetically pleasing and impressive (though they may sometimes have looked incongruous in rural areas). In the 1960s two factories in Dundalk, both by Ronald Tallon, won prizes from the Royal Institute of the Architects of Ireland: the General Electricity Company factory (1964), which won a gold medal, and Carroll's factory (1967).

Banks were slower to adopt the new idiom, perhaps because they thought it lacked *gravitas*. In the 1970s two imposing buildings were commissioned: the Bank of Ireland head office (1972–9, R. Tallon) and the Central Bank (1975, Sam Stephenson). The first is a sensitive and imposing adaptation of the style of Mies van der Rohe to Georgian Dublin. The second is a piece of virtuosity where great, apparently unsupported, spans are achieved by suspending the different floors from cables tied back, at roof level, to the central core. The latter, and Stephenson's Bord na Móna headquarters, wrapped in a wall of glass (1979), go some way to excuse him for the offence caused to Dubliners by the façade he designed for the E.S.B. offices in Lower Fitzwilliam Street in 1969, and the Wood Quay civic offices of 1976. Even his bank was controversial: its height disturbed the skyline of Dublin.[36]

Cinemas, being a new building type, enthusiastically embraced the new architecture, art deco as happily as the more austere International style. Rothery sees the new cinemas of the 1930s in Belfast and neighbourhood (and particularly the work of J. McBride Neill, such as the Curzon in Belfast and the Tonic in Bangor) as more International style than the Dublin cinemas such as the art deco Theatre Royal, the largest cinema in Ireland (which was further compromised by an 'atmospheric' interior of gothic arches). But Jones & Kelly's Green Cinema in Dublin had a distinguished International style

[33] Ibid., p. 18; Hugh Campbell, 'Irish identity and the architecture of the new state' in Becker, Olley, & Wang, *20th-century architecture*, pp 83–8: 86.

[34] 1930/12 (4 June 1930); made permanent by 1933/18 (27 July 1933).

[35] Rothery, *Ire. & the new architecture*, pp 144–8; Campbell, 'Irish identity and the architecture of the new state', p. 86.

[36] His partner Arthur Gibney designed the prize-winning Irish Management Institute building at Sandyford, south of Dublin (1971–4).

façade, and Michael Scott applied the lessons of contemporary Dutch architecture at the Ritz in Athlone in 1938.[37]

Between 1962 and 1973 the various buildings associated with R.T.É (R. Tallon) were erected. Even the higher culture succumbed to the new style with the Ulster Museum extension (1963–71, Francis Pym). For the most part, owing to lack of resources, new cultural buildings were adaptations of existing buildings. In 1967 an art gallery was established in the restored Kilkenny Castle and in 1981 the great hall of University College Dublin in Earlsfort Terrace was converted into the national concert hall, both by the office of public works. Meanwhile, there were plans to restore the Royal Hospital, Kilmainham, and convert it into a cultural centre, which were realised in 1986. The architectural activity of the 1960s to the 1980s responded to increased patronage from such bodies as art galleries. It may also reflect the financial advantages of joining the culturally aware European Economic Community.

Another sphere that took to the modern form, if hesitatingly, was the educational, and at all levels. R. S. Wilshere pioneered an innovative if cautious approach in the twenty-six schools he designed between 1926 and 1939 for the Belfast corporation. His McQuiston memorial school (now the school of music) of 1935–6 is notable. Rothery sees this educational programme as exceptional in public patronage in Northern Ireland, where the government tended to favour instead the neo-classicism of Thornely's Stormont or West's law courts. Governments in the south, on the contrary, he sees as more open to the introduction of modern architecture.[38] We have seen this in the hospital building and (at local level) in the new housing in Dublin. It was also manifested in the new vocational schools, if only in their stripped classicism and art deco flourishes. Robinson, Keefe's technical school, Marino, Dublin (1935–6), was a fine example until spoiled by recent alterations.

The 1960s was a pivotal decade in the development of Irish architectural consciousness. It was mainly the universities that led the way, followed before long by private schools such as Wesley College and Alexandra College (Dublin; M. Hogan of Ryan & Hogan). Others were to follow in the 1970s. The Trinity College Berkeley Library (1967) by Paul Koralek, a British architect who had won the competition for the building, set the pace. Whether or not his 'brutal' (i.e. untreated concrete) architecture will survive, it was fashionable at the time and seemed, in a curious way, to fit in with the college's eighteenth- and nineteenth-century masterpieces. In 1970 an arts building (Andrzej Wejchert) and restaurant (Robin Walker, of Scott, Tallon, Walker) for University College Dublin were completed on the new campus at Belfield, and in 1972 the administrative building (Wejchert) and the

---

[37] Rothery, *Ire. & the new architecture*, pp 186–95.   [38] Ibid., pp 153–5.

library (Spence Partners) were added. In 1980 the new arts building at Trinity College (Koralek) was built.

Outside Dublin, examples of the modern form included a new extension at University College Galway (1971, R. Tallon, of Scott, Tallon, Walker), the National Institute for Higher Education at Limerick, and the Sir William Whitla Hall, Queen's University, Belfast (1939–49, John McGeagh).

If modernist architecture was regarded as suitable for hospitals, factories, and the like, and even for ancient institutions of learning, there were doubts among some of the clergy about its suitability for ecclesiastical buildings. Traditional styles, principally byzantine, but also gothic and renaissance, persisted into the 1950s: the Church of St Francis of Assisi, Cork (1951, Jones & Kelly), and of the Immaculate Virgin Mary, Clonskeagh, Dublin (1958, Jones & Kelly). The latter's design was chosen in preference to those by the premium winners in a competition. Two fine cathedrals in traditional styles had also been built, both by Ralph Byrne: Mullingar (1936) and Kilmore in Cavan town (1946). In 1930 F. G. Hicks won a prize for his Italianate Church of St Thomas, Cathal Brugha Street, Dublin. The last major manifestation of traditionalism was Galway cathedral (1965, J. J. Robinson). Two churches in the north Dublin suburbs by Robinson, Keefe could be regarded as marking a transition to the modern: Christ the King, Cabra (1933), and Corpus Christi, Drumcondra (1941).

The first church in the modern idiom was designed in 1927 by an American, Barry Byrne of Chicago, who had been with Frank Lloyd Wright from 1902 to 1908 (that is, during Wright's first profoundly significant phase), and erected at Turner's Cross, Cork. It created a sensation and was compared to a cinema. There was then a long gap till the next, Holy Rosary, Ennis Road, Limerick (1951, Corr & McCormick). In 1953 Corr & McCormick built their next church in Ennistymon, County Clare, after winning the first competition (1947) for a modern church. Then followed a succession of modern churches in a great variety of imaginative shapes from the rectilinear to the round, from the flat-roofed to intersecting roofs. Among the highly praised are St Brigid's, Curragh Camp (1959, G. McNicholl); Corpus Christi, Knockanure, County Kerry (1964, R. Tallon of Scott, Tallon, Walker); St Dominic's, Athy, County Kildare (1965, Thompson, Partners); the prize-winning St Aengus, Burt, County Donegal (1965, L. McCormick); and Christ Prince of Peace, Fossa, County Kerry (1977–9, McCormick, Partners).

It should be noted that the spate of church building since the early 1950s, as against the paucity of new churches in the 1920s and 1930s, reflects the rise in prosperity over the period. Many of these churches were built in rural areas and small towns. Moreover, their design, layout, and decor reflects the advance in Ireland of the liturgical movement, especially after the second Vatican council.

THE first two decades after independence witnessed the consolidation of a home-based Irish painting and an attempt to give a distinctive expression to Irish landscape and the Irish way of life. Though Irish artists still worked in Britain, and most spent some time on the Continent, almost all returned to settle in Ireland. John Butler Yeats died in 1922, but his son Jack survived till 1957. Jack's style had recently altered. For one thing, he was painting in oils rather than water-colours or ink. His paint was smooth, cool, and delicate. In an oblique way he conveyed the momentous events in Irish history that had taken place in the years before independence, starting with 'Bachelor's Walk—In memory' (1915)—a flower girl dropping a rose where civilians were shot down after the gun-running at Howth.[39] This was followed by 'The funeral of Harry Boland' (1922) and 'Communicating with prisoners' (1924). At about this time Yeats's style changed again. It has been variously described as expressionistic, romantic, visionary, and painterly. What is certain is that he began to use paint freely and loosely, often leaving the viewer at a loss not only to understand what the picture was meant to signify, but also to recognise the figures. Typical of these pictures are 'A race in Hy Brazil' (1937); the more sombre product of war years, 'Tinkers' encampment: the blood of Abel' (1940); a somewhat jollier 'Above the fair' (1946); the mysterious 'On through the silent lands' (1951); and a truly romantic work, based on the poem by Caroline Norton, 'The Arab's farewell to his steed': 'My beautiful, my beautiful!' (1953).

Like Yeats, Sir John Lavery (1856–1941) and Sir William Orpen (1878–1931) were both working in Ireland. Both had been war artists. Orpen was also artist to the Versailles peace conference in 1919 and produced an antiwar picture which, in a revised version, is in the Imperial War Museum, London. Orpen taught in the metropolitan college of art and influenced the generation of Keating, Whelan, and Tuohy. Lavery painted some commemorative pictures ('The lying in state of Michael Collins' (1922)) for the Free State government and designed its bank-notes (his wife was the model for Erin). He settled in County Kilkenny, but by 1920 he had passed his prime, as had Orpen.

Other artists who had reached maturity before 1921 were Mary Swanzy (1882–1978), Paul Henry (1876–1958), Grace Henry (1868–1953), W. J. Leech (1881–1968), and the Ulster painter William Conor (1881–1968). Mary Swanzy was notably cosmopolitan. She was admitted among the avant-garde in Paris as one of themselves, and an English critic spoke of her individual, imaginative brand of cubism as being like illustrations of a disordered dream. In the late 1930s she settled in London, but maintained her links with Ireland. However, it was not till 1968 that she received recognition (at the age of 86) with a retrospective exhibition in Dublin. Paul Henry had

[39] Above, vi, 142–3, 179.

been a student in Paris in the 1890s, and on his return (finding the Dublin art world to be somewhat reactionary) he established the Society of Dublin Painters in 1920 to give young artists a venue at which to show their work. For two decades the Society's gallery displayed the best of avant-garde painting in Ireland. Besides Henry and his wife Grace, early members included Mary Swanzy and Jack Yeats.[40] Through his own work Henry managed to impose his image of the Connemara landscape on the Irish (and foreign) consciousness with his simple formula of clouds rising dramatically from behind mountains of uniform blue reflected in charming lakes. In fact his paintings are far more subtle than their travel-poster version suggests. His wife Grace was possibly the first Irish-based artist to become aware of the cubist movement. There is nothing distinctively Irish in her style, apart from the occasional peasant genre painting. On the whole, Grace Henry reflects an Irish view of continental Europe. Swanzy had done the same and so had Leech. Indeed, Leech settled in England in 1916. He showed regularly at the R.H.A., but beyond that his connections with Ireland were slight. As for William Conor, the poet John Hewitt considered that he should be placed with Paul Henry and Jack Yeats as one of the first to record the people in painterly terms, without the trappings of stage-Irishry. Perhaps, but not without sentimentality; and yet he was a good observer of people, as witness 'The Twelfth' (1918).

The painters in their twenties or early thirties in 1921—such as James Sleator (1885–1950), Seán Keating (1889–1977), Leo Whelan (1892–1956), Charles Lamb (1893–1964), Patrick Tuohy (1894–1930), and Maurice Mac-Gonigal (1900–79)—were not only influenced by Orpen's teaching but had an urge to celebrate independence with a distinctive Irish art, historically, in portraiture, in landscape, and in genre. Few succeeded in a big way; most succeeded in small ways. Keating was the most successful. He dominated Irish painting for two decades when Jack Yeats was too obscure for popular taste. He captured the spirit of Irish nationalism in his romantic portrayal of Aran fishermen and even more so in his fighting men, whether sportsmen ('The Tipperary hurler' (1932)) or gunmen ('Men of the west' (1916) and 'Men of the south' (1922)). He had no time for continental modernism, though by the time he became president of the R.H.A. in 1950 'Living art'[41] was already established and he could only deride it. In short, Keating and his fellows were crypto-socialist-realists. Keating's 'Night's candles are burnt out' (1928–9) has all the ingredients of socialist realism: the family looking to the future, the entrepreneur confronting the armed man, the drinking workman, and the skeleton of times past; the candle age; and the priest, irrelevantly, reading his breviary in the presence of the building of the Shannon hydro-electric scheme.

[40] Kennedy, *Ir. art & modernism*, p. 20.   [41] Below, p. 606.

MacGonigal too could paint socially relevant pictures, such as 'Dockers' (1933–4), showing the men possibly contemplating a strike or just depressed by the depression. Sleator, Whelan, and Tuohy were good portrait painters and they could also capture the lower-middle-class domestic scene. Tuohy's commissioned portrait of James Joyce's father, John Stanislaus (1923–4), is quite a triumph and might have been entitled 'Impatience on the verge of irritability'. Lamb, on the other hand, was more romantic both in his land-scapes and his studies of peasants and fishermen, though less so than Keat-ing, and he had charm. These were the artists who dominated the Irish art scene from independence till the 1940s. They had control of the R.H.A. and of the national college of art. For an artist to achieve recognition he or she had to be admitted to their number or at least exhibit at their annual exhib-ition. The painter who could have led Irish art into the mainstream of Euro-pean painting while preserving a distinctive Irish character was Jack Yeats. But he had just begun to float away on visions of his own. The younger generation of artists influenced by the modernist movement on the Continent were in rebellious mood in the early 1940s. However, before coming to them a word must be said about the White Stag group, which settled in Ireland in 1939.

The group was founded by the Czech émigré Basil Rákóczí (1908–79) and Kenneth Hall (1913–46) in London in 1935 for the study of subjectivity in art and psychology. Both were pacifists, so when war became imminent they moved to Ireland and settled first in County Mayo and later in Dublin, where they held a number of mixed exhibitions in 1940 and gave lectures on creative psychology and also on cubism. In that year they exhibited works by Picasso, Gris, Rouault, Dufy, Gleizes, and other modern painters, as well as works by Evie Hone and Mainie Jellett. Nano Reid and Patrick Scott joined the group in 1941. In 1944 the group held a major exhibition of non-representational art, under the title 'Subjective art'. The critic Herbert Read wrote an introduction to the catalogue and was to have given a lecture, but was mysteriously prevented from doing so (the text was, however, read). The exhibition and Read's text were on the whole well received by the press, which probably marks the acceptance of modernism in art by the Irish public, though the Living Art exhibition of the previous year would probably claim the credit for having laid the foundations. In 1945, the war over, the group dispersed.[42]

The first Irish Exhibition of Living Art (I.E.L.A.), to give it its proper title, was held in Dublin in 1943. Although the artists involved had exhibited at the R.H.A., there had been little enthusiasm for their work. Matters had come to a head in 1942 when Louis le Brocquy, who had exhibited at the

---

[42] For the White Stag group, see Kennedy, *Ir. art & modernism*, ch. 5; Dorothy Walker, *Modern art in Ireland* (Dublin, 1997), ch. 1.

R.H.A. since 1937, had two paintings rejected, on top of one the previous year. One of the pictures, 'The Spanish shawl' (1941), though odd (yet interesting) in its depiction of human relationships, is far from avant-garde. A committee was set up under the chairmanship of Mainie Jellett, consisting of (among others) Evie Hone, Louis le Brocquy, and Norah McGuinness, to establish an alternative to the R.H.A. (Strangely, the president of the R.H.A. was a patron, which should caution against making too much of the divide between the two organisations.) The I.E.L.A. survived into the 1980s. In 1972, true to its spirit, the whole committee resigned and handed over the management to a younger generation with ideas of its own. Living Art (a somewhat pretentious title—all art is living, except the other fellow's) was a genuine alternative to the R.H.A. It not only encouraged young and adventurous artists, even if their work was not always of a high artistic or creative standard; it introduced the public to foreign art. Jellett died the year after the first exhibition, but not before she had struck an appropriate note when addressing young painters and students: 'Let us open our eyes and our minds and form our own honest opinions.'[43] Coming after the solipsistic interwar years, Living Art contributed to that refocusing.

In this context mention should also be made of two other exhibiting bodies, the Ulster Academy (founded in 1920), and An tOireachtas. The former tended to be rather provincial. The latter, primarily an annual Gaelic festival, held an art exhibition from 1941 on. Initially it was dominated by members of the R.H.A., but in later years it broadened its scope and held a balance between the R.H.A. and the I.E.L.A. In 1934 the Ulster Unit was founded as a forum for young artists, often excluded by the Ulster Academy, to meet and exhibit their work. It proved ephemeral, but staged an exhibition in 1934, and was notable for espousing an aesthetic based on contemporary trends.

Even before the I.E.L.A., Victor Waddington was selling modern Irish, British, and continental art in the 1930s. Other Dublin galleries followed: the Dawson (Leo Smith, later Taylor) in the 1940s, Hendriks in the 1950s, and Oliver Dowling's in the 1970s. The artists behind the formation of the I.E.L.A. were, needless to say, trained on the Continent in modernist art, not always of the highest order. However, the first Irish painter to be deeply touched by modernism was May Guinness (1863–1955) who took up painting seriously in her forties and studied in Paris some time between 1905 and 1910. She was much influenced by the *Fauves*, particularly Matisse, and in the 1920s she studied cubism under André Lhôte, returning later to a free form of fauvism. Meanwhile Evie Hone (1894–1955) and Mainie Jellett (1897–1944) had been studying with Lhôte before moving on to the even

---

[43] Mainie Jellett in *Commentary*, May 1942, p. 7, quoted in Kennedy, *Ir. art & modernism*, pp 115–16.

more academic cubist, Albert Gleizes. Jellett persevered in this form of semi-abstraction, which she thought more spiritual than representational painting, and applied it to religious subjects. It certainly lent itself to coloration. On her return to Ireland Jellett became a fervent advocate of cubism. Hone, on the other hand, soon abandoned cubism for a more fluent style much influenced by the paintings of Rouault, which resembled stained glass, to which she soon turned. A fourth student (and they were all of them women) to study under Lhôte was Norah McGuinness (1901–80). Like Hone she soon modified her cubism but retained its ambiguity of perspective. She appropriated Dublin Bay and the Liffey basin as her artistic territory. One other artist temporarily affected by modernism, who later repudiated it, was Harry Kernoff (1900–74). Though an academician and influenced by academicians, his work was individual, never academic.

The next generation, which came to maturity in the 1940s, included Nano Reid (1900–81), Patrick Collins (1910–94), Colin Middleton (1910–83), William Scott (1913–89), Tony O'Malley (1913–), Louis le Brocquy (1916–), Gerard Dillon (1916–71), Derek Hill (1916–2000), George Campbell (1917–79), and Daniel O'Neill (1920–74). Scott was a Scotsman, but he received his artistic education first in Ulster, regularly exhibited in Ireland, and regarded himself as an Irishman. He was a semi-abstract painter with a homely touch, glorying in the outlined essences of eggs, lemons, and kitchen utensils. He had the distinction of a retrospective exhibition at the Tate Gallery in 1972. (Jack Yeats shared the London National Gallery with William Nicholson in 1942.)

If we count Scott and Reid (who was born in Drogheda) as northern, half the artists named above were northerners, and northerners continue to be well represented among Irish painters. John Betjeman compared Reid to the poet John Clare. Whether this was judicious or not, she was one of the most poetic of Irish painters, treating paint and imagery freely, with a lyrical abandon. Middleton, on the other hand, tried out almost every modern style from expressionism through surrealism to Nicholsonian abstraction, where the delicacy of his line rivals Ben Nicholson's. But he is at his most characteristic in visionary or humorous pictures. Humour was also a characteristic of Dillon, whose deceptively simple pictures of rural life are not only subtle compositions but also studies of human estrangement. O'Neill was a strange mixture of realism—childbirth, suckling—and romanticism, with a very distinctive (and weird) sickly, yellow-green tinge on his subjects' faces.

Campbell, though born in County Wicklow, had a diversity of interests and styles that associated him with Ulster painters. Though traditional in style he was accepted by Living Art as one of their own. Collins painted intriguing nudes and semi-abstract landscapes set in a frame within a frame. O'Malley is likewise a semi-abstract landscape painter, though he has produced informal abstractions too. It is not surprising that he made a home for many years in St Ives, Cornwall, where he found a soulmate in the English artist Peter Lanyon.

Of the southern painters of that time le Brocquy was far and away the most successful, gaining an international reputation. After his contretemps with the R.H.A., he was soon elected a member. He was regarded by British critics as a British painter in 1947. In 1956 he won the Premio Prealpina at the Venice Biennale for 'A family' (1951), and in 1958 he was included in '50 ans de l'art moderne' in Brussels. Three characteristics have persisted in his work: a preference for white or grey; the portrayal of the estranged or isolated, from a style of almost abstract forms (Beings or Presences) to heads of famous Irish literary figures (Yeats, Joyce, Beckett) seen through a mist, and finally to disturbing faces ('Heads') seen through glass with blood-stained hands pressed against the glass; and consequential on this, the treatment of humans as objects rather than as persons. Le Brocquy also drew on the imagery of ancient Celtic sculpture, and on imagery inspired by ancient writings such as 'Táin Bó Cúailnge', which (in Thomas Kinsella's translation) he illustrated in 1969. In addition, he designed tapestries, such as 'Adam and Eve in the garden' (1951–2) and 'Allegory' (1950), as well as textiles.

The next generation includes Patrick Scott (1921–), Cecil King (1921–86), Deborah Brown (1927–), Camille Souter (1929–), T. P. Flanagan (1929–), Patrick Pye (1929–), Barrie Cooke (1931–), Anne Madden (1932–), Basil Blackshaw (1932–), and Carmel Mooney (1936–). By now—the late 1950s and early 1960s—the 'new' art had established itself as a distinct tradition, separate from, though not exclusive of, the R.H.A. All these artists exhibited at the I.E.L.A. as a matter of course, though they also exhibited at the R.H.A. They may have used an artistic idiom alien to the academy, but even the academicians would have realised that, up to the 1960s at least, there was something distinctively Irish in their work. This can be illustrated in the progress of Patrick Scott's painting.

Scott had exhibited with the White Stag group, and even then his work was rather abstract. 'The sun' (1964)—a recurring theme—can be seen as a circle and irregular rectangles or as a red sun over fields or strips of bogland. Throughout the 1950s his work continued along these lines, ending in the 'soft-edge' 'Bog' series. The shimmering light over a bog is suggested by soft forms in tempera on unprimed canvas. In 1960 Scott represented Ireland at the Venice Biennale and also won the Guggenheim national award for 'Bog grasses'. Throughout the 1960s his work became more abstract in appearance—lines, squares, circles, and curves—and he began to use gold leaf. But the Irish resonance remained, with suggestions of gold ornaments, and, of course, the sun. Like le Brocquy, Scott designed tapestry.

Another artist who 'turned abstract' in the 1960s was Deborah Brown. She began a delicious series of paintings using free brush-strokes in the early

1960s. Hitherto her work had been semi-abstract. Cecil King, who had come late to art, plunged straight into abstraction of a most severe geometrical kind and remained with it, making elegant variations in shapes and colours. The shapes, however, were not very varied; the circus trapeze was the main inspiration. Anne Madden's work in the 1960s looks abstract, but in fact is based on the forms of clouds hanging over mountains in western Ireland, or ancient Irish monuments such as megaliths.

As for the rest, they were representational artists. Even when their work was semi-abstract, it was clear what they were trying to represent. Camille Souter, English but brought up in Ireland from the age of one, comes the closest to being abstract. But however abstract her pictures seem to be, they capture the essence of her subject—her beloved Calary (County Wicklow) in winter, the view from a window, fish, meat. In 1961 she represented Ireland at the Paris Biennale. Barrie Cooke is also English by birth and spent his early years as an artist in the United States. However, he has made Ireland his home and has captured the lushness of the Nore valley in his semi-abstract landscapes. He is also interested in the more exotic aspects of Irish lore such as the sheela-na-gigs. T. P. Flanagan and Basil Blackshaw, northern Irish painters, are more straightforwardly representational, though still not in the academic, Orpenesque manner. Flanagan's landscapes are subtle and poetic, much admired by Seamus Heaney; Blackshaw's landscapes have a feeling of space achieved by the subtle use of line. He also paints rather unflattering portraits. Mooney at that time painted landscapes and natural objects, such as birds, trees, and flowers, going through cycles from loosely naturalistic through semi-abstract to abstract.

Two other painters from this period stand somewhat apart, but for very different reasons: Patrick Pye because he is, strangely, one of the few Irish painters engaged in religious subjects, his style influenced as much by early Italian as by modern works; and James Dixon (1887–1970) the only Irish primitive painter of note, famous for his versions of life on and around Tory island. He was encouraged, if not influenced, by the English painter Derek Hill, who made Tory his home, and was a painter of expressive portraits.

There were at least three other artists of this period who might not be regarded as in the mainstream of modern art but deserve mention: Patrick Swift (1927–83), Edward McGuire (1932–86), and Patrick Hickey (1927–98). Swift was heavily influenced by Lucien Freud and slightly by Francis Bacon. He was an excellent portraitist, but his most characteristic works were intimate depictions of domestic scenes with plants, birds, and still-life objects. McGuire was a portraitist par excellence. His portraits are realistic, his sitter usually in front of a window, with appropriate background and props. Hickey had the distinction of setting up the Graphic Studio, Dublin, in 1961, with Leslie McWeeney, Anne Yeats, and Liam Miller, and was himself an outstanding lithographer. He represented Ireland at many print biennales. He was also a painter in oils and watercolours, particularly of landscapes, which sometimes have a lugubrious look that suits his choice of colour.

Graphics have become a feature of Irish pictorial art since the founding of the Graphic Studio (1962). The studio is both a facility for printmakers and a training institution, not just for art students but also for established professional painters, who are encouraged to learn the various techniques of printmaking (except for silk-screen). Besides obtaining support from the arts council, the studio encourages sponsorship (in return for prints). The result is that a great number of Irish painters have also been printmakers, which made sense for a country with limited financial resources. One of the prominent figures in the studio from 1982 till her premature death was American-born Mary Farl Powers (1948–92).

In the 1960s there appeared what developed into a national institution, the international exhibition 'Rosc'. It was the brain-child of Michael Scott and the American critic and museum director J. J. Sweeney, and was unique among international exhibitions. It did not compare or compete with the exhibitions of contemporary art held in Venice, Kassel, Paris, or São Paulo, yet it attracted the leading living artists. The idea was that an international jury should choose the best work produced by fifty artists in the four years prior to the exhibition. The first exhibition was held in 1967, and between then and 1980 three more were held. Rosc gave a great boost to art in Ireland for both artists and the public. But, like so many artistic ventures in Ireland, it was not without its share of controversy: in this case, over the expense, and the exclusion of Irish artists. The latter issue was eventually resolved. Under the chairmanship of P. J. Murphy the Guinness Hop Store was obtained as one of the venues for Rosc, commencing in 1984. Rosc continued to bring international art to Dublin till the late 1980s, since when its role has been taken over by the Irish Museum of Modern Art (1991).[44]

A more direct boost for contemporary Irish art came in the form of institutional patronage. Although this was not new, the spread of modernist architecture in the 1960s and 1970s was accompanied by a greater propensity on the part of institutions such as universities, commercial firms, and especially banks, to commission and sometimes to collect such work. One such collection, which began to be built up by the Bank of Ireland in the early 1970s, was of exceptional importance for its time and as an example of corporate patronage.[45] Items from the collection are frequently exhibited abroad. Both painting and sculpture have benefited from such patronage.

By the 1960s Irish artists were well and truly under the influence of international trends and fashions, though they retained their Irish individuality.

[44] Walker, *Modern art in Ire.*, pp 133–8.
[45] Edward McParland, 'The bank and the visual arts' in F. S. L. Lyons (ed.), *Bicentenary essays: Bank of Ireland 1783–1983* (Dublin, 1983), pp 97–139: 129–34.

Of this generation one can name Brian Bourke (1936–), Roy Johnston (1936–), David Crone (1937–), Micheal Farrell (1940–2000), Theo McNab (1940–), Robert Ballagh (1943–), Sean Scully (1945–), and Tim Goulding (1945–).

Bourke is a very individual painter, sometimes self-mocking, often sombre in his landscapes and unflattering in his portraits. He has been described as a nihilist; if so, he is one with a sense of humour as well as of the absurd. In 1965 he represented Ireland at the Paris Biennale. Johnston, by contrast, is an abstract artist working with paint, reliefs, formed canvases, and free-standing pieces. He likes to work with permutations of forms ('systems'), often monochrome and yet sensuous. Johnston, though an Ulster painter, reflects none of the turmoil in the province. Crone reflects it very vividly. He has evolved a style that conveys the devastation to lives and property: the compositions themselves appear to disintegrate. Farrell too refers to the 'troubles' in various ways. In his 'Pressé' series the spurting fruit juice is cleverly transformed to suggest the spurting of blood. He has also presented the state of Ireland symbolically and satirically as Miss O'Murphy, mistress of Louis XV, after the painting by Boucher. Though his work until the mid 1970s was mostly abstract, it embodied Celtic motifs. Farrell has exhibited in international collective exhibitions in Europe and the United States, where he has won prizes. He is a printmaker and has designed tapestries. McNab is a graphic artist, as well as a painter; he also works in reliefs. His work is abstract, sensuous, and explores the perception of space. He too has repre-sented Ireland abroad.

Ballagh is a socially and politically motivated artist, self-taught, whose work is largely representational. Paradoxically, what instruction he received (from Micheal Farrell) was in abstract painting. He paints with wit and humour, producing pastiches of the masters, some with political import, such as 'Liberty at the barricades' (1971; after Delacroix) or 'The third of May' (1970; after Goya)—both of which are in print form to reach a wide public. Not surprisingly, he is attracted to the wit of Sterne and has done a series on Tristram Shandy. Even less surprisingly he is preoccupied with the state of the nation, but obliquely, like Farrell. His 'Miami murders' (1976) is a picture of a framed photograph of the Miami showband, three of whom were killed in County Down returning to the Republic from a concert—the glass is shattered by a bullet.

Ballagh might be loosely described as a pop artist; certainly his aim is populist. Goulding too fits into that category, at least in some of his phases, best reflected in his banners. Like Ballagh and so many Irish artists of this period he is largely self-taught, and like him has had considerable success abroad, but nothing like the success of Sean Scully. Scully, though spending most of his life abroad, has never severed his links with Ireland. His paint-ings are abstract, cool, and elegant in form and colour; they quietly assert themselves in any company. He has taught in British art schools and at Harvard. Among his many awards, he won the John Moore (Liverpool) prize, the only Irishman in our period to do so.

As to the next generation, it would be foolish to make firm predictions. Nevertheless, some artists born in the 1950s or just before, who deserve mention as showing promise and having fulfilled it by the 1980s, include Ciarán Lennon (1947–), Martin Gale (1949–), John Aiken (1950–), Charles Tyrrell (1950–), Felim Egan (1952–), and Brian Henderson (1952–) (Aiken, a sculptor, and Egan are from Northern Ireland). With the exceptions of Gale (who has a predilection for painting the bovine) and Henderson (whose work in the 1970s reflected an interest in Gaelic ecology), the others fitted in to the latest phase of the international modernist tradition. By 1980 they had just begun to gain international recognition at 'A sense of Ireland', a group of exhibitions held in London that year.

Thus within the space of sixty years Irish painting had transformed itself from a British- and continental-orientated school (though with very definite Irish characteristics) into an insular, nationalistic school, and had finally broken free of both. It can be said that painting, like literature, reflects the mind of the society in which it is produced more directly than either sculpture or architecture. Whether this is a valid generalisation or not, it is true of Irish painting from 1921 to the early 1980s. The early part of our period (with exceptions, of course) reflected the perfectly understandable inward-looking attitude of Irish patriots who had won freedom and could take their place freely among the nations of the earth. But, in painting at least, this bred insularity among gifted painters who may have thought that they had established an Irish school of painting that would survive developments on the Continent. Other painters saw that, notwithstanding the insularity of many politicians, they could not ignore what was going on in the outside world. And the great Rosc exhibitions and the successes of Irish artists abroad must surely have broadened the Irish consciousness.

As for sculpture, in 1921 many of the older generation were still very active. In 1936 Oliver Sheppard (1865–1941) could still produce a noble bust of Patrick Pearse, which graces Dáil Éireann. He also designed two medals for the Tailteann games, held in 1924 and 1928 to promote sport in the Free State, and named after the ancient Irish festival Óenach Tailten. His greatest triumph was when his 'The death of Cú Chulainn' (1911–12), a Rodinesque masterpiece, was installed in the G.P.O. to commemorate the rising of 1916.[46]

The memorial to 1916 by Albert Power (1881–1945) in Limerick (1919–39) was not so successful, but his bust of W. B. Yeats (1939) admirably captures the intellectual intensity of the man. He produced a charming statue

---

[46] Above, vi, 488, and plate 42.

of Pádraic Ó Conaire (1935) for Galway. However, he was more at home with natural objects such as trout jumping ('Leenane, Connemara trout', 1944). Jerome Connor (1876–1943) was of the same generation. Though he earned his reputation in the United States he came to Ireland in 1925 to work on the *Lusitania* memorial for Cobh, but went bankrupt. A memorial to the insurrection of 1798 for Tralee, 'Pikeman' or 'Croppy boy', was left to Power to complete. Meanwhile, up to his death, he was doing 'little pieces of free work' that had a vitality lacking in his commissions.

Another homecoming took place in 1939 when Andrew O'Connor (1874–1941) arrived to make a statue of Daniel O'Connell for the National Bank of Ireland, 34 College Green, Dublin (now a branch of the Bank of Ireland). He was an American of Scottish parentage, but claimed Irish ancestry. He was held in high esteem in the United States for his monumental sculpture. He had made a maquette for a monument to Commodore John Barry (a version of which stands in Wexford harbour) with a frieze of 'The sufferings of Ireland' (1906). The O'Connell statue was finished in the year of arrival, and while owing much to Rodin's 'Balzac', it is worthy of the Liberator. Another commission for Ireland was at first to have been a war memorial for the victims of the first world war. However, by popular request it was changed into a 'Monument to Christ the King', as a testimony to catholic fidelity to the ancestral faith. It was intended to be placed overlooking Dún Laoghaire harbour, the then 'gateway to Ireland'. The maquette was exhibited in Paris in 1926; but, though the monument was cast, it was not installed till much later, and it now stands in a garden overlooking the harbour. It is exceptional in that it depicts Christ in three phases of the Crucifixion. First in desolation, the expiring Christ; the consoling Christ with his arms outstretched; and, on the third side, Christ triumphant, upright on the cross. O'Connor died in Ireland, and it is a pity he could not have lived to see his monument erected. But, perhaps, it was too advanced for the times in Ireland (and possibly still is).

A sculptor who has been somewhat neglected except in his native Cork but deserves recognition is Joseph Higgins (1885–1925). He was a modernist before his time, in so far as he grasped the importance of the material in which he worked and did not attempt to disguise it but drew out its potentials for his creative purposes. This is well demonstrated in his head of Michael Collins (1922), where the handling of the wood brings out the strength of character of the man.

As often happens in art we have to skip a generation before coming again to artists of substance. All the sculptors to be discussed from now on came to maturity after 1921. Of those born at the turn of the century, two stand out. One is F. E. McWilliam (1909–92) from Ulster. He was the first Irish sculptor to understand the modern movement in sculpture. He spent most of his working life in Britain but never broke his links with Ireland, where he regularly exhibited. In 1964 he was awarded an honorary doctorate by the Queen's University of Belfast, and was made a fellow of University College London in 1971. He also achieved international recognition, exhibiting in international exhibitions and being represented in foreign galleries at a time when no other Irish sculptor was heard of, even so near home as on the Isle of Man. He tended to follow the fashions, more so than most 'British' sculptors. He oscillated between the surreal and the abstract, but even his abstract was in a way surreal. His contact with his native Ulster was manifested in his 'Women of Belfast' series, vivid portraits of women contorted by bomb blasts (1972).

Nobody could have been more different from McWilliam than his contemporary Séamus Murphy (1907–75), born in County Cork. Apart from studies in Paris, his career was confined to Ireland. His work was hardly touched by modernism. He was primarily a stonemason, a carver of monuments, as he claims in his book *Stone mad*. But he made some fine sculpture, particularly portrait busts.

The next generation includes Oisín Kelly (1915–81), Hilary Heron (1923–77), Laurence Campbell (1911–64), and Friedrich Herkner (1902–86). Kelly, like Murphy, claimed to be nothing more than a craftsman. A craftsman he certainly was. He was master of his materials, which were very varied. He chose simple subjects—country people, birds, cattle. His one major sculpture was 'The children of Lir' (1966) in the Garden of Remembrance, Parnell Square, Dublin. Hilary Heron also embraced the modernist emphasis on 'truth to materials', but for a different reason from Kelly, to whom it came naturally. For Heron, it was part of the modern movement, with which she came in contact in the late 1940s. She worked mostly in wood, though her 'Crazy Jane' series, a humorous, semi-abstract interpretation of Yeats's poems, is in metal. Most of her work is semi-abstract, though she also produced fine portraits, such as her 'James Connolly' of 1946. Laurence Campbell might be said to have captured the spirit of modernism rather than being a strict modernist. His formalised style, with telling touches of realism, is illustrated in his memorial to Seán Heuston (1943) in the Phoenix Park, Dublin. Friedrich Herkner, an Austrian, who taught for years at the National College, was more modernist in that he was more abstract than Campbell (the continental as against the Irish approach, perhaps); take, for example, his 'Mother Éire' (1939) for the New York world fair.

Modernist sculpture in its fully abstract form was brought to Ireland by Gerda Frömel (1931–75), a Czech, who had studied in Germany and, understandably, did not wish to return to her native country in the 1950s. In 1956 she settled in Ireland and practised a form of abstraction tempered with suggestions of ancient tradition. This blended well with Irish sculpture of the time. Two other Irish sculptors of the same period also studied in Germany: Edward Delaney (1930–   ) and Ian Stuart (1926–   ). Delaney never absorbed the modern idiom. He has remained figurative in a traditional twentieth-century manner, dating from Rodin and Brosseau, of loosely handling metal. He has adorned Dublin with intriguing monuments to Thomas Davis in College Green and Wolfe Tone at one corner of St Stephen's Green. Stuart started as a figurative sculptor working in wood. His subjects were, for the most part, religious. In the late 1950s his work became more abstract and he turned to metal and painted wood. In the 1960s he entered a phase of minimalism (the reduction of sculpture to very simple shapes, repeated and spaced in order to build up a composition) under the influence of American sculptors, principally David Smith. He began to make monumental works, some to be set in the open, of polished aluminium or painted plywood. Stuart won many prizes and exhibited abroad. He was for a long time the foremost Irish sculptor.

Both Stuart and Delaney influenced the next generation of Irish sculptors. Stuart influenced Brian King (1942–   ) and Michael Bulfin (1939–   ); Delaney influenced John Behan (1938–   ). Early on, King was a minimalist (he has subsequently gone in other directions). His minimalism has been compared to the music of Bach, which is not a far-fetched comparison. He thinks in terms of mass and space, of objects and the intervals between them, and the resulting rhythms. In this he is quintessentially a sculptor. During the vogue for 'earth art' he carved the actual landscape in the Dublin mountains into geometrical shapes with the precision he brought to his other sculpture. In 1969, at the age of 27, he won the major award of the exhibition at the Paris Biennale, the first Irishman to do so. In 1972 he became the first president of the newly constituted committee of the Irish Exhibition of Living Art.

Bulfin too is an abstract sculptor, but not a minimalist. His sculpture owes something to the imagery of science and technology, to physical links more than to pertinent gaps and intervals, as in the early work of Brian King. In 1970 he represented Ireland at the Paris Biennale. If, by the late 1960s, Irish sculptors were in the mainstream of international art, and recognised as being so, they could also use modernised versions of traditional modes. John Behan's work combines both approaches. For instance, his mother-and-child theme appears in a range of styles from the semi-abstract manner of Moore to near-constructivism. The same is true of the bull series, but here the range extends from the representational noble bull (1967) through an angry abstract bull (1969) to a serene and dignified one (1979). Behan is also a painter, draughtsman, and printmaker, and his works in these media exhibit the same range of styles as the sculpture.

An artist who belongs to this period, if not to this generation, is Deborah Brown. She came late to sculpture—as did Behan. Her structures are made of fibreglass and look like foam or cloud. They are more than reliefs and less than sculpture in the round. In 1972 she interlaced some of her work with barbed wire; in the Irish artist's tradition of oblique political comment, from Jack Yeats through Farrell, Crone, Ballagh, and countless others, this was her reflection on 'the troubles'.

In the early 1980s sculpture was thriving in Ireland. There were plenty of up-and-coming sculptors such as Clifford Rainey, Michael Warren, and John Burke. Outdoor exhibitions of art were held in public places and attracted wide interest. Though modest and often humorous public sculpture cropped up here and there, of varying degrees of quality (and even comprehensibility—rough-hewn boulders were popular), there were few monumental works. The insurrections of 1798 and 1916–21 had already been commemorated, while the Irish who died in the two world wars were largely ignored except in Northern Ireland; as noted above, Lutyens's memorial gardens outside Dublin were not restored till the 1980s.[47] Even church commissions, which had been favourable to sculptors in the 1960s and 1970s, as being in the spirit of the liturgical movement, were scarcer. One sculptor who produced most of her work for churches was German-born Imogen Stuart. Her simplified style can be most expressive, as in the stations of the cross in the Church of the Redeemer, Dundalk. But if church commissions were fewer, sculpture itself was flourishing. It was adventurous. Neither blindly following international trends nor subservient to nationalist pressures—though receptive (as was painting) to the political situation in which the whole island, not just Northern Ireland, found itself—it went a way of its own.

This can best be illustrated in the works of Michael Craig-Martin (1941–) and James Coleman (1934–). They have many things in common. They have both spent most of their active life abroad but have maintained their links with Ireland (where both were born, one in Dublin, the other in Roscommon). In a way they are not sculptors (they do not sculpt, though they put things together), yet nor are they painters. They inhabit a no-man's-land. Craig-Martin's work uses objects, such as glasses of water, which he may or may not have made—that is irrelevant. He occasionally paints ordinary things, such as spoons, of vast dimensions, on walls. Coleman is even more eccentric. In the late 1960s he was producing what may be called dynamic works, as, for example, 'Cubes' (1969): about a dozen cubes dancing frenetically in a small space. But his work, like so many others, has political implications, reflecting the times. His 'Strongbow' (1978) consisted of a replica of the effigy on the tomb of the invader of Ireland, behind which stood a television screen with two hands, one green, the other orange, clapping in varying tempos while those of Strongbow remain clasped and

---

[47] A campaign for a memorial to merchant seamen who died in the second world war was commenced about 1970 by the Maritime Institute of Ireland. It was hampered by lack of funds, but two decades later a memorial had been erected on City Quay, Dublin.

tranquil. Three-dimensional art of this kind is neither stagnant nor unrelated to its Irish roots.

As with painting, we have seen that in the sixty years since independence Irish sculpture had passed, after a rather insular and nationalistic phase, to a broader, more international style. Without developing a national style—and what nation does nowadays, in sculpture, at least?—it has maintained its contacts with Irish sculptural tradition and with contemporary events.

AT the time of independence stained glass in Ireland was thriving. An Túr Gloine (Sarah Purser's studios) and the Harry Clarke and Thomas Earley studios, as well as others, were active.[48] Clarke (1889–1931) made a charming window for a private house, illustrating various episodes from Keats's 'The eve of St Agnes' (1924). He also produced windows for the Oblate Fathers in Raheny, County Dublin, and for the catholic church at Ballinrobe, County Mayo. In 1928 he produced eight more for the Jesuit Fathers' retreat house at Rathfarnham, Dublin (now in the catholic cathedral, Tullamore, County Offaly). Between 1928 and 1930 he completed a major work, the 'Geneva window', illustrating fourteen scenes from Irish literature. It was intended for the League of Nations building in Geneva but was never installed. After a sojourn in the municipal gallery, Dublin, it went to America.

Michael Healy (1873–1941) was also busy completing his brilliant series of ten windows (some three-light) for the cathedral at Loughrea, County Galway. He continued this work till shortly before his death. Meanwhile, between 1915 and 1930 he produced three windows for the church of St Catherine and St James, Donore Avenue, Dublin, including the fascinating and majestic 'St Victor'. In 1925 he created five windows for the convent, Ballyhaunis, County Mayo—the west of Ireland, home of Edward Martyn,[49] has many good examples of Irish stained glass. Healy had produced an early window for the college chapel of Clongowes Wood, County Kildare, in 1916 and another in 1920. In 1936 he was commissioned to produce a series of the 'Seven dolours of Our Lady'. He had finished three before his death. The others were completed by Evie Hone, adapting her style as far as she could to his, but no greater immediate contrast of styles in Irish stained glass is to be found.

Healy, along with Clarke, belonged to what might be called the Beardsley school of illustration, in which colouring was broken down into small areas outlined in black. Clarke used this method to great effect in his illustrations of fairy tales. A similar effect is produced in stained glass by what is known as aciding. Hone and, before her, Wilhelmina Geddes (1887–1955) used more traditional methods of handling glass. Thanks to the efforts of Nicola Gordon Bowe, Geddes is coming to be recognised for the considerable artist she was. One reason for her neglect is that most of her work is overseas.

[48] Above, vi, 473, 491–3.   [49] Above, vi, 490–91.

What is in Ireland is confined mainly to Northern Ireland. She worked in An Túr Gloine till 1922, when she had to leave Ireland because of ill-health. She settled in London and continued working till the 1930s. Of her works in Ireland there is the original and dazzling 'The leaves of the tree were for the healing of the nations' in St John's Church of Ireland church, Malone Road, Belfast.[50]

We have already considered Evie Hone's career as painter. When she tired of the cubism of Lhôte and Gleizes, she turned to stained glass, and it might be said of Hone that she restored stained glass to its original medieval splendour. She had been attracted to it, not only by a study of the windows of the great French cathedrals, but also by her admiration for the painting of Georges Rouault. Rouault was the son of a stained-glass-maker and his works look like cartoons for stained-glass panels. In 1935, having worked in Geddes's studios in London, Hone was admitted to the Purser studios. There she was greatly helped by Healy, and later she set up a studio of her own at Rathfarnham. Initially influenced by French glass, she came to assimilate the imagery of Irish medieval carvings. Her major works include five windows each for the Jesuit house, Tullabeg, County Offaly (1946), and for the University Hall chapel in Hatch Street, Dublin (1947). The Tullabeg windows (now in the Jesuit house at Manresa, Clontarf, County Dublin)—four scenes from the gospels and the Sacred Heart with Jesuit saints—are among her finest works. There are four fine windows in the catholic church at Kingscourt, County Cavan. But the height of Hone's achievement is the chancel window in Eton College chapel (1949–52), completed shortly before her death. It was a huge undertaking, a nine-light window, with the main themes the Crucifixion, above, and the Last Supper, below.[51]

Another member of An Túr Gloine who deserves mention is Hubert V. McGoldrick (1897–1967). The early 1920s was a time when memorial windows for the victims of various wars were in demand. In his first commission, for the Church of Ireland church at Gowran, County Kilkenny—said to be his best work—McGoldrick catered for this need with great sensitivity and compassion, with a window entitled 'Sorrow and joy' (1920). He also contributed a fine window to Loughrea catholic cathedral and to the Muckross Dominican convent in Dublin. Ill-health forced him to give up work in glass in 1953, but he contributed to a rare form of glass mosaic (with large pieces, rather than tesserae) known as *opus sectile*.

Sarah Purser died in 1943, and An Túr Gloine as a cooperative was dissolved in 1944. However, McGoldrick and Catherine (Kitty) O'Brien, who had taken over the running of it in 1940, kept on the studios and rented

---

[50] Nicola Gordon Bowe, David Caron, and Michael Wynne, *Gazetteer of Irish stained glass* (Blackrock, Dublin, 1988), pp 24–5, 100–02.

[51] See also Walker, *Modern art in Ire.*, pp 27–30.

them out until O'Brien (who owned them) died in 1963. Among those who rented the studios were Patrick Pollen (who later bought them) and Patrick Pye. They kept on the tradition of modern Irish stained glass, even if the heroic days had passed. Earley's studios continued to flourish till the late 1960s, and Clarke's closed in 1973. Overall, the impact of Irish stained glass has been considerable, not only in Ireland and Britain but in North America, Australia, and New Zealand.[52]

[52] Bowe, Caron, & Wynne, *Gazetteer*, p. 24.

CHAPTER XXI

Music in independent Ireland since 1921

ONE of the most stirring and memorable phrases in 'The minstrel boy' is
that in which the warrior bard unhesitatingly proclaims in bold crotchets the
'land of song'. The combination of national sentiment and pride in a singular
musical heritage found in these vigorous verses by Thomas Moore is telling.
The ten volumes of lyric verse with musical settings by Sir John Stevenson
that Moore published between 1807 and 1834 had found wide favour in
polite society on both sides of the Irish Sea; and while their musical value
was viewed with increasing disdain by subsequent generations of musicians,
their success in focusing attention on Ireland's rich treasure of folksong was
never in doubt. The fruits of Moore's labours, along with the burgeoning
interest in cultural archaeology to which the poet was beholden, advanced the
notion of the Irish as a nation of people especially gifted in musical expression. Indeed, the excellence of the musical heritage contributed significantly
to the cultural arguments in favour of Ireland's separate nationhood. The
store of traditional song was adequate corroboration of the country's claim to
be regarded among the most musically endowed of the western world; the
testimony was sufficiently strong for the claim to be accepted without reservation. Thus it is all the more surprising to recognise the penurious condition of the art on the eve of the realisation of independent statehood. This
sorry circumstance was at variance with the proud assertion to be the 'land of
song'.

The debilitated condition that the art revealed in 1921 offers, in microcosm, an interesting reflection of a broader national picture. The conflicts
within Irish society found echo in a fractured musical tradition. Just as the
heterogeneous composition of the society gave the lie to claims of racial
unity, so also did the two distinct principal musical practices deny the proposal that Ireland was united in its musical expression.[1] The music of Gaelic

---

[1] The terms 'Gaelic' and 'European' are used as a convenient pairing to distinguish these
two radically different musical impulses.

Ireland was the more celebrated of the two, being valued particularly for its characteristic quality and because it was undeniably Irish, a relevant consideration in a jingoistic age. It was also localised and largely innocent of learned scrutiny. This was truly the art of the people; a venerable oral tradition, predominantly monophonic, small in structure, with a repository of melody of undeniable beauty. It was lauded by its champions as the very embodiment of the nation's spirit. While the nineteenth century had concerned itself with the discovery and dissemination of this living culture, the increasing rate of social change perforce shifted the focus in the twentieth century to preservation. Ireland's experience in this regard proved similar to that of other emerging western nations: the indigenous praxis that flourished within the intimacy of a local community showed itself to be fragile in the face of rapid change, particularly in rural society. Accordingly, this native expression was both the more celebrated and the more endangered of the two cultures. The protectionist outlook understandably engendered by such a fragile flowering was inimical to natural development, and the constant emphasis on distinctiveness had the unfortunate consequence of making the tradition insular.

The antithesis of this experience was provided by the second practice, the European (or cosmopolitan) aesthetic. This was a broader-based expression, which through the preceding centuries had shown itself capable of adapting to varying circumstances and translating smoothly across shifting political boundaries. The demands it made of performer and audience ensured that it found currency in Ireland primarily among the educated classes and in urban areas. In earlier centuries divisions between these two traditions had to some extent been bridged, as the case of the harper-composer Carolan (1670–1738) shows;[2] and even in the twentieth century it would be too simplistic to argue that the division between the separate cultures was absolutely denoted by class and geography. However, by the beginning of the century in large measure the Gaelic and European expressions were fostered by disparate communities each within its distinct heartland.

An account of music in Ireland in the twentieth century is in no small measure a history of the attempt to find a common ground between these different traditions. Again, parallels with broader events can be discerned. An emerging nation might deem it preferable to proffer a distinct but unified representation rather than fractured traditions that pointed to underlying divisions. So also it would ideally cultivate the broader aesthetic and aspire to partake in this global culture through its own peculiar contribution while at the same time preserving the indigenous music. The succeeding decades discover spasmodic efforts to fructify art music (as distinct from popular music) through the employment of structures and characteristics of the

---

[2] Above, iv, 562–3.

native practice. The individual artists who proposed such a marriage laboured largely without the support of a creative tradition; therefore, the proposition of employing indigenous idioms advanced some prospect of making a distinctive contribution to the literature. It also offered a tribute and a context to an increasingly imperilled heritage.

By 1921 the indigenous tradition was more lauded than practised. The decline in the principal heritage of folksong was intimately connected with the waning condition of the native language. Generations of dedicated collectors had laboured in the knowledge that time was the greatest enemy; they chronicled an expression as exquisite as it was moribund. The sterling work of these antiquarians who sought to capture for posterity a culture fast disappearing was afforded a measure of formal recognition by the new state with the establishment in 1935 of the Coimisiún Béaloideasa Éireann (the Irish Folklore Commission). The commission, under the direction of Professor J. H. Delargy, was charged with the collection of folklore in the widest sense. While advice on the collection of folksong was promptly sought, the evidence would suggest that music was not afforded a particular emphasis in the work of the commission. On 29 November 1935 Colm Ó Lochlainn, a Dublin printer and devotee of traditional singing and from 1939 a lecturer in Irish folk music in University College, Dublin, presented a paper to a small committee appointed to consider the recording of folksong, but in large measure his recommendations were ignored. The unpublished final report, presented when the commission was brought to a close in March 1970, discloses that some 1,600 items of melody and songs in staff-notation had been gathered, with another 1,200 items of melody on disc or tape. Much work remained to be done with this material when U.C.D. was subsequently invited to take charge of the commission's collection.

Interest in traditional music tended to be cyclical. During one such wave in 1951, coinciding with the start of the fleadh cheoil (music festival) phenomenon with accompanying céilí dances that attracted thousands, a department of Irish folk music was established in U.C.D. Donal O'Sullivan, the former editor of the *Journal of the Irish Folk Song Society* and author of the leading study of Carolan's life and music, was director of studies. However, the promise inherent in this venture quickly abated through lack of support. Ironically the ending of the commission's work coincided with just such a period of renewed interest in the indigenous musical heritage. The Folk Music Society was inaugurated in April 1971, and official recognition of this resurgence came in the last quarter of that year when the minister for education approved a further pilot scheme that resulted in two collectors gathering a further 600 songs, a return that places the musical commitment of the commission in perspective. In the following year the minister authorised the establishment of an archive of Irish folk music that was also transferred to the department of folklore in U.C.D., in November 1974. A civil servant,

Breandán Breathnach, was seconded and appointed the custodian of this musical archive till his retirement in February 1977. Breathnach was a committed advocate of traditional music and had edited the occasional journal *Ceol* which appeared between 1963 and 1986, and had published in 1971 his short introduction to the musical inheritance, *Folk music and dances of Ireland*. A man of trenchant opinion, he had not been slow to berate central authority for what he regarded as the less than wholehearted support for the culture. He was equally forthright in condemning individuals and organisations purporting to represent the authentic tradition when, in his view, they were in reality more concerned with popularisation. Comhaltas Ceoltóirí Éireann, founded by traditional performers in 1950 with the objective of promoting traditional music in all its forms, came in for particular criticism. Breathnach was scathing in his attacks on the organisation's encouragement for ballad groups, which he saw as the inevitable consequence of the passing of control from practitioners to 'the articulate and literate who were mostly ignorant of the subject they professed to be promoting'.[3] His overall opinion of the work of Comhaltas and his despondency with the current state of traditional music are given voice in a characteristically blunt passage:

In a period when the collector of folk music is competing with the undertaker one finds that a national organisation dedicated to the promotion of Irish traditional music does not possess a habitation, a reference library, an archive of song and music, a manuscript collection, a publication or a gramophone record. It is, however, taking an active part in promoting the tourist industry. Sadly it must be recorded that Comhaltas Ceoltóirí Éireann is an organisation with a great future behind it.[4]

In the interests of balance it should be stated that Comhaltas has been diligent in promoting a local network of branches and, through social events, competitions, and its journal *Treoir* (1967–), has provided a focus for music-making. The movement has proved adept at employing technological developments to advance its interests: this is attested by an impressive catalogue of recordings, particularly in the period from 1957 when Gael-Linn produced its first 78 rpm records of traditional music and song.

Antagonism between proponents of differing approaches is a feature of Irish musical life. The inertia of the 1930s was a factor of the absence of consensus regarding the direction of the art; the period was most notable for the acrimonious debate between the progressive and protectionist schools, conducted largely through the pages of the short-lived periodical *Ireland Today* (1936–8). The polemic centred on a series of articles by Aloys Fleischmann (1910–92) and Éamonn Ó Gallchobhair (1906–82), the latter being a disciple of the extreme insular view as earlier promulgated through the writings of the Rev. Dr Richard Henebry (1863–1916) who had argued that

---

[3] 'As we see it' in *Ceol*, ii, no. 3 ([c.1964]), pp 60–61.   [4] Ibid., p. 61.

'the more we foster modern music the more we help to silence our own'.[5] The debate was not conclusive; it served principally to deflect energy from the creative sphere. Ultimately the division became outmoded. But the exchange points to the unhappy fruits of a ruptured tradition: this can be seen in the continuing existence of separate competitive festivals, Feis Ceoil (exclusively musical, but including music from the broader tradition), and An tOireachtas (a smaller assembly concerning itself with a range of native cultural traditions), inaugurated within a day of each other in May 1897.[6] The latter in effect became the cultural congress of the Gaelic League, established in 1893. That such a divided course was necessary speaks volumes for the underlying aesthetic schism. A similar tendency can be noted in the twentieth century in the propensity to create too many organisations with overlapping objectives, all of which are liable to suffer in the competition for limited attention and scarce resources.

Irish traditional music undeniably remains a minority expression. But despite the celebration and the acclaim, much of which emanated from foreign scholars, it can be argued that this heritage is more endangered now than it was a century ago.[7] It is an indictment of the claim to be a musical people that a glorious native practice, freely invoked in the nineteenth century to endorse the nation's claim to sovereignty, should largely be forgotten when that political aim was attained; the contrast between the emphasis placed on culture by the intelligentsia that prepared the path to independence and its low priority in the new state that ultimately emerged is particularly evident in the case of music. Furthermore, the sole note of success, the popularisation of traditional music since mid century, has been achieved by adulterations that leave many people without a clear view of what traditional style and repertoire really are. A reevaluation of the contribution of Seán Ó Riada (1931–71) is in this respect overdue. The popular perception of him as the quintessential national composer does not conform with the record. His initial works engage with the technical departures widely evident in early twentieth-century music; the acclaimed work for strings, 'Nomos No. 1: Hercules dux ferrariae' (1957), freely mixes serial and tonal elements. Ó Riada's Irish note appears relatively late in his life. His film scores, 'Mise Eire' ('I am Ireland') (1959) and 'Saoirse?' ('Freedom?') (1961), earned him the mantle of

[5] Richard Henebry, *Irish music* (Dublin, [1903]), p. 15.

[6] The impetus for the creation of Feis Ceoil came from papers delivered to the National Literary Society by the musician Dr Annie Patterson (1868–1934) and by the poet and schools-inspector Alfred Perceval Graves (1846–1931). Gaelic League delegates withrew at the planning stage when it was decided that the festival would be entirely musical, and would entertain music from the broader tradition. See also above, vi, 515.

[7] For the view that the heyday of Irish traditional music was over by the 1950s see Reg Hall, 'Heydays are shortlived' in Fintan Vallely, Hammy Hamilton, Eithne Vallely, and Liz Doherty (ed.), *Crosbhealach an cheoil 1996: the crossroads conference. Tradition and change in Irish traditional music* (Dublin, 1999), pp 77–81.

the truest representative of the traditional note. In fact Ó Riada and his group Ceoltóirí Chulainn undoubtedly gave an impetus to the interest in the heritage, but at a price. Such a group, with its harpsichord, chromatic inflections, and concerted approach, owed as much to the ballad group and the céilí band as to the tradition that it sought to celebrate. Increased befuddlement was the legacy of Ó Riada's proselytising. The propagating fervency generated confusion from diffusion. And it was ever thus; the whole course of the art in Ireland has been dominated by the question of what constitutes Irish music.

This question is apparent even in a consideration of the popular music idiom. Increasingly throughout this period the range of music available in Ireland through concerts, the sound media, and in dance halls was what could be expected of a developing western state in an age of open communication. It is, however, observable that much of the native popular idiom consciously exploited elements of traditional music; indeed, popular musicians showed themselves more adept at this than did the exponents of art music, despite the fact that the latter had wrestled with the issue for considerably longer. A long-lived and highly successful group, the Chieftains, whose career began in the 1960s, was foremost among the groups following Ó Riada's path of evangelisation. While this group may not have found favour with purists, it irrefutably engendered international interest in a form of Irish music. The 1960s also saw another version of popularisation in the rise to fame of Tommy Makem and the Clancy Brothers, who together set a standard for the many balladeers. A younger group, Clannad, from County Donegal, also won wide approval with a style based on the indigenous musical idiom and one that employed the Irish language. Yet another approach was shown in the history of Horslips, regarded by many as Ireland's most important rock band, who achieved spectacular domestic success in the 1970s through an irreverent marriage of traditional elements with a basic rock style.

More recently a succession of individuals and groups have demonstrated how completely Irish youth can assimilate a cosmopolitan popular culture; the achievements of the group U2 and the solo singer Sinead O'Connor both confirm this and moreover show how Irish musicians can set the parameters of that culture. This point is endorsed by Ireland's record of success in the bland but enduring annual Eurovision Song Contest. Meanwhile, the persistent appeal of country-and-western music illustrates how the Irish diaspora helped to shape the twentieth-century musical experience. Country-and-western music owes much to Irish traditional music; the demand for 'ethnic' recordings among immigrant populations meant that much Irish traditional music which might otherwise have been lost was recorded in the United States in the first half of the twentieth century. However, in America such music was also transformed, with the development of ensemble playing in the 1920s and 1930s before it appeared in Ireland.[8]

Openness to worldly influence is a relatively recent phenomenon. A tendency toward insularity, both economic and cultural, is often a feature of a successful emerging nationalism, and such a protective spirit was evident in Ireland in the decades following the achievement of independence. This was particularly marked during the 1930s and 1940s, when isolationists received support from a fundamentalist lobby which argued that popular foreign music could undermine the native moral code. In spring 1943 this powerful combination resulted in Radio Éireann introducing a proscription on the broadcasting of dance music, a loose term that came to be understood to encompass 'swing', 'jive', and 'hot jazz', the latter evidently adjudged a particular source of evil. Also prohibited was any music with a vocal chorus sung by a 'crooner', another broad category that appeared worryingly inclusive to concerned contemporaries. P. J. Little, the minister for posts and telegraphs, charged with responsibility for the broadcasting station, was particularly concerned that commercial programmes such as that sponsored by the hospital sweepstakes (established in 1930) were disseminating an alien culture inimical to the ethos of a service that was intended to be national, despite the fact that only Irish concerns were allowed to promote such programmes. Business houses took the opposite view: experience taught that the more popular the content of the fifteen-minute programme, the better the public response to the sponsoring product or service. Little strongly discouraged the broadcasting of jazz, giving rise to a proscription better described as a taboo than a ban. The term appeared in a contemporary report in the *Irish Times*, which noted that further measures might well follow:

A tendency working against modern composers outside the jazz school, which has been noticeable for some time past, may crystallise shortly, resulting in the taboo also cutting out from the lunch-hour broadcasts representative composers such as Stravinsky, Milhaud, etc. On top of the dance-music ban, which was aimed at making Radio Éireann less lowbrow, the discrimination to be operated against modern 'straight' composers will also make the station less highbrow.[9]

Despite public protest the restriction was imposed and remained operative till 1948. The same drive to curb the growing interest in jazz and modern dance resulted in the passing of the public dance halls act of 1935,[10] by which public dancing could take place only in licensed halls under official supervision. Although the act did facilitate Irish dancing, this was céilí dancing at the expense of set dancing, to which parish priests took particular

[8] Catherine Curran, 'Changing audiences for traditional Irish music' in *Crosbhealach an cheoil*, pp 56–63: 56–7.
[9] *Irish Times*, 18 May 1943, p. 1.
[10] 1935/2 (19 Feb. 1935).

exception. Crossroads dancing, which had been part of the life of rural Ireland, was badly affected. Thus a measure designed to exclude foreign influences contributed to the undermining of an Irish folk music tradition. The point has been made that 'although the decline of Irish music as a folk music was exacerbated by emigration and rural decline in general, it was also aided by the spirit of the catholic church and the increasing conservatism of the Fianna Fáil government in the 1930s'.[11]

THE nature of a distinctive Irish music was an issue also engaged by the minority who subscribed to the broader art music tradition. In preceding centuries spokesmen for the Anglo-Irish establishment would have argued that their own expression had equal right to be considered Irish music, although there was in truth little distinctiveness in the earliest emanations from this tradition. And those who advocated the more cosmopolitan tradition were also to the fore in attesting the merit of the folk music uncovered by the antiquarians. The treasure revealed through successive collecting activities was widely celebrated and appeared to offer a unique source to creative artists desirous of formulating a distinctive Irish voice in music. But there were few such in Ireland in 1921. Art music too had suffered in the political trauma of the preceding decades and could not boast the infrastructure necessary to nurture a school of composition. In fact the European aesthetic had never recovered from the removal of the appurtenances of power following the act of union in 1800. Deprived of patronage and society, the practice of the art declined. The heroic efforts of individual musicians, along with occasional celebrity concerts and the enterprise of a handful of enthusiastic amateur societies, continued to provide the little music available in the country in 1921 in a manner consistent with much of the nineteenth century. The uncertain political prospects following the strong drive for home rule in the 1880s had vitiated even this fitful endeavour. Dublin, Cork, and the smaller urban centres continued to monopolise what limited activity there was.

Some encouragement could be taken from the commitment of the Royal Dublin Society, which in 1886 commenced its annual series of chamber recitals in the capital designed 'to aid in the development of an enlightened musical taste in Dublin'.[12] These continued into the twentieth century, and one of the original instigators, Michele Esposito (1855–1929), remained an occasional contributor to what was the most consistent musical enterprise of the age. Indeed Esposito's unstinting energy represents the most auspicious contribution in a torpid period. It would be difficult to overestimate his influence on the musical life of the city at the turn of the century. His work

---

[11] Curran, 'Changing audiences for traditional Irish music', p. 57.

[12] Cited in A. Hughes, 'The Society and music' in James Meenan and Desmond Clarke (ed.), *The Royal Dublin Society: 1731–1981* (Dublin, 1981), p. 265. See also above, vi, 510.

as professor of pianoforte in the Royal Irish Academy of Music offered further grounds for optimism, as did the influence of the municipal schools of music in Dublin and Cork. But viewed in perspective these isolated endeavours could have but limited impact on the general enervation. Furthermore, by 1921 Esposito had already made the burden of his contribution and had little time to serve before he finally returned to his native Naples in 1928; and the schools of music were not sufficiently large to foster a broad revival, while their influence extended only within the range of their respective cities. Even further disruption in the minimal musical life seemed assured when the new state sought and secured Leinster House, the home of the Royal Dublin Society and hitherto the venue for its recitals, as the meeting place for the dáil in 1922. The Royal Irish Academy of Music (based in Westland Row from the 1870s) discussed the desirability of incorporating a concert hall in its premises, but nothing was done until the Dagg Hall (converted from the former band room) was opened in 1945, with seating for 200.[13]

The 'land of song' had no permanent orchestra and few suitable auditoriums with which to commence an independent musical life after 1921. An unstable domestic situation reduced further the visits of foreign soloists and ensembles, resulting in a deficiency that could not be supplied through native endeavour. The only opportunity to encounter live opera came with the occasional performance staged by travelling opera companies. Such a penurious situation was not wholly surprising. Music had been afforded little emphasis through the preceding period when public attention had been occupied by dramatic events at home and abroad. Not only was the environment inimical to a flourishing musical life, more crucial was the fundamental lack of musical discernment in the population. This is not a criticism but rather a reflection of the low priority afforded music education. A people extolled for its musical sensibility had in truth little opportunity to engage with the literature of European art music or, in many instances, with its own native music. The want of education lay at the heart of the musical malaise and those who sought to furnish the young state with an expression of which it could be proud quickly identified the development of a systematic scheme of music education as the essential prerequisite.

Esposito had been among the first to address this question when from his position as the seminal influence in the Royal Irish Academy of Music he initiated a scheme of local centre examinations in practical music, which for the first time proposed a uniform standard. The examinations were first held in 1894 in a limited number of centres, but it is testimony to Esposito's perseverance that within decades they were being taken by students in the

[13] Richard Pine and Charles Acton (ed.), *To talent alone: the Royal Irish Academy of Music 1848–1998* (Dublin, 1998), pp 357–9.

most remote rural districts. As a teaching institution, the academy gave a distinguished lead in the excellence of its string school and in a surpassing school of pianoforte personally directed by Esposito. That the academy was charged with the education of the children of genteel families says much about the social context of music; the generous bequest of Miss Elizabeth Coulson in 1861 stipulated that it was to be used 'for the instruction in instrumental music to the children of respectable Irish parents'.[14] The capital's other such institution, the Municipal School of Music, catered for a different constituency and initially had separate aims. It had been founded after the artisans exhibition of 1885 which had featured many of the amateur bands of the city. There was appreciable interest in this form of music-making among the working class of Dublin, but the exhibition revealed a want of instruction in wind playing and a universally poor standard of performance. At a meeting held on 2 September 1888 in the Workmen's Club, members of the associated bands sought the creation of a municipal teaching institution under the aegis of the Royal Irish Academy of Music that would offer tuition at moderate charges to its members. The definite class distinction was evident in the aims set out when the new school opened on 15 October 1890, charged with making 'provision for the musical instruction of the working classes'.[15] The decided emphasis on wind playing is clear from the record of 1902 that shows 205 pupils all studying woodwind, brass, or percussion. However, the greater appeal of more refined instruments, along with the association of wind playing with lower social status, evidently played a part in the municipal school's decision in 1904 to offer classes in piano, strings, and vocal studies. This departure was also a result of the placing of the school under the authority of the Dublin Technical Instruction Committee, thus removing it from the early control exercised by its older neighbour. By 1918 only thirty-four students in the burgeoning school were taking woodwind, brass, or percussion; there could be no clearer demonstration of how far the institution had strayed from its original purpose. The influence of this institution has long been impeded by a lack of space available for its teaching: in 1954 it could accommodate only 1,400 pupils.

The position of the capital's principal music schools in 1921 signalled the growing desire for technical instruction and the willingness to meet this demand; but equally it provides an example of the characteristically Irish duplication of effort and multiplicity of institutions. Moreover, it pointed up the geographical imbalance in endeavour; smaller urban centres and rural areas had no such advantages; even the Municipal School of Music in Cork, which had been founded in 1878, could at first cater for only 180 pupils,

[14] Cited in W. J. M. Starkie, 'The Royal Irish Academy of Music' in Aloys Fleischmann (ed.), *Music in Ireland: a symposium* (Cork, 1952), p. 107.
[15] John McCann, 'The Dublin Municipal School of Music' in ibid., p. 113.

although this was significantly increased in succeeding decades. The concentration of estimable institutions in Dublin that occasioned the imbalance in the opportunity for an education in music was further emphasised by the creation of the Leinster School of Music in 1904 and the Read School of Pianoforte Playing in 1915.

The belief in the primacy of education was continued by Esposito's pupil, John Larchet (1884–1967), who was to exercise a telling influence on the course of music in Ireland. Larchet's career is especially significant in that he was the first musician of stature in the modern era whose education and working life were spent exclusively at home. In 1921 he was appointed professor of music in U.C.D., a post he retained till 1958. The position conferred on him the opportunity to comment with authority on the current state of the art. In a seminal article written two years after his appointment, Larchet catalogued the sorry situation of music in the country. The very title 'A plea for music' reveals his despondent reaction to the low priority afforded the art, and Larchet clearly identified what he termed the 'fundamentally unsound' system of musical education as the principal reason for this impoverishment.[16] Consistent with these early sentiments, he was to devote his life to the formation of a vigorous musical training, with special emphasis on the availability of music at primary and secondary levels. Larchet was particularly well placed to effect change in this area, as along with his position in U.C.D. he was also to succeed Esposito as senior professor of composition, harmony, and counterpoint in the Royal Irish Academy of Music, thus allowing him ready access to the most accomplished students in both academic and technical disciplines. He was joined in this crusade by a younger colleague, Aloys Fleischmann, who was appointed to the chair of music in University College Cork in 1934 where he had an even longer tenure, retiring in 1980. Fleischmann had an inclusive view of music and focused his energy and that of his department on making some experience of music available to as many as possible. At first the universities were somewhat constricted in their influence. Larchet's post in Dublin was not converted to a full-time position till 1944, while the limited influence of the department in U.C.C. can be gauged from the fact that between the creation of a lectureship in music in 1906 and 1928 only one student graduated. Of the remaining institutions, University College Galway did not offer music as a subject; St Patrick's College, Maynooth, had the oldest department in the country but it was constrained through its exclusive focus on sacred music; while the country's most venerable educational centre, Trinity College, was not well placed in 1921 to promote a revival, being (as far as music was concerned) an examining body rather than a teaching establishment.

[16] 'A plea for music' in William Fitz-Gerald (ed.), *The voice of Ireland* (Dublin and London, [1924]), p. 508.

The initially debilitated educational situation necessarily meant that a large proportion of the population was unversed in the literature of the European aesthetic. This had consequences for those endeavouring to promote the performance of music. The elements required for a healthy musical life were all lacking to some degree: it was first essential to cultivate a discerning audience; suitable venues for performance were in short supply; and even executants were not readily available in all instruments, there being a notable shortage of wind instrumentalists. The latter deficiency was a singular index of decline, given the country's, and especially Dublin's, earlier reputation as a centre for the sale and repair of instruments.[17] The occasional celebrity concerts promoted by agencies such as that of Harold Holt continued to exercise appeal but were not designed to accommodate a more general revival. Committed individuals also periodically sought to provide the leadership necessary for a musical resurgence. The much vaunted Irish Musical League was initiated in 1926 by Hester Travers Smith and others, with the purpose of shifting the focus of attention from the celebrity to the music. While the celebrity concert had been the mainstay of Dublin musical life in the first quarter of the century, it also inured audiences to novelty and absolved a community from the responsibility to provide its own music. However, Travers Smith's venture foundered quickly because it failed to attract sufficient financial support to realise its ambitions.

While the failure is revealing about the general apathy, it also puts in perspective the difficulties facing those desirous of promoting an active musical life, and in particular the persistence and singular contribution of the Royal Dublin Society. Despite losing the use of its erstwhile home to the dáil in 1922, the society continued its creditable commitment to music by presenting concerts at first in the Abbey and later in the Theatre Royal. This was inevitably a disruptive time, and it was autumn 1925 before the society could promote a series in its new members' hall in Ballsbridge. The list of artistes and ensembles who accepted the invitation to perform in the new hall is testimony to the society's continuing commitment to music. Many of the leading string quartets of the age appeared, including the Lener, Arnold Rosé, Pro Arte, and Prague; while Cortot, Rubinstein, Schnabel, and Gieseking were just some of the more accomplished pianists who appeared. Convention, plus considerations of cost and the limited size of the hall, ensured that emphasis remained firmly on chamber music. Occasional orchestral concerts were given by native musicians, and there were some notable visits from a reduced complement of the Hallé Orchestra under Hamilton Harty. Through these endeavours the Royal Dublin Society established its estimable record as the principal patron of the art in the new state, but the commitment was inevitably focused on a defined group within a limited geographical area.

A broader musical regeneration would inevitably require central initiative. The first official recognition of music from the new state came in 1922, but in an unusual manner. General Richard Mulcahy, the first minister for defence, faced with an army of a size necessary to sustain a civil war, but unsupportable in the longer term, proposed, consistent with his vocationalist philosophy, to make of the army a 'works of public service',[18] concentrating its manpower and skills on a series of projects that would be of benefit to the country and that equally would furnish soldiers with the experience necessary to pursue careers outside the army. The range of enterprises identified by Mulcahy says much for his prescience: it included the fostering of the Gaelic tongue, the reafforestation of the country, and promotion of equestrian sport, as well as the creation of an army school of music that was intended to aid in a national musical revival. To further the latter project and on the advice of Larchet, Mulcahy appointed in 1923 two Germans, Wilhelm Fritz Brase (1875–1940) and Friedrich Christian Sauerzweig (1881–1953), to direct the new school. Both were accomplished musicians whose energies were to extend well beyond the duty of creating bands of quality for the army. Brase in particular was diligent in promoting music in the capital, and it was at his suggestion that the Dublin Philharmonic Society was formed in 1927. During the following decade this large body, comprising orchestra and chorus with both professional and amateur musicians, presented an annual series of concerts in the capital. Audiences were offered an enterprising repertoire including many works never before heard in the country; the society was also diligent in providing talented Irish vocalists and instrumentalists with a platform. A didactic aspect to its work was evident in the excellent printed programmes produced for the concerts, each carrying informative illustrated notes on the works to be performed. The initial success enjoyed by the society represented the first large-scale musical enterprise in the Free State and demonstrated the fecund possibilities inherent in the combination of native industry and foreign guidance, which in itself was a considerable achievement in a chauvinistic age. However, public support proved fickle and the society faced increasing problems in sustaining its ambitious annual series. It was forced to cease its activities in 1936.

The high level of religious observance in Ireland might suggest a role for the principal churches as significant patrons of music. However, the record shows otherwise, with the Roman Catholic church being especially culpable. Despite its ever dwindling community, the Church of Ireland has preserved its support for music, notably in Christ Church and St Patrick's, the cathedrals of the capital, where a venerable commitment to music as part of

---

[18] Mulcahy papers, U.C.D., A.D. P7/B/322.

worship is continued to this day. In contrast it is striking that the most notable single initiative within the catholic tradition, the creation of the Palestrina Choir in St Mary's pro-cathedral, Dublin, in 1902, was due primarily to the munificence of Edward Martyn rather than to any decision of the hierarchy.[19] While individual bishops and priests have encouraged the role of music of quality within the liturgy, the modest general standard of sacred music throughout the country is a reflection of the low priority afforded music by the church. Individual endeavour was again to the fore in the formation of Our Lady's Choral Society in 1946. This large amateur group, reminiscent of the separate religious choral societies that emerged in the middle of the previous century, was formed from the combined catholic church choirs of the archdiocese of Dublin, with the backing of Archbishop John Charles McQuaid. The performance of Elgar's 'The dream of Gerontius' given in 1951, with the Hallé Orchestra under Sir John Barbirolli, was characteristic of its purpose. Composers have, however, been encouraged by the Irish commission for liturgy to set the mass particularly in a style sufficiently simple for communal singing. Interestingly, even in this form it is possible to discern some, such as Thomas C. Kelly (1917–85), in his 'Mass for peace' (1976), who employ a broader palette, and others such as Seóirse Bodley (1933–   ), in another 'Mass for peace' written in the same year, who fashion a response in a distinctly Irish idiom. The 'Ó Riada mass' (1968), bearing the composer's name, and his later 'Aifreann nua' (1970) are consistent with the latter approach.

It was a further example of central enterprise that did most to facilitate the broad revival of music in the country. It was some time before the potential of the state broadcasting service that tentatively commenced operation on 1 January 1926 was fully appreciated. Recent political turmoil meant that radio came relatively late to Ireland, and as a consequence it remained a state-controlled instrument; too close a concentration on politics, and even on news, was adjudged contentious in the wake of troubled times. Entertainment was the primary function, albeit with a decidedly national flavour, with music afforded the predominant place. This in turn, owing to technical limitations, and the fact that recording was as yet in its infancy, meant live music. Vincent O'Brien, renowned as a leading figure in church music and as the conductor of the Palestrina Choir, was appointed part-time director of music, and together with a string trio he provided much of the music heard in the earliest transmissions from 2RN, the attractive call-sign adopted by the new station. This contribution was supported by a wide range of visiting solo performers and artistes: vocalists, traditional musicians, choirs, and military bands were all regularly heard by the relatively small audience with access to crystal sets. The early schedules were accordingly dominated by

[19] Above, vi, 516–17.

shorter musical items. By June 1926 the permanent station ensemble had grown to a respectable seven members, notwithstanding the stringent financial regulations governing the service's operations. Enlisting the assistance of other instrumentalists, O'Brien embarked in November 1927 on the courageous design of presenting the station's first public symphony concert in Dublin's Metropolitan Hall. While a disappointing attendance militated against an immediate repeat, the enterprise did signal the broadcasting service's tacit acceptance of its formative role in the musical life of the nation.

Following the passing of the wireless telegraphy act,[20] the government appointed an advisory body in 1927 to advise and assist the appropriate minister, J. J. Walsh, in the conduct of the broadcasting service. Protracted lobbying by members of this committee sympathetic to the cause of music attained an appreciable success in 1933 with the augmentation of the station orchestra to nineteen instrumentalists. With the exception of the four military bands of the army school of music, this constituted the only permanent professional ensemble in the state and was thus regarded with some pride as the national orchestra, although it was not named as such. In addition, the achievement represented a significant amelioration in music's erstwhile sorry condition: the small orchestra afforded the basis necessary to present competently the symphonic repertoire on a regular basis; it also offered the prospect of home employment to native executants; and it provided the essential vehicle for the ideas of young composers. In May 1936 a board of assessors led by Sir Hamilton Harty conducted auditions that resulted in an increased orchestra of twenty-four members. The reconstructed ensemble comprised a flute, oboe, clarinet, bassoon, French horn, trumpet, trombone, and timpanist, along with the complement of strings and a piano.

Broadcasting also proved a powerful didactic medium. A scheme of schools' concerts was inaugurated during the 1930s with the orchestra or an army band bringing live music to children in centres throughout the country. This worthwhile endeavour was complemented by a series of illustrated broadcasts with talks by musicians (such as Sauerzweig), the eminent academic Walter Starkie, the champion of traditional music Carl Hardebeck, and leading critic Harold White. The effect was to introduce a wider public to the hitherto esoteric world of music.

Discovering competent conductors for the station orchestra proved a formidable problem. The army bands provided the sole source of experienced direction. Consequently, from July 1936 a succession of officers who had trained under Brase, unrivalled as the preeminent conductor of his generation resident in Ireland, was transferred on secondment to the department of posts and telegraphs, under whose auspices the broadcasting service operated. The most notable of those to take charge of the new Irish radio

[20] 1926/45 (24 Dec. 1926).

orchestra was Lieutenant (later Captain) Michael Bowles (1909–98). Within six months of Bowles's arrival in 1941, Vincent O'Brien retired from his part-time position on age grounds, leaving Bowles to combine the dual roles of acting music director and principal conductor. With the support of P. J. Little, the minister with responsibility for broadcasting, Bowles instigated a fortnightly series of public symphony concerts commencing in the autumn of 1941. The departure proved far more popular than O'Brien's earlier initiative, and the audience demand was sufficiently strong to occasion an immediate move from the original venue in the Round Room of the Mansion House, with its capacity of just 800, to the more spacious Capitol Theatre. Each series, held annually up to and including 1947, consisted of ten Sunday afternoon concerts conducted by Bowles and a concluding spring concert given under the direction of a distinguished visiting conductor. Sir Adrian Boult took the rostrum for the first of these in 1942 and was succeeded by Constant Lambert.

Bowles demonstrated patent perspicacity in deciding the orchestral curriculum. Like the Dublin Philharmonic before him, he presented enterprising programmes including first Irish performances of four of the symphonies of Sibelius, the popular piano concerto by John Ireland, and E. J. Moeran's violin and cello concertos. The orchestra also gave weekly studio concerts that were transmitted live on Friday nights and an occasional series entitled 'Contemporary Irish composers', which provided a unique platform for the emerging generation. Such industry found its reward in the further augmentation of the orchestra to forty instrumentalists. It also served to emphasise the pivotal role of the broadcasting service in musical affairs. However, these developments also resurrected the debate about the extent to which an orchestra established as a broadcasting medium, and funded from a radio licence, should serve a broader role as a national facility. Bowles had no doubts; under his direction the service, functioning under the title Radio Éireann since 1937, confirmed its undisputed position as the principal patron of music in the state. This was underscored by the creation in 1948 of a second orchestral body, the Light Orchestra, a small ensemble of twenty-two instrumentalists established to complement its older sister by concentrating on broadcasting the lighter orchestral repertoire with special emphasis on arrangements of native airs. Five years earlier the service had established Cór Radio Éireann, a chamber choir of twenty-four trained singers operating on a part-time basis; in 1953 this body was reconstituted as a professional choir of ten singers with a permanent conductor. A greater commitment to choral music had been signalled the previous year with the formation of a larger amateur body, the Radio Éireann Choral Society under Dr Hans Waldemar Rosen, which was available to perform the larger works of the repertoire.

An infelicitous and complex dispute with the station authorities resulted in Bowles's departure in 1948. It was an unfortunate end for an energetic public servant who in a relatively short period had helped secure Radio Éireann's position at the centre of Irish musical life. The fact that Bowles was replaced by a succession of foreign conductors raised chauvinistic feelings that had never been far below the surface. The sensibilities of a newly autonomous people, allied to a difficult economic situation, suggested that preferential treatment should be afforded to native talent. Yet many of the leading musical institutions felt it necessary to look abroad at least initially to discover the experience required to generate a revival. The principal schools of music felt that they had little option but to enlist foreign teachers. The singular contribution of the Italian Michele Esposito has already been mentioned. He was but one of many visiting musicians who worked in the Royal Irish Academy of Music; the reputation of the string school was founded on the commitment (among others) of the Italians Guido Papini and Achille Simonetti, and Adolf Wilhelmj (son of the acclaimed German violinist and composer August Wilhelmj), while the most influential member of the vocal staff was likewise an immigrant musician, Adelio Viani. Similarly in Cork, the Milanese Ferrucio Grossi set the standard for string teaching and performance between 1902 and 1930. Grossi was one of many foreigners to settle in Cork. The work of the Fleischmann family from Munich deserves particular mention: Aloys G. Fleischmann was noted for his work in the field of sacred music, while the reputation of his wife, Tilly, was founded on her prodigious keyboard facility. Their impact on music in Cork was surpassed by that of their son, also named Aloys, who from his time of appointment to the chair of music in the university at the age of 24 exercised a guiding influence on the art in the city and was an assiduous advocate for the cause of music in the country. The catholic church was likewise dependent on foreign schools of music, notably those at Regensburg, Aachen, and the Lemmens Institute at Malines (Mechelen), to fill many of the positions of organist in cathedral towns; this did not provoke controversy, as the small department in Maynooth was not equipped to supply the required graduates. However, the appointment of the Germans, Brase and Sauerzweig, to direct the fledgling army school of music occasioned open hostility. Vitriolic correspondence in leading newspapers suggested that native musicians were well capable of performing these duties. That the national broadcasting service, hitherto largely partisan in its recruitment policy, chose to replace Bowles with immigrant conductors led to a resurgence of what Vaughan Williams, considering a similar eruption in Britain, referred to as the 'keep out the foreigner movement'.[21] The eminent Jean Martinon was the first of a succession of visiting conductors to take charge in the following years. Among others appointed were Edmond Appia, Sixten Eckerberg, Hans Schmidt-Isserstedt, Norman del Mar, Jean Fournet, Milan Horvat, and Tibor Paul. A similar movement

[21] Ralph Vaughan Williams, *National music* (2nd ed., Oxford, 1987), p. 55.

was apparent in the instrumental ranks of the symphony orchestra after the departure of Bowles. The long-time leader, Terry O'Connor, a member of the original string trio, retired and was replaced by the Florentine Renzo Marchionni, who remained with the orchestra till 1959. Indeed, the majority of the instrumentalists recruited at the end of the 1940s, when the orchestra was augmented to sixty-one players, came from abroad. It was a situation that led to entreaties from eminent musicians as late as the 1960s that the orchestras of the broadcasting service be Irish in the fullest sense of the term; the symphony orchestra at that time having half of its complement of instrumentalists from abroad.[22]

Such debate did not detract from the service's contribution to the musical life of the country. It is interesting to note that the expenditure sheets for 1955 show that the orchestras accounted for almost 30 per cent of the station's annual salary bill. That the station was the principal source of patronage was largely taken for granted. Persistent petitions from Cork that an orchestra be located there were answered in a novel and politic manner with the establishment of a string quartet in 1959. An existing English ensemble, the Raphael Quartet, was engaged and based in Cork, where its members also taught in the Cork school of music. In subsequent years this group was succeeded by other quartets including the Academica and the Vanbrugh. Thus by 1960 Radio Eireann, with its orchestras, choirs, and quartet, was making an impressive contribution relative to its size.

Other musical ventures, notably the productions of the principal opera companies, also benefited from the station's munificent policy. Opportunities to encounter live opera were rare in the years after 1921. Itinerant companies such as the Carl Rosa, the O'Mara, and the splendidly named Moody–Manners Opera Company toured occasionally. It was the singer Joseph O'Mara of the O'Mara Opera Company who produced the first performance of Godfrey Molyneux Palmer's opera 'Sruth na Maoile' ('The waters of Moyle') in the Gaiety Theatre in July 1923. The work was supported by the revivalist policy of the Gaelic League and was given under the direction of Vincent O'Brien. It is based on the legend of the children of Lir, with a libretto in Irish by the Rev. Thomas Ó Ceallaigh of Sligo, who had earlier supplied the text for another singularly Irish statement, Robert O'Dwyer's 'Eithne'. The music is not wholly original, enlisting traditional airs including that most closely associated with the subject, 'Silent, O Moyle'. An organist and composer, Molyneux Palmer was born in Middlesex in 1882 but had settled in Ireland in 1910. This work evinces his ready espousal of the dominant nationalist mode; indeed, there is no little irony in the fact that immigrant musicians were to the fore in proposing an insular

---

[22] See Joseph Groocock, *A general survey of music in the Republic of Ireland* (Dublin, 1961), p. 78.

aesthetic in the early decades of the century. 'Sruth na Maoile' was repeated in August of the following year in a week-long festival of Irish opera given in the Theatre Royal as part of the revived Tailteann games. O'Mara was again prominent in this venture, which included performances of Stanford's 'Shamus O'Brien'—a work initially so popular that it was disowned by its creator, only becoming available for presentation after his death earlier that year—and a new large opera, 'Shaun the Post', by the Dublin critic and teacher Harold White, who wrote under the nom de plume 'Dermot Macmurrough'. Based on Boucicault's 'Arrah-na-Pogue', this too employs traditional airs such as the 'Derry air', although compared with 'Sruth na Maoile' its design is more capacious. Although 'Shaun the Post' was subsequently performed by the Carl Rosa Company, these two works represented the swan-song of the Gaelic League's involvement in the form, and indeed of the very attempt to fashion an indigenous opera.

A more inclusive view of the form was proposed in 1928 by Signor Adelio Viani when he established the Dublin Operatic Society as the first resident enterprise designed to serve the opera-loving public of the metropolis. As so often with Irish musical ventures, early success was not sustained, primarily because of the difficulty facing the society in engaging and paying for an adequate orchestra. A subsequent organisation, the Dublin Grand Opera Society, established in 1941, prospered, not least because from 1948 it engaged members of the broadcasting orchestras for its spring and winter seasons. Similarly, the innovative Wexford autumn season, inaugurated in 1951 (a singularly significant year in Ireland's artistic life), profited from the full cooperation of Radio Éireann. While the Dublin Grand Opera Society has an established and valued role presenting the standard works of the repertoire in the Gaiety Theatre, the Wexford festival has earned international critical acclaim for its enterprise in staging intimate productions of lesser known operas in a homely setting. Owing much to the energies of a local medical practitioner, Dr T. J. Walsh, the festival has, from its first production of Balfe's 'The rose of Castile', expanded to present three operas each season, along with a range of associated artistic events. Successive councils and committees have been consistent in offering opportunities to younger Irish artistes to work alongside the many distinguished vocalists, conductors, and producers who come from abroad. In the very year when the Wexford festival was created, the baritone Michael O'Higgins, a noted teacher of voice, founded the Thirteens Musical Society, which concentrated on producing in Dublin the operas of Mozart and specialised also in the performance of rare early and modern choral music. Many aspiring vocalists of later generations have had a first experience of operatic performance with Irish National Opera, a touring body that has been succeeded since 1986 by the Opera Theatre Company. Functioning with the support of the arts council, this company tours at home and abroad, making opera more accessible and contributing to the reversal of the urban bias that had hitherto been a debilitating feature of music in Ireland.

It is the creative record that ultimately offers the truest measure of a nation's musical health; and it is this record that provides the most damning indicator of Ireland's musical condition in 1921. The reasons for the sorry situation are clear, and they are the inevitable fruits of the country's history. A people deprived of any reasonable musical infrastructure was manifestly not equipped to foster imaginative endeavour. Even more critical was the fact that a fractured expression militated against a coherent tradition of composition. To correct the first required will, central support, and experienced direction, all of which were forthcoming to a greater or lesser degree; that there is now an active and growing interest in composition is itself adequate testimony to the advances instituted by those who set themselves the task of addressing the development of the necessary infrastructure. The creation of a distinct voice from a sundered tradition proved far more problematic, and the question occasioned a debate that lasted for much of the period under examination here.

Disparate philosophical approaches can be recognised in the early compositions emerging from the new state. The insular and cosmopolitan practices corresponded to, and reflected, differing political responses to the new polity. Those who adhered to the former sought in some measure of cultural isolation the protection with which to nourish a distinctive note, free of external influence. The alternative approach proposed to develop an expression that was characteristic but one equally nourished from the broader tradition of art music. The segregationist view, as outlined by one of its most vocal champions, Éamonn Ó Gallchobhair, won considerable approval in the early decades; but ultimately this approach proved untenable. Others who championed this cause were imbued with the zeal of the convert. Robert O'Dwyer (1862–1949), a teacher and occasional composer, was born in Bristol but moved to Ireland in 1897, where his advocacy of traditional music and the success of his opera 'Eithne' led to his appointment in 1914 as professor of Irish music in U.C.D. This work in Irish was consistent with the aims of the Gaelic revival as promulgated by the Gaelic League and was written for An tOireachtas of 1909.[23] Another more industrious and controversial advocate of an insular culture possessed even more exotic antecedents: Carl Hardebeck (1869–1945) could point to Dutch ancestry on his father's side; his mother came from Wales, and he was born in London. He moved to Belfast in 1893, where his regard for the Irish language led him to esteem traditional vocal

---

[23] A series of performances of 'Eithne' at the Gaiety Theatre, Dublin, during May 1910 is frequently designated the premiere of O'Dwyer's opera: see e.g. *The new Grove dictionary of music and musicians*, ix, ed. Stanley Sadie (London, 1980), p. 316; above, vi, 521. The actual premiere was in Dublin in August 1909.

music, and he was to devote his life to the preservation and propagation of this heritage. He is valued for his work as a collector and arranger of traditional airs rather than for his record as an original artist. But to advance the notion of a continuance of tradition, through an expression based on the glorious heritage of folksong, was more populist than realistic. The weight of tradition proved a heavy burden. A linear style, constructed in short forms, was technically unsuited to support a broader musical emanation. Folksong is simply not the stuff of extended composition; it fails the essential criterion in that it is not capable of development. It is therefore not surprising that there is no original enduring work of quality representative of this approach.

Those who espoused the alternative practice opted for a lonely but ultimately a more rewarding progress. Even within this discipline two distinct approaches can be discerned: the first espoused the modern European idiom without reservation, while its counterpart sought to imbue this aesthetic with a perceptible local flavour. There was no conflict between the two: both were determined to be anything other than parochial; it was merely that the second school wished its internationalism to sport a green mantle.

Frederick May (1911–85) was the most outstanding of the first generation of composers in the new state who embraced the broader style with a will. He was born in Dublin, studied with Larchet at the Royal Irish Academy of Music, and took a primary degree in music at Trinity College in 1931. His interest in modern creative techniques brought him to the Royal College of Music in London, where he came under the influence of Gordon Jacob and Vaughan Williams. A further period of study in Vienna, with the composer and musicologist Egon Wellesz, confirmed May in his espousal of the European aesthetic. These formative experiences, singular for an Irish musician of the time, consolidated a progressive approach that led to a succession of early compositions including the string quartet in C minor (1936) and 'Songs from prison' (1941), the latter being an ambitious creation for baritone solo and enlarged orchestra largely based on the text of the revolutionary German poet and dramatist Ernst Toller. These challenging works constitute two of the most ambitious statements of the century by a native composer and were innovative to a degree that ensured they would find limited understanding in Ireland. May's initial determination to forge a national idiom that would be cognizant of wider technical and musical developments evoked little sympathy, and this produced an increasing disenchantment that deflected him from composition. Instead, he contributed a number of articles to the influential periodical *The Bell*. Those of a younger generation, who saw May as a pioneer possessed of a prodigious talent lying fallow, urged him to resume composition, but with the exception of 'Sunlight and shadow' (1955) he produced only ephemeral pieces, including modish arrangements of native airs that were guaranteed a payment from Radio Éireann under a commissioning scheme instituted in 1943. The Irish public remains largely unconscious of May's admittedly small output and of the significance of his role as the harbinger of a new creative impetus. His success lay in the venture to establish a distinctive voice that was neither insular nor indentured to the past.

Brian Boydell (1917–2000) was a colleague who shared May's perspective and consistently championed his music. He too had enjoyed a comprehensive education, having studied in Ireland, in England, and in Germany at the Evangelical Church Music Institute of Heidelberg University. He demonstrated an eclectic range both in his general and musical interests, and he proved a prolific composer. His works, from the solemn 'In memoriam Mahatma Gandhi' (1948) and the string quartet no. 1 (1949), with its characteristic flashes of humour, reveal a personality that is, if anything, even more pertinaciously cosmopolitan than that of his friend. His oeuvre is wholly consistent in making no concession to parochialism. Boydell also made an eloquent contribution to extending musical horizons through his work as a broadcaster and as a teacher: the Royal Irish Academy of Music gave him his first securely paid post as a struggling young professional musician in the 1940s, and he subsequently served as professor of music in Trinity College for a period of some twenty years commencing in 1962. He was sometime conductor of the Dublin Orchestral Players, an amateur body founded in 1939 by Constance Hardinge and Havelock Nelson to afford young players the opportunity to gain orchestral experience. This body has been diligent in presenting contemporary Irish work. A tireless advocate of his art, Boydell was also one of the founding members of the Music Association of Ireland in 1948. A successor to the short-lived Musical Association of Ireland (1939), the new organisation quickly established its position as the country's principal champion of the cause of music and the music profession. At its first general meeting in January 1949 it was decided to issue a monthly bulletin, the responsibility for which fell to the young pianist Anthony Hughes who, some nine years later, was to succeed Larchet as professor of music at U.C.D. Despite a chequered history revealing a somewhat spasmodic record of application, the Music Association has persevered in its objectives and has contributed to the enhanced status of the art and its practitioners.

One of the association's original objectives was the erection of a national concert hall. For decades many had petitioned unsuccesfully for a major auditorium for the country. The want of such a facility long precluded the presentation of larger ventures; the Phoenix Hall, in which Radio Éireann had presented its twice weekly symphony concerts in the period from 1948, had a capacity of only 800. Other venues were also used, but it was not till 1974 that the government decided on the great hall at Earlsfort Terrace, erected for the great exhibition of 1865 (and later the hall of the Royal University of Ireland and its eventual successor U.C.D.) as the location for the National Concert Hall. The extensive conversion was completed in 1981 and the hall, with a capacity of 1,250, was opened in September of that year. This splendid centre has provided a focus for a diverse range of musical and artistic events, although its limited stage space does pose problems for larger visiting ensembles.

Another to the fore in the establishment of the Music Association of Ireland, and one whose career offers parallels with that of his friend Boydell, was Aloys Fleischmann,[24] whose compositions present an interesting variation on the broader creative mode adopted by May and Boydell. Born in 1910, he was some seven years older than Boydell and a year senior to May. He was, if not a disciple, a supporter of the path traced by May, but his particular interest lies in the manner in which he compromised with the insistent demands for a popularly recognisable national expression. In this respect Fleischmann straddles both schools described above. His background and his schooling, divided between Ireland and his native Germany, are fittingly symbolic of the cosmopolitan approach he frequently elucidated in prose. But the youthful certainty that engendered a trenchantly anti-parochial approach mellowed in later decades, to the point where some of his most accessible achievements resulted directly from nationalist inspiration. 'The humours of Carolan' (1941) for string orchestra and 'Clare's dragoons' (1945) scored for baritone, chorus, war pipes, and orchestra are unequivocally populist. The partisan disposition of the latter is explained by the fact that it was commissioned by Radio Éireann for the Thomas Davis and Young Ireland centenary concert given in the Capitol Theatre, Dublin, on 9 September 1945. The text is based on a poem by the nineteenth-century Young Irelander Thomas Davis and was dedicated to Fleischmann's contemporary, Donal O'Sullivan, whose influence as an advocate of traditional music was decisive in furthering the composer's interest in the nationalist idiom. It is ominous that 'Clare's dragoons' is the work that most readily springs to mind in a consideration of Fleischmann's creative output. Successful and dramatic though it is, it can neither be proposed as his finest work nor even as representative of his style. That it is so highly regarded relative to his other compositions is rather, first, a measure of the Irish public's unpreparedness to embrace works of a demanding technical and philosophical nature, and, second, an indicator of a chauvinistic proclivity in the imaginative perceptions of a recently independent people. The conjunction of low musical literacy and desire for an identifiable national expression ensured that those who espoused the modern technical developments of art music were at first a beleaguered minority. However, wider access to musical education, more opportunity to encounter music through live concerts, broadcasts, and recordings, and a burgeoning general self-confidence occasioning a

---

[24] See Ruth Fleischmann (ed.), *Aloys Fleischmann (1910–92): a life for music in Ireland remembered by contemporaries* (Dublin, 2000).

greater openness to external influences have improved their position. This melioration was given concrete expression with the successful foundation in 1969 of the Dublin Twentieth-Century Music Festival, which introduced contemporary trends to Irish audiences while also providing a welcome platform to emerging native composers. A progressive attitude to new music is also discernible in the creation in 1986 of the Contemporary Music Centre funded by the arts council. This splendid resource, successor to the Irish Composers' Centre, promotes modern Irish creative writers and provides information on current developments in Ireland and abroad.

It is inevitable that the name of John Larchet[25] will attend any discussion of composition in Ireland in the modern era. This arises not so much from his imaginative prowess as from his seemingly ubiquitous influence. It was Ireland's fortune in these formative years that it chose for its principal chairs of music pedagogues with a creative flair. Larchet was the father figure to the practice of composition in all its divers approaches. That he was a principal advocate of an Irish note in music did not prevent him offering support to pupils such as May and Boydell who had a different vision. Given his persuasion, it is not surprising to find that he was a miniaturist, his small output comprising short compositions and arrangements. His attractive lyrical style is evident in the two pairings for string orchestra, 'Dirge of Ossian' and 'Macananty's reel' (1940) and 'Carlow tune' and 'Tinkers' wedding' (1952), while the popular 'By the waters of Moyle' (1957) provides an example of Larchet's mature orchestral writing. Bearing the subtitle 'Nocturne for orchestra', it is constructed in a characteristic ternary form and scored for small ensemble. Its use of the traditional air 'Arrah, my dear Eveleen', better known by Moore's title 'Silent, O Moyle', offers illustration of Larchet's distinctive voice and helps explain why he was particularly pleased with the compliment offered by his friend and fellow academic, Walter Starkie, who said of two early songs, 'Padraic the fiddler' (1919) and 'An Ardglass boat song' (1920), that they 'are true evocations of the Irish spirit'.[26]

The referential quality of opera offered the ideal medium for a distinctive national expression; the century's earliest works in this form—O'Brien Butler's 'Muirgheis' (1903), Robert O'Dwyer's 'Eithne', and Molyneux Palmer's 'Sruth na Maoile'—were consciously Irish operas dealing with indigenous themes. Harold White's 'Shaun the Post' (as noted above) and a number of short works for stage by Éamonn Ó Gallchobhair were also of this tradition. That the century furnished so few operas is a factor both of the low rate of creative enterprise and of the long reliance on the infrequent presentations of touring companies. A renewed concentration on the form was engendered by

[25] Above, p. 631.
[26] 'John F. Larchet' in H. Allen, G. Bantock, E. J. Dent, H. Wood, and A. Eaglefield-Hull (ed.), *A dictionary of modern music and musicians* (London, [1924]), p. 288.

the emergence of native companies; the second half of the century has accordingly seen greater willingness on the part of composers living in Ireland to turn their attention to opera. The last completed work of Ina Boyle (1889–1967) was 'Maudlin of Paplewick' (1964–6), a short pastoral opera for smaller forces to her own libretto after Ben Jonson's 'The sad shepherd'. 'Patrick' (1962) by A. J. Potter (1918–80) was conceived for the relatively new medium of television; his three-act work 'The wedding' (1979) was premiered posthumously in 1981 in the Abbey Theatre. The enthusiasm of James Wilson (1922–) for the voice has found fruition in 'Twelfth night', first produced at the Wexford festival in 1969, and in its successor 'Letters to Theo' (1982) based on the correspondence between the Van Gogh brothers. His urbane interests are also evident in the two operas for children, 'The hunting of the snark' (1963) and 'The king of the golden river' (1987). Gerald Barry's three-act 'The intelligence park' (1981–90) is the most ambitious recent creation, while the many works for stage by Gerard Victory (1921–95) make him the most prolific Irish composer in the form.

The history of opera composition in the twentieth century manifests the departure from insular preoccupations; the inclination was evident from the 1940s. Many creative voices were to adopt Larchet's line in seeking to represent a distinctive national idiom through a synthesis of the indigenous character with the prevailing European tradition. This desire is personified in the singular response of Arthur Knox Duff (1899–1956), whose works betray the influence of the miniaturists of the early twentieth-century English school. Duff's educational progression was similar to that of Larchet: he had been a student both in the Royal Irish Academy of Music and at Trinity College. Like Larchet, he worked in smaller forms. His achievements point to the formidable relationship between imaginative enterprise and practical circumstances. The works that brought him notice as a composer, 'Meath pastoral' and the 'Irish suite for strings', both written in 1940, were products of his collaboration with the Dublin String Orchestra, a specialist group founded and directed by Terry O'Connor. An affection for the secular music of the renaissance is evinced in Duff's two late suites 'Echoes of Georgian Dublin' (1955 and 1956), which won wide appeal but are essentially elegant pastiche. Duff was not possessed of a great original talent, but his wistful pastoralism represents a unique strain in twentieth-century Irish composition. Thomas Kelly[27] and Walter Beckett (1914–96) are two more orthodox disciples of the Larchet school. The Wexford-born Kelly was an occasional composer whose attractive style and modest purpose were determinedly focused on constructing a native expression. Beckett's music discloses a broader range of influence, including that of Vaughan Williams and particularly of Delius. The latter's presence is revealed in many of the works written during the 1940s

[27] Above, p. 634.

and more recently in the short song cycle for mezzo-soprano or baritone and piano, 'Goldenhair' (1980). The 'Irish rhapsody no. 1' for full orchestra, written and premiered in 1957, is more representative. Cast in one continuous movement, its whole approach attests the conscious desire to devise an unmistakably Irish idiom.

The enervating debate concerning the relative merits of a national and cosmopolitan expression continued through the decades, but it was not such a critical factor in the outlook of the second generation of composers, who benefited from a combination of the pioneering work of their predecessors, the improving circumstances of musical life, and a consequent sea-change in public perception. While the principal figures all reveal individual personality, they are united in a greater confidence in engaging with the available technical resources of the broader expression. The greater access to education was one factor in the burgeoning confidence. Like Frederick May, both Selina (Ina) Boyle and Archibald (A. J.) Potter studied in London with Ralph Vaughan Williams. Both were versatile and prolific, exploring a wide range of forms and styles while adhering to the tonal system. The majority of Boyle's work emanates from the first half of her life, with the pastoral 'Colin Clout' (1921) and the early symphony 'Glencree' (1927) provoking a warm response when performed in Dublin and London. She was resident in County Wicklow, where A. J. Potter, born in Belfast, also came to live. Potter was especially catholic in the range of his creative interests, and many of his works, from the early 'Overture to a kitchen comedy' (1950) through two symphonies to the late arrangements for brass and military band, provide evidence of his characteristic humour. Gerard Victory was even more prolific and demonstrated a wide range in his technical approach to composition. The requiem 'Ultima rerum' (1981) for soloists, chorus, and full orchestra was his most ambitious statement. As director of music in Radio Telefís Éireann, Victory did much to promote the cause of contemporary Irish music. His successor in this post when he retired in 1982 was John Kinsella (1932–   ), one of the most progressive members of the modern school of Irish composition. His creative achievement is notable in that he is largely self-taught. An extensive catalogue of works, including two symphonies and two violin concertos, reflects also Kinsella's especial penchant for chamber music. Some echo of the central debate can be perceived in the compositional history of Seóirse Bodley. An early experimental tendency has given way to later works of a more accessible nature, such as the symphony no. 3 'Ceol', commissioned for the opening of the National Concert Hall in 1981.

Ireland proved inspirational to a number of English composers. Arnold Bax (1883–1953) and Ernest Moeran (1894–1950) were the principal figures who shared a love for the country and for its music. Bax was primarily concerned to absorb the spirit of the nation and to have this inform his creativity. This desire refers to one particular early phase of his life that saw the tone-poems 'Cathleen ni Hoolihan' (1905), 'Into the twilight' (1908), 'In the faery hills' (1909), and 'Roscatha' (1910), all of which demonstrated Bax writing 'Irishly', as he said himself. Moeran's enthralment was perhaps less perfervid but ultimately more sustained. His violin concerto (1941) remains his finest tribute to his adopted land and especially to his beloved Kerry. Both composers were well versed in the ways of Ireland and they embraced its character ardently; but the Irish note was for them an exotic and was not central to their creative personalities.

While a fractured tradition has precluded the natural emergence of a recognisable school of composition, the creative endeavour apparent in Ireland in the 1980s and 1990s is a measure of the improvement in the circumstances of music. The observer is encouraged not only by the greater numbers contributing to increased activity but also by the fact that this generation is drawn from all corners of the land. Gerald Barry (1952–) from County Clare and Raymond Deane (1953–) from Achill Island, both of whom have studied with Stockhausen, are two of the most prominent voices. John Buckley (1951–) comes from County Limerick; his 'Concerto for chamber orchestra' (1981) was commissioned by the New Irish Chamber Orchestra, one of the most energetic of the newer performing groups. Somewhat more senior are Frank Corcoran (1944–) from Tipperary and Jerome de Bromhead (1945–) from Waterford. Both Eric Sweeney (1948–) and Roger Doyle (1949–) are Dublin-born; the former is based in Waterford, where he teaches and has done much to encourage the performance of twentieth-century music. Yet another active composer, Jane O'Leary (1946–), works from her adopted home in Galway; she settled in Ireland in 1972 from her native Connecticut and like Sweeney has contributed to the presentation of contemporary music through her work since 1976 as director of the active chamber group, Concorde. The industry displayed by these and younger colleagues attests to Ireland's growing maturity as a musical nation.

This vigour has been matched by a corresponding improvement in the circumstances of music. This is manifest in increased participation in music-making: the Cork Symphony Orchestra (1934) and the Dublin Symphony Orchestra (1966) are two active amateur bodies, while the Dublin Baroque Players (1965) and Hibernian Orchestra (1981) explore a more specialised repertoire. The Irish Chamber Orchestra (1970) constitutes the sole professional orchestral ensemble independent of the broadcasting service. There also exist national and regional orchestras of young players performing to a high standard. The commitment to choral work demonstrated by Radio Telefís Éireann has contributed to a spectacular revival in this area, which finds a celebratory focus each year in the Cork international choral and folk dance festival, founded in 1954. The global character of this annual celebration is also a feature of the separate international festivals of organ and piano that take place in Dublin. The addition of the biennial Dublin international organ festival (1980) and the triennial international piano competition which commenced in 1988, Dublin's millennium year, have helped raise the country's artistic profile. The National Concert Hall is available to benefit both these competitions: this long-awaited facility has been further enhanced with the inauguration in 1991 of a splendid pipe organ built by the Bray-based firm of Kenneth Jones.

BY the end of our period in the mid 1980s the prospects for music in Ireland had improved considerably. Composers had largely broken free of the burden of tradition and their disparate work looked promising for the future. That no recognisable creative school had emerged was just one legacy of earlier division; but then the desirability of such a school is debatable. This heartening animation was directly related to improved financial circumstances. Individual endeavour with directed central support had done much to address the earlier penury. Apart from the continuing involvement of the broadcasting service, the establishment of the arts council, another child of 1951, proved the single most important initiative. Many of the commendable departures in subsequent years relied on a measure of support from this body. It operated to promote both art music and the indigenous practice; the latter profited by the appointment of a traditional music officer in 1981 and the establishment in 1987 of the Irish Traditional Music Archive.

The place of the arts in Irish education (1979), a report commissioned by the arts council from Ciaran Benson, opens with the bold statement: 'The arts have been neglected in Irish education.' This remains true. Notwithstanding the advances in music education and especially in access to technical training for the committed student, the majority of first- and second-level schools can offer their pupils little opportunity to become acquainted with the art, though it is heartening that in 1980 over 20,000 candidates took Royal Irish Academy of Music examinations.[28] Without the required resources and commitment, the country will not realise a level of literacy necessary to promote a universal musical resurgence. A paucity of venues for music-making is another legacy of earlier stasis; and the problem remains that those that do exist are concentrated in the larger urban areas. It would however be difficult to exaggerate the vitalising influence of the National Concert Hall. Also the ready access to broadcasts has gone some way towards redressing the geographical imbalance; through its transmission of live and recorded music, its illustrated talks, through its orchestras, choirs, and quartet, and through its commissions, and in the willing support it has afforded various extraneous ventures, the national broadcasting service has shouldered an inordinate responsibility for music-making in the country. The renaming of its principal ensemble as the National Symphony Orchestra in 1990

[28] Pine & Acton, *To talent alone*, pp 311–12.

provides clear acceptance of this inherited obligation. However, that the service continues to constitute the major patron is indicative of a fundamental weakness in Irish musical life. Conversely, the accepted didactic potency of the broadcast media has only intermittently been employed in the service of remedying the generally low level of musical literacy.

This has been a preparative period; the musicians of the twentieth century have perforce laid the foundations for a more vigorous future. In working to this end, a disproportionate burden has fallen to isolated individuals and agencies. It is a tribute to this commitment that despite the fitful application, the uneven achievement, and the enduring imperfections, the outlook for music in Ireland appears far more promising than the observer could have hoped for in 1921.

CHAPTER XXII

Music in Northern Ireland since 1921

ROY JOHNSTON

To the ordinary Ulster family, living on the land or in the towns, music in 1921 meant hymns and psalms in church on Sunday, and in the rest of the week the popular music of the day, learned by hearing it from others or from sheet music played on the family piano. The pianists in the family would have learned technique and theory from a teacher by private tuition, and been given music to play from the progressive instructional material put out by the examining bodies; they might be working also on set pieces for the competitive musical festivals. To the family's encounter with music there would be added the music that was heard at dances, to an increasing extent the music that was a necessary accompaniment to the silent film in the local picture-house, and the songs learned at school. Music at primary school meant singing and was taught by tonic sol-fa; emphasis was laid on the heritage of songs from England, Scotland, Wales, and Ireland as collected in *The national song book*, widely used in northern schools. It was through its Irish section that the national music (Bunting's term) was most likely to be known. The oral tradition by now carried heavy overlays of later accretion of rural and industrial work-songs, and of songs that for various reasons were unlikely to be printed. The piano was a symbol of respectability, and its purchase took precedence over many things in the setting up of house: the newly-weds might not be musical, but it would be expected that their children would be 'sent to music'. If a male member of a family was in a band (women generally played the piano and were home-bound, men played in bands; both sang in choirs), the house might also contain a flute, a brass instrument, bagpipes, or a button accordion.

The church choir and the amateur band were forms of communal music-making common to town and countryside. It was in the towns that the more highly organised forms of musical activity were to be found, and where the professional musician was most likely to find a living: children learned other instruments besides the piano, amateur musical societies put on concerts and operettas, choral music played a greater part in the churches. It was there that the American invasion of the ballroom with jazz and ragtime was to be encountered, and where the voices of Caruso, Galli-Curci, and John McCormack were likely to be heard on the gramophone. The concentration in the Belfast conurbation of the majority of the population provided by sheer weight of numbers the most likely ground for the emergence of the concert and opera life, which by the latter half of the nineteenth century had become a feature of western industrialised society.[1] Other northern towns had not been ignored by the international virtuosi and the touring opera companies; but it was a hard reality that the 'musicality' of a town (however perceived) mattered less in the preparation of an itinerary than a six-figure population. Belfast's relations with Dublin were cordial enough: the two cities might be the same size by the turn of the century, but the newer was content to acknowledge the deeper and wider musical life of the elder and, while not dependent, to draw upon it frequently for concert soloists and other services.

Size apart, it seems likely that Belfast did not differ much in its musical life from such another provincial town as Cork, and indeed the general Ulster picture just sketched contained no major features to mark it out from similar communities in the rest of Ireland, notwithstanding those influences to be expected from its Calvinism and the Scots origin of many of its people. Any expectation that Northern Ireland might develop characteristics of its own as a musical expression of its independence was decisively counteracted by external forces. Within the next seven decades it was to absorb, like the western world in general, the impact of changes in its musical experience that transformed the 1921 scene out of all recognition and culminated in the enormous worldwide transmission of music by mass recording technology. This cultural revolution was conditioned not by traditional appetites for music but by the demands of the 'youth-quake', its content not confined to music of western or of any culture.

Just as in the third quarter of the nineteenth century concert life had settled in Europe in general into the pattern it was to maintain, so by the 1990s it was possible to see on both sides of the Irish border a not dissimilar stage of equilibrium reached in the development of music in general. It was evident in education, in concert life, in opera, in jazz, in traditional music, in a common saturation by pop music, in the presence of music promoted by broadcasting and arts council. In some of these aspects development had proceeded from 1921 in much the same way and at much the same pace in both parts of the island. In other aspects, the splitting of the government of the island and the separation of one part from Britain had caused musical development to take different paths, activated by different stimuli and proceeding at different rates of growth.

[1] For music in nineteenth-century Belfast, see above, vi, 502–3, 510–11, 518–19.

Tied to the Westminster economy, the new northern statelet would be unable to avoid the industrial slump of the 1930s or participation in the second world war; but on the credit side it would be eligible for its share of some pioneering social initiatives. By virtue of its possession of appurtenances of self-government, it was better placed than some to receive regional benefits and make use of them. In music these were to include such major agents of development as broadcasting and government subsidy of the arts through an arts council.

With the coming of a measure of self-government, a civil service and a judiciary would be created. Major institutions such as the university, hitherto regional, would find a quasi-national dimension thrust upon them. Existing functions such as health and education would find themselves responsible neither to Dublin nor to Westminster but to new government departments closer at hand, with new prospects of mutual dialogue and influence. Provincial newspapers would learn the skills of reporting a parliament. While much of the image of independence was more apparent than real, it gave an enhanced *amour-propre* in some quarters, especially in the newly created institutions directly serving the state. In music there was something of an enhanced receptivity caused by this and by an increase in the musical public, hitherto largely mercantile and professional, that had sustained the concert life of Belfast since its beginnings in the eighteenth century.

In Belfast the year 1921 entered in unwonted silence. There was no singing of 'Auld lang syne' round the clock tower of the Albert memorial on New Year's eve, for the city was under curfew. For the remainder of the 1920/21 season, concerts began early and encores were dispensed with. By and large, the concert life of Belfast ran in the mode into which it had settled fifty years before. The Philharmonic Society, founded in 1874, put on three or four subscription concerts a year in the Ulster Hall, at each of which a major choral work was performed[2] by the society's amateur chorus and its orchestra, which was largely amateur with a stiffening of professionals. The orchestra also played concerts on its own; there were occasional chamber concerts and celebrity recitals. Other towns in Northern Ireland had musical societies that gave concerts of the same kind; as Belfast lacked the resources necessary for a fully professional orchestra, so these towns were unresourced in comparison with Belfast.

Musically speaking, the separation of the six northern counties from the rest of the island caused less disruption and realignment than in many other fields of the polity. The repertory of concert hall and opera house was international enough in character and appeal to transcend political boundaries. Musical activity existed on a local or, at largest, provincial scale; there was no national symphony orchestra or opera company. The Irish itineraries

[2] See Malcolm Ruthven, *Belfast Philharmonic Society, 1874–1974* (Belfast, 1974), pp 60–63.

of visiting artists and touring companies continued to include the major cities of the whole island. As it happened, at the time of partition the musical life of Belfast was being nourished less from Dublin than from the north of England. E. Godfrey Brown, who conducted the Belfast Philharmonic and its orchestra, came from Barrow-in-Furness. John Vine, singing teacher and founder and conductor of choirs, came from the north of England; so did Tom Corrin, who was to become the new ministry of education's first inspector of music in schools. In the absence of a professional symphony orchestra, an academy of music, or a university chair of music, musical taste was dominated from the organ loft. The leaders of public music-making—Brown, Vine, Charles Brennan of St Anne's cathedral, the composer and critic Norman Hay—all had posts as organists and choirmasters.

Agents of the great twentieth-century shift from active to passive participation in music were already on the scene. If the gramophone was still too pricey for the lower classes, it was proving a domestic competitor for the ubiquitous piano. The importance of the concert and the theatre as main sources of music and public entertainment was challenged by the cinema: in any town or village, a hall could be adapted with minimal outlay and capital expenditure to show films, and a profit could be ensured to the entrepreneur from admission prices low enough to attract audiences from a wider social spectrum than theatre or concerts. Throughout Northern Ireland in the 1920s, the principal source of employment for professional instrumental players was in the picture-houses, where the music for the silent films was supplied by anything from a single pianist (usually a woman) to a sizeable orchestra.[3]

The Philharmonic Society's orchestra and the Belfast Symphony Orchestra which Godfrey Brown founded were part-time and largely amateur bodies, with a core of professional players. A permanent full-time orchestra for the city was an idea close to Brown's heart, but he recognised the difficulties. In Belfast, as in Dublin, most of the good instrumentalists were fully employed in picture-houses and theatres. Disturbances sometimes prevented army and police bandsmen (who supplied brass and woodwind) from attending on concert nights. Amateurs and semi-professionals needed more rehearsal than could be afforded.[4]

Help was nearer at hand than many, including perhaps Brown himself, recognised. The announcements in September 1924 of the season's programmes of Philharmonic and celebrity concerts (given by internationally famous solo artists on tour such as Melba and Kreisler, and continuing under successive promoters well into the 1950s) were overshadowed by the

[3] By 1928 in Britain cinemas provided 75–80 per cent of 'paid musical employment' (Cyril Ehrlich, *The music profession in Britain since the 18th century* (Oxford, 1985), p. 199).
[4] Letter from E. Godfrey Brown to Sir Charles Brett, 3 May 1920 (P.R.O.N.I., D970).

imminent commencement of broadcasting from the new station in Linenhall Street in Belfast. The inaugural programme of music on the evening of Monday 15 September was listened to as far away as Dublin,[5] and tribute was paid to the 'operators' who 'broadcasted the music very efficiently'.[6] As a region, Northern Ireland qualified to be allocated a B.B.C. orchestra, permanently based in Belfast and composed of full-time professional musicians. Godfrey Brown, while retaining his conductorship of the Philharmonic orchestra and chorus, was appointed director of music. Within a few years orchestral concerts run by the B.B.C., with an orchestra augmented on occasion to seventy players and upwards, included some of the finest players that money could bring to Belfast.[7]

Brown began with some adventitious advantages. The new station shared with its counterparts in Great Britain John Reith's obligation not to depart from a high moral tone. It had also peculiar to itself the extreme touchiness of its divided population; but music was blessedly neutral. Local programmes were supposed to be complementary to London programmes, but since the new technology would be beset for some considerable time with teething problems, Belfast, with its call sign 2BE, was left to its own devices and resources for most of the schedules.[8] Brown could flood the air with music to his heart's content. By mid October of the opening year the first part of the Philharmonic's performance of Mendelssohn's 'Elijah' was being broadcast from the Ulster Hall.

In 1925 a new critical voice began to appear in the *Belfast Telegraph*. E. Norman Hay came from Coleraine; he had an Oxford doctorate in music and a handful of impressive compositions to his name, performed both at home and in Great Britain. Under the house pseudonym 'Rathcol', his output of criticism and the style of his weekly column on general musical topics reached a wide audience and placed him in a more influential position in the formation of musical taste than that enjoyed either by his predecessors or by his successors.

In the early 1930s the highly industrialised city of Belfast felt the force of the national slump. Professional musicians in the north at large had to face an additional disaster. With the arrival of the talking films in 1929 the boom in employment of musicians in the cinemas was over. The pianists were paid off, the orchestras disbanded. Nor could they look forward, like the shipyard workers, to a return of work when the slump would end: the silent films were gone for good. Some found work in Godfrey Brown's adventurous musicmaking. As early as 1928 the *B.B.C. handbook* for the year had noted preco-

---

[5] The Dublin commentator who complained about the English accent of the announcer was presumably not aware that it belonged to the young Tyrone Guthrie.

[6] *Belfast Telegraph*, 16 Sept. 1924.

[7] E. Godfrey Brown in Aloys Fleischmann (ed.), *Music in Ireland* (Cork, 1952), p. 264.

[8] Rex Cathcart, *The most contrary region: the B.B.C. in Northern Ireland, 1924–84* (Belfast, 1984), p. 20.

cious development in Northern Ireland: a permanent station orchestra, a station military band, its own dance band and chamber music quartet. Brown could tap into financial resources far beyond what he could have hoped for, especially in those straitened days, from any form of purely local management. His main orchestra played a symphonic repertoire of breadth and depth, as a glance through the programmes shows. For soloists of national reputation, vocal and instrumental, the best were simply summoned from London.

Even more remarkable was the extent of the extramural work to which Brown committed his players. The philharmonic societies of Bangor, Lisburn, Ballymena, and Derry, using their own choruses and Brown's orchestra, or with local orchestras stiffened with Brown's professionals, had their concerts broadcast from their town halls. Brown persuaded the Belfast corporation and the Y.M.C.A. to join with the B.B.C. in promoting concert series in the Ulster Hall and Wellington Hall. The corporation was also persuaded to allow a series, which ran all the year round, of weekly afternoon broadcast concerts in the art gallery of its new municipal museum.

In 1929/30 came the first of four remarkable seasons. The B.B.C. orchestra played a series of twelve concerts in the Wellington Hall and a spring series of thirteen in the Ulster Hall, as well as children's and provincial concerts, and it provided the professional core of the orchestra of the six Belfast Philharmonic concerts.[9] The assiduous Belfast concertgoer could have attended three dozen concerts; if stamina was sufficient to take in a visit to the museum on Wednesday afternoons, that total was more than doubled. The following season the new pattern expanded to include six concerts in Bangor. Brown had also begun having guest conductors. Sir Henry Wood (a personal friend) and Adrian Boult both came several times in the next three seasons, and so did Fritz Brase from Dublin. For the Philharmonic, Arthur Bliss came to conduct his new 'Morning heroes' and Vaughan Williams his 'Sancta civitas'. Elgar, Brown's favourite composer, was at last persuaded in 1932 to come over and conduct 'The dream of Gerontius'. Norman Hay was given the baton on the occasions when his own music was being performed.

There had never been so much orchestral music in Belfast, or of such a standard. Average attendances in the Ulster Hall were 1,100 (capacity 1,200) and even in the museum 500–600.[10] Nor had it ever cost the concertgoer so little. Virtually the whole cost was met by the B.B.C. The museum concerts were free.[11] Seats at the Ulster Hall and Wellington Hall concerts cost 6d.

---

[9] Its name changed several times. It began as the '2BE Orchestra' and progressed through 'B.B.C. Wireless Symphony Orchestra', increasing in size as it went.

[10] Speech by Godfrey Brown, reported in *Belfast Telegraph*, 28 May 1932.

[11] Wednesday was early closing day. In his concern to extend the social range of his audiences Brown was following his own bent as much as the B.B.C.'s; his 1920 letter to Brett (above, p. 653, n. 4) had proposed Friday night concerts in a hall on the Shankill Road 'to interest another class of people'.

and 1*s*. For comparison, the Grand Opera House was charging up to 4*s*. 9*d*. for the Carl Rosa opera company and the D'Oyly Carte, the Philharmonic up to 8*s*. 6*d*., and the celebrity concerts up to half-a-guinea (10*s*. 6*d*.).

In such a plentiful provision of orchestral music, the virtual absence of opera went apparently unlamented. The Carl Rosa, frequent annual visitors for a two- or three-week season in the 1920s, visited Belfast in only three years during the 1930s, for a total in the decade of five weeks. The apparent buoyancy of the orchestral concert, however, introduces a distortion into an overall picture that is more truly represented by the paucity of opera. The Carl Rosa was undergoing energetic rationalisations at the hands of the Phillips family (H. B. Phillips, who took over the company in 1924, came from Derry and began his musical career as a choirboy in St Columb's cathedral). The Phillipses were doing all that could be done, in their way, at that time, to make the Carl Rosa a viable touring opera company. But there were economic forces at work against which the skills and style of the old-world manager were ineffective. It was becoming more and more evident that the arts would require public subsidy to survive, let alone develop. But matters continued as they were to the outbreak of the second world war, the problems masked for part of that time in Northern Ireland, and especially in Belfast, by Godfrey Brown's exploitation of the munificence of his faraway masters in the B.B.C.

The fragility of the bubble was demonstrated in the 1933/4 season when concert admission prices were raised to 1*s*. 3*d*. and 2*s*. 4*d*. Immediately, the Ulster Hall and Wellington Hall audiences fell by more than half. The first waves of rationalisation had hit the B.B.C.: the reliance of broadcasting on music as its staple was giving way to talks, features, drama, variety, and outside broadcasts. The museum concerts were discontinued. In the 1934/5 season both they and the spring seasons stopped, and the main Ulster Hall series was reduced from six concerts to four. With an attenuation also of the Wellington Hall concerts from eight to four, the great days were over.

Godfrey Brown's work for music was recognised by the award of an O.B.E. in the 1936 new year honours. That summer Hitler entered the Rhineland, Mussolini's Abyssinian campaign ended victoriously, and the Spanish civil war began. At the Philharmonic's 'Messiah' on Friday 11 December in the Ulster Hall the performance was interrupted for a relay of the broadcast of Edward VIII's abdication speech; it resumed with the bass aria 'Why do the nations so furiously rage together?'[12]

In 1937 Godfrey Brown was succeeded as director of music at the B.B.C. by B. Walton O'Donnell, conductor in London of the B.B.C. military band. In O'Donnell's second season, 1938/9, the Belfast corporation withdrew its support completely and there were no Ulster Hall concerts. In August 1939,

---

[12] *Belfast Telegraph*, 12 Dec. 1936.

after a short illness, O'Donnell died. A fortnight later Britain and France declared war on Germany. The B.B.C. put its whole operation on a war footing. B.B.C. Northern Ireland was reduced to a skeleton staff.[13] It fell to Godfrey Brown to conduct the orchestra in its final studio concert, before handing notices terminating their engagements to the forty permanent players.[14] After a few weeks, David Curry formed a light orchestra and started Saturday night concerts in the Wellington Hall. A trickle of midday recitals began with local artists. In December the Philharmonic managed a 'Messiah' in the Grosvenor Hall, the Ulster Hall being taken over for food control administration. In May 1940, of all unlikely and welcome visitors, the Carl Rosa came for a week, their first visit in six years.

There came the news in July 1940 of the death on active service of Tom Corrin, since 1925 inspector of music in Northern Ireland schools. The teaching of music in the elementary schools had been almost entirely in singing, and based on tonic sol-fa; its hegemony was by no means unchallenged but it was supported by long usage and the Curwen publishing empire. Corrin's programme in 1932 preached new orthodoxy: 'Eye training may be carried out from the earliest stages in staff notation solely; the sol-fa time notation need not be introduced at all.'[15] Corrin was popular with teachers and pupils, and organised, with Godfrey Brown, orchestral concerts for schoolchildren. He also frequented the north's musical festivals, which began allocating him a day to conduct, non-competitively, the massed school choirs of the area. Norman Hay thought the world of him, and argued in his column for 'a body of musical organisers on an area basis, to be trained for two years in the art of teaching under Corrin'.[16] Hay, in failing health himself, died at Portstewart in September 1943.

In music, there had always been cross-border traffic, notwithstanding the lack of common institutions. Fritz Brase and Vincent O'Brien were invited to conduct in Belfast, Godfrey Brown in Dublin. Solo artists knew the studios of both B.B.C. and Radio Éireann. Since the wartime restrictions on the passage of the Irish Sea affected the whole island, this internal traffic increased. What is remarkable is not how little public music-making there was in Northern Ireland in the war years, but how much: in particular, how many artists of quality made the crossing from Britain, with all its restrictions and hazards.

By far the most fertile seed for the future was planted as early as 1940, when the Pilgrim Trust made a grant of £750 to the joint committee for adult education at Queen's University for the promotion of 'Music for the

---

[13] Cathcart, *Most contrary region*, p. 106.
[14] Brown in Fleischmann, *Mus. in Ire.*, p. 264.
[15] N.I. ministry of education, *Programme of instruction for public elementary schools* (Belfast, 1932), p. 24.
[16] *Belfast Telegraph*, 9 Jan. 1932.

People' and 'Art for the People'. Encouraged by the success of pilot schemes, the joint committee approached the trust for assistance in establishing for Northern Ireland a council on the lines of the Council for the Encouragement of Music and the Arts (C.E.M.A.) that had been set up in Great Britain.[17] The trust agreed to contribute £1,500 for two years on condition that the government of Northern Ireland would give a similar sum each year and take over responsibility for the scheme at the end of the second year. The government agreed, and C.E.M.A. (Northern Ireland) held its first meeting on 1 February 1943. In its first year of reporting, music recitals promoted by C.E.M.A. (N.I.) took place not only in Belfast but in Armagh, Ballymena, Coleraine, Derry, Dungannon, Enniskillen, Larne, Newry, Omagh, Portadown, and Portrush.[18]

As the war neared its end C.E.M.A. (N.I.) was learning to walk; but it would have to run. Full orchestral concerts and opera were sorely missed and not to be had in Northern Ireland, but the skies and the seas were safe again. C.E.M.A. (N.I.) brought Sadlers Wells Opera for a three-week season in the summer of 1945. When peace returned, the B.B.C. showed no sign of reconstituting its Northern Ireland orchestra. The more welcome was the enterprise of C.E.M.A. (N.I.) in bringing Sir Malcolm Sargent and the Liverpool Philharmonic orchestra to play to packed houses in April 1946, and in July the London Philharmonic. Smyth's of Belfast, local promoters of pre-war celebrity concerts, brought the Hallé orchestra under John Barbirolli to the echoing spaces of the King's Hall, and another local organisation, the Young Philanthropists, brought the Dublin Grand Opera Society for a week in September to the Hippodrome. It appeared that C.E.M.A. (N.I.) was now in a position to withdraw, like C.E.M.A. in Great Britain, into the hortatory function explicit in its title. But not yet: detecting a curiosity for ballet, it brought the Ballets Jooss and Rambert, and encouraged Patricia Mulholland to set up her own Irish Ballet to perform throughout the north.

When the B.B.C. returned to producing local programmes, music was given a place; and local singers, choirs, and bands were to be heard again on their own wavelength. In 1947 two notable appointments to the station staff were made. E. W. G. Boucher and Havelock Nelson came from Dublin, the former to be head of music; they were to exercise great influence on music and music-making in Northern Ireland both within the B.B.C. and in the community at large until, and after, they retired in the 1980s. Andrew Stuart, appointed regional controller in 1949, pressed for and got a Northern Ireland Light Orchestra of sixteen part-time professional players. Under David Curry it gave its first broadcast in July 1949. It fulfilled a broadcasting role

[17] *C.E.M.A. (N.I.), 1st report: 1 Feb. 1943–31 Mar. 1944* (Belfast, 1944).
[18] Ibid.

and also provided the professional core of Godfrey Brown's Philharmonic orchestra; but it was a case of half a loaf being better than no bread.

In 1947 Ivor Keys was appointed the first full-time lecturer in music at Queen's University. In 1949 a second lectureship was created and the degree of bachelor of music was established in the faculty of arts. In 1951 Keys became the first incumbent of the Hamilton Harty chair of music. Under his active guidance and example (he was a considerable pianist) a university music society came into being, promoting concerts and giving concerts itself.

In his missionary curricular work in the schools before the war, Tom Corrin had laboured alone. His postwar successor, Tim Turner, worked in a more congenial climate. The 1947 education act[19] offered new opportunities, which some local education authorities were willing to grasp. Belfast appointed Douglas Dawn as its adviser in music in 1951. He spent twelve years developing, organising, and encouraging, and at the carol concert in December 1955 his youth orchestra made its first public appearance.

In the 1920s Norman Hay had energetically advocated an Ulster college of music. There were difficulties and a lack of enabling legislation. It was in the period of Dawn's successor, Leonard Pugh, that Belfast decided to establish its own City of Belfast School of Music with, eventually, government sanction. If Leonard Pugh was building on the foundation laid by Douglas Dawn, his vision of a flexible interrelation of the school of music with the schools was his own. The teaching of music at higher levels was intimately linked with the teaching of music in the schools, and the staff of the school of music worked partly in the day schools and partly in the school of music.

IN Northern Ireland in the 1920s the responsibility for the recovery, preservation, and promotion of traditional music rested largely on the urban musician with a classical training. Recordings and radio duly arrived, and by the outbreak of the second world war had already done a great deal of the work of rescue. When the B.B.C. in Northern Ireland first decided to do something about traditional music, it promulgated an 'Ulster airs' scheme (launched in 1936), in which it commissioned arrangements from Ulster composers. Norman Hay had reservations about the arrangement principle, and (impressed by the song-collecting work of his fellow-townsman Sam Henry) pleaded strongly in his column for the recording of the songs and singers of the countryside in their traditional styles before they vanished from the earth. The B.B.C. also encouraged David Curry to make arrangements of traditional airs and dances for a small group of orchestral instruments; as 'Irish rhythms' they became a very popular series of radio programmes. In Belfast the uilleann pipe tradition was kept alive by Richard O'Mealy, Francis McPeake, and others; and it was from a Belfast base that Carl Hardebeck

[19] 1947, c. 3 (27 Mar. 1947).

continued his researches into the music of the Gaeltacht, after his brief tenure of the professorship of Irish music in Cork. Hardebeck lived and died in comparative obscurity. Seán Ó Baoill, who had been his friend and amanuensis, was commissioned by the B.B.C. in the 1950s to make a recording survey of folk music in Northern Ireland. Over 200 vocal and instrumental items were recorded and two notable series of broadcasts, 'Music on the hearth' and 'As I roved out', drew on the results of the survey and spread the music widely.

Jazz found a ready reception in Northern Ireland. What is remarkable about the visit of Will Marion Cook's Southern Syncopated Orchestra of black musicians in November 1921 is not that it happened, but that it took place during the season, in the Ulster Hall, and lasted for a fortnight with performances twice daily. As elsewhere in Ireland, the popularity of jazz was nourished by gramophone records, by the visits of notable jazz musicians and jazz-influenced dance bands, and by the improvisatory nature of the art-form, which encouraged people to try it themselves. In the second world war, some of the U.S. soldiers who passed through on their way to the war in Europe played jazz with local groups.[20] On a visit to Belfast in 1954 the Chris Barber band, one of the best-known of the British traditional jazz groups, discovered Ottilie Patterson, a young blues singer who went on to achieve international success with the band.[21] By the 1960s Northern Ireland was established on the jazz-band touring circuit and received visits from all the major bands and solo musicians. The outstanding activity in the locally based jazz scene was the club at Queen's University, which organised the successful 'Jazz at the Whitla' concerts. It was on this foundation that the substantial jazz component of the Belfast Festival at Queen's was laid.

The best-known of Ulster-born composers was Hamilton Harty. To the 1920s and 1930s belong the Handel and John Field arrangements, the piano concerto for Michele Esposito, and the poem for orchestra 'The children of Lir', which had its origin in a holiday in north Antrim, near the Sea of Moyle mentioned in the legend. Harty died in 1941, and in 1946 his library was presented to Queen's University. The scores of his own music that it contained, with later supplementation, formed the comprehensive Harty archive. The other parts of his library formed the nucleus of the music section of the main university library.[22] Although he was an eclectic com-poser, a native accent was always present in his work. A revival of interest in Harty's music in the 1980s was led by the commercial recordings made by the Ulster Orchestra. The same orchestra revived in performance some of the music of Norman Hay, also an eclectic composer in his earlier and best

[20] Solly Lipsitz in Michael Longley (ed.), *Causeway: the arts in Ulster* (Belfast, 1971), p. 132.
[21] Ibid., p. 133.
[22] David Greer (ed.), *Hamilton Harty, his life and music* (Belfast, 1978), p. 152.

days. 'Paean', for contralto, chorus, and string orchestra, had been performed at the Three Choirs festival at Worcester, and the tone poem 'Dunluce' at the Henry Wood promenade concerts. Other works awaiting revival include his 'Wind among the reeds' of 1921, 'To wonder', and the string quartet of 1918 published by the Carnegie Trust. When the B.B.C. initiated its 'Ulster airs' scheme, Hay accepted the editorship and made some arrangements himself.

The 'Ulster airs' scheme elicited arrangements from Charles Brennan, who also wrote music for the organ; from Redmond Friel, a Derry composer who placed much of his considerable output with bodies in the Republic;[23] and from two Ulster-born composers based at that time in London, Howard Ferguson and Joan Trimble. Much of Joan Trimble's work was written for two pianos, the medium in which she and her sister Valerie made their concert career. In 1957 she was commissioned to write 'Blind Raftery', an opera for television. Howard Ferguson showed himself able to write original songs of great power, but composed best on a broader canvas, with his octet of 1933, partita (1936) which exists in orchestral and two-piano versions, piano sonata (1940), and piano concerto (1951). After two extended choral works, 'Amore langueo' (1956) and 'The dream of the rood' (1959), he decided to abandon composition and turned his attention to musicology and the editing of early keyboard music. Havelock Nelson, born in Cork but of Ulster ancestry and long domicile, showed versatility and wrote in many forms. The bulk of his work was choral and vocal, but he also wrote orchestral suites, ballets, a sinfonietta (1950), a piano concertina (1956), and chamber music as well as instrumental music for plays and broadcasts.

During the second world war the Belfast tenor James Johnston, well known in Northern Ireland as a concert and oratorio soloist, made a reputation in opera in Dublin. After the war he sang principal roles at both Sadlers Wells and Covent Garden, earning a salute from one authority as 'a singer to whom postwar British opera owed a great deal'.[24] International reputations were made in the postwar years by the soprano Heather Harper and the flautist James Galway.

Godfrey Brown retired in March 1950, after thirty-eight years with the Belfast Philharmonic. The Philharmonic orchestra was an ad hoc body, convened for each of the season's half-dozen concerts. C.E.M.A. (N.I.) again forsook the touchline for the field of play. With the help of its grant from the Belfast corporation it created a post of choral and orchestral conductor for the city of Belfast, the holder's services to be placed at the disposal of the Philharmonic. The conductor would also form and conduct a permanent semi-professional orchestra in Belfast, as well as carrying out other duties for

---

[23] See Fleischmann, *Mus. in Ire.*, pp 170–75.
[24] Lord Harewood in Alan Blyth (ed.), *Opera on record* (3 vols, London, 1979–84), i, 255.

C.E.M.A. (N.I.). A new City of Belfast Orchestra gave its first concert in October 1950. The objects of the exercise were achieved; yet, perhaps because Godfrey Brown cast so long a shadow, the new orchestra could not fill the Ulster Hall. When its conductor Denis Mulgan left after five years, the post was wound up, and the decision taken to offer a season of rehearsals and performances to a guest conductor.[25] The man who added this appointment to his portfolio of work in London and elsewhere was Maurice Miles. Over the next few seasons capacity audiences greeted the City of Belfast Orchestra at most of its concerts, in the Ulster Hall and elsewhere.

The recollection sometimes encountered, that the Carl Rosa (and for that matter the D'Oyly Carte) 'used to come faithfully every year', is not founded in fact. Over the four decades 1921–60 the total experience of touring opera was:

Carl Rosa	39 weeks
D'Oyly Carte	13 weeks
other companies	29 weeks
TOTAL	81 weeks

In thirteen of the forty years there was no visit from a touring company. When Carl Rosa tours resumed in the 1940s they did not include Northern Ireland. The company's first reappearance in Belfast in eleven years was in 1951. Financial crises forced Mrs Phillips (who had taken over on the retirement of her husband) to make the pilgrimage to the arts council, as C.E.M.A. in Great Britain had renamed itself. A Carl Rosa trust was formed, and was able to launch an autumn tour of fourteen weeks in 1953, which included Belfast. So did the tours of 1955 and 1956, but after that Northern Ireland saw the Carl Rosa no more.

Until the late 1950s no other agency performed large-scale opera, ever the most expensive of art forms; economic circumstances had made touring by major companies virtually impossible. Sadlers Wells, after two postwar visits, found it too expensive to come regularly. Even within the island, the Dublin Grand Opera Society appearance of 1946 had not been followed up. The arts council of Great Britain was not inclined to allocate a disproportionate amount of its limited resources to the underwriting of a national touring opera company, after its experience with the Carl Rosa.[26] Havelock Nelson, indefatigable in the encouragement of local music-making by example and precept, saw a place for locally produced opera in the C.E.M.A. (N.I.) strat-

[25] *C.E.M.A. (N.I.) report, 1954–5* (Belfast, 1955), p. 4.
[26] The Carl Rosa's relationship with Mrs Phillips and the arts council had not proved easy. The arts council ultimately withdrew its support, and the Royal Carl Rosa Opera Company, after 85 years of existence, gave its last performance in London in Sept. 1960.

egy of bringing the arts to the provincial towns. He began in June 1950 with a Haydn one-act opera, 'La canterina', performed by local soloists and his Studio String Orchestra. Two years later the little enterprise took to itself the name of Studio Opera Group, and throughout the 1950s it explored the repertory of short chamber operas and performed them, in English, before audiences in Belfast and on tour throughout Northern Ireland and in the Republic of Ireland. In 1961 the group broke new ground with a production of 'The marriage of Figaro', and soon showed itself capable of performing the full-length chamber operas of Mozart and Rossini. It went on to demonstrate a notable specialism in the works of Benjamin Britten, giving several Irish premieres. In thirty years, rarely using other than local resources and always under Dr Nelson's direction, it made seventy-seven presentations (not including tour performances) of thirty-nine operas by twenty-five composers.

The Studio Opera Group could tour, and did so for many years without public subsidy; opera-lovers had access to an increasing body of commercial recordings; but for the live experience of the major repertoire performed with full professional resources, they had to travel beyond Northern Ireland. The Dublin example had shown that a local foundation was viable, and in 1957, on the initiative principally of John Patterson and John Lewis-Crosby, the Grand Opera Society of Northern Ireland (G.O.S.N.I.) came into being. It provided a local amateur chorus, and hired the Grand Opera House and an orchestra. Of the two productions in its first season in 1958, 'Carmen' was sung in English, conducted by Havelock Nelson with a cast that included James Johnston; 'Rigoletto' had an Italian conductor, production, and cast. G.O.S.N.I. went through its vicissitudes, but succeeded in establishing a practice of regular locally produced major opera. By 1970 a Northern Ireland Opera Trust (N.I.O.T.) had been formed: half the governing board were nominees of the Arts Council of Northern Ireland (as C.E.M.A. (N.I.) had now become), and a full-time administrator was employed to look after both the Grand Opera Society and the Studio Opera Group.

In 1965 the B.B.C. Northern Ireland Orchestra was at last enlarged from twenty-one players to thirty and changed from a part-time body into a full-time one.[27] The effect on the City of Belfast Orchestra, unfortunately, which was doing so well under Maurice Miles and was now deprived of the essential help of the B.B.C. professionals, was catastrophic, and it performed for the last time on 25 March. The arts council made another bold decision. It committed half its total annual resources to the creation of an Ulster Orchestra[28] and established in 1966, under its own direct management, a full-time professional orchestra of forty players. In its first six months it played 100 concerts to 45,000 people: but notwithstanding its energetic annual

[27] E. W. G. Boucher in *Causeway*, p. 142.
[28] *Arts Council of Northern Ireland (A.C.N.I.) report, 1965–6* (Belfast, 1966), p. 5.

schedules, it never came near to replacing the City of Belfast Orchestra in public affection. Its size prevented it from playing the romantic nineteenth-century repertoire, which attracted large audiences. Northern Ireland found itself with one small-to-medium-sized orchestra that broadcast but did not play outside concerts, and another that played concerts but did not broadcast. The arts council suggested a merger, but the B.B.C. found difficulty in agreeing. The anomalous situation continued, with the Ulster Orchestra creating a disproportionate demand on arts council finances.

INSTRUMENTAL music was now forging ahead in the schools. The new secondary schools set up under the 1947 education act offered the double challenge of devising a curriculum that would be free of the examination straitjacket, and of creating a supply of teachers to implement it. Much more time was available for music than in the grammar schools, and it was taught enthusiastically both by the existing teachers who were qualified in the subject and by the semi-specialists from the training colleges who, having taken the general course as qualified teachers, went on for a further year to specialise in the teaching of music. The grammar schools took steps to catch up. A level of musical interest and literacy was created on which the new music advisory services of the local education authorities, following Belfast's lead, could build. They created youth orchestras, bands, and ensembles and began to penetrate the primary schools with peripatetic teachers and tutors. There were independent initiatives, of which the Ulster Junior Orchestra, founded in 1963, and the Ulster College of Music, under Daphne Bell, were notable. In Belfast, Leonard Pugh combined the posts of senior music adviser and principal of the school of music. The school of music had no students in full-time attendance but provided the base from which the teaching staff influenced the musical life of young people ranging from nursery school to diploma standard. The cost of instruments had been a serious impediment to the spread of instrumental music. In 1973 a radical reorganisation of local government placed education in the hands of five area boards, financed by central government. Delivered from dependence on local opinion and the rates, and enjoying allocations of manpower and funds beyond the dreams of their predecessors, the area boards were enabled to press ahead.

By the time the 1973 reorganisation took place, the troubles had begun. Music, in the schools and the community at large, benefited from being one of the activities that spanned the divide and through which experience of working together could take place. The troubles caused surprisingly little disruption in musical activity. Both sides of the community continued to comprise the Ulster Hall and Grand Opera House audiences and made input into opera, oratorio, recital, and youth orchestra. Traditional music at once united the two sides by the universality of its emotional content, and separated them by its origin in the Gaelic tradition. The troubles had their creative precipitate in traditional music as in other branches of the arts, and some of the music created reflected the bitterness of feelings in the struggle. Country-and-western, based as an industry chiefly in Nashville, Tennessee, and as a musical genre based in part at least on a Scots-Irish emigrant traditional music, offered an alternative to those who had repudiated the Gaelic tradition. It was set alongside the not-inconsiderable corpus of music emanating from the protestant tradition and the Orange marching bands.

The outbreak of the troubles came in the midst of the pop music revolution. In the 1950s popular music had come to mean the music, and the style of music, most widely played on radio, jukebox, and gramophone. It differed from post-first-world-war popular music principally in being somewhat louder through amplification; it was no threat to the unamplified sound of the human voice or the instrumental group, much less the band or orchestra; it was possible to engage in conversation without shouting while dancing to it. Asked for a definition, many would have said simply that it was music not to be taken seriously. The cataclysmic worldwide transformation of popular music brought about in the aftermath of the arrival of rock-and-roll in the mid 1950s has been well documented, and it suffices here to note that in Northern Ireland as elsewhere there were misgivings about the extent of the takeover by the new popular music, its blatant sexuality, its appeal to an age group not well understood and beginning to be feared by its elders, the provocative and outlandish behaviour and attire of its performers, above all its identification with protest movements worldwide. As the 'youth-quake', which it nurtured and which was nurtured by it, developed, the fragility of accepted musical norms was demonstrated: the inadequacy of unamplified sound to reach a mass live audience (the 'Baumol effect');[29] the impossibility of avoiding the new music in most public places, especially those frequented by the young; the assault on the traditional aesthetic autonomy. This music was not amenable to the notion that music transcends the social, political, and everyday because of its abstract or non-representational nature; popular but clamouring to be taken seriously, it addressed all three in the most direct and disturbing terms. To control it was impossible; it was too powerful, too international, too pervasive; it had to be lived with. In the early days of the troubles and possibly thereafter, it added a further dimension of alarmed anxiety to the prevalent communal feeling of insecurity; the fear of a link through music into international subversion, however, proved groundless. Also, the raucousness of much of the 1960s music deafened the ears to its content and to that of the other less violent musics of the pop revolution; it became possible eventually, for other generations besides the young to accept, listen, appreciate, choose, and apply perspective.

[29] So called from its consideration by W. J. Baumol and W. G. Bowen in *Performing arts: the economic dilemma* (New York, 1966).

To the expression, or the emergence, of a popular music of Northern Ireland character, of either or both communities, the pop revolution was both enemy and friend. Two countries, Britain and the United States, dominated performance and record distribution, and those individuals or groups who wished to have their music performed widely had perforce to place it with those countries and conform to their norms of expression in such matters as rhythm, instrumentation, and use of amplification. That said, the culture was nothing if not international, and any country, sect, or grouping could make its voice heard if it accepted the norms and was successful in achieving a fusion with its own musical message. New groups superseded dance bands in Northern Ireland and a few, such as the Undertones, Stiff Little Fingers, and the singer Van Morrison, had success in the wider world.

Traditional music, however, was far from being extinguished by the pop revolution. With the action came the reaction, and the very recording techniques and methods of distribution that had furthered the spread of pop became available to other genres, to serve a renewed curiosity and appetite, which were also in reaction. Taken with parallel advances in information technology and scholarly method, it became possible to study, store, perform, and disseminate traditional music with an integrity and purity previously unknown; the new techniques were particularly valuable in recording and preserving authentic music played and sung by living exponents. It would not be long before the front of the stage was at last taken over by those who were members of the tradition themselves.

Although the educative role of the musical festivals diminished in importance with the progress of the subject in the schools, they continued in being as the main competitive arena at the learning stage. To the public at large, however, 'festival' came to mean something different, a non-competitive concentration of special events and performances, musical and otherwise, over a brief period of time. Such festivals proliferated, large and small, in the 1970s and 1980s. The longest established were the North West Arts Festival, based in Derry, and the Belfast Festival, which began in 1962 and was based at Queen's University. Although the Belfast Festival attracted artists and companies of high standing, it did not become a place of international pilgrimage as did the Edinburgh Festival, to which it claimed to be second only in size in the British Isles. Its strength lay in the range, number, and quality of the events it provided in a large variety of auditoria. The university provided most of the auditoria, the arts council most of the financial support. In music it included jazz and traditional music as well as orchestral and chamber music and opera; it was weak in contemporary and new music. Its drama and dance components were greatly enhanced by the programme provided for it by the Grand Opera House when that was reopened in 1980.

As a concert hall, the Great Hall at Queen's was superseded after the war by the Whitla Hall. A complex of rooms elsewhere in the university became the home of the music department. The Harty Room provided an attractive small recital venue, used by the university and by the Sunday afternoon local performers and audience of the Performers' Club, founded by the singing teacher Frank Capper. A nearby church was acquired and converted into a medium-sized auditorium as the Elmwood Hall; this became the most recent home of Northern Ireland's main promoter of chamber music recitals since the early days of the century, the B.M.S. The initials originally stood for British Music Society, of which it was the local branch. On the demise of that body it continued as the Belfast Music Society. The Elmwood Hall also became the headquarters of the Ulster Orchestra. Both B.M.S. and Performers' Club were for the general public. University students could participate within Queen's in its orchestra and choir, and enlarge their experience in three university-based festivals: the Sonorities Festival of twentieth-century music and the Festival of Early Music, which took place in alternate years, and the main festival, which occurred each year. Several of the members of the music department enriched Northern Ireland musical life with their compositions during their stay, including two of the Harty professors, Raymond Warren and Adrian Thomas, and there was created a post of composer-in-residence.

Although nothing like a school of composers grew up in Queen's University or elsewhere in Northern Ireland, the level of compositional activity remained high, and showed itself sensitive to the trends in new music in Europe and farther afield. Philip Hammond, acknowledging many influences, wrote chamber music and music for the piano and for voices; as the arts council's director of music he actively encouraged the composition of new music. David Byers, whose 'Moon shadows' was written to B.B.C. commission, wrote well for the voice, and was adventurous in applying his skills and imagination to a variety of ensembles and combinations reflecting his wide interest in contemporary styles; when he became senior music producer at B.B.C. Northern Ireland following E. W. G. Boucher, he was at pains both to promote new music and to revive the music of Norman Hay and others. The compositions of Eibhlish Farrell of Rostrevor and Kevin O'Connell from Derry indicated that the creative spirit was not confined to Belfast.

In the mid 1960s there came into being the New University of Ulster at Coleraine and Derry, and the Ulster Polytechnic at Jordanstown outside Belfast. In 1983 they combined to form the University of Ulster. The university's B.Mus. degree stressed the integration of performance and academic work. A pre-degree course took the form of a part-time certificate in foundation studies and was either taken for its own sake or as a preparation for degree work. As at Queen's, extramural courses were available, and a musical campus life flourished at Coleraine and Derry as well as at Jordanstown. In the expansion of composition activity in Northern Ireland in recent years a feature has been the appearance of a number of young composers from the University of Ulster, including Ian Wilson and Michael Alcorn. In the college of education, the position was reached by the 1980s where all students took basic musical studies. The three-year general course of professional teacher training, leading to a bachelor of education (validated as a degree by Queen's), could be taken with music as a main subject, and there was a four-year honours course. In-service courses for serving teachers included a B.Ed. with music, and there was a postgraduate certificate in education.

With the university auditoria, the Ulster Hall and other places, Belfast in the 1970s could satisfactorily house a range of musical events that was wide—but not wide enough. The Grand Opera House, designed by Frank Matcham and opened in 1895, was converted to a cinema in 1961 but remained available for occasional seasons of drama, ballet, and opera. It was closed in 1972 and sold to property developers. N.I.O.T. seasons of opera thereafter took place in the A.B.C. Cinema from 1973 to 1977, and concert performances of opera were given in 1978 and 1979 in other venues. The Grand Opera House had been shaken by nearby bombings but not bombed itself, and it was structurally sound.[30] The arts council, aware of the place of the building in the community in its better days and of the real danger of its demolition by developers, put down a resolution calling on the government to make available funds to save it. It was a situation not unfamiliar to the arts council of Great Britain, which had had to stand by while developers bought up and destroyed theatres in London and other places. But the arts council of Northern Ireland, unlike its counterpart, had the power under its articles of association as a limited company to acquire and manage a theatre. With funds made available by government, it bought the Grand Opera House and restored it, with the original Victorian design and detail preserved and the necessary additional work of modernisation carried out in harmony. In 1980 it was reopened as a modern working theatre, housing a full variety of events. These included opera and ballet: Opera Northern Ireland put on its productions there, as did local musical societies, and there were visits from Scottish opera.

In the inflationary 1970s, the running costs of the Ulster Orchestra became such that the arts council commissioned a report on its future. Acting on the main recommendation, the arts council recommended negotiations with the B.B.C. and the players' unions. Progress was slow, and near the end of the decade the arts council had decided to set up an independent orchestra. Things took a different turn when in 1979 the B.B.C. in London proposed a severe contraction of its own nationwide orchestral resources, shortly

[30] It has however been severely damaged on two occasions by I.R.A. car-bombs since its reopening.

followed by specific proposals that included the winding up of their Northern Ireland orchestra. This concentrated the mind wonderfully: in a new atmosphere negotiations recommenced, and in effect the merger of the B.B.C. Northern Ireland Orchestra and the Ulster Orchestra went through. The new Ulster Orchestra, with a basic establishment of fifty-five full-time players and Bryden Thomas as principal conductor, came into being under an independent board of management and gave its first concert in May 1981. Funded mainly by the arts council and B.B.C., it drew financial support also from Belfast city council and from private sponsorship, of which that from the tobacco firm, Gallaher's, formed the largest element. Now sufficiently large to play the romantic repertoire (with augmentation as necessary), it was soon filling the Ulster Hall to capacity again; it was a return to, and indeed an improvement on, the great days of Godfrey Brown and Maurice Miles, both of whose orchestras had contained a proportion of amateur players. In its first decade the Ulster Orchestra made a considerable reputation beyond Northern Ireland with its commercial recordings, beginning with the works of Hamilton Harty and Arnold Bax. It also toured the Republic, Great Britain, and continental Europe, and played a Henry Wood promenade concert in the Albert Hall.

It was time for the arts council to turn the beam of rationalisation on the other big spender, opera. At a time when the trend of N.I.O.T. was towards professionalisation in nearly every area of activity, Havelock Nelson's Studio Opera Group remained essentially amateur. The two bodies shared less common ground than the orchestras had, but the difficult merger was achieved in 1984. N.I.O.T. and Studio Opera were wound up and Opera Northern Ireland was formed, with the declared aims of maintaining a high standard of local operatic performances of all kinds, of mounting tours, and of providing opportunities for local singers to appear in opera. A Belfastman, Kenneth Montgomery, who had established himself as a conductor on the international circuit, was appointed artistic and musical director. Opera Northern Ireland established itself quickly as a mainline British opera company, using the professional talents it deemed necessary to such an image. As an independent venture, attracting no grant from the arts council funds and using largely Northern Ireland singers and players, there came into being in 1986 Castleward Opera, which put on an opera season each June in the attractive environment of Castleward, the big house by the shores of Strangford Lough. Turning to good account the limitations of a tiny theatre (the converted stables), and relying on a great deal of voluntary labour freely given, it soon established a niche for itself as a Northern Ireland institution. In the final decades of the twentieth century the amateur societies rose in importance under the stimulus of the annual Waterford competitive festival, performing with increased vitality and sophistication a repertoire ranging from Viennese operetta and Gilbert and Sullivan to the most recent available musicals.

By the early 1990s many of the aspirations of Norman Hay and Godfrey Brown for the welfare of music in Northern Ireland had been realised. Major areas of musical activity were safely in the hands of specialised institutions sustained by the public purse. If it might be a matter of regret to them that there appeared to be less of a role for the inspired individual, they could take comfort from the proliferation of independent bodies large and small—most of them, but not all, clients of the arts council of Northern Ireland—and from the survival of such bodies as the B.M.S. and the Performers' Club with a foot in either camp. Alongside the prodigious growth of pop, there were infinitely more opportunities for classical music, opera, traditional music, and jazz to be experienced both in reproduction and, more surprisingly, in live performance. The advances in music education from nursery to university were great, and irreversible. The growth of instrumental music in schools had not caused vocal music to disappear. Traditional music flourished throughout Northern Ireland; it had its place in the education system, and the arts council since 1975 had employed a full-time traditional arts officer. The appointment of a jazz officer to the arts council had recognised the need to encourage an enduringly healthy level of activity. But if there were grounds for satisfaction there were important areas where there could be no complacency. The twin flagship enterprises, the Ulster Orchestra and Opera Northern Ireland, could not exist without the assistance of large amounts of grant from public funds, irrespective of private sponsorship and healthy box-office returns, and were particularly vulnerable to rising costs; these were in fact to cause the demise of Opera Northern Ireland in October 1998. The most significant fact to emerge from a retrospective glance at the turn of the century was the discomfiture of the Cassandras. Every technical innovation, from the gramophone and wireless to the synthesiser, was to have been the death of music and musical appreciation, yet the opposite had been the case.

CHAPTER XXIII

The mass media in twentieth-century Ireland

H. R. CATHCART with MICHAEL MULDOON

TWENTIETH-century Ireland, lying between two of the most developed economies in the world, has been subjected to, or as some would have it seduced by, the cultures of both. The process has been facilitated by the fact that English is the shared dominant language of the United States, Great Britain, and Ireland. The barrier to communication of geographical distance between the peoples has proved relative. Increasingly rapid modes of transport, which brought Ireland and Britain close to each other in the nineteenth century, have in the twentieth century steadily reduced the gap between Ireland and 'the next parish' across the Atlantic Ocean. The easy movement of people, temporary or permanent, made possible by these revolutionary changes has strengthened the links between the communities and has ensured that the cultural impact of the two major powers on the relatively small Irish population has been profound. The development of the mass media of communication—newspapers, cinemas, radio, and television—has guaranteed that the impact has been, and remains, prompt, continuous, and pervasive.

IN the final quarter of the nineteenth century the urban population of Ireland became in many respects a province of British popular culture. The economic progress that increased the potential of the lower middle and working classes as consumers and afforded them more leisure time was common to both islands' cities and towns. The popularity of sports and games, of seaside resorts, of variety theatres, of circuses and fairgrounds soared. A striking dimension of these activities as now presented was the degree to which they were organised and made respectable. Violence and crude behaviour in action on the field and in words on the stage were reduced; drinking in music halls and gambling at sports were discouraged. The upper classes could feel comfortable with the changes and encourage them. Among the games they organised were soccer, cricket, and rugby. In Ireland this transformation in leisure activities was commonly associated with the Anglo-Irish establishment. It provoked a profound reaction among those who felt that it was the final stage in the process of anglicisation. In 1884 the Gaelic Athletic Association was founded to ensure that parallel reforms took place in the organisation of the sports and games traditionally associated with the Irish countryside, to preserve and promote them in the face of the English challenge. The association drew together a broad spectrum of nationalist opinion, with Archbishop Croke of Cashel and Michael Davitt as its first patrons and some elements of the Irish Republican Brotherhood as its early instigators: these included a leading fenian, Alderman James Nowlan of Kilkenny, who was president of the G.A.A. from 1901 to 1921. The association developed a rural mass following, and also made considerable progress in urban areas. In the towns and cities a similar broad front came together in the Gaelic League, founded in 1893, to turn the tide of anglicisation not alone by maintaining the Irish language but by fostering traditional Irish popular culture: music, singing, dancing, and storytelling. The recreational pursuits of a rural society were called on to challenge the newly emerging forms of commercialised urban entertainment. The league, with its middle-class ethos, imposed a degree of order on what was spontaneous in the countryside in order to increase its attractiveness and acceptability in the towns. Moreover, it initially eschewed party politics.[1]

It was into a society that was beginning to experience overt cultural conflict that the technical innovations that were to provide the basis of the mass media of the twentieth century were introduced. The cinematograph and the phonograph, recent products of scientific investigation into the nature of vision and sound, initially found their place on the bill in the palaces of variety. The first films shown in Ireland were screened on 20 April 1896 in the Star of Erin Music Hall, subsequently known as the Olympia Theatre, Dublin. The occasion proved disappointing because the moving pictures of everyday scenes were difficult to see. However, within a few months improved projection methods ensured that the cinematograph surpassed in popularity all other music-hall acts. Thereafter the showing of films spread rapidly to many venues in town, seaside, and fairground. Although the films were silent, they soon proved successful enough to prompt the opening of specialised picture houses or palaces; somewhat earlier the playing of sound recordings had left the stage to become a domestic activity, at least till the sound could be wedded to film or broadcast over the air. It was in 1909 that the first Irish specialised picture house or cinema was opened by James Joyce: the Volta in Mary Street, Dublin. By that date the programmes available to the audience were more sophisticated and consisted of one- or two-reel silent melodramas and travelogues made in Britain, on the Continent of Europe, or in the United States.

[1] See Marcus de Búrca, *The G.A.A.: a history* (Dublin, 1980); see also above, vi, 402–4.

It is coincidental that yacht racing in 1898 provided the occasion for perhaps the earliest film shot in Ireland and for one of the first public experiments in wireless telegraphy in the world: the former at a regatta in Belfast Lough and the latter when Marconi, acting for a newspaper, transmitted race results back to land from a regatta in Dublin Bay. Film of local scenes and events was a feature of Irish cinema shows almost from the beginning, although it became a subsidiary part of the whole programme. Wireless telegraphy was soon used in a broadcast fashion by ships in distress at sea, but apart from an ingenious effort by the leaders of the 1916 rising to circumvent British censorship by transmitting the news of their action in morse code for the outside world to pick up, the development of sound broadcasting as we know it had to await the emergence of radio telephony from the first world war. Before then, however, both newspapers and cinemas had begun the drive to reach the masses.

The potential for the rapid mass production of newspapers lay in rotary presses and linotype setting, and although the technology had been exploited in the United States earlier in the century, it was not till 1896 that entrepreneurs on the eastern side of the Atlantic seized the opportunity presented. The *Daily Mail*, launched by Alfred and Harold Harmsworth, proved the harbinger of a revolution in British—and Irish—newspapers. The paper's distinctiveness lay in the way it was laid out and organised financially. The experience of earlier popular weekly papers such as *Tit Bits* and *Pearson's Weekly* was exploited and the presentation of news and features was short, simple, and snappy. Sports coverage was significant. The paper was designed perhaps more to entertain than to inform. Advertisements, exploiting the new consumer potential of the working and lower middle classes, were transformed into attractive, eye-catching productions and soon provided the major part of the recurrent revenue of the paper. The *Daily Mail*, 'the penny newspaper for one halfpenny', took a little time to build its circulation, to catch and pass the circulation of weekly and Sunday newspapers such as the *News of the World*. It did not, however, initially adopt the circulation-boosting sensationalism that characterised this last paper.

The British weeklies and Sundays had significant circulations in Ireland before the *Daily Mail* arrived, and the *News of the World* had already achieved notoriety. Its practice of reporting in detail divorce proceedings in British courts and sexual crimes created great offence in church quarters in Ireland, as indeed it did in Britain. More than any other facet of British popular culture, this could be represented as an invasion of alien mores. It provoked a movement for the censorship of newspapers, periodicals, and books that was, with varying degrees of fortune, to remain influential. Vigilance committees were set up in urban areas throughout the country, and through direct action and intimidation they attempted to impede the circulation of offending literature. In 1911, for example, a consignment of *News of the World* was publicly shredded on arrival at Limerick railway station. Newsagents in many towns were compelled to cease stocking offending papers. The propaganda was belligerent: '... it is a fight against a bad press—against papers that fill their columns, issue after issue, with vile, filthy, immoral matter, unfit to be read by our Irish men and women... the evil publications... are foreign to every ideal and aspiration of the clean-minded Celt, and mostly inspired by hatred of the catholic faith and catholic morality.'[2] Such sentiments were conjoined in many quarters with a determination to create a purely Gaelic and catholic Ireland. Perhaps the most vociferous campaign to this end was pursued by the weekly *Leader*, edited by D. P. Moran. Moran defended 'Irish-Ireland' and spearheaded the effort to drive out English popular newspapers and other literature. He repeatedly called for government action.[3]

It was opportune that, as this movement began to emerge, an Irish entrepreneur should launch a newspaper of mass appeal that was intended to take cognisance of the Gaelic catholic mind and its preconceptions. William Martin Murphy took the *Daily Mail* as his model and was at pains to establish that Alfred Harmsworth, soon to be Lord Northcliffe, had no plans to extend his publishing operations to Ireland. Northcliffe in fact gave every advice and assistance. Murphy acquired the latest rotary presses and linosetting equipment and with this technology produced the new *Irish Independent* on 2 January 1905. Not a party organ, it was 'to be independent in fact as well as in name'. Murphy had plenty of experience of running unsuccessful papers 'as a "side show" to politics' and was determined to break that mould and create a profit-making paper of universal appeal. The first editorial of his new halfpenny daily announced that the paper 'will place our country's interests above those of party, and will not seek to exploit any section or individual... While uncompromising in its support for the national rights of Ireland, the *Irish Independent* will be neither offensive nor aggressive in its style of advocacy, and as a newspaper will be found acceptable by every class and creed.'[4] The new style of presentation owed much to the *Daily Mail*: bright advertisements, photographs, features signed by literary and political figures, a women's page, and competitions. Much space was given to church news, both at home and abroad, and every effort was directed towards making the *Irish Independent* the favourite daily of the catholic clergy.

The *Irish Independent* very soon became the most successful Irish daily newspaper, and its circulation figures reached 100,000 a day by 1917. It could be said to have become by then, in terms of Ireland, a mass medium.[5] Murphy's achievement with his daily had its limitations: it did not penetrate

[2] Editorial in *Irish Rosary*, Feb. 1913, quoted in Adams, *Censorship*, p. 16.

[3] Adams, *Censorship*, p. 18.

[4] *Irish Independent*, 2 Jan. 1905.

[5] L. M. Cullen, 'Establishing a communications system: news, post, and transport' in Brian Farrell (ed.), *Communications and community in Ireland* (Dublin and Cork, 1984), p. 28.

the countryside effectively. In December 1905, however, he founded the *Sunday Independent*, which gained a very large rural readership. It was and remained a custom of the Irish countryman till the 1950s to buy a national paper only on Sundays while supporting a local paper during the week. In a similar way film shows did not reach most rural areas till the 1950s, although very many country dwellers travelled on foot, by bicycle, and by car to the nearest town cinema long before that. Daily cinema shows were an urban phenomenon and, of course, frequent attendance was particularly a city pursuit. It is calculated, for example, that up to a third of Belfast's population attended weekly in the silent era. Nevertheless, it was probably in the 1930s with the advent of the 'talkies' that film became a mass medium in Ireland. In 1935 there were about 165 cinemas in the Irish Free State that gave performances on at least five days of the week, and their seating capacity was estimated at the time as 100,000. It was a year in which more than 80 per cent of the films shown were U.S.-produced and the balance were British. There was no Irish production. The cinema provided an unending diet of foreign fare. It had not always been so.

In the decade before independence was achieved in the Free State, expatriates had demonstrated that feature films with Irish themes could be made in Ireland of a comparable standard to films imported from elsewhere. The way had been led by the American Kalem company, which among film production enterprises in the United States first pioneered the use of foreign locations. One of Kalem's top directors, of Irish parentage, was Sidney Olcott, who brought production teams to Ireland between 1910 and 1914. He made a number of films, of which perhaps his adaptations of the plays 'The colleen bawn' and 'The shaughraun' by the nineteenth-century romantic dramatist Dion Boucicault were the most notable. Olcott's time in the country was not uneventful, for he ran into the opposition of a local parish priest in Kerry. More seriously, he came under the surveillance of the security forces as a consequence of his sympathy for the cause of Irish nationalism. This commitment was manifest in his films 'Rory O'More' (1911), 'Arrah-na-Pogue' (1911) (on the 1798 rising), 'For Ireland's sake' (1912), and finally 'Bold Emmet, Ireland's martyr'. The last was withdrawn by government instruction promptly after its launch in 1915 because it was claimed that it interfered with wartime recruitment for the British army. Olcott was the precursor of others who fell foul of the authorities. In 1914 Walter MacNamara, an Irishman who had returned from the United States, produced 'Ireland a nation', a feature film combining historical reconstruction of the 1798 rebellion and its aftermath with newsreel footage of John Redmond, Eamon de Valera, and others. After a delay caused by the loss of the first print of the film, which went down with the *Lusitania* in May 1915, the film in a censored form was allowed two showings in Dublin (January 1917) and then banned. In 1916 the most important development in Irish film production of this era, the Film Company of Ireland, began operations. Again, the entrepreneur responsible, James Mark Sullivan, was a returned emigrant from the United States. The Film Company at first made a number of romantic films in Irish settings but then turned to an epic theme, the land struggle, as depicted in a novel by Charles Kickham that was highly popular among the nationalist population. 'Knocknagow' was an immense success with Irish filmgoers in 1918. In 1920 it prompted the company to adapt another well-known Irish novel, *Willy Reilly and his dear colleen bawn*, by William Carleton. This film proved an even greater commercial success at home and abroad than 'Knocknagow'. Unfortunately, in 1920 the Film Company of Ireland went out of business, a victim of the civil disruption resulting from the struggles for independence. The company had been firmly aligned with the nationalist cause and might have been expected to inspire others to follow its example when independence was achieved. This did not happen. There was almost no effort in the new state to produce films that would provide some counterbalance to the mass of imported fare.[6]

At least the new state emerged with one mass medium attuned to the new era. The *Irish Independent* became the prime communication medium of the new establishment in the Irish Free State. It took the place of the *Irish Times*, a daily with a fraction of its circulation, which had fulfilled a similar role for the former unionist establishment. To some extent the *Irish Independent* arrived at this new eminence by default. Its founder, William Martin Murphy, had consistently pursued a policy of critical appraisal of the Irish parliamentary party and of its efforts to achieve home rule; at the same time his paper had shown singular disfavour to republicans and had castigated the leaders of the 1916 rising. Subsequently the *Irish Independent* had, however, found itself aligned with Sinn Féin in the crisis over conscription. Mindful of the paper's influence, the prime minister, Lloyd George, tried to win Murphy's support for a partitionist policy, but the latter was opposed to such a course, and the attempt failed. Murphy died in June 1919, before any settlement was in sight. He had, however, laid down the policy that his newspapers would pursue in the post-treaty era by his well-established alignment with the catholic church. The church threw the full weight of its power and influence behind the provisional government in 1922, and the *Irish Independent* and *Sunday Independent* adopted the same stance.[7]

THE new state was committed to the gaelicisation of Irish society, and it set about achieving this through the educational system.[8] A thoroughly gaeli-

---

[6] For film in this period see Kevin Rockett, 'The silent period' in Kevin Rockett, Luke Gibbons, and John Hill (ed.), *Cinema and Ireland* (London and Sydney, 1987), pp 3–50.
[7] Donal McCartney, 'William Martin Murphy: an Irish press baron and the rise of the popular press' in Farrell, *Communications & community*, pp 30–38.
[8] Below, pp 726–31.

cised population would be insulated against the products of foreign culture, but this was an objective that even the most optimistic Irish language supporters knew would not take place in the short or even medium term. In the mean time, it was not practical to exclude foreign influences by banning American movies and British newspapers and books, but censorship could bring about the removal of the most undesirable features of these alien media. The agenda had long been set by the Irish Vigilance Association, which had organised not very effective campaigns for a decade or more under British rule. With an independent government, the association's time had come, and it expected legislation that would ban 'immoral' books and films, as well as any media appearing to promote or condone birth control, procreation outside wedlock, or divorce.[9]

The government acted remarkably promptly. The censorship of films act was passed in 1923 while the country was still coping with the consequences of civil war. The act required that all films intended for public showing had to be viewed by a censor, who was to be a full-time official. The censor was required to pass a film 'unless he is of the opinion that such picture or some part thereof is unfit for general exhibition in public by reason of its being indecent, obscene, or blasphemous; or because the exhibition thereof in public would tend to inculcate principles contrary to public morality or would be otherwise subversive of public morals'.[10] The censor's operations were to prove draconian, for many films were rejected that had met the standards set in the United States by the Hays office and in Britain by the board of film censors. The primary sensitivity in Ireland was to all dimensions of overt sex on screen, but there were much wider dimensions of the films shown that alarmed the guardians of the people's traditional way of life. The catholic hierarchy was for long exercised by the values displayed, and implicitly extolled, in the American films that dominated Irish screens. The first film censor, who held office from 1923 to 1940, shared the bishops' concern, remarking that he feared the Los Angelisation of the Irish people more than their anglicisation.[11] The bishops' condemnation was reiterated year after year throughout the 1920s and 1930s in their Lenten pastorals. Consumerism (often characterised more generally as 'materialism'), immodest clothes, cosmetics, and modern popular music with its characteristic dancing were all portrayed as evil, undermining the very fabric of national life.

Some of these were ills that were eventually to manifest themselves in a new medium of communication that emerged on the international scene at the same time as the Irish Free State was established. It was a medium,

[9] Adams, *Censorship*, pp 27–8.
[10] 1923/23 (16 July 1923).
[11] James Montgomery, 'The menace of Hollywood' in *Studies*, xxxi (1942), pp 420–28, cited in Brian Farrell, 'Communications and community: problems and prospects' in Farrell, *Communications & community*, pp 119, 133.

however, that was amenable to government control. Experiments with wireless telephony in Britain had revealed to companies manufacturing radio equipment that there was a large potential market for receivers among the public if transmitting stations provided music and talk for people to 'listen in' to. The British government, at the same time as it was engaged in devising and negotiating the Anglo–Irish treaty, was trying to decide how it would legislate for sound broadcasting in the United Kingdom. In the immediate aftermath of independence, while the British government's decision was still pending, the leading British manufacturing company, Marconi, approached the new Irish post office to seek permission to establish a radio station to provide programmes, in order that it might sell receivers in the Irish Free State. The postmaster general had no intention of granting the right to a foreign company; in any case there was a civil war waging and all civil radio operations were for the time being illegal.

The Irish P.M.G., J. J. Walsh, came under local pressure to provide for broadcasting. He was eventually persuaded to copy the model of the British Broadcasting Company, and negotiated with Irish entrepreneurs to establish an I.B.C. There was a significant difference in the situation in the two jurisdictions: whereas the B.B.C. was an amalgam of the interests of British radio manufacturers, Ireland had no radio manufacturers, and at least two of the companies involved in Walsh's preliminary negotiations had no particular interest in radio, merely wishing to exploit the business opportunity presented. When the dáil learned of the project, it established a parliamentary committee to examine Walsh's proposals. The committee, having exposed the dubious activities of one of the companies Walsh had been negotiating with, came to favour a government broadcasting service. Walsh was strongly opposed to this idea, on the grounds that his department could not possibly manage what would be an entertainment medium, in which his officials would have to decide between different artistes and choose music for listeners. The committee and other members of the dáil, however, foresaw a role for radio in national reconstruction as a provider of educational and informational programmes. They included some who believed Irish radio could be an instrument of gaelicisation, and at the launch of the Dublin station, 2RN, on 1 January 1926, Douglas Hyde in his inaugural talk confirmed their view when he declared:

Our enterprise today marks the beginning ... of a new era in which our nation will take its place amongst the other nations of the world. A nation has never been made by act of parliament. A nation cannot be made by act of parliament; no, not even by a treaty. A nation is made from inside itself; it is made first of all by its language, if it has one; by its music, songs, games, and customs ... So, while not forgetting what is best in what other countries have to offer us, we desire to especially emphasise what we have derived from our Gaelic ancestors ... This much I have said in English for any strangers who may be listening-in. Now I address my own countrymen.[12]

Hyde went on in Irish; thus giving a somewhat misleading impression to those who heard him elsewhere by courtesy of B.B.C. relay, and certainly overestimating the Irish-language capacity of his fellow-countrymen. The state radio service came into being against the firm resistance of the government's finance ministry and with the extreme reluctance of the post office. Both would have preferred a commercial service under government control. The department of finance proved in the event to be parsimonious, and paltry programme budgets ensured that performers in the programmes had virtually to be confined to those in the Dublin area. Consequently the pool of traditional music artistes from which the station could draw was limited. In any case, the audience expected, and undoubtedly would only pay the licence fee for, a service similar to that provided by other European stations: a diet of live light classical and parlour music with an occasional improving talk or lesson.[13] This, conjoined with the fact that the radio signal was mainly picked up by the overwhelmingly English-speaking listeners-in who lived within twenty miles (32 km) of the transmitter, ensured that the presumptions of Hyde were not fulfilled for most of the first decade of 2RN's existence. Nevertheless, concessions were made to the gaelicisation policy. There was a traditional-music progamme by a singer, piper, or fiddler on most weekday nights and an Irish-language lesson once a week.

Apart from these last components the service provided by the B.B.C.'s station in Belfast was much the same. It did, in fact, feature traditional Irish musicians from time to time. The Belfast station, 2BE, went on the air some sixteen months before 2RN. It was officially launched on 15 September 1924. The two stations in the early years maintained cordial relations with each other and even attempted joint programmes. As Belfast had much more generous budgets than 2RN, it was possible for many leading performers from Dublin to be invited to broadcast from the B.B.C. station. These included, for example, Colonel Fritz Brase, the Irish army's head of music, who conducted the B.B.C.'s local orchestra; the director of 2RN, Séamus Clandillon, and his wife, Maighréad Ní Annagáin, both well-known traditional Irish singers, who gave a recital, and a number of actors and actresses from the Abbey Theatre, Dublin, who played leading roles in radio drama productions. The Abbey Theatre broadcast whole seasons of plays from 2BE years before it gave its first performance via Radio Éireann.[14]

[12] Quoted in Maurice Gorham, *Forty years of Irish broadcasting* (Dublin, 1967), p. 24.
[13] Above, p. 627.
[14] Rex Cathcart, *The most contrary region* (Belfast, 1984), pp 40–41. See also above, pp 657, 659–60.

Broadcasting in post-partition Ireland reflected both the international style of broadcasting and the relations between the governments, south and north. While these relations were not harmonious, they were not necessarily antagonistic. Each political entity was absorbed in its own problems, and both governments were endeavouring to consolidate their regimes. The population, north and south, endeavoured to cope with the cultural consequences of partition, and the evidence suggests that the unionist majority in the north took some time to size up its position. The cultural policy of the local B.B.C. reflected this. Broadcasting in this period was not likely to assume any kind of political stance because it was not concerned with current affairs; and, constrained as it was by competition from the press, it provided only a minimal news service.

Newspapers in Northern Ireland, however, did reflect through their particular political and sectarian prisms the course of events. The unionist community was served by the *Belfast News Letter*, the *Northern Whig*, and the *Belfast Evening Telegraph*. Of these only the last had a circulation that in relative terms suggested a mass medium. Its 70,000 or more copies sold daily in 1920 compared with not quite half that figure for each of the morning papers. The *Irish News*, which catered for the catholic community, scarcely reached the circulation of the establishment's morning papers.

The Bairds of the *Telegraph*, the Hendersons of the *News Letter*, and the Cunninghams of the *Northern Whig* were all pillars of the unionist regime, and they ensured that their editors were as committed to unionism as they were. In recognition of services rendered in the establishment of Northern Ireland two of the proprietors, Robert Baird and Trevor Henderson, were knighted by George V when he opened the new Northern Ireland parliament in June 1921. No Cunningham was so honoured, perhaps because the *Northern Whig*'s support was sometimes tempered with criticism. As for the editors, two (Thomas Moles of the *Telegraph* and Robert J. Lynn of the *Whig*) were remarkable in that they combined their newspaper role with membership of both the Westminster and Northern Ireland parliaments; they also both served in their time as deputy speakers of the local parliament. They could scarcely have given more of their lives to the unionist cause. Naturally their papers were similarly dedicated.

The northern unionist press was not slow to draw attention to Irish Free State policies that appeared to be fostering a Gaelic catholic state. Legislation for censorship, for example, was presented as an infringement of the liberty of protestants and of other non-catholics in the Free State; this in spite of the fact that protestants, clerical and lay, took part in framing and enforcing the legislation.

A new drive to control 'the cross-Channel unclean press' and 'immoral and dangerous literature' was launched by the catholic hierarchy in the Irish Free State in 1924. The campaign was strongly backed by the Catholic Truth

Society and the Irish Vigilance Association (founded in 1911 by the Dominicans). In response the government set up a 'committee of inquiry on evil
literature'. In its submission to the committee, the Catholic Truth Society
gave estimates of the weekly circulation of the seven English Sunday papers
to which they most objected. Of these, the *News of the World* had by far the
largest at 132,444, while the combined total of sales for the seven was
352,802. The society's main concern was undoubtedly with these mass circulation newspapers rather than with imported books.[15] While the government
took time to draw up legislation in response, armed bands held up trains
carrying Sunday newspapers, sacked them, and burned the papers. When the
censorship of publications act was eventually passed in 1929, it went much
further than an attack on the imported popular press. In addition to banning
any publication advocating birth control, it set up a censorship board with
the responsibility for banning books or publications, including newspapers,
that it considered to be indecent or obscene. It had a wide remit, which was
interpreted widely. Whether owing to the inadequacy of the board's support
in full-time personnel or to a narrow-minded punitive disposition on the part
of its members, works were banned simply on the basis of underlined passages, long or short, submitted by the public as offensive. Little or no account
appears to have been taken of the context, and as a result many of the major
works of contemporary literature were banned. These included works of most
notable Irish writers published in the 1930s, 1940s, and 1950s. Paradoxically,
the attempt to exclude alien influences had ended up silencing the nation's
own creative voices.[16]

The record of the post-treaty Cumann na nGaedheal government's attempts to fulfil the cultural objectives of the Irish revolutionary movement
was mixed. Certainly, there were reforms in the educational system, with the
aim of reviving the Irish language.[17] However, the government did not come
into power on the surge of a popular mass movement; rather, the civil war
that followed its accession shattered any cohesion in national cultural objectives and dissipated what popular enthusiasm there was for them. And there
was a failure to subsidise radio, newspapers, or film-making. The task of
restoring Irish was simply left to the nation's teachers.

THE foundation of a new political party in 1926 among those who had
opposed the Anglo–Irish treaty was the prelude to changes that were to affect
profoundly the press and radio in Ireland. Eamon de Valera sought to organise Irish republicanism into a constitutional movement and to give it a

[15] Adams, *Censorship*, pp 28–9, citing figures from the C.T.S. pamphlet *The problem of
undesirable printed matter* (Dublin, 1927); Terence Brown, *Ireland: a social and cultural history
1922–79* (Glasgow, 1981), pp 68–9.
[16] Above, pp 488–90, 505.
[17] Below, pp 726–31.

national voice. The outcome was Fianna Fáil and the *Irish Press*. The *Irish Press* was launched on 5 September 1931, and in its first editorial was contemptuously dismissive of its competitors, the *Irish Independent* and the *Irish Times*:

Until today the Irish people have had no daily paper in which Irish issues were made predominant. There has been nothing comparable in Ireland to the great English, French, and American dailies, which look naturally out upon the world from their national territories and speak authoritatively for their peoples ... The *Irish Press* makes good that deficiency. Henceforth other nations will have a means of knowing that Irish opinion is not merely an indistinct echo of the opinions of a section of the British press ...

It declared: 'We are a national organ in all that term conveys ... Our ideal, culturally, is an Irish Ireland aware of its own greatness, sure of itself, conscious of the spiritual forces which have formed it into a distinct people having its own language and customs and a traditionally Christian way of life.' What divided Fianna Fáil and the *Irish Press* from the Cumann na nGaedheal government was a civil war and the issues for which that war was fought. In republican eyes the treaty had compromised Irish independence by retaining links with Britain and by accepting partition. Moreover, in the truncated nation state that it had accepted, the government had since 1922 singularly failed to construct an adequate cultural and economic base. This set an agenda for the Fianna Fáil party to achieve in government and for the *Irish Press*, whether the party was in or out of power.

The launch of the *Irish Press* was achieved in the face of considerable obstacles. In the first instance, raising the necessary capital in the midst of the great depression had required much energy and ingenuity. De Valera travelled to the United States to raise money among the expatriate community, but his success was limited. It was only when he unfroze the large sums held in American banks as a consequence of the bonds sold by the first dáil that he gained access to the necessary funds. Holders of the bonds were persuaded to transfer the investment to the *Irish Press*. The paper's difficulties were not over when publication began. Its circulation was obstructed by rivals. Their newsagents would not handle it and their managements prevented copies being carried by the specially chartered early morning trains used for distribution. Finally, shortly after the launch the Cumann na nGaedheal government successfully sued the *Irish Press* for libel. Public reaction to the prosecution, it was suspected, contributed in a small way to Fianna Fáil's winning the general election in 1932. From then on for the next sixteen years de Valera and his party ruled the twenty-six counties, and the *Irish Press* effectively became the mouthpiece of the government. The combination of new voice and new government gained a circulation for the paper that exceeded 100,000 within five years. It is not surprising that the sales were substantially achieved with a new readership; the *Irish Press* did not win readers from its rivals to any great extent.

In the advertisements by which they sought to raise capital for the *Irish Press* the promoters used two quotations from authors committed to catholic–Gaelic reconstruction: 'We are in a condition of mental bondage... We are in the stranglehold of an alien press', and 'Day after day what remains of our nationality is being sapped by the increasing stream of publications which is pouring in on us from the other side of the Irish Sea... In matters of the spirit we are more and more becoming England's slaves.'[18] The advertisements also pointed out that 'we are at present importing every day not less than 250,000 copies of English daily papers which are markedly hostile to Irish sentiment, culture and philosophy'.[19] In the light of such complaints it was not surprising that the Fianna Fáil government implemented a proposal strongly advocated for some time by Fr R. S. Devane, S.J., the author of the first quotation. Promptly on gaining power it imposed a tariff on all imported daily newspapers. Imports fell by half.

A marked feature of the *Irish Press* was its extensive coverage of Gaelic sport. This was an innovation that proved very popular and obliged the *Irish Independent* to respond in kind. The Gaelic Athletic Association had also benefited from 2RN's outside broadcasts of its major matches. In this sports coverage Irish broadcasters were pioneers; for in the beginning, until 1927, the B.B.C. was prevented from engaging in such activities because British newspapers still enjoyed a monopoly, claiming that they were disadvantaged by live coverage of public events, including sport. It is difficult to gauge the popularity gained by 2RN in its early coverage of Gaelic games but it was necessarily limited because the number of licence-holders in 1932 was still below 30,000, most of whom owned crystal sets, which confined listening to individuals with earphones. In that year, however, a new high-powered transmitter was opened in Athlone that was capable of reaching most of the population. From then on Radio Éireann's audiences for hurling and Gaelic football rose. Numbers of listeners-in were boosted as the sales of valve sets increased, permitting groups to listen, in homes or in public places.

To meet the capital and recurrent costs of the new transmitter it was decided to provide air time for sponsored programmes. As the signal was expected to reach Britain, it was hoped to attract British sponsors. The International Broadcasting Company, London, was given the franchise to find them. The outcome was unfortunate for the Fianna Fáil government on two counts: the sponsored programmes included much modern light music on records and, of course, the products advertised were often foreign. The whole enterprise was deemed to be inimical to the government's avowed policy of promoting Irish industries and Irish goods. It was, in addition, at odds with the commitment to Irish music. The church and Gaelic lobbies

---

[18] R. S. Devane and T. F. O'Rahilly, quoted in *Nation*, 15 Sept. 1928.
[19] Ibid.

attacked. They were at one in their condemnation of 'jazz', in which they included swing and crooning. The government used its direct control of broadcasting to reduce the amount of such music and backed down on the promotion of non-Irish goods. It even accepted a ban on cosmetics advertisements.

In 1935 a somewhat battered Fianna Fáil government endeavoured to transform Radio Éireann into a more effective instrument of its policies. The minister for finance, Seán MacEntee, said: 'With regard to the broadcasting service, I think that those... who have experience of the service since it was inaugurated here, must admit that it has not been on the whole satisfactory to the public or to the government'.[20] He went on to announce the appointment of a new director, T. J. Kiernan (drawn, like his predecessor, from the civil service), who, he confidently predicted, would open up a new era. His optimism proved to be justified on several counts, not least because within two years the number of licence-holders had exceeded 100,000.

Shortly after taking up office, Kiernan was joined by the man who had edited the *Irish Press* since it was launched in 1931: Frank Gallagher became deputy director. The appointment effectively ensured a coincidence of purpose between the radio service and the newspaper, for Gallagher was a very committed member of Fianna Fáil. Before his arrival, however, Kiernan had begun to reform the schedule of programmes. Broadcasting in Irish received a new look: language lessons gave way to plays, sketches, and lectures in the language. Kiernan increased the number of outside broadcasts taken along telephone lines, not only to improve coverage of G.A.A. events but also to implement his 'regional scheme' which was designed to counteract the domination of Dublin in programming. County committees were formed for the purpose of planning local programmes, usually consisting of musical items, often of the traditional kind. The scheme ran for two or three years but produced mediocre results. It was notable for raising the expectation of the Galway committee that it might lead to a local all-Irish language radio station, an outcome not to materialise till nearly forty years later. Kiernan had more success with his farming programmes, in which likewise he reached into the countryside, replacing the official government voice with the farmer's own.

Kiernan's policy towards traditional music involved severe criticism of the low standards of musicianship among soloists, which the public often found acceptable. He was determined to be more selective in the choice of performers and reduced considerably the number of programmes in which they appeared. Instead he encouraged the development of céilí bands and made increased programme space for them. Kiernan was not an isolationist, in spite of his strong nationalist outlook. He hoped to build a powerful short-wave receiver so that overseas broadcasts could be relayed to Irish listeners.

[20] *Seanad Éireann deb.*, xix, 1461 (27 Mar. 1935).

His plan was frustrated by lack of funds. He sought to develop with B.B.C. Northern Ireland a pool of Irish programmes, but this too ran into insuperable difficulties.

B.B.C. Northern Ireland's policy, in relation both to the region it served and to the Free State, changed under the new director, George Marshall, who arrived in 1932. Marshall, who was allowed considerable autonomy, was extremely cautious. Experience and circumstances made him so. He probably arrived in Belfast with an inflated notion of the effect of radio, for he had been associated in 1926 with Ronald Knox's broadcast of a fictitious account of large-scale riots in London, which had provoked a nationwide scare. Marshall's first years in Belfast made him realise how volatile the situation was, as serious disturbances took place in 1932 and 1935. He was determined that broadcasting should not precipitate civil strife. So he made sure that no manifestations of the orange or the green, either political or cultural, were allowed air time. When the unionist press in Belfast discovered that the B.B.C.'s programme director was in Dublin negotiating with Radio Éireann, it forcefully condemned this collaboration with a government opposed to the existence of Northern Ireland. Marshall denied he was planning to create a pool of programmes with his Dublin opposite number. He was well aware of how sensitive the unionist press had become to political changes in the Free State. Indeed, coincident with this affair there had been a unionist call for the Northern Ireland government to take over the local B.B.C. in order that it could be used to reply to what was declared to be anti-unionist propaganda issuing from the Irish state broadcasting service. The unionist government, however, had no intention of upsetting the status quo, and the prime minister, Craigavon, spoke in glowing terms of the wider achievements of the B.B.C. when he attended the opening of the new powerful transmitter at Lisnagarvey on 20 March 1936. The B.B.C.'s signal could now be received throughout Northern Ireland with an overspill into the Free State. The I.R.A. declared that this development was part of an imperialist plot to undermine Irish nationality.

From time to time in the 1930s the I.R.A. intimidated cinema owners in the Free State and in nationalist areas in Northern Ireland where certain British films were being shown. Sometimes they used armed intervention and sometimes more subtle means. The official state censor, by contrast, had no powers to cut or ban for political reasons. However, British films were seldom perceived by nationalists as a political or cultural threat. Most were simply unpopular; this was the case even in the heart of unionist Belfast, for the films were cheaply and poorly made to take advantage of the quota system by which a proportion of films shown in British cinemas had to be British productions. Irish governments were to show no disposition to impose such a prescription in Ireland, which would have created space for a native film industry. Catholic and Gaelic pressure groups appealed to the Fianna Fáil government to act, at least to impose a levy on cinema revenues to provide the means of financing Irish films, so as to counter the prevailing influence of American films and create employment.

The 1930s afforded enough examples of films made in Ireland to encourage the belief that an industry was possible. The most renowned was the documentary 'Man of Aran' (1934). It was a British production, the work of an American director, Robert Flaherty. Flaherty lived on Aran for some time reconstructing the life of its inhabitants with his film in mind. The most dramatic sequences in the film are of the hunt of the basking shark. This was an activity which had not taken place locally for generations and for which the skills were lost. Flaherty created the scenes at great risk to the participants. The film, nevertheless, impressed most viewers with its authenticity, especially those who attended the premiere in Dublin on 6 May 1934. The attendance included Eamon de Valera, other members of the government, and many prominent figures in national life, including W. B. Yeats. The film quickly won international acclaim. It should be said that there were critics who objected to its failure to depict the catholic faith of the islanders; indeed, the Catholic Film Society of London made a rival film, 'Aran of the saints'. Members of the Irish-language lobby, on the other hand, were mollified because the government provided the money for Flaherty to make a low-budget short film in Irish to be shown alongside his masterpiece. It featured a traditional Irish storyteller. The film proved of little consequence; perhaps because the script was written by a civil servant in the government department of education.[21]

Two feature films of note were produced by Irish companies in the 1930s. Their significance lies not in their filmic quality but in the achievement they represented for all those who participated in their making. Neither director was a professional and each worked on a shoestring budget. Both films dealt with themes from the war of independence. In 1933–4 the dramatist Denis Johnston took the distinguished short story 'Guests of the nation' by Frank O'Connor and turned it into a silent film. His cast consisted of experienced actors, many of whom were later to become eminent. As Johnston was completing his production in Dublin, a group of complete amateurs was endeavouring to recreate in narrative form their experiences as I.R.A. men in the war with the 'Black-and-Tans'. In the light of the tasks they undertook, such as building a production studio in their spare time, their achievement was remarkable. Their production, 'The dawn' (1936), was in sound. Neither this film nor 'Guests of the nation' compared in any way with the production standards of those on the commercial circuits. They were nevertheless enthusiastically received by Irish audiences, for whom they represented honest attempts to portray aspects of the immediate past. As such they were a relief

---

[21] Kevin Rockett, 'Documentaries' in Rockett, Gibbons, & Hill, *Cinema & Ire.*, pp 72–3.

from the stereotypes of Irish people ever present in American films and occasionally in British productions. 'Guests of the nation' and 'The dawn' indicated that there was a will in Ireland to make films if only the government would help find a way.

In 1938 the Fianna Fáil government at last responded to pressure and established an inquiry into film in Ireland. This came at a time when a new concern was being expressed. It appeared that a chain of cinemas controlled by a British production company was expressing an interest in buying into chains in Ireland. The government was alerted to the prospect of foreigners exerting even more influence and drawing out even more profits. Those who were apt to abuse cinema owners, often in anti-Semitic terms, as purveyors of foreign culture now became their defenders. Events in 1939, however, soon overtook both the inquiry and the intentions of the foreign cinema chain. The second world war began and the prospects for an Irish film industry and for a foreign takeover of Irish cinemas were deferred for its duration. The inquiry into film resulted in a report in 1943 but the government did not bother to publish it.[22] At the same time an inquiry into the possibility of an Irish-language radio station in the Galway region suffered the same fate.

THE impact of the 1939–45 war ('the emergency') on Irish cinemas, radio, and newspapers was severely constricting. Government controls were imposed as the economy was compelled to become ever more self-sufficient and as efforts were made to give effect to the official policy of neutrality. Thus newspapers not only had to cope with much-diminished, rationed supplies of newsprint but also with a rigorous censorship; this affected the press in general and not just the pro-British *Irish Times* under the editorship of the redoubtable R. M. Smyllie.[23] Even weather details could not be printed. Constraints on the economy affected government priorities profoundly, and as a consequence the radio service suffered. The hours of broadcasting were curtailed and an already small staff was reduced. Censorship of what was still a government service, however, was not a problem. There was no ban on listening to foreign radio stations. But for those who did not yet have access to an electricity supply, difficulties were experienced by listeners who, whether they sought to follow Radio Éireann programmes or to pick up the B.B.C. or German broadcasts in English (or even in Irish), were confronted with ever greater shortages in the servicing or replacing of the batteries that powered their wireless sets. Cinema-going remained throughout the war years a prime leisure activity of the population. Censorship of films for the

[22] Rockett, 'An Irish film studio', ibid., pp 95–126: 95–6.
[23] For wartime censorship, see Donall Ó Drisceoil, *Censorship in Ireland, 1939–45* (Cork, 1996).

duration of the war was extended to the political field and came into action immediately in 1939 when 'The spy in black', then showing in Dublin, was banned on the grounds that it might offend the German government. Although the United States did not enter the war for some time, American films were no less subject to the censor's blade than British productions. Thus, Chaplin's 'The great dictator' was not seen by Irish cinema-goers till after 1945. The impact of censorship was inevitably one-sided, as apart from the broadcasts of William Joyce ('Lord Haw-Haw') and others like him, there were relatively few opportunities for Nazi or indeed Italian fascist propaganda to reach Ireland. In the interests of the policy of neutrality, it was the more easily accessible coverage from the Allied side that was curbed.

It was to counter the effects of Irish censorship and the broadcasts of 'Haw-Haw' that the British ministry of information sought to use the airwaves to appeal to Irish listeners with special programmes and thus induce them to listen to British news bulletins. To this end the ministry issued a directive to the B.B.C. A key part was played by the B.B.C.'s director in Northern Ireland, George Marshall, who was given censorship powers by the B.B.C. over all programmes concerning Ireland. This became his prime occupation during the war, as Belfast had ceased to be an important programme production centre with the end of regional broadcasting in 1939.

The war demonstrated the power of radio as an instrument of government policy. The impact of Churchill's broadcasts to the British peoples was paralleled by that of de Valera's and Lemass's broadcasts to the Irish people. No more dramatic demonstration was needed than that provided by de Valera's broadcast reply in May 1945 to Churchill's attack via the B.B.C. on the Irish wartime policy of neutrality. It was therefore not surprising that in the post-war period de Valera favoured the expansion of Radio Éireann's services. Enhanced transmissions would enable the nation to overcome the isolation that had been its lot during the war. They would permit the nation to project itself to other nations and to the Irish overseas, especially in the U.S.A. The short-wave transmitter required to achieve these purposes was purchased, but it was never brought into service, owing to difficulties in procuring a wavelength. The developments within Radio Éireann that were intended to provide improved programmes for listeners abroad were, by contrast, implemented, and the home listener gained a much better service as a result.

The end of isolation was not welcomed by all. As newsprint became more easily available, British newspapers attempted to recover their Irish market. By 1949 the sales of dailies were rising, although they were not much above a third of their immediate prewar level. Expansion was inhibited by the tariff that had been imposed in 1933 as a result of the campaign led by (among others) Fr Devane. Devane now began a new agitation. He was particularly exercised by the fact that sales of British Sunday newspapers, which had never been subject to tariffs, were soaring ahead. He wanted tariffs on all imported literature, with licences and quotas introduced for some. 'We must break through this alien system of intellectual tutelage or (shall we say?) mental servitude', he declared.[24] His pleas fell on stony ground, but at least in respect of the Sunday papers the launch of the *Sunday Press* in 1949 proved that a new Irish paper could compete on equal terms with its British counterparts. In the 1950s it attained a circulation of half a million copies and thus became the most successful Irish newspaper ever published. Its major achievement was that it truly penetrated the countryside, besides winning a large urban working-class readership: that is, it reached the constituency to which Fianna Fáil appealed.

'RADIO Éireann gained [in 1947]—and never lost—a proper news service, a symphony orchestra, a light orchestra, staff scriptwriters, outside broadcast officers, and, among other things, a professional repertory company.'[25] There was a transformation in the programmes as a result. The quality of drama and music transmitted was greatly enhanced. Nowhere was progress more apparent than in outside broadcasting, where, as new flexible recording technologies became available, programmes were able to reflect life in countryside and town in a natural, more spontaneous way. Most notably, it was possible to bring traditional music and folklore to the microphone as never before, and in so doing secure performances on disc and tape for audiences in future generations. In other dimensions of the service, change involved opportunities for a greater professionalism. This proved particularly true in orchestral music. Adrian Boult had paid tribute to the small pre-war radio orchestra, but the new full complement of sixty-one players in the years after 1947 permitted a much wider repertoire and the recruitment of additional continental talents. However, progress was inhibited by the need for a satisfactory concert hall in which the orchestra could perform in a fully extended way. The need, diagnosed by Boult in 1937, remained unsatisfied for some decades to come.

In 1947 Séamus Ó Braonáin, whose tenure as director of the radio service had begun shortly after the outbreak of the second world war, retired. During the 'emergency' he had had to act in effect as a censor for broadcasting, and the curbs on Radio Éireann's freedom occasionally gave rise to concern. Moreover, his were years when a certain opportunism permitted the Fianna Fáil government to exploit for its own and other ends the emergency powers that it took to protect the country's neutrality.[26] It is clear that this state of affairs continued under the coalition government that succeeded Fianna Fáil. Towards the end of 1950 the coalition minister for posts and telegraphs was involved in a very controversial appointment of a postmistress

---

[24] R. S. Devane, *The imported press. A national menace: some remedies* (Dublin, 1950), p. 25.
[25] Gorham, *Forty years*, p. 162.
[26] Ibid., pp 131–2, 155.

in a County Wicklow village, but while 'the battle of Baltinglass' featured prominently and at length in newspapers at home and abroad, it was scarcely mentioned on radio news.[27] When Fianna Fáil came back into power, the new minister for posts and telegraphs, Erskine Childers, mindful of the criticisms of Radio Éireann, sought formally to create distance between himself and the broadcasting service without resorting to legislation. He established an executive council, Comhairle Radio Éireann, of five prominent lay people to run the radio service. The Comhairle began operating on 1 January 1953, with a newly appointed professional director, Maurice Gorham. Gorham, an Irishman, was an experienced broadcaster who had served in the B.B.C. for many years. Further innovations appeared, including the Thomas Davis lecture series dealing with historical and cultural issues at a scholarly level, first broadcast in 1953 and still in progress. Gorham now sought to run a fairly autonomous public service, although the then secretary of the department of posts and telegraphs, Leon Ó Broin, was later to expose the real limitations within which the Comhairle worked:

The legal position was that the members of the Comhairle could only function as a civil service broadcasting unit within the department, and to enable them to do even that much they had to be given temporary appointments within the civil service. And not merely were they responsible to the minister but, like all other members of the staff, they were under the permanent head of the department who, as accounting officer, had to account for all expenditure on broadcasting and everything else to the minister for finance and the public accounts committee of the dáil.[28]

While the B.B.C. under its charter had a substantial measure of real autonomy from government, its regional administration in Northern Ireland did not behave as if it was free from Northern Ireland government influence. The regional director, Marshall, stated in public in 1947 that 'B.B.C. programme policy in Northern Ireland is not to admit any attack on the constitutional position of Northern Ireland',[29] which effectively deprived the main opposition party of any opportunity on air to discuss or even to allude to the main plank in its political platform—the issue of the partition of the island. Moreover, the news editor was forbidden to include any items from south of the border in local news bulletins. Marshall retired in 1948, however, and from that date forward there was a gradual liberalisation of local programming. The opportunity for regional control of local programming was rejected in 1952, as no party believed in the power-sharing that was the essential prerequisite. Local B.B.C. officials thereafter pursued a policy of attempting to build a consensus by developing dialogue between the unionist and national-

---

[27] *Irish Times*, 9 Feb. 1951.
[28] Leon Ó Broin, 'The mantle of culture' in Louis McRedmond (ed.), *Written on the wind: personal memories of Irish radio 1926–76* (Dublin, 1976), p. 14.
[29] Cathcart, *The most contrary region*, pp 137–8.

ist communities and by reporting on their common social and economic problems. The constraint on the broadcasters was that they were effectively required to emphasise the positive in community relations while ignoring the negative. Any hint of the latter brought immediate and loud protests from the Northern Ireland government or from unionist organisations. Within this constraint B.B.C. Northern Ireland sought to reflect the region it served, and its outside broadcasting units, like those working in Radio Éireann, made extensive use of recordings of everyday life, folklore, and traditional music. The Irish language at no time featured, however, in spite of representations from local enthusiasts.

While radio, north and south, was extending its audience, the cinemas were winning ever larger numbers of patrons throughout the island. During the early 1950s attendance in rural areas was being promoted by mobile 16 mm units such as those owned by Cineroadshows Ltd. In the cities the chief beneficiary of expansion was now J. Arthur Rank Ltd, the British film production company, which bought out cinema chains in Dublin in 1945 and 1946. Rank extended to Ireland the vertical control that it already exercised in Britain, which ensured that the films it made were distributed and shown. Later, in 1955, the Rank organisation, as Odeon Ltd, took over the main cinemas in Belfast. Although the ownership of first-run cinemas in Dublin and later in Belfast effectively gave to Rank the decision on which films would be shown in the twenty-six counties and Northern Ireland, there was in fact no marked reduction in the number of American films shown in favour of British. The dominance of the Rank organisation did mean, however, that all efforts to promote an Irish film industry would effectively be dependent on its goodwill. In the meantime, when the Fianna Fáil government decided to commemorate on film the life of one of the leading figures in the pantheon of Irish nationalist heroes, Thomas Davis, it was obliged to turn to Rank. 'A nation once again' (1946) was substantially a British product, and when shown in Ireland in 1946 it appeared for the most part on British-owned screens.

The pressure for an Irish film industry was renewed as the 1939–45 war drew to an end. The success with which Irish locations were being used in popular British and American films, such as 'Henry V' (1944), 'Odd man out' (1947), 'The quiet man' (1952), and 'Moby Dick' (1956), was both a persuasive argument in favour of development and a distraction. A group of Irish entrepreneurs was led to develop the Ardmore film studio complex in Bray, County Wicklow, primarily designed to facilitate British and American film-makers. The Ardmore studios, opened by the Fianna Fáil minister for industry and commerce, Seán Lemass, on 12 May 1958, received considerable financial support from government.[30]

[30] For Ardmore, see Rockett, 'An Irish film studio', pp 95–126, and below, pp 696–8.

In 1953 there emerged from within the Irish-language lobby an organisation that was to make an original contribution to Irish culture. Gael-Linn was founded on the initiative of Donall Ó Moráin with the intention of using the mass media to promote the Irish language. It was financed from football pools and demonstrated a versatility, enthusiasm, and capacity to appeal especially to youth that might have profoundly affected the fortunes of the language movement, had it been manifested earlier. As it was, Gael-Linn was to find itself in a society that had less and less enthusiasm for Gaelic values. Gael-Linn's first notable contribution was to Ireland's film culture. From 1956 to 1964 it produced a regular newsreel in Irish, which was shown widely in cinemas throughout the country. In 1959 it was responsible for 'Mise Éire' ('I am Ireland'), a historical documentary which used archive film to present the nationalist struggle down to 1918. The film, enriched with incidental music composed by Seán Ó Riada, made a considerable impact. 'Saoirse?' ('Freedom?'), which followed in 1961, dealt with the more controversial period leading to the outbreak of civil war and did not achieve the same degree of success. Gael-Linn went on sponsoring films as the cinemas began to experience declining fortunes. Its promotion of live and recorded traditional and contemporary Irish folk music helped to transform that scene. Eventually Gael-Linn was even to attempt a project hitherto deemed impractical: it launched a newspaper in Irish.

The 1950s were a period of relative stability for the major national newspapers. Their historical allegiances continued unabated: the *Irish Independent* and its associated Sunday and evening papers were now aligned with Fine Gael, the party derived from Cumann na nGaedheal, and with the catholic hierarchy; the *Irish Press* and the *Sunday Press* with Fianna Fáil and less overtly with the catholic position; and finally the *Irish Times*, while it still espoused a liberal unionist stance, sustained a critical view of the Irish establishment, clerical and lay. On to this scene in 1954 entered a new paper, the *Evening Press*. Under the editorship of Douglas Gageby it sought to distance itself from its stablemate, the daily *Irish Press*, and dissociate itself from the latter's perpetual expression of solidarity with the Fianna Fáil party and with Fianna Fáil governments. The *Evening Press* quickly achieved a large circulation throughout the country—100,000 within five years—and its non-party alignment heralded the direction that Irish newspapers would have to take if they were to expand or even sustain their readerships. The arrival of television in the south and north was to confirm this style as the norm. In Northern Ireland the Canadian newspaper magnate Roy Thomson (later Lord Thomson) bought out the *Belfast Telegraph* in 1961, and while its basic orientation was to support the union in a liberal way, it ceased to be aligned in any narrow sense with the Unionist party. Its rise to complete dominance of circulation figures in the region owed much to this stance and to a general commercial orientation that was designed to minimise the danger of alienating any section of the Northern Ireland readership. The *News Letter* and the *Irish News*, on the other hand, remained associated with political parties and so in time were to find it more difficult to remain viable.

B.B.C. television signals were received on the east coast of Ireland as early as 1953. In that year, in recognition of its Northern Ireland regional responsibilities, a temporary transmitter was set up by the B.B.C. to provide the Belfast conurbation with programmes. The particular demand there from the unionist population was for live coverage of the coronation in that year. On 21 July 1955 the Divis transmitter opened to give 80 per cent of Northern Ireland the B.B.C. signal. As the 1950s progressed, the forest of television masts in the Dublin area and in the other overspill areas along the border grew ever more dense, and their numbers were further swollen by the arrival of a second British service, independent and commercial. The popular demand for a national service became compelling. Late in 1957 the government indicated that it envisaged a service run by commercial interests, and when a television commission was established in 1958, this proposed arrangement was modified only to the extent that a public authority was promised to control the service. The government was pressed to make decisions and take action, especially after Northern Ireland obtained its second service, Ulster Television, in 1959.

The broadcasting authority bill was published on 1 January 1960. It proposed to establish an autonomous broadcasting service combining television and radio under a public authority consisting of not more than nine and not fewer than seven members, appointed by the government for five years. Broadcasting was to be financed by licences and advertising.

The bill contained clauses enjoining the authority to preserve objectivity and impartiality in its treatment of news and current affairs, but without excluding party political broadcasts. It was to have regard for the special position of Irish advertisers and Irish products and could fix preferential rates for them. It should also bear constantly in mind the national aims of restoring the Irish language and preserving and developing the national culture, and should endeavour to promote the attainment of these aims.[31]

The bill became law on 12 April 1960. Remarkably, the new television service was launched on 31 December 1961. Telefís Éireann arrived in a society that was beginning to experience profound change. In 1958 the 'Programme for economic expansion', a five-year plan, had been launched in an effort to extricate the Republic from its current dire economic plight. The strategy involved encouraging exports and foreign investment. Free trade replaced the discredited drive to autarky. As industry and services developed, they

---

[31] Gorham, *Forty years*, p. 302; see 1960/10 [R.I.], sect. 17.

absorbed an increasing majority of the working population, while the rural population declined even as agriculture improved. In the circumstances the place of urban life in the national psyche could not continue to remain at a discount. The free movement of ideas was the corollary to that of goods. The barriers, restrictions, and compulsions that were so much a part of Irish society were to be steadily eroded or removed. The Republic's participation in international bodies challenged complacency at home; and the hierarchy's participation in the second Vatican council (1962–5) had a similar impact on the catholic church. There is no doubt that television stimulated the whole process of change by promoting the free movement of ideas. It provided the critical assessment of national policies and institutions that had been disallowed in earlier broadcasting. It encouraged an openness in dialogue on private mores, a presentation of alternative lifestyles, that had not hitherto been part of national life. It forced newspapers, previously disposed in the case of the *Irish Independent* to be excessively concerned to respect the conservative norms of Irish religion (both catholic and protestant), and in the case of the *Irish Press* the conservative norms of Irish nationalism, to follow its path. They were slow at first to respond because they presumed on the unchanging allegiance of their respective political constituencies.

One national newspaper matched the pace of television. It was compelled to do so in order to survive. It was the achievement of Douglas Gageby, who took over the editorship of the *Irish Times* in 1963, to transform this erstwhile protestant unionist voice into a critical national forum for a modernising Ireland. In doing so, he turned the fortunes of the paper round, doubling its circulation within a decade to reach 70,000 readers, most of whom were drawn from the higher social classes. By 1974 the *Irish Independent* had begun to lose readers, while the *Irish Press* had started on a disastrous downward slide. The *Evening Press*, by contrast, which Gageby had created, held its own.

Television took over the role of the cinema in promoting the Los Angelisation of Ireland. When it was not showing American films, it was showing American situation comedy, crime, or cowboy series. From the beginning, however, Telefís Éireann strove to provide a significant level of locally produced programmes. In the 1960s the proportion reached over one-half, though subsequently the level dropped. In 1964–5 twenty-eight producers were producing twenty-two hours of programmes a week, which was high productivity in comparative international terms. Reflecting the nation to itself, somewhat more faithfully than newspapers had done in the past, was achieved through programme series such as 'The late, late show' and 'The Riordans'. The process provoked some adverse reaction, but it proceeded. Current-affairs programming evolved to become investigative journalism with 'Seven days' in 1967. Many dimensions of social and political life came under critical scrutiny. Politicians, particularly those in government, began to manifest unease.

The broadcasting authority's specific cultural remit was to promote the Irish language. Initially, this presented problems for television. In the opinion of an early controller of programmes (Gunnar Rugheimer, a Swede), the members of the authority who were presumed to have a special interest in this field were not constructive; indeed one, Earnán de Blagdh (Ernest Blythe), was positively opposed in principle, for example, to a television series designed to teach Irish, which went ahead in any case.[32] It was only when Donall Ó Moráin of Gael-Linn joined the authority and a number of fluent Irish-speakers were trained as producers that Irish programming could make real progress. By 1972–3 Irish-language programmes, excluding news, occupied 2.15 per cent of total transmission time and bilingual programmes another 4.12 per cent. On 2 April 1972 transmission of an Irish-language radio service began in the west from Raidió na Gaeltachta. The authority was at pains to state that this innovation did not detract from its responsibilities in television, but it did point out to the broadcasting review committee (1973–4) that the duty to preserve the language and develop the national culture had to be reconciled with audience acceptance. Audiences for Irish-language programmes were small and therefore had an adverse effect on the sale of advertising time, which depended on estimated totals of viewers.[33]

The competition for advertising revenue in the Irish economy became acute with the advent of television. Newspapers were particularly affected: during the economic boom of the 1960s their revenue remained buoyant, but after the oil crisis of 1973 they were all in trouble. The *Irish Independent* lost readers but eventually managed to diversify, which helped to soften the blow. The *Irish Press* was pushed deeper into difficulties, while the *Irish Times* experienced a substantial decline in circulation. The decline occurred shortly after Douglas Gageby had retired from the editorship and the company had become a trust; the paper was saved by Gageby's return. The *Irish Independent* group was shored up when in 1973 the Irish and American entrepreneur, A. J. O'Reilly, became a substantial shareholder and member of the board of directors.

If the impact of television on newspapers was considerable, its impact on cinemas was almost fatal. Cinema-going was directly affected by the steady rise in television-viewing. It was not that all viewers gave up going to the cinema, it was the fact that the habit of weekly or twice-weekly attendance was broken, and this created a vast surplus of seats. Eventually hundreds of cinemas throughout the island closed. Odeon Ltd in Dublin and Belfast shut down their circuits. A few city cinemas found a new viability through conversion to multi-screen complexes. Diminished seating space with multiple

---

[32] Author's interview with Gunnar Rugheimer, controller of programmes 1963–6, 27 Nov. 1972. De Blagdh held that such a series was inappropriate for Telefís Éireann and an insult to the language.

[33] *Broadcasting review committee report, 1974* (R. 120), pp 86–7.

choice of programmes satisfied a clientèle that now only went to the films from time to time. Radio displayed greater resilience. One sign of this occurred in the 1960s when the state radio service began to experience competition from pirate radio stations. Legislative attempts to curb the pirates were made in 1968 and 1972,[34] and some prosecutions were undertaken. However, under legislation passed in 1988 a new policy was adopted and licences were granted to a number of local and community radio stations.[35]

THE fortunes of film in Ireland from the mid 1960s to the mid 1980s were mixed. Starting with Martin Ritt's classic 'The spy who came in from the cold' (1965) and ending with Pat O'Connor's 'Cal' (1984), some eighty-two international feature films[36] were made wholly or partly in Ireland by a catalogue of directors that reads like a 'Who's who' of late twentieth-century A-list film-makers. Stanley Kubrick, John Boorman, John Huston, David Lean, Roger Corman, Sergio Leone, Robert Altman, Sam Fuller, Michael Crichton, and rising star Neil Jordan directed films in Ireland that appeared in cinemas around the world. These productions boasted a galaxy of major film stars, among them Sean Connery, Lee Marvin, Robert Mitchum, Julie Christie, James Mason, Michael Caine, Peter Sellers, Peter O'Toole, Richard Harris, Richard Burton, Gene Wilder, Katharine Hepburn, Julie Andrews, Noel Coward, Paul Newman, and Roger Moore.

For its part, the native film industry was plagued with feuds. Yet it was during this period that the fledgling Irish film industry took strong root, in preparation for its first real flowering in the 1990s. Among the key developments were the rise and fall of the troubled National Film Studios (Ardmore); the first published government report on Irish film production; two film industry acts, and the creation of Bord Scannán na hÉireann (the Irish Film Board). There was also a major challenge to the Irish film censor, thanks to the proliferation of Irish film societies that allowed members to view otherwise cut or banned films. Almost sixty Irish films were made during this period.[37] These were mainly 16 mm shorts and documentaries, with a sprinkling of features, but still remarkable for revealing the first efforts of home-grown Irish film talent, including directors Joe Comerford, the late Kieran Hickey, Bob Quinn, Tommy McArdle, Cathal Black, Thaddeus O'Sullivan, screenwriters Neil Jordan and Frank Deasy, and actors of international stature such as Stephen Rea, Liam Neeson, Gabriel Byrne, and Patrick Bergin, as well as producers such as David Collins and John Kelleher.

[34] 1968/35 (6 Aug. 1968); 1972/5 (3 Apr. 1972).
[35] 1988/18 (3 July 1988).
[36] Calculated from listings in Arthur Flynn, *Irish film: 100 years* (Bray, 1996).
[37] Calculated from listings in Kevin Rockett, *The Irish filmography: fiction films 1896–1996* (Dublin, 1996).

By 1963 the Ardmore studios were in receivership. This enterprise had been established less to encourage Irish producers than to induce foreign film producers to make use of the studio facilities, which were considered well equipped and professionally managed. Seán Lemass had emphasised 'the employment and export, rather than cultural, value of the studios'.[38] But even within these terms the results were controversial. Restrictive agreements were reached between Ardmore and the A.C.T.T., the British film technicians' union, by which Ardmore would be regarded as a British studio for the purpose of obtaining Eady funding[39] as long as only A.C.T.T. members were employed on the productions. The consequent exclusion of Irish technicians from employment, and from the chance of gaining experience, led to bitter labour disputes, and attracted scathing criticism from independent Irish film-makers. To add insult to injury, the Industrial Credit Corporation had been persuaded to create a subsidiary, the Irish Film Finance Corporation (I.F.F.C.), which would invest in these productions. There was no specific provision for Irish film production or for the employment of Irish technicians. Paradoxically, British producers, already in receipt of Eady finance, now had access to I.F.F.C. money, which left the Irish state supporting British films made in Ireland from which Irish people were excluded.[40] Louis Marcus, an accomplished Irish film-maker of highly regarded documentaries, and recipient of an Oscar for a short film about Waterford Glass, was the most vocal and coherent critic of what he termed 'the irrelevance of Ardmore studios', contending that the £750,000 invested at Ardmore by the government was of 'negligible benefit to an Irish film industry'.[41]

As a commercial enterprise the studios proved to be a catastrophe. Debts were written off by the government agencies, and receivership continued till the studios were sold in 1966 to a private consortium of British businessmen. Beset by mismanagement and other irregularities they again went into receivership in 1972, when they were purchased by a new company, Ardmore Studios International, whose board members included Bing Crosby and John Huston. However, within four months Ardmore's third receiver was appointed, and in 1973 the minister for industry and commerce, Justin Keating, arranged for them to be sold to R.T.É. Two years later Keating renamed Ardmore the National Film Studios of Ireland (N.F.S.I.) and appointed the English film director and Irish resident, John Boorman, as chairman.

---

[38] Rockett, 'An Irish film studio', p. 99.

[39] The Eady fund (financed from a statutory levy on cinema seats and reallocated to British film producers in proportion to their success at the box office) amounted to some £250,000 each year. Since just two companies, Rank and A.B.C. (better known as Pathé), controlled the bulk of cinema outlets, they were able to scoop up the proceeds of this fund by the simple expedient of making weekly magazine shorts that were shown in all their cinemas. See Louis Marcus, *The Irish film industry* (Dublin, [1967]), pp 25–6.

[40] Rockett, 'An Irish film studio', pp 100–01.

[41] Marcus, *Ir. film industry*, p. 15.

Boorman was later to become a controversial figure both as chairman of the studios and as a first member of the Irish film board. He produced three films at the new N.F.S.I.: 'Zardoz' (1973), 'The hard way' (1979), and 'Excalibur' (1981). He was also instrumental in attracting major productions to Ireland, including Stanley Kubrick's 'Barry Lyndon' (1975), Michael Crichton's 'The great train robbery' (1979), and Sam Fuller's 'The Big Red One' (1978).

By 1982 studio losses again led government to withdraw support, and Ardmore/N.F.S.I. was again placed in receivership by the then minister for industry and commerce, Albert Reynolds. In August 1984 the studios found their way into private hands when they were purchased by Pakistani-born businessman Mahmud Sipra. However, the renamed Sipra studios never saw any film production, for Sipra's other ventures began to collapse within the year, and once again the 'for sale' notice was hung on the studio gates. The studios were eventually to be sold in 1986 to an Irish/American consortium that included the Irish enterprise agency, the National Development Corporation.

In 1968 Taoiseach Jack Lynch established the film industry committee, with John Huston as chairman. Other members included Irish film-makers Louis Marcus, Patrick Carey, and Tom Hayes, Lord Killanin, Louis Heelan of the I.C.C., and representatives of Rank's and A.B.C.'s Irish subsidiaries. Within a year the committee had produced the first report on the film industry to be published by government.[42] Among its recommendations were pre-production financing of up to £10,000 for international commercial features budgeted at £200,000, full support for more modest-scale features budgeted at £50,000, and support for short film productions (where Irish film-makers had most experience) with subventions of £55,000–£75,000. It was assumed that the film-makers would be Irish, rising from the ranks of documentary, television, and commercial productions. The committee also recommended that the making of television commercials by Irish technicians should be encouraged (in 1973 the Irish Film Workers Association and the Irish Transport and General Workers Union succeeded in blocking the use of imported crews to shoot Irish commercials).

The committee's objectives were summed up best in the words of its chairman John Huston, who was expressly interested in 'nourishing and developing an Irish film industry, independent of the rest of the world, in order to air the talent of Éire'.[43] Through the lobbying and pressure applied by the Society of Film-Makers of Ireland, legislation was brought forward with surprising alacrity. The film industry bill of 1970 accepted several of the recommendations of the committee and proposed a seven-member board to

---

[42] *Report of the film industry committee* (Prl 145) (Dublin, 1968).
[43] Quoted in Rockett, 'An Irish film studio', p. 125, n. 47.

administer the funding. However, the bill failed to obtain a second reading. Almost a decade would pass before another film bill would emerge. In 1978 an independent report, commissioned the previous year by Desmond O'Malley, minister for industry and commerce, made two remarkable recommendations: an independent film board should be set up, and it should be allocated a budget of £4.1 million.[44] Competition for control of these proposed funds ensued between the N.F.S.I. and independent film-makers. The latter hoped for access to the funds through an independent administration. The government responded with the Irish Film Board Act of 1980, which set up an independent administration (An Bord Scannán na hÉireann) to oversee funding; a further act authorised the minister for finance to take up shares in the N.F.S.I. Ltd.[45] At the same time, however, many of the more specific requests of the indigenous film-makers were ignored.

The first investment decision of the newly formed film board plunged the film community into further discord. When only three appointments to the seven-member board had been made (Louis Heelan of the I.C.C. (chairman), Robin O'Sullivan, director of the Cork film festival, and John Boorman of the N.F.S.I), the board decided to invest half its 1981 budget of £200,000 in one film: Neil Jordan's first feature, 'Angel'. The decision was particularly controversial because Boorman was the film's executive producer and Jordan, a gifted and award-winning writer, had only a documentary about the making of Boorman's film 'Excalibur' to his credit. Independent film-makers dissociated themselves from the board's decision and boycotted the screening of 'Angel' at the third international festival of film and television in the Celtic countries. Ill-judged comments by Boorman and Jordan fuelled the controversy. Heelan resigned from the board, and so, eventually, did Boorman, but the episode caused deep rifts and 'a long-term negative effect on Irish film production'.[46]

Muiris MacConghail, then R.T.É. head of features, was subsequently appointed chairman of the board for a four-year term, an appointment welcomed by the independent film-makers. Further appointments, of Tiernan MacBride, chairman of the Association of Film Producers of Ireland, and Michael Algar, chairman of the Irish Film and Television Guild, signalled a clear change of direction, while Louis Marcus's appointment in 1982 as chief executive consolidated the independent film-makers' control of the board. But while the new board supported Irish projects, none of them attracted much critical acclaim or commercial success. Worthy in their own right, they were often ponderous and somewhat lacklustre, confusing solemnity with seriousness. Ironically, Jordan's 'Angel' (1982) was particularly well

---

[44] Ibid., p. 116.
[45] Irish Film Board Act, 1980 (1980/36, 17 Dec. 1980); National Film Studios of Ireland Ltd Act, 1980 (1980/37, 17 Dec. 1980).
[46] Rockett, 'An Irish film studio', p. 119.

received, winning him a B.A.F.T.A. award for the most promising new talent, and launching him on a career as a director and screenwriter of international stature, a future Oscar winner, and a future member of the Irish film board.

In *Cinema and Ireland* (1987), the seminal work on Irish film, Kevin Rockett remarks that

from the mid 1970s onwards Irish fiction films began exploring a more secular and historically reflective society. A more complex notion of the past was examined; the family became a location of instability and fragmentation; sexuality was examined if . . . obliquely and hesitantly; repressive catholic education was relived on the screen; the use of landscape as an idealised backdrop for Irish arcadian beauty was partly discarded; working-class experience made its appearance for the first time; experiments in film form challenged narrative's traditional supremacy.[47]

For the first time Irish film-makers were being given the opportunity, if in a rather limited fashion, to tell their stories in their own voices. With one or two notable exceptions, personal expression and the relentless questioning of romantic and received notions of Irish life, rather than commercial viability or technical accomplishment, were the hallmark of the work of Irish film-makers at this period.

This new filmic articulation of contemporary Irish life was facilitated by a number of different factors. One was the rise of film clubs and film societies such as the Project Cinema Club and the Irish Film Theatre. Such societies afforded the chance to see films made in Ireland by Irish film-makers who were working outside the Hollywood mainstream. Films in these venues escaped the mutilation or outright banning that mainstream films often suffered at the hands of the Irish film censor, who showed scant regard for either film culture or artistic integrity.[48] The making of such films was also encouraged by the arts council's commitment to independent 16 mm production, and by the establishment of the arts council film-script award in 1977. In addition, Irish students in art colleges in London and Dublin began using film as a means of expression previously reserved for literature, drama, or the traditional plastic arts of painting and sculpture. A film culture and a film community were gradually coming together in Ireland.

Documentary film-making in Ireland flourished during this period, giving rise to many fine films, and some very able film-makers. Eamon de Buitléar and Gerrit van Gelderen distinguished themselves in the field of natural history, while David Shaw-Smith explored the world of traditional Irish crafts. Peter Lennon's 'The rocky road to Dublin' (1968) broke new ground in its approach to the twin themes of history and sexuality, provoking one journalist, Fergus Linehan, to remark that 'this, one would hope, is one of the kinds of picture which would emerge from a native film industry'.[49] Perhaps the most prolific and consistently thought-provoking documentarist was Louis Marcus, who from the 1960s to the mid 1990s made over thirty documentaries. These included several Irish-language films for Gael-Linn, such as 'An tine bheo' ('The bright flame') (1966), to commemorate the fiftieth anniversary of the Easter rising. Marcus also produced 'Heritage of Ireland' (1978), a major English-language television series for R.T.É. His work reexamined interpretations of Irish history and its attendant myths. As he noted at the time: 'Ireland is, of course, not so much obsessed with history, which I don't think it wants to know about, but with various mythologies which change from time to time . . . our interpretation of this history has been utterly simplistic and naive.'[50]

It was this spirit of critical reevaluation of what it meant to be living in what T. S. Eliot called 'the present moment of the past'[51] that also preoccupied and informed the fictive film-making of the period. Working their way through short films to feature-length productions, the handful of directors who emerged at that time applied this new scrutiny to rural and urban life in both contemporary and historical Ireland. In 'Swan Alley' (1969), 'Emtigon' (1970), 'Down the corner' (1977), 'Traveller' (1981), 'Withdrawal' (1982), and the experimental 'Waterbag' (1984), Joe Comerford explored variously the lives of junkies, itinerants, the urban poor, and the disintegrating family. Through these films, he found apposite metaphors for the shifting political and social realities of Irish life. The late Kieran Hickey plumbed the depths of repression and violence in contemporary middle-class Irish society with films such as 'Exposure' (1978), 'Criminal conversation' (1980), and 'Attracta' (1983). Cathal Black's 'Wheels' (1976), 'Our boys' (1981), and 'Pigs' (1984) took on the themes of fragmented family, the brutality of education under the Christian Brothers, and urban violence and alienation. Rural life was explored in the context of traditional superstition in Tommy McArdle's 'The kinkisha' (1977), and was ruthlessly deromanticised in Bob Quinn's Irish-language film 'Poitín' (1978). Quinn worked extensively through the medium of Irish, having made the first independently produced Irish-language film, 'Caoineadh Airt Uí Laoire' ('Lament for Art O'Leary') (1975), which was sponsored by the Workers' party. The film juxtaposes the present with the past in an innovative and challenging film style, but comes down on the side that favours the romance of defiant heroism over realpolitik.

In the early 1980s history was the principal preoccupation of films such as 'Maeve' by Pat Murphy and John Davies (1981), Tommy McArdle's 'It's

---

[49] 'An eye on ourselves', *Irish Times*, 13 May 1968, quoted in Rockett, 'Documentaries', p. 85.
[50] Interview with Kevin Rockett, *IFT News*, iii, no. 12 (Dec. 1980), p. 11.
[51] T. S. Eliot, 'Tradition and the individual talent' in id., *The sacred wood* (7th ed., London, 1950), pp 47–59: 59.

handy when people don't die' (1982), John Davies's 'Acceptable levels' (1983), and Pat Murphy's 'Anne Devlin' (1984). Social and personal history, narrative and myth, were given both conventional and novel treatment in these works.

In terms of international accessibility perhaps the two most successful films of the period were Neil Jordan's 'Angel' (1982), an Irish Film Board/ Channel Four venture, and Pat O'Connor's 'Cal' (1984), a U.K. production under David Puttnam. Both directors explored, in very different ways, the corrosive and brutalising effects of the violence that accompanied 'the troubles' in Northern Ireland. Jordan's fortunes have already been discussed, but O'Connor, who also made the trenchant and acclaimed R.T.É./B.B.C. co-production 'Ballroom of Romance' (1982), based on a story by William Trevor,[52] was the only other Irish film director to achieve international (Hollywood) status.

While many of these films found an appreciative if limited local audience, for the most part they made little impact outside Ireland. Film is an uneasy (some would say unholy) alliance between art and commerce. If films fail to perform in the marketplace, investors are reluctant to invest, and investment is as much the lifeblood of film-making in Dublin as it is in Hollywood. For Irish film-makers who wished to challenge received interpretations of Irish history, and to view contemporary issues through 'Irish eyes', it was necessary to have control of production; but the pressure to make films with international mass audience appeal, which would attract larger budgets, meant compromising that control. This dilemma was to have an enormous impact on the Irish film industry. As film historian Kevin Rockett has observed, 'if the errors of the past are to be avoided then artistic control of Irish-theme films must remain in Ireland, while Irish film-makers need to fully appreciate the necessary compromises of international co-productions'.[53]

POLITICIANS may have conceded a considerable measure of autonomy to the broadcasters in the act of 1960, but the concession was reluctantly made and undoubtedly was soon regretted. The broadcasters quickly acquired the confidence to mount programmes critical of government performance and policy, to counterpose spokesmen for interests adversely affected by government policy to the ministers responsible, and not to be intimidated when party whips refused to conform to programme arrangements. The broadcasters were aware that they could only be formally constrained by a written direction as prescribed under section 31 of the act, which provided that 'the minister may direct the authority in writing to refrain from broadcasting any

---

[52] Above, p. 536.
[53] Kevin Rockett, 'Breakthroughs' in Rockett, Gibbons, & Hill, *Cinema & Ire.*, pp 127–44: 143.

particular matter or matter of any particular class, and the authority shall comply with the direction'. They assumed that the government would normally be reluctant to act in this way for fear of adverse publicity. The presumption did not prevent the taoiseach, Seán Lemass, from declaring in 1966:

Radio Telefís Éireann was set up by legislation as an instrument of public policy, and as such is responsible to the government. The government have overall responsibility for its conduct, and especially the obligation to ensure that its programmes do not offend against the public interest or conflict with national policy as designed in legislation. To this extent the government reject the view that Radio Telefís Éireann should be, either generally or in regard to its current affairs and news programmes, completely independent of government supervision ...[54]

Lemass's observations were an angry reaction to the way in which a policy statement made to farmers by the minister for agriculture in a television news bulletin was immediately challenged on air by the president of the National Farmers' Association. In fact ministers were not slow to exert direct personal pressure on the chairman of the authority, as occurred in 1967 when a current affairs team was prevented from travelling to North Vietnam. Friction between ministers and R.T.É. remained fairly constant and was frequently sharpened by the investigative 'Seven days' programmes. R.T.É. itself made a move that was perceived as a bid to restrain the 'Seven days' team. The team was placed under the control of the head of news, a former editor of the *Irish Press*. In the event this did not prevent conflict with the government. When in 1969 'Seven days' mounted a programme on the extortionate activities of moneylenders among Dublin's poor and implied that the scale of the problem was not recognised by the police, opposition deputies in the dáil seized their chance to challenge the minister for justice on the subject. The minister criticised the contents of the programme in some detail, and the disparities revealed between his perceptions and what the broadcasters claimed were such that the government set up a judicial inquiry into the programme. The inquiry found that the broadcasters had made exaggerated assertions and that some of their research methods were unsatisfactory. As one expert commentator remarked, 'something better is manifestly required [to resolve conflicts between the government and the authority]... than the cumbersome and enormously expensive machinery of a judicial inquisition'.[55] Circumstances arising from the civil disturbances in Northern Ireland from 1968 onwards occasionally prompted ministers

---

[54] *Dáil Éireann deb.*, ccxxiv, 1045–6 (12 Oct. 1966).

[55] Leon Ó Broin, 'Anatomy of a programme: the Irish "7 days" enquiry' in *EBU Review*, no. 127 (May 1971), p. 49. See also Ó Broin, 'Amending Irish broadcasting law' in *EBU Review*, xxvi, no. 5 (Sept. 1975), pp 39–41; xxvii, no. 1 (Jan. 1976), pp 38–40; xxviii, no. 2 (Mar. 1977), pp 48–9.

to exercise their statutory right to control the broadcasters by written direction.

ALONE of all the media, the *Irish Times* gave comprehensive coverage of political affairs in Northern Ireland before the outbreak of 'the troubles'. In 1967 it began to provide a fuller account of the proceedings in the Stormont parliament than was available even in the Northern Ireland newspapers, and as the civil rights movement developed, its activities were followed in detail. The *Irish Independent*, which had long had a northern editor, contributing mainly to its northern editions, soon extended its coverage. The broadcasting services, British and Irish, had not been notable for current-affairs programmes on Northern Ireland. British producers were inhibited by the possibility of a repeat performance of the unionist uproar that greeted the first in a series of filmed reports on Northern Ireland by Alan Whicker in 1959. It was a tactic that the unionist government had used and exploited on a number of occasions but never with such effectiveness, for the remaining programmes in the series were abandoned by the B.B.C.[56] A British government commission in 1977 indicted British broadcasters for their failure to draw the public's attention to the impending crisis. R.T.É. had in the mid 1960s been primarily concerned to cover positive developments in the relations between the two parts of Ireland. Constructive dialogue was promoted by joint programming between R.T.É. and B.B.C. Northern Ireland.

It was, however, television that sensationally alerted viewers across the world to the clashes between the civil rights demonstrators and the instruments of the Stormont government's authority, the Royal Ulster Constabulary. Film, particularly that taken by R.T.É. and Ulster Television, of the police attack in Duke Street, Derry, on 5 October 1968, was carried on news bulletins in many countries and provoked strong reactions against the unionist regime, most significantly in the British government. As the confrontations and conflict grew sharper, journalists from Irish and British newspapers and broadcasting services poured into Belfast. Eventually, permanent studio arrangements were established there by the Dublin and London television and radio services; the Irish national newspapers set up local offices in Belfast with teams of reporters and photographers.

In the early phase of 'the troubles' B.B.C. Northern Ireland and Ulster Television were acutely anxious not to inflame their viewers and make the situation worse. Local news and current-affairs programmes were cautiously handled and efforts were made to influence and control television teams coming into the province. This proved easier in the centralised B.B.C.. When the independent television companies, Thames and Granada, were deemed to be taking advantage of a position in which Ulster Television was

[56] Cathcart, *The most contrary region*, pp 190–93.

opting out of showing current-affairs programmes on the local situation, the Independent Broadcasting Authority intervened to insist that programmes should be made to be shown throughout the system.

British television coverage of the prolonged crisis was affected initially by the intervention of British troops and subsequently by the introduction of direct rule from Westminster. These moves represented deeper involvement by the government, politicians, and the public in Great Britain; and the governments, particularly (but not exclusively) those that were Conservative, increasingly resisted the efforts of broadcasters to report on the scene impartially, insisting that in a 'war situation' the B.B.C. and I.T.V. must get on side. Programmes in which there appeared members of the Provisional I.R.A. (and other organisations violently opposed to the British presence) proved unacceptable, and the government threatened legal action to bring them to an end. Programmes portraying security forces in anything other than a favourable light stimulated the fury of right-wing politicians and the popular British press. In 1979 the government referred two B.B.C. broadcasts to the director of public prosecutions, invoking the 1976 prevention of terrorism act.[57] Although it was decided not to prosecute, letters were exchanged between the attorney general and the chairman of the B.B.C. After 1981, no interviews with members of proscribed organisations were broadcast. This brought British broadcasters broadly into line with conditions as they then were in the Republic.[58]

As viewers in the Republic have always been able to see British television coverage of the Northern Ireland situation, that coverage is both a source of information and newsworthy in itself. The British government's efforts to influence and restrict television coverage of Northern Ireland, which were often reported on very critically in Irish newspapers, were not as drastic as those of the Irish government in relation to Irish broadcasting. The tension that had previously existed between the government and broadcasters became acute over R.T.É. programmes in which members of the Provisional and Official I.R.A., or the political wings of these bodies, presented their positions. The Fianna Fáil government's first reaction in June 1971 was to refuse to participate in a radio programme in which 'subversives' were involved. This was followed three months later by a 'Seven days' programme in which recorded interviews with 'subversives' were followed by studio discussion. This provoked the minister for posts and telegraphs to issue a written directive to the R.T.É. authority 'to refrain from broadcasting any matter... that could be calculated to promote the aims or activities of any organisation which engages in, promotes, encourages, or advocates the attaining of any particular objective[s] by violent means'.[59] The directive was

---

[57] 1976, c. 8 (25 Mar. 1976).   [58] Cathcart, *The most contrary region*, pp 237–40.
[59] *Dáil Éireann deb.*, cclvi, 1361 (4 Nov. 1971).

devoid of precision, and therefore very difficult to interpret. The authority sought clarification, but judged that the direction was not intended to prevent it fulfilling its duty to provide impartial news coverage of the violent events in Northern Ireland. In November 1972, however, a paraphrased version of an interview with the head of the Provisional I.R.A. was used in a radio news bulletin, and as a result the minister dismissed the whole R.T.É. authority.

In February 1973 the Fianna Fáil government was replaced by a coalition government, which responded promptly to this drastic action with draft legislation to secure the tenure of future members of the authority. Henceforth, as in the case of judges, dismissal would require action by both houses of the oireachtas, thus denying to ministers an arbitrary power. The coalition minister, Conor Cruise O'Brien, did not reverse the ban imposed by his predecessor on the appearance of 'subversives' on television or radio; rather, he defined and extended it to include all the organisations in Northern Ireland and in the Republic that used violence as public statements of their policies. He did, however, ensure that the ban required the regular approval of the oireachtas.[60] O'Brien was personally responsible for a very controversial initiative by which he proposed to use a new second national television channel to relay transmissions of B.B.C. Northern Ireland or of Ulster Television, or a mixture of both, to the whole Republic. This concept of 'open broadcasting' had as its corollary the arrangement for the transmission of R.T.É. programmes in Northern Ireland, and the whole scheme was designed to promote mutual awareness and understanding throughout both parts of Ireland. The project met with fierce opposition not alone from broadcasters but especially from the traditional nationalist and Gaelic lobbies, who perceived 'open broadcasting' as the final surrender to anglicisation. In the propaganda battle the secretary of the Gaelic League, Maolsheachlainn Ó Caollai, was prompted to call into service a modish concept derived from Marxist sources, 'cultural imperialism', to denigrate O'Brien's project. The combined opposed forces were entirely successful in seeing 'open broadcasting' off. Their victory was signalled by a 2:1 defeat of the proposal in a national opinion survey. It proved somewhat Pyrrhic in that the service eventually provided by R.T.É. on its second channel responded neither to the objectives nor the expectations of the Irish-language enthusiasts or of traditional nationalists. It did ensure, however, that the choice of foreign programmes, which altogether predominated in the service, was made by R.T.É. executives, not by broadcasting executives outside the state. The measure of disillusion of the Gaelic lobby is perhaps to be detected in the fact that the proposals of the state-appointed committee charged with con-

---

[60] Broadcasting Authority (Amendment) Act, 1976 (1976/37, 21 Dec. 1976), sections 2 and 16.

sidering the future of the Irish language, published not long afterwards, failed even to mention national television in its report. Henceforth, the drive among enthusiasts was to be for a special Irish-language service for the Gaeltacht similar to that already provided on radio.[61]

As R.T.É. entered the 1980s, the organisation found itself in a remarkably similar position to that experienced by the young Radio Éireann in the early 1930s. It enjoyed neither the confidence of politicians nor that of the powerful traditional lobbies. In both cases this stemmed from the nature of the financial arrangements that the state imposed on the broadcasting services, and the failure of governments to address the issues involved in sustaining services designed to maintain and develop all dimensions of Irish culture in the face of the flood of influences from abroad. R.T.É. in the 1980s, however, had a measure of autonomy that had been wholly denied to its predecessor in the 1930s. It proved successful both in its capacity to attain profitability and in the premise on which this had to be based: that is, in its capacity to achieve a high audience share. Neither of these achievements, however, protected R.T.É. from the designs of unsympathetic, disaffected politicians, who were increasingly determined to provide directly competitive alternative commercial services. When these almost immediately proved nonviable, the politicians moved once again to attack R.T.É. by skimming off its profits to subsidise the rivals. The rhetoric that was used to justify these political actions was that the new services would provide greater choice for viewers and listeners. The reality was that the politicians were set on the deliberate taming of public-service broadcasting.

Within R.T.É. there was a conviction that the application of section 31 of the broadcasting act was inhibiting news and current-affairs broadcasting. While this was undoubtedly the case, there would appear to have been deeper forces at work achieving a somewhat similar effect in newspapers, where there was no external censorship. In 1980–81 the sequence of hunger strikes in Northern Ireland by incarcerated members of the Provisional I.R.A. won an unparalleled degree of attention from all the media in Ireland and in the United Kingdom. A remarkable breadth of sympathy for the strikers was engendered even among moderate nationalists, and perhaps an equal and opposite reaction among those who favoured Northern Ireland's union with Britain. The evidence suggests that this episode was to prove the last point at which the mass media exerted a powerful influence on their various publics through the coverage of Northern Ireland's crisis. Thereafter, the coverage and consequential influence was to decline. That this was not solely the result of censorship (in the case of television) is suggested by developments that occurred in the newspaper coverage of Northern Ireland. There was a marked contraction in the number of journalists and photographers assigned to the

[61] *Committee on Irish language attitudes research: main report* (Dublin, 1975), pp 343–5.

north. It would appear that the long-running nature of the crisis was simply diminishing its newsworthiness in both the editors' and the public's eyes. Internal considerations increasingly preoccupied the Republic's media, while within Northern Ireland the media themselves were facing new challenges. The B.B.C. set up Radio Foyle in Derry, the second city of the north, in 1979 and the station soon achieved a striking degree of credibility among most sections of a very divided community. In Belfast the Irish-language lobby began to win a modest degree of success in pressing the B.B.C. to provide radio programmes in Irish for the general listener and for schools. Eventually television programmes would follow. 'Twisting the tail of the British lion' was proving more effective than lobbying Irish governments, for government-financed Irish broadcasts for schools in the Republic had finally been abandoned in the mid 1970s. Another form of contradiction was manifest in the campaign for increased broadcast coverage of G.A.A. sports activities in Northern Ireland (which was successful), while at the same time in the Republic the G.A.A. authorities were seriously considering whether to press for reduced coverage because it was believed that television in particular was adversely affecting attendances at matches.

Traditional nationalists and Irish-language enthusiasts in Northern Ireland find an obvious target for criticism in the forces that resist their objectives. British rule is the obstruction. In the Republic of Ireland, however, this focus is internally absent, and it is difficult for enthusiasts to escape the conclusion that the main obstacle to gaelicisation is the freely exercised choice of their fellow citizens. Nor do the lobbies any longer have the opportunity of pressing the command economy of the state to serve their purposes. It has always been highly significant in any case that the main target of their attacks has been British domination and influence, and that confrontation with the United States has been avoided, although arguably it is American popular culture that has exercised the more corrosive effect on traditional Irish society and its values as the century has advanced, as in so many other regions of the world. However, it must be recognised that, despite the failure to revive the Irish language, the success of the G.A.A. and the traditional-music movement have helped to shape aspects of modern Irish society.

As Ireland in 1984 faced towards the end of the twentieth century, the pressure from overseas cultural influences seemed, as a result of the revolutionary advances in communications and in the organisation of the mass media, to be likely to overwhelm those who struggled to preserve and develop distinctive local identities and cultures. Cable television ensured that the signals of services that had hitherto been inadequately or not at all received could be picked up efficiently and distributed throughout at least the urban areas of the island. Satellite television would offer direct services or could be received through cable. The organisations behind much satellite television proved, because of the vast capital sums involved, to be multinational media empires built on the acquisition of publication enterprises in all their manifestations, from newspapers and commercial terrestrial television stations to the latest information technological companies. Their activities are unimpeded in states where the political rhetoric sustains the principle of freedom of action for the entrepreneurs and freedom of choice for the public in the cultural market. The question must then be how far and how soon will these conglomerates absorb or transform the Irish media.

THE twentieth century has been the first century of the media of mass communication. No countries and no peoples have been able to escape their impact through isolation. The history of the changes that have been coterminous with the century has, as far as Ireland is concerned, only begun to be written. Thus, there are as yet no histories of national news-papers or of the role played by the international news agencies in their coverage, no histories of the rise and fall of popular cinema culture through-out the island, no comprehensive history of television in the Republic of Ireland. There *are* histories of Irish radio, of Irish film culture, of the B.B.C. in Northern Ireland, and an anecdotal survey of the development of news-papers.[62] It is true that specific issues have prompted a welter of research into limited aspects of media development, such as censorship in the Republic and various dimensions of the Northern Ireland crisis. As far as traditional culture is concerned an important beginning has been made in the history of the recording of Irish music, but no account exists of the significant evolution of Gael-Linn.

The theme that must be the overarching concern of historians of Ireland is the way in which the media have contributed to the political and cultural evolution of the island. Small countries are almost inevitably the victims of their greater neighbours, and physical invasion is not a necessary precondi-tion for cultural invasion and domination. The concern to preserve historical identity is found very widely, but the defences that states have erected to protect themselves from outside influences and cultural penetration by alien forces have proved less and less effective as the century has advanced. The question of effectiveness must raise itself in the case of Irish governments, which have been somewhat unimaginative in the policies they have pursued to preserve and develop Irish culture and identities. In the examination of their policies, historians need assessments of the possibilities that existed and were not grasped. An historical analysis of the Irish economy and of public finances in order to establish the degree to which there were opportunities that existed and were not seized, or with a view to showing how extensive or

---

[62] Gorham, *Forty years*; Rockett, Gibbons, & Hill, *Cinema & Ire.*; Cathcart, *The most contrary region*; Jonathan Bardon, *Beyond the studio: a history of BBC Northern Ireland* (Belfast, 2000); Hugh Oram, *The Irish newspaper book: a history of newspapers in Ireland, 1649–1983* (Dublin, 1983). See also below, pp 969–70.

limited were the opportunities for governments to pursue constructive policies, is a prime essential. Comparative studies with other small European states could be suggestive.

Whatever the difficulties, the challenge to explore the role of the media in Irish history remains. A society that has manifestly been transformed in the course of the twentieth century invites the attention of historians to the agencies of change; and although media researchers may affirm that the influence of any medium is inextricably entwined with other social influences, it is still important to attempt to unravel the processes by which change occurs. The historian must ask how the country passed from a stage in which a Fianna Fáil taoiseach in 1943 could propound as his national ideal the idyll of a peasant society, with its traditional music and dancing at the crossroads, to a stage in 1992 where another taoiseach, of the same republican party, professing unchanged values, could have made a successful career in the 1960s and 1970s promoting dancehalls in which 'country and western' music was the normal fare. At this, the most superficial, yet in reality the most profound, level, the much proclaimed cultural values of the country had, it would appear, been subverted in half a century. And yet at a second glance perhaps the change was not so great. For the taoiseach who stood for traditional music had been born in America; while the 'country and western' music of his successor was, in essence, Irish traditional music transported across the Atlantic, repackaged, and returned.[63]

---

[63] Albert Reynolds (taoiseach 1992–4) owned a chain of rural dancehalls. See Fintan O'Toole, 'Land across the waves: Ireland and America' in Martin Parr, *A fair day: photographs from the west of Ireland* (Wallasey, 1984), pp 6–12: 9, and pp 626–7, 665 above.

CHAPTER XXIV

Pre-university education, 1921–84

D. H. AKENSON with SEAN FARREN and JOHN COOLAHAN

DURING most of the twentieth century there was no such thing as an Irish educational system. Instead, one must speak of education in the two parts of Ireland. Although the two systems sprang from a common stem, they diverged sharply, each being moulded according to the social and political contours of its own constituency. This essay will describe the evolution of the two systems and then will highlight some of the contrasts between them. But in noting the contrasts the reader should realise that this requires paying more attention to them than did educational policy-makers in either area. To a remarkable extent each system evolved without reference to the other. Thus, the comparisons between the two emergent systems should not be taken as indicating any causal links. The educational system of the south evolved with little reference to events elsewhere, while the northern system was greatly influenced by British examples, but was almost totally unaffected by southern practices.

When on 7 June 1921 the Northern Ireland cabinet was formally named, Charles Stewart Henry Vane-Tempest-Stewart, seventh marquis of Londonderry, became minister for education for Northern Ireland. Londonderry (like his counterpart in the south) inherited three educational systems, primary, intermediate, and technical. The first two were ailing seriously and all three needed coordination and overall policy direction. Londonderry's task was a difficult one. The region was seriously disturbed. Further, there never had been a major arm of the education service in Belfast, so he was charged with creating a new civil service cadre. He managed as best he could with those civil servants whom he could entice away from Dublin, with Scottish and English recruits, and with newcomers from the ranks of the recent university graduates. Although the ministry was established in June 1921 there were delays in obtaining information and personnel from the southern government, the leaders of which were reluctant to cooperate with the northern government formed under the 'partition act'. Not until 1 February 1922 were full powers for education in Northern Ireland transferred to the northern ministry.

Even after obtaining full legal control of the northern educational machines, Londonderry's ministry had troubles, for about one-third of the catholic elementary school teachers refused to recognise the northern ministry, a stance facilitated by the southern government's continuing to pay their salaries.[1] This campaign continued till October 1922, when the provisional government in the south withdrew its subventions. The resistance by the catholic primary teachers exacerbated the general tension between the ministry of education and the catholics that had risen in the spring of 1922, when most catholic intermediate school headmasters had their students take the examinations as set in the south, not those of the Belfast ministry. Originally the northern ministry had asked the Dublin officials to conduct the examinations, but then withdrew this request when they became aware of the emphasis that the Dublin authorities planned to give to the Irish language in the examinations; thus, one of the few promising opportunities for cross-border cooperation was lost.

Lord Londonderry's ministry had some good fortune which partially offset its difficulties. In the first place, when the northern government was constituted, a single ministry of education was created to embrace the three formerly separate branches of schooling. Thus, the problem of coordinating the branches effectively was solved. Second, the ministry was fortunate in the quality of the personnel associated with it. As permanent secretary, Londonderry recruited Lewis McQuibban, a Scottish civil servant highly experienced in drafting educational legislation. In charge of the primary schools— much the most important branch—was A. N. Bonaparte Wyse, who had been recognised generally as the most promising administrator in the service of the former commissioners of national education in Dublin. Wyse, a catholic, became permanent secretary of the ministry in 1927. Also, Robert McKeown, a prominent businessman and Belfast M.P., served with great ability as parliamentary secretary. McKeown was especially important because Lord Londonderry's seat was in the senate, and therefore the chief duty of defending the ministry in the commons fell to McKeown.

When in 1922 the ministry of education turned to drafting a major educational reform measure, it was almost inevitable that this measure should include provision for rate aid to the various levels of schooling and for local lay involvement in controlling the schools. In 1919 and 1920 Ulster unionist M.P.s had supported two bills in the London parliament that would have provided rate aid for primary, intermediate, and technical education, and another bill that would have provided rate aid to the Belfast primary schools

---

[1] See Donald Harman Akenson, *Education and enmity: the control of schooling in Northern Ireland, 1920–1950* (Newton Abbot, 1973), pp 44–7; Phoenix, *Northern nationalism*, pp 178–9.

and local civic control of those schools. That these three measures had been blocked by the hierarchy of the catholic church in Ireland certainly did nothing to lessen the unionists' adherence to the bills' principles. Further, a conference of the leading professional educators in Northern Ireland (the 'Belfast coordination conference'), held in 1921, had recommended that county councils and borough councils be required to levy rates to aid education. The predispositions to provide rate aid, and to invoke some element of local lay control, were reinforced by reference to English precedents, in particular the 'Balfour act' of 1902.[2] Indeed, the sixth marquis of Londonderry, the father of Northern Ireland's first education minister, had been president of the English board of education during 1902–5, the very years in which English education was being brought under local civic control. Finally, an official formulation of reform ideas, including local aid and control, had been articulated by the Lynn committee, a body appointed by Lord Londonderry in September 1921, which issued an interim report in late June 1922.[3]

The Londonderry act of 1923[4] provided the basic framework for Ulster education till 1947 and is therefore worth some attention. The least important changes introduced were in terminology. The former national schools became known as 'primary schools' and as 'public elementary schools', and it became common to refer to the former intermediate institutions as 'secondary schools'. In substantive matters the most important provision of the Londonderry act was to establish 'regional education committees' as subcommittees of county councils and of county borough councils. Confusingly, while these committees controlled educational policy in their respective areas, they neither controlled the individual schools (which were under various forms of management committees or, in the case of voluntary schools, individual managers), nor did they set the education rates, which were set by the county and county-borough councils.

As if this system were not awkward enough, it was criss-crossed with three categories of primary schools, differentiated according to their form of management and how much government money they received. The first class of schools were those totally under the control of local education authorities, whether built by the authorities ('provided schools') or those handed over to the local authorities by their former managers ('transferred schools'). In these schools, teachers were paid by the ministry, and all other expenses, including capital expenditure, were covered by a combination of central and local government funds. The second class of schools comprised those under special management committees, usually called 'four-and-two committees', four of whose members were named by the existing managers or trustees and

[2] 2 Edw. VII, c. 42 (18 Dec. 1902).
[3] The catholic clergy had refused to nominate representatives to the Lynn committee; see Akenson, *Education & enmity*, pp 51–8; Phoenix, *Northern nationalism*, p. 242.
[4] 13 & 14 Geo. V, c. 21 (22 June 1923).

two by the local education authorities. These schools received complete sub-vention of their teachers' salaries and one-half of maintenance expenses from the local rates. In addition they were eligible for discretionary grants for capital construction both from the ministry and from the local rates. The third class of schools were those that remained completely independent of local control. These schools continued to receive full payment of teachers' salaries by the ministry of education and one-half of maintenance expenses from the rates, but they received no capital expenditure grants from any public source.

The Londonderry act made it possible for the managers of secondary schools to transfer them to the control of the regional or county borough education committees, and permitted those authorities, with the cooperation of the relevant rating authority, to construct new secondary schools. These plans, however, were more dream than reality, for in fact very few secondary schools chose to come under the supervision of local authorities, and few authorities had sufficient resources to build their own schools. Nevertheless, Londonderry's ministry effected one signal improvement in secondary educa-tion. It replaced the old system of payment-by-examination-results with a system of inspection of each school. At the same time, secondary-school teachers' salaries were raised considerably.

As for technical education, the act added another layer of complications. Instead of having the regional education committee oversee the technical schools, it was necessary, for political reasons, to perpetuate the technical edu-cation responsibilities of the urban district councils. Thus in the towns tech-nical education was locally supervised and rate-aided by urban district councils, but in the rural areas it was supported from the county rates and supervised by one of the regional education committees. Perhaps the least complex provisions of the Londonderry act were those making effective throughout Northern Ireland compulsory education from 6 to 12 years of age for all children, and to 14 for those not employed in certain scheduled occupations.

In framing his education act, Lord Londonderry was guided by certain vaguely ecumenical goals. He wished that Ulster's catholic and protestant children could be educated together, and if that were not feasible he firmly believed that the educational system should be equitable as between religious groups. In practice his act changed the secondary and technical school systems very little, but it did alter considerably the arrangements for those primary schools that opted to come fully under local control. In order to prevent these locally controlled and fully governmentally financed schools from being bent to the purposes of any denomination, the Londonderry act contained two important provisions: first that no form of religious instruc-tion, including Bible reading, could be paid for by public funds or conducted during compulsory school hours, and secondly that local appointment committees could not take religion into account when appointing a primary-school teacher.[5]

These two requirements rankled with many of the protestant clergy, who wanted not only full governmental support for local schools but the power to appoint only protestants as teachers and to require these teachers to give Bible instruction outside the hours of compulsory secular instruction. An attack on the Londonderry act was led by the Rev. William Corkey, convenor of the elementary education board of the general assembly of the Presbyterian Church in Ireland. Corkey's chief assistants were the Rev. James Quinn (anglican) and the Rev. W. H. Smyth (methodist), and this triumvirate was instrumental in forming the 'united education committee of the protestant churches' to lobby the government. The clergy demanded 'protestant teachers to teach protestant children' and at least a half-hour of Bible instruction in all 'provided' and 'transferred' primary schools each day. The clerical campaign against the Londonderry act was mounted in late 1924, and in the spring of 1925 it reached a high pitch just at the time Sir James Craig was seeking to show his strength on the boundary issue by achieving a complete victory in the election for the Northern Ireland parliament scheduled for April 1925. Faced with this divisive electoral threat Craig promised the protestant clerics an amending bill.[6]

The actual meaning of the amending act of 1925[7] has never been fully explained, but a 'concordat' between the ministry and the protestant clerics drawn up thereunder in late June 1925 stated: that local education authorities could require teachers to give Bible instruction in the time set aside for religious teaching, but that Bible instruction was not to be included in the hours of compulsory school attendance. These provisions satisfied many protestant clergymen; and by 1930, 430 formerly voluntary protestant elementary schools had been transferred to local civic control.

But the Rev. Messrs Corkey, Quinn, and Smyth were not yet satisfied. In the first place, although the 1925 education act removed the prohibition on religious discrimination in the appointment of teachers, the ministry of education still claimed that appointment boards were prohibited by the Government of Ireland Act, 1920, from religious discrimination. More important, some regional education committees, although predisposed to require daily Bible reading, refused to allow a legal requirement that such teaching be given to be inserted in the deeds of transfer whereby the former voluntary managers handed their schools over to the regional committees. From this refusal, many protestant clergy concluded that at some awful date in the future the regional education committees might suddenly cease requiring Bible instruction to be given, and thus schools that had once been protestant

---

[5] Akenson, *Education & enmity*, pp 64–71.   [6] Ibid., pp 79–84.
[7] 15 & 16 Geo. V, c. 1 (13 Mar. 1925).

bastions would become godless, secular institutions. Related to these protestant fears was the demand that protestant clergy be appointed to sit on all
civic education committees.

Thus a new agitation began in 1927 under the continuing auspices of the
united education committee of the protestant churches. The chief clerical
agitators were the same, although now the ministry of education was under
the headship of Lord Charlemont (Lord Londonderry had resigned early in
1926) and the permanent secretaryship of A. N. Bonaparte Wyse. As in the
previous agitation, the clergy bided their time and then struck when the
government was vulnerable, this time as the May 1929 general election approached. The Orange order also threw its weight behind the campaign.
Whether the government surrendered to the clerical agitators or simply
granted them a boon is unclear, but the result was that Lord Craigavon (Sir
James had become a viscount in 1927) made arrangements that resulted in
the education act of 1930.[8] Under this act clergymen were appointed to the
regional and county borough education committees, and control of the
committees of management of transferred schools was effectively given to
the former denominational managers. Further, management committees of
provided and transferred schools were given the right to narrow the list
of candidates for teaching posts to three, from which the regional or county
borough education committee would pick one. Because each transferred
school was, under the 1930 act, controlled by the former denominational
interests, it was now possible to limit the three candidates selected to those
of the same denomination as the former denominational managers. Significantly, the 1930 act made it a binding duty of local education authorities to
provide Bible instruction in provided and transferred schools if the parents
of ten or more children asked that such instruction be given. In such cases
the schoolchildren were not compelled to attend the Bible lessons, but the
teachers were compelled to give the instruction as part of their normal work-
load.

There was one provision of the 1930 act that appears anomalous at first
glance: the provision empowering the ministry of education to pay half the
capital cost of constructing new voluntary schools and half the cost of enlarg-
ing existing ones. This focuses our attention on the position of the catholics
and the primary schools. The authorities of the catholic church continually
refused to countenance anything but clerical control over the schools; so
whereas the provisions for provided and transferred schools were matters for
contention between the government and the protestant clergy, the provisions
for the voluntary primary schools were negotiated between the government
and the catholic leaders. But why did Lord Craigavon's government make
such a large concession—raising the school-constructing grant from nothing

[8]   20 & 21 Geo. V, c. 14 (17 June 1930).

to 50 per cent of capital costs—at this time? The answer is that, in contrast to the period before the passage of the 1925 education act, the catholic authorities and catholic politicians were now vigorously defending their interests. Abandoning the unproductive policy of refusing to negotiate with the northern government, the church leaders adopted a new realism. One sign of this realism was the Christian Brothers' adhesion in 1926–7 to the northern government's elementary education system, an arrangement that yielded approximately £10,000 each year. The assertiveness and size of the nationalist party under Joseph Devlin increased almost annually from his entry into parliament in 1925 and was a development that greatly aided the church's cause. Thus, when it became clear that in 1930 Lord Craigavon was certain to introduce an education bill that would benefit the protestant churches, the catholic clergy and lay teachers pressed vigorously for a quid pro quo for their voluntary primary schools. Most important, Bishop Daniel Mageean threatened to contest the constitutionality of the proposed 1930 education measure as an illegal endowment of the protestant religion. This was a very shrewd threat, for in reality the 1930 amending measure went beyond the powers of the government of Ireland act; this illegality was not officially admitted, however, till the 1940s. For the moment, the threat was enough. Craigavon introduced the capital expenditure grants to voluntary schools, and the menace of legal action was withdrawn. The 1930 act, therefore, was an apparently equitable compromise between severely conflicting protestant and catholic claims.[9]

The decade after the passage of the 1930 education act was relatively quiet. The depression years hurt the morale of the schoolteachers but no severe problems developed. During the 1930s the ministry of education pressed its campaign to amalgamate small elementary schools, especially neighbouring boys' and girls' schools when either had an average attendance of under fifty. In the case of the protestant primary schools the ministry was fairly successful, but the catholic clergy and political leaders zealously fought amalgamations on moral grounds. In the face of this opposition the ministry adopted a double standard, forcing protestant schools to merge but allowing separate catholic schools to continue even when their enrolments were well below fifty.

Near the end of the decade the Northern Ireland government followed the English example and raised the school-leaving age to 15, effective as from the school year 1939–40. However, whereas the English act of 1936[10] had applied to all children, the Northern Ireland measure of 1938[11] allowed children engaged in certain forms of 'beneficial employment' to leave at 14. In actual

---

[9] Akenson, *Education & enmity*, pp 104–11.
[10] 26 Geo. V & 1 Edw. VIII, c. 41 (31 July 1936).
[11] 1 & 2 Geo. VI, c. 20 (24 Nov. 1938).

fact, both the English and the Northern Irish measures were prevented from coming into force by the onset of the second world war.

The war was directly destructive to the northern educational system in terms of buildings and personnel, but these debilitating effects were more than offset by the war's focusing the attention of the population on the need for educational reform. Crucially, the positive aspect of the war experience was reinforced by English events. The second world war yielded major reforms in England, and the northern government was tied directly to England by its social parity policy and by a predisposition of the unionist leadership to emulate English actions as models. Not surprisingly, then, the Northern Ireland educational reform act of 1947[12] closely paralleled England's reform measure, the Butler act of 1944.[13]

'The general assembly is convinced that any less a measure of reform in Northern Ireland than that now secured for England would be disastrous to the well-being of the people of Northern Ireland', was a resolution passed by the presbyterian church's general assembly in June 1944, a resolution whose tone was approved by most protestants and by many influential catholics as well.[14] The government, responding to reform pressures, produced a white paper, *Educational reconstruction in Northern Ireland*, in December 1944. The most important proposals were, firstly, to raise the school-leaving age to 15 with no exemptions, and secondly, to introduce a break between primary and post-primary education at the age of 11-plus. At that age children were to be divided into two streams, a few into academic secondary schools and the majority into non-selective secondary institutions. Thirdly, the number of local education authorities was to be reduced from eighteen to eight, one for each county and county-borough council. These authorities were now to assume jurisdiction over technical education, a branch of education previously having its own separate local administrative structure. In its fourth and potentially most divisive proposal, the white paper recommended that the capital construction grant for voluntary primary schools, and for former voluntary primary schools that were converted into non-academic secondary schools, be raised from the existing 50 per cent to 65 per cent. Although there were still in operation a large number of protestant voluntary elementary schools, this fourth recommendation was generally, and correctly, interpreted as a concession to the catholics. Voluntary academic secondary schools were to be eligible for a 65 per cent capital construction grant if they gave up 80 per cent of their places to children sponsored by the local education authorities, but this provision affected protestants and catholics equally.

The education act of 1947 was shaped and guided through parliament by Lieutenant-colonel Samuel H. Hall-Thompson, who had become minister

---

[12] 1947, c. 3 (27 Mar. 1947).   [13] 7 & 8 Geo. VI, c. 31 (3 Aug. 1944).
[14] Akenson, *Education & enmity*, pp 157–8.

for education in March 1944.[15] As has so often been the case in Northern Ireland's educational affairs, the major educational provisions of the act (in this case the extension of the school-leaving age and the separation of children into two discrete school systems, non-academic 'intermediate schools' and academic 'grammar schools', at age 11-plus) attracted relatively little comment. But matters touching religion received great attention. Not only were many protestant leaders opposed to the government's proposal to raise the voluntary schools capital grants to 65 per cent, but ancillary matters angered them even more. The measure required that, in each school under government control, a collective act of worship was to begin each school day, and religious instruction was to be part of the compulsory curriculum. The inclusion of these requirements meant that the government, as a matter of civil liberty, had to make provision for those teachers who could not in conscience participate in such worship or give religious instruction. In mid 1945 the government and the protestant churches seemed to have formulated an agreed conscience clause; but something went awry, exactly what is uncertain, and a frightful row erupted. Charges and counter-charges that the other was reneging or acting unethically rang from both sides. In the final event the government rammed through a conscience clause that gave effective protection to teachers with religious scruples. The clause was unacceptable to the more excitable protestant clergymen.

Even more disturbing to some protestant clergymen was the government's insistence on repealing all previous statutes that had regulated the conditions of religious instruction in public elementary schools. This insistence was largely a result of the opinion of the attorney general for Northern Ireland, John C. MacDermott, that the religious provisions of the 1925 and 1930 acts were *ultra vires* and that the transfer deeds written under those acts were illegal if they included provisions compelling teachers paid with public funds to give Bible instruction. To the minds of some protestant leaders this opinion raised the possibility of catholics, in certain border areas where they commanded a majority, gaining control of the local education authority and then prohibiting the reading of the Bible in schools originally built with protestant funds and subsequently turned over to public management on the express contractual condition that Bible reading would always form a part of the curriculum.

Merely because Hall-Thompson and the unionist government were under attack from the protestant side, it should not be supposed that catholics were happy. Far from being grateful for the increase in capital grants to voluntary schools, the catholic viewpoint was that the proper figure for these grants was not 65 per cent but 100 per cent.

---

[15] Harkness, *N.I. since 1920*, p. 98.

Despite the pressures from the protestant right wing and from the nationalist representatives, Sir Basil Brooke's cabinet held firm and Hall-Thompson's bill was passed with little trimming to either side. The measure was an impressive achievement. Indeed, the evolution of education in Northern Ireland from 1947 to the mid 1960s can be summarised as the working-out in practice of the ideals of the Hall-Thompson act. In administrative terms the act implied four interwoven structural reforms: the reorganisation of the primary school to take children only up to age 11-plus; the necessity of establishing a new kind of practical post-primary school, the intermediate schools, not to be confused with 'intermediate schools' of the pre-1922 era, which were academic grammar schools; the need to expand academic grammar-school places; and the raising of the leaving age to 15. All these changes were interrelated, and the problem of effecting them simultaneously was much greater than the mere sum of the difficulties of meeting each separate goal. Reorganisation of the primary schools proceeded slowly, and not till the 1960s were the majority of the elementary schools organised as units specialising in the training of children under the age of 12. The establishment of a network of intermediate schools proceeded just as slowly. By the end of the academic year 1950–51, only twelve intermediate schools were in operation and all of these were converted primary and technical schools.[16] Not until 1952 was the first specially designed intermediate school opened. Rural areas stubbornly resisted this new form of education; the farmers preferred having their children educated in nearby all-age elementary schools. By 1958, however, fifty-five intermediate schools were in operation, and 129 by 1964.

As a corollary of the difficulties in reorganising the primary schools and constructing the intermediate schools, it was necessary to postpone the raising of the leaving age to 15 from 1951 to 1953 and finally to 1957, when it at last became operative. For the grammar schools the new education act brought a rapid increase in enrolments. This was partly a result of the new scholarship system, partly a product of lowering the entrance age from 12-plus to 11-plus, and partly because of a secular trend towards increased demand for grammar-school places. Thus, the grammar schools had somewhat over 17,000 pupils on their rolls in 1947–8, about 29,000 in 1957–8, and over 44,000 in early 1969.

PARADOXICALLY, when the new government of the Irish Free State began managing its own system of education, it honoured precedents set by the old Dublin administration much more than did the Northern Ireland government. As far as the structure, as distinct from the content, of education was concerned, the Irish revolution was less a revolution than a change of management. Understandably, the revolutionary dáil, the provisional government, and the new Irish Free State government successively gave lower

---

[16] Akenson, *Education & enmity*, pp 180–83.

priority to education than to other matters more central to the state's survival. When in January 1919 the constitution of Dáil Éireann was approved, it did not include provision for an education minister, although there was a ministership for the Irish language. For most of the provisional government period (1922) there were two ministers for education, one for the provisional government and another for the dáil, and neither appears to have been able to give full attention to educational questions. Only when Eoin MacNeill took over both portfolios in the autumn of 1922 was one man placed in charge, and only then did clear, firm central leadership become possible.[17] MacNeill, however, was often busy with other affairs and attended the dáil too infrequently to deal effectively with educational matters, or so many deputies complained. Then in November 1924 he was appointed to the boundary commission, an onerous duty which effectively took him away from his department for a full year.

Under a provisional government order of 19 January 1922 nine government departments were defined, one of these being education. On 31 January the commissioners of national education were convened by Patrick Bradley, the new chief executive for primary education, and told that their services were no longer needed. The same thing happened to the commissioners of intermediate education, although somewhat more gently. The abolition of these two boards removed the only independent forum whereby lay citizens could influence the formulation of educational policy. Although there were calls, notably from the Irish National Teachers' Organisation, for the establishment of an independent education advisory council, it was not till 1950, when the 'council of education' was formed, that a substitute was available.[18] Implicitly, therefore, the new government of the Free State concentrated the educational authority of the central government in the hands of the civil servants. But who comprised the civil service of the new Ireland? Of the more than 21,100 civil servants in the new state, only 131 had been personnel of the revolutionary dáil; all the rest were former United Kingdom staff. Inevitably, imperial procedures, slightly modified to correspond to the new situation, prevailed.

The natural predisposition at the centre to preserving the existing educational system was reinforced by religious imperatives that operated at both national and local levels. The Irish revolution and its aftermath greatly strengthened the powers of the catholic church. In the first place, the

---

[17] Donald Harman Akenson, *A mirror to Kathleen's face: education in independent Ireland 1922–1960* (Montreal and Dublin, 1975), p. 27.
[18] The establishment of such a council was resisted by W. T. Cosgrave, Eamon de Valera, and most of the catholic bishops. However, church resistance weakened in face of papal support for corporatist principles, and the council was formed following an election pledge in 1948 by Fine Gael. However, only 3 of its 30 members were primary teachers; most were managers and officials with a bias towards the status quo. See ibid., pp 29–31, 70, 106–8.

detachment of Northern Ireland from the south, whatever its constitutional implications, greatly increased the leverage of the catholic church in the south, since partition removed much of the protestant counterweight to the church's influence. Secondly, the civil war reinforced the catholic church's powers, because a tacit alliance was forged between the new Irish government and the religious authorities. Thirdly, the new Free State government was much more responsive to Irish domestic lobbies, among them the churches, protestant as well as catholic, than the United Kingdom legislature had been. By and large the leaders of the main churches in the Free State were satisfied with the existing educational arrangements, for local management of national and intermediate schools was almost entirely in religious hands; this applied to protestant as well as catholic schools.[19]

Coordination and improvement, not radical reform, became the watchwords of the education authorities of the new state, and within this limited ambit they were quite successful. The key to the coordination policy was the ministers and secretaries act of 1924,[20] which reorganised the Irish Free State government and gave the minister for education control of technical instruction, a field that previously had been controlled by the minister for agriculture. Now one minister controlled all three major branches of schooling and was able to coordinate them so that no curricular gaps remained. (Incidentally, the 1924 act called the old national schools 'primary schools' and denominated the former intermediate schools 'secondary schools', a usage that became common, but far from universal; hereafter the two sets of terms are used as pairs of synonyms.)

Significantly, in 1924 the new regime abolished the system of payment by results, whereby academic secondary schools previously had won grants according to their pupils' marks in nationwide examinations. Now the straitjacket of the results system was replaced by a capitation grant paid for each pupil following an approved course, a change that provided an opportunity for imaginative teachers to vary somewhat the school curriculum according to the requirements of their individual classes.

Near the end of the Cosgrave administration, another set of improvements in post-primary schooling was effected as a result of the vocational education act of 1930.[21] This act, besides renaming the technical schools 'vocational schools', filled in the gaps in the vocational education network by replacing the former patchwork system with one that covered rural as well as municipal districts. Also, each vocational education authority, a group now appointed by the appropriate local government unit, was required, not merely permitted, to strike a rate in aid of local vocational institutions.

The educational improvement that affected the greatest number of children was the compulsory attendance act of 1926.[22] This measure was badly

[19] Ibid., p. 116.   [20] 1924/16 (21 Apr. 1924).   [21] 1930/29 (21 July 1930).
[22] 1926/17 (27 May 1926).

needed, for in 1918 only 68.9 per cent of the average number of children on the national school rolls throughout Ireland were in daily attendance; whereas, to use a graphic comparison, in the remote and windswept Orkney Islands, the area of Scotland with the lowest attendance, 83 per cent of the children attended school every day. After two unsuccessful attempts to overcome difficulties, first with the Garda Síochána and secondly with the department of finance, the department of education was finally able to draft a successful bill, which passed through the legislature in the winter and spring of 1925–6. This new act, unlike its predecessor of 1892, blanketed the country with effective agencies to enforce compulsory attendance. In each of the eight largest urban areas, school attendance committees were to enforce the school attendance laws, and in the rest of the Irish Free State a local garda officer was assigned to enforce them. Children were required to attend school approximately from their sixth till their fourteenth birthday. School attendance for most children would be in a national school, but the act permitted the minister for education to certify other schools or home education as acceptable in individual cases. The new act had an obvious effect, for attendance—measured in terms of numbers of children in average daily attendance as a percentage of the average number on the rolls—rose from 77.0 per cent in 1925–6 to 82.9 per cent in 1930–31.[23]

Reflect now on both what had been done by the new government and what had not. The three major systems of schooling—primary, academic secondary, and vocational—had been concentrated under a single ministry and administratively dovetailed. The previously inadequate compulsory attendance laws had been tightened, the vocational schools network fully articulated, and the grants system for academic secondary schools signally improved. However, none of these changes involved any significant change in the basic institutions of education or in their control. The new government's policy of coordination and improvement implicitly affirmed the desirability of operating three distinct school systems and tacitly affirmed the nature and the legitimacy of the powers that controlled these systems.

In addition, the improvements of the 1920s increased educational efficiency but did not commit the state to any great increase in educational investment, and the levels of educational investment stayed low into the 1960s. The total public expenditure for all levels of education, including university, as a percentage of gross national product at factor cost was as follows for representative years:

1926–7	3.1
1931	3.3
1941	3.2

[23] Akenson, *A mirror to Kathleen's face*, pp 65–8.

1951	3.1
1961	3.5

To place this expenditure in perspective, it is useful to compare it as a percentage of national income in the early 1960s with that of Great Britain and Northern Ireland.[24]

Republic of Ireland	3.4
England and Wales	3.9
Northern Ireland	5.4
Scotland	6.5

Actually, the Republic's relatively modest expenditures were smaller comparatively than these percentages indicate, for each of the other governmental areas in Great Britain and Ireland was considerably wealthier than the Republic, and thus each was spending considerably more per child than were the Irish, even after religious philanthropy is taken into account.

Why was the south so relatively parsimonious? Firstly, a sequence of economic circumstances hurt the schools. Even in the buoyant economic climate of the 1920s the process of creating the new state absorbed any surplus funds that might have been available. Then came the great depression of the 1930s, the economic dislocation of the second world war in the 1940s, and finally the trade fluctuations of the early 1950s. Secondly, mechanisms for smoothly channelling increased funds to the schools were lacking. The decision on whether or not to initiate a primary or academic secondary school building programme in a given area was in private hands, usually those of the religious authorities. In the case of the primary schools, one-third of the cost of construction normally had to come from voluntary sources, and the entire cost of secondary school construction fell on voluntary charity. The religious authorities resisted any change that would have undercut the theory that the schools were private property. Indeed, in the early 1950s the catholic bishops condemned a proposal by the Irish National Teachers' Organisation that the state underwrite a great proportion of capital expenses for primary school construction. Similarly, the religious authorities opposed direct local-authority rate aid to either primary or secondary schools, presumably because receipt of such aid might alter the managerial arrangements. Thirdly, it should be added that this relatively low expenditure on education was related to the state's collective system of values. Such a statement may sound vacuous, or derogatory, but it really is neither. What it means is simply that the community preferred to spend its money on things other than education. This is clearly indicated by charting

[24] Ibid., p. 84.

education's percentage of the total public-sector budget for representative years:[25]

1926–7	14.1
1931	16.1
1941	12.1
1951	9.3
1961	9.5

Given that the total public-sector budget grew markedly over time (from £34.0 million in 1926–7 to £214.7 million in 1961), it is clear that the state could have spent more money on education if it had wanted to do so, but that it deliberately chose not to do so. This was a choice which educationists are apt to deplore, but which may well have been wise when the state's entire welfare is considered: for example, in many areas a new hospital may have benefited more people than a new school would have done.

But assuming that the state's money was probably well spent in acquiring services other than education, it should not be inferred that the school systems did not need more funds than they received. Primary education provides the best example on this point. In 1952 the parliamentary secretary to the taoiseach admitted that there were 460 national schools below modern health standards, for which replacements had not yet been authorised. In 1963–4 fewer than half of the primary schools had drinking water in the school or on the school site, and under half had either a chemical or a flush toilet. As late as 1963–4, nearly two-thirds of the primary schools were heated by open fires. Statistics for 1960 revealed that over 40 per cent of the republic's primary-school buildings either had been formally declared obsolete by the office of public works or had been standing for eighty years or more.[26]

Accepting, then, that the Irish revolution neither revolutionised patterns of educational investment nor altered arrangements for the control of educational institutions, it remains to note that the relationship of individual social classes to the school systems was hardly changed at all. To a considerable extent an Irish child's chances in life were determined by the level of education he or she received, primary education being for labourers, academic secondary schooling for clerks and the mercantile trades, and university training for the better off, aspiring professionals, and higher-ranking civil servants. The crucial screening device was the network of academic secondary schools which, like St Peter, sometimes opened the door to higher things,

[25] Ibid., p. 85.
[26] Ibid., pp 87–8. However, on the eve of the second world war there were many similar deficiencies in schools in N.I., which was a generation behind England and Wales in provision of accommodation (Buckland, *Factory of grievances*, p. 102).

but more often denied such delights to those at the gates. Unlike primary education, which was a universal right, academic secondary training was a privilege. The secondary schools were private institutions, and admission to them was governed more by the economics of the market-place than by a calculus of merit. The secondary schools were not free (although the catholic teaching orders implicitly subsidised them through giving of their own services below market cost) and therefore were economically and socially discriminatory, which is to say that the secondary school system reinforced existing class divisions. A middle-class child of modest ability was almost certain of finding a place in a secondary school, while a working-class child of similar ability had a much smaller chance of admission. However, such shortcomings were not confined to Ireland.

Like the Victorian English, the post-revolutionary Irish accepted the proposition that such social inequalities were both just and inevitable, while simultaneously creating a scholarship ladder whereby a few very bright children of the working class could acquire a secondary schooling and thus earn their way into a higher station on the social ladder. In 1921 the revolutionary dáil authorised each county and county-borough council to strike a penny in the pound rate to provide scholarships for primary school pupils to academic secondary or technical schools, a programme that was ratified by the Irish Free State government in 1923, and subsequently expanded in 1944. In addition, there were state 'intermediate scholarships' awarded on the basis of a student's prowess in the new intermediate school certificate, taken usually at about age 16, as distinct from the leaving certificate taken at the close of secondary education at about 18. How many children did these scholarship programmes benefit? Take 1950–51 as a representative year: in that year 48,559 pupils were attending academic secondary schools. The average size of the secondary schools was 115 pupils and the average number of pupils holding scholarships in each school was 5.3. Undoubtedly individual cases of charity by individual headmasters augmented these governmental scholarships but certainly not enough to upset the existing social class arrangements.[27]

At this point our discussion breaks sharply: whereas conservatism in structure was the keynote of the post-revolutionary educational system, a truly revolutionary change occurred in content, namely the recasting of the curriculum in an effort to revive the Irish language. Even before independence, the commissioners of national education had begun to make provision for the teaching of Irish as well as English in Irish-speaking and bilingual areas; the aim, however, was to provide children with a basic education rather than to preserve the language.[28] The general story of the Irish-language revival movement is told elsewhere;[29] for the purposes of this essay the crucial point

---

[27] Akenson, *A mirror to Kathleen's face*, pp 77–9.   [28] Above, vi, 535–6.
[29] Above, pp 538–73.

is that after independence the schools became the chief instrument of the revival. This use of the schools was essentially extra-educational: although acquiring the language was an intellectual exercise of some value for the individual student, the Irish language was taught not chiefly to develop the mind of the individual child but to establish the political and cultural identity of the new state. As Eoin MacNeill said in the dáil, 'the business and main functions of the department of education in this country are to conserve and to build up our nationality'.[30] Very rarely in dáil debates or in educationists' writings is the argument found that the Irish language is good for the child; instead it is presented as being good for the nation and therefore necessary for the child.

The importance the new government placed on Irish is indicated by its issuance on 1 February 1922, soon after taking office, of Public Notice Number Four, whose theme sentence stated: 'the Irish language shall be taught or used as a medium of instruction for not less than one full hour each day in all national schools where there is a teacher competent to teach it.'[31] This order became effective on St Patrick's Day, 1922.

Actually, despite the new government's considerable enthusiasm for the language, the running was being made by extra-governmental bodies, in particular the 'national programme conference' on primary education. This group, which first met in January 1921, was formed at the instigation of the Irish National Teachers' Organisation and included a representative, although far from comprehensive, panel of educational, governmental, and revivalist bodies. So influential was this group's report that, having been signed in late January 1922, its programme came into effect in April. The programme may be summarised under four heads, the first of which clashes in tone with the other three. At its very first meeting the programme conference agreed that 'in the case of schools where the majority of the parents of the children object to having either Irish or English taught as an obligatory subject, their wishes should be complied with'.[32] This recommendation was the only one to be printed in bold-face type in the final report. Secondly, the conference recommended that Irish be taught to all schoolchildren, subject to the above proviso, for at least one hour per day, and that certain subjects were to be taught only through the Irish language: singing in all standards and history and geography from the third standard upwards. Thirdly, certain subjects necessarily had to be cut from the primary-school curriculum, notably drawing, elementary science, and nature study. Fourthly, and most startling, in the two grades of infant classes the Irish language only was to be used even if the children's home language was English.

[30] *Dáil Éireann deb.*, xiii, 187 (11 Nov. 1925).
[31] Akenson, *A mirror to Kathleen's face*, p. 42.
[32] National programme conference, *National programme of primary instruction* (Dublin, 1922), p. 4.

Alarmed now by the enthusiasms of some of the language revivalists, the teachers obtained a promise from the minister for education that they would not be penalised if they were unable to carry out immediately the extensive demands of the new programme. They were given to understand that the programme was an ideal, which could be in complete operation in five years' time at the very soonest. For the present the department of education agreed to the principle of using Irish as a medium of instruction only when the teachers were able to use it effectively, and only when the pupils were able to benefit from its use. But this principle melted away under the zealotry of school inspectors and departmental officials, and soon the teachers were highly agitated. Therefore, in 1924 the Irish National Teachers' Organisation decided to reconvene the national programme conference. This so frightened the minister and the officials of the department of education that they seized control of the invitation list and themselves selected the individuals who would 'represent' the various parties. Only the I.N.T.O. was permitted to select its own representatives. With considerable candour Eoin MacNeill explained why this tactic was necessary: because the government would find it very awkward if the conference, or even a significant minority, opposed the government's language policy. Even so, the 'second national programme conference' backed away a good deal from the first conference's recommendations. In particular, the second report stated that when a teacher was only marginally competent in Irish, the language had to be used for one hour only per day in infants' classes, not throughout the school day. As teachers became more competent they were to introduce more Irish, till finally all infant classes would be entirely in Irish. As a concession to those parents who wished their children to learn the proper use of English, that language was to be taught to infants in special classes conducted outside regular school hours. As for the higher grades, the basic principle of the first programme conference remained untouched: that where a teacher was competent to teach through Irish and the children to learn, it should be the language of instruction. To establish the educational hegemony of the Irish language, two courses were prescribed: the one, the 'low Irish high English' plan, being adopted where necessary, the other, the 'high Irish low English' option, being the scheme towards which all primary schools were to strive. A remarkable pseudo-mathematical formula encapsulated this plan: 'the sum of Irish plus English equals a constant quantity.'[33] The second programme was implemented in mid 1926 by John Marcus O'Sullivan, who had replaced Eoin MacNeill as minister for education early in 1926, and the teachers were satisfied.

---

[33] *Report of the second national programme conference (1925–6), made for the information of the minister for education* (Dublin, 1926), p. 28.

But with the change of government and the appointment of Thomas Derrig as de Valera's minister for education, the pace again swiftened. In mid 1934 Derrig summoned I.N.T.O. representatives and told them that he was not happy with the primary teachers' efforts in the language revival. A bargain was struck with the teachers whereby, in return for the teachers' placing more emphasis on the language, the academic standards demanded in other subjects were lowered. The English-language course in all national schools was reduced to the level of the 'low English high Irish' course, and rural science as a required subject disappeared. The level of mathematics instruction also was reduced. Then, in 1943 the primary school certificate, which had been introduced as a voluntary exercise in 1928–9, was made compulsory. The certificate placed a heavy emphasis on the Irish language—Irish, English, and arithmetic being the only subjects tested—and discriminated in favour of Irish-speaking children. A 40 per cent mark was necessary for a pass on each of these tests, except for children from the predominantly Irish-speaking districts, who had only to score 30 per cent on the English-language section. As a result of these developments the Irish language was emphasised above all other subjects in the curriculum.[34]

A variety of ancillary devices were developed to help support the revivalist efforts. For example, in 1933–4 the de Valera government introduced a grant of £2 a year to the parents of each child in an Irish-speaking district whose home language was Irish and who was attending a national school. Earlier, in 1926, the department of education had established the first of six secondary boarding schools, denominated 'preparatory colleges', for Irish-speaking young persons who wished to become primary-school teachers. In the training colleges that gave a two-year course for academic secondary-school graduates who wished to teach primary school, Irish became the language of work. By 1927 four of the five training colleges were teaching the majority of their subjects through Irish, and from 1931 onwards the bilingual certificate was a prerequisite to receiving the training-college diploma. Teachers already in service were pressed to acquire competence in Irish, and from 1935 onwards all teachers who had been below the age of 30 as of July 1922 had to obtain the ordinary certificate of competence to teach Irish or lose their salary increments.

Although the primary schools were seen as the major implement in the language revival, the academic secondary schools were not ignored. When in 1924 the old payment-by-results system was replaced by the intermediate and leaving certificate examinations, the pupils were permitted to take either English or Irish as an examination subject. A year later the department of education made a pass in Irish compulsory for the intermediate certificate, and in 1934 compulsory for the leaving certificate. The scoring system on the

[34] Akenson, *A mirror to Kathleen's face*, pp 48–9.

examinations encouraged Irish and discouraged English, both by giving more points for the Irish than the English language (for example, in the late 1940s 50 per cent more points on the intermediate examination could be earned in Irish literature than in English literature) and by giving bonus points for answers in non-linguistic subjects that were written in the Irish language. Thus, in the 1940s a student who answered the science papers in Irish received a 10 per cent bonus on that section of the examination. From 1927–8 every secondary school receiving a government grant had to teach Irish and, according to a 1932 decree, all pupils had to take the subject if they were to be recognised for grant-earning purposes. A complex system of financial bonuses was established for secondary schools that taught all or part of their courses through the medium of Irish.

Obviously a great deal of effort and money was expended in using the schools as an instrument of the Irish-language revival and, equally obviously, certain benefits accrued from these efforts and expenditures. Unfortunately, no precise accounting of time and money is possible; firstly, because the Irish government has repeatedly refused to allow any financial or educational audit of the programme, and secondly, because most of the items on the linguistic balance sheet are intangible, their valuation being more a matter of individual belief than objective accounting. Nevertheless, it is at least possible to adumbrate the benefits and costs, if not to tally their total precisely. On the benefit side of the ledger, the first item is crucial: the extensive educational efforts did, indeed, save the Irish language from virtual extinction. In 1911, 17.7 per cent of the entire population of the twenty-six counties could speak Irish. The percentage of Irish speakers in the same area, under the new government, expressed as a function of the number of persons 3 years of age and over, was as follows.[35]

1926	19.3
1936	23.7
1946	21.2
1961	27.2

Admittedly the areas in which Irish was used as the native language continually shrank during this period, but at least Irish as a second language was making headway. Secondly, the acquisition by all schoolchildren of a second language was a valuable intellectual exercise. Thirdly, the children's acquisition of the ethnic language, which once had been the native language, undoubtedly gave many children a valuable induction into their ancestral culture.

Now for the other side of the ledger. The actual financial expenditure on the schools' linguistic efforts is difficult to determine. Using data available for

[35] Ibid., p. 54.

the fiscal year 1928–9, the present author has calculated that the total direct incremental expense for the schools' work in the revival was somewhat above £162,000; this at a time when the Irish Free State had a gross national product of somewhat over £159 million. Secondly, in addition to direct financial expenditure the language revival probably involved indirect economic costs, because the time spent on Irish meant that the children were less well schooled in other areas, a loss that presumably reduced somewhat collective economic productivity. How much, however, is entirely problematical. The third, and much the most important, cost of the revival was borne directly by the children. Since they spent so much time on Irish they learned less English, arithmetic, history, and science than they otherwise would have done. During the 1930s the I.N.T.O., despairing of ever convincing the government of the necessity of evaluating the Irish-language policy, initiated a survey of its own. This survey, published in 1941,[36] was ingenious, for it produced a maximum of data at a minimum of expense: the I.N.T.O. designed a questionnaire about the educational effects of the Irish-language policy, to be completed only by those teachers who had actually taught through the medium. At the infant level, the study indicated that the use of Irish was intellectually inhibitive and, often, terrifying to a young child. The infant, already confused and frightened by entering a new environment,was cut off in most cases from the home language (English) and deprived of one of the few tools available for dealing with the new and alien environment. Some children, the teachers reported, were both mentally and physically hurt by the strain of the linguistic code. Less severe, but still significant, were the effects on the ordinary grades. Only in two subjects, singing and needlework, did the teachers adjudge that children learned as well when taught through the medium of Irish as when taught through English. Significantly, the validity of the I.N.T.O. survey was confirmed by a much more sophisticated study published in 1966 by the Rev. Dr John MacNamara.[37] This study indicated that an average of 42 per cent of the average primary-school week was spent on Irish-language lessons, plus whatever time was spent teaching other subjects through the medium. As a result, in English-language skills at age 12-plus the children were about seventeen months behind English children of the same age and social background and about eleven months behind in arithmetical skills.

Here we are at a dead end, for whether or not the benefits exceed the costs, whether the acquisition of Irish outweighs the loss in other subjects, is almost entirely a matter of individual perspective. Each individual's answer will depend chiefly on the degree of faith in the value of the Irish language. But faith, after all, is what revivals are all about.

[36] I.N.T.O., *Report of committee of inquiry into the use of Irish as a teaching medium to children whose home language is English* (Dublin, 1941).
[37] John MacNamara, *Bilingualism and primary education: a study of Irish experience* (Edinburgh, 1966).

To return briefly to matters of educational structure, the 1960s were years of considerable change; indeed, in comparison with the previous passivity of the department, they were almost years of revolution. The appointment of Patrick Hillery as minister for education in June 1959 was crucial, for under his regime education was transformed from a political albatross into a subject of continual public interest and continual debate. During Hillery's administration a radical change was made in the financing of the secondary schools: early in 1964 the government announced that in the future academic secondary schools would be eligible to receive grants of up to 60 per cent of capital costs for expansion and for new buildings. Happily, the bishops withdrew their former objections to such grants and the scheme was smoothly implemented. Further, the national economic plan published in 1964[38] stated that the school-leaving age would be raised to 15 by 1970 (in the event the extension had to be postponed until the academic year 1972–3). In order to meet the obviously growing need for post-primary school places, Hillery announced in May 1963 a plan for 'comprehensive schools' to enrol children from ages 12–13 to ages 15–16. Those schools would provide an opportunity for obtaining the intermediate certificate, but would not rival existing academic secondary schools: they would be established only in areas where post-primary opportunities were lacking. The state would provide the entire cost of building these new schools and would directly pay the teachers' salaries. By early 1970 four comprehensives were in operation and five more were scheduled to open soon. Their remit had been extended to cover the full range of second-level education, and not just the junior cycle.

Both a symbol and a lever for the new approach to education was Hillery's appointment in 1962 of a team of social scientists to study Irish education. The team's monumental report, *Investment in education*, appeared in two volumes in 1965.[39] For the first time a major governmental commission approached education not from a theo-philosophical viewpoint but as a social and economic activity. Behind all the tables and detailed recommendations was a single, obvious conclusion: that if the republic were to compete in the emerging European market-place it would have to allocate more resources to education and would have to spend that money more effectively.

The investment report served as a perfect backdrop for the September 1966 announcement by Donogh O'Malley, who had become minister in July 1966, that beginning in 1967 free post-primary education up to intermediate certificate level would be available for all children in academic secondary, vocational, and comprehensive schools.[40] The heart of O'Malley's plan was the payment of a £25 annual grant per child to each academic secondary

[38] *Second programme for economic expansion*, pt II (Pr 7670) (Dublin, 1964).
[39] *Investment in education: report of the survey team appointed by the minister for education in October 1962*, i (Pr 8311), ii (Pr 8527) (Dublin, 1965–6).
[40] John Coolahan, *Irish education: its history and structure* (Dublin, 1981), p. 195.

school that agreed to stop charging school fees. Strictly speaking, this plan did not make post-primary education costless, for not only did most parents still have to pay for books and school supplies, but a small minority of secondary schools refused to adopt the new scheme. Nevertheless, most children had access to a post-primary school they could attend without fee, a development that presumably has somewhat reduced the social class discrimination in post-secondary schooling.

Also in 1966 O'Malley was responsible for establishing the Kennedy committee to investigate industrial and reformatory schools, whose origins went back to the pre-independence era. Numbers had declined since their peak (seventy-one industrial schools throughout the island in 1898, plus a handful of reformatory schools), but many remained, all run by the religious orders. Following a damning report, the schools were gradually phased out during the 1970s. In recent years the treatment of children in such schools has become a matter of controversy. Contrary to the general impression, the bulk of the pupils were neither juvenile offenders nor orphans, but children whose parents were experiencing difficulties in coping. Nor were such schools run on charitable lines; government provided funds on a capitation basis, though inspection by the department of education seems to have been minimal. It is difficult to avoid the impression that the schools lasted as long as they did because of a tacit agreement between church and state that the system was a cheap and convenient way to exercise social control in this field.[41]

All these reforms suggested that, having entered the era of political independence in a mood of educational conservatism, the state was preparing itself for entry into the European Economic Community in a spirit of innovation.

BY the mid 1960s the differences between the southern and northern educational systems were great. Undoubtedly these contrasts told a good deal about the differing character of the two political systems and cultural milieus, but within the scope of the present chapter all that can be done is to draw attention to the similarities and contrasts and leave it to the reader to speculate on their interpretation.

At once the most basic and the most paradoxical contrast in the development of the two systems was that whereas Northern Ireland was established in a counter-revolutionary spirit, its educational development was more radical, more nearly revolutionary, than was that of the south, an ostensibly revolutionary government. To some extent this paradox was related to the availability of appropriate models for each government to emulate. The Northern Ireland government immediately began measuring itself against British standards and thus departed radically from Irish traditions. The Irish

---

[41] See Mary Raftery and Eoin O'Sullivan, *Suffer the little children: the inside story of Ireland's industrial schools* (Dublin, 1999).

Free State, on the other hand, had no suitable models, and in education, as in so many other areas, looked to the Irish past for guidance about future practice. In educational matters preservation of the immediate past was desirable, because the primary- and academic secondary-school systems were denominational networks, operating along lines congenial to the leaders of the principal churches, and thus to most of the citizens.

Also behind the basic paradox was a contrast in protestant and catholic attitudes towards the state. Although both catholics and protestants had at various times shown themselves suspicious of state control of education, by the beginning of the twentieth century it was the catholic clergy who were standing out against a greater degree of state control and lay involvement in the management of schools. The main protestant denominations, by contrast, were more well disposed, and had already introduced a lay element into boards of management of most secondary schools.[42] The predominantly protestant north was much more apt to respond to social problems in general, and educational problems in particular, by invoking state mechanisms, whereas in the south the state was introduced only as a last resort.

Similarly, protestants were less afraid of civic involvement in educational affairs and believed in the necessity of aid from central or local government funds to all public schools, a position explicitly condemned by the catholic hierarchy. This belief in financial aid and civic control, it must be emphasised, antedated the establishment of the northern government: it was not a unionist dodge to seize control of denominational schools under a unionist government. Taken together, the protestant affinity for state action and the acceptance of the need for local civic involvement in financing and control of the schools help in part to explain why, in relation to its southern neighbour, Northern Ireland was so educationally radical during its early years.

The debates of the northern and southern parliaments relating to education reveal another difference: that within the northern polity the subject of education received much more attention than it did in the south. One reason, of course, was that the north was a much more sharply divided community religiously, so education inevitably was a much more contentious topic and therefore received much greater attention than in the south. But that was not the sole reason, for in addition to quarrelling more about the topic of education, the northerners were more willing to pay for it. As noted earlier, the north spent a considerably higher proportion of its national income on education than did the south, Further, because per capita income in the north was higher than in the south, the amount spent per head was much greater. For example, in 1967–8 the Republic's public education budget was £50 million, the north's £58 million, a sum that amounted to £17 per head in the Republic and £38 per head in Northern Ireland.[43]

---

[42] Above, vi, 537–8; Akenson, *Education & enmity*, p. 12.   [43] *Hibernia*, 25 Aug. 1972.

Finally, two points that the two school systems had in common stand out: each system was simultaneously generous to religious minorities and intolerant and discriminatory towards them. The generosity of the southern government to protestants is well known. Fewer protestants than catholic children were required to constitute a recognised school; special transportation arrangements were made for them; a special grants scheme was developed for protestant post-primary schools that otherwise would not qualify for aid under the O'Malley plan. The northern government's benevolence was less publicised but nonetheless real: it allowed the catholic schools to operate by a special set of rules. Although after partition the northern majority was strongly committed to the constitutional principle that local schools should be supported in large part from the rates and placed under local civic control, the northern government continued to underwrite the greater part of the expenses of the catholic schools even though the school heads refused to accept any civic interference in their prerogatives. Further, in matters such as school amalgamations, the regulations were rigidly applied to protestant institutions but quietly ignored for catholic schools, a practice that produced the same result as the republic's special provisions for small protestant schools, but without the attendant publicity. Granted, in each case it was an open question whether the government's generosity was motivated solely by Christian charity.

Were these policies discriminatory? Yes. Ever since partition the catholic primary schools in the north received less than full financial support from governmental sources, whereas most protestant schools were fully underwritten by state and local funds. Thus the parents of a catholic child had to pay a somewhat higher proportion of their child's educational expenses than had the protestants. But much the same happened throughout the post-independence period to protestant parents in the south. Whereas every catholic child in the twenty-six counties had a primary school within walking distance, the protestant did not, thus involving the cost of transportation or of boarding. In 1934 the southern government began a system of transportation grants to the protestants, but these never covered the full cost of transport.[44] Further, when in the mid 1960s Donogh O'Malley mooted his scheme of free post-primary education, it was not applicable to most protestant schools, because the protestant schools, being staffed almost entirely with salaried lay teachers, could not afford to abolish school fees for a grant of only £25 per child. Ultimately the government made a special bloc grant to the protestant secondary schools, but this was insufficient to allow the schools to abolish fees. Thus, through the years typical southern protestant parents, like their northern catholic counterparts, paid a higher portion of their children's educational costs than did their fellow citizens of the majority religion.

[44] Akenson, *A mirror to Kathleen's face*, p. 117.

Were these policies intolerant? Yes again, unhappily. In each case the minority was tolerated as a religious minority, its religious practices and scruples respected in educational matters, but it was not accorded full toleration as a cultural minority. And in each case the Irish language in the primary schools was the nub of the issue. In the north the Irish language was virtually extinct as a primary language long before partition. Even in the historic province of Ulster, which contained several Irish-speaking areas excluded from the hegemony of the government of Northern Ireland, as early as 1851 only 6.8 per cent of the inhabitants could speak Irish. Hence, there were legitimate educational doubts about the value of introducing into the schools a language whose connections with the actual cultural contours of Northern Ireland were minimal. But the Irish-language question was not argued solely, or even chiefly, on educational grounds. It was an emotional issue because, despite the role played by individual protestants, including Douglas Hyde, W. B. Yeats, and Lady Gregory, in championing Irish, during the late nineteenth century gaelicism, catholicism, and Irish nationalism had become interwoven. Thus, unionists had a difficult time recognising the possibility that for some students the Irish language might be at least as useful a cultural acquisition as French or Latin. On the other side, many nationalists held an almost mystic belief in the virtues of the Irish tongue. The comments of the archbishop of Armagh, Dr MacRory, in 1929, illustrate this viewpoint:

It is the language that is adapted to us. It must be so. If there is anything in heredity it must be so. It was the system for two thousand of years, and our forefathers—and you know the brains of our forefathers—gradually modified the form of our Irish speech. It stands to reason—it is scientifically true that the Irish language must be better suited for ... us than any other language.[45]

Behind the prejudices of both sides were some basic cultural differences. The protestant population was descended chiefly from English and Scottish antecedents and had been English-speakers for centuries, whereas catholics were more likely to have been bilingual or Irish-monoglots at least till the late eighteenth century. Moreover, there is reliable evidence that even in English-speaking areas, as late as the mid-twentieth century, there persisted other relevant cultural differences between the catholic and protestant groups. Catholics attached much more importance to 'Irishness', were more impervious to outside cultural influences, and were more apt to cherish old customs and manners than were the protestants.[46] Given such cultural dissimilarity, the Irish language would have become a subject of contention even if it had possessed no political connotations.

[45] *Irish News*, 5 Feb. 1929.
[46] Rosemary Harris, 'Social relations and attitudes in a N. Irish rural area—Ballygawley' (M.A. thesis, University of London, 1954), pp 157–73.

Under the former commissioners of national education in the late Victorian period Irish had been permitted as an optional subject in all standards in primary schools throughout Ireland; a bilingual programme was approved in 1904 for districts in which Irish was the primary language; and organisers of Irish-language instruction were employed.[47] When the Northern Ireland government took over control of primary education in the north, the bilingual programme was dropped. Although the post of organiser of the Irish language remained on the books of the northern ministry of education for the year 1922–3, thereafter it was abolished, the parliamentary secretary reporting to members of parliament that 'I can assure them that there is no such thing as an organiser of Irish language'.[48] Until 1926 the language could be taught in the third standard and upwards as an additional subject, which earned the teacher special fees from the ministry of education, but in that year this opportunity was limited to the fifth and sixth standards.[49] The ministry's reasoning was that because Irish had to be taught by the same instructional methods as a foreign language it should be placed on the same plane as any other foreign language, these subjects being allowed only in the advanced standards. The new rules momentarily reduced the number of elementary schools teaching Irish as an extra subject from 140 in 1926–7 to 66 in 1928–9, but the number had recovered to 119 by 1932–3.[50] Irish could, of course, also be taught after regular school hours, without earning any grant.

During the depression years the Irish-language grants came under further scrutiny. They had always been vulnerable to attack in the unionist-dominated parliament: one unionist member went so far as to assert that 'the only people interested in this language are the people who are the avowed enemies of Northern Ireland'.[51] The extra fees paid for Irish by the ministry were averaging about £1,500 annually.[52] Hence, when the budget was introduced in April 1933 one economy that was effected was the abolition of the Irish-language grant. The parliamentary secretary J. H. Robb explained that the budget cut was justifiable, first because only a small minority of schools under catholic management took advantage of the grants, and secondly because in any case the improvements in facilities for secondary education meant that the teaching of language 'apart from the mother tongue' was being transferred from the elementary schools into the secondary schools.[53] Under the new regulation Irish still could be taught as an optional subject, usually (but not always) limited to standard III and above, and many elementary schools persevered. On 31 December 1940 Irish was being taught in 128 public elementary schools to 11,570

[47] Above, vi, 405–6, 535–6.   [48] *Hansard N.I. (commons)*, iii, 664 (2 May 1923).
[49] Ibid., vii, 1246, 1255 (13 May 1926).   [50] Ibid., xv, 919 (16 Mar. 1933).
[51] Ibid., xv, 773 (9 Mar. 1933).   [52] Ibid., xv, 919 (16 Mar. 1933).
[53] Ibid., xv, 1077 (25 April 1933).

children,[54] meaning, in effect, that slightly more than one out of every seven catholic elementary schoolchildren was learning the Irish language. Certainly the northern government's attitude toward the catholic minority's attraction to the Irish language was intolerant if not downright obstructionist.

John Hanna Robb was accurate in stating that the secondary schools were taking up the slack language programme. The ministry of education report for 1931–2 said simply that Irish was taught in all secondary schools under catholic management. The position of Irish in the secondary curriculum was the same as that of any language other than English; that is, at the discretion of the school managers, Irish could be taught as part of the ordinary school curriculum and it was one of the subjects recognised in the secondary school certificate examinations. Twenty-nine preparatory and secondary schools were teaching Irish as of 31 December 1940, and although no precise figures were available on the number of students studying the language, the parliamentary secretary of the ministry of education estimated that a large majority of the 4,259 students enrolled in these schools were learning Irish. The inclusion of Irish as part of the normal foreign language alternative in the secondary schools awakened no significant opposition from the unionist benches and seems to have satisfied the nationalist members.

Under the Londonderry act of 1923 Irish, among other languages, was permitted in the curriculum of the technical schools, but it was never an important part of the technical schools' work. Apparently there was very little demand for the teaching of Irish in technical schools, and even when it was demanded some technical education committees, notably in Fermanagh and Tyrone, resisted the demand. Thus, in 1945 only seventy of the 980 pupils examined by the technical examinations committee presented Irish as one of their subjects.

But equally, the southern government in its vigorous affirmation of the Irish language trod roughshod over the cultural values of its protestant minority. Protestantism in the south, no less than catholicism in the north, was not merely a religious system but a constellation of cultural characteristics. Just as catholicism in the north was tied to an affirmation of 'Irishness' and the Irish language, protestantism in the south was tied to the English language and to an affirmation of the culture associated with English literature and social thought. Despite the highly publicised enthusiasm of a few protestant language-revivalists, an enthusiasm that has persisted to the present day, Irish had never been the language of a significant proportion of protestants, and most protestants viewed the compulsory revival of the language via the primary schools as incompatible with their own cultural traditions. Inevitably the compulsory Irish programme downgraded the English-language culture, which was central to the protestant identity. During the 1920s

---

[54] Ibid., xxv, 619 (12 Mar. 1942).

leading protestants argued against heavy compulsion on two related grounds. Firstly, they argued that the formularies of the protestant religion, the Bible and the prayer book, were in English, and because of the close ties of protestants and the English language any attack on the language was an attack on their church. (This was, of course, to overlook long-standing versions of both Bible and prayer book in Irish.) Secondly, and more important, many protestant leaders believed in the supremacy of English-language culture, especially its literature, and valued English as an international language. For many the language was their cultural lifeline to the outside world.[55]

Protestant schoolteachers fought the compulsory Irish programme by word rather than deed, for they believed their position in Irish society to be too tenuous to allow vigorous opposition to the government. The government for its part modified individual regulations to make it easier for protestants to satisfy them, and attempted to find texts that would be acceptable: it was pointed out that many Irish-language texts contained catholic overtones, as reflected (for example) in the invocation of saints in customary greetings. Even so, as late as 1951, a subcommittee of the anglican board of education found that no set of readers on the department of education's list, either in Irish or in English, was wholly acceptable.[56]

Although most protestant parents followed their children's headmasters and reluctantly accepted the new regimen, many preferred to have their children educated in private schools or sent them to Britain or Northern Ireland for schooling. In 1934 Thomas Derrig, minister for education, tried to prosecute parents who sent their children to a private school in County Wexford, on the grounds that since no Irish was taught in the school they were delinquent under the terms of the 1926 compulsory attendance act. The 1926 act did not prescribe Irish in every school but did give the minister power to issue or refuse a certificate of suitability. Derrig won the case in the court of first instance but then lost it on appeal. Not a man to give up, in 1942 Derrig brought forward a school-attendance bill which in practice would have prohibited protestants from sending their children outside the state to be educated, since it would have required that each child on returning home had to pass a state-determined test, which certainly would have included an examination in the Irish language. This remarkable assault on minority civil rights passed through the legislature but was referred to the supreme court by Douglas Hyde, president of Ireland, himself a protestant Irish-speaker.[57] The court ruled that it was repugnant to the constitution and the matter dropped. But in the south as in the north, the position remained clear: the educational system was one in which religious denominationalism was affirmed, but cultural pluralism abridged.

---

[55] Akenson, *A mirror to Kathleen's face*, p. 119. [56] Ibid., p. 123.
[57] Ibid., pp 128–30.

WHILE ominous reminders of a deep communal cleavage persisted, the early 1960s had heralded an expectation of improving community relations throughout Northern Ireland. Under the premiership of Terence O'Neill, tentative steps were being taken to bridge the divide that had long separated the protestant-unionist and catholic-nationalist communities. Within this spirit of growing reconciliation the 1968 education act[58] was a notable measure, which addressed in a manner generally regarded as satisfactory the long-standing grievances of the catholic church on the matter of public funding for its schools. Specifically, voluntary primary and intermediate schools that accepted a management board, two-thirds of whose members were to be nominated by the former private managers (essentially the old four-and-two concept, now called 'maintained status'), would receive 80 per cent capital construction grants and 100 per cent grants for maintenance and equipment. Any new voluntary schools, whatever their academic level, were to be recognised for grant purposes only under the new terms, but existing voluntary schools had the option of continuing under the old scheme or coming under the new. After initial hesitation, this new plan commended itself to many catholic clerical managers of voluntary primary and intermediate schools (by this time, the overwhelming majority of protestant voluntary primary and intermediate schools had already been transferred to civic control). The legislation thus marked the beginning of a more positive relationship between the catholic church and the department of education, which would culminate two decades later in the establishment of the publicly funded council for catholic maintained schools.

The year 1968, however, also witnessed growing public agitation arising out of the civil rights campaign, which was focusing on allegations of discrimination against the catholic-nationalist population and, consequently, was heightening political tension. Street demonstrations and the ensuing violence soon dissipated the spirit of reconciliation and hope, and eventually precipitated the 'troubles', which characterised life in Northern Ireland over the following decades. The most significant result of the early phase of this period was the British cabinet's decision in 1972 to abolish Northern Ireland's devolved system of government, and the assumption of direct control over the administration of all government departments. While the British government's key political objective was to seek agreement between local political parties on a system of shared responsibility for government, this was not achieved except for a very short period of five months from January to May in 1974. Within the system of British 'direct rule', education, along with all other departments of the administration, was placed in the charge of a minister appointed by the government in London. From 1972 to 1979 the ministers were members of the Labour party, while during the

[58] 1968, c. 2 (26 Mar. 1968).

remainder of the period under review they were drawn from the Conservative party.

Against the background of escalating violence and civil unrest, the 1960s closed with several major issues emerging to occupy the attention of education's policy-makers and administrators. Some of these paralleled developments already taking place in England, on whose system Northern Ireland's was closely modelled; others derived from local conditions. They included the raising of the school-leaving age from 15 to 16; the reorganisation of local administrative structures; the new comprehensive model for second-level schooling; the issues surrounding transfer from primary to second-level education; curriculum reform; and the role of education in a deeply divided society. To these issues would be added, later in the 1970s and 1980s, an attempted reorganisation of teacher education, reform of public examinations, and eventually, in the 1989 education reform order, a wholesale restructuring of the legislative framework within which education was provided.

FOLLOWING the adoption of a government report on the structure, role, and responsibilities of local councils, the Macrory report,[59] Northern Ireland's six county and two borough education authorities were abolished, to be replaced in 1973 by five area boards, designated 'education and library boards'. To these regional authorities was committed all responsibility for public-sector schools, those now termed 'controlled' schools. To this was added responsibility for supporting 'maintained' schools: those (mainly catholic) schools whose management structures now included public representation from the area boards. Responsibility for the provision of further education, youth, and library services was also committed to these authorities.

The composition of the area boards reflected a desire to address one of the main political charges that had overshadowed the old local authorities: that whether under unionist or nationalist control they had been biased towards the needs of their respective communities. With only 40 per cent of the membership of the new area boards coming from the district councils in the areas served, and 60 per cent nominated by the minister for education, the scope for such bias was likely to be more constrained than in the past. Since the establishment of the boards also coincided with the assumption of direct rule by the British government, nominations to the 60 per cent (which had to include church and teacher as well as lay interests) were likely to have resulted in even more disinterested control than would have been the case had the administration remained in the hands of Northern Ireland politicians. Over the next two decades the boards would gradually develop support structures for curriculum development, for in-service training, for

[59] *Report of the review body on local government in Northern Ireland, 1970* [Cmd 546] (Belfast, 1970).

school-building and maintenance programmes, as well as for a range of other more minor activities. In the course of these developments the boards gained a wide degree of respect and support from across the entire education service.

At primary level the major influence of the early part of this period was the Plowden report, *Children and their primary schools* (1967).[60] Among the report's key emphases were a holistic approach to the curriculum and the absence of a prescriptive programme. The Northern Ireland version of this approach was evident in the new programme for primary schools published in 1974, which explictly eschewed setting out what should be taught and how teachers should organise their work. The emphasis was on the teacher, in partnership with colleagues, taking professional responsibility for his or her work. Within that approach considerable encouragement was to be given to experimentation and 'the pooling of knowledge and experience'.[61]

Although this emphasis remained official policy throughout the remainder of the decade, it was gradually to be replaced by a more guided and, eventually, a quite prescriptive approach. The Northern Ireland Council for Educational Development, established in 1980, published a series of more precise guidelines than those of 1974. Produced in response to requests from teachers themselves and as a result of inspectors' observations, and still within the non-prescriptive remit of the 1974 approach, these guidelines heralded the beginning of a return to centralised control of the curriculum. They strongly advocated a more explicitly planned and documented approach to the curriculum within each school, together with examples of 'good practice'.

Second-level education underwent a further period of rapid expansion during the 1970s, owing both to the continuing rise in enrolments from the primary sector and the raising of the school-leaving age to 16 in 1972. The latter affected the secondary intermediate sector most particularly, since it added one cohort to schools that previously had had only four age-groups. The grammar-school sector, which continued to cater for 11–18 year olds, was not so directly affected. The most dramatic development at this level was the attempt to introduce comprehensive-type schooling along English and Welsh lines.

The 1964 white paper on education had left unresolved the issues of selection for second-level education and whether or not a comprehensive system, also at second level, should be adopted. In 1969 a working party (the Burges committee) was established to address both questions. In its report the working party recommended that selection at 11 be abolished and that

[60] *Children and their primary schools: a report of the central advisory council for education* (London, 1967) (Plowden report).
[61] Department of education (N.I.), *Primary education teachers' guide* (Belfast, 1974), p. 1.

preparations be made for a non-selective intake into second-level schools.[62] It was not till July 1976 that proposals for a reorganised secondary system appeared in a consultative document from the department of education.[63] These proposals detailed local arrangements whereby existing schools could be linked to ensure integration and continuity across the pre- and post-16 phases of full-time education. Public debate was intense, with considerable pressure being mounted by grammar-school interests to oppose any change in the existing structures or forms of secondary education. Following widespread consultation, the department of education decided against imposing a comprehensive system, opting instead to allow the education boards to propose plans for any comprehensive schools they might wish to establish in their areas. In the event no such plans appeared, and apart from a small number of initiatives and experiments, no general programme of comprehensive education was introduced in Northern Ireland.

At curricular level the most notable development was the adoption of the certificate of secondary education (C.S.E.) as the main terminal qualification for intermediate schools. Syllabuses for C.S.E. examinations had been developed in England and Wales on very flexible bases in order to take account of the wide range of pupil abilities in intermediate schools (secondary moderns in England and Wales). These syllabuses offered a variety of modes for assessing pupils, including project and course work, alongside traditional examinations. Teachers were deeply involved in syllabus planning and in the assessment of course and project work. The contrast with the end-of-session examinations held for the general certificate of education (G.C.E.) (ordinary level), the main examination taken in grammar schools, was stark. As in England and Wales, the adoption of the C.S.E. in Northern Ireland had a profound effect on the thinking that led to the replacement of both C.S.E. and G.C.E. (ordinary level) with the general certificate of secondary education (G.C.S.E.) in 1987. The G.C.S.E. contained features of the approaches to assessment used in the two examinations it replaced. Both kinds of secondary schools were now preparing their pupils for the same terminal examination, and in so doing were to a greater extent than before providing a broadly similar pattern of second-level education. This similarity would become even more marked with the introduction of a common curriculum after the implementation of the 1989 reforms.

SERIOUS and sustained debate among educationists as to the role of education in addressing social and political divisions did not develop until the political and security crises of the early 1970s forced a critical reexamination

---

[62] *Reorganisation of secondary education in Northern Ireland: a report of the advisory council for education in Northern Ireland* [Cmd 574] (Belfast, 1973) (Burges committee).

[63] Department of education (N.I.), *Reorganisation of secondary education in Northern Ireland: a consultative document* (Belfast, H.M.S.O., 1976).

of many fundamental assumptions about the nature of society in Northern Ireland. The educational dimension to the ensuing debate attempted to determine the responses that schools and education generally should and could make to assist in overcoming those divisions.

For some, the most appropriate response lay in an integrated system of education in which protestant and catholic pupils would be educated together, a solution that echoed the official view of those who had established the national school system in 1831, and had motivated Lord Londonderry's ill-fated education act of 1923. The Burges committee considered the matter, but while endorsing the goal of an integrated system decided that it could only come about in a voluntary way and not as a result of official determination. The only change in official attitudes towards integrated education at this time was signalled in an initiative taken during the period of the short-lived 'power-sharing' executive in 1974. The minister for education in that executive, Basil McIvor, issued a consultative document on the possibility of creating interdenominational boards of management for existing schools.[64] With the downfall of the executive the initiative died, but even if the executive had survived it is doubtful how much progress would have been made. Cardinal William Conway, archbishop of Armagh, on behalf of the catholic authorities rejected the idea out of hand, though it received a positive reception from other quarters, with teachers' unions and the main political parties, unionist and nationalist, welcoming it. In a considered comment the Catholic Advisory Council on Education argued that the catholic church regarded education as an essentially religious matter; hence the necessity for catholic schools.[65] The council added that even if its schools contributed in any way to communal strife, means should be sought to deal with the problem other than by bringing pressure to bear on catholic schools to amalgamate with others.

The achievement of integrated education was, therefore, left to the efforts of voluntary groups, several of which had emerged at this time to campaign for the establishment of such schools.[66] Initially, progress was slow, but by the early 1980s the first successes had been achieved with the opening of several integrated primary and secondary schools. Thereafter progress was quite rapid, and by 1990 almost 4,000 pupils were enrolled in integrated schools across Northern Ireland, and a council for integrated education had been established to oversee the establishment and development of this new sector.

---

[64] *Shared management of schools: a discussion document* (Belfast, 1974).
[65] Catholic Advisory Council on Education, *Catholic education* (Belfast, 1974).
[66] Elizabeth Benton, 'Integrated education' in *Scope: a review of voluntary and community work in Northern Ireland*, xxix (1979), pp 12–14; Seamus Dunn, *Integrated schools in Northern Ireland: a report for the standing advisory commission on human rights* (Belfast, 1986).

Notwithstanding the progress made by the proponents of integrated education, it was obvious that large-scale integration could not be realised in the short term. Consequently, it was argued that a range of initiatives directed at improving cross-community relationships was necessary. Irrespective of the integrated education issue, it was becoming accepted that curricular and other initiatives were required to address the ignorance and misconceptions held by the communities in Northern Ireland about each other. The Burges committee had recommended such an approach, arguing that 'every encouragement be given to teaching within schools which can lead to better understanding of other religious beliefs and that there be an increase in the arrangements already in existence by which schools of different denominational character . . . collaborate in extra-curricular activities'.[67]

Although they were not the only initiatives at this time, two projects in the field of cultural studies highlighted the response to this debate and gave a lead to those seeking a role for schools in addressing the deteriorating community and political relations in Northern Ireland. Indeed, it is to both projects that many of the ideas that were to inform official decisions about the common curriculum, adopted in 1989, can be traced. The first was the *Schools curriculum project*,[68] directed by John Malone at Queen's University; the second the *Schools cultural studies project*,[69] directed by Malcolm Skilbeck at the New University of Ulster. While the aim of the *Schools curriculum project* focused on strengthening the moral purposes of education, its relevance to the inclusion of different local cultural traditions within the curriculum lay in the considerable emphasis it placed on using 'children's own personal and community knowledge and experience as the basis for moral and social education'.[70] In practice, this led to the study of local communities and local developments within Northern Ireland. What was new in the project was the use of local studies as a means of promoting pupils' understanding of and tolerance for lifestyles different from their own. The project also encouraged teachers to develop and use materials on topics 'as diverse as the linen industry in Dunmurry, the Clogher Valley Railway in Tyrone, and the redevelopment of the Lower Falls in Belfast, using as far as was possible original and varied sources, including official documents, ordnance survey memoirs, correspondence, railway timetables, street directories, photographs, slides, films, tapes, interviews, questionnaires and posters'.[71] The scope of the project's work was not confined to Northern Ireland. Borrowing ideas

---

[67] *Reorganisation of secondary education in Northern Ireland*, p. 21.

[68] Robert Crone and John Malone, *Continuities in education: the Northern Ireland schools' curriculum project, 1973–1978* (Windsor, 1979).

[69] Alan Robinson, *The schools' cultural studies project: a contribution to peace* (Coleraine, 1981).

[70] John Malone and Robert Crone, 'New approaches to innovation in schools' in *The Northern Teacher*, xii, no. 1 (1975–6), pp 16–20.

[71] Ibid.

that Bruner[72] had developed in his *Man: a course of study* project, Malone included the study of lifestyles remote in time and place from those of most of the pupils. His actual choice was life on 'different types of islands—offshore, tropical, colonial, mythological', with the aim of affording pupils 'the opportunity of becoming acquainted with people who look at and interpret the world in very different ways from themselves'.[73]

The *Schools cultural studies project* was very ambitious in terms of its aims, its nature, and its scope. The point has been made that 'the project was an educationist's response to the conflict in Northern Ireland and was concerned with increasing levels of tolerance, personal awareness, and mutual understanding among young people in both controlled (mainly protestant) schools and maintained (catholic) secondary intermediate schools (11–16 years), and, to a lesser extent, in primary schools (particularly 8–11 years)'.[74] Like Malone's project, the *Cultural studies project* was ultimately concerned with values education. It chose as the means towards that end the development of a *Cultural and social studies programme* for use in secondary schools, and of an *Education trails project* for use in primary schools. Central to the philosophy of the project was Skilbeck's explicitly reconstructionist view of education. In a key article outlining his views on education in Northern Ireland, he used the term 'democratic-reconstructionism' 'to identify and establish a role, a task, or a purpose for the school, in relation to the culture of which it is a part'. Arguing the need for a 'reconstructionist' as opposed to a 'transmission' role for education in Northern Ireland, Skilbeck described culture in Northern Ireland as 'militant . . . highly ideological in character, expansionist, aggressive and sectarian'.[75] He argued that to escape from its intercommunal conflicts Northern Ireland required a more open and more tolerant society. The programme of cultural studies developed by this project was intended to promote these objectives by inviting teachers and pupils to acquire an understanding not simply of their own and other cultures, but of the whole process of cultural evolution, of cultural identity, and of the way in which people from different traditions perceive and relate to each other.

The pioneering work of Skilbeck and Malone eventually gained official recognition when the themes of 'education for mutual understanding' and 'cultural heritage' became required features of the new Northern Ireland curriculum. Under the terms of the 1989 education order a requirement to include a set of cross-curricular 'educational themes' was made, two of which were cultural heritage and education for mutual understanding. The inclusion of cultural heritage was to enable pupils to know about, understand, and

[72] Jerome Bruner, *Toward a theory of instruction* (Cambridge, Mass., 1966).
[73] Malone & Crone, 'New approaches to innovation in schools'.
[74] Robinson, *The schools' cultural studies project*, p. 11.
[75] Malcolm Skilbeck, 'Education and cultural change' in *Compass: journal of the Irish Association for Curriculum Development*, v, no. 2 (1976), pp 3–23.

evaluate 'the common experiences of their cultural heritage; the diverse and distinctive aspects of their culture; the interdependence of cultures'.[76] The scope of the theme was to be universal in the sense that it envisaged the exploration of cultures from the most local to the most distant in order that pupils should appreciate their diversity, distinctiveness, and interdependence. 'Education for mutual understanding' was intended to be 'about fostering self-respect, respect for others, and the improvement of relationships between people of differing cultural traditions'.[77] The theme's objectives include that of developing 'knowledge and understanding of conflict in a variety of contexts and of approaches to its resolution by non-violent means'. Together, the two themes have provided a clear imperative for curriculum planners to strive to ensure that never again will pupils in either of Northern Ireland's two main communities fail to address each other's origins and beliefs, or their relationships to one another.

The same openness to change began to characterise official treatment of the Irish language during the period under review. As noted above, since the early decades of the twentieth century when the language-revival movement became ideologically part of the movement for political independence, Irish had been almost exclusively a nationalist preserve. Offered only in catholic-run schools, and officially ignored or treated with disdain, Irish survived in Northern Ireland essentially because of the voluntary efforts of enthusiasts.[78] Among those enthusiasts was a group of parents who in the early 1970s took a decision that had profound effects on the status and development of Irish within the education system. They decided to establish their own school, Bunscoil Phobal Feirste ('Belfast primary school'), to provide Irish-medium education at primary level. Official recognition was slow to be achieved. At first a degree of cold hostility greeted the development and for many years the school was entirely dependent on voluntary donations. Then in 1984 official recognition conferred grant-maintained status on the Bunscoil and Irish-medium education became an accepted part of the educational service of Northern Ireland. Thereafter progress was quite rapid, and by the early 1990s fourteen such schools (all but two at primary level) were in operation. In addition, there were nineteen Irish-medium pre-school groups operating with the aim of preparing children for Irish-medium primary schools.[79]

Indeed, Irish was slowly emerging from its exclusive association with the catholic-nationalist community and acquiring a degree of common ownership

[76] Department of education (N.I.), *The Northern Ireland curriculum, educational (cross-curricular) themes* (Belfast, 1992), p. 8.
[77] Ibid., p. 5.
[78] L. S. Andrews, 'The Irish language in the educational system of Northern Ireland: some political and cultural perspectives' in R. M. O. Pritchard (ed.), *Motivating the majority: modern languages in Northern Ireland* (London, 1991).
[79] Sean Farren, 'Language policy in a divided community' in Tina Hickey and Jenny Williams (ed.), *Language, education and society in a changing world* (Dublin, 1996), pp 54–62.

across the communal divide in Northern Ireland, thus, as one commentator put it, advancing the language 'beyond the immediate tribal stereotypes'.[80] When the new programmes of study were being drafted for first- and second-level education under the terms of the 1989 order, a special working party on Irish-medium education was established, a further sign of the recognition that Irish was receiving.

The 1989 education reform order[81] was Northern Ireland's version of the legislation adopted in England and Wales in 1988.[82] A major measure, the order introduced, among other innovations, statutory requirements for the primary and secondary curricula, formal assessment at each of four stages between ages 5 and 16, significant changes in the role and responsibilities of school boards, increased parental involvement in those boards, and measures to ensure greater accountability by schools for the education they provided. Apart from the initiatives discussed above, much of the rationale for the measure arose out of debates affecting education in England and Wales rather than in Northern Ireland. The most notable feature of its passage through parliament was the extent to which almost all Northern Ireland's M.P.s, unionists and nationalists, cooperated (unsuccessfully) in opposition to some of its provisions. That in itself was a novelty, given the political controversies that had surrounded educational legislation in earlier years.

THE changes in education in the Irish Republic in the 1960s, referred to above,[83] such as state grants for secondary schools, the introduction of comprehensive schools, and 'free' secondary education, were reflective of new economic, political, and social forces that were to steer the education system in new directions for the following decades. Educational policy and provision received a higher priority and acquired a new momentum, and this was to alter greatly the profile of Irish education from its condition during the first four decades of independence.

The *Programme for economic expansion* of 1958 and the economic programmes that flowed from it in 1959 and 1963 signalled a more dynamic approach to economic development. They promoted the process whereby industry, manufacturing, and the services sector ousted agriculture as the major source of employment. A more liberal free-trade approach, allied to a strong campaign to attract foreign capital investment, fuelled an economic recovery, with growth rates of about 4 per cent per annum in the early 1960s. The government's new drive for economic development assigned a significant part to education. The *Second programme for economic expansion* of 1963–4 significantly now viewed education as an economic investment rather

---

[80] James Hawthorne, 'What is a cultural tradition?' in *Fortnight* (supplement) (Nov. 1989).
[81] Education Reform (Northern Ireland) Order, 1989, S.I. 1989/2406 (N.I. 20).
[82] Education Reform Act, 1988, c. 40 (29 July 1988).   [83] Above, pp 732–3.

than as merely a consumer service, stating that 'even the economic returns from investment in education and training are likely to be as high in the long run as those from investment in physical capital'.[84] Investment in 'human capital' and drawing on the 'pool of talent' became the educational-economic slogans of the day. Economic development and education were now seen to be reciprocally linked. The prosperity of a modern technological and industrially oriented society depended on the availability of an educated workforce. Increased economic growth and production, in turn, allowed for greater financial resources to be made available to education. Thus, a benign circle was seen to operate in the relationship between the economy and education. Public expenditure on education as a percentage of G.D.P. grew from 3 per cent in 1960–61 to 6 per cent in 1974, and to 6.3 per cent in 1984. Educational expenditure, as a percentage of total public expenditure, expanded from 10 per cent in 1960 to 16 per cent in 1971. In the following decade this percentage fluctuated, but by 1984 it had again reached 16 per cent, from which point it continued to expand, reaching 20 per cent by 1992.[85]

As well as sharing in the international economic buoyancy and its economic orthodoxy of investment in human capital in the 1960s, the Republic also became much more open to other international influences and organisations. Ireland was a founder member of the O.E.C.D. and the Council of Europe and was admitted to the United Nations in 1955. Hopes were high of joining the E.E.C. in the early 1960s. Irish representatives began to take more active roles in international bodies, participating in various international conferences and symposia. A notable instance was participation in an O.E.C.D. conference in Washington in 1961 on economic growth and investment in education.

Another major international institution was undergoing changes in the early 1960s which would have a significant impact on life in Ireland. This was the catholic church, which, through the second Vatican council, was mapping out new directions for itself in the modern world. Because of the traditional strong allegiance in the Republic to the catholic church and the important role played by the church in Irish education, the repercussions of some of the new attitudes defined by Vatican II would gradually influence the control and management of schooling in Ireland and also affect personnel and curricular issues.

In many countries in post-war Europe the slogan 'equality of educational opportunity' gained general currency. This also began to permeate educational and social attitudes in Ireland in the 1960s, and raised a challenge to the traditional elitism of the system. In the context of the changing times,

---

[84] *Second programme for economic expansion*, pt. II (Pr 7676) (Dublin, 1964), i, para. 14.
[85] John Coolahan, *Irish education: its history and structure* (Dublin, 1981), p. 138; *Education for a changing world* (Pn 2009) (Dublin, 1995), statistical appendix.

parents became more alert to the links between educational certification and worthwhile employment opportunities. The introduction of a national television station in 1961, as well as the increasing interest taken by newspapers in educational issues, helped to inform public opinion on educational debate. Ireland also experienced a breakdown of an older paternalist ethos in educational debate, with parents, teachers, students, and the general public now utilising the more tolerant and pluralist climate of debate. In a scholarly environment the expansion of research and teaching in the universities of the behavioural sciences, such as psychology and sociology, helped to focus the attention of planners and educationists on problems involved in addressing educational inequality. Various teacher organisations and other discussion groups provided fora where debate, proposals, and criticism on educational issues took place.

As might be expected in the context of increasing public expenditure on education and a greater public concern about the subject, the interest by politicians in education gathered momentum. In earlier decades the ministry of education portfolio did not carry with it significant political status, and ministers were apt to view the role in a largely non-interventionist, non-directive way. In October 1959 a new taoiseach, Seán Lemass, signalled that education was going to assume a new importance in government policy, and announced an 'immediate policy to increase the facilities for post-primary education'.[86] A succession of young, dynamic, ambitious politicians were appointed to the education portfolio, and the image began to be used of the minister as 'captain of the ship, planning and pointing the way'.[87] A striking feature of a changed approach to educational policy was the unprecedented degree of analysis of and reportage on the educational system which was in place by the mid 1960s, including the *Investment in education* report of 1965.[88] This formed the backdrop for a reforming era in education.

AT primary level, almost half the schools dated from the nineteenth century and were poorly maintained. The great majority were very small: two-thirds were one- or two-teacher schools. The facts revealed by the *Investment in education* report underlined how out of alignment many schools were with modern educational, health, and comfort requirements. A major policy initiative was commenced in 1965 on the closure or amalgamation of small schools. Overall, the number of one- and two-teacher schools declined from 3,194 in 1962 to about 2,000 by 1973 and to 900 by 1984.[89] As might be expected, this

---

[86] *Dáil Éireann deb.*, clxxvii, 470–71 (28 Oct. 1959).

[87] Seán O'Connor, *A troubled sky: reflections on the Irish education scene, 1957–68* (Dublin, 1986).

[88] Above, p. 732.

[89] John Coolahan, 'Educational policy for national schools, 1960–85' in D. G. Mulcahy and D. O'Sullivan (ed.), *Irish educational policy* (Dublin, 1989), p. 42.

policy aroused controversy, particularly in the early years; many communities viewed their local school as symbolic of their continued well-being, and its closure as amounting to a vote of no confidence in their future. The department can be criticised for inadequate consultation and for a failure to discuss the advantages of new arrangements with parents. Nevertheless, painful decisions were made, and in the long run, parents could see how their children benefited. The department of education also adopted a more progressive policy when old schools were being replaced or new ones were built to suit changes in population trends. New standards of design, space, decor, and furnishings were approved, which reflected a more attractive image of the school as a living and working environment for teachers and pupils.

Linked to the rationalisation of school provision was a policy on improving pupil–teacher ratios, which traditionally had been very high in Irish schools. This proved a more difficult problem than originally expected, as it coincided with a steady increase in the primary-school-going population. Thus, while progress was made, it was not dramatic: the national average pupil–teacher ratio declined from 34.3 : 1 in 1961 to 32.8 by 1972, reaching 30.7 : 1 in 1977.[90] Official policy also moved against the employment of untrained teachers, who had formed a minority of the teaching force. The colleges of education were expanded and modernised, and produced a larger cadre of teachers of high academic quality. Moves afoot in the 1960s towards granting university degree status to primary-school teachers reached fruition in 1974 when the B.Ed. degree was established, with the colleges being linked to the universities for their awards. Official policy also favoured the rapid promotion of children through the primary school so that the ordinary transfer age to the post-primary sector was dropped to 12.

A very significant development was the decision in the mid 1960s to introduce a new curriculum for primary schools, which would replace that devised in the 1920s. The new curriculum was to involve a radical shift of ideological position and methodological approach. On the lines of the contemporary Plowden report in England, the curriculum adopted a child-centred ideology and urged that school work should be closely aligned to the cognitive and affective stages of young children's development. Individual and small-group learning were encouraged, with an emphasis on heuristic pedagogy. Following various pilot schemes and consultation with relevant interests, the new curriculum was implemented nationwide in 1971. Its wide range of subjects and its encouragement to the teachers to adapt it to suit local school and environmental circumstances represented a landmark in the history of Irish primary education. A more generous scheme of equipment grants was introduced for schools to assist in the implementation of the new curriculum.

[90] Ibid., p. 34.

The existing management system of primary schools had its roots deep in church–state conflicts in the nineteenth century. By the 1960s the almost universal form of management was that of a single manager of the school, who was an authority figure within one of the religious denominations. In the course of the 1960s this system came under new scrutiny and voices were raised against it in some political parties. The second Vatican council had encouraged the greater participation of parents in the life of schools, and gradually such thinking bore fruit in Ireland. In 1969 the catholic hierarchy declared itself in favour of closer cooperation between clergy, parents, and teachers in primary schooling. Eventually, in 1973 the government moved forward with specific proposals for new management boards for schools, and in 1975 the first change in the management of primary schools since the 1830s took place. While the boards of management still favoured clerical influence, parents and teachers were now also partners on the boards. Improved capitation grants for primary pupils were used as an incentive to promote the establishment of management boards. The overall result of the various changes initiated in the 1960s was to alter greatly the configuration and character of primary education in Ireland and place it on a path of worthwhile development, following many decades of public neglect.

In line with the gradual acceptance of a more central voice for parents in the schooling of their children in the early 1970s was the emergence of two interesting 'bottom-up' movements by parents. Some groups of parents campaigned for the establishment of multidenominational primary schools for their children. In the early years they faced opposition from churches and an obstructionist attitude by the state. However, their perseverance paid off and the right to multidenominational schools was accepted. A small number of such schools became established in urban areas. Interestingly also, as the state was seen to slacken its enthusiasm for Irish-medium schools, groups of parents pushed for the establishment of all-Irish primary and, subsequently, postprimary schools. They subsequently became an accepted part of the landscape of Irish schooling, and are coordinated by the Gaelscoileanna organisation.

An important area of educational provision that received only very limited state support before 1960 was the area of special education. The 1960s saw greater official interest in and support for education provision adapted to the needs of children who, because of mental, physical, sensory, or emotional disabilities, were unable or found it very difficult to participate in ordinary schooling. The approach taken was largely that of special schools, special classes, or special provision by travelling teachers. Improved teacher-training courses for special eduation were developed. Reports on various aspects of the provision of special education were published. In line with international trends, moves towards integrating such pupils into mainstream schooling were favoured, but the provision of the necessary resources and training was slower in coming. Significant progress on the education of children of the travelling people was also made in the 1970s, which provided a basis for more extensive work in later years.

THE government viewed reforms in post-primary education as a particular priority in the context of its economic and social policy. The *Investment in education* report highlighted poor levels of pupil participation, linked to socio-economic status and geographical location. As noted above, even before the publication of the report, the minister for education, in a major policy speech in May 1963, stated that the government would establish a new kind of school—comprehensive schools—which would be coeducational, open to all classes and levels of ability, offering a broad, balanced curriculum, and managed by committees representative of key educational interests. The first comprehensive schools were opened in 1966, and the concept was further developed by government in 1970 with the introduction of community schools, which added a broader community dimension to the role of the comprehensive school. The 1963 statement also indicated the intention of raising the status of the vocational schools, which had hitherto offered two-year courses of an applied character, so that they too could offer the intermediate certificate examination (age 15, 16), and the leaving certificate examination (age 17, 18), which had hitherto been the preserve of the academic secondary schools. This process continued through the 1960s, as did the general promotion of technical and scientific education. Thus, four types of school—secondary, vocational, comprehensive, and community—were now offering the full range of post-primary schooling.

A landmark development in fostering greater pupil participation was the introduction of free post-primary education in 1967, coupled with a free school-transport system. These measures caught the imagination of parents, and participation increased by over 50 per cent within six years, helped also by the raising of the compulsory age for schooling to 15 in 1972. The enrolled pupils in post-primary schools increased from 143,000 in 1965 to 340,000 in 1985. The retention rate for pupils staying on to complete post-primary education increased from 33 per cent to 70 per cent over the same period. This huge bulge in participation gave rise to a big school-building programme and the employment of many new teachers, all of which created a buzz of excitement in educational circles.

Although the structural changes stole the limelight, there were several important policy changes in school curricula. The comprehensive type of curriculum, with its balance of academic and practical subjects, was the favoured view of the government, and all schools were encouraged to adopt it, as far as possible. Science teaching was given a more experimental base, and extra grants were made available for science laboratories. Mathematics courses were changed into a 'new maths' mode. The teaching of modern languages was modernised with language laboratories, film strips, and tape recorders, giving a more communicative emphasis in place of grammar–translation methods. The promotion of modern languages received more emphasis after accession to the E.E.C. in 1973. Literature texts included the works of more living authors. From the mid 1960s onwards most other subjects were revised, and some new subjects introduced.

A research study on the leaving certificate examination was published in 1970 which highlighted some deficiencies; improvements were subsequently made. A ministerial committee published a report on the intermediate certificate in 1975. However, its radical proposals for change were not adopted. With some modifications, the format of the examinations as public examinations, externally marked and relying heavily on written terminal examination papers, continued. The initiation in 1969 of a 'points system' as a mode of selection for university entrance, based on student performance levels in the leaving certificate examination, was to develop and greatly influence teaching in the upper levels of the post-primary schools and introduce a very high level of competitiveness within schools.

The rapidly expanding and changing pupil clientele in post-primary schools highlighted the need for curricular reform. Through the 1970s and early 1980s a good deal of curriculum development work and experimentation took place, without affecting mainstream schooling.[91] In 1984 a non-departmental body, the Curriculum and Examinations Board (C.E.B.) was set up. It was the intention that this ad hoc agency would be given a statutory basis and made responsible for curricular and examination issues. This did not come to pass and, with a change of government in 1987, the C.E.B. was abolished and replaced by an advisory body, the National Council for Curriculum and Assessment (N.C.C.A.). The department of education established a psychological service for post-primary schools in 1965, and from 1968 schools could appoint guidance and counselling teachers. The average pupil–teacher ratio was reduced to 15 : 1. Pupils also benefited from a school television service, introduced in 1964. Thus, post-primary schooling, which had been the preserve of a minority till the early 1960s, had become available to all, its character had greatly altered, and the curriculum and ancillary services had been modernised and enriched by a more proactive government policy.

The different categories of teachers—primary, vocational, and secondary—traditionally enjoyed different salary scales, and operated within different schemes of conciliation and arbitration for salary purposes. In the 1960s government was keen to establish a common salary scale and a common scheme for conciliation and arbitration. The Ryan tribunal on teacher salaries reported in favour of such changes in 1968. The issues arising from this report were not well handled, and a period of great dissension, involving

[91] D. G. Mulcahy, *Curriculum and policy in Irish post-primary education* (Dublin, 1981).

teachers' strikes, followed. After protracted negotiations, in 1972 a common salary scale with allowances for qualifications and responsibilities was introduced.[92] Moves to an all-graduate teaching profession were undertaken in those years, resulting in degree arrangements for primary teachers, as well as for specialist post-primary teachers such as teachers of woodwork, metalwork, home economics, and art. These significant changes for the teaching profession came close to being carried further in 1974–5 with the proposed establishment of a regulatory teaching council, on the lines of the legal and medical professions. However, not all teachers agreed on such a move, and the initiative was dropped from the political agenda.

Teacher education underwent significant changes in line with the needs of a changing school system. As well as changes in pre-service education, a greater availability of in-service education opportunities appeared. In-service education was to become an established area of support for teachers. The opening of the first regional teacher centres in 1972 signalled a new emphasis in this field. Teacher unions grew in strength, in organisational efficiency, and in influence through the 1970s and 1980s. They employed this strength effectively in the early and mid 1980s when they successfully opposed government decisions on school entry age and on a salary arbitration award.

IN retrospect, it can be concluded that the two decades from the mid 1960s to the mid 1980s witnessed many worthwhile reforms in education. Besides the development of new kinds of post-primary schools, the massive increase in pupil participation, and the post-primary curriculum reforms, there was also the rationalisation of small primary schools, the new primary curriculum, an improved primary-school building programme, and the introduction of boards of management. It is noteworthy that there were no significant ideological disagreements about the measures adopted. The closest matters came to conflict concerned the policy of closing small schools, when local political interests were under pressure. In reality, there was a large degree of all-party agreement and considerable continuity between the policies of different governments.

The general approach taken by policy-makers was not to issue grand designs of overall reform by means of green or white papers, but rather to proceed by pragmatic gradualism. Maximum scope was retained by the public service for ad hoc planning and for altering direction easily without public controversy. It was the preferred mode of the department of education to move things forward on a gradual path, testing responses, slowing down or speeding up developments as circumstances permitted. It was also the case that while many individual reforms can be identified, they were devised

---

[92] For a detailed examination of development in post-primary education, see John Coolahan, *The A.S.T.I. and post-primary education in Ireland 1909–84* (Dublin, 1984), pp 273–308.

within the existing administrative and structural parameters. The highly centralised mode of administration adopted after independence was sustained, and little challenging of the position of key power-brokers in the system occurred.[93] With no fundamental administrative restructuring being undertaken, what resulted was that new responsibilities arising from the changing and expanding education system were accumulated by the central administration, which remained largely unaltered in its tradition, structure, and mode of administration. Two attempts at a form of regionalisation of education administration were made in 1974 and 1985, but these were strongly rebuffed by existing management interests.

The first Irish white paper on education, the *White paper on educational development*, was published in 1980,[94] but it disappointed greatly in its lack of clear policy directions for the way forward, and it had little impact. In 1984, the government published its *Programme for action in education, 1984–1987*.[95] This was a more targeted document, and betokened a more open approach to policy issues. However, it coincided with a period of great crisis in the national finances, and the time was not propitious for major initiatives that had serious financial implications. It was not till the 1990s that more comprehensive and radical green and white papers on education would be produced, which would propose a fundamental restructuring of the administration of Irish education and seek, for the first time, to put a satisfactory legislative framework in place for the education system.

[93] Séamas Ó Buachalla, *Education policy in twentieth century Ireland* (Dublin, 1988), pp 205–75.
[94] *White paper on educational development, laid by the government before each house of the oireachtas, December 1980* (Prl 9373) (Dublin, 1980).
[95] *Programme for action in education, 1984–1987* (Pl 2153) (Dublin, 1984).

CHAPTER XXV

Higher education in Ireland, 1908–84

JOHN COOLAHAN

THE history of Irish higher education in the twentieth century falls into a number of distinct periods, and this will be reflected in the structure of the present chapter. The first period corresponds to the years following the passing of the Irish universities act of 1908 down to the Anglo–Irish treaty of 1921. A second period dates from the treaty to the end of the second world war in 1945. The postwar years to 1959 mark another era. A fourth period, from about 1960 to the early 1980s, was a time of great expansion and development. During the first three periods the fortunes of the individual university institutions are followed within the general political and economic context. During the final era higher education became much more diversified, greater public attention was focused on the issues, and the developments are best dealt with in a general, trans-institutional way.

THE Irish universities act of 1908[1] was a most significant landmark in the history of university education in Ireland and a natural starting-point for study of twentieth-century higher education. It emerged as the latest legislative attempt to settle a highly contentious political and academic problem stretching back over seventy years. Despite its long gestation, aspects of the act were not initially expected to last. Yet it has proved to be a very durable settlement through subsequent decades of great political change. Shortly after his appointment as chief secretary in 1907 Augustine Birrell took a firm grip of the university issue, reflected on the recent reports of the Robertson and Fry commissions, examined other contemporary proposals, took soundings from key interested parties, and made up his mind on the solution that he considered most appropriate and that had the greatest chance of success. A key feature of his thinking was to leave the long-established University of Dublin with its single college, Trinity College, intact and undisturbed. On the other hand, he decided to abolish the other Irish university, the Royal

---

[1] 8 Edw. VII, c. 38 (1 Aug. 1908); above, vi, 566–70.

University. This had been a purely examining and degree-awarding body, and its passing was regretted by few. In its place two new universities were established. Queen's College, Belfast, was now raised to the status of 'The Queen's University of Belfast'. In Dublin, the National University of Ireland was established on a federal model with three constituent colleges; University College, Dublin (U.C.D.), University College, Cork (U.C.C.), and University College, Galway (U.C.G.). Trinity, Queen's, Belfast, and the N.U.I. represented diverse religious and political traditions within Irish society.

The terms of settlement and financial arrangements arrived at in the relative calm of 1908 were put under extraordinary strain by the unprecedented effects of a world war that transformed pre-war Edwardian society. The Irish independence movement produced political upheaval throughout the country. The general election of 1918 saw the overwhelming defeat of the Irish parliamentary party, which had been a key agency in the 1908 university settlement. All university institutions were buffeted and affected by these years of warfare and political change. It was particularly difficult for the university authorities to lay the foundations for the necessary regulations, staffing arrangements, academic courses, examination procedures, buildings, facilities, and equipment, so as to get the new institutions off to a good start.

Despite the difficulties and unpropitious circumstances, significant progress was made. The bases were laid that ensured the success of the three universities of Ireland. They were all non-denominational universities, though each had its own religious atmosphere. They were open to students of all denominations or none, and to both sexes. The student body grew from about 2,700 in 1909–10 to about 4,700 by 1920–21, an increase of 74 per cent. Each of the universities was preoccupied with its own concerns in those early years. Moreover, those in authority in the various institutions differed in their political and religious affiliations, and this worked against the development of close ties between the universities. Lack of cooperation became the norm within the changed political environment in Ireland that followed partition and the winning of Irish independence.

THE National University of Ireland was established under the universities act of 1908. It was incorporated by charter in December 1908, and on the dissolution of the royal university on 31 October 1909 it came into full operation. At the first meeting of the university senate on 17 December 1908 Archbishop William Walsh was unanimously elected chancellor. He had taken a keen interest in educational affairs, and was known to have nationalist sympathies. When he died in 1921 he was succeeded as chancellor by Eamon de Valera, the then president of Dáil Éireann, who continued in the post for fifty-four years till his death in 1975.[2]

---

[2] Donal McCartney, *The National University of Ireland and Eamon de Valera* (Dublin, 1983).

Under the terms of the universities act the income of the royal university from the church surplus fund at £20,000 a year was divided between Queen's University and the national university. Queen's was also to receive an annual grant of £18,000 as well as a building grant of £60,000. The new college in Dublin, U.C.D., was to receive an annual grant of £32,000, the Cork college £18,000, and Galway £12,000. The Cork and Galway colleges were based in the old queen's colleges buildings. The new University College, Dublin, took over the town houses used by the old catholic university and the premises in Earlsfort Terrace that had been used by the non-teaching Royal University. It was recognised, however, that these were quite inadequate for the new college, and a building grant of £110,000 was allocated to U.C.D.

The three constituent colleges of the new federal N.U.I. had different historical traditions and experiences, and at first the prospects for welding them into a federation seemed poor. U.C.G. was in a particularly weak position, with only about 100 students; it had been under the shadow of abolition. On the other hand, Sir Bertram Windle, the distinguished and forceful president of U.C.C., had ambitions to establish his college as the independent university of Munster. U.C.D. was the inheritor of diverse traditions, had no satisfactory college base, and faced the competition of the long-established and prestigious Trinity College, located in the same city at a distance of a quarter of a mile. As expected, St Patrick's College, Maynooth, wasted no time in applying to be accepted as a recognised (as distinct from a constituent) college of the N.U.I. This was accepted by the senate of the N.U.I. in February 1910, with recognition backdated to 1 November 1909.[3]

The senate of the N.U.I. exercised several key functions in relation to the constituent colleges. It was the appointing body for presidents, professors, and statutory lecturers, following recommendations to it from the governing bodies of the colleges. A board of studies was set up to evaluate courses of study proposed by the colleges. The senate also appointed external examiners to monitor examination standards. It was the senate that awarded the academic qualifications to successful students on the completion of their courses. A significant step was taken in June 1910 when the senate designated Irish as a compulsory subject for matriculation with effect from 1913. This was a controversial issue: the standing committee of the catholic bishops, while welcoming the prospect of the restoration of the Irish language had expressed fears in 1909 that making Irish compulsory for matriculation in the N.U.I. might induce some catholics to resort instead to Trinity College. Accordingly, the senate's decision was regarded as a signal victory for the cultural nationalists.[4]

---

[3] Minutes of senate of N.U.I., 23 Feb. 1910, p. 62.
[4] Minutes of senate of N.U.I., 23 June 1910, p. 119; see also above, vi, 407–8, 568.

The Dublin commissioners who had been charged with the framing of statutes for the new university had completed their work by July 1911. The power of making statutes was then transferred to the senate, subject to approval of the national legislature. Good working relationships were built up between the senate and the authorities within individual colleges. The great problem for the N.U.I. colleges did not relate to appointments or academic issues but to inadequate funding, which seriously impeded expansion and development. This problem became more acute in the case of U.C.D., which, assisted by its location in the capital city, grew most impressively in student numbers.

In its initial years U.C.D. operated in very inadequate premises; plans to build a new college for 1,000 students on the Earlsfort Terrace site were never fully implemented.[5] The U.C.D. authorities could be excused for casting envious eyes at the grandiose Royal College of Science nearby, which had been built by the government for fewer than 200 students and opened in 1911. The inadequate capital grant to U.C.D. was matched by inadequate current grants. However, despite the unsatisfactory environment for teaching and learning, student numbers expanded significantly in the early years, growing from 695 in 1910–11 to 1,317 by 1920–21.[6]

U.C.C. and U.C.G. were better off for university buildings and college campuses, but their student numbers were low. President Windle of U.C.C. was successful in gaining some endowments, notably from the Honan family. By the time of Windle's retirement in 1919, he had brought about many improvements in the college, notably in laboratory provision for physics, chemistry, engineering, and biology, as well as a large-scale revamping of the facilities for the medical school. He also improved administrative facilities as well as social and club amenities for students.[7]

U.C.G., with student numbers of under 100 in 1909, was in a particularly vulnerable position. The college found itself with little money for reequipment and development, and sent a special deputation to Lloyd George, then chancellor of the exchequer, who agreed to double any money raised locally. The case was put to the county councils for Connacht and County Clare, which agreed to raise and contribute funds. These funds, with the additions from the exchequer, went to establish new professorial chairs.[8]

TRINITY College had successfully withstood repeated attempts to change its constitution so that it might form the focus of a single federal university for

---

[5] U.C.D., *University College Dublin and its building plans* (Dublin, 1959), pp 10–11.

[6] James Meenan, '"The universities". I—University College Dublin' in *Stat. Soc. Ire. Jn.*, xvii (1942–7), pp 460–81: 463. '1910–11', '1920–21' denote academic years.

[7] Denis Gwynn, 'Sir Bertram Windle, 1858–1929—a centenary tribute' in *University Review—Jubilee issue, 1908–1958*, ii, nos 3–4, pp 48–58.

[8] Thomas Dillon, 'The origin and early history of the national university, part II' in *University Review*, i, no. 6 (1955), pp 12–28: 25.

the whole country. Its ancient traditions, splendid buildings, and city-centre location, its investments and endowments as well as its contacts at home and abroad, marked it out clearly as the most privileged university institution in the country. Yet it too was to face difficulties and challenges as the years unfolded, and its strategic decision to remain apart may have hindered the realisation of its full potential in the new Ireland that was emerging. Trinity was strongly unionist in politics and protestant in ethos. It opposed home rule and was hostile to the physical-force movement represented by the 1916 rebellion. However, any problems of adjustment lay in the future. In the years immediately before the first world war, a number of positive changes were under way. In 1909 Magee College in Derry, instead of linking up with the new Queen's University of Belfast, decided to negotiate an arrangement whereby its students spent the sophister years at Trinity and were permitted to enter for the B.A. degree there. In 1911 letters patent were issued which made many important reforms in the administration of the university. The board and council were reconstituted, changes were introduced in the selection of fellows, and the board was given a certain degree of autonomy. An ordinance of 1920 carried reforms further, removed many outdated restrictions, and laid down new regulations for the election of fellows that remained in force for many subsequent years.[9] Also in 1911 the college benefited from an endowment by Lord Iveagh of £24,450, which went to the building of laboratories for experimental physics and botany.

The first world war had a serious effect on life within Trinity College. As was the case with other colleges, the rise in prices and reduced money values caused difficulties, but it suffered in more grievous ways than other colleges. It identified closely with the war effort, and staff and students joined up in considerable numbers. Most strikingly, it experienced a huge drop in student numbers, which declined from 1,250 in 1914 to 700 in 1917–18. It has been calculated that the loss of income to the college amounted to nearly £50,000.[10] The resultant straitened circumstances prompted the college authorities to seek a state grant for the first time. In November 1920 the Geikie royal commission supported Trinity's request and recommended an immediate non-recurrent grant of £113,000 and an annual subsidy of £49,000.[11] However, the government of Ireland bill had been introduced into parliament before the Geikie report was published. Provost Bernard obtained a clause in the bill assuring an annual grant of £30,000 to the college, chargeable on the exchequer of Southern Ireland. Meanwhile, between 1919 and 1923 Trinity managed to secure a series of ad hoc grants from the British

[9] K. C. Bailey, *A history of Trinity College Dublin, 1892–1945* (Dublin, 1947), pp 26–31.

[10] Ibid., p. 38; R. B. McDowell and D. A. Webb, *Trinity College, Dublin, 1592–1952* (Cambridge, 1982), p. 420.

[11] *Royal commission on the University of Dublin* (Geikie commission) [Cmd 1078], H.C. 1920, xiii, 1189; [Cmd 1167], H.C. 1921, xi, 487.

government totalling £56,000. But the Anglo–Irish treaty of 1921 contained no clause relating to any government subvention for Trinity College, and Trinity was uneasy about its future prospects within the new state.

THE new Queen's University of Belfast was situated in a city that had grown remarkably in the previous sixty years, from a population of 100,000 in 1849 when the original queen's college opened, to 400,000 in 1909, when the new university got under way. About half the student body in 1909 came from Belfast. From an early stage efforts were made to attract catholic students to the university. Five catholics were appointed to the university senate. The immediate appointment of a catholic dean of residence, the establishment of a lectureship in scholastic philosophy, provision for 'Celtic' as a subject (this term was preferred to 'Irish'), and links between the Mater hospital and the medical school were factors that achieved this; for several years there were more catholics than Church of Ireland students in Queen's University. Queen's had close links with the presbyterian Royal Belfast Academical Institution, and many presbyterians found the ethos of Queen's very congenial. A tradition was therefore established early on for a good mixture of students from all denominations.

The senate of Queen's lost no time in getting to work to utilise the building grant of £60,000 that had been allocated to it. Work on new buildings began in the autumn of 1911, and Queen's was fortunate to have met its most urgent building requirements before the outbreak of war in 1914. Personnel of Queen's participated both directly and indirectly in the war effort. But in contrast with Trinity College, student numbers increased during the war years by over 50 per cent, from 584 in 1914 to 888 at the close of the war.[12] This reflected the huge population increase in the Belfast area and the lack of any rival university institution in the city. Expansion continued in the postwar years, with the faculties of medicine and science benefiting most.

Queen's now suffered, as was the case with the other university institutions, from lack of money and inadequate facilities. The university sought to establish close ties between town and gown. The commerce faculty established evening classes, and classes were also conducted in association with the municipal teaching institute. However, public support from the city was slow in coming, though some gifts and donations were made. Current grants were increased by £8,000 on a temporary basis in 1919, and capital grants from the government amounting to £18,000 in 1919–20 helped Queen's to purchase Stranmillis House and grounds in 1919, which, however, was later sold to the new Northern Ireland ministry of education for use as a teacher-

---

[12] T. W. Moody and J. C. Beckett, *Queen's, Belfast, 1845–1949: the history of a university* (2 vols, London, 1959), p. 458.

training college. In 1920 Queen's purchased Queen's Elms (for use later as student residences) and Cherryvale as an athletic ground.[13] New courses were set up in the postwar years, thanks to a new faculty of science and technology, a school of dentistry, and a faculty of agriculture.

Conscious of the political momentum towards home rule, Queen's was anxious to obtain guarantees for its future in any new legislation. This was secured in section 64 of the government of Ireland act of 1920. The college's parliamentary representation in both Westminster and the planned Northern Ireland parliament was guaranteed, and so was its academic independence. The annual grant of £26,000 was secured, as well as the annual grant of £10,000 from the church temporalities fund. At the time of the passing of the act Queen's had 1,000 enrolled students.[14]

AFTER the Anglo–Irish treaty, university affairs slipped from public attention. Lack of public interest went hand in hand with financial neglect by the state of university education. For most of the period from 1922 to 1945 the economic condition of the Irish Free State was not conducive to high government spending, while in Northern Ireland government spending was constrained by Britain. In any case, university education was regarded as a minority aspiration for those among the better-off who sought a safe future for their children through access to careers that required a university degree. For the vast majority of parents the university played no part in their thinking. They knew little about it, it seemed socially and culturally remote, and it was out of the question to take on the financial burdens of sending their children there. The universities in turn adopted a very low public profile. Their leaders very rarely saw fit to communicate with the general public, no significant campaign was launched to inform or help educate public opinion about the role of the university, and very little effort was made to improve and disseminate information about courses. This was despite the fact that two ministers for education in the 1920s, Eoin MacNeill and John Marcus O'Sullivan, held university chairs. As a result, the universities, particularly those in the south, came to experience great financial problems, which affected their academic well-being. This became dramatically apparent as the universities entered the 1940s.

In the Irish Free State, the adoption of a new constitution in 1937 involved changes in the universities' parliamentary representation. Their dáil seats were withdrawn and seats in the second chamber, the senate, were substituted. Since that time the University of Dublin and the National University have both been entitled to three seats in the senate, elected by their respective graduates.

[13] Ibid., pp 465–71.   [14] Ibid., p. 466.

THE policy of a low public profile was pursued most assiduously by Trinity College. As McDowell and Webb comment, the policy 'was in part dictated by the logic of facts, but it was to some extent followed deliberately'.[15] Trinity found itself in a particularly awkward situation. For centuries it had been associated with protestant interests and the British connection and it now found itself in a state that had come into being through a catholic, nationalist, populist movement. Though formal declarations of tolerance and mutual respect were made, long-held attitudes did not change all at once. Following the signing of the treaty the board of Trinity passed a resolution that stated: 'The true interests of Trinity College can only be furthered by Irish peace, and in building up happier conditions in Ireland the board believes that Trinity men should take an active and sympathetic part.' Yet there were Trinity men who continued to look back; who could 'remain physically in Ireland but emigrate mentally'.[16] Old loyalties continued to find public and symbolic expression in the form of flags, emblems, and toasts, especially while the Irish Free State remained in the commonwealth.

Following rather strained negotiations with the department of finance and the government in 1923, Trinity made no further submission to the government for financial assistance till 1946. To a very large extent the college's income derived from endowments, property, investments, and student fees. While for the interwar years it could be said that Trinity suffered from 'a moderate but not acute atmosphere of financial stringency',[17] the condition became acute in the early 1940s, prompting a reappraisal of the need for state support.

The number of students at Trinity remained largely static between 1920–21 and 1944–5, at about 1,400.[18] Women had first been admitted in 1904, and the percentage of women students increased during these decades from 19 per cent in 1921–2 to 27 per cent in 1944–5.[19] Not surprisingly, Trinity drew many of its students from Dublin. Of the student intake in 1943–4, 33.7 per cent were from Dublin, with a further 17.3 per cent from the rest of Leinster. Interestingly, the number of students from Ulster increased over the years, amounting to 33 per cent of entrants in 1943–4. The number of overseas students remained relatively small, amounting to 5.8 per cent in 1928–9 and 4.1 per cent in 1943–4. The college offered relatively generous support schemes for students in the form of exhibitions, prizes, and scholarships. However, student fees were significantly higher in Trinity than in the

[15] McDowell & Webb, *Trinity College*, p 429.
[16] Ibid., pp 430, 432.
[17] Ibid., p. 429.
[18] James Meenan, ' "The universities". II—The University of Dublin: Trinity College' in *Stat. Soc. Ire. Jn.*, xvii (1942–7), pp 594–607: 597.
[19] Ibid., p. 598.

N.U.I. colleges. Medicine was the most expensive faculty in both universities.

The general course of studies in Trinity did not change greatly during the period under review. In 1925 a school of commerce was instituted. A number of diploma courses were introduced, such as those in geography (1929), painting (1934), social studies (1934), and public administration (1941). In 1927 the Trinity College Educational Endowment Fund was established. Other efforts were made to draw the community associated with Trinity closer together. In 1928 the Hall of Honour, commemorating the 450 staff and students who lost their lives in the first world war, was opened. The first meeting of the Trinity College Association, representative of alumni from all over the world, was held in the same year, while the bicentenaries of two distinguished past students, Edmund Burke and Oliver Goldsmith, were observed by the college with due ceremony. In 1937 a new octagonal reading room was completed, to which the hall of honour formed the entrance; it was opened by Eamon de Valera, then head of government. On the eve of a new world war, in 1939, the Dixon Hall was opened, reflective of the role of the medical (physics) school in the college. Following the establishment of the diploma in public administration, evening courses were offered from 1942. This brought an influx of students of a new type, who provided additional support for student sports clubs and societies. In 1941 the first students' representative council was set up in the college.

The outbreak of the second world war led to a decline in student numbers in Trinity, but not to the extent experienced during the 1914–18 war. Irish neutrality was respected, but many failed to share its rationale. Some staff took leave of absence to engage in the war effort. This, coupled with the deaths of some of the remaining staff and the difficulties involved in obtaining replacements, placed severe strain on staff resources as the war dragged on.

Trinity's relative isolation from the main currents of national life was further emphasised by the opposition of the catholic church to parents sending their children there. In February 1944 the archbishop of Dublin, John Charles McQuaid, intensified this opposition by declaring it a matter of mortal sin if parents in the Dublin diocese sent their children to Trinity without the special permission of the archbishop in each case.

THE three constituent colleges of the National University of Ireland, after an initial fall in student numbers in the early 1920s, experienced considerable growth in the subsequent twenty years. In 1920–21 student numbers were about 2,245. In 1925–6 they had dropped to 1,881, but as table 1 indicates, sustained growth occurred thereafter. The growth in all colleges was striking, although in the case of Cork and Galway it was from a small base. The near tripling of numbers in U.C.D. was the most impressive. However, such

TABLE 1. *Student numbers in constituent colleges of the N.U.I., 1925–45*

	1925–6	1930–31	1938–9	1945–6
U.C.C.	534	617	942	1,084
U.C.G.	242	555	669	757
U.C.D.	1,105	1,542	2,121	3,039

Source: James Meenan, 'The universities—III' in *Stat. Soc. Ire. Jn.*, xviii (1947–52), p. 351.

growth presented daunting problems for administrators, staff, and students. The largest student body was housed in the most unsatisfactory university premises. Professor Michael Tierney, who was to become president of U.C.D. in 1947, graphically described the situation in a 1944 article:

...the college is easily the worst housed institution of its size and kind in the world. It presents a brave front in its new building at Earlsfort Terrace; but there is very little more than front. Behind it stand the gaping ruins of the royal university, pitifully unworthy of even a comparatively poor secondary school, but with crumbling walls and leaky rooms still forced to perform most incongruously and inadequately the function of library buildings and examination halls...As a university building it comes as near disembodiment as to make very little difference.[20]

Despite such unpropitious conditions, U.C.D. ranked sixth in terms of full-time students among twenty-four universities in Britain and Ireland in 1939. In the early years, women students formed a significant proportion of the student body: as much as 36 per cent by 1931. However, by 1943–4 they made up only 24 per cent of full-time students. The proportion of women in the student body tended to be higher in U.C.C. and U.C.G. than in U.C.D. For instance, in 1938–9 the percentage of women in the former two colleges was about 30 while in U.C.D. it was 24. In 1947–8 the proportions were much the same, at 32 per cent in Cork and Galway and 25 per cent in U.C.D.

U.C.G. and U.C.C. tended to draw more on their immediate hinterland for students than did U.C.D., or indeed Trinity. For instance, in 1947–8 53 per cent of U.C.C. students came from Cork city or from within a thirty-mile radius. In Galway the percentage was 51 from the city or from a similar radius. However, in U.C.D. only 32 per cent came from the city or within a thirty-mile radius, with over 66 per cent from other parts of Ireland or Britain.

[20] Michael Tierney, 'Universities: English and Irish' in *I.E.R.*, lxiii (1944), pp 145–54: 153–4.

None of the N.U.I. colleges had residential accommodation. The vast majority of students took lodgings or 'digs' within the university cities. Student debating societies and cultural and sports clubs helped the social and intellectual development of students. The relatively small student body, particularly in Galway and Cork, fostered a sense of intimacy.

As far as academic life was concerned, it is noteworthy that each of the three N.U.I. colleges saw a decline in the numbers of art students. Table 2 gives an indication of this trend and the strengths of the various faculties. Another striking feature was the growing strength of the medical and dentistry faculties in all three colleges. Engineering and architecture also did relatively well, but science, commerce, and agriculture did not progress satisfactorily and in some colleges suffered a decline. The strength of the

TABLE 2. *Distribution of full-time N.U.I. students by faculty (%)*

	1929–30	1938–9	1947–8
U.C.C.			
Arts	42.3	29.8	22.3
Science	16.7	11.7	14.9
Law	2.0	0.6	0.8
Medicine/dentistry	22.3	35.5	37.4
Engineering/architecture	7.3	9.3	8.4
Commerce	7.0	6.7	9.5
Agriculture/dairy science	2.4	6.4	6.7
U.C.G.			
Arts	38.0	37.0	27.0
Science	10.5	8.8	13.1
Law	2.0	1.5	0.3
Medicine/dentistry	12.0	25.2	33.0
Engineering/architecture	9.2	15.3	15.8
Commerce	28.3	12.2	8.4
Agriculture	—	—	2.4
U.C.D.			
Arts	51.3	32.8	31.5
Science	9.2	8.3	9.0
Law	1.5	2.6	0.5
Medicine/dentistry	17.5	31.6	32.5
Engineering/architecture	6.2	12.2	14.9
Commerce	12.8	8.4	5.0
Agriculture	1.5	4.1	4.9
Veterinary science	—	—	1.7

Source: Meenan, 'The universities—III', p. 353.

professional subjects—medicine, dentistry, engineering, and architecture—was more than adequate for supplying the country's needs for graduates in those disciplines. In many cases the main field of employment lay abroad, and the high level of emigration among graduates gave rise to controversy about the return to Irish society for the investment in their education. In order to improve employment prospects for N.U.I. graduates, the senate established the National University Appointments Committee in May 1935. However, it seems that this initiative made little impact. Arguably, the neglect of science, commerce, and agriculture reflected the underdeveloped state of the Irish economy. There was no overseeing body to draw attention to trends or to foster public awareness about the need for developing particular lines of study. Consumer choice ruled, and for many middle-class parents entry to the professions, whether at home or abroad, was the desired aim for their children.

The N.U.I. colleges relied for their income almost exclusively on state aid and student fees. They benefited scarcely at all from endowments. As late as 1947–8, it has been calculated, the three colleges were in receipt of the paltry sum of £1,600 in endowments.[21] Municipal, business, and professional bodies never took the N.U.I. colleges to their hearts or supported them in the way that many red-brick universities were supported in England. Scholarships for students, too, were limited and many of them had not altered in value since they were originally established in 1908–9.

The college that experienced the greatest increase in numbers and was the worst housed was U.C.D. In 1926 the Royal College of Science in Merrion Street was transferred to U.C.D., which improved the amenities for science and engineering. Also in 1926, as a result of the agriculture and dairy science act,[22] the Albert Agricultural College at Glasnevin was transferred to U.C.D., leading to the establishment of the faculty of agriculture there, funded by the department of agriculture. The improvement in space was only temporary, and the significant rise in student numbers from 1,200 to 3,000 between 1926–7 and 1944–5 put additional pressure on inadequate accommodation. In 1932 the faculty of medicine was transferred from its old home in Cecilia Street to Earlsfort Terrace. No new building grant had been made available since the initial one, but in 1926, when student numbers were about 1,160, the annual grant was raised to £82,000. The new figure included costs involved in taking over the College of Science and its staff. The grant remained fixed at that level until the mid 1940s, by which time student numbers had reached 3,000. The problems of cramped and overcrowded lecture halls were further aggravated by the absence of sports and recreational facilities. In 1934 the college purchased Belfield House and grounds,

[21] James Meenan, 'The universities—III' in *Stat. Soc. Ire. Jn.*, xviii (1947–52), p. 357.
[22] 1926/32 (17 July 1926).

a few miles south of the city in Stillorgan, to provide a sports centre and playing fields. The environment of the college itself was improved in 1941 by the Guinness family's grant of the Iveagh Gardens, located at the rear of Earlsfort Terrace and Newman House.

U.C.D. made efforts to provide courses other than full-time degree courses. Thus, in 1925, the important step of providing night degree courses in commerce and arts was taken. Diploma courses were also introduced for library studies (1928), social science (1935), and public administration (1941). These courses were a success with the public, but the night degree courses, in particular, placed heavy pressures on staff. They also tended to exacerbate an existing trend that emphasised teaching at the expense of research. It was a tribute to scholars on the staff that a considerable range of academic publication was produced despite the difficulties. Salaries, too, became increasingly unattractive over time in the N.U.I. as well as in other university institutions. In the mid 1940s it was ascertained that, apart from an increase given in 1919–20 to cope with high inflation, staff salaries had not been substantially raised since the foundation of the N.U.I. in 1908.[23]

Like U.C.D., University College Cork benefited from the provisions of the agriculture and dairy science act of 1926. The college's small annual grant of £20,000 was increased to £40,000, and it received a capital sum of £15,000. Arising from the act, a faculty of dairy science was established, for which the college received additional grants. An athletic ground was procured for student use. U.C.C. also made efforts to meet the needs of a wider section of the community. A bureau of economic research was set up, and largely through the efforts of Professor Alfred O'Rahilly, a scheme of extension lectures was initiated in 1930. In addition, U.C.C. took the enterprising step of establishing Cork University Press.

UNIVERSITY College Galway, the smallest of the colleges, with student numbers growing from 242 in 1925–6 to 757 in 1945–6, benefited from an increase in its annual government subsidy from £14,000 to £28,000. To U.C.G. was assigned, more particularly than the other N.U.I. colleges, the task of promoting the Irish language by engaging in university teaching through the medium of Irish. The University College Galway Act, 1929,[24] also required that, provided there was suitability in other respects, competence to teach through Irish should be a requirement for staff appointments.

The administrative machinery of the federal National University proceeded smoothly, and there is no doubt that in the difficult early decades academic cooperation, the maintenance of standards through the board of studies, and a sense of solidarity were cultivated by the federal structure. By

---

[23] James Meenan, '"The universities". I', p. 479.
[24] 1929/35 (17 Dec. 1929).

the mid 1940s, however, there was evidence of some restlessness with the federal system on the part of U.C.D., whose student numbers had reached 3,000.[25]

DESPITE the inadequate funding of university institutions and research, new ground was broken in 1940 by the establishment in Dublin of the Institute of Advanced Studies. This was very much the brainchild of the taoiseach, Eamon de Valera, although he had support for the idea from the Irish studies committee of the Royal Irish Academy. It was considered that Ireland was a particularly appropriate location for research in Celtic studies. There was much scholarly work to be done on unpublished and unedited Irish manuscripts, on phonetics, linguistics, and dialectology; and there was a need for dictionaries and standardised grammars. Both de Valera and the Irish studies committee considered that it would be best to establish a scholarly institute, independent of existing universities but working in cooperation with them. The bill to establish the Institute of Advanced Studies met with parliamentary opposition from some influential T.D.s who considered that such an institute was unnecessary and would prove detrimental to the interests of the existing universities. Indeed, as chancellor of the National University of Ireland since 1921, de Valera might have been expected to favour U.C.D. as the location for the new centre; but U.C.D. was widely perceived to have strong Fine Gael connections. De Valera steered the bill through to a successful conclusion,[26] and from 1940 on Ireland had a new and distinguished research institution, which has continued to contribute much to scholarship.

In addition to the school of Celtic studies the act established a school of theoretical physics, linked to the Dunsink observatory. A number of internationally distinguished mathematicians were interested in such a development. De Valera, a keen mathematician himself, considered that the school would not be expensive to run and would provide an appropriate environment through which Ireland could be seen to make worthwhile research contributions in the field of mathematics. In 1947 a school of cosmic physics was added to the institute.

THE establishment of Northern Ireland as a distinct political entity had the effect of fostering closer links between Queen's University and the north-eastern corner of Ireland. Queen's came to be regarded generally as the north's university. Traditionally associated with unionism and presbyterianism, Queen's tried to uphold liberal standards in its academic and student affairs. Bearing in mind the intensity of religious and political divisions in Northern Ireland, it is significant that Queen's won support from all denom-

[25] Michael Tierney, 'Universities: English and Irish', p. 153.
[26] 1940/13 (19 June 1940).

inations, and succeeded well in keeping national politics out of the conduct of university affairs. The conferring of honorary degrees by Queen's in 1929 on the heads of catholic, anglican, and presbyterian churches symbolised the university's efforts to win the support of the different denominations.

The position of Northern Ireland within the United Kingdom served to strengthen ties with universities in Britain, and only tenuous links were maintained with universities south of the border. Although the great industrial and commercial families of the north were reluctant to act as patrons, the university did benefit from three significant bequests. In 1922 it received a bequest of £57,000 from Henry Musgrave; in 1924 T. C. White made an endowment of £60,000; and in 1933 the Whitla bequest amounted to £35,000 and a fine house. Sir William Whitla's memory was honoured in the building of the Whitla Hall in 1942.[27]

The increase in student numbers after the first world war placed considerable pressure on the university, and financial difficulties greatly impeded development. Appeals to the government were received sympathetically but yielded nothing. Eventually in 1928 the annual grant from government was raised by £4,000. In an effort to build on this and also to cultivate links with graduates a Graduates' Association was launched in 1929. Then in 1930 the lord mayor of Belfast launched the Queen's University Guild, hoping to elicit more public support for the college. However, these initiatives did not prove a financial success; nor did a further public appeal for funds in 1938. Vice-chancellor Richard Livingstone met with slightly more success in the early 1930s with his appeals to local authorities, which agreed to make an aggregate annual payment of £5,000 a year. In 1937 a new scheme of grading, promotion, and salary scales was introduced for staff, which brought conditions generally into line with those prevailing in England.[28] The following year, 1938, the government increased its annual grant by £20,000 and the local authorities also increased their support. These were desirable and necessary developments in the years immediately before the second world war, but the war was to place new stresses and strains on resources.

By 1939 student numbers had increased from 1,000 in 1920 to 1,500, although the proportion of women students had fallen from about 34 per cent in 1924 to about 25 per cent a decade later. Student numbers expanded significantly through the war years, to reach just over 2,000 in 1945. This resulted in cramped teaching conditions and heavier teaching loads as thirty-two staff members were released for war service.[29]

Significant academic developments took place during the interwar years. A faculty of applied science and technology was established. In October 1924 the first appointments to a new faculty of agriculture were made, with new

---

[27] Moody & Beckett, *Queen's, Belfast*, pp 468, 493, 501.
[28] Ibid., p. 501.   [29] Ibid., p. 522.

buildings becoming available in 1924. In 1926 a faculty of theology was agreed on, following which in 1928 an honours status was accorded to the course in scholastic philosophy. The Queen's education department assisted the Northern Ireland authorities in the provision of teachers, and close links were forged between Queen's and the new Stranmillis College for teacher education. A thaw in the political climate, which saw some nationalist politicians take their places in the Northern Ireland parliament, was reflected in the establishment of an honours school for Celtic studies in 1927. New professional faculties were set up, including dentistry and law. Belfast was now the centre of a distinct judicial system, highlighting the need for the academic and professional study of law in Northern Ireland. Accordingly, in 1926 a separate inn of court was set up in Belfast. Another important initiative came in 1928 with the appointment of a lecturer and director of extramural studies, with the aim of extending some of the benefits of university education outside the Belfast area.

As the war years drew to a close, it was apparent that new planning and development would be necessary for the postwar era. In November 1944 the decision was taken to fill existing staff vacancies. The British university grants committee (U.G.C.) was invited to visit Queen's to assist the planning process. The committee visited early in 1945 and had its report written by March 1945.[30] The report gave hope for a new era of development. In April 1945 new property was purchased and buildings adjacent to Queen's were secured. The year 1945, the centenary of the establishment of the original queen's colleges, saw the launching of a centenary fund to try to raise £250,000. It seemed clear that the Queen's University of Belfast was poised for an era of expansion.

THE most striking feature of university education in the fifteen years from 1945 to 1959 was the growth in student numbers, combined with a deepening crisis over accommodation, resources, and staffing. The total number of full-time students in the N.U.I. constituent colleges and in T.C.D. increased from 4,978 in 1938–9 to 6,796 in 1948–9 and to 8,653 in 1959–60.[31] This represented an increase of 74 per cent on the pre-war figure. However, there had been no significant expansion in accommodation for decades, nor had staffing arrangements been reformed in line with the needs of the day. The outcome was intense overcrowding in most campuses, overstretching of staff, and limited promotion of research.

Of all the colleges, University College Dublin was the one under greatest pressure. Accommodation designed for fewer than 1,000 students had to cope with about 3,000 in the immediate postwar years. By 1946–7 the college finances 'had run into desperate straits'. In 1947 the government paid

[30] Ibid., p. 526.
[31] Commission on higher education, *Report* (Pr 9389) (Dublin, 1967), table 12, i, 31.

off an outstanding college debt of £85,000, and in 1948 the annual parliamentary grant was increased from £82,000 to £147,000 and to £231,000 by 1952.[32] As early as 1946 U.C.D. had prepared a memorandum on its need for new buildings and presented it to the government. For a number of years, the college authorities sought building space in the neighbourhood of its Earlsfort Terrace site. However, it emerged that there was no real possibility of significant expansion in that area. From 1949, under President Michael Tierney, the strategic decision was made to look further afield and to acquire property in the area of the college's grounds in Belfield, Stillorgan. Over the next decade, six contiguous properties on the Stillorgan Road were purchased, making a total of 252 acres (102 hectares). Various plans were drawn up for new buildings. However, aspiration and realisation did not coincide, and as the 1950s passed the overcrowding problem in the old site grew still more intense. Although not to the same critical extent, the colleges at Cork and Galway were experiencing similar problems.

Eventually, the minister for education appointed a commission to examine the accommodation needs of the N.U.I. colleges, chaired by Justice Cearbhall Ó Dálaigh. The commission issued reports on the individual colleges and a final report in May 1959. The final report noted that the problem of accommodation was a long-standing one that had been neglected:

The result has been that the colleges have become more and more overcrowded, and arrears of building have been accumulating...Already breakdown point has been reached in the colleges. Twenty years ago the colleges were full. Since that time accommodation has remained virtually unaltered, but student numbers have been growing and the field of university studies expanding. Today, the situation is that university teachers and students have to work under very trying and, in some cases, almost impossible conditions.[33]

This was an indictment of general neglect, but the dilemma of U.C.D. was picked out for special mention. The accommodation there was 'wholly inadequate'. The report endorsed U.C.D.'s submission for extra accommodation as 'reasonable' but 'modest', and in respect of research facilities the submission was deemed to be 'not adequate'. The only satisfactory solution to the problems was the 'transfer of the entire college to a new site', and the Belfield campus was recommended.[34]

The proposals for extra accommodation for U.C.C. were also fully endorsed, but again the commission considered that the provision sought for research requirements was not sufficient.[35] Concerning U.C.G. the

---

[32] Michael Tierney (ed.), *Struggle with fortune: a miscellany for the centenary of the Catholic University of Ireland, 1854–1954* (Dublin, 1954), p. 188.
[33] 'Final report on accommodation needs' in *Report of the commission on accommodation needs of the constituent colleges of the N.U.I.* (Pr 5089) (Dublin, [1959]), pp 126, 128.
[34] 'Report on the accommodation needs of U.C.D.', ibid., p. 44.
[35] 'Report on the accommodation needs of U.C.C.', ibid., pp 55, 56.

commission held that the college, 'throughout all its facilities, is in urgent and immediate need of additional accommodation'.[36] The final report made the important proposal that a university development committee should be established for the execution of the proposed building programmes. Such a body would constitute a useful link between the colleges and the government and 'in time, might also be called upon to advise on long-term plans for development and on problems of coordination'. This proposal was not implemented but may have been influential in promoting the establishment of a commission on higher education in the following year, 1960. Meanwhile, the Ó Dálaigh commission criticised the colleges for not publicising their problems sufficiently: 'The emergence of a university accommodation problem of this magnitude must come to many as a surprise and even a shock, and we cannot but feel that the colleges might have done more to bring their needs to the knowledge of the public.'[37]

Now, however, action could no longer be postponed, and in June 1959 the government decided to accept the recommendation of the commission and to transfer U.C.D. to its new site at Belfield, Stillorgan. The shift to the modern, spacious campus was largely completed by the early 1970s. On a smaller and less dramatic scale, the 1960s also saw expansion of buildings and facilities in U.C.C. and U.C.G., as the N.U.I. colleges were all gradually equipped for a new era in Irish university education.

The postwar years saw the establishment of new extramural courses in the N.U.I. colleges, aimed at the general adult public in the university cities. Student numbers on these courses grew from 105 in 1948–9 to 693 in 1952–3. There was also a significant increase in the postwar years in the numbers of part-time students studying for evening degrees and diplomas. In 1938–9 there had been 265 part-time students, about 5 per cent of the total. In 1948–9 the number had increased to 593 or 8 per cent of the total. By 1959–60 there were 918 part-time students, about 13 per cent of the student body of 7,128 in the N.U.I. colleges.[38] Evening degrees had become popular since the early 1950s and by 1959–60 about 50 per cent of part-time students were taking undergraduate degree courses. Women students formed only 20 per cent of the total part-time students by 1959–60. The proportion of women full-time students in the N.U.I. colleges and Trinity actually declined from 30 per cent in 1948–9 to 26 per cent by 1959–60.[39] Postgraduate degree students in the N.U.I. colleges remained small in number, growing from 134 in 1948–9 to 227 in 1959–60.[40]

[36] 'Report on the accommodation needs of U.C.G.', ibid., p. 112.
[37] 'Final report on accommodation needs', ibid., p. 125.
[38] Commission on higher education, *Report*, i, 26, 47.
[39] Ibid., p. 33, and table 40, p. 59.   [40] Ibid., table 41, p. 60.

A striking celebratory event in this period was the commemoration by U.C.D. of the centenary of the foundation of the catholic university in 1854, from which the college traced its descent. The occasion was a resplendent affair. The president of U.C.D. edited a volume of centenary essays, *Struggle with fortune*, which provided an opportunity for retrospective reflection at a time when planning and pressure for new developments were under way.[41]

At about the same time, an N.U.I. graduates' association was established, in 1953, which it was hoped would help to develop a sense of solidarity among graduates. The association had Dublin and regional branches, and aimed at raising funds for the advancement of scholarship and research, as well as providing a meeting place for graduates and a data centre for employment opportunities. Although it was a praiseworthy initiative, it failed to galvanise widespread enthusiasm—it was even unpopular with President Michael Tierney—and its impact was limited.

An issue that caused increasing unease in N.U.I. circles was the mode of academic appointments. Unlike most other universities in Britain and Ireland, there were no formal specialist academic selection committees with external representation to evaluate the relative merits of candidates and report to the consultative and appointing bodies. The existing system was cumbersome for candidates and gave rise to doubt whether the best candidate was always the successful one.[42]

A controversy concerning university appointments arose in U.C.D., which led to a visitation to the college by government-appointed visitors. In 1949 U.C.D. had adopted the practice of appointing 'assistant lecturers', and in 1953 the grade of 'college lecturers' was introduced. Appointments to these positions, which were renewable on a yearly basis, were made without reference to the senate of the N.U.I. The posts were usually not advertised, and were regarded as promotional posts within the colleges. Within this system of 'internal' appointments there went a policy of leaving some professorships and almost all the university statutory lectureships unfilled, so that by 1959 there were ten professorships and thirty-four university lectureships vacant. In 1959 the government agreed to a petition by Justice John Kenny that visitors should be appointed to investigate the situation. The visitors found that appointments to assistant lectureships and college lectureships were invalid, and found the governing body in breach of duty in not taking proper steps to fill university lectureships when they became vacant. The government brought in legislation to deal with the situation and legitimise earlier

---

[41] Denis Gwynn and James Hogan, 'Some afterthoughts on the Newman centenary celebrations' in *University Review*, i, no. 2 (autumn 1954), pp 3–9: 4; Tierney, *Struggle with fortune*.

[42] Canvassing as such was forbidden, but the practice had arisen for candidates to call on all members of the relevant faculty, academic council, governing body, and senate. Aloys Fleischmann, 'University appointments' in *University Review*, i, no. 11 (1957), pp 3–16: 5, 14.

appointments. The visitors' report caused something of a shock to the public and to the convocation of the N.U.I.[43]

Why had the U.C.D. authorities acted in ways that risked legal action? Lack of familiarity with the terms of the college charter, a desire to circumvent the slow and complicated method of election by the senate, and considerations of professorial power all probably played their part. But one other matter was raised by Justice Kenny in his retrospective review of the visitation. Although not put explicitly to the board of visitors, there was a sense in U.C.D. that the college ought to be autonomous and not beholden to a federal system for the making of appointments. This underlying sense had been expressed in 1953 by President Michael Tierney when he said: '[U.C.D.] is a university forced by many different pressures, applied for the better part of a century, to masquerade as a college'.[44]

The problems revealed by the commission on N.U.I. accommodation, the unease about appointment procedures, and the absence of a body akin to the British U.G.C. to act as an intermediary between the colleges and government departments all pointed to the desirability of a thorough appraisal of all third-level education. In 1958 Ireland adopted its first economic programme, and increasingly it was realised that investment in education was crucial to economic and social development. In 1960 the government was to take the significant step of establishing the first major commission on higher education since the foundation of the state, appointing Ó Dálaigh, who had just chaired the commission on university accommodation, as its chairman.

In Trinity College, the total number of students increased from 1,579 in 1938–9 to 2,525 in 1948–9 and to 2,674 in 1959–60.[45] The immediate postwar years witnessed a significant expansion in numbers, particularly of foreign students, but during the 1950s numbers remained fairly constant. There were considerable problems in providing the facilities for a modern university. Following a deputation to the taoiseach, Eamon de Valera, in February 1947, a grant of £35,000 was secured. Further calls were made to the coalition government in 1948, 1949, and 1950 without success. Meanwhile U.C.D. was receiving increases in its annual grants; for instance, an extra £100,000 was awarded in 1951, while Trinity obtained only £10,000. A Trinity deputation met the taoiseach, John Costello, and the minister for finance, Patrick McGilligan, in March 1951, but this resulted only in a rather bitter exchange of views. On de Valera's return to power in 1951 Trinity was granted an increase of £40,000 with a further building grant of £10,000.[46]

[43] John Kenny, 'The visitation in University College, Dublin' in *University Review*, ii, no. 11 (1961), pp 9–29; and *Report of board of visitors*, pp 7–9.
[44] Kenny, 'Visitation', p. 26.
[45] Commission on higher education, *Report*, i, table 12, p. 31; table 22, p. 44.
[46] McDowell & Webb, *Trinity College*, p. 470.

Trinity also experienced a significant administrative change in 1952 with A. J. McConnell's election as the new provost. This was followed by what has been termed 'a palace revolution' in the general reorganisation of administrative offices, procedures, and personnel.[47] Under the new regime a more outgoing approach was adopted and closer contacts were established with government. The Moyne Institute of Preventive Medicine was opened in 1953, and new extensions were made to the engineering buildings. The Trinity Trust, established in 1955, was successful in raising funds to improve various buildings and facilities. Planning began for a major fund-raising campaign to build a new library, which was completed and opened in 1967. Student life was enriched by the provision of a new theatre and sports grounds. The late 1950s witnessed reforms in academic courses, involving a shift away from a general education towards more specialised studies.[48] Also at that time, decisions were made regarding the professionalisation of administrative positions which helped lay the foundations for the period of unprecedented expansion that took place in subsequent decades.

THE postwar years saw significant improvements in the financing of Queen's University, Belfast. Following the visit of the university grants commission in 1945, the annual grant was raised by £80,000 and a capital grant of £50,000 was made available. The university also benefited from an increase in the grants from local councils and an increase in fees. Expansion and improvement of buildings took place and there was a large increase in the recruitment of new staff.[49] A second visit from the U.G.C. led to further increases in government support that continued the momentum for expansion. Through the U.G.C. the university came more closely into line with contemporary developments taking place in English universities.[50]

The Education Act (Northern Ireland), 1947,[51] was influenced by the 1944 Butler education act in England. One outcome of the 1947 act was to increase participation in secondary schooling and to open up access to higher education for those pupils who performed well in tests and examinations. This increased the demand for teachers; numbers in teacher-education institutions increased significantly through the 1950s, from 660 in 1949–50 to 1,662 in 1959–60. The prospective expansion of higher education meant that the years leading up to the formal celebration of the centenary of Queen's in September 1949 were years of achievement and promise. The centenary fund raised £292,000, of which the government donated £130,000.

At about this time the question arose as to whether Magee College in Derry, which had established an association with T.C.D. following the Irish

[47] J. V. Luce, *Trinity College, Dublin: the first 400 years* (Dublin, 1992), p. 149.
[48] Ibid., p. 170.   [49] Moody & Beckett, *Queen's, Belfast*, pp 526, 530.
[50] Ibid., p. 528.   [51] 1947, c. 3 (27 Mar. 1947).

universities act of 1908, should be developed as a second centre for university studies in Northern Ireland. The Acheson committee was established to report on the matter. Its recommendations, in 1950, were extremely cautious. Proposals by the college authorities for departments of science and social studies at Magee were rejected, since in the committee's opinion facilities at Queen's were sufficient to cope with any expansion in these areas. The main recommendation of the committee was to strengthen the provision for the arts subjects already on offer at Magee. This was conditional on Magee college separating its theological studies from its other academic work. Subsequent legislation in 1953 divided the college into two institutions, Magee Theological College and Magee University College.[52] However, the college did not develop courses up to degree level as envisaged, and it retained its links with Trinity College, as well as more tenuous links with Queen's. Student numbers increased at Magee from seventy-two in 1952 to 245 in 1963.

Although student numbers in Queen's reached 2,361 in 1949–50, a decline set in during the 1950s and it was not till 1957–8 that this figure was reached again, when 2,409 students were enrolled. Thereafter, steady expansion took place so that the 3,000 mark was reached in 1959–60, and by 1963–4 over 4,000 students (4,135) attended Queen's on a full-time basis. Through the Higher Technological Studies Act, 1954,[53] a joint authority was established between Queen's and the Belfast College of Technology, which led to shared teaching of higher technological studies in the Ashby Institute near Queen's University. Queen's remained by far the most important provider of higher education in Northern Ireland up to 1960, but subsequent decades were to witness many new institutional developments that changed greatly the shape of higher education.

WHILE higher education did not feature prominently in public consciousness during the first four decades after independence, the following twenty years witnessed considerable analysis and appraisal, and a level of action on a range of fronts that transformed the provision and profile of higher education. The transformation involved great expansion of existing institutions and the establishment of many new ones; the setting up of a planning and budgetary agency to oversee many of those institutions; the foundation of a course validation and award-giving body for the non-university sector; and the establishment of a clearing house for higher education applications. The number of full-time students increased from about 9,000 in 1960 to 51,000 in 1984, and through student unions and representation on college bodies the

---

[52] *Report of the committee on the possible development of Magee University College* [Cmd 175] (Belfast, 1950) (Acheson report); 1953, c. 1 (7 July 1953).
[53] 1954, c. 29 (21 Dec. 1954).

voice of students was added to the higher education debate. An impressive
diversification of courses took place in response to the changing needs of
individuals and society. Government became much more actively involved
in higher education policy, which was now regarded as having much wider
social and economic significance. The universities' monopoly of higher education ceased, leading to wider roles for some existing institutions and to
the establishment of many new ones. The impressive expansion of higher
education was not always matched by consistency of government policy, and
this sometimes gave rise to uncertainty and unease in higher education
circles. Nevertheless, the decades since 1960 have to be regarded as a period
of unprecedented achievement. Policy became more coordinated, focusing on
the general higher education sector, rather than on individual institutions.
The approach taken in this section reflects that pattern, and deals with the
overall development of higher education during this period.

By 1960 the government had accepted that the whole question of higher
education, which would form a crucial element in the planned socio-economic
development of the state, needed to be examined. With this end in view, the
minister for education, Patrick Hillery, appointed a twenty-eight-person
commission on higher education in 1960. Its terms of reference were very
wide, and in effect included the surveying of every feature of higher education: 'Having regard to the education needs and to the financial and other
resources of the country, to inquire into and to make recommendations
in relation to university, professional, technological, and higher education
generally...'[54]

This was the first comprehensive survey of higher education in Ireland,
and the first commission since independence to examine the academic and
administrative issues involved. Perhaps it was the wide scope, and the vast
range of issues that were considered, that caused the delays in completing the
commission's work, and raised problems about some of its proposed solutions. The commission took seven years to conclude and present its report, a
very long time at a period when many educational issues were pressing for
resolution.

It is worth noting that while the commission was engaged in its deliberations, several other educational inquiries were set up and a number of
important decisions were taken by government. Just as the commission was
the first major survey of higher education, the 'Investment in education'
inquiry, jointly established by the Irish government and the O.E.C.D. in
1962, was the first comprehensive survey of the first- and second-level
systems. In 1963 a joint study was also undertaken with the O.E.C.D. on
scientific research and technology in relation to Irish economic development.
Furthermore, in 1963 the minister for education announced his intention of

---

[54] Commission on higher education, *Report* (Pr 9389) (Dublin, 1967), i, pp 1, xxviii.

establishing regional technical colleges, and in 1966 the minister (now Donogh O'Malley) set up a steering committee on technical education to advise on regional technical colleges. In December 1966 the minister brought his major proposal for merging T.C.D. with U.C.D. to the cabinet, which deferred a decision pending the conclusion of the commission's report. By this stage, the delay in concluding that report was giving rise to political controversy and acrimony.

The report, as published in 1967, comprised part I, *Presentation and summary*, and the *Report* proper in two volumes amounting to 400,000 words. Its thirty-two chapters were by far the most thorough examination ever made of higher education in Ireland. First, the commission set out and assessed the structure of the existing provision for higher education. This produced a rather dismal picture but one that influenced the commission greatly in its recommendations for the future. The piecemeal character of the system and the lack of planning machinery came in for criticism. The commissioners considered that increasing numbers of students, low entry standards, and inadequate staffing and accommodation, placed academic standards in jeopardy. They were not impressed by what was being achieved in the areas of postgraduate studies and research, and they criticised the appointments system within the N.U.I., and the constitution and administrative structures of the higher education institutions.[55] In general, they considered that the inadequacies revealed were 'so grave as to call for a concentrated effort to remove them'.

In trying to establish a guiding principle by which to evaluate future development, the commission set down 'a view of the university': 'The university is not a professional academy, or congregation of professional academies, existing merely to provide a training for the several professions... The university is a place for the study and communication of basic knowledge... The university adds to existing knowledge and advances it beyond its present frontiers.'[56] The commission went on to draw a distinction between pure and applied learning and education in the scientific or philosophical principles on the one hand, and training in techniques and practice on the other. It stated that 'study of first principles is the distinctive function of the university, and herein lies the university's major obligation in professional training'.

In a later section dealing with the university and technology, the commission argued that the responsibility for technological education should not lie with the university.[57] Throughout the report there was a consistent view that the university was concerned with first principles and experimental research,

[55] Commission on higher education, *Presentation and summary of report* (Pr 9326) (Dublin, 1967), pp 22–3. By the 1970s the N.U.I. colleges had introduced specialist assessment boards for appointments, which reported to the various consultative and appointing bodies.
[56] Commission on higher education, *Report* (1967), i, 122.
[57] Ibid., pp 143–4, 184.

as distinct from professional training and applied research. This view, coupled with concern about safeguarding standards, which seemed to be at risk under existing conditions, underlay many of the specific recommendations of the commission. They formed the pivotal axis of the report's analysis and its recommendations for the future. The commissioners' solution was to maintain the existing universities for what they saw as their proper role, and to protect standards, by proposing a new type of third-level institution—the 'new college'—and diverting some of the professional work to other existing institutions for applied research. The 'new college' was devised essentially to help meet the growing demand for third-level places, to enrich the intellectual and cultural life of the provinces, and to provide forms of higher education, lower in standard and with a different emphasis from that of the university.

Interestingly, the commission ruled out the desirability of a technological university, nor did it recommend a raising of the colleges of technology under the Dublin vocational education committee (V.E.C.) to the status of advanced colleges of technology, on the lines of the contemporary British polytechnics. It did, however, recommend the setting up of a technological authority that would have responsibilities for ensuring that advanced technological education, training, and research were provided in relation to the needs of Irish industry. In keeping with its views on the distinctions between pure and applied learning, that is, 'between research and training', the commission recommended the establishment of a separate national college of agricultural and veterinary sciences 'as a fully integrated teaching and research organisation of university standing'. And while the university should be concerned with original research in the fields of law and business, the practical and vocational training in these fields should be provided outside the university.

Among other significant recommendations was the dissolution of the N.U.I. in favour of independent university status for the constituent colleges. However, the commission was strongly in favour of greater cooperation between the universities and recommended the establishment of a statutory council of Irish universities, with a right to determine policy in a number of academic areas. It also recommended the setting up of a statutory commission for higher education, with overall planning and budgetary responsibilities, which 'would be the keystone of the future structure of higher education'. New governing structures for the universities and other higher education institutions should be introduced, along with new appointment procedures, the promotion of research and postgraduate studies, improvements in staff–student ratios, a student grants scheme, and improved student facilities.[58] The recommendations concerning students coincided with a

---

[58] Commission on higher education, 'Conclusion' in *Report* (Pr 9588) (Dublin, 1967), ii, 855–60.

period of worldwide unrest by university students, who sought more democratic structures and better facilities.

The commission's report, finally completed in February 1967, had been
impatiently awaited. Reaction was mixed, for the time-lag since the commission had begun its deliberations meant that the debate had, in some respects,
moved on. Public attention quickly focused on a number of specific issues,
and the controversy surrounding them tended to distract attention from the
overall plan.[59] Many of the criticisms related to the basic core of the commission's analysis. The distinction between research and training, and the exclusion of the latter from the university, was seen by many as a basic error.

The 'new colleges' proposal had been, to some extent, preempted by the
government's decision to establish regional technical colleges. In September
1966 a steering committee on technical education had been appointed to
advise the government generally on technical education and, in particular, on
building arrangements for the colleges. The committee presented an interim
report in January 1967 and a final report in April 1967, in order to take the
commission's recommendations into account. The role recommended for the
regional colleges was broad—'to educate for trade and industry over a broad
spectrum of occupations ranging from craft to professional level, notably in
engineering and science but also in commercial, linguistic, and other special-
ities'. The colleges were to be capable of 'continuing adaptation to social,
economic, and technological changes'.[60]

The steering committee expressed disagreement with the commission's
views on entry standards and on the levels of academic attainment proposed
for the 'new colleges'. In general, it endorsed the government's plans for
regional technical colleges and largely ignored consideration of how they
might mesh with the commission's colleges. The steering committee recommended the establishment of regional education councils 'having accountability, in as much as it would be possible, for all education in each of the
regions', and also recommended the establishment of a national council for
educational awards (N.C.E.A.) with responsibility for syllabus and course
validation in technical education, on the lines of the C.N.A.A. in Britain.
Although similarities existed between the commission's proposal for a technological authority and the steering committee's N.C.E.A. proposal, the
steering committee's report pointed more firmly towards a binary third-level
framework on British lines, while the commission's report saw the universities and the 'new colleges' fitting into a university model, with less emphasis on technical and technological education.

---

[59] The rejection by government of two key recommendations of the commission concerning
the university question in Dublin and the 'new colleges' has led some to suppose that the
commission's report had little effect. This, however, is unfair to the report, many of whose
other recommendations were implemented in subsequent years.

[60] Steering committee on technical education, *Report* (Prl 371) (Dublin, 1967), p. 11.

An issue that gave rise to greater public debate concerned the future structure of university education. Here government thinking diverged from that of the commission. The commission had recommended the dissolution of the N.U.I. in favour of independent status for its constituent colleges, while leaving Trinity College as it was, but the minister for education, O'Malley, rejected this advice. On 18 April 1967 he made the dramatic announcement that it was the government's intention to establish a single multidenominational university in Dublin, to contain two colleges based on U.C.D. and Trinity. O'Malley argued that his proposal made economic, educational, and social sense. It certainly caught the attention of the general public. The minister's perspective was not, however, shared by many interested parties, and very divergent views were expressed in the ensuing controversy, concerning what became popularly known as 'the merger proposals'.

On 5 July 1968 the new minister for education, Brian Lenihan, announced the government's detailed proposals on the reorganisation of the universities. The N.U.I. was to be dissolved, with U.C.C. and U.C.G. gaining independent status. Trinity and U.C.D. were to form a single multidenominational university based on the two colleges. The statement set out a division of faculties between the colleges. Maynooth College was to become an associated college of this new university. In line with the commission's report, a conference of Irish universities was to be set up to deal with academic issues common to all universities. Also in line with the report, a permanent authority to deal with financial and organisational problems of higher education was to be established.

This latter proposal was the first (and, as it turned out, the last) to be implemented. In the following month, August 1968, the higher education authority (H.E.A.) was established on an ad hoc basis; it was given statutory recognition in 1971. Its terms of reference were wide-ranging in respect of the budgetary and planning aspects of higher education. The minister informed the authority at its first meeting on 12 September 1968 that it was 'an autonomous body' and 'in no way an executive arm of the government or of any department of state'. The first task deputed to the authority was to advise the ministers on the nature of the legislation required to put into effect the 'decisions already taken by the government on higher education'. Accordingly, the H.E.A. opened discussions with university interests and sought their opinions on the proposed changes.

In the meantime, the minister sought the H.E.A.'s advice on the setting up of a body to award national qualifications for technicians and technologists; on the nature of a third-level educational institution that the government was committed to establishing at Limerick; and on future provision for teacher training. In March 1969 the H.E.A. endorsed the steering committee's recommendation for a national council for educational awards for non-university institutions, and recommended the establishment of a 'pioneering' institute of higher education in Limerick on polytechnic lines. In November 1970 the H.E.A. gave its view on a proposal by the city of Dublin's vocational education committee to establish a new centre on a single campus in Ballymun, Dublin, for higher-technician, technological, higher-commercial, and management departments. While supporting the general idea of such a centre, the H.E.A. considered that it should develop separately under its own governing body. This was to evolve in 1976 into the National Institute of Higher Education, Dublin, modelled on the Limerick institute, which had enrolled its first students in 1972.

Even in its first report (1970), the H.E.A. clearly saw higher education in Ireland developing on a binary model. There were references to the 'university' and 'non-university sectors', and to 'the distinctive parts to be played by each'. The opening of the first regional colleges in 1970 pointed up the necessity for an early establishment of an accrediting and awarding body for the non-university institutions. The N.C.E.A. was set up on an ad hoc basis in 1972, and it seemed that a full binary system of higher education was now firmly in place. On the question of teacher training, the commission's report in 1967 had urged that teacher education be raised in status, and one of the recommendations of the H.E.A.'s report on the subject in July 1970 was that a Foras Oideachais (teaching foundation) should be established to promote aspects of teacher education and teaching as a profession. The H.E.A. report also urged that primary teaching should become a degree subject, under the proposed N.C.E.A.

In December 1971 the H.E.A. presented its report on university reorganisation to the minister for education. The report took note of the high level of opposition to the single-university proposal for Dublin. By April 1970 representatives of the N.U.I. and T.C.D. had come together and worked out a set of joint proposals, referred to as the N.U.I./T.C.D. agreement, which was presented to the H.E.A. The H.E.A. considered that the government proposals of 1967–8 had concentrated the minds of the college authorities and created a context for cooperative planning in the hope of avoiding a fate that neither institution desired. Furthermore, the removal by the catholic hierarchy in 1970 of the ban on catholic attendance at Trinity had opened up new possibilities, and Trinity itself had decided to limit its intake of foreign students to 10 per cent of the total. It was also the case that the continuing increase in student numbers alleviated some of the apparent wastage of resources in unnecessary duplication. The H.E.A. report declared that 'in view of these fundamentally altered circumstances we have felt impelled to reassess the entire situation'.

The H.E.A.'s favoured solution was for two universities in Dublin linked by a statutory conjoint board. Certain faculties should be developed in one institution only, with special joint arrangements for medicine and engineering. The H.E.A. did not favour giving statutory status to a conference of

Irish universities, which it felt should be established by the universities themselves, on a voluntary basis. As for U.C.G. and U.C.C., the H.E.A. supported the government's intention to establish them as independent universities.[61]

The government made no public response to the H.E.A. report or to the N.U.I./T.C.D. agreement. Nor was action taken to implement either its own earlier decisions or the recommendations of the H.E.A. However, some coordination of subject areas took place between T.C.D. and U.C.D., the most significant of which was the location of veterinary studies exclusively in U.C.D., while dentistry and pharmacy became Trinity's preserve. The great increase in student numbers taking place in the late 1960s and early 1970s, assisted by a new means-tested student grant scheme, introduced in 1968, put many courses on a more viable and cost-effective footing.

The arrival of the Fine Gael–Labour coalition government in 1973 heralded several new changes of direction. An early initiative was that by which the minister for education, Richard Burke, requested the universities to investigate the possibility of awarding degrees to primary teachers. The discussions proved successful and a new professional degree course, the B.Ed., was established in 1974. The larger colleges of education, St Patrick's, Drumcondra, and Our Lady of Mercy, Carysfort, both in Dublin, and Mary Immaculate College in Limerick, became recognised colleges of the National University of Ireland, while the Church of Ireland College and the Marino and Sion Hill Colleges became associated with Trinity College in the new degree arrangements. Later in the 1970s St Angela's College of Home Economics in Sligo became a N.U.I. recognised college and was linked for degree purposes with U.C.G. Other categories of teachers, in such fields as physical education, art, and rural science, also had their courses restructured and upgraded to degree status. The new Thomond College in Limerick, and the national college of art and design, which had been established on a statutory basis in 1971, were the main providers of these courses. The courses were validated, and awards conferred by the N.C.E.A. The Royal College of Surgeons in Ireland also became a recognised college of the N.U.I. in 1977.

The degree-awarding power of the N.C.E.A. came into question under the coalition government. On 16 December 1974 the minister for education announced wide-ranging government proposals for the future of higher education, which contrasted markedly with the proposals of the previous administration. The statement indicated that the central issue in planning was 'whether to continue and to develop the existing binary system, or to initiate the establishment of a fully comprehensive system of higher education'. The government had decided 'to initiate the establishment of the

[61] Higher Education Authority, *Report on university reorganisation* (Prl 2276) (Dublin, 1972).

structures necessary to secure a comprehensive system of higher education in Ireland'. Among specific proposals there were to be three universities in the state—the National University of Ireland, comprising U.C.C. and U.C.G.; the University of Dublin (Trinity College); and a university constituted from the existing U.C.D. Maynooth would have the option of becoming a constituent college of any of the three universities. These proposals were, of course, directly contrary to those of the previous government. The National Institute of Higher Education at Limerick would become a recognised college of the national university, as would Thomond College, and the N.I.H.E. in Dublin would become a recognised college of one of the Dublin universities. The N.C.E.A. would become a council for technological education with responsibilities for coordinating and awarding non-degree third-level qualifications. The range of bodies designated under the H.E.A. would be extended, and a conference of Irish universities, meeting on an ad hoc basis since June 1974, would be made permanent. The two proposed Dublin universities would acquire a conjoint board, and a division of faculties between the two was set out.[62]

The clear aim of this policy was a concentration of higher-level institutions within a framework of three universities. Other third-level institutions would be linked to one or other of these universities for all degrees and postgraduate work. The status of the N.C.E.A. would be reduced. The overall role of the H.E.A. would be expanded as the key overseeing body of the third-level institutions. The conference of Irish universities and the conjoint board of the two Dublin universities were intended to improve coordination and cooperation between the universities.

While the emphasis of the new policy was clear, this government shared the previous government's failure to set out a detailed rationale, or an overall conception of what constituted university education. The public was presented with decisions on restructuring, but without the benefit of argumentation on which they were based. Like the Fianna Fáil recommendations for higher education, the coalition proposals were highly controversial; like them, they were destined for the most part not to be implemented. However, degree-awarding powers were removed from the N.C.E.A. This created some immediate problems. The most awkward of these faced Thomond College and N.I.H.E., Limerick, which were now forced to adapt their courses in line with U.C.C.'s requirements in the case of Thomond, and U.C.G.'s in the case of N.I.H.E. In a less controversial move, the establishment in 1976 of a central agency, the Central Admissions Office (C.A.O.) to process student applications to universities and some of the other third-level institutions, facilitated students in their applications to a rapidly changing range of third-level institutions and courses.

---

[62] Press release of Minister Richard Burke on new government proposals, 16 Dec. 1974.

THE middle 1970s could be characterised as a period of drift or confusion concerning the future structure of higher education. The government's 1974 plans were not given legislative form. Indeed, in July 1976 the government amended its policy and announced proposals for the setting up of five universities, based on T.C.D., U.C.D., U.C.C., U.C.G., and Maynooth, with scope for associated and recognised colleges linked to them. A working party, chaired by the minister for education, took on the task of preparing the necessary legislation. The return of a Fianna Fáil government, following the general election of 1977, led to a further change of policy whereby the 'comprehensive' model was abandoned and the 'binary' model reinstated. The emphasis of legislation now shifted towards giving statutory status to the new institutions. Degree-awarding powers were restored to the N.C.E.A. under new legislation in 1979. Thomond College was given statutory status in 1980. In the same year the National Institutes of Higher Education in Limerick and Dublin were established as independent institutions looking to the N.C.E.A. for the validation of their courses and the awarding of their qualifications.[63] The new legislation gave more power to the minister for education over these institutions than over the existing universities, which operated under an older conception of academic freedom. The series of legislative enactments in 1979–80 put the seal on the binary approach and gave the new institutions the sense that their foundations were secure. However, a decade later, in 1989, the N.I.H.E.s were raised to the status of independent universities, the first established since the state's foundation.

Meanwhile, the V.E.C. colleges were also experiencing change. The third-level colleges of the City of Dublin V.E.C. underwent significant expansion and reorganisation in the 1970s. The plan of the V.E.C. to have the new college in Ballymun under its control failed to win government approval. However, in April 1976 the V.E.C. reached an agreement with Trinity College, whereby Trinity would confer degrees on students who had successfully completed approved degree courses in the Dublin V.E.C. colleges. Another significant development was the reconstitution of the six colleges of the V.E.C. in 1978 as the Dublin Institute of Technology (D.I.T.). The new regional technical colleges, which had opened during the period 1970–77, operated under the aegis of their local vocational education committees, in conformity with the 1930 vocational education act.[64]

In 1980 the government issued a white paper on educational development with chapter 10 devoted to higher education. The opening paragraphs indicated that the government was determined that its own priorities would be paramount in the allocation of funding, and there were signs of impatience

---

[63] 1979/30 (20 Nov. 1979); 1980/34 (10 Dec. 1980); 1980/25 (14 July 1980); 1980/30 (3 Dec. 1980).
[64] 1930/29 (21 July 1930).

with the H.E.A.'s status as an independent agency between government and the higher education institutions. The announcement that a bill was to be introduced at an early date for the dissolution of the N.U.I. and the establishment of its constituent colleges as independent universities was not carried through. The plan to provide four new regional technical colleges for the greater Dublin area also remained unrealised, a casualty of the serious crisis in the public finances during the early 1980s.[65]

In 1984 the minister for education, Gemma Hussey, published a *Programme for action in education, 1984–87*. Chapter 6 was devoted to higher education. Its proposals reflected a concern to secure greater productivity and economies in higher education. To improve the 'throughput' of students, it was proposed to explore the possibility of a four-term academic year, cutting back four-year degree courses to three years, the introduction of a unit cost system of funding, and a rationalisation of courses within and between institutions. Priority in financial support was to be given to technological studies, and links between higher education and industry were to be intensified. It was also stated that legislation would be brought forward to establish independent universities.[66] Little of this was carried out, but the concern with the cost of higher education and the emphasis on applied studies continued to influence public policy.

Arising from all the initiatives from the early 1960s to the early 1980s, some key features can be summarised. The number of full-time students in state-aided higher education institutions had more than trebled in the twenty-year period from 1964–5, when they numbered 16,327, to 1984–5, when they amounted to 50,945. In 1964–5, 82 per cent of the students were in the universities, but twenty years later this had changed greatly, with the universities accounting for 50 per cent, and the other 50 per cent distributed over more than thirty non-university institutions, which now formed part of the differentiated higher education sector. The proportion of women students had increased from about 30 per cent in 1964–5 to 46 per cent in 1984–5. The number of postgraduate degree students grew from about 650 to 3,094, over the two decades.[67] The percentage of current income derived by the universities from student fees declined from 31 per cent in 1964 to 17 per cent in 1984.

Despite the great expansion in student numbers and the introduction of grant schemes, significant disparities continued to exist in the participation of different social classes in higher education. The rate of admission to higher education in 1980 was 20 per cent of the age cohort, but an analysis of

[65] Government of Ireland, *White paper on educational development* (Prl 9373) (Dublin, 1980), pp 70–84.

[66] Department of education, *Programme for action in education, 1984–1987* (Dublin, 1984).

[67] Commission on higher education, *Report*, i, 26; H.E.A., *Report, accounts and student statistics, 1984–1985* (Dublin, 1986), p. 38.

the socio-economic status of higher education entrants in that year revealed significant inequalities, with certain social groups over-represented and a corresponding under-representation of economically weaker groups. Similar disparities affected participation in the professional faculties; and the geographical location of students' homes was revealed as a factor inhibiting or facilitating participation.[68] Demand for places in the professional faculties led to the introduction of a points system for entry to such faculties in the late 1960s, which has subsequently become a much publicised aspect of entry to higher education. A *numerus clausus* policy was introduced for high-status professional faculties in universities, which led to very keen competition among aspiring applicants. The fields of study followed by students have altered somewhat; in 1980 fewer than 15 per cent of new entrants enrolled in the humanities. Most higher education institutions benefited from new buildings and expanded resources and equipment. Governing structures became more democratic. There was a great increase in numbers of academic staff and a consequent expansion of research. Administration became more professionalised. Student unions helped in the establishment of better facilities and services for students, and new agencies such as the H.E.A., the N.C.E.A., and the C.A.O. proved their value in their respective fields.

The costs involved in this great expansion of higher education, during years of difficulty in the national economy, caused considerable financial strains, and one result was that the state assumed a much more directive role in higher education. Government was anxious to see higher education become more widely available, as well as to ensure that it was responsive to the perceived economic and social goals of society, and that the financial investment in it would yield satisfactory dividends for the public good. The establishment of the non-university sector gave the government its opportunity to assume a more direct role; and influences and pressures were applied that in turn affected the policies pursued within the universities. Subjects that received priority support were technology, engineering, business studies, electronics, information technology, and applied science. Institutions were encouraged to establish links with industry, and did so, as well as seeking sponsorship from the private sector. Technology parks and ancillary industries began to be established on campuses. The utilitarian emphasis raised concern among academics that pure research together with the humanities and social sciences were being undervalued. Such concerns were part of an international pattern, for most western governments adopted similar approaches. Overall, by 1984, Irish higher education had been transformed from the condition described by the commission on higher education in the

---

[68] Rates of admission varied considerably by county, with the rate for Carlow (29%) being twice as high as that for Laois (14.5%): the national average was 20% (Patrick Clancy, *Participation in higher education: a national survey* (Dublin, 1982), pp 52–7).

early 1960s. The system had expanded and diversified impressively, a new dynamism and innovatory spirit was in evidence, and a confidence existed about future prospects for development.

THE early 1960s was a period in which major appraisals of higher education were undertaken in these islands. In the Republic the commission on higher education was at work and in Britain the Robbins committee presented its major report in 1963. Later that year the committee on higher education in Northern Ireland (the Lockwood committee) was established. Its terms of reference were 'to review the facilities for university and higher education in Northern Ireland, having regard to the report of the Robbins committee and to make recommendations'.[69] The committee had completed its work by 1965, in what was the first comprehensive survey of arrangements for higher education undertaken in Northern Ireland. From the outset the committee indicated how influenced it was by the Robbins report. 'We have accepted the main aims and principles of the Robbins committee and we have based our proposals for the future development of higher education in Northern Ireland on them.' Among these guidelines was an acceptance of the 'pool of talent' idea, whereby it was suggested that it was in society's interest to draw on the talents of all citizens by making courses in higher education available to all who were qualified by ability and attainment to pursue them and who wished to do so. As a further guiding principle the Lockwood committee set out a view of the university that sought a 'compromise' between the traditional role of disinterested pursuit of knowledge and a harnessing of the university's activities to the economic betterment of society: 'They [the universities] must now seek a viable and vigorous compromise between, on the one hand, the pursuit of truth and the disinterested gaining, preservation, and dissemination of knowledge and, on the other, responsibility, through the professions and industry and commerce, to communities in which they exist and to the wider interests of society and the world at large.'[70]

One of the central questions addressed by the Lockwood committee was whether a second university should be established in Northern Ireland and, if so, where it should be located. The committee strongly recommended the setting up of a second university and added, 'an immediate decision to establish it is, therefore, in our view essential'. However, such an institution should not simply be a duplicate of Queen's University. The latter, in the committee's view, should in the future place a strong emphasis on technology and engineering in addition to its provision for medicine, law, and the arts. It should also extend its postgraduate courses. The new university should con-

---

[69] *Report of the committee on higher education in Northern Ireland* (Lockwood committee) [Cmd 475] (Belfast, 1965), p. 21.
[70] Ibid., p. 66.

centrate on the biological and allied sciences, and on agriculture, which should be transferred from Queen's. The proposed educational spectrum for the new institution was set out: the biological and related pure and applied sciences; environmental and social sciences; the humanities, and teacher education.

Three main locations were already in competition for the proposed university—Derry, Armagh, and Coleraine. The committee's decision to recommend Coleraine became a most controversial one. Nationalist and catholic opinion considered that Derry had a compelling claim, and the decision was received as a blow to that entire community. A further recommendation of the committee—that Magee College in Derry be discontinued—was regarded as another snub to the city. Lockwood envisaged that there would be a need for places for about 13,000 university students in Northern Ireland, 7,000 in Queen's, and between 5,000 and 6,000 in the new institution at Coleraine, which was to be called the New University of Ulster.

Another major recommendation of the Lockwood committee was that a new institution—an 'Ulster College'—should be set up in the Belfast area, to include a new regional college of technology, as well as a cluster of existing non-university colleges. The committee saw great merit in such an amalgamation, which ideally should be on the same campus. The Ulster College would be multifunctional and provide a wide range of courses at non-degree level. The existing teacher-training colleges were to be retitled 'colleges of education' and become linked to the universities. The committee also urged the setting up of machinery to coordinate the work of the higher education institutions.

The government responded quickly to the Lockwood report and accepted most of its recommendations. In the most controversial area, opposition to Coleraine as the location for the new university was resisted, but government demurred from the recommendation to discontinue Magee College. Rather, the possibility of incorporating it within the new university was to be further explored.[71] Queen's University was not neglected. The agriculture faculty was not transferred to the new university; and considerable capital expenditure was put into the expansion of Queen's in the 1960s, as student numbers increased from 4,135 in 1963–4 to 6,513 in 1969–70. Queen's was integrated into the British student application system, U.C.C.A., in 1967. Also, in 1965, responsibility for the provision of university finance was transferred from the ministry of finance to the ministry of education, which continued to receive advice from the U.G.C.

Building went ahead on the new university site at Coleraine, so that the first students, 392 in all, were enrolled in October 1968. This was the first

---

[71] Government of Northern Ireland, *Higher education in Northern Ireland* [Cmd 480] (Belfast, 1965), p. 2.

new 'green field' university foundation on the island of Ireland since the mid nineteenth century. The New University of Ulster received its charter in September 1970, and in October of that year Magee College became an integral part of the university. Two years later, in 1972, Magee lost its degree students to the Coleraine campus, but was itself reconstituted as the Institute for Continuing Education. The number of students at the New University rose quickly in the early years, so that when part-time students were added to full-time students the number reached 1,384 full-time equivalents in 1970–71. However, enrolment through the 1970s never reached expectations. The highest total, 1,913, was recorded in 1976–7, after which a decline set in with numbers falling to 1,836 by 1980–81.[72] The Lockwood committee target for that date had been 5,000 to 6,000 students.

The progress of the Ulster College was more impressive during these years. The Ulster College act of 1968[73] set in place the necessary legislative framework. The new regional technical college became the central institution on the campus at Jordanstown, about seven miles north of Belfast. Linked with it were the Belfast College of Art, the Belfast College of Domestic Science, and the Ulster College of Physical Education. Many advanced courses were also transferred to the Ulster College from the Belfast College of Technology and the Belfast College of Commerce. When the Ulster College opened in September 1971 it had the equivalent of 1,464 full-time students, of whom 76 per cent were at the higher education level. By 1980–81 the student body had grown to 5,686, of whom 93 per cent were at higher education level. In 1977 the Ulster College had its degrees validated and conferred by the Council for National Academic Awards (C.N.A.A.). In 1978 the official name of the Ulster College was changed to the Ulster Polytechnic and it continued to display 'commendable energy and initiative'.[74]

Northern Ireland students also benefited from the availability of courses of the Open University (O.U.), which had been established in 1969. Funded by the ministry of education, by 1971–2 the O.U. had 1,162 students in Northern Ireland. A number of study centres were established and in 1974 Northern Ireland became a separate region of the O.U. with its own regional director. By that year student numbers had grown to 1,521, a figure that remained fairly constant down to the end of this period.

Teacher education was an issue of recurring public concern in the period 1960–84. By 1963–4 there were over 2,000 teacher-education students, of whom almost three-quarters were women. The Lockwood committee had recommended closer links between the colleges of education and the univer-

---

[72] Higher education review group (Chilver), *The future of higher education in Northern Ireland* (Belfast, 1982), table 8.2, p. 148.
[73] 1968, c. 14 (4 July 1968).
[74] *The future of higher education* (Chilver), pp 5, 87.

sities, and in 1968 the Institute of Education at Queen's University was established and the degree of B.Ed. for teachers was introduced. At the New University of Ulster the education centre became a key component from the outset. In 1971 the Lelièvre committee was set up to report on the education, initial training, and probation of teachers. Its recommendations (December 1973) were influenced by the 1972 report of the James committee in England. The Lelièvre report gave its backing to the establishment of an all-graduate teaching profession. It set out a wide range of proposals on course content and duration, the induction of teachers, establishment of teacher tutors, the development of teacher centres, and the setting up of a panel of supply teachers. In line with the James report, it laid great stress on the importance of in-service education for teachers. It also recommended the institution of a council for the education of teachers.[75] However, little of this agenda was achieved. In 1975 a working party submitted a report on 'a teaching council for Northern Ireland', but the department of education did not adopt the proposal. What it did establish, in 1976, was an advisory council on the supply of teachers. This was at a time when the decline in the pupil population was reducing the demand for teachers, and limitations were being placed on numbers allowed into teacher-education courses. The problems became acute, and the minister for education requested the review group on higher education (Chilver committee), set up in 1978, to present an interim report focusing on teacher education. The report was published in May 1980, and stated: 'As a general principle teacher education should be conducted in multi-disciplinary institutions where future students can be educated together alongside and mix academically and socially with students in other disciplines.'[76]

The review group recommended 'a consolidation of present arrangements for teacher education'. It urged the amalgamation of St Joseph's and St Mary's colleges of education with Queen's University education department and Stranmillis College to form the Belfast Centre for Teacher Education. The three partners should operate from a single site, the Stranmillis College site, 'while retaining safeguards for the distinctive ethos of each of the colleges of education'. The proposals were opposed by the churches, still very sensitive to the issue of denominational teacher education, and they were not adopted by government, although St Joseph's and St Mary's colleges did amalgamate. With the decline in numbers of students studying to become teachers, most institutions developed courses for in-service teacher education.

[75] *Report of the committee on the education, initial training, and probation of teachers* (Belfast, 1973), pp 46–8.
[76] Higher education review group (Chilver), *The future structure of teacher education in Northern Ireland* (Belfast, 1980), p. 65.

In 1965 the Lockwood committee had recommended the establishment of a higher-education coordinating mechanism, but nothing had been done. An advisory committee on the coordination of higher education, set up in 1974 with representatives from the ministry and the institutions, did not work satisfactorily. The student participation projections of the Lockwood committee had not been borne out. The committee had envisaged a full-time student enrolment in Northern Ireland higher education institutions of between 19,000 and 21,000 by 1980–81: the reality turned out to be 13,600. The political strife that had broken out in the late 1960s created a difficult climate for normal developments. Very few external students came to study in Northern Ireland colleges, while large numbers of indigenous students studied outside Northern Ireland; in 1980–81 the figure was about 5,000.

In 1978 the government set up a review group (the Chilver committee) to review the broad field of higher education in Northern Ireland for the 1980s and 1990s. As a guiding principle the review group argued that 'there is a need for higher education in Northern Ireland to become more deeply involved in industry, commerce, the professions, and the general life of the community'. One of the main questions addressed in the review group's report was the future of the New University of Ulster, which had failed to grow as planned. Having examined the relevant issues, the report concluded: 'The New University of Ulster has not achieved the role which was envisaged when it was set up in 1968.' It went on to state: 'The arguments for closure or continuance of N.U.U. are finely balanced. After the most careful consideration, we believe that—on balance—N.U.U. should be retained but only provided the university implements fundamental changes in its policies and activities in ways which lead to the development of a new style of institution.'[77] The way ahead was seen in catering for mature students, engaging in distance education and in activities seen as more relevant to the needs of Northern Ireland. The university should lose most of its degree work. Queen's University, on the other hand, should develop further along existing lines, paying close attention to attaining the highest standards and becoming more innovative in its traditional subject areas. The Ulster Polytechnic was praised for its energy and initiative in developing a wide range of courses, and it was urged to consolidate and place more emphasis on vocational courses. The Open University was urged to do more to recruit students who resided at a distance from the major educational institutions. The report recommended the establishment of an independent coordinating body to advise the minister on the overall requirements for higher education.

The government gave its reaction to the Chilver report very quickly because of the uncertainty of the issues concerning the new university. It took a more radical approach than the review group and decided on a merger of the new university with the polytechnic to form a new university institution. The talents of the two institutions were thought to be complementary, and the merger was expected to give rise to a clear alternative to Queen's that would have a 'distinctively practical and applied emphasis'.[78] The planned university would operate on three campuses: Coleraine; Magee College, Derry; and Jordanstown. The staff of the new university opposed the plan, but (faced with a government ultimatum on withdrawal of funds) accepted the inevitable. A steering committee was appointed forthwith to prepare for the merger. The new university began to function in autumn 1984 under the title 'The University of Ulster'. Thus, after two decades of much debate and varied initiatives in the higher education system, the end result was two universities, with different emphases, and considerable coordination and interlinkage between all the higher education institutions in Northern Ireland.

[78] Government of Northern Ireland, *Higher education in Northern Ireland: the future structure* (Belfast, 1982), p. 10.

CHAPTER XXVI

Emigration and immigration in the twentieth century: an overview

J. J. SEXTON

UNTIL relatively recently in its demographic history, Ireland was unique among European countries in experiencing almost continuous population decline through emigration over a long period.[1] Table 1, which gives population totals for the period from 1841 to 1993, shows that the population of the entire island stood at over 8 million in 1841. By 1851, because of the outflows and deaths associated with the great famine it had fallen to just over 6.5 million. By the beginning of the twentieth century it had fallen to just under 4.5 million. Thereafter the decline continued, but at a much slower pace. By the mid 1920s the population of the island had fallen to about 4.2 million and it remained at approximately this level till the early 1960s. Thereafter it began to rise again to an estimated total population level for the whole island of nearly 5.2 million by 1993.

Turning specifically to the trends for the Republic of Ireland, the figures in table 1 show that in the aftermath of the famine during the second half of the nineteenth century the population of the twenty-six counties fell by over 50 per cent from 6.5 million in 1841 to about 3.2 million at the turn of the century. When national independence was achieved in 1922, the population had fallen to about 3 million and it remained at or slightly below this level till the early 1950s. The period 1951 to 1961 was again characterised by very high emigration which precipitated a further significant fall in the population; the lowest level ever recorded, 2,818,000, occurred in 1961.

With the advent of increased economic growth in the 1960s, the pace of emigration from the Republic began to diminish. During this decade the net outflow declined to a level lower than the natural increase in the population (see table 2a) and the population began to rise. The subsequent decade of the

---

[1] For detailed consideration of emigration in the nineteenth and early twentieth centuries, see above, v, 562–622; vi, 606–52.

TABLE I. *Population of Ireland since 1841* (in thousands)

Year	Ireland (26 counties)	Northern Ireland (6 counties)	Ireland total
1841[1]	6,529	1,649	8,178
1851[1]	5,112	1,443	6,555
1861	4,402	1,396	5,798
1871	4,053	1,359	5,412
1881	3,870	1,304	5,174
1891	3,469	1,236	4,705
1901	3,222	1,237	4,459
1911	3,140	1,251	4,391
1926	2,972	1,257	4,229
1936	2,968	1,280[2]	4,248
1946	2,955	n.a.	n.a.
1951	2,961	1,371	4,332
1961	2,818	1,425	4,243
1971	2,978	1,536	4,514
1981	3,443	1,532	4,975
1986	3,541	1,567	5,107
1987	3,546	1,575	5,121
1988	3,531	1,578	5,109
1989	3,510	1,583	5,093
1990	3,506	1,589	5,095
1991	3,526	1,601	5,127
1992	3,549	1,618	5,167
1993	3,563	1,632	5,195

[1]Armed forces excluded. [2]The figure for Northern Ireland relates to 1937.
Sources: *Census Ire., 1991*, i, 30, Pl 9877 (Dublin, 1993); C.S.O., *Economic series, April 1995* (Dublin, 1995), p. 11; Registrar general's office, N.I.

1970s was even more remarkable in that a confluence of events, both economic and social,[2] caused a reversal of the traditional pattern of emigration. The outflow fell significantly and former emigrants began to return in substantial numbers, with their families. As a result, an overall net inflow of population materialised. This, when combined with a rising natural increase, caused the population to increase rapidly. By 1981 the total population had increased to 3,443,000, nearly half a million (or almost 16 per cent) higher than the level ten years earlier.

[2] These circumstances are described more fully below.

TABLE 2a.   *Components of population change for Republic of Ireland (26 counties) for intercensal periods, 1901–91*

Intercensal period	Population change	Natural increase (births less deaths)	Net migration
Annual averages			
1901–11	−8,214	17,940	−26,154
1911–26	−11,180	15,822	−27,002
1926–36	−357	16,318	−16,675
1936–46	−1,331	17,380	−18,711
1946–51	+1,119	25,503	−24,384
1951–61	−14,226	26,652	−40,877
1961–71	+15,991	29,442	−13,451
1971–81	+46,516	36,127	+10,389
1981–91	+8,231	28,837	−20,606
Rates per 1,000 average population			
1901–11	−2.6	5.6	−8.2
1911–26	−3.7	5.2	−8.8
1926–36	−0.1	5.5	−5.6
1936–46	−0.4	5.9	−6.3
1946–51	+0.4	8.6	−8.2
1951–61	−4.9	9.2	−14.1
1961–71	+5.5	10.2	−4.6
1971–81	+14.5	11.3	+3.2
1981–91	+2.4	8.3	−5.9

Sources: *Commission on emigration, reports* (1954); *Census Ire.*, 1991, i.

The recession of the early 1980s caused emigration from the Republic to reemerge, gradually at first, but on an increasing scale as the decade progressed. The annual average net outflow throughout the decade was nearly 21,000 (or 6 per 1,000 population) and while this was still lower than the natural increase, it caused a deceleration in population growth. By 1991 the population had increased by only a further 80,000 to 3,526,000, some 2.5 per cent higher than the 1981 level. The early 1990s involved yet another change as net emigration virtually disappeared. While this was partly the result of a reasonably creditable growth performance, it was mainly caused by a deterioration in external labour markets, particularly in the U.K. This had the effect of deterring many potential emigrants from leaving and induced many of those abroad to return home. These changes caused a modest acceleration in population growth. In the period between 1991 and 1994 the total population increased by nearly 45,000 to reach a level of 3,571,000 in the latter year.

TABLE 2b. *Components of population change for Northern Ireland (6 counties) for intercensal periods, 1901–91*

Intercensal period	Population change	Natural increase (births less deaths)	Net migration
Annual averages			
1901–11	1,358	7,900	−6,542
1911–26	402	7,574	−7,172
1926–37	2,108	7,349	−5,241
1937–51	6,513	11,317	−4,805
1951–61	5,412	14,635	−9,223
1961–71	11,102	17,356	−6,254
1971–81	−387	10,755	−11,142
1981–91	6,900	11,506	−4,606
Rates per 1,000 average population			
1901–11	1.1	6.4	−5.3
1911–26	0.3	6.0	−5.7
1926–37	1.7	5.8	−4.1
1937–51	4.9	8.5	−3.6
1951–61	3.9	10.5	−6.6
1961–71	7.5	11.7	−4.2
1971–81	−0.3	7.0	−7.3
1981–91	2.9	7.4	−4.5

Source: C.S.O., *Statistical abstract, 1994* (Pn 1044) (Dublin, 1995), based on data from the registrar general's office, N.I.

The population trends for Northern Ireland are somewhat different. While the six counties of what is now Northern Ireland also suffered substantial population losses through emigration in the second half of the nineteenth century, these were not on the same relative scale as those in the rest of the country. The population decreased from 1.65 million in 1841 to 1.24 million in 1901, a reduction of almost 25 per cent or almost half of the decline in the twenty-six counties. Thereafter the population of Northern Ireland stabilised and actually showed significant increases in the period between the mid 1920s and the early 1970s, largely because the Northern Ireland economy had a sizeable industrial base which expanded significantly during this period (see below). By 1971 the Northern Ireland population had risen to 1.54 million. It remained constant at approximately this level till the late 1980s, when it began to rise again, to reach an estimated 1,632,000 by 1993.

The variation in population trends between the two parts of the country can be attributed primarily to differences in the relative extent of emigration, even though this in turn relates essentially to differences in economic performance. An examination of the data in tables 2a and 2b (especially the rates per 1,000 average population) show that emigration was consistently of a lower order of magnitude in Northern Ireland from the beginning of the period under consideration till the 1960s. In contrast the data relating to the natural increase in the population for both jurisdictions are very similar over this entire time span.

While the initial surge in Irish emigration in the nineteenth century was linked to massive crop failures, its continuance thereafter can be attributed to economic and social causes.[3] To put it in its simplest terms, the primary reason for continued Irish emigration was an inability to generate a level of economic growth sufficient to absorb an expanding population into employment. Allied with this, however, was the fact that the potential Irish emigrant had relatively easy access to developed external labour markets, which, for the most part, offered ample employment opportunities. Thus there were 'push' and 'pull' factors involved.

By the middle of the nineteenth century Ireland was one of the most densely populated countries in Europe. This was partly owing to the use of the potato as a basic food which, in Irish climatic conditions, could be produced in considerable volume from relatively small areas of land. However, when viewed in retrospect, the sole dependence by so many on this source meant that the great famine of the late 1840s, which was precipitated by the destruction of the crop by potato blight, was a disaster waiting to happen. While this event was the trigger that caused emigration to escalate, subsequent socio-economic conditions ensured that it continued. Ireland's experience during the industrial revolution may not have been as bleak as it has been painted,[4] but the country possessed virtually none of the natural resources (e.g. coal) which were then necessary to achieve very high levels of economic growth. The country remained largely agrarian in character, with the result that the potential for employment expansion was quite limited. This, when coupled with the high birth rate, ensured a continuation of the population outflow.[5] Broadly speaking this situation prevailed till the late 1950s.

---

[3] Above, v, 562–622; vi, 606–52.

[4] For a discussion of the influence of nationalist historiography on the economic history of the eighteenth and nineteenth centuries, see L. M. Cullen, 'Irish economic history: fact and myth' in L. M. Cullen (ed.), *The formation of the Irish economy* (Cork, 1969), pp 113–24.

[5] However, a contributory factor during this period was the reduction in the cost of travel. Before and during the great famine the cost of a passage to America prevented the poorest sections of the population from leaving Ireland. But with the introduction of steam vessels and the fall in price of a transatlantic crossing, as well as the flow of money from family and friends in America to assist the emigration of those staying behind, this constraint diminished. For a further discussion on this aspect see Cormac Ó Gráda and B. M. Walsh, *Irish emigration: patterns, causes and effects* (Dublin, 1992).

In Ulster, however, the development of textiles (especially linen) and ship-building and associated industries in the latter half of the nineteenth century provided a basis for economic expansion that contributed significantly to reducing the migratory outflows. At a later stage the continued growth of those sectors contributed to the modest increases in population that occurred during the first half of the twentieth century. Emigration rose during the 1950s in response to postwar recovery opportunities in Britain and the United States, Canada, and Australia. It dropped in the 1960s, which was a decade of inward investment and the development of new industries such as artificial fibres. However, by this time the older staple industries were in decline.[6] The simultaneous outbreak of civil unrest in Northern Ireland in the late 1960s and the subsequent prolonged 'troubles' were further contributing factors that gave rise to a static population at a time when the population of the Republic was growing rapidly, especially in the 1970s.

The destinations to which Irish migrants have tended to go have changed significantly over time. The large numbers of emigrants who left in the nineteenth century, and in the early part of the twentieth century, went mainly to North America.[7] Figures on gross outward movements from the twenty-six counties over the period from 1901 to 1931 (given in table 3) indicate that nearly 90 per cent of emigrants during this period went to the United States. However, these flows came to an abrupt end at the beginning of the 1930s because of the great depression that followed the stock market crash of 1929. Employment opportunities in the United States dried up, and not only did the outflow cease but many former emigrants returned. From this point onwards the great majority of Irish emigrants headed for the United Kingdom. These flows received a further stimulus during the years of the second world war as large numbers of (mainly male) Irish took advantage of the employment opportunities afforded by the British war effort. The estimates given in table 3 show that nearly 175,000 Irish nationals migrated to Great Britain between 1941 and 1946, with (understandably) negligible flows to other parts of the world, in a period of war.

Figures for the immediate post-second-world-war period indicate that between 1946 and 1951 nearly 83 per cent of Irish emigrants went to the United Kingdom. The British census of 1966 recorded the largest ever number of Irish-born in Britain.[8] By the mid 1980s, however, while the U.K. was still the most popular destination for Irish emigrants, they now tended to travel to a wider range of countries. External migration figures for the Republic published by the Central Statistics Office in May 1994 (see table 4) indicate that over 60 per cent of those who emigrated between 1987

[6] Paul Compton, *Demographic review Northern Ireland 1995* (Belfast, 1995), p. 17.
[7] Above, v, 568–9; vi, 608–9, 641.
[8] Liam Ryan, 'Irish emigration to Britain since world war II' in Richard Kearney (ed.), *Migrations: the Irish at home and abroad* (Dublin, 1990), pp 45–67: 49.

TABLE 3.   *Estimated gross migratory outflows from the Republic of Ireland (26 counties) since 1901* (thousands)

Period	Destination			Total gross outflow	Net migration
	Great Britain	U.S.A.	Other overseas		
1901–11	14	240	12	266	−262
1911–22	9	97	10	116	n.a.
1926–31	n.a.	104	15	n.a.	−123
1931–6	n.a.	2	2	n.a.	−44
1936–41	n.a.	3	2	n.a.	−57
1941–6	173	—	—	173	−130
1946–51	119	17	8	144	−120
1951–61	n.a.		68	n.a.	−409
1961–71	n.a.		49	n.a.	−135
1971–81	155		21	176	+104
1981–91	263	62	111	436	−206

Source: J. J. Sexton, B. M. Walsh, D. Hannan, and D. McMahon, *The economic and social implications of emigration* (N.E.S.C. report no. 90, Dublin, 1991). The sources used in the N.E.S.C. study were the reports of the commission on emigration (1954), the C.S.O. annual *Statistical abstract* (various issues), and data derived from censuses and labour force surveys. The N.E.S.C. report should be consulted for further details of the compilations involved.

and 1993 went to the U.K., over 10 per cent to other E.U. countries, some 15 per cent to the United States, and a similar proportion to other destinations. A notable feature of these data is the increasing share accounted for by E.U. countries other than the U.K. This was 21 per cent in 1993, compared with less than 8 per cent in 1987. And within the U.K. changes have taken place in the regional destinations for migrants, as work on Northern Ireland has shown. Historically, a core–periphery relationship brought emigrants to greater London, the inner south-east, the west midlands, greater Manchester, Merseyside, and (more particularly for protestants) Scotland. By the 1990s, reflecting changes in the British economy, the south of England was drawing the bulk of emigrants. Northern Ireland was not the only U.K. region to be affected by the pull of the south: the population of Scotland and parts of the north of England actually declined in the 1970s and 1980s as migrants moved south.[9]

[9] Compton, *Demographic review*, pp 22–3.

803

TABLE 4. *Republic of Ireland: estimated out-migration and in-migration classified by country of destination/origin, 1987–93 (thousands)*

Year (ending April)	Out-migration					In-migration					Net migration
	U.K.	Rest of E.U.	U.S.A.	Rest of world	Total	U.K.	Rest of E.U.	U.S.A.	Rest of world	Total	
1987	21.8	3.1	9.9	5.4	40.2	8.1	2.2	3.0	4.0	17.2	−23.0
1988	40.2	2.8	7.9	10.2	61.1	9.9	2.6	3.4	3.4	19.2	−41.9
1989	48.4	3.9	8.2	10.0	70.6	14.2	3.6	3.1	5.8	26.7	−43.9
1990	35.8	5.1	7.7	7.6	56.3	17.6	5.0	3.9	6.9	33.3	−22.9
1991	23.0	3.1	4.8	4.4	35.3	18.7	4.2	4.3	6.1	33.3	−2.0
1992	17.3	7.7	3.8	5.9	34.6	22.7	6.6	4.6	6.9	40.8	+6.1
1993	17.1	7.3	5.9	6.0	36.3	17.5	6.7	5.0	5.7	34.8	−1.5

Source: C.S.O., *Annual population and migration estimates, 1987–1994* (Dublin, 1994).

It is clear thus far that the Irish expatriate community underwent a very substantial expansion throughout the nineteenth century. By the early 1900s it was spread across the globe, especially in English-speaking countries, and most particularly in the United States. Table 5 gives data derived from population censuses in other countries of destination from post-famine times to the present day. Already by 1871 the total number of Irish-born persons in the countries in question was over 3 million, mainly as a result of the very large migratory flows to the United States. Thereafter, as the level of emigration from Ireland decreased (and as a result of ageing and mortality among former emigrants) the expatriate community began to decline. By 1901 the total had fallen to just over 2.5 million, of which over 1.5 million were in the United States, 100,000 in Canada, over 180,000 in Australia, and 630,000 in Great Britain.

Both the size and the geographical distribution of this community changed greatly during the twentieth century. The final column of figures in table 5 shows that by 1991 the total number of Irish-born persons residing abroad had fallen to 1.14 million, a decrease of 55 per cent compared with 1901. This was mainly owing to a very large decline in the United States, where the numbers had fallen to below 190,000. The numbers in Canada and Australia had also decreased, albeit less dramatically, to about 40,000 and 80,000 respectively. However, the size of the expatriate community in Great

TABLE 5. *Population of Ireland (32 counties) and geographical distribution of Irish-born persons, 1871–1991* (thousands)

Country	1871	1901	1991
Population in Ireland	5,412	4,459	5,127
Irish-born people living in:			
U.S.A.	1,856	1,615	187[1]
Canada	223	102	42[2]
Australia	214	184	77
U.K.	774	632	837
Total for countries listed	3,067	2,533	1,143

[1]The figure for the U.S.A. relates to 1990. It involves an estimate for those born in Northern Ireland (on the basis of 1980 census data).
[2]The 1991 population total for Canada involves an estimate for those born in Northern Ireland.
Sources: Donal Garvey, 'The history of migration flows in the Republic of Ireland' in *Population Trends*, xxix (1985), pp 22–30; above, v, 609, vi, 640; tabulations provided by the U.S. bureau of the census, Statistics Canada, the Australian bureau of statistics and the office of population censuses and surveys, London.

Britain rose by about a third between 1901 and 1991, from 630,000 to 840,000. These changes were, of course, consistent with the trend of migration throughout the twentieth century, both in regard to the magnitudes in different periods (which were considerably smaller than in the 1800s) and also the changed pattern of destination outlined above.

The preceding analysis covered only those Irish-born persons who were resident in the countries referred to, even if these were obviously the most important in numerical terms. There are significant numbers of Irish resident in other countries. Information published by the E.U. Commission[10] indicates that in E.F.T.A. countries other than the U.K. (i.e. current E.U. member states plus Norway, Switzerland, and Iceland) there were about 30,000 persons of Irish nationality resident on 1 January 1991. The largest number (over 10,000) was in Germany. When this additional element is considered together with the figures in table 5, it suggests a total at or about 1.2 million Irish-born persons resident outside Ireland in 1991. It is not possible to estimate by how much this total should be increased if account were taken of Irish persons residing in countries other than those covered (e.g. in Africa, Asia, the Middle East, etc.).

The existence of this external network (especially in earlier periods when it was much larger) meant that many emigrants were assured of assistance on arriving in the host country in the form of employment and accommodation, and in a more general way in facilitating their assimilation into the host societies. This constituted a powerful attraction, irrespective of the state of the Irish economy, and gave rise to what is termed the 'traditional' aspect of Irish emigration.[11]

In earlier periods emigration was a singularly permanent event for most emigrants. The fact that most of them went to North America and other distant countries, had few means, and aspired to unskilled work, meant that there was little prospect of even a temporary return. The difficulties and costs associated with long-distance sea travel imposed further constraints. The most that the majority of emigrants could aspire to was a once-in-a-lifetime return visit, if that. The pattern began to change in the post-famine period when fares fell, allowing some migrants to return, mostly as visitors.[12] Subsequently, further changes have taken place. As the analysis will show, since the 1970s emigrants have become better equipped educationally and can take advantage of better job opportunities. The facilities afforded by the speed, convenience, and relatively inexpensive nature of air travel, means that the emigrant is, for the most part, a highly mobile person who tends to return to Ireland at fairly frequent intervals, either for holidays or leisure

[10] Eurostat, *Migration statistics, 1994.*
[11] Even in the economically buoyant 1970s, when there was a sizeable net inflow of population, an estimated 176,000 persons migrated from the Republic alone.
[12] Above, vi, 633–4.

purposes, or for intermittent periods of work. This greater mobility has contributed to the fact that, when viewed collectively, emigrants are now more responsive to changes in relative economic conditions, a feature that helps to explain some of the volatility evident in migration flows in recent years. It has also caused an increase in the extent of ethnic tourism.[13]

A striking feature of Irish emigration affecting both parts of the country has been the presence of religious differentials. Thanks to historically higher marital fertility among catholics, the relative size of the catholic population in Northern Ireland has grown from *c.*33.5 per cent in 1926 to *c.*38.5 per cent in 1981, with most of the growth taking place since 1951. This proportion would have been higher had it not been for the greater propensity of catholics to emigrate. While firm figures do not exist, estimates made in the 1960s for the intercensal periods 1937–51 and 1951–61 suggested that with only about one-third of the population catholics accounted for 55–8 per cent of the emigration. Subsequently, in the intercensal periods 1961–71 and 1971–81 catholics accounted for around 60 per cent of emigrants. Despite these emigration rates, higher fertility among catholics would still have outweighed losses through emigration, bringing into prospect the likelihood of a catholic majority in Northern Ireland. However, from the late 1960s catholic marital fertility began to fall, and although there is still a gap between catholic and protestant fertility (the latter, as well as the former, is higher than the U.K. average) the two levels have tended to converge, thus calling into question earlier predictions of an imminent catholic majority. Nevertheless, given the volatility of emigration rates, the future demographic balance is difficult to predict with any confidence.[14]

In the Republic too, emigration patterns in the twentieth century have revealed religious differentials. The most striking instance was the very large outflow of protestants in the period when independence was being achieved. Taking the Church of Ireland alone (whose members made up about 80 per cent of all protestants in the state), between 1911 and 1926 numbers fell by over one-third, from *c.*249,500 to 164,200. The drop was only partly caused by an exodus of personnel linked with the British army, civil service, and police; there can be little doubt that the main factor was a sense of apprehension among some in the protestant communities arising from the transition to independence and the upheavals that attended that event. In the two decades

---

[13] The proportion of total expenditure in the Republic by overseas visitors who came 'to visit relatives' in 1994 was 24 per cent. This proportion exceeded 30 per cent in the late 1980s, after periods of high emigration. For further details see the C.S.O. statistical release *Tourism and travel 1994* (Dublin, 1995).

[14] Denis P. Barritt and Charles F. Carter, *The Northern Ireland problem: a study in group relations* (2nd ed., London, 1972), pp 107–8; Paul Compton and John Coward, *Fertility and family planning in Northern Ireland* (Avebury, 1989), pp 6, 60, 80, 214; E. F. Jardine, 'Demographic structure in Northern Ireland and its implications for constitutional preference' in *Stat. Soc. Ire. Jn.*, xxvii, pt 1 (1994), pp 193–220.

after 1926, when the catholic population stabilised and even showed a slight increase, protestant numbers continued to decline at about double their rate in the half century before 1911. In part, this decline was owing to a lower marriage rate and lower fertility than that of catholics, but southern protestants also continued to have higher emigration rates than catholics, and emigration was particularly marked among young adults.

Down to the 1950s emigration was the main cause of the decline in the southern protestant population. However, emigration in the Republic as a whole declined in the 1960s, and protestant emigration rates fell below catholic levels. But since their death rate remained well above their birth rate, there was little prospect of growth in their numbers. A relevant factor here was the impact of Pope Pius X's *Ne temere* decree concerning marriages between catholics and non-catholics, which came into effect in 1908. In such cases written promises were required from both partners that children would be raised as catholics. In 1970 the requirement was relaxed, though not abandoned. A study for the Forum for Peace and Reconciliation found that 'mixed marriages' had a profound effect on birth numbers and rates associated with the minority religious communities in the Republic and was a significant factor contributing to the decline in numbers.[15] Notwithstanding these difficulties, the decline in numbers of the minority religious communities began to level off in the 1970s, and the 1991 census recorded an increase over 1981 from 128,000 to 148,000, even though this rise related to what might be called 'non-traditional' religious groupings, other than the Church of Ireland, presbyterians, and methodists.[16]

TURNING to gender differences, if Irish migration flows are viewed over a long period there does not appear to be any material difference in the balance between males and females, even though this can vary substantially from time to time.[17] The outflows in the 1980s, for example, involved a significant majority of males, principally because throughout that decade the prospects for females in the Irish labour market were relatively more advantageous.[18] In the 1960s, on the other hand, females constituted the majority among emigrants. In Northern Ireland females traditionally showed a greater propensity for emigration than males; this has become more marked since the mid 1970s.

[15] Above, vi, 119; J. J. Sexton and Richard O'Leary, 'Factors affecting population decline in minority religious communities in the Republic of Ireland' in *Building trust in Ireland* (Studies commissioned by the Forum for Peace and Reconciliation, Belfast, 1996), pp 255–332.

[16] *Commission on emigration and other population problems 1948–54: reports* (Pr 2541) (Dublin, 1954), pp 200–01; Kurt Bowen, *Protestants in a catholic state* (Dublin, 1983), ch. 2; *Census of Ireland, 1991, v: religion* (Pn 2034) (Dublin, 1995), p. 8.

[17] Above, v, 573–4, vi, 612–13. For the impact of emigration on the age and gender of the remaining population, see above, p. 75.

[18] If the position is viewed in terms of net outflows, the total for males between 1981 and 1991 was nearly 30 per cent higher than that for females.

As for age, Irish migration has tended to apply predominantly to young people, that is, those aged under 25 years, even though when economic conditions in Ireland are severely depressed emigration can extend to the immediately older age groups. In the latter circumstances the emigration flows can include significant numbers of children as more family groups migrate. Figures quoted in the 1991 N.E.S.C. study on emigration indicate that over the period from the middle of the nineteenth century to the late 1940s up to 50 per cent of Irish emigrants were aged between 15 and 24 years. More recent data suggest that this proportion has increased. Central Statistics Office (C.S.O.) gross outflow estimates for the period from 1987 to 1993 (see table 6) reveal that over 56 per cent of emigrants from the Republic were in this age category, with a further 30 per cent accounted for by the 25 to 44 age group.[19]

In earlier periods the traditional stereotype of the Irish emigrant characterised a person who was largely unskilled, or at best possessed rudimentary manual skills. The information available for past decades would appear to support this view. Data given in the 1954 commission on emigration report indicates that in the period from the early 1920s to 1950 over 70 per cent of male emigrants were unskilled or came from an agricultural background. Nearly 90 per cent of female migrants were classified in activities related to domestic service and the hotel and catering industry.

The circumstances that fostered emigration in the early decades after independence had much in common with those in the previous half century. Munster continued to be the province of greatest emigration, although figures for Connacht were also high. In all of the intercensal periods 1926–36, 1936–46, and 1946–51, over half the total net emigration came from just six counties: Cork, Kerry, Galway, Mayo, and Donegal constituted five of the six in every period, with Tipperary making the sixth in 1926–36, and Limerick in the two later periods. The highest rates of net emigration (the number leaving per 1,000 of population per year) were found in Ulster (three counties), at 10.3 in 1926–36, and subsequently in Connacht for the later periods (10.3 and 15.1 respectively).

The commission on emigration noted that the counties with the highest emigration rates tended to share certain characteristics. They all contained large and heavy-density rural populations, high proportions of small agricultural holdings, and low-valuation agricultural land per head of population. These areas were conspicuously failing to provide a living for the numbers who survived childhood. In such areas emigration touched most families. In other parts of the country, such as Leinster, emigration to a greater extent

---

[19] Even though these data do not provide a more detailed age subdivision, other sources indicate that the great majority of emigrants in this age class were aged between 25 and 34 years.

TABLE 6. *Republic of Ireland: estimated out-migration and in-migration by age group, 1987–93 (thousands)*

Year ending April	Out-migration						In-migration						Net migration
	0–14	15–24	25–44	45–64	65+	Total	0–14	15–24	25–44	45–64	65+	Total	
1987	2.8	24.0	11.8	1.7	0.0	40.2	3.1	5.1	6.1	1.8	1.1	17.2	−23.0
1988	8.3	31.2	18.3	3.2	0.0	61.1	3.0	5.4	7.2	2.2	1.4	19.2	−41.9
1989	7.8	37.0	21.9	3.8	0.0	70.6	4.4	7.7	10.6	2.2	1.8	26.7	−43.9
1990	6.7	30.8	16.9	1.9	0.0	56.3	5.2	10.1	14.0	2.7	1.4	33.3	−22.9
1991	4.6	19.9	10.5	0.4	0.0	35.3	5.2	9.3	14.6	2.5	1.7	33.3	−2.0
1992	0.2	22.1	11.2	1.0	0.1	34.6	6.2	12.7	16.4	4.1	1.4	40.8	+6.1
1993	0.2	23.3	11.5	1.3	0.0	36.3	5.6	10.4	14.4	3.6	0.9	34.8	−1.5

Source: as table 4.

reflected class differences. The unskilled and unemployed might regard Britain as a land of opportunity, but to farmers with fifty acres or more and the middle classes of the towns and villages, emigration often conjured up pictures of Irish ghettos.[20]

From the 1960s onwards, when economic conditions began to improve, the nature of emigration changed gradually as a greater element of choice presented itself. The fact that the composition of the emigrant flows from the Republic in this period began to involve a majority of females is indicative of this change. Unfortunately, no information on the occupations of emigrants is available for the 1960s or the 1970s. However, British data does shed light on the occupations taken up by emigrants. Whereas in the 1950s and 1960s Irish men had entered building and construction work in disproportionate numbers, and women had tended to take up nursing and office work, by the 1970s emigrants were employed in a wider range of occupations. There were significant numbers of Irish-born persons in the professions: in 1971 more Irish-born doctors and dentists were working in Britain than in the Republic. There were also 10,000 teachers, of whom 1,000 were working in higher education. From the 1960s on, Irish-born emigrants also began to become more involved in local government and parliament. Other signs of assimilation included a high rate of intermarriage. Data available in 1970 indicated that almost half the Irish-born in Britain had a spouse who was not born in Ireland. In only 36 per cent of marriages did both partners come from Ireland. Such developments helped undermine the idea of the 'Irish ghetto' in Britain. However, the Irish-born were still over-represented among those with social problems. One explanation for this was that disproportionately high numbers of Irish emigrants were drawn from the most crime-prone group: single men in the age group 18–30, with poor education and low socio-economic status.[21]

In Northern Ireland too, the educational profile of emigrants has improved in recent years. In fact by 1991 emigrants from Northern Ireland were better qualified than the population at large. Higher education opportunities constituted one of the main reasons for emigration, according to a survey conducted in that year of over 5,000 emigrants (table 7). Only about 6 per cent of those questioned identified the 'troubles' and discrimination as the principal reasons for emigration, although it is possible that some respondents were less than fully frank.[22]

Further data on the occupational backgrounds of emigrants become available for the late 1980s, on the basis of the gross outflow estimates derived from recent labour-force surveys. However, these data do not allow direct

[20] *Commission on emigration*, pp 130–31; Ryan, 'Irish emigration to Britain', pp 50–54.
[21] Ryan, 'Irish emigration to Britain', pp 61–5.
[22] Compton, *Demographic review*, pp 123–7.

TABLE 7.   *Reasons for migrants leaving Northern Ireland (%)*

	Principal reason	Second reason
For higher education	32.3	4.9
Job-related factors, as follows:	30.0	9.5
To take up a new job	13.6	3.5
To search for a new job	7.9	3.4
To search for a first job	5.8	2.1
Job transfer	2.7	0.5
To get away from the province	14.1	20.4
Family/personal reasons	13.2	5.4
The 'troubles'	4.9	6.7
Discrimination	1.1	1.5
Other reasons and not stated	4.4	4.4
No second reason	0.0	47.2

N = 5,358
Source: 1991 migrant traveller survey, in Compton, *Demographic review*, p. 127.

comparisons with earlier periods, as information on the actual occupations of those who left is not available. A reasonable indication of the background of these more recent emigrants can, however, be obtained by classifying them in terms of the social group of the head of the household in which they previously resided (which would involve a close association with occupation in any case). This is, perhaps, a more appropriate way to approach the problem, as many emigrants would be so young as to have spent only a brief period in the labour force (some of them would not even have entered it) and, therefore, classifications based on previous occupations would not be very meaningful.

The relevant figures, expressed as migration rates per 1,000 population, for the year ended April 1988, are given in table 8. The data indicate that the then migratory outflow was broadly representative of the structure of society in the Republic. There was no marked predominance for any one particular group, at least not to the same degree that appeared to prevail in earlier periods. There is some evidence, however, of a tendency for the professional, managerial, and non-manual groups to be over-represented and, rather surprisingly, for those from farming backgrounds to be under-represented. If the farming community is excluded, the figures indicate a greater uniformity among the different social group categories for males, while for females the figures suggest a somewhat lower propensity to emigrate when the family background is manual or unskilled.

The apparently greater propensity to emigrate among those from higher social backgrounds in recent years seems to be borne out by other statistics. Information available on the experience of graduates from third-level

TABLE 8. *Gross migratory outflow in 1987/8 (R.I.) by the social group of the household head in which the emigrant previously resided (rates per 1,000 population)*

	Males	Females	Persons
Farmers, agricultural	12.4	12.4	12.4
Professional and associate professional	19.3	14.4	16.8
Employers, managers	19.9	16.2	18.1
Salaried, intermediate non-manual	15.3	13.4	14.3
Other non-manual	21.3	14.5	18.0
Skilled, semi-skilled manual	18.9	12.1	15.6
Unskilled	19.1	10.6	15.2
TOTAL	19.1	12.8	15.9

Source: as table 3. These figures are special tabulations derived from the C.S.O. *Labour force survey 1988* (Pl 6640) (Dublin, 1989). The total figures include persons for whom the social group of the relevant households' head was unknown.

education indicates a rising incidence of emigration for this group throughout the 1980s. The figures given in table 9, which describe the labour market situation of such persons some nine months after leaving higher education, show that the proportion that had emigrated rose from about 8 per cent in 1980 to nearly 30 per cent in the later stages of that decade. The incidence of emigration among third-level graduates declined from 1990 onwards as the situation in external labour markets deteriorated. Over the period in question the proportion who found employment in the Republic fell from 80 per cent to about 65 per cent. Particularly striking are the 'interchanges' between unemployment and emigration throughout the period.[23] In fact, relatively few third-level graduates emigrated until the mid 1980s (when labour market conditions in Ireland and the United Kingdom began to diverge), but from that point on the emigration option was increasingly taken up.

While the incidence of emigration among highly qualified persons has been a matter of public debate, it is important to bear in mind that the great majority of emigrants are not from this group. It can be readily inferred from the more broadly based social-background information in table 8 that the majority possess basic second-level qualifications. The outflows also continue to involve significant numbers of poorly qualified persons who are singularly ill equipped to meet the challenges that migration brings. Problems with the last mentioned group arose particularly during the second half of the 1980s, when sizeable numbers of very young and unskilled Irish people emigrated and found the labour market situation abroad as difficult as it was at home.

[23] Above, p. 463.

TABLE 9. *Labour market status (Republic of Ireland) of third-level award recipients who left full-time education, approximately one year after graduation, 1980–93 (%)*

Status	1980	1985	1989	1990	1991	1992	1993
At work in Ireland	80.0	67.4	64.3	67.5	65.5	65.3	67.1
Unemployed	11.6	16.9	7.2	12.2	16.2	15.9	14.6
Emigrated to find work	8.4	15.7	28.5	20.3	18.4	18.8	18.3
TOTAL	100.0	100.0	100.0	100.0	100.1	100.0	100.0
Domestic unemployment rate	12.7	20.0	10.1	15.3	19.8	19.6	17.9

The years indicated are the years in which the award recipients graduated; labour market status relates to the position in the spring of the year following graduation; the 'unemployed' category includes those accommodated on manpower schemes; and the 'domestic unemployment rate' is the number of unemployed graduates taken as a proportion of those graduates of the same year who were in the Irish labour force when the surveys were taken.

Sources: Higher Education Authority: first destination of award recipients in higher education, *(1992)* (Dublin, 1994); J. J. Sexton, B. M. Walsh, D. Hannan, and D. McMahon, *The economic and social implications of emigration* (N.E.S.C. report no. 90, Dublin, 1991).

Many of them ended up dependent on social welfare systems and other support agencies in host countries, particularly in the larger urban centres of the United Kingdom.[24] A contributing factor here was the fact that the traditional social linkages forged through previous emigration, which in the past had provided support for migrants,[25] had diminished over the preceding decades when emigration was relatively low.

IT is instructive to consider recent trends in migration for the Republic in somewhat more detail, not only because they differ from those for earlier periods, but also because they serve to illustrate important causative factors in a more explicit fashion. Relevant data are given in table 10, which shows annual figures for employment, unemployment, and net external migration for the period from 1971 to 1994.

As noted above, the structure of the economy changed little till the late 1950s. At that point, however, the introduction of economic planning (of which the expansion of the industrial base through the promotion of inward investment was an important ingredient) boosted economic growth and employment. The population outflows began to diminish and by the early 1970s net emigration had dwindled to zero. Remarkably a net inflow began to

[24] A detailed discussion of these issues is contained in J. J. Sexton, B. M. Walsh, D. Hannan, and D. McMahon, *The economic and social implications of emigration* (N.E.S.C. report no. 90, Dublin, 1991), ch. 7.
[25] Above, v, 599–607; vi, 609–10.

TABLE 10.   *Annual estimates of total numbers at work, unemployed and net migration (Republic of Ireland), 1971–94* (thousands)

Year (April)	At work	Unemployed	Labour force	Unemployment rate	Net external[1] migration
1971	1,049	61	1,110	5.5	−5
1972	1,052	69	1,121	6.2	+11
1973	1,067	64	1,132	5.7	+13
1974	1,082	62	1,144	5.4	+16
1975	1,073	85	1,158	7.3	+20
1976	1,064	105	1,169	9.0	+16
1977	1,083	105	1,188	8.8	+10
1978	1,110	99	1,209	8.2	+7
1979	1,145	88	1,233	7.1	+16
1980	1,156	91	1,247	7.3	−8
1981	1,146	126	1,272	9.9	+2
1982	1,146	147	1,293	11.4	−1
1983	1,124	183	1,307	14.0	−14
1984	1,103	204	1,307	15.6	−9
1985	1,079	226	1,305	17.3	−20
1986	1,081	227	1,308	17.4	−28
1987	1,090	232	1,323	17.6	−23
1988	1,090	218	1,308	16.7	−42
1989	1,088	201	1,289	15.6	−44
1990	1,134	176	1,310	13.4	−23
1991	1,134	209	1,342	15.5	−2
1992	1,143	217	1,360	16.0	+6
1993	1,148	230	1,378	16.7	−2
1994	1,182	218	1,400	15.6	−6

[1]The net migration figures relate to the year ending April.

Sources: C.S.O., *The trend of employment and unemployment 1979–85* (Pl 5793) (Dublin, 1988); C.S.O., *The trend of employment and unemployment 1986–88* (Pl 7550) (Dublin, 1991); C.S.O., *Labour force survey 1994* (Pn 2098) (Dublin, 1995); C.S.O., *Annual population and migration estimates 1987–1994* (Dublin, 1994).

materialise, mainly consisting of former emigrants and their families. Apart from the enhanced growth performance, a number of further reasons for this change can be identified. Membership of the European Community in 1973 provided an additional economic stimulus, particularly in the agricultural sector in the early years after entry. The 1970s also witnessed significant advances in the social sphere as welfare and health support systems were brought to levels comparable with those in other European countries. In the late 1970s very high levels of employment growth were achieved.

There was, however, a fragility associated with these improvements in economic fortune, as they depended on maintaining not only high but sustained growth if the burgeoning population was to be accommodated in employment. The global recession that followed the second oil price shock in 1979–80 brought expansion in the economy to an abrupt end. The recession of the early 1980s hit the Republic particularly hard, not only in its intensity, but in its duration. However, not all those problems could be attributed to external effects. They derived to a significant extent from injudicious fiscal and public-expenditure policies followed in the late 1970s, which involved tax cuts and sizeable increases in public expenditure and public-sector employment. While these may have created an impressive surge in employment growth, they left the Irish economy with an enormous increase in the size of the public debt. The problems associated with correcting this resulted in the country languishing in recession until well into the second half of the 1980s, long after other western economies had recovered and had begun to achieve some employment expansion. Table 10 shows that employment fell by nearly 80,000 (or almost 7 per cent) between 1980 and 1985, thus negating the gains of the late 1970s. The rate of unemployment rose from just over 7 per cent to nearly 18 per cent. This created a sharp divergence in labour market conditions between the Republic and other countries, particularly the United Kingdom, which led to a resumption of emigration. The trend emerged slowly at first as the economic difficulties were initially regarded as transient. However, as the prospect of early recovery receded and employment opportunities in the United Kingdom improved, the outward movement commenced in earnest. It appeared to acquire a momentum of its own, even after economic conditions had improved. The net outflow reached almost 45,000 in 1988/9 (12 per 1,000 population), a level that equated with earlier periods of very high emigration.

The economy finally began to improve after 1986. Between 1986 and 1990 real G.N.P. grew by almost 21 per cent and employment rose by nearly 55,000. The latter, when combined with the continuing net outflow (as conditions were still buoyant in the United Kingdom) caused unemployment to fall significantly, to 13.4 per cent. However, the renewed onset of world recession in 1990 again caused this expansion to end. In the early 1990s annual average G.N.P. growth declined to between 2 and 3 per cent and total employment remained virtually static. With the emigration option no longer attractive because of adverse labour market conditions abroad, the pressure of labour-force growth caused unemployment to escalate.[26] By April 1993 the

[26] The age structure of the Republic's population by the mid 1990s was such that, in the absence of net emigration, the potential for labour-force increase had become very substantial (even before any allowance was made for rising female participation in the workforce). The numbers of births increased rapidly throughout the 1970s (until they peaked in 1980) and the effects of this became evident in the labour force in the form of a large inflow from the

unemployment rate had risen to 16.7 per cent. The position was compounded by a return flow of former emigrants, mainly from the United
Kingdom where the effects of this recession were particularly severe. In
contrast to the large migratory outflows that characterised the later 1980s,
the estimates for the early 1990s indicated a situation of near nil net migration.

It is relevant to note, however, that unlike the early 1980s (which can be
regarded as a similar stage in the economic cycle), the recession in the first
years of the 1990s did not precipitate an employment decline. Modest output
growth was maintained and employment continued to drift slowly upwards.
When economic circumstances improved in 1993 total employment rose rapidly—by as much as 35,000 between 1993 and 1994. By the mid 1990s, in the
expectation of a continuing upturn in the world economy, most economic
analysts were forecasting significant employment gains in the Republic's
economy over the coming years, heralding the imminent arrival of the 'Celtic
tiger'.

Before leaving the subject of external migration it is appropriate to consider briefly the changes that have taken place as a result of internal migration. In Northern Ireland the nineteenth-century trend, which lasted down
to the 1950s, was one of increasing population concentrations in and around
the city of Belfast, at the expense in particular of the region west of the River
Bann. Since the 1970s, the latter region has experienced some resurgence.
Although it still loses population disproportionately through out-migration,
this is counterbalanced by a higher rate of natural increase. Moreover, the
population of Belfast city and the greater Belfast urban region has declined,
despite growth in the surrounding districts. The only substantial inter-
regional migration in recent years has been the outflow from Belfast, mainly
to the region east of the Bann. The 1991 census revealed that two-thirds of
the population were living in this eastern region.[27]

In the Republic somewhat similar trends are apparent. In the first half of
the century, Dublin city and suburbs constituted an area of net inward
migration, and showed considerable growth: between 1926 and 1951 the
proportion of the population living in the greater Dublin area rose from
under 15 per cent to over 20 per cent. In the commission on emigration
report of 1954 this trend was designated 'unnatural' by some, who fretted at

educational system which far exceeded the outflows for other reasons (e.g. retirement). By the
mid 1990s the labour force had the capacity to expand by between 20,000 and 25,000 each year
(i.e. by 1.5 to 2 per cent), a situation set to continue till the end of the decade. This is
reaffirmed by the figures given in table 10, which indicate that the labour force began to
increase rapidly after net emigration ceased in the early 1990s. The position may change in the
twenty-first century, however, when the effects of the sharp fall in the number of births from
1980 on will begin to affect the flows into the workforce.

[27] Compton, *Demographic review*, pp 20, 24, 30.

Dublin's growth while the population of the state as a whole continued to decline. Paradoxically, Dublin showed virtually no growth during the 1950s, and the inner city registered a decline, a pattern that was to continue. By 1986 the inner-city population was less than one-third of its 1936 size, though corporation housing schemes and 'urban renewal' plans were about to restore some demographic vitality. However, in the 1960s and 1970s growth resumed within a 20–25-mile radius of the city, so that by the latter decade a city-region was beginning to come into existence. As in the case of Belfast, some of this growth has arisen because of an outflow from the city to villages and towns within the commuting zone. By 1986 almost 30 per cent of the Republic's population lived in this city-region.[28]

HERETOFORE most of the emphasis in this chapter has been on analysing external migration in terms of outflows, that is, relating to those who leave Ireland. This is because in earlier periods net emigration was virtually synonymous with the gross outward flow, as the numbers migrating into Ireland were negligible (at least in relative terms). The position can be readily inferred from the near equality of the gross outflow and net external migration figures for the period from 1901 to 1911, given in table 3. However, for the reasons already outlined, within the last thirty years inward migration has become a much more important phenomenon. In Northern Ireland significant inward migration appeared in the 1960s, a decade of economic buoyancy and inward investment. The influx was chiefly from Britain, and comprised mainly students pursuing higher education, and people entering government service. However, although inflows have continued, exceeding outflows in the early 1990s, they were on a more restricted scale than in most other parts of the United Kingdom.[29] In the Republic, when the migratory inflow exceeded the outward movement in the 1970s, the return of former emigrants (and their families) constituted the dominant element. There is now always inward migration of significant proportions, even in times when the net migratory balance is highly negative, and every emigrant can now be regarded as a potential candidate to return at some time in the future. Throughout the 1980s, despite the scale of the migratory outflows, sizeable inward movements occurred. The estimates given in table 3 indicate that between 1981 and 1991 gross immigration amounted to some 230,000. Such sizeable movements clearly have a significant impact when viewed in economic and social terms, and it is, therefore, desirable to try and identify the salient features involved.

---

[28] Above, pp 430–31; *Commission on emigration: minority report by Most Rev. C. Lucey*, pp 335–7, 359; Arnold Horner, 'From city to city-region' in F. H. A. Aalen and Kevin Whelan (ed.), *Dublin city and county: from prehistory to present* (Dublin, 1992), pp 327–58.

[29] Compton, *Demographic review*, p. 17.

Table 6, it will be recalled, shows annual estimates of the gross migratory inflow to the Republic for the period from 1987 to 1993. A notable aspect of these data is the large increase in the inward movement in the early 1990s. The gross inflow was just over 17,000 in 1987 but this figure had risen to nearly 41,000 by 1992. The reasons for this have been discussed above.

These figures also exhibit a marked stability in the age distribution of the gross inflow over the years indicated. Those aged 25 years or over constituted some 55 per cent of the total inflow, with a significant concentration in the 25–44-year age band. That age band can be associated with the family formation stage of the life-cycle, and the significant numbers included in this category suggest that return migration tends to be associated with family-related events, such as when children begin to reach school-going age. The fact that between 15 and 20 per cent of inward migrants were young children under 15 lends further support to the view that many of the incoming migrants came as family groups. About a third of the gross inflow was in the youth category 15–24 years—a very much smaller proportion than that featuring in the gross outflows.

Inward migration, however, does not consist entirely of returning emigrants or their families. The inward flows also include non-nationals coming to reside in Ireland. These mainly comprise persons coming to take up employment, students coming to attend third-level institutions, and dependants of persons in these groups. The numbers involved may be small relative to the total population, but as noted above in respect of Northern Ireland they are a significant element in the context of the gross inward movements. Further information detailing the characteristics of foreign residents in the Republic is given below.

It is also of interest to assess past inward migration flows in terms of occupational profiles. Table 11 contains an occupational classification of immigrants who entered the Republic's labour force over the period 1983 to 1988. The table also distinguishes between those who had found work in Ireland and those who were unemployed.[30] The figures show that those who entered employment after immigration were heavily concentrated in the highly skilled areas, with about 40 per cent classified in professional and technical occupations (which would normally require third-level

---

[30] These data, which are taken from the 1991 N.E.S.C. report on emigration (above, n. 24), represent aggregations of annual figures for the period 1983–8, derived from successive labour-force surveys. The figures for any one year relate to those who were resident in Ireland at the time of the labour-force survey, having been resident abroad one year earlier. The status categories 'at work' and 'unemployed', as well as the occupations, relate to the situation as recorded in these years and do not necessarily reflect the situation of respondents at the end of the period (i.e. in 1988). The figures (particularly the percentages) should, therefore, be interpreted as portraying the 'average' position over the period 1983–8. The data could, of course, be shown for individual years but, in view of the small numbers involved, would be subject to sizeable sampling variability.

TABLE 11. *Persons who migrated into the Republic of Ireland, 1983–8, by occupation*

	At work on survey dates		Unemployed on survey dates	
	(1000s)	(%)	(1000s)	(%)
Agricultural	1.4	4.6	0.2	1.2
Industrial, transport occupations	5.0	16.3	4.2	25.0
Labourers, unskilled	0.8	2.6	2.2	13.2
Clerical, commercial	5.2	17.0	3.1	18.5
Service occupations	3.3	10.8	1.7	10.2
Professional, technical, etc.	11.8	38.6	1.6	9.6
Other	3.1	10.1	3.7	22.2
TOTAL (1983–8)	30.6	100.0	16.8	100.0

Source: as table 3.

qualifications). This is a very high figure: about twice the corresponding proportion in the domestic non-agricultural labour force. For the un-employed group on the other hand, there was a much greater spread among the different occupational categories, with significant proportions associated with industrial occupations, unskilled work, and with the miscellaneous 'other' category.

These results suggest that in the period in question the migratory inflow consisted essentially of two very distinct groups. In the first place, there were those with skills and qualifications who appear to have found employment readily. Indeed, many in this category would have acquired a job before they entered the country. This group also contained a significant minority of non-nationals, including, for example, those taking up employment in multi-national enterprises, which by then accounted for a substantial part of the industrial sector in the Republic. This particular inflow could, therefore, be viewed as economically beneficial, as the individuals concerned tended to fill vacancies in strategic areas of the economy. There was, however, a further substantial group who clearly had had unsatisfactory experiences abroad. On the basis of the evidence, they appear to have fared no better on return in the way of acquiring work, and indeed, probably had difficulties even before they emigrated originally. While the nature of the estimates does not allow a more detailed analysis, other evidence suggests that many such persons were young and unskilled.

It is important to bear in mind, however, that the foregoing analysis relates to a period when the economy was in a depressed state. While the analysis can be taken as representing the broad features of twentieth-century inward migration flows (in so far as the labour force is concerned) the picture is unlikely to have been as gloomy in circumstances of greater economic buoyancy. The large inflows that occurred in periods when the economy was growing rapidly are indicative of persons entering primarily to take up employment, rather than persons returning to escape the rigours of unfavourable circumstances in labour markets abroad. In summary, while the occupational profiles of the two groups involved would be unlikely to show significant change, the relative size of the 'unemployed' inflow would be much smaller.

It is appropriate to complete this review of immigration by providing some information on the numbers of persons in Ireland who were born elsewhere and on the numbers of resident non-nationals. In Northern Ireland the number is small: in fact this is the most homogeneous region in the United Kingdom, with over 90 per cent of residents in the last three censuses being born there. Immigration from the Republic is noticeably slight. In 1971 three per cent of Northern Ireland residents (46,400) were born in the Republic; by 1991 the figure (35,400) was 2.2 per cent.[31] The number of persons in the Republic who were born in other countries is fairly large. Data derived from the 1986 census of population indicates that some 6.5 per cent of the then total population (234,000 out of a total population of 3.45 million) were born abroad. Within this group over 140,000 persons (63 per cent) were born in Great Britain. While these figures serve to reaffirm the scale of earlier inward movements, they do not provide much guidance on the magnitude of inflows in any current sense, as many of the persons concerned would have entered the country many years earlier. Indeed, many would have entered for the first time as children on the return of their (former emigrant) parents.

This issue can be viewed in other ways; for example, in terms of nationality, by considering the numbers of non-nationals residing in the country. Such information can be obtained from the annual series of labour-force surveys. Using this source, table 12 shows that out of the total population of 3.5 million in April 1992 nearly 95,000 were non-nationals. The latter total comprised almost 61,000 who were nationals of the United Kingdom; over 12,000 had come from other E.U. member states; over 9,000 were United States passport-holders, and nearly 13,000 had come from other countries.

Even when viewed in relative terms the numbers involved, constituting about 2.5 per cent of the total population, are small when compared with many other European countries, some of which have large immigrant populations. In Germany there were some 5.5 million non-nationals in 1991, constituting nearly 7 per cent of the total population; in France the number in the same year was over 3.5 million, or 6 per cent of the total; in the United Kingdom, the number was nearly 2.5 million, or 4 per cent. By comparison

---

[31] Compton, *Demographic review*, pp 18–19, 99.

TABLE 12. *Republic of Ireland: population classified according to nationality in 1992* (thousands)

Nationality	Males	Females	Persons
Irish	1,719.8	1,734.5	3,454.2
United Kingdom	28.7	32.2	60.9
Other E.U.	6.0	6.1	12.2
U.S.A.	4.0	5.3	9.3
Other	6.6	6.0	12.5
TOTAL	1,765.1	1,784.0	3,549.1

The reference dates of the survey relate to the spring of each year.
Source: Special tabulation derived from the C.S.O., *Labour force survey 1992* (Pn 0832) (Dublin, 1994).

with these countries, the Irish population, both north and south, has remained remarkably homogeneous. On the other hand, in some southern European countries, such as Spain and Portugal, the numbers of non-nationals constituted only about 1 per cent of the total population in the year in question.[32]

Table 13 provides summary information from the 1992 labour-force survey on the economic status of non-nationals in the Republic. These data indicate that of the 80,000 non-nationals aged 15 years or over, some 40,000 (about one-half) were in the labour force, some 13,000 were in full-time education,

TABLE 13. *Republic of Ireland: population aged 15 years and over in 1992 by nationality and principal economic status* (thousands)

Nationality	Labour force	Students	Other	Total
Irish	1,319.9	293.7	924.5	2,538.2
United Kingdom	27.3	4.9	19.4	51.7
Other E.U.	5.5	3.3	2.6	11.3
U.S.A.	2.9	1.9	2.6	7.3
Other	4.8	2.9	2.1	9.8
TOTAL	1,360.3	306.7	951.2	2,618.2

The labour force includes those employed and unemployed.
Source: as table 12.

[32] Note that the figures quoted are official census-based data that do not necessarily cover all illegal or undocumented immigrants. There are also indications that the number of immigrants to the southern states of the E.U. has increased in recent years, mainly because of illegal inflows from North Africa and the Middle East.

and a further 27,000 were not gainfully employed. A significant proportion of the last-mentioned category would be women engaged in home duties.

IN considering policies adopted by governments to counter emigration it is important to bear in mind that in an Irish context the phenomenon is a symptom deriving from fundamental imbalances in the economy. Basically it has to be viewed in the same light as unemployment; it has been demonstrated that the two conditions or outcomes are to a large degree interchangeable, depending on the relative state of the Irish vis-à-vis external economies: this applies to both parts of Ireland. The first question that needs to be addressed concerning emigration is whether it derives primarily from high population growth (in the sense that the numbers of persons entering the labour market are such that it is extremely difficult to provide employment for all of them) or whether society has not sufficiently applied itself to achieving higher but attainable growth rates leading to increased levels of employment creation. If the first premise is accepted, then policy remedies should be directed primarily to the supply side, for example measures to control population expansion. Even though the very high birth rates that existed in Ireland in previous periods suggest that such approaches may have been appropriate, social and religious attitudes ruled them out. It must be recognised, however, that the low marriage rates that prevailed in earlier times, and the propensity to marry late in life, represented a degree of 'self-adjustment' in the Irish population to the existing economic and social conditions.[33]

For the most part in recent decades initiatives by governments in the Republic to counter the migratory outflows have taken the form of multi-purpose broadly based expansion programmes designed to boost employment. Some of these have met with a significant degree of success. The analyses presented earlier in this paper illustrate the advances that were made in the 1960s and in the 1970s, first in reducing and then at least temporarily eliminating the net outflows.

Given the high levels of emigration that have prevailed in the past, it might well be asked why more 'emigration-specific' policies were not followed. It could be said that an element of specificity existed in the form of certain earlier development plans that were targeted on underdeveloped regions where emigration (and unemployment) were high.[34] However, given that emigration tends to be closely intertwined with other socio-economic phenomena, it is difficult to conceive of specific measures that would not have adverse effects elsewhere in the economy. The actual employment effects that would follow from some of the initiatives suggested are also questionable. Recent data from Northern Ireland suggest that there is now

[33] For discussion of these issues in the period before 1921, see above, vi, 627–9.
[34] Above, pp 439–41.

little obvious relation there between propensity to migrate and spatial economic structure. Many of the most deprived areas produced fewer emigrants
than might have been expected in simple population terms.[35]

There are, however, certain areas where specific emigration-related policies
could have been followed. One is the question of donor countries providing
some assistance for their emigrants. This is an area where, despite the large
outflows in the past, little was done by successive governments in the Republic, largely because of political fears that such initiatives would be interpreted
as an admission of failure.[36] A few organisations were set up in the 1950s, and
more in the 1960s, but these were mostly sponsored by the catholic church.
While recent experience has shown that greater numbers of Irish emigrants
are now reasonably well qualified (and therefore better able to cope with the
problems of migrating), there have also been significant outflows of less-well
prepared young people, who departed with few resources and with an inadequate knowledge of life and conditions in the centres to which they went.
There are signs of change, however. The Republic's government did take
limited steps to assist underprivileged Irish emigrants in the United Kingdom
during the late 1980s through the allocation of grants to voluntary agencies.
The question of extending voting rights to emigrants has been raised. There
are also now more extensive transitional administrative procedures within the
European Union to facilitate and assist workers in finding employment outside their home country.

The relatively high rates of emigration that have recently prevailed among
skilled persons, particularly higher-education award holders, raise further
issues. Inevitably the question arises as to whether third-level educational
facilities should be provided to the degree that they are when sizeable
numbers of graduates emigrate. However, any disadvantages that arise therefrom are mitigated, to the extent that many qualified former emigrants return
with enhanced skills and thus make a significant contribution to the economic and social development of the country. In this wider context the
Republic's government has tended to strive to accommodate the 'social'
demand for higher education within the community. For this reason the
debate on this issue has centred on how to share the financing and the
education and training involved between the recipient and the general taxpayer.[37]

It should be borne in mind that a substantial proportion of both current
and capital higher education expenditure in the Republic (especially in the

[35] Compton, *Demographic review*, p. 130.
[36] This contrasts with the policies followed by some other donor countries (e.g. Turkey, the former Yugoslavia), which were prepared to work with host countries in attempting to control flows and to alleviate the plight of recently arrived migrants.
[37] A significant step in favour of general taxpayer support was taken in 1995 with the government decision to abolish third-level fees for undergraduate students.

non-university sector) is now met from E.U. funds.[38] This can, in a sense, be deemed to represent some recompense for the advantages that accrue to other member states arising from the dispersal of many third-level students across E.U. countries. Another factor to bear in mind is the attendance of sizeable numbers of students from the Republic at third-level institutions in Northern Ireland and in Britain, a phenomenon that emerged during the 1980s.

It is also of interest to make some brief reference to the legal provisions relating to the position of non-nationals in the Republic, particularly in so far as these apply to citizens of non-E.U. states. Accession to the European Community in 1973 meant that nationals of other E.U. member states had to be afforded the same rights as Irish citizens concerning rights of residence, access to employment and education, and eligibility for social welfare and health support. However, the basic legal framework covering non-E.U. foreign nationals in Ireland continued to be the 1935 aliens act.[39] Under the terms of this legislation, such persons arriving in Ireland are required to register with the immigration authorities. Initially they may be allowed to remain in the country for a period of up to three months. Permission to remain for a period of one year may subsequently be granted on application to the minister for justice if it can be demonstrated that the applicant will not become dependent on the state. These permissions can be renewed on application.

In view of the relatively small numbers involved down to the mid 1990s there was no strong impetus to formulate a comprehensive policy on the position of foreign residents in the Republic. Generally speaking it can be said that the official attitude towards granting residence and work permits to non-E.U. nationals has tended to be restrictive, except in certain circumstances where, for example, special skills were required.[40] Another important consideration has been the desire on the part of the Irish government not to allow the free movement provisions with the United Kingdom to be used as a means of facilitating the inflow of non-Irish (or now non-E.U.) nationals into the U.K. Here it may be noted that passports have not normally been

[38] However, the extent to which these subventions will continue when the current tranche of E.U. structural funds support ends is very uncertain.

[39] 1935/14 (10 Apr. 1935). In 1999 the supreme court found that discretionary powers granted by the act to the minister for justice in respect of deportation orders were unconstitutional (*Irish Times*, 21 May 1999). This followed the incorporation into Irish law of various international conventions concerning the examination of applications for asylum (Refugee Act, 1996 (1996/17, 26 June 1996)).

[40] In recent years citizenship and residence rights have been granted in cases where substantial financial investments were made in the state under the terms of a business migration scheme introduced in 1986. The operation of this measure has given rise to much controversy and adverse comment. Concern has centred on the nature of some of the investments and whether all the required criteria were met, particularly those relating to the obligations for applicants to reside in the state.

required to enter Britain from Ireland. In 1939 wartime emigration controls
required identity documents and visas to be produced by those seeking to
enter Britain and Northern Ireland, but these controls were abandoned in
1952, except for aliens.[41] The situation was not materially changed by the
fallout from the passing of the Republic of Ireland act (1948) and the subsequent British response (the Ireland act of 1949), because the latter declared
that the Republic was not to be regarded as a foreign country, nor were its
citizens to be regarded as aliens in the United Kingdom.[42]

[41] *Commission on emigration*, app. vii, pp 267–8.
[42] 1948/22 (21 Dec. 1948); 12, 13 & 14 Geo. V, c. 41 [U.K.] (2 June 1949); above, pp 273–7.

CHAPTER XXVII

Women, emancipation, and politics, 1860–1984

MARY CULLEN

T HE women's emancipation movement that emerged in Ireland in the second half of the nineteenth century was part of a wider phenomenon in western society. At a time when greater rights and opportunities for middle- and working-class men were being demanded, there were those who contended that women too had rights and should be accorded greater autonomy or even full equality with men. Such a claim was not entirely new, but the nineteenth century witnessed sustained pressure on a number of different fronts.

While laws, regulations, and customs differed from country to country, the restrictions imposed on women's autonomy in the early nineteenth century were essentially similar. With some aristocratic and royal exceptions, women were excluded from positions of formal power. They could not hold public office, sit on representative parliamentary bodies, or vote in parliamentary elections. Virtually all well-paid employments, including the expanding professions, were closed to them, as were the universities. For those middle- and upper-class women who had to earn their own living, the only socially acceptable employments were poorly paid and low-status occupations such as governessing or needlework. At secondary level, girls' education aimed largely at accomplishment-level learning. While the family was regarded as women's 'sphere', within it laws placed authority and control of resources firmly in male hands. Under English common law, operative in Ireland, married women 'had no civil existence: they owned no personal property, they could neither sue nor be sued, they could not divorce their husbands, or claim any rights over their children'.[1] If a woman left her husband, his duty to maintain her lapsed but (assuming that her property was not held in trust) he retained control of her property, including any income she might earn after separation. In sex-related offences such as adultery, prostitution, and illegitimate births women were the guilty and punishable party in the eyes of society.

[1] Jane Rendall, *The origins of modern feminism: women in Britain, France, and the United States, 1780–1860* (London, 1985), p. 4.

Among the intellectual and philosophical influences that contributed to the emergence of the women's emancipation movement, historians have noted the European enlightenment, the French revolution, and evangelical religion. Enlightenment emphasis on a common rational human nature encouraged women's claims, despite little support from male thinkers. So did the French revolution's calls for liberty, equality, and fraternity, again despite male scepticism. Evangelical religion, influential across all denominations, stressed a mother's responsibility for the moral welfare of the family, and by extension the wider community. This gave religious backing to improved female education and a concept of women as in some ways morally superior to men. Other philosophical developments, too, encouraged challenges to accepted models of male–female relations, particularly within left-wing and socialist movements. The radical tradition that emphasised utility as the guiding force in political economy was one such influence, giving primacy to the principle of the greatest happiness of the greatest number. The cooperative movement produced, in the joint work of an Irish woman and an Irish man, one of the most cogently argued cases for the full equality of the sexes in all spheres of life, including the political.[2] Within the Marxist tradition Engels's contention,[3] that the ideology of the father-dominated family originated in male control of private property, challenged claims that patriarchal authority protected women and children. Theories of evolution gave scientific support to arguments that women's moral and intellectual character could be improved by better education, upgraded legal status, and the shouldering of political and civil responsibility in place of being shielded from 'the world' in a perpetual childhood. Drawing on these various sources, nineteenth-century emancipationists used two main lines of argument in support of their cause. The first began with the individual, irrespective of sex, and claimed women's full emancipation as a human right based on the rational human nature shared by all persons. The second started from a concept of difference and complementarity between male and female. It saw the contribution of women to society as *different* from that of men, but equally important and equally essential. To make their contribution women needed and had the right to participate in society at all levels.

---

[2] William Thompson, *Appeal of one-half of the human race, women, against the pretensions of the other half, men, to retain them in political, and thence in civil and domestic slavery* (London, 1983; first published 1825). In the 'Introductory letter' to Anna Wheeler, Thompson regrets that she, the source of its ideas, did not write the book herself; and adds that a 'few only therefore of the following pages are the exclusive produce of your mind and pen, and written with your own hand. The remainder are our joint property, I being your interpreter and the scribe of your sentiments' (p. xxiii).
[3] Friedrich Engels, *The origin of the family, private property and the state* (Harmondsworth, 1985), ch. 2.

ORGANISED action in Ireland emerged first among small groups of middle-class protestant women. Many of these pioneers came from the considerable number of women, married and single, who had already found their way to contribute to society outside the confines of the immediate family circle. Inspired by religious zeal and humanitarian concern, and mandated by the now recognised responsibility of women as custodians of morality and dispensers of charity, well-off women in the late eighteenth and nineteenth centuries poured energy and commitment into work for the moral and physical betterment of the poor.

This philanthropy developed beyond the activity of benevolent individuals to the formation of organisations to carry out specific work. Women moved from fund-raising for charities run by men to establishing and running their own societies.[4] Magdalen asylums—refuges for prostitutes, that gave shelter, protection, and encouragement to find alternative means of support—were among the first enterprises. So were visiting the poor in their homes and visiting prisons to teach women inmates to read, write, and sew. This was followed by aftercare in the form of refuges where ex-prisoners could learn domestic skills and be prepared for a new life, often through emigration. Creation of employment for poor women was a constant activity through the setting up of local industries and sale of the products. Foundations included orphanages, hospitals, schools, and asylums. Such work brought philanthropists into interaction with the 'public' sphere of administration, where they could observe its workings and analyse its inadequacies. They learned for themselves how the poor lived. Work with prostitutes, the sick poor, and impoverished mothers trying to earn money to feed and clothe their children, demolished the myth that women were a favoured species supported and 'protected' by men.

The philanthropists laid the foundations for many services that were later taken over by the state. As governments became more involved in education, health services, and provision for the poor, women's exclusion from the public political process came to be seen as a serious restriction on their work. Some became convinced that women needed access to public decision-making if they were to be effective in their mission to help the underprivileged and raise the moral level of society.

A minority of philanthropic women moved beyond the idea of alleviating the symptoms of poverty, and helping the poor to cope within the existing system, to tackling causes of social inequality and injustice. Working and organising in groups also encouraged analysis of their own position as women in society. Some gained political experience of campaigning to change the law by participation in such movements as the abolition of slavery and the

---

[4] See Maria Luddy, *Women and philanthropy in nineteenth-century Ireland* (Cambridge, 1995), for a comprehensive coverage.

temperance movement. Claiming the rights and duties of citizenship for other excluded groups highlighted women's own lack of civil rights. The slowness of some male colleagues to support women's full citizenship or to treat women as equal partners in other campaigns was often educational. The notorious refusal of the English anti-slavery movement to allow American women delegates to participate in the world anti-slavery convention in London in 1840 was a major impetus behind the first women's rights convention held in Seneca Falls, New York State, in 1848, and the lesson was not lost on women in other countries.[5] While only a minority of women went on to organise campaigns for female citizenship, a larger number with experience in philanthropy comprised a pool of female knowledge and concern about a broad range of social problems. Many of them shared the conviction that what women had to offer society was valuable and badly needed, and they were ready to move into new areas of activity opened up by feminist action.[6]

As to the relevance of religion, the Christian churches on the one hand tended to approve women's spiritual mission while on the other in varying degrees they emphasised submission to authority and self-effacement as virtues particularly pleasing in females. In general terms the more importance a church gave to private judgement and the less hierarchical its authority structure, the more it appears to have favoured, or the less it hindered, demands for emancipation. Protestantism generally allowed the individual conscience more autonomy than did catholicism. While no church gave women equal status with men in decision-making roles,[7] the quaker doctrine of the inner light appears to have been particularly favourable. The catholic church, whose exclusively male priesthood reserved to itself the right to interpret God's revelation and will for the laity, and which had no remembered tradition of women preachers or teachers, lay at the other extreme. For catholic women to assert claims to personal autonomy and equal citizenship must have involved a more radical challenge to their church than was required of women from other denominations. Moreover in Ireland the perception that women's emancipation was a foreign, and specifically an English, import posed problems for nationalist women, most of whom were catholics.

Any assessment of catholic women's engagement with women's issues in nineteenth-century Ireland must take into account the growing appeal of the

---

[5] The American quaker feminist, Lucretia Mott, travelled to Ireland immediately after attending the London convention and visited quaker communities in Dublin and Belfast.

[6] In English, the term 'feminism', meaning support for the emancipation of women, first came into use, following French usage, in the 1890s; see *O.E.D.*, and Karen Offen, 'Defining feminism: a comparative historical approach', in *Signs: journal of women in culture and society*, xiv, no. 1 (1988), pp 119–57: 126.

[7] See David Hempton and Myrtle Hill, 'Women and protestant minorities in eighteenth-century Ireland' in Margaret MacCurtain and Mary O'Dowd (ed.), *Women in early modern Ireland* (Dublin, 1991), pp 197–211.

religious orders after the relaxation of the penal laws. While middle-class catholic lay women were involved in the philanthropic movement from its beginnings in the eighteenth century, by the middle of the nineteenth their work had largely been taken over by nuns. The number of nuns in Ireland grew from 120 in 1800 to 1,500 in 1851 and over 8,000 in 1901; exact numbers are difficult to ascertain because some women religious were classified as nurses or teachers.[8] By 1926 the number exceeded 9,000 in the twenty-six counties of the Irish Free State. The number of convents grew from 11 in 1800 to 91 in 1850 and to 368 in 1900.

The Poor Clares (1629), Dominicans (1644), and Carmelites (1690) were already established. The Ursulines came to Cork in 1771 at the request of Nano Nagle, and subsequently from the late eighteenth century to the middle of the nineteenth there was a growth of new Irish congregations working for the most part with the poor. Most of these began as groups of lay philanthropists which later transformed themselves into religious congregations. Nano Nagle's Presentation Sisters, founded first as the Sisters of the Charitable Institution of the Sacred Heart of Jesus in Cork in 1775, Mary Aikenhead's Irish Sisters of Charity (1815), Frances Ball's Irish branch of the Loreto order (1822), and Catherine McAuley's Sisters of Mercy (1831) all made this transition. Margaret Aylward's first major undertaking (1850) was the establishment of the Ladies' Association of Charity of St Vincent de Paul to undertake the visitation of the sick poor in north Dublin city; this lay group formed the core management of St Brigid's outdoor orphanage and poor schools. A most reluctant foundress, Aylward came under pressure from Archbishop Paul Cullen to transform her fellow workers into a religious community. Accordingly, in order to ensure the continuation of these charities, Aylward established the Holy Faith congregation (sanctioned 1867).[9] Certain bishops played a key role in respect of new foundations: in 1807 Bishop Daniel Delany of Kildare and Leighlin initiated the restoration of the ancient Order of St Bridget, while Thomas Furlong, bishop of Ferns, facilitated the foundation of the Sisters of St John of God in 1871 by a group of Irish women who had been members of the Sisters of Bon Secours in Paris.

From the middle of the nineteenth century there was an influx of French teaching congregations, which recruited Irish women. These included the Sacred Heart (1842), the Faithful Companions of Jesus (1843), St Louis (1859), St Joseph of Cluny (1860), and the Marists (1873). Such congrega-

---

[8] Tony Fahey, 'Nuns in the catholic church in Ireland in the nineteenth century' in Mary Cullen (ed.), *Girls don't do honours: Irish women in education in the nineteenth and twentieth centuries* (Dublin, 1987), pp 7–30: 7. The term 'nun' strictly applies to members of religious orders with solemn vows. Many Irish women religious belonged to congregations with simple vows.

[9] Jacinta Prunty, *Margaret Aylward 1810–1889: lady of charity, sister of faith* (Dublin, 1999).

tions supplemented the work of the Dominicans and Ursulines, who had a long record of catering for the education of the daughters of better-off catholics. The new indigenous Irish foundations, by contrast, were more preoccupied with the education and catechesis of the poor.

The contribution of nuns to Irish life was impressive. They undertook an enormous range and variety of social work. Schools, orphanages, refuges, asylums, and hospitals were among the institutions founded and run by nuns to serve the needs of the poor, and later of the better-off. By the end of the nineteenth century they had established an immense network of institutions, which had become indispensable to the functioning of the Irish church and society.[10] By welfare-state standards the regimes in some of these institutions, such as the refuges for 'fallen women', were harsh. However, the commitment, orderliness, and cleanliness the nuns brought to their undertakings raised standards across the board and did much to make nursing in particular an acceptable career for middle-class women. Their work was regarded with respect and admiration by English feminists.

Recent scholarship has been reassessing the vocation of nun in the context of the work and choices available to Irish women.[11] The historical context was the challenge faced by the catholic church in retaining the adherence of rapidly expanding populations, especially among the poor in cities and towns. This gave the opportunity for a new form of religious life for women in which they moved outside the convent enclosure and engaged in active ministry. The founding mothers were women of formidable character and vision, but also of wealth and social standing who, as single women or widows, had control over the use of their property, and could decide to use their money and position to establish the new organisations. These organisations had an obvious attraction for women who wanted to contribute to society in substantial ways outside the confines of their immediate family, and to exercise initiative and management skills not usually allowed to women. Their growth also reflected the relatively low marriage rate in post-famine Ireland.

In many respects the way of life of nuns might appear well suited to the emergence of feminist awareness. Nuns lived in all-women communities with

---

[10] See Mary Peckham, 'Catholic female congregations and religious change in Ireland, 1770–1870' (Ph. D. thesis, University of Wisconsin–Madison, 1993); Maria Luddy, 'Prostitution and rescue work in nineteenth-century Ireland' in Maria Luddy and Cliona Murphy (ed.), *Women surviving: studies in Irish women's history in the 19th and 20th centuries* (Dublin, 1990), pp 51–84.

[11] See Caitriona Clear, *Nuns in nineteenth-century Ireland* (Dublin, 1987); ead., 'Walls within walls: nuns in nineteenth-century Ireland' in Chris Curtin, Pauline Jackson, and Barbara O'Connor (ed.), *Gender in Irish society* (Galway, 1987), pp 134–51; ead., 'The limits of female autonomy: nuns in nineteenth-century Ireland' in Luddy & Murphy, *Women surviving*, pp 15–50; Tony Fahey, 'Female asceticism in the catholic church: a case study of nuns in nineteenth-century Ireland' (Ph. D. thesis, University of Illinois, 1981); id., 'Nuns in the catholic church'.

female authority figures, and were engaged in demanding work, which required organisation and cooperation. They ran their own convents and institutions. The fact that they were in varying degrees under the authority of the bishop and there was always the possiblility, and sometimes the reality, of clerical regulation might have acted as a stimulus to assertions of female autonomy. Yet only one Irish nun appears to have produced anything resembling a critical analysis of women's position in society, and even she (the outspoken Margaret Anne Cusack, the 'Nun of Kenmare') accepted that God had ordained the subordination of wives to husbands, and appears to have subscribed to the view that women were in some respects less intelligent than men.[12]

Nor did convents produce critiques of poverty and inequality in society or proposals for social revolution. On the contrary nuns won the grudging approval of state officials (who were sometimes ill-disposed to the very idea of catholic nuns) because they were seen to train the young of the poorer classes to accept social inequality. In the education of young women of more privileged backgrounds there is the apparent paradox of nuns, the successors of pioneering women who themselves broke through the conventions of appropriate female behaviour, training generations of young Irish women of all classes, including later generations of novices, to conform to a model of feminine meekness and docility as well as piety. It appears that once the founding mothers had won their first battles, the women who followed them did not have to challenge convention as did lay women who organised and ran philanthropic institutions. It also has to be remembered that most women entered religious life primarily for religious reasons; the constant struggle to overcome self and self-will that was an integral part of religious life scarcely encouraged radical critiques of contemporary society. Moreover, although the phenomenon of nuns undertaking a wide range of social, educational, and philanthropic roles now seems unremarkable, in the nineteenth century the tradition that women could only contribute to the catholic church's mission through their role in the family, or in enclosed orders, still commanded much support among the church authorities. From this perspective, the main challenge facing the religious orders was to gain acceptance from the church authorities for their role.[13] This they achieved, thanks in part to the contribution the religious orders were able to make in helping to impose post-Tridentine catholic standards on the whole of catholic Ireland.

The early stages of feminist organisation in Ireland have yet to be fully researched. However, by the 1860s action was emerging around the issues of married women's property, education and employment for middle-class

---

[12] Margaret Anne Cusack (Sr M. Francis Clare), *Women's work in modern society* (Kenmare, 1874), p. 11, and appendix.
[13] Peckham, 'Catholic female congregations'; Séamus Enright, unpublished research. See also Fahey, 'Nuns in the catholic church', pp 21–2.

women, double sexual standards, and the parliamentary vote on the same terms as men. Membership of the first groups was small, middle-class, and protestant, with quakers particularly prominent. Two of the leading pioneers, who appear to have been to the fore in all areas of action, were Anna Haslam (1829–1922)[14] in Dublin and Isabella Tod (1836–96)[15] in Belfast. Haslam, born Anna Fisher, came from a quaker family in Youghal involved in philanthropy and the anti-slavery movement. She helped in a soup kitchen during the famine of the 1840s and with her sister set up a crochet and knitting industry for poor women. Isabella Tod, born in Edinburgh, was a presbyterian with a background in philanthropy and a lifelong commitment to women's involvement in the temperance movement. Both shared with other feminist pioneers relative financial independence and freedom from family opposition. Tod was unmarried while Haslam had no children; her husband was her lifelong co-worker in the women's movement.

The position of married women under common law was a crucial issue. Lack of control over inherited or earned property was fundamental. This affected the lives of women of all social classes, those of married women directly and those of single women indirectly. It severely limited married women's control over their own lives, and, linked with women's exclusion from most lucrative occupations, encouraged girls' education to aim at acquiring the accomplishments that would lead to marriage, rather than towards intellectual development and economic independence. The property of wealthy wives could be protected by the system of trusts developed by the courts of equity to circumvent the common law. This empowered trustees to 'protect' a woman's property against her husband, but did not necessarily give control to the woman herself and did not disturb the principle of patriarchal marriage. In any case, trusts were only feasible where substantial property was involved.

Isabella Tod and Anna Haslam were both involved in this campaign. Tod organised a Belfast branch of the London-based Married Women's Property Committee for reform of the law; she was the only woman to give evidence before the select committee of the house of commons in 1868. She explained that 'educated' women in Belfast and Dublin had taken up property-law reform primarily to help the many poor married women working in the linen mills in the Belfast area. The pay was too low to make such work worth their while unless their husbands' 'ill-health or bad conduct' made it imperative. The law left their earnings, and those of their children, at the mercy of their husbands. Tod argued that protection orders were not the answer and that the only satisfactory solution was a woman's full legal right to her own

[14] Mary Cullen, 'Anna Maria Haslam' in Mary Cullen and Maria Luddy (ed.), *Women, power and consciousness in 19th-century Ireland: eight biographical studies* (Dublin, 1995), pp 161–96.
[15] Maria Luddy, 'Isabella M. S. Tod', ibid., pp 197–230.

earnings. She explained that middle-class women of limited means also needed this right since it was difficult for them to pay for a protective settlement or to find suitable trustees. She pointed out that a women's committee had been established in Dublin, and petitions in favour of reform had been organised in both Dublin and Belfast.[16] Tod went on to serve on the executive committee of the central Married Women's Property Committee in England during 1873–4.[17] Opponents of the campaign argued that married women's control of their own property would undermine the authority of husbands, to the consequent peril of the family and society. Reform proceeded gradually, with successive acts of parliament in 1870, 1874, 1882, and 1907, by which time the principle of spouses' separate property had been established.[18]

There was also Irish participation in the campaign to repeal the contagious diseases acts, which had been passed in the 1860s amid fears that venereal disease was undermining the health of the British army and navy.[19] They provided for state regulation of prostitution in certain designated areas, of which three were in Ireland: Cork, Queenstown (Cobh), and the Curragh in County Kildare. The acts allowed the arrest of a woman on suspicion of being a prostitute and, if she was found to be suffering from venereal disease, her detention in a lock-hospital for up to nine months. Work for prostitutes had always been high on the agenda of philanthropic women. While the objective was to 'rescue' the 'fallen' woman and help her to a better life, the emancipationists understood the economic realities underpinning prostitution and its link to the low level of payment in all 'respectable' female employments. They opposed state regulation of prostitution on two main grounds. The first was that in practice it gave state sanction to a major threat to family life. The second was that it applied a double standard, which did not interfere with the men involved but treated the women as commodities to be periodically cleansed and recycled as 'clean harlots for the army and navy'.[20]

The Ladies' National Association (L.N.A.) and the National Association for the Repeal of the Contagious Diseases Acts, both founded in England in 1869, had branches in Ireland. First Tod and subsequently Haslam were members of the L.N.A. executive, and branches were established in Belfast,

---

[16] *Special report from the select committee on the married women's property bill* [4417], H.C. 1867–8, cccxxxix, 74–5.

[17] Lee Holcombe, *Wives and property: reform of the married women's property law in nineteenth-century England* (Oxford, 1983), p. 242.

[18] 33 & 34 Vict., c. 93 (9 Aug. 1870); 37 & 38 Vict., c. 50 (30 July 1874); 45 & 46 Vict., c. 75 (18 Aug. 1882); 7 Edw. VII, c. 18 (21 Aug. 1907).

[19] See Luddy, 'Prostitution and rescue work', p. 69; ead., 'Women and the contagious diseases acts, 1864–1886' in *History Ireland*, i, no. 1 (spring 1993), pp 32–4.

[20] Evidence of Josephine Butler (*Report of the royal commission upon the administration and operation of the contagious diseases acts, vol. ii, minutes of evidence*, p. 440, H.C. 1871 (408–1), xix).

Dublin, and Cork. Numbers were never large. The members appear to have been exclusively protestant, with quakers as usual to the fore. Campaigning and speaking at public meetings on an issue explicitly related to women's sexuality broke new ground for middle-class women, who were expected to know little about prostitution and venereal disease, much less make public speeches about them. The smallness of the numbers involved reflects the strength of the taboo, as does the existence of separate women's committees side by side with mixed-sex committees. Haslam, typically, took part in both, becoming secretary of the mixed-sex committee set up in Dublin in 1870, and treasurer of the women's committee set up a year later. Meetings and demonstrations were held in Belfast and Dublin over the years, and petitions were organised.

Participation provided experience of the rough-and-tumble of public polit-ics from which so many men were anxious to shield women's delicacy. In 1878 the English social reformer Josephine Butler addressed a public meeting at the Rotunda in Dublin, which had to be abandoned when it was disrupted by heckling medical students demanding that women be ejected. Haslam and her husband promptly organised another meeting, which Butler successfully addressed, winning over many of the former hecklers. The contagious dis-eases acts were eventually repealed in 1886. Anna Haslam's comment that the eighteen-year campaign 'threw the suffrage movement back for ten years as we were all so absorbed in it'[21] indicates how small was the number of active emancipationists; so many of the same people were involved in the different campaigns.

EDUCATION was another key area for women's emancipation, not merely for the improved employment opportunities it would bring, but as developing and confirming women's intellectual abilities. Educational provision for girls beyond primary level was limited. In 1871 the number of boys and girls attending primary schools was almost equal, while there were no women at all in the universities. Secondary schools were not yet fully differentiated as a separate category, but all educational establishments that taught at least one of the subjects Latin, Greek, modern languages, or mathematics were defined in the census reports as providing 'superior' education. Among those receiv-ing a superior education males outnumbered females by more than five to three, but it was differences in the kind and quality of the education of the two sexes that was the first concern of feminists. Few girls studied Greek, Latin, or mathematics. The vast majority receiving a superior education did so on the basis of learning French, and the census commissioners were scep-tical about the standards involved: 'From time immemorial the acquirement of some knowledge—very superficial for the greater part—of foreign living

---

[21] Interview with Francis Sheehy Skeffington in *Irish Citizen*, 21 Mar. 1914, p. 347.

languages has entered into the instructions of females rather as an accomplishment—like music, or drawing, or embroidery—than as a study.'[22] The reforming pioneers included Margaret Byers (1832–1912), a presbyterian from County Down, who founded the Ladies Collegiate School (later called Victoria College) in Belfast in 1859; Anne Jellicoe (1823–80), a quaker from Queen's County (Laois), closely involved in founding the Queen's Institute for the Training and Employment of Educated Women (1861), Alexandra College (1866), the Governess Association of Ireland (1869), and Alexandra School (1873), all in Dublin; and Isabella Tod, who was involved in setting up both the Ladies' Institute in Belfast in 1867 and the Ulster Schoolmistresses' Association in 1881.[23]

Anne Jellicoe's work highlights some of the problems encountered in raising standards. The Queen's Institute organised training for sewing machinists, law writers, telegraph clerks, and commercial clerks. It also provided classes in ornamental writing, lithography, and wood and metal engraving.[24] The list indicates the limited range of careers seen by the pioneers as realistic aspirations for genteel women. And there were barriers to be overcome to achieve entry even to some of these. The Queen's Institute lobbied successfully for the opening of examinations for commercial certificates to women on the same terms as men in 1861 and for the opening of the first civil service jobs to women as telegraph clerks in 1870.[25] The basic education of the supposedly 'educated' students of the Institute was found to be so poor that Jellicoe proceeded to the foundation in 1866 of Alexandra College for the Higher Education of Women, with the primary purpose of producing teachers and governesses who could raise standards in girls' education. In turn, deficiencies in the education of the students entering the college led to the founding of Alexandra High School in 1873 to act as a feeder. Not surprisingly both Jellicoe and Byers had to turn to male dons and graduates to provide teaching in the early stages of their projects.

The prospectus of Alexandra College offered 'an education more sound and solid, more systematically imparted and better tested than is at present easily to be obtained by women of the middle and upper classes in this

---

[22] *Census Ire., 1871*, pt iii, general report, p. 176 [C 1377], H.C. 1876, lxxxi.

[23] See Eileen Breathnach, 'Women and higher education in Ireland (1879–1914)' in *The Crane Bag*, iv, no. 1 (1980), pp 47–54; ead., 'Charting new waters; women's experience in higher education, 1879–1908' in Cullen, *Girls don't do honours*, pp 55–78; Anne V. O'Connor, 'The revolution in girls' secondary education in Ireland 1860–1910', ibid., pp 31–54; Anne V. O'Connor and Susan M. Parkes, *Gladly learn and gladly teach: Alexandra College and School 1866–1966* (Tallaght, 1984); Anne V. O'Connor, 'Anne Jellicoe' in Cullen & Luddy, *Women, power & consciousness*, pp 125–60.

[24] Jellicoe's own first aim had been to improve the employment of poorer women, but it appears that her colleagues, who saw the education of middle-class women as the first priority, carried the day.

[25] O'Connor & Parkes, *Gladly learn*, p. 7.

country'. Victoria College in Belfast aimed 'to afford girls the same opportunities for sound scholarship that were given to their brothers in the best boys' schools'. These new developments were based on a belief in 'public examinations as a means of raising standards, the inclusion of mathematics and Latin in the curriculum, a close liaison between secondary schools and university, and the belief that the education of boys and girls should, as far as possible, be the same'.[26]

The universities, too, were pressed to admit women. The first response was the provision of special classes for females, but the reformers wanted full admission to degrees and classes on the same terms as men. Meanwhile they achieved some important objectives through the intermediate education act in 1878 and the royal university act in 1879.[27] Both acts were designed to wean middle-class catholics away from home rule by extending opportunities for male catholics to obtain qualifications. In each case a purely examining and award-giving body was established; no compulsory attendance at any specified institutions was required. The emancipationists, who, with Isabella Tod to the fore, kept a careful watch on legislation to further women's interests, recognised the potential and in each case carried out a successful lobby of politicians in London, with the result that when passed both acts had been amended to extend their provisions to girls and women. The intermediate board held competitive examinations yearly. Pupils were awarded prizes and exhibitions, and schools received per capita payments according to the number of subjects passed by their pupils. For girls' schools access to intermediate examinations allowed the testing of standards alongside those of boys' schools, and gave an incentive to introduce such subjects as Latin and mathematics. Qualifications achieved by competitive examination also opened the way to new employment possibilities. This was particularly relevant to the growth of clerical work in the civil service and the expanding commercial sector.

Meanwhile in the secondary education of catholic girls a trend had emerged towards fee-paying convent schools to meet the social aspirations of the catholic middle classes. At the top of the social hierarchy were convent boarding schools, affordable only by the well-off, and these were dominated numerically and socially by the French religious teaching orders from the 1850s on. The majority of convent boarding schools were run by these orders, and they set the general tone and educational standards. French language, emphasis on politeness, order, general good conduct, and the development of good taste (le goût) in literature and art were among the French traditions emphasised. For the less wealthy, two of the Irish teaching orders, the Mercy and Presentation, provided fee-paying day schools for those who

---

[26] O'Connor, 'The revolution in girls' secondary education', p. 35.
[27] 41 & 42 Vict., c. 66 (16 Aug. 1878); 42 & 43 Vict., c. 65 (15 Aug. 1879).

could not afford boarding schools. In addition, some convent national schools provided subjects beyond the basic three Rs, thereby allowing some upward social mobility for poorer girls. The catholic middle classes were quick to see the employment potential of the intermediate examinations for their daughters and to demand that the convent schools prepare their pupils for them. The nuns responded: the number of convent schools entering pupils was 29 in 1893 and 45 in 1898.[28] The nationalist press added a political dimension by urging the convents to compete for results with their protestant counterparts. The catholic bishops, initially unenthusiastic for the most part, saw where things were heading and began to voice encouragement instead of disapproval.

At university level the problem for women, excluded from the universities, was to find the teaching to prepare them for the royal examinations. Alexandra College in Dublin immediately begun to provide classes and Victoria College in Belfast followed, as did a number of other northern institutions. Organisations were set up to protect what had been achieved and to push forward. The Ulster Schoolmistresses' Association (1881) and the Dublin-based Central Association of Schoolmistresses and Other Ladies Interested in Education (1882) merged to form an umbrella organisation, to which a Cork branch and corresponding members in Derry and Galway were added. Pressure on the universities to admit women to degree courses increased. The queen's colleges were the first to respond: Belfast in 1882, Cork in 1886, and Galway in 1888 (Galway's concession somewhat marred by the catholic bishop forbidding catholic women to attend). In Dublin both Trinity College and the catholic university, renamed 'University College' in 1882 and under Jesuit control from 1883, held out against full admission for many years. In spite of the difficulties the first nine women graduated from the royal university in 1884, to general feminist acclaim.[29]

Catholic institutions were slower to provide the teaching necessary to prepare girls for university. In Dublin many catholic women studied at Alexandra College; for their part, both the Loreto and Dominican sisters were eager to set up university establishments. Archbishop William Walsh was persuaded by the Dominicans to cooperate in the opening of a catholic women's college, St Mary's University College and High School in Dublin in 1893. The Loreto order on its own initiative promptly established a university centre at St Stephen's Green in 1894. In the same year the Ursulines in Cork began to provide university teaching.[30]

By the early years of the twentieth century the long-expected resolution of the Irish university situation was imminent.[31] The royal university had been

---

[28] O'Connor, 'The revolution in girls' secondary education', pp 42–4, 48.
[29] Breathnach, 'Charting new waters', pp 58–62.
[30] Ibid., pp 68–9.   [31] Above, vi, 565–6.

intended as a stop-gap pending a final solution, and women had no assurance of their position in new structures, which would almost certainly make attendance at specified institutions a prerequisite for degrees. Two government commissions were set up, the Robertson in 1901 on the royal university and the Fry in 1906 on Trinity College. The women educationists gave their views to both. The Central Association of Irish School Mistresses and the more recent Irish Association of Women Graduates (1902) pressed for fully coeducational institutions, arguing that this was the only way for women to share in the higher standards made possible by endowments, and the only way for women's degrees to be accepted as equal with men's. The women's colleges, both protestant and catholic, understandably wanted to survive as recognised teaching colleges affiliated to the universities, and argued the benefits of the collegiate life they could provide. The pros and cons of single-sex education were vigorously debated. But the campaign for coeducation was led by the women's colleges' own alumnae, who were adamant they did not want women 'to be shut into women's colleges'.[32] Then, while the arguments were in progress, both University College and Trinity College finally agreed to admit women. The enthusiasm with which students from both catholic and protestant women's colleges took advantage of this development further weakened the single-sex case.

The Irish universities act of 1908[33] set up two new institutions, the National University of Ireland—comprising University College, Cork, and University College, Galway (formerly queen's colleges), together with University College, Dublin—and the Queen's University of Belfast, the third former queen's college. Attendance was compulsory. Women's colleges were not given recognised college status in either university, but women were admitted on equal terms with men to the teaching, degrees, honours, and offices of both.

Access to degrees did not remove all barriers to the admission of women to the higher professions. In the United Kingdom the rise of 'scientific' medicine, monopolised by men, had culminated in the medical registration act of 1858. This made registration a prerequisite for medical practice, and registration required a qualification from one of the specified British examining or licensing bodies, thus excluding women. Feminist campaigning led to an act of parliament of 1876, which allowed, but did not require, United Kingdom governing bodies to award medical degrees to women.[34] There was some Irish participation in this campaign: Anna Haslam was one of those involved. The cause had the support not only of Irish feminists but also of some Irish doctors. Hence it was that the Royal College of Physicians of Ireland became

---

[32] Breathnach, 'Charting new waters', p. 71.
[33] 8 Edw. VII, c. 38 (1 Aug. 1908).
[34] 21 & 22 Vict., c. 90 (2 Aug. 1858); 39 & 40 Vict., c. 41 (11 Aug. 1876).

the first institution in the United Kingdom to admit women to the examinations for their licentiate; the first contingent of pioneering English and Scottish women were registered as licentiates in 1877. This allowed them to gain admission to the medical register and hence to practise.[35] Full admission to all professions had to wait until the Sex Disqualification (Removal) Act, 1919.[36]

MEANWHILE organised efforts to obtain the parliamentary vote had been under way in Ireland since the 1860s.[37] The explicit exclusion of women by the introduction of the words 'male person' in the reform act of 1832,[38] which extended the parliamentary franchise to middle-class men, was in itself evidence of developing feminist claims. Anna Haslam was one of the signatories to the famous petition for women's suffrage presented to the United Kingdom parliament by John Stuart Mill and Henry Fawcett in 1866. This asked for the inclusion of women in the 1867 reform act which extended the franchise to householders in boroughs and to rural and urban occupiers, subject to a property qualification.[39] Its rejection sparked off organised action in England and Ireland. During the late 1860s and early 1870s public and drawing-room meetings were held in various parts of Ireland. In the Dublin area Anne Robertson of Blackrock was a leading organiser, while in 1871 in Belfast Isabella Tod established the Northern Ireland Society for Women's Suffrage, affiliated to the London Women's Suffrage Society. Tod became one of the most effective public speakers for suffrage and other feminist causes, and was in demand for public meetings in both Ireland and England. Anna Haslam and her husband founded the Dublin Women's Suffrage Association (D.W.S.A.) in 1876.

The numbers involved in the suffrage campaign remained small until the end of the century, and Anna Haslam noted that it 'never penetrated much beyond the outskirts of Dublin, Belfast, and one or two other towns'. The D.W.S.A. itself, the organisation about which most is known, had only forty-three members in 1896.[40] Its membership was predominantly middle-class, protestant, and quaker, and included men as well as women. Haslam's husband, Thomas J. Haslam, also a quaker and a life-long collaborator with his

---

[35] 'The close of a long struggle', *Englishwoman's Review*, viii (15 Apr. 1877), pp 150–51; J. D. H. Widdess, *A history of the Royal College of Physicians of Ireland 1654–1963* (Edinburgh and London, 1963), pp 210–11.

[36] Below, p. 863.

[37] For the suffrage movement see Rosemary Cullen Owens, *Smashing times: a history of the Irish women's suffrage movement 1889–1922* (Dublin, 1984); Cliona Murphy, *The women's suffrage movement and Irish society in the early twentieth century* (New York, 1989).

[38] 2 & 3 Will. IV, c. 88 (7 Aug. 1832).

[39] 30 & 31 Vict., c. 102 (15 Aug. 1867).

[40] Anna Haslam, 'Irishwomen and the local government act' in *Englishwoman's Review*, xxix, 15 Oct. 1898, p. 224; Cullen Owens, *Smashing times*, p. 25.

wife in the women's movement, published three issues of a periodical, the *Women's Advocate*, in April, May, and July 1874. The first issue argued the classic enlightenment case for suffrage as 'the moral right of properly qualified women to some share in the enactment of the laws which they are required to obey'. The second gave practical advice on how to organise local groups for effective political action, advice followed by the association itself over many years under the energetic secretaryship of Anna Haslam, who continued as secretary and central organiser till 1913 when she became life president. Members worked to educate public opinion by writing to the newspapers and organising drawing-room and public meetings, the latter whenever the opportunity of high-profile or effective speakers arose. The D.W.S.A. maintained contact with the movement in England and sent delegates, regularly both Haslams, to suffrage and other feminist congresses. It kept a watchful eye on political developments in Ireland as well as in Britain to exploit favourable opportunities to lobby. It organised petitions to the house of commons. It sent deputations and wrote letters to Irish M.P.s urging them to introduce or support bills or amendments to bills to enfranchise women. It wrote to 'influential' women around the country exhorting them to lobby M.P.s. It noted with approval advances in the various emancipation campaigns, understandably since Haslam was involved in most or all of them.

Private members' bills for women's suffrage were introduced regularly from 1884, when women were yet again refused inclusion in a reform act.[41] This act extended the franchise to all male agricultural labourers who were householders, though a property qualification for lodgers still excluded a substantial proportion of men. Women's suffrage regularly attracted considerable support, sometimes majorities, in the house of commons, but never translated into legislation. This was partly because the Conservative party, generally opposed to women's suffrage, was in government almost continuously from 1885 to 1906; and partly because the Conservative majority in the house of lords could quash any measure that passed the commons.

Suffrage activity was sometimes interrupted by members' participation in other feminist campaigns. It was also interrupted by the land war. The D.W.S.A., for instance, held no executive meeting between April 1882 and June 1883. Although it distracted from the suffrage campaign, the land movement was to afford a unique opportunity for middle-class nationalist women to exercise political leadership in the Ladies' Land League.[42]

[41] 48 Vict., c. 3 (6 Dec. 1884).
[42] For the Ladies' Land League see Anna Parnell, *The tale of a great sham*, ed. with introduction by Dana Hearne (Dublin, 1986). The author made unsuccessful efforts to have this account (written in 1907) published in her lifetime. *The tale of a great sham* is a scathing criticism of the Land League leaders and league policy. See also T. W. Moody, 'Anna Parnell and the Land League' in *Hermathena*, cxvii (1974), pp 5–17; Margaret Ward, *Unmanageable*

Participation in community-based politics was nothing new for Irish women. During the nineteenth century some had also been active, as individuals, in such organisations as the repeal association, Young Ireland, and the fenians. On the unionist side, by the end of the century there were women's unionist associations. Isabella Tod, a particularly committed unionist, organised a Liberal Women's Unionist Association in Belfast, while Anna Haslam established a branch in Dublin.[43] As far as the Land League was concerned, women had taken an early part in the league's activities. They were essential participants—and often in the van—in the boycotting, preventing of evictions, and repossession of holdings that were the sanctions behind the league's policy.[44] Women who were tenant farmers in their own right (mostly widows) were eligible for league membership, and some took an active part. But the Ladies' Land League, an organisation of middle-class women which for a time ran a national campaign composed largely of men, was a new venture.

Michael Davitt, while in America, had been impressed by what he saw of the Ladies' Land League, an effective fund-raising and propaganda organisation initiated by Fanny Parnell, sister of Anna and Charles, in October 1880. He suggested a similar organisation in Ireland to dispense league funds to evicted families and families of arrested men (the typical work of a women's auxiliary organisation), but also to keep the league going in the expected event of the male leaders being imprisoned. In spite of the misgivings of the rest of the male leadership, including C. S. Parnell, the Ladies' Land League was established—on the male leaders' initiative—in January 1881 with Anna Parnell as organising secretary.

There appears to have been some lack of clarity as to what exactly the male leaders wanted the Ladies' Land League to do, and what the women understood them to want. In the event the women found themselves in charge of spending league funds according to existing league policy, that of 'rent at the point of a bayonet'. The women came to believe that this was a counterproductive policy, since in most cases the rent was eventually paid, at great expense to the league and little benefit to the cause: in other words, 'a great sham'. When the male leaders were imprisoned and the Land League suppressed in October 1881 the women found themselves in charge of the entire movement. This included administering a new policy, the 'No rent

revolutionaries: women and Irish nationalism (Dingle and London, 1983); Jane McL. Côté, *Fanny and Anna Parnell: Ireland's patriot sisters* (London, 1991); Dana Hearne and Jane McL. Côté, 'Anna Parnell' in Cullen & Luddy, *Women, power & consciousness*, pp 263–88.

[43] Patrick Buckland, *Irish unionism: one. The Anglo-Irish and the new Ireland 1885–1922* (Dublin and New York, 1972), p. 150; Maria Luddy, 'Women and politics in nineteenth-century Ireland' in Maryann G. Valiulis and Mary O'Dowd (ed.), *Women and Irish history* (Dublin, 1997), pp 89–108: 104–5.

[44] Janet K. TeBrake, 'Irish peasant women in revolt: the Land League years' in *I.H.S.*, xxviii, no. 109 (May 1992), pp 63–80.

manifesto' issued from Kilmainham, calling for the suspension of rent payments until the leaders were released. The Ladies' Land League's conduct of affairs at this point became the subject of some dispute. It appears that the women were not aware that the manifesto was essentially a political face-saver, which the men did not expect to be put into effect. Accordingly, they tried to implement a policy that was enormously expensive, and for which it would probably have been impossible to gain effective support from the tenants as a body. Anna Parnell came to believe that the male leadership had involved the women on false pretences.

When the men were released in May 1882 the Ladies' Land League leaders wanted to disband and hand back the management of league policy to the men. According to Anna Parnell, the men wanted the women to continue to do the unpopular work of handling the tenants' claims, as 'a perpetual petticoat screen behind which they [the men] could shelter, not from the government, but from the people'.[45] Her brother, however, is recorded as having been anxious for the Ladies' Land League to be suppressed. In any case, by this time the Ladies' Land League was a proscribed organisation. C. S. Parnell ensured that there would be no repetition of such clashes by excluding women from the Irish National League with which he replaced the Land League in October 1882.[46]

Despite all this the Ladies' Land League left a legacy of pride and achievement as a pioneering development in women's political organisation in Ireland. By July 1881 there were over 400 branches of various sizes throughout the country, with rank-and-file membership drawn largely from the catholic tenant-farmer class. The central leadership was composed mainly of middle-class women, catholic and protestant. At central and local level women filled public leadership positions. Some travelled around the country organising local activities, conduct regarded as a particular breach of conventional middle-class female behaviour. They organised the building of land league huts for the dispossessed, addressed huge outdoor public meetings, and defied official suppression of the Ladies' Land League. Some were arrested and went to prison.

Catholic members of the Ladies' Land League had to brave considerable criticism for invading a male sphere. The catholic archbishop of Dublin, Edward McCabe, in a pastoral letter read in all the parishes of his diocese, spoke of the modesty and chastity by which Irish women had brought glory to their country and which were now 'to be laid aside' on a false 'pretext of charity'. He urged his flock not to tolerate in their sodalities 'the woman who so far disavows her birthright of modesty as to parade herself before the

[45] Parnell, *Tale of a great sham*, pp 16, 155.
[46] T. W. Moody, *Davitt and Irish revolution 1846–82* (Oxford, 1981), pp 532, 545; Hearne & McL. Côté, 'Anna Parnell', pp 283–4; above, vi, 48.

public gaze'.[47] This was balanced by Archbishop T. W. Croke of Cashel, who commended the women as praiseworthy nationalists.

In the closing years of the century the suffrage movement was back in full action and achieved some tangible results. In the 1880s local government reform was on the political agenda in Britain and Ireland. English women had won the municipal franchise in 1869 and the omens were promising for an Irish initiative. A campaign led by Isabella Tod and the local women's suffrage society succeeded in winning the municipal franchise for female householders in Belfast in 1887. Eligibility of women to serve as poor law guardians now moved to the top of the suffragists' agenda. Women ratepayers already had the vote for guardians on the same terms as men, while in Britain women were also eligible for election as guardians. The office of poor law guardian had obvious interest for women philanthropists anxious to participate in policy-making. Anna Haslam attributed the Irish suffragists' earlier neglect of this issue to the fact that election to the boards had early on become an arena for political contests between male nationalists and unionists. It was conducted so much on 'party lines and with so little regard to the well-being of our destitute poor, that we were fairly excusable for taking little interest in it'.[48] Now it gave them their first major breakthrough. The Belfast M.P. William Johnston, who had introduced the Belfast municipal franchise bill, introduced a bill that became law as the Poor Law Guardians (Ireland) (Women) Act, 1896.[49] It provided that no person otherwise qualified 'shall be disqualified by sex or marriage' from being elected or serving as a guardian. The D.W.S.A. wrote to the newspapers and published leaflets explaining how women could ensure that they were properly registered to vote and to stand for election. Individual women all around the country were exhorted to seek out suitable candidates and urge them to go forward. By 1898 there were seventeen women poor law guardians, and by 1900 nearly 100; enough to hold a conference to share experience and ideas.

Isabella Tod died in 1896, without seeing the full results of her work. During her lifetime Tod had one of the highest profiles of any Irish feminist and was one of the leaders in every aspect of feminist activity. For the next generation it was Anna Haslam whose name became synonymous with pioneering Irish feminism. Haslam lived till 1922, retained her boundless energy, enthusiasm, and organising ability, and continued as an active suffragist well into the second decade of the twentieth century.

The next success came with the 1898 local government act, which set up county councils and urban and rural district councils. Women gained all the

[47] Côté, *Fanny and Anna Parnell*, pp 169–70.
[48] Haslam, 'Irishwomen and the local government act' in *Englishwoman's Review*, xxix (15 Oct. 1898), p. 221.
[49] 59 Vict., c. 5 (31 Mar. 1896).

remaining local government franchises on the same terms as men, as well as eligibility to become district councillors and town commissioners. Eligibility for membership of county and borough councils was withheld till 1911. These developments were seen by the D.W.S.A. as 'the most signal political revolution that has taken place in the history of Irishwomen. We have, in round numbers, somewhere about one hundred thousand women ratepayers who are now invested with powers which they never possessed before'. Again the D.W.S.A. published letters and leaflets to explain what had been achieved and how to excercise it. Anna Haslam saw the 1898 act as a political educator that would greatly strengthen the drive for the parliamentary vote. She envisaged the spread of the suffrage movement far beyond its current limits in Dublin, Belfast, and one or two other towns. 'For the great majority of our countrywomen in all our rural districts their political education commences with the present year.' The experience of participation in local government will 'make them not only desire the parliamentary vote, but willing to take some little trouble in order to obtain it'.[50] In response to these developments the D.W.S.A. changed its name first to the Dublin Women's Suffrage and Local Government Association and then to the Irish Women's Suffrage and Local Government Association (I.W.S.L.G.A.). While these local government advances were real achievements in themselves, Irish women were essentially catching up with what women in England had already gained; serious opposition, though real, was limited. The right to vote for and sit in parliament was unlikely to be so readily won. This became the central feminist campaign of the next two decades.

BY the turn of the century a new generation of educated Irish women, beneficiaries of the achievement of the earlier feminists, was emerging on the public scene. By 1881 in the age group 15–24 the literacy rate of females had overtaken and outstripped that of males, and in school attendance rates for the 5–9 age group girls had nearly caught up with boys.[51] By 1901 at secondary level, though boys outnumbered girls by nearly two to one, the curriculum in girls' schools was more academically demanding than it had been. And while the census recorded 3,101 male undergraduates to just 91 females, the very existence of women undergraduates and graduates, as well as a women graduates association (founded in 1902), was an important development for the women's movement and the suffrage campaign. In the new ferment of cultural and political activity and the surge of optimism and self-help, many women became actively involved in the language and cultural

[50] Local Government (Ireland) Act, 61 & 62 Vict., c. 37 (12 Aug. 1898); *Englishwoman's Review*, xxix (15 Oct. 1898), pp 223–5.
[51] David Fitzpatrick, ' "A share of the honeycomb": education, emigration, and Irishwomen' in Mary Daly and David Dickson (ed.), *The origins of popular literacy in Ireland: language change and educational development 1700–1920* (Dublin, 1990), pp 167–87: 169.

movements, in politics, organised labour, and agricultural improvement. When they found themselves excluded from an organisation, a regular response was to establish a women's organisation. An implicit feminist awareness appears to have informed most of these developments even when the objectives were not explicitly feminist.

The structure of Irish society suggested that the majority of feminist activists would continue to be middle-class women. Few working-class women worked in situations conducive to feminist politicisation and organisation. Outside the north-east, large-scale factory work was limited. Census reports continued to record most women as housewives classified under 'indefinite and non-productive' occupations. The big areas of paid employment were still domestic service, agriculture, and cloth and garment manufacture. Young women from the poorer classes expressed their dissatisfaction with what Ireland had to offer them by emigrating in large numbers. Employment opportunities for educated middle-class women remained few. Teaching was by far the largest professional occupation: the 1911 census recorded 11,667 schoolmistresses and assistants, and 2,265 teachers, lecturers, and governesses. Clerical work was beginning to expand, with 2,804 women in the civil service as 'officers and clerks' and 7,849 commercial clerks. Nuns, at 8,887, came next. Nursing, developing as a career for educated women, had moved out of domestic service to professional status with 4,516 women in 'subordinate medical service' and 1,006 'hospital certificated nurses', showing the trend towards training and recognised qualifications.[52] Among the 'higher' professions only medicine was effectively open to women, and the number entering was small; only 33 were recorded as 'physicians, surgeons, and general practitioners'.

The first fully autonomous organisation of nationalist women, Inghinidhe na hÉireann (Daughters of Ireland),[53] was founded in Dublin in October 1900 with Maud Gonne as the first president.[54] An ad hoc women's committee had come together to organise a 'patriotic children's treat' to counter an official free children's outing marking Queen Victoria's visit to Ireland in 1900. This committee went on to form a permanent national women's organisation. The objectives of the Inghinidhe were:

The reestablishment of the complete independence of Ireland.

To encourage the study of Gaelic, of Irish literature, history, music and art, especially among the young, by organising the teaching of classes for the above subjects.

---

[52] For the history of nursing see Pauline Scanlon, *The Irish nurse, a study of nursing in Ireland: history and education 1718–1981* (Manorhamilton, 1991).

[53] For Inghinidhe na hÉireann, see Ward, *Unmanageable revolutionaries*, pp 40–87.

[54] Maud Gonne (1866–1953), daughter of an English army officer, became a convert to Irish nationalism. She had the self-confidence to seek entry to organisations such as the Irish National League; and on finding women excluded, she and others established their own.

To support and popularise Irish manufacture.

To discourage the reading and circulation of low English literature, the singing of English songs, the attending of vulgar English entertainments at the theatres and music hall, and to combat in every way English influence which is doing so much injury to the artistic taste and refinement of the Irish people.

To form a fund called the National Purposes Fund, for the furtherance of the above objects.[55]

The Inghinidhe brought to their work a style and flair that epitomised the enthusiasm and high spirits of the broad cultural-nationalist milieu of the period. Among the members were poets, writers, actresses, and feminists, including such diverse personalities as Jennie Wyse Power, formerly of the Ladies' Land League; Alice Milligan, the presbyterian nationalist and poet, who with the poet Anna Johnston ('Ethna Carbery') edited the nationalist paper *Shan Van Vocht* in Belfast from 1896 to 1899; and Constance Markievicz, daughter of the landed Gore-Booth family in Sligo, and a convert to nationalism and socialism.

From 1908 to 1911 the Inghinidhe published the first Irish women's paper, *Bean na hÉireann*, a 'woman's paper advocating militancy, separatism, and feminism',[56] which attracted a wide spectrum of readers and writers of both sexes. They also ran children's classes, organised céilís, and staged *tableaux vivants* and plays, including W. B. Yeats's 'Cathleen Ni Houlihan', written for Maud Gonne to play the title role. Their work in these areas contributed to the emergence of the Abbey Theatre, some of whose leading actresses, including Máire Nic Shiubhlaigh and Helena Molony, were members. On the political side, the Inghinidhe were also active in the foundation in 1905 of Sinn Féin,[57] the first nationalist organisation in which women held executive office alongside men. In pursuit of their political aims the Inghinidhe also patrolled the streets of Dublin to dissuade young Irish women from consorting with British soldiers.

In the area of rural development 1910 saw the foundation of what was to become the largest and most long-lived of all Irish women's organisations, the United Irishwomen (later known as the Irish Countrywomen's Association). The first branch was founded in 1910 by Anita Lett, a farmer, in Bree, County Wexford, following a lively correspondence in the pages of the *Irish Homestead* on the drabness of rural life for young women. A major impetus came from interaction with the cooperative movement of Sir Horace Plunkett and the Irish Agricultural Organisation Society (1894). Registered as a friendly society and affiliated to the I.A.O.S., the United Irishwomen sought to supply a dimension missing from the work of the former. The aim was to

---

55 Ward, *Unmanageable revolutionaries*, p. 51.
56 Its editor Helena Molony, quoted in Cullen Owens, *Smashing times*, pp 45–6.
57 The name 'Sinn Féin' was devised by a woman, Máire Butler, in 1905 (below, viii, 376).

animate country living by encouraging rural women, of all classes, religions and politics, to develop a 'healthy and progressive community life' which would reduce both emigration and the flight from country to city.

The society was organised on hierarchical lines with an executive in Dublin. Branches were to be established at parish level and affiliated to county organisations, and through these to the central body. Officeholders were drawn from the middle and upper classes, protestant and catholic, with the catholic Lady Fingall serving as president from 1912 to 1942 in succession to the protestant Anita Lett. But the society aimed at a membership of all classes and denominations and saw itself as 'strongly national' from the start.[58]

The United Irishwomen's work covered agriculture and industry, domestic economy, and social and intellectual development. Some of its first campaigns targeted health education for women and the provision of qualified district nurses and doctors. Other activities included instruction in household economy, horticulture, bee-keeping, poultry and egg production, and the holding of local shows. Dances, music, and drama were also important; and by 1912 there were twenty-one branches in Counties Antrim, Carlow, Clare, Donegal, Galway, Kildare, Kilkenny, Limerick, Louth, Mayo, Wicklow, and Wexford.

While the society did not describe itself as a feminist organisation, it did aim to have women's voices and actions felt in the development of the new Ireland. According to its first organiser, writing in 1911, the United Irishwomen

consider it essential that women in Ireland should make their wishes known if they want them to be gratified, and they feel that they have somewhat neglected their own and each other's interests by not putting them before the public more prominently than they have done. For this reason they intend to seek for better representation on public bodies, so as to be able to make their point of view known in public affairs.[59]

Organisation and activity were disrupted by the first world war, the 1916 rising, the war of independence, and the civil war. But expansion began again in the 1920s, and in 1935 the society reorganised and changed its name to the Irish Countrywomen's Association.

Meanwhile the suffrage campaign was expanding rapidly, fulfilling Anna Haslam's prophecy. Internationally it was becoming a large-scale movement and adopting new campaigning methods. In the later decades of the nine-

---

[58] Muriel Gahan, 'Bantracht na Tuaithe 1910–1970' in *Irish Countrywoman: the journal of Bantracht na Tuaithe* (Dec. 1970), pp 21–44: 24; Sarah McNamara, *Those intrepid United Irishwomen: pioneers of the Irish Countrywomen's Association* (Limerick, 1995).
[59] Ellice Pilkington, 'The United Irishwomen—their work' in Horace Plunkett, Ellice Pilkington, and George Russell, *The United Irishwomen: their place, work and ideals* (Dublin, 1911), pp 19–35: 33.

teenth century large-scale street demonstrations with banners, slogans, and colours had appeared in countries where governments tolerated such public expressions of dissent. Some women moved to more assertive methods, first to passive civil disobedience such as refusing to pay tax, then to heckling and disrupting public meetings, and finally to physical violence such as damaging public property. This final level of what was termed 'militancy' emerged in Britain and Ireland where suffrage had for so long appeared within reach but had not yet been attained. The name 'suffragette' was coined to distinguish the 'militants' from the 'constitutional' suffragists who believed the cause was best served by campaigning strictly within the law. In England militancy was associated with the Women's Social and Political Union (W.S.P.U.), founded in 1903 and led by the Pankhursts, in contrast to the constitutional National Union of Women's Suffrage Societies (N.U.W.S.S.).

In Ireland the Irish Women's Franchise League (I.W.F.L.) was founded in 1908 as a society prepared to use militant methods if necessary, by a group led by Hanna Sheehy Skeffington[60] and Margaret Cousins.[61] Both women had begun their suffrage careers in the I.W.S.L.G.A., and their respect and affection for Anna Haslam remained strong. But although the I.W.S.L.G.A. was explicitly non-aligned to any political party, and had many nationalist members, the new group wanted a suffrage society that was more assertive and more distinctly Irish. The I.W.F.L. (also non-aligned to any political party) modelled its militancy on that of the English W.S.P.U., whose 'spirited frontal attack on their government' the Irish women greatly admired.[62] But it was committed to complete independence of any English organisation. It grew rapidly, and it appears that a large proportion of catholic suffragists joined its ranks.

Further new suffrage organisations followed, and the movement attained a numerical strength and scale far beyond that of any earlier feminist campaign. Membership was still predominantly middle-class and protestant, but a growing proportion—about one-third—were catholics.[63] In 1912 it was

---

[60] Hanna Sheehy Skeffington (1877–1946) came from a Dublin catholic nationalist family. Her father, David Sheehy, was nationalist M.P. for Galway South (1885–1900) and Meath South (1903–18). An M.A. of the royal university and founder of the Irish Association of Women Graduates (1902), she had argued for coeducational colleges in the new university system. She and her husband Francis Skeffington, both socialists, feminists, and pacifists, adopted the joint name Sheehy Skeffington. See Leah Levenson and Jerry H. Natterstad, *Hanna Sheehy Skeffington: Irish feminist* (Syracuse, 1986); Maria Luddy, *Hanna Sheehy Skeffington* (Dublin, 1995); Margaret Ward, *Hanna Sheehy Skeffington* (Dublin, 1997).

[61] Margaret Gillespie (1878–1954) came from a protestant unionist family in Roscommon, but both she and her husband, James Cousins of Belfast, were nationalists. They both converted to theosophy and emigrated to India in 1915, where Margaret Cousins became a pioneer of the Indian women's movement. See J. H. Cousins and M. E. Cousins, *We two together* (Madras, 1950).

[62] Ibid, p. 164.

[63] Dana Hearne, 'The development of Irish feminist thought: a critical historical analysis of *The Irish Citizen* 1912–1920' (Ph. D. thesis, York University, Ontario, 1992).

calculated (perhaps optimistically) that there were over 3,000 active suffragists in Ireland. The largest groups were the long-established I.W.S.L.G.A. with 700–800 members; the I.W.F.L. with over 1,000; an Irish branch of the Conservative and Unionist Women's Franchise Association with 660, and the Irish Women's Suffrage Society (I.W.S.S.) in Belfast, with several hundred.[64] There was also the umbrella Irish Women's Suffage Federation (I.W.S.F.), founded in 1911 to link the smaller groups in a network. The Federation included the Irish Women's Reform League (I.W.R.L.), founded by Louie Bennett with a remit that included the social and economic interests of working-class women as well as the vote. By 1913 there were well over a dozen societies affiliated to the I.W.S.F., including nine in Ulster as well as the Munster Women's Franchise League (M.W.F.L.), which had its own branches.[65] Some groups had specific political or religious affiliations, and in 1915 the Irish Catholic Women's Suffrage Association was founded, which had about 167 members in 1917.

Political developments in the early twentieth century created tensions within the suffrage movement. The 1911 limitation on the powers of the house of lords improved the prospects for legislation on both home rule and women's suffrage. Suffragists now had to contemplate the likelihood of two parliaments. A women's suffrage act passed by the U.K. parliament might enfranchise women in both Britain and Ireland, but it was important that women should have the vote for any home rule parliament. Despite their politically mixed composition, the suffrage societies maintained a united policy of supporting all measures of female suffrage. Unionist suffragists opposed home rule, but if it should come wanted it to include votes for women. So did British suffragists, since this would make it more difficult to refuse the vote for women in the U.K.[66] The attitude of the Irish home rule M.P.s was important to all suffragists, since it could be crucial to the success of a U.K. as well as a home rule suffrage measure.

Nationalist women experienced some tensions over the suffrage issue. The nationally minded I.W.F.L. was to the fore in pressing that female suffrage be included in any home rule bill, and also urged Irish M.P.s to support any U.K. suffrage bill that came before parliament. Certain other nationalist women, often themselves suffragists, argued that on principle nationalists should not give legitimacy to the U.K. parliament's claim to authority over Ireland by asking it for the vote. They also argued that women should wait until the home rule bill was safely passed before pressing for women's suffrage in a new Irish parliament. The Inghinidhe na hÉireann paper *Bean na hÉireann* posited a golden era in Ireland's past when women and men had

---

[64] *Irish Citizen*, 25 May 1912, p. 7.
[65] Cullen Owens, *Smashing times*, p. 43.
[66] Margaret Ward, 'Conflicting interests: the British and Irish suffrage movements' in *Feminist Review*, 1 (summer 1995), p. 132.

been fully equal, and argued that equality would automatically be restored once independence was achieved. Another claim was that, by virtue of their equal status with men in the Gaelic League, Sinn Féin, and the industrial movement, women already effectively had the franchise in Irish Ireland. Such optimism was criticised by 'suffrage first' activists as doomed to disillusionment. Hanna Sheehy Skeffington cautioned that until 'the parliamentarian and the Sinn Féin woman alike possess the vote, the keystone of citizenship, she will count but little with either party'.[67] Unionist women also faced political choices. The Ulster Women's Unionist Council (U.W.U.C.) was established in January 1911 to support the Ulster Unionist Council's opposition to home rule. Within a year it recorded 40,000–50,000 members. While the U.W.U.C. insisted that maintenance of the union took priority over any other commitment, the political experience gained by its members appears to have been a positive one for the suffrage movement in the longer run.[68]

While many members of the Irish parliamentary party individually supported women's franchise, they fell into line whenever Redmond decided that backing it might harm the prospects for home rule. Looking back Hanna Sheehy Skeffington commented that to 'the powerful Irish party and its machine, backed by such organisations as the sectarian Ancient Order of Hibernians of Joseph Devlin . . . we were a pestilential red herring across the trail of home rule'.[69] The situation was similar to that in the United States, where some had opposed women's suffrage on the grounds that it might delay votes for freed male slaves, or in Britain, where it might hold up extensions of the franchise to new classes of men. The suffragists' frustration was not lessened by the knowledge that Redmond himself and the Liberal prime minister Asquith were both personally opposed to women's franchise.

Because newspaper coverage of suffrage and other feminist concerns was so inadequate, in 1912 a fortnightly suffrage paper, the *Irish Citizen*, was founded in association with the I.W.F.L., with Francis Sheehy Skeffington and James Cousins as editors, carrying on its masthead the motto: 'For men and women equally the rights of citizenship; from men and women equally the duties of citizenship.' The *Irish Citizen* supported the suffrage-first position, but it carried news on all suffrage activity and provided a forum for debate on a range of feminist concerns. This debate demonstrated the continuing broad agenda of the Irish feminist movement. Working-class

---

[67] *Bean na hÉireann*, i, no. 13 (Nov. 1910), p. 6.
[68] Diane Urquhart, ' "The female of the species is deadlier than the male"? The Ulster Women's Unionist Council, 1911–1940' in Janice Holmes and Diane Urquhart (ed.), *Coming into the light: the work, politics and religion of women in Ulster 1840–1940* (Belfast, 1994), pp 93–123: 97, 102.
[69] Hanna Sheehy Skeffington, 'Reminiscences of an Irish suffragette' (1941) in Andrée Sheehy Skeffington and Rosemary Owens (ed.), *Votes for women: Irish women's struggle for the vote* (Dublin, 1975), p. 13.

women's conditions and their need for trade union organisation; equal pay; domestic and sexual violence against women and children; and the need for women jurors, lawyers, police and judges were among the issues discussed. The paper continued till 1920 and became one of the best sources of information on the women's movement during that period.

In 1912 one of a series of 'conciliation' bills, which by agreement between the main political parties would have conceded a limited female franchise, confined to householders, was defeated when the Irish party failed to support it. Redmond feared its passing might jeopardise the Liberal government, thus endangering home rule. The English W.S.P.U. retaliated by declaring opposition to home rule itself on the principle 'No suffrage—no home rule'. Irish suffragists increased the pressure on the Irish party to have suffrage included in the home rule bill then before parliament. The I.W.F.L. had already begun to use more militant methods against the Irish party, heckling and disrupting its public meetings. Redmond remained obdurate, and the combined suffrage movement responded with a mass meeting in Dublin. Mary Hayden, professor of Irish history at U.C.D., chaired the meeting in the Antient Concert Rooms. The hall was packed with suffragists of all creeds and politics as well as nationalist and labour women. The meeting sent an agreed resolution to cabinet ministers and to all Irish M.P.s:

That while expressing no opinion on the general question of home rule, this mass meeting of delegates from the Irish suffrage societies and other women's organisations, representing all shades of political and religious opinion, profoundly regrets the proposal to establish a new constitution in Ireland on a purely male franchise, and calls upon the government to amend the home rule bill in committee by adopting the local government register (which includes women) as the basis for the new parliament.[70]

When this still failed to elicit a response the I.W.F.L. moved up the scale of militancy to an organised breaking of windows in Dublin Castle and other public buildings. Several Irish suffragists had already been imprisoned for militant suffrage activities in England, and the Dublin incidents now led to a number of suffragists being arrested, charged, fined, refusing to pay, and being sent to prison. Down to this point, public reaction to the Irish suffrage movement had been mixed. Now the I.W.F.L.'s militant tactics, which were regarded as unwomanly, attracted widespread criticism. Nationalists also worried about the implications for home rule. Of course, many of the critics opposed votes for women even when advocated by constitutional suffragists. The constitutional I.W.S.L.G.A. publicly criticised the I.W.F.L.'s militancy as counterproductive, but it rejected the double standards that attacked the I.W.F.L. for largely symbolic actions which would hardly have raised an

[70] Cullen Owens, *Smashing times*, p. 53.

eyebrow if carried out by any male organisation. Anna Haslam, herself a liberal unionist and now aged 83, visited Hanna Sheehy Skeffington in Mountjoy prison. 'Don't think I approve—but here's a pot of verbena I brought you. I am not here in my official capacity, of course—the Irish Women [*sic*] Suffrage and Local Government Association strongly disapprove of violence as pulling back the cause. But here's some loganberry jam—I made it myself'.[71]

During Prime Minister Asquith's visit to Dublin in July 1912 three members of the English W.S.P.U. travelled to Dublin without the knowledge of the Irish suffragists. One of them threw a hatchet, 'small ... blunt and meant symbolically, but that didn't help much', according to Hanna Sheehy Skeffington, at Asquith's carriage. It missed him and grazed Redmond. The following day two of the women set fire to curtains at a box in the Theatre Royal, and this was followed by a small explosion. Amid public outrage Mary Leigh and Gladys Evans were each sentenced to five years penal servitude. Refused political prisoner status, they went on hunger strike and were forcibly fed. The I.W.F.L. was annoyed at this unauthorised intervention in Ireland, but did not condemn the action itself; the League was, however, blamed by a hostile press and members of the public for the W.S.P.U.'s activities. Some members resigned and there were serious physical attacks on their public meetings. The *Irish Citizen* defended the Englishwomen, and Sheehy Skeffington and others in prison at the same time went on sympathetic hunger strike.

Militancy died down in Dublin towards the latter part of 1913, but it flared up in the north. Suffrage societies in the north had tended to be quite small and non-militant, and the I.W.F.L. had found it difficult to get a foothold there because it was seen as a nationalist body. However, the English W.S.P.U. established a branch in Belfast to press for the inclusion of women's suffrage in the Ulster Unionist Council's plan to set up a provisional government if home rule became a reality. But in March 1914 Sir Edward Carson made it clear that he was no more prepared than Redmond to commit himself to the potentially divisive policy of votes for women. The W.S.P.U. retaliated with violence that went beyond the largely symbolic actions of the I.W.F.L., setting fire to privately owned unionist property and planting a bomb at Lisburn cathedral. Between March and August 1914 thirteen women were arrested.[72]

At the same time the suffrage movement was interacting with socialism and the labour movement. For many socialists, the initiative in social revolution must come from the workers, not the middle or upper classes. Socialist

[71] Murphy, *Women's suffrage movement*, ch. 5; Sheehy Skeffington, 'Reminiscences', pp 20–21.
[72] Cullen Owens, *Smashing times*, pp 70–71.

feminism had emerged most strongly in Germany under the leadership of Clara Zetkin and in association with the Social Democratic Party (S.P.D.) in the 1890s.[73] Socialist feminists argued that working-class women would not benefit from the removal of discrimination based on sex unless the class issue was first resolved.

The nineteenth-century Irish emancipation movement, like the American and British movements, had developed within a liberal-individualist ethos. It sought the vote for women on the same terms as men, which in the mid nineteenth century still meant a property qualification. For socialist feminists this turned the campaign into a 'bourgeois' one, concerned mainly with emancipation for middle-class women. In the early decades of the twentieth century some links developed between the nationalist and syndicalist trade union movement, led by James Larkin and James Connolly, and the suffrage organisations sympathetic to nationalism and socialism, the I.W.F.L. and the I.W.R.L. Connolly was a feminist by conviction, who unequivocally supported women's right to the franchise and their right to use it against him if they wished, and who encouraged militant demands for the vote. The Irish Socialist Republican party he had founded in 1896 had included universal suffrage in its manifesto. Later, he became national organiser of the Socialist Party of Ireland, of which both Sheehy Skeffingtons were members. Connolly was regularly available to speak on I.W.F.L. platforms.[74]

In the early 1900s some of the young feminists in the suffrage movement had socialist and labour sympathies. Louie Bennett's I.W.R.L. explicitly linked labour issues with suffrage, and both *Bean na hÉireann* and the *Irish Citizen* advocated the organisation of women workers. Trade unions were more difficult to organise among women than among men. Homemaking, the majority occupation, was ill adapted to unionisation, and so were those major areas of women's paid employment, domestic service and agriculture. Marriage added a further complication. A young single employed woman might want equal pay with men, but once she married higher pay for men might become preferable. Factory work was the most favourable to unionisation, but many women in the clothing industries worked at home as outworkers.

Moves to develop women's trade unions in Ireland had begun at least as early as 1880[75] and had attracted the support of middle-class feminists, including Anna Haslam. In the aftermath of the Trade Union Congress held in Dublin in 1880, two unions were formed, the Dublin Tailoresses'

[73] Richard J. Evans, *The feminists: women's emancipation movements in Europe, America and Australasia, 1840–1920* (London and New York, 1977), p. 160.
[74] Peter Berresford Ellis, *A history of the Irish working class* (London, 1972), p. 173; Levenson & Natterstad, *Hanna Sheehy Skeffington*, pp 51–2.
[75] See Theresa Moriarty, *Work in progress: episodes from the history of Irish women's trade unionism* (Dublin and Belfast, 1994).

Society and the Bookfolders and Sewers' Union, but both were shortlived. In 1893 the Textile Operatives Society of Ireland was established in Belfast. Mary Galway, who became its secretary in 1897, later became the first woman vice-president of the Irish Trade Union Congress. In August 1911 3,000 Dublin women struck for better pay at Jacob's biscuit factory. In the same year the Irish Women Workers Union (I.W.W.U.) was established in Dublin as a general union for all women workers. Towards the end of the first world war it grew rapidly: by 1918 its members included printers, laundresses, and general workers.

The I.W.W.U. emerged within the socialist and nationalist labour movement led by Larkin and Connolly, and with the encouragement and support of many feminists. Constance Markievicz and Hanna Sheehy Skeffington were platform speakers at the I.W.W.U.'s inaugural meeting. Markievicz reminded her audience that they could achieve nothing without organisation, and urged them, amid laughter, to join the union, which would help them to gain the vote 'and make men of you all'.[76] The first general secretary was Delia Larkin, sister of James, who was succeeded by Helena Molony,[77] and in 1917 by Louie Bennett.[78]

During the 1913 lockout Sheehy Skeffington and other I.W.F.L. members helped in the soup kitchen in Liberty Hall, presided over by Markievicz, while Bennett and the I.W.R.L. gave support to strikers' families. The Irish Citizen Army, set up by Larkin and Connolly to protect the workers, enrolled women on equal terms with men. All this encouraged debates about adult suffrage as opposed to women's suffrage, and forged bonds between labour and feminism, at least at leadership level. It is less clear how close the links were at rank and file level. Looking back in 1930 Helena Molony wrote that the women's movement had 'passed over the head of the Irish working woman and left her untouched'.[79]

The growing political tension over home rule saw the emergence of a new women's organisation and more problems for feminists. The Ulster Women's Unionist Council engaged in vigorous propaganda and demonstrations against home rule, and (when women were barred from signing the Ulster

[76] Mary Jones, *These obstreperous lassies: a history of the Irish Women Workers Union* (Dublin, 1988), p. 3.

[77] Helena Molony (1883–1967), nationalist, feminist, and Abbey Theatre actress, devoted most of her life to the union. Sent to prison in 1911 for throwing a stone at a shop window during protests at the state visit of George V, she was imprisoned again for her part in the 1916 rising, and from prison persuaded her friend Louie Bennett to take over the leadership of the I.W.W.U.

[78] Louie Bennett (1870–1956) came from a protestant, unionist, middle-class Dublin family. She became a feminist, pacifist, and campaigner for social and economic justice, with a commitment to Irish nationalist objectives, though opposing the use of physical force. She founded the Irish Women's Reform League (I.W.R.L.) in 1911 and was involved in setting up the Irish Women's Suffrage Federation (I.W.S.F.). Like Molony, she devoted her life to the I.W.W.U. In 1931 she became the first woman president of the Irish Congress of Trade Unions.

[79] Cullen Owens, *Smashing times*, p. 92.

covenant in September 1912) organised a women's declaration which collected more signatures than the men's covenant. When the Ulster Volunteer Force was set up in 1913, the U.W.U.C. actively supported it. It appears that far larger numbers of women could be rallied for unionist causes than for either nationalism or suffrage.[80] On the nationalist side in April 1914 Cumann na mBan (Association of Women) was established in Dublin as an auxiliary to the Irish Volunteers. Cumann na mBan's constitution stated its aims as:

1. To advance the cause of Irish liberty.
2. To organise Irishwomen in furtherance of this object.
3. To assist in arming and equipping a body of Irishmen for the defence of Ireland.
4. To form a fund for these purposes to be called the 'Defence of Ireland Fund'.[81]

Both the U.W.U.C. and Cumann na mBan attracted many women who supported women's suffrage. Argument among nationalist feminists over priorities broke out immediately. The issue was how, rather than whether, suffrage should be achieved. Cumann na mBan women supported the separatist view that England's difficulty in the imminent war would be Ireland's opportunity, and argued that national freedom must come first, with the emancipation of women following that of the nation. The I.W.F.L. and the *Irish Citizen* maintained that suffrage must remain the first priority; they also adopted a pacifist position. *Irish Citizen* editorials insisted that feminists should not compromise on women's rights, and deplored the fact that nationalist women accepted a status subordinate to that of the men in the Volunteers. Cumann na mBan retorted that they were not the servants of the Volunteers but their colleagues and co-workers.

Britain's entry into war in August 1914 faced unionist feminists with their own questions about priorities. In Britain most suffrage societies, including the militant W.S.P.U., suspended campaigning and lined up behind the war effort. In Ireland, suffrage groups linked to British organisations tended to suspend suffrage activity and turn to relief work. For many suffragists who looked to the U.K. parliament for the vote, war work gave women the opportunity to prove their entitlement to the vote by their ability to carry out men's work. The I.W.S.L.G.A., whose members included both nationalists and unionists, subscribed to a Red Cross hospital bed, collected funds to help refugees, and tried to coordinate feminist action on issues other than suffrage. Allegiances were often strained. Individual members of Cumann na mBan cooperated with Lady Aberdeen (wife of the viceroy) and the

[80] Urquhart, '"The female of the species"', pp 100, 102; Luddy, 'Women and politics in nineteenth-century Ireland', p. 105.
[81] Ward, *Unmanageable revolutionaries*, p. 93.

Women's National Health Association (1907) to form an Irish branch of the Red Cross after the outbreak of war;[82] but when the Munster Women's Franchise League donated an ambulance to the war effort, Mary MacSwiney, a nationalist and member of Cumann na mBan, resigned. The I.W.F.L. and the *Irish Citizen* continued to urge that suffrage must remain the first priority.

A home rule bill passed in September 1914, but with its operation suspended till the war ended, and with the future of the Ulster counties still unclear. When John Redmond, hoping to promote home rule, adopted a policy of support for Britain, the Irish Volunteers split, with the majority following Redmond into the National Volunteers and many from there to the trenches, and the minority retaining the original name and the hope that Ireland's opportunity might be imminent. Cumann na mBan also split, but in their case the majority rejected Redmond's policy and opted for the separatist side.

The relationship between feminists, war, and pacifism was now to the fore. Women, and particularly feminists, had long been active in peace movements. In Ireland, for example, Anna Haslam's first public activity had been in the Olive Leaf circle, a quaker peace organisation. Now a women's peace movement emerged from the international women's movement, with which Irish feminists had long-established contacts. In 1888 the International Council of Women had been established to link national councils of women's organisations in different countries. Not all were supporters of women's suffrage, and so a separate International Woman Suffrage Alliance (usually called the International Alliance) was founded in 1904. Since its early years the I.W.S.L.G.A. had maintained links with the movement, and in 1906 Thomas Haslam was a delegate from the I.W.S.L.G.A. to the International Alliance congress in London.[83] In 1913 Hanna Sheehy Skeffington from the I.W.F.L., Louie Bennett from the I.W.S.F., and Lady Dockrell from the I.W.S.L.G.A. attended the congress in Budapest.[84] By 1914 the International Alliance had extended its membership to women's organisations in twenty-four countries around the world. By 1920 its aims had expanded to include, besides suffrage, equal pay, the right to work, the improved legal status of wives and mothers, abolition of slavery and child marriage, and the control of dangerous drugs.

As war approached the Alliance was divided over whether to take a strictly pacifist stance. The International Committee of Women for Permanent Peace (I.C.W.P.P.), known from 1919 as the Women's International League

[82] John C. Gordon and Ishbel M. Gordon, '*We twa*': *reminiscences of Lord and Lady Aberdeen* (2 vols, London, 1925), ii, 230.
[83] Arnold Whittick, *Woman into citizen* (London, 1979), pp 22–32, 51.
[84] Rosemary Cullen Owens, 'Women and pacificism in Ireland, 1915–1932' in Valiulis & O'Dowd, *Women & Ir. hist.*, pp 220–38: 220–21.

(W.I.L.), was founded by pacifist feminists after an international congress at the Hague in April 1915.[85] Pacifism was a controversial issue both for feminists who supported their own government's participation in the war and for those who upheld the right of armed insurrection. In Ireland as elsewhere, pacifist feminists were in a minority. At this period they appear to have been drawn largely from the I.W.F.L. and the I.W.S.F., with vigorous support from the *Irish Citizen*. An Irish committee was established, which nominated seven delegates to attend the Hague conference. The British government, like others, was opposed to pacifism and tried to obstruct attendance. Of the Irish delegates only Louie Bennett obtained a permit and she, like most of the English women, was prevented from attending by the British admiralty's banning of passenger traffic on the crucial day. The Irish committee continued in being, at first as part of the British branch. However, it sought separate representation, and in January 1916 an independent Irish branch was set up, with the name 'Irishwomen's International League' (I.I.L.), which by December was recognised by the I.C.W.P.P. Its objectives were to work for the 'complete enfranchisement of women', a 'just and reasonable' settlement of the Irish question by promoting 'goodwill and a better understanding', and cooperation with women of other countries with the aim of 'permanent international peace'.[86]

In the turmoil of political events the suffrage movement inevitably declined in numbers and vigour, yet the close relationship between the I.W.F.L., Cumann na mBan, and the republican male leaders led to the public endorsement of women's full citizenship in the 1916 proclamation. R. M. Fox in 1935 looked back to the days when the I.W.F.L. and the *Irish Citizen* 'formed a rallying point for all the best and most progressive elements in Dublin... In its pages the anti-conscription struggle, and other vital issues, received attention... Madame Markievicz, Connolly, Pearse, MacDonagh, and many other pioneers of the rebellion used the platform of the Franchise League to express their views'.[87]

The 1916 proclamation asserted that the 'Irish Republic is entitled to, and hereby claims, the allegiance of every Irishman and Irishwoman. The Republic guarantees religious and civil liberty, equal rights, and equal opportunities to all its citizens.' Kathleen Clarke recalled how on the night the proclamation was signed her husband told her 'it represented the views of all except one, who thought equal opportunities should not be given to women.' She went on: 'Except to say that Tom [Clarke] was not that one, my lips are sealed.'[88] James

[85] Jill Liddington, *The long road to Greenham: feminism and anti-militarism in Britain since 1820* (London, 1989), p. 106.

[86] Cullen Owens, 'Women and pacificism in Ireland', pp 224, 227.

[87] R. M. Fox, *Rebel Irishwomen* (Dublin, 1967; 1st ed. 1935), p. 75.

[88] Kathleen Clarke, *Revolutionary woman: Kathleen Clarke 1878–1972, an autobiography*, ed. Helen Litton (Dublin, 1991), p. 69.

Connolly, too, indicated that only one of the seven signatories had disagreed with the commitment to equality.[89] The proclamation, together with women's participation in the rising, accordingly became the basis for nationalist women's demand for full equality of citizenship in an independent Ireland.

Despite the confusion resulting from the countermanding of the orders for Easter Sunday, over 200 women took part in the 1916 rising, most of them in Dublin. A few were involved in active combat, others in liaison and dispatch-carrying, more in nursing, first aid, and cooking, and yet others in bringing food, arms, and equipment to the various posts.[90] The particularly difficult task of acting as Pearse's envoy during the surrender was carried out by Elizabeth O'Farrell, a member of the Inghinidhe na hÉireann branch of Cumann na mBan. In general, Citizen Army women appear to have found it easier to be accepted as equals by their male colleagues, and to take an active part in the fighting. Constance Markievicz fought as second-in-command to Michael Mallin at St Stephen's Green and the College of Surgeons. She was court-martialled and sentenced to death, though this was commuted to a life sentence. Helena Molony took part in the attack on Dublin Castle, and she too was imprisoned after the rising. Dr Kathleen Lynn, another leading feminist member of the Citizen Army, served as medical officer. Cumann na mBan women had a more mixed experience, some finding that they were not readily allowed to join the men and those that did discovering that they were apt to be treated very much as auxiliaries.

In the later months of 1916 women such as Kathleen Clarke played a central role in the emergence of Sinn Féin as an umbrella organisation for a broad range of nationalists. They organised help for the republican prisoners and relief for their families, developed an amnesty movement, and raised the profile of the rising and kept it constantly before the public eye. As the revitalised Sinn Féin became established, 'nation-first' and 'suffrage-first' feminists came together to press their male colleagues to share leadership with women. Cumann na mBan no longer believed that nationalist men would of their own accord accept women as equal political partners. Like Sinn Féin, Cumann na mBan grew significantly in numbers during this period.

The I.W.F.L., while maintaining its suffrage-first position, was also concerned to assert women's rights within the new nationalist structures. Hanna Sheehy Skeffington, whose husband had been summarily executed by British soldiers during the rising, was also becoming a leading public speaker in support of nationalist claims for full independence. The two organisations found a new unity of purpose in which they also cooperated with the

---

[89] Fox, *Rebel Irishwomen*, p. 76.

[90] Ward, *Unmanageable revolutionaries*, pp 108–14; Ruth Taillon, *When history was made: the women of 1916* (Belfast, 1996).

I.W.W.U.,[91] now under the leadership of Louie Bennett, who remained an uncompromising pacifist but who was also a strong supporter of Irish independence and a committed feminist.

A new organisation, Cumann as dTeachtaire (Society of Delegates), comprising women delegates to all republican bodies and conferences, was set up to press for adequate representation for women in republican structures, to promote women's rights in general, and where possible to cooperate with other women's organisations. Accordingly, during 1918 Cumann na mBan, the I.W.W.U., and the I.W.F.L. combined in opposition to conscription, and the I.W.S.L.G.A. joined them to oppose the regulation of prostitution in the Defence of the Realm Consolidation Act, 1914 (5 Geo.V, c. 8 (27 Nov. 1914)). Nationalist women, and the I.W.W.U. in particular, played an important part in the resistance to conscription. Their refusal to accept industrial conscription (the recruitment of women to fill the jobs vacated by conscripted men) was essential to the success of the campaign.

At this time too the first instalment of parliamentary suffrage was finally achieved. In February 1918 the Representation of the People Act, 1918,[92] a compromise acceptable to the Liberal and Conservative parties, was passed. This gave a limited measure of female suffrage, confined to women over 30 who themselves or whose husbands were householders or occupiers of land or premises of a minimum yearly value of £5, a restriction that reflected the fears of most political parties as to how women would use their votes in the coming election. Both the Irish parliamentary party and the unionists tried to prevent the extension of the limited franchise act to Ireland. In view of their record on women's suffrage both had reason to feel apprehensive. In November 1918 a further act[93] made women eligible for election to parliament. When the general election was held in December 1918, suffragists of all political hues came together to honour the veteran Anna Haslam who finally cast her vote after over forty years of campaigning. The I.W.S.L.G.A. now changed its name again, to the Irish Women Citizens and Local Government Association (I.W.C.L.G.A.), and continued to promote women's citizenship.[94]

For republican women the election results brought mixed messages. On the one hand it appeared that women's votes and campaign work had had a significant impact on the outcome. Also, the combined efforts of Cumann na mBan, the I.W.W.U., the I.W.F.L., and Sinn Féin had succeeded in getting Constance Markievicz (herself in Holloway Prison—'an excellent election

[91] Beth McKillen, 'Irish feminism and nationalist separatism, 1914–1923' in *Éire-Ireland*, xvii (1982), no. 3, pp 61–7; no. 4, pp 72–7: 72.

[92] 7 & 8 Geo. V, c. 64 (6 Feb. 1918).

[93] 8 & 9 Geo. V, c. 47 (21 Nov. 1918).

[94] Meeting, 12 Nov. 1918 (*Reports of the Irish Women's Suffrage and Local Government Association 1896–1918* (Dublin, 1919), pp 8–9).

address', as she wrote to her supporters) returned for a seat in Dublin, the first woman to be elected to the Westminster parliament. Yet to have returned only one woman was a poor result. It had proved difficult to get the parties to adopt women candidates. Only Sinn Féin ran any women: Markievicz, and Winifred Carney in Belfast, though Louie Bennett had declined an offer to stand for Labour. Nor did the feminists believe that the men in Sinn Féin had pulled their weight in trying to get women elected. The *Irish Citizen* expressed the feeling of betrayal: 'Under the new dispensation the majority sex in Ireland has secured one representative. This is the measure of our boasted sex equality. The lesson the election teaches is that reaction has not died out with the Irish party.'[95]

It appears that unionist women also felt let down by the lack of recognition from male colleagues; the U.W.U.C. was becoming increasingly dissatisfied with control by the male council. The unionist political campaign had been suspended during the war, but the women's organisation sought to keep it going through the efforts of individual members. The U.W.U.C. also actively supported the extension of conscription to Ireland, and during the 1918 election campaign worked to get the unionist women's vote out.[96]

When the Sinn Féin members boycotted Westminster and set up Dáil Éireann and alternative government structures in 1919, again there were some welcome, if very few, female advances. When the dáil met after the release of the republican prisoners and de Valera was elected president, Markievicz was appointed minister for labour, a European first for women. This too had to be fought for, as Kathleen Clarke recounts:

I asked her how she had managed it, as I had noticed that the present leaders were not over-eager to put women into places of honour or power, even though they had earned the right to both as well as the men had, having responded to every call made upon them throughout the struggle for freedom. She told me she had had to bully them; she claimed she had earned the right to be a minister as well as any of the men, and was equally well fitted for it, educationally and every other way, and if she was not made a minister she would go over to the Labour party.[97]

Clarke herself was chosen to chair the north-city republican courts in Dublin. In the 1920 local elections Sinn Féin swept the board despite the introduction of a proportional representation voting system. In Dublin five women were elected to the corporation: Jennie Wyse Power, Kathleen Clarke, Hanna Sheehy Skeffington, Margaret McGarry, and Anne Ashton.[98] Again the result was gratifying, but fell far short of real equality.

---

[95] *Irish Citizen* (Apr. 1919), p. 656.
[96] Urquhart, '"The female of the species"', pp 104–7.
[97] Clarke, *Revolutionary woman*, pp 170, 176.
[98] Marie O'Neill, *From Parnell to de Valera: a biography of Jennie Wyse Power 1858–1941* (Dublin, 1991), p. 119.

As the war of independence escalated in 1920, the services of Cumann na mBan were essential in the ensuing guerrilla war. A much more active role was taken than had been possible in 1916, and the importance of this contribution was recognised by male colleagues. The work in support of the West Cork I.R.A., for instance, was described as 'indispensable to the army, nursing the wounded and sick, carrying dispatches, scouting, acting as intelligence agents, arranging billets, raising funds, knitting, washing, cooking for the active service men, and burying our dead'.[99] This participation gave added authority to the demand for women to be accorded full citizenship in the future settlement.

For the feminist movement the war of independence was seriously disruptive. A major loss was the *Irish Citizen*, which had managed to survive thus far despite lack of funds and personnel. Louie Bennett offered to take it over and turn it into a trade union paper, but Hanna Sheehy Skeffington refused. During 1920 it appeared irregularly and carried repeated requests for new writers. The last issue was for September–December 1920, and contained a review by Sheehy Skeffington of the current position of feminism. She compared Ireland (now in 'a state of war') with other European countries during the recent war, in which 'the woman's movement merged into the national movement, temporarily at least, and women became patriots rather than feminists, and heroes' wives or widows rather than human beings, so now in Ireland the national struggle overshadows all else'. Feminism, she said, could only mark time. But in the meantime there could be no woman's paper

without a woman's movement, without earnest and serious-minded women readers and thinkers—and these in Ireland have dwindled perceptibly of late, partly owing to the cause above mentioned, and partly because since a measure, however limited, of suffrage has been granted, women are forging out their own destiny in practical fields of endeavour... We still believe we have a mission and a message for Irishwomen as a purely feminist paper and emboldened in that belief we shall carry on.

Soon after this, the police smashed the printing equipment and publication ceased.[100]

In the general elections held in May 1921 under the government of Ireland act, the Sinn Féin candidates in the twenty-six counties were all returned unopposed. They included six women: Markievicz, Kathleen Clarke, Margaret Pearse (mother of Patrick), Mary MacSwiney, Katherine O'Callaghan, and Dr Ada English. In the treaty debates all six opposed the treaty and voted against it. In March 1922 O'Callaghan, invoking the 1916 proclamation and women's role in the war of independence, proposed that women be immediately admitted to the parliamentary franchise on the same terms as men. Anti-treaty deputies showed support for this position, while pro-treaty

[99] Tom Barry, quoted in Ward, *Unmanageable revolutionaries*, p. 144.
[100] *Irish Citizen* (Sept.–Dec. 1920), p. 2; Ward, *Hanna Sheehy Skeffington*, p. 238.

deputies opposed it, apparently for fear of its effects on the prospects of the treaty in any election in which younger women had the vote. In the event the dáil rejected the proposal by 47 to 38 votes, and the election was held in June with women under 30 still disfranchised. The delay was only temporary, and within months full political and civil rights were extended to women in article 3 of the constitution of the Irish Free State: 'Every person, without distinction of sex, domiciled in the area of the jurisdiction of the Irish Free State [Saorstát Éireann] at the time of the coming into operation of this constitution, who was born in Ireland . . . shall . . . enjoy the privileges and be subject to the obligations of such citizenship.' Taken in conjunction with the U.K. Sex Disqualification (Removal) Act, 1919,[101] which outlawed disqualification on grounds of sex or marriage for civil professions and jury service, the Free State constitution established the full formal equality of the sexes in the new state. Women in Northern Ireland and Great Britain had to wait till 1928 for similar equality.

Thus by 1922 the women's emancipation movement had succeeded in removing virtually all legal barriers to women's personal autonomy and citizenship. However, during the campaigns there had been signs that formal equality might not remove less visible barriers of custom, tradition, and entrenched paradigms of male and female roles. How the new constitutional position of women would translate into practice remained to be seen.

IN the decades following the Anglo-Irish treaty, attitudes became if anything more resistant to women moving into 'non-traditional' roles and occupations. Here both the Irish Free State and Northern Ireland were in line with the general European trend in the 1920s and early 1930s. In reaction against the extension of women's roles during the first world war, and in order to safeguard employment for men, the prevailing mood now looked back to pre-war values, stressing the role of women in the home. The teachings of both the catholic and protestant churches, north and south, reinforced this. In neither part of Ireland was there a powerful socialist or liberal movement to act as a counteracting force, while the all-male church authorities could call on a body of educated intellectuals and a propaganda network that included control of the primary and secondary educational systems, and the weekly sermon in the parish church.[102]

Accordingly, north and south, the majority of Irish women continued to work as houseworkers and child-rearers in their own homes, and their unpaid work continued to be regarded by officialdom as economically 'non-productive'. Most of those in 'gainful employment' worked in occupations

---

[101] 9 & 10 George V, c. 71 (23 Dec. 1919).
[102] See Liam O'Dowd, 'Church, state and women: the aftermath of partition' in Curtin, Jackson, & O'Connor, *Gender in Ir. society*, pp 3–36.

characterised by low pay and status. In 1926 the largest areas of women's employment in the Irish Free State were still domestic service, agriculture, and textile and clothing manufacture.[103] Participation in professional work had increased; teaching and nursing were now dominated by women, though neither brought the financial rewards or public prestige of such male-dominated professions as medicine and law. The law had only recently been opened to women by the 1919 removal of sex disqualification act, and there were very few women lawyers. In Northern Ireland the pattern was much the same. Women comprised over two-thirds of teachers in Dublin and Belfast, but only 13 per cent of Dublin doctors and 14 per cent of Belfast doctors were women. There were still fewer in other professions. Only 2 per cent of dentists in Dublin and 1 per cent in Belfast were women, and there were no female engineers or surveyors in either city. Belfast had no female accountants, though there were a few in Dublin.[104]

Women's participation in public political life followed this general pattern. Politics in both parts of the island remained overwhelmingly a male preserve. In the Irish Free State and the Republic of Ireland between 1923 and 1969 women comprised between 1.9 per cent and 2.9 per cent of the total number of dáil candidates, and between 1.9 per cent and 3.4 per cent of elected deputies. There were five women in the dáil in 1923 and only three in 1943. Numbers did not begin to rise significantly till the 1980s. By 1989 14.1 per cent of candidates and 7.8 per cent of elected deputies (thirteen in all) were women.[105] In Northern Ireland, the first woman was elected to the Northern Ireland parliament in 1921, but in all only seventeen women stood as candidates between 1921 and 1972, no more than nine of whom were ever elected, mostly for the Q.U.B. seats. The first woman to be elected to the U.K. parliament for Northern Ireland was Patricia Ford (Down North) in 1953. In the Irish Free State such low participation on the part of women may seem surprising, in view of the high profile achieved by nationalist women between 1916 and 1922. But that relative breakthrough had not taken place within the established political structures, rather within a revolutionary movement, where traditional taboos regarding acceptable female behaviour were more readily broken, at least temporarily. Once the revolutionary movement became the new ruling establishment, the usual historical pattern suggests that equal participation by the sexes in the public political life of the new state would have been problematic even in the most favourable circumstances. As it was, one of the most striking features of post-treaty politics in

---

[103] Mary E. Daly, 'Women in the Irish workforce from pre-industrial to modern times' in *Saothar*, vii (1981), pp 74–82: 77.

[104] O'Dowd, 'Church, state and women', p. 22.

[105] Frances Gardiner, 'Political interest and participation of Irish women 1922–1992: the unfinished revolution' in *Canadian Journal of Irish Studies*, xviii, no. 1 (July 1992), pp 15–39: 18.

the Irish Free State was the sudden disappearance from the public political arena of many of the women who had become prominent there. Some of these women opposed the treaty, and some did not recognise the legitimacy of the new state and therefore refused to participate in its political structures. However, most of them continued to participate in republican, socialist, feminist, or pacifist activities, though these have received little attention from historians.

The general election in June 1922 gave pro-treaty Sinn Féin fifty-eight seats against thirty-six for anti-treaty Sinn Féin. Only two women were elected, both in strongly anti-treaty areas: Mary MacSwiney in Cork and Kate O'Callaghan in Limerick. Of the five women elected to Dáil Éireann in 1923, four—Constance Markievicz, Mary MacSwiney, Kathleen Lynn, and Caitlín Brugha—opposed the treaty and did not take their seats, which left Margaret Collins-O'Driscoll, sister of Michael Collins and member of Cumann na nGaedheal, as the only woman deputy in the dáil. MacSwiney and Lynn lost their seats in the 1927 election and Caitlín Brugha left politics. Constance Markievicz remained active in local politics as a member of Rathmines urban district council, and was particularly concerned with housing, public-health, and child-welfare issues. She published a pamphlet in 1924 reconciling James Connolly's socialist views with catholic teaching. She joined Fianna Fáil in 1926, drawn by its programme of national economic self-sufficiency and tariff barriers, and was elected to the dáil in June 1927 but died in July before Fianna Fáil entered the dáil.

Hanna Sheehy Skeffington opposed the treaty and was active in Sinn Féin and the Women's Prisoners' Defence League set up by Maud Gonne and Charlotte Despard in 1922. Attracted by the return to participation in the dáil, she became a member of the Fianna Fáil executive, but resigned when de Valera signed the oath of allegiance. She then threw her energy into socialist republicanism and feminism, as assistant editor of *An Phoblacht*, and in organisations including the Friends of Soviet Russia and the Women's International League of Peace and Freedom (W.I.L.P.F.). She supported the idea of a women's political party in the 1930s and stood as a dáil candidate for the Women's Social and Progressive League in 1943.

The two prominent nationalist-feminist women who stayed in public political life moved further towards a republican position as time went on. Kathleen Clarke opposed the treaty, joined Fianna Fáil, won and lost a dáil seat in the two elections of 1927, and became a Fianna Fáil senator in 1928. Disillusioned by what she saw as Fianna Fáil's abandonment of its policies on partition and the Irish language, she openly criticised the 1937 constitution for its attitude to women; an unsuccessful attempt was made to expel her from the party for this protest. She became the first woman to be elected lord mayor of Dublin and served a two-year term, 1939–41. She subsequently resigned from Fianna Fáil, stood unsuccessfully for both the dáil and seanad as an independent, and for Clann na Poblachta in 1948.

Jennie Wyse Power, one of the small minority in Cumann na mBan who supported the treaty, became a senator, nominated by Dublin corporation and appointed by W. T. Cosgrave. Disappointed with Cumann na nGaedheal's stand on the boundary commission in 1924, she voted against the government. She resigned from the party, became an independent senator, and later, attracted by the Fianna Fáil policy of dismantling the treaty, joined that party and was elected as a Fianna Fáil senator in 1934. She remained an outspoken supporter of feminist causes throughout her career.[106]

The women who entered the dáil did so through a system where, in terms of winning and retaining a seat, party support was more important than commitment to feminist issues. An assessment written in 1978 noted that, while the women T.D.s were competent and successful, as evidenced by regular reelection, they generally toed the party line; none 'has ever defied the party whip, taken a major initiative on women's rights or championed any significant legislation against the wishes of the party'.[107] By contrast, in the seanad some of the women senators were prepared, when necessary, to oppose a government over feminist issues.[108] These included Eileen Costello (Cumann na nGaedheal senator, 1922–34), Kathleen Clarke (Fianna Fáil senator, 1928–36), and, in particular, Jennie Wyse Power, from 1922 to 1936 successively a Cumann na nGaedheal, Independent, and Fianna Fáil senator.

When the civil war broke out Cumann na mBan split, as did the I.R.A., but unlike the I.R.A. a large majority voted to take the anti-treaty side. As in the war of independence, Cumann na mBan again took an active role, carrying arms and dispatches, finding safe houses, and hiding I.R.A. men. Some hundreds were arrested and imprisoned in Kilmainham gaol. When the war ended Cumann na mBan did not recognise the legitimacy of the Free State government.[109] It declined in numbers and experienced further divisions in the 1930s over the question of a workers' republic. Individual members such as Sheila Humphries joined Saor Éire, the socialist republican organisation founded in 1931, while others, such as Mary MacSwiney, regarded socialist republicanism as unduly divisive. Maud Gonne MacBride, Charlotte Despard, Rosamond Jacob, Norah Connolly O'Brien, and Helena Molony (together with Hanna Sheehy Skeffington) were among republican women active in organisations such as the Friends of Soviet Russia, the Indian–Irish Independence League, and the League against Imperialism and for National Defence. Cumann na mBan participated in marches and demonstrations in

---

[106] See Clarke, *Revolutionary woman*; O'Neill, *From Parnell to de Valera: Jennie Wyse Power*.

[107] Maurice Manning, 'Women in Irish national and local politics 1922–77' in Margaret MacCurtain and Donncha Ó Corráin (ed.), *Women in Irish society: the historical dimension* (Dublin, 1978), pp 92–102: 96. Manning concedes that most male T.D.s also kept to the party line.

[108] Mary Clancy, 'Aspects of women's contribution to the oireachtas debate in the Irish Free State, 1922–1937' in Luddy & Murphy, *Women surviving*, pp 206–32: 209–10.

[109] Ward, *Unmanageable revolutionaries*, pp 171–200.

support of several of these causes, but appears to have remained generally aloof from feminist opposition to discriminatory policies in the Irish Free State.

A number of republican women continued to be active in the peace movement during the 1920s. From the outset there had been different emphases placed on the relationship between 'peace' and 'freedom' by members of the I.I.L., specifically as to whether pacifism was compatible with support for a defensive war or resistance to oppression. The 1921 treaty and the civil war increased these internal tensions. Most of the Free State supporters resigned from the I.I.L., while republicans such as Hanna Sheehy Skeffington, Rosamond Jacob, Maud Gonne MacBride, and Charlotte Despard remained active members, alongside pacifists such as Louie Bennett, Helen Chenevix, and Lucy Kingston who held that pacifism ruled out the use of force in any circumstances. Tensions continued throughout the 1920s and were apparent when the W.I.L.P.F. held its fifth international congress in Dublin in 1926 at the invitation of the Irish committee. It was a major public event, with 2,000 people attending the public meeting in the Mansion House addressed by Jane Addams, the American president of W.I.L.P.F., on the subject of 'Next steps towards world peace'. Topics discussed included colonial and economic imperialism, women and world peace, the relationship between majorities and minorities, and conciliation, arbitration, and disarmament. The Irish section presented a report on minority problems in Ireland. The tensions within the I.I.L. led to further dissension when some of the republican women used the opportunity of a large international presence for demonstrations in support of republican political prisoners. Continuing disagreements over precisely what pacifism involved in practice eventually led to the disintegration of the I.I.L. in 1931; some members continued to participate in W.I.L.P.F. as individuals, and some were active in the disarmament movement of the 1930s.[110]

As far as specifically feminist interests were concerned, the national and international climate in post-war Europe did little to encourage the emergence of a new generation of activists. By and large it was groups founded earlier that carried on the campaign. Both the I.W.C.L.G.A. and the women's graduate associations (the I.A.W.G. had split in 1914 into the National University, Dublin University, and Queen's University women graduate associations) were to the fore. Cross-party cooperation continued, and while numbers were smaller than in the suffrage campaign, many high-profile women were involved. For instance, both Senator Jennie Wyse Power and Mary Hayden, professor of modern Irish history at University College, Dublin, were longstanding members of the I.W.C.L.G.A. Hayden also served as president of the National Council of Women and of the N.U.W.G.A. Hanna Sheehy

---

[110] Cullen Owens, 'Women and pacifism', pp 231–7.

Skeffington, Mary Macken, professor of German, and Agnes O'Farrelly, professor of modern Irish, were all prominent members of the latter.[111] Contact with the international women's movement continued. The International Alliance had lobbied at the Paris peace conference after the armistice to have women's interests taken into account. It set up an office in Geneva and worked to have women's equality recognised and supported by the authority of the League of Nations, which was bound by its charter to uphold equal opportunity for women in its own appointments. In 1926 the Alliance changed its name to the International Alliance of Women for Suffrage and Equality. In the Irish Free State the National Council of Women in Ireland was founded in 1924 to affiliate to both the International Council of Women and the International Alliance, and 'to promote joint action ... and to stimulate thought and cooperation on all questions of social interest'. Affiliates to the National Council included the two graduate associations; the Women's National Health Association (1907); the I.W.W.U.; the I.W.C.L.G.A.; the United Irishwomen (1910); Saor an Leanbh (the Irish branch of Save the Children, founded in 1920); the Irish Matrons' Association (1904); the Irish Girls' Friendly Society (1877); and the Irish Union of Assistant Mistresses in Secondary Schools. Northern affiliates included the Belfast Women Citizens Union (1911), first established as a suffrage society.[112]

Feminists soon found themselves in conflict, first with the Cumann na nGaedheal governments in the 1920s and later with the Fianna Fáil governments in the 1930s, as each in turn tried to dismantle aspects of the political and economic equality of the sexes guaranteed by the 1922 constitution.[113] There was no shortage of issues to concern feminists. Women's liability for jury service had been established only in 1919 by the removal of sex disqualification act. In 1924 the government proposed to remove women from jury service on the grounds that 'the woman juror has not been an outstanding success'. It was alleged that 'the insertion of women's names in the jury book leads to nothing but trouble; the women do not turn up, or they get themselves excused, or they are objected

[111] Maryann G. Valiulis, 'Engendering citizenship: women's relationship to the state in Ireland and the United States in the post-suffrage period' in Valiulis & O'Dowd, *Women & Ir. hist.*, pp 159–72: 160; Caitriona Beaumont, 'Women and the politics of equality: the Irish women's movement, 1930–1943', ibid., pp 173–88: 175–6.

[112] It is not clear precisely when these associations became affiliates, but they were listed as such in the National Council's submission to the commission on vocational organisation in 1940.

[113] See Clancy, 'Aspects of women's contribution'; Caitriona Beaumont, 'Irish women and the politics of equality in the 1930s' in *Phoebe*, iii, no. 1 (spring 1991), pp 26–31; ead., 'Women and the politics of equality'; Maryann G. Valiulis, 'Defining their role in the new state: Irishwomen's protest against the juries act of 1927' in *Canadian Journal of Irish Studies*, xviii, no. 1 (July 1992), pp 43–60; ead., 'Power, gender, and identity in the Irish Free State' in *Journal of Women's History*, vi, no. 4/vii, no. 1 (winter/spring 1995), pp 117–36; Gardiner, 'Political interest and participation of Irish women'.

to'.[114] Although this proposal apparently incurred no opposition in dáil or seanad, the feminist organisations saw it as likely to stifle the growth of women's citizenship before it could take root. The I.W.C.L.G.A. argued that women had no right to evade the duties of citizenship, and that to allow them to do so was unfair to men and degrading to women. The Women's Independent Association claimed that it was a reactionary step, which would discourage women's acceptance of civic responsibility. Kevin O'Higgins, minister for justice, dismissed the 1919 act as a measure that only applied in Ireland 'because we were at that time part and parcel of the political system of Great Britain'.[115] This was a revealing comment in view of earlier expectations of some nationalist feminists that their male colleagues would give women full equality in an independent Ireland. The feminists won a limited compromise in that the 1924 juries act[116] retained women as jurors while allowing any woman who was qualified and liable for jury service to opt to be registered as exempt.

In 1927 the government returned to the subject. Awareness of its significance had increased since 1924. The I.W.C.L.G.A. was again in action, as well as the Women's Equality League and the I.W.W.U., and on this occasion they found allies in the dáil, seanad, and other political and civic groups. O'Higgins claimed that the vast majority of women would be grateful to be relieved of jury service, that the system could work without them, that women had obligations to home and children, and that the state would save money by not having to provide separate bathroom facilities. He described the women who opposed him as unrepresentative 'self-appointed spokeswomen'. Ultimately, it seemed, he and the government knew what was best for women: 'We find ourselves frequently in the position of preventing people getting something which they pretend they want, and which would not be good for them. Politically and economically, that seems to be our chronic position. In this matter I am really the champion of women in the state, but I never expect to get any gratitude for that.'[117]

Certainly the feminists were not grateful. Instead they suggested that the bill was in breach of article 3 of the constitution. They asked whether, if the duties of citizenship were curtailed, the rights would also be cut, and they saw sinister implications in the extension of this benevolence to women but not to men. They urged that petty economies should not be put in the balance against common justice and public duty, and that arguments based on women's unwillingness to serve were dishonest in the light of women's very recent access to jury service and of the regular practice in the courts by which women jurors were asked to stand aside. Again the result was a compromise, but the new position was significantly worse than in 1924. The 1927

[114] Valiulis, 'Defining their role', p. 43.
[115] Quoted in Clancy, 'Aspects of women's contribution', p. 221.
[116] 1924/18 (23 May 1924).
[117] Quoted in Valiulis, 'Defining their role', p. 45.

act[118] placed all women in the category of persons exempted but entitled to serve on application, which made it highly unlikely that many women would see this as part of their duties as citizens.

In 1926 the Civil Service Regulation (Amendment) Act[119] amended a 1924 act[120] to legalise a sex bar by allowing competitive examinations for positions in the civil service to be confined to people 'qualified in respect of sex, age, health, character, knowledge and ability for such situation'. In the dáil there was no opposition to the bill, and Margaret Collins-O'Driscoll actively supported it. The I.W.C.L.G.A., the National University Women Graduates Association, and other women's organisations campaigned against it, as did Senators Eileen Costello and Jennie Wyse Power. Wyse Power reminded the seanad that no men 'in a fight for freedom ever had such loyal cooperation from their women as the men who now compose the present executive council', and who now proposed such discriminatory legislation.[121] The bill was defeated in the seanad, but was passed by the dáil after the required constitutional delay and became law.

The question of divorce also arose in the 1920s. In 1925 the government moved that standing orders be changed so as to prevent the introduction of divorce bills. The United Kingdom matrimonial causes act of 1857,[122] which had allowed divorce to be pursued through the courts, had not been extended to Ireland, and divorce required legislative approval for a private members bill. Opposition came chiefly from male protestants in the seanad. It is not clear whether or to what extent divorce was seen as a feminist concern at this time. The government action was in line with catholic teaching, and in the interests of the socially and politically powerful farming class, for whom divorce raised difficult questions concerning property. Moreover, most married women were dependent on their husbands for their livelihood and thus were unlikely to be enthusiastic for divorce. Some of the double standards involved in the provisions were noted by feminists. In relation to the definition of a wife's domicile as that of her husband even if they lived in different continents, Lucy Kingston, a quaker member of the I.W.C.L.G.A., commented that the dáil debate was 'very unsatisfactory. No divorce (*a vinculo matrimonia*) but judicial separation without remarriage possible. Divorce possible only if husband changes domicile—not possible at all therefore to the wife.'[123]

Birth control literature was banned under the censorship of publications act of 1929.[124] There appears to have been no discussion in the oireachtas of

---

[118] 1927/23 (26 May 1927).   [119] 1926/41 (22 Sept. 1926).
[120] 1924/5 (21 Mar. 1924).
[121] Speech of 17 Dec. 1925, quoted in Clancy, 'Aspects of women's contribution', p. 218.
[122] 20 & 21 Vict., c. 85 (28 Aug. 1857).
[123] Daisy Lawrenson Swanton, *Emerging from the shadow: the lives of Sarah Anne Lawrenson and Lucy Olive Kingston, based on personal diaries, 1883–1969* (Dublin, 1994), p. 97.
[124] 1929/21 (16 July 1929); above, pp 118–19.

the merits or demerits of contraception. There was feminist concern about the bill, but it is not clear to what extent the women's organisations saw birth control as a feminist issue. Both the I.W.C.L.G.A. and the Irish branch of the W.I.L.P.F. took part in the public debate on birth control that preceded the censorship measure, and the former campaigned against some aspects of the bill. Lucy Kingston's diaries suggest that birth control was debated in the context of control of world population, and when the bill appeared she noted it as 'an insidious move against birth control'.[125]

The year 1932 witnessed a major political shift when Fianna Fáil came to power under Eamon de Valera. It quickly became apparent that this would produce little change in attitudes to women. Shortly before the 1932 general election, when Cumann na nGaedheal was still in government, the department of education informed the Irish National Teachers Organisation (I.N.T.O.) that it proposed to introduce compulsory retirement on marriage for women national teachers. The election intervened and the I.N.T.O. executive complained to the new Fianna Fáil government that the regulation was unconstitutional, contending that married women were especially suitable as teachers of young children and were favoured by parents.[126] The government proceeded with the ban, arguing that married women teachers meant some loss either to the school or the home, and that the double-income families of comparatively well-paid teachers gave rise to jealousy. Both the government and the I.N.T.O. referred the question to the catholic hierarchy, which decided to express no opinion, effectively giving it tacit approval.

Sexuality issues arose again with the criminal law amendment bill of 1934. The 1931 Carrigan report on sexual offences, which was not published but was in part reported in the *Irish Press*, contained several proposals, including raising the age of consent in respect of carnal knowledge to 18, making prostitutes' clients as well as prostitutes liable to prosecution, setting up a women's police force, recruiting more women probation officers, and placing jury service for women on the same terms as for men. The subsequent government bill (which passed in 1935)[127] raised the age of consent from 13 to 15 in cases of unlawful carnal knowledge classed as felonies, and from 16 to 17 in cases classed as misdemeanours. Ignoring the commission's other recommendations, it proposed to control prostitution by imposing a fine of up to 40s. for a first conviction for soliciting, and imprisonment for up to six months for subsequent offences. It also banned the sale or importation of contraceptives.

---

[125] Clancy, 'Aspects of women's contribution', p. 212 and n. 25; Swanton, *Emerging from the shadow*, pp 107–13. Kingston noted that at W.I.L.P.F. meetings there was 'almost unanimity in resolution to take part in future conferences and appoint commission on subject' (ibid., p. 109).

[126] T. J. O'Connell, *History of the Irish National Teachers' Organisation 1868–1968* (Dublin, 1968), p. 281.

[127] 1935/6 (28 Feb. 1935).

In the oireachtas the three women T.D.s made no intervention on any of the issues in the bill, but there was opposition in the seanad, which set up a special committee to examine it. Kathleen Clarke opposed the ban on contraception, on the grounds that it would be counterproductive. Oliver St John Gogarty in the seanad and R. J. Rowlette in the dáil argued in favour of contraception, both pointing to the pressures on the poor and the dangers of infanticide. The seanad committee deleted the ban, but the house then accepted a government amendment to reinstate it. On prostitution the committee proposed to replace 'every common prostitute' with a wording that made men as well as women chargeable for soliciting or importuning a member of the opposite sex. The government opposed the proposal and the seanad accepted the government amendment by a single vote. The seanad accepted its own committee's proposal to raise the age of consent from 15 to 18 in the case of indecent assault, but subsequently yielded to government representations and agreed to drop it.[128]

Outside the oireachtas there was a strong feminist response. A Joint Committee of Women's Societies and Social Workers was established in March 1935. The attendance at the early meetings included W. R. O'Hegarty, Hanna Sheehy Skeffington and her sister Mary Kettle, Helen Chenevix, Louie Bennett, and Maud Gonne MacBride. The committee was composed of delegates from independent societies and had two aims: to study social legislation affecting women and children and to recommend necessary reforms.[129] Early affiliates included the Irish Girls Friendly Society, the Girl Guides, the Irish Countrywomen's Association (I.C.A.), the Irish Matrons' Association, Saor an Leanbh, the Irish School Mistresses Association, the I.W.W.U., the National Council of Women in Ireland, the Dublin University Women Graduates Association, the I.W.C.L.G.A., the Women's National Health Association, the Mothers' Union, the Holy Child Association, the S.P.C.C., and the Legion of Mary.[130] Many of these, as noted above, were also affiliates of the National Council of Women.

The joint committee immediately lobbied to have the bill amended in line with the Carrigan proposals, although it does not appear to have protested against the ban on contraceptives. Again, the reason for not taking up the contraceptive issue is not clear. The 1930s witnessed a strengthening of the catholic ethos in the Irish Free State, which created difficulties for some feminists. Lucy Kingston noted that she had worked 'comfortably' with catholics on committees and mixed socially with them prior to 1932, the year

[128] Clancy, 'Aspects of women's contribution', pp 212–15; *Seanad Éireann deb.*, xix, 793–8, 1247 (12 Dec. 1934, 6 Feb. 1935).
[129] Clancy, 'Aspects of women's contribution' p. 216. See also Hilda Tweedy, *A link in the chain: the story of the Irish Housewives' Association 1942–1992* (Dublin, 1992).
[130] Michael G. Broderick, 'Women and Bunreacht na hÉireann: aspects of the debate in May and June 1937' (M. Phil. thesis, T.C.D., 1994), app. A, p. 82.

of the eucharistic congress in Dublin, but afterwards, and through the 1940s and 1950s, she was more aware of tensions on certain issues, especially when anti-communism was at its height.[131] But it may be that contraception did not become a serious feminist demand until the introduction of the contraceptive pill in the 1960s made available an effective woman-controlled method of birth control.

Later in 1935, in the context of economic depression and high male unemployment, the conditions of employment bill proposed to control the entry of women to various skilled trades. Seán Lemass, minister for industry and commerce, used the protectionist argument that some types of work were unsuitable for women. There was no opposition from the three women T.D.s. In the seanad both Jennie Wyse Power and Kathleen Clarke opposed the bill, the former recalling the dashed hopes of the young girls who had been dismissed from their employment after the 1916 rising, and the latter calling on the united trade union movement to support equal pay. In response to the accusation that 'the feminists have run riot' over the conditions of employment bill, Clarke replied that, although she was sympathetic to the feminist movement, her opposition was specifically based on the 1916 proclamation.[132]

The women's organisations lobbied vigorously, and the I.W.W.U. representatives met Lemass to try to influence the bill. They found neither government nor male trade unionists in general sympathetic to their case. Under pressure, the I.C.T.U. reluctantly passed a resolution supporting 'equal democratic opportunities for all citizens and equal pay for equal work'.[133] In spite of the objections, the conditions of employment act as passed[134] authorised the minister to prohibit the employment of women in any form of industrial work and to impose a limit on the female proportion of the workforce in any particular industry. In a case where the minister made such regulations it was illegal for an employer to breach them.

The problems experienced by the I.W.W.U. in opposing this legislation highlight some of the difficulties faced by a women's trade union. The union wanted to support both the interests of the labour movement as a whole and women's interests within that movement. The very question of a separate women's union was controversial. But male trade unionists generally had little interest in the problems of women's employment, and many were mainly concerned with any threat to men's employment. Wage differentials in favour of men were defended, though the fact that lower pay for women could lead employers to favour them in preference to men was deplored.

---

[131] Swanton, *Emerging from the shadow*, pp 124–5.
[132] Clancy, 'Aspects of women's contribution', pp 220–21.
[133] Jones, *These obstreperous lassies*, pp 127–30.
[134] 1936/2 (14 Feb. 1936).

Women workers themselves were not united on all issues. Many women agreed with the prevailing ethos that women's place was ideally in the home, with an adequate family wage paid to the male breadwinner. In the light of these complexities it is not difficult to understand why the views on such issues expressed at different times by I.W.W.U. leaders appeared contradictory.

Undoubtedly the contribution of the I.W.W.U. to the labour movement as a whole was positive and substantial. It insisted on raising issues of sex equality and led the way in the unionisation of Irish women. It defended the right of women to work in all employments while accepting that men and women had different roles and functions in society. It won many victories for its members, and played a leading part in winning improvements in working conditions, including paid holidays, shorter working hours, and tea breaks, for all workers, men as well as women.[135]

In 1937 the draft of de Valera's proposed new constitution incorporated several of the principles underlying the various pieces of legislation that the feminist organisations had been challenging since the birth of the state. Article 3 of the 1922 constitution had given full and equal citizenship 'without distinction of sex', while article 14 stated that 'all citizens of the Irish Free State [Saorstát Éireann] without distinction of sex, who have reached the age of twenty-one years and who comply with the provisions of the prevailing electoral laws, shall have the right to vote for members of Dáil Éireann...'. The new draft constitution replaced this unambiguous equality with a qualifed one. Its text read that the 'acquisition and loss of Irish nationality and citizenship shall be determined in accordance with law' (article 9.1), while 'every citizen who has reached the age of twenty-one years, and who is not placed under disability or incapacity by this constitution or by law, shall be eligible for membership of Dáil Éireann' (16.1.1). A similar qualification was attached to the right to vote (16.1.2).

Article 41.2.1 recognised the work of housewives: 'In particular, the state recognises that by her life within the home, woman gives to the state a support without which the common good cannot be achieved.' But the use of the singular 'woman' rather than some or many 'women', and 'life' rather than 'work', went beyond recognition of the value to society of the work done by so many women to express an ideology that placed all women on the basis of their sex in a 'private' or domestic sphere. Article 41.2.2 followed with an undertaking that 'the state shall, therefore, endeavour to ensure that mothers shall not be obliged by economic necessity to engage in labour to the neglect of their duties in the home.' Article 45.4.1 pledged the state 'to

[135] For discussion of some of these issues see Mary E. Daly, 'Women, work and trade unionism in Ireland' in MacCurtain & Ó Corráin, *Women in Ir. society*, pp 71–81; Ellen Hazelkorn, 'The social and political views of Louie Bennett 1870–1956' in *Saothar*, xiii (1988), pp 32–44; Jones, *These obstreperous lassies.*

safeguard with especial care the economic interests of the weaker sections of the community, and, where necessary, to contribute to the support of the infirm, the widow, the orphan and the aged'. Article 40.1 guaranteed equality before the law for all citizens but added the qualification that this 'shall not be held to mean that the state shall not in its enactments have due regard to differences of capacity, physical and moral, and of social function'. Article 45.4.2 was more explicit: 'The state shall endeavour to ensure that the inadequate strength of women and the tender age of children shall not be abused, and that women or children shall not be forced by economic necessity to enter avocations unsuited to their sex, age or strength.'[136]

Taken together, and interpreted in the light of government policy towards women over the previous fifteen years, these clauses appeared to feminists as an attempt to reverse much of what women had achieved in 1922. The Joint Committee of Women's Societies lobbied de Valera to reinstate equal citizenship 'without distinction of sex', but he argued that, now that women were fully equal, they no longer needed a clause that reminded them that they had not always been so. Since their fear was that they might not in fact remain so for much longer, they were not impressed. Eventually de Valera agreed to the reinstatement, and gave a commitment that no other article would be used to curtail women's citizenship (article 9.1.3). He refused to change the other suspect clauses, and the feminists turned to a campaign to win public support.

In letters to the newspapers Mary Kettle, who chaired the joint committee, explained the need for an explicit commitment to women's equality in the light of recent history. Women who read articles 40, 41, and 45 in context would realise that if they became law 'no woman who works—be it in trade, factory, or profession—will have any security whatever'. Article 40.1 would give the state 'dangerous' powers of legislating on sex or class lines, while 41.2.2 could sanction further limitation of women's work opportunities. The committee wanted article 45.4.2 deleted on similar grounds and asked who was to make decisions under these articles. With technology eliminating heavy work in industry, it was in the home that many women faced really heavy work. The suspicion was that protection would not be used to help women where they needed it, but to exclude them from work where they threatened the interests of men.[137] For her part, Hanna Sheehy Skeffington roundly asserted that the equal citizenship of 1916 was 'being scrapped for a fascist model, where women are relegated to permanent inferiority, their vocations and choice of callings limited because, apparently, of an implied permanent invalidism as the weaker sex'. The changes were in line with the

---

[136] *Bunreacht na hÉireann (dréacht)* (Dublin, [1937])
[137] For the feminist response to the draft constitution, see Broderick, 'Women and Bunreacht na hÉireann', ch. 5; Beaumont, 'Women and the politics of equality'.

Cosgrave government's policy on jury service, the civil service, and the 1936 employment act. Now the 1916 proclamation was being nullified. Having been a colleague of de Valera for many years, she claimed that concerning women, he and other cabinet members shared the 'fascist ideal now working under Mussolini and Hitler'.[138]

Articles 40, 41, and 45 were of particular concern to the joint committee. What did it mean that mothers should not be forced by economic necessity to work, and could it be used to deny employment to married women? The joint committee was also suspicious of the clauses concerning women's employment. It particularly wanted the removal of phrases such as 'the inadequate strength of women'. Again de Valera defended his wording vigorously. Like Kevin O'Higgins before him he claimed he was doing women a service for which he deserved gratitude rather than reproach. He seemed particularly concerned about women's 'inadequate strength', a phrase he managed to repeat six times in one paragraph of a dáil speech.[139]

An I.W.W.U. delegation eventually succeeded in winning a commitment to amend article 45.4.2, which eventually read: 'The state shall endeavour to ensure that the strength and health of workers, men and women, and the tender age of children shall not be abused and that citizens shall not be forced by economic necessity to enter avocations unsuited to their sex, age or strength.' Having won this, the I.W.W.U. dropped its opposition and withdrew from the campaign to amend the constitution.

The seanad had been abolished in 1936, so oireachtas debate was confined to the dáil. Of the three women deputies, Margaret Pearse made no contribution, Bridget Redmond did so only under pressure, and, perhaps most significantly, Helena Concannon, a member of the National University Women Graduates Association, itself a leading participant in the feminist campaign, supported the draft constitution, putting her party before feminist politics. The joint committee continued its campaign but gained no further changes. Feminists were now a small group of activists, and no significant body of public opinion emerged to support their case. Of the newspapers, editorials in the *Irish Times* and the *Irish Independent* took a neutral, if not negative, stance on feminist concerns, while the *Irish Press* vigorously supported de Valera.[140] The feminists campaigned for a no vote in the subsequent referendum on the constitution, which in the event was passed by a fairly narrow majority.

The joint committee's work gives an indication of the issues on which the constituent organisations joined forces, if not of the full range of the latter's

---

[138] Broderick, 'Women and Bunreacht na hÉireann', p. 28, quoting *Irish Independent*, 11 May 1937.

[139] Ibid., pp 32, 36–7.

[140] Ibid., ch. 7; Jones, *These obstreperous lassies*, p. 142; Clancy, 'Aspects of women's contribution', p. 224.

concerns. The committee continued to campaign for women police, a long-standing feminist aim. In 1936 it lobbied for a 50 per cent representation of women in the new seanad, to be chosen on vocational rather than party lines. During the 1940s it worked to amend the married women's maintenance act and the law on adoption, to replace institutional care of deprived children by a boarding-out system, and for the appropriate training of social workers.

During the debates over the constitution the idea of a women's political party was mooted, and as a result a meeting of women's associations on 24 November 1937 founded the Women's Social and Political League to 'promote and protect the political, social and economic status of women and to further their work and usefulness as citizens'. It aimed to organise women voters, to secure equal opportunities and pay, put forward independent women candidates for the dáil, seanad, and other public bodies, and secure the appointment of women to government commissions. The women members of the dáil had shown that they did not see themselves as campaigners for women's rights. The new party would try to change this, and to challenge entrenched ideas of separate spheres for women and men. In the event the problems of sustaining a political party, including the ban on civil servants joining one, proved too formidable. In 1938 the league changed its name to 'Women's Social and Progressive League', but continued to work for the same objectives.[141]

During the 1938 general election campaign the league raised a range of feminist concerns. These included women's jury service, pay differentials between men and women in secondary-school teaching, the civil service, and the professions in general, and the enforced retirement of women primary-school teachers at 60, recently introduced by the Fianna Fáil government to provide more jobs for a surplus of trained teachers,[142] which deprived women teachers of full pension rights. In the 1943 general election the league put forward its president Hanna Sheehy Skeffington as an independent candidate, and backed three other women candidates, but none of them was elected.

Between 1939 and 1943 the commission on vocational organisation was at work. In April 1940 representatives of several women's organisations set up a committee to prepare a memorandum and give evidence if required. Three organisations, the National Council of Women in Ireland, the Joint Committee of Women's Societies, and the Catholic Women's Federation of Secondary School Unions, presented a joint memorandum and gave oral evidence together. They proposed the direct representation of 'home-makers' on vocation-based assemblies at local or national level. Home-makers, most of whom were female, included those returned in the census as engaged in home

---

[141] Beaumont, 'Irish women and the politics of equality', pp 27–9.
[142] O'Connell, *History of the I.N.T.O.*, pp 284–5.

duties (1,301 men and 552,176 women) and domestic servants (2,282 men and 86,102 women), altogether comprising over 25 per cent of the adult population.

Despite the 1937 constitution's emphasis on the importance to society of the contribution of women in the home, the commission refused to endorse this proposal. Its chairman, Michael Browne, bishop of Galway, was disparaging when W. R. O'Hegarty, Lucy Franks, and Mrs V. Dempsey appeared before the commission. He noted that it was 'quite easy to organise a number of philanthropic ladies of leisure' but more difficult 'in the case of most working women and domestic servants...'. When challenged on the 'ladies of leisure', he said that he had used the expression in the technical sense meaning those who did not have to work for a living, to which O'Hegarty replied that many of the committee members worked for their living. The bishop's response is indicative of the attitudes the women's movement encountered during these years.[143]

The Irish Countrywomen's Association also presented a memorandum to the commission, advocating the provision of village halls and more cooperation between the departments of primary and vocational education and of agriculture, as well as the direct representation of countrywomen in any scheme of vocational organisation. The association, when still known as the United Irishwomen, had been growing again since the mid 1920s,[144] largely owing to the work of Lucy Franks, who was a founder member in 1928 of the Associated Countrywomen of the World. From 1926 the Royal Dublin Society provided space for U.I. exhibitions and craft demonstrations. An annual summer school began in 1929 and An Grianán, a residential college at Termonfeckin in County Louth, was established in 1953. In 1935 a new and more democratic structure was adopted, which replaced the central executive and branches by self-managing guilds and a national council of guilds. The organisation could no longer be registered as a friendly society and was no longer affiliated to the Irish Agricultural Organisation Society. To avoid confusion with the United Ireland party (Fine Gael) of 1933, the U.I. became the Irish Countrywomen's Association. It grew in size, and by the 1990s had 1,000 guilds and over 22,000 members. Continuing the original commitment to 'a healthy and progressive community life' and to making rural life lively and enjoyable, it combined development of members' skills from housewifery to art and drama, with research and lobbying on such issues as rural water supply and electrification.[145] It was an affiliate of the

---

[143] Minutes of evidence to the commission on vocational organisation, 12 Dec. 1940 (N.L.I., MS 930, xi, 3065–80). See also Caitriona Clear, '"The women cannot be blamed": the commission on vocational organisation, feminism, and "home-makers" in independent Ireland in the 1930s and 40s' in Mary O'Dowd and Sabine Wichert (ed.), *Chattel, servant or citizen: women's status in church, state and society* (Belfast, 1995), pp 179–86.

[144] Gahan, 'Bantracht na Tuaithe', pp 21–8.   [145] Ibid.

Joint Committee of Women's Societies, and its interest in some specifically feminist concerns, such as the jury service issue, continued.

In 1942 a new organisation, the Irish Housewives' Association (I.H.A.), was founded by a group of young married women, all protestant and middle class. Some had links with the preceding generation of feminists; members included Andrée Sheehy Skeffington, daughter-in-law of Hanna, and Susan Manning, a sister of Louie Bennett. Membership soon crossed religious divides, but despite strenuous efforts did not succeed in crossing class barriers: the I.H.A. remained a largely middle-class organisation.

The I.H.A.'s first concern was the fair and efficient provision of food and other scarce commodities during the second world war. Its work and substantial research, and particularly that on the milk and beef industries, led to the founding of the Consumers' Association of Ireland. Its agenda soon included specifically feminist goals, as shown in the statement of objectives from its 1946 constitution:

(a) to unite housewives so that they shall recognise, and gain recognition for, their right to play an active part in all spheres of planning for the community; (b) to secure all such reforms as are necessary to establish a real equality of liberties, status, and opportunity for all persons; (c) the aims and general policy shall be to defend consumers' rights as they are affected by supply, distribution and price of essential commodities, to suggest legislation or take practical steps to safeguard their interests, as well as generally to deal with matters affecting the home; (d) to take steps to defend consumers against all taxation on necessary food, fuel and clothing.[146]

The I.H.A. also took part in the campaign to elect Hanna Sheehy Skeffington to the dáil in 1943. In 1947 the I.W.C.L.G.A. merged with the I.H.A., thus bringing the latter into affiliation with the International Alliance of Women (I.A.W.).

During the 1950s government attempts to claw back aspects of women's equal citizenship passed their peak. The 1956 civil service commissioners act[147] explicitly continued the marriage and sex bars. However, Irish society was about to enter a period of dramatic change, which was to have profound consequences for women and the women's movement. During the economic boom of the 1960s, the population grew and emigration trends were reversed. The proportion of women completing second-level education and going on to third-level increased. Under the influence of the second Vatican council, Irish catholicism was also changing. One analysis sees Irish catholics moving away from a 'legalistic acceptance of the church's rules and regulations to a more protestant, do-it-yourself type of religious ethic in which they are making up their own minds about what is right and wrong'. Another suggests that 'Irish people have become more optimistic, more adventurous...and

[146] See Tweedy, *A link in the chain*, p. 18.   [147] 1956/45 (19 Dec. 1956).

more ready to accept criticism from themselves and from others.'[148] The link between unquestioning acceptance of catholic church teaching and genuine 'Irishness' was diminishing.

At the same time Irish demographic patterns began to approach the European norm. Marriage age fell, marriage rates rose, and the number of children per family dropped, while the percentage of married women in employment outside the home grew, though it remained well below the western European average. More Irish women than ever before had a direct interest in issues such as equal pay and employment for married women. The advent of the contraceptive pill, which gave women control over their fertility, prompted a new interest in birth control; this despite the fact that even after Vatican II the catholic church still frowned on artifical methods of contraception.

The year 1968 saw the start of a new campaign to press for full equality of citizenship. The impetus came from the international women's movement. Irish Housewives' Association delegates had attended International Alliance of Women's conferences over the years, with Hilda Tweedy serving on the I.A.W. board from 1961 to 1964 and from 1973 to 1989. The 1961 alliance congress was held in Dublin, where the changed times found President de Valera acting as patron to the congress while Archbishop McQuaid of Dublin made the Institute of Catholic Sociology available as a venue for plenary sessions.

The I.A.W. had developed links with the United Nations, as it had earlier with the League of Nations.[149] In 1967 the U.N. commission on the status of women issued a directive to women's international organisations to instruct affiliated groups to examine the status of women in their own countries and, where necessary, urge governments to set up national commissions. In Ireland the Federation of Business and Professional Women's Clubs, recently established in 1965, and the I.H.A. both received this instruction and jointly called a meeting of women's organisations in January 1968. An ad hoc committee was set up to work for a national commission. Permanent members of the committee included, besides the two aforementioned bodies, representatives of the Association of Widows in Ireland, the I.C.A., the Soroptimists, the two associations of women graduates, and the Women's International Zionist Organisation.

The ad hoc committee identified issues for particular attention, including equal pay for equal work, discrimination against married women in employment and taxation, and girls' education. In October 1968 a memorandum was sent to the taoiseach, Jack Lynch, and after a year's lobbying by the commit-

---

[148] Tom Inglis, *Moral monopoly: the catholic church in modern Irish society* (Dublin, 1987), p. 225; Whyte, *Ch. & state*, p. 357.

[149] Whittick, *Woman into citizen*, p. 167.

tee the government set up the first commission on the status of women. It
met in 1970 to 'examine and report on the status of women in Irish society,
to make recommendations on the steps necessary to ensure the participation
of women on equal terms with men in the political, social, cultural and
economic life of the country, and to indicate the implications generally—
including the estimated cost—of such recommendations'. The ad hoc committee ensured that the commission would be composed of equal numbers of
women and men, and chaired by a woman of the committee's choice, Dr
Thekla Beere.[150]

The commission's report, published in 1973, noted the stereotyped role
that was assigned to women, and the transmission to both boys and girls in
their formative years of firm views about distinct and separate roles for the
sexes.[151] Girls were encouraged to think in terms of a relatively short period
of gainful employment, followed by marriage and responsibilities for home
care and child rearing. Yet the women workers interviewed were dissatisfied
with jobs involving repetitive action and low skill levels. They wanted recognition as individual workers rather than as 'a group of women workers'.[152]
The report recommended the removal of discrimination based on sex and
marriage in access to employment, pay, taxation, social security, and pension
schemes. It advocated improved provision for deserted wives, unmarried
mothers, widows, and wives of prisoners. It proposed equal liability of the
sexes for jury service, the appointment of more women to statutory and other
bodies, coeducation, and encouragement to study 'non-traditional' subjects.
It advocated marriage-counselling services, and family-planning advice
centres that would respect the moral and personal attitudes of every married
couple.

The setting up of the commission and the publication of the report suggested a dramatic change in the attitude of Irish governments to the role of
women in society. These moves, however, had largely come about through
U.N. pressure. It did not follow that Irish governments either actively desired the proposed reforms or would take steps to put them into effect.
Accordingly, in 1973 the women's organisations established the Council for
the Status of Women to ensure the implementation of the report's recommendations. The council was subsequently granted government funding and
consultative status on draft legislation concerning women. By 1980 it had
over thirty-five member organisations.

Even as the existing women's organisations were achieving this unprecedented public recognition, a new wave of the women's movement was

[150] Tweedy, A link in the chain, pp 35–47. Thekla Beere was the first woman secretary of an
Irish government department.
[151] Commission on the status of women, report (Prl 2760) (Dublin, 1973).
[152] Eunice McCarthy, 'Women and work in Ireland: the present, and preparing for the
future' in MacCurtain & Ó Corráin, Women in Ir. society, pp 103–17: 107–8.

appearing on the public scene in Ireland. The Irish Women's Liberation Movement (I.W.L.M.) began in 1970 with a meeting in Bewley's café in Westmoreland Street, Dublin, of five women who were all involved in left-wing radical activities in the 1960s. Their inspiration came from the women's liberation movement in the United States.[153] So low was the public profile of feminism in Ireland at the time that the younger women did not at first regard the longer-established women's groups as feminist, but as part of the establishment. Whereas the existing feminist organisations used a gradualist approach, operating through committees, mandated leaders, and lobbying, the women's liberation movement aimed at sweeping change by means of a non-hierarchical movement intended both to change women themselves and to jolt and shock public opinion into awareness of discrimination. The new international wave of feminism contained a number of strands, including the liberal feminist emphasis on equal rights, the 'radical' feminist insistence on the importance of sexuality, and a new socialist feminism that linked Marxism to radical feminist insights. All these strands were present in Ireland.

Three groups were prominent in the I.W.L.M.: 'political women (mainly left-wing and republican activists), women in the media, and professional/university-educated women.'[154] From the outset the movement achieved unprecedented publicity. In March 1971 'The late, late show', the television series that had become compulsive viewing, devoted a whole show to 'women's lib.'. This was followed in April by a public meeting that packed the Mansion House in Dublin; long queues of women formed to express their views. Then came the 'contraceptive train' in May, when a group of thirty women travelled by train to Belfast where they purchased condoms and other contraceptives and brought these back to Dublin amid maximum publicity.

The first stated objectives of the new movement were very similar to those of the longer established groups. The 1970 I.W.L.M. manifesto, *Chains or change? The civil wrongs of Irish women*, set out a number of areas of discrimination: inequities in law; the lack of equal pay for equal work; differences in the education of boys and girls which effectively closed many areas of well-paid employment to women; discrimination at work and job bars to women; inequitable treatment of widows, deserted wives, unmarried mothers, and single women; laws against family planning, and lack of child-care facilities, playgrounds, retraining; unfair taxation of women. These concerns were essentially the same as those addressed in the report of the first commission on the status of women. Finally it pointed to the advantages of 'living in sin' as

---

[153] June Levine, *Sisters: the personal story of an Irish feminist* (Swords, 1982), p. 139.
[154] Linda Connolly, 'The women's movement in Ireland 1970–1995: a social movement's analysis' in *Irish Journal of Feminist Studies*, i, no. 1 (Mar. 1996), pp 43–77. For a contemporary assessment, see Catherine Rose, *The female experience: the story of the woman movement in Ireland* (Dublin, 1975).

opposed to marriage: women could keep their jobs; they would not have to pay extra tax; they could retain their business identity; and they could leave a bad relationship.

As the original group expanded, internal differences emerged. Socialist women wanted 'the entire fabric of society changed from the bottom up' while others wanted piecemeal reforms. Some favoured action while others wanted discussion and consciousness-raising. Some argued for setting up a national movement immediately while others doubted the group's ability to run one. All were talking a new language, a 'language of personal political power'.[155] In an account written several years later, the point was made that

[a] sober, sensible, structured organisation would never have given the jolt that was necessary, would never have grabbed the headlines, would never have shocked men and women into awareness of the inferior legal and social status of women. They may have disliked much of what was going on, but they could not ignore it. Most importantly, the movement provided a breeding ground for the many pressure groups which emerged throughout the seventies.[156]

Yet publicity and style by themselves could not have accounted for the impact made by women's liberation if its message had not struck a chord with many women in all parts of the country. In highlighting discrimination against women the new movement identified the individual as the central focus for change, with personal awareness leading to personal liberation and then to change in society. This appears to have been the new factor that made the message relevant to so many women in the Ireland of the 1960s and 1970s, in a way never achieved by the older established organisations. Women's consciousness-raising groups and action groups began to spring up around the country. 'The personal is political' expressed the belief that individuals' perceptions of personal oppression must be accepted as real experiences but then must be analysed and the underlying social structures changed.

Having achieved the initial response the central I.W.L.M. group faced the problem of how to proceed. Was it to be a mass movement or a small pressure group? If a mass movement, how would it be organised—indeed, should it be organised? Should it confine itself specifically to women's issues or take on others? Under these pressures the central I.W.L.M. gradually disintegrated, and 1975 saw the foundation of Irish Women United (I.W.U.), another attempt to establish a nationwide women's movement. Few members of the I.W.L.M. were involved in this strongly left-wing grouping, which had links to the Movement for a Socialist Republic, the Communist Party of Ireland, an emerging gay women's movement, and the trade union move-

[155] Levine, *Sisters*, p. 143.
[156] Office of the minister of state for women's affairs, *Irishwomen into focus 1: the road to equal opportunity: a narrative history* (Dublin [1987]), p. 11.

ment, as well as having a strong student membership.[157] Its charter covered many of the established goals, though it expressed these in a socialist language and context. It broke new ground in sex-related areas, being more explicit with regard to contraception and adding abortion and lesbian rights to its main demands, which included the removal of all legal and bureaucratic obstacles to equality; free legal contraception, with birth-control clinics and the right to free, legal, and safe abortion; equality in education, with state-funded, secular, co-educational schools with community control, and women's studies programmes at second and third level; equal pay for equal work and a minimum wage for low-paid, mainly female jobs; state funding for women's centres; the right of all women to a self-determined sexuality. This charter is particularly interesting, since now for the first time the majority in the Irish women's movement came from catholic backgrounds. Despite the taboos on public discussion of sex and sexuality in the Republic, and catholic teaching that 'unnatural' birth control and single-sex relationships were sinful, these issues were now appearing in feminist manifestos. Liberation for Irish Lesbians (L.I.L.) was founded in 1978.

Internal tensions caused I.W.U. in its turn to fragment in 1977, even as all-Ireland feminist conferences in Belfast and Dublin and the trade union women's forum were endorsing the need for an all-Ireland women's movement. Although this was to prove elusive—and there were major difficulties in reconciling national organisation with the ideal of an unstructured mass movement—the highly publicised activities of both groups also helped the longer-established women's organisations in getting many of the recommendations of the commission on the status of women put into effect; the 1970s saw growing mutual recognition and cooperation between old and new feminists with fruitful results.

THE Civil Service (Employment of Married Women) Act, 1973, removed the power to bar married women from competing for appointments, and ended the requirement that women had to retire from the civil service on marriage. In a 1974 test case the supreme court ruled that the ban on the importation of contraceptives was illegal. In 1976 a new juries act overturned the 1927 compromise and made qualification and liability for jury service the same for both sexes. European Community membership put pressure on Irish governments to introduce equality legislation. Sex-differentiated pay scales were removed in 1973 and marriage-differentiated scales in 1974. The Anti-Discrimination (Pay) Act, 1974, brought the principles of 'equal pay for like work' and 'equal pay for work of equal value' into Irish labour law. The Employment Equality Act, 1977, prohibited discrimination on grounds of sex or marital status in recruitment, training, or provision of opportunities for

---

[157] Connolly, 'The women's movement in Ireland', pp 53–62.

promotion. The Unfair Dismissals Act, 1977, prohibited dismissal on grounds of pregnancy except in specified circumstances, and the Maternity Protection of Employees Act, 1981, introduced the right to fourteen weeks paid maternity leave. The Health (Family Planning) Act, 1979, allowed the sale of contraceptives, but only to married couples;[158] not till 1992 was it permissible to sell contraceptives to unmarried persons aged 17 or over.

In 1976 the Family Law (Maintenance of Spouses and Children) Act made it possible to apply to the courts for maintenance, while the Family Home Protection Act of that year provided that a spouse could not normally sell the family home without the consent of the other spouse. Within the social welfare system various differences between the treatment of women and men were removed. In addition, the Social Welfare Act, 1973, introduced an unmarried mother's allowance. The Social Welfare Act, 1974, gave the legal title to children's allowances to mothers rather than fathers, and the Social Welfare Act (no. 2) 1974, introduced an allowance for wives of prisoners.[159]

Both I.W.L.M. and I.W.U. members contributed to the emergence of an impressive range of single-issue organisations during the 1970s. A network of self-help services developed, provided for women by women, often recruiting those who had themselves come for help. The Women's Progressive Association (1971), which became the Women's Political Association in 1973, fostered entry to public and political life. ALLY (1971) established a service for pregnant women, single or married. The following year saw the foundation of AIM for family law advice and reform; of Family Planning Services, a company providing contraceptives; and of Cherish, an organisation for single parents; and in Cork a federation of women's organisations was established. ADAPT, an association for deserted wives and husbands, came into being in 1973. Women's Aid, to help victims of domestic violence, was set up in 1974, and the Dublin Rape Crisis Centre in 1977.[160] Public attention was directed towards issues that had remained almost invisible in Irish society, including rape, incest, and family violence, and the status of single mothers. Government interest and financial support were sought. Where these were obtained, some organisations inevitably took on some of the trappings of establishment bureaucracy, a paradox that created its own problems.

Striking testimony to the developments of the decade came with the recognition by the existing political parties that there was now a women's vote that could be harnessed in support of feminist candidates. For the first time

---

[158] Second commission on the status of women, *Report to government January 1993* (Pl 9557) (Dublin, 1993), pp 363–90; 1973/17 (31 July 1973); 1976/4 (2 Mar. 1976); 1974/15 (1 July 1974); 1977/16 (1 June 1977); 1977/10 (6 Apr. 1977), sect. 6: 2 (f); 1981/2 (26 Mar. 1981); 1979/20 (23 July 1979).
[159] 1976/11 (6 Apr. 1976); 1976/27 (12 July 1976); 1973/10 (27 June 1973); 1974/12 (12 June 1974); 1974/14 (27 June 1974).
[160] Office of the minister of state for women's affairs, *Irishwomen into focus 1*, pp 17–21.

candidates with a high profile in the women's movement were selected by the main parties to stand for election to the dáil. Graduating from the Women's Political Association, women such as Nuala Fennell, Gemma Hussey, and Monica Barnes were elected in 1982 as Fine Gael T.D.s. Hussey was appointed minister for education, and Fennell minister of state for women's affairs in the coalition Fine Gael–Labour government of 1982–7. The rising profile of women in public life was to be signalled dramatically in 1990 with the election of Mary Robinson, a distinguished lawyer and well-known feminist, as the first woman president of the Republic.

However, by the 1980s economic recession, rising unemployment and emigration, cutbacks in government spending, and an accompanying moral fundamentalism had created something of a backlash. This was particularly apparent in the area of sexuality, where the 1980s saw referenda in the Republic on abortion and divorce. Abortion had been a taboo subject generally in Irish society. Under the 1861 offences against the person act[161] abortion was illegal in Ireland, and the fact that some thousands of women travelled each year to Britain for abortions was quietly ignored. There had been little discussion of or support for abortion in the Irish women's movement when a small 'Women's right to choose' group emerged in 1979, aiming to decriminalise abortion and provide pregnancy-counselling services that would include information on abortion. Few Irish feminists supported abortion at all, and fewer still did so publicly. Nevertheless, a preemptive anti-abortion campaign was mounted by a number of conservative and religious groups and individuals. The Pro-Life Amendment Campaign was set up in Dublin in 1981 to amend the constitution so as to render any future legalisation of abortion in Ireland unconstitutional.[162] The campaign secured the support of the leaders of the two largest political parties, Garret FitzGerald of Fine Gael and Charles Haughey of Fianna Fáil. Subsequently, in a referendum held in September 1983, the amendment, stating that the state 'acknowledges the right to life of the unborn and, with due regard to the equal right to life of the mother, guarantees in its laws to respect, and, as far as practicable, by its laws to defend and vindicate that right', was carried by a majority of 2 to 1. It thus became article 40.3.3 of the constitution. This did not finally settle the matter; the right to disseminate literature about abortion clinics in Britain, and the right to travel outside the state to make use of abortion services were both subsequently challenged in the courts. However, a further referendum in 1992 confirmed these limited rights,[163] although an amendment providing for abortion to be carried out in Ireland where 'the life, as distinct from the health' of a pregnant woman was at risk was

[161] 24 & 25 Vict., c. 100 (6 Aug. 1861), sects. 58–9.
[162] See Emily O'Reilly, *Masterminds of the right* (Dublin [1992]).
[163] Eighth Amendment of the Constitution Act (7 Oct. 1983); Thirteenth Amendment (23 Dec. 1992); Fourteenth Amendment (23 Dec. 1992).

defeated. While there is still no universally agreed position on abortion among Irish feminists, the experience of these years has moved the focus of attention to the decision of the woman involved and away from that of religious and medical 'experts'.

In 1986 a referendum to change the constitution to permit divorce was introduced and supported by the government, by the civil libertarians, and by the women's movement in general. Despite the indications of opinion polls, the proposed amendment was defeated. The reasons for defeat have been much debated. One key issue, particularly important to farming families, was family property. Moreover, separation procedures were not yet fully in place, and wives remained economically vulnerable in the event of marriage break-down. Like the 1983 abortion referendum, the 1986 divorce referendum was seen at the time as a setback for the women's movement. However, it too was to be followed by another referendum in 1995 which narrowly accepted divorce. On both abortion and divorce it is clear that Irish public opinion is becoming more complex.

The 1980s also saw further expansion and diversification in the women's movement. There was no longer any central organisation, but instead a diverse and widely spread movement. One development was the emergence of women's studies, which began to produce a growing body of analysis and research within and across the established disciplines. Feminist publishing houses played an important part, with Arlen House emerging first in 1975, followed in 1978 by Irish Feminist Information, which became Attic Press in 1980. From this period on, women's studies was to develop in a plethora of forms and locations, from community or locally based women's educational projects, to university courses at different levels.

The development of women's studies interacted with the emergence of working-class women's groups, the successors to the largely middle-class women's consciousness-raising groups of the 1970s and early 1980s. The new working-class groups were locally based, and have generally been described as community groups. This development was one that many believed to have the potential to bring about effective change in society. For the first time Irish working-class women in substantial numbers became active feminists and began to speak and write for themselves, some challenging the established feminist agenda on the grounds that for the most part it benefited only middle-class women. This was one facet of the new leadership role being taken by women in community activity generally, and particularly in the poorer housing estates.

The 1980s also witnessed 'an unprecedented blossoming of cultural expression by women'.[164] One sign of this was seen when the third

---

[164] Ailbhe Smyth, 'The women's movement in the Republic of Ireland 1970–1990' in Ailbhe Smyth (ed.), *Irish women's studies reader* (Dublin, 1993), pp 245–69: 250.

international interdisciplinary congress on women (held in Dublin in 1987), included, side by side with the usual programme of academic papers, a major festival of art and music. These developments have sparked off more debate as to the meaning, validity and value of concepts such as 'women's art' and 'women's writing'.

Nor were the churches immune from the effects of feminism. In the catholic church the consciousness-raising of the new wave of feminism met the new 'release of spiritual energies among priests, laity, and religious women and men' sparked off by the second Vatican council in the 1960s.[165] Sexist language in the liturgy, the absence of women from decision-making roles in the church, and traditional stereotypes of female conduct all came in for scrutiny. In a departure from their traditional role, nuns have been very much to the fore in these challenges. Prominent also has been a small but growing number of lay female theologians. In the protestant churches, where the role of the laity of both sexes was afforded greater recognition from the reformation onwards, the feminist challenge was not quite so searching, but in the Church of Ireland women's ordination became an important issue, and was adopted in 1990, some years ahead of the Church of England. Women's ordination also began to be debated in some catholic circles.

In Northern Ireland the position of women differed in some ways from that of women in the Republic, although it was not necessarily the same as that in Great Britain. Marriage bars in the civil service, teaching, and the banks, though removed in the late 1960s (some years earlier than in the south), contributed to the difference between the 29 per cent of married women 'economically active' in Northern Ireland (1971 figures) compared with 42 per cent in Great Britain, and only 8 per cent in the Republic (1970 figures). Family planning and contraceptives were free, as in Britain, but not easily accessible for rural and working-class women; and for some women ecclesiastical opposition was a problem. The average number of children per family has been 2.2 since 1983, and catholic families remain larger than protestant families, although these differences are declining.[166] Not all U.K. legislation was extended to Northern Ireland. Exceptions included abortion: Northern Ireland women, as well as their counterparts in the south, travelled to Britain for abortions.

In Northern Ireland the new wave of the women's movement emerged against the background of the civil rights movement of the 1960s, and developed during the years of conflict that followed. Divided loyalties and pressure not to be seen to criticise the men on one's own side made feminist

---

[165] See Margaret MacCurtain, 'Moving statues and Irish women' in Smyth, *Ir. women's studies reader*, pp 203–13.
[166] Above, pp 429–30, 806–7.

assertion particularly difficult. The main churches and political parties in Northern Ireland all tended to be conservative and patriarchal in their attitudes to women, although the Unionist Party of Northern Ireland was the first party in Ireland to elect a woman, Anne Dickson, as its leader, in September 1976. Participation in the political developments of the 1960s and early 1970s, first in housing allocation campaigns and then in the civil rights movement, brought many women to feminist awareness.[167] In both these movements women played a more central role than has generally been acknowledged: 'the combination of the civil rights movement, the street politics, and the more local community development campaigns all helped to develop the political acumen so necessary for these early feminist groups.'[168] Inevitably, most, though by no means all, of the early activists were drawn from the catholic community; in general protestant women did not have the same incentives to challenge the status quo.

THE early 1970s saw scattered individual groups emerge, followed after 1975 by more vigorous growth, debate, and argument, and more contact between groups in Northern Ireland and those in the Republic. The Northern Ireland Women's Rights Movement (N.I.W.R.M.) was founded in 1975 to ensure that new U.K. sex discrimination legislation[169] was extended to Northern Ireland. This objective was achieved in 1976. The N.I.W.R.M. drew up a charter of women's demands, and aimed to coordinate a wide range of organisations. Perhaps because of its conventional structure (unlike the women's collectives, it had a constitution and a committee) it survived despite internal tensions. From it several groups broke away, including the Socialist Women's Group (S.W.G.) and the Women's Aid groups. The former flourished in the late 1970s and was committed to a socialist republic as a prerequisite for the success of feminism, and to putting feminism on the agenda of the left. Women's Aid groups had developed in Belfast, Coleraine, and Derry in the 1970s, and elsewhere, including Newry, North Down, and Omagh in the 1980s: a Northern Ireland Women's Aid Federation was set up in 1977. Such groups drew attention to the incidence of domestic violence against women. This problem cut across political allegiances and was exacerbated in Northern Ireland by the number of weapons held, legitimately or illegitimately, by men. In 1976 a Women's Law and Research

[167] Eilish Rooney, 'Political division, practical alliance: problems for women in conflict' in *Journal of Women's History*, vi, no 4 (winter/spring 1995), pp 40–48: 41–2. For a personal story of one woman's experience see Margaret Ward, 'From civil rights to women's rights' in Michael Farrell (ed.), *Twenty years on* (Dingle, 1988), pp 122–33.

[168] See Catherine B. Shannon, 'Women in Northern Ireland' in O'Dowd & Wichert, *Chattel, servant or citizen*, pp 238–47; Monica McWilliams, 'Struggling for peace and justice: reflections on women's activism in Northern Ireland' in *Journal of Women's History*, vi, no. 4 (winter/spring 1995), pp 13–39: 25.

[169] Sex Discrimination Act (U.K.), 1975 (12 Nov. 1975, c. 65).

Group was established from a number of existing groups to research and campaign on legislation affecting women. Also during the 1970s lesbian groups became better organised; a lesbian helpline was established in 1978.[170]

Within the nationalist tradition there were other problems and divisions. The old question of the primacy of the national struggle or the rights of women reemerged. The Belfast Women's Collective (1977–80) registered its opposition to imperialism but stopped short of supporting the republican movement, while Women Against Imperialism (1978–81) put the republican programme at the top of its agenda. For some nationalist women the treatment of republican women prisoners in Armagh prison, and particularly strip-searching, was primarily a feminist issue; for other feminists it was essentially a republican issue.

A women-led initiative to end political conflict, known as the 'Peace women', later the 'Peace people', emerged in 1976 and attracted huge support across the religious and political divide, leading at the end of the year to the award in Oslo of the 'people's peace prize' to its leaders, Máiréad Corrigan, Betty Williams, and Ciarán McKeown. Women's groups were initially enthusiastic, but later became more critical. The movement subsequently declined in numbers and influence, amid internal and external disagreements over its definition of violence and understanding of precisely what constituted 'peace'.

During the 1980s efforts continued to turn the spotlight on issues of primary concern to women. The Northern Ireland Abortion Campaign (N.I.A.C.) was set up in 1980, and the issue was taken over by the Northern Ireland Association for Law Reform on Abortion (N.I.A.L.R.A.) from 1984. The Belfast Rape Crisis Centre was set up in 1982, followed by the Northern Ireland Rape Crisis Association. And 1984 saw the appearance of the *Women's News*, a newspaper designed for women. [171]

The 1980s also saw what has been described as 'feminist activism as an agent of change'. This involved campaigning to include gender inequality and women's concerns in all discussions of solutions to the problems of Northern Ireland, and continuing efforts to build a feminist movement that crossed political, religious, and class divides. This has been particularly apparent in the participation of working-class women, a strong element in the Northern Ireland women's movement from the start. The early prominence of women in tenant and community organisations led to a vigorous growth of locally based women's groups, and active participation in such organisations and networks as the Women's Information Group (1980) and the Women's

---

[170] Eileen Evason, *Against the grain: the contemporary women's movement in Northern Ireland* (Dublin, 1991), pp 16–36.
[171] Ibid., pp 36–45.

Resource and Development Agency (1983).[172] The greater involvement of protestant women has been a feature in recent years, and increasingly community women's groups from both sides of the political divide have been meeting each other with the aim of understanding and coming to terms with difference. From the 1980s on there have also been renewed efforts to bring feminists, north and south, together. There appears now to be greater recognition of the fact that diversity of interests and identities are realities that have to be faced; and that there is a common interest in insisting that feminist perspectives and concerns are present when future political, social, and economic directions in both parts of Ireland are under discussion.

THE dramatic changes that have taken place in the status and role of women in Ireland since the mid nineteenth century are clearly part of an international movement that has in some respects carried women far beyond the aims of most early campaigners for women's emancipation—even if some visions have yet to be realised. As this survey has shown, Irish women played a full part in promoting reform in Ireland, at times contributed to reform in the United Kingdom, and took part in international organisations. Future objectives and strategies have to be devised in the context of contemporary political, social, and economic structures: generations of women are growing up who have little acquaintance with the struggles of the past. As feminists in Ireland, both north and south, face into the twenty-first century, there is a growing perception of the need for a forum for debate about the nature, the meaning, and the future directions of feminism itself.

[172] McWillliams, 'Struggling for peace and justice', pp 29–30.

BIBLIOGRAPHY

J. R. HILL AND J. E. BARDON

INTRODUCTION

THE pressures and constraints affecting the bibliography of volume VI of the *New history*—particularly the enormous quantity and variety of primary and secondary source material available for the period—apply also here. A similar departure from the original bibliographical plan of the *New history* has therefore been necessary. It has been impossible to include sections on manuscript sources, official and other records, contemporary writing, newspapers, maps, and other visual material; the space necessary to do so comprehensively would be many times greater than that at our disposal. Instead, the sections of 'bibliographies and guides' have been extended to provide fuller assistance towards further reading in all types of source material. References to a few of the more important sources can also be found in the footnotes to the main text.

Among secondary works, the passage of time has made accessible more records, and made possible more detachment in assessing actors, episodes, and trends in this period. Scholarly studies in political and economic history and in other fields are therefore multiplying. Moreover, despite the substantial changes and developments in Ireland in recent years, some of the fundamental issues present in 1922 are still active, the most conspicuous being the partition of the island. The original conception for this volume was that, as far as possible, the history of south and north since 1922 should be taken together and considered comparatively—an ideal most closely approached, as far as politics are concerned, in the chapters above by J. H. Whyte. Even before 1969, however, the existence of two jurisdictions with separate political cultures, economic structures, social climates, and external alignments was producing two separate bodies of historical writing—a trend greatly reinforced by the onset of the 'troubles' in that year. We have therefore followed the example of others—notably the annual lists of 'Writings on Irish history' (section I)—and produced separate bibliographies for 'Ireland' and Northern Ireland, almost identical in structure, with the latter including a section on the 'troubles'. A few works, because of their general relevance, appear in both parts. Composite works do not appear in a separate section of their own, but under the appropriate subject headings. In most cases their constituent articles are not listed separately; a few exceptions have been made for articles of particular importance.

We are grateful to other scholars in several fields, including Professor Kevin B. Nowlan, Dr Peter Denman, Dr Máire Ní Annracháin, and Dr David Craig, director of the National Archives of Ireland, for their advice and suggestions. Special thanks are due to Sarah Ward-Perkins and John McHugh for help in checking bibliographical items.

The bibliography was substantially revised and updated in 2000, following which it has not been possible to include more than a handful of subsequent publications. It is proposed to develop an on-line version of 'Writings on Irish history' (below, p. 899) with the assistance of the Irish Research Council for the Humanities and Social Sciences; in the meantime, readers are referred to the Royal Historical Society Bibliography of British and Irish history on-line (below, p. 898).

CONTENTS

Ireland

Northern Ireland

IRELAND

I BIBLIOGRAPHIES AND GUIDES

Adams, Valerie (ed.). *An Irish genealogical source: a guide to church records.* Belfast, 1994.

Barrington, Clare. *Irish women in England: an annotated bibliography.* Dublin, 1997.

Bishop, A. W., and Ferguson, Kenneth. *Index to the Irish Sword, vols i to xviii, 1949–1992; compiled for vols i to x by A. W. Bishop; continued to end of vol. xviii and prepared for publication by Kenneth Ferguson.* [Dublin], 1992.

Blessing, Patrick J. *The Irish in America: a guide to the literature and the manuscript collections.* Washington, D.C., 1992.

Brady, Anna. *Women in Ireland: an annotated bibliography.* New York, 1988.

British Library. *The British Library general catalogue of printed books to 1975.* 366 vols. London, 1979–88. CD-ROM, London, 1992. 1976–82, 50 vols, London, 1983; 1982–5, 26 vols, London, 1986; 1986–7, 22 vols, London, 1988; 1988–9, 28 vols, London, 1990.

——*Catalogue of printed maps, charts, and plans.* 15 vols. London, 1967. Ten-year supplement (1965–74), London, 1978.

Burchell, R. A. The historiography of the American Irish. In *Immigrants and Minorities,* i, no. 3 (1982), pp 281–305.

Chambers, Bernadette. A note on the archives of the department of foreign affairs. In *Ir. Archives,* new ser., ii, no. 2 (autumn 1995), pp 44–8.

Cole, Jean, and Church, Rosemary. *In and around record repositories in Great Britain and Ireland.* 3rd ed., Huntingdon, 1992. Previous ed. published as *In and around record offices in Great Britain and Ireland,* 1987.

Cullen, L. M. Irish Manuscripts Commission survey of business records. In *Ir. Econ. & Soc. Hist.,* x (1983), pp 81–91.
     See below Donnelly, Brian.

de Hae, Risteárd. *Clár litridheacht na Nua-Ghaeilge 1850–1936.* 3 vols. Dublin, 1938–40.

Denson, Alan. *Printed writings by George Russell (AE): a bibliography*. Evanston, Ill., 1961.

Donnelly, Brian. Irish Manuscripts Commission survey of business records. In *Ir. Econ. & Soc. Hist.*, xi (1984), pp 122–4; xii (1985), pp 117–19; xiii (1986), pp 117–19; xiv (1987), pp 80–82; xv (1988), pp 99–100; xvi (1989), pp 95–7; xvii (1990), pp 93–4; xviii (1991), pp 54–5; xix (1992), pp 77–9; xx (1993), pp 72–4; xxi (1994), pp 72–4.

——National Archives survey of business records. In *Ir. Econ. & Soc. Hist.*, xxii (1995), pp 88–9; xxiii (1996), pp 120–21; xxiv (1997), pp 105–6; xxv (1998), pp 88–9; xxvi (1999), pp 81–2; xxvii (2000), pp 73–6. In progress.

——Records of the Royal College of Physicians. In *Ir. Archives*, i (1989), pp 31–4.

——and Ó hÓgartaigh, Margaret. Medical archives for the socio-economic historian. In *Ir. Econ. & Soc. Hist.*, xxvii (2000), pp 66–72.

——and Warke, Oonagh (ed.). Maritime history sources issue. In *Ir. Archives*, ii, no. 1 (1992).

Dooley, Terence. *Source for the history of landed estates in Ireland*. Dublin, 2000.

Doughan, David, and Souchez, Denise. *Feminist periodicals, 1855–1984: an annotated critical bibliography of British, Irish, commonwealth, and international titles*. Brighton, 1987.

Downs, R. B. *British and Irish library resources: a bibliographical guide*. Revised ed., London, 1981.

Eager, A. R. *A guide to Irish bibliographical material: a bibliography of Irish bibliographies and sources of information*. 2nd ed., revised and enlarged. Westport, Conn., and London, 1980.

Edwards, John. *The Irish language: an annotated bibliography of socio-linguistic publications, 1772–1982*. New York and London, 1983.

Études Irlandaises: a bilingual journal of Irish history, civilisation, and literature. Index [1972–92]. Sainghin-en-Mélantois, [1993].

Ferguson, Paul. *Irish map history: a select bibliography of secondary works 1850–1983 on the history of cartography in Ireland*. Dublin, 1983.

Ferriter, Diarmaid. Oral archives in Ireland: a preliminary report. In *Ir. Econ. & Soc. Hist.*, xxv (1998), pp 91–5.

Finneran, Richard J. (ed.). *Anglo-Irish literature: a review of research*. New York, 1976. Supplement, 1983. (Modern Language Association of America.)

Flynn, Mary E. Ten-year retrospective bibliography of Irish labour history, 1963–1972. In *Saothar*, xiv (1989), pp 143–57.

——A retrospective bibliography of Irish labour history, 1960–1972. In *Saothar*, xvi (1991), pp 144–58.

See below, O'Connell, Deirdre.

Forth, G. J. (ed.). *A biographical register and annotated bibliography of Anglo-Irish colonists in Australia*. Warrnambod, 1992.

Gmelch, George, and Gmelch, S. B. Ireland's travelling people: a comprehensive bibliography. In *Journal of the Gypsy Lore Society*, i, no. 3 (1977), pp 159–69.

Grenham, John. *Tracing your Irish ancestors: the complete guide*. 2nd ed., Dublin, 1999. First published 1992.

Harmon, Maurice. *Select bibliography for the study of Anglo-Irish literature and its backgrounds*. Dublin, 1977.

Hartigan, Maureen (compiler), and Hickman, Mary J. (ed.). *The history of the Irish in Britain: a bibliography*. London, 1986.

Hayes, R. J. (ed.). *Manuscript sources for the history of Irish civilisation*. 11 vols. Boston, 1965. First supplement [1965–75]. 3 vols, Boston, 1979.

——*Sources for the history of Irish civilisation: articles in Irish periodicals*. 9 vols. Boston, 1970.

Helferty, Seamus, and Refaussé, Raymond (ed.). *Directory of Irish archives*. 3rd ed., Dublin, 1999. 1st ed., 1988; 2nd ed., 1993.

Herries Davies, Gordon L. *The history of Irish science: a select bibliography*. 2nd ed., Dublin, 1985.

Holzapfel, Rudolf P. *A survey of Irish literary periodicals from 1900 to the present day*. Dublin, 1964.

Horgan, Dominique. In our keeping: the archives of the Congregation of the Irish Dominican Sisters, Cabra [Dublin]. In *Catholic Archives*, xiv (1994), pp 60–64.

Horton, Charles. The records of the Freemasons in Ireland. In *Familia*, ii (1986), pp 65–9.

Hunter, Jennifer. Irish Labour History Society archives and museum. In *Saothar*, xxii (1997), pp 123–5.

Inglis, K. S. Catholic historiography in Australia. In *Historical Studies*, viii (1958), pp 233–53.

Irish Historical Studies: supplement 1. Dublin, 1968. Includes index (by Esther Semple) for vols i–xv (1938–67).

Irish Manuscripts Commission. *Guide to the Genealogical Office, Dublin*. Dublin, 1998.

Irish University Review: a journal of Irish studies, xv, no. 2 (autumn 1985). Includes index for vols i–xv (1970–85).

Jefferson, George. *Liam O'Flaherty: a descriptive bibliography of his works*. Dublin, 1993.

Joannon, Pierre. Liste des ouvrages consacrés a l'histoire, la politique, les institutions de l'Irlande. Published annually in *Études Irlandaises*, 1974–81. Continued as 'Bibliographie selective: histoire, politique, institutions Irlandaises', 1982– . In progress.

Kamen, Ruth H. *British and Irish architectural history: a bibliography and guide to sources of information*. London, 1981.

Kelly, Katherine, *et al. An indexed bibliography of Irish marine literature from 1939–1997*. Dublin, 1997.

Lester, Dee Gee. *Irish research: a guide to collections in North America, Ireland, and Great Britain*. New York, 1987.

Library Associations of Ireland. *Directory of libraries in Ireland*. 2nd ed., Dublin and Belfast, 1988. 1st ed. 1983.

Libraries of Dublin: proceedings of a conference held on 14–16 October 1988, as part of the city's millennium celebrations. Dublin, 1989.

Lohan, Rena. *Guide to the archives of the Office of Public Works*. Dublin, 1994.

MacLysaght, Edward. *Bibliography of Irish family history*. 2nd ed. Blackrock, 1982.

McParland, Edward. A bibliography of Irish architectural history. In *I.H.S.*, xxvi, no. 102 (Nov. 1988), pp 161–212.

MacWhite, Eoin. Guide to Russian writings on Irish history, 1917–63. In *Melbourne Slavonic Studies*, no. 3 (1969), pp 40–96.

Malcomson, A. P. W. PRONI and its archives. In *Ir. Econ. & Soc. Hist.*, xxiii (1996), pp 117–19.

Maltby, Arthur, and McKenna, Brian. *Irish official publications: a guide to Republic of Ireland papers with a breviate of reports, 1922–1972.* Oxford, 1980.

Marman, Ed. (ed.). *Éire-Ireland: the comprehensive index, 1966–1988.* Index issue, vols i–xxiii (1992).

Martin, G. H., and MacIntyre, Sylvia. *A bibliography of British and Irish municipal history.* Leicester, 1972.

Metress, Séamus P. *The Irish-American experience: a guide to the literature.* Washington, D.C., 1981.

Milne, Kenneth. The Church of Ireland: a critical bibliography. Part vi: 1870–1992. In *I.H.S.*, xxviii, no. 112 (Nov. 1993), pp 376–84.

Mitchell, Brian. *A guide to Irish parish registers.* Baltimore, Md., 1988.

Nolan, William. *Tracing the past: sources for local studies in the Republic of Ireland.* Dublin, 1982.

——and Simms, Anngret (ed.). *Irish towns: a guide to sources.* Dublin, 1998.

Ó Catháin, Séamus. The Irish folklore archive. In *History Workshop*, xxxi (1991), pp 145–8.

O'Connell, Declan. The Irish in Australia: some recent work. In *Saothar*, viii (1982), p. 115.

O'Connell, Deirdre. A bibliography of Irish labour history ... [from 1973]. Published annually in *Saothar*, 1979– . In progress.
See above, Flynn, Mary E.

——Electronic sources for labour history. In *Saothar*, xxiv (1999), pp 123–4.

O'Hanrahan, Brenda. *Donegal authors: a bibliography.* Dublin, 1982.

O'Higgins, Paul. *A bibliography of periodical literature relating to Irish law.* Belfast, 1966. First supplement, Belfast, 1973. Second supplement, Belfast, 1983.

——*A bibliography of Irish trials and other legal proceedings.* Abingdon, 1986.

Ó hOgartaigh, Margaret. Archival sources for the history of professional women in late nineteenth and early twentieth-century Ireland. In *Ir. Archives*, new ser., vi, no. 1 (1999), pp 23–5.

Osborough, W. N. Recent writing on modern Irish legal history. In *Zeitschrift für neuere Rechtsgeschichte*, viii (1986), pp 180–94.

O'Sullivan, S. The work of the Irish Folklore Commission. In *Oral History*, ii, no. 2 (1974).

O'Toole, James. *Newsplan: report of the Newsplan project in Ireland.* Revised ed., ed. Sara Smyth. London and Dublin, 1998.
Listing of Irish newspaper holdings in the U.K. and Ireland.

Pattison, I. R. (ed.). *A bibliography of vernacular architecture.* Vol. iii: 1977–1989. Aberystwyth, 1992.

Ward-Perkins, Sarah (ed.). *Select guide to trade union records in Dublin: with details of unions operating in Ireland to 1970.* Dublin, 1996.

Prochaska, Alice. *Irish history from 1700: a guide to sources in the Public Record Office.* London, 1986.

Rafroidi, Patrick; Alluin-Popot, Raymonde; Deboulonne, Marie-Jocelyne; Escarbelt, Bernard; Neville, Grace; and Rafroidi, Anne. The year's work in Anglo-Irish literature. Published annually in *Études Irlandaises*, 1974–80. Continued as 'The year's work in Irish-English literature', 1981–6. Continued as 'Irish literature in English: the year's work', 1987– . In progress.

Refaussé, Raymond. Church of Ireland parish registers in the Representative Church Body Library, Dublin. In *Ir. Geneal.*, ix (1994), pp 73–5.

—— The Representative Church Body Library and the records of the Church of Ireland. In *Archiv. Hib.*, xlix (1995), 115–24.

—— *Church of Ireland records*. Dublin, 2000.

Rouse, Sarah. *Into the light: an illustrated guide to the photographic collections in the National Library of Ireland*. Dublin, 1998.

Royal Historical Society. *Annual bibliography of British and Irish history: publications of 1975* [etc.]. Hassocks, Sussex, and Atlantic Highlands, N.J., 1976– . Annual. Ed. G. R. Elton, 1975–84; D. M. Palliser, 1985–7; Barbara English and J. J. N. Palmer, 1988–92; Katharine F. Beedham, Barbara English, and J. J. N. Palmer, 1993; Barbara English and J. J. N. Palmer, 1994; Austin Gee, 1995–9. Publications of 1989– published in Oxford and New York. In progress.

Ryan, James. *Irish records: sources for family and local history*. Salt Lake City, Utah, and Glenageary, Co. Dublin, 1988.

—— (ed.). *Irish church records: their history, availability, and use in family and local history research*. Glenageary, Co. Dublin, 1992.

Schneider, Jürgen, and Sotscheck, Ralf. *'Irland': eine Bibliographie selbständiger deutschsprachiger Publikationen: 16. Jahrhundert bis 1989*. Darmstadt, 1988.

Select bibliography of writings on Irish economic and social history, published in 1973 [etc.]. Published annually in *Ir. Econ. & Soc. Hist.*, 1974– . In progress.

Shannon, Michael O. (ed.). *Modern Ireland: a bibliography on politics, planning, research and development*. London, 1981.

Sheehy, David. The current state of catholic archives in Ireland: an overview. In *Catholic Archives*, xv (1995), pp 62–6.

Smythe, Colin, and others (ed.). International Association for the Study of Anglo-Irish Literature [later International Association for the Study of Irish Literature] annual bibliography bulletin, 1973– . Published annually in *Irish University Review*, xv (1975) [etc.]. In progress.

Studies: an Irish quarterly review. General index of vols i–l (1912–61). Roscrea, 1967.

Tierney, Mark. Calendar of 'Irlande', vols 1–3 in the collection 'Europe' 1918–29, in the Archives Diplomatiques, Paris. In *Collect. Hib.*, xxi–xxii (1979–80), pp 203–5; [vols 4–6], xxiv (1982), pp 116–46; [vols 19, 22, and 26 in the collection 'Europe', 1930–40], xxvi (1984), pp 129–56.

Wade, Allan. *A bibliography of the writings of W. B. Yeats*. 3rd ed., revised by Russell K. Alspach. London, 1968.

Watson, George. *The new Cambridge bibliography of English literature*. 5 vols. Cambridge, 1969–77.

Weaver, Jack W., and Lester, Dee Gee. *Immigrants from Great Britain and Ireland: a guide to manuscript and archival sources in North America*. Westport, Conn., 1986.

White, Stephen. Soviet writings on Irish history, 1917–80: a bibliography. In *I.H.S.*, xxiii, no. 90 (Nov. 1982), pp 174–86.

Wiles, James, and Finnegan, Richard. *A select list of Irish government publications, 1972–1992*. Dublin, 1994.

Woods, C. J. A guide to Irish biographical dictionaries. In *Maynooth Review*, vi (1980), pp 16–34.

Writings on Irish history, 1936– . Dublin, 1938– . Published annually in *I.H.S.* to 1979; lists for 1979–83 published in microfiche by Irish Committee for Historical Sciences; lists from 1984 published as annual/biennial booklets by I.C.H.S. in association with *I.H.S.*, and (1986–7) with A New History of Ireland. In progress.

Yurdan, Marilyn. *Irish family history*. London, 1990.
Guide to archives and research procedures.

II SECONDARY WORKS

A GENERAL HISTORY

Augusteijn, Joost (ed.). *Ireland in the 1930s: new perspectives*. Dublin, 1999.

Beckett, J. C. *A short history of Ireland*. London, 1952. 6th ed., 1979.

—— *The making of modern Ireland, 1603–1923*. London and New York, 1966; paperback ed., London and Boston, 1981.

Bottigheimer, K. S. *Ireland and the Irish: a short history*. New York, 1982.

Boyce, D. George. *Ireland 1828–1923: from ascendancy to democracy*. Oxford, 1992.

Carroll, Joseph T. *Ireland in the war years 1939–1945*. Rev. ed., San Francisco, 1998. First published 1975.

Connery, Donal S. *The Irish*. London, 1968. Revised ed. 1972.

Coogan, Tim Pat. *Disillusioned decades: Ireland 1966–87*. Dublin, 1987.

Curtis, Edmund. *A history of Ireland*. 6th ed., London and New York, 1950. 1st ed. 1936.

Elvert, Jürgen. *Geschichte Irlands*. Munich, 1993.

Fanning, Ronan. *Independent Ireland*. Dublin, 1983.

Fennell, Desmond. *The state of the nation: Ireland since the sixties*. Swords, 1983.

Finnegan, Richard B., and McCarron, Edward T. *Ireland: historical echoes, contemporary politics*. Boulder, Colo., 2000.

Foster, Roy. *Modern Ireland 1600–1972*. London, 1988; paperback ed., 1989.

—— (ed.). *The Oxford history of Ireland*. Oxford, 1992. Previous ed. published as *The Oxford illustrated history of Ireland*, 1989.

Fréchet, René. *Histoire de l'Irlande*. Paris, 1992.

Girvin, Brian, and Roberts, Geoffrey (ed.). *Ireland and the second world war:politics, society, and remembrance*. Dublin, 2000.

Gol'man, L. I., and others. *Istoriya Irlandii*. Moscow, 1981.

Gray, Tony. *The Irish answer: an anatomy of modern Ireland*. London, 1966.

—— *Ireland this century*. London, 1996.

—— *The lost years: the emergency in Ireland, 1939–45*. London, 1997.

Harkness, David W. *Ireland in the twentieth century: divided island*. Basingstoke, 1996.

Hoppen, K. Theodore. *Ireland since 1800: conflict and conformity*. London and New York, 1989. 2nd ed. 1999.
Johnson, Paul. *Ireland, land of troubles: a history from the twelfth century to the present day*. London, 1980.
Keogh, Dermot. *Twentieth-century Ireland: nation and state*. Dublin, 1994.
Lee, J. J. *Ireland 1912–1985: politics and society*. Cambridge, 1989.
—— (ed.). *Ireland, 1945–70*. Dublin, 1979. (Thomas Davis Lectures.)
—— and Ó Tuathaigh, Gearóid (ed.). *The age of de Valera*. Dublin, 1982.
Lydon, James. *The making of Ireland from ancient times to the present*. London, 1998.
Lyons, F. S. L. *Ireland since the famine*. London, 1971; paperback ed., 1973.
MacDonagh, Oliver. *Ireland: the union and its aftermath*. Rev. ed., London, 1977. Previous ed. 1968.
MacManus, Francis (ed.). *The years of the great test, 1926–39*. Cork, 1967.
Moody, T. W., and Martin, F. X. (ed.). *The course of Irish history*. Rev. and enlarged ed., ed. F. X. Martin. Cork, 1994. Previous eds 1967, 1984.
Morrison, George. *The emergent years: independent Ireland 1922–62*. Dublin, 1984.
Murphy, John A. *Ireland in the twentieth century*. Dublin, 1975; new impression, 1989.
Norman, E. R. *A history of modern Ireland*. Harmondsworth, 1971.
O'Farrell, Patrick. *England and Ireland since 1800*. London, 1975.
O'Faolain, Sean. *The Irish*. Harmondsworth, 1990. First ed. 1947.
O'Hegarty, P. S. *A history of Ireland under the union, 1801 to 1922*. London, 1952.
Ranelagh, John O'Beirne. *A short history of Ireland*. Cambridge, 1994. First published 1983.
Tobin, Fergal. *The best of decades: Ireland in the nineteen sixties*. Dublin, 1996. First published 1984.
Townshend, Charles. *Ireland: the twentieth century*. London, 1999.

B SPECIAL FIELDS AND TOPICS

1 POLITICAL HISTORY

Allen, Kieran. *Fianna Fáil and Irish labour: 1926 to the present*. London, 1997.
Allison, Jonathan. *Yeats' political identities: selected essays*. Ann Arbor, 1996.
Anderson, Malcolm, and Bort, Eberhard. *The Irish border: history, politics, culture*. Liverpool, 1999.
Arnold, Bruce. *What kind of country: modern Irish politics 1968–1983*. London, 1984.
Bax, M. *Harp strings and confessions: machine style politics in the Irish republic*. Assen, 1976.
Beaverbrook, W. M. *The decline and fall of Lloyd George*. London, 1963.
Bell, Geoffrey. *Troublesome business: the Labour party and the Irish question*. London, 1982.
Bell, J. Bowyer. *The secret army: the I.R.A. 1916–1979*. 4th ed., Swords, 1989.
—— *The I.R.A., 1968–2000: analysis of a secret army*. London and Portland, Or., 2000.
—— *The gun in politics: an analysis of Irish political conflict, 1916–1986*. New Brunswick, N.J., 1987.
—— *In dubious battle: Dublin and Monaghan bombings, 1972–74*. Dublin, 1996.

Bew, Paul. Moderate nationalism and the Irish revolution, 1916–1923. In *Hist. Jn.*, lxii (1999), pp 729–49.

—— Hazelkorn, Ellen; and Patterson, Henry. *The dynamics of Irish politics.* London, 1989.

—— and Patterson, Henry. *Seán Lemass and the making of modern Ireland, 1945–66.* Dublin, 1982.

Boland, Kevin. *'We won't stand (idly) by'.* Dublin, 1972.

—— *The rise and decline of Fianna Fáil.* Dublin, 1982.

Bowman, John. *De Valera and the Ulster question 1917–1973.* Oxford, 1982.

Boyce, D. George. *Englishmen and Irish troubles.* Aldershot, 1994. First ed. 1972.

—— *Nationalism in Ireland.* 3rd ed., London, 1995. First ed. 1982.

—— (ed.). *The Irish question in British politics, 1868–1986.* Basingstoke and London, 1988. 2nd ed. 1996.

—— (ed.). *The revolution in Ireland, 1879–1923.* Dublin, 1988.

Broderick, Eugene. The Blueshirts in Waterford, 1932–1934. Parts 1 and 2. In *Decies*, xlviii (1993), pp 54–63; xlix (1994), pp 55–61.

—— The corporate labour policy of Fine Gael, 1934. In *I.H.S.*, xxix, no. 113 (May 1994), pp 88–99.

Bromage, Mary C. *Churchill and Ireland.* Notre Dame, Ind., 1964.

—— *De Valera and the march of a nation.* London, 1956.

—— Ireland's nationalist leadership, a 20th century prototype? In *Emory University Quarterly*, xxii (1966), 36–45.

de Bruyne, Arthur. *Eamon de Valera en de Ierse Republiek.* Antwerp, 1954.

Busteed, M. A. *Voting behaviour in the Republic of Ireland: a geographical perspective.* Oxford, 1990.

Butler, John (ed.). Lord Oranmore's journal, 1913–27. In *I.H.S.*, xxix, no. 116 (Nov. 1995), pp 553–93.
Southern unionist.

Canning, Paul. *British policy towards Ireland 1921–1941.* Oxford, 1985.

Carroll, Joseph T. U.S.–Irish relations, 1939–45. In *Ir. Sword*, xix (1993–4), pp 99–105.

Carty, R. K. *Party and parish pump: electoral politics in Ireland.* Waterloo, Ontario, 1981. Dingle, 1983.

Clarkson, J. D. *Labour and nationalism in Ireland.* New York, 1925.

Coakley, John. Minor parties in Irish political life, 1922–1989. In *Econ. & Soc. Rev.*, xxi, no. 3 (1990), pp 269–97.

—— and Gallagher, Michael (ed.). *Politics in the Republic of Ireland.* Galway, 1992. 3rd ed., London, 1999.

Cohan, Al. *The Irish political elite.* Dublin, 1972.

—— The used vote and electoral outcomes: the Irish general election of 1973. In *British Journal of Political Science*, v (1975), pp 363–83.

Collins, Stephen. *Spring and the Labour story.* Dublin, 1993.

—— *The Cosgrave legacy.* Dublin, 1996.

—— *Fianna Fáil since Lemass.* Dublin, 2000.

Coogan, Tim Pat. *Ireland since the rising.* Westwood, Conn., 1976. First ed. London, 1966.

—— *The I.R.A.* London, 1970; revised and updated ed., 2000.

Coombes, David (ed.). *Ireland and the European Communities: ten years of membership.* Dublin, 1983.

Cronin, Mike. *The Blueshirts and Irish politics.* Dublin, 1997.

——and Regan, John M. (ed.). *Ireland: the politics of independence 1922–1949.* Basingstoke and New York, 2000.

Cronin, Seán. *Washington's Irish policy, 1916–1986.* Dublin, 1987.

Cullingford, Elizabeth. *Yeats, Ireland and fascism.* New York, 1981.

Curran, Joseph M. *The birth of the Irish Free State 1921–1923.* University, Ala., 1980.

Davis, E. E., and Sinnott, R. *Attitudes in the Republic of Ireland relevant to the Northern Ireland problem*, i. General Research Series, E.S.R.I., Dublin, 1979.

Davis, Troy D. *Dublin's American policy: Irish–American diplomatic relations, 1945–1952.* Washington, 1998.

Dillon, Martin. *Twenty-five years of terror.* Rev. ed., London, 1996. Originally published as *The enemy within*, 1994.

The I.R.A. bombing campaigns in Britain.

Dooge, James (ed.). *Ireland in the contemporary world: essays in honour of Garret FitzGerald.* Dublin, 1986.

Dooley, Terence. *The plight of Monaghan protestants, 1912–1926.* Dublin, 2000.

Douglas, R. M. The swastika and the shamrock: British fascism and the Irish question. In *Albion*, xxix (1997), pp 57–75.

Downey, James. *Them and us: Britain, Ireland and the Northern question, 1969–1982.* Dublin, 1983.

Drudy, P. J. (ed.). *Ireland: land, politics and people.* Cambridge, 1982. (Irish Studies, II).

——(ed.) *Ireland and Britain since 1922.* Cambridge, 1986. (Irish Studies, V.)

——and McAleese, Dermot (ed.). *Ireland and the European Community.* Cambridge, 1984. (Irish Studies, III.)

Dunphy, Richard. *The making of Fianna Fáil power in Ireland, 1923–1948.* Oxford, 1995.

Dwyer, T. Ryle. *Michael Collins and the treaty: his differences with de Valera.* Dublin, 1981.

——*De Valera's darkest hour, 1919–1932.* Dublin, 1982.

English, Richard. *Radicals and the republic: socialist republicanism in the Irish Free State, 1925–1937.* Oxford, 1994.

Faligot, Roger. *La resistance irlandaise: 1916–1992.* 2nd ed., Rennes, 1995.

Fanning, Ronan. Leadership and transition from the politics of revolution to the politics of party: the example of Ireland, 1914–1939. In *Reports: 14th International Congress of Historical Sciences* (New York, 1977), iii, 1741–68.

——London and Belfast's response to the declaration of the Republic of Ireland, 1948–49. In *International Affairs*, lviii (1981–2), pp 95–114.

——Kennedy, Michael; Keogh, Dermot; and O'Halpin, Eunan (ed.). *Documents on Irish foreign policy, vol. i: 1919–1922.* Dublin, 1998. *Vol. ii: 1923–1926.* Dublin, 2000.

Farrell, Brian (ed.). *The Irish parliamentary tradition.* Dublin, 1973.

Farry, Michael. *The aftermath of revolution: Sligo, 1921–23.* Dublin, 2000.

Fianna Fáil, an chéad tréimhse: the story of Fianna Fáil, first phase. Dublin, 1960.

FitzGerald, Garret. *Towards a new Ireland*. Dublin and London, 1972.

Fitzpatrick, David. *Revolution? Ireland 1917–23*. Dublin, 1990.

—— *The two Irelands, 1912–1939*. Oxford, 1998.

Foley, Conor. *Legion of the rearguard: the I.R.A. and the modern Irish state*. London, 1992.

Foster, R. F. Together and apart: Anglo-Irish agreements, 1886–1986. In *History Today*, xxxvi (May 1986), pp 6–9.

Fraser, Thomas G. *Partition in Ireland, India and Palestine: theory and practice*. London, 1984.

Gallagher, Michael. *Electoral support for Irish political parties 1927–1973*. London, 1976.

—— The pact general election of 1922. In *I.H.S.*, xxi, no. 84 (Sept. 1979), pp 404–21.

—— The impact of lower preference votes on Irish parliamentary elections, 1922–1977. In *Econ. & Soc. Rev.*, xi (1979), pp 19–32.

—— *The Irish Labour party in transition 1957–82*. Manchester, 1982.

—— *Political parties in the Republic of Ireland*. Dublin, 1985.

—— (ed.). *Irish elections 1922–44: results and analysis*. Limerick, 1993.

Gallogly, Dan. Patrick Finegan and the birth of the Irish Free State 1909–1923. In *Breifne*, viii (1996), pp 625–71.

Garvin, Thomas. The destiny of the soldiers: tradition and modernity in the politics of de Valera's Ireland. In *Political Studies*, xxvi (1978), pp 328–47.

—— *The evolution of Irish nationalist politics*. Dublin, 1981.

—— *Nationalist revolutionaries in Ireland 1858–1928*. Oxford, 1987.

—— *1922: the birth of Irish democracy*. Dublin, 1996.

—— The aftermath of the civil war. In *Ir. Sword*, xx (1997), pp 387–95.

Geiger, Till, and Kennedy, Michael. Select Documents L: The lost origins of Ireland's involvement in Europe: the Irish response to the Briand plan, 1929–30. In *I.H.S.*, xxxii, no. 126 (Nov. 2000), pp 232–45.

Girvin, Brian. *Between two worlds: politics and economy in independent Ireland*. Dublin, 1989.

—— and Sturm, Roland (ed.) *Politics and society in contemporary Ireland*. Aldershot, 1986.

Greaves, Desmond. *The Irish case against partition: full facts and programme of action*. London, 1956.

Gwynn, Denis. *The Irish Free State, 1922–7*. London, 1928.

—— *The history of partition, 1912–1925*. Dublin, 1950.

Hancock, W. K. *Survey of British commonwealth affairs. Vol. i*. London and New York, 1937.
Chapters on 'Saorstát Éireann' and 'Ireland unappeased'.

Harkness, D. W. *The restless dominion: the Irish Free State and the British commonwealth of nations, 1921–31*. New York, 1970. First published 1969.

—— Patrick McGilligan, man of commonwealth. In *Journal of Imperial and Commonwealth History*, viii, no. 1 (1979), pp 117–35.

Harrison, Henry. *Ireland and the British empire, 1937: conflict or collaboration?* London, 1937.

Hart, Peter. The geography of revolution in Ireland, 1917–23. In *Past & Present*, no. 155 (1997), pp 142–76.

Hart, Peter. *The I.R.A. and its enemies: violence and community in Cork, 1916–23.* Oxford, 1998.

—— The social structure of the Irish Republican Army, 1916–23. In *Hist. Jn.*, xlii (1999), pp 207–31.

Harvey, Brian. *Cosgrave's coalition.* 2nd ed. [Wembley], 1980. Previous ed., 1978.

Hazelkorn, Ellen, and Patterson, Henry. The new politics of the Irish republic. In *New Left Review*, no. 207 (1994), pp 49–71.

Hechter, Michael. *Internal colonialism: the Celtic fringe in British national development, 1536–1966.* Berkeley and London, 1975.

Hederman, Miriam. *The road to Europe: Irish attitudes 1948–61.* Dublin, 1983.

Hepburn, A. C. *The conflict of nationality in modern Ireland.* New York and London, 1980.

Herz, Dietmar. *Frieden und stabilität: die Nordirland-politik der Republik Irland 1969–1987.* Bochum, 1989.

Hesketh, Tom. *The second partitioning of Ireland?: the abortion referendum of 1983.* Dún Laoghaire, 1990.

Hogan, Gerald, and Walker, Clive. *Political violence and the law in Ireland.* Manchester and New York, 1989.

Holmes, Michael; Rees, Nicholas; and Whelan, Bernadette. *The poor relation: Irish foreign policy and the third world.* Dublin, 1993.

Horgan, John. *Labour: the price of power.* Dublin, 1986.

—— Arms dumps and the I.R.A., 1923–32. In *History Today*, xlviii, no. 2 (1998), pp 11–16.

Hussey, Gemma. *At the cutting edge: cabinet diaries 1982–1987.* Dublin, 1990.

Jackson, Alvin. *Ireland 1798–1998: politics and war.* Oxford, 1999.

Joannon, Pierre (ed.). *De Gaulle and Ireland.* Dublin, 1991.

Keatinge, Patrick. *The formulation of Irish foreign policy.* Dublin, 1973.

—— *A place among the nations: issues of Irish foreign policy.* Dublin, 1978.

—— *Ireland and E.C. membership evaluated.* London, 1991.

Kee, Robert. *The green flag: a history of Irish nationalism.* London, 2000. First published 1972.

Kelly, James J. *Orders from the captain?* Dublin, 1971.

Kennedy, Michael. *Ireland and the League of Nations 1919–1946: international relations, diplomacy and politics.* Blackrock, 1996.

—— *Division and consensus: the politics of cross-border relations in Ireland, 1925–1969.* Dublin, 2000.

—— and O'Halpin, Eunan. *Ireland and the Council of Europe: from isolation towards integration.* Strasbourg, 2000.

—— and Skelly, Joseph M. (ed.). *Irish foreign policy, 1919–1966: from independence to internationalism.* Dublin, 2000.

Kenny, Shane. *Go dance on somebody else's grave.* Dublin, 1990.

Charles Haughey and government, 1980s.

Keogh, Dermot. *Ireland and Europe, 1919–1948.* Dublin, 1988.

—— *Ireland and Europe 1919–1989: a diplomatic and political history.* Cork and Dublin, 1990.

—— Ireland, the Vatican, and the cold war: the case of Italy, 1948. In *Hist. Jn.*, xxxiv (1991), pp 931–52.

—— The diplomacy of 'dignified calm': an analysis of Ireland's application for membership of the EEC 1961–1963. In *Journal of European Integration History*, iii, no. 1 (1997), pp 81–101.

—— (ed.) *Ireland and the challenge of European integration.* Cork, 1989.

Kline, Benjamin. Churchill and Collins, 1919–22: admirers or adversaries? In *Hist. Ire.*, i, no. 3 (1993), pp 38–43.

Komito, Lee. Voters, politicians and clientelism: a Dublin survey. In *Administration*, xxxvii (1989), pp 171–96.

Kostick, Conor. *Revolution in Ireland: popular militancy 1917 to 1923.* London, 1996.

Laffan, Michael. 'Labour must wait': Ireland's conservative revolution. In P. J. Corish (ed.), *Radicals, rebels & establishments* (Belfast, 1985; *Hist. Studies*, xv), pp 203–22.

—— *The partition of Ireland 1911–1925.* Dundalk, 1983.

—— *The resurrection of Ireland: the Sinn Féin party, 1916–1923.* Cambridge, 1999.

Lawlor, Sheila. *Britain and Ireland 1914–1923.* Dublin and Totowa, N.J., 1983.

Lijphart, Arend, and Irwin, Galen A. Nomination strategies in the Irish STV system: the dáil elections of 1969, 1973, and 1977. [Followed by] Cohan, A. S., rejoinder. In *British Journal of Political Science*, ix (1979), pp 362–70.

Macardle, Dorothy. *The Irish republic: a documented chronicle of the Anglo–Irish conflict and the partitioning of Ireland, with a detailed account of the period 1916–25.* London, 1937. 2nd and 3rd eds 1937–8; 4th ed., London, 1951.

McCabe, Ian. *A diplomatic history of Ireland 1948–49: the republic, the commonwealth, and NATO.* Dublin, 1991.

MacDermott, Eithne. *Clann na Poblachta.* Cork, 1998.

MacDonagh, Oliver. What was new in the New Ireland forum? In *Crane Bag*, ix, no. 2 (1985), pp 166–70.

McDowell, R. B. *Crisis and decline: the fate of the southern unionists.* Dublin, 1997.

MacEoin, Uinseann. *Survivors: the story of Ireland's struggle as told through some of her outstanding living people.* Dublin, 1980.

—— *The IRA in the twilight years, 1923–1948.* Dublin, 1997.

McEvoy, F. J. Canada, Ireland and the commonwealth: the declaration of the Irish Republic, 1948–9. In *I.H.S.*, xxiv, no. 96 (Nov. 1985), pp 506–27.

McGarry, Fearghal. *Irish politics and the Spanish civil war.* Cork, 1999.

McKay, Enda. Changing with the tide: the Irish Labour party, 1927–1933. In *Saothar*, xi (1986), pp 27–38.

McLoughlin, Barry. Proletarian academics or party functionaries? Irish communists at the International Lenin School, Moscow, 1927–1937. In *Saothar*, xxii (1997), pp 63–79.

McMahon, Deirdre. *Republicans and imperialists: Anglo-Irish relations in the 1930s.* New Haven and London, 1984.

MacMillan, Gretchen M. *State, society and authority in Ireland: the foundations of the modern state.* Dublin, 1993.

Maher, Denis J. *The tortuous path: the course of Ireland's entry into the EEC 1948–1973.* Dublin, 1986.

Mair, Peter. *The changing Irish party system: organisation, ideology, and electoral competition.* London, 1987.

Mandle, W. F. *The Gaelic Athletic Association & Irish nationalist politics 1884–1924*. London and Dublin, 1987.

Manning, Maurice. *The Blueshirts*. Dublin, 1970. 2nd ed. 1987.

—— *Irish political parties: an introduction*. Dublin, 1972.

Mansergh, Martin (ed.). *The spirit of the nation: the speeches and statements of Charles J. Haughey (1957–1985)*. Cork, 1986.

Martin, F. X., and Byrne, F. J. (ed.). *The scholar revolutionary: Eoin MacNeill, 1867–1945, and the making of the new Ireland*. Shannon, 1973.

Maume, Patrick. Anti-Machiavel: three Ulster nationalists in the age of de Valera. In *Ir. Political Studies*, xiv (1999), pp 43–63.
    Eoin MacNeill, Louis V. Walsh, Aodh de Blacam.

Maye, Brian. *Fine Gael 1923–1987: a general history with biographical sketches of leading members*. Dublin, 1993.

Mitchell, Arthur. William O'Brien, 1881–1968 and the Irish Labour movement. In *Studies*, lx (1971), pp 311–31.

—— *Labour in Irish politics, 1890–1930: the Irish labour movement in an age of revolution*. Dublin, 1974.

—— *Revolutionary government in Ireland: Dáil Éireann 1919–22*. Dublin, 1995.

Molohan, Cathy. *Germany and Ireland 1945–1955: two nations' friendship*. Dublin, 1999.

Morgan, Austen, and Purdie, Bob (ed.). *Ireland: divided nation, divided class*. London, 1980.

Morris, Ewan. 'God save the king' versus 'The soldier's song': the 1929 Trinity College national anthem dispute and the politics of the Irish Free State. In *I.H.S.*, xxxi, no. 121 (May 1998), pp 72–90.

Moss, Warner. *Political parties in the Irish Free State*. New York, 1968. Facsimile reprint of first ed., 1933.

Moynihan, Maurice (ed.). *Speeches and statements by Eamon de Valera 1917–1973*. Dublin, 1980.

Munger, Frank. *The legitimacy of opposition: the change of government in Ireland in 1932*. London, 1975.

Murray, Patrick. Eamon de Valera's indispensible secretary: Kathleen O'Connell, 1888–1956. In *Éire-Ireland*, xxx, no. 4 (1995), pp 111–33.

Murray, Sean, *et al. The Irish case for communism: the building of the Marxist-Leninist party (1930–35)*. Cork, 1979.

Ó Brádaigh, Ruairí. *Dílseacht: the story of Comdt General Tom Maguire and the second (All Ireland) dáil*. Dublin, 1997.

O'Brien, Conor Cruise. *To Katanga and back: a U.N. case history*. New York, 1962.

—— The embers of Easter, 1916–1966. In O. D. Edwards and Fergus Pyle (ed.), *1916: the Easter rising* (London, 1968), pp 225–40.

—— *States of Ireland*. London, 1972.

—— *Herod: reflections on political violence*. London, 1978.

—— *Godland: reflections on religion and nationalism*. Cambridge, Mass., 1988.

O'Brien, Jack. *The unionjacking of Ireland*. Cork, 1993.

Ó Broin, Leon. *Revolutionary underground: the story of the Irish Republican Brotherhood 1858–1924*. Dublin, 1976.

O'Byrnes, Stephen. *Hiding behind a face: Fine Gael under FitzGerald*. Dublin, 1986.

O'Carroll, J. P., and Murphy, John A. (ed.). *De Valera and his times: political development in the Republic of Ireland*. Cork, 1983.

O'Connor, Emmet. Jim Larkin and the Communist Internationals, 1923–9. In *I.H.S.*, xxxi, no. 123 (May 1999), pp 357–72.

O'Connor Lysaght, D. R. (ed.). *The communists and the Irish revolution*. Dublin, 1993. Part 1: the Russian revolutionaries on the Irish national question, 1889–1924; includes works by Lenin, Trotsky, and others.

Ó hEithir, Breandán. *The begrudger's guide to Irish politics*. Dublin, 1986.

O'Farrell, Patrick. *Ireland's English question: Anglo–Irish relations, 1534–1970*. London, 1971.

O'Grady, Joseph P. Ireland, the Cuban missile crisis, and civil aviation: a study in applied neutrality. In *Éire-Ireland*, xxx, no. 3 (1995), pp 67–89.

O'Halloran, Clare. *Partition and the limits of Irish nationalism*. Dublin, 1987.

O'Keefe, Patrick D. Clann na Poblachta: its origin and growth. Parts 1–2. In *Tipperary Historical Journal 1993*, pp 19–30; *1994*, pp 1–8.

O'Kelly, Michael. Gender and voter appeal in Irish elections, 1948–1997. In *Econ. & Soc. Rev.*, xxxi, no. 3 (2000), pp 249–65.

O'Leary, Cornelius. *Irish elections 1918–1977: parties, voters and proportional representation*. Dublin, 1979.

O'Mahony, T. P. *The politics of dishonour: Ireland, 1916–1977*. Dublin, 1977.

Orridge, Andrew. The Blueshirts and the 'economic war': a study of Ireland in the context of dependency theory. In *Political Studies*, xxxi, no. 3 (1983), pp 351–69.

Pakenham, Frank. *Peace by ordeal: an account, from first hand sources, of the negotiation and signature of the Anglo–Irish treaty, 1921*. London, 1962; previous ed., 1951.

Patterson, Henry. *The politics of illusion: a political history of the I.R.A.* London, 1997. Previously published as *The politics of illusion: republicanism and socialism in modern Ireland*, 1989.

——Seán Lemass and the Ulster question, 1959–65. In *Journal of Contemporary History*, xxxiv (1999), 145–59.

Pearce, Donald R. (ed.). *The senate speeches of W. B. Yeats*. Bloomington, Ind., 1960.

Penniman, Howard. *Ireland at the polls: the dáil elections of 1977*. Washington, 1978.

Phillips, W. Alison. *The revolution in Ireland*. London, 1923.

Powell, Frederick W. *The politics of Irish social policy, 1600–1990*. Queenston (Ont.), 1992.

Prager, Jeffrey. *Building democracy in Ireland: political order and cultural integration in a newly independent nation*. Cambridge, 1986.

Rafter, Kevin. *The Clann: the story of Clann na Poblachta*. Dublin, 1996.

Ranelagh, John O'Beirne. The I.R.B. from the treaty to 1924. In *I.H.S.*, xx, no. 77 (Mar. 1976), pp 26–39.

Regan, John M. Looking at Mick again: de-militarising Michael Collins. In *Hist. Ire.*, iii, no. 3 (1995), pp 17–22.

——*The Irish counter-revolution 1921–1936: treatyite politics and settlement in independent Ireland*. Dublin, 1999.

Rohan, Michael. University representation, 1918–1938. In *Administration*, xxix (1981), pp 260–89.

Rose, A. J. Partition and Ireland. In *Australian Quarterly*, xxvii (1955), pp 67–81.

Rose, Kieran. *Diverse communities: the evolution of lesbian and gay politics in Ireland.* Cork, 1994.

Rumpf, Erhard, and Hepburn, A. C. *Nationalism and socialism in twentieth century Ireland.* Liverpool, 1977.

Sacks, P. M. *The Donegal mafia: an Irish political machine.* New Haven and London, 1976.

Schmitt, D. *The irony of Irish democracy.* Lexington and London, 1973.

Sharp, Paul. *Irish foreign policy and the European Community: a study of the impact of interdependence on the foreign policy of a small state.* Aldershot, 1990.

Skelly, Joseph M. *Irish diplomacy at the United Nations, 1945–1965: national interests and the international order.* Dublin, 1997.

Sloan, Geoffrey R. *The geopolitics of Anglo–Irish relations in the twentieth century.* London and Washington, 1997.

Smith, Raymond. *The quest for power: Haughey and O'Malley.* Dublin, 1986.

Spender, J. A. *Great Britain, empire and commonwealth, 1886–1935.* London, 1936.

Swart, W. J. The League of Nations and the Irish question: master frames, cycles of protest, and 'master frame alignment'. In *Sociological Quarterly,* xxxvi (1995), pp 465–81.

Taylor, Rex. *Assassination: the death of Sir Henry Wilson and the tragedy of Ireland.* London, 1961.

Towey, Thomas. The reaction of the British government to the 1922 Collins–de Valera pact. In *I.H.S.,* xxii, no. 85 (Mar. 1980), pp 65–76.

Townshend, Charles. *Political violence in Ireland: government and resistance since 1848.* Oxford, 1983.

——(ed.). *Consensus in Ireland: approaches and recessions.* Oxford, 1988.

Uris, Jill, and Uris, Leon. *Ireland, a terrible beauty: the story of Ireland today.* London, 1976.

Varley, Tony, and Moser, Peter. Clann na Talmhan: Ireland's last farmers' party. In *Hist. Ire.,* iii, no. 2 (1995), pp 39–43.

Walsh, Dick. *The party: inside Fianna Fáil.* Dublin, 1986.

Walsh, Pat. *Irish republicanism and socialism: the politics of the republican movement 1905 to 1994.* Belfast, 1994.

Williams, T. D. (ed.). *The Irish struggle 1916–1926.* London, 1966.

Younger, Calton. *A state of disunion: Arthur Griffith, Michael Collins, James Craig, and Eamon de Valera.* London, 1972.

2 CONSTITUTIONAL, ADMINISTRATIVE, AND LEGAL HISTORY

Abbott, Richard. *Police casualties in Ireland 1919–1922.* Cork, 2000.

Allen, Gregory. *The Gárda Síochána: policing independent Ireland 1922–82.* Dublin, 1999.

Andrews, J. H. The *Morning Post* line. In *Ir. Geography,* iv (1960), pp 99–106. Forecasts findings of Irish boundary commission, 1925.

Arkins, Audrey M. Legislative and executive relations in the Republic of Ireland. In *West European Politics,* xiii, no. 3 (1990), pp 90–102.

Bannon, Michael J. *A hundred years of Irish planning.* Dublin, 1984.

Barrington, T. J. *The Irish administrative system.* Dublin, 1980.

Bartholomew, Paul C. *The Irish judiciary*. Dublin, 1971.

Beth, Loren P. *The development of judicial review in Ireland, 1937–1966*. Dublin, 1967.

Blackwell, John, and Convery, F. J. (ed.). *Promise and performance: Irish environmental policies analysed*. Dublin, 1983.

Bourke, Marcus. *Murder at Marlhill: was Harry Gleeson innocent?* Dublin, 1993. Harry Gleeson, d. 1941.

Brady, Conor. *Guardians of the peace*. Dublin, 1974. London, 2000.

Brennan, Niamh. A political minefield: southern loyalists, the Irish Grants Committee and the British government, 1922–31. In *I.H.S.*, xxx, no. 119 (May 1997), pp 406–19.

Brewer, John D.; Lockhart, William; and Rodgers, Paula. *Crime in Ireland, 1945–95: here be dragons*. Oxford, 1997.

Bromage, Mary C. Consolidation of the Irish revolution, 1921–22: de Valera's plan. In *University Review*, v (1968), pp 23–35.

Byrne, Raymond, and McCutcheon, J. Paul. *The Irish legal system*. 2nd ed., Dublin, 1996. Previous eds 1986, 1989.

Campbell, Colm. *Emergency law in Ireland, 1918–1925*. Oxford, 1994.

Carey, Tim. *Mountjoy: the story of a prison*. Cork, 2000.

Casey, James. Republican courts in Ireland, 1919–22. In *Ir. Jurist*, v (1970), pp 321–42.

Casey, James P. *The office of the attorney general in Ireland*. Dublin, 1980.

Carty, Anthony. *Was Ireland conquered? International law and the Irish question*. London, 1996.

Caudle, P. R. K. *Social security in Ireland and western Europe*. Dublin, 1964.

—— *Social policy in the Irish republic*. London, 1967.

Chubb, Basil. *A source book of Irish government*. 2nd ed., Dublin, 1983. Previous ed. 1964.

—— *The politics of the Irish constitution*. Dublin, 1991.

—— *The government and politics of Ireland*. 3rd ed. London, 1992. Previous eds 1970, 1982.

Clifford, Angela. *The constitutional history of Éire/Ireland*. Belfast, 1987.

Colley, Michael. *The communicators: the history of the Public Relations Institute of Ireland, 1953–1993*. Dublin, 1993.

Cooke, Pat. *A history of Kilmainham gaol, 1796–1924*. Dublin, 1995.

Cousins, Mel. The introduction of children's allowances in Ireland, 1939–1944. In *Ir. Econ. & Soc. Hist.*, xxvi (1999), pp 35–53.

Daly, Mary E. An Irish-Ireland for business?: the Control of Manufactures Acts, 1932 and 1934. In *I.H.S.*, xxiv, no. 94 (Nov. 1984), pp 246–72.

—— *The buffer state: the historical roots of the department of the environment*. Dublin, 1997.

—— The state in independent Ireland. In Richard English and Charles Townshend (ed.), *The state: historical and political dimensions* (London, 1999), pp 66–94.

Davitt, Cahir. The civil jurisdiction of the courts of justice of the Irish Republic, 1920–1922. In *Ir. Jurist*, iii (1968), pp 112–30.

Dawson, Norma; Greer, Desmond; and Ingram, Peter (ed.). *One hundred and fifty years of Irish law*. Dublin and Belfast, 1996.

Dawson, Robert M. *The development of dominion status, 1900–36*. London, 1937. Includes documents concerning the Irish Free State.

Dean, D. W. Final exit? Britain, Éire, the commonwealth and the repeal of the external relations act, 1945–1949. In *Journal of Imperial and Commonwealth History*, xx (1992), pp 391–418.

Delany, Hilary. *The courts acts 1924–1991*. Dublin, 1994. (Irish Statutes Annotated, 3).

Delany, V. T. H. *The administration of justice in Ireland*. 4th ed., Dublin, 1975. First ed. 1962.

Dooney, Seán. *The Irish civil service*. Dublin, 1976.

——and O'Toole, John. *Irish government today*. Dublin 1992. 2nd ed. 1998.

Duggan, John P. *The Irish Free State diplomatic service, 1922–1937*. Blackrock, 1994.

Dulin, C. I. *Ireland's transition: the postal history of the transitional period, 1922–1925*. Dublin, 1992.

Dunne, Derek, and Kerrigan, Gene. *Round up the usual suspects: Nicky Kelly & the Cosgrave coalition*. Dublin, 1984.

Earl, Lawrence. *The battle of Baltinglass*. London, 1952.

Elvert, Jürgen. Der 'Republic of Ireland bill' vom 18 April 1949: einige Überlegungen zur irischen Sezession vom British Commonwealth of Nations. In *Historische Mitteilungen der Ranke-Gesellschaft*, v (1992), pp 114–29.

Fairfield, Letitia (ed.). *The trial of Peter Barnes and others (the I.R.A. Coventry explosion of 1939)*. London, 1953. (Notable British Trial series.)

Fanning, Ronan. *The Irish department of finance 1922–1958*. Dublin, 1978.

Farrell, Brian. *Chairman or chief? the role of taoiseach in Irish government*. Dublin, 1971.

——(ed.). *De Valera's constitution and ours*. Dublin, 1988. (Thomas Davis Lectures).

Fay, Patrick. The amendments to the constitution committee 1926. In *Administration*, xxvi (1978), pp 331–51.

Fedorowich, Kent. The problems of disbandment: the Royal Irish Constabulary and imperial migration, 1919–29. In *I.H.S.*, xxx, no. 117 (May 1996), pp 88–110.

Finlay, Ian. *The Labour Court, 'not an ordinary court of law': a history of fifty years of the Labour Court from 1946 to 1996*. Dublin, 1996.

FitzGerald, Garret. *Planning in Ireland*. Dublin and London, 1968.

Foley, J. Anthony, and Lalor, Stephen (ed.). *Gill & Macmillan annotated constitution of Ireland 1937–1994, with commentary*. Dublin, 1995.

Gageby, Douglas. *The last secretary general: Sean Lester and the League of Nations*. Dublin, 1998.

Gallagher, Frank. Dáil Éireann. By David Hogan [Frank Gallagher]. In *Parliamentary Affairs*, viii (1955), pp 215–29.

Garvin, Thomas. *The Irish senate*. Dublin, 1969.

——*1922: the birth of Irish democracy*. Dublin, 1996.

Girvin, Brian. Social change and moral politics: the Irish constitutional referendum 1983. In *Political Studies*, xxxiv, no. 1 (1986), pp 61–81.

Grogan, Vincent. Irish constitutional development. In *Studies*, xl (1951), pp 385–98. See also *Capuchin Annual, 1940*, pp 64–79.

Hadden, Tom, and Boyle, Kevin. *The Anglo–Irish agreement: commentary, text and official review*. London, 1989.

Hand, Geoffrey J. MacNeill and the boundary commission. In F. X. Martin and F. J. Byrne (ed.), *The scholar revolutionary: Eoin MacNeill, 1867–1945* (Shannon, 1973), pp 254–9.

Harrison, William M. European postcoloniality: *the Saorstát Éireann/ Irish Free State official handbook*, 1932. In *Éire-Ireland*, xxx, no. 1 (1995), pp 35–42.

Henchy, Séamus. Precedent in the Irish supreme court. In *Modern Law Review*, xxv (1962), pp 544–58.

Hill, Ronald J., and Marsh, Michael (ed.). *Modern Irish democracy: essays in honour of Basil Chubb*. Blackrock, 1993.

Hoctor, Daniel. *The department's story: a history of the department of agriculture*. Dublin, 1971.

Hogan, Gerard. The supreme court and the reference of the offences against the state bill, 1940. In *Ir. Jurist*, xxxv (2000), pp 238–79.

Hopkinson, Michael (ed.). *The last days of Dublin Castle: the Mark Sturgis diaries*. Dublin and Portland, Ore. 1999.

Humphreys, Richard F. The constitution of Ireland: the forgotten textual quagmire. In *Ir. Jurist*, xxii, pt 2 (winter 1987), pp 169–78.
Irish-language versions of the constitution.

Institute of Public Administration. *City and county management, 1929–90: a retrospective*. Dublin, 1991.

Ivory, Gareth. Fianna Fáil, constitutional republicanism, and the issue of consent: 1980–1996. In *Éire-Ireland*, xxxii, nos 2–3 (1997), pp 93–116.

Joyce, Joe, and Murtagh, Peter. *Blind justice*. Dublin, 1984.

Keane, Ronan. Fundamental rights in Irish law: a note on the historical background. In James O'Reilly (ed.), *Human rights and constitutional law: essays in honour of Brian Walsh* (Dublin, 1992), pp 25–35.

Kelly, Adrian. Catholic action and the development of the Irish welfare state in the 1930s and 1940s. In *Archiv. Hib.*, liii (1999), pp 107–17.

Kelly, J. M. *Fundamental rights in the Irish law and constitution*. Dublin, 1961.

Kelly, James. *The thimbleriggers: the Dublin arms trials of 1970*. Dublin, 1999.

Kenny, Anthony. *The road to Hillsborough: the shaping of the Anglo-Irish agreement*. Oxford, 1986.

Keogh, Dermot. The Jesuits and the 1937 constitution. In *Studies*, lxxviii, no. 309 (1989), pp 82–95.

Knight, James, and Baxter-Moore, Nicholas. *Republic of Ireland—the general elections of 1969 and 1973*. London, 1973.

Kohn, Leo. *The constitution of the Irish Free State*. London, 1932.

Korpi, Walter. *Welfare state development in Europe since 1930: Ireland in a comparative perspective*. Dublin, [1993]. (Geary Lecture.)

Kotsonouris, Mary. *Retreat from revolution: the dáil courts, 1920–1924*. Blackrock, 1994.

Laver, Michael, and Shepsle, K. A. (ed.). *Cabinet ministers and parliamentary government*. Cambridge, 1994.
Chapters on Ireland.

Litton, Frank (ed.). The constitution of Ireland 1937–1987. In *Administration*, xxxv, no. 4 (1987), pp 1–225.
Special commemorative issue.

Long, Bill. *Bright light, white water: the story of Irish lighthouses and their people.* Dublin, 1993.

Lowe, W. J., and Malcolm, E. The domestication of the Royal Irish Constabulary, 1836–1922. In *Ir. Econ. & Soc. Hist.*, xix (1992), pp 27–48.

Lynch, Patrick. The economist and public policy. In *Studies*, xlii (1953), pp 241–74.

—— and James Meenan (ed.). *Essays in memory of Alexis Fitzgerald.* Dublin, 1987.

Lysaght, Charles E. The Irish peers and the house of lords. In *Northern Ireland Legal Quarterly*, xviii (1967), 277–301.

McBride, Lawrence W. *The greening of Dublin Castle: the transformation of bureaucratic and judicial personnel in Ireland, 1892–1922.* Washington, D.C., 1991.

McColgan, John. *British policy and the Irish administration, 1920–22.* London, 1983.

McCracken, J. L. *Representative government in Ireland: a study of Dáil Éireann, 1919–48.* Oxford, 1958.

McCullagh, David. *A makeshift majority: the first inter-party government, 1948–51.* Dublin, 1998.

MacIntyre, Tom. *Through the Bridewell gate: a diary of the Dublin arms trial.* London, 1971.

McMahon, Deirdre. The chief justice and the governor general controversy in 1932. In *Ir. Jurist*, xvii (1982), pp 145–67.

MacMillan, Gretchen. British subjects and Irish citizens: the passport controversy, 1923–24. In *Éire-Ireland*, xxvi, no. 3 (1991), pp 25–50.

—— *State, society and authority in Ireland: the foundations of the modern state.* Dublin, 1993.

McNiffe, Liam. *A history of the Garda Síochána.* Dublin, 1997.

Mackay, James A. *Irish postmarks since 1840.* Dumfries, 1982.

Mackey, Rex. *Windward of the law.* London, 1965. 2nd ed. 1986.
Sketches of Irish life by a barrister.

Mansergh, Nicholas. *The Irish Free State: its government and politics.* London, 1934.

—— *Survey of British commonwealth affairs: problems of external policy, 1931–9: problems of war-time cooperation and post-war change, 1939–52.* 2 vols. London, 1952–8.

—— *The commonwealth and the nations: studies in British commonwealth relations.* London, 1966.

—— *The unresolved question: the Anglo–Irish settlement and its undoing, 1912–1972.* London, 1991.

—— *Nationalism and independence: selected Irish papers.* Ed. Diana Mansergh. Cork, 1997.

Meghen, P. J. *A short history of the public service in Ireland.* Dublin, 1962.

Micks, W. L. *An account of the constitution, administration, and dissolution of the congested districts board for Ireland from 1891 to 1923.* Dublin, 1925.

Mitchell, Arthur. *Revolutionary government in Ireland: Dáil Éireann, 1919–22.* Dublin, 1995.

Murphy, Gary. *Towards a corporate state? Seán Lemass and the realignment of interest groups in the policy process, 1948–1964.* Dublin, 1997.

Murphy, Tim, and Twomey, Patrick (ed.). *Ireland's evolving constitution, 1937–1997: collected essays*. Oxford, 1998.

Murray, Brian. The supreme court and the constitution in the nineteen-eighties. In *Studies*, lxxix, no. 314 (1990), pp 160–75.

O'Brien, Justin. *The arms trial*. Dublin, 2000.

O'Brien, Miriam Hederman. Whatever happened to rates?: a study of Irish tax policy on domestic dwellings. In *Administration*, xxxvii (1989), pp 334–45.

O'Callaghan, Margaret. Old parchment and water: the boundary commission of 1925 and the copperfastening of the Irish border. In *Bullán*, iv, no. 2 (winter 1999/spring 2000), pp 27–55.

Ó Ceallaigh, Daltún. *Sovereign people or crown subjects? the case for articles 2 and 3 and against sections 1 and 75*. Dublin, 1993.

Ó Cearúil, Micheál. *Bunreacht na hÉireann: a study of the Irish text*. Dublin, 1999.

O'Donnell, Peadar. *There will be another day*. Dublin, 1963.
  History of land annuities.

O'Grady, Joseph P. The Irish Free State passport and the question of citizenship, 1921–4. In *I.H.S.*, xxvi, no. 104 (Nov. 1989), pp 396–405.

O'Halpin, Eunan. The civil service and the political system. In *Administration*, xxxviii (1991), pp 283–302.

O'Leary, Brendan. An taoiseach: the Irish prime minister. In *West European Politics*, xiv, no. 2 (1991), pp 133–62.

O'Leary, Cornelius. *The Irish republic and its experiment with proportional representation*. Notre Dame, Ind., 1961.

O'Mahony, Paul. *Crime and punishment in Ireland*. Dublin, 1993.

Osborne, Mark. In the commonwealth? In *The Bell*, x (1945), pp 577–84.

Osborough, W. N. Law in Ireland, 1916–26. In *Northern Ireland Legal Quarterly*, xxiii, no. 1 (1972), pp 48–81.

—— *Borstal in Ireland, 1906–74*. Dublin, 1975.

—— *Studies in Irish legal history*. Dublin and Portland, Or., 1999.

O'Sullivan, D. *The Irish Free State and its senate*. London, 1940.

Prone, Terry. *Irish murders: 2*. Dublin, 1994.

Quinn, Gerard; Ingram, Attracta; and Livingstone, Stephen (ed.). *Justice and legal theory in Ireland*. Dublin, 1995.

Rea, J. Irish state forestry: government policy. In *Irish Forestry*, xlii (1985), pp 7–15.

Report of the Irish boundary commission. With an introduction by Geoffrey J. Hand. Shannon, 1969. Originally published London, 1925.

Reynolds, Brian A. *William T. Cosgrave and the foundation of the Irish Free State, 1922–25*. Kilkenny, [1998?].

Riordan, Susannah. 'A political blackthorn': Seán MacEntee, the Dignan plan, and the principle of ministerial responsibility. In *Ir. Econ. & Soc. Hist.*, xxvii (2000), pp 44–62.

Roche, Desmond. *Local government in Ireland*. Dublin, 1982.

Sammon, Patrick J. *In the land commission: a memoir 1933–1978*. Dublin, 1997.

Sexton, Brendan. *Ireland and the crown 1922–1936: the governor generalship of the Irish Free State*. Blackrock, 1989.

Shinn, Ridgway. Changing the king's title, 1926: an asterisk to 'O'Higgins' comma'. In *Ir. Jurist*, xvi (1981), pp 114–40.

Staunton, Enda. The boundary commission debacle 1925: aftermath and implications. In *Hist. Ire.*, iv, no. 2 (1996), pp 42–5.

Towey, Thomas. Hugh Kennedy and the constitutional development of the Irish Free State, 1922–1923. In *Ir. Jurist*, xii (1977), pp 355–70.

Townshend, Charles. Martial law: legal and administrative problems of civil emergency in Britain and the empire, 1800–1940. In *Hist. Jn.*, xxv, no. 1 (1982), pp 167–95.

——Policing insurgency in Ireland, 1914–1923. In David Anderson and David Killingray (ed.), *Policing and de-colonisation: politics, nationalism and the police, 1917–1965* (Manchester, 1992), pp 22–41.

——The meaning of Irish freedom: constitutionalism in the Free State. In *Transactions of the Royal Historical Society*, 6th ser., viii (1998), pp 45–70.

Tulloch, Hugh. A. V. Dicey and the Irish question, 1870–1922. In *Ir. Jurist*, xv (1980), pp 137–65.

Ward, Alan J. *The Irish constitutional tradition: responsible government and modern Ireland, 1782–1992*. Dublin, 1994.

Wylie, J. C. W. *Irish land law*. London, 1975. 2nd ed., 1986.

3   ECCLESIASTICAL HISTORY

Acheson, Alan. *A history of the Church of Ireland, 1691–1996*. Dublin, 1997.

Augustine, Fr., O.F.M. *Ireland's loyalty to the mass*. London, 1933; 2nd ed. 1938.

Barkley, John Montieth. *The Irish Council of Churches, 1923–83*. Belfast, 1983.

Battersby, William. *The Hospitallers at Kilmainham, Kells, 1196–1996*. Navan, 1996.

de Bhaldraithe, Eoin. Mixed marriages and Irish politics: the effect of 'Ne Temere'. In *Studies*, lxxvii, no. 307 (1988), pp 284–99.

Blanshard, Paul. *The Irish and catholic power: an American interpretation*. Westport, Conn., 1972. First published Boston, 1953.

Bolster, Evelyn. *The Knights of Saint Columbanus*. Dublin, 1979.

Bowen, Desmond. *History and the shaping of Irish protestantism*. New York, 1995.

Bowen, Kurt. *Protestants in a catholic state: Ireland's privileged minority*. Dublin, 1983.

Brown, Lindsay. The presbyterians of County Monaghan. Pt 1: the unfolding story. In *Clogher Rec.*, xiii, no. 3 (1990), pp 7–54.

Brown, Stewart J., and Miller, David W. (ed.). *Piety and power in Ireland, 1760–1960: essays in honour of Emmet Larkin*. Belfast, 2000.

Burke Savage, Roland. The church in Dublin: 1940–1965. In *Studies*, liv (1965), pp 297–338.
    Study of Archbishop J. C. McQuaid.

Butler, Thomas C. *John's Lane: history of the Augustinian friars in Dublin, 1280–1980*. Dublin, 1983.

Canning, Bernard J. *Bishops of Ireland 1870–1987*. [Ballyshannon, 1987].

Clarke, Desmond M. *Church and state: essays in political philosophy*. Cork, 1984.

Cole, R. Lee. *History of methodism in Ireland, 1860–1960*. Belfast, 1960.

Cooney, Dudley A. Levistone. *'Artless, earnest and serious': 250 years of methodism in Laois, 1748–1998*. [n.p.], 1998.

Cooney, John. *John Charles McQuaid: ruler of catholic Ireland*. Dublin, 1999.

Corish, Patrick J. The Catholic Truth Society of Ireland: the first fifty years, 1899–1949. In Catholic Truth Society of Ireland (ed.)., *First fifty years, 1899–1949* (Dublin, 1949), pp 11–26.

—— (ed.). *A history of Irish catholicism*. 16 fascs. Dublin and Melbourne, 1967–72.

—— *The Irish catholic experience: a historical survey*. Dublin, 1985.

—— *Maynooth College, 1795–1995*. Dublin, 1995.

Costello, Declan. The priest and public affairs. In *Christus Rex*, xxiii, no. 4 (1969), pp 293–8.

Cuddy, Edward. The Irish question and the revival of anti-catholicism in the 1920s. In *Catholic Historical Review*, lxvii (1981), pp 236–55.

Curran, Olive C. (ed.). *History of the diocese of Meath 1860–1993*. [Mullingar], 1995.

Dooley, Terence. Monaghan protestants in a time of crisis, 1919–22. In R. V. Comerford, Mary Cullen, Jacqueline Hill, and Colm Lennon (ed.), *Religion, conflict and coexistence in Ireland: essays presented to Monsignor Patrick J. Corish* (Dublin, 1990), pp 235–51.

Dowdall, Raymund M. *Memories of recent Irish Dominicans, 1930–1940*. Dublin, 1967.

Dunne, Eamonn. Action and reaction: catholic lay organisations in Dublin in the 1920s and 1930s. In *Archiv. Hib.*, xlviii (1994), pp 107–18.

Faherty, Padhraic. *Pitch my tent in the Lord: memories of Fr Michael Morahan, S.J.* Barna, Co. Galway, 1993.
1914–92; missionary priest.

Fennell, Desmond. *The changing face of catholic Ireland*. London, 1968.

FitzGerald, Billy. *Father Tom: an authorized portrait of Cardinal Tomás Ó Fiaich*. London, 1990.

Ford, Alan; McGuire, James; and Milne, Kenneth (ed.). *As by law established: the Church of Ireland since the reformation*. Dublin, 1995.

Forristal, Desmond. *Edel Quinn, 1907–1944*. Dublin, 1994.

Gallogly, Daniel. *The diocese of Kilmore 1800–1950*. Monaghan, 1999.

Griffin, Victor. *Mark of protest*. Dublin, 1993.
Autobiography of dean of St Patrick's cathedral, Dublin, b. 1924.

Hodgins, Jack. *Sister island: the history of CMS in Ireland, 1814–1994*. Dunmurray, Co. Antrim, [1994].
Church Missionary Society.

Hogan, Edmund M. *The Irish missionary movement: a historical survey, 1830–1980*. Dublin, 1990.

Holy Cross College, Clonliffe, Dublin, 1859–1959: College history and centenary record. Dublin, 1962.

Hurley, Michael (ed.). *Irish anglicanism, 1869–1969: essays … presented to the Church of Ireland, on the occasion of the centenary of its disestablishment, by a group of methodist, presbyterian, quaker and Roman Catholic scholars*. Dublin, 1970.

Inglis, Tom. *Moral monopoly: the rise and fall of the catholic church in modern Ireland*. 2nd ed., Dublin, 1998. First published as *Moral monopoly: the catholic church in modern Irish society* (Dublin, 1987).

Jeffery, Frederick. *Irish methodism: an historical account of its traditions, theology, and influence*. Belfast, 1964.

John's Lane, 1862–1962: centenary of the church of St Augustine and St John the Baptist, Dublin. Dublin, 1962.

Kelly, James, and Keogh, Dáire (ed.). *History of the catholic diocese of Dublin.* Dublin, 2000.

Kenny, Mary. *Goodbye to catholic Ireland: a social, personal and cultural history from the fall of Parnell to the realm of Mary Robinson.* London, 1997; revised ed., 2000.

Keogh, Dermot. *The Vatican, the bishops and Irish politics 1919–1939.* Cambridge, 1986.

—— *Ireland and the Vatican: the politics and diplomacy of church–state relations, 1922–1960.* Cork, 1995.

—— *Jews in twentieth-century Ireland: refugees, anti-semitism and the holocaust.* Cork, 1998.

Kiggins, Thomas. *Maynooth mission to Africa: the story of St Patrick's, Kiltegan.* Dublin, 1991.

St Patrick's missionary society, 1920– .

Liechty, Joseph. *Roots of sectarianism in Ireland: chronology and reflections.* Belfast, 1993.

MacCarthy, R. B. *Ancient and modern: a short history of the Church of Ireland.* Dublin, 1995.

McDowell, R. B. *The Church of Ireland, 1869–1969.* London, 1975.

McEvoy, John. *Carlow College 1793–1993: the ordained students and teaching staff of St Patrick's College, Carlow.* Carlow, 1993.

McGarry, J. G. Cardinal William Conway, 1913–1977. In *The Furrow*, xxviii (1977), pp 271–3.

McGlade, Joseph. The missions: Africa and the Orient. In P. J. Corish (ed.), *A history of Irish catholicism* (16 fascs, Dublin and Melbourne, 1967–72), vi, fasc. 8 (1967).

McGrath, Thomas G. The Tridentine evolution of modern Irish catholicism, 1563–1962: a re-examination of the 'devotional revolution' thesis. In *Recusant History*, xx (1991), pp 512–23.

Maguire, Martin. The organisation and activism of Dublin's protestant working class, 1883–1935. In *I.H.S.*, xxix, no. 113 (May 1994), pp 65–87.

Mac Réamoinn, Seán (ed.). *Pobal: the laity in Ireland.* Dublin, 1986.

McRedmond, Louis. *To the greater glory: a history of the Irish Jesuits.* Dublin, 1991.

Milne, Kenneth. *The Church of Ireland: a history.* Dublin, 1966.

Moffitt, Miriam. *The Church of Ireland community of Killala & Achonry 1870–1940.* Blackrock, 1994. (Maynooth Studies in Local History.)

Murphy, Brian S. The stone of destiny: Fr John Fahy (1894–1969), Lia Fáil and smallholder radicalism in modern Irish society. In Gerard Moran (ed.), *Radical Irish priests 1660–1970* (Dublin, 1998), pp 185–218.

Murray, Patrick. *Oracles of God: the Roman Catholic church and Irish politics, 1922–37.* Dublin, 2000.

Newsinger, John. Revolution and catholicism in Ireland, 1848–1923. In *European Studies Review*, ix, no. 4 (1979), pp 457–80.

O'Doherty, J. F. Maynooth, 1895–1945. In *I.E.R.*, lxvi (1945), pp 208–23.

Ó hÉideáin, Eustás (ed.). *The Dominicans in Galway, 1241–1991.* Galway, 1991.

O'Leary, Don. *Vocationalism and social catholicism in twentieth-century Ireland*. Dublin, 2000.

O'Neill, Rose. *A rich inheritance: Galway Dominican nuns, 1644–1994*. Galway, 1994.

O'Neill, Thomas P. Dr J. C. McQuaid and Eamon de Valera: insights on church and state. In *Breifne*, viii (1992–3), pp 327–37.

O'Riordan, Seán. *The Furrow*: 1950–1990: a personal review of 'a varied programme'. In *The Furrow*, xli (1990), pp 71–80.

The Passionists. *Centenary of the Passionists in Ireland, 1856–1956*. Dublin, 1956.

Phillips, W. Alison (ed.). *History of the Church of Ireland from the earliest times to the present day*. 3 vols. Oxford, 1933–4.

Power, Louis. *+ Kevin: a portrait of Archbishop Kevin McNamara*. Dublin, 1993.

Purcell, Mary. *The story of the Vincentians: a record of the achievements in Ireland and Britain of the priests and lay-brothers of the Congregation of the Mission, founded by St Vincent de Paul*. Dublin, 1973.

—— *A time for sowing: the St John of God brothers in Ireland: a centenary record 1879–1979*. Dublin, 1979.

Ryan, Liam. Church and politics: the last twenty-five years. In *The Furrow*, xxx, no. 1 (Jan. 1979), pp 3–18.

Rynne, Catherine. *Knock, 1879–1979*. Dublin, 1979.

Scantlebury, Charles. The Jesuit houses in Ireland. In *Irish Jesuit Directory and Yearbook, 1944*, pp 144–64.

Shiels, W. J., and Wood, Diana (ed.). *The churches, Ireland and the Irish*. Oxford, 1989. (Studies in Church History, 25.)

Shillman, Bernard. *A short history of the Jews in Ireland*. Dublin, 1945.

Silke, John J. *The diocese of Raphoe: a brief history: Ráth Bhoth: stair na deoise i mbeagán focal*. Letterkenny, 2000.

Stanford, William Bedell. *A recognised church: the Church of Ireland in Éire*. Dublin, [1944].

Suenens, Léon-Joseph. *A heroine of the apostolate (1907–1944), Edel Quinn, envoy of the Legion of Mary to Africa*. Dublin, 1954. Originally published as *Une héroine de l'apostolat* (Bruges, 1952).

—— *The hidden hand of God: the life of Veronica O'Brien and our common apostolate*. Dublin, 1994. Legion of Mary and charismatic renewal.

Szuchewycz, B. G. The rhetoric of religious innovation: perceptions and reactions to the catholic charismatic renewal in Ireland. In *Canadian Journal of Irish Studies*, xix, no. 1 (1993), pp 37–53.

Thompson, Joan. The Women's Auxiliary of the Irish Baptist Foreign Mission, 1929–1950/1. In *Journal of the Irish Baptist Historical Society*, x (1977), pp 4–18.

Warke, R. A. *Ripples in the pool*. Dublin, 1993. Church of Ireland bishop of Cork, Cloyne and Ross, b. 1930.

Weafer, John A. Change and continuity in Irish religion, 1974–1984. In *Doctrine and Life*, xxxvi, no. 10 (Dec. 1986), pp 507–17.

—— The Irish laity: some findings of the 1984 national survey. In *Doctrine and Life*, xxxvi, no. 5 (May–June 1986), pp 247–53.

Weafer, John A. Vocations: a review of national and international trends. In *The Furrow*, xxxix, no. 8 (Aug. 1988), pp 501–11.
White, Jack. *Minority report: the protestant community in the Irish republic.* Dublin, 1975.
Whyte, J. H. *Church and state in modern Ireland 1923–1979.* Dublin, 1980.
First ed. (covering period 1923–70) published 1971.
Wigham, Maurice J. *Irish quakers: a short history of the Religious Society of Friends in Ireland.* Dublin, 1992.

4 MILITARY HISTORY

Adams, Thomas A. *Irish naval service.* Kendal, 1982.
Allen, Trevor J. *The storm passed by: Ireland and the battle of the Atlantic, 1940–41.* Blackrock, 1996.
Barlow, Dorothy. Aiken's mission to the United States in 1941: a reinterpretation. In *Études Irlandaises*, xix, no. 1 (1994), pp 121–37.
Barry, Michael. *Great aviation stories.* 2 vols. Fermoy, 1993, 1997.
Berardis, Vicenzo. *Neutralitá e indipendenza dell'Éire.* Roma, 1950.
Berger, Alexander. *Die Gefangenen der grunen Insel: Tatsachenbericht aus Irland.* Zurich, 1964.
German airmen interned in Ireland during the second world war.
Bourke, Joanna. Effeminacy, ethnicity and the end of trauma: the sufferings of 'shell-shocked' men in Great Britain and Ireland, 1914–39. In *Journal of Contemporary History*, xxxv, no. 1 (2000), pp 57–69.
Bredin, A. E. C. *A history of the Irish soldier.* Belfast, 1987.
Brophy, Kevin T. *Walking the line: scenes from an army childhood.* Edinburgh, 1994. Galway, c.1950s.
Brunicardi, Daire. The marine service. In *Ir. Sword*, xix (1993–4), pp 77–85.
Buttimer, John. The great withdrawal. In *An Cosantóir*, xxxix (1979), pp 365–9.
Withdrawal of last British unit in 1922.
Canny, Liam. Pariah dogs: deserters from the Irish defence forces who joined the British armed forces during 'the emergency'. In *Studia Hib.*, xxx (1998–9), pp 231–49.
Carter, Carolle J. *The shamrock and the swastika: German espionage in Ireland in World War II.* Palo Alto, California, 1977.
Cole, Robert. 'Good relations': Irish neutrality and the propaganda of John Betjeman, 1941–43. In *Éire-Ireland*, xxx, no. 4 (1995), pp 33–46.
Coogan, Tim Pat, and Morrison, George. *The Irish civil war.* London, 1999.
Cunliffe, Marcus. *The Royal Irish Fusiliers, 1793–1968.* 2nd ed., Oxford, 1970.
Deasy, Liam. *Brother against brother.* Dublin, 1982.
Irish civil war.
Doherty, Richard. *Clear the way! a history of the 38th (Irish) brigade, 1941–1947.* Dublin, 1993.
—— *Irish generals: Irish generals in the British army in the second world war.* Belfast, 1993.
—— *Irishmen and women in the second world war.* Dublin, 1999.
—— and Truesdale, David. *Irish winners of the Victoria Cross.* Dublin, 2000.

Door, Noel. The development of U.N. peace-keeping concepts over the past fifty years: an Irish perspective. In *Ir. Sword*, xx (1996), pp 16–31.

Doorly, Mary Rose. *Hidden memories: the personal recollections of survivors and witnesses to the Holocaust living in Ireland*. Dublin, 1994.

Duggan, John P. *Neutral Ireland and the Third Reich*. Revised ed., Dublin, 1989; previous ed., 1985.

——*A history of the Irish army*. Dublin, 1990.

Dukes, Jim. The emergency services. In *Ir. Sword*, xix (1993–4), pp 66–71.

Dungan, Myles. *Distant drums: Irish soldiers in foreign armies*. Belfast, 1993. Anthology.

Dwyer, T. Ryle. *Irish neutrality and the U.S.A. 1939–47*. Dublin, 1977.

——*Guests of the state: the story of Allied and Axis servicemen interned in Ireland during World War II*. Dingle, 1994.

Fanning, Ronan. The United States and Irish participation in N.A.T.O.: the debate of 1950. In *Irish Studies in International Affairs*, i (1979), pp 38–48.

——Neutral Ireland? In *An Cosantóir*, xlix, no. 9 (Sept. 1989), pp 45–8.

Farrell, Theo. Professionalisation and suicidal defence planning by the Irish army, 1921–1941. In *Journal of Strategic Studies*, xxi, no. 3 (1998), pp 67–85.

Fisk, Robert. *In time of war: Ireland, Ulster and the price of neutrality 1939–45*. Dublin, 1996. First published 1983.

Fitzgerald, D. J. L. *History of the Irish Guards in the second world war*. Aldershot, 1949.

Fitzgerald, Seamus. The Arklow war graves. In *Arklow Historical Society Journal 1992–3*, pp 22–3.

Fitzpatrick, David. 'Unofficial emissaries': British army boxers in the Irish Free State, 1926. In *I.H.S.*, xxx, no. 118 (Nov. 1996), 206–32. (Select documents, XLVI.)

Forde, Frank. *The long watch: World War Two and the Irish mercantile marine*. Revised ed., Dublin, 2000. First published 1981.

Franchi, Nicola. La guerra d'Abissinia visita dallo Stato Libero d'Irlanda. In *Storia delle Relazioni Internazionali*, ix (1995 for 1993), pp 127–41. The Free State and the Abyssian war.

Fraser, T. G., and Jeffery, Keith (ed.). *Men, women and war*. Dublin, 1993 (*Hist. Studies*, xviii).

Gavin, Joseph, and O'Sullivan, Harold. *Dundalk: a military history*. Dundalk, 1987.

Girvin, Brian, and Roberts, Geoffrey. The forgotten volunteers of World War II. In *Hist. Ire.*, vi, no. 1 (1998), pp 46–51.

————(ed.). *Ireland and the second world war: politics, society and remembrance*. Dublin, 2000.

Harrington, Niall C. *Kerry landing*. Dublin, 1992. An episode in the Irish civil war, 1922.

Harris, R. G. *The Irish regiments: a pictorial history, 1683–1987*. Tunbridge Wells, 1989.

Hart, Peter. *The I.R.A. and its enemies: violence and community in Cork, 1916–1923*. Oxford, 1998.

——The social structure of the Irish Republican Army, 1916–1923. In *Hist. Jn.*, xlii (1999), 207–31.

Hawkins, Richard. 'Bending the beam': myth and reality in the bombing of Coventry, Belfast and Dublin. In *Ir. Sword*, xix (1993–4), pp 131–43.

Harvey, Dan, and White, Gerry. *The barracks: a history of Victoria/Collins barracks, Cork*. Cork, 1997.

[Hayes, Karl; Conran, Phil; Kearns, A. P.; and Smyth, Damian.] *A history of the Royal Air Force and United States Naval Air Service in Ireland, 1913–1923*. Killiney, 1988.

Healy, James. The civil war hunger-strike—October 1923. In *Studies*, lxxi (1982), pp 213–26.

Holt, Edgar. *Protest in arms: the Irish troubles, 1916–23*. London, 1960.

Hopkinson, Michael. *Green against green: the Irish civil war*. Dublin, 1988.

——The civil war from the pro-treaty perspective. In *Ir. Sword*, xx (1997), pp 287–92.

The Irish defence forces and the U.N.: the proceedings of a seminar . . . In *Ir. Sword*, xx (1996), pp 1–113.

Jeffery, Keith. *The British army and the crisis of empire, 1918–22*. Manchester, 1984.

Kearns, A. P. The air corps 1939–1945. In *An Cosantóir*, xlix, no. 9 (Sept. 1989), pp 13–19.

Keatinge, Patrick. *A singular stance: Irish neutrality in the 1980s*. Dublin, 1984.

Kelleher, George D. *Gunpowder to guided missiles—Ireland's war industries*. Inniscarra, Co. Cork, 1993.

Kennedy, Michael. Prologue to peacekeeping: Ireland and the Saar, 1934–5. In *I.H.S.*, xxx, no. 119 (May 1997), pp 420–28.

Keogh, Dermot. De Valera, Hitler & the visit of condolence May 1945. In *Hist. Ire.*, v, no. 3 (1997), pp 58–61.

——and Nolan, Aengus. Anglo-Irish diplomatic relations and World War II. In *Ir. Sword*, xix (1993–5), pp 106–30.

Kerrigan, Paul. *Castles and fortifications in Ireland, 1485–1945*. London, 1995.

Kinsella, Anthony. The British military evacuation [1922]. In *Ir. Sword*, xx (1997), pp 275–86.

Kochavi, Arieh J. Britain, the United States and Irish neutrality 1944–5. In *European History Quarterly*, xxv, no. 1 (1995), pp 93–115.

Litton, Helen. *The Irish civil war: an illustrated history*. Dublin, 1996.

Long, Patrick. Organisation and development of the pro-treaty forces, 1922–1924. In *Ir. Sword*, xx (1997), pp 308–30.

Macardle, Dorothy. *Tragedies of Kerry 1922–1923*. 16th ed., Dublin, 1998. First published 1924.

MacCarron, Donal. *Wings over Ireland: the story of the Irish air corps*. Leicester, 1996.

——*Step together! The story of Ireland's emergency army as told by its veterans*. Dublin, 1999.

McCarthy, P. J. The R.A.F. and Ireland, 1920–22. In *Ir. Sword*, xvii (1989), pp 174–88.

McCullen, John. The Irish National War Memorial Gardens. In *Irish Garden*, ii, no. 3 (1993), pp 30–32.

Designed and laid out in the 1930s by Sir Edwin Lutyens.

McDonald, Henry. *Irishbatt: the story of Ireland's Blue Berets in the Lebanon.* Dublin, 1993.

McDonald, Thomas. The defence forces—history outlined. In *An Cosantóir*, xxvii (1967), pp 608–16.

McGarry, Fearghal. *Irish politics and the Spanish civil war.* Cork, 1999.

MacGinty, Tom. *The Irish navy: a story of courage and tenacity.* Tralee, 1995.

McIvor, Aidan. *A history of the Irish naval service.* Blackrock, 1994.

McKenna, T. Thank God we're surrounded by water. In *An Cosantóir*, xxxiii, no. 4 (Apr. 1973), pp 103–23.

Mac Unfraidh, Gearóid. *Clocha ceangailte: léargas ar UNFIL sa Liobáin.* Dublin, 1994. Irish U.N. forces in Lebanon, 1975– .

Mangan, Colm. Plans and operations. In *Ir. Sword*, xix (1993–4), pp 47–56. The emergency, 1939–45.

Morrison, George. *The Irish civil war.* Dublin, 1981.

Murphy, Brian P. The Irish civil war 1922–1923: an anti-treaty perspective. In *Ir. Sword*, xx (1997), pp 293–307.

Neeson, Eoin. *The civil war 1922–23.* Revised ed., Dublin, 1989. Previously published as *The civil war in Ireland* (Cork, 1969).

O'Carroll, Donal. The emergency army. In *Ir. Sword*, xix (1993–4), pp 19–46.

Ó Conchubhair, Padraic. The Irish tricolour. In *I.B.L.*, xxvii (1940), pp 159–60.

O'Connell, J. J. The vulnerability of Ireland in war. In *Studies*, xxvii (1938), pp 125–35.

O'Donnell, P. D. Dublin's military barracks: three centuries. In *An Cosantóir*, xli, no. 3 (1981), pp 73–7; no. 7 (1981), pp 102–7.

Ó Gadhra, Nollaig. *Civil war in Connacht 1922–23.* Cork, 1999.

O'Halpin, Eunan. The army in independent Ireland. In Thomas Bartlett and Keith Jeffery (ed.)., *A military history of Ireland* (Cambridge, 1996), pp 407–30.

——*Defending Ireland: the Irish state and its enemies since 1922.* Oxford, 2000. Originally published 1999.

O'Riordan, Michael. *Connolly column: the story of the Irishmen who fought in the ranks of the International Brigades in the national-revolutionary war of the Spanish people, 1936–39.* Dublin, 1979.

Parsons, Denis. Mobilisation and expansion, 1939–40. In *Ir. Sword*, xix (1993–4), pp 11–18.

Quigley, Aidan. Air aspects of the emergency. In *Ir. Sword*, xix (1993–4), pp 86–90.

Quigley, Martin. *A U.S. spy in Ireland.* Dublin, 1999. Second world war.

Quinn, John. *Down in a free state: wartime aircrashes and forced landings in Éire 1939–1945.* Belfast, 1999.

Raymond, R. J. David Gray, the Aiken mission and Irish neutrality, 1940–41. In *Diplomatic History*, ix (1985), pp 55–71.

Robertson, David. *Deeds not words: Irish soldiers, sailors and airmen in two world wars.* Multyfarnham, Co. Westmeath, 1998.

Rosenberg, J. L. The 1941 mission of Frank Aiken to the United States: an American perspective. In *I.H.S.*, xxii, no. 86 (Sept. 1980), pp 162–77.

Salmon, Trevor. *Unneutral Ireland: an ambivalent and unique security policy.* Oxford, 1989.

Scannell, James. Arklow's 1941 narrow escape. In *Arklow Historical Society Journal 1990–91*, pp 24–9; *1992–3*, pp 17–18.

Share, Bernard. *The emergency: neutral Ireland, 1939–45.* Dublin, 1978.

Smith, M. L. R. *Fighting for Ireland? the military strategy of the Irish republican movement.* London, 1995.

Smith, Raymond. *The fighting Irish in the Congo.* Dublin, 1962.

Staunton, Enda. Frank Ryan & collaboration: a reassessment. *Hist. Ire.*, v, no. 3 (1997), pp 49–51.

—— The case of Biafra: Ireland and the Nigerian civil war. In *I.H.S.*, xxxi, no. 124 (Nov. 1999), pp 513–34.

Stephan, Enno. *Geheimauftrag Irland. Deutsche Agenten im irischen Untergrundkampf, 1939–1945.* Hamburg, 1961. English translation by Arthur Davidson as *Spies in Ireland* (London, 1963).

Stradling, Robert A. *The Irish and the Spanish civil war, 1936–1939: crusades in conflict.* Manchester, 1999.

Townshend, Charles. *Britain's civil wars: counterinsurgency in the twentieth century.* London, 1986.

Valiulis, Maryann Gialanella. *Almost a rebellion: the Irish army mutiny of 1924.* Cork, 1985.

Young, Peter. The way we were. In *An Cosantóir*, xlix, no. 9 (Sept. 1989), pp 3–38.

—— Defence and the new Irish state, 1919–1939. In *Ir. Sword*, xix (1993–4), pp 1–10.

Younger, Calton. *Ireland's civil war.* London, 1968.

5 HISTORICAL GEOGRAPHY AND DEMOGRAPHY

Aalen, F. H. A. *Man and the landscape in Ireland.* London, 1978.

—— Whelan, Kevin; and Stout, Matthew (ed.). *Atlas of the Irish rural landscape.* Cork, 1997.

Andrews, J. H.; Simms, Anngret; Clarke, H. B.; and Gillespie, Raymond (ed.). *Irish Historic Towns Atlas.* Dublin, 1986– . (R.I.A.) In progress. *I: Kildare.* By J. H. Andrews (1986). *III: Bandon.* By Patrick O'Flanagan (1988). *IV: Kells.* By Anngret Simms with Katharine Simms. (1990). *V: Mullingar.* By J. H. Andrews with K. M. Davies. (1992). *VI: Athlone.* By Harman Murtagh (1994). *VII: Maynooth.* By Arnold Horner (1995). *IX: Bray.* By K. M. Davies (1998). *X: Kilkenny.* By John Bradley (2000). I, III–IV ed. J. H. Andrews and Anngret Simms; V–VI ed. J. H. Andrews, Anngret Simms, and H. B. Clarke; VII, IX ed. J. H. Andrews, Anngret Simms, H. B. Clarke, and Raymond Gillespie; X ed. Anngret Simms, H. B. Clarke, and Raymond Gillespie.

Bannon, Michael J. The making of Irish geography, III: Patrick Geddes and the emergence of modern town planning in Dublin. In *Ir. Geography*, xi (1978), pp 141–8.

—— *Planning: the Irish experience 1920–1988.* Dublin, 1989.

—— Dublin town planning competition: Ashbee and Chettle's 'New Dublin—a study in civics'. In *Planning Perspectives*, xiv, no. 2 (1999), pp 145–62.

Brunt, Barry. *The Republic of Ireland*. London, 1988. [Regional planning.]

Buttimer, Neil; Rynne, Colin; and Guerin, Helen (ed.). *The heritage of Ireland*. Cork, 2000.

Carter, R. W. G., and Parker, A. J. (ed.). *Ireland: contemporary perspectives on a land and its people*. London, 1989.

Collins, Timothy (ed.). *Decoding the landscape: papers read at the inaugural conference of the Centre for Landscape Studies…at University College Galway…1990 and subsequent meetings*. Galway, 1994.

Deasy, J. J. Some notes on coastal afforestation in Co. Wexford. In *Irish Forestry*, iii (1946), pp 29–39.

Delany, Ruth. *By Shannon shores: an exploration of the river*. Dublin, 1987.

Duffy, Patrick J., and Keenan, James. *Landscapes of south Ulster: a parish atlas of the diocese of Clogher*. Belfast, 1993.

Duffy, Seán (ed.). *Atlas of Irish history*. Dublin, 1997. 2nd ed. 2000.

Evans, E. Estyn. *The personality of Ireland: habitat, heritage and history*. Revised ed., Dublin, 1992. First published 1973; revised 1981.

Feehan, John. *Laois: an environmental history*. Stradbally, 1983.

Flanagan, Deirdre, and Flanagan, Laurence. *Irish place names*. Dublin, 1994.

Freeman, T. W. Migration movements and the distribution of population in Éire. (With discussion.) In *Stat. Soc. Ire. Jn.*, xvi, 92nd session (1938–9), pp 89–104.

—— The changing distribution of population in Donegal, with special reference to the congested areas. (With discussion.) In *Stat. Soc. Ire. Jn.*, xvi, 94th session (1940–41), pp 31–46.

—— The changing distribution of population in Kerry and West Cork. In *Stat. Soc. Ire. Jn.*, xvi, 95th session (1941–2), pp 28–43.

—— The congested districts of the west of Ireland. In *Geographical Review*, xxxiii, no. 1 (1943), pp 1–15.

—— *Ireland: its physical, historical, social, and economic geography*. London, 1950; 4th ed., 1969; reprint, with revisions, 1972.

Geary, R. C. Some reflections on Irish population questions. In *Studies*, xliii (1954), pp 168–77.

Goldstrom, J. M., and Clarkson, L. A. (ed.). *Irish population, economy, and society: essays in honour of the late K. H. Connell*. Oxford, 1981.

Graham, B. J., and Proudfoot, L. J. (ed.). *An historical geography of Ireland*. New York and London, 1993.

Herries Davies, G. L. The Geographical Society of Ireland. In *Ir. Geography: golden jubilee issue* (1984), pp 1–23.

Heslinga, M. W. *The Irish border as a cultural divide: a contribution to the study of regionalism in the British Isles*. 3rd ed., Assen, 1979. First published 1962.

Horner, Arnold. Planning the Irish transport network: parallels in nineteenth- and twentieth-century proposals. In *Ir. Geography*, x (1977), pp 44–57.

—— Changes in population and in the extent of the built-up area in the Dublin city-region. In *Ir. Geography*, xxiii (1990), pp 50–55.

Hourihan, Kevin. Urban population density patterns and change in Ireland, 1901–79. In *Econ. & Soc. Rev.*, xiii (1982), pp 125–47.

Hourihan, Kevin. Population change in Irish cities, 1981–86: county boroughs, suburbs, and daily urban systems. In *Ir. Geography*, xxv (1992), pp 160–68.

Johnson, James H. Population change in Ireland, 1961–1966. In *Ir. Geography*, v (1968), pp 470–77.

—— *The human geography of Ireland.* New York, 1994.

Kennedy, Robert E. *The Irish: emigration, marriage, and fertility.* Berkeley, Calif., and London, 1973.

King, Russell, and Shuttleworth, Ian. Ireland's new wave of emigration in the 1980s. In *Ir. Geography*, xxi (1988), pp 104–8.

Kockel, Ullrich (ed.). *Landscape, heritage and identity: case studies in Irish ethnography.* Liverpool, 1995.

Lyon, Stanley. The census of population 1946. In *Stat. Soc. Ire. Jn.*, xvii, 99th session (1945–6), pp 579–93.

Mac Cártaigh, Domhnall. Marriage and birth rates for Knockainy parish, 1882–1941. In *Cork Hist. Soc. Jn.*, xlvii (1942), pp 4–8.

MacLaughlin, Jim (ed.). *Location and dislocation in contemporary Irish society: emigration and Irish identities.* Cork, 1997.

Mitchell, Frank. *Reading the Irish landscape.* Dublin, 1998. Revised and redesigned ed. of *The Irish landscape* (1976). 2nd ed., *The Shell guide to reading . . .* , 1986.

—— The influence of man on vegetation in Ireland. In *Journal of Life Sciences*, iii, pt. 1 (1982), pp 7–14.

—— Frank Mitchell—a man and the landscape [interviewed by Gabriel Cooney]. In *Archaeology Ireland*, iii (1989), pp 91–5.

Mulrennan, Monica E. Changes since the nineteenth century to the estuary-barrier complexes of north County Dublin. In *Ir. Geography*, xxvi (1993), pp 1–13.

Nolan, William (ed.). *The shaping of Ireland: the geographical perspective.* Cork, 1986. (Thomas Davis Lectures.)

O'Brien, John A. (ed.). *The vanishing Irish.* London, 1954.

Ó Gráda, Cormac, and Walsh, B. M. *Irish emigration: patterns, causes and effects.* Dublin, 1992.

Prunty, Jacinta. *Dublin slums 1800–1925: a study in urban geography.* Dublin, 1999.

Richards-Orpen, J. Strip farms in the Graiguenamanagh basin. In *Ir. Geography*, i (1946), pp 77–80.

Shaw, D. H. Mortality experience among the lower income families in Éire. In *Stat. Soc. Ire. Jn.*, xvii, 99th session (1945–6), pp 489–503.

Smyth, William J., and Whelan, Kevin (ed.). *Common ground: essays on the historical geography of Ireland presented to T. Jones Hughes.* Cork, 1988.

Stephens, Nicholas, and Glasscock, Robin E. (ed.). *Irish geographical studies in honour of E. Estyn Evans.* Belfast, 1970.

Sweeney, John. A three-century storm climatology for Dublin, 1715–2000. In *Ir. Geography*, xxxiii (2000), pp 1–14.

Turnock, David. *An historical geography of railways in Great Britain and Ireland.* Aldershot, *c.* 1998.

Verrière, Jacques. *La population de l'Irlande.* Paris, 1979.

Walsh, J. A. Population change in the Republic of Ireland in the 1980s. In *Geographical Viewpoint*, xix (1991), pp 89–98.

6 ECONOMIC AND SOCIAL HISTORY

Aalen, F. H. A. *The Iveagh Trust: the first hundred years, 1890–1990*. Dublin, 1990.
—— Ireland. In C. Pooley (ed.)., *The comparative study of housing strategies in Europe, 1880–1930* (Leicester, 1992), pp 132–65.
Annett, Anthony M. Elections and macroeconomic outcomes in Ireland, 1948–91. In *Econ. & Soc. Rev.*, xxv (1994), pp 21–47.
Ardagh, John. *Ireland and the Irish: portrait of a changing society*. Harmondsworth, 1995. First published London, 1994.
Arensberg, C. M. *The Irish countryman: an anthropological study*. Prospect Heights, Ill., 1988. First published New York, 1937; reprint, 1959.
—— and Kimball, S. T. *Family and community in Ireland*. 2nd ed., Cambridge, Mass., 1968. 1st ed. 1940.
Austin, Valerie A. The céilí and the public dance hall act, 1935. In *Éire-Ireland*, xxviii, no. 3 (1993), pp 7–16.
Bacon, Peter; Durkan, Joe; and O'Leary, Jim. *The Irish economy: policy and performance, 1972–81*. Dublin, 1982.
Baillie, I. F., and Sheehy, S. J. (ed.). *Irish agriculture in a changing world*. Edinburgh, 1971.
Baker, Michael H. C. *Irish railways since 1916*. London, 1972.
Baker, Susan. The nuclear power issue in Ireland: the role of the Irish anti-nuclear movement. In *Irish Political Studies*, iii (1988), pp 3–17.
Barry, Frank (ed.). *Understanding Ireland's economic growth*. Basingstoke, 1999.
Bell, Philip W. *The sterling area in the postwar world: internal mechanism and cohesion 1946–1952*. Oxford, 1956.
Bielenberg, Andy. *Locke's Distillery: a history*. Dublin, 1993.
—— Watching the future...? Keating, Siemens & the Shannon scheme. In *Hist. Ire.*, v, no. 3 (1997), pp 43–7.
Birdwell-Pheasant, Donna. The early twentieth-century stem family: a case study from County Kerry. In Marilyn Silverman and P. H. Gulliver (ed.), *Approaching the past: historical anthropology through Irish case studies* (New York, 1992), pp 205–35.
—— Irish households in the early twentieth century: culture, class, and historical contingency. In *Journal of Family History*, xviii (1993), pp 19–38.
Birnie, J. E. Irish farming labour productivity: comparisons with the U.K., 1930s–1990. In *Ir. Econ. & Soc. Hist.*, xxiv (1997), pp 22–41.
Bolger, Patrick. *The Irish co-operative movement: its history and development*. Dublin, 1977.
Bourke, Edward J. *Shipwrecks of the Irish coast, vol. 3: 1582–2000*. Dublin, 2000.
Boyd, Andrew. *The rise of the Irish trade unions, 1729–1970*. Tralee, 1972; 2nd ed., 1985.
Boylan, Patricia. *All cultivated people: a history of the United Arts Club, Dublin*. Gerrards Cross, 1988.
Bradley, Dan. *Farm labourers: Irish struggle, 1900–1976*. Belfast, 1988.
Brady, John. Social welfare in Meath. In *Ríocht na Midhe*, iii, no. 1 (1963), pp 57–63.
Breathnach, Proinnsias. The development of the Irish fish farming industry. In *Ir. Geography*, xxv (1992), pp 182–7.

Breen, Richard. Farm servanthood in Ireland, 1900–40. In *Econ. Hist. Rev.*, xxxvi, no. 1 (1983), pp 87–102.

——, Hannan, Damian; Rottman, David; and Whelan, Christopher. *Understanding contemporary Ireland: state, class and development in the Republic of Ireland.* Dublin, 1990.

Bristow, J. A., and Tait, A. A. (ed.). *Economic policy in Ireland.* Dublin, 1968.

Brodie, Malcolm. *100 years of Irish football.* Belfast, 1980.

Brody, Hugh. *Inishkillane: change and decline in the west of Ireland.* London, 1973.

Brown, Stephen J. Racialism in Ireland? In *I.E.R.*, lv (1940), pp 367–76.
A continuation of his articles on racial theory: ibid., lv (1940), pp 132–42, 226–37.

Brown, Terence. *Ireland: a social and cultural history 1922–79.* Glasgow, 1981. Revised ed. (*1922–85*), London, 1987.

Byrne, Liam. *History of aviation in Ireland.* Belfast, 1980.

Campbell, John. *An association to declare: a history of the Preventive Staff Association.* Dublin, 1996. [Customs and excise.]

Casserley, H. C. *Outline of Irish railway history.* Newton Abbot, 1974.

Clarke, Howard B. (ed.). *Irish cities.* Cork, 1995. (Thomas Davis lectures.)

Clarke, Peter. *The Royal Canal: the complete story.* Dublin, 1992.

Clune, M. A. *Connacht triumphs: fifteen years of high endeavour and brilliant achievement in Gaelic football, 1931–1945.* Dublin, 1946.

Cody, Seamus; O'Dowd, John; and Rigney, Peter (ed.). *The parliament of labour: 100 years of the Dublin Council of Trade Unions.* Dublin, 1986.

Coill Dubh, 1952–1992. [Coill Dubh, Co. Kildare, 1993.]
Village set up by Bord na Móna to house workers.

Coleman, Marie. *I.F.U.T.: a history.* Dublin, 2000.
Irish Federation of University Teachers.

Collins, Michael. *Rail versus road in Ireland, 1900–2000: a century of change in Irish railways, road and rail passenger services and vehicles.* Newtownards, 2000.

Connery, Donald S. *The Irish.* London, 1968. Revisied ed. 1972.

Corcoran, Michael. *Through streets broad and narrow: a history of Dublin trams.* Leicester, 2000.

Court, Artelia. *Puck of the Droms: the lives & literature of the Irish tinkers.* Berkeley, Calif., 1985.

Cronin, Mike. *Sport and nationalism in Ireland: Gaelic games, soccer and Irish identity since 1884.* Dublin, 1999.

Cronin, Willie. Memories of fifty years in the Irish woollen trade. In *Capuchin Annual, 1944*, pp 88–100.

Crotty, Raymond D. *Irish agricultural production: its volume and structure.* Cork, 1966.

—— *Ireland in crisis: a study in capitalist colonial underdevelopment.* Dingle, 1986.

Cullen, L. M. (ed.). *The formation of the Irish economy.* Cork, 1969. (Thomas Davis Lectures.)

—— *Six generations: life and work in Ireland from 1790.* Cork, 1970.

—— *Princes & pirates: the Dublin Chamber of Commerce 1783–1983.* Dublin, 1983.

—— *An economic history of Ireland since 1660.* London, 1987. 1st ed. 1972.

Daly, Mary E. *A social and economic history of Ireland since 1800.* Dublin, 1981.

—— An alien institution: attitudes towards the city in nineteenth- and twentieth-century Irish society. In *Études Irlandaises*, x (1985), pp 181–94.

—— The employment gains from industrial protection in the Irish Free State during the 1930s: a note. (With reply by D. S. Johnson.) In *Ir. Econ. & Soc. Hist.*, xv (1988), pp 71–5, 76–80.

—— *Industrial development and Irish national identity, 1922–1939*. Dublin, 1993.

—— Integration or diversity? Anglo–Irish economic relations, 1922–39. In S. J. Connolly (ed.), *Kingdoms united? Great Britain and Ireland since 1500*. Dublin, 1999.

D'Arcy, Fergus A. *Horses, lords and racing men: the Turf Club, 1790–1990*. The Curragh, Kildare, 1991.

—— and Hannigan, Ken (ed.). *Workers in union: documents and commentaries on the history of Irish labour*. Dublin, 1988.

de Búrca, Marcus. *The G.A.A.: a history*. 2nd ed. Dublin, 1999. First published 1980.

Delany, Ruth. *The Grand Canal of Ireland*. Newton Abbot, 1973. 2nd ed. Dublin, 1995.

—— *A celebration of 250 years of Ireland's inland waterways*. Revised ed., Belfast, 1992. First published 1986.

—— *Ireland's Royal Canal: 1789–1992*. Dublin, 1992.

—— *The shoemaker's canal*. Dublin, 1992.

Delany, V. T. H., and Delany, D. R. *The canals of the south of Ireland*. Newton Abbot, 1966.

Dennison, S. R., and MacDonagh, Oliver. *Guinness, 1886–1939: from corporation to the second world war*. Cork, 1998.

Devereux, Eoin. Community development—problems in practice: the Muintir na Tíre experience, 1931–1958. In *Administration*, xxxix (1992), pp 351–69.

Dooley, Terence A. M. *The decline of the 'big house' in Ireland: a study of Irish landed families*. Dublin, 2001.

Doyle, Oliver. G.A.A. football finals, 1953–4. In *Ir. Railway Rec. Soc. Jn.*, xviii, no. 123 (1994), pp 322–30.
Quicker travel time with introduction of steam engines.

—— and Hirsch, Stephen. *Railways in Ireland 1834–1984*. Dublin, 1983.

Duncan, G. A. The public finances of the Irish Free State, 1932–8. In *Economic History*, iii (1939), pp 259–67.

—— The social income of the Irish Free State, 1926–38 (with discussion). In *Stat. Soc. Ire. Jn.*, xvi, 93rd session (1939–40), pp 1–16.

—— The first year of the war: its economic effects on the twenty-six counties of Ireland. In *Economic Journal*, li (1941), pp 389–99.

—— Banking in Ireland. In R. S. Sayers (ed.), *Banking in the British commonwealth* (Oxford, 1952), pp 303–19.

—— Eason, J. C. M; and Lyon, Stanley. The trade statistics of the Irish Free State. (With discussion.) In *Stat. Soc. Ire. Jn.*, xvi, 91st session (1937–8), pp 1–20.

Dunlevy, Mairead. *Dress in Ireland*. London, 1989.

Dunn, Joseph. *No tigers in Africa! recollections and reflections on 25 years of Radharc*. Dublin, 1986. [Television series.]

Dwyer, D. J. The leather industries of the Irish Republic, 1922–55: a study in industrial development and location. In *Ir. Geography*, iv (1961), pp 175–89.

Dwyer, D. J. and Symons, L. J. The development and location of the textile industries in the Irish Republic. In *Ir. Geography*, iv, no. 6 (1963), pp 415–31.

Eason, J. C. M. An analysis giving a comparison of national expenditure, sources of revenue, and the debt, for the years 1929–30 and 1939–40 (with discussion). In *Stat. Soc. Ire. Jn.*, xvi, 94th session (1940–41), pp 123–39.

Eaton, M. R. J. *Irish banking, currency and credit*. Dublin, 1954.

Ellis, Peter Berresford. *A history of the Irish working class*. London, 1996. First published 1972.

Fanning, Ronan. Economists and governments: Ireland, 1922–52. In *Hermathena*, cxxxv (1983), pp 138–56.

Farmar, Tony. *Heitons: a managed transition: Heitons in the Irish coal, iron and building markets 1818–1996*. Dublin, 1996.

Ferguson, Kenneth. *Fox's of Grafton Street 1881–1981: history of a family tobacco shop*. Dublin, 1981.

Ferriter, Diarmaid. *A nation of extremes: the Pioneers in twentieth-century Ireland*. Dublin, 1999.

Fifty years of Liberty Hall. Dublin, 1959. [Irish Transport and General Workers' Union.]

Fitzgibbon, Constantine. *The Irish in Ireland*. Newton Abbot, 1983.

Fogarty, Michael; Ryan, Liam; and Lee, Joseph. *Irish values & attitudes: the Irish report of the European values system study*. Dublin, 1984.

Foley, Anthony, and McAleese, Dermot (ed.). *Overseas industry in Ireland*. Dublin, 1991.

Forbes, A. C. The forestry revival in Éire. In *Irish Forestry*, iv (1947), pp 11–26.

Furlong, Nicholas. *The greatest hurling decade: Wexford and the epic teams of the '50s*. Dublin, 1993.

Geary, R. C. Irish economic development since the treaty. In *Studies*, xl (1951), pp 399–418.

Gibbon, Peter. Arensberg and Kimball revisited. In *Economy and Society*, ii (1973), pp 479–98.

——and Curtin, Chris. Irish farm families: facts and fantasies. In *Comparative Studies in Society and History*, xxv (1983), pp 375–80.

Gibson, N. J., and Spencer, J. E. (ed.). *Economic activity in Ireland: a study of two open economies*. Dublin, 1977.

Gibson, William H. *Early Irish golf: the first courses, clubs and pioneers*. Naas, 1988.

Gilligan, H. A. *A history of the port of Dublin*. Dublin, 1988.

Girvin, Brian. *Between two worlds: politics and economy in independent Ireland*, Dublin, 1989.

Goldthorpe, J. H., and Whelan, C. T. (ed.). *The development of industrial society in Ireland: the third joint meeting of the Royal Irish Academy and the British Academy, Oxford, 1990*. Oxford, 1992.

Goodman, James. *Single Europe, single Ireland: uneven development in process*. Dublin, 2000.

Graham, B. J., and Hood, Susan. Town tenant protest in late nineteenth- and early twentieth-century Ireland. In *Ir. Econ. & Soc. Hist.*, xxi (1994), pp 39–57.

Gray, Tony. *St Patrick's people: new look at the Irish*. London, 1996.

Greaves, C. D. *The Irish Transport and General Workers Union: the formative years, 1909–1923*. Dublin, 1982.

Hall, F. G. *The Bank of Ireland, 1783–1946*. Dublin and Oxford, 1949.

Hearn, Mona. *Below stairs: domestic service remembered in Dublin and beyond, 1880–1922*. Dublin, 1993.

Heverin, Aileen. *The Irish Countrywomen's Association: a history 1910–2000*. Dublin, 2000.

Hill, Jacqueline, and Lennon, Colm (ed.). *Luxury and austerity*. Dublin, 1999. (*Hist. Studies*, xxi.)

Hogan, Oliver. *Clanna Gael-Fontenoy: the history of Dublin's G.A.A. club. Vol. I (1887–1950)*. Dublin, [1995].

Hogan, Sarsfield. *A history of Irish steel*. Dublin, 1980.

Honohan, Patrick, and Ó Gráda, Cormac. The Irish macroeconomic crisis of 1955–56: how much was due to monetary policy? In *Ir. Econ. & Soc. Hist.*, xxv (1998), pp 52–80.

Horgan, John. The port of Cork. In *Stat. Soc. Ire. Jn.*, xix, 109th session (1955–6), pp 42–57.

Humphries, Madeleine. An issue of confidence: the decline of the Irish whiskey industry in independent Ireland, 1922–1952. In *Journal of European Economic History*, xxiii (1994), pp 93–113.

An iascaireacht in Inis Óirr: sraith léachtaí idir stair dian cur síos, a thug Gobnait ní Chonghaile agus Sorcha ní Chonghaile; gcomóradh 50 bliain Scoil Chaomhá in Inis Óirr 1942–1992. [Inis Óirr], 1994.
Fishing in the Aran Islands.

Ireland, John de Courcy. *Ireland's sea fisheries: a history*. Dublin, 1981.

——— *Ireland and the Irish in maritime history*. Dún Laoghaire, 1986.

Jacobson, D. S. The political economy of industrial locations: the Ford motor company at Cork, 1912–26. In *Ir. Econ. & Soc. Hist.*, iv (1977), pp 36–55.

Jarvie, Grant (ed.). *Sport in the making of Celtic cultures*. London, 1999.

Johnson, David J. *The interwar economy in Ireland*. Dundalk, 1985.

——— The economic performance of the independent Irish state. In *Ir. Econ. & Soc. Hist.*, xviii (1991), pp 48–53.

Jones, D. S. Land reform legislation and security of tenure in Ireland after independence. In *Éire-Ireland*, xxxii–xxxiii (1997–8), pp 116–43.

Kavanagh, Catherine. Public capital and private sector productivity in Ireland, 1958–1990. In *Journal of Economic Studies*, xxiv, nos 1–2 (1997), pp 72–94.

Kearns, Kevin C. Development of the Irish peat fuel industry. In *American Journal of Economy and Society*, xxxvii (1978), pp 179–93.

——— *Dublin's vanishing craftsmen: in search of the old masters*. Belfast, 1987.

——— *Dublin tenement life: an oral history*. Dublin, 1994.

Kearns, Séamus. Picture postcards as a source for social historians. In *Saothar*, xxii (1997), pp 128–33.

Keating, Carla (ed.). *Plunkett and co-operatives: past, present and future*. Cork, 1983.

Keating, Paul, and Desmond, Derry. *Culture and capitalism in contemporary Ireland*. Aldershot, 1993.

Keeble, David; Offord, John; and Walker, Sheila. *Peripheral regions in a community of twelve member states*. Luxembourg, 1988.

Kennedy, Kieran A. The national accounts for Ireland in the nineteenth and twentieth centuries. In *Scandinavian Economic History Review*, xliii (1995), pp 101–14.

—— (ed.). *Ireland in transition: economic and social change since 1960*. Cork, 1986. (Thomas Davis Lectures.)

—— (ed.). *From famine to feast: economic and social change in Ireland, 1847–1997*. Dublin, 1998. (Thomas Davis Lectures.)

—— and Dowling, Brendan R.. *Economic growth in Ireland: the experience since 1947*. Dublin, 1975.

—— Giblin, Thomas; and McHugh, Deirdre. *The economic development of Ireland in the twentieth century*. London, 1988.

Kennedy, Liam. *The modern industrialisation of Ireland, 1940–1988*. Dublin, 1989.

—— Farm succession in modern Ireland: elements of a theory of inheritance. In *Econ. Hist. Rev.*, xliv (1991), pp 477–99.

Kennedy, Michael. Towards co-operation: Seán Lemass and north–south economic relations: 1956–65. In *Ir. Econ. & Soc. Hist.*, xxiv (1997), pp 42–61.

Kennedy, Walter. *Shipping in Dublin port, 1939–45*. Edinburgh, 1998.

Kent, Edmond. A review of agricultural policy in Éire, 1932–8. In *Irish Monthly*, lxviii (1940), 661–74.

King, Carla (ed.). *Famine, land and culture in Ireland*. Dublin, 2000.
    Essays on land in Ireland from the great famine to the present.

Lamb, J. G. D., and Bowe, P. *A history of gardening in Ireland*. Dublin, 1995.

Lane, Pádraig G. The Lambert Brookhill estate: a record of Mayo property, 1694–1946. In *Cathair Na Mart: journal of the Westport Historical Society*, xvi (1997), pp 45–61.

Lawlor, Anthony T. *Irish maritime survey: a guide to the Irish maritime world, 1945*. Dublin, 1945.

Lewis, Colin A. *Hunting in Ireland: an historical and geographical analysis*. London, 1975.

—— Irish horse breeding and the Irish draught horse, 1917–78. In *Agricultural History Review*, xxxi (1983), pp 37–49.

Liddle, L. H. Passenger steamers on the Irish Sea, 1919–39, i. In *Ir. Railway Rec. Soc. Jn.*, xviii, no. 123 (1994), pp 314–21.

Lindsay, Deirdre. *Dublin's oldest charity: the Sick and Indigent Roomkeepers Society, 1790–1990*. Dublin, 1990.

Lisney, Harry. Rating and valuation (with discussion). In *Stat. Soc. Ire. Jn.*, xvi, 92nd session (1938–9), pp 73–88.

Lynch, Patrick. The Irish economic prospect. In *Studies*, xliv (1955), pp 5–16.

Lyons, F. S. L. (ed.). *Bicentenary essays: Bank of Ireland 1783–1983*. Dublin, 1983.

McCarthy, Charles. *The decade of upheaval: Irish trade unions in the nineteen sixties*. Dublin, 1973.

—— *Trade unions in Ireland, 1894–1960*. Dublin, 1977.

McCarthy, J. C. History of pig breeding in Ireland. In *Éire, Department of Agriculture, Journal*, lxiii (1966), pp 55–60.

McCarthy, John F. (ed.). *Planning Ireland's future: the legacy of T. K. Whitaker.* Dublin, 1990.

MacCarthy, R. B. *The Trinity College estates, 1800–1923: corporate management in an age of reform.* [Dundalk], 1992.

McDonald, Rosemarie. Horses and hospitals: the Irish sweepstakes. In *Éire-Ireland,* xxix, no. 1 (1994), pp 24–34.

McGowan, Pádraig. *Money and banking in Ireland: origins, development, and future.* Dublin, 1990.

MacGréil, Micheál. *Prejudice and tolerance in Ireland.* Dublin, 1977.

—— *Prejudice in Ireland revisited.* Dublin, 1996.

McGuire, E. B. *Irish whiskey: a history of distilling, the spirit trade, and excise controls in Ireland.* Dublin and New York, 1973.

Maguire, Martin. *Servants to the public: a history of the Local Government and Public Services Union, 1901–1990.* Dublin, 1998.

Mahony, Edmund. *The Galway blazers: memoirs.* Galway, 1979.
Foxhunting in Ireland.

Malins, Edward, and Bowe, Patrick. *Irish gardens and demesnes from 1830.* London, 1980.

Manning, Maurice, and McDowell, Moore. *Electricity supply in Ireland: the history of the E.S.B.* Dublin, 1984.

Matsuo, Taro. *Comparative aspects of Irish and Japanese economic and social history.* Tokyo, 1993.

Meenan, James. *The Irish economy since 1922.* Liverpool, 1970.

Merrigan, Matt. *Eagle or cuckoo? the story of the A.T.G.W.U. in Ireland.* Dublin, 1989.

Micks, W. L. *An account of the constitution, administration, and dissolution of the congested districts board for Ireland from 1891 to 1923.* Dublin, 1925.

Middlemass, Tom. *Irish standard gauge railways.* Newton Abbot, 1981.

Mitchison, Rosalind, and Roebuck, Peter (ed.). *Economy and society in Scotland and Ireland, 1500–1939.* Edinburgh, 1988.

Mjoset, Lars. *The Irish economy in a comparative institutional perspective.* Dublin, 1992.

Moore, John S. *Motor makers in Ireland.* Belfast, 1982.

Moynihan, Maurice. *Currency and central banking in Ireland, 1922–1960.* Dublin, 1975.

Mulligan, Fergus. *One hundred and fifty years of Irish railways.* Belfast, 1983.

Mullins, Richard J. *A history of Portarlington generating station & Clonsast bog development.* n.p., 1993.
Co. Laois, 1936–88.

Murphy, Antoin E. (ed.). *Economists and the Irish economy: from the eighteenth century to the present day.* Dublin, 1984.

Murphy, Gary. 'Fostering a spurious progeny?' the trade union movement and Europe, 1957–64. In *Saothar,* xxi (1996), pp 61–70.

Murphy, K. J., and Nunan, D. B. A time series analysis of farmland price behaviour in Ireland, 1901–86. In *Econ. & Soc. Rev.,* xxiv (1993), pp 125–53.

Neary, J. Peter, and Ó Gráda, Cormac. Protection, economic war and structural change: the 1930s in Ireland. In *I.H.S.,* xxvii, no. 107 (May 1991), 250–66.

Neeson, Eoin. *A history of Irish forestry*. Dublin, 1991.

Nelson, E. C., and Brady, Aidan (ed.). *Irish gardening and horticulture*. Dublin, 1979.

Nevin, Donal (ed.). *Trade unions and change in Irish society*. Dublin, 1980. (Thomas Davis Lectures.)

—— (ed.). *Trade union century*. Cork, 1994. (Thomas Davis Lectures.)

——*James Larkin: lion of the fold*. Dublin, 1998.

New Ireland Assurance Company. *Achievement: the twenty-eight years' story of the New Ireland Assurance Company Ltd*. Dublin, 1947.

——*New Ireland comes of age, 1918–1939: the history and development of a great Irish institution*. Dublin, 1939.

Nock, O. S. *Irish steam: a twenty year survey 1920–1939*. Newton Abbot, 1982.

Nolan, William. New fields and farms: migration policies of state land agencies, 1891–1980. In W. J. Smyth and Kevin Whelan (ed.)., *Common ground:essays ...presented to T. Jones Hughes* (Cork, 1988), pp 296–319.

Norton, James E. *History of the South County Dublin Harriers and some neighbouring harrier packs*. Dublin, 1991.

O'Beirne, Gerald. *Siemens in Ireland, 1925–2000*. Dublin, 2000.

O'Brien, Flann. The dance hall. In *The Bell*, i, no. 5 (Feb. 1941), pp 44–52.

O'Brien, George. The impact of the war on the Irish economy. In *Studies*, xxxv (1946), pp 25–39.

——Ireland's position in the world today. In *Cambridge Journal*, i (1948), pp 429–38.

—— The economic progress of Ireland, 1912–1962. In *Studies*, li (1962), pp 9–26.

Ó Ceallaigh, Séamus. *Story of the G.A.A.* Limerick, 1977.

O'Connell, T. J. *History of the Irish National Teachers' Organisation, 1868–1968*. Cover title: *100 years of progress: the story of the Irish National Teachers' Organisation, 1868–1968*. Dublin, [1970?].

O'Connor, Emmet. *Syndicalism in Ireland 1917–1923*. Cork, 1988.

——*A labour history of Waterford*. Waterford, 1989.

——*A labour history of Ireland, 1824–1960*. Dublin, 1992.

——Jim Larkin and the Communist Internationals, 1923–9. In *I.H.S.*, xxxi, no. 123 (May 1999), pp 357–72.

O'Connor, Robert, and Guiomard, C. Agricultural output in the Free State area before and after independence. In *Ir. Econ. & Soc. Hist.*, xii (1985), pp 89–97.

——and Henry, E.W. Estimates of gross and net output and income arising in agriculture in all Ireland and in the Free State area...between 1900–01 and 1926–27. In *Ir. Econ. & Soc. Hist.*, xxiii (1996), pp 45–72.

O'Donoghue, Thomas A. Sport, recreation and physical education: the evolution of a national policy of regeneration in Éire, 1926–48. In *British Journal of Sports History*, iii (1986), pp 216–33.

O'Dowd, Anne. *Spalpeens and tattie hokers: history and folklore of the Irish migratory agricultural worker in Ireland and Britain*. Dublin, 1990.

Ó Giolláin, Diarmuid. *Locating Irish folklore: tradition, modernity, identity*. Cork, 2000.

O'Gorman, Ronnie (ed.). *Thanks for the memories, 1954–1994: 40 years of the Galway international oyster festival*. Galway, 1994.

Ó Gráda, Cormac. Determinants of Irish agriculture. In *International Migration Review*, xx (1986), pp 650–56.

—— Irish agricultural history: recent research. In *Agricultural History Review*, xxxviii (1990), pp 165–73.

—— Irish agriculture north and south since 1900. In Bruce Campbell and Mark Overton (ed.), *Land, labour and livestock: historical studies in European agricultural productivity* (Manchester, 1991), pp 439–56.

—— *Ireland: a new economic history, 1780–1939*. Oxford, 1994.

—— Money and banking in the Irish Free State, 1921–1939. In Charles Feinstein (ed.), *Banking, currency, and finance between the wars* (Oxford, 1995), pp 414–33.

—— *A rocky road: the Irish economy since the 1920s*. Manchester, 1997.

O'Hagan, J. W. An analysis of the relative size of the government sector: Ireland 1926–52. In *Econ. & Soc. Rev.*, xii (1980), pp 17–35.

—— (ed.). *The economy of Ireland: policy and performance*. 6th ed. Dublin, 1991; 1st ed., 1978.

O'Hanlon, Thomas J. *The Irish: portrait of a people*. London, 1976.

O'Hare, Aileen; Whelan, Christopher; and Commins, Patrick. The development of an Irish census-based social class scale. In *Econ. & Soc. Rev.*, xxii, no. 2 (1991), pp 135–56.

O'Leary, Eoin. The convergence performance of Ireland among E.U. countries: 1960 to 1990. In *Journal of Economic Studies*, xxiv, nos 1–2 (1997), pp 43–58.

Ollerenshaw, Philip. The business and politics of banking in Ireland, 1900–1943. In Philip Cottrell, Alice Teichova, and Takeshi Yuzawa (ed.), *Finance in the age of the corporate economy: the third Anglo-Japanese business history conference* (Aldershot, 1997), pp 52–78.

O'Mahony, David. *The Irish economy: an introductory description*. Revised ed., Cork, 1970. Previous eds 1964, 1967.

O'Malley, Eoin. *Industry and economic development: the challenge for the latecomer*. Dublin, 1989.

Ó Nualláin, Labhrás. A comparison of the economic position and trend in Éire and Northern Ireland. In *Stat. Soc. Ire. Jn.*, xvii, 99th session (1945–6), pp 504–40.

Oram, Hugh. *The advertising book: the history of advertising in Ireland*. Dublin, 1986.

—— *Dublin airport: the history*. Dublin, 1990.

O'Reilly, Emily. *Masterminds of the right*. Dublin, 1992.
  Irish opponents of divorce and abortion.

Ó Riain, Mícheál. *On the move: Córas Iompair Éireann, 1945–95*. Dublin, 1995.

O'Rourke, Kevin. Burn everything British but their coal: the Anglo–Irish economic war of the 1930s. In *Journal of Economic History*, li (1991), pp 357–66.

—— The costs of international economic disintegration: Ireland in the 1930s. In *Research in Economic History*, xv (1995), pp 215–59.

—— and Polak, Ben. Property transactions in Ireland, 1708–1988: an introduction. In *Ir. Econ. & Soc. Hist.*, xxi (1994), pp 58–71.
  Time series derived from Registry of Deeds records.

O'Sullivan, Donal. *Dublin Bay: a century of sailing, 1884–1984: a centenary celebration by the Dublin Bay Sailing Club*. Dublin, 1984.

O'Sullivan, Patrick. Ireland and the Olympic games. In *Hist. Ire.*, vi, no. 1 (1998), pp 40–45.

O'Toole. Fintan. *Black hole, green card: the disappearance of Ireland*. Dublin, 1994.

Peillon, Michel. *Contemporary Irish society: an introduction*. Dublin, 1982.

Pomfret, J. E. *The struggle for land in Ireland, 1880–1923*. Princeton, N.J., 1930.

Power, Con. *Under the hammer: property in Ireland—a history of the Irish Auctioneers & Valuers Institute, 1922–97*. Dublin, 1997.

Press, Jon. *The footwear industry in Ireland, 1922–1973*. Dublin, 1989.

Quinn, Anthony P. *Credit unions in Ireland*. 2nd revised ed. Dublin, 1999. 1st ed. 1994.

Redmond, Sean. *The Irish Municipal Employees' Trade Union 1883–1983*. Dublin, 1983.

Robinson, H. W. *A history of accountants in Ireland*. Dublin, 1983. First published 1964.

Rowan, Paul. *The team that Jack built*. Edinburgh, 1994.
Jack Charlton and Irish soccer.

Rudd, Niall. *Pale green, light orange: a portrait of bourgeois Ireland, 1930–1950*. Dublin, 1994.

Ryall, Tom. *Kilkenny: the G.A.A. story 1884–1984*. Kilkenny, 1984.

Ryan, Mary; Browne, Seán; and Gilmour, Kevin (ed.). *No shoes in summer*. Dublin, 1995.
Early 20th-century Ireland; anthology.

Sands, Christopher. *The Gresham for style*. Dublin, 1994.
Gresham Hotel, Dublin.

Sexton, J. J.; Walsh, B. M.; Hannan, D.; and McMahon, D. *The economic and social implications of emigration*. Dublin, 1991.

Share, Bernard. *The flight of the Iolar: the Aer Lingus experience, 1936–86*. Dublin, 1986.

—— In our own image: the branding of industrial Ireland. In *Hist. Ire.*, vi, no. 4 (1998), pp 31–5.

Shiel, Michael J. *The quiet revolution: the electrification of rural Ireland, 1946–1976*. Dublin, 1984.

Shields, B. F. The Irish census of distribution [1933]. In *Royal Stat. Soc. Jn.*, ci, pt 1 (1938), pp 188–201.

—— An analysis of the legislation, published accounts and operating statistics of the Great Southern Railways Co., 1924–1937. In *Stat. Soc. Ire. Jn.*, xvi, 91st session (1937–8), pp 87–111.

—— An analysis of the financial and operating statistics of the Great Southern Railways Co. and Great Northern Railway Co., 1938–44. In *Stat. Soc. Ire. Jn.*, xvii, 99th session (1945–6), pp 541–64.

Shepherd, Ernie, and Beesley, Gerry. *The Dublin & South Eastern Railway: an illustrated history*. Leicester, 1998.

Shillman, Bernard. *Trade unionism and trade disputes in Ireland*. Dublin, 1960.

Simms, Anngret, and Andrews, J. H. (ed.). *Irish country towns*. Cork, 1994. (Thomas Davis Lectures.)

—— —— *More Irish country towns*. Cork, 1995. (Thomas Davis Lectures.)

Skehill, Caroline. *The nature of social work in Ireland: a historical perspective*. Lewiston, New York, 1999.

Smith, Louis P., and Healy, Sean. *Farm organisations in Ireland: a century of progress*. Dublin, 1996.

Smith, Raymond. *The clash of the ash: a popular history of the national game (1884–1972)*. Dublin, 1972.

—— *The football immortals: a popular history of Gaelic football (1884–1984)*. 4th ed. Dublin, 1983.

—— *The greatest hurlers of our time*. Dublin, 1990.

—— *The centenary Co-operative Creamery Society Ltd: a century of co-operative endeavour, 1898–1998*. Dublin, 1998.

Smyth, Ailbhe (ed.). *The abortion papers: Ireland*. Dublin, 1992.

Somerville-Large, Peter. *Irish voices: an informal history 1916–1966*. London, 2000. First published as *Irish voices: fifty years of Irish life, 1916–1966* (London, 1999).

Sweeney, Garry. *In public service: a history of the Public Service Executive Union, 1890–1990*. Dublin, 1990.

Sweetman, Rosita. *'On our knees': Ireland 1972*. London, 1972. Interviews with contemporaries, north and south.

Thacker, Christopher. *The genius of gardening: the history of gardens in Britain and Ireland*. London, 1994.

Thomas, William A. *The stock exchanges of Ireland*. Liverpool, 1986.

Thornley, David. Ireland: the end of an era? In *Studies*, liii (1964), pp 1–17.

Villiers-Tuthill, Kathleen. The Connemara railway 1895–1935. In *Hist. Ire.*, iii, no. 4 (1995), pp 35–40.

Vaizey, John. *The brewing industry, 1886–1951*. London, 1960.

Waller, Michael H., and Waller, M. P. *British & Irish tramway systems since 1945*. Shepperton, 1991.

Walsh, Brendan. Tests for macroeconomic feedback from large-scale migration based on the Irish experience, 1948–87: a note [and a rejoinder]. In *Econ. & Soc. Rev.*, xx (1989), pp 257–66, 278–9.

Walsh, J. A. Adoption and diffusion processes in the mechanisation of Irish agriculture. In *Ir. Geography*, xxv (1992), pp 33–53.

Waters, John. *Jiving at the crossroads*. Belfast, 1991.

Webb, Marcus (ed.). *Hockey in Trinity: the story of Dublin University Hockey Club, 1893–1993*. Dublin, 1993.

Weir, R. B. In and out of Ireland: the Distillers Company Ltd and the Irish whiskey trade, 1900–39. In *Ir. Econ. & Soc. Hist.*, vii (1980), pp 45–65.

West, T. Sir Horace Plunkett 1854–1932. In *Irish Banking Review 1994*, pp 14–23.

Whelan, Bernadette. *Ireland and the Marshall plan 1947–1957*. Dublin, 2000.

White, Terence de Vere. Social life in Ireland 1927–1937. In *Studies*, liv (1965), pp 74–82.

—— *The Anglo-Irish*. London, 1972.

Witoszek, Nina, and Sheeran, Pat. *Talking to the dead: a study of Irish funerary traditions*. Amsterdam, 1998.

Wolf, James. 'Withholding their due': the dispute between Ireland and Great Britain over unemployed insurance payments to . . . Irish wartime volunteer workers. In *Saothar*, xxi (1996), pp 39–45.

7 HISTORY OF WOMEN

Beale, Jenny. *Women in Ireland: voices of change*. Dublin, 1986.

Beaumont, Caitriona. Irish women and the politics of equality in the 1930s. In *Phoebe*, iii, no. 1 (spring 1991), pp 26–31.

——Women, citizenship and catholicism in the Irish Free State, 1922–1948. In *Women's History Review*, vi (1997), pp 563–84.

Benton, Sarah. Women disarmed: the militarisation of politics in Ireland 1913–23. In *Feminist Review*, l (1995), pp 148–72.

Blackwell, John. *Women in the labour force*. Dublin, 1986. 2nd ed., 1989

Bolger, Patrick (ed.). *And see her beauty shining there: the story of the Irish Country-women*. Dublin, 1986.

Breathnach, Eileen. Women and higher education in Ireland (1879–1914). In *Crane Bag*, ix, no. 1 (1980), pp 47–54.

Brown, Alice, and Galligan, Yvonne. Views from the periphery: changing the political agenda for women in the Republic of Ireland and in Scotland. In *West European Politics*, xvi (1993), pp 165–89.

Clarke, Kathleen. *Revolutionary woman: Kathleen Clarke 1878–1972; an autobiography*. Ed. Helen Litton. Dublin, 1991.

Clear, Caitriona. *Women of the house: women's household work in Ireland 1922–1961: discourses, experiences, memories*. Dublin, 2000.

Connolly, Linda. The women's movement in Ireland 1970–1995: a social movements analysis. In *Irish Journal of Feminist Studies*, i, no. 1 (Mar. 1996), pp 43–77.

Côté, Jane McL. *Fanny and Anna Parnell: Ireland's patriot sisters*. London, 1991.

Cullen, Mary (ed.). *Girls don't do honours: Irish women in education in the 19th and 20th centuries*. Dublin, 1987.

——and Luddy, Maria (ed.). *Women, power and consciousness in 19th-century Ireland: eight biographical studies*. Dublin, 1995.

Curtin, Chris; Jackson, Pauline; and O'Connor, Barbara (ed.). *Gender in Irish society*. Galway, 1987.

Daly, Mary (ed.). *Women together against poverty: the experience of travelling women and settled women in the community*. Dublin, 1988.

Daly, Mary E. Women in the Irish workforce from pre-industrial to modern times. In *Saothar*, vii (1981), pp 74–82.

——Women in the Irish Free State, 1922–1939: the interaction between politics and ideology. In *Journal of Women's History*, vi & vii (1995), pp 99–116.

——*Women and work in Ireland*. [Dublin], 1997.

Darcy, R. The election of women to Dáil Éireann: a formal analysis. In *Irish Political Studies*, iii (1988), pp 63–76.

Dunphy, Richard. Gender and sexuality in Ireland. In *I.H.S.*, xxxi, no. 124 (Nov. 1999), pp 549–57.
Review article.

Eager, Clare. Splitting images—women and the Irish civil service. In *Seirbhís Phoiblí*, xii, no. 1 (Apr. 1991), pp 15–23.

Evans, Richard J. *The feminists: women's emancipation movements in Europe, America and Australasia, 1840–1920*. London and New York, 1977. Revised ed. 1979.

Fox, R. M. *Rebel Irishwomen*. Dublin, 1967. First published 1935.

Gahan, Muriel. Bantracht na Tuaithe 1910–1970. In *Irish Countrywoman: the journal of Bantracht na Tuaithe* (Dec. 1970), pp 21–44.

Gardiner, Frances. Political interest and political participation of Irish women 1922–1992: the unfinished revolution. In *Canadian Journal of Irish Studies*, xviii, no. 1 (July 1992), pp 15–39.

Garrett, Paul Michael. The abnormal flight: the migration and repatriation of Irish unmarried mothers. In *Social History*, xxv, no. 3 (2000), pp 330–43.

Hazelkorn, Ellen. The social and political views of Louie Bennett 1870–1956. In *Saothar*, xiii (1988), pp 32–44.

Holcombe, Lee. *Wives and property: reform of the married women's property law in nineteenth-century England*. Oxford, 1983.

Jones, Mary. *These obstreperous lassies: a history of the Irish Women Workers Union*. Dublin, 1988.

Kirkpatrick, Kathryn (ed.). *Border crossings: Irish women writers and national identities*. Tuscaloosa, Alabama, and Dublin, 2000.

Levenson, Leah, and Natterstad, Jerry H. *Hanna Sheehy Skeffington: Irish feminist*. Syracuse, 1986.

Levine, June. *Sisters: the personal story of an Irish feminist*. Swords, 1982.

Luddy, Maria. Women and the contagious diseases acts, 1864–1886. In *Hist. Ire.*, i, no. 1 (spring 1993), pp 32–4.

—— *Women and philanthropy in nineteenth-century Ireland*. Cambridge, 1995.

—— *Hanna Sheehy Skeffington*. Dublin, 1995.

—— and Murphy, Cliona (ed.). *Women surviving: studies in Irish women's history in the 19th and 20th centuries*. Dublin, 1990.

MacCurtain, Margaret, and Ó Corráin, Donncha (ed.), *Women in Irish society: the historical dimension*. Dublin, 1978.

McCoole, Sinéad. *Guns & chiffon: women revolutionaries and Kilmainham gaol 1916–1923*. Dublin, 2000. 1st ed. 1997.

Macdona, Anne (ed.). *From Newman to new woman: UCD women remembered*. Dublin, 2001.

McKillen, Beth. Irish feminism and nationalist separatism, 1914–1923. In *Éire-Ireland*, xvii, no. 3 (1982), pp 52–67; no. 4 (1982), pp 72–90.

McNamara, Sarah. *Those intrepid United Irishwomen: pioneers of the Irish Countrywomen's Association*. Limerick, 1995.

Mahoney, Rosemary. *Whoredom in Kimmage: Irish women coming of age*. Boston, 1993.

Matthews, Ann. Women and the civil war. In *Ir. Sword*, xx (1997), pp 379–86.

Mitchell, Geraldine. *Deeds not words: the life and work of Muriel Gahan, champion of rural women and craftworkers*. Dublin, 1997.

Moriarty, Theresa. *Work in progress: episodes from the history of Irish women's trade unionism*. Dublin and Belfast, 1994.

Murphy, Cliona. *The women's suffrage movement and Irish society in the early twentieth century*. New York, 1989.

O'Connor, Pat. *Emerging voices: women in contemporary Irish society*. Dublin, 1998.

O'Doherty, Martina A. Dreams, drear, and degradation: the representation of early twentieth-century Irishwomen in selected plays of Teresa Deevy (1894–1963). In *Women's Studies Review*, vii (2000), pp 99–122.

O'Dowd, Anne. Women in rural Ireland in the nineteenth and early twentieth centuries: how the daughters, wives and sisters of small farmers and landless labourers fared. In *Rural History*, v (1994), pp 171–83.

BIBLIOGRAPHY

O'Dowd, Mary, and Wichert, Sabine (ed.). *Chattel, servant or citizen: women's status in church, state and society*. Belfast, 1995. (*Hist. Studies*, xix.)

O'Leary, Eoin. The Irish National Teachers' Organisation and the marriage bar for women national teachers. In *Saothar*, xii (1987), pp 47–52.

O'Neill, Marie. *From Parnell to de Valera: a biography of Jennie Wyse Power, 1858–1941*. Dublin, 1991.

O'Sullivan, Patrick (ed.). *Irish women and Irish migration*. London and New York, 1995. (The Irish World Wide, iv.)

Owens, Rosemary Cullen. *Smashing times: a history of the Irish women's suffrage movement, 1889–1922*. Dublin, 1984.

Rendall, Jane. *The origins of modern feminism: women in Britain, France, and the United States 1780–1860*. Basingstoke, 1985.

Rose, Catherine. *The female experience: the story of the woman movement in Ireland*. Galway, 1975.

Ryan, Louise. A question of loyalty: war, nation, and feminism in early twentieth-century Ireland. In *Women's Studies International Forum*, xx, no. 1 (1997), pp 21–32.

—— 'Furies' and 'die-hards': women and Irish republicanism in the early twentieth century. In *Gender & History*, xi (1999), 256–75.

Sawyer, Roger. *We are but women: women in Ireland's history*. London and New York, 1993.

Sheehy Skeffington, Andrée, and Owens, Rosemary C. (ed.). *Votes for women: Irish women's struggle for the vote*. Dublin, 1975.

Smyth, Ailbhe (ed.). *Irish women's studies reader*. Dublin, 1993.

Swanton, Daisy Lawrenson. *Emerging from the shadow: the lives of Sarah Anne Lawrenson and Lucy Olive Kingston, based on personal diaries 1883–1969*. Dublin, 1994.

Taillon, Ruth. *When history was made: the women of 1916*. Belfast, 1996.

TeBrake, Janet. Irish peasant women in revolt: the Land League years. In *I.H.S.*, xxviii, no. 109 (May 1992), pp 63–80.

Tweedy, Hilda. *A link in the chain: the story of the Irish Housewives Association, 1942–1992*. Dublin, 1992.

Valiulis, Maryann G. Defining their role in the new state: Irishwomen's protest against the juries act of 1927. In *Canadian Journal of Irish Studies*, xviii, no. 1 (July 1992), pp 43–60.

—— Power, gender and identity in the Irish Free State. In *Journal of Women's History*, vi & vii (winter/spring 1995), pp 117–36.

—— and O'Dowd, Mary (ed.). *Women & Irish history: essays in honour of Margaret MacCurtain*. Dublin, 1997.

Ward, Margaret. *Unmanageable revolutionaries: women and Irish nationalism*. London, 1995. 1st ed. Dingle, 1983.

—— From civil rights to women's rights. In Michael Farrell (ed.), *Twenty years on* (Dingle, 1988), pp 122–33.

—— *Hanna Sheehy Skeffington: a life*. Dublin, 1997.

Whelan, Bernadette (ed.). *Women and paid work in Ireland, 1500–1930*. Dublin, 2000.

Wills, Clair. Rocking the cradle?—Women studies and the family in twentieth-century Ireland. In *Bullán*, i, no. 2 (autumn 1994), pp 97–106.
   Review article.

8   HISTORY OF ENGLISH LANGUAGE AND LITERATURE

Agnew, Úna. Patrick Kavanagh: early religious work and devotional influences on his work. In *Clogher Rec.*, xv, no. 1 (1994), pp 51–73.

—— *The mystical imagination of Patrick Kavanagh*. Dublin, 1998.

Alldritt, Keith. *W. B. Yeats: the man and the milieu*. London, 1997.

Alspach, Russell K. *Yeats and Innisfree*. Dublin, 1965.

Attridge, Derek (ed.). *The Cambridge companion to James Joyce*. Cambridge, 1990.

Brown, Terence. *Ireland: a social and cultural history, 1922–79*. London, 1981. Revised ed. (*1922–1985*), London, 1987.

—— New literary histories. In *I.H.S.*, xxx, no. 119 (May 1997), pp 462–70. Review article.

—— *The life of W. B. Yeats*. Oxford and Dublin, 1999.

Cahalan, James. *The Irish novel: a critical history*. Dublin, 1988.

—— *Liam O'Flaherty: a study of the short fiction*. Boston, 1991.

Cairns, David, and Richards, Shaun. *Writing Ireland: colonialism, nationalism and culture*. Manchester, 1988.

Clarke, Austin. *Poetry in modern Ireland*. With illustrations by Louis Le Brocquy. Dublin, 1951. 2nd ed. 1961.

Clissman, Anne. *Flann O'Brien: a critical introduction*. Dublin, 1975.

Clune, Anne, and Hurson, Tess (ed.). *Conjuring complexities: essays on Flann O'Brien*. Belfast, 1997.

Connolly, Peter. *No bland facility: selected writings on literature, religion and censorship*. Ed. James H. Murphy. Gerrards Cross, 1991.

Costello, Peter. *The heart grown brutal: the Irish revolution in literature from Parnell to the death of Yeats, 1891–1939*. Dublin and Totowa, N.J., 1977.

Craig, Patricia. *The Oxford book of Ireland*. Oxford, 1998.

Cronin, Anthony. *Dead as doornails*. Dublin, 1976; revised ed., Dublin, 1999. Postwar literary Dublin.

—— *'No laughing matter': the life and times of Flann O'Brien*. London, 1989.

Cronin, John. *The Anglo-Irish novel. Vol. 2: 1900–1940*. Belfast, 1990. published 1992 as *Irish fiction, 1900–1940*.

Dalsimer, Adele. *Kate O'Brien: a critical study*. Dublin, 1990.

Deane, Séamus. *Celtic revivals: essays in modern Irish literature, 1880–1980*. London, 1985.

—— *A short history of Irish literature*. London and Notre Dame, Ind., 1986.

—— *Irish writers, 1886–1986*. Dublin, 1986.

—— *Strange country: modernity and nationhood in Irish writing since 1790*. Oxford, 1997.

—— (ed.) *The Field Day anthology of Irish writing*. 3 vols. Derry, 1991.

Dolan, T. P. (ed. and compiler). *A dictionary of Hiberno-English: the Irish use of English*. Dublin, 1998.

Donleavy, J. P. *The history of the Ginger Man*. London, 1994.

Dorgan, Theo (ed.). *Irish poetry since Kavanagh*. Dublin, 1996. (Thomas Davis Lectures.)

Egan, Desmond. Peter Connolly (1927–1987). In *The Furrow*, xxxviii (1987), pp 428–35.
Professor of English, St Patrick's College, Maynooth.

Ellmann, Richard. *Yeats, the man and the masks*. New York, 1948. Other eds. 1958, 1961.

——*James Joyce*. 2nd revised ed., Oxford, 1983. First published 1959.

——and Feidelson, Charles (ed.). *The modern tradition*. Oxford, 1965.

Fairhall, James. *James Joyce and the question of history*. Cambridge, 1993.

Fallon, Brian. *An age of innocence: Irish culture, 1930–1960*. Dublin, 1999.

Foster, John Wilson. *Colonial consequences: essays on Irish literature and culture*. Dublin, 1991.

Foster, R. F. *W. B. Yeats: a life. I: The apprentice mage, 1865–1914*. Oxford, 1997.

Garratt, Robert F. *Modern Irish poetry: tradition and continuity from Yeats to Heaney*. Berkeley and London, [1986?].

Garvin, John. *James Joyce's disunited kingdom and the Irish dimension*. Dublin, 1976.

Gibbon, Monk (ed.). *The living torch: A.E.* [George William Russell]. With an introductory essay. London, 1937.

Gogarty, Oliver St John. *William Butler Yeats: a memoir*. With a preface by Myles Dillon. Dublin, 1963.

Gonzales, Alexander G. (ed.). *Modern Irish writers: a bio-critical sourcebook*. Westport, Conn., and London, 1997.

Harmon, Maurice. *Sean O'Faolain: a critical introduction*. Notre Dame, Ind., and London, 1966. Revised ed. 1984.

——The era of inhibitions: Irish literature 1920–60. In *Emory University Quarterly*, xxii (1966), pp 18–28.

——*Austin Clarke, 1896–1974: a critical introduction*. Dublin, 1989.

——*Sean O'Faolain*. London, 1994.

Higgins, Michael D. The gombeen man in Irish fact and fiction. In *Études Irlandaises*, x (Dec. 1985), pp 31–52.

Hone, Joseph M. *W. B. Yeats, 1865–1939*. 2nd ed., London, 1962. First published 1942.

Howes, Majorie. *Yeats's nations: gender, class, and Irishness*. Cambridge, 1996.

Igoe, Vivien. *A literary guide to Dublin: writers in Dublin: literary associations and anecdotes*. London, 1994.

Jeffares, A. Norman. *W. B. Yeats: man and poet*. London, 1949.

——*Anglo-Irish literature*. Dublin, 1982.

Joyce, P. W. *English as we speak it in Ireland*. With introduction and revised bibliography by T. P. Dolan. Portmarnock, 1979. First ed. 1910.

Kavanagh, Peter. *Sacred keeper: a biography of Patrick Kavanagh*. The Curragh, Co. Kildare, 1979.

——(ed.) *Patrick Kavanagh: man & poet*. Orono, Me., 1986.

Kearney, Colbert. *The writings of Brendan Behan*. Dublin, 1977.

Kennelly, Brendan (ed.). *The Penguin book of Irish verse*. 2nd ed. Harmondsworth, 1981. First ed. 1970.

Kenner, Hugh. *The stoic comedians: Flaubert, Joyce and Beckett*. Berkeley, 1974.

Kenny, Herbert A. *Literary Dublin: a history*. 2nd ed., Dublin, 1991. First ed. 1974.

Kiberd, Declan. *Anglo-Irish attitudes*. Derry, 1984.

—— *Idir dhá chultúr*. Dublin, 1993.

—— *Inventing Ireland: the literature of the modern nation*. London, 1995. 2nd ed. 1996.

—— *Irish classics*. London, 2000.

Kiely, Benedict. *Drink to the bird: a memoir*. London, 1999. 1st ed. 1991.

Kinsella, Thomas (ed.). *The new Oxford book of Irish verse*. Oxford, 1989. First published 1986.

Komesu, Okifumi, and Sekine, Masaru (ed.). *Irish writers and politics*. Gerrards Cross, 1990.

Lee, Hermione. *Elizabeth Bowen*. London, 1981; revised ed., London, 1999.

Levenson, Leah. *The four seasons of Mary Lavin*. Dublin, 1998.

Lloyd, David. *Anomalous states: Irish writing and the post-colonial moment*. Dublin, 1993.

Logan, John (ed.). *With warmest love: lectures for Kate O'Brien, 1984–93*. Limerick, 1994.

Longley, Edna. *The living stream: literature & revisionism in Ireland*. Newcastle upon Tyne, 1994.

Lucy, Seán (ed.). *Irish poets in English: the Thomas Davis lectures on Anglo-Irish poetry*. Cork, 1973. (Thomas Davis Lectures.)

Lyons, J. B. A Gogarty/Gregory correspondence, 1910–30. In *Galway Arch. Soc. Jn.*, xlix (1997), pp 141–58.

McCartney, Anne. *Francis Stuart: face to face: a critical study*. Belfast, 2000.

McCormack, W. J. *From Burke to Beckett: ascendancy, tradition and betrayal in literary history*. Cork, 1994. Previously published as *Ascendancy and tradition in Anglo-Irish literary history from 1789 to 1939*. Oxford, 1985.

—— *Dissolute characters: Irish literary history through Balzac, Sheridan, Le Fanu, Yeats and Bowen*. Manchester and New York, 1993.

—— Convergent criticism: the biographia literaria of Vivian Mercier and the state of Irish literary history. In *Bullán*, ii, no. 1 (summer 1995), pp 79–100.

McHugh, Roger, and Harmon, Maurice. *Short history of Anglo-Irish literature from its origins to the present day*. Dublin, 1982.

MacKenna, Dolores. *William Trevor: the writer and his work*. Dublin, 1999.

McKeon, Jim. *Frank O'Connor: a life*. Edinburgh, 1998.

MacMahon, Bryan. *The master: an autobiography*. Swords, 1992.

MacNeice, Louis. *The poetry of W. B. Yeats*. London, 1967.

Magee, W. K. *A memoir of A. E.: George William Russell*. By John Eglinton [pseud.]. London, 1937.

Maddox, Brenda. *George's ghosts: a new life of W. B. Yeats*. London, 1999.

Mahon, Derek (ed.). *Modern Irish poetry*. London, 1972.

Masefield, John. *Some memories of W. B. Yeats*. Dublin, 1940. Reprinted Shannon, 1971.

Mason, Ellsworth, and Ellmann, Richard (ed.). *The critical writings of James Joyce*. New York, 1959. Reprinted with foreword by Guy Davenport, 1996.

Matthews, Steven. *Irish poetry: politics, history, negotiation: the evolving debate, 1969 to the present*. Basingstoke, 1997.

Mercier, Vivian. *The Irish comic tradition*. Oxford, 1962.

—— The Irish short story and oral tradition. In Ray B. Browne, W. J. Roscelli, and R. Loftus (ed.), The *Celtic cross: studies in Irish culture and literature* (Lafayette, Ind., 1964), pp 98–116.

Mercier, Vivian. *Modern Irish literature: sources and founders*. Ed. Eilís Dillon. Oxford, 1994.

Montague, John (ed.). *Faber book of Irish verse*. London, 1974.

Muldoon, Paul (ed.). *Faber book of contemporary Irish poetry*. London, 1986.

Nolan, Emer. *James Joyce and nationalism*. London, 1995.

O'Brennan, Kathleen. Alice Furlong—some memories. In *I.B.L.*, xxx (1948), pp 105–6.

O'Brien, Conor Cruise. *Writers and politics*. London, 1965.

O'Connor, Frank. A. E.: a portrait. In *The Bell*, i, no. 2 (1940), pp 49–57.

—— The old age of a poet. In *The Bell*, i, no. 5 (1941), pp 7–18. W. B. Yeats.

O'Donnell, Peadar. *The gates flew open*. London, 1932. Cork, 1966.

O'Faolain, Sean. *Vive moi! an autobiography*. Boston, 1964.

O'Keeffe, Timothy (ed.). *Myles: portraits of Brian O'Nolan*. London, 1973.

Ó Muirithe, Diarmaid (ed.). *The English language in Ireland*. Dublin and Cork, 1977; reprinted 1978. (Thomas Davis Lectures.)

—— *A dictionary of Anglo-Irish: words and phrases from Gaelic in the English of Ireland*. Blackrock, 1996.

Oshima, Shotaro. *W. B. Yeats and Japan*. Tokyo, 1965.

Pyle, Hilary. *James Stephens: his work and an account of his life*. London, 1965.

Porter, Raymond, and Brophy, James (ed.). *Modern Irish literature: essays in honour of W. Y. Tindall*. New York, 1972.

Quinn, Antoinette. *Patrick Kavanagh: born-again romantic*. Dublin, 1991.

Rafroidi, Patrick, and Brown, T. (ed.). *The Irish short story*. Lille, 1979.

Rauchbauer, Otto (ed.). *Ancestral voices: the 'big house' in Anglo-Irish literature: a collection of interpretations*. Dublin, 1992.

Reynolds, Lorna. *Kate O'Brien: a literary portrait*. Gerrards Cross, 1987.

Rivoallan, A. *Littérature irlandaise contemporaine*. Paris, 1939.

Ryan, John. *Remembering how we stood: bohemian Dublin at the mid-century*. Dublin, 1975.

Ryan, Ray (ed.). *Writing in the Irish Republic: literature, culture, politics 1949–1999*. Basingstoke and New York, 2000.

Salvadori, Corinna. *Yeats and Castiglione: poet and courtier*. Dublin, 1965.

Sampson, Denis. *Brian Moore: the chameleon novelist*. Dublin, 1998.

Sheeran, Patrick F. *The novels of Liam O'Flaherty: a study in romantic realism*. Dublin, 1976.

Spoo, Robert. *James Joyce and the language of history*. New York and Oxford, 1994.

Telfer, Giles W. L. *Yeats' idea of the Gael*. Dublin, 1965.

Tierney, Michael. A prophet of mystic nationalism—A. E. [George William Russell]. In *Studies*, xxvi (1937), pp 568–80.

Tomelty, Joseph. Patrick McGill. In *Irish Bookman*, i, no. 12 (1947), pp 25–32.

Trevor, William. *A writer's Ireland: landscape in literature*. London, 1984.

Ussher, Arland. *Three great Irishmen: Shaw, Yeats, Joyce*. London, 1952.

Vance, Norman. *Irish literature: a social history*. Oxford, 1990. 2nd ed. Dublin, 1999.

Walshe, Éibhear (ed.). *'Ordinary people dancing': essays on Kate O'Brien*. Cork, 1993.

—— *Sex, nation and dissent in Irish writing*. Cork, 1997. Gay and lesbian literature.

Warner, Alan. *A guide to Anglo-Irish literature*. Dublin and New York, 1981.

Watson, George. *Irish identity and the Irish literary revival*. 2nd ed., Washington, 1994. First published 1979.

Weekes, Anne O. *Irish women writers: an uncharted tradition*. Lexington, Ky., 1991.

Whitaker, Thomas R. *Swan and shadow: Yeats's dialogue with history*. Chapel Hill, N.C., 1964.

9 HISTORY OF IRISH LANGUAGE AND LITERATURE

Bartlett, Thomas; Curtin, Chris; O'Dwyer, Riana; and Ó Tuathaigh, Gearóid (ed.). *Irish studies: a general introduction*. Dublin and Totowa, N. J., 1988.

Butler, Matthew. *Fifty golden years: history of the Gaelic League in Waterford*. Waterford, 1944.

Caird, Donald. A view of the revival of the Irish language. In *Éire-Ireland*, xxv, no. 2 (1990), pp 96–108.
The Church of Ireland and language revival.

Comerford, R. V. Nation, nationalism and the Irish language. In Thomas E. Hachey and L. J. McCaffrey (ed.), *Perspectives on Irish nationalism* (Lexington, Ky., 1989), pp 20–41.

Corkery, Daniel. *The fortunes of the Irish language*. Cork, 1968.

de Blaghd, Earnán. *The state and the language*. Dublin, [1950]; 2nd ed., 1951.

Delap, Breandán. *Úrscéalta stairiúla na Gaeilge*. Dublin, 1993.
Twentieth-century Irish fiction.

Denvir, Gearóid. *Cadhan aonair: saothar liteartha Mháirtín Uí Chadhain*. Dublin, 1987.
Máirtín Ó Cadhain (1906–70), writer.

——One hundred years of Conradh na Gaeilge. In *Éire-Ireland*, xxx, no. 1 (1995), pp 105–29.

——*Litríocht agus pobal*. Indreabhán, Co. Galway, 1997.

——(ed.). *Aistí Phádraic Uí Chonaire*. Indreabhán, Co. Galway, 1978.
Pádraic Ó Conaire (1882–1928), writer .

de Paor, Louis. *Faoin mblaoisc bheag sin: an aigneolaíocht i scéalta Mháirtín Uí Chadhain*. Dublin, 1991.
Máirtín Ó Cadhain, writer.

de Paor, Pádraig. *Tionscnamh filíochta Nuala Ní Dhomhnaill*. Dublin, 1997.
Nuala Ní Dhomhnaill (1952–), poet.

Durkacz, V. E. *The decline of the Celtic languages: a study of linguistic and cultural conflict in Scotland, Wales, and Ireland from the reformation to the twentieth century*. Edinburgh, 1983.

Fischer, Joachim, and Dillon, John (ed.). *The correspondence of Myles Dillon 1922–1925: Irish–German relations and Celtic studies*. Dublin, 1999.

Greene, David. Fifty years of writing in Irish. In *Studies*, lv (1966), pp 51–9.

——The Irish language movement. In Michael Hurley (ed.). *Irish anglicanism 1869–1969* (Dublin, 1970), pp 110–19.

Hindley, Reg. *The death of the Irish language: a qualified obituary*. London and New York, 1990.

——Clear Island (Oileán Chléire) in 1958: a study in geolinguistic transition. In *Ir. Geography*, xxvii (1994), pp 97–106.

Johnson, Nuala C. Building a nation: an examination of the Irish Gaeltacht commission report of 1926. In *Journal of Historical Geography*, xix (1993), pp 157–68.

Jordan, John (ed.). *The pleasures of Gaelic literature*. Cork, 1977.

Kimpton, Bettina N. Rúndiamhair na súl: cumhacht agus traidisiún in *An tsraith ar lár*. In *Oghma*, vi (1994), pp 106–10.

Mac Aodha Bhuí, Iarla. *Diarmaid Ó Súilleabháin: saothar próis*. Dublin, 1992.
Diarmaid Ó Súilleabháin (1932–85), writer.

Mac Aonghusa, Proinsias, and de Bhaldraithe, Tomás. *Dáithi Ó hUaithne: cuimhní cairde*. Dublin, 1994.
David Greene (1915–81), Irish language scholar.

MacAulay, Donald. *The Celtic languages*. Cambridge, 1992.

McCone, Kim, *et al.* (ed.). *Stair na Gaeilge: in ómós do Pádraig Ó Fiannachta*. Maynooth, 1994.
Essays in honour of Pádraig Ó Fiannachta, professor of Irish, St Patrick's College, Maynooth.

Mac Conghail, Muiris. *The Blaskets: people and literature*. Dublin, 1987. 2nd ed. 1994.

Mac Congáil, Nollaig (ed.). *Scríbhneoireacht n gConallach*. Dublin, 1990.
Irish literature.

Mac Craith, Mícheál. *An t-oileán rúin agus muir an dáin: staidéar ar fhilíocht Mháirtín Uí Dhireáin*. Dublin, 1993.
Máirtín Ó Direáin (1910–88), poet.

Mac Giolla Léith, Caoimhín (ed.). *Cime mar chách: aistí ar Mháirtín Ó Direáin*. Dublin, 1993.

Mac Giolla Phádraig, Brian. Gléasadh oideachas nua: na coláistí Gaedhilge. In *Éire: Bliainiris Ghaedheal, 1943*, pp 61–70.
Colleges to prepare Irish-speakers for teaching, etc.

Mac Mathúna, Liam. *Dúchas agus dóchas: scéal na Gaeilge i mBaile Átha Cliath*. Dublin, 1991.
Irish-language revival in Dublin.

Mag Shamhráin, Antain. *Litríocht, léitheoireacht, critic: príomhghnéithe na critice in 'Irisleabhar Mhá Nuad', 1966–1978*. Dublin, 1986.
Irish-language periodical.

——Ní mise Robert Schumann. In *Oghma*, iv (1992), pp 82–9.

de Mórdha, Mícheál (ed.). *Bláithín = Flower*. An Daingean, 1998.
Robin Flower (1881–1946).

Murphy, Gerard. Irish in our schools, 1922–45. In *Studies*, xxxvii (1948), pp 420–28.

Ní Annracháin, Máire. An tsuibiacht abú, an tsuibiacht amú. In *Oghma*, vi (1994), pp 11–22.
Twentieth-century Irish literature.

——Biddy agus an Bandia. In P. Riggs, B. Ó Conchúir, and S. Ó Coileáin (ed.), *Saoi na héigse: aistí in ómós do Sheán Ó Tuama* (Dublin, 2000), pp 339–57.
Poetry of Biddy Jenkinson.

——Seanphoirt, gléas úr: athnuachan an traidisiúin liteartha sa Ghaeilge san fhichiú h-aois. In *Léachtaí Cholm Cille*, xxxi (2001), pp 110–27.

Twentieth-century Irish literature.

——and Nic Dhiarmada, Bríona (ed.). *Téacs agus comhthéacs: gnéithe de chritic na Gaeilge*. Cork, 1998.
Literary criticism and literature in Irish.

Ní Chéilleachair, Máire (ed.). *Tomás Ó Criomhthain 1855–1937*. An Daingean, 1998.
Author of *An t-oileánach* (*The islandman*) (1934).

Nic Dhiarmada, Bríona. Immram sa tsícé: filíocht Nuala Ní Dhomhnaill agus próiseas an indibhidithe. In *Oghma*, v (1993), pp 78–94.
Nuala Ní Dhomhnaill, poet.

Ní Dhonnchadha, Aisling. *An gearrscéal sa Ghaeilge 1898–1940*. Dublin, 1981.
The short story in Irish.

Nic Eoin, Máirín. *An litríocht réigiúnach*. Dublin, 1982.
Regional literature.

——*Eoghan Ó Tuairisc: beatha agus saothar*. Dublin, 1988.
Eoghan Ó Tuairisc (1919–82), writer.

——*Ó An t-oileánach go dtí Kinderszenen*: an toise dírbheathaisnéiseach i bprósscríbhneoireacht na Gaeilge. In *The Irish Review*, no. 13 (winter 1992/3), pp 14–21.
Autobiography and fiction.

Ní Ghacháin, Mairéad. *Lúise Gabhánach Ní Dhufaigh agus scoil Bhríde*. Dublin, 1993.
Louise Gavan Duffy (1884–1969), founder of Irish-language secondary school for girls.

Nic Ghiolla Phádraig, Máire; Brady, Joseph; and Parker, Anthony. The hidden Dublin: an analysis of the distribution of Irish-speakers in the Dublin metropolitan region. In *Administration*, xxxvii (1989), pp 7–24.
Based on 1971 and 1981 census.

Nic Pháidín, Caoilfhionn. *Fáinne an Lae agus an athbheochan, 1898–1900*. Dublin, 1998.
Irish-language periodical.

Nugent, Martin. *Drámaí Eoghain Uí Thuairisc*. Maynooth, 1984.

Ó hAodha, Donncha A. An branar á chur: *An branar gan cur* agus an nouveau roman. In *Oghma*, vi (1994), pp 45–56.
Fiction in Irish.

O'Brien, Frank, and Mac Dhubháin, Aodh (ed.). *Filíocht Ghaeilge na linne seo: staidéar criticiúil*. Dublin, 1968. [Poetry in Irish].

Ó Buachalla, Breandán. Canóin na creille: an file ar leaba a bháis. In Máirín Ní Dhonnchadha (ed.), *Nua-léamha: gnéithe de chultúr, stair agus polaitíocht na hÉireann c.1600–c.1900* (Dublin, 1996), pp 149–69.
Poetry in Irish.

Ó Buachalla, Séamas. Educational policy and the role of the Irish language from 1831 to 1981. In *European Journal of Education*, xix, no. 1 (1984), pp 75–92.

Ó Cadhain, Máirtín. *'Páipéir bhána agus páipéir bhreaca'*. Dublin, 1969.
Essays and lectures on the Irish language.

O'Callaghan, Margaret. Language, nationality and cultural identity in the Irish Free State, 1922–7: the *Irish Statesman* and the *Catholic Bulletin* reappraised. In *I.H.S.*, xxiv, no. 94 (Nov. 1984), pp 226–45.

Ó Ciosáin, Éamon. *An t-Éireannach 1934–1937: nuachtán sóisialach Gaeltachta.* Dublin, 1993.
Socialist newspaper.
Ó Coileáin, Seán. *Seán Ó Ríordáin, beatha agus saothar.* Dublin, 1982.
Seán Ó Ríordáin (1917–77), poet.
Ó Cruadhlaoich, Gearóid. An nua-fhilíocht Ghaeilge: dearcadh dána. In *Innti*, x (1986), pp 63–66.
Poetry in Irish.
Ó Cuív, Brian. *Irish dialects and Irish-speaking districts: three lectures.* Dublin, 1951.
——(ed.). *A view of the Irish language.* Dublin, 1969. (Thomas Davis Lectures.)
Ó Doibhlin, Breandán. *Aistí critice agus cultúir.* Dublin, [c.1973].
——*Aistí critice agus cultúir II.* Belfast, 1997.
Ó Droighneáin, Muiris. *Taighde i gcomhair stair litridheachta na Nua-Ghaeidhilge.* Dublin, 1936.
History of Irish literature from 1882.
Ó Dúbhda, Peadar. *Stair na craoibhe: Dún Dealgan (1899–1939).* Dundalk, 1940.
Ó Dúill, Gréagóir. Infinite grounds for hope? Poetry in Irish today. In *Poetry Ireland*, xxxix (1993), pp 10–27.
Ó Fiannachta, Pádraig (ed.). *An nuafhilíocht. Léachtaí Cholm Cille*, xvii (Maynooth, 1986).
Poetry in Irish.
——*Litríocht na Gaeltachta. Léachtaí Cholm Cille*, xix (Maynooth, 1989).
Literature of the Gaeltacht.
——*An t-úrscéal sa Ghaeilge. Léachtaí Cholm Cille*, xxi (Maynooth, 1991).
The novel in Irish.
——Nessa Ní Shéaghdha (1916–93). In *Éigse*, xxvii (1993), pp 139–40.
Irish-language scholar.
Ó Giollagáin, Conchúr (ed.). *Stairsheanchas Mhicil Chonraí: ón Máimín go Ráth Chairn.* Indreabhán, Co. Galway, 1999.
Reminiscences of the Meath Gaeltacht.
Ó Glaisne, Risteárd. *Gaeilge i gColáiste na Tríonóide, 1592–1992.* Dublin, 1992.
The Irish language in Trinity College.
Ó Háinle, Cathal. *Promhadh pinn.* Maynooth, 1978.
Essays on Irish literature.
——(ed.). *Gearrscéalta an Phiarsaigh.* Dublin, 1979.
Short stories of Patrick Pearse.
——(ed.). *Criostalú: aistí ar shaothar Mháirtín Uí Chadhain.* Dublin, 1998.
Ó Laoghaire, Diarmuid (ed.) *Náisiún na hÉireann: mar a bhí agus mar atá.* Dublin, 1993.
Irish language and culture.
O'Leary, Philip. *The prose literature of the Gaelic revival 1881–1921: ideology and innovation.* University Park, Penn., 1994.
Ó Lúing, Seán. Robin Flower (1881–1946). In *Studies*, lxx, nos 278–9 (1981), pp 121–34.
——*Saoir theagan.* Dublin, 1989.
Irish language, twentieth century.

Ó Muirithe, Diarmaid. *A dictionary of Anglo-Irish: words and phrases from Gaelic in the English of Ireland*. Blackrock, 1996.

Ó Néill, Séamus and Ó Dubhthaigh, Bernárd (ed.). *Colaiste Uladh: leabhar cuimhne iubhaile leith-chéad bliain, 1906–1956*. Wexford, 1956.
Irish-speaking college, Cloghaneely, Co. Donegal.

Ó Riagáin, Pádraig. *Language maintenance and language shift as strategies of social reproduction: Irish in the Corca Dhuibhne Gaeltacht, 1926–1986*. Dublin, 1992.
Dingle peninsula.

—— *Language policy and social reproduction: Ireland, 1893–1993*. Oxford, 1997.

Ó Siadhail, Pádraig. *Stair dhrámaíocht na Gaeilge 1900–1970*. Indreabhán, Co. Galway, 1993.
Drama in Irish.

Ó Tuama, Seán (ed.). *The Gaelic League idea*. Cork, 1972. (Thomas Davis Lectures.)

—— *Filí faoi sceimhle: Seán Ó Riordáin agus Aogán Ó Rathaille*. Dublin, 1978.
Poetry in Irish.

—— *Cúirt, tuath agus bruachbhaile: aistí agus dréachtaí liteartha*. Dublin, 1990.
Irish literature.

Ó Tuathaigh, Gearóid. Language, literature and culture in Ireland since the war. In J. J. Lee (ed.), *Ireland 1945–70* (Dublin, 1979), pp 111–23.

—— Ó Laoire, Liam; and Ua Súilleabháin (ed.). *Pobal na Gaeltachta: a scéal agus a dhán*. Galway, 2000.
History of the Gaeltacht.

Poetry Ireland Review, xxxix (autumn 1993). Special issue: contemporary poetry in Irish.

Prút, Liam. *Máirtín Ó Direáin: file tréadúil*. Maynooth, 1982.

Riggs, Pádraigín. *Pádraic Ó Conaire: deoraí*. Dublin, 1994.

—— Adhlacadh ma mháthar. In P. Riggs, B. Ó Conchúir, and S. Ó Coileáin (ed.), *Saoi na héigse: aistí in ómós do Sheán Ó Tuama* (Dublin, 2000), pp 327–37.

Titley, Alan. *Máirtín Ó Cadhain: clár saothair*. Dublin, 1975.

—— *An t-úrscéal Gaeilge*. Dublin, 1991.
The novel in Irish.

—— *Chun doirne: rogha aistí*. Belfast, 1996.
Irish literature.

Uí Mhorónaigh, Eibhlín, and Prút, Liam (ed.). *Ó ghlúin go glúin: scéal Chonradh na Gaeilge in Aonach Urmhumhan, 1901–93*. [Dublin], 1993.
The Gaelic League in Nenagh, Co. Tipperary.

10 HISTORY OF EDUCATION

Akenson, D. H. *A mirror to Kathleen's face: education in independent Ireland 1922–1960*. Montreal and Dublin, 1975.

Bailey, K. C. *A history of Trinity College Dublin, 1892–1945*. Dublin, 1947.

Bowden, Brian. *200 years of a future through education: a history of the Masonic Girls' Charity*. [Dublin, 1992].
1792–1992.

Boyd, Andrew. *Fermenting elements: the labour colleges in Ireland, 1924–1964*. Belfast, 1999.

Broderick, Terri, and Duggan, Regina. *Origins and development of St Mary's School for Deaf Girls, Cabra.* Dublin, [1996].

Casteleyn, Mary. *A history of literacy and libraries in Ireland.* Aldershot, 1984.

Centenary of the death of Edmund Ignatius Rice, founder of the Christian Brothers of Ireland. Dublin, 1944.

Clancy, Patrick. *Participation in higher education: a national survey.* Dublin, 1982.

Coldrey, Barry. 'A strange mixture of caring and corruption': residential care in the Christian Brothers orphanages and industrial schools during their last phase, 1940s to 1960s. In *History of Education*, xxix, no. 4 (2000), pp 343–55.

Coolahan, John. *Irish education: its history and structure.* Dublin, 1981.

—— *The ASTI and post-primary education in Ireland 1909–84.* Dublin, 1984.

—— The commission on higher education, 1967, and third-level policy in contemporary Ireland. In *Irish Educational Studies*, ix, no. 1 (1990), pp 1–12.

Crean, Edward J. *Breaking the silence: the education of the deaf in Ireland, 1816–1996.* Dublin, 1997.

Cunningham, John. *St Jarlath's College, Tuam, 1800–2000.* Tuam, 1999.

Dillon, Thomas. The origin and early history of the national university, part II. In *University Rev.*, i, no. 6 (1955), pp 12–28.

Donovan, Patrick. *The Christian Brothers in New Ross, first century, 1849–1949.* Wexford, 1952.

Dowling, Patrick J. *A history of Irish education: a study in conflicting loyalties.* Cork, 1971.

Drudy, Sheelagh, and Lynch, Kathleen. *Schools and society in Ireland.* Dublin, 1993.

Duncan, G. A. The law school [in Trinity College, Dublin] during the last half century. In *Hermathena*, lviii (1941), pp 30–39.

Durcan, Thomas J. *History of Irish education from 1800 (with special reference to manual instruction).* Bala, Merioneth, 1972.

Durkan, Regina. The colleges of education. In *Social Studies*, vii (1983), pp 211–21.

Farragher, Seán P., and Wyer, Annraoi. *Blackrock College 1860–1995.* Dublin, 1995.

Farren, Sean. *The politics of Irish education 1920–65.* Belfast, 1995.

Fenton, Seamus. *It all happened.* Dublin, 1948.
    Reminiscences of a school inspector.

Fitzpatrick, Georgina. *St Andrew's College 1894–1994: ardens sed virens.* Blackrock, 1994.

Fleming, John; Murray, Donal; and O'Grady, Sean. *St Munchin's College Limerick, 1796–1996.* Limerick, 1996.

Fleischmann, Aloys. University appointments. In *University Rev.*, i, no. 11 (1957), pp 3–16.

Foley, Tadhg (ed.). *From Queen's College to National University: essays on the academic history of QCG/ UCG/ NUI Galway.* Dublin, 1999.

Griffey, Nicholas. *From silence to speech: fifty years with the deaf.* Dublin, 1994.
    Education of the deaf in Ireland.

Gwynn, Denis, and Hogan, James. Some afterthoughts on the Newman centenary celebrations. In *University Rev.*, i, no. 2 (autumn 1954), pp 3–9.

Hoare, Peter A. Writing our history: the project for a history of libraries in Britain and Ireland. In *Library History*, xi (1995), pp 86–95.

Hyland, Áine, and Milne, Kenneth (ed.). *Irish educational documents. Vol. 2: a selection of extracts . . . relating to the history of education from 1922 to 1991*. Dublin, 1991.

Irish National Teachers' Organisation: eighty years of progress. Dublin, 1948.

Johnson, Nuala C. Nation-building, language and education: the geography of teacher recruitment in Ireland 1925–55. In *Political Geography*, xi (1992), pp 170–89.

Jones, Valerie. The attitudes of the Church of Ireland Board of Education to textbooks in national schools, 1922–1967. In *Irish Educational Studies*, xi (1992), pp 72–81.

Kenny, John. The visitation in University College, Dublin. In *University Rev.*, ii, no. 11 (1961), pp 9–29.

Logan, John (ed.). *Teachers' union: the T.U.I. and its forerunners 1899–1994*. Dublin, 1999.

Luce, J. V. *Trinity College, Dublin: the first 400 years*. Dublin, 1992.

McCartney, Donal. *The National University of Ireland and Eamon de Valera*. Dublin, 1983.

—— *UCD. A national idea: the history of University College, Dublin*. Dublin, 1999.

McDowell, R. B., and Webb, D. A. *Trinity College Dublin 1592–1952: an academic history*. Cambridge, 1982.

McElligott, T. J. *Education in Ireland*. Dublin, 1966.

McGee, Eugene. *St Mel's of Longford: 1865–1990*. Longford, 1996.

McMillan, Norman (ed.). *Prometheus's fire: a history of scientific and technological education in Ireland*. Carlow, 2000.

MacNamara, John. *Bilingualism and primary education: a study of Irish experience*. Edinburgh, 1966.

McQuaid, John Charles. *Higher education for catholics*. Dublin, 1961.

—— *Catholic education: its functions and scope*. Dublin, 1962.

Mac Shamhráin, A. S. Ideological conflict and historical interpretation: the problem of history in Irish primary education, c.1900–1930. In *Irish Educational Studies*, x (1991), pp 229–43.

Meenan, James. The universities. I—University College Dublin. II—The University of Dublin: Trinity College. The universities—III. In *Stat. Soc. Ire. Jn.*, xvii (1942–7), pp 460–81, 594–607, xviii (1947–52), pp 349–61.

Motherway, Anthony. Developing the history curriculum in the primary school, 1922–1986. In *Irish Educational Studies*, vii, no. 2 (1988), pp 35–46.

Mulcahy, D. G. *Curriculum and policy in Irish post-primary education*. Dublin, 1981.

—— and O'Sullivan, Denis (ed.). *Irish educational policy: process and substance*. Dublin, 1989.

Murphy, James H. (ed.). *Nos autem: Castleknock College and its contribution*. Dublin, 1996.

Murphy, John A. *The College: a history of Queen's/University College Cork, 1845–1995*. Cork, 1996.

Nic Craith, Mairéad. Primary education on the Great Blasket island, 1864–1940. In *Kerry Hist. Soc. Jn.*, xxviii (1995), pp 77–137.

Ó Buachalla, Séamas (ed.). *A significant Irish educationalist: the educational writings of P. H. Pearse*. Dublin and Cork, 1980.

Ó Buachalla, Séamas. *Education policy in twentieth-century Ireland.* Dublin, 1988.

O'Byrne, Mairin. Libraries and librarianship in Ireland. In *Administration*, xvi (1968), pp 148–54.

O'Cleirigh, Noel. *Ninety years of technical education in an Irish maritime town: the story of Arklow Community College, 1905–1995.* Arklow, 1995.

O'Connor, Anne V., and Parkes, Susan M. *Gladly learn and gladly teach: Alexandra College and School 1866–1966.* Tallaght, 1984.

O'Connor, Seán. Post-primary education: now and in the future. In *Studies*, lvii, no. 227 (1968), pp 233–51.

——*A troubled sky: reflections on the Irish education scene, 1957–1968.* Dublin, 1986.

O'Donoghue, Thomas A. The Roman Catholic ethos of Irish secondary schools, 1924–62, and its implications for teaching and school organisation. In *Journal of Educational Administration and History*, xxii, no. 2 (1990), pp 27–37.

——*The catholic church and the secondary school curriculum in Ireland, 1922–1962.* Frankfurt am Main, 2000.

O'Hara, Bernard. *Regional Technical College Galway: the first 21 years.* Galway, 1993.

O'Sullivan, John M. Dr Denis J. Coffey, president of University College, Dublin, 1909–40. In *Studies*, xxxiv (1945), pp 145–57.

O'Sullivan, M. D. The centenary of Galway College (the text of a lecture delivered in 1949). In *Galway Arch. Soc. Jn.*, li (1999), 24–42.

Parkes, Susan M. *Kildare Place: the history of the Church of Ireland Training College, 1811–1969.* Dublin, 1984.

Purser, Olive. *Women in Dublin University, 1904–1954.* Dublin, 1954.

Quane, Michael. D'Israeli school, Rathvilly [Co. Carlow, 1826–1939]. In *R.S.A.I. Jn.*, lxxviii (1948), pp 11–23.

Raftery, Mary, and O'Sullivan, Eoin. *Suffer the little children: the inside story of Ireland's industrial schools.* Dublin, 1999.

Robinson, Lennox. How the county libraries began. In *The Bell*, i, no. 1 (1940), pp 2–32.

Ryan, Desmond. St Enda's—fifty years after. In *University Rev.*, ii, nos 3–4 (1958), pp 82–90.

Ryan, Liam. Social dynamite: a study of early school leavers. In *Christus Rex*, xxi, no. 1 (Jan. 1967), pp 7–44.

Sheehan, Thomas W. Éire modernizes teacher education. In *Catholic Educational Review*, xliv (1946), pp 529–34.
    1922–44.

Tierney, Michael. Universities: English and Irish. In *I.E.R.*, lxiii (1944), pp 145–54.

——(ed.). *Struggle with fortune: a miscellany for the centenary of the Catholic University of Ireland, 1854–1954.* [Dublin, 1954].

West, Trevor. *Midleton College, 1696–1996: a tercentenary history.* Midleton, Co. Cork, 1996.

White, G. K. *A history of St Columba's College, 1843–1974.* [Dublin], 1980.

Whiteside, Lesley. *A history of the King's Hospital.* 2nd ed., Palmerstown, Dublin, 1985. First published 1975.

Wigham, Maurice J. *Newtown School Waterford, 1798–1998: a history.* Waterford, 1998.

11 HISTORY OF IDEAS

Bell, Desmond. Culture and politics in Ireland: postmodern revisions. In *History of European Ideas*, xvi (1993), pp 141–6.

Boyce, D. George. *Nationalism in Ireland*. 3rd ed., London, 1995. 1st ed. 1982.

Cronin, Mike. 'Putting new wine into old bottles': the Irish right and the embrace of European social thinking in the early 1930s. In *European History Quarterly*, xxvii (1997), pp 93–125.

Cronin, Seán. *Irish nationalism: a history of its roots and ideology*. Dublin, 1980.

Curtin, Chris; Kelly, Mary; and O'Dowd, Liam (ed.). *Culture and ideology in Ireland*. Galway, 1984.

Dowling, Michele. 'The Ireland that I would have': de Valera and the creation of an Irish national image. In *Hist. Ire.*, v, no. 2 (1997), pp 37–41.

English, Richard. 'Paying no heed to public clamour': Irish republican solipsism in the 1930s. In *I.H.S.*, xxviii, no. 112 (Nov. 1993), pp 426–39.

——Green on red: two case studies in early twentieth-century Irish republican thought. In D. G. Boyce, Robert Eccleshall, and Vincent Geoghegan (ed.), *Political thought in Ireland since the seventeenth century* (London and New York, 1993), pp 161–89.

——Reflections on republican socialism in Ireland: Marxian roots and Irish historical dynamics. In *History of Political Thought*, xvii (1996), pp 555–70.

Fallon, Brian. *An age of innocence: Irish culture, 1930–1960*. Dublin, 1999.

Flynn, M. K. *Ideology, mobilization and the nation: the rise of Irish, Basque and Carlist nationalist movements in the nineteenth and early twentieth centuries*. Basingstoke, 2000.

Foster, R. F. *Paddy and Mr Punch: connections in Irish and English history*. London, 1995. First published 1993.

Garvin, Tom. The return of history: collective myths and modern nationalisms. In *The Irish Review*, no. 9 (1990), pp 16–30.

Gibbons, Luke. Identity without a centre: allegory, history and Irish nationalism. In *Cultural Studies*, vi (1992), pp 358–75.

Goldring, Maurice. *Pleasant the scholar's life: Irish intellectuals and the construction of the nation state*. London, 1993.

Graham, B. J. (ed.). *In search of Ireland: a cultural geography*. London and New York, 1997.

Graham, Colin. 'Liminal spaces': post-colonial theories and Irish culture. In *The Irish Review*, no. 16 (1994), pp 29–43.

Hazelkorn, Ellen. Why is there no socialism in Ireland? Theoretical problems of Irish Marxism. In *Science and Society*, liii, no. 2 (1989), pp 136–64.

Hogan, Gerard. Irish nationalism as a legal ideology. In *Studies*, lxxv, no. 300 (1986), pp 528–38.

Hoppen, K. Theodore. Ireland, Britain, and Europe: twentieth century nationalism and its spoils. In *Hist. Jn.*, xxxiv (1991), pp 505–18.
Review article.

Hutton, Seán, and Stewart, Paul (ed.). *Ireland's histories: aspects of state, society and ideology*. London and New York, 1991.

Jameson, Fredric. *Nationalism, colonialism and literature: modernism and imperialism.* Derry, 1988. (Field Day Pamphlet.)

Kearney, Richard. *Transitions: narratives in modern Irish culture.* Dublin, 1988.

——Postmodernity, nationalism and Ireland. In *History of European Ideas*, xvi (1993), pp 147–55.

Keating, Paul, Cultural values and entrepreneurial action: the case of the Irish republic. In Joseph Melling and Jonathan Barry (ed.), *Culture in history: production, consumption and values in historical perspective* (Exeter, 1992), pp 92–108.

Kennedy, Liam. Modern Ireland: post-colonial society or post-colonial pretensions? In *The Irish Review*, no. 13 (winter, 1992/3), pp 107–21.

Lee, J. J. Aspects of corporatist thought in Ireland: the commission on vocational organisation, 1939–43. In Art Cosgrove and Donal McCartney (ed.), *Studies in Irish history presented to R. Dudley Edwards* (Dublin, 1979), pp 324–46.

Livesey, James, and Murray, Stuart. Post-colonial theory and modern Irish culture. In *I.H.S.*, xxx, no. 119 (May 1997), pp 452–61. Review article.

Lloyd, David. *Ireland after history.* Cork, 1999.

Longley, Edna (ed.). *Culture in Ireland: division or diversity?* Belfast, 1991.

Lyons, F.S.L. *Culture and anarchy in Ireland, 1880–1939.* Oxford, 1979.

McBride, Lawrence W. (ed.). *Images, icons, and the Irish nationalist imagination.* Dublin, 1999.

McCarthy, Conor. *Modernisation, crisis and culture in Ireland, 1969–1992.* Dublin, 2000.

MacDonagh, Oliver. *States of mind: a study of Anglo-Irish conflict 1780–1980.* London, 1985. Originally published 1983.

Morrissey, Thomas. The paradox of James Connolly, Irish Marxist socialist (1868–1916), and the papal social encyclicals (1891–1991). In *Milltown Studies*, new ser., xviii (1991), pp 24–40.

O'Brien, Conor Cruise. *Ancestral voices: religion and nationalism in Ireland.* Dublin, 1994.

O'Connor, Emmet. *Syndicalism in Ireland, 1917–1923.* Cork, 1988.

O'Dowd, Liam. Intellectuals in 20th century Ireland and the case of George Russell (A.E.). In *Crane Bag*, ix, no. 1 (1985), pp 6–25.

Ó Drisceoil, Proinsias (ed.). *Culture in Ireland—regions, identity and power: proceedings of the Cultures of Ireland Group conference . . . 1992.* Belfast, 1993.

O'Halloran, Clare. *Partition and the limits of Irish nationalism: an ideology under stress.* Dublin, 1987.

O'Mahony, Patrick, and Delanty, Gerard. *Rethinking Irish history: nationalism, identity and ideology.* Ed. Jo Campling. Basingstoke, 1998.

Ó Murchadha, Felix. Violence, reconciliation, pluralism: a critique of Irish nationalism. In *Canadian Journal of Irish Studies*, xix, no. 2 (1993), pp 1–12.

Outram, Dorinda. Negating the natural: or why historians deny Irish science. In *The Irish Review*, no. 1 (1986), pp 45–9.

Pratschke, John. Economic philosophy and ideology in Ireland. In *Studies*, lxxiv, no. 294 (1985), pp 145–54.

Ruane, Joseph. Ireland, European integration, and the dialectic of nationalism and postnationalism. In *Études Irlandaises*, xix, no. 1 (1994), pp 183–93.

——Colonial legacies and cultural reflexivities. In *Études Irlandaises*, xix, no. 2 (1994), pp 107–19.

Sailer, Susan (ed.). *Representing Ireland: gender, class, nationality*. Gainesville, Fla., 1997.

Smyth, Jim. Nationalist nightmares and postmodernist utopias: Irish society in transition. In *History of European Ideas*, xvi (1993), pp 157–63.

12 LEARNED SOCIETIES

Budd, Declan, and Hinds, Ross. *The Hist and Edmund Burke's club, an anthology of the College Historical Society, 1747–1997*. Dublin, 1997.

Daly, Mary E. *The spirit of earnest inquiry: the Statistical and Social Inquiry Society of Ireland*. Dublin, 1997.

Dixon, F. E. The Old Dublin Society, 1934–84. In *Dublin Hist. Rec.*, xxxvii (1984), pp 82–7.

Freeman, T. W. Early years of the Geographical Society of Ireland. In *Ir. Geography*, xvii (1984), pp 32–8.

Meenan, James (ed.). *Centenary history of the Literary and Historical Society of University College, Dublin, 1855–1955*. Tralee, [1956].

——and Clarke, Desmond (ed.). *RDS: the Royal Dublin Society, 1731–1981*. Dublin, 1981.

Ó Raifertaigh, Tarlach (ed.). *The Royal Irish Academy: a bicentennial history, 1785–1985*. Dublin, 1985.

Phelan, Margaret. Kilkenny Archaelogical Society, 1945–1994. In *Old Kilkenny Rev.*, xlvi (1994), pp 96–104.

White, Terence de Vere. *The story of the Royal Dublin Society*. Tralee, [1955].

13 MEDICAL, SCIENTIFIC, AND TECHNICAL HISTORY

Barrington, Ruth. *Health, medicine and politics in Ireland, 1900–1970*. Dublin, 2000. 1st ed. 1987.

Barry, J. M. *The Victoria Hospital, Cork: a history*. Cork, 1992.

Berrios, German E., and Freeman, Hugh (ed.). *150 years of British psychiatry, 1841–1991*. London, 1991.
Two chapters on Ireland. See also below under Freeman.

Bowler, Peter J., and Whyte, Nicholas (ed.). *Science and society in Ireland: the social context of science and technology in Ireland, 1800–1950*. Belfast, 1997.

Browne, Alan (ed.). *Masters, midwives and ladies-in-waiting: the Rotunda Hospital, 1745–1995*. Dublin, 1995.

Burke, Helen. *The Royal Hospital, Donnybrook: a heritage of caring, 1743–1993*. Dublin, 1993.

Carr, James C. (ed.). *A century of medical radiation in Ireland—an anthology*. [Dublin], 1995.

Coakley, Davis. *Baggot Street: a short history of the Royal City of Dublin Hospital*. Dublin, 1995.

Coon, Carleton Stevens. *The races of Europe*. New York, 1939.
Section on Ireland based on measurements of 10,000 adult males, made under aegis of anthropology division, Harvard University.

Cooney, Mark. The Army Medical Corps: some recollections of its early days. In *An Cosantóir*, xxvii (1967), pp 529–35.

Cooper, C. and Whelan, N. *Science, technology and industry in Ireland*. Dublin, 1973.

Curran, P. L. (ed.). *Towards a history of agricultural science in Ireland: commemorating the golden jubilee of the Agricultural Science Association, 1942–1992*. Dublin, 1992.

de Courcy, John. *A history of structural engineering in Ireland, 1908–1983*. Dublin, 1983.

Deeny, James. *To cure & to care: memoirs of a chief medical officer*. Dun Laoghaire, 1989. [Originator of the 'mother and child' scheme.]

Farmar, Tony. *Holles Street 1894–1994: the National Maternity Hospital—a centenary history*. Dublin, 1994.

Feeney, John K. *The Coombe Lying-In Hospital*. Dublin, 1983.

Fleetwood, John F. *The history of medicine in Ireland*. 2nd ed., Dublin, 1983. First published 1951.

Freeman, Edward T. *Centenary of the Mater Misericordiae Hospital, 1861–1961*. Dublin, 1963.

Freeman, Hugh, and Berrios, German E. (ed.). *150 years of British psychiatry. Vol. 2: The aftermath*. London, 1996.
    Contains chapters on Ireland, north and south. See also above under Berrios.

Friis, Henning. *Development of social research in Ireland*. Dublin, 1965.

Gatenby, Peter. *Dublin's Meath Hospital 1753–1996*. Dublin, 1996.

Henry, Hanora M. *Our Lady's Psychiatric Hospital, Cork: history of the mental hospital in Cork spanning 200 years*. The Lough, Co. Cork, 1989.

Henry, Patrick J. *Sligo: medical care in the past, 1800–1965*. Manorhamilton, 1995.

Herries Davies, G. L. Irish thought in science. In Richard Kearney (ed.), *The Irish mind* (Dublin, 1985), pp 294–310.

Houston, Ken (ed.). *Creators of mathematics: the Irish connection*. Dublin, 2000.

Hughes, Noel J. *Irish engineering 1760–1960*. [Dublin], 1982.

Scheper-Hughes, Nancy. *Saints, scholars, and schizophrenics: mental illness in rural Ireland*. Berkeley, Cal., and London, 1979. New ed., 2001.

Johnson, Roy. Science and technology in Irish national culture. In *Crane Bag*, vii (1983), pp 58–63.

Jones, Greta. The Rockefeller Foundation and medical education in Ireland in the 1920s. In *I.H.S.*, xxx, no. 120 (Nov. 1997), pp 564–80.

—— and Malcolm, Elizabeth (ed.). *Medicine, disease and the state in Ireland, 1650–1940*. Cork, 1999.

Lyons, J. B. *The quality of Mercer's: the story of Mercer's Hospital, 1734–1991*. Dun Laoghaire, 1991.

—— *A pride of professors: the professors of medicine at the Royal College of Surgeons in Ireland 1813–1985*. Dublin, 1999.

—— (ed.). *2000 years of Irish medicine*. Dublin, 2000.

Lysaght, Seán. *Robert Lloyd Praeger: the life of a naturalist*. Dublin, 1998.

McDonald, Rosemarie. Horses and hospitals: the Irish sweepstakes. In *Éire-Ireland*, xxix, no. 1 (1994), pp 24–34.

McKee, Eamonn. Church–state relations and the development of Irish health policy: the mother-and-child scheme, 1944–53. In *I.H.S.*, xxv, no. 98 (Nov. 1986), pp 159–94.

Malcolm, Elizabeth. *Swift's hospital: a history of St Patrick's Hospital, Dublin, 1746–1989.* Dublin, 1989.

Meenan, F. O. C. *St Vincent's Hospital, 1834–1994: an historical and social portrait.* Dublin, 1995.

Mitchell, David. *A 'peculiar' place: the Adelaide Hospital, Dublin: its times, places and personalities, 1839–1989.* Tallaght, 1989.

Nelson, E. Charles. *Shamrock: botany and history of an Irish myth.* Aberystwyth and Kilkenny, 1991.

O'Brien, Eoin (ed). *Essays in honour of J. D. H. Widdess.* Dublin, 1978.

——(ed). *The Charitable Infirmary, Jervis Street, 1718–1987: a farewell tribute.* Monkstown, 1987.

——Browne, Lorna; and O'Malley, Kevin. *The House of Industry hospitals 1772–1987: the Richmond, Whitworth and Hardwicke (St Laurence's hospital): a closing memoir.* Monkstown, 1988.

O'Connell, T. C. J. Whither Irish surgery. In *Irish Journal of Medical Science*, 6th ser., no. 169 (1940), pp 1–20.

O'Dowd, Liam (ed.). *The state of social science research in Ireland.* Dublin, 1988.

Ó Gráda, Cormac. The Rotunda Hospital and the people of Dublin, 1745–1995. In *Éire-Ireland*, xxx, no. 1 (1995), pp 49–76.

Robins, Joseph. *Fools and mad: a history of the insane in Ireland.* Dublin, 1986.

Ryan, J. Philip. *The Chemical Association of Ireland, 1922–1936.* Blackrock, 1997.

Scaife, W. Garrett. *From galaxies to turbines: science, technology and the Parsons family.* Bristol, 2000.

Scanlan, Pauline. *The Irish nurse: a study of nursing in Ireland: history and education 1718–1981.* Manorhamilton, 1991.

Shields, Lisa (ed.). *The Irish meteorological service: the first fifty years 1936–1986.* Dublin, 1987.

Solomons, Bethel. *One doctor in his time.* London, 1955.

Whyte, Nicholas. *Science, colonialism and Ireland.* Cork, 1999.

Widdess, J. D. H. *A history of the Royal College of Physicians of Ireland 1654–1963.* Edinburgh and London, 1963.

——*The Royal College of Surgeons in Ireland and its medical school 1784–1984.* 3rd ed., Dublin, 1983.

14 LOCAL AND FAMILY HISTORY

ARKLOW. *Maritime Arklow.* By Frank Forde. Dún Laoghaire, 1988.

ARAN ISLANDS. *The book of Aran: the Aran Islands, Co. Galway.* Ed. John Waddell, J. W. O' Connell, and Anne Korff. Kinvara, Co. Galway, 1994.

BALLINASLOE. *The parish of Ballinasloe: its history from earliest times to the present.* By Patrick Egan. Galway, 1994. Facsimile of ed. published Dublin, 1960.

BALLYHAHILL. *Recollections of our native valley: a history of the parish of Loughill-Ballyhahill and the Owvaun Valley.* By Gerard Curtin. Ballyhahill, Co. Limerick, 1996.

BLACKROCK. *The book of Blackrock.* By Liam Mac Cóil. 2nd ed., Blackrock, 1981. First published 1977.

BLASKET ISLANDS. *Blasket memories: the life of an Irish island community*. Ed. Pádraig Tyers. Cork, 2000.

CAPPAGHGLASS. *Cappaghglass*. By Peter Somerville-Large. London, 1985.

CAPPAMORE. *Cappamore: a parish history*. Cappamore Historical Society, Cappamore, Co. Limerick, 1992.

CAVAN. *Cavan: essays on the history of an Irish county*. Ed. Raymond Gillespie. Blackrock, 1995.

CLARE. *Clare and its people: a concise history*. By Brian Dinan. Cork and Dublin, 1987.

CONNACHT. *Seaweed memories: in the jaws of the sea*. By Heinrich Becker. Dublin, 2000.

People of the Connacht coast: anthology.

Connell, Paul; Cronin, Denis; and Ó Dálaigh, Brian (ed.). *Irish townlands: studies in local history*. Dublin, 1998.

CORK. *Cork: history and society. Interdisciplinary essays on the history of an Irish county*. Ed. Patrick O'Flanagan and Cornelius G. Buttimer. Dublin, 1993. (Irish County History Series.)

—— *The first hundred years: Cork County Council*. By Edward Marnane. Cork, 1999.

CRUSHEEN (CO. CLARE). *The parish of Inchicronan (Crusheen)*. By Thomas Coffey. Whitegate, Co. Clare, 1993.

DONEGAL. *Donegal: history and society. Interdisciplinary essays on the history of an Irish county*. Ed. William Nolan, Liam Ronayne, and Mairead Dunlevy. Dublin, 1995. (Irish County History Series.)

DUBLIN. *A history of the port of Dublin*. By H. A. Gilligan. Dublin, 1988.

—— *Four roads to Dublin: the history of Rathmines, Ranelagh and Leeson Street*. By Deirdre Kelly. Dublin, 1995.

—— *Dublin: the first thousand years*. By Peter Somerville-Large. Belfast, 1988. First published 1979.

—— *Stoneybatter: Dublin's inner suburban village*. By Kevin C. Kearns. Dublin, 1989.

—— *Dublin street life and lore: an oral history*. By Kevin C. Kearns. Dublin, 1991.

—— *Dublin city and county: from prehistory to present: studies in honour of J. H. Andrews*. Ed. F. H. A. Aalen and Kevin Whelan. Dublin, 1992. (Irish County History Series.)

DÚN LAOGHAIRE. *Between the mountains and the sea: Dún Laoghaire–Rathdown County*. By Peter Pearson. Dublin, 1998.

DURROW. *Durrow in history: a celebration of what has gone before*. Ed. Michael Byrne. Tullamore, 1994.

Evans, M. D., and Ó Duill, Eileen (ed.). *Aspects of Irish genealogy: proceedings of the 1st [etc.] Irish genealogical congress*. n.p., 1993, 1996, 1999.

GALWAY. *Galway: history and society. Interdisciplinary essays on the history of an Irish county*. Ed. Gerard Moran. Dublin, 1996. (Irish County History Series.)

—— *A history of Galway County Council: stair Comhairle Chontae na Gaillimhe*. By Gabriel O'Connor. Galway, 1999.

—— *Tribes to tigers: a history of Galway Chamber of Commerce and Industry*. By Kieran Woodman. Galway, 2000.

Gillespie, Raymond, and Hill, Myrtle (ed.). *Doing local history: pursuit and practice*. Belfast, 1998.

GRANARD. *Window on a catholic parish: St Mary's, Granard, Co. Longford, 1933–68.* By Francis Kelly. Blackrock, 1996. (Maynooth Studies in Local History.)

Grehan, Ida. *Irish family histories.* Schull, Co. Cork, 1993.

Grenham, John. *Clans and families of Ireland: the heritage and heraldry of Irish clans and families.* Dublin, 1993.

INISHOWEN. *Our Inis Eoghain heritage: the parishes of Culdaff and Cloncha.* By Brian Bonner. Dublin, 1972. 2nd ed. Pallaskenry, Co. Limerick, 1984.

KELLS. *The story of Kells.* By Leo Judge. Kells, 1993.

KILKENNY. *Kilkenny: history and society. Interdisciplinary essays on the history of an Irish county.* Ed. William Nolan and Kevin Whelan. Dublin, 1990. (Irish County History Series.)

—— *Kilkenny County Council: a century of local government.* By Tom Boyle. Ed. Michael O'Dwyer. Kilkenny, 1999.

LAOIS. *Laois: history and society. Interdisciplinary essays on the history of an Irish county.* Ed. Pádraig Lane and William Nolan. Dublin, 1999. (Irish County History Series.)

—— *Laois County Council: the first 100 years.* Ed. Teddy Fennelly. [Portlaoise], 1999.

LEITRIM. *Ó aois go h-aois, céad bliain ag fás. From age to age: one hundred years of growth 1899–1999, centenary of local government in County Leitrim.* By Denis O'Donovan. n.p. [1999].

LIMERICK. *The story of Limerick.* By Robert W. Jackson. Dublin and Cork, 1973.

LISTOWEL. *Listowel and its vicinity.* By J. Anthony Gaughan. Cork, 1973.

LONGFORD. *Longford: essays in county history.* Ed. Raymond Gillespie and Gerard Moran. Dublin, 1991.

LOUTH. *History of local government in the county of Louth: from earliest times to the present time.* By Harold O'Sullivan. Dublin, 2000.

MAYNOOTH. *Cannonballs and croziers: a history of Maynooth.* By John Drennan. Maynooth, 1994.

—— *Má Nuad: Maynooth: a short historical guide.* By Mary Cullen. 2nd ed., Maynooth, 1995. Previous ed. 1979.

MAYO. *Where the sun sets: Ballycroy, Belmullet, Kilcommon & Kiltane, County Mayo.* By Seán Noone. Naas, 1991.

—— *Public spirited people: Mayo County Council, 1899–1909.* By Joe McDermott. Castlebar, 1999.

—— *Mayo's lost islands: the Inishkeas.* By Brian Dornan. Dublin, 2000.

MEATH. *A history of Meath County Council, 1899–1999: a century of democracy in Meath.* By Denis Boyle. [Navan], 1999.

OFFALY. *Offaly: history and society. Interdisciplinary essays on the history of an Irish county.* Ed. William Nolan and Timothy P. O'Neill. Dublin, 1998. (Irish County History Series.)

RATHKEALE. *All Ireland is in and about Rathkeale.* By Patrick J. O'Connor. Coolanoran, Newcastle West, Co. Limerick, 1996.

THOMASTOWN. *In the valley of the Nore: a social history of Thomastown, Co. Kilkenny, 1840–1983.* By Marilyn Silverman and P. H. Gulliver. Dublin, 1986.

TIPPERARY. *Tipperary: history and society. Interdisciplinary essays on the history of an Irish county.* Ed. William Nolan and Thomas McGrath. Dublin, 1985. (Irish County History Series.)

—— *History of south Tipperary.* By Patrick C. Power. Cork and Dublin, 1989.

—— *Tipperary S.R. County Council 1899–1999: a century of local democracy.* By Brendan Long. Clonmel, 1999.

TORY ISLAND (CO. DONEGAL). *The Tory islanders: a people of the Celtic fringe.* By Robin Fox. Cambridge, 1978.

—— Population, society and economy on Tory Island, Co. Donegal. By D. Scott and S. Royle. In *Ir. Geography*, xxv (1992), pp 169–76.

WATERFORD. *A history of Waterford city and county.* By Patrick C. Power. Cork, 1990.

—— *Waterford: history and society. Interdisciplinary essays on the history of an Irish county.* Ed. William Nolan and Thomas Power. Dublin, 1992. (Irish County History Series.)

—— *A history of Waterford and its mayors from the 12th century to the 20th century.* Ed. Eamonn McEneaney. Waterford, 1995.

—— *Comhairle Chontae Phortláirge, 1899–1999.* By Brian McNally and Maurice McHugh. [Lismore, 1999].

WEXFORD. *Wexford: history and society. Interdisciplinary essays on the history of an Irish county.* Ed. Kevin Whelan and William Nolan. Dublin, 1987. (Irish County History Series.)

WICKLOW. *Wicklow: history and society. Interdisciplinary essays on the history of an Irish county.* Ed. Ken Hannigan and William Nolan. Dublin, 1994. (Irish County History Series.)

—— *For the betterment of the people: a history of Wicklow County Council.* By Brian Donnelly. [Wicklow], 1999.

WOODBROOK (CO. ROSCOMMON). *Woodbrook.* By David Thomson. London, 1991. First published 1974.
Personal observations of Woodbrook estate.

15 HISTORY OF THE IRISH ABROAD

Akenson, D. H. *The United States and Ireland.* Cambridge, Mass., 1973.

—— *The Irish in Ontario: a study in rural history.* Kingston, 1984.

—— *Half the world from home: perspectives on the Irish in New Zealand, 1860–1950.* Wellington, N.Z., 1990.

—— *The Irish diaspora: a primer.* Belfast, 1993.

Bielenberg, Andy (ed.). *The Irish diaspora.* Harlow, 2000.

Birmingham, Stephen. *Real lace: America's Irish rich.* London, 1987. First published New York, 1973.

Buckland, Patrick, and Belchem, John (ed.). *The Irish in British labour history.* Liverpool, 1993.

Bull, Philip; Devlin-Glass, Frances; and Doyle, Helen (ed.). *Ireland and Australia, 1798–1998: studies in culture, identity and migration.* Sydney, 2000.

Byron, Reginald. *Irish America.* Oxford, 1999.

Callahan, Bob (ed.). *The big book of American Irish culture.* New York, 1987.

Clark, Dennis. *The Irish in Philadelphia*. Philadelphia, 1974; first published 1973.
—— *Hibernia America: the Irish and regional cultures*. New York and London, 1986.
—— *The Irish in Pennsylvania*. University Park, Pa., 1991.
Cleary, J. M. The Irish and modern Wales. In *The Furrow*, vii (1956), 205–10.
Coffey, Michael. *The Irish in America*. New York, 1997.
Comyn, James. *Summing it up: memoirs of an Irishman at the English bar*. Dublin, 1991.
—— *Watching brief: further memoirs of an Irishman at law in England*. Dublin, 1993.
—— *Leave to appeal: further legal memoirs*. Dublin, 1994.
    Born 1921; Q.C. and high court judge.
Coogan, Tim Pat. *Wherever green is worn: the story of the Irish diaspora*. London, 2000.
Delaney, Enda. The churches and Irish emigration to Britain, 1921–60. In *Archiv. Hib.*, l (1998), pp 98–114.
—— *Demography, state and society: Irish migration to Britain, 1921–1971*. Liverpool, 2000.
Devine, T. M. (ed.). *Irish immigrants and Scottish society in the nineteenth and twentieth centuries*. Edinburgh, 1991.
Doyle, David, and Edwards, O. D. (ed.). *America and Ireland, 1776–1976: the American identity and the Irish connection*. Westport, Conn., and London, 1980.
Drudy, P. J. (ed.). *The Irish in America: emigration, assimilation and impact*. Cambridge, 1985.
Faherty, William B. *Dream by the river: two centuries of St Louis catholicism, 1766–1967*. St Louis, 1973.
Fedorowich, Kent. Reconstruction and resettlement: the politicisation of Irish migration to Australia and Canada, 1919–29. In *E.H.R.*, cxiv (1999), pp 1143–78.
Freeman, Joshua B. *In transit: the Transport Workers Union in New York city, 1933–1966*. New York and Oxford, 1989.
    Mike Quill (1905–66) and Irish republicanism.
Greeley, A. M. *That most distressful nation: the taming of the American Irish*. Chicago, 1972.
Handley, J. E. *The Irish in modern Scotland*. Cork, 1947.
Hatton, Timothy J. and Williamson, Jeffrey (ed.). *Migration and the international labour market 1850–1939*. London, 1994.
Hickman, Mary. *Religion, class and identity: the state, the catholic church and the education of the Irish in Britain*. Aldershot, 1995.
—— Reconstructing and deconstructing 'race': British political discourses about the Irish in Britain. In *Ethnic and Racial Studies*, xxi, no. 2 (1998), 288–307.
Jackson, John Archer. *The Irish in Britain*. London, 1963.
Kearney, Richard (ed.). *Migrations: the Irish at home and abroad*. Dublin, 1990.
Kiernan, Colm (ed.). *Ireland and Australia*. Dublin and Cork, 1984. (Thomas Davis Lectures.)
—— *Australia and Ireland, 1788–1988: bicentenary essays*. Dublin, 1986.
McCaffrey, Lawrence. *The Irish diaspora in America*. Bloomington, Ind., 1972. 2nd ed., Washington, D.C., 1984. Revised ed. 1997.
—— (ed.) *Irish nationalism and the American contribution*. New York, 1976.
—— *The Irish catholic diaspora in America*. Washington, D.C., 1997.

MacKenzie, H. A. *The Irish in Cape Breton*. Antigonish, Nova Scotia, 1979.

MacLoughlin, William. The Hibernian-Argentinian: a forgotten branch of the Irish diaspora. In *Ir. Geneal.*, ix (1997), pp 423–5.

Mannion, John. *Irish settlements in eastern Canada*. Toronto, 1974.

Martin, F. X., and O'Reilly, Clare (ed.). *The Irish Augustinians in Rome, 1656–1994, and Irish Augustinian missions throughout the world*. Dublin and Rome, 1994.

Miller, Kerby A., and Wagner, Paul. *Out of Ireland: the story of Irish emigration to America*. London, 1994.

O'Brien, John, and Travers, Pauric (ed.). *The Irish emigrant experience in Australia*. Dublin, 1991.

O'Connor, Kevin. *The Irish in Britain*. London, 1972.

O'Driscoll, Robert, and Reynolds, Lorna (ed.). *The untold story: the Irish in Canada*. 2 vols. Toronto, 1988.

O'Farrell, Patrick. *The Irish in Australia*. Sydney, 1987; rev. ed., 1992.

—— *Vanished kingdoms: the Irish in Australia and New Zealand: a personal excursion*. Sydney, 1990.

O'Sullivan, Patrick (ed.). *Patterns of migration*. London, 1997. First published 1992. (The Irish World Wide, i.)

—— *The Irish in the new communities*. Leicester, 1992. (The Irish World Wide, ii.)

—— *The creative migrant*. Leicester, 1994. (The Irish World Wide, iii.)

—— *Religion and identity*. New York and London, 1996. (The Irish World Wide, v.)

Reece, Bob (ed.). *The Irish in Western Australia*. Nedlands, 2000. (University of Western Australia.)

Ryan, Liam. Irish emigration to Britain since World War II. In Richard Kearney (ed.), *Migrations: the Irish at home and abroad* (Dublin, 1990), pp 45–67.

Smith, F. B. (ed.). *Ireland, England and Australia: essays in honour of Oliver MacDonagh*. Canberra and Cork, 1990.

Tennant, Lorraine. The Irish emigrant database. In *Scotch-Irish Studies*, i, no. 1 (2000), pp 120–24.

Thernstrom, Stephan. *The other Bostonians, 1880–1970*. Cambridge, Mass, 1973.

Winston, Nessa. *Between two places: a case study of Irish-born people living in England*. Dublin, 2000.

16 HISTORY OF ARCHITECTURE, PAINTING, AND DECORATIVE ARTS

Adam, Peter. *Eileen Gray, architect-designer: a biography*. London, 1987. Revised ed. 2000.

Arnold, Bruce. *A concise history of Irish art*. Revised ed., London, 1977. First published 1969.

—— *Mainie Jellett and the modern movement in Ireland*. New Haven and London, 1991.

—— *Jack Yeats*. New Haven and London, 1998.

Becker, Annette; Olley, John; and Wang, Wilfred (ed.). *20th-century architecture: Ireland*. Munich and New York, 1997.
    With biographies of architects.

Benington, Jonathan. *Roderic O'Conor*. Blackrock, 1992.

Bodkin, Thomas. *Hugh Lane and his pictures*. 2nd ed., Dublin, 1934. First published 1932.

—— *Tuarascáil ar na h-ealaíona in Éirinn. Report on the arts in Ireland*. Dublin, 1949.

Bowe, Nicola Gordon. *The life and work of Harry Clarke*. Blackrock, 1989.

—— Caron, David; and Wynne, Michael. *Gazetteer of Irish stained glass*. Blackrock, 1988.

—— and Cumming, Elizabeth. *The arts and crafts movements in Dublin & Edinburgh, 1885–1925*. Dublin, 1998.

Bhreathnach-Lynch, Sighle. The church and the artist: practice and patronage, 1922–45. In *Irish Arts Review Yearbook 1991/2*, pp 130–34.

—— The Academy of Christian Art (1929–1946): an aspect of catholic cultural life in newly independent Ireland. In *Éire-Ireland*, xxxi, nos 3–4 (1996), pp 102–16.

Butler, Patricia. *Three hundred years of Irish watercolours and drawings*. London, 1997. Originally published 1990.

Casey, Christine, and Rowan, Alistair. *North Leinster: the counties of Longford, Louth, Meath and Westmeath*. Harmondsworth, 1993. (The Buildings of Ireland, ii.)

Crookshank, Anne. *Irish art from 1600 to the present day*. Dublin, 1979.

—— *Irish sculpture from 1600 to the present day*. Dublin, 1984.

Cullen, Fintan. *Visual politics: the representation of Ireland, 1750–1930*. Cork, 1997.

—— (ed.). *Sources in Irish art: a reader*. Cork, 2000.

Curran, C. P. Michael Healy: stained glass worker, 1873–1941. In *Studies*, xxxi (1942), pp 65–82.

—— Evie Hone: stained glass worker, 1894–1955. In *Studies*, xliv (1955), pp 129–42.

Deane, John F. *Toward harmony: Tony O'Malley*. Dublin, 1993.

Denson, Alan. *An Irish artist: W. J. Leech, R.H.A. (1881–1968)*. 2 vols. Kendal, 1968–9.

Douglas, Roy; Harte, Liam; and O'Hara, Jim. *Drawing conclusions: a cartoon history of Anglo–Irish relations, 1798–1998*. Belfast, 1998.

Fallon, Brian. *Irish art: 1830–1990*. Belfast, 1994.

Fenlon, Jane; Figgis, Nicola; and Marshall, Catherine (ed.). *New perspectives: studies in art history in honour of Anne Crookshank*. Blackrock, 1987.

Ferran, Denise. *William John Leech: an Irish painter abroad*. Dublin and London, 1996.

Fitz-Simon, Christopher. *The arts in Ireland: a chronology*. Dublin, 1982.

Garner, Philippe. *Eileen Gray: design and architecture 1878–1976*. Cologne, 1993.

Glin (Desmond FitzGerald, knight of); Griffin, David J.; and Robinson, Nicholas. *Vanishing country houses of Ireland*. 2nd ed., Dublin, 1989. Previous ed. 1988.

Gowrie, Grey. *Derek Hill: an appreciation*. London, 1987.

Graby, John (ed.). *150 years of architecture in Ireland: R.I.A.I., 1839–1989*. Dublin, 1989.

—— and O'Connor, Deirdre (ed.). *Dublin*. London, 1993. Architecture guidebook.

Grimes, Brendan. *Irish Carnegie libraries: a catalogue and architectural history*. Dublin, 1998.

Guinness, Desmond. The Irish Georgian Society: the first thirty year [1958–88]. In *Ir. Georgian Soc. Bull.*, xxi (1988), pp 3–30.

Harbison, Peter; Potterton, Homan; and Sheehy, Jeanne. *Irish art and architecture from prehistory to the present*. London, 1978.

Hicks, F. G. An architect's reminiscences. In *Ir. Builder*, lxxxviii (1946), p. 748.

Hill, Judith. *Irish public sculpture: a history*. Dublin, 1998.

Hurley, Richard, and Cantwell, Winifred. *Contemporary Irish church architecture*. Dublin, 1985.

Kelly, Anne. *Cultural policy in Ireland*. Dublin, 1989.

Kennedy, Brian P. *Alfred Chester Beatty and Ireland, 1950–1968: a study in cultural politics*. Dun Laoghaire, 1988.

—— The failure of the cultural republic: Ireland, 1922–39. In *Studies*, lxxxi, no. 321 (1992), pp 14–22.

—— (ed.). *Art is my life: a tribute to James White*. Dublin, 1991.
Director of the National Gallery of Ireland 1964–80.

—— and Gillespie, Raymond (ed.). *Ireland: art into history*. Dublin, 1994.

Kennedy, S. B. *Irish art and modernism 1880–1950*. Belfast, 1991.

—— *Paul Henry*. New Haven and London, 2000.

Kinmouth, Claudia. *Irish country furniture, 1700–1950*. Newhaven, 1993.

Knowles, Roderic. *Contemporary Irish art: a documentation*. Dublin, 1982.

Larmour, Paul. *The arts and crafts movement in Ireland*. Belfast, 1992.

Lynam, Gena. Daniel O'Neill (1920–1974): landscape and figure painter. In *Irish Arts Review Yearbook*, xv (1999), pp 134–41.

McConkey, Kenneth. *A free spirit: Irish painting 1860–1960*. Woodbridge, 1990.

McCrum, Sean, and Lambert, Gordon (ed.). *Living with art: David Hendriks*. Dublin, 1985.

McDonald, Frank. *The destruction of Dublin*. Dublin, 1985.

—— *The construction of Dublin*. Kinsale, 2000.

MacGreevy, Thomas. Michael Healy: personal reminiscences. In *Capuchin Annual 1944*, pp 113–15, 441.

McParland, Edward. The bank and the visual arts. In F. S. L. Lyons (ed.), *Bicentenary essays: Bank of Ireland 1783–1983* (Dublin, 1983), pp 97–140.

Madden, Anne. *Seeing his way: Louis le Brocquy: a painter*. Dublin, 1994.

Mallon, Declan. *Nano Reid*. Drogheda, 1994.

Murphy, Paula. *O'Conor: Roderic O'Conor, 1860–1940*. Dublin, 1992.

O'Beirne, Tomas. *A guide to modern architecture in Dublin*. Dublin, 1978.

O'Byrne, Robert. *After a fashion: a history of the Irish fashion industry*. Dublin, 2000.

—— *Hugh Lane 1875–1915*. Dublin, 2000.

O'Connor, Ciaran, and O'Regan, John (ed.). *Public works: the architecture of the office of public works, 1831–1987*. Dublin, 1987.

O'Donovan, Donal. *God's architect: a life of Raymond McGrath*. Bray, 1995.

O'Grady, John. *The life and work of Sarah Purser*. Blackrock, 1996.

Office of Public Works. *Monuments in the past: photographs 1870–1936*. Dublin, 1991.

Pearson, Peter, *The heart of Dublin: resurgence of an historic city*. Dublin, 2000.

Pegum, Caroline, with Brown, Terence; Gibney, Arthur; and O'Doherty, Michael. *Building for government: the architecture of state buildings, O.P.W.: Ireland 1900–2000*. Dublin, 1999.

Power, Sinéad. The development of the Ballymun housing scheme, Dublin, 1965–1969. In *Ir. Geography*, xxxiii (2000), pp 199–212.

Pyle, Hilary. *Jack B. Yeats: a biography*. Revised ed., London, 1989. First published 1970.

Rifkin, Ned. *Sean Scully: twenty years, 1976–1995*. London, 1995.

Robinson, Lennox. *Palette and plough: a pen-and-ink drawing of Dermod O'Brien*. Dublin, 1948.

Rothery, Sean. *Ireland and the new architecture, 1900–1940*. Dublin, 1991.

——*A field guide to the buildings of Ireland: illustrating the smaller buildings of town & countryside*. Dublin, 1997.

Rowan, Ann Martha. A database of Irish architects 1700–1950. In *Ir. Georgian Soc. Bull.*, xxxvi (1994), pp 75–7; xxxviii (1996–7), pp 40–64; continued in *Irish Architectural and Decorative Studies: the Journal of the Irish Georgian Society*, i (1998), pp 176–93; ii (1999), pp 198–206; iii (2000), pp 167–75. In progress.

Shaffrey, Maura. Sackville Street/O'Connell Street. In *GPA Irish Arts Review Yearbook 1988* (Belfast, 1988), pp 144–56.

Shaffrey, Patrick, and Shaffrey, Maura. *Buildings of Irish towns: treasures of everyday architecture*. Dublin, 1983.

——*Irish countryside buildings: everyday architecture in the rural landscape*. Dublin, 1985.

Sheehy, Jeanne. *The rediscovery of Ireland's past: the Celtic revival 1830–1930*. London, 1980.

Thiessen, Gesa E. *Theology and modern Irish art*. Blackrock, 1999.

Turpin, John. *A school of art in Dublin since the eighteenth century: a history of the National College of Art and Design*. Dublin, 1995.

——Nationalist and unionist ideology in the sculpture of Oliver Sheppard and John Hughes, 1895–1939. In *The Irish Review*, no. 20 (1997), pp 62–75.

——*Oliver Sheppard (1865–1941): symbolist sculptor of the Irish cultural revival*. Dublin, 2000.

Walker, Dorothy. *Modern art in Ireland*. Dublin, 1997.

Extensive bibliography, including exhibition catalogues.

——L'art de vivre: the designs of Eileen Gray (1878–1976). In *Irish Arts Review Yearbook*, xv (1999), pp 118–25.

White, James. *Jack B. Yeats: drawings and paintings*. London, 1971

——*Brian Bourke: a catalogue of his work*. The Curragh, 1982.

——*Pauline Bewick: painting a life*. Dublin, 1985.

——*Gerard Dillon : an illustrated biography*. Dublin, 1984.

Williams, Jeremy. *A companion guide to architecture in Ireland, 1837–1971*. Blackrock, 1994.

Wynne, Michael. *Irish stained glass*. Dublin, 1977.

17 HISTORY OF MUSIC AND THEATRE

Alvarez, A. *Beckett*. London, 1973. 2nd ed. 1992.

Armstrong, W. A. *Seán O'Casey*. London, 1967. Tokyo, 1991.

Bentley, Eric. *Bernard Shaw*. New York, 1985.

Breathnach, Breandán. *Folk music and dances of Ireland*. Revised ed., Cork, 1977. First published Dublin, 1971.

Brown, Ivor. *Shaw in his time*. London, 1965.

Canfield, Curtis (ed.). *Plays of changing Ireland*. New York, 1936.

Clarke, B. K, and Ferrar, H. *The Dublin drama league, 1918–41*. Dublin, 1979.

Clarke, Michael. The sacred and religious records of John McCormack. In *I.E.R.*, lxviii (1946), pp 384–94.

Cowasjee, Saros. *Seán O'Casey: the man behind the plays*. Edinburgh, 1963.

Cowell, John. *No profit but the name: the Longfords and the Gate Theatre*. Dublin, 1988.

Cronin, Anthony. *Samuel Beckett: the last modernist*. London, 1996.

Curtis, Bernard B. (ed.). *Centenary of the Cork School of Music: progress of the school 1878–1978*. Cork, 1978.

de Blaghd, Earnán. *The Abbey Theatre*. Dublin, 1963.

de Búrca, Séamus. *The Queen's Royal Theatre, Dublin, 1829–1969*. Dublin, 1983.

Delany, James. Church music reform. In *I.E.R.*, lxviii (1946), pp 232–42.

Devine, Francis. *Dermot Doolan and the organisation of Irish actors and performing artists, 1947–1985*. Dublin, 1997.

Dowling, Vincent. *Astride the moon: a theatrical life*. Dublin, 2000.

Dukes, Fred. *Campanology in Ireland: a study of bells, bell-founding, inscriptions and bell-ringing*. Blackrock, 1994.

Duncan, G. A. *The Abbey Theatre in pictures*. Dublin, 1963.

Ellis, Sylvia. *The plays of W. B. Yeats: Yeats and the dancer*. Basingstoke, 1995.

Ervine, St John. *Bernard Shaw: his life, work and friends*. London, 1956.

Esslinger, Pat M. The Irish alienation of Seán O'Casey. In *Éire-Ireland*, i, no. 1 (1966), pp 18–25.

Fallon, Gabriel. F. J. McCormick: an appreciation. In *Studies*, xxxvi (1947), pp 181–6.

—— *Sean O'Casey: the man I knew*. London, 1965.

Farrell, Michael. Series of articles on local and regional theatre in *The Bell*, i, no. 2 (1940), pp 76–84; i, no. 4 (1941), pp 78–86; i, no. 6 (1941), pp 83–8; ii, no. 5 (1941), pp 79–87; xi (1946), pp 998–1003.

Farrelly, Peter. *600 years of theatre in Kilkenny, 1366–1966*. Kilkenny, [1994].

Fitz-Simon, Christopher. *The Irish theatre*, London, 1983.

—— *The boys: a double biography*. London, 1994.
    Micheál MacLiammóir and Hilton Edwards.

Fleischmann, Aloys (ed.). *Music in Ireland: a symposium*. Cork, 1952.

Fleischmann, Ruth (ed.). *Aloys Fleischmann (1910–92): a life for music in Ireland remembered by contemporaries*. Cork, 2000.

Freyer, Grattan, and Harris, Bernard (ed.). *The achievement of Seán Ó Riada*. Chester Springs, Pa., 1981.

Gillen, Gerard, and White, Harry (ed.). *Music and the church*. Dublin, 1993.

—— *Music and Irish cultural history*. Blackrock, 1995.

Greaves, C. Desmond. *Sean O'Casey: politics and art*. London, 1979.

Grene, Nicholas. *The politics of Irish drama: plays in context from Boucicault to Friel*. Cambridge, 1999.

Griffiths, Trevor, and Jones, Margaret Llewellyn (ed.). *British and Irish women dramatists since 1958: a critical handbook*. Buckingham, 1993.

Grindle, W. H. *Irish cathedral music: a history of music at the cathedrals of the Church of Ireland*. Belfast, 1989.

Groocock, Joseph. *A general survey of music in the Republic of Ireland*. Dublin, 1961.

Harrington, John P. *The Irish Beckett*. Syracuse, 1991.

Hogan, Robert. *After the Irish renaissance: a critical history of Irish drama since 'The plough and the stars'*. Minneapolis, 1967.

—— (ed.). *Feathers from the green crow: Sean O'Casey 1905–1925*. Columbia, Mo., 1962; London, 1963.

—— and Burnham, Richard. *The years of O'Casey, 1921–1926: a documentary history*. Newark and Gerrards Cross, 1992.

Holroyd, Michael. *Bernard Shaw*. 4 vols. London, 1988–92.

Hunt, Hugh. *The Abbey: Ireland's national theatre, 1904–1978*. Dublin, 1979.

—— *Sean O'Casey*. Dublin, 1980.

Innes, Christopher (ed.). *The Cambridge companion to George Bernard Shaw*. Cambridge, 1998.

Johnston, Denis. *Orders and desecrations: the life of the playwright Denis Johnston*. Ed. Rory Johnston (Dublin, 1992).

Junker, Mary. *Beckett: the Irish dimension*. Dublin, 1995.

Kaufmann, R. J. *G. B. Shaw: a collection of critical essays*. New Jersey, 1965.

Keane, John B. *Selfportrait*. Cork, 1964.

Knowlson, James. *Damned to fame: the life of Samuel Beckett*. London, 1996.

Krause, David. *Sean O'Casey: the man and his work*. Revised and enlarged ed., New York, 1975. First published 1960.

Laffan, Pat, and O'Grady, Faith (ed.). *Donal McCann remembered*. Dublin, 2000.

McCarthy, Marie. *Passing it on: the transmission of music in Irish culture*. Cork, 1999.

MacLíammóir, Micheál. *All for Hecuba: an Irish theatrical autobiography*. London, 1946. 3rd revised ed. 1961.

—— *Theatre in Ireland*. Dublin, 1964.

MacNamara, Brinsley. *Abbey plays, 1899–1948: including the productions of the Irish Literary Theatre*. Dublin, 1949.

Maxwell, D. E. S. *A critical history of modern Irish drama, 1891–1980*. Cambridge and New York, 1984.

Mercier, Vivian. *Beckett/Beckett*. London, 1990. First published New York, 1977.

Mitchell, Arthur. George Orwell and Sean O'Casey: two prickly characters intersect. In *Hist. Ire.*, vi, no. 3 (1998), pp 44–6.

Moore, John Rees. *Masks of love and death: Yeats as dramatist*. Ithaca, N.Y., 1971.

Ó hAodha, Micheál. *Plays and places*. Dublin, 1961.

—— *The importance of being Micheál: a portrait of MacLiammóir*. Dingle, 1990.

—— *Siobhán: a memoir of an actress*. Dingle, 1994.

Siobhán McKenna (1922–86).

Ó Canainn, Tomás, and Mac an Bhua, Gearóid. *Seán Ó Riada: a shaol agus a shaothar*. Dublin, 1993.

O'Connor, Ulick. *Brendan Behan*. London, 1993. Originally published 1970.

O'Driscoll, Robert (ed.). *Theatre and nationalism in twentieth-century Ireland*. London, 1971.

—— and Reynolds, Lorna (ed.). *Yeats and the theatre*. London, 1975.

O'Mahony, Mathew J. *Progress guide to Anglo-Irish plays*. Dublin, 1960.

O'Sullivan, Donal (ed.). *Irish folk music, song, and dance*. Dublin, 1952; revised reprint, 1961, 1969.

Pearson, Hesketh. *Bernard Shaw: his life and personality*. London, 1961.

Pilling, John (ed.). *The Cambridge companion to Beckett*. Cambridge, 1994.

Pine, Richard, and Cave, Richard. *The Dublin Gate Theatre, 1928–1978*. Cambridge, 1984.

——and Acton, Charles (ed.). *To talent alone: the Royal Irish Academy of Music, 1848–1998*. Dublin, 1998.

Pountney, Rosemary. *Theatre of shadows: Samuel Beckett's drama 1956–1976*. Gerrards Cross, 1988.

Power, Vincent. *Send 'em home sweatin': the showband story*. Revised ed., Cork, 2000. First published Dublin, 1990.

Prattie, David. *The complete critical guide to Samuel Beckett*. London and New York, 2000.

Rafroidi, Patrick; Popot, Raymonde; and Parker, William. *Aspects of the Irish theatre*. Lille, 1972.

Robinson, Lennox. *Ireland's Abbey Theatre: a history, 1899–1951*. London, 1951. Portwashington, N.Y., 1968. [Contains records, with casts, of all first performances].

——(ed.). *The Irish theatre: lectures delivered during the Abbey Theatre festival held in Dublin in August 1938*. London, 1939. New York, 1971.

Ryan, Philip B. *Jimmy O'Dea, the pride of the Coombe*. Swords, 1991. First published 1990.

——*Noel Purcell: a biography*. Swords, 1992.

Schrank, Bernice, and Demastes, William (ed.). *Irish playwrights, 1880–1995: a research and production sourcebook*. Westport, Conn., and London, 1997.

Shields, Hugh. *Narrative singing in Ireland: lays, ballads, come-all-yes and other songs*. Blackrock, 1993.

Smith, Gus, and Hickey, Des. *John B.: the real Keane*. Cork, 1992.

Strauss, Erich. *Bernard Shaw: art and socialism*. London, 1942.

Vallely, Fintan (ed.). *The companion to Irish traditional music*. Cork, 1999.

——Hamilton, Hammy; Vallely, Eithne; and Doherty, Liz (ed.). *Crosbhealach an cheoil 1996: the crossroads conference. Tradition and change in Irish traditional music*. Dublin, 1999.

Welch, Robert. *The Abbey Theatre, 1899–1999: form and pressure*. Oxford, 1999.

White, Harry. *The keeper's recital: music and cultural history in Ireland, 1770–1970*. Cork, 1998.

18 HISTORIOGRAPHY

Beckett, J. C. *The study of Irish history*. Belfast, 1963.

Bogdanor, Vernon. Remembering and forgetting: the complexities of Irish history. In *20th Century British History*, vii (1996), pp 253–61.

Boyce, D. George, and O'Day, Alan (ed.). *The making of modern Irish history: revisionism and the revisionist controversy*. London and New York, 1996.

Brady, Ciaran (ed.). *Interpreting Irish history: the debate on historical revisionism, 1938–1994*. Blackrock, 1994.
Anthology of essays on the character and purpose of Irish historical writing.

Brett, David. *The construction of heritage*. Cork, 1996.

Cadogan, Tim. Supporting roles: a century of Cork's other historical journals. In *Cork Hist. Soc. Jn.*, xcvi (1991), pp 159–64.

Clarke, Aidan. Robert Dudley Edwards (1909–88). In *I.H.S.*, xxvi, no. 102 (Nov. 1988), pp 121–7.

Clarkson, L. A. The writing of Irish economic history since 1968. In *Econ. Hist. Rev.*, xxxiii (1980), pp 100–11.

Coughlan, Anthony. James Hogan, revolutionary, historian, political scientist (1898–1963). In *Hist. Ire.*, vii, no. 1 (1999), 9–10.

CRONE. John Smyth Crone. 1858–1945. [Obituary.] In *I.B.L.*, xxx, no. i (1946), pp 1–3.

Cronne, H. A.; Moody, T. W.; and Quinn, D. B. James Eadie Todd as historian and teacher. In eid. (ed.), *Essays in British and Irish history in honour of James Eadie Todd* (London, 1949), pp ix–xv.

Cullen, Mary. Women's history in Ireland. In Karen Offen, Ruth Pierson, and Jane Rendall (ed.)., *Writing women's history: international perspectives* (London, 1991), pp 429–41.

CURTIS. Edmund Curtis. [Obituary.] In *Anal. Hib.*, no. 16 (1946), pp 387–9.

Dickson, David. McDowell at eighty. In *Hist. Ire.*, i, no. 4 (1993), pp 9–12.
Interview with R. B. McDowell.

Drake, Michael. Professor K. H. Connell. In *I.H.S.*, xix, no. 73 (Mar. 1974), pp 83–5.

Dunlevy, Mairead. Ada K. Longfield (Mrs H. G. Leask) 1899–1987. In *R.S.A.I. Jn.*, cxviii (1988), pp 169–70.

Dunne, Tom. New histories: beyond 'revisionism'. In *The Irish Review*, no. 12 (1992), pp 1–12.

Edwards, R. W. Dudley. T. W. Moody and the origins of *Irish Historical Studies*: a biographical memoir. In *I.H.S.*, xxvi, no. 101 (May 1988), pp 1–2.

Fitzpatrick, David. Women, gender and the writing of Irish history. In *I.H.S.*, xxvii, no. 107 (May 1991), pp 267–73.
Review article.

Gray, Peter. Our man at Oxford. In *Hist. Ire.*, i, no. 3 (1993), pp 9–12.
Interview with Roy Foster.

Foster, R. F. We are all revisionists now. In *The Irish Review*, no. 1 (1986), pp 1–5.

—— *Francis Stewart Leland Lyons, 1923–1983*. London, 1986.

—— History, locality and identity: a lecture to mark the centenary of the Society. In *Cork Hist. Soc. Jn.*, xcvii (1992), pp 1–10.

—— *The Irish story: telling tales and making it up in Ireland*. London, 2001.

Graham, Tommy. A man with a mission. In *Hist. Ire.*, i, no. 1 (1993), pp 52–5.
Interview with Brendan Bradshaw.

Harkness, David. Nicholas Mansergh: historian of modern Ireland. In *Études Irlandaises*, xix, no. 2 (1994), pp 87–95.

Harris, Mary. Whose history? In *Hist. Ire.*, viii, no. 4 (2000), pp 16–19.
Interview with Maria Luddy, director, Women's History Project.

Howe, Stephen. *Ireland and empire: colonial legacies in Irish history and culture.* Oxford, 2000.

Jackson, Alvin. Twentieth-century foxes? Historians and late modern Ireland. In *I.H.S.*, xxxii, no. 126 (Nov. 2000), pp 272–7.
Review article.

Kennedy, Liam. Ireland in the light of the West Country: David S. Johnson (1943–98). In *Ir. Econ. & Soc. Hist.*, xxv (1998), pp vii–xii.

Keogh, Dermot. Ireland and the historiography of European integration. In *Lettre d'Information des Historiens de l'Europe Contemporaine*, vii, nos 1–2 (1992), pp 37–62.

Laffan, Michael. Insular attitudes: the revisionists and their critics. In Máirín Ní Dhonnchadha and Theo Dorgan (ed.), *Revising the rising* (Derry, 1991), pp 106–21.

Lee, J. J. Some aspects of modern Irish historiography. In Ernst Schulin (ed.)., *Gedenkschrift Martin Guhring: studien zur Europäischen geschichte* (Wiesbaden, 1968), pp 431–43.

——(ed.). *Irish historiography, 1970–79.* Cork, 1981.

Lyons, F. S. L. The dilemma of the Irish contemporary historian. In *Hermathena*, cxv (1973), pp 45–56.

McCaffrey, L. J. The American Committee for Irish Studies. In *I.H.S.*, xv, no. 60 (Sept. 1967), pp 446–9.

MacCurtain, Margaret. Late in the field: catholic sisters in twentieth-century Ireland and the new religious history. In *Journal of Women's History*, vi & vii (1995), pp 49–63.

McGuire, James. T. Desmond Williams (1921–87). In *I.H.S.*, xxvi, no. 101 (May 1988), pp 3–7.

Macken, Mary M. In memoriam: Mary T. Hayden; died 12 July 1942. In *Studies*, xxxi (1942), pp 369–71.

McMahon, Deirdre. 'A worthy monument to a great man': Piaras Béaslaí's Life of Michael Collins. In *Bullán*, ii, no. 2 (winter/spring 1996), pp 55–65.

Martin, F. X. Theodore William Moody. In *Hermathena*, cxxxvi (1984), pp 5–7.

Moody, T. W. The first forty years. In *I.H.S.*, xx, no. 80 (Sept. 1977), pp 377–83. *Irish Historical Studies.*

——(ed.). *Irish historiography, 1936–70.* Dublin, 1971.

Mulvey, Helen F. Ireland's commonwealth years, 1922–1949. In Robin W. Winks (ed.), *The historiography of the British empire-commonwealth: trends, interpretations, and resources* (Durham, N. Carolina, 1966), pp 326–43.

——Theodore William Moody (1907–84): an appreciation. In *I.H.S.*, xxiv, no. 94 (Nov. 1984), pp 121–30.

Nutt, Kathleen. Irish identity and the writing of history. In *Éire-Ireland*, xxix, no. 2 (1994), pp 160–72.

O'Connor, Emmet. Reds and the green: problems of the history and historiography of communism in Ireland. In *Science & Society*, lxi, no. 1 (1997), pp 113–18.

O'Flaherty, Kathleen. James Hogan: 1898–1963. In *Studies*, liii (1964), pp 57–60.

O'Halpin, Eunan. Historical revisit: Dorothy Macardle, *The Irish republic* (1937). In *I.H.S.*, xxxi, no. 123 (May 1999), pp 389–94.

Osborough, W. N. (ed.). *The Irish Legal History Society: inaugural addresses*. Blackrock, 1989.

—— In search of Irish legal history: a map for explorers. In *Long Room*, xxxv (1990), pp 28–38.

Our society, 1891–1941. In *Cork Hist. Soc. Jn.*, xlvi (1941), pp 1–5.
Account of the Cork Historical and Archaeological Society.

Rees, Russell. *Ireland, 1905–25: vol. 1: text and historiography*. Newtownards, Co. Down, 1998.

Shaw, Francis. The canon of Irish history—a challenge. In *Studies*, lxi (1972), pp 113–53.

Tierney, Michael. Eoin Mac Neill: a biographical study. In Eoin Mac Neill, *Saint Patrick*, ed. John Ryan (Dublin, 1964), pp 9–34.

Townsend, Susan C. Yanaihara Tadao and the Irish question: a comparative analysis of the Irish and Korean questions, 1919–36. In *I.H.S.*, xxx, no. 118 (Nov. 1996), pp 195–205.

Walker, Brian M. Ireland's historical position: 'colonial' or 'European'. In *The Irish Review*, no. 9 (1990), pp 36–40.

—— *Dancing to history's tune: history, myth and politics in Ireland*. Belfast, 1996.

Whelan, Kevin. Watching the detective. In *Hist. Ire.*, ii, no. 2 (1994), pp 10–12.
Interview with L. M. Cullen.

19 HISTORY OF PRINTING, PUBLISHING, AND THE MASS MEDIA

Adams, Michael. *Censorship: the Irish experience*. Dublin, 1968.

Barrington, Brendan (ed.). *The wartime broadcasts of Francis Stuart 1942–1944*. Dublin, 2000.

Burns-Bisogno, Louisa. *Censoring Irish nationalism: the British, Irish, and American suppression of republican images in film and television, 1909–1995*. Jefferson, N.C., 1997.

Byrne, Gay, and Purcell, Deirdre. *The time of my life*. Dublin, 1989.

Clarke, Paddy. *'Dublin calling': 2RN and the birth of Irish radio*. Dublin, 1986.

Colley, Michael. *The communicators: the history of the Public Relations Institute of Ireland, 1953–1993*. Dublin, 1993.

Cormack, M. Minority languages, nationalism and broadcasting: the British and Irish examples. In *Nations and Nationalism*, vi, no. 3 (2000), pp 383–98.

Donahue, Hugh C. Tradition and technology in Irish publishing. In *Éire-Ireland*, xxvii, no. 3 (1992), pp 7–17.

Farrell, Brian (ed.). *Communications and community in Ireland*. Dublin and Cork, 1984. (Thomas Davis Lectures.)

Flynn, Arthur. *Irish film: 100 years*. Bray, Co. Wicklow, 1996.

Gibbons, Luke. *Transformations in Irish culture*. Cork, 1996.

Gorham, Maurice. *Forty years of Irish broadcasting*. Dublin, 1967.

Gray, Tony. *Mr Smyllie, Sir*. Dublin and gigginstown, Co. Westmeath, 1991.
R. M. Smyllie, editor of *Irish Times* 1934–1954.

Hayley, Barbara, and McKay, Enda (ed.). *Three hundred years of Irish periodicals*. Dublin and Gigginstown, Co. Westmeath, 1987.

Horgan, John. *Irish media: a critical history since 1922*. London and New York, 2001.
Extensive bibliography.

In praise of Ireland: photographs from the Source collection, Dublin. Introduction by
Jane Ewart-Biggs. Dublin, 1987.

Kelly, Mary J., and O'Connor, Barbara (ed.). *Media audiences in Ireland: power and
cultural identity*. Dublin, 1997.

Kennedy, Brian P. Seventy-five years of *Studies*. In *Studies*, lxxv, no. 300 (1986),
pp 361–73.

Kinane, Vincent. *A history of the Dublin University Press, 1734–1976*. Dublin, 1994.

Lewis, Gifford. *The Yeats sisters and the Cuala* [Press]. Blackrock, 1994.

Lynch, Brian. The first agricultural broadcasts on 2RN. In *Hist. Ire.*, vii, no. 2
(1999), pp 42–5.

McGuinne, Dermot. *Irish type design: a history of printing types in the Irish character*.
Blackrock, 1992.

McKeane, Ian. Michael Collins and the media—then and now. In *Hist. Ire.*, iii, no. 3
(1995), pp 23–6.

McLoone, Martin. *Irish film: the emergence of a contemporary cinema*. London, 2000.

—— and MacMahon, John (ed.). *Television and Irish society: 21 years of Irish television*. Dublin, 1984.

McRedmond, Louis (ed.). *Written on the wind: personal memories of Irish radio
1926–76*. Dublin, 1976.

Marcus, Louis. *The Irish film industry*. Dublin, [1967].

Martin, F. X. The Thomas Davis lectures, 1953–67. In *I.H.S.*, xv, no. 59 (Mar.
1967), pp 276–302.

Ó Broin, Leon. Amending Irish broadcasting law. In *EBU Review*, xxvi, no. 5
(Sept. 1975), pp 39–41; xxvii, no. 1 (Jan. 1976), pp 38–40; xxviii (Mar. 1977),
pp 48–9.

O'Donnell, E. E. *Father Browne's Dublin: photographs, 1925–50*. Dublin, 1993.

O'Donoghue, David. *Hitler's Irish voices: the story of German radio's wartime Irish
service*. Belfast, 1998.

Ó Drisceoil, Donal. *Censorship in Ireland, 1939–1945: neutrality, politics and society*.
Cork, 1996.

Ó Glaisne, Risteárd. *Raidió na Gaeltachta*. Indreabhán, Co. Galway, 1982.

Ó Neill, Séamus. The Gúm. In *The Bell*, xii (1946), pp 136–40.
Government firm publishing Irish-language material.

Oram, Hugh. *The newspaper book: a history of newspapers in Ireland, 1649–1983*.
Dublin, 1983.

O'Toole, Michael. *More kicks than pence: a life in Irish journalism*. Swords, 1992.
Irish Press, 1960s–90s.

Quinlan, Tom. Ferreting out evil: the records of the committee on evil literature. In
Ir. Archives, iii, no. 2 (1996), pp 35–41.

Rockett, Kevin. *The Irish filmography: fiction films, 1896–1996*. Dublin, 1996.

—— Gibbons, Luke; and Hill, John (ed.). *Cinema and Ireland*. London and Sydney,
1987.

Savage, Robert J. *Irish television: the political and social origins*. Cork, 1996.

Schofield, Carey. *Ireland: photographs 1840–1930*. London, 1994.

Smyth, Patrick, and Hazelkorn, Ellen (ed.). *Let in the light: censorship, secrecy and democracy*. Dingle, 1993.

Walker, Graham. 'The Irish Dr Goebbels'. Frank Gallagher and Irish republican propaganda. In *Journal of Contemporary History*, xxvii (1992), pp 149–65.

Woodman, Kieran. *Media control in Ireland, 1923–83*. Carbondale, Ill., 1985.

20   BIOGRAPHY

ABERDEEN. *'We twa': reminiscences of Lord and Lady Aberdeen*. By John C. Gordon and Ishbel M. Gordon. 2 vols. London, 1925.

—— *Ishbel: Lady Aberdeen in Ireland*. By Maureen Keane. Newtownards, 1999.

ANDREWS. *Dublin made me*. By C. S. Andrews. Dublin, 1979.

—— *Man of no property*. By C. S. Andrews. Dublin, 1982.

BAILEY. *Throttle full open: a life of Lady Bailey, Irish aviatrix*. By Jane Falloon. Dublin, 1999.

BARRY. *The Tom Barry story*. By Meda Ryan. Dublin, 1982.

BLANEY. *Neil Blaney: a soldier of destiny*. By Kevin Rafter. Dublin, 1993.

BOLAND. *Harry Boland: a biography*. By Jim Maher. Cork, 1998.

—— *Harry Boland: a man divided*. By Andrew Brasier and John Kelly. Dublin, 2000.

BRADY. *Doctor of millions: the rise and fall of stamp king Dr Paul Brady*. By Séamus Brady. Tralee, 1965.
Encouraged speculation in postage stamps.

BREEN. *My fight for Irish freedom*. By Dan Breen. New ed., Dublin, 1981. First published Dublin, 1924; revised and expanded ed., 1964.

BROWNE. *Against the tide*. By Noël Browne. Dublin, 1986.

—— *Thanks for the tea, Mrs Browne: my life with Noël*. By Phyllis Browne. Dublin, 1998.

—— *Noël Browne: passionate outsider*. By John Horgan. Dublin, 2000.

BRUGHA. *Cathal Brugha: a shaol is a thréithe*. By Tomás Ó Dochartaigh. Dublin, 1969.

BUTLER. Far-seeing gifts: Hubert Butler, 1900–1991. By W. J. McCormack. In *Éire-Ireland*, xxvi, no. 1 (1991), pp 95–100.

CARNEY. *Silent radical: Winifred Carney, 1887–1943*. Dublin, 2000.

CHARTRES. *John Chartres: mystery man of the treaty*. By Brian P. Murphy. Blackrock, 1995.

CHILDERS. *The riddle of Erskine Childers*. By Michael McInerney. Dublin, 1971.

—— *Damned Englishman: a study of Erskine Childers (1870–1922)*. By Tom Cox. New York, 1975.

—— *The riddle of Erskine Childers*. By Andrew Boyd. London, 1977.

—— *Erskine Childers*. By Jim Ring. London, 1996.

CHILDERS. *Erskine H. Childers, president of Ireland: a biography*. By John N. Young. Gerrards Cross, 1985.

CHURCHILL. *Churchill, a founder of modern Ireland*. By Anthony J. Jordan. Dublin, 1995.

CLARE. Wallace George Clare, 1895–1963. In *Ir. Geneal.*, iii (1964), pp 281–6.
Founder of Irish Genealogical Research Society.

COLLINS. *Michael Collins.* By Desmond Ryan. n.p., n.d. First published as *The invisible army* (London, 1932).

—— *Michael Collins.* By Rex Taylor. London, 1958. 2nd ed. 1970.

—— *Michael Collins: the lost leader.* By Margery Forester. London, 1971; reissued Dublin, 1989.

—— *Michael Collins.* By Leon Ó Broin. Dublin, 1980.

—— *Michael Collins: a biography.* By Tim Pat Coogan. London, 1990.

—— *Michael Collins.* By Colm Connolly. London, 1996.

—— *Michael Collins and the women in his life.* By Meda Ryan. Cork, 1996.

—— *Michael Collins: a life.* By James A. Mackay. Edinburgh, 1996.

—— *Michael Collins: the final days.* By Justin Nelson. Dublin, 1997.

—— *Michael Collins: the secret file.* By A. T. Q. Stewart. Belfast, 1997.

—— *Big fellow, long fellow: a joint biography of Collins and de Valera.* By T. Ryle Dwyer. Dublin, 1998.

CONNOLLY. *Memoirs of Senator Joseph Connolly (1885–1961): a founder of modern Ireland.* Ed. J. Anthony Gaughan. Blackrock, 1996.

COSGRAVE. *William T. Cosgrave and the foundation of the Irish Free State.* By Brian A. Reynolds. Kilkenny, 1999.

COX. *Arthur Cox, 1891–1965.* By Eugene McCague. Dublin, 1994.
Lawyer and missionary priest.

CURTIS. *From empire to imperial commonwealth: a biography of Lionel Curtis.* By Deborah Lavin. Oxford and New York, 1995.

DE VALERA. *De Valera* By Denis Gwynn. London, 1933.

—— *De Valera.* By Tomás Ó Neill and Pádraig Ó Fiannachta. 2 vols. Dublin, 1968, 1970.
In Irish: for comparison with the English version (next entry) see J. H. Whyte in *I.H.S.*, xvii, no. 68 (Sept. 1971), pp 593–5.

—— *Eamon de Valera.* By the earl of Longford and T. P. O'Neill. London, 1974. First published 1970.

—— *The life and times of Eamon de Valera.* By Constantine Fitzgibbon. Dublin, 1973.

—— *Eamon de Valera 1882–1975.* By M. McInerney. Dublin, 1976.

—— *Eamon de Valera.* By T. Ryle Dwyer. Dublin, 1980.

—— *Éamon de Valera.* By Owen Dudley Edwards. Cardiff, 1987.

—— *De Valera: the man and the myths.* By T. Ryle Dwyer. Swords, 1991.

—— *De Valera: Long fellow, long shadow.* By Tim Pat Coogan. London, 1993, 1995.

—— *Eamon de Valera.* By Pauric Travers. Dundalk, 1994.

DE VALERA. *Sinéad: scéal Shinéad Bean de Valera.* By Caitlín Uí Thallamhain. Dublin, 1979.

DILLON. *James Dillon: a biography.* By Maurice Manning. Dublin, 1999.

DILLON. *John Dillon: a biography.* By F. S. L. Lyons. London, 1968.

DOUGLAS. *Memoirs of Senator James G. Douglas (1887–1954): concerned citizen.* Ed. J. Anthony Gaughan. Dublin, 1998.

DUFF. *Frank Duff.* By Leon Ó Broin. Dublin, 1982.

FITZGERALD. *Garret: the enigma. Dr Garret FitzGerald*. By Raymond Smith. Dublin, 1985. 2nd ed. 1986.

—— *All in a life: an autobiography*. By Garret FitzGerald. Dublin, 1991.

GAVAN DUFFY. *George Gavan Duffy, 1882–1951: a legal biography*. By G. M. Golding. Blackrock, 1982.

GREAVES. *C. Desmond Greaves, 1913–1988*. By Anthony Coughlan. Dublin, 1990.

GRIFFITH. *Arthur Griffith*. By Padraic Colum. Dublin, 1959.

—— *Arthur Griffith*. By Richard P. Davis. Dundalk, 1976.

—— *Arthur Griffith*. By Calton Younger. Dublin, 1981.

—— *Arthur Griffith*. By Brian Maye. Dublin, 1997.

HAUGHEY. *The boss: Charles J. Haughey in government*. By Joe Joyce and Peter Murtagh. Swords, 1983.

—— *The statesman: a study of the role of Charles J Haughey in the Ireland of the future*. By John M. Feehan. Cork, 1985. [See also id., *An apology to the Irish people* (Cork, 1988)].

—— *Charlie: the political biography of Charles J. Haughey*. By T. Ryle Dwyer. Dublin, 1987.

—— *The Haughey file: the unprecedented career and last years of the boss*. By Stephen Collins. Dublin, 1992.

—— *Haughey's thirty years of controversy*. By T. Ryle Dwyer. Cork, 1992.

—— *Haughey: his life and unlucky deeds*. By Bruce Arnold. London, 1993.

—— *Short fellow: a biography of Charles J. Haughey*. By T. Ryle Dwyer. Dublin, 1995; revised ed., Dublin, 1999.

HEALY. *T. M. Healy*. By Frank Callanan. Cork, 1996.

HYDE. *Douglas Hyde: a maker of modern Ireland*. By Janet Dunleavy and Gareth Dunleavy. Berkeley, Calif., 1991.

INGLIS. *Downstart: the autobiography of Brian Inglis*. By Brian Inglis. London, 1990.

JOHNSON. *Thomas Johnson, 1872–1963: first leader of the Labour party in Dáil Éireann*. By J. Anthony Gaughan. Dublin, 1980.

LARKIN. *James Larkin, Irish labour leader 1876–1947*. By Emmet Larkin. London, 1965; repr. 1977.

LEMASS. *Seán Lemass*. By Brian Farrell. Dublin, 1983.

—— *Seán Lemass: a biography*. By Michael O'Sullivan. Dublin, 1994.

—— *Seán Lemass: the enigmatic patriot*. By John Horgan. Dublin, 1997.

—— *Seán Lemass*. By Robert Savage. Dundalk, 1999.

LENIHAN. *For the record*. By Brian Lenihan. Dublin, 1991.

—— *Lenihan: his life and loyalties*. By James Downey. Dublin, 1998.

LYNCH. *Jack Lynch: a biography*. By T. P. O'Mahony. Tallaght, Co. Dublin, 1991.

LYNCH. *No other law: the story of Liam Lynch and the Irish Republican Army, 1916–23*. By Florence O'Donoghue. Dublin, 1986. First published 1954.

MACBRIDE. *Seán MacBride: a biography*. By Anthony J. Jordan. Dublin, 1993.

MCDYER. *Father McDyer of Glencolumcille: an autobiography*. By James McDyer. Dingle, 1997. First published 1982.

MAC EOIN. *The Sean Mac Eoin story*. By Padraic O'Farrell. Dublin, 1981.

MACNEILL. *Eoin MacNeill: scholar and man of action*. By Michael Tierney. Ed. F. X. Martin. Oxford, 1980.

MAC STIOFÁIN. *Memoirs of a revolutionary*. By Seán Mac Stiofáin. London, 1975. Chief of staff of Provisional I.R.A., 1970–72.

MACSWINEY. *Soul of fire: a biography of Mary MacSwiney*. By Charlotte H. Fallon. Cork, 1986.

MAHR. Adolf Mahr. In *Archaeology Ireland*, vii, no. 3 (1993), pp 29–30. Director of National Museum of Ireland, 1927–39.

MARKIEVICZ. *Terrible beauty: a life of Constance Markievicz, 1868–1927*. By Diana Norman. London, 1987; Dublin, 1988.

MELLOWS. *Liam Mellows and the Irish revolution*. By C. Desmond Greaves. London, 1971.

MORIARTY. *Joan Denise Moriarty: founder of Irish national ballet*. Ed. Ruth Fleischmann. Cork, 1998.

MULCAHY. *Portrait of a revolutionary: General Richard Mulcahy and the founding of the Irish Free State*. By Maryann Gialanella Valiulis. Blackrock, 1992.

O'BRIEN. *Conor: a biography of Conor Cruise O'Brien*. By D. H. Akenson. 2 vols. Kingston, Ontario, 1994.

—— *To laugh or to weep: a biography of Conor Cruise O'Brien*. By Anthony J. Jordan. Dublin, 1994.

—— *Memoir: my life and themes*. By Conor Cruise O'Brien. Dublin, 1999.

O'BRIEN. *We shall rise again*. By Nora Connolly O'Brien. London, 1981.

Ó BROIN. *Just like yesterday: an autobiography*. By Leon Ó Broin. Dublin, 1986.

Ó DÁLAIGH. *Immediate man: cuimhní ar Chearbhall Ó Dálaigh*. Ed. Aidan Carl Mathews. Portlaoise, 1983.

O'DONNELL. *Peadar O'Donnell: Irish social rebel*. By Michael McInerney. Dublin, 1974.

—— *Peadar O'Donnell*. By Peter Hegarty. Cork, 1999.

O'FAOLAIN. *Sean O'Faolain: a life*. By Maurice Harmon. London, 1994.

O'FLANAGAN. *They have fooled you again: Michael O'Flanagan (1876–1942), priest, republican, social critic*. By Denis Carroll. Blackrock, 1993.

O'HIGGINS. *Kevin O'Higgins*. By Terence de Vere White. Dublin, 1986. First published London, 1948; 2nd ed., Tralee, 1966.

O'HIGGINS. *A double life*. By Thomas F. O'Higgins. Dublin, 1996.

O'MALLEY. *Ernie O'Malley: I.R.A. intellectual*. By Richard English. Oxford, 1998.

O'RAHILLY. *Alfred O'Rahilly, vol 1: academic. 2: public figure. 3, pt 1: social reformer. 3, pt 2: controversialist; catholic apologist*. By J. Anthony Gaughan. 4 vols. Dublin, 1986–93.

O'REILLY. *Oh really O'Reilly: a biography of Dr A. J. F. O'Reilly*. By C. H. Walsh. Blackrock, 1992.

—— *The player: the life of Tony O'Reilly*. By Ivan Fallon. London, 1994.

PECK. *Dublin from Downing Street*. By John Peck. Dublin, 1978.

REYNOLDS. *Albert Reynolds: the Longford leader: the unauthorised biography*. By Tim Ryan. Dublin, 1994.

ROBINSON. *Mary Robinson: the life and times of an Irish liberal*. By Michael O'Sullivan. Dublin, 1993.

—— *Mary Robinson: the authorised biography*. By Olivia O'Leary and Helen Burke. London, 1998.

RYAN. *Frank Ryan: the search for the republic.* By Seán Cronin. Dublin, 1980.

SHEEHY SKEFFINGTON. *Skeff: a life of Owen Sheehy Skeffington, 1909–1970.* By Andrée Sheehy Skeffington. Dublin, 1991.

SPRING. *Dick Spring: a safe pair of hands!* By Tim Ryan. Dublin, 1993.

SWIFT. *John Swift: an Irish dissident.* By John P. Swift. Dublin, 1991.
Socialist and trade unionist.

WALSH. *Recollections of a rebel.* By J. J. Walsh. Tralee, 1944.

YEATS. *The Yeats sisters: a biography of Susan and Elizabeth Yeats.* By Joan Hardwick. London, 1996.

—— *Family secrets: William Butler Yeats and his relatives.* By William M. Murphy. Dublin, 1995.

C BIOGRAPHICAL AND OTHER WORKS OF REFERENCE

Bennett, Douglas. *Encyclopedia of Dublin.* Dublin, 1991.

Boylan, Henry. *A dictionary of Irish biography.* 3rd ed. Dublin, 1998. First published 1978.

Breathnach, Diarmuid, and Ní Mhurchú, Máire. *Beathaisnéis 1882–1982.* 5 vols. Dublin, 1992–7.
Biographical dictionary of writers in Irish.

Cairnduff, Maureen (ed.). *Who's who in Ireland: 'the influential 1000'.* Dún Laoghaire, 1984. 2nd ed., updated, 1991. 3rd ed., updated, ... *plus 200 rising stars,* 1999.

Cleeve, Brian. *Dictionary of Irish writers.* 3 vols, Cork, 1967–71. Revised ed. published in 1 vol. as Anne M. Brady and Brian Cleeve, *A biographical dictionary of Irish writers* (Gigginstown, Co. Westmeath, 1985).

The concise dictionary of national biography: from earliest times to 1985. 3 vols. Oxford and New York, 1992.

Connolly, S. J. (ed.). *The Oxford companion to Irish history.* Oxford, 1998.

Cordasco, Francesco. *Dictionary of American immigration history.* Metuchen, N.J., and London, 1990.

Cullen, Donal. *Ireland on the ball: a complete record of the international matches of the Republic of Ireland soccer team, March 1926 to June 1993.* Dublin, 1993.

Eaton, George. *Introducing Ireland: a critical guide with biographies of over 450 leaders.* Cork and Dublin, 1989.

Encylopaedia of Ireland. Ed. Victor Meally and others. Dublin, 1968.

Farrelly, Jim. *Who's who in Irish politics: the top 500.* Dublin, [1990].

Fewer, T. N. *Waterford people: a biographical dictionary.* Callaghane, Waterford, 1998.

Glazier, Michael (ed.). *The encyclopedia of the Irish in America.* Notre Dame, 1999.

Harrison, Richard S. *A biographical dictionary of Irish quakers.* Dublin, 1997.

Herlihy, Jim. *The Royal Irish Constabulary: a complete alphabetical list of officers and men, 1816–1922.* Dublin, 1999.

Hickey, D. J., and Doherty, J. E. *A dictionary of Irish history since 1800.* Dublin, 1980.

———— *A chronology of Irish history since 1500.* Dublin, 1989.

Hogan, Robert (ed.). *Dictionary of Irish literature.* Revised and expanded ed. 2 vols. London, 1996. Previous ed., Westport, Conn., and Dublin, 1979.

Kehoe, A. M. *History makers of 20th century Ireland: 10 concise biographies*. Dublin, 1989.

McCormack, W. J. (ed.). *The Blackwell companion to modern Irish culture*. Oxford, 1999.

MacLysaght, Edward. *Irish families: their names, arms, and origins*. Dublin, 1957. 4th ed., revised and enlarged, Blackrock, 1985.

—— *More Irish families: a new revised and enlarged edition of Irish families*. Galway and Dublin, 1960.

McNamara, Maedhbh, and Mooney, Paschal. *Women in parliament: Ireland 1918–2000*. Dublin, 2000.

McRedmond, Louis (ed.). *Modern Irish lives: dictionary of 20th-century biography*. Dublin, 1996.

Moody, T. W.; Martin, F. X.; and Byrne, F. J. (ed.). *A new history of Ireland, viii: a chronology of Irish history to 1976*. Oxford, 1982.

—— —— —— *A new history of Ireland, ix: maps, genealogies, lists*. Oxford, 1984.

Ó Céirín, Kit, and Ó Céirín, Cyril. *Women of Ireland: a biographical dictionary*. Kinvara, Galway, 1996.

O'Clery, Conor. *Phrases make history here: a century of Irish political quotations, 1886–1986*. Dublin, 1986.

—— *Ireland in quotes: a history of the 20th century*. Dublin, 1999.

O'Day, Alan, and Stevenson, John (ed.). *Irish historical documents since 1800*. Dublin, 1991.

O'Farrell, Padraic. *Who's who in the Irish war of independence and civil war, 1916–1923*. Dublin, 1997.

O'Leary, Cornelius. *Irish elections, 1918–1977*. Dublin, 1979.

Room, Adrian. *A dictionary of Irish place-names*. Belfast, 1986. Revised ed., 1994.

Share, Bernard. *Irish lives*. Dublin, 1971.

Snoddy, Theo. *Dictionary of Irish artists: 20th century*. Dublin, 1996.

Vallely, Fintan (ed.). *The companion to Irish traditional music*. Cork, 1999.

Vaughan, W. E., and Fitzpatrick, A. J. (ed.). *Irish historical statistics: population, 1821–1971*. Dublin, 1978. (A New History of Ireland, Ancillary Publications II.)

Walker, Brian M. (ed.). *Parliamentary election results in Ireland, 1918–1992*. Dublin and Belfast, 1992. (A New History of Ireland, Ancillary Publications V.)

Welch, Robert. *The Oxford companion to Irish literature*. Oxford, 1996.

NORTHERN IRELAND

I BIBLIOGRAPHIES, CATALOGUES, AND GUIDES

Bardon, Jonathan. *A guide to local history sources in the Public Record Office of Northern Ireland*. Belfast, 2000.

Bell, Robert. *Northern Ireland political periodicals, 1966–1992: a bibliography of the holdings of the Linen Hall Library*. Belfast, 1994.

Collett, Rosemary J. *Northern Ireland statistics: a guide to principal sources*. Belfast, 1979.

Crossey, Ciarán. Labour history sources in the Linen Hall Library, Belfast. In *Saothar*, xxii (1997), pp 29–44.

Darby, J. P. *Register of research into the Irish conflict.* Belfast, 1972.

Deutsch, R. R. *Northern Ireland, 1921–74: a select bibliography.* New York and London, 1975.

Gracey, J. W., and Howard, P. Northern Ireland political literature, 1968–70: a catalogue of the collection in the Linen Hall Library. In *Ir. Booklore*, i (1971), pp 44–82.

Loughran, Grainne, and McCavana, Marian. *The radio catalogue: BBC Northern Ireland archives at the Ulster Folk and Transport Museum.* Belfast, 1993.

Malcomson, A. P. W. The publication programme of the Public Record Office of Northern Ireland. In *Ir. Booklore*, i (1971), pp 210–21.

Maltby, Arthur. *The government of Northern Ireland, 1922–72: a catalogue and breviate of parliamentary papers.* Dublin, 1974.

Maxwell, Ian. *Tracing your ancestors in Northern Ireland: a guide to ancestry research in the Public Record Office.* Edinburgh, 1997.

O'Neill, Robert K. *Ulster libraries: archives, museums & ancestral heritage centres.* Belfast, 1997.

Parkhill, Trevor. Labour records in the P.R.O.N.I. (sources). In *Saothar*, vii (1981), pp 100–06.

Public Record Office of Northern Ireland. Accessions of records of interest to the social and economic historian, 1989– . In *Ir. Econ. & Soc. Hist.*, xvii (1990), p. 95; xviii (1991), p. 56; xx (1993), pp 74–5; xxi (1994), pp 74–5; xxii (1995), pp 89–90; xxiii (1996), p. 122; xxiv (1997), pp 107–8; xxv (1998), p. 90; xxvi (1999), pp 83–4; xxvii (2000), pp 75–6; xxviii (2001), pp 74–5; xxix (2002), pp 72–4. In progress.

——*A guide to cabinet conclusions, 1921–1943.* Belfast, 1993.

Rolston, Bill, and others. *A social science bibliography of Northern Ireland 1945–1983: material published since 1945 relating to Northern Ireland since 1921.* Belfast, 1983.

Rose, Richard. Ulster politics: a select bibliography of political discord. In *Political Studies*, xx (1972), pp 206–12.

Shannon, Michael Owen. *Northern Ireland.* Santa Barbara, Calif., 1992.

Smyth, Peter. Thirty years on. In *Irish Archives Bulletin*, v (1975), pp 31–40.

Whyte, John H. *Interpreting Northern Ireland.* Oxford, 1990.
 Guide to and assessment of works on the community divide, with extensive bibliography (pp 269–96).

II SECONDARY WORKS

A GENERAL HISTORY

Arthur, Paul, and Jeffery, Keith. *Northern Ireland since 1968.* 1st ed. Oxford, 1988. 2nd ed., Oxford, 1996.

Bardon, Jonathan. *A history of Ulster.* Belfast, 1992.

——*A shorter illustrated history of Ulster.* Belfast, 1996.

Buckland, Patrick. *A history of Northern Ireland.* Dublin, 1981.

Farrell, Michael. *Northern Ireland: the Orange state.* London, 1976.

Fitzpatrick, David. *The two Irelands, 1912–1939.* Oxford and New York, 1998.

Foster, R. F. *Modern Ireland 1600–1972*. London, 1988.

Harkness, David. *Northern Ireland since 1920*. Dublin, 1983.

Heath, Anthony; Breen, Richard; and Whelan, Christopher (ed.). *Ireland north and south: perspectives from social science*. Oxford, 1999.

Hennessey, Thomas. *A history of Northern Ireland, 1920–1996*. Dublin and Basingstoke, 1997.

Lee, J. J. *Ireland 1912–1985: politics and society*. Cambridge, 1989.

Longford, Frank Pakenham, earl of, and McHardy, Anne. *Ulster*. London, 1981.

Lyons, F. S. L. *Ireland since the famine*. London, 1971. Revised ed., 1973.

Moody, T. W. *The Ulster question, 1603–1973*. Dublin and Cork, 1974.

—— and Beckett, J. C. (ed.). *Ulster since 1800: a political and economic survey*. London, 1954.

de Paor, Liam. *Divided Ulster*. 2nd ed., Harmondsworth, 1971. First published 1970.

Shearman, Hugh. *Northern Ireland, 1921–1971*. Belfast, 1962; 2nd ed., 1971.

Stewart, A. T. Q. *The narrow ground: aspects of Ulster, 1609–1969*. London, 1977. Belfast, 1997.

Wichert, Sabine. *Northern Ireland since 1945*. London, 1991. 2nd ed., 1999.

Wilson, Thomas (ed.). *Ulster under home rule: a study of the political and economic problems of Northern Ireland*. London, 1955.

—— *Ulster: conflict and consent*. Oxford, 1989.

B   SPECIAL FIELDS AND TOPICS

1   POLITICAL HISTORY

Arthur, Paul. *The People's Democracy 1968–1973*. Belfast, 1974.

—— *Government and politics of Northern Ireland*. 2nd ed., London and New York, 1984. 1st ed., 1980.

Aughey, Arthur. *Under siege: Ulster unionism and the Anglo–Irish agreement*. Belfast, 1989.

Ball, Stuart, and Seldon, Anthony (ed.). *The Heath government, 1970–1974: a reappraisal*. Harlow and London, 1996.

Barritt, D. P., and Carter, C. F. *The Northern Ireland problem: a study in group relations*. London, 1962. 2nd ed., London, 1972.

Bell, Geoffrey. *The protestants of Ulster*. London, 1976.

Bew, Paul. A protestant parliament and a protestant state: some reflections on government and minority in Ulster 1921–43. In Art Cosgrove and J. I. McGuire (ed.), *Parliament and community* (Belfast, 1983). (*Hist. Studies*, xiv.)

—— Darwin, Kenneth, and Gillespie, Gordon (ed.). *Passion and prejudice: nationalist/unionist conflict in Ulster in the 1930s and the origins of the Irish Association*. Belfast, 1993.

—— Gibbon, Peter; and Patterson, Henry. *Northern Ireland 1921–1994: political forces and social classes*. London, 1995. First published as *The state in Northern Ireland 1921–72: political forces and social classes* (Manchester, 1979).

—— and Norton, Christopher. The unionist state and the outdoor relief riots of 1932. In *Econ. & Soc. Rev.*, x (1979), pp 255–65.

—— and Patterson, Henry. *The British state and the Ulster crisis: from Wilson to Thatcher.* London, 1985.

Bowman, John. *De Valera and the Ulster question 1917–1973.* Oxford, 1982.

Boyce, D. George. *The Irish question and British politics, 1868–1986.* London, 1988.

Boyd, Andrew. *Holy war in Belfast.* Tralee, 1969. 3rd ed., Belfast, 1987.

Bryan, Dominic. *Orange parades: the politics of ritual, tradition and control.* London, 2000.

Buckland, Patrick. *Irish unionism, 1885–1923: a documentary history.* Belfast, 1973.

—— *Irish unionism: two—Ulster unionism and the origins of Northern Ireland, 1886–1922.* Dublin and New York, 1973.

—— The history of Ulster unionism, 1886–1939. In *History*, lx (1975), pp 211–23.

—— *The factory of grievances: devolved government in Northern Ireland 1921–39.* Dublin and New York, 1979.

Budge, Ian, and O'Leary, Cornelius. *Belfast: approach to crisis: a study of Belfast politics 1613–1970.* London, 1973.

Campbell, T. J. *Fifty years of Ulster, 1890–1940.* Belfast, 1941. Later published as *Irish action: nationalist politics in northern Ireland in the Stormont period...* By T. J. Campbell and Eddie McAteer. Belfast, 1979.

Carlton, Charles (ed.). *Bigotry and blood: documents on the Ulster troubles.* Chicago, 1977.

Carroll, Joseph T. *Ireland in the war years 1939–45.* Newton Abbot, 1975.

Churchill, Winston S. *The world crisis: the aftermath.* London, 1929.

Costello, Francis. King George V's speech at Stormont (1921): prelude to the Anglo–Irish truce. In *Éire-Ireland*, xxii, no. 3 (1987), pp 43–57.

Coulter, Colin. The character of unionism. In *Irish Political Studies*, ix (1994), pp 1–24.

Cunningham, Michael J. *British government policy in Northern Ireland, 1969–89: its nature and execution.* Manchester and New York, 1991.

Dixon, Paul. 'A house divided cannot stand': Britain, bipartisanship and Northern Ireland. In *Contemporary Record*, ix (1995), pp 147–87.

Dooley, Terence. Protestant migration from the Free State to Northern Ireland, 1920–25: a private census for Co. Fermanagh. In *Clogher Rec.*, xv, no. 3 (1996), pp 87–132.

Doyle, John. *'Ulster like Israel can only lose once': Ulster unionism, security and citizenship, 1972–97.* Dublin, 1997.

Edwards, Ruth Dudley. *The faithful tribe: an intimate portrait of the loyal institutions.* London, 1999.

Elliott, Marianne. *The catholics of Ulster: a history.* London, 2000.

Elvert, Jürgen (ed.). *Nordirland in Geschichte und Gegenwart.* Stuttgart, 1994.

—— Nordirland als dreifache Peripherie [N.I. as threefold periphery]. In Hans-H. Nolte (ed.), *Europäische innere Peripherien im 20 Jahrhundert* (Stuttgart, 1997), pp 113–30.

Fisk, Robert. *In time of war: Ireland, Ulster and the price of neutrality 1939–45.* London, 1983.

Follis, Bryan A. *A state under siege: the establishment of Northern Ireland, 1920–25.* Oxford, 1995.

Fox, Colm. *The making of a minority: political developments in Derry and the north 1912–25.* Londonderry, 1997.

Fraser, T. G. *Partition in Ireland, India and Palestine: theory and practice.* London, 1984.

Fraser, T. G. (ed.). *The Irish parading tradition: following the drum*. Basingstoke, 2000.

Gallagher, Frank. *The indivisible island: the history of the partition of Ireland*. London, 1957.

Greer, Alan. *Rural politics in Northern Ireland: policy networks and agricultural development since partition*. Aldershot, 1996.

Guelke, Adrian. *Northern Ireland: the international perspective*. Dublin and New York, 1988.

Haddick Flynn, Kevin. *Orangeism: the making of a tradition*. Dublin, 1999.

Harbinson, John F. *The Ulster Unionist party 1882–1973: its development and organisation*. Belfast, 1973.

Harrison, Henry. *Ulster and the British empire, 1939*. London, 1939.

Hastings, Max. *Ulster 1969: the fight for civil rights in Northern Ireland*. London, 1970.

Hepburn, A. C. The Belfast riots of 1935. In *Social History*, xv, no. 1 (1990), pp 75–96.

Holt, Edgar. *Protest in arms: the Irish troubles 1916–1926*. London, 1960.

Hopkinson, Michael A. The Craig–Collins pact of 1922: two attempted reforms of the Northern Ireland government. In *I.H.S.*, xxvii, no. 106 (Nov. 1990), pp 145–58.

Hughes, Eamonn (ed.). *Culture and politics in Northern Ireland, 1960–1990*. Milton Keynes, 1991.

Johnson, D. S. The Belfast boycott, 1920–22. In J. M. Goldstrom and L. A. Clarkson (ed.), *Irish population, economy and society: essays in honour of the late K. H. Connell* (Oxford, 1981), pp 287–307.

Jones, Thomas. *Whitehall diary, vol. 3: Ireland 1918–1925*. Ed. Keith Middlemass. London, 1971.

Kenna, G. B. (Rev. John Hassan, C. C.). *Facts and figures of the Belfast pogrom, 1920–1922*. Dublin, 1922.

Kennedy, Dennis. *The widening gulf: Northern attitudes to the independent Irish state 1919–49*. Belfast, 1988.

Killen, John. *John Bull's famous circus: Ulster history through the postcard 1905–1985*. Dublin, 1985.

—— *The unkindest cut: a cartoon history of Ulster, 1900–2000*. Belfast, 2000.

Kingsley, Paul. *Londonderry revisited: a loyalist analysis of the civil rights controversy*. Belfast, 1989.

Laffan, Michael. *The partition of Ireland 1911–1925*. Dundalk, 1983.

Loughlin, James. Northern Ireland and British fascism in the inter-war years. In *I.H.S.*, xxix, no. 116 (Nov. 1995), pp 537–52.

—— *The Ulster question since 1945*. Basingstoke, 1998.

Lynn, Brendan. *Holding the ground: the nationalist party in Northern Ireland 1945–72*. Aldershot, 1997.

McAuley, J. W., and McCormack, P. J. The protestant working class and the state in Northern Ireland since 1930: a problematic relationship. In Sean Hutton and Paul Stewart (ed.), *Irish histories: aspects of state, society and ideology* (London, 1991), pp 114–28.

McCartney, Clem, and Bryson, Lucy. *Clashing symbols? A report on the use of flags, anthems and other national symbols in Northern Ireland*. Belfast, 1994.

McCluskey, Conn. *Up off their knees: a commentary on the civil rights movement in Northern Ireland*. [Belfast], 1989.

McIntosh, Gillian. Symbolic mirrors: commemorations of Edward Carson in the 1930s. In *I.H.S.*, xxxii, no. 125 (May 2000), pp. 93–112.

McKay, Susan. *Northern protestants: an unsettled people*. Belfast, 2000.

MacNeill, Ronald. *Ulster's stand for union*. London, 1922.

Mitchell, Paul, and Wilford, Rick (ed.). *Politics in Northern Ireland*. Oxford, 1998. Boulder, Colo., 1999.

Morgan, Austen. *Labour and partition: the Belfast working class, 1905–1933*. London, 1991.

Murphy, Gerard. *John Hume and the SDLP: impact and survival in Northern Ireland*. Dublin, 1998.

Newsinger, John. Ulster and the downfall of the Labour government 1974–79. In *Race and Class*, xxxiii (1991), pp 45–57.

Norton, Christopher. The Left in Northern Ireland 1921–1932. In *Labour History Review*, lx, no. 1 (1995), pp 3–20.

——The Irish Labour party in Northern Ireland 1949–1958. In *Saothar*, xxi (1996), pp 47–59.

O'Brien, Conor Cruise. *States of Ireland*. London, 1972, 1974.

O'Connor, Fionnula. *In search of a state: catholics in Northern Ireland*. Belfast, 1993.

O'Leary, Brendan, and McGarry, John. *The politics of antagonism: understanding Northern Ireland*. London, 1996. First published 1993.

O'Neill, Terence. *Ulster at the crossroads*. With an introduction by John Cole. London, 1969.

Osborne, Robert D. The Northern Ireland parliamentary electoral system: the 1929 reapportionment. In *Ir. Geography*, xii (1979), pp 42–56.

Pakenham, Frank. *Peace by ordeal: an account, from first hand sources, of the negotiation and signature of the Anglo–Irish treaty, 1921*. London, 1962; previous ed., 1951.

Phoenix, Eamon. *Northern nationalism: nationalist politics, partition and the catholic minority in Northern Ireland 1890–1940*. Belfast, 1994.

Probert, Belinda. *Beyond orange and green: the political economy of the Northern Ireland crisis*. London, 1978.

Purdie, Bob. *Politics in the streets: the origins of the civil rights movement in Northern Ireland*. Belfast, 1990.

Quinn, Raymond J. *A rebel voice: a history of Belfast republicanism, 1925–1972*. Belfast, 1999.

Roche, Patrick J., and Barton, Brian (ed.). *The Northern Ireland question: nationalism, unionism and partition*. Aldershot and Brookefield, Vt., 1999.

Rowthorn, Bob, and Wayne, Naomi. *Northern Ireland: the political economy of conflict*. Cambridge, 1988.

Walker, G[raham]. S. The Commonwealth Labour party in Northern Ireland, 1942–7. In *I.H.S.*, xxiv, no. 93 (May 1984), pp 69–91.

——*The politics of frustration: Harry Midgley and the failure of Labour in Northern Ireland*. Manchester, 1985.

Walker, G[raham]. S. *Intimate strangers: political and cultural interaction between Scotland and Ulster in modern times*. Edinburgh, 1995.

Wallis-Davy, Frédérique. La discussion européenne en Irlande du Nord de 1957 à 1973: le clivage unionistes–nationalistes. In *Lettre d'Information des Historiens de l'Europe Contemporaine*, x, nos 1–4 (1995), pp 75–87.

Whyte, J. H. Intra-unionist disputes in the Northern Ireland house of commons, 1921–72. In *Econ. & Soc. Rev.*, v (1973), pp 99–105.

——How much discrimination was there under the unionist regime, 1921–68? In Tom Gallagher and James O'Connell (ed.), *Contemporary Irish studies* (Manchester, 1983), pp 1–35.

Wilson, Alec. *PR urban elections in Ulster, 1920*. London, 1972. Facsimile of 1st ed. (Belfast, 1920).

2 CONSTITUTIONAL, ADMINISTRATIVE, AND LEGAL HISTORY

Andrews, J. H. The *Morning Post* line. In *Ir. Geography*, iv, no. 2 (1960), pp 99–106. Forecasts findings of the Irish boundary commission, 1925.

Birrell, Derek. The Northern Ireland civil service—from devolution to direct rule. In *Public Administration*, lvi (1978), pp 305–19.

——The Westminster parliament and Northern Ireland business. In *Parliamentary Affairs*, xliii, no. 4 (1990), pp 435–47.

——and Murie, Alan. *Policy and government in Northern Ireland: lessons of devolution*. Dublin, 1980.

Bloomfield, Ken. *Stormont in crisis: a memoir*. Belfast, 1994.

Boal, F. W., and Buchanan, Ronald. The 1969 Northern Ireland election. In *Ir. Geography*, vi, no. 1 (1969), pp 78–84.

Boyle, Kevin; Hadden, Tom; and Hillyard, Paddy. *Law and state: the case of Northern Ireland*. London, 1975.

——*Ten years on in Northern Ireland: the legal control of political violence*. London, 1980.

Brady, John. The New Ireland Forum: the search for a political solution in Northern Ireland. In *Studies*, lxxxiii, no. 292 (1984), pp 318–23.

Brett, C. E. B. *Housing a divided community*. Dublin, 1986.

Brewer, John D.; Guelke, Adrian; Hume, Ian; Moxon-Browne, Edward; and Wilford, Rick. *The police, public order and the state: policing in Great Britain, Northern Ireland, the Irish Republic, the USA, Israel, South Africa and China*. Basingstoke, 1988.

——and Magee, Kathleen. *Inside the R.U.C.: routine policing in a divided society*. Oxford, 1991.

Calvert, Harry. *Constitutional law in Northern Ireland*. London, 1968.

Cecil, Rosanne; Offer, John; and St Leger, Fred. *Informal welfare: a sociological study of care in Northern Ireland*. Aldershot, 1987.

Chambers, Gerald. *Equality and inequality in Northern Ireland: pt 2: the workplace*. London, 1987.

Connolly, Michael. Policy differences within the United Kingdom: the case of housing policy in Northern Ireland 1979–89. In *Public Administration*, lxix, no. 3 (1991), pp 303–24.

Cormack, R. J., and Osborne, R. D. (ed.). *Religion, education and employment: aspects of equal opportunity in Northern Ireland.* Belfast, 1983.

Darby, John, and Morris, Geoffrey. *Intimidation in housing.* Belfast, 1974.

Devlin, Paddy. *The fall of the Northern Ireland executive.* Belfast, 1975.

Donohue, Laura K. Regulating Northern Ireland: the Special Powers Acts, 1922–1972. In *Hist. Jn.,* xli (1998), pp 1089–1120.

Elliott, Sydney, and Wilford, Richard. *The 1982 Northern Ireland assembly election.* Glasgow, 1983.

English, Richard. The state and Northern Ireland. In Richard English and Charles Townshend (ed.), *The state: historical and political dimensions* (London, 1999), pp 95–108.

Farrell, Michael. *Arming the protestants: the formation of the Ulster Special Constabulary and Royal Ulster Constabulary, 1920–27.* London, 1983.

Finn, John E. *Constitutions in crisis: political violence and the rule of law.* Oxford, 1991. Northern Ireland and West Germany.

Gaffikin, Frank, and Morrissey, Mike. Poverty and politics in Northern Ireland. In Paul Teague (ed.), *Beyond the rhetoric: politics, the economy and social policy in Northern Ireland* (London, 1987), pp 136–59.

Graham, Donald. Discrimination in Northern Ireland: the failure of the Fair Employment Agency. In *Critical Social Policy* (summer 1984), pp 40–54.

Green, Arthur J. *Devolution and public finance: Stormont from 1921 to 1972.* Glasgow, 1979.

Greer, S. C. The supergrass system in Northern Ireland. In Paul Wilkinson and Alasdair Stewart (ed.), *Contemporary research on terrorism* (Aberdeen, 1987), pp 510–35.

Hadden, Tom, and Hillyard, Paddy. *Justice in Northern Ireland: a study in social confidence.* London, 1973.

—— and Boyle, Kevin. *The Anglo–Irish agreement: commentary, text, and official review.* London, 1989.

Hadfield, Brigid (ed.). *Northern Ireland: politics and the constitution.* Buckingham and Philadelphia, 1992.

Hezlet, Arthur. *The B Specials: a history of the Ulster Special Constabulary.* London, 1973.

Hillyard, Paddy. Law and order. In John Darby (ed.), *Northern Ireland: the background to the conflict* (Belfast, 1983), pp 32–60.

Kennedy, Liam. *Two Ulsters: a case for repartition.* Belfast, 1986.

Kenny, Anthony. *The road to Hillsborough: the shaping of the Anglo–Irish agreement.* Oxford, 1986.

Knight, James. *Northern Ireland: the elections of 1973.* London, 1974.

—— *Northern Ireland: the election of the constitutional convention, May 1975.* London, 1975.

—— *The election of the Assembly, 20 October 1982.* London, [1983?].

—— and Baxter-Moore, Nicholas. *Northern Ireland: the elections of the twenties.* London, 1972.

——— *Northern Ireland local government election, 30th May 1973.* London, n.d.

Kyle, Keith. Sunningdale and after: Britain, Ireland, and Ulster. In *The World Today*, xxxi, no. 11 (Nov. 1975), pp 439–50.

Lawrence, R. J. *The government of Northern Ireland: public finance and public services 1921–1964*. Oxford, 1965.

—— Politics and public administration in Northern Ireland. In *Administration*, xvi (1968), pp 112–20.

McColgan, John. 'Ulster's midwife': Sir Ernest Clark and the birth of the Northern Ireland administration. In *Administration*, xxxviii (1990), pp 41–69.

McSheffrey, Gerald. *Planning Derry: planning and politics in Northern Ireland*. Liverpool, 2000.

McVeigh, Jim. *Executed: Tom Williams and the I.R.A.* Belfast, 1999.
Tom Williams, hanged 1942.

Maltby, Arthur. *The government of Northern Ireland*. Dublin, 1974.

Mansergh, Nicholas. *The government of Northern Ireland: a study in devolution*. London, 1936.

—— The government of Ireland act, 1920, its origins and purposes: the working of the 'official' mind. In J. G. Barry (ed.), *Historical Studies IX: papers read before the Irish Conference of Historians, Cork, 29–31 May 1971* (Belfast, 1974), pp 19–48.

—— *The unresolved question: the Anglo–Irish settlement and its undoing 1912–72*. New Haven and London, 1991.

Moore, Steven. *Behind the garden wall: a history of capital punishment in Belfast*. Antrim, 1995.

Morrison, Danny. *And then the walls came down: a prison journal*. Cork, 1999.

Neill, D. G. Housing and social aspects of town and country planning in Northern Ireland. In *Administration*, ii (1954), pp 49–60.

O'Callaghan, Margaret. Old parchment and water: the boundary commission of 1925 and the copperfastening of the Irish border. In *Bullán*, iv, no. 2 (winter 1999/ spring 2000), pp 27–55.

O'Leary, Cornelius; Elliott, Sydney; and Wilford, R. A. *The Northern Ireland assembly 1982–1986: a constitutional experiment*. Belfast, 1988.

Oliver, John Andrew. *Working at Stormont: memoirs*. Dublin, 1978.

Oliver, Patrick J. The evolution of constitutional policy in Northern Ireland over the past fifteen years. In Desmond Rea (ed.), *Political co-operation in divided societies: a series of papers relevant to the conflict in Northern Ireland* (Dublin, 1982), pp 60–91.

—— The Stormont administration. In *Contemporary Record*, v, no. 1 (1991), pp 71–104.

Palley, Claire. *The evolution, disintegration and possible reconstruction of the Northern Ireland constitution*. London, 1972.
Reprinted from the *Anglo-American Law Review*.

Queckett, A. S. *The constitution of Northern Ireland*. 3 vols. Belfast, 1928–46.

Report of the Irish boundary commission. With an introduction by Geoffrey J. Hand. Shannon, 1969. Orginally published London, 1925.

Ryder, Chris. *The RUC: a force under fire*. London, 1989. 2nd ed. 1992. Revised ed. 1997. Further revised ed. published as *The RUC 1922–2000: a force under fire*. London, 2000.

——*Inside the Maze: the untold story of the Northern Ireland prison service*. London, 2000.

Shannon, Colm. *Building a better Belfast*. Belfast, 1991.

Sinclair, R. J. K., and Scully, F. J. N. *Arresting memories: captured moments in constabulary life*. Belfast, 1982.
Photographs of R.I.C. and R.U.C. personnel and activities.

Spjut, R. J. The Northern Ireland constitutional settlement of 1973 and the loyalist opposition. In *Ir. Jurist*, xii (1977), pp 243–60.

Taylor, Peter. *Stalker: the search for the truth*. London, 1987.

Tonge, Jonathan, From Sunningdale to the Good Friday agreement: creating devolved government in Northern Ireland. In *Contemporary British History*, xiv, no. 3 (2000), pp 39–60.

Ulster Unionist Party. *Devolution and the Northern Ireland assembly: the way forward*. Belfast, 1984.

Watt, David (ed.). *The constitution of Northern Ireland: problems and prospects*. London, 1981.

Weitzer, Ronald J. *Policing under fire: ethnic conflict and police–community relations in Northern Ireland*. Albany, N.Y., 1995.

3 ECCLESIASTICAL HISTORY

Barkley, John Monteith. *St Enoch's congregation, 1872–1972: an account of presbyterianism in Belfast through the eyes of a congregation*. Belfast, 1972.

Brooke, Peter. *Ulster presbyterianism: the historical perspective 1610–1970*. Dublin, 1987.

Carson, George. *The first one hundred years: a short history of Kells presbyterian church, Kells, Co. Antrim*. Kells, 1974.

Cole, R. L. *History of methodism in Ireland, 1860–1960*. Belfast, 1960.

Davey, J. E. *1840–1940: the story of a hundred years: an account of the Irish presbyterian church from the formation of the general assembly to the present time*. Belfast, 1940.

Davey, Ray. *A channel of peace: the story of the Corrymeela community*. London, 1993.
Ecumenical centre, Co. Antrim.

Dunlop, John; Clifford, Gerard; and Elliott, Eric. Pastoral dimensions of the Northern Ireland conflict. In *The Furrow*, xxxiii (1982), pp 36–50.

Eames, Robin. *Chains to be broken*. London, 1992.

Ellis, I. M. *Vision and reality: a survey of twentieth-century Irish inter-church relations*. Belfast, 1992.

Evans, Ernest. The Irish catholic church and the Northern Ireland conflict. In *Conflict*, xi, no. 4 (1991), pp 267–78.

Gallagher, Eric, and Worrall, Stanley. *Christians in Ulster, 1968–1980*. Oxford, 1982.

Harris, Mary. *The catholic church and the foundation of the Northern Ireland state, 1912–1930*. Cork, 1993.

Holmes, Finlay. *The Presbyterian Church in Ireland: a popular history*. Blackrock, 2000.

Jefferies, Henry A., and Devlin, Ciarán (ed.). *History of the diocese of Derry from earliest times*. Dublin, 2000.

Liechty, Joseph, and Clegg, Cecelia. *Moving beyond sectarianism: religion, conflict and reconciliation in Northern Ireland*. Dublin, 2001.

Mawhinney, Brian, and Wells, Ronald. *Conflict and Christianity in Northern Ireland.* Berkhamsted, 1975.

Megahey, Alan. *The Irish protestant churches in the twentieth century.* Basingstoke, 2000.

Murray, Raymond. *Archdiocese of Armagh: a history.* Strasbourg, 2000.

Noll, Mark; Bebbington, D. W.; and Rawlyk, G. A. (ed.). *Evangelicalism: comparative studies of popular protestantism in North America, the British Isles, and beyond, 1700–1990.* Oxford, 1994.

Presbyterian Church in Ireland. *A history of congregations in the Presbyterian Church in Ireland 1610–1982.* Belfast, 1982.

——*A history of congregations... a supplement of additions, emendations and corrections with an index prepared by R. Buick Knox.* Belfast, 1982.

Rafferty, Oliver P. *Catholicism in Ulster 1603–1983: an interpretative history.* London, 1994.

Warke, J. Baptists in Belfast: the twentieth-century challenge of urban growth and decline. In *Journal of the Irish Baptist Historical Society*, xx (1987–8), pp 12–19.

4 MILITARY HISTORY

Arthur, Max (ed.). *Northern Ireland: soldiers talking.* London, 1987.

Barton, Brian. *The blitz: Belfast in the war years.* Belfast, 1999. 1st ed. 1989.

——*Northern Ireland in the second world war.* Belfast, 1995.

Barzilay, David. *The British army in Ulster.* 4 vols. Belfast, 1973–81.

Blake, J. W. *Northern Ireland in the second world war.* Belfast, 2000. First published 1956.

Callaghan, Kevin, with Gorry, Terry. *A price on my head.* Wigan, 1993. British army bomb disposal in N.I.

Clark, H. W. S. *Guns in Ulster.* Belfast, 1967.

Dane, Mervyn. *The Fermanagh 'B' Specials.* Enniskillen, 1970.

Davison, Robson S. The Belfast blitz. In *Ir. Sword*, xvi (1985), pp 65–83.

Dewar, Michael. *The British army in Northern Ireland.* London, 1985; 2nd ed., 1996.

Faligot, Roger. *Britain's military strategy in Ireland: the Kitson experiment.* Dingle and London, 1983.

Fleming, George. *Magennis VC: the story of Northern Ireland's only winner of the Victoria Cross.* Dublin, 1998.

Hamill, Desmond. *Pig in the middle: the army in Northern Ireland, 1969–1984.* London, 1985.

Holland, Jack. *The American connection: US guns, money, and influence in Northern Ireland.* New York, 1987. Swords, 1989.

Jeffery, Keith. Security policy in Northern Ireland: some reflections on the management of violent conflict. In *Terrorism and Political Violence*, ii, no. 1 (1990), pp 21–34.

Kelley, Kevin. *The longest war: Northern Ireland and the IRA.* Dingle and London, 1982.

Kitson, Frank. *Low intensity operations: subversion, insurgency, peacekeeping.* London, 1971.

Murray, Raymond. *The SAS in Ireland.* Cork, 1990.

Reynolds, Oliver. A captain at large in the province: impressions of Northern Ireland 1968–9. In *Army Quarterly and Defence Journal*, cxx, no. 2 (1990), pp 182–6.

Ryder, Chris. *The Ulster Defence Regiment: an instrument of peace?* London, 1991. Revised ed., 1992.

Taylor, Peter. *Beating the terrorists? Interrogation at Omagh, Gough and Castlereagh.* Harmondsworth, 1980.

5 HISTORICAL GEOGRAPHY AND DEMOGRAPHY

Anderson, James, and Shuttleworth, Ian. Sectarian readings of sectarianism: interpreting the Northern Ireland census. In *The Irish Review*, no. 16 (1994), pp 74–93.

Andrews, J. H.; Simms, Anngret; Clarke, H. B., and Gillespie, Raymond (ed.). *Irish Historic Towns Atlas.* Dublin, 1986–   . (R.I.A.) In progress. *II: Carrickfergus.* By Philip Robinson (1986). *VIII: Downpatrick.* By R. H. Buchanan and Anthony M. Wilson (1997).

Boal, F. W. Territoriality on the Shankill–Falls divide, Belfast. In *Ir. Geography*, vi, no. 1 (1969), pp 30–50.

—— Territoriality and class: a study of two residential areas in Belfast. In *Ir. Geography*, vi, no. 3 (1971), pp 229–48.

—— Doherty, Paul, and Pringle, D. G. *The spatial distribution of some social problems in the Belfast urban area.* Belfast, 1974.

—— and Douglas, J. Neville (ed.), with the assistance of J. A. E. Orr. *Integration and division: geographical perspectives on the Northern Ireland problem.* London, 1982.

Compton, Paul A. *Northern Ireland: a census atlas.* Dublin, 1978.

—— (ed). *The contemporary population of Northern Ireland and population-related issues.* Belfast, 1981.

—— The changing religious demography of Northern Ireland: some political implications. In *Studies*, lxxviii, no. 312 (1989), pp 393–402.

—— Demography: the 1980s in perspective. In *Studies*, lxxx, no. 318 (1991), pp 157–68.

—— *Demographic review Northern Ireland 1995.* Belfast, 1995.

—— and Coward, John. *Fertility and family planning in Northern Ireland.* Aldershot, 1989.

Gallagher, Lyn, and Rogers, Dick. *Castle, coast and cottage.* Belfast, 1986. 2nd ed., 1992.

Heslinga, Marcus W. *The Irish border as a cultural divide: a contribution to the study of regionalism in the British Isles.* With a foreword by E. Estyn Evans. Assen, 1971.

Jardine, E. F. Demographic structure in Northern Ireland and its implications for constitutional preference. In *Stat. Soc. Ire. Jn.*, xxvii, pt 1 (1993–4), pp 193–220.

Jones, Emrys. The distribution and segregation of Roman Catholics in Belfast. In *Sociological Review*, iv (1956), pp 167–89.

—— *A social geography of Belfast.* London, 1965.

Mogey, John M. *Rural life in Northern Ireland: five regional studies made for the Northern Ireland Council of Social Service.* London, 1947.

Shuttleworth, Ian. Population change in Northern Ireland, 1981–1991: preliminary results of the 1991 census of population. In *Ir. Geography*, xxv, no. 1 (1992), pp 83–8.

Stockdale, Aileen. Recent trends in urbanisation and rural repopulation in Northern Ireland. In *Ir. Geography*, xxiv, no. 2 (1991), pp 70–80.

6 ECONOMIC AND SOCIAL HISTORY

Aughey, Arthur (ed.). *Northern Ireland in the European Community: an economic and political analysis*. Belfast, 1989.

Arnold, R. M. The Belfast and Co. Down Railway: its decline and fall. In *Ir. Railway Rec. Soc. Jn.*, iv (1955), pp 1–12.

Baker, Susan. Agenda setting, pressure groups and public policy: electricity generation and lignite use in Northern Ireland. In *Public Administration*, lxix, no. 3 (1991), pp 392–98.

Barritt, Denis P., and Carter, Charles F. *The Northern Ireland problem: a study in group relations*. 2nd ed., London, 1972.

Beattie, Geoffrey. *We are the people: journeys through the heart of protestant Ulster*. London, 1992.
A protestant growing up in N.I., 1960s.

Brown, Stephen. Retail change in Belfast city centre: 1950–1970. In *Ir. Geography*, xxiii, no. 2 (1990), pp 107–19.

Camblin, Gilbert. *The town in Ulster*. Belfast, 1951.

Cameron, Bobby. *Before this generation passes: the story of a Short's apprentice*. Antrim, 2000.

Capper, Wilfrid. *Caring for the countryside: a history of 50 years of the Ulster Society for the Preservation of the Countryside*. n.p., [1995].

Chambers, George. *Faces of change: the Belfast and Northern Ireland chambers of commerce and industry 1783–1983*. Belfast, 1983.

Colhoun, Mabel. *The shirt industry of the north west of Ireland*. Derry, n.d.

Corlett, John. *Aviation in Ulster*. Belfast, 1981.

Cradden, Terry. *Trade unionism, socialism and partition: the labour movement in Northern Ireland, 1939–1953*. Belfast, 1993.

Crafts, N. F. R. The golden age of economic growth in postwar Europe: why did Northern Ireland miss out? In *Ir. Econ. & Soc. Hist.*, xxii (1995), pp 5–25.

Currie, James Russell. *The Northern Counties Railway: vol. 2: heyday and decline, 1903–72*. Newton Abbot, 1974.

Devine, Francis. *Navigating a lone channel: Stephen McGonagle, trade unionism and labour politics in Derry*. Dublin, 2000.

Devlin, Paddy. *Yes, we have no bananas: outdoor relief in Belfast, 1920–39*. Belfast, 1981.

Ditch, John. *Social policy in Northern Ireland between 1939–50*. Aldershot, 1988.

Evason, Eileen. *On the edge: a study of poverty and long-term unemployment in Northern Ireland*. London, 1985.

Farrell, Michael. *The poor law and the workhouse in Belfast, 1838–1948*. Belfast, 1978.

Gibson, N. J., and Spencer, J. E. (ed.). *Economic activity in Ireland: a study of two open economies*. Dublin, 1977.

Greer, P. Eugene. *Road versus rail: documents on the history of public transport in Northern Ireland 1921–48*. Belfast, 1982.

Gribbon, H. D. *The history of water power in Ulster*. Newton Abbot, 1969.

Gudgin, Graham; Hart, Mark; Fagg, John; D'Arcy, Eamonn; and Keegan, Ron. *Job generation in manufacturing industry 1973–1986*. Belfast, 1989.

——and O'Shea, Geraldine (ed.). *Unemployment forever? The Northern Ireland economy in recession and beyond*. Belfast, 1993.

Hamilton, Paul. *Up the Shankill*. Belfast, 1979.

Hammond, David (ed.). *Steelchest, Nail in the Boot and the Barking Dog: the Belfast shipyard: a story of the people told by the people*. Belfast, 1986.

Hanna, Eamon (ed.). *Poverty in Ireland: Social Study Conference*. Portlaoise, 1988.

Harris, Richard I. D. *Regional economic policy in Northern Ireland, 1945–1988*. Aldershot, 1991.

——Jefferson, C. W.; and Spencer, J. E. (ed.). *The Northern Ireland economy: a comparative study in the economic development of a peripheral region*. London and New York, 1990.

Harris, Rosemary. *Prejudice and tolerance in Ulster: a study of neighbours and 'strangers' in a border community*. Manchester, 1972.

——Community relationships in Northern and Southern Ireland: a comparison and a paradox. In *Sociological Review*, xxvii (1979), pp 41–53.

Hunter, R. A.; Ludgate, R. C.; and Richardson, J. *Gone but not forgotten: Belfast trams, 1872–1954*. Whitehead, 1979.

Isles, K. S., and Cuthbert, Norman. *An economic survey of Northern Ireland*. Belfast, 1957.

Johnson, D. S. The economic history of Ireland between the wars. In *Ir. Econ. & Soc. Hist.*, i (1974), pp 49–61.

——Cattle smuggling on the Irish border, 1932–38. In *Ir. Econ. & Soc. Hist.*, vi (1979), pp 41–63.

——Northern Ireland as a problem in the economic war, 1932–38. In *I.H.S.*, xxii, no. 86 (Sept. 1980), pp 144–61.

——Partition and cross-border trade in the 1920s. In Peter Roebuck (ed.), *Plantation to partition: essays in Ulster history in honour of J. L. McCracken* (Belfast, 1981), pp 229–46.

Kennedy, Liam. *The modern industrialisation of Ireland 1940–1988*. Dundalk, 1989.

——and Ollerenshaw, Philip (ed.). *An economic history of Ulster 1820–1940*. Manchester, 1985.

King, Sophia, H., and McMahon, Sean (ed.). *Hope and history: eyewitness accounts of life in twentieth-century Ulster*. Belfast, 1996.

Love, Walter (ed.). *From yesterday with Love*. Belfast, 1982.

McCormick, W. P. *The railways of Northern Ireland and their locomotives*. 2nd ed., [Millisle, Co. Down,] 1980. First published, n.p., 1946.

McCutcheon, W. A. *The industrial archaeology of Northern Ireland*. Belfast, 1980.

McNamee, Peter, and Lovett, Tom. *Working class community in Northern Ireland*. Belfast, 1987.

McNeill, Donald B. *Irish passenger steamship services, vol 1: North of Ireland*. Newton Abbot, 1969.

Messenger, Betty. *Picking up the linen threads: a study in industrial folklore*. Belfast, 1980.

Mogey, J. M. *Rural life in Northern Ireland*. London, 1947.

Moody, T. W., and Beckett, J. C. *Ulster since 1800*. 2 vols. London, 1955, 1957.

Morgan, Michael. Postwar social change and the catholic community in Northern Ireland. In *Studies*, lxxvii, no. 308 (1988), pp 422–33.

Moss, Michael, and Hume, John R. *Shipbuilders to the world: 125 years of Harland & Wolff, Belfast, 1861–1986*. Belfast, 1986.

Mulholland, Marc. 'One of the most difficult hurdles': the struggle for recognition of the Northern Ireland Committee of the I.C.T.U., 1958–1964. In *Saothar*, xxii (1997), pp 81–94.

Munck, Ronnie, and Rolston, Bill. *Belfast in the thirties: an oral history*. Belfast, 1987.

Murray, Michael. *The politics and pragmatism of urban containment: Belfast since 1940*. Aldershot, 1991.
City planning.

Rowthorn, Bob, and Wayne, Naomi. *Northern Ireland: the political economy of conflict*. Cambridge, 1988.

Simpson, John. Economic development: cause or effect in the Northern Ireland conflict? In John Darby (ed.), *Northern Ireland: the background to the conflict* (Belfast, 1983), pp 79–109.

Symons, Leslie (ed.). *Land use in Northern Ireland: the general report of the survey compiled in the department of geography, the Queen's University of Belfast*. London, 1963.

Walker, Brian M. *Sentry Hill: an Ulster farm and family*. Belfast, 1981.

7   WOMEN'S HISTORY

Bleakley, David. *Saidie Patterson: Irish peacemaker*. Belfast, 1980.

Buckley, Suzann, and Lonergan, Pamela. Women and the troubles. In Yonah Alexander and Alan O'Day (ed.)., *Terrorism in Ireland* (London, 1984), pp 75–85.

Byrne, Anne, and Leonard, Madeleine (ed.). *Women and Irish society: a sociological reader*. Belfast, 1997.

Evason, Eileen. Women and Northern Ireland. In *Cahiers du Centre d'Études Irlandaises*, xi (1987), pp 145–54.

——*Against the grain: the contemporary women's movement in Northern Ireland*. Dublin, 1991.

Fairweather, Eileen; McDonough, Roisín; and McFadyean, Melanie. *Only the rivers run free: Northern Ireland: the women's war*. London, 1984.

Fearon, Kate. *Women's work: the story of the Northern Ireland Women's Coalition*. Belfast, 1999.

Ferris, Mary. *Women's voices: an oral history of women's health in Northern Ireland 1900–90*. Dublin, 1992.

Jones, Greta. Marie Stopes in Ireland—the mother's clinic in Belfast, 1936–47. In *Social History of Medicine*, v, no. 2 (1992), pp 255–77.

Holmes, Janice, and Urquhart, Diane (ed.). *Coming into the light: the work, politics and religion of women in Ulster, 1840–1940*. Belfast, 1994.

Kilmurray, Avila. Women in the community in Northern Ireland: struggling for their half of the sky. In *Studies*, lxxvi, no. 302 (1987), pp 177–84.

Kinghan, Nancy. *United we stood: the official history of the Ulster Women's Unionist Council, 1911–1974*. Belfast, 1975.

MacCurtain, Margaret, and Ó Corráin, Donncha (ed.). *Women in Irish society: the historical dimension*. Dublin, 1978.

McLaughlin, Eithne. Women and work in Derry city: a survey. In *Saothar*, xiv (1989), pp 35–45.

McWilliams, Monica. Struggling for peace and justice: reflections on women's activism in Northern Ireland. In *Journal of Women's History*, vi, no. 4 (winter/spring 1995), pp 13–39.

Morrissey, Hazel. Betty Sinclair: a woman's fight for socialism, 1910–1981. In *Saothar*, ix (1983), pp 121–31.

Roulston, Carmel. Women on the margin: the women's movement in Northern Ireland, 1973–1988. In *Science and Society*, liii, no. 2 (1989), pp 219–36.

Shannon, Catherine. The woman writer as historical witness: Northern Ireland 1968–1994. An interdisciplinary perspective. In M. G. Valiulis and Mary O'Dowd (ed.), *Women and Irish history: essays in honour of Margaret MacCurtain* (Dublin, 1997), pp 239–59.

Trewsdale, Janet M., and Trainor, Mary. *Womanpower no. 1: a statistical survey of women and work in Northern Ireland*. Belfast, 1979.

Urquhart, Diane. *Women in Ulster politics 1890–1940: a history not yet told*. Dublin and Portland, Oregon, 2000.

Ward, Margaret. *Unmanageable revolutionaries: women and Irish nationalism*. Dingle, 1983.

8 HISTORY OF ENGLISH LANGUAGE AND LITERATURE

Andrews, Elmer. *The poetry of Seamus Heaney: a reader's guide to essential criticism*. Duxford, Cambridge, 1998.

Bell, Sam Hanna; Robb, Nesca A.; and Hewitt, John (ed.). *The arts in Ulster: a symposium*. London, 1951.

Bresland, Ronald W. *The backward glance: C. S. Lewis and Ireland*. Belfast, 1999.

Brown, Terence. *Louis MacNeice: sceptical vision*. Dublin, 1975.

——*Northern voices: poets from Ulster*. Dublin, 1975.

Corcoran, Neil. *The poetry of Seamus Heaney: a critical study*. London, 1998.

Craig, Patricia. Moore's maladies: Belfast in the mid-twentieth century. In *University Rev.*, xviii, no. 1 (spring 1988), pp 22–3.

——(ed.). *The rattle of the north: an anthology of ulster prose*. Belfast, 1992.

Curtis, Tony (ed.). *The art of Seamus Heaney*. 3rd ed., Dublin, 1994. 1st ed. 1982.

Dawe, Gerald, and Longley, Edna (ed.). *Across a roaring hill: the protestant imagination in modern Ireland: essays in honour of John Hewitt*. Belfast, 1985.

——and Foster, John Wilson (ed.). *The poet's place: Ulster literature and society: essays in honour of John Hewitt, 1907–1987*. Belfast, 1991.

Deane, Seamus. The writer and the troubles. In *Threshold*, no. 25 (1974), pp 13–17.

Foster, John Wilson. *Forces and themes in Ulster fiction*. Dublin and London, 1974.

Grant, Patrick. *Breaking enmities: religion, literature and culture in Northern Ireland, 1967–1997*. Basingstoke, 1999.

Hayes, Maurice. *Whither cultural diversity?* Belfast, 1990.

Heaney, Seamus. Place and displacement: recent poetry from Northern Ireland—the Peter Laver memorial lecture. In *The Wordsworth Circle*, xvi, no. 2 (spring 1985), pp 48–56.

Kirkland, Richard. 'The shanachie of Belfast and its red-brick Gaeltacht': Cathal O'Byrne. In *Bullán*, iv, no. 2 (winter 1999/spring 2000), pp 67–82. Literature in English.

Leith, Linda. Subverting the sectarian heritage: recent novels of Northern Ireland. In *Canadian Journal of Irish Studies*, xviii, no. 2 (Dec. 1992), pp 88–106.

Longley, Edna. Progressive bookmen: politics and northern protestant writers since the 1930s. In *The Irish Review*, no. 1 (1986), pp 50–57.

—— *Louis MacNeice: a study*. London, 1988.

Longley, Michael (ed.). *Causeway: the arts in Ulster*. Belfast and Dublin, 1971.

Macafee, Caroline I. (ed.). *A concise Ulster dictionary*. Oxford, 1996. Dialect dictionary for Ulster.

McDonald, Peter. *Louis MacNeice: the poet in his contexts*. Oxford, 1991.

—— *Mistaken identities: poetry and Northern Ireland*. Oxford, 1997.

McIlroy, Brian. Poetry imagery as political fetishism: the example of Michael Longley. In *Canadian Journal of Irish Studies*, xvi, no. 1 (July 1990), pp 59–64.

O'Brien, Darcy. *W. R. Rodgers*. Lewisburg, Pa., 1970.

O'Donoghue, Bernard. *Seamus Heaney and the language of poetry*. New York and London, 1994.

Olinder, Britta. John Hewitt: Ulsterman of planter stock. In Heinz Kosok (ed.), *Studies in Anglo-Irish literature* (Bonn, 1982), pp 376–89.

Ormsby, Frank (ed.). *A rage for order: poetry of the Northern Ireland troubles*. Belfast, 1992.

Rafroidi, Patrick. Literary echoes of the present troubles in Northern Ireland. In Horst Drescher and Hermann Volker (ed.), *Nationalism in literature—literarischer nationalismus: literature, language, and national identity* (Frankfurt, 1989), pp 281–7.

Rolston, Bill. Escaping from Belfast: class, ideology and literature in Northern Ireland. In *Race and Class*, xx (1978), pp 41–62.

—— Mothers, whores and villains: images of women in novels of the Northern Ireland conflict. In *Race and Class*, xxxi, no. 1 (1989), pp 41–57.

Scanlan, Margaret. The unbearable present: Northern Ireland in four contemporary novels. In *Études Irlandaises*, x (Dec. 1985), pp 145–61.

Stallworthy, Jon. *Louis MacNeice*. London, 1995.

Todd, Loreto. *Words apart: a dictionary of Northern Ireland English*. Gerrards Cross, 1990.

Unrau, John. Desperate ironies: Ulster poets on the troubles. In *West Virginia University Philological Papers*, xxxiii (1987), pp 93–103.

Vendler, Helen. *Seamus Heaney*. London, 1998.

Williams, Michael. Richard Rowley: an introductory bibliography. In *Ir. Booklore*, iv (1978), pp 48–52.

Wills, Clair. *Improprieties: politics and sexuality in Northern Irish poetry*. Oxford, 1993.

9 HISTORY OF IRISH LANGUAGE AND LITERATURE

Andrews, L. S. The Irish language in the educational system of Northern Ireland: some political and cultural perspectives. In R. M. O. Pritchard (ed.), *Motivating the majority: modern languages in Northern Ireland* (London, 1991).

Farren, Sean. Language policy in a divided community. In Tina Hickey and Jenny Williams (ed.), *Language, education and society in a changing world* (Dublin, 1996), pp 54–62.

Holmer, N. M. *The Irish language in Rathlin Island, Co. Antrim*. Dublin, 1942.

Hughes, A. J. Manx speaker Ned Maddrell and Irish Gaelic author Liam MacNeachtain. In *Seanchas Ardmhacha*, xv, no. 2 (1993), pp 125–9.

Mac Póilín, Aodán. *The Irish language in Northern Ireland*. Belfast, 1997.

——Language, identity and politics in Northern Ireland. In *Ulster Folklife*, xlv (1999), pp 106–32.

Maguire, Gabrielle. *Our own language: an Irish initiative*. Clevedon, 1991.

Irish language in Belfast, 1960s– .

O'Reilly, Camille. *The Irish language in Northern Ireland: the politics of culture and identity*. London, 1999.

Stockman, Gerard. The sounds of Ulster Irish: a guide for non-Irish speakers. In *Ulster Folklife*, xl (1994), pp 39–48.

10 HISTORY OF EDUCATION

Allen, Robert. *The presbyterian college, Belfast, 1853–1953*. Belfast, 1954.

Akenson, Donald Harmon. *Education and enmity: the control of schooling in Northern Ireland 1920–1950*. Newton Abbot, 1973.

Benton, Elizabeth. Integrated education. In *Scope: a review of voluntary and community work in Northern Ireland*, xxix (1979), pp 12–14.

Campbell, J. J. *Catholic schools: a survey of a Northern Ireland problem*. Belfast, 1964.

Caul, Leslie. *Schools under scrutiny: the case of Northern Ireland*. Basingstoke, 1990.

Corkey, William. *Episode in the history of protestant Ulster 1923–47: story of the struggle of the protestant community to maintain Bible instruction in their schools*. Belfast, [1959?].

Crone, Robert, and Malone, John. *Continuities in education: the Northern Ireland Schools Curriculum Project, 1973–1978*. Windsor, 1979.

Darby, John; Murray, D.; Batts, D.; Dunn, S.; Farren, S.; and Harris, J. *Schools apart? Education and community in Northern Ireland*. Coleraine, 1977. Reprinted with Seamus Dunn, John Darby, and Kenneth Mullan, *Schools together?* (1984) in 1 vol. as *Schools apart? Schools together?* (Coleraine, 1989); 2nd ed., *Education and community in Northern Ireland* (Coleraine, [1999?]).

Dunn, Seamus. *Integrated schools in Northern Ireland. A report for the standing advisory commission on human rights*. Belfast, 1986.

—— *Education and the conflict in Northern Ireland: a guide to the literature*. Coleraine, 1986.

——Darby, John; and Mullan, Kenneth. *Schools together?* Coleraine, 1984. See above under Darby.

Farren, Sean. Unionist-protestant reaction to educational reform in Northern Ireland, 1923–1930. In *History of Education*, xiv (1985), pp 227–36.

——A lost opportunity: education and community in Northern Ireland, 1947–1960. In *History of Education*, xxi (1992), pp 71–82.

—— *The politics of Irish education 1920–65*. Belfast, 1995.

Gallagher, A. M. *Education and religion in Northern Ireland.* Coleraine, 1989.

Henderson, J. W. *Methodist College, Belfast, 1868–1938.* Belfast, 1939.

Holmes, R. F. G. *Magee 1865–1965: the evolution of the Magee Colleges.* Belfast, 1965.

Jamieson, John. *The history of the Royal Belfast Academical Institution, 1810–1960.* Belfast, 1959.

Killen, John. *A history of the Linen Hall library, 1788–1988.* Belfast, 1990.

McGrath, Michael. The narrow road: Harry Midgley and catholic schools in Northern Ireland. In *I.H.S.*, xxx, no. 119 (May 1997), pp 429–51.

McNeilly, Norman. *Exactly fifty years: the Belfast Education Authority and its work, 1923–73.* Belfast, [1974].

Malone, John, and Crone, Robert. New approaches to innovation in schools. In *The Northern Teacher*, xii, no. 1 (1975–6), pp 16–20.

Moffat, Chris (ed.). *Education together for a change: integrated education and community relations in Northern Ireland.* Belfast, 1993.

Moody, T. W., and Beckett, J. C. *Queen's, Belfast, 1845–1949: the history of a university.* 2 vols. London, 1959.

Murray, Dominic. *Worlds apart: segregated schools in Northern Ireland.* Belfast, 1985.

Robinson, Alan. *The schools cultural studies project: a contribution to peace.* Coleraine, 1981.

Skilbeck, Malcolm. Education and cultural change. In *Compass: journal of the Irish Association for Curriculum Development*, v, no. 2 (1976), pp 3–23.

St Joseph's College of Education. Belfast, 1971.

Walker, Brian, and McCreary, Alf. *Degrees of excellence: the story of Queen's, Belfast, 1845–1995.* Belfast, 1994.

11 HISTORY OF IDEAS

Arthur, Paul. Northern Ireland: religion, national identity and distorted history. In *Parliamentary History*, xii (1993), pp 312–20.

Bruce, Steve. *The edge of the union: the Ulster loyalist political vision.* Oxford, 1994.

Clayton, Pamela. *Enemies and passing friends: settler ideologies in twentieth-century Ulster.* East Haven, Conn., and London, 1996.

Feldman, Allen. *Formations of violence: the narrative of the body and political terror in Northern Ireland.* Chicago, 1991.

Hepburn, A. C. (ed.). *The conflict of nationality in modern Ireland.* London, 1980.

Jackson, Alvin. Unionist myths 1912–1985. In *Past & Present*, no. 136 (1992), pp 164–85.

Loughlin, James. *Ulster unionism and British national identity since 1885.* London, 1995.

McBride, Ian. *The siege of Derry in Ulster protestant mythology.* Dublin, 1997.

McIntosh, Gillian. *The force of culture: unionist identities in twentieth-century Ireland.* Cork, 1999.

McKinley, Michael. 'Dangerous liaisons?' The Provisional I.R.A., Marxism, and the communist governments of Europe. In *History of European Ideas*, xv, nos 1–3 (1992), pp 443–9.

Miller, David W. *Queen's rebels: Ulster loyalism in historical perspective.* Dublin, 1978.

Roche, P. J., and Barton, Brian. (ed.). *The Northern Ireland question: myth and reality.* Aldershot, 1991.

Todd, Jennifer. Unionist political thought, 1920–1972. In D. G. Boyce, R. Eccleshall, and V. Geoghegan (ed.), *Political thought in Ireland since the seventeenth century* (London and New York, 1993), pp 190–211.

Walker, Brian M. *Dancing to history's tune: history, myth and politics in Ireland.* Belfast, 1996.

——— *Past and present: history, identity and politics in Ireland.* Belfast, 2000.

12 MEDICAL, SCIENTIFIC, AND TECHNICAL HISTORY

Bennett, J. A. *Church, state and astronomy in Ireland: 200 years of Armagh observatory.* Belfast, 1990.

Blaney, Roger. *Belfast: 100 years of public health 1888–1988.* Belfast, 1988.

Clarke, Richard. *The Royal Victoria Hospital, Belfast: a history 1797–1997.* Belfast, 1997.

Jones, Greta. Marie Stopes in Ireland: the mothers' clinic in Belfast, 1936–1947. In *Social History of Medicine*, v (1992), pp 255–77.

Love, Harold. *The Royal Belfast Hospital for Sick Children: a history, 1948–1998.* Belfast, 1998.

McCutcheon, Alan. *Wheel and spindle: aspects of Irish industrial history.* Belfast, 1977.

Prior, Lindsay. *The social organisation of death: medical discourse and social practices in Belfast.* London, 1989.

Prior, Pauline. *Mental health and politics in Northern Ireland.* Aldershot, 1993.

Rae, John Bell. *Harry Ferguson and Henry Ford.* Belfast, 1980.

Sheehan, Maura. The evolution of technical efficiency in the Northern Ireland manufacturing sector, 1973–1985. In *Scottish Journal of Political Economy*, xliv (1997), pp 59–81.

13 LOCAL AND FAMILY HISTORY

ARMAGH. *Armagh: historic photographs of the primatial city.* By Roger Weatherup. Belfast, [1993?].

——— *The chosen Fews: exploding myths in south Armagh.* By Darach MacDonald. Cork, 2000.

People of the Fews region.

BALLYMENONE (CO. FERMANAGH). *Passing the time: folklore and history of an Ulster community.* By Henry Glassie. Dublin, 1982.

BALLYMONEY. *Ballymoney: sources for local history.* Belfast, 1975. (P.R.O.N.I.)

BELFAST. *Belfast: the origin and growth of an industrial city.* Ed. J. C. Beckett and R. E. Glasscock. London, 1967.

——— *St Joseph's centenary 1872–1972: story of a dockside parish.* By Fred Heatley. Belfast, 1972.

——— *Belfast: an illustrated history.* By Jonathan Bardon. Belfast, 1982.

——— *Images of Belfast.* By Robert Johnstone and Bill Kirk. Dundonald, 1983.

BELFAST. *Province, city and people: Belfast and its region*. Ed. R. H. Buchanan and B. M. Walker. Antrim, 1987.

—— *Belfast: portraits of a city*. By Robert Johnstone. London, 1990.

—— *Belfast*. By W. A. Maguire. Keele, 1993. (Town and City Histories.)

—— *Belfast: a pocket history*. By Jonathan Bardon. Belfast, 1996.

—— *A past apart: studies in the history of catholic Belfast 1850–1950*. By A. C. Hepburn. Belfast, 1996.

COLERAINE. *The port of Coleraine*. By Robert Anderson. Coleraine, 1978.

Crawford, W. H., and Foy, R. H. (ed.). *Townlands in Ulster: local history studies*. Belfast, 1998.

DERRY/LONDONDERRY. The 1940s and 60s in Derry. By Nell McCafferty. In Sharon Gmelch (ed.), *Irish life* (Dublin, 1979), pp 145–60.

—— *Siege city: the story of Derry and Londonderry*. By Brian Lacy. Belfast, 1990.

—— *Derry and Londonderry: history and society. Interdisciplinary essays on the history of an Irish county*. Ed. Gerard O'Brien. Dublin, 1999. (Irish County History Series.)

—— *Ulster's historic city: Derry, Londonderry*. By T. H. Mullin. Coleraine, 1986.

DONAGHMORE (CO. TYRONE). *Domhnach Mór (Donaghmore): an outline of parish history*. By Éamon Ó Doibhlin. Omagh, 1969. 2nd ed., 1988.

DOWN. *Down: history and society. Interdisciplinary essays on the history of an Irish county*. Ed. Lindsay Proudfoot. Dublin, 1997. (Irish County History Series.)

DUNDONALD. *A history of Dundonald, County Down*. By Peter Carr. Dundonald, 1987.

FERMANAGH. *The Fermanagh story: a documented history of the County Fermanagh*. By Peadar Livingstone. Enniskillen, 1969; 2nd printing, 1974.

LIMAVADY. *Limavady and the Roe valley*. By T. H. Mullin. Limavady, 1983.

LISBURN. *Lisburn: the town and its people*. By Brian Mackey. Belfast, 2000.

NEWRY. *Frontier town: an illustrated history of Newry*. By Tony Canavan. Belfast, 1989.

RATHLIN ISLAND (CO. ANTRIM.) *Rathlin—disputed island*. By H. Wallace Clark. Portlaw, 1971.

TYRONE. *Tyrone: history and society*. Ed. Charles Dillon and Henry A. Jefferies. Dublin, 2000. (Irish County History Series.)

UPPERLANDS (CO. LONDONDERRY.) *Linen on the green: an Irish mill village 1730–1982*. By H. Wallace Clark. Belfast, 1982. 2nd ed., 1983.

14 HISTORY OF THE IRISH ABROAD

Devine, T. M. (ed.). *Irish immigrants and Scottish society in the nineteenth and twentieth centuries*. Edinburgh, 1991.

—— and McMillan, J. F. (ed.). *Celebrating Columba: Irish–Scottish connections 597–1997*. Edinburgh, 1999.

Elliott, Bruce. *Irish migrants in the Canadas: a new approach*. Kingston, Montreal, and Belfast, 1988.

Handley, J. E. *The Irish in modern Scotland*. Cork, 1947.

Houston, Cecil J., and Smyth, W. J. *The sash Canada wore: a historical geography of the Orange Order in Canada*. Toronto, 1980.

Jones, M. A. The Scotch-Irish. In Stephan Thernstrom, Oscar Handlin, and Ann Orlov (ed.), *Harvard encylopaedia of American ethnic groups* (Cambridge, Mass., and London, 1980), pp 896–908.

O'Driscoll, Robert, and Reynolds, Lorna (ed.). *The untold story: the Irish in Canada.* 2 vols., Toronto, 1988.

Paisley, Ian Richard Kyle. *America's debt to Ulster: a bi-centennial publication, 1776–1976.* Belfast, 1976.

Pennefather, R. S. The Orange Order and the United Farmers of Ontario, 1919–23. In *Ontario History*, lxxix (1977), pp 169–84.

Walker, W. M. Irish immigrants in Scotland: their priests, politics and parochial life. In *Hist. Jn.*, xv, no. 4 (1972), pp 649–67.

15 HISTORY OF ARCHITECTURE, PAINTING, AND DECORATIVE ARTS

Becker, Annette; Olley, John; and Wang, Wilfred (ed.). *20th-century architecture: Ireland.* Munich and New York, 1997.
With biographical notes on architects.

Boyd, Brian. *A heritage from stone: a review of architecture in Ulster from prehistory to the present day.* Belfast, 1986.

Brett, Charles E. B. *Court and market houses of the province of Ulster.* Belfast, 1975.

—— *Buildings of County Antrim.* Belfast, 1996.

—— *Buildings of County Armagh.* Belfast, 1999.

Catto, Mike. *Art in Ulster 2: a history of painting, sculpture and printmaking, 1957–1977.* With selected biographical notes by Theo Snoddy. Belfast, 1977.

Chabanais, Paula, and Goldberg, David. Sidney Smith: painter and moralist (1912–1982). In *Irish Arts Review Yearbook 1994*, pp 235–44.
Belfast artist.

Dixon, Hugh. *An introduction to Ulster architecture.* Belfast, 1975.

Evans, David. *An introduction to modern Ulster architecture.* Belfast, 1977.

—— and Larmour, Paul. *Queen's: an architectural legacy.* Belfast, 1995.

Gailey, Alan. *Rural houses of the north of Ireland.* Edinburgh, 1984.

Glendinning, Miles, and Muthesius, Stefan. *Tower block: modern public housing in England, Scotland and Northern Ireland.* New Haven, 1994.

Greer, Alan. Sir James Craig and the construction of parliament buildings at Stormont. In *I.H.S.*, xxxi, no. 123 (May 1999), pp 373–88.

Hewitt, John. The arts: architecture, painting, sculpture. In T. W. Moody and J. C. Beckett (ed.), *Ulster since 1800* (London, 1954), pp 214–23.

—— *John Luke (1906–1975).* [Dublin], 1978.

—— *Art in Ulster 1: paintings, drawings, prints and sculpture for the last 400 hundred* [sic] *years to 1957.* With biographies of the artists by Theo Snoddy. Belfast, 1977.

Kelly, Liam. *Thinking long: contemporary art in the north of Ireland, 1977–95.* Kinsale, 1996.

Kennedy, John, and Wheeler, Gordon (ed.). *Parliament buildings, Stormont: the building, its setting, uses and restoration, 1922–1998.* Belfast, 1999.

Loftus, Belinda. *Mirrors: William III & Mother Ireland.* Dundrum, Co. Down, 1990.

Rolston, Bill. *Politics and painting: murals and conflict in Northern Ireland.* London, 1991.
—— *Drawing support: murals in the north of Ireland.* Belfast, 1992.
—— *Drawing support 2: murals of war and peace.* Belfast, 1995.
Walker, Dorothy. *Modern art in Ireland.* Dublin, 1997.
    Extensive bibliography and exhibition catalogues.
Wilson, Judith C. *Conor: the life and work of an Ulster artist.* Dundonald, 1981.
    William Conor, 1881–1968.

16 HISTORY OF MUSIC AND THEATRE

Allen, Gregory. The blind bard of Belfast: Carl Gilbert Hardebeck (1869–1945). In *Hist. Ire.*, vi, no. 3 (1998), pp 38–43.
Andrews, Elmer. *The art of Brian Friel.* Basingstoke, 1995.
Bell, Sam Hanna. *The theatre in Ulster: a survey...from 1902 until the present day.* Dublin, 1972.
Delaney, James, Church music reform. In *I.E.R.*, lxviii (1946), pp 232–42.
Greacen, R. Drama up north. In *The Bell*, xiii (1947), pp 53–7.
Greer, David (ed.). *Hamilton Harty: his life and music.* Belfast, [1979].
—— (ed.) *Hamilton Harty: early memories.* Belfast, 1979.
Huntingdon, Gale, and Herrman, Lani (ed.). *Sam Henry's 'Songs of the people'. Folk songs of Northern Ireland published in the Coleraine Chronicle 1923–39.* Athens, Ga., 1990.
Kennedy, D. The theatre in Ulster. In *Bann*, xx (1953).
Klein, Michael. Life and theatre in Northern Ireland. In *Red Letters: a journal of cultural politics*, xvi (spring/summer 1984), pp 26–31.
Maxwell, D. E. S. *Brian Friel.* Lewisburg, 1973.
O'Malley, Mary. *Never shake hands with the devil.* Dublin, 1990.
    Lyric theatre, Belfast, 1951–   .
Pilkington, Lionel. Violence and identity in Northern Ireland: Graham Reid's *The death of Humpty Dumpty.* In *Modern Drama*, xxx, no. 1 (1990), pp 15–29.
—— Theatre and cultural politics in Northern Ireland: the *Over the bridge* controversy, 1959. In *Éire-Ireland*, xxx, no. 4 (1995), pp 76–93.
Pine, Richard. *Brian Friel and Ireland's drama.* London, 1990.
—— *The diviner: the art of Brian Friel.* Dublin, 1999.
Richtarik, Marilynn J. *Acting between the lines: the Field Day Theatre Company and Irish cultural politics 1980–1984.* Oxford, 1994.
Rosenfield, R. Theatre in Belfast: achievement of a decade. In *Threshold*, ii, no. 1 (1958), pp 66–77.
Ruthven, Malcolm. *Belfast Philharmonic Society, 1874–1974.* Belfast, 1974.

17 HISTORIOGRAPHY

Bell, J. Bowyer. The chroniclers of violence in Northern Ireland: the first wave interpreted. In *Review of Politics*, xxxiv (1972), pp 147–57.
—— The chroniclers revisited: the analysis of tragedy. In *Review of Politics*, xxxvi (1974), pp 521–43.

Clarkson, L. A. The writing of Irish economic and social history since 1968. In *Econ. Hist. Rev.*, xxxiii (1980), pp 100–111.

Foster, R. F. *Paddy and Mr Punch: connections in Irish and English history.* London, 1993.

Harkness, David W. Ireland since 1921. In J. J. Lee (ed.), *Irish historiography 1970–79* (Cork, 1981), pp 132–53.

Lynch, John. 'Ceasefire in the Academy'? In *Hist. Ire.*, ii, no. 4 (1994), pp 11–14. Interview with Paul Bew.

Moody, T. W. Thirty-five years of Irish historiography. In T. W. Moody (ed.), *Irish historiography, 1936–70* (Dublin, 1971), pp 137–50.

Morgan, Hiram. A scholar and a gentleman. In *Hist. Ire.*, i, no. 2 (1993), pp 55–8. Interview with A. T. Q. Stewart.

——The life of Brian. In *Hist. Ire.*, viii, no. 2 (2000), pp 43–6. Interview with Brian Walker.

Mulvey, Helen F. Thirty years' work in Irish history (IV): twentieth-century Ireland, 1914–70. In *I.H.S.*, xvii, no. 66 (Sept. 1970), pp 151–84.

——Twentieth-century Ireland, 1914–70. in T. W. Moody (ed.), *Irish historiography 1936–70* (1971), pp 103–36.

Walker, Graham. Old history: protestant Ulster in Lee's *Ireland*. In *The Irish Review*, no. 12 (1992), pp 65–71.

18   HISTORY OF PRINTING, PUBLISHING, AND THE MASS MEDIA

Auld, John. Picture houses in east Belfast. In *Journal of the East Belfast Historical Society*, i, no. 1 (1981), pp 11–23.

Bardon, Jonathan. *Beyond the studio: a history of BBC Northern Ireland.* Belfast, 2000.

Bell, Robert; Johnstone, Robert; and Wilson, Robin (ed.). *Troubled times: Fortnight magazine and the troubles in Northern Ireland 1970–91.* Belfast, 1991. With chronology of events, 1970–90.

Brodie, Malcolm. *The Tele: a history of the Belfast Telegraph.* Belfast, 1995.

Butler, David. Documenting the troubles: a question of perspective. In *Irish Communications Review*, ii (1992), pp 35–45.

Cathcart, Rex. *The most contrary region: the BBC in Northern Ireland 1924–1984.* Belfast, 1984.

Darby, John. *Dressed to kill: cartoonists and the Northern Ireland conflict.* Belfast, 1983.

Keenan, Joe (ed.). '*The Labour Opposition of Northern Ireland': complete reprint of the first Labour newspaper in Northern Ireland, 1925–26.* Belfast, 1992.

Killen, John. *John Bull's famous circus: Ulster history through the postcard, 1905–1985.* Dublin, 1985.

MacQuitty, William. *A life to remember.* London, 1991. Founding manager-director of Ulster Television.

Maguire, W. A. *A century in focus: photography and photographers in the north of Ireland, 1839–1939.* Belfast, 2000.

Miller, David. *Don't mention the war: Northern Ireland, propaganda and the media.* London and Boulder, Colo., 1994.

Phoenix, Eamon (ed.). *A century of northern life: the Irish News and 100 years of Ulster history, 1890s–1990s*. Belfast, 1995.

Rolston, Bill (ed.). *The media and Northern Ireland: covering the troubles*. Basingstoke, 1990.

Sullivan, Rose. The silent picture houses of west Belfast. In *Outline*, i (1975), pp 33–43.

19 BIOGRAPHY

ADAMS. *Falls memories*. By Gerry Adams. Dingle, 1982.

—— *Gerry Adams: a biography*. By Colm Keena. Cork, 1990.

BELL. *Sam Hanna Bell: a biography*. By Seán McMahon. Belfast, 1999.

BLOOMFIELD. *Stormont in crisis: a memoir*. By Ken Bloomfield. Belfast, 1994.

Brett, Charles E. B. *Long shadows cast before: nine lives in Ulster, 1625–1977*. Edinburgh, 1978.

BROOKEBOROUGH (BROOKE). *Brookeborough: the making of a prime minister*. By Brian Barton. Belfast, 1988.

CALLAGHAN. *A house divided: the dilemma of Northern Ireland*. By James Callaghan. London, 1973.

CARSON. *The life of Carson*, iii. By Ian Colvin. London, 1936.

—— *Sir Edward Carson*. By Alvin Jackson. Dundalk, 1993.

—— *Edward Carson*. By A. T. Q. Stewart. Belfast, 1997. Previous ed., Dublin, 1981.

CHURCHILL. *Winston S. Churchill*. 8 vols. London, 1966–88. Vols 1–2 by R. S. Churchill; vols 3–8 by Martin Gilbert. 13 companion vols.

CRAIGAVON (CRAIG). *Not an inch: a study of Northern Ireland and Lord Craigavon*. By Hugh Shearman. London, 1942.

—— *Craigavon, Ulsterman*. By St John Ervine. London, 1949.

—— *James Craig, Lord Craigavon*. By Patrick Buckland. Dublin, 1980.

DEVLIN. *The price of my soul*. By Bernadette Devlin. London, 1969.

—— *Bernadette: the story of Bernadette Devlin*. By George W. Target. London, 1975.

DEVLIN. *Straight left: an autobiography*. By Paddy Devlin. Belfast, 1993. Co-founder of S.D.L.P., 1970.

FAULKNER. *Faulkner: conflict and consent in Irish politics*. By David Bleakley. London, 1974.

—— *Memoirs of a statesman*. By Brian Faulkner. London, 1978.

GALLAGHER. *Acorns and oakleaves—a Derry childhood: growing up in Derry 1920–45*. By Charles Gallagher. n.p. [1983].

HERMON. *Holding the line: an autobiography*. By John Hermon. Dublin, 1997.

HUME. *John Hume: statesman of the troubles*. By Barry White. Belfast, 1984.

—— *John Hume: man of peace*. by G.M.F. Drower, London, 1996.

—— *John Hume: the biography*. By Paul Routledge. London, 1997.

HURD. *An end to promises: sketch of a government, 1970–74*. By Douglas Hurd. London, 1979.

MCAUGHTRY. *The sinking of the Kenbane Head*. By Sam McAughtry. Belfast, 1977.

MCCANN. *War and an Irish town*. By Eamonn McCann. Harmondsworth, 1974; 2nd ed., 1980. 3rd (revised) ed., London, 1993.

O'Brien, Gerard, and Roebuck, Peter (ed.). *Nine Ulster lives*. Belfast, 1992.

O'DOHERTY. *The volunteer: a former I.R.A. man's true story*. By Shane O'Doherty. London, 1993.

OLIVER. *Working at Stormont*. By John Oliver. Dublin, 1978.

O'NEILL. *The autobiography of Terence O'Neill, prime minister of Northern Ireland 1963–1969*. By Terence O'Neill. London, 1972.

PAISLEY. *Paisley: man of wrath*. By Patrick Marrinan. Tralee, 1973.

—— *Paisley*. By Ed Moloney and Andy Pollak. Swords, 1986.

—— *Ian Paisley, my father*. By Rhonda Paisley. Basingstoke, 1988.

PRIOR. *A balance of power*. By James Prior. London, 1986.

REES. *Northern Ireland: a personal perspective*. By Merlyn Rees. London, 1985.

SHEA. *Voices and the sound of drums: an Irish autobiography*. By Patrick Shea. Belfast, 1981.

TRIMBLE. *Trimble*. By Henry McDonald. London, 2000.

WILSON. *Marie: a story from Enniskillen*. By Gordon Wilson and Alf McCreary. London, 1991.

WILSON. *Harold Wilson*. By Austen Morgan. London, 1992.

—— *Harold Wilson*. By Ben Pimlott. London, 1992.

20 THE TROUBLES

Adams, Gerry. *The politics of Irish freedom*. Dingle, 1986.

Anderson, Don. *Fourteen May days: the inside story of the loyalist strike of 1974*. Dublin, 1994.

Arthur, Paul. *The People's Democracy 1968–73*. Belfast, 1974.

—— and Jeffery, Keith. *Northern Ireland since 1968*. Oxford, 1988; 2nd ed. 1996.

Aunger, Edmund A. *In search of political stability: a comparative study of New Brunswick and Northern Ireland*. Montreal, 1981.

Barritt, Denis P. *Northern Ireland: a problem to every solution*. London, 1982.

—— and Carter, Charles F. *The Northern Ireland problem: a study in group relations*. London, 1962; 2nd ed. 1972.

Belfrage, Sally. *The crack: a Belfast year*. London, 1987.

Bell, John Bowyer. The escalation of insurgency: the Provisional I.R.A.'s experience, 1969–71. In *Review of Politics*, xxxv (1973), pp 398–411.

—— *The Irish troubles: a generation of violence, 1967–1992*. Dublin, 1993.

—— *The I.R.A. 1968–2000: analysis of a secret army*. London, 2000.

Bell, Robert; Johnstone, Robert; and Wilson, Robin (ed.). *Troubled times: Fortnight magazine and the troubles in Northern Ireland*. Belfast, 1991.

Beresford, David. *Ten men dead: the story of the 1981 Irish hunger strike*. London, 1987.

Bew, Paul, and Patterson, Henry. *The British state and the Ulster crisis: from Wilson to Thatcher*. London, 1985.

Bishop, Patrick, and Mallie, Eamonn. *The Provisional I.R.A.* London, 1987.

Black, R.; Pinter, F.; and Overy, R. *Flight: a report on population movement in Belfast during August 1971*. Belfast, [1971].

Boulton, David. *The UVF, 1966–73: an anatomy of loyalist rebellion*. Dublin, 1973.

Boyd, Andrew. *Have the trade unions failed the North?* Dublin, 1984.

Boyle, Kevin, and Hadden, Tom. *Ireland: a positive proposal*. Harmondsworth, 1985.

Bruce, Steve. *God save Ulster! The religion and politics of Paisleyism.* Oxford and New York, 1986.
—— *The red hand: protestant paramilitaries in Northern Ireland.* Oxford, 1992.
Burton, Frank. *The politics of legitimacy: struggles in a Belfast community.* London, 1978.
Calvert, Harry. *The Northern Ireland problem.* London, 1972.
Campbell, Brian; McKeown, Laurence; and O'Hagan, Felim (ed.). *Nor meekly serve my time: the H Block struggle 1976–1981.* Belfast, 1994.
Conroy, John. *War as a way of life: a Belfast diary.* London, 1988.
Coogan, Tim Pat. *On the blanket: the H-block story.* Dublin, 1980.
—— *The troubles: Ireland's ordeal 1969–96 and the search for peace.* 2nd ed., London, 1996. 1st ed. London, 1995.
Cox, Michael; Guelke, Adrian; and Stephen, Fiona (ed.). *A farewell to arms? From 'long war' to long peace in Northern Ireland.* Manchester and New York, 2000.
Cox, W. Harvey. Who wants a united Ireland? In *Government and Opposition,* xx, no. 1 (winter 1985), pp 29–47.
——Northern Ireland: dirty wars and constitutional dilemmas. In *Parliamentary Affairs,* xlv, no. 4 (1992), pp 693–6.
Cunningham, Michael J. *British government policy in Northern Ireland, 1969–89: its nature and execution.* Manchester, 1991.
Curran, Frank. *Derry: countdown to disaster.* Dublin, 1986.
Cusack, Jim, and McDonald, Henry. *U.V.F.* Dublin, 1997; revised ed. 2000.
Darby, John. *Conflict in Northern Ireland: the development of a polarised community.* Dublin and New York, 1976.
—— *Intimidation and the control of conflict in Northern Ireland.* Dublin, 1986.
—— (ed). *Northern Ireland: the background to the conflict.* Belfast, 1983.
—— and Williamson, A. (ed.). *Violence and the social services in Northern Ireland.* London, 1978.
Davis, Richard. Nelson Mandela's Irish problem: republican and loyalist links with South Africa, 1970–1990. In *Éire-Ireland,* xxvii, no. 4 (1992), pp 47–68.
—— *Mirror hate: the convergent ideology of Northern Ireland paramilitaries, 1966–1992.* Aldershot, 1994.
de Baroid, Ciaran. *Ballymurphy and the Irish war.* London, 1990. Revised ed., 2000.
Deutsch, Richard, and Magowan, Vivien. *Northern Ireland: a chronology of events 1968–74.* 3 vols. Belfast, 1973–5.
Dillon, Martin. *The Shankill Butchers: a case study in mass murder.* London, 1989.
—— and Lehane, Denis. *Political murder in Northern Ireland.* Harmondsworth, 1973.
Drake, C. J. M. The Provisional IRA: a case study. In *Terrorism and Political Violence,* ii, no. 2 (1991), pp 43–60.
Edwards, Owen Dudley. *The sins of our fathers: roots of conflict in Northern Ireland.* Dublin, 1970.
Egan, Bowes, and McCormack, Vincent. *Burntollet.* London, 1969. 2nd ed., London, 1969.
Farrell, Michael (ed.). *Twenty years on.* Dingle, 1988.
Fisk, Robert. *The point of no return: the strike which broke the British in Ulster.* London, 1975.

Flackes, W. D. *Northern Ireland: a political directory, 1968–79*. Dublin and New York, 1980. New ed. (*1968–83*), London, 1983.

—— and Elliott, Sydney. *Northern Ireland: a political directory, 1968–1988*. Belfast, 1989.

Galliher, John F., and DeGregory, Jerry. *Violence in Northern Ireland: understanding protestant perspectives*. Dublin, 1985.

Gilligan, Oscar (ed.). *The Birmingham six: an appalling vista*. Dublin, 1990.

Goldring, Maurice. *Belfast: from loyalty to rebellion*. London, 1991.

Guelke, Adrian. Political impasse in South Africa and Northern Ireland: a comparative perspective. In *Comparative Politics*, xxiii, no. 2 (1991), pp 143–62.

Hall, Michael. *20 years: a concise chronology of events in Ireland from 1968–1988*. Belfast, 1988.

Hannigan, John A. The Armalite and the ballot box: dilemmas of strategy and ideology in the Provisional I.R.A. In *Social Problems*, xxxiii (1985), pp 31–40.

Hastings, Max. *Ulster 1969: the fight for civil rights in Northern Ireland*. London, 1970.

Holland, Jack, and McDonald, Henry. *I.N.L.A.: deadly divisions*. London, 1994.

Hull, Roger H. *The Irish triangle: conflict in Northern Ireland*. Princeton, 1976.

Jeffery, Keith (ed.). *The divided province: the troubles in Northern Ireland 1969–1985*. London, 1985.

Jenkins, Richard. Northern Ireland: in what sense 'religions' in conflict? In Richard Jenkins, H. Donnan, and G. McFarlane, *The sectarian divide in Northern Ireland today* (London, 1986), pp 1–21.

Kenny, Anthony. *The road to Hillsborough: the shaping of the Anglo–Irish agreement*. Oxford, 1986.

Keogh, Dermot, and Haltzel, Michael (ed.). *Northern Ireland and the politics of reconciliation*. Cambridge, 1993.

McCann, Eamonn. *War and an Irish town*. Harmondsworth, 1974; 2nd ed. London, 1980. 3rd (revised) ed., London, 1993.

—— with Sheils, Maureen, and Hannigan, Bridie. *Bloody Sunday in Derry: what really happened*. Dingle, 1992. New ed., Dingle, 2000.

McClean, Raymond. *The road to Bloody Sunday*. Dublin, 1983. Revised ed., Derry, 1997.

McCluskey, Conn. *Up off their knees: a commentary on the civil rights movement in Northern Ireland*. Galway, 1989.

McCreary, Alf. *Survivors*. Belfast, 1976.

McElroy, Gerard. *The catholic church and the Northern Ireland crisis, 1968–1986*. Dublin, 1990.

McGuffin, John. *Internment*. Tralee, 1973.

McGuire, Maria. *To take arms: a year in the Provisional IRA*. London, 1973.

McKeown, Ciaran. *The passion of peace*. Belfast, 1984.

McKittrick, David, and McVea, David. *Making sense of the troubles*. Belfast, 2000. Revised ed., London, 2001.

—— Kelters, Seamus; Feeney, Brian; and Thornton, Chris. *Lost lives: the stories of the men, women and children who died as a result of the Northern Ireland troubles*. Edinburgh and London, 1999.

Magee, John. *Northern Ireland—crisis and conflict*. London and Boston, 1974.

Moxon-Browne, Edward. The water and the fish: public opinion and the Provisional IRA in Northern Ireland. In Paul Wilkinson (ed.), *British perspectives on terrorism* (London, 1981), pp 41–72.

——*Nation, class and creed in Northern Ireland*. Aldershot, 1983.

Munck, Ronnie. The making of the troubles in Northern Ireland. In *Journal of Contemporary History*, xxvii, no. 2 (1992), pp 211–29.

Nelson, Sarah. *Ulster's uncertain defenders: protestant political, paramilitary and community groups and the Northern Ireland conflict*. Belfast, 1984.

Newsinger, John. Ulster and the downfall of the Labour government 1974–79. In *Race and Class*, xxxiii, no. 2 (1991), pp 45–57.

O'Dowd, Liam; Rolston, Bill; and Tomlinson, Mike (ed.). *Northern Ireland: between civil rights and civil war*. London, 1980.

O'Duffy, Brendan, and O'Leary, Brendan. Violence in Northern Ireland, 1969–June 1989. In John McGarry and Brendan O'Leary (ed.), *The future of Northern Ireland* (Oxford, 1990), pp 318–41.

O'Malley, Padraig. *The uncivil wars: Ireland today*. Belfast, 1983.

——*Biting at the grave: the Irish hunger strikes and the politics of despair*. New York, 1990.

Ó Maolchatha, Aogan. Political violence and criminality: the case of the 1981 Irish hunger strike. In *Journal of Political and Military Sociology*, xvii, no. 1 (1989), pp 151–4.

Pipe, Caroline K. *The origins of the present troubles in Northern Ireland*. London and New York, 1997.

——and McInnes, Colin. The British army in Northern Ireland 1969–1972: from policing to counter-terror. In *Journal of Strategic Studies*, xx, no. 2 (1997), pp 1–24.

Pringle, Peter and Jacobson, Philip. *Those are real bullets, aren't they? Bloody Sunday, Derry, 30 January 1972*. London, 2000.

Purdie, Bob. *Politics in the streets: the origins of the civil rights movement in Northern Ireland*. Belfast, 1990.

Roche, Patrick J., and Barton, Brian (ed.). *The Northern Ireland question: myth and reality*. Aldershot, 1991.

Rose, Peter. *How the troubles came to Northern Ireland*. Basingstoke, 2000.

Rose, Richard. *Governing without consensus: an Irish perspective*. London, 1971.

——*Northern Ireland: a time of choice*. London, 1976.

Ruane, Joseph, and Todd, Jennifer. *The dynamics of conflict in Northern Ireland: power, conflict and emancipation*. Cambridge, 1996.

Soule, John W. Problems in applying counterterrorism to prevent terrorism: two decades of violence in Northern Ireland reconsidered. In *Terrorism*, xii, no. 1 (1989), pp 31–46.

Sunday Times Insight Team. *Ulster*. Harmondsworth, 1972.

Sweeney, George. Irish hunger strikes and the cult of self sacrifice. In *Journal of Contemporary History*, xxviii, no. 3 (1993), pp 421–37.

Taylor, Peter. *Families at war: voices from the troubles*. London, 1989.

——*Provos: the I.R.A. and Sinn Féin*. London, 1997.

—— *Loyalists: Ulster's protestant paramilitaries.* London, 1999.

Urban, Mark. *Big boys' rules: the secret struggle against the I.R.A.* London, 1992.

Utley, T. E. *Lessons of Ulster.* London, 1975.

Wallis, Roy; Bruce, Steve; and Taylor, David. *'No surrender!' Paisleyism and the politics of ethnic identity in Northern Ireland.* Belfast, 1986.

Watson, Rhoda. *Along the road to peace: fifteen years with the Peace People.* Belfast, 1991.

White, Robert W. The Irish Republican Army: an assessment of sectarianism. In *Terrorism and Political Violence*, ix, no. 1 (1997), pp 20–55.

Whyte, J. H. *Interpreting Northern Ireland.* Oxford, 1990.

Wilson, Andrew J. *Irish America and the Ulster conflict: 1968–1995.* Belfast, 1995.

Wilson, Harold. *The Labour government, 1964–70: a personal record.* Harmondsworth, 1974.

Wilson, Thomas. *Ulster: conflict and consent.* Oxford, 1989.

Wright, Frank. Protestant ideology and politics in Ulster. In *European Journal of Sociology*, xiv (1973), pp 213–80.

—— *Northern Ireland: a comparative analysis.* Dublin, 1987.

—— Northern Ireland and the British–Irish relationship. In *Studies*, lxxviii, no. 310 (1989), pp 151–62.

—— Is Northern Ireland Britain's Algeria? In *Études Irlandaises*, xvi, no. 2 (1991), pp 119–31.

C BIOGRAPHICAL AND OTHER WORKS OF REFERENCE

Compton, Paul A. *Northern Ireland: a census atlas.* Dublin, 1978.

Deutsch, Richard, and Magowan, Vivien. *Northern Ireland: a chronology of events 1968–74.* 3 vols. Belfast, 1973–5.

Elliott, Sydney. *Northern Ireland parliamentary election results, 1921–72.* Chichester, 1973.

Flackes, W. D. *Northern Ireland: a political directory, 1968–79.* Dublin and New York, 1980. New ed. (*1968–83*), London, 1983.

—— and Elliott, Sydney. *Northern Ireland: a political directory, 1968–1988.* Belfast, 1989. 5th ed. (*1968–1999*), Belfast, 1999.

McNamara, Maedhbh, and Mooney, Paschal. *Women in parliament: Ireland 1918–2000.* Dublin, 2000.

Newmann, Kate (comp.). *Dictionary of Ulster biography.* Belfast, 1993.

Vaughan, W. E., and Fitzpatrick, A. J. (ed.). *Irish historical statistics: population 1821–1971.* Dublin, 1978. (A New History of Ireland, Ancillary Publications II.)

Walker, B. M. (ed.). *Parliamentary election results in Ireland, 1918–92.* Dublin and Belfast, 1992. (A New History of Ireland, Ancillary Publications V.)
Includes elections for Westminster, Belfast, Dublin, and Strasbourg.

INDEX

All persons of rank are indexed primarily under the family name, cross references being given from the title.

The following special abbreviations are used:

abp	archbishop	P.	protestant
bp	bishop	pl.	plate
I.F.S.	Irish Free State	P.R.	proportional representation
L.L.	lord lieutenant	R.C.	Roman Catholic
(m)	map	R.I.	Republic of Ireland
n	note	(t)	table
N.I.	Northern Ireland		

'M.P.' denotes a member for a British constituency of the U.K. parliament; 'N.I. M.P.' denotes a member for a Northern Ireland constituency of the U.K. parliament, of the N.I. parliament, or of the subsequent N.I. representative bodies.

1. Sir James Craig, N.I. prime minister, inspecting police cyclists, 1921

2. A unit of the Irish army taking over Richmond Barracks, Dublin (British troops on left), 1922

3. A unit of the Irish army entering Athlone military barracks (British sergeant on right)

4. R.I.C. men sorting tunics during evacuation of Dublin Castle, 1922

5. First squad of Garda Síochána entering Dublin Castle

6. British sympathisers waving flags, 1922

7. Destruction of the Four Courts, Dublin, including the Public Record Office, at the start of the civil war, 30 June 1922

8. View of destroyed Four Courts, Dublin, from Merchants' Quay

9. Buildings destroyed in O'Connell Street, Dublin, July 1922

10. First issue of Irish postage stamps: British stamps, overprinted 'Rialtas Sealadach na hÉireann' ('Provisional government of Ireland'), 17 Feb. 1922

11. Charlotte Despard, veteran feminist and socialist (on left of back seat), and Maud Gonne MacBride (on right) on Red Cross work, 4 July 1922; driver, Andy Woods of Donnybrook

12. Funeral of Michael Collins, O'Connell Street, Dublin (view from Nelson's Pillar), Aug. 1922

13. National army troops on southern front, en route for attack on Irregulars, chatting to children, 1922/3

14. The *Argenta*, moored in Larne Lough to hold internees, 1922–4

15. Corpus Christi procession, Cashel, Co. Tipperary: benediction being given inside the gates of the old cathedral, early 1920s

16. Group outside Royal Irish Academy, Dawson St., Dublin, 1923, including W. T. Cosgrave, Desmond FitzGerald, Hugh Kennedy (chief justice), Eoin O'Duffy, Kevin O'Higgins, W. B. Yeats

17. Dublin Horse Show: Governor-general T. M. Healy greets woollen workers from Co. Longford, 14 Aug. 1923

18. Members of boundary commission, late 1924. Left to right: F. B. Bourdillon (secretary), J. R. Fisher, Richard Feetham, Eoin MacNeill, C. Beerstecher (Feetham's private secretary)

19. Funeral from Armagh cathedral of Cardinal Michael Logue, archbishop of Armagh, 25 Nov. 1924

20. Sir James Craig, N.I. prime minister, and Sir Richard Dawson Bates, minister of home affairs, with supporters at Strabane, Co. Tyrone, 1926

21. Removal of remains of Countess Markievicz from mortuary chapel, Glasnevin, Dublin, 1927; those present include Patrick J. Ruttledge, Frank Aiken, Eamon de Valera

22. A priest addresses nationalists from a lorry in Termonamongan, Co. Tyrone, 1928

23. Baker St. in the Pound Loney area of the lower Falls Road, Belfast, 12 Oct. 1932, piled with cobblestones for use during rioting

24. 'Ingenious cattle
smuggler: "A merry
Christmas, my worthy
friend!"', cartoon by
Seán Coughlan (1933)

25. 'I see the Maguire
boys are home for
Christmas', cartoon
by Rowel Friers

26. 'I really will have to learn the language, Sally. Whenever he answers me back in Irish I can't make up my mind whether to pat him on the back or clip his ear', cartoon by 'Maskee' (William Beckett)

27. 'Will yiz shut up, all o' yiz, while your father's explainin' me position under the New [1937] Constitution!', cartoon by 'C. E. K' (Charles E. Kelly)

28. British troops leaving Spike Island, Co. Cork, 1939, as part of the return of the 'treaty ports' to Dublin control

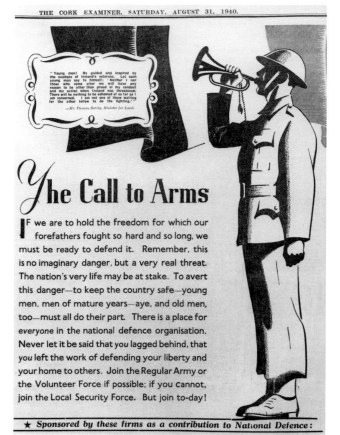

29. 'The call to arms', advertisement placed by department of defence, *Cork Examiner*, 31 Aug. 1940, p. 9

30. John Andrews, N.I. prime minister, with A. J. Kelly, assistant secretary to the cabinet, 1942

31. The first American troops to arrive in Co. Londonderry form up in front of their barracks, Jan. 1942

32. Sir Basil Brooke, N.I. prime
minister, with Herbert Morrison,
British home secretary, on an
American air base in N.I., July
1943

33. Surrendered German U-boats
at Lisahally, Lough Foyle, 1945

34. 'Ulster holds the Fort!', poster for the 1949 N.I. general election, showing Sir Basil Brooke (created Viscount Brookeborough, 1952)

35. U.S. travel agents in Cork, Oct. 1951

36. Second Wexford Opera Festival, Oct. 1952, featuring Donizetti's 'L'elisir d'amore'. Back row, left to right: Charles E. Kelly of *Dublin Opinion*; Elvira Ramella ('Adina'); Nicola Monti ('Nemorino'); Dr Tom Walsh, founder of the festival. In front: Cristiano Dallamangus ('Dr Dulcamara')

37. Tercentenary of death of Giovanni Battista Rinuccini (1592–1653), papal nuncio to Ireland, Dec. 1953. Left to right: P. J. Corish, professor of ecclesiastical history, St Patrick's College, Maynooth; John Charles McQuaid, archbishop of Dublin; Donal Cregan, president of Castleknock College, Co. Dublin; Seán T. O'Kelly, president of Ireland; Michael Tierney, president of U.C.D.; Gerald Patrick O'Hara, papal nuncio; Mrs O'Kelly; Eamon de Valera, taoiseach; R. Dudley Edwards, professor of modern Irish history, U.C.D.

38. Clifden children awaiting Fr Peyton, 30 Apr. 1954 (Patrick Peyton, native of Attymass, Ballina, Co. Mayo)

39. The freedom of the cities of Belfast and Derry presented to Winston Churchill at the Mansion House, London, 16 Dec. 1955. Left to right: Viscount Brookeborough, Viscount Montgomery, Churchill, Viscount Alanbrooke, Earl Alexander, Sir Gerald Templer

40. The N.I. cabinet, Oct. 1958; those present include A. R. G. Gordon, J. L. O. Andrews, Robert Moore, Terence O'Neill, Lord Brookeborough, Cecil Bateman (cabinet secretary), W. W. B. Topping, Lord Glentoran

41. Sir John Hunt inspecting the Combined Cadet Force at Portora Royal School, Enniskillen, c.1960

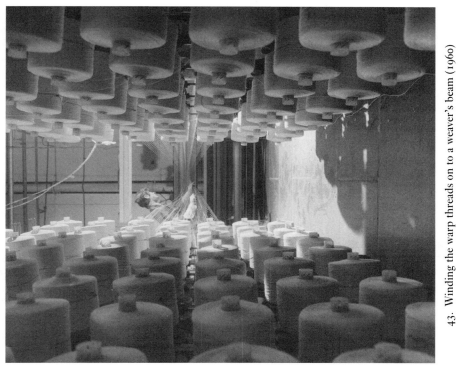

43: Winding the warp threads on to a weaver's beam (1960)

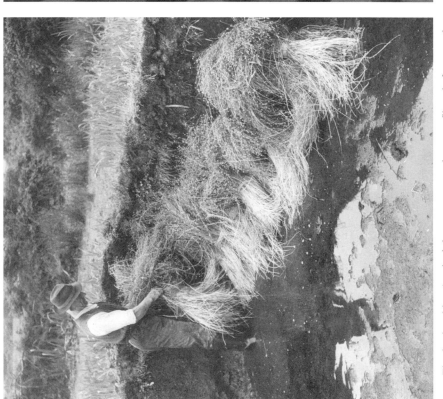

42: Flax is placed in a 'retting' dam to rot away the outer fibres before scutch‐ing, hackling, and cleaning in preparation for the spinning room (1960)

44. Cutting and stacking turf for Bord na Móna (1962)

45. A Royal Dublin Society spring show of the 1960s

46. Cahermee fair, 13 July 1964: a general view of the annual horse fair, held at Buttevant, Co. Cork, attended by U.K. and Continental buyers

47. Crowning the Queen of the Carberies at the opening of the festival in Leap, west Cork, 2 Aug. 1964: the Rev. P. O'Connell, P.P., crowns 17-year-old Frances Daly, with Sheila and Ann O'Mahony, ladies-in-waiting; on right, Commdt-gen. Tom Barry, who performed the opening ceremony

48. Launch of the first edition (1967) of T. W. Moody and F. X. Martin (ed.), *The course of Irish history*. Left to right: unidentified, F. X. Martin, professor of medieval history, U.C.D.; T. W. Moody, professor of modern history, T.C.D.; Jack Lynch, taoiseach

50. Edward Augustine McGuire (1901–92), senator, businessman, sportsman, and chairman of the National Gallery of Ireland

49. Richard James Hayes (1902–76), director of the National Library of Ireland 1940–67, cryptographer, and bibliographer

51 (*above left*). 'Everyone march': poster advertising the first major march organised by People's Democracy, from the students' union at Queen's University, Belfast, 16 Oct. 1968

52 (*above right*). 'The Falls burns, Malone Road fiddles': one of the first People's Democracy silk-screen posters, produced immediately after the Aug. 1969 riots in Belfast

53 (*right*). 'Smash Stormont': People's Democracy silk-screen poster by John McGuffin, 1969, showing the parliament of the 'Unionist junta' crushed by a red hand (evoking both Ulster and socialist revolution)

54. Rioting in Annadale St., Belfast, May 1970

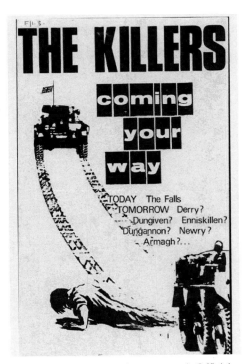

55. 'The Killers: coming your way': Official Sinn Féin poster, produced after the 36-hour curfew imposed on the Falls Road, Belfast, 3–4 July 1970

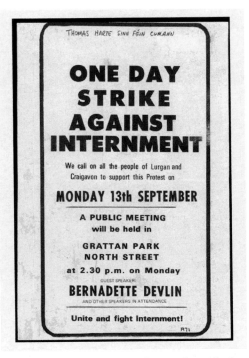

56. Sinn Féin poster calling for one-day strike in Lurgan and Craigavon, Co. Armagh, against internment, 13 Sept. 1971

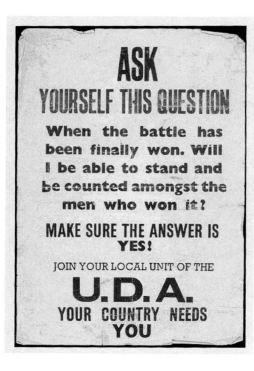

57 (*above left*). Ulster Defence Association recruiting poster, issued shortly after its formation in Sept. 1971

58 (*above right*). Ulster Vanguard poster for rally at Ormeau Park, Belfast, 18 Mar. 1972

59 (*left*). 'Willie Whitewash—"I'll soon have this job finished"': Ulster Vanguard poster produced shortly after the introduction of direct rule (Mar. 1972)

60. Wrecked cars at Eden Quay, Dublin, after two bomb explosions in the city centre killed two people and injured 127, 1 Dec. 1972, ending the dáil crisis over the Offences against the State (Amendment) Bill

61. Tipperary full forward Donie Cassidy (left) rounding Cork back Sean O'Gorman during the Munster Under-21 hurling final, Aug. 1980

62. Nurses' reunion, silver jubilee of St Mary's Orthopaedic Hospital, Gurranabraher, Cork, 30 Aug. 1980. Included are Miss Maura O'Connell, matron, Nurses Winifred Murphy and Delia Phelan, former matrons

63. Inauguration of the National Concert Hall, Dublin, Sept. 1981

64. Taoiseach Garret FitzGerald addressing the New Ireland Forum, flanked by John Hume (left) and Peter Barry, minister for foreign affairs (right)

65. The McGimpsey brothers Christopher and Michael, Unionists, at the New Ireland Forum, 19 Jan. 1984, session no. 11

66. Charles Haughey, leader of Fianna Fáil, signing copies of the New Ireland Forum report, 2 May 1984

67. Parliament Buildings, Belfast, 1932, Arnold Thornely architect

68. Government Buildings (College of Science), Dublin, 1922, Aston Webb architect

69. Church of Christ the King, Cork, 1937, Barry Byrne architect

70. Dublin Airport terminal building, Co. Dublin, 1939, Desmond FitzGerald architect

71. Arus Mhic Diarmada (Busárus), Dublin, 1953, Michael Scott architect

72. Bank of Ireland, Baggot Street, Dublin, 1972–9, R. Tallon architect; photograph courtesy of Bank of Ireland Group

73. Berkeley Library, Trinity College, Dublin, 1967, Paul Koralek architect

74. 'A Connemara landscape', by Paul Henry

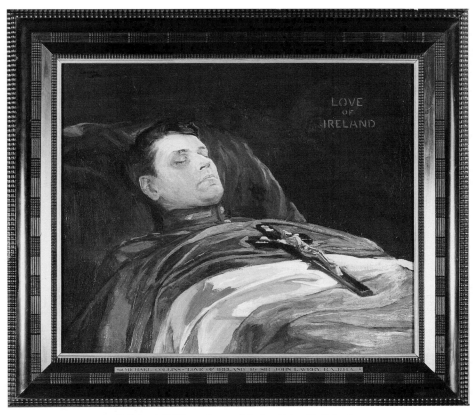

75. 'Michael Collins—Love of Ireland', by Sir John Lavery

76. 'On through the silent lands', by Jack B. Yeats

77. 'Men of the south', by Sean Keating

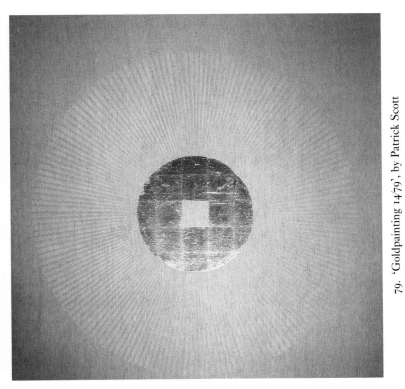

79. 'Goldpainting 1479', by Patrick Scott

78. 'Study of a girl's head', by Louis le Brocquy

80. 'Pressée politique with floor piece' ('Pressée irlandaise'), by Micheal Farrell

81. 'Miami murders', by Robert Ballagh

82. 'Portrait of James Joyce', by Basil Blackshaw

84. Pádraic Ó Conaire, sculpture by Albert Power

83. Patrick Pearse, sculpture by Oliver Sheppard

86. Daniel O'Connell, sculpture by Andrew O'Connor; photo courtesy of Bank of Ireland Group

85. 'The pikeman', sculpture by Jerome Connor

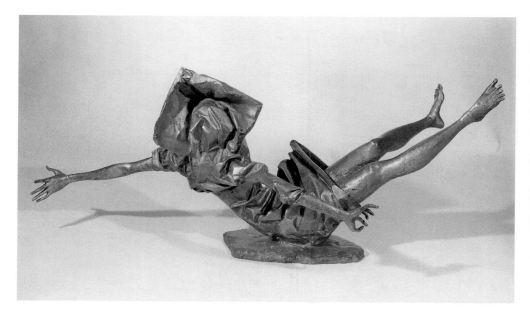

87. 'Woman caught in bomb–blast', sculpture by F. E. McWilliam

88. 'The children of Lir', sculpture by Oisin Kelly

89. James Connolly, sculpture by Hilary Heron

90. 'Barbed wire I', sculpture by Deborah Brown

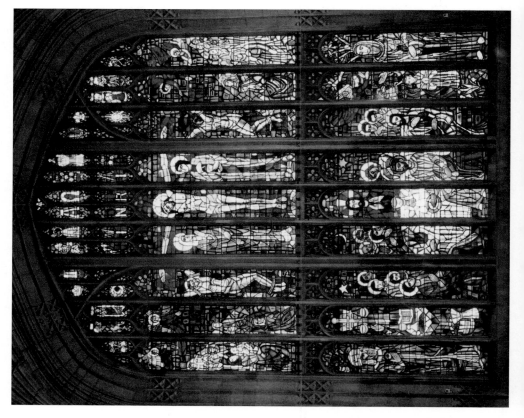

91 (*right*). 'The flight into Egypt', stained glass, by Michael Healy

92 (*far right*). 'Crucifixion and last supper', stained glass, by Evie Hone